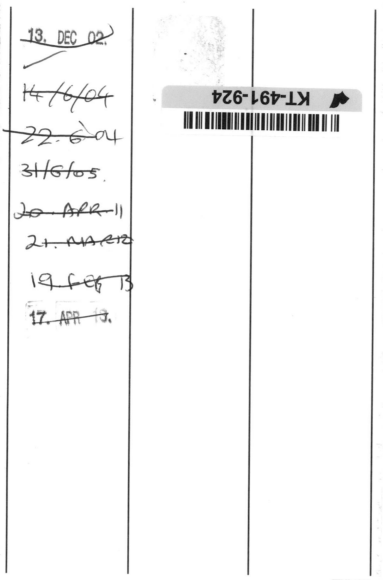

Hilgard's Introduction to Psychology

Thirteenth Edition

Publisher	Earl McPeek
Executive Editor	Carol Wada
Market Strategist	Kathleen Sharp
Developmental Editor	Janie Pierce-Bratcher
Project Editor	Michele Tomiak
Art Director	David A. Day
Production Manager	Andrea Archer

Cover art: Robert Delaunay, *Formes circulaires,* 1912, Kunstmuseum, Bern, Switzerland

ISBN: 0-15-508044-X
Library of Congress Catalog Card Number: 99-64304

Address for Domestic Orders
Harcourt Brace College Publishers, 6277 Sea Harbor Drive, Orlando, FL 32887-6777
800-782-4479

Address for International Orders
International Customer Service
Harcourt Brace & Company, 6277 Sea Harbor Drive, Orlando, FL 32887-6777
407-345-3800
(fax) 407-345-4060
(e-mail) hbintl@harcourtbrace.com

Address for Editorial Correspondence
Harcourt Brace College Publishers, 301 Commerce Street, Suite 3700, Fort Worth, TX 76102

Web Site Address
http://www.harcourtcollege.com

Harcourt Brace College Publishers will provide complimentary supplements or supplement packages to those adopters qualified under our adoption policy. Please contact your sales representative to learn how you qualify. If as an adopter or potential user you receive supplements you do not need, please return them to your sales representative or send them to: Attn: Returns Department, Troy Warehouse, 465 South Lincoln Drive, Troy, MO 63379.

Printed in the United States of America

0 1 2 3 4 5 6 7 8 048 9 8 7 6 5 4 3

Hilgard's Introduction to Psychology

Thirteenth Edition

Rita L. Atkinson
University of California, San Diego

Richard C. Atkinson
University of California, San Diego

Edward E. Smith
University of Michigan

Daryl J. Bem
Cornell University

Susan Nolen-Hoeksema
University of Michigan

Contributing Editor: Carolyn D. Smith

Harcourt College Publishers

Fort Worth   Philadelphia   San Diego   New York   Austin   Orlando   San Antonio
Toronto   Montreal   London   Sydney   Tokyo

Preface

A Tradition Begins

More than 45 years ago, Ernest (Jack) Hilgard began writing the first edition of what would become one of the most prestigious textbooks in history. Professor Hilgard had been teaching popular courses in introductory psychology at Yale and Stanford since 1928 and for decades had been courted by publishers to write a textbook. He simply did not feel that he had time to write his own textbook until he gave up the chairmanship of the Stanford Psychology Department in 1951 to become Dean of the Graduate Division at Stanford (in 1951 it was less time-consuming to be dean than chair of a department). In addition, he felt that the field was ready for a new introductory textbook, partly because Robert Woodworth's text, which had dominated the field for years, had last been published in 1947 with no prospects for revision.

In writing *Introduction to Psychology,* Hilgard sought to engage students by raising important psychological questions and by teaching them how to answer these questions. He states, "In planning my own book, I resolved to have the student very much in mind, just as I had done in my lecturing. I never approved fully of frontal lecturing that talked at the students instead of engaging them in seeking their own answers to some of the questions that were raised, or encouraging them to interrupt with questions when my expository remarks were unclear. In the outlining of the book and in its writing, I tried to remain faithful in this commitment to involve the student's participating interest."

One way in which Hilgard piqued the intrinsic interest of students was to focus the first chapter of the book on developmental psychology, particularly young adult development. This text also devoted more space than did other textbooks to the application of psychology to personal and social problems. He knew that students were interested in the problems faced by clinical and coun-

seling psychologists and by vocational and industrial psychologists, and he felt that they would be more motivated to learn fundamental concepts in psychology if they understood how those concepts could be used to overcome important problems. Finally, he introduced "critical discussion" sections that addressed controversial issues in detail, a feature that was brand new to psychology textbooks.

In addition to appealing to students' interests, Hilgard sought to provide a comprehensive and rigorous review of current theory and research in psychology. He accomplished this goal, covering more scholarly material than any previous introductory text, while presenting research in language that students could grasp.

The first edition of *Introduction to Psychology* was received enthusiastically and sold 145,000 copies. In subsequent editions Hilgard added chapters on biology, sensation and perception, statistics, and psychological measurement. His revisions were lauded, and the third edition of the book sold 415,000 copies. Eventually the book was translated into French, German, Hebrew, Italian, Portuguese, Spanish, and Chinese.

Hilgard retired to Emeritus Professor status at Stanford in 1969, but continued to revise the textbook for 18 years. Two years earlier he had begun taking on coauthors to ensure that the rapidly expanding subfields of psychology were covered by experts. Richard Atkinson became a coauthor in 1967, bringing his expertise in cognitive and biological psychology. In 1971 Rita Atkinson, a clinical psychologist, joined the team, revising the chapters in her area and coordinating the efforts of the authors. Daryl Bem joined the team in 1975 and eventually took responsibility for the material on development, personality, and social psychology. In 1979 Edward Smith began contributing his expertise in cognitive psychology. Finally, in 1992 Susan Nolen-Hoeksema joined the team to revise the material on health and clinical psychology.

The decision to change the title to *Hilgard's Introduction to Psychology* was made in preparation for the twelfth edition in an effort to honor the contributions of Ernest Hilgard to this book and to the teaching of introductory psychology. The contributing authors remain committed to Hilgard's goals of presenting a comprehensive and scholarly overview of psychology in a clear and engaging manner. Due to the continued efforts of this team of authors, Hilgard's text has continued to enjoy a reputation for "scholarly sophistication," "extensive coverage," and "plain language" (Pfeiffer, 1980, p. 119). Instructors have come to know that they can rely on this textbook to provide a critical analysis of the major issues in historical and contemporary psychology in a manner that students find interesting and comprehensible.

Hilgard's Introduction to Psychology remains one of the best-selling introductory psychology textbooks in the world.

The Thirteenth Edition

In order to capture the dynamic nature of contemporary psychology and to inspire students to learn more about the field, we have added several features to this classic text. We believe that these new features are consistent with the heritage of this book and result in a scholarly, state-of-the-art, well-written learning tool. Features that have not been changed include part outlines, chapter outlines, chapter summaries, and suggested readings. Following is a list of the text's new features:

Contemporary Voices in Psychology boxes contain essays written specifically for this text by leading researchers in psychology. These researchers argue their findings on controversial/cutting-edge issues such as *Are we naturally selfish?* (Chapter 1); *Are positive emotions good for us?* (Chapter 11); *Is Freud still alive?* (Chapter 13); and *Is ADHD overdiagnosed?* (Chapter 15). For a complete list of these essays and their authors, please see the detailed table of contents or the book's back cover.

Frontiers of Psychological Research boxes replace the previous editions' "Critical Discussions" boxes; the general purpose of this feature, however, remains the same: to examine the research that is expanding the limits of our knowledge about the field of psychology. Examples include *Effects of Daycare* (Chapter 3), *A Herbal Remedy for Memory Loss?* (Chapter 8), *Neurotransmitters and Personality* (Chapter 13), and *Altruism* (Chapter 18). For a complete list of topics covered in these boxes, please see the detailed table of contents.

All graphs have been newly rendered by a psychologist. Richard W. Bowen of Loyola University Chicago researched and re-plotted each graph according to its original data when available.

Critical thinking questions are found at the end of each chapter. These address current and/or everyday issues and require that students consider the information supplied in the chapter, think reasonably and logically, and rely on their own experiences and ideas to arrive at the answers.

Key terms are boldfaced in the text and now are also listed at the end of each chapter with page references.

In addition to these changes, we have made numerous content updates and revisions. Our goal in doing so is to provide students with a solid background in psychology by providing the best of both the classic and the new. While continuing to emphasize (and in many cases enhance) the book's focus on relationships between biological and psychological phenomena, we have added numerous discussions that reflect the contemporary interest in cognitive theory in such areas as personality and dreaming. Following are just a few of content changes you will find in the thirteenth edition:

■ In response to requests by several reviewers, we have moved the material on the history of psychology out of the appendix and placed it in Chapter 1, with an introductory section on nativism versus empiricism.

■ The chapters on sensation and perception have been thoroughly updated and now included expanded discussion of the visual cortex, Gestalt principles, and motion perception.

- In keeping with the text's emphasis on biological-psychological relationships, we have added numerous discussions of biological aspects of psychological phenomena throughout each chapter. For example, you will find new sections on the opponent-process model of sleep (Chapter 6), the role of the amygdala in emotional memory (Chapter 8), and new drug therapies for schizophrenia and anxiety disorders (Chapter 16).

- Chapters 12 and 13 have been extensively revised to include recent theories of intelligence and cognitive theories of personality. The cognitive perspective also appears in Chapter 6 in the discussion of theories of dreaming.

- Several other topics of current interest have been included in this edition. Among them are sleep deprivation (Chapter 6), issues in the treatment of children (Chapter 16), and altruism (Chapter 18).

Supporting Materials

For the Student

Study Guide and Unit Mastery Program

Prepared by Fred W. Whitford, Montana State University

Whether you teach your course by conventional lecture or by unit mastery methods, this guide will help your students master the content of your introductory psychology course. The study guide helps students to distinguish between crucial material and less important details; it also points out notable figures in the field along with the meanings of specific psychological terms and concepts. And finally, this guide allows students to test themselves along the way. Subsections include Learning Objectives, Important Names, Vocabulary and Details, Ideas and Concepts, and Sample Quizzes.

The Explorer

Prepared by John Mitterer of Brock University

This accompanying CD-ROM is an innovative learning tool that allows students to explore and understand the realm of psychology in an interactive, multimedia environment. *The Explorer* allows students to interactively explore dynamic processes illustrated in the text with a wave of the mouse. In addition to further explorations of graphic material from *Hilgard's Introduction to Psychology,* Thirteenth Edition, *The Explorer* allows students to repeat experiments on classic psychological phenomena, such as the Stroop effect and the Müller-Lyer illusion. Links to Web pages from *The Explorer* give students the power and currency of the World Wide Web. In addition, this CD-ROM allows students to test their mastery of the material in a series of test questions, based on the material in *Hilgard's Introduction to Psychology,* Thirteenth Edition.

Website

Students will find an abundance of useful information about learning in general as well as learning psychology at www.harbrace.com/psych/atkinson/index.html. We offer **Online Quizzes** and **Web Search Assignments** for each chapter. This site will also contain the **Contemporary Voices in Psychology** boxes found in the book along with links to further information on the authors and issues therein.

For the Instructor

Instructor's Manual and Unit Mastery Guide

Prepared by Fred W. Whitford, Montana State University

As in previous editions, this instructor's manual contains many activities, assignments, questions, and suggestions for your introductory psychology course. New to this edition are Internet URLs for relevant lecture ideas, discussion questions, and class activities/assignments. Subsections include Chapter Outline, Notable Quotes, Chapter Terms, Lecture Ideas, Essay Questions, Writing Activities an Discussion Questions, Class Activities and Assignments, Film Suggestions, and Example Quizzes.

Test Bank

Prepared by N. Jay Bean, Vassar College

This ancillary provides you with more than 150 multiple-choice items and 5 essay questions for each chapter, as well as more than 75 questions for the Statistical Appendix. Each question is rated according to difficulty and is referenced to the text. Items that address new material in the text are marked with an asterisk.

Computerized Test Bank

Prepared by ESA

Computerized versions of the test bank are available in 3.5-inch floppies or CDs in either Windows or Macintosh formats so you can customize the questions provided in the printed test bank. The test item software *EXAMaster+™* offers three unique features. *EasyTest* creates a test from a single screen in just a few easy steps. You choose the parameters, then either select questions from the database or let *EasyTest* randomly select them. *FullTest* offers a range of options that includes selecting, editing, adding, or linking questions or graphics; random selection of questions from a wide range of criteria; creating criteria; blocking questions; and printing up to 99 different versions of the same test and answer sheet. *EXAMRecord™* records, curves, graphs, and prints out grades according to criteria you select and can display the grade distribution as a bar graph or a plotted graph. For the instructor without access to a computer, Harcourt College Publishers offers *RequesTest*. By calling 1-800-447-9457, a software specialist will compile questions according to your criteria and will mail or fax the test master within 48 hours.

PowerPoint Presentation

Prepared by Gordon K. Hodge, University of New Mexico

Bring psychology to life with this easy-to-use, fully customizable, overhead lecture software consisting of approximately 300 slides conveniently organized according to the text outline. Illustrations and video clips appear frequently, perfectly depicting essential concepts found in the book.

Overhead Transparencies

These full-color acetates and accompanying guide provide more than 100 images for use in your introductory psychology course.

On-Line Course Management

We are proud to offer an exciting new software package that helps you build sophisticated Web-based learning environments for your students. This fully customizable software package can be used to create on-line courses or to simply post office hours or supplementary materials to the Web. You can design your own Web sites that provide a full array of educational tools, including communication, testing, student tracking, access control, database collaboration tools, on-line searching and navigation tools, and much more. We provide the foundation, you customize the program to suit your and your students' needs. If you are interested in moving your courses to the Web, please contact your local Harcourt sales representative for more information on this exciting new resource.

Web Site

The psychology home page, www.harbrace.com/psych/, contains vast amounts of useful information about learning as well as links to other interesting psychology sites. **Shockwave Animations** provide you and your students with a sampling of the multimedia experience that is on the *Explorer CD-ROM*. Browse **Our Favorite Links** for information on topics such as social psychology, the science of psychology, sign language, cow eye dissection, optical illusions, life spans, and more. **Everyday Psychology** provides information on how psychology fits into the "real" world with topics including stress management, coping with insomnia, establishing routines, and mastering difficult material. *Hilgard's Introduction to Psychology, Thirteenth Edition* Web page, www.harbrace.com/psych/atkinson/index.html, contains an abundance of teaching aids, including **"Tips on Teaching Introductory Psychology"** from Eric Landrum's *Guide to Teaching Introductory Psychology*. From this site you can also download **Overhead Transparencies**, examine **Teaching Strategies**, and visit **Related Links** for each chapter.

Films for the Humanities and Sciences

These videos are available upon adoption of a Harcourt introductory psychology textbook. Choose from films in the areas of biopsychology, developmental psychology, abnormal psychology, social psychology, etc. Qualifying criteria apply. For more information, please contact your local Harcourt representative.

The Whole Psychology Catalog, Fifth Edition

Prepared by Michael B. Reiner, Kennesaw State College

Easily supplement your course with work and assignments from *The Whole Psychology Catalog*. This ancillary has perforated pages containing experiential exercises, questionnaires, and visual aids. Each activity is classified by one of eight learning goals central to the teaching of psychology. Also included in the fifth edition is an informative section on using the World Wide Web.

Software Technical Support

Technical support is available for all of our software products by simply calling 1-800-447-9457. Service is available Monday through Friday, 7 a.m. to 6 p.m., central standard time.

Acknowledgments

First, we would like to acknowledge our colleagues and peers who contributed substantially to this revision. **Richard W. Bowen** of Loyola University–Chicago donated extensively to this project as he donated his time and expertise to rendering the graphs as accurately as possible. He re-plotted each of the graphs from the original research when available—a job most intimidating to anyone but a graphing psychologist. **James T. Enns** of the University of British Columbia took time away from his hectic schedule at UBC's Vision Lab to assist in the updating and revision of the sensation and perception chapters (4 and 5); his extensive knowledge in these areas is apparent in each chapter's subtle reorganization and extensive revision. Chapter 2: Biological Basis of Psychology benefits greatly from the efforts of **Kent Berridge** of University of Michigan, who provided the groundwork for the revision of the chapter, and from those of **Josephine F. Wilson** of Wittenberg University, who lends clarity to the discussions on action potentials, dopamine and seratonin, and the organization of the brain. The Contemporary Voices in Psychology boxes became a reality through the persuasiveness and perseverance of **Carla Grayson** of the University of Michigan; she went out of her way to contact and commission the feature's more than 30 contributors. And, last but certainly not least, **Carolyn D. Smith,** a professional writer and editor, has done a wonderful job of bringing our (and the aforementioned contributors') many voices together; she masterfully smoothed our transitions and ensured a consistent textual flow.

As always, we extend our sincere appreciation to the introductory psychology instructors who provided helpful, knowledgeable feedback through pre-revision and manuscript reviews for this thirteenth edition. Following are some of those who participated in this capacity: N. Jay Bean, Vassar College; Richard W. Bowen, Loyola University–Chicago; James F. Calhoun, University of Georgia; Janice Chapman, Bossier Parrish Community College; Stanley Coren, University of British Columbia; Emma Lou Linn, St. Edwards University; Mitchell M. Metzger, Penn State University–Shenango; Frank Muscarella, Barry University; Gayle Norbury, University of Wisconsin–Milwaukee; Shane Pitts, Birmingham-Southern College; Mark Plonsky, University of Wisconsin–Stevens Point; Harold Schiffman, Duke University; J. Anthony Shelton, Liverpool John Moores University; Elaine K. Thompson, Georgian Court College; Lynne S. Trench, Birmingham-Southern College; Frank J. Vattano, Colorado State University; and Ann L. Weber, University of North Carolina at Asheville.

We would also like to recognize the following instructors who contributed to previous editions through insightful manuscript reviews and stimulating telephone discussions: James Ackil, Western Illinois University; Cynthia Allen, Westchester Community College; Eileen Astor-Stetson, Bloomsburg University; Gordon D. Atlas, Alfred University; Raymond R. Baird, University of Texas, San Antonio; N. Jay Bean, Vassar College; John B. Best,

Eastern Illinois University; Randolph Blake, Vanderbilt University; Terry Blumenthal, Wake Forest University; Richard W. Bowen, Loyola University; Thomas Brothen, University of Minnesota; James P. Buchanan, University of Scranton; James F. Calhoun, University of Georgia; Charles S. Carver, University of Miami; Avshalom Caspi, University of Wisconsin; Paul Chara, Loras College; Stephen Clark, Vassar College; Richard Eglfaer, Sam Houston State University; Gilles Einstein, Furman University; Judith Erickson, University of Minnesota; G. William Farthing, University of Maine; Mary Ann Fischer, Indiana University Northwest; Barbara L. Fredrickson, Duke University; William Rick Fry, Youngstown State University; Richard Gist, Johnson County Community College; W. B. Perry Goodwin, Santa Clara University; Bill Graziano, Texas A&M University; Paul Greene, Iona College; Elizabeth Hillstrom, Wheaton College; David Holmes, University of Kansas; William L. Hoover, Suffolk County Community College; Ralph Hupka, California State University; Fred A. Johnson, University of the District of Columbia; Wesley P. Jordan, St. Mary's College of Maryland; Grace Kannady, Kansas City Kansas Community College; Richard A. Kasschau, University of Houston; Charles Ksir, University of Wyoming; Joan Lauer, Indiana University/Purdue University; Elissa M. Lewis, Southwest Missouri State University; Marc A. Lindberg, Marshall University; Richard Lippa, California State University, Fullerton; Joseph Lowman, University of North Carolina; James V. Lupo, Creighton University; Michael Martin, University of Kansas; Fred Maxwell, Southwest Missouri State University; Mary Benson McMullen, Indiana University; Steven E. Meier, University of Idaho; Chandra Mehrotra, College of Saint Scholastica; Sheryll Mennicke, University of Minnesota; Thomas Miller, University of Minnesota; Thomas Miller, University of Oklahoma; Jannay Morrow, Vassar College; Dean Murakami, American River College; Gregory L. Murphy, University of Illinois at Urbana-Champaign; David Neufeldt, Hutchinson Community College; Michael O'Hara, University of Iowa; Paul V. Olczak, SUNY, Geneseo; Carrol Perrino, Morgan State University; Jacqueline B. Persons, Oakland, California; David Pitlenger, Marietta College; Steve Platt, Northern Michigan University; Tom Posey, Murray State University; Janet Proctor, Purdue University; David Raskin, University of Utah; Cheryl A. Rickabaugh, University of Redlands; Steven Robbins, Haverford College; Tim Robinson, Gustavus Adolphus College; Irvin Rock, University of California, Berkeley; Brian H. Ross, University of Illinois at Urbana-Champaign; Jack Rossman, Macalister College; Gene Sackett, University of Washington; D. Kim Sawrey, University of North Carolina, Wilmington; Robert Smith, George Mason University; Steven Smith, Texas A&M University; Joan Stanton, Wheaton College; Tim Strauman, University of Wisconsin, Madison; Francine Tougas, University of Ottawa; Stuart Valins, SUNY, Stonybrook; Frank Vattano, Colorado State University; Paul J. Wellman, Texas A&M University; and Carsh Wilturner, Green River College.

As always, we are indebted to the staff at Harcourt College Publishers, who have once again made this book a reality. Many thanks to Executive Psychology Editor Carol Wada, whose encouragement essentially drove this project. Janie Pierce-Bratcher, our Development Editor, did an amazing job of pulling together not only our work but also that of the five contributing experts and the 36 essay contributors. Picture and Rights Editor Caroline Robbins and freelance Photo/Permissions Editor Cheri Throop worked tirelessly to secure photos and permissions on a very condensed schedule. Senior Project Editor Michele Tomiak skillfully shuttled this project through production with amazing speed and accuracy, and always with a kind word. This fabulous design is the creation of Senior Art Director David Day, who graciously smiled, laughed, and persevered when everyone on the project had differing opinions about the design. Production Manager Andrea Archer absolutely bent over backward to keep the book on schedule and within budget. And finally, we extend special thanks to Market Strategist Kathleen Sharp (Shark) who worked tirelessly before and after publication to encourage everyone to "Rediscover the Classic" that is *Hilgard's Introduction to Psychology*.

Contents in Brief

Contents

Part 3

Consciousness and Perception   108

Part 4

Learning, Remembering, and Thinking   232

PART 7

PART 8

Social Behavior   604

Frontiers of Psychological Research

Contemporary Voices in Psychology

A WORD TO THE STUDENT

A central topic in psychology is the analysis of learning and memory. Almost every chapter of this book refers to these phenomena; Chapter 7 ("Learning and Conditioning") and Chapter 8 ("Memory") are devoted exclusively to learning and memory. In this section we review a method for reading and studying information presented in textbook form. The theoretical ideas underlying this method are discussed in Chapter 8; the method is described here in greater detail for readers who wish to apply it in studying this textbook.

This approach for reading textbook chapters, called the PQRST method, has been shown to be very effective in improving a reader's understanding of and memory for key ideas and information. The method takes its name from the first letter of the five steps one follows in reading a chapter—Preview, Question, Read, Self-recitation, Test. The steps or stages are diagrammed in the figure. The first and last stages (Preview and Test) apply to the chapter as a whole; the middle three stages (Question, Read, Self-recitation) apply to each major section of the chapter as it is encountered.[*]

Stage P (Preview) In the first step, you preview the entire chapter by skimming through it to get an idea of major topics. This is done by reading the chapter outline and then skimming the chapter, paying special attention to the headings of main sections and subsections and glancing at pictures and illustrations. The most important aspect of the preview stage is to read carefully the summary at the end of the chapter once you have skimmed through the chapter. Take time to consider each point in the summary;

questions will come to mind that should be answered later as you read the full text. The preview stage will give you an overview of the topics covered in the chapter and how they are organized.

Stage Q (Question) As noted earlier, you should apply Stages Q, R, and S to each major section of the chapter as it is encountered. The typical chapter in this textbook has five to eight major sections, each section beginning with a heading set in large letters. Work through the chapter one section at a time, applying Stages Q, R, and S to each section before going on to the next section. Before reading a section, read the heading of the section and the headings of the subsections. Then turn the topic headings into one or more questions that you should expect to answer while reading the section. Ask yourself: "What are the main ideas the author is trying to convey in this section?" This is the Question Stage.

Stage R (Read) Next, read the section carefully for meaning. As you read, try to answer the questions you asked in Stage Q. Reflect on what you are reading, and try to make connections to other things you know. You may choose to mark or underline key words or phrases in the text. Try, however, not to mark more than 10 to 15 percent of the text. Too much underlining defeats the intended purpose, which is to make key words and ideas stand out for later review. It is probably best to delay taking notes until you have read the entire section and encountered all the key ideas, so you can judge their relative importance.

Stage S (Self-Recitation) After you have finished reading the section, try to recall the main ideas and recite the information. Self-recitation is a powerful means of fixing the material in your memory. Put the ideas into your own words and recite the information (preferably aloud or, if you are not alone, to yourself).

---

[*]The PQRST method as described here is based on the work of Thomas and H. A. Robinson (1982) and Spache and Berg (1978); their work, in turn, is based on the earlier contributions of R. P. Robinson (1970). In some sources, the name SQ3R is used instead of PQRST. The S, the Q, and the three Rs stand for the same five steps, but are relabeled as Survey, Question, Read, Recite, and Review. We find PQRST to be easier to remember than SQ3R.

Check against the text to be sure that you have recited the material correctly and completely. Self-recitation will reveal blanks in your knowledge and help you organize the information in your mind. After you have completed one section of the chapter in this way, turn to the next section and again apply Stages Q, R, and S. Continue in this manner until you have finished all sections of the chapter.

Stage T (Test) When you have finished reading the chapter, you should test and review all of the material. Look over your notes and test your recall for the main ideas. Try to understand how the various facts relate to one another and how they were organized in the chapter. The test stage may require that you thumb back through the chapter to check key facts and ideas. You should also reread the chapter summary at this time; as you are doing so, you should be able to add details to each entry in the summary. Don't put off the test stage until the night before an examination. The best time for a first review of the chapter is immediately after you have read it.

Research indicates that the PQRST method is very helpful and definitely preferable to simply reading straight through a chapter (Thomas & Robinson, 1982). Self-recitation is particularly important; it is better to spend a significant percentage of study time in an active attempt to recite than it is to devote the entire time to reading and rereading the material (Gates, 1917). Studies also show that a careful reading of the summary of the chapter before reading the chapter itself is especially productive (Reder & Anderson, 1980). Reading the summary first provides an overview of the chapter that helps organize the material as you read through the chapter. Even if you choose not to follow every step of the PQRST method, special attention should be directed to the value of self-recitation and reading the chapter summary as an introduction to the material.

The PQRST method and various other study skills, including taking lecture notes and preparing for and taking examinations, are discussed in an excellent book entitled *Building Better Study Skills: Practical Methods for Succeeding in College,* published by the American College Testing Program, Iowa City, Iowa. As its subtitle indicates, this book focuses on practical methods for achieving personal and academic success in college.

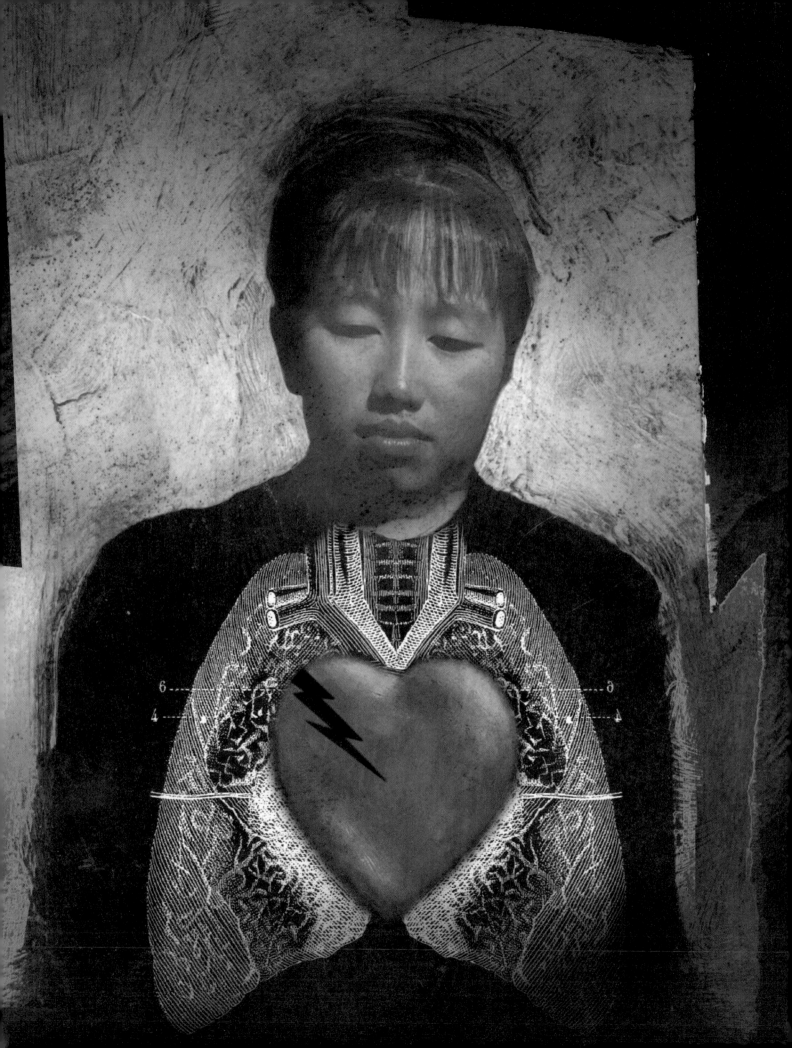

One

Psychology as a Scientific and Human Endeavor

CHAPTER 1   The Nature of Psychology

A Note to the Student

A method for effectively reading a textbook is described in the section immediately before this chapter; you may wish to read that section before starting this chapter.

Chapter 1
The Nature of Psychology

*P*sychology asks questions that touch virtually every aspect of our lives. It asks questions like these: How does the way your parents raised you affect the way you raise your own children? What is the best treatment for drug dependency? Can a man care for an infant as capably as a woman can? Can you remember a traumatic experience in more detail under hypnosis? How should a nuclear power plant be designed to minimize human error? What effects does prolonged stress have on the immune system? Is psychotherapy more effective than drugs in treating depression? Psychologists are conducting research to find answers to these and many other questions.

Psychology also affects our lives through its influence on laws and public policy. Psychological theories and research have influenced laws dealing with discrimination, capital punishment, pornography, sexual behavior, and personal responsibility for actions. For example, laws pertaining to sexual deviancy have changed markedly in the past 45 years as research has shown that many sexual acts that were previously considered perversions are "normal" in the sense that most people engage in them.

Because psychology affects so many aspects of our lives, even people who do not intend to specialize in it need to know something about this dynamic field. An introductory course in psychology should give you a better understanding of why people think and act as they do, as well as provide insights into your own attitudes and reactions. It should also help you evaluate the many claims made in the name of psychology. Everyone has seen newspaper headlines like these:

■ New form of psychotherapy facilitates recovery of repressed memories

■ Anxiety controlled by self-regulation of brain waves

■ Proof of mental telepathy found

■ Hypnosis effective in the control of pain

■ Emotional stability closely related to family size

■ Homosexuality linked to parental attitudes

■ Transcendental meditation facilitates problem solving

■ Multiple personality linked to childhood abuse

There are two things you need to know to evaluate such claims. First, you need to know what psychological facts are already firmly established. If the new claim is not compatible with those facts, there is reason to be cautious. Second, you need to have the knowledge required to determine whether the arguments in support of the new claim meet the standards of scientific evidence; if they do not, again there is reason for skepticism. This book tries to meet both of these needs. First, it reviews the current state of knowledge in psychology—that is, it tries to present the most important findings in the field so that you know the established facts. Second, it examines the nature of research—that is, how a psychologist designs a

research program that can provide strong evidence for or against a hypothesis, so that you know the kind of evidence needed to back up a new claim.

In this chapter we begin by considering the kinds of topics that are studied in psychology. After a brief review of psychology's historical origins, we discuss the perspectives that psychologists adopt in investigating these topics. Then we describe the research methods used in psychological investigation, including the ethical guidelines that have been proposed for such research. We end with a description of some of the major subfields of psychology.

The Scope of Psychology

Psychology can be defined as *the scientific study of behavior and mental processes.* An astonishing variety of topics fits this definition, as can be seen in the brief examples presented here. (All of these topics will be discussed in more detail at various points in this book.)

Brain Damage and Face Recognition   It is no surprise that when people suffer brain damage, their behavior is affected. What is surprising is that when the damage is in a specific part of the brain, the person's behavior may change in one way while appearing normal in all other ways. In some such cases, for example, people are unable to recognize familiar faces as a result of damage to a particular region on the right side of their brain—yet they can do just about everything else normally. A famous example of this condition, termed "prosopagnosia," was described by neurologist Oliver Sacks (1985)* in his book *The Man Who Mistook His Wife for a Hat*. In another case, a person with prosopagnosia complained to a waiter that someone was staring at him, only to be informed that he was looking in a mirror! Such cases tell us a lot about the way the normal brain works.

---

*Throughout this book you will find references, cited by author and date, that document or expand the statements made here. Detailed publishing information on these studies appears in the reference list at the end of the book.

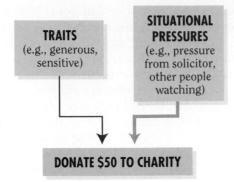

FIGURE 1-1

Trait Attribution. *In deciding whether a substantial donation to charity is caused by the giver's traits or by the situation, we are biased toward believing that a trait was the critical factor.*

They indicate that some psychological functions—like face recognition—are localized in particular parts of the brain.

Attributing Traits to People Suppose that in a crowded department store a person soliciting for a charity approaches a customer and implores her to make a contribution; the woman proceeds to write a $50

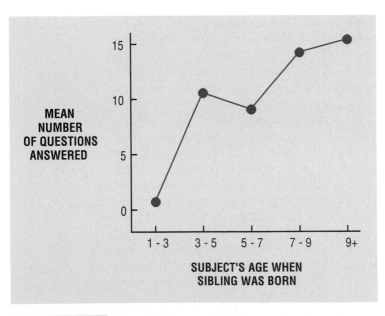

FIGURE 1-2

Recall of an Early Memory. *In an experiment on childhood amnesia, college-age participants were asked 20 questions about the events surrounding the birth of a younger sibling. The average number of questions answered is plotted as a function of the participant's age when the sibling was born. If the birth occurred before the participant's fourth year of life, no participant could recall a thing about it; if the birth occurred after that, recall increased with the participant's age at the time of the event. (After Sheingold & Tenney, 1982)*

check to the charity. Would you think the woman was generous? Or would you think she had been pressured into making the donation because so many people witnessed her action? Experiments designed to study situations like this one have shown that most people would consider the woman generous. We tend to see other people's actions as caused by their personal traits, not by the situations in which they find themselves—even though some situational pressures can be so great that they cause just about everybody to act in predictable ways (see Figure 1-1).

Childhood Amnesia Most adults can recall events from their early years, but only up to a certain point. Almost no one can accurately recall events from the first 3 years of life. Consider a significant event like the birth of a sibling. If the birth occurred after you were 3 years old, you may have some memory of it. But if the birth occurred before age 3, you probably would remember very little about it, if anything at all (see Figure 1-2). This phenomenon is called *childhood amnesia*. It is particularly striking because our first three years are so rich in experience: We develop from helpless newborns to crawling, babbling infants to walking, talking children. But these remarkable transitions leave little trace in our memory.

Obesity Roughly 35 million Americans are obese—that is, their weight is 30% or more above the level that would be appropriate for their body structure and height. Obesity is dangerous—it increases vulnerability to diabetes, high blood pressure, and heart disease. Psychologists are interested in what factors lead people to eat too much. One factor seems to be a history of deprivation. If rats are first deprived of food, then allowed to eat until they return to their normal weight, and finally allowed to eat as much as they want, they eat more than rats that have no history of deprivation.

Effects of Media Violence on Children's Aggression The question of whether watching violence on television causes children to be more aggressive has long been controversial. Although many observers believe that televised violence affects children's behavior, others have suggested that watching violence might have a *cathartic* effect—that is, it

Psychologists are interested in what causes people to eat too much. Among the possible causes they have studied are genetic factors and environmental influences such as a tendency to overeat in the presence of certain stimuli.

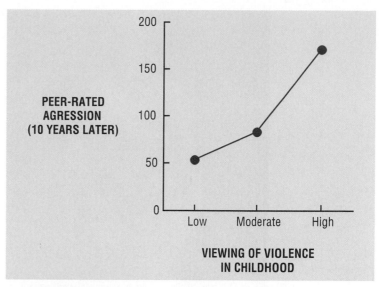

FIGURE 1-3

The Relationship Between Childhood Viewing of Violent Television and Adult Aggression.   *A classic study shows that preference for viewing violent TV programs by boys at age 9 is related to aggressive behavior as rated by peers at age 19. (After Eron, Huesmann, Lefkowitz, & Walder, 1972)*

might actually reduce aggression by allowing children to express it vicariously, thereby "getting it out of their system." But research evidence does not support this view. In one experiment, one group of children watched violent cartoons while another group watched nonviolent cartoons for the same amount of time. The children who watched violent cartoons became more aggressive in their interactions with peers, whereas the children who viewed nonviolent cartoons showed no change in aggressive behavior. These effects can persist over time: The more violent programs a boy watches at age 9, the more aggressive he is likely to be at age 19 (see Figure 1-3).

The Historical Origins of Psychology

The roots of psychology can be traced to the great philosophers of ancient Greece. The most famous of them, Socrates, Plato, and Aristotle, posed fundamental questions about mental life: What is consciousness? Are people inherently rational or irrational? Is there really such a thing as free choice? These questions, and many similar ones, are as important today as they were two thousand years ago. They deal with the nature of the mind and mental processes, and as we will see in the next section, they are key elements of the cognitive perspective in psychology.

Other psychological questions deal with the nature of the body and human behavior, and they have an equally long history. Hippocrates, often called the "father of medicine," lived around the same time as Socrates. He was deeply interested in **physiology,** *the study of the functions of the living organism and its parts.* He made many

Psychological studies provide evidence that violent television programming may have harmful effects on young viewers.

The ancient Greek philosopher Socrates posed fundamental questions about mental life. Many of these questions are as important today as they were in Socrates's time.

important observations about how the brain controls various organs of the body. These observations set the stage for what became the biological perspective in psychology.

Nativism Versus Empiricism

One of the earliest debates about human psychology is still raging today. It centers on the question of whether human capabilities are inborn or acquired through experience. The *nativist* view holds that human beings enter the world with an inborn store of knowledge and understanding of reality. Early philosophers believed that this knowledge and understanding could be accessed through careful reasoning and introspection. In the 17th century, Descartes supported the nativist view by arguing that some ideas (such as God, the self, geometric axioms, perfection, and infinity) are innate. Descartes is also notable for his conception of the body as a machine that can be studied much as other machines are studied. This is the root of modern *information-processing* perspectives on the mind, discussed later in the chapter.

The *empiricist* view holds that knowledge is acquired through experiences and interactions with the world. Although some of the early Greek philosophers held this view, it is most strongly associated with the 17th-century English philosopher John Locke. According to Locke, at birth the human mind is a *tabula rasa,* or blank slate, on which experience "writes" knowledge and understanding as the individual matures. This perspective gave birth to *associationist psychology.* Associationists denied that there were inborn ideas or capabilities. Instead, they argued that the mind is filled with ideas that enter by way of the senses and then become associated with one another through such principles as similarity and contrast. Current research on memory and learning is related to early association theory.

These days, the debate between nativism and empiricism is referred to as the *nature-nurture* debate. Although some psychologists would still argue that human thought and behavior is the result primarily of biology or primarily of experience, most psychologists take a more integrated approach, acknowledging that biological processes (such as heredity or processes in the brain) affect thoughts, feelings, and behavior, but that experience leaves its mark on these as well. We will encounter the nature-nurture issue at numerous points in later chapters.

The Beginnings of Scientific Psychology

Although philosophers and scholars continued to be interested in the functioning of both the mind and the body through the centuries, scientific psychology is usually considered to have begun in 1879, when Wilhelm Wundt established the first psychological laboratory at the University of Leipzig in Germany. The impetus for the establishment of Wundt's lab was the belief that mind and behavior, like planets or chemicals or human organs, could be the subject of scientific analysis. Wundt's own research was concerned primarily with the senses, especially vision, but he and his co-workers also studied attention, emotion, and memory.

Wundt relied on introspection as a method of studying mental processes. **Introspection** refers to *the observation and recording of the* nature of one's own perceptions, thoughts, and feelings—for example, reflections on one's immediate sensory impressions of a stimulus such as the flash of a colored light. The introspective method was inherited from philosophy, but Wundt added a new dimension to the concept. Pure self-observation was not sufficient; it had to be supplemented by experiments. Wundt's experiments systematically varied some physical dimension of a stimulus, such as its intensity, and used the introspective method to determine how these physical changes modified the participant's conscious experience of the stimulus.

The reliance on introspection, particularly for very rapid mental events, proved unworkable. Even after extensive training in introspection, different people produced very different introspections about simple sensory experiences, and few conclusions could be drawn from these differences. As a result, introspection is not a central part of the current cognitive perspective. And as we will see, some psychologists' reactions to introspection played a role in the development of other modern perspectives.

Structuralism and Functionalism

During the 19th century chemistry and physics made great advances by analyzing complex compounds (molecules) into their elements (atoms). These successes encouraged psychologists to look for the mental elements that combined to create more complex experiences. Just as chemists analyzed water into hydrogen and oxygen, perhaps psychologists could analyze the taste of lemonade (perception) into elements such as sweet, bitter, and cold (sensations).The leading proponent of this approach in the United States was E. B. Titchener, a Cornell University psychologist who had been trained by Wundt. Titchener introduced the term **structuralism**—meaning *the analysis of mental structures*—to describe this branch of psychology.

But some psychologists opposed the purely analytic nature of structuralism. William James, a distinguished psychologist at Harvard University, felt that less emphasis should be placed on analyzing the elements of consciousness and more on understanding its fluid, personal nature. His approach

Archives of the History of American Psychology, The University of Akron.

Wilhelm Wundt established the first psychological laboratory at the University of Leipzig. Here he is shown in the laboratory with his associates.

was named **functionalism,** which refers to *studying how the mind works so that an organism can adapt to and function in its environment.*

Nineteenth-century psychologists' interest in adaptation stemmed from the publication of Charles Darwin's theory of evolution. It was argued that consciousness had evolved only because it served some purpose in guiding the individual's activities. To find out how an organism adapts to its environment, functionalists argued that it was necessary to observe actual behavior. Thus, functionalism broadened the scope of psychology to include behavior as an object of study. But both structuralists and functionalists still regarded psychology as the science of conscious experience.

Behaviorism

Structuralism and functionalism played important roles in the early development of psychology. Because each viewpoint provided a systematic approach to the field, they were considered competing *schools of psychology.* By 1920, however, both were being displaced by three newer schools: behaviorism, Gestalt psychology, and psychoanalysis.

Of the three new schools, behaviorism had the greatest influence on scientific psychology in North America. Its founder, John B. Watson, reacted against the view that conscious experience was the province of psychology. Watson made no assertions about consciousness when he studied the behavior of animals and infants. He decided not only that animal psychology and child psychology could stand on their own as sciences, but also that they set a pattern that adult psychology might follow.

For psychology to be a science, Watson believed, psychological data must be open to public inspection like the data of any other science. Behavior is public; consciousness is private. Science should deal only with public facts. Because psychologists were growing impatient with introspection, the new behaviorism caught on rapidly; many younger psychologists in the United States called themselves "behaviorists." (The Russian physiologist Ivan Pavlov's research on the conditioned response was regarded as an important area of behavioral research, but it was Watson who was responsible for behaviorism's widespread influence.)

Watson argued that nearly all behavior is a result of conditioning and that the environment shapes behavior by reinforcing specific habits. For example, giving a child a cookie to stop him or her from whining will reinforce (reward) the habit of whining. The conditioned response was viewed as the smallest unit of behavior, from which more complicated behaviors could be created. All types of complex behavior patterns arising from special training or education were regarded as nothing more than an interlinked fabric of conditioned responses.

Behaviorists tended to discuss psychological phenomena in terms of stimuli and responses, giving rise to the term *stimulus-response (S-R) psychology*. Note, however, that S-R psychology itself is not a theory or perspective but a set of terms that can be used to communicate psychological information. S-R terminology is often used in psychology today.

Gestalt Psychology

Around 1912, at about the same time that behaviorism was catching on in America, Gestalt psychology was appearing in Germany. *Gestalt* is a German word meaning "form" or "configuration," and it was used to refer to the approach favored by Max Wertheimer and his colleagues Kurt Koffka and Wolfgang Köhler, all of whom immigrated to the United States.

The Gestalt psychologists were interested primarily in perception, and they believed that perceptual experiences depend on the

William James, John B. Watson, and Sigmund Freud were key figures in the early history of psychology. James developed the approach known as functionalism, while Watson was the founder of behaviorism and Freud originated the theory and method of psychoanalysis.

patterns formed by stimuli and on the *organization* of experience. What we actually see is related to the background against which an object appears, as well as to other aspects of the overall pattern of stimulation (see Chapter 5). Thus, the whole is different from the sum of its parts, since the whole depends on the relationships among the parts. For example, when we look at Figure 1-4 we see it as a single large triangle—as a single form or Gestalt—rather than as three small angles.

The Gestalt psychologists were interested in the perception of motion, in how people judge size, and in the appearance of colors under changes in illumination. These interests led them to a number of perception-centered interpretations of learning, memory, and problem solving that helped lay the groundwork for current research in cognitive psychology.

Psychoanalysis

Psychoanalysis is both a theory of personality and a method of psychotherapy. It originated with Sigmund Freud around the turn of the 20th century.

At the center of Freud's theory is the concept of the **unconscious**—that is, *the thoughts, attitudes, impulses, wishes, motivations, and emotions of which we are unaware.* Freud believed that the unacceptable (i.e., forbidden or punished) wishes of childhood are driven out of conscious awareness and become part of the unconscious, where they continue to influence our thoughts, feelings, and actions. Unconscious thoughts are expressed in various ways, including dreams, slips of the tongue, and physical mannerisms. During therapy with patients Freud used the method of *free association,* in which the patient is instructed to say whatever comes to mind as a way of bringing unconscious wishes into awareness. The analysis of dreams serves the same purpose.

In classical Freudian theory the motivations behind unconscious wishes almost always involved sex or aggression. It is for this reason that Freud's theory was not widely accepted when it was first proposed. But while most contemporary psychologists do not completely accept Freud's view of the unconscious, they tend to agree that individuals are not fully aware of some important aspects of their behavior.

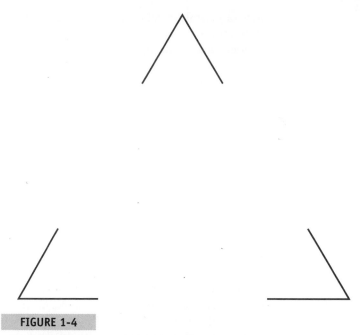

FIGURE 1-4

A Gestalt Image. *When we look at the three angles of an equilateral triangle, we see a single large triangle rather than three small angles.*

Modern Developments

Despite the important contributions of Gestalt psychology and psychoanalysis, until World War II psychology was dominated by behaviorism, particularly in the United States. After the war interest in psychology increased. Sophisticated instruments and electronic equipment became available, and a wider range of problems could be examined. It became evident that earlier theoretical approaches were too restrictive.

This viewpoint was strengthened by the development of computers in the 1950s. Computers were able to perform tasks—such as playing chess and proving mathematical theorems—that previously could be done only by human beings. They offered psychologists a powerful tool for theorizing about psychological processes. In a series of papers published in the late 1950s, Herbert Simon (who was later awarded a Nobel prize) and his colleagues described how psychological phenomena could be *simulated* using the computer. Many psychological issues were recast in terms of *information-processing systems.* The notion of the human being as a processor of information provided a more dynamic approach to psychology than S-R theory. Similarly, the information-processing approach made it possible to formulate some of the ideas of Gestalt psychology and psychoanalysis in a more precise fashion. In this way, earlier ideas about the nature of the mind could be expressed in concrete terms and checked against actual data. For example, we can think of the operation of memory as analogous to the way a computer stores and retrieves information. Just as a computer can transfer information from temporary storage in its internal memory chips (RAM) to more permanent storage on the hard disk, so, too, our short-term memory can act as a way-station to long-term memory (Atkinson & Shiffrin, 1971; Raaijmakers & Shiffrin, 1992).

Another important influence on psychology in the 1950s was the development of modern linguistics. Linguists began to theorize about the mental structures required to comprehend and speak a language. A pioneer in this area was Noam Chomsky, whose book *Syntactic Structures,* published in 1957, stimulated the first significant psychological analyses of language and the emergence of the field of psycholinguistics.

At the same time, important advances were occurring in neuropsychology. Various discoveries about the brain and the nervous system revealed clear relationships between neurological events and mental processes. In recent decades, with the aid of advances in biomedical technology, rapid progress has been made in research on these relationships. In 1981 Roger Sperry was awarded a Nobel prize for his work demonstrating the links between specific regions of the brain and particular thought and behavioral processes, which we discuss in Chapter 2.

The development of information-processing models, psycholinguistics, and neuropsychology has produced an approach to psychology that is highly cognitive in orientation. But while its principal concern is the scientific analysis of mental processes and structures, cognitive psychology is not exclusively concerned with thought and knowledge. As we will see throughout this book, this approach has been expanded to many other areas of psychology, including motivation, perception, personality, and social psychology.

In sum, during this century the focus of psychology has come full circle. After rejecting conscious experience as ill-suited to scientific investigation and turning to the study of overt, observable behavior, psychologists are once again theorizing about covert aspects of the mind, but this time with new and more powerful tools.

Contemporary Psychological Perspectives

Now that we have explored the historical background of psychology, let us examine some of the discipline's major contemporary perspectives. What is a perspective? Basically, it is an approach, a way of looking at a topic. Any topic in psychology can be approached from a variety of perspectives. Indeed, this is true of any action a person takes. Suppose you walk across the street. From a biological perspective, this act can be described as involving the firing of the nerves that activate the muscles that move your legs. From a behavioral perspective, the act can be described without reference to anything within your body; rather, the green light is a stimulus to which you respond by crossing the street. One may also take a cognitive perspective of crossing the street, focusing on the mental processes involved in producing the behavior. From a cognitive perspective, your action might be explained in terms of your goals and plans: Your goal is to visit a friend, and crossing the street is part of your plan for achieving that goal.

Although there are many possible ways to describe any psychological act, the five perspectives described in this section represent the major approaches to the modern study of psychology (see Figure 1-5). Because these five perspectives are discussed throughout the book, here we provide only a brief description of some main points for each of them. Also keep in mind that these approaches need not be mutually exclusive; rather, they may focus on different aspects of the same complex phenomenon.

The Biological Perspective

The human brain contains well over 10 billion nerve cells and an almost infinite number of interconnections between them. It may well be the most complex structure in the universe. In principle, all psychological events can be related to the activity of the

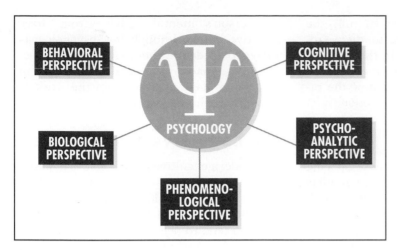

FIGURE 1-5

Perspectives in Psychology.
The analysis of psychological phenomena can be approached from several perspectives. Each offers a somewhat different account of why individuals act as they do, and each can make a contribution to our conception of the total person. The Greek letter psy, Ψ, is sometimes used as an abbreviation for "psychology."

brain and nervous system. The biological approach to the study of human beings and other species attempts to relate overt behavior to electrical and chemical events taking place inside the body. Thus, research from this perspective seeks to specify the neurobiological processes that underlie behavior and mental processes. The biological approach to depression, for example, seeks to understand this disorder in terms of abnormal changes in levels of neurotransmitters, which are chemicals produced in the brain that make communication between nerve cells possible.

We can use one of the problems described earlier to illustrate this perspective. The study of face recognition in patients with brain damage indicates that particular regions of the brain are specialized for face recognition. The human brain is divided into right and left hemispheres, and the regions devoted to face recognition seem to be located mainly in the right hemisphere. It turns out that there is considerable hemispheric specialization in humans; for example, in most right-handed people the left hemisphere is specialized for understanding language and the right hemisphere is specialized for interpreting spatial relations. The biological perspective has also assisted in the study of memory. It emphasizes the importance of certain brain structures, including the hippocampus, which is involved in consolidating memories. Childhood amnesia may be partly due to an immature hippocampus, since this structure is not fully developed until a year or two after birth.

The Behavioral Perspective

As described in our brief review of the history of psychology, the behavioral perspective focuses on observable stimuli and responses. For example, an S-R analysis of your social life might focus on which people you interact

By studying the brain activity of animals, researchers gain insight into the human brain. In this single-cell recording experiment, a microelectrode, which monitors the electrical activity of a single neuron, is implanted in the visual system of a monkey.

with (these would be the social stimuli), the kinds of responses you make to them (rewarding, punishing, or neutral), the kinds of responses they in turn make to you (rewarding, punishing, or neutral), and how the rewards sustain or disrupt the interaction.

We can use our sample problems to further illustrate this approach. With regard to obesity, some people may overeat (a specific response) only in the presence of specific stimuli, and learning to avoid these stimuli is part of many weight-control programs. With regard to aggression, children are more likely to express aggressive responses, such as hitting another child, when such responses are rewarded (the other child withdraws) than when their responses are punished (the other child counterattacks).

Historically, the strict behavioral approach did not consider the individual's mental processes at all, and even contemporary behaviorists usually do not conjecture about the mental processes that intervene between the stimulus and the response. Nevertheless, psychologists other than strict behaviorists will often record what a person says about his or her conscious experiences (a verbal report), and draw inferences about

the person's mental activity from these objective data. Although few psychologists today would define themselves as strict behaviorists, many modern developments in psychology have evolved from the work of the earlier behaviorists (Skinner, 1981).

The Cognitive Perspective

The modern cognitive perspective is in part a return to the cognitive roots of psychology and in part a reaction to the narrowness of behaviorism and the S-R view (both of which tend to neglect complex human activities like reasoning, planning, decision making, and communication). Like the 19th-century version, the modern study of cognition is concerned with mental processes such as perceiving, remembering, reasoning, deciding, and problem solving. Unlike the 19th-century version, however, modern cognitivism is not based on introspection. Instead, it assumes that (1) only by studying mental processes can we fully understand what organisms do, and (2) we can study mental processes in an objective fashion by focusing on specific behaviors (just as behaviorists do) but interpreting them in terms of

If the aggressive child has her way and the other child yields the swing, the aggressive behavior will be rewarded and the child will be more likely to behave aggressively in the future.

Events that happen early in childhood usually are not remembered. This little girl probably will not remember the events surrounding the birth of her baby brother.

underlying mental processes. In making these interpretations, cognitive psychologists often rely on an analogy between the mind and a computer. Incoming information is processed in various ways: It is selected, compared and combined with other information already in memory, transformed, rearranged, and so on. Consider the phenomenon of childhood amnesia described at the beginning of the chapter. Perhaps we cannot remember events from the first few years of life because of a major developmental change in the way we organize our experience in memory. Such changes may be particularly pronounced around age 3 because at that point there is a major increase in our language abilities, and language offers us a new way of organizing our memories.

The Psychoanalytic Perspective

As mentioned earlier, the psychoanalytic conception of human behavior was developed by Sigmund Freud in Europe at about the same time behaviorism was evolving in the United States. In some respects psychoanalysis was a blend of the 19th-century versions of cognition and physiology. In particular, Freud combined cognitive notions of consciousness, perception, and memory with ideas about biologically based instincts to forge a bold new theory of human behavior.

The basic assumption of Freud's theory is that much of our behavior stems from unconscious processes, meaning beliefs, fears, and desires that a person is unaware of but that nonetheless influence his or her behavior. Freud believed that many of the impulses that are forbidden or punished by parents and society during childhood are derived from innate instincts. Because each of us is born with these impulses, they exert a pervasive influence that must be dealt with in some manner. Forbidding them merely forces them out of awareness into the unconscious. They do not disappear, however; they may manifest themselves as emotional problems, symptoms of mental illness, or, on the other hand, socially approved behavior such as artistic and literary activity. For example, if you feel a lot of anger toward a person whom you cannot afford to alienate, your anger may become

unconscious, perhaps being expressed in a dream about that person.

Freud believed that we are driven by the same basic instincts as animals (primarily sex and aggression) and that we are continually struggling against a society that stresses the control of these impulses. Thus, the psychoanalytic perspective suggests new ways of looking at some of the problems described at the beginning of the chapter. For example, Freud claimed that aggressive behavior stems from an innate instinct. While this proposal is not widely accepted in human psychology, it is in agreement with the views of some biologists and psychologists who study aggression in animals.

The Phenomenological Perspective

The phenomenological approach has traditionally been associated with social psychologists, who are particularly interested in how we perceive, understand, and interpret our social worlds. Within the domain of personality psychology, this approach is favored by *humanistic* psychologists. Humanistic psychologists reject the assumptions about human nature made by the psychoanalytic and behavioral approaches. Instead, they emphasize the unique human qualities that distinguish healthy people from both disturbed patients and animals. For example, according to humanistic theories an individual's principal motivational force is a tendency toward growth and self-actualization. All of us have a basic need to develop our potential to the fullest, to progress beyond where we are now. Although we may be blocked by environmental and social obstacles, our natural tendency is toward actualizing our potential. For example, a woman in a traditional marriage who had been raising her children for 10 years may come to feel a strong desire to pursue an outside career, perhaps to develop a long-dormant interest in science that she feels the need to actualize.

Phenomenological or humanistic psychology has been more aligned with literature and the humanities than with science. For this reason, it is difficult to give detailed descriptions of what the phenomenological perspective would say about our sample problems, such as face recognition and childhood amnesia, because these are not the kinds of problems that phenomenologists study. Phenomenological and humanistic psychologists have contributed most to the study of personality, and we will discuss their approach more fully in Chapter 13.

Relationships Between Psychological and Biological Perspectives

The behaviorist, cognitive, psychoanalytic, and phenomenological perspectives all rely on concepts that are purely psychological (such as perception, the unconscious, and self-actualization). Although these perspectives sometimes offer different explanations for the same phenomenon, those explanations are always psychological in nature. The biological perspective is different. In addition to using psychological concepts, it employs concepts (such as neurotransmitters and hormones) drawn from physiology and other branches of biology.

There is a way, though, in which the biological perspective makes direct contact with the psychological perspectives. Biologically oriented researchers attempt to explain psychological concepts and principles in terms of their biological counterparts. For example, researchers might attempt to explain the normal ability to recognize faces solely in terms of neurons and their interconnections in a certain region of the brain. Such attempts are termed **reductionism** because they involve *reducing psychological notions to biological ones.* Throughout this book we will present examples in which reductionism has been successful; that is, situations in which what was once understood at only the psychological level is now understood at least in part at the biological level.

If reductionism can be successful, why bother with psychological explanations at all? To put it another way, is psychology just something to do until the biologists figure everything out? The answer is no.

First, psychological findings, concepts, and principles direct biological researchers in their work. Given that the brain contains billions of brain cells and countless interconnections between these cells, biological researchers cannot hope to find something of interest by arbitrarily selecting some brain cells to study. Rather, they must have a way of directing their search to relevant groups of brain cells. Psychological findings can supply this direction. For example, if psychological research indicates that our ability to discriminate among spoken words (that is, to tell when they differ) obeys different principles from our ability to discriminate among different spatial positions, biological psychologists might look in different regions of the brain for the neural basis of these two kinds of discrimination capacities (the left hemisphere for word discrimination and the right hemisphere for spatial-position discrimination). As another example, if psychological research indicates that learning a motor skill is a slow process that is hard to undo, biological psychologists can direct their attention to brain processes that are relatively slow but that permanently alter connections between neurons (Churchland & Sejnowski, 1988).

Second, our biology always acts in concert with our past circumstances and current environment. For example, obesity can be the result of both a genetic predisposition to gain weight (a biological factor) and the learning of bad eating habits (a psychological factor). The biologist can seek to understand the former, but it is still up to the psychologist to explore and explain the past experiences and current circumstances that influence a person's eating habits.

Nevertheless, the push for reductionism goes on at an ever-increasing rate. For many topics in psychology, we now have both psychological explanations and knowledge about how the relevant psychological concepts are implemented or executed in the brain (for example, what particular parts of the brain are involved and how they are interconnected). This kind of biological knowledge typically falls short of total reductionism, but it is still very important. Memory researchers, for example, have long distinguished between short-term memory and long-term memory (which are psychological notions), but now they also know something about how these two kinds of memory are actually coded differently in the brain. Hence, for many of the topics discussed in this book, we will review what is known at the biological level as well as at the psychological level.

Indeed, a central theme of this book, and of contemporary psychology in general, is that psychological phenomena can be understood at both the psychological and biological levels, where the biological analysis shows us how the psychological notions can be implemented in the brain. Both levels of analysis are clearly needed (although for some topics, including many dealing with social interactions, only psychological analyses have much to say).

How Psychological Research Is Done

Now that we have some idea of the topics studied by psychologists and the perspectives from which they may approach the study of those topics, we can consider the research strategies they use to investigate them. In general, doing research involves two steps: (1) generating a scientific hypothesis and (2) testing that hypothesis.

Generating Hypotheses

The first step in any research project is to generate a **hypothesis**—*a statement that can be tested*—about the topic of interest. If our concern is childhood amnesia, for example, we might generate the hypothesis that people can retrieve more memories of their early life if they are back in the same place where the incidents originally occurred. How does a researcher arrive at such a hypothesis? There is no single answer. A person who is an astute observer of naturally occurring situations may have an advantage in coming up with hypotheses. For example, you might have noticed that you can remember more about your high-school years when you are back home; this could generate the hypothesis just mentioned. It also helps to be very familiar with the relevant scientific literature—that is, previously published books and articles about the topic of interest.

The most important source of a scientific hypothesis, however, often is a scientific **theory,** *an interrelated set of propositions about a particular phenomenon.* For example, one theory of sexual motivation (discussed in Chapter 10) proposes that there is a genetic predisposition toward heterosexuality or homosexuality. This leads to the testable scientific hypothesis that pairs of identical twins—who have identical genes—should be more likely to have the same sexual orientation than pairs of fraternal twins, who share only about half their genes. A

competing theory emphasizes childhood events as the source of an individual's sexual orientation, and generates a competing set of hypotheses that can also be tested. As we will see throughout this book, the testing of hypotheses derived from competing theories is one of the most powerful ways of advancing scientific knowledge.

The term *scientific* means that the research methods used to collect the data are (a) unbiased, in that they do not favor one hypothesis over another; and (b) reliable, in that they allow other qualified people to repeat the observations and obtain the same results. The various methods to be considered in this section have these two characteristics. Although some of these methods are better suited to certain perspectives than others, each method can be used with each perspective. The major exception is that some phenomenological psychologists reject scientific methods entirely.

Psychologists sometimes join forces with scientists in other disciplines, especially biology, to study psychological phenomena. For a description of some of these interdisciplinary approaches, see the Frontiers of Psychological Research feature on pages 16–17.

Experiments

The most powerful scientific method is the experiment. The investigator carefully controls conditions—often in a laboratory—and takes measurements in order to discover relationships among variables (a **variable** is *something that can occur with different values*) (see Table 1-1). For example, an

---

TABLE 1-1

Terminology of Experimental Research

hypothesis: a statement that can be tested.

variable: something that can occur with different values.

independent variable: a variable that is independent of what the participant does.

dependent variable: a variable whose values ultimately depend on the value of the independent variable.

experimental group: a group in which the condition under study is present.

control group: a group in which the condition under study is absent.

measurement: a system for assigning numbers to variables.

FRONTIERS OF PSYCHOLOGICAL RESEARCH

Interdisciplinary Approaches

Increasingly, researchers in other disciplines are joining forces with psychologists to forge new approaches to the study of psychological phenomena. These approaches promise to be of great importance in the next few decades. Of particular interest are cognitive neuroscience, evolutionary psychology, cognitive science, and cultural psychology. Here we briefly describe each of these approaches, with examples of the kinds of research being done in each field.

Cognitive Neuroscience

Cognitive neuroscience focuses on cognitive processes, relying heavily on the methods and findings of neuroscience (the branch of biology that deals with the brain and nervous system). In essence, it attempts to discover how mental activities are executed in the brain. The key idea is that cognitive psychology provides hypotheses about specific cognitive capacities—such as recognizing faces—and neuroscience supplies proposals about how these specific functions might be executed in the brain.

What is particularly distinctive about cognitive neuroscience is its reliance on new techniques for studying the brains of normal participants (as opposed to brain-damaged ones) while they are performing a cognitive task. These neuroimaging or brain-scanning techniques create visual images of a brain in action, with an indication of which regions of the brain

show the most neural activity during a particular task. An example is studies of how people remember information for either brief or long periods. When people are asked to remember information for a few seconds, neuroimaging results show increases in neural activity in regions in the front of the brain; when they are asked to remember information for a long period, there is an increase in activity in an entirely different region, one closer to the middle of the brain. Thus, different mechanisms seem to be used for the short-term and long-term storage of information (Smith & Jonides, 1994; Squire et al., 1993).

Evolutionary Psychology

Evolutionary psychology is concerned with the biological origins of cognitive psychological mechanisms. In addition to psychology and biology, the other disciplines involved in this approach include anthropology and psychiatry. The key idea behind evolutionary psychology, is that, like biological mechanisms, psychological mechanisms must have evolved over millions of years through a process of natural selection. This implies that those mechanisms have a genetic basis and have proved useful in the past in increasing the organism's chances of surviving and reproducing. To illustrate, consider a liking for sweets. Such a preference can be thought of as a psychological mechanism, and it has a genetic

basis. Moreover, we have this preference because it increased our ancestors' chances of survival: The fruit that tasted the sweetest had the highest nutritional value, so by eating it they increased the chances of continued survival of the relevant genes (Symons, 1992).

There are a couple of ways in which adopting an evolutionary perspective can affect the study of psychological issues. For one thing, from an evolutionary perspective certain topics are of particular importance because of their link to survival or successful reproduction. Such topics include how we select our mates and how we handle our aggressive feelings (Buss, 1991). An evolutionary perspective can also provide some new insights into familiar topics. We can illustrate this point with the example of obesity. We noted earlier that a history of deprivation can lead to overeating in the future. Evolutionary psychology provides an interpretation of this puzzling phenomenon. Until comparatively recently in human history, people experienced deprivation only when food was scarce. An adaptive mechanism for dealing with scarcity is overeating when food is available. Hence, evolution may have favored individuals with a tendency to overeat following deprivation.

Cognitive Science

Cognitive science describes areas of psychological research that (a) are concerned with cognitive processes

experiment might seek to discover the relationship between the variables of memory and sleep (e.g., whether one's ability to recall childhood events decreases with lack of sleep). To the extent that memory changes systematically with sleep, an orderly relationship between these two variables has been

found to exist.

The ability to exercise precise control over a variable distinguishes the experimental method from other methods of scientific observation. For example, if the hypothesis being tested is that individuals will perform better on a mathematics problem if they are

like perceiving, reasoning, and problem solving; and (b) overlap with other disciplines that are interested in these processes, such as computer science. The field's major objectives are to discover how information is represented in the mind (mental representations) and what types of computations can be carried out on these representations to bring about perceiving, remembering, reasoning, and so on. In addition to psychology, the disciplines involved are anthropology, linguistics, philosophy, neuroscience, and artificial intelligence. (The latter is a branch of computer science that is concerned with developing computer programs that can simulate human thought processes.)

A central idea behind cognitive science is that the human cognitive system can be understood as though it were a giant computer engaged in a complex calculation. Just as a computer's complex calculation can be broken down into a set of simpler computations, such as storing, retrieving, and comparing symbols or representations, so a person's action can be broken down into a set of elementary mental components. Moreover, those components may involve storing, retrieving, and comparing symbols. There is a further parallel between a computer's calculations and mental computations. A computer's activity may be analyzed at different levels—including the level of hardware, with its empha-

sis on chips, and the level of representation-and-algorithm, with its emphasis on data structures and processes. Similarly, human cognitive activity may also be analyzed at the level of "hardware," or neurons, and the level of mental representations and processes. The ideas of mental computation and levels of analysis, then, are among the cornerstones of cognitive science (Osherson, 1990).

Cultural Psychology

Scientific psychology in the West has often assumed that people in all cultures have exactly the same psychological processes. Increasingly, this assumption is being challenged by proponents of cultural psychology, an interdisciplinary movement involving psychologists, anthropologists, sociologists, and other social scientists. Cultural psychology is concerned with how the culture in which an individual lives—its traditions, language, and worldview—influences that person's mental representations and psychological processes.

Here is an example. In the West—North America and much of Western and Northern Europe—we think of ourselves as separate and autonomous agents with unique abilities and traits. In contrast, many cultures in the East—including those of India, China, and Japan—emphasize the interrelationships among people rather than their individuality. Moreover, Easterners tend to pay more at-

tention to social situations than Westerners do. These differences lead Easterners to explain the behavior of another person differently than do Westerners. Rather than explaining a piece of behavior solely in terms of a person's traits, Easterners explain it in terms of the social situation in which it occurred. This has profound implications for trait attribution, one of the sample problems discussed at the beginning of the chapter. These differences between East and West in explaining behavior can also have educational implications. Because of their emphasis on collectivism rather than individualism, Asian students tend to study together more than American students. Such group study may be a useful technique, and it may be part of the reason why Asian students outperform their American counterparts in mathematics and some other subjects. In addition, when an American student is having difficulty in mathematics, both the student and the teacher tend to attribute the difficulty to the individual abilities of the student; when a comparable case arises in a Japanese school, student and teacher are more likely to look to the situation—the student-teacher interaction in the instructional context—for an explanation of the poor performance (Stevenson, Lee & Graham, 1993).

offered more money for a good performance, the experimenter might randomly assign participants to one of three conditions: One group is told that they will be paid $10 if they perform well; the second group is told that they will be paid $5 if they perform well; the third group is not offered any money for their

performance. The experimenter then measures and compares the actual performance of all three groups to see if, in fact, more money produces better performance.

In this study, the amount of money offered is called the **independent variable** because it is *a variable that is independent of what the* *participant does.* Performance on the task is called the **dependent variable** because it is *a variable that is hypothesized to depend on the value of the independent variable.* Thus, the independent variable is the variable that the experimenter manipulates, and the dependent variable is the variable that the experimenter observes. The dependent variable is almost always some measure of the participant's behavior. The phrase "is a function of" is used to express the dependence of one variable on another. For this experiment, we could say that the participants' performance on the tasks is a function of the amount of money they had been offered. The groups that are paid money are usually called the **experimental groups,** or *groups in which the condition under study is present.* The group that was not paid would be called the **control group,** or *the group in which the condition under study is absent.* In general, a control group serves as a baseline against which experimental groups can be compared.

One important feature of the experiment just described is random assignment of participants to conditions. If this is not done, the experimenter cannot be certain that something other than the independent variable might have produced the results. For example, an experimenter should never let participants choose which group they would like to be in. Although most participants might choose to be in the highest-paid group, those who are made nervous by pressure might choose to be in a "casual" group that was not paid. In any case, the problem is that the groups would now contain different kinds of people and the differences in their personalities, rather than the amount of money offered, might be the reason that one group does better than another. Or suppose that an experimenter runs all the paid groups first and runs the no-payment groups afterward. This introduces a host of potential problems. Perhaps performance varies as a function of the time of day (morning, afternoon, or evening); maybe those who participate later in the experiment are closer in time to their midterm exams than earlier participants. In addition to these uncontrolled variables, there may be many others of which the experimenter is unaware. All such problems are resolved by randomly assigning participants to conditions.

The experimental method can be used outside the laboratory as well. For example, in research on obesity it is possible to investigate the effects of different methods of weight control by trying these methods on separate

A researcher in a sleep laboratory monitors the brain activity of a sleeping woman.

but similar groups of obese individuals. The experimental method is a matter of logic, not location. Still, most experiments take place in laboratories, chiefly because in a laboratory setting it is possible to measure behavior more precisely and to control the variables more completely. And again, it is often random assignment that is at issue: If two obesity clinics use different methods and achieve different results, we cannot conclude with confidence that the different methods are responsible because the clinics might attract different kinds of people to their programs.

The experiments described so far examine the effect of one independent variable on one dependent variable. Limiting an investigation to only one independent variable, however, is too restrictive for some problems. *Multivariate experiments*—that is, studies involving the manipulation of several variables—are frequently used in psychological research. Thus, in the hypothetical study just described, in which participants were offered different amounts of money for solving math problems, the experimenter might also vary the level of difficulty of the problems. Now there would be six groups of participants, each combining one of three different amounts of money with one of two levels of difficulty (easy versus difficult).

Measurement Psychologists using the experimental method often find it necessary to make statements about amounts or quantities. Sometimes variables can be measured by physical means—for example, hours of sleep deprivation or dosage of a drug. At other times variables have to be scaled in a manner that places them in some sort of order. In rating a patient's feelings of aggression, for example, a psychotherapist might use a five-point scale ranging from "never" through "rarely," "sometimes," "often," and "always." Thus, for purposes of precise communication, experiments require some form of **measurement,** *a system for assigning numbers to variables.*

Experiments usually involve making measurements on many participants, not just one. The results therefore consist of data in the form of a set of numbers that can be summarized and interpreted. To accomplish this task, one needs to use **statistics,** *the discipline that deals with sampling data from a population of individuals and then drawing infer-*

ences about the population from those data. Statistics plays an important role not only in experimental research but in other methods as well.* The most common statistic is the **mean,** which is simply *the technical term for an arithmetic average.* It is the sum of a set of scores divided by the number of scores in the set. In studies involving experimental and control groups, there are two means to be compared: a mean for the scores of the participants in the experimental group and a mean for the scores of the participants in the control group. The difference between these two means is, of course, what the experimenters are interested in. If the difference between the means is large, it can be accepted at face value. But what if the difference is small? What if the measures used are subject to error? What if a few extreme cases are producing the difference? Statisticians have solved these problems by developing tests for determining the significance of a difference. A psychologist who says that the difference between the experimental group and the control group is "statistically significant" means that a statistical test has been applied to the data and that the observed difference is unlikely to have arisen by chance or because there were a few extreme cases.

Correlation

Not all problems can be easily studied using the experimental method. There are many situations in which the investigator has no control over which participants go in which conditions. For example, if we want to test the hypothesis that anorexic people are more sensitive to changes in taste than normal-weight people, we cannot select a group of normal-weight participants and require half of them to become anorexic! Rather, we select people who are already anorexic or already of normal weight and see if they also differ in taste sensitivity. More generally, we can make use of the correlational method to determine whether some variable that is not under our control is associated, or correlated, with another variable of interest.

In the example just given, there were only two values of the weight variable—

*This discussion is designed to introduce the problems of measurement and statistics. A more thorough discussion is provided in Appendix I.

anorexic and normal. It is more common to have many values of each variable and to determine the degree to which values on one variable are related to values on another. This is done by using a descriptive statistic called the **correlation coefficient,** *an estimate of the degree to which two variables are related.* The correlation coefficient, symbolized by *r,* is expressed as a number between −1 and 1. A perfect relationship is indicated by 1 (+1 if the relationship is positive and −1 if the relationship is negative); if there is no relationship at all, this is indicated by 0. As *r* goes from 0 to 1 (or from 0 to −1), the strength of the relationship increases.

A correlation can be either + or −. The sign of the correlation indicates whether the two variables are positively correlated (the values of the two variables either increase together or decrease together) or negatively correlated (as the value of one variable increases, the value of the other decreases). For example, suppose that the number of times a student is absent from class correlates −.40 with the final course grade (the more absences, the lower the grade). On the other hand, the correlation between the number of classes attended and the course grade would be +.40. The strength of the relationship is the same, but the sign indicates whether we are looking at classes missed or classes attended.*

To get a clearer picture of a correlation coefficient, consider the hypothetical study presented in Figure 1-6. As shown in Figure 1-6a, the study involves patients with brain damage leading to problems in face recognition (prosopagnosia). What is of interest is whether the degree of deficit, or error, in face recognition increases with the amount of brain tissue that is damaged. Each point on the graph in Figure 1-6a represents the percentage of errors made by one patient on a test of face recognition. For example, a patient who had only 10% brain damage made 15% errors on the face-recognition test, but a patient who had 55% brain damage made 95% errors. If errors in face recognition *always* increased along with amount of brain damage, the points in the graph would consistently increase in moving from left to right; if the

points had all fallen on the diagonal line in the figure, the correlation would have been *r* = 1.0—a perfect correlation. A couple of points fall on either side of the line, though, so the correlation is about .90. Such a high correlation indicates that there is a very strong relationship between amount of the brain damage and errors in face recognition. In Figure 1-6a, the correlation is positive because more errors are associated with more brain damage.

If, instead of focusing on errors, we plot the percentage of correct responses on the face recognition test, we end up with the diagram in Figure 1-6b. Now the correlation is negative—about −.90—because *fewer* correct responses are associated with *more* brain damage. The diagonal line in Figure 1-6b is simply the inverse of the one in Figure 1-6a.

Finally, consider the diagram in Figure 1-6c. Here we have graphed errors on the face-recognition test as a function of the patients' height. Of course, there is no reason to expect a relationship between height and face recognition, and the graph shows that there is none. The points neither consistently increase nor consistently decrease in moving from left to right, but rather bounce around a horizontal line. The correlation is 0.

In psychological research, a correlation coefficient of .60 or more is considered to be quite high. Correlations in the range from .20 to .60 are of practical and theoretical value and are useful in making predictions. Correlations between 0 and .20 must be judged with caution and are only minimally useful in making predictions.

Tests   The familiar use of the correlational method involves tests that measure aptitudes, achievement, or other psychological traits. A test presents a uniform situation to a group of people who vary in a particular trait (such as mathematical ability, manual dexterity, or aggression). The variation in scores on the test can be correlated with variations on another variable. For example, people's scores on a test of mathematical ability can be correlated with their subsequent grades in a college math course; if the correlation is high, then the test score may be used to determine which of a new group of students should be placed in advanced sections of the course.

Correlation and Causation   There is an important distinction between experimental

*The numerical method for calculating a correlation coefficient is described in Appendix I.

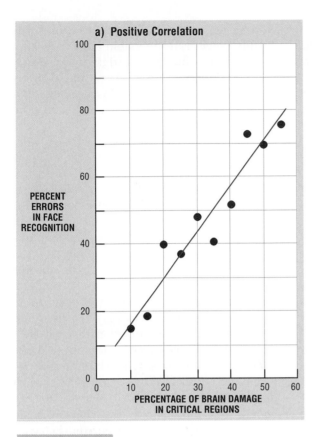

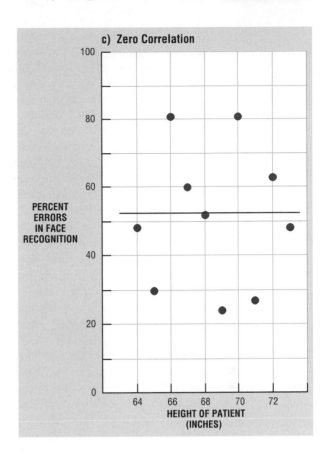

FIGURE 1-6

Scatter Diagrams Illustrating Correlations. *These hypothesized data are based on 10 patients, all of whom have some damage in regions of the brain known to be involved in face recognition. In Figure 1-6a the patients are ordered along the horizontal axis with respect to the amount of brain damage, with the patient represented by the leftmost point having the least brain damage (10%) and the patient represented by the rightmost point having the most brain damage (55%). Each point on the graph represents a single patient's score on a test of face recognition. The correlation is a positive .90. In Figure 1-6b the same data are depicted, but we now focus on the percentage of correct responses (rather than errors). Now the correlation is a negative .90. In Figure 1-6c the patients' performance on the face recognition test is graphed as a function of their height. Now the correlation is 0.*

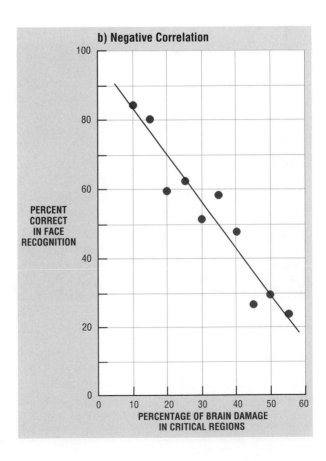

and correlational studies. In a typical experimental study, one variable (the independent variable) is systematically manipulated in order to determine its *causal* effect on some other variable (the dependent variable). Such cause-and-effect relationships cannot be inferred from correlational studies. This point can be illustrated with a couple of examples. Studies have shown that the more TV violence a young boy watches, the more aggressive he is. But does watching violent TV cause the aggression or do more aggressive boys choose to watch more violent TV? If all we have is a correlation, we cannot say which variable is cause and which is effect. (As noted earlier in the chapter, however, other studies do demonstrate a causal relationship between watching violent TV and behaving aggressively. Note that they are able to do this because they used random assignment of participants to conditions.)

It is also possible for two variables to be correlated when neither is the cause of the other. For example, many years before careful medical studies demonstrated that cigarette smoking actually causes cancer, it was known that there was a correlation between smoking and lung cancer. That is, it was already known that people who smoked were more likely to contract cancer. But—as the tobacco companies rushed to point out—this left open the possibility that some third cause was responsible. For example, if people who live in smoggy urban areas are more likely to smoke than people who live in rural areas with cleaner air, it could be air pollu-

tion rather than smoking that causes the higher cancer rates in smokers.

In short, when two variables are correlated, variation in one of them may possibly be the cause of variation in the other, but without further experiments no such conclusion is justified.

Observation

Direct Observation   In the early stages of research, the most efficient way of making progress toward an explanation may be to simply observe the phenomenon under study as it occurs naturally. Careful observation of animal and human behavior is the starting point for a great deal of research in psychology. For example, observation of primates in their native environment may tell us things about their social organization that will help in later laboratory investigations (see Figure 1-7). Motion pictures of newborn babies reveal details of their activity shortly after birth and the types of stimuli to which they respond. It is important to note that investigators observing naturally occurring behavior must be trained to observe and record events accurately in order to avoid letting their own biases influence what they report.

Observational methods may be used in a laboratory if the problem being studied is partly a biological one. For example, in their classic study of the physiological aspects of human sexuality, William Masters and Virginia Johnson (1966) developed techniques for directly observing sexual responses in the laboratory. The data included (a) observations of behavior, (b) recordings of physiological changes, and (c) responses to questions about the participant's sensations before, during, and after sexual stimulation. While the researchers agreed that human sexuality has many dimensions besides the biological one, their observations of the anatomical and physiological aspects of sexual response have been very helpful in understanding the nature of human sexuality, as well as in solving sexual problems.

FIGURE 1-7

Baboons Observed in Their Natural Habitat. *Field studies can often tell us more about social behavior than experimental studies. Professor Shirley Strum has observed the same troop of baboons in Kenya for more than 20 years, identifying individual animals and making daily recordings of their behaviors and social interactions. Her data have provided remarkable information about the mental abilities of baboons and the role of friendships in their social system.*

The Survey Method   Some problems that are difficult to study by direct observation may be studied by indirect observation through the use of questionnaires or interviews. That is, rather than observe people engaging in a particular behavior, such as exercising regularly, researchers simply ask them if they engage in

Survey researchers ask individuals or, as in this case, couples about their attitudes and behavior. For survey results to be valid, the respondents must be representative of the larger population being studied.

that behavior. Since people may be trying to present themselves in a favorable light (for example, by saying that they exercise more than they actually do), this method is more open to bias than direct observation. Still, the survey method has produced many important results. For example, before Masters and Johnson conducted their research on human sexual response, most of the available information on how people behave sexually (as opposed to how laws, religion, or society said they should behave) came from extensive surveys conducted by Alfred Kinsey and his associates 20 years earlier. Information from thousands of interviews was analyzed, resulting in the publication of two pioneering works: *Sexual Behavior in the Human Male* (Kinsey, Pomeroy, & Martin, 1948) and *Sexual Behavior in the Human Female* (Kinsey, Pomeroy, Martin, & Gebhard, 1953).

Surveys have also been used to discover people's political opinions, product preferences, healthcare needs, and so on. The Gallup poll and the U.S. census are probably the most familiar surveys. An adequate survey requires that a carefully pretested questionnaire be presented to a sample of people who have been selected by methods designed to ensure that they are representative of the larger population being studied.

Case Histories   Still another form in indirect observation is to obtain a partial biography of a particular individual. This involves asking people to recall relevant experiences from their past. For example, if the research is con-

cerned with the childhood antecedents of adult depression, the researcher might begin by asking questions about earlier life events. These **case histories** are *biographies designed for scientific use,* and they are important sources of data for psychologists studying individuals.

A major limitation of case histories is that they rely on the person's memories and reconstructions of earlier events, which are frequently distorted or incomplete. Sometimes other data can be used to corroborate information obtained in a case history. For example, written records, such as death certificates, can be used to check on specific dates, or relatives of the person being interviewed can be asked to report their own memories of the relevant events. Even so, their limitations make case histories less useful for testing a theory or proving a hypothesis than for suggesting hypotheses that can then be tested in more rigorous ways or checked with a larger sample of participants. In this way, scientists use the case history in much the same way that a therapist or physician might when trying to formulate a diagnosis and treatment of a particular individual.

Ethics of Psychological Research

Because psychologists study living beings, they need to be sensitive to ethical issues that can arise in the conduct of research. Accordingly, the American Psychological Association (APA) and its counterparts in Canada and Great Britain have established guidelines for the treatment of both human participants and animal subjects (American Psychological Association, 1990). In the United States, federal regulations require any institution that conducts federally funded research to establish an internal review board, which reviews proposed studies to ensure that participants will be treated properly.

The first principle governing the ethical treatment of human participants is **minimal risk.** The federal guideline specifies that, in most cases, *the risks anticipated in the research should be no greater than those ordinarily encountered in daily life.* Obviously, a person should not be exposed to physical harm or injury, but deciding how much psychological stress is ethically justified in a research project is not always so clear-cut.

In everyday life, of course, people may be impolite, lie, or make other people anxious. Under what circumstances is it ethically justifiable for a researcher to treat a participant in such ways in order to meet the goals of a research project? These are the kinds of questions that the review boards consider on a case-by-case basis.

The second principle governing the ethical treatment of human participants is **informed consent**, meaning that *participants must enter a study voluntarily and be permitted to withdraw from it at any time without penalty if they so desire.* They must also be told ahead of time about any aspects of the study that could be expected to influence their willingness to cooperate. Like the principle of minimal risk, informed consent is not always easy to implement. In particular, informed consent is sometimes at odds with another common requirement of research: that participants be unaware of the hypotheses being tested in a study. If a researcher plans to compare participants who learn lists of familiar words with participants who learn lists of unfamiliar words, no ethical problem arises by simply telling participants ahead of time that they will be learning lists of words: They do not need to know how the words vary from one participant to another. Nor are any serious ethical issues raised if participants are given a "surprise quiz" on words they didn't expect to be tested on. But what if the researcher seeks to compare participants who learn words while in a neutral mood with participants who learn words while they are angry or embarrassed? Clearly the research would not yield valid conclusions if participants had to be told ahead of time that they would be intentionally angered (by being treated rudely) or embarrassed (by being led to believe that they had accidentally broken a piece of equipment). Accordingly, the guidelines specify that if such a study is permitted to proceed at all, participants must be *debriefed* about it as soon as possible afterwards. The reasons for keeping them in ignorance—or deceiving them—about the procedures must be explained, and any residual anger or embarrassment must be dealt with so that they leave with their dignity intact and their appreciation for the research enhanced. The review board must be convinced that the debriefing procedures are adequate to this task.

A third principle of ethical research is the **right to privacy.** *Information about a person acquired during a study must be kept confidential and not made available to others without his or her consent.* A common practice is to separate the names and other information used to identify participants from the data collected in the study. The data are then identified only by code or case numbers. In that way, no one other than the experimenter has access to how any particular participant responded.

Even if all of these ethical conditions are met, it is still necessary for the researcher to weigh the costs of the study against the potential benefits—not the economic costs, but the costs in human terms. Is it really necessary to conduct a study in which participants will be deceived or embarrassed? In other words, will the potential findings be worth the human costs? Only if the researcher is certain that the study will uncover worthwhile information—either practical or theoretical—can the research be fully justified.

Another area in which ethical standards must be observed is research using animals. About 7 to 8% of psychological studies employ animals (mostly rodents and birds), and very few of these involve painful or harmful procedures. Nevertheless, concern over the use, care, and treatment of animal subjects has increased in recent years, and both federal and APA guidelines require that any painful or harmful procedures imposed upon animals must be thoroughly justified in terms of the knowledge to be gained from the study. Specific rules also govern the living conditions and maintenance of laboratory animals.

Aside from these specific guidelines, a central principle of research ethics is that those who participate in psychology studies should be considered as full partners in the research enterprise. Some of the research discussed in this text was conducted before the ethical guidelines just described were formulated and would not be permitted by most review boards today.

Major Subfields of Psychology

In this chapter we have gained a general understanding of the nature of psychology by looking at its topics, perspectives, and methods. We can further our understanding by looking at what different kinds of psychologists do.

About half the people who have advanced degrees in psychology work in colleges and universities. In addition to teaching, they may devote much of their time to research or counseling. Other psychologists work in schools, hospitals or clinics, research institutes, government agencies, or business and industry. Still others are in private practice and offer their services to the public for a fee. We now turn to a brief description of some of the subfields of psychology.

Biological Psychology Biological psychologists (also referred to as physiological psychologists) seek to discover the relationship between biological processes and behavior.

Experimental Psychology Experimental psychologists usually conduct research from a behaviorist or cognitive perspective and use experimental methods to study how people (and other animals) react to sensory stimuli, perceive the world, learn and remember, reason, and respond emotionally.

Developmental, Social, and Personality Psychology These three subfields overlap. Developmental psychologists are concerned with human development and the factors that shape behavior from birth to old age. They might study a specific ability, such as how language develops in children, or a particular period of life, such as infancy.

Social psychologists are interested in how people perceive and interpret their social world and how their beliefs, attitudes, and behaviors are influenced by others. They are also concerned with social relationships between and among people, and with the behavior of groups.

Personality psychologists study the thoughts, emotions, and behaviors that define an individual's personal style of interacting with the world. Accordingly, they are interested in differences between individuals, and they

also attempt to synthesize all the psychological processes into an integrated account of the total person.

Clinical and Counseling Psychology The largest number of psychologists are clinical psychologists; they apply psychological principles to the diagnosis and treatment of emotional and behavioral problems—including mental illness, drug addiction, and marital and family conflict.

Counseling psychologists serve many of the same functions as clinical psychologists, although they often deal with less serious problems. They often work with high school or university students.

School and Educational Psychology Because serious emotional problems often make their first appearance in the early grades, many elementary schools employ psychologists whose training combines courses in child development, education, and clinical psychology. These school psychologists work with children to evaluate learning and emotional problems. In contrast, educational psychologists are specialists in learning and teaching. They may work in the schools, but more often they are employed by a university's school of education, where they do research on teaching methods and help train teachers.

Industrial and Engineering Psychology Industrial psychologists (sometimes called organizational psychologists) typically work for a company. They are concerned with such problems as selecting people who are most suitable for particular jobs or developing job training programs. Engineering psychologists (sometimes called human factors engineers) seek to improve the relationship between people and machines; they help design machines that minimize human errors. One way in which these help improve human-machine interaction is by designing machines with the most efficient placement of gauges and controls, which leads to improved performance, safety, and comfort.

We Are Biologically Selfish

George C. Williams, *State University of New York, Stony Brook*

George C. Williams

Yes we are selfish, in a special biological sense, but an important one that should be borne in mind in discussing human affairs, ethical philosophy, and related topics (Williams, 1996: Chs. 3 & 9). We are selfish in the special way that our genes demand. They are maximally selfish because, if they were not, they would not exist. The genes that get passed on through many generations are those that are best at getting themselves passed on. To do this they must be better than any alternatives at making bodies, human or otherwise, that transmit genes more profusely than other members of their population. Individuals can win this genetic contest mainly by surviving to maturity and then competing successfully for the resources (food, nest sites, mates, etc.) needed for their own reproduction.

In this sense we are necessarily selfish, but this need not imply that we are never expected to be unselfish in the sense in which this term is normally understood. Individuals can and often do assist others in gaining resources and avoiding losses or dangers. For a biological understanding of such behavior, the important observations lie in the circumstances in which the apparent benevolence occurs. The most obvious example of helpful behavior is that performed by parents for their own offspring. Its obvious explanation is that parents would not successfully transmit their genes if they did not help their own young in special ways: mammalian mothers must nurse their babies; birds must bring food to their nestlings; a plant must pack an optimum quantity of nutrients into each of its seeds. Yet this kind of provisioning is never a generalized helpfulness of adults toward young. There are always mechanisms at work by which parents can usually identify their own offspring and confine their helpfulness to them alone.

If all reproduction is sexual and mates are seldom closely related to each other, each offspring has half of each parent's genes. From a parent's perspective, a son or daughter is genetically half as important as itself, and an offspring's reproduction is half as important as its own, for getting genes transmitted. Yet the same kind of partial genetic identity is true of all relatives, not just offspring. It may serve the genetic selfishness of an individual to behave helpfully toward relatives in general, not merely offspring. Such behavior arises from what is termed *kin selection*, natural selection for the adaptive use of cues that indicate degrees and probabilities of relationship. To whatever extent there is evidence of genealogical connections, an individual is expected to favor relatives over nonrelatives and close relatives (parents, offspring, siblings) over more distant ones.

A male bird whose mate laid eggs in his nest can be favored in evolution if he incubates the eggs and feeds the later hatchlings. But what about possible cuckoldry? Can he really be sure that his mate was not inseminated by a neighboring male so that one or more of those eggs are not actually his own offspring? Extra-pair mating by female birds, with or without consent, does happen in many species. Males in such species are especially watchful of their mates' behavior and diligent in chasing rival males from their territories. It is expected that males, in species in which an average of 10% of the eggs are fertilized by rivals, will be less conscientious toward their nestlings than in species in which cuckoldry never happens.

Kin selection is one factor that causes what looks like unselfish behavior. Reciprocation between unrelated individuals, with immediate or likely future profit to each participant, is another. So is that which is caused by the selfish deception or manipulation of another's kin-selected or other altruistic or cooperative instincts. Female birds, like males, cannot be certain that nestlings are their own, because *egg dumping* (Sayler, 1992), the laying of an egg in another bird's nest while its owner is briefly away feeding, happens in many species. One female gains genetically by exploiting the parental instincts of another. The species in which deception and manipulation are most extensively developed is our own, by virtue of our language capability. Henry V, according to Shakespeare, addressed his army as "We band of brothers." Feminist leaders speak of the "sisterhood." Deception and manipulation of others' emotions can, of course, be for either a worthy or an unworthy cause.

Why We Aren't Born Selfish

Frans B. M. de Waal, *Emory University*

"How selfish soever man may be supposed, there are evidently some principles in his nature, which interest him in the fortune of others, and render their happiness necessary to him, though he derives nothing from it, except the pleasure of seeing it."

Adam Smith, 1759

When Lenny Skutnik dove into the icy Potomac in Washington, DC, in 1982, to rescue a plane-crash victim, or when Dutch civilians sheltered Jewish families during World War II, life-threatening risks were taken on behalf of complete strangers. Similarly, Binti Jua, a lowland gorilla at Chicago's Brookfield Zoo, rescued an unconscious boy who had fallen into her enclosure, following a chain of actions no one had taught her.

Such examples make a deep impression mainly because they benefit members of our own species. But in my work on the evolution of empathy and morality, I have found evidence so rich of animals caring for one another and responding to each other's distress that I am convinced that survival depends not only on strength in combat but also at times on cooperation and kindness (de Waal, 1996). For example, it is common among chimpanzees that a bystander approaches the victim of an attack to gently wrap an arm around his or her shoulder.

Despite these caring tendencies, humans and other animals are routinely depicted by biologists as complete egoists. The reason is theoretical: all behavior is supposed to have evolved to serve the actor's own interests. It is logical to assume that genes that fail to benefit their carrier are at a disadvantage in the process of natural selection. But is it correct to call an animal selfish simply because its behavior evolved for its own good?

The process by which a behavior came to exist over millions of years of evolution is irrelevant when considering why an animal here and now acts in a particular way. Animals only see the immediate consequences of their actions, and even those are not always clear to them. We may think that a spider builds a web to catch flies, but this is true only at the functional level. There is no evidence that spiders have any idea what webs are for. In other words, a behavior's purpose says nothing about its underlying motives.

Only recently has the concept of "selfishness" been robbed of its vernacular meaning and applied outside the psychological domain. Even though the term is now seen by some as synonymous with self-serving, selfishness implies the *intention* to serve oneself, hence knowledge of what one stands to gain from a particular behavior. A vine may serve its own interests by overgrowing a tree, but since plants lack intentions and knowledge, they cannot be selfish except in a meaningless, metaphorical sense. For the same reason, it is impossible for genes to be selfish.

Charles Darwin never confused adaptation with individual goals, and endorsed altruistic motives. In this he was inspired by Adam Smith, the moral philosopher and father of economics. It says a great deal about the distinction between self-serving actions and selfish motives that Smith, known for his emphasis on self-interest as the guiding principle of economics, also wrote about the universal human capacity of sympathy.

The origins of this inclination are no mystery. All species that rely on cooperation show group loyalty and helping tendencies. These tendencies evolved in the context of a close-knit social life in which they benefited relatives and companions able to repay the favor. The impulse to help was, therefore, never totally without survival value to the ones showing the impulse. But the impulse became divorced from the consequences that shaped its evolution, permitting its expression even when payoffs were unlikely, such as when strangers were the beneficiaries.

To call all behavior selfish is like describing all life on earth as converted sun energy. Both statements have some general value but offer little help in explaining the diversity we see around us. Some animals survive through ruthless competition, others through mutual aid. A framework that fails to distinguish the contrasting mind-sets involved may be of use to the evolutionary biologist: It has no place in psychology.

An adult male chimpanzee, defeated in a fight with a rival, screams while being comforted by a juvenile with an embrace. Such "consolations" have as yet not been reported for other animals. The behavior seems a form of empathy without tangible benefit to the performer.

SUMMARY

1. Psychology is the scientific study of behavior and mental processes.

2. The roots of psychology can be traced to the fourth and fifth centuries B.C. The Greek philosophers Socrates, Plato, and Aristotle posed fundamental questions about the mind, while Hippocrates, the "father of medicine," made many important observations about how the brain controlled other organs. One of the earliest debates about human psychology focused on the question of whether human capabilities are inborn (the nativist view) or acquired through experience (the empiricist view). Scientific psychology was born in the latter part of the 19th century with the idea that mind and behavior could be the subject of scientific analysis. The first experimental laboratory in psychology was established by Wilhelm Wundt at the University of Leipzig in 1897.

3. Among the early "schools" of psychology were structuralism (the analysis of mental structures), functionalism (studying how the mind works so that an organism can adapt to and function in its environment), behaviorism (the study of behavior without reference to consciousness), Gestalt psychology (which focuses on the patterns formed by stimuli and on the organization of experience), and psychoanalysis (which emphasizes the role of unconscious processes in personality development and motivation).

4. Modern developments in psychology include information-processing theory, psycholinguistics, and neuropsychology.

5. The study of psychology can be approached from several perspectives. The biological perspective relates actions to events taking place inside the body, particularly the brain and nervous system. The behavioral perspective considers only external activities that can be observed and measured. The cognitive perspective is concerned with mental processes such as perceiving, remembering, reasoning, deciding, and problem solving, and with relating these processes to behavior. The psychoanalytic perspective emphasizes unconscious motives stemming from sexual and aggressive impulses. The phenomenological perspective focuses on the person's subjective experiences and motivation toward self-actualization. A particular topic often can be analyzed from more than one of these perspectives.

6. The biological perspective differs from the other viewpoints in that its principles are partly drawn from biology. Often biological researchers attempt to explain psychological principles in terms of biological ones; this is known as reductionism. Behavioral phenomena are increasingly being understood at both the biological and psychological levels.

7. Doing psychological research involves generating a hypothesis and then testing it using a scientific method. When applicable, the experimental method is preferred because it seeks to control all variables except the ones being studied. The independent variable is the one that is manipulated by the experimenter; the dependent variable (usually some measure of the participant's behavior) is the one being studied to determine whether it is affected by changes in the independent variable. In a simple experimental design, the experimenter manipulates one independent variable and observes its effect on one dependent variable. An essential element of experimental design is the random assignment of participants to experimental and control groups.

8. In many experiments the independent variable is something that is either present or absent. The simplest experimental design includes an experimental group (with the condition present for one group of participants) and a control group (with the condition absent for another group of participants). If the manipulation of the independent variable results in a difference between the experimental and control groups that is found to be statistically significant, we know that the experimental condition had a reliable effect; that is, the difference is not due to chance factors or a few extreme cases.

9. In situations in which experiments are not feasible, the correlational method may be used. This method determines whether a naturally occurring difference is associated with another difference of interest. The degree of correlation between two variables is measured by the correlation coefficient, r, a number between -1 and 1. The absence of any relationship is indicated by 0; a perfect relationship is indicated by 1. As r goes from 0 to 1, the strength of the relationship increases. The correlation coefficient can be positive or negative, depending on whether one variable increases with another ($+$) or one variable decreases as the other increases ($-$).

10. Another way of conducting research is to use the observational method, in which one observes the phenomenon of interest. Researchers must be trained to observe and record behavior accurately. Phenomena that are difficult to observe directly may be observed indirectly by means of surveys (questionnaires and interviews) or by reconstructing a case history.

11. The basic ethical principles governing the ethical treatment of human participants are minimal risk, informed consent, and the right to privacy. Any painful or harmful procedures imposed upon animals must be thoroughly justified in terms of the knowledge to be gained from the study.

12. Among the major subfields of psychology are biological psychology; experimental psychology; developmental, social, and personality psychology; clinical and counseling psychology; school and educational psychology; and industrial and engineering psychology.

KEY TERMS

psychology (p. 3)
physiology (p. 5)
introspection (p. 6)
structuralism (p. 7)
functionalism (p. 7)
unconscious (p. 9)
reductionism (p. 14)
hypothesis (p. 15)
theory (p. 15)
variable (p. 15)
independent variable (p. 17)

dependent variable (p. 18)
experimental group (p. 18)
control group (p. 18)
measurement (p. 19)
statistics (p. 19)
mean (p. 19)
correlation coefficient (p. 20)
case history (p. 23)
minimal risk (p. 23)
informed consent (p. 24)
right to privacy (p. 24)

CRITICAL THINKING QUESTIONS

1. Consider the question, "What are the determinants of an individual's sexual orientation?" How would the different perspectives outlined in this chapter approach this question? Which of the methods discussed in the chapter would each perspective be likely to use in attempting to answer it?

2. Figure 1-3 displays the results of a classic study showing that preference for viewing violent TV programs by boys at age 9 is related to aggressive behavior at age 19. Why does this study fail to demonstrate that watching violence on TV makes boys more aggressive? What kind of evidence would one need to make such an argument?

FURTHER READING

The topical interests and theories of any contemporary science can often be understood best according to its history. Several useful books are Hilgard, *Psychology in America: A Historical Survey* (1987); Wertheimer, *A Brief History of Psychology* (4th ed., 2000); and Schultz, *A History of Modern Psychology* (5th ed., 2000). Also of interest is Kimble, Wertheimer, and White's *Portraits of Pioneers in Psychology* (1991).

The various conceptual approaches to psychology are discussed in Medcof and Roth (eds.), *Approaches to Psychology* (1988); Anderson, *Cognitive Psychology and Its Implications* (3rd ed., 1990); Peterson, *Personality* (1988); Royce and Mos (eds.), *Humanistic Psychology: Concepts and Criticism* (1981); and Lundin, *Theories and Systems of Psychology* (3rd ed., 1985).

The methods of psychological research are presented in Wood, *Fundamentals of Psychological Research* (3rd ed., 1986); Snodgrass, Levy-Berger, and Haydon, *Human Experimental Psychology* (1985); Ray and Ravizza, *Methods Toward a Science of Behavior and Experience* (3rd ed., 1988); and Elmes, Kantowitz, and Roediger, *Research Methods in Psychology* (3rd ed., 1989). For more of an emphasis on the thinking skills needed to do psychological research, see Stanovich's *Thinking Straight About Psychology* (1992).

A simple but elegant introduction to basic concepts in statistics is Phillips, *How to Think About Statistics* (revised ed., 1992). A good introduction to cognitive neuroscience is provided by Kosslyn and Koenig, *Wet Mind: The New Cognitive Neuroscience* (1992). For an introduction to evolutionary psychology, see Barkow, Cosmides, and Tooky, *The Adapted Mind* (1990).

A general introduction to cognitive science is given in Gardner, *The Mind's New Science: A History of the Cognitive Revolution* (1985) and in Osherson, *Invitation to Cognitive Science* (Vols. 1–3) (1990). For an introduction to cultural psychology see Shewder's *Cultural Psychology* (1990).

To find out more about career opportunities in psychology and the training required to become a psychologist, write to the American Psychological Association (1400 North Uhle Street, Arlington, Va., 22201) for a copy of the booklet, *A Career in Psychology.*

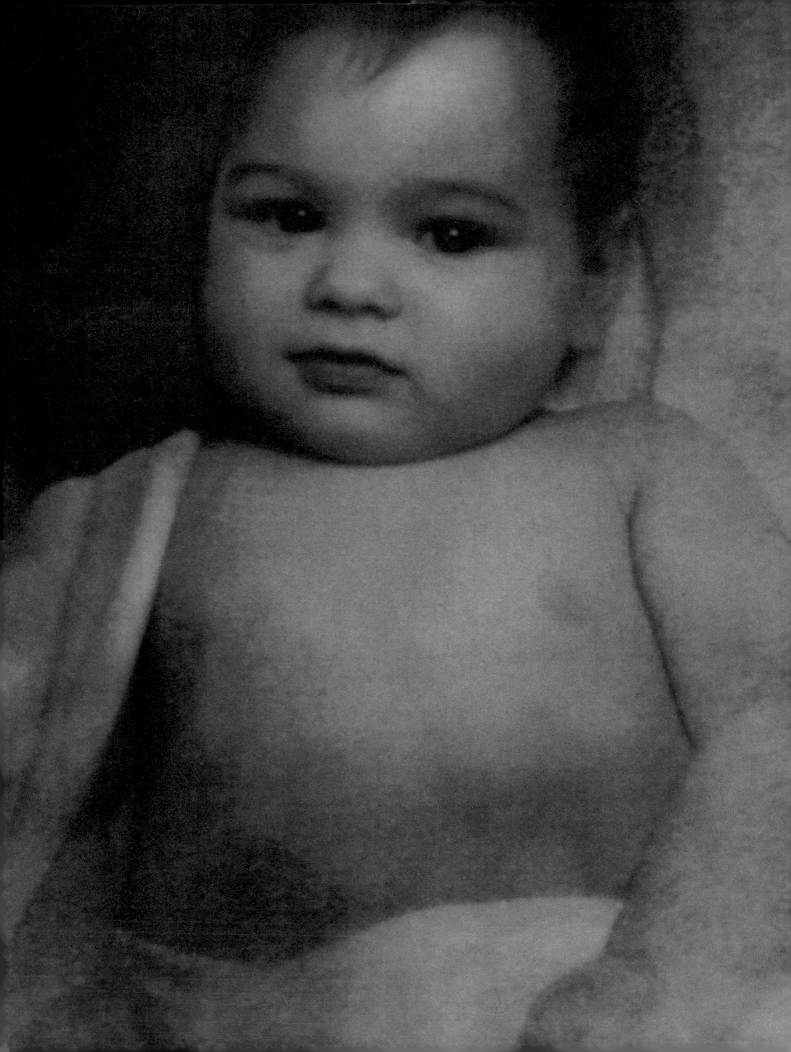

Biological and Developmental Processes

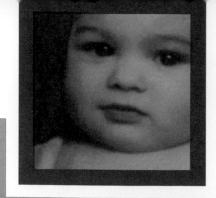

Chapter 2
Biological Foundations of Psychology

All behavior, from blinking an eye to playing basketball to writing a computer program, depends on the integration of many different processes within the body. This integration is provided by the nervous system, with help from the endocrine system. Consider, for example, all the processes that must be coordinated to enable you to stop your car at a red light. First you must see the light; this means that the light must register on a set of sensory organs—in this case, your eyes. Neural impulses from your eyes are relayed to your brain, where the stimulus is analyzed and compared with information about past events that is stored in your memory. This process enables you to recognize that a red light in this context means "stop." The process of moving your foot to the brake pedal and pressing it is initiated by the motor areas of the brain that control the muscles of your leg and foot. In order to send the proper signals to these muscles, the brain must know where your foot is as well as where you want it to go. The brain maintains a register of the position of all the parts of your body relative to one another, which it uses to direct the movements of those parts. You do not stop the car with one sudden movement of your leg, however. A specialized part of your brain receives continuous feedback from your leg and foot muscles so that you are aware of how much pressure is being exerted and can alter your movements accordingly. At the same time, your eyes and some of your other senses tell you how quickly the car is stopping. If the light turned red as you were speeding toward the intersection, some of your endocrine glands would also be activated, leading to increased heart rate, faster respiration, and other metabolic changes associated with fear; these processes increase your reaction time in an emergency. Thus, stopping at a red light happens quickly and seems automatic; yet it involves a variety of complex messages and adjustments. The information for these activities is transmitted by large networks of nerve cells.

Our nervous system, sense organs, muscles, and glands enable us to be aware of and to adjust to our environment. Our perception of events depends on how our sense organs detect stimuli and how our brain interprets information coming to it from the senses. Much of our behavior is motivated by such needs as hunger, thirst, and avoidance of fatigue or pain. Our ability to use language, to think, and to solve problems depends on a brain that is incredibly complex. Indeed, the specific patterns of electrical and chemical events in the brain are the basis of our most intricate thought processes. For these reasons, virtually all aspects of behavior and mental functioning can be better understood with some knowledge of the underlying biological processes. This chapter provides an overview of those processes.

Neurons, the Building Blocks of the Nervous System

The basic unit of the nervous system is the **neuron,** *a specialized cell that transmits neural impulses or messages to other neu-* *rons, glands, and muscles.* It is important to understand neurons because they hold the secrets of how the brain works and, in turn, the nature of human consciousness. We know the role they play in the transmission of nerve impulses, and we know how some neural circuits work; but we are just beginning to unravel their more complex functioning in memory, emotion, and thought.

There are two types of neurons in the nervous system: very tiny neurons known as *local neurons* and larger neurons called *macroneurons.* Although the majority of neurons are local neurons, we have only recently begun to understand how they function. In fact, for a long time many investigators believed that these tiny neurons were not neurons at all or that they were immature neurons incapable of transmitting information. Today we know that local neurons do indeed pass messages to other neurons. However, they tend to exchange messages with neighboring neurons and do not transmit information over long distances in the body as macroneurons do.

Macroneurons, on the other hand, have been studied extensively, and therefore our discussion in this chapter will focus on these neurons. Although macroneurons differ markedly in size and appearance, they have certain common characteristics (see Figure 2-1). Projecting from the cell body are a number of short branches called *dendrites* (from the Greek word *dendron,* meaning "tree"). The dendrites and cell body receive neural impulses from adjacent neurons. These messages are transmitted to other neurons (or to muscles and glands) by a slender tubelike extension of the cell called an *axon.* At its end, the axon branches into a number of tiny branches that end in small swellings called *terminal buttons.*

The terminal button does not actually touch the adjacent neuron. There is a slight gap between the terminal button and the cell body or dendrites of the receiving neuron. This junction is called a *synapse,* and the gap itself is called the *synaptic gap.* When a neural impulse travels down the axon and arrives at the terminal buttons, it triggers the secretion of a **neurotransmitter,** *a chemical that diffuses across the synaptic gap and stimulates the next neuron,* thereby transmitting the impulse from one neuron to the next. The axons from a great many neurons synapse on the dendrites and cell body of a single neuron (see Figure 2-2).

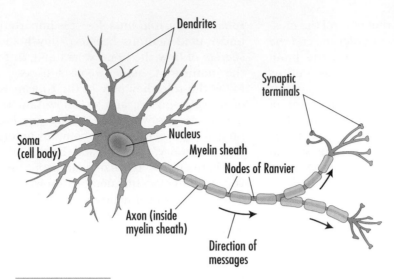

FIGURE 2-1

Schematic Diagram of a Neuron   *Arrows indicate the direction of the nerve impulse. Some axons are branched; the branches are called* collaterals. *The axons of many neurons are covered with an insulating myelin sheath that helps increase the speed of the nerve impulse.*

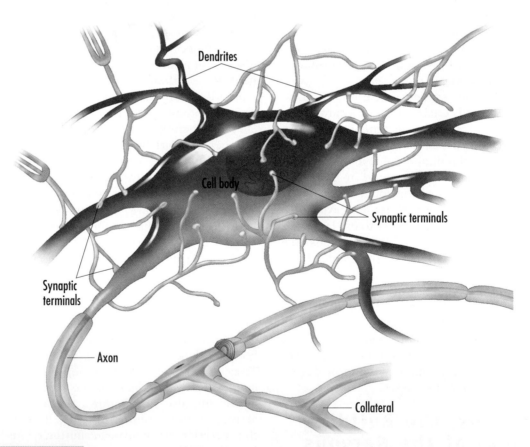

FIGURE 2-2

Synapses at the Cell Body of a Neuron   *Many different axons, each of which branches repeatedly, synapse on the dendrites and cell body of a single neuron. Each branch of an axon ends in a swelling, called a* terminal button, *that contains called* neurotransmitters. *When released, neurotransmitters transmit the nerve impulse across the synapse to the dendrites or cell body of the receiving cell.*

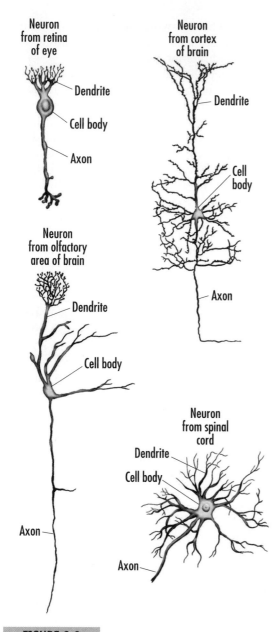

Neuron from retina of eye

- Dendrite
- Cell body
- Axon

Neuron from cortex of brain

- Dendrite
- Cell body
- Axon

Neuron from olfactory area of brain

- Dendrite
- Cell body
- Axon

Neuron from spinal cord

- Dendrite
- Cell body
- Axon

FIGURE 2-3

Shapes and Relative Sizes of Neurons *The axon of a spinal cord neuron (not shown in its entirety in the figure) may be several feet long.*

Although all neurons have these general features, they vary greatly in size and shape (see Figure 2-3). A neuron in the spinal cord may have an axon three to four feet long running from the end of the spine to the muscles of the big toe; a neuron in the brain may cover only a few thousandths of an inch.

Neurons are classified into three categories, depending on their general function. *Sensory neurons* transmit impulses received by receptors to the central nervous system. The receptors are specialized cells in the sense organs, muscles, skin, and joints that detect physical or chemical changes and translate these events into impulses that travel along the sensory neurons. *Motor neurons* carry outgoing signals from the brain or spinal cord to muscles and glands. *Interneurons* receive the signals from the sensory neurons and send impulses to other interneurons or to motor neurons. Interneurons are found only in the brain, eyes, and spinal cord.

A **nerve** is *a bundle of elongated axons belonging to hundreds or thousands of neurons.* A single nerve may contain axons from both sensory and motor neurons. The cell bodies of neurons are generally found grouped together throughout the nervous system. In the brain and spinal cord, a group of cell bodies of neurons is referred to as a **nucleus** (plural: *nuclei*). A group of neuronal cell bodies found outside the brain and spinal cord is called a **ganglion** (plural: *ganglia*).

In addition to neurons, the nervous system consists of a large number of nonneural cells, called *glial cells,* that are interspersed among—and often surround—neurons. Glial cells outnumber neurons by 9 to 1 and take up more than half the volume of the brain. The name *glia,* derived from the Greek work for glue, suggests one of their functions— namely, to hold neurons in place. In addition, they provide nutrients to the neurons and appear to "keep house" in the brain by gathering and packaging up waste products and gobbling up dead neurons and foreign substances, thereby maintaining the signaling capacity of neurons (Sontheimer, 1995). Uncontrolled proliferation of glial cells is the cause of almost all brain tumors.

Estimates of the number of neurons and glial cells in the human nervous system vary widely, and scientists do not agree on the best estimate. For the brain alone, the estimates range from 10 billion to 1 trillion neurons; whatever the estimate for neurons, the number of glial cells is about 9 times that number (Groves & Rebec, 1992).

Action Potentials

Information moves along a neuron in the form of a neural impulse called an **action potential**—*an electrochemical impulse that travels from the dendritic area down to the end of the axon.* Each action potential is the result of movements by electrically charged molecules, known as *ions,* in and out of the

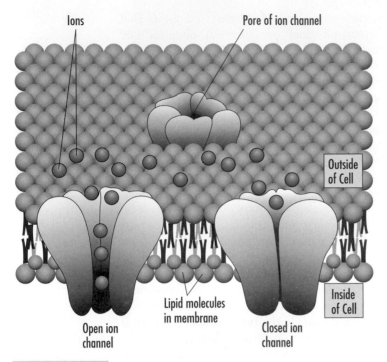

Ions

Pore of ion channel

Outside of Cell

Inside of Cell

Lipid molecules in membrane

Open ion channel

Closed ion channel

FIGURE 2-4

Ion Channels *Chemicals such as sodium, potassium, calcium, and chloride pass through the cell membrane via doughnut-shaped protein molecules called* ion channels.

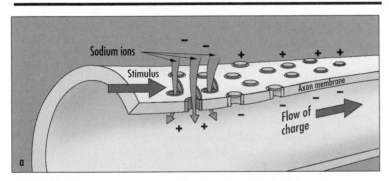

Sodium ions

Stimulus

Axon membrane

Flow of charge

a

Sodium ions

Stimulus

Axon membrane

Flow of charge

Potassium ions

b

FIGURE 2-5

Action Potential *(a) During an action potential, sodium gates in the neuron membrane open and sodium ions enter the axon, bringing a positive charge with them. (b) After an action potential occurs at one point along the axon, the sodium gates close at that point and open at the next point along the axon. When the sodium gates close, potassium gates open and potassium ions flow out of the axon, carrying a positive charge with them. (Modified from Starr & Taggart, 1989)*

neuron. The following electrical and chemical processes lead to an action potential.

The cell membrane of the neuron is *semipermeable*, which means that some chemicals can pass through the cell membrane easily and others are not allowed to pass through except when special passageways in the membrane are open. These passageways, called *ion channels,* are doughnut-shaped protein molecules that form pores across the cell membrane (see Figure 2-4). These protein structures regulate the flow of ions such as sodium (Na^+), potassium (K^+), calcium (Ca^{++}), and chloride (CL^-) in and out of the neuron. Each ion channel is selective, permitting only one type of ion to flow through it when it is open.

When a neuron is not transmitting information, it is referred to as a *resting neuron*. In a resting neuron, separate protein structures, called *ion pumps*, help maintain an uneven distribution of various ions across the cell membrane by pumping them into or out of the cell. For example, the ion pumps transport Na^+ out of the neuron whenever it passes into the neuron, and pumps K^+ back into the neuron whenever it gets out. In this way the resting neuron maintains high concentrations of Na^+ outside the cell and low concentrations inside it. The overall effect of these ion channels and pumps is to electrically polarize the cell membrane of the resting neuron, making the inside of the neuron more negative than the outside.

When the neuron is stimulated, the voltage difference across the cell membrane is reduced. If the voltage drop is large enough, Na^+ channels open briefly at the point of stimulation and Na^+ ions flood into the cell. This process is called *depolarization.* Now the inside of that area of the cell membrane becomes positive relative to the outside. Neighboring Na^+ channels sense the voltage drop and open, causing the adjacent area to depolarize. This process of depolarization, repeating itself down the length of the axon, is a neural impulse. As the impulse travels down the axon, the Na^+ channels close behind it and the various ion pumps are activated to quickly restore the cell membrane to its resting state (see Figure 2-5). The importance of Na^+ channels is shown by the effect of local anesthetic agents such as Novocaine or Xylocaine: These prevent Na^+ channels from opening, thus stopping the action potential and preventing sensory signals from reaching the brain (Ragsdale et al., 1994).

The speed of the neural impulse as it travels down the axon can vary from about 2 to 200 miles per hour, depending on the diameter of the axon; larger ones generally are faster. The speed can also be affected by whether or not the axon is covered with a *myelin sheath.* This sheath consists of specialized glial cells that wrap themselves around the axon, one after another, with small gaps between them (refer back to Figure 2-1). These tiny gaps are called *nodes of Ranvier.* The insulation provided by the myelin sheath allows the nerve impulse to jump from one node of Ranvier to the next in a process known as *saltatory conduction,* which greatly increases the speed of transmission of the action potential down the axon. (*Saltatory* comes from the Latin word *saltare,* which means "to leap." In saltatory conduction, the action potential leaps from one node of Ranvier to another.) The myelin sheath is particularly prevalent in areas of the nervous system where rapid transmission of the action potential is critical—for example, along axons that stimulate skeletal muscles. In *multiple sclerosis,* a disorder in which symptoms first become evident between the ages of 16 and 30, the immune system attacks and destroys the body's own myelin sheaths, producing severe motor-nerve dysfunction.

Synaptic Transmission

The synaptic junction between neurons is extremely important because it is there that nerve cells transfer signals. A single neuron discharges, or *fires,* when the stimulation reaching it via multiple synapses exceeds a certain threshold. The neuron fires in a single, brief pulse and then becomes inactive for a few thousandths of a second. The strength of the neural impulse is constant and cannot be triggered by a stimulus unless it reaches the threshold level; this is referred to as the *all-or-none principle* of neural action. The nerve impulse, once started, travels down the axon to its many axon terminals.

As mentioned earlier, neurons do not connect directly at a synapse; there is a slight gap across which the signal must be transmitted (see Figure 2-6). When an action potential moves down the axon and arrives at the terminal buttons, it stimulates *synaptic vesicles* located in the terminal buttons. The synaptic vesicles are small spherical structures that contain neurotransmitters; when they are

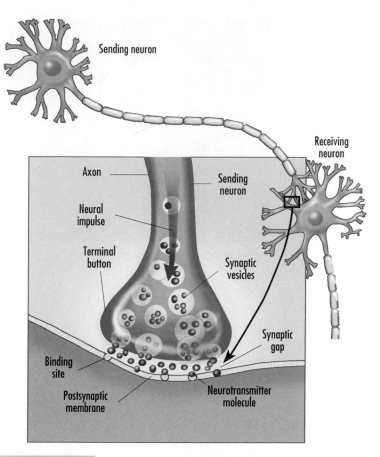

FIGURE 2-6

Release of Neurotransmitters Into a Synaptic Gap   *The neurotransmitter is carried to the presynaptic membrane in synaptic vesicles, which fuse with the membrane and release their contents into the synaptic gap. The neurotransmitters diffuse across the gap and combine with receptor molecules in the postsynaptic membrane.*

stimulated, they discharge the neurotransmitters into the synapse. The neurotransmitters diffuse across the synaptic gap and bind to *receptor sites* in the cell membrane of the receiving neuron. The neurotransmitter and the receptor site fit together like the pieces of a jigsaw puzzle or a key and a lock. This lock-and-key action causes a change in the permeability of ion channels in the receiving neuron. When bound to their receptors, some neurotransmitters have an *excitatory effect,* meaning that they allow positively charged ions, such as Na^+, to enter, thereby depolarizing the receiving neuron and making the inside of the cell more positive relative to the outside. Other neurotransmitters are *inhibitory,* meaning that they make the inside of the receiving neuron more negative relative to the outside, either by allowing positively charged ions, such as K^+, to leave the neuron or by letting negatively charged ions, such as

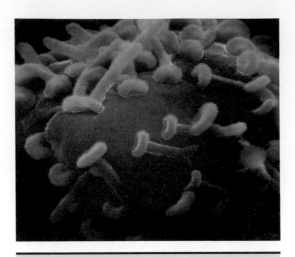

An electron micrograph of a neuron densely packed with synapses.

Cl$^+$, enter the cell. Thus, the excitatory effect increases the likelihood that the neuron will fire, whereas the inhibitory effect decreases the likelihood of firing.

A given neuron may receive neurotransmitters from many thousands of synapses with other neurons. Some of these neurons release neurotransmitters that are excitatory, while others release neurotransmitters that are inhibitory. Depending on their pattern of firing, different axons release their neurotransmitter substances at different times. If—at a particular moment and at a particular place on the cell membrane—the excitatory effects on the receiving neuron become large relative to the inhibitory effects, depolarization occurs and the neuron fires an all-or-none impulse.

Once a neurotransmitter substance is released and diffuses across the synaptic gap, its action must be very brief in order to maintain precise control. This is achieved in one of two ways. For some neurotransmitters, the synapse is almost immediately cleared by *reuptake,* a process in which the neurotransmitter is reabsorbed by the synaptic terminals from which it was released. Reuptake cuts off the action of the neurotransmitter and spares the axon terminals from having to manufacture more of the substance. The effect of other neurotransmitters is terminated by *degradation,* a process in which enzymes in the membrane of the receiving neuron react with the neurotransmitter to break it up chemically and make it inactive.

Neurotransmitters

More than 70 different neurotransmitters have been identified, and others surely will be discovered. Moreover, some neurotransmitters can bind to more than one type of receptor, causing different effects. For example, the neurotransmitter glutamate can activate at least 16 different types of receptor molecules, allowing neurons to respond in distinct ways to this same neurotransmitter (Westbrook, 1994). Certain neurotransmitters are excitatory at some sites and inhibitory at other sites because two different types of receptor molecules are involved. In this chapter we obviously can't discuss all of the neurotransmitters that are found in the nervous system, so we will focus on a few that have an important influence on behavior.

Acetylcholine Acetylcholine is found at many synapses throughout the nervous system. It is usually excitatory, but it can also be inhibitory, depending on the type of receptor molecule in the membrane of the receiving neuron. Acetylcholine is particularly prevalent in an area of the forebrain called the hippocampus, which plays a key role in the formation of new memories (Squire & Zola, 1996). This neurotransmitter plays a prominent role in Alzheimer's disease, a devastating disorder that affects many older people, causing impairment of memory and other cognitive functions. It has been demonstrated that neurons in the forebrain producing acetylcholine tend to degenerate in Alzheimer patients, thereby reducing the production of acetylcholine; the less acetylcholine is produced, the more serious the memory loss.

Acetylcholine is also released at every synapse where a neuron terminates at a skeletal muscle fiber. The acetylcholine is directed onto small structures called *end plates,* which are located on the muscle cells. The end plates are covered with receptor molecules that, when activated by acetylcholine, trigger a molecular linkage inside the muscle cells that causes them to contract. Certain drugs that affect acetylcholine can produce muscle paralysis. For example, botulinum toxin, which forms from bacteria in improperly canned foods, blocks the release of acetylcholine at nerve-muscle synapses and can cause death when the muscles used in breathing become paralyzed. Some nerve gases developed for warfare, as well as many pesticides, cause paralysis by destroying the enzyme that degrades acetylcholine once the neuron has fired; when the degradation process fails, there is an uncontrolled buildup of acetylcholine in the nervous system and normal synaptic transmission becomes impossible.

Norepinephrine   Norepinephrine (NE) is produced mainly by neurons in the brain stem. Two well-known drugs, cocaine and amphetamines, prolong the action of NE by slowing down its reuptake process. Because of the delay in the reuptake, the receiving neurons are activated for a longer period; this is what causes these drugs' stimulating psychological effects. In contrast, lithium is a drug that speeds up the reuptake of NE, causing a person's mood level to be depressed. Any drug that causes NE to increase or decrease in the brain is correlated with an increase or decrease in the individual's mood level.

Dopamine   Dopamine is chemically very similar to norepinephrine. Release of dopamine in certain areas of the brain produces intense feelings of pleasure, and current research is investigating the role of dopamine in the development of addictions. Too much dopamine in some areas of the brain may cause schizophrenia, while too little in other areas may lead to Parkinson's disease. Drugs used to treat schizophrenia, such as thorazine or clozapine, block the receptors for dopamine. In contrast, L-dopa, the drug most commonly prescribed to treat Parkinson's disease, increases dopamine in the brain.

Serotonin   Serotonin belongs to the same family of chemicals, called *monoamines,* as dopamine and norepinephrine. Like norepinephrine, serotonin plays an important role in the regulation of mood. For example, low levels of serotonin have been associated with feelings of depression. Specific antidepressant drugs have been developed, called *serotonin reuptake inhibitors,* that increase serotonin levels in the brain by blocking the uptake of serotonin by neurons. Prozac, Zoloft, and Paxil, drugs that are commonly prescribed to treat depression, are serotonin reuptake inhibitors. Serotonin is also important in the regulation of sleep and appetite, and therefore is also used to treat the eating disorder *bulimia.* The mood-altering drug LSD creates its effects by causing an excess of serotonin in the brain. LSD's chemical structure is similar to that of serotonin, and there is evidence that LSD accumulates in certain brain cells, where it mimics the action of serotonin and overstimulates the cells.

GABA   Another prominent neurotransmitter is gamma-aminobutyric acid (GABA). This substance is a major inhibitory transmitter; in fact, the majority of the synapses in the brain use GABA (Feldman, Meyer, & Quenzer, 1997). The drug picrotoxin blocks GABA receptors and produces convulsions because without GABA's inhibiting influence, muscle movement cannot be controlled. The tranquilizing effects of certain drugs, known as *benzodiazepines,* used to treat patients suffering from anxiety are a result of GABA's inhibitory action (see Chapter 15).

Glutamate   The excitatory neurotransmitter glutamate is present in more neurons of the central nervous system than any other transmitter. There are at least three subtypes of glutamate receptors, and one in particular is believed to play a role in learning and memory. It is called the NMDA receptor, after the chemical (N-methyl D-aspartate) that is used to detect it. Neurons in the hippocampus (an area near the center of the brain) are particularly rich in NMDA receptors, and there is evidence that this area is critical in the formation of new memories.

The NMDA receptor is unlike other receptors, in that successive signals from two different neurons are required in order to activate it. The signal coming from the first neuron sensitizes the cell membrane in which the NMDA receptor is embedded. Once the cell membrane is sensitized, a second signal (glutamate transmitters coming from another neuron) will activate the receptor. When such converging signals occur, the NMDA receptor allows a very large number of calcium ions to flow into the neuron. That influx of ions appears to cause a long-term change in the membrane of the neuron, making it more responsive to the initial signal when it recurs at a later time—a phenomenon known as long-term potentiation, or LTP (see Figure 2-7).

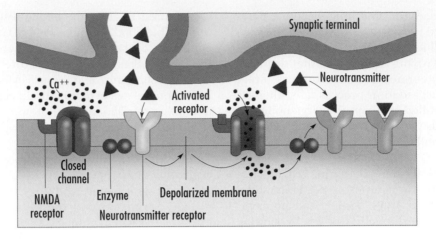

FIGURE 2-7

NMDA Receptors and LTP   *This diagram illustrates a possible mechanism by which NMDA receptors could effect a long-term change in the strength of a synaptic connection (LTP). When neurotransmitters (blue triangles) are released from the first signaling neuron, they activate non-NMDA receptors in the receiving neuron (1) that partially depolarize the cell membrane (2). This partial depolarization sensitizes the NMDA receptors so that they can now be activated by glutamate transmitters coming from the second signaling neuron (3). Activating the NMDA receptors causes their associated calcium channels to open (4). As the calcium ions flow into the cell, they interact with various enzymes (5), presumably in ways that restructure the cell membrane (6). This restructuring makes the receiving neuron more sensitive to neurotransmitters from the first neuron, so that in time it can activate the receiving neuron on its own, thus inducing LTP.*

Such a mechanism, in which two divergent signals strengthen a synapse, provides a possible explanation of how separate events become associated in memory. For example, learning someone's name requires that you make an association between the person's appearance and his or her name. LTP strengthens synapses so that the sight of the person will prompt you to recall the person's name. The NMDA mechanism thus offers an intriguing theory to explain how events are associated in memory—a theory that is being actively pursued in current research (Malinow et al., 1994; Zalutsky & Nicoll, 1990).

Research on neurotransmitters and receptors has led to many practical applications. Some of these are discussed in the "Frontiers of Psychological Research" feature on the following page.

The Organization of the Nervous System

Divisions of the Nervous System

All parts of the nervous system are interrelated. But for purposes of discussion, the nervous system can be separated into two major divisions, each of which has two subdivisions (see Figure 2-8). The **central nervous system** includes *all the neurons in the brain and*

FIGURE 2-8

The Organization of the Nervous System

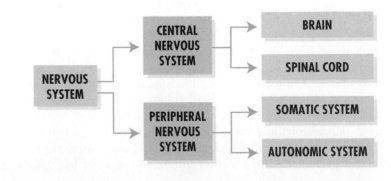

FRONTIERS OF PSYCHOLOGICAL RESEARCH

Molecular Psychology

As discussed in the text, when the neural impulse reaches the end of an axon, neurotransmitters are released that cross the synaptic gap and combine with receptors in the membrane of the receiving neuron. The lock-and-key action of the neurotransmitter and its receptor changes the electrical properties of the target cell, making firing either a bit more likely (excitation) or a bit less likely (inhibition). To serve its function, every key requires a lock and every neurotransmitter requires a receptor. Many commonly used drugs interact with receptor molecules in very much the same way as neurotransmitters. Molecules of these drugs are shaped enough like those of the neurotransmitters to work as if they were keys to the locks of receptors.

A good example of look-alike molecules is a class of drugs called *opiates,* which includes heroin and morphine. In molecular shape, opiates resemble a group of neurotransmitters called *endorphins,* which have the effect of blocking pain. The discovery that opiates mimic naturally occurring substances in the brain has prompted considerable research on the chemical control system that copes with stress and pain. Individuals who appear to be indifferent to pain may have an unusual ability to increase the production of these natural painkillers when they are needed.

Research with one of the endorphins, called enkephalin, has helped explain why a painkiller like morphine can be addictive. Under normal conditions, enkephalin binds to a certain number of opiate receptors. Morphine relieves pain by binding to the receptors that are left unfilled. Too much morphine can cause a drop in enkephalin production, leaving opiate receptors unfilled. The body then requires more morphine to fill the unoccupied receptors and to reduce pain. When morphine is discontinued, the opiate receptors are left unfilled, causing painful withdrawal symptoms.

The fact that the brain synthesizes substances that resemble opiates has been invoked to explain all sorts of effects. Joggers tout the theory that physical exertion increases enkephalin production to induce a "runner's high." Acupuncturists say that their needles actuate enkephalins, which then act as natural anesthetics. Some evidence to support this claim comes from observations that acupuncture-like stimulation appears to reduce pain responses and actuate enkephalin neural systems even when it is administered to animals (Chen, Geller, & Adler, 1996). Since animals are unlikely to show placebo effects, such studies are perhaps the strongest grounds for concluding that acupuncture directly activates neural enkephalin systems, although how it does this remains unclear.

Drugs that influence mental functioning and mood, such as opiates, are referred to as *psychoactive drugs.* By and large, they produce their effects by altering one of the various neurotransmitter-receptor systems. Different drugs can have different actions at the same synapse. One drug might mimic the effect of a specific neurotransmitter, another might occupy the receptor site so that the normal neurotransmitter is blocked out, and still others might affect the reuptake or degradation processes. The drug action will either increase or decrease the effectiveness of synaptic transmission.

Two drugs, chlorpromazine and reserpine, have proved useful in treating schizophrenia (a mental illness discussed in Chapter 15). Both drugs act on the norepinephrine and dopamine systems, but their antipsychotic action is due primarily to their effect on the neurotransmitter dopamine. It appears that chlorpromazine blocks dopamine receptors and that reserpine reduces dopamine levels by destroying storage vesicles in the synaptic terminals. The effectiveness of these drugs in treating schizophrenia has led to the formulation of the *dopamine hypothesis,* which states that schizophrenia is caused by an excess of dopamine activity in critical cell groups within the brain. The key evidence for this hypothesis is that antipsychotic drugs seem to be clinically effective to the extent that they block the transmission of impulses by dopamine molecules.

Research on neurotransmitter-receptor systems has increased our understanding of how drugs work. In the past, psychoactive drugs were discovered almost entirely by accident and their development took years of research. Now, as we gain more knowledge about neurotransmitters and receptors, new drugs can be designed and developed in a systematic way. For example, during the past 10 years a great deal has been learned about the molecular basis of interneural communication. The emerging picture is that thousands of different types of molecules are involved—not just transmitter and receptor molecules but also the enzymes that manufacture and degrade them and various other molecules that modulate their action. Of course, each time a new molecule is identified, we have discovered the potential for at least two diseases or forms of mental illness; some people will surely have too much of that molecule and others too little. Research on these problems has proved so productive that the field has been given the name *molecular psychology* (Franklin, 1987). The basic idea behind this new discipline is that mental processes and their aberrations can be analyzed in terms of the molecular interplay that takes place between neurons.

spinal cord. The **peripheral nervous system** consists of *the nerves connecting the brain and spinal cord to other parts of the body.* The peripheral nervous system is further divided into the **somatic system,** which *carries messages to and from the sense receptors, muscles, and the surface of the body,* and the **autonomic system,** *which connects with the internal organs and glands.*

The *sensory nerves* of the somatic system transmit information about external stimulation from the skin, muscles, and joints to the central nervous system; they make us aware of pain, pressure, and temperature variations. The *motor nerves* of the somatic system carry impulses from the central nervous system to the muscles, where they initiate action. All the muscles we use in making voluntary movements, as well as involuntary adjustments in posture and balance, are controlled by these nerves. The nerves of the autonomic system run to and from the internal organs, regulating such processes as respiration, heart rate, and digestion. The autonomic system, which plays a major role in emotion, is discussed later in the chapter.

Most of the nerve fibers connecting various parts of the body to the brain are gathered together in the *spinal cord,* where they are protected by the bony spinal vertebrae. The spinal cord is remarkably compact—barely the diameter of your little finger. Some of the simplest stimulus-response reflexes are carried out at the level of the spinal cord. One example is the knee jerk, the extension of the leg in response to a tap on the tendon that runs in front of the kneecap. Doctors use this test, performed with a small rubber hammer, to determine the efficiency of the spinal reflexes. The function of this reflex is to ensure that the leg will extend when the knee is bent by the force of gravity; this enables the organism to remain standing. When the knee tendon is tapped, the attached muscle stretches and a signal from sensory cells embedded in the muscle is transmitted through sensory neurons to the spinal cord. There the sensory neurons synapse directly with motor neurons, which transmit impulses back to the same muscle, causing it to contract and the leg to extend. Although this response can occur solely in the spinal cord without any assistance from the brain, it can be influenced by messages from higher nervous centers. For example, if you grip your hands just before your knee is tapped, the extension movement will be exaggerated. And if you consciously try to inhibit the reflex just before the doctor taps the tendon, you can do so. Thus, while the basic mechanism is built into the spinal cord, it can be modified by messages from higher brain centers.

The Organization of the Brain

There are a number of ways to conceptualize the brain. Figure 2-9 presents one way to think about the brain. This approach divides the brain into three regions based on location: (1) the **hindbrain,** which includes *all the structures located in the hind, or posterior, part of the brain, closest to the spinal cord;* (2) the **midbrain,** which is located in *the middle of the brain;* and (3) the **forebrain,** which includes *the structures located in the front, or anterior, part of the brain.* The Canadian investigator Paul MacLean proposed another framework for organizing the brain that is based on the function of the brain structures rather than on their location. According to MacLean, we can think of the human brain as composed of three concentric layers: (1) the *central core,* which regulates our most primitive behaviors; (2) the *limbic system,* which controls our emotions, and (3) the *cerebrum,* which regulates our higher intellectual processes. Figure 2-10 shows how these layers fit together; compare it with the more detailed cross-section in Figure 2-11. We will use MacLean's organizational framework as we discuss the various structures in the brain and their functions.

The Central Core

The **central core,** also known as the *brainstem,* controls involuntary behaviors such as coughing, sneezing, or gagging, as well as "primitive" behaviors that are under voluntary control, such as breathing, vomiting, sleeping, eating, drinking, temperature regulation, and sexual behavior. The brainstem includes all the structures in the hindbrain and midbrain and two structures in the forebrain, namely, the hypothalamus and the thalamus. This means that the central core of the brain stretches from the hindbrain to the forebrain. In this chapter we will limit

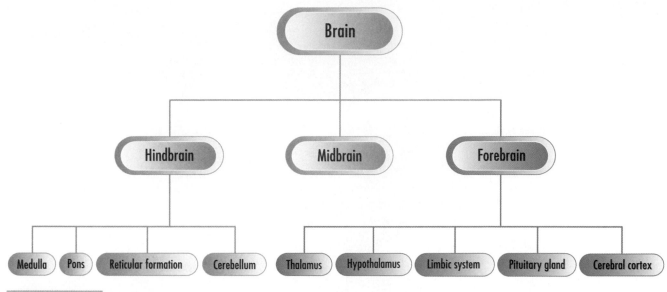

FIGURE 2-9

Locational Organization of Major Brain Structures   *The hindbrain includes all the structures located in the posterior part of the brain. The midbrain is located in the middle of the brain, and the forebrain includes structures located in the anterior part of the brain.*

our discussion to five brainstem structures—the medulla, the cerebellum, the thalamus, the hypothalamus, and the reticular formation—which are responsible for the regulation of the most important primitive behaviors necessary for survival. Table 2-1 lists the functions of these five structures as well as the functions of the cerebral cortex, the corpus callosum, and the hippocampus.

The first slight enlargement of the spinal cord as it enters the skull is the *medulla,* a narrow structure that controls breathing and some reflexes that help maintain upright posture. Also at this point, the major nerve tracts

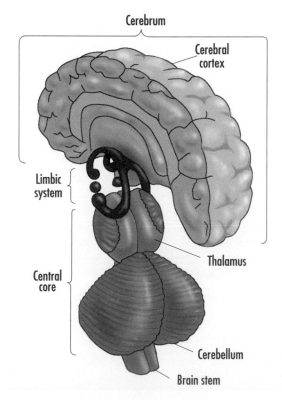

FIGURE 2-10

Functional Organization of the Human Brain *The central core and the limbic system are shown in their entirety, but the left cerebral hemisphere has been removed. The cerebellum of the central core controls balance and muscular coordination; the thalamus serves as a switchboard for messages coming from the sense organs; the hypothalamus (not shown but located below the thalamus) regulates endocrine activity and life-maintaining processes such as metabolism and temperature control. The limbic system is concerned with actions that satisfy basic needs, and with emotion. The cerebral cortex (an outer layer of cells covering the cerebrum) is the center of higher mental processes, where sensations are registered, voluntary actions initiated, decisions made, and plans formulated.*

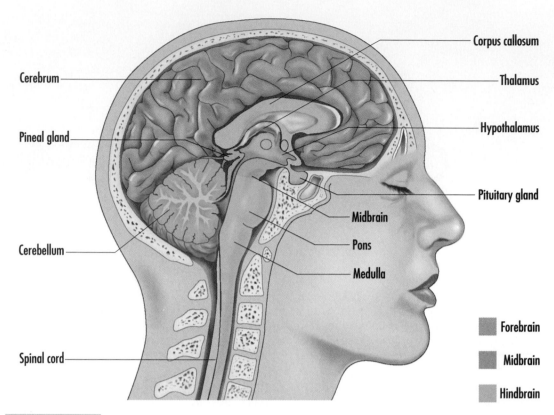

Corpus callosum

Cerebrum

Thalamus

Hypothalamus

Pineal gland

Pituitary gland

Midbrain

Pons

Medulla

Cerebellum

Spinal cord

Forebrain

Midbrain

Hindbrain

FIGURE 2-11

The Human Brain   *This schematic drawing shows the main structures of the central nervous system. (Only the upper portion of the spinal cord is shown.)*

coming up from the spinal cord cross over so that the right side of the brain is connected to the left side of the body and the left side of the brain to the right side of the body.

The Cerebellum   Attached to the rear of the brain stem slightly above the medulla is a convoluted structure called the *cerebellum*. It is concerned primarily with the coordination

TABLE 2-1

Parts of the Human Brain

Structure	Function
Cerebral cortex	Consists of several cortical areas: the primary motor area, the primary somatosensory area, the primary visual area, the primary auditory area, and the association areas.
Corpus callosum	Connects the two hemispheres of the cerebrum.
Thalamus	Directs incoming information from the sense receptors to the cerebrum; plays a role in the control of sleep and wakefulness.
Hypothalamus	Mediates eating, drinking, and sexual behavior; regulates endocrine activity and maintains homeostasis; plays a role in emotion and response to stress.
Reticular formation	Plays a role in controlling arousal and in ability to focus attention on particular stimuli.
Hippocampus	Plays a special role in memory; also involved in emotional behavior.
Cerebellum	Concerned primarily with the coordination of movement.
Medulla	Controls breathing and some reflexes that help the organism maintain an upright posture.

of movement. Specific movements may be initiated at higher levels, but the coordination of those movements depends on the cerebellum. Damage to the cerebellum results in jerky, uncoordinated movements.

Some surprising new evidence has identified direct neural connections between the cerebellum and frontal parts of the brain involved in language, planning, and reasoning (Middleton & Strick, 1994). These connecting circuits are much larger in human beings than in monkeys and other animals. This and other evidence suggests that the cerebellum may play a role in the control and coordination of higher mental functions as well as in the coordination of movements.

The Thalamus   Located just above the midbrain inside the cerebral hemispheres are two egg-shaped groups of nerve cell nuclei that make up the *thalamus.* One region of the thalamus acts as a relay station, directing incoming information from the sense receptors (vision, hearing, etc.) to the cerebrum. Another region of the thalamus plays an important role in the control of sleep and wakefulness.

The Hypothalamus   The *hypothalamus* is a much smaller structure located just below the thalamus. Centers in the hypothalamus regulate eating, drinking, and sexual behavior. The hypothalamus also regulates endocrine activity and maintains homeostasis. **Homeostasis** refers to *the normal level of functioning that is characteristic of the healthy organism,* such as normal body temperature, heart rate, and blood pressure. When an organism is under stress, homeostasis is disturbed and processes are set into motion to correct the disequilibrium. For example, if we are too warm, we perspire; and if we are too cool, we shiver. Both of these processes tend to restore normal temperature and are controlled by the hypothalamus.

The hypothalamus also plays an important role in the sensation of emotions and in our response to stress-producing situations. Mild electrical stimulation of certain areas in the hypothalamus produces feelings of pleasure; stimulation of adjacent regions produces sensations that are unpleasant. Through its influence on the pituitary gland, which lies just below it (see Figure 2-11), the hypothalamus controls the endocrine system and, thus, the production of hormones. This control is particularly important when the body must mobilize a complex set of physiological processes (known as the "fight-or-flight response") to deal with emergencies. The hypothalamus has been described as the brain's "stress center" in recognition of this function.

The Reticular Formation   A network of neural circuits that extends from the lower brain stem up to the thalamus, traversing some of the other central core structures, is called the *reticular formation.* This network of neurons plays an important role in controlling arousal. When an electric current of a certain voltage is sent through electrodes implanted in the reticular formation of a cat or dog, the animal goes to sleep; stimulation by a current with a more rapidly changing waveform awakens the sleeping animal.

The reticular formation also plays a role in our ability to focus attention on particular stimuli. All of the sense receptors have nerve fibers that feed into the reticular system. The system appears to act as a filter, allowing some sensory messages to pass to the cerebral cortex (that is, to conscious awareness) while blocking others. Thus, our state of consciousness at any moment appears to be influenced by a filtering process taking place in the reticular formation.

The Limbic System

Around the central core of the brain is the **limbic system,** *a set of structures that are closely interconnected with the hypothalamus and appear to impose additional controls over some of the instinctive behaviors regulated by the hypothalamus and the brain stem* (refer back to Figure 2-10). Animals that have only rudimentary limbic systems, such as fish and reptiles, carry out activities such as feeding, attacking, fleeing, and mating by means of stereotyped behaviors. In mammals, the limbic system seems to inhibit some of these instinctive patterns, allowing the organism to be more flexible and better able to adapt to changes in the environment.

One part of the limbic system, the *hippocampus,* plays a special role in memory. The effects of surgical removal of the hippocampus have demonstrated that it plays a critical role in storing new events as lasting

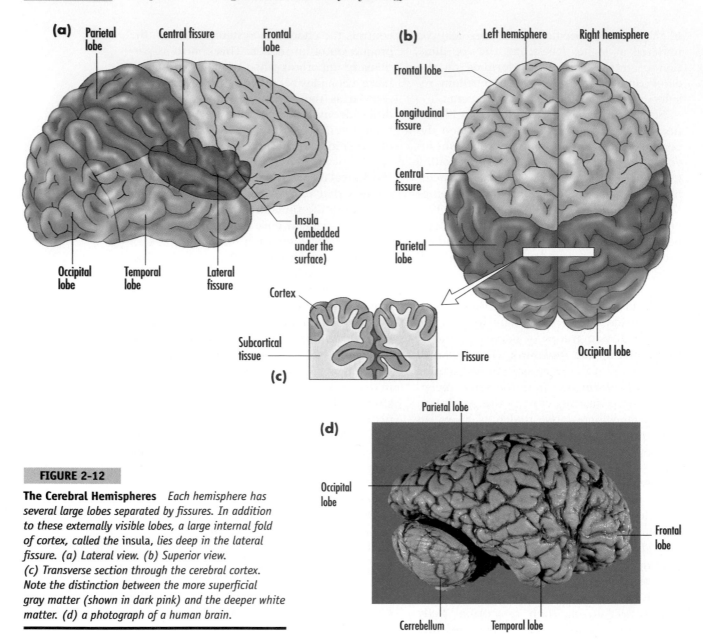

(a) Parietal lobe · Central fissure · Frontal lobe · Occipital lobe · Temporal lobe · Lateral fissure · Insula (embedded under the surface)

(b) Left hemisphere · Right hemisphere · Frontal lobe · Longitudinal fissure · Central fissure · Parietal lobe · Occipital lobe

(c) Cortex · Subcortical tissue · Fissure

(d) Parietal lobe · Occipital lobe · Cerrebellum · Temporal lobe · Frontal lobe

FIGURE 2-12

The Cerebral Hemispheres *Each hemisphere has several large lobes separated by fissures. In addition to these externally visible lobes, a large internal fold of cortex, called the* insula, *lies deep in the lateral fissure. (a) Lateral view. (b) Superior view. (c) Transverse section through the cerebral cortex. Note the distinction between the more superficial gray matter (shown in dark pink) and the deeper white matter. (d) a photograph of a human brain.*

memories, yet is not necessary for the retrieval of older memories. Upon recovery from such an operation, patients have no difficulty recognizing old friends or recalling earlier experiences; they are able to read and perform skills learned earlier in life. However, they have little, if any, recall of events that occurred during the year before the operation, and they cannot remember events occurring after the operation at all. For example, they will fail to recognize a new person with whom they may have spent many hours earlier in the day. They will do the same jigsaw puzzle week after week, never remembering having done it before, and will read the same newspaper over and over without remembering the contents (Squire & Zola, 1996).

The limbic system is also involved in emotional behavior. Monkeys in which some regions of the limbic system are damaged react with rage at the slightest provocation, suggesting that the destroyed area normally has an inhibiting influence. Monkeys with damage to other areas of the limbic system no longer express aggressive behavior and show no hostility, even when attacked. They simply ignore the attacker and act as if nothing had happened.

Describing the brain in terms of three concentric structures—the central core, the limbic system, and the cerebrum (discussed in the next section)—must not lead us to think of these structures as independent of one another. They are actually analogous to a network of interrelated computers. Each has specialized functions, but they must work together to produce the most effective result. Similarly, the analysis of information coming from the senses requires one kind of computation and decision process (for which the cerebrum is well adapted), which differs from the kind required for controlling a reflexive sequence of activities (the limbic system). Finer adjustments of the muscles (as in writing or playing a musical instrument) require another kind of control system, which is provided by the primary motor area on the cortex in the forebrain. All these activities are organized into an integrated system that keeps the organism functioning smoothly.

The Cerebrum

The **cerebrum**—*the brain's two cerebral hemispheres*—is more highly developed in humans than in any other organism. Its outer layer is called the *cerebral cortex* (or simply *cortex*) from the Latin word for "bark." The cortex of a preserved brain appears gray because it consists largely of nerve cell bodies and unmyelinated fibers—hence the term "gray matter." The inside of the cerebrum, beneath the cortex, is composed mostly of myelinated axons and appears white.

Each of the sensory systems sends information to specific areas of the cortex. Motor responses, or movements of body parts, are controlled by another area of the cortex. The rest of the cortex, which is neither sensory nor motor, consists of *association areas*. These areas occupy the largest portion of the human cortex and are concerned with memory, thought, and language.

Before discussing some of these locations, we need to establish a few landmarks to use in describing specific areas of the cerebral hemispheres. The two hemispheres are basically symmetrical, with a deep division between them running from front to rear. We therefore refer to the right and left hemispheres. Each hemisphere is divided into four lobes: *frontal, parietal, occipital,* and *temporal.* The divisions between these lobes are shown in Figure 2-12. The frontal lobe is separated from the parietal lobe by the *central fissure,* which runs from near the top of the head sideways to the ears. The division between the parietal

lobe and the occipital lobe is less clear-cut; for our purposes, we can say that the parietal lobe is at the top of the brain behind the central fissure and that the occipital lobe is at the rear of the brain. The temporal lobe is set off by a deep fissure at the side of the brain, the *lateral fissure.*

The Primary Motor Area The *primary motor area* controls voluntary movements of the body; it lies just in front of the central fissure (see Figure 2-13). Electrical stimulation at certain spots on the motor cortex causes specific parts of the body to move; when these same spots on the motor cortex are injured, movement is impaired. The body is represented on the motor cortex in approximately upside-down form. For example, movements of the toes are controlled from an area near the top of the head, while tongue and mouth movements are controlled from near the bottom of the motor area. Movements on the right side of the body are governed by the motor cortex of the left hemisphere; movements on the left side are governed by the right hemisphere.

The Primary Somatosensory Area In the parietal lobe, separated from the motor area by the central fissure, lies an area that, when stimulated electrically, produces a sensory experience somewhere on the opposite side of the body. It is as though a part of the body were being touched or moved. This is called the *primary somatosensory area* (body-sense area). Heat, cold, touch, pain, and the sense of body movement are represented here.

Most of the nerve fibers in the pathways that radiate to and from the somatosensory and motor areas cross to the opposite side of the body. Thus, sensory impulses from the right side of the body go to the left somatosensory cortex, and the muscles of the right foot and hand are controlled by the left motor cortex.

In general, the amount of somatosensory or motor area associated with a particular part of the body is related to its sensitivity and use. For example, among four-footed mammals, the dog has only a small amount of cortical tissue representing the forepaws, whereas the raccoon—which makes extensive use of its forepaws in exploring and manipulating its environment—has a much larger cortical area to control the forepaws, including regions for separate fingers. The

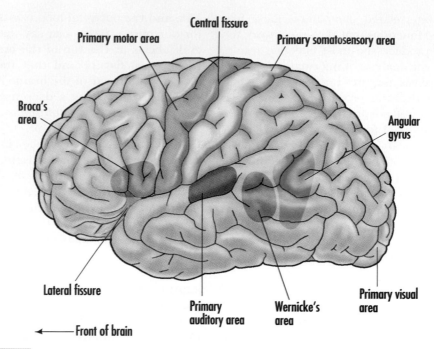

FIGURE 2-13

Specialization of Function in the Left Cortex   *A major part of the cortex is involved in generating movements and analyzing sensory inputs. These areas (which include motor, somatosensory, visual, auditory, and olfactory areas) are present on both sides of the brain. Other functions are found on only one side of the brain. For example, Broca's area and Wernicke's area are involved in the production and understanding of language, and the angular gyrus is involved in matching the visual form of a word with its auditory form; these functions exist only on the left side of the human brain.*

rat, which learns a great deal about its environment by means of its sensitive whiskers, has a separate cortical area for each whisker.

The Primary Visual Area   At the back of each occipital lobe is an area of the cortex known as the *primary visual area*. Figure 2-14 shows the optic nerve fibers and neural pathways leading from each eye to the visual cortex. Notice that some of the optic fibers from the right eye go to the right cerebral hemisphere, whereas others cross over at a junction called the *optic chiasm* and go to the opposite hemisphere; the same arrangement holds true for the left eye. Fibers from the right sides of both eyes go to the right hemisphere of the brain, and fibers from the left sides of both eyes go to the left hemisphere. Thus, for example, damage to the visual area of the left hemisphere will result in blind fields in the left sides of both eyes, causing a loss of vision to the right side of the environment. This fact is sometimes helpful in pinpointing the location of a brain tumor or other abnormalities.

The Primary Auditory Area   The *primary auditory area*, located on the surface of the temporal lobe at the side of each hemisphere, plays a role in the analysis of complex auditory signals—particularly the temporal patterning of sound, as in human speech. Both ears are represented in the auditory areas on both sides of the cortex; however, connections to the contralateral, or opposite, side are stronger. This means that the right ear sends information to both the right and left primary auditory areas, but it sends more information to the auditory area on the left side of the brain. The opposite is true of the left ear.

Association Areas   As mentioned earlier, the areas of the cerebral cortex that are not directly concerned with sensory or motor processes are called *association areas*. The *frontal association areas* (the parts of the frontal lobes in front of the motor area) appear to play an important role in thought processes required for problem solving. In monkeys, for example, damage to the frontal

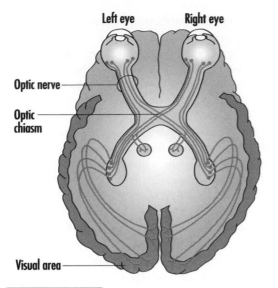

FIGURE 2-14

Visual Pathways *Nerve fibers from the inner, or nasal, half of the retina cross over at the optic chiasm and go to opposite sides of the brain. Thus, stimuli falling on the right side of each retina are transmitted to the right hemisphere, and stimuli falling on the left side of each retina are transmitted to the left hemisphere.*

lobes destroys the ability to solve a delayed-response problem. In this kind of problem, food is placed in one of two cups while the monkey watches, and the cups are covered with identical objects. An opaque screen is then placed between the monkey and the cups; after a specified period the screen is removed and the monkey is allowed to choose one of the cups. Normal monkeys can remember the correct cup after delays of several minutes, but monkeys with frontal lobe damage cannot solve the problem if the delay is more than a few seconds. Normal monkeys have neurons in the frontal lobe that fire action potentials during the delay, thus possibly mediating their memory of an event (Goldman-Rakic, 1996).

The *posterior association areas* are located near the various primary sensory areas and appear to consist of subareas that each serve a particular sense. For example, the lower portion of the temporal lobe is related to visual perception. Lesions (that is, brain damage) in this area cause deficiencies in the ability to recognize and discriminate between different forms. A lesion here does not cause loss of visual acuity, as would a lesion in the primary visual area of the occipital lobe; the individual "sees" the form and

traces its outline, but cannot identify the shape or distinguish it from a different form (Goodglass & Butters, 1988).

Pictures of the Living Brain

A number of techniques have been developed to obtain detailed pictures of the living human brain without causing the patient distress or damage. Before these techniques were perfected, the precise location and identification of most types of brain injury could be determined only by exploratory neurosurgery, a complicated neurological diagnosis, or an autopsy after the patient's death. The new techniques depend on sophisticated computer methods that have become feasible only recently.

One such technique is *computerized axial tomography* (CAT or CT). In this procedure a narrow X-ray beam is sent through the patient's head and the amount of radiation that gets through is measured. The revolutionary aspect of this technique is that measurements can be made on hundreds of thousands of different orientations (or axes) through the head. These measurements are fed into a computer to construct a cross-sectional picture of the brain that can be photographed or displayed on a television monitor. The cross-sectional "slice" *(tomo* is an ancient Greek word meaning "slice" or "cut") can be shown at any level and angle desired.

A newer and even more powerful technique is *magnetic resonance imaging* (MRI). Scanners use strong magnetic fields, radio-frequency pulses, and computers to compose an image. In this procedure the patient lies in a doughnut-shaped tunnel surrounded by a large magnet that generates a powerful magnetic field. When a selected part of the body is placed in a strong magnetic field and exposed to a certain radio-frequency pulse, the tissues emit a signal that can be measured. As with the CT scanner, hundreds of thousands of measurements can be made and then manipulated by a computer to produce a two-dimensional image of the part of the body under study. Scientists usually call this technique "nuclear magnetic resonance" because it measures variations in the energy level of hydrogen atom nuclei caused by the radio-frequency pulses. However, many physicians leave out the term "nuclear" because they

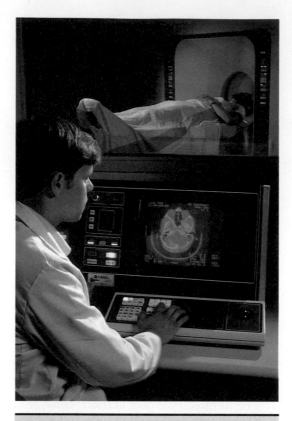

A technician administering a magnetic resonance imaging procedure. An image of the patient's brain appears on the computer screen.

Red areas indicate maximum brain activity; blue areas show minimum activity.

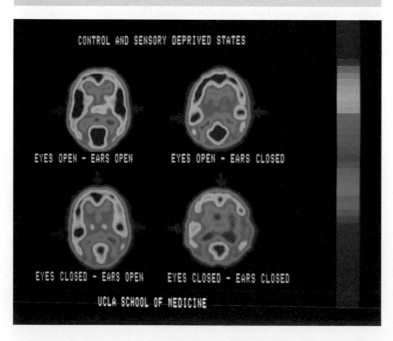

CONTROL AND SENSORY DEPRIVED STATES

EYES OPEN - EARS OPEN   EYES OPEN - EARS CLOSED

EYES CLOSED - EARS OPEN   EYES CLOSED - EARS CLOSED

UCLA SCHOOL OF MEDICINE

fear that the public may perceive it as referring to nuclear radiation.

MRI offers greater precision than the CT scanner in the diagnosis of diseases of the brain and spinal cord. For example, an MRI cross-section of the brain shows features characteristic of multiple sclerosis that are not detected by a CT scanner; previously, diagnosis of this disease required hospitalization and a test in which dye is injected into the canal around the spinal cord. MRI is also useful in detecting abnormalities in the spinal cord and at the base of the brain, such as herniated disks, tumors, and birth malformations.

While CT and MRI provide a picture of the anatomical details of the brain, it is often desirable to assess levels of neural activity at different locations in the brain. A computer-based scanning procedure called *positron emission tomography* (PET) provides this information. This technique depends on the fact that every cell in the body requires energy to conduct metabolic processes. In the brain, neurons use glucose (obtained from the bloodstream) as their principal source of energy. A small amount of a radioactive tracer compound can be mixed with glucose so that each molecule of glucose has a tiny speck of radioactivity (that is, a *label*) attached to it. If this harmless mixture is injected into the bloodstream, after a few minutes the brain cells begin to use the radio-labeled glucose in the same way that they use regular glucose. The PET scan is essentially a highly sensitive detector of radioactivity. The neurons that are most active require the most glucose and therefore will be the most radioactive. The PET scan measures the amount of radioactivity and sends the information to a computer that draws a cross-sectional picture of the brain, using different colors to represent different levels of neural activity. The measurement of radioactivity is based on the emission of positively charged particles called "positrons" —hence the term "positron emission tomography."

Comparing PET scans of normal individuals with those of people with neurological disorders indicates that a variety of brain problems (epilepsy, blood clots, brain tumors, and so on) can be identified using this technique. The PET scan has also been used to compare the brains of schizophrenics with those of normal individuals and has revealed differences in metabolic levels in certain cortical

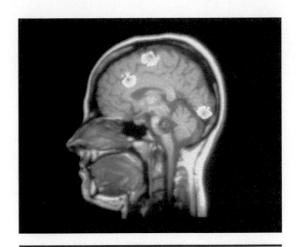

This PET image shows three areas in the left brain that are active during a language task.

areas (Andreasen, 1988). It has also been used to investigate the brain areas that are activated during higher mental functions such as listening to music, doing mathematics, or speaking—the goal being to identify the brain structures involved (Posner, 1993).

CT, MRI, and PET are proving to be invaluable tools for studying the relationship between the brain and behavior. These instruments provide an example of how progress in one field of science forges ahead because of technical developments in another (Raichle, 1994; Pechura & Martin, 1991). For example, PET scans can be used to study differences in neural activity between the two cerebral hemispheres. These hemispheric differences in activity are known as *brain asymmetries*.

Asymmetries in the Brain

At first glance, the two halves of the brain look like mirror images of each other. But when brains are measured during autopsies, the left hemisphere is almost always larger than the right hemisphere. Also, the right hemisphere contains many long neural fibers that connect widely separated areas of the brain, whereas the left hemisphere contains many shorter fibers that provide large numbers of interconnections within a limited area (Hellige, 1993).

As early as 1861, the French physician Paul Broca examined the brain of a patient who had suffered speech loss. He found damage in an area of the left hemisphere just above the lateral fissure in the frontal lobe. This region,

known as *Broca's area* (see Figure 2-13), is involved in the production of speech. Destruction of the equivalent region in the right hemisphere usually does not result in speech impairment. The areas involved in understanding speech and being able to write and understand written words are also usually located in the left hemisphere. Thus, a person who suffers a stroke that damages the left hemisphere is more likely to show language impairment than one in whom damage is confined to the right hemisphere. A few left-handed people have speech centers located in the right hemisphere, but the great majority have language functions in the left hemisphere, as do most right-handed individuals.

Although the left hemisphere's role in language has been known for some time, only recently has it been possible to investigate what each hemisphere can do on its own. In a normal individual the brain functions as an integrated whole; information in one hemisphere is immediately transferred to the other via a broad band of connecting nerve fibers called the *corpus callosum*. This connecting bridge is a problem in some forms of epilepsy because a seizure starting in one hemisphere may cross over and trigger a massive discharge of neurons in the other hemisphere. In an effort to prevent such generalized seizures, neurosurgeons have surgically severed the corpus callosum in individuals with severe epilepsy. The operation has proved successful in some cases, resulting in a decrease in seizures. In addition, there appear to be no undesirable aftereffects; the patients seem to function as well as individuals whose hemispheres are still connected.

Split-Brain Research It took some very special tests to demonstrate how mental functions are affected by separating the two hemispheres. But before describing these, we need a little more background information. We have seen that the motor nerves cross over as they leave the brain, so that the left cerebral hemisphere controls the right side of the body and the right hemisphere controls the left. We noted also that the area for the production of speech (Broca's area) is located in the left hemisphere. When the eyes are fixated directly ahead, images to the left of the fixation point go through both eyes to the right side of the brain and images to the right of the fixation point go to the left side of the brain (see Figure 2-15). Thus, each hemisphere has a view of the half of the visual field in which "its" hand normally functions; for example, the left hemisphere sees the right hand in the right visual field. In the normal brain, stimuli entering one hemisphere are rapidly communicated to the other, so that the

brain functions as a unit. Now let us take a look at what happens when the corpus callosum is severed—leaving a split brain—and the two hemispheres cannot communicate with each other.

Roger Sperry, who pioneered work in this field, was awarded the Nobel prize in 1981. In one of Sperry's test situations, a person who has undergone a split-brain operation is seated in front of a screen that hides his hands from view (see Figure 2-16a). His gaze is fixed on a spot at the center of the screen. The word "nut" is flashed on the left side of the screen for one-tenth of a second. Remember that this visual signal goes to the right side of the brain, which controls the left side of the body. With his left hand, the person can easily pick up a nut from a pile of objects hidden from view. But he cannot tell the experimenter what word flashed on the screen because speech is controlled by the left hemisphere and the visual image of "nut" was not transmitted to that hemisphere. When questioned, he seems unaware of what his left hand is doing. Since the sensory input from the left hand goes to the right hemisphere, the left hemisphere receives no information about what the left hand is feeling or doing. All information is fed back to the right hemisphere, which received the original visual input of the word "nut."

It is important that the word be flashed on the screen for no more than one-tenth of a second. If it remains longer, the person's eyes move so that the word is also projected to the left hemisphere. If people can move their eyes freely, information goes to both cerebral hemispheres; this is one reason why the deficiencies caused by severing the corpus callosum are not readily apparent in a person's daily activities.

Further experiments demonstrate that a split-brain patient can communicate through speech only what is going on in the left hemisphere. Figure 2-16b shows another test situation. The word "hatband" was flashed on the screen so that "hat" went to the right hemisphere and "band" to the left. When asked what word he saw, the person replied, "band." When asked what kind of band, he made all sorts of guesses—"rubber band," "rock band," "band of robbers," and so forth—and only hit on "hatband" by chance. Tests with other word combinations (such as "keycase" and "suitcase") have

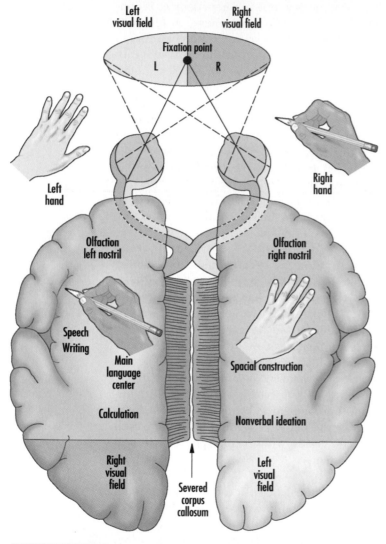

FIGURE 2-15

Sensory Inputs to the Two Hemispheres *With the eyes fixated straight ahead, stimuli to the left of the fixation point go to the right cerebral hemisphere, and stimuli to the right go to the left hemisphere. The left hemisphere controls movements of the right hand, and the right hemisphere controls the left hand. Hearing is largely crossed in its input, but some sound representation goes to the hemisphere on the same side as the ear that registered it. The left hemisphere controls written and spoken language and mathematical calculations. The right hemisphere can understand only simple language; its main ability seems to involve spatial construction and pattern sense.*

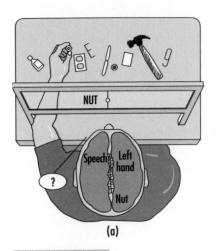
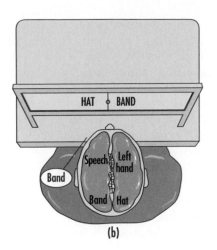
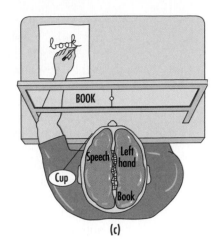

(a)   (b)   (c)

Testing the Abilities of the Two Hemispheres   *(a) A split-brain patient correctly retrieves an object by touch with the left hand when its name is flashed to the right hemisphere, but he cannot name the object or describe what he has done. (b) The word "hatband" is flashed so that "hat" goes to the right cerebral hemisphere and "band" goes to the left hemisphere. The patient reports that he sees the word "band" but has no idea what kind of band. (c) A list of common objects (including "book" and "cup") is initially shown to both hemispheres. One word from the list ("book") is then projected to the right hemisphere. When given the command to do so, the left hand begins writing the word "book," but when questioned, the patient does not know what his left hand has written and guesses "cup."*

shown similar results. What is perceived by the right hemisphere is not transferred to the conscious awareness of the left hemisphere. With the corpus callosum severed, each hemisphere seems oblivious to the experiences of the other.

If split-brain patients are blindfolded and a familiar object (such as a comb, toothbrush, or keycase) is placed in their left hand, they appear to know what it is; for example, they can demonstrate its use by appropriate gestures. But they cannot express this knowledge in speech. If asked what is going on while they are manipulating the object, they have no idea. This is true as long as any sensory input from the object to the left (speaking) hemisphere is blocked. But if the patient's right hand inadvertently touches the object or if the object makes a characteristic sound (like the jingling of a keycase), the speaking hemisphere immediately gives the correct answer.

Although the right hemisphere cannot speak, it does have some linguistic capabilities. It recognized the meaning of the word "nut" in our first example, and it can write a little. In the experiment illustrated in Figure 2-16c, split-brain patients are first shown a list of common objects such as a cup, a knife, a book, and a glass. This list is displayed long enough for the words to be pro-

jected to both hemispheres. Next, the list is removed, and one of the words (for example, "book") is flashed briefly on the left side of the screen so that it goes to the right hemisphere. When patients are asked to write what they saw, their left hand will begin writing the word "book." If asked what their left hand has written, they have no idea and will guess at any of the words on the original list. They know that they have written something because they feel the writing movements through their body. But because there is no communication between the right hemisphere that saw and wrote the word and the left hemisphere that controls speech, they cannot tell you what they wrote (Sperry, 1970, 1968; see also Hellige, 1990, and Gazzaniga, 1995).

Hemispheric Specialization   Studies with split-brain patients indicate that the two hemispheres function differently. The left hemisphere governs our ability to express ourselves in language. It can perform complicated logical activities and is skilled in mathematical computations. The right hemisphere can comprehend only very simple language. It can, for example, respond to simple nouns by selecting objects such as a nut or a comb, but it cannot comprehend more abstract linguistic forms. If it is presented with simple commands like "wink," "nod," "shake head," or "smile," it seldom responds.

The right hemisphere, however, has a highly developed spatial and pattern sense. It is superior to the left hemisphere in constructing geometric and perspective drawings. It can assemble colored blocks to match a complex design much more effectively than the left hemisphere. When split-brain patients are asked to use their right hand to assemble blocks to match a design shown in a picture, they make numerous mistakes. Sometimes they have trouble keeping their left hand from automatically correcting the mistakes being made by the right hand.

Studies with normal individuals tend to confirm the different specializations of the two hemispheres. For example, verbal information (such as words or nonsense syllables) can be identified faster and more accurately when flashed briefly to the left hemisphere (that is, in the right visual field) than to the right hemisphere. In contrast, identification of faces, facial expressions of emotion, line slopes, or dot locations occurs more quickly when these are flashed to the right hemisphere (Hellige, 1990). Also, studies using electroencephalograms (EEG) indicate that electrical activity from the left hemisphere increases during a verbal task, whereas during a spatial task, electrical ac-

tivity increases in the right hemisphere (Springer & Deutsch, 1989; Kosslyn, 1988).

One should not infer from this discussion that the two hemispheres work independently of each other. Just the opposite is true. The hemispheres differ in their specializations, but they continually integrate their activities. It is this interaction that gives rise to mental processes that are greater than and different from each hemisphere's special contribution. As one researcher describes it,

> These differences are seen in the contrasting contributions each hemisphere makes to all cognitive activities. When a person reads a story, the right hemisphere may play a special role in decoding visual information, maintaining an integrated story structure, appreciating humor and emotional content, deriving meaning from past associations and understanding metaphor. At the same time, the left hemisphere plays a special role in understanding syntax, translating written words into their phonetic representations and deriving meaning from complex relations among word concepts and syntax. But there is no activity in which only one hemisphere is involved or to which only one hemisphere makes a contribution. (Levy, 1985, p. 44)

Language and the Brain

A great deal of our information about brain mechanisms for language comes from observations of patients suffering from brain damage. The damage may be due to tumors, penetrating head wounds, or the rupture of blood vessels. The term **aphasia** is used to describe *language deficits caused by brain damage.*

As discussed earlier, Broca observed that damage to a specific area on the side of the left frontal lobe was linked to a speech disorder called *expressive aphasia.* People with damage to Broca's area have difficulty enunciating words correctly and speak in a slow, labored way. Their speech often makes sense, but it includes only key words. Nouns are generally expressed in the singular, and adjectives, adverbs, articles, and conjunctions are likely to be omitted. However, these individuals have no difficulty understanding either spoken or written language.

In 1874 a German investigator, Carl Wernicke, reported that damage to another site in the cortex—also in the left hemisphere, but located in the temporal lobe—is linked to a language disorder called *receptive*

Studies with split-brain patients have shown that the two hemispheres specialize in different aspects of mental functioning. The right hemisphere, for example, is superior in constructing geometric and perspective drawings, leading to the belief that artists have a highly developed "right brain."

aphasia. People with damage in this location, known as *Wernicke's area,* are unable to comprehend words: They can hear words, but they do not know their meaning. They can produce strings of words without difficulty and with proper articulation, but they make errors in usage and their speech tends to be meaningless.

On the basis of an analysis of these defects, Wernicke developed a model to explain how the brain functions in producing and understanding language. Although his model is 100 years old, its general features still appear to be correct. Norman Geschwind built on these ideas in developing a theory that has come to be known as the Wernicke-Geschwind model (Geschwind, 1979). According to this model, Broca's area stores articulatory codes, which specify the sequence of muscle actions required to pronounce a word. When these codes are transmitted to the motor area, they activate the muscles of the lips, tongue, and larynx in the proper sequence and produce a spoken word. Wernicke's area, on the other hand, is where auditory codes and the meanings of words are stored. For a word to be spoken, its auditory code must be activated in Wernicke's area and transmitted to Broca's area, where it activates the corresponding articulatory code. In turn, the articulatory code is transmitted to the motor area to activate the muscles that produce the spoken word.

If a word spoken by someone else is to be understood, it must be transmitted from the auditory area to Wernicke's area. There the spoken form of the word is matched with its auditory code, which in turn activates the word's meaning. When a written word is presented, it is first registered in the visual area and then relayed to the angular gyrus, which associates the visual form of the word with its auditory code in Wernicke's area; once the word's auditory code has been found, so has its meaning. Thus, the meanings of words are stored along with their acoustical codes in Wernicke's area. Broca's area stores articulatory codes, and the angular gyrus matches the written form of a word to its auditory code. Neither of these areas, however, stores information about word meaning. The meaning of a word is retrieved only when its acoustical code is activated in Wernicke's area.

The Wernicke-Geschwind model explains many of the language deficits shown by aphasics. Damage that is limited to Broca's area disrupts speech production but has less effect on the comprehension of spoken or written language. Damage to Wernicke's area disrupts all aspects of language comprehension, but the person can still articulate words properly (even though the output is meaningless) because Broca's area is intact. The model also predicts that individuals with damage in the angular gyrus will not be able to read, but will have no difficulty speaking or comprehending speech. Finally, if damage is restricted to the auditory area, a person will be able to read and speak normally, but he or she will not be able to comprehend speech.

The Autonomic Nervous System

We noted earlier that the peripheral nervous system consists of two divisions. The somatic system controls the skeletal muscles and receives information from the skin, muscles, and various sensory receptors. The autonomic system controls the glands and the smooth muscles, which include the heart, the blood vessels, and the lining of the stomach and intestines. These muscles are called "smooth" because that is how they look when examined under a microscope. (Skeletal muscles, in contrast, have a striped appearance.) The autonomic nervous system derives its name from the fact that many of the activities it controls are autonomous, or self-regulating, and continue even when a person is asleep or unconscious; examples include digestion and circulation.

The autonomic nervous system has two divisions, *sympathetic* and *parasympathetic,* whose actions are often antagonistic. Figure 2-17 shows the contrasting effects of the two systems on various organs. For example, the parasympathetic system constricts the pupil of the eye, stimulates the flow of saliva, and slows the heart rate; the sympathetic system has the opposite effect in each case. The normal state of the body (somewhere between extreme excitement and vegetative placidity) is maintained by the balance between these two systems.

The sympathetic division tends to act as a unit. During emotional excitement, it simultaneously speeds up the heart, dilates the arteries of the skeletal muscles and heart,

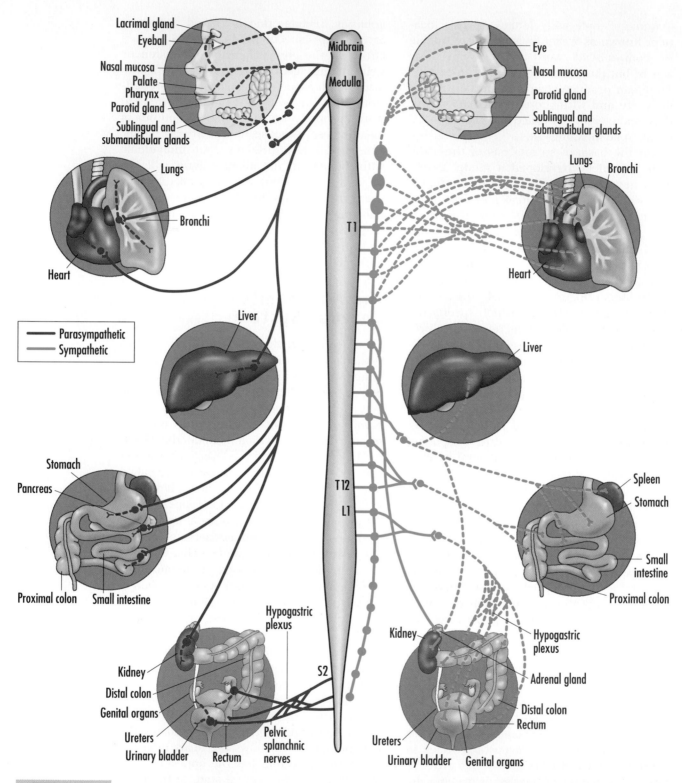

FIGURE 2-17

Motor Fibers of the Autonomic Nervous System *In this diagram the sympathetic division is indicated in blue and the parasympathetic division in red. Solid lines indicate preganglionic fibers; dashed lines indicate postganglionic fibers. Neurons of the sympathetic division originate in the thoracic and lumbar regions of the spinal cord; they form synaptic junctions with ganglia lying just outside the cord. Neurons of the parasympathetic division exit from the medulla region of the brain stem and from the lower (sacral) end of the spinal cord; they connect with ganglia near the organs stimulated. Most internal organs are innervated by both divisions, which function in opposition to each other.*

constricts the arteries of the skin and digestive organs, and causes perspiration. It also activates certain endocrine glands to secrete hormones that further increase arousal.

Unlike the sympathetic system, the parasympathetic division tends to affect one organ at a time. Whereas the sympathetic system is dominant during violent and excited activity, the parasympathetic system is dominant during periods of quiescence. It participates in digestion and, in general, maintains the functions that conserve and protect bodily resources. For example, a decreased heart rate and slowed breathing, which are maintained by the parasympathetic nervous system, require far less energy than a fast heartbeat and rapid breathing, which are by-products of activation of the sympathetic nervous system.

While the sympathetic and parasympathetic systems are usually antagonistic, there are some exceptions to this principle. For example, the sympathetic system is dominant during fear and excitement; however, a not-uncommon parasympathetic symptom during extreme fear is involuntary discharge of the bladder or bowels. Another example is the complete sex act in the male, which requires erection (parasympathetic) followed by ejaculation (sympathetic). Thus, although the two systems are often antagonistic, they interact in complex ways.

The Endocrine System

We can think of the nervous system as controlling the fast-changing activities of the body through its ability to directly activate muscles and glands. (*Glands* are organs located throughout the body that secrete special substances, such as sweat, milk, or a particular hormone.) The endocrine system acts more slowly, indirectly affecting the activities of cell groups throughout the body. It does so by means of **hormones,** *chemicals secreted by the endocrine glands into the bloodstream and transported to other parts of the body, where they have specific effects on cells that recognize their message* (see Figure 2-18). Hormones act in various ways on cells of different types. Each target cell is equipped with receptors that recognize only the hormone molecules that act on that cell; the receptors pull

those molecules out of the bloodstream and into the cell. Some endocrine glands are activated by the nervous system, while others are activated by changes in the internal chemical state of the body.

One of the major endocrine glands is the *pituitary.* This gland is partly an outgrowth of the brain and lies just below the hypothalamus (refer back to Figure 2-11). The pituitary has been called the "master gland" because it produces the largest number of different hormones and controls the secretion activity of other endocrine glands. One of the pituitary hormones has the crucial job of controlling the body's growth. Too little of this hormone can create a dwarf, while too much can produce a giant. Other hormones released by the pituitary trigger the action of other endocrine glands, such as the thyroid, the sex glands, and the outer layer of the adrenal gland. Courtship, mating, and reproductive behavior in many animals are based on a complex interaction between the activity of the nervous system and the influence of the pituitary on the sex glands.

The relationship between the pituitary gland and the hypothalamus illustrates the complex interactions that take place between the endocrine system and the nervous system. In response to stress (fear, anxiety, pain, emotional events, and so forth) certain neurons in the hypothalamus secrete a substance called corticotropin-release factor (CRF), which is carried to the pituitary through a channel-like structure. The CRF stimulates the pituitary to release adrenocorticotrophic hormone (ACTH), the body's major stress hormone. ACTH, in turn, is carried by the bloodstream to the adrenal glands and various other organs, causing the release of some 30 hormones, each of which plays a role in the body's adjustment to emergency situations.

The adrenal glands play an important role in determining mood, energy level, and ability to cope with stress. The inner core of the adrenal gland secretes epinephrine and norepinephrine (also known as adrenaline and noradrenaline). Epinephrine acts in a number of ways to prepare the organism for an emergency. In conjunction with the sympathetic division of the autonomic nervous system, it affects the smooth muscles and sweat glands. It also causes constriction of the blood vessels in the stomach and intestines

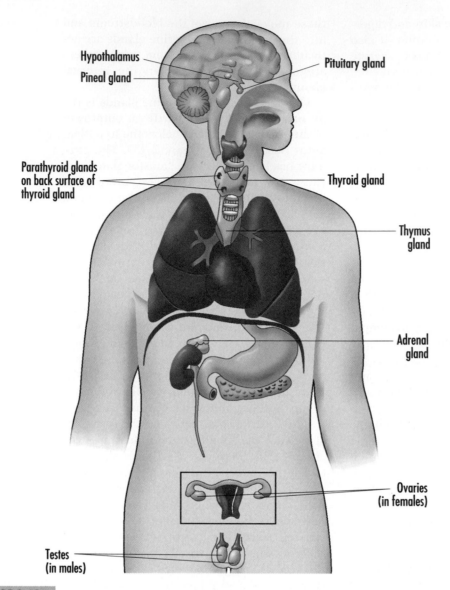

FIGURE 2-18

Some of the Endocrine Glands   *Hormones secreted by the endocrine glands are as essential as the nervous system to the integration of the organism's activity. The two systems differ, however, in the speed with which they can act. A nerve impulse can travel through the organism in a few hundredths of a second. Seconds, or even minutes, may be required for an endocrine gland to produce an effect; the hormone, once released, must travel to its target site via the bloodstream—a much slower process.*

and makes the heart beat faster. Norepinephrine also prepares the organism for emergency action. It stimulates the pituitary to release a hormone that acts on the outer layer of the adrenal glands; this hormone, in turn, stimulates the liver to increase the blood-sugar level so that the body has the energy required for quick action.

The hormones of the endocrine system and the neurotransmitters of neurons perform similar functions: They both carry messages between cells. A neurotransmitter carries messages between adjacent neurons, and its effects are highly localized. In contrast, a hormone may travel a long distance through the body and act in various ways on many different types of cells. Despite these differences, the basic similarity between these chemical messengers is shown by the fact that some of them serve both functions. Epinephrine and norepinephrine, for example, act as neurotransmitters when they are released by neurons and as hormones when they are released by the adrenal gland.

Genetic Influences on Behavior

To fully understand the biological foundations of psychology, we need to know something about genetic influences as well as biological structures and processes. The field of **behavior genetics** *combines the methods of genetics and psychology to study the inheritance of behavioral characteristics* (Plomin, Owen, & McGuffin, 1994). We know that many *physical* characteristics—height, bone structure, hair and eye color, and so on—are inherited. Behavioral geneticists are interested in the degree to which *psychological* characteristics, including mental ability, temperament, emotional stability, and the like, are transmitted from parent to offspring (Bouchard, 1984, 1995). Recent research has even suggested that intelligence may have a genetic component. Researchers led by Robert Plomin of London's Institute of Psychiatry have identified a specific gene that contributes to intelligence (Plomin et al., 1998). However, findings like these are not conclusive. As we will see in this section, environmental conditions have a lot to do with the way a particular genetic factor is expressed in an individual as he or she matures.

Chromosomes and Genes

The hereditary units that we receive from our parents and transmit to our offspring are carried by **chromosomes,** *structures found in the nucleus of each cell in the body.* Most body cells contain 46 chromosomes. At conception, the human being receives 23 chromosomes from the father's sperm and 23 chromosomes from the mother's ovum. These 46 chromosomes form 23 pairs, which are duplicated each time the cells divide (see Figure 2-19).

Each chromosome is composed of many individual hereditary units called genes. A **gene** is *a segment of a deoxyribonucleic acid (DNA) molecule.* As shown in Figure 2-20, the DNA molecule looks like a twisted ladder or a double-stranded helix (spiral).

Each gene gives coded instructions to the cell, directing it to perform a specific function (usually to manufacture a particular protein). Although all cells in the body carry

the same genes, the specialized nature of each cell is due to the fact that only 5% to 10% of the genes in any given cell are active. In the process of developing from a fertilized egg, each cell switches on some genes and switches off all others. When "nerve genes" are active, for example, a cell develops as a neuron because the genes are directing the cell to make the products that allow it to perform neural functions (which would not be possible if irrelevant genes, such as "muscle genes," were not switched off).

Genes, like chromosomes, exist in pairs. One gene of each pair comes from the sperm chromosomes, and one gene comes from the ovum chromosomes. Thus, a child receives only half of each parent's total genes. The total number of genes in each human chromosome is around 1,000, perhaps higher. Because the number of genes is so high, it is extremely unlikely that two human beings would inherit the exact same set of genes, even if they were siblings. The only exception is identical twins, who, because they developed from the same fertilized egg, have exactly the same genes.

Dominant and Recessive Genes   Either gene of a gene pair can be *dominant* or *recessive.*

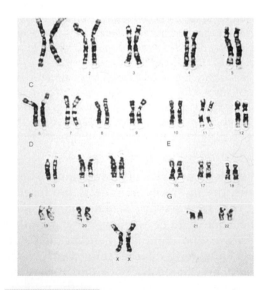

Chromosomes   *This photo (greatly enlarged) shows the 46 chromosomes of a normal human female. In a human male pairs 1 through 22 would be the same as those in the female, but pair 23 would be XY rather than XX.*

Structures of the DNA Molecule *Each strand of the molecule is made up of an alternating sequence of sugar (S) and phosphate (P); the rungs of the twisted ladder are made up of four bases (A, G, T, C). The double nature of the helix and the restriction on base pairings make possible the self-replication of DNA. In the process of cell division, the two strands of the DNA molecule come apart, with the base pairs separating; one member of each base pair remains attached to each strand. Each strand then forms a new complementary strand using excess bases available in the cell; an A attached to a strand will attract a T, and so forth. By this process, two identical molecules of DNA come to exist where previously there was one.*

When both members of a gene pair are dominant, the individual manifests the form of the trait specified by these dominant genes. When one gene is dominant and the other recessive, the dominant gene again determines the form of the trait. Only if the genes contributed by both parents are recessive is the recessive form of the trait expressed. In the case of the genes determining eye color, for example, blue is recessive and brown is dominant. Thus, a blue-eyed child may have two blue-eyed parents, or one blue-eyed parent and one brown-eyed parent (who carries a recessive gene for blue eyes), or two brown-eyed parents (each of whom carries a recessive gene for blue eyes). A brown-eyed child, in contrast, never has two blue-eyed parents. Some other characteristics that are carried by recessive genes are baldness, albinism, hemophilia, and susceptibility to poison ivy.

Most human characteristics are not determined by the actions of a single gene pair, but there are some striking exceptions in which a single gene has enormous importance. Of special interest from a psychological viewpoint are diseases like phenylketonuria (PKU) and Huntington's disease (HD), both of which involve deterioration of the nervous system and associated behavioral and cognitive problems. Geneticists have identified the genes that cause both of these disorders.

PKU results from the action of a recessive gene inherited from both parents. The infant cannot digest an essential amino acid (phenylalanine), which then builds up in the body, poisoning the nervous system and causing irreversible brain damage. PKU children are severely retarded and usually die before reaching the age of 30. If the PKU disorder is discovered at birth and the infant is placed on a diet that controls the level of phenylalanine, the chances of survival with good health and intelligence are fairly high. Until the PKU gene was located, the disorder could not be diagnosed until an infant was at least 3 weeks old. Now it is possible to determine whether a fetus has the PKU gene so that the proper diet can begin at birth.

HD is caused by a single dominant gene. The long-term course of the disease involves degeneration of certain areas in the brain; the ultimate outcome is death. Individuals with HD gradually lose the ability to talk and to control their movements, and show marked deterioration in memory and mental ability. The disease usually strikes when a person is 30 to 40 years old; before then there is no evidence of the disease. Once HD strikes, the individual will typically live another 10 to 15 years with progressive deterioration.

Now that the Huntington gene has been isolated, geneticists can test individuals at risk for the disease and determine whether or not they carry the gene. As yet, there is no cure for HD, but the protein produced by the gene has been identified and may provide a key to treating the disease.

Sex-Linked Genes A normal female has two similar-looking chromosomes in pair 23, called X chromosomes. A normal male has one X chromosome in pair 23 and one that looks slightly different, called a Y chromosome (refer back to Figure 2-19). Thus, the normal female chromosome pair is represented by XX and the normal male pair by XY.

Women, who have two X chromosomes, are protected from recessive traits carried on the X chromosome. Men, who have only one X chromosome and one Y chromosome, express more recessive traits because a gene that is carried on one of these chromosomes will not be countered by a dominant gene on the other. A variety of genetically determined characteristics and disorders are linked to the 23rd chromosome pair and hence are called *sex-linked traits* or *disorders*. For example, color blindness is a recessive sex-linked trait. A man will be color blind if the X chromosome he receives from his mother carries the gene for color blindness. Females are less likely to be color blind, because a color-blind female has to have both a color-blind father and a mother who is either color blind or carries a recessive gene for color blindness.

The famous folk singer Woody Guthrie died of Huntington's disease at the age of 55.

Genetic Studies of Behavior

Some traits are determined by single genes, but most human characteristics are determined by many genes; they are *polygenic*. Traits such as intelligence, height, and emotionality do not fall into distinct categories but show continuous variation. Most people are neither dull nor bright; intelligence is distributed over a broad range, with most individuals located near the middle. Sometimes a specific genetic defect can result in mental retardation, but in most cases a person's intellectual potential is determined by a large number of genes that influence the factors underlying different abilities. Of course, as we will see shortly, what happens to this genetic potential depends on environmental conditions (Plomin, Owen, & McGruffin, 1994).

Selective Breeding   One method of studying the inheritance of particular traits in animals is *selective breeding*. Animals that are high or low in a certain behavioral or physical trait are mated with each other. For example, in an early study of the inheritance of learning ability in rats, females that did

poorly in learning to run a maze were mated with males that did poorly; females that did well were mated with males that did well. The offspring of these matings are tested on the same maze. After a few rodent generations, "bright" and "dull" strains of rats were produced (see Figure 2-21).

Selective breeding has been used to demonstrate the inheritance of a number of behavioral characteristics. For example, dogs have been bred to be excitable or lethargic; chickens, to be aggressive and sexually active; fruit flies, to be more attracted or less attracted to light; and mice, to be more attracted or less attracted to alcohol. If a trait is influenced by heredity, it should be possible to change it through selective breeding. If selective breeding does not alter a trait, we assume that the trait is dependent primarily on environmental factors (Plomin, 1989).

Twin Studies   Since it is obviously unethical to carry out breeding experiments with human beings, we must look instead at similarities in behavior among individuals who are related. Certain traits often run in families. But family members are not only linked genetically; they also share the same environment. If musical talent "runs in the family," we do not know whether inherited ability or parental emphasis on music is the primary influence. Sons of alcoholic fathers are more likely than sons of nonalcoholic fathers to develop alcoholism. Do genetic tendencies or environmental conditions play the major role? In an effort to answer questions of this sort, psychologists have turned to studies of twins, especially twins who have been adopted and raised in separate environments.

Identical twins develop from a single fertilized egg and therefore share exactly the same genes (they are referred to as *monozygotic* because they come from a single zygote, or fertilized egg). Fraternal twins develop from different egg cells and are no more alike genetically than ordinary siblings; they are referred to as *dizygotic* because they come from two zygotes. Studies that compare identical and fraternal twins help sort out the influences of environment and heredity. Identical twins are found to be more similar in intelligence than fraternal twins, even when they are separated at birth and reared in different homes (see Chapter 13). Identical twins are also more similar than fraternal twins in some personality characteristics and in susceptibility to schizophrenia (see Chapter 15).

One surprising finding from studies of adopted children suggests that genetic influences may actually become stronger as people age. The psychological traits of young children are not particularly similar to those of either their biological parents or their adoptive parents. As they grow older, one might expect them to become more like their adoptive parents in traits such as general cognitive ability and verbal ability, and even less like their biological parents. But contrary to this expectation, as adopted children approach age 16 they actually become more similar to their biological parents than to their adoptive parents in these traits (Plomin, Fulker, Corley, & Defries, 1997), suggesting an emerging role of genetic influences.

Molecular Genetics of Behavior In recent years, some researchers have suggested that certain human traits, such as some aspects of personality, are influenced by specific genes, which are thought to affect particular neurotransmitter receptors (Zuckerman, 1995). In most studies of this sort, family members who have a certain psychological trait are identified and compared with family members who lack that trait. Using techniques of molecular genetics, the researchers attempt to find genes or chromosome segments that are correlated with the presence of the trait under study. For example, a combination of traits referred to as "novelty seeking" (that is, a tendency to be impulsive, exploratory, and quick-tempered, as measured by scores on personality scales) has been reported to be linked to a gene that controls the D4 receptor for dopamine (Benjamin et al., 1996).

Occasionally this type of analysis has been applied to very specific behavioral traits. For example, as mentioned earlier, sons of alcoholic fathers are more likely to be alcoholics themselves than are people chosen at random. It was recently reported that when they drink alcohol, sons of alcoholics also tend to release greater amounts of endorphin (the natural opiate neurotransmitter related to reward) than other people (Gianoulakis, Krishnan, & Thavundayil, 1996), suggesting the possibility that there may be a biological predisposition toward alcoholism.

But these analyses can sometimes be misleading and must be viewed with caution. For example, it was once claimed that a gene for

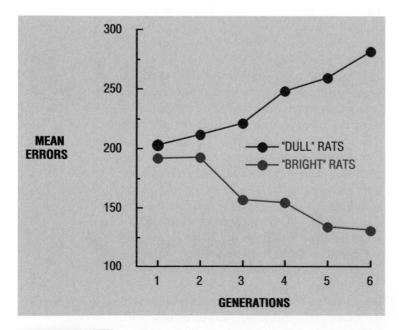

FIGURE 2-21

Inheritance of Maze Learning in Rats *Mean error scores of "bright" (green line) and "dull" (purple line) rats selectively bred for maze-running ability.* (After Thompson, 1954)

Identical twins are referred to as monozygotic *because they develop from a single fertilized egg; fraternal or* dizygotic *twins develop from different egg cells and therefore are no more similar genetically than ordinary siblings.*

the D2 dopamine receptor occurred only in severe alcoholics and thus was a genetic basis for alcoholism. More recent studies of this gene, however, indicate that it also occurs in individuals who pursue many other types of pleasure and may be linked to drug abuse, obesity, compulsive gambling, and other forms of "unrestrained behavior" (Blum, Cull, Braverman, & Comings, 1996). Our understanding of the role of this gene, and of its relationship to behavior, clearly has changed in the few years since its discovery and may change again as further evidence emerges. This highlights the need to await further confirmation before concluding that the genetic basis for behavior of any kind has been identified. In several cases, what appeared at first to be a clear genetic explanation has later been found to be spurious.

Environmental Influences on Gene Action   The inherited potential with which an individual enters the world is very much influenced by the environment he or she encounters. This interaction will be made clear in later chapters, but two examples will suffice to illustrate the point here. The tendency to develop diabetes is hereditary, although the exact method of transmission is unknown. Diabetes

is a disease in which the pancreas does not produce enough insulin to burn carbohydrates and thus provide energy for the body. Scientists assume that genes determine the production of insulin. But people who carry the genetic potential for diabetes do not always develop the disease; for example, if one identical twin has diabetes, the other twin will develop the disorder in only about half the cases. Not all of the environmental factors that contribute to diabetes are known, but one variable that is fairly well established is obesity. An overweight person requires more insulin to metabolize carbohydrates than a thin person. Consequently, an individual who carries the genes for diabetes is more likely to develop the disorder if he or she is overweight.

A similar situation is found in the case of schizophrenia. As we will see in Chapter 15, there is substantial evidence that this disorder has a hereditary component. If one identical twin is schizophrenic, chances are high that the other twin will exhibit some signs of mental disturbance. But whether or not the other twin develops full-blown schizophrenia will depend on a number of environmental factors. Thus, genes may predispose a person to schizophrenia, but the environment in which he or she grows up shapes the actual outcome.

IS AGGRESSIVE BEHAVIOR BIOLOGICALLY OR ENVIRONMENTALLY BASED?

How Biology Influences Human Aggression

L. Rowell Huesmann, *University of Michigan*

L. Rowell Huesmann

Neuroanatomical, neurophysiological, endocrine, and other physiological abnormalities affect the likelihood of aggressive behavior. While these factors do not seem to cause violent behavior directly in humans, children's biological differences interact with their early exposure to different learning environments (or biosocial interactions) to create individual differences in their social behavior.

Biosocial interactions early in life seem to be particularly critical for the development of habitual aggressive behavior. Anger is first experienced well before a child is a year old, and physical aggression (hitting, pushing) is common among 2-year-olds. On the average, the more aggressive a 6-, 7-, or 8-year-old is, the more aggressive the adult (Huesmann, Eron, Lefkowitz, & Walder, 1984). Biological differences influence how young children behave and learn as well as how individuals respond emotionally to certain situations that often stimulate violence.

What are some of the biological factors that may predispose some people toward behaving aggressively?

First, a variety of neuroanatomical differences seem to influence aggression. Along with the prefrontal cortex, the *hypothalamus* and the *amygdala* appear to be particularly important loci for anatomical differences affecting aggression. Electrical stimulation and lesions in these nuclei can increase or decrease one's propensity to behave aggressively (see Moyer, 1976). Anatomical differences in any of these areas caused by trauma, tumors, etc. affect aggressive tendencies. However, whether noticeable changes in aggressiveness actually occur seems to depend on situational factors as well. For example, electrical stimulation studies with animals have shown that the same stimulation that triggers aggression against a small opponent may not trigger aggression against a larger opponent.

Second, individuals with lower levels of serotonin—a neurotransmitter involved in inhibiting impulsive responses to frustration—in their brain seem to be more at risk to behave aggressively (Knoblich & King, 1992). If serotonin is depleted in animals (e.g., through a diet or drugs), the treated animals then behave more aggressively. Linnoila and colleagues (1983) have found that men imprisoned for impulsive violent crimes have lower levels of serotonin than nonimpulsive violent offenders. In addition, children with low serotonin levels are more likely to behave aggressively (see Knoblich & King, 1992).

Third, higher levels of testosterone intrauterine and in early childhood seem to cause the development of a neurophysiology more predisposed to aggression. Higher levels of testosterone at any moment seem to increase the likelihood of an individual behaving aggressively at that moment. Reinisch (1981) found that girls whose mothers were treated with a hormone similar to testosterone while they were pregnant grow up to be more aggressive than comparable control subjects. Similarly, adolescent boys who have more testosterone behave more aggressively when provoked (Olweus et al., 1988). However, the effects are not one way. Recent studies have also found that dominating another or aggressing against another increases testosterone in both males and females (Booth et al., 1989).

Other biological factors in addition to the three I have mentioned undoubtedly also play a role in aggression (e.g., characteristic arousal level), but these three serve well to illustrate how biology interacts with environment to affect aggressiveness. What causes the biological differences? Genetic variation is clearly important. Studies of twins raised apart from birth show a much higher correlation for aggression between identical twins than between fraternal same-sex twins (e.g., Tellegen et al., 1988). Large longitudinal studies of boys adopted at birth have also shown a concordance between the natural father and an adopted son having been convicted of a violent crime (Mednick et al., 1987). These genetic influences may well express themselves through the biological differences I have discussed—testosterone, serotonin, or limbic system neuroanatomy—or through another mechanism. Whatever the exact origin, these biological predispositions undoubtedly influence how interactions with the environment mold the child's social scripts, beliefs, and schemas, and how people respond cognitively and emotionally to provoking and frustrating environmental stimuli.

The Importance of Learning in Aggression

Russell Geen, *University of Missouri-Columbia*

The roles of learned and innate factors in human aggression cannot be described in an either-or way. Virtually every psychologist who investigates the problem recognizes that both factors are involved and that differences in viewpoint involve the relative emphasis placed on each.

Evidence for the importance of learning in aggression comes from two major sources. One consists of controlled studies of behavior in experimental and natural settings. Experimental studies have shown that aggression is susceptible to influence by rewards and punishments in the same way as many other operant behaviors. In addition, human aggression varies according to how much the aggressor thinks that such behavior will lead to desirable outcomes and to the worth of those outcomes to the aggressor (Perry, Perry, & Boldizar, 1990). That behavior is a function of the expectancy of rewards and the value of those rewards to the person has long been accepted as a basic premise of social learning theory. Research has also shown that aggressive antisocial behavior can be traced back to early experiences in the home involving family members. One group of researchers who have studied this problem concludes that "the basic training for patterns of antisocial behavior prior to adolescence takes place in the home, and family members are the primary trainers" (Patterson, Reid, & Dishion, 1992). Children begin by learning that fighting, yelling, and throwing temper tantrums can be effective means of securing desired outcomes from other family members, and such behavior eventually generalizes to larger-scale aggressive antisocial behavior both in and outside the home.

The other source of evidence for social learning of aggression is found in studies that reveal differences in violence as a function of cultural and social variables. There is, for example, considerable evidence of systematic variation in the occurrence of violent acts across different national cultures. Residents of some countries also show a more pervasive tendency to think of violence as means of solving problems than persons living in other nations (Archer & McDaniel, 1995). Other studies indicate the existence of regional subcultural differences in aggression within the United States. For example, homicide rates among white non-Hispanic males living in rural or small-town environments in the southern part of the country have been shown to be higher than corresponding rates in similar setting in other regions, a finding that has been attributed to different local norms for aggressive behavior (Cohen & Nisbett, 1994).

To set nature against nurture in a discussion of human aggression is to create a false dichotomy. Geen (1990) has suggested that both learning and heredity are best understood as background variables that create a level of potential for aggression without being proximal antecedents. Aggressive behavior is a response to situational conditions that provoke and arouse the person to attack. Even when a person is disposed to aggress and capable of behaving aggressively, a specific situation must elicit the act. The probability that such behavior will occur, and also the inten-

Russell Geen

sity of the behavior, will vary according to both the nature of the provocation and the level of potential for aggression set by the several background variables. Certainly people born with dispositions to be violent will be more aggressive when attacked than those lacking such dispositions, and people who have acquired strong aggressive tendencies through social learning will react more aggressively than those who have not. Heredity and social learning are complementary factors in human aggression.

SUMMARY

1. The basic unit of the nervous system is a specialized type of cell called a neuron. Local neurons are tiny cells that communicate only with neighboring neurons, while the larger macroneurons are capable of transmitting neural impulses over long distances. Projecting from the cell body of a macroneuron are a number of short branches called dendrites and a slender tubelike extension called the axon. Stimulation of the dendrites and cell body leads to a neural impulse that travels down the length of the axon. Sensory neurons transmit signals from sense organs to the brain and spinal cord; motor neurons transmit signals from the brain and spinal cord to muscles and glands. A nerve is a bundle of elongated axons belonging to hundreds or thousands of neurons.

2. A stimulus moves along a neuron as an electrochemical impulse that travels from the dendrites to the end of the axon. This traveling impulse, or action potential, is caused by depolarization, an electrochemical process in which the voltage difference across cell mechanisms is changed at successive points along the neuron.

3. Once started, an action potential travels down the axon to many small swellings at the end of the axon called terminal buttons. These terminal buttons release chemical substances, called neurotransmitters, that are responsible for transferring the signal from one neuron to an adjacent one. The neurotransmitters diffuse across the synapse, a small gap between the juncture of the two neurons, and bind to neuroreceptors in the cell membrane of the receiving neuron. Some neurotransmitters have an excitatory effect, whereas others are inhibitory. If the excitatory effects on the receiving neuron become large relative to the inhibitory effects, depolarization occurs and the neuron fires an all-or-none impulse.

4. There are many different kinds of neurotransmitter-receptor interactions, and they help explain a range of psychological phenomena. The most important neurotransmitters include acetylcholine, norepinephrine, dopamine, serotonin, gamma-aminobutyric acid (GABA), and glutamate.

5. The nervous system is divided into the central nervous system (the brain and spinal cord) and the peripheral nervous system (the nerves connecting the brain and spinal cord to other parts of the body). Subdivisions of the peripheral nervous system are the somatic system (which carries messages to and from the sense receptors, muscles, and the surface of the body) and the autonomic system (which connects with the internal organs and glands).

6. The human brain is composed of three concentric layers: the central core, the limbic system, and the cerebrum. The central core includes the medulla, which is responsible for respiration and postural reflexes; the cerebellum, which is concerned with motor coordination; the thalamus, a relay station for incoming sensory information; and the hypothalamus, which is important in emotion and in maintaining homeostasis. The reticular formation, which crosses through several of the other central core structures, controls the organism's state of arousal and consciousness.

7. The limbic system controls some of the instinctive behaviors regulated by the hypothalamus, such as feeding, attacking, fleeing, and mating. It also plays an important role in emotion and memory.

8. The cerebrum is divided into two cerebral hemispheres. The convoluted surface of these hemispheres, the cerebral cortex, plays a critical role in higher mental processes such as thinking, learning, and decision making. Certain areas of the cerebral cortex are associated with specific sensory inputs or control of specific movements. The remainder of the cerebral cortex consists of association areas, which are concerned with memory, thought, and language.

9. A number of techniques have been developed to obtain detailed pictures of the human brain without causing the patient undue distress or damage. These include computerized axial tomography (CAT or CT), magnetic resonance imaging (MRI), and positron emission tomography (PET).

10. When the corpus callosum (the band of nerve fibers connecting the two cerebral hemispheres) is severed, significant differences in the functioning of the two hemispheres can be observed. The left hemisphere is skilled in language and mathematical abilities. The right hemisphere can understand some language but cannot communicate through speech; it has a highly developed spatial and pattern sense.

11. The term *aphasia* is used to describe language deficits caused by brain damage. People with damage to Broca's area have difficulty enunciating words correctly and speak in a slow, labored way. People with damage to Wernicke's area can hear words but do not know their meaning.

12. The autonomic nervous system consists of the sympathetic and parasympathetic divisions. Because it controls the action of the smooth muscles and the glands, the autonomic system is particularly important in emotional reactions. The sympathetic division is active during excitement and the parasympathetic system is dominant during periods of quiescence.

13. The endocrine glands secrete hormones into the bloodstream that travel through the body, acting in various ways on cells of different types. The pituitary has been called the "master gland" because it controls the secretion activity of other endocrine glands. The adrenal glands play an important role in determining mood, energy level, and ability to cope with stress.

14. An individual's hereditary potential, which is transmitted by the chromosomes and genes, influences his or her psychological and physical characteristics. Genes are segments of DNA molecules, which store genetic information. Some genes are dominant, some recessive, and some sex-linked. Most human characteristics are polygenic; that is, they are determined by many genes acting together rather than by a single gene pair.

15. Selective breeding (mating animals that are high or low in a certain trait) is one method of studying the influence of heredity. Another means of sorting out the effects of environment and heredity is twin studies, in which the characteristics of identical twins (who share the same heredity) are compared with those of fraternal twins (who are no more alike genetically than ordinary siblings). Behavior depends on the interaction between heredity and environment: An individual's genes set the limits of his or her potential, but what happens to that potential depends on the environment in which he or she grows up.

KEY TERMS

neuron (p. 33)
neurotransmitter (p. 34)
nerve (p. 34)
nucleus (p. 35)
ganglion (p. 35)
action potential (p. 35)
central nervous system (p. 40)
peripheral nervous system (p. 40)
somatic system (p. 42)
autonomic system (p. 42)
hindbrain (p. 42)

midbrain (p. 42)
forebrain (p. 42)
central core (p. 43)
homeostasis (p. 45)
limbic system (p. 45)
cerebrum (p. 46)
aphasia (p. 54)
hormone (p. 56)
behavior genetics (p. 59)
chromosome (p. 59)
gene (p. 59)

CRITICAL THINKING QUESTIONS

1. Only about one-tenth of the cells in your brain are neurons (the rest are glial cells). Does this mean that you use only one-tenth of your brain when you think? Perhaps not. What other possibilities are there?

2. Local anesthetics, such as the one you might receive in a dentist's office, work by blocking Na^+ gates in the neurons near the point of injection. Of course, dentists and physicians typically inject them in a part of the body near the source of pain. What do you think such a drug would do if it were injected into the brain? Would it still block pain and touch, and nothing else? Or would its effect be different?

3. Why is your brain symmetrical (meaning that the left and right sides look alike)? You have a left and a right motor cortex, a left and a right hippocampus, a left and a right cerebellum, and so on. In each case, the left side is a mirror image of the right side (just as your left eye is a mirror image of your right eye, your left ear a mirror image of your right ear, etc.). Can you think of any reason why your brain is symmetrical in this way?

4. In "split-brain" patients, whose corpus callosum has been cut, the left and right sides of the brain seem to work independently after the operation. For example, a word shown to one side may be read and responded to without the other side knowing what the word was. Does such a person have two minds, each capable of knowing different things? Or does the patient still have only one mind?

5. It seems that every year the discovery of a new "gene for alcoholism," or for drug dependence, schizophrenia, sexual orientation, impulsiveness, or some other complex psychological trait, is reported. But it often turns out after further studies that the gene is related to the trait in some people but not in everyone. And often the gene also turns out to be related to other behavioral traits in addition to the one to which it was originally linked. Can you think of any reasons why genes might affect psychological traits in this way? In other words, why isn't there a perfect one-to-one match between the presence of a gene and the strength of a particular psychological trait?

FURTHER READING

Introductions to physiological psychology are Carlson, *Foundations of Physiological Psychology* (3rd ed., 1995); Groves and Rebec, *Introduction to Biological Psychology* (4th ed., 1992); Kolb and Whishaw, *Fundamentals of Human Neuropsychology* (4th ed., 1996); Schneider and Tarshis, *An Introduction to Physiological Psychology* (3rd ed., 1986); Rosenzweig and Leiman, *Physiological Psychology* (2nd ed., 1989); and Kalat, *Biological Psychology* (6th ed., 1998).

For a review of the molecular basis of neural processes, see Alberts et al., *Molecular Biology of the Cell* (3rd ed., 1994), or Levitan and Kaszmarek, *The Neuron: Cell and Molecular Biology* (1997). Also see Squire, *Memory and Brain* (1987) for a discussion of the neural basis of memory and cognition; and Crick, *The Astonishing Hypothesis: The Scientific Search for the Soul* (1994) for a discussion of human consciousness in terms of neural mechanisms.

A survey of genetic influences on behavior is provided by Plomin, De Fries, and McClearn, *Behavioral Genetics: A Primer* (2nd ed., 1990). For a review of psychoactive drugs and their effects on the body, brain, and behavior, see Julien, *A Primer of Drug Action* (6th ed., 1992) and Julien, *Drugs and the Body* (1988).

For a survey of research on the function of the two cerebral hemispheres, see Springer and Deutsch, *Left Brain, Right Brain* (4th ed., 1993), and Hellige, *Hemispheric Asymmetry: What's Right and What's Left* (1994).

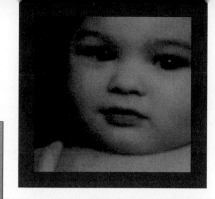

Chapter 3
Psychological Development

*O*f all mammals, human beings require the longest period of maturation and learning before they are self-sufficient. In general, the more complex an organism's nervous system, the longer it takes for the organism to reach maturity. A lemur (a primitive primate) can move about on its own shortly after birth and is soon able to fend for itself; an infant monkey is dependent on its mother for several months, a chimpanzee for several years. But even a chimpanzee—one of our closest relatives—will be a functioning adult member of its species long before a human of the same age.

Developmental psychologists are concerned with how and why different aspects of human functioning develop and change across the life span. They focus on physical development, such as changes in height and weight and the acquisition of motor skills; cognitive development, such as changes in thought processes, memory, and language abilities; and personality and social development, such as changes in self-concept, gender identity, and interpersonal relationships. The development of particular psychological abilities and functions is treated in more detail in later chapters. In this chapter we provide a general overview of psychological development across the life span and consider two central questions: (1) How do biological factors interact with events in the child's environment to determine the course of development (often called the *nature-nurture question*)? and (2) Is development best understood as a gradual, continuous process of change or as a series of abrupt, qualitatively distinct stages?

Nature and Nurture

The question of whether heredity ("nature") or environment ("nurture") is more important in determining the course of human development has been debated for centuries. The 17th-century British philosopher John Locke rejected the prevailing notion that babies were miniature adults who arrived in the world fully equipped with abilities and knowledge and simply had to grow in order for these inherited characteristics to appear. On the contrary, Locke believed that the mind of a newborn infant is a *tabula rasa* (Latin for "blank slate"). What gets written on this slate is what the baby experiences— what he or she sees, hears, tastes, smells, and feels. According to Locke, all knowledge comes to us through our senses. It is provided entirely by experience; there is no built-in knowledge.

Charles Darwin's theory of evolution (1859), which emphasizes the biological basis of human development, led many theorists to place renewed emphasis on heredity. With the rise of behaviorism in the 20th century, however, the environmentalist position once again gained dominance. Behaviorists like John B. Watson and B. F. Skinner argued that human nature is completely malleable: Early training can turn a child into any kind of adult, regardless of his or her heredity. Watson stated this argument in its most extreme form:

> Give me a dozen healthy infants, well-formed, and my own specified world to bring them up in, and I'll guarantee to take any one at random and train him to be any type of specialist I might select—doctor, lawyer, artist, merchant-chief, and, yes, even beggar-man and

Both John Locke and Charles Darwin influenced the nature-nurture debate, but in different ways. Locke emphasized the role of the senses in the acquisition of knowledge, arguing that knowledge is provided only by experience. Darwin emphasized the biological basis of human development, leading to renewed interest in the role of heredity.

thief, regardless of his talents, penchants, tendencies, abilities, vocations, and race of his ancestors. (1930, p. 104)

Today most psychologists agree not only that both nature and nurture play important roles but that they interact continuously to guide development. For example, we will see in Chapter 12 that the development of many personality traits, such as sociability and emotional stability, appears to be influenced about equally by heredity and environment; similarly, we will see in Chapter 15 that psychiatric illnesses can have both genetic and environmental determinants.

Even forms of development that seem to be determined by innate biological timetables can be affected by environmental events. At the moment of conception, a remarkable number of personal characteristics are already determined by the genetic structure of the fertilized ovum. Our genes program our growing cells so that we develop into a person rather than a fish or a chimpanzee. They determine our sex, the color of our skin, eyes, and hair, and our overall body size, among other things. These genetically determined characteristics are expressed through the process of **maturation**—*an innately determined sequence of growth and change that is relatively independent of external events.* Thus, the human fetus develops according to a fairly fixed schedule, and fetal behavior, such as turning and kicking, also follows an orderly sequence that depends on

the stage of growth. However, if the uterine environment is seriously abnormal in some way, maturational processes can be disrupted. For example, if the mother contracts rubella during the first three months of pregnancy (when the fetus's basic organ systems are developing according to the genetically programmed schedule), the infant may be born deaf, blind, or brain-damaged, depending on which organ system was in a critical stage of development at the time of infection. Maternal malnutrition, smoking, and consumption of alcohol and drugs are other environmental factors that can affect the normal maturation of the fetus.

Motor development after birth also illustrates the interaction between genetically programmed maturation and environmental influences. Virtually all children go through the same sequence of motor behaviors in the same order: rolling over, sitting without support, standing while holding onto furniture, crawling, and then walking. But they go through the sequence at different rates, and developmental psychologists have long wondered whether learning and experience play an important role in such differences. Although early studies suggested that the answer was no (McGraw, 1935/1975; Dennis & Dennis, 1940; Gesell & Thompson, 1929), more recent studies indicate that practice or extra stimulation can accelerate the appearance of motor behaviors to some extent. For example, newborn infants have a stepping

Virtually all children go through the same sequence of motor behaviors in the same order, but they go through the sequence at different rates.

  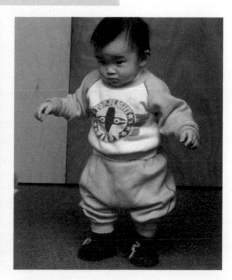

reflex; if they are held in an upright position with their feet touching a solid surface, their legs will make stepping movements that are similar to walking. A group of infants who were given stepping practice for a few minutes several times a day during the first two months of life began walking five to seven weeks earlier than babies who had not had this practice (Zelazo, Zelazo, & Kolb, 1972).

The development of speech provides another example of the interaction between genetically determined characteristics and experience. In the course of normal development, all human infants learn to speak, but not until they have attained a certain level of neurological development; with rare exceptions, infants less than a year old cannot speak in sentences. But children reared in an environment in which people talk to them and reward them for making speech-like sounds talk earlier than children who do not receive such attention. For example, children reared in middle-class American homes begin to talk at about 1 year of age. Children reared in San Marcos, a remote village in Guatemala, have little verbal interaction with adults and do not utter their first words until they are over 2 years old (Kagan, 1979). Note that it is the *rate* at which children acquire the skills that is affected by the environment, not the ultimate skill level.

Stages of Development

In explaining the sequence of development, several psychologists have proposed that there are discrete, qualitatively distinct steps or stages of development. Many of us use this concept informally. We think of the life span as being divided into the stages of infancy, childhood, adolescence, and adulthood. Parents might say that their adolescent is going through a "rebellious stage." Developmental psychologists, however, have a more precise concept in mind: The concept of stages implies that (a) behaviors at a given stage are organized around a dominant theme or a coherent set of characteristics; (b) behaviors at one stage are qualitatively different from behaviors at earlier or later stages; and (c) all children go through the same stages in the same order. Environmental factors may speed up or slow down development, but the order of stages does not vary; a child cannot enter a later stage without going through an earlier one first. As we will see later in the chapter, however, not all psychologists agree that development proceeds according to a fixed sequence of qualitatively distinct stages.

Closely related to the concept of stages is the idea that there may be **critical periods** in human development—*crucial time periods in a person's life during which specific events occur if development is to proceed* normally. Critical periods have been identified for some aspects of physical development of the human fetus. For example, the period six to seven weeks after conception is critical for normal development of the sex organs. Whether the primitive sex organ develops into a male or female sexual structure depends on the presence of male hormones, regardless of the XX or XY arrangement of chromosomes. The absence of male hormones means that female sexual organs will develop in either case. If male hormones are injected later in development, they cannot reverse the changes that have already taken place.

During postnatal development there is a critical period for the development of vision. If children who are born with cataracts have them removed before the age of 7, their vision will develop fairly normally. But if a child goes through the first seven years without adequate vision, extensive permanent disability will result (Kuman, Fedrov, & Novikova, 1983).

The existence of critical periods for *psychological* development is less well established. It is probably more accurate to say that there are *sensitive periods*—periods that are optimal for a particular kind of development. If a certain behavior is not well established during this sensitive period, it may not develop to its full potential. For example, the first year of life appears to be a sensitive period for the formation of close interpersonal attachments (Tizard & Rees, 1975). The preschool years may be especially significant for intellectual development and language acquisition (Curtiss, 1977, 1989; Cardon et al., 1992). Children who have not had enough exposure to language before age 6 or 7 may fail to acquire it altogether (Goldin-Meadow, 1982). The experiences of the child during such sensitive periods may shape his or her future course of development in a manner that will be difficult to change later.

Capacities of the Newborn

At the end of the 19th century, psychologist William James suggested that the newborn child experiences the world as a "buzzing, blooming confusion," an idea that was still prevalent as late as the 1960s. We now know that newborn infants enter the world with all of their sensory systems functioning and are well prepared to learn about their new environment.

Because babies cannot explain what they are doing or tell us what they are thinking, developmental psychologists have had to design some ingenious procedures to study the capacities of young infants. The basic method is to change the baby's environment in some way and observe the responses. For example, an investigator might present a tone or a flashing light and see if there is a change in heart rate or if the baby turns its head or sucks more vigorously on a nipple. In some instances the researcher will present two stimuli at the same time to determine whether infants look longer at one than at the other. If they do, it indicates that they can tell the stimuli apart and may indicate that they prefer one over the other. In this section we describe some of the findings of research on infant capacities, beginning with studies of infants' vision.

Vision

As we will see in Chapter 5, newborns have poor visual acuity, their ability to change focus is limited, and they are very nearsighted. It is not until they are 2 years of age that they see as well as an adult (Courage & Adams, 1990). But, despite the immaturity of their visual system, newborns spend a lot of time actively looking about. They scan the world in an organized way and pause when their eyes encounter an object or some change in their visual field. They are particularly attracted to areas of high contrast, such as the edges of an object. Instead of scanning the entire object, as an adult would, they keep looking at areas that have the most edges. They also prefer complex patterns over plain ones and patterns with curved lines over patterns with straight lines.

The possibility that there is an inborn, unlearned preference for faces initially aroused great interest, but later research showed that infants are not attracted to faces per se but to stimulus characteristics such as curved lines, high contrast, edges, movement, and complexity—all of which faces possess (Banks & Salapatek, 1983; Aslin, 1987). Newborns look mostly at the outside contour of a face, but by 2 months they focus on the inside of the face—the eyes, nose, and mouth (Haith, Bergman, & Moore, 1977). At this point parents may notice with delight that the baby has begun to make eye contact.

Hearing

Newborn infants will startle at the sound of a loud noise. They will also turn their head toward the source of a sound. Interestingly, the head-turning response disappears at about 6 weeks and does not reemerge until 3 or 4 months, at which time the infants will also search with their eyes for the source of the sound. The temporary disappearance of

Although infants love to explore the faces of those who care for them, research has shown that they are attracted not to faces per se but to such characteristics as curved lines, movement, and complexity.

the head-turning response probably represents a maturational transition from a reflexive response controlled by subcortical areas of the brain to a voluntary attempt to locate the source of the sound. By 4 months, infants will reach toward the source of a sound in the dark; by 6 months, they show a marked increase in their responsiveness to sounds that are accompanied by visual stimuli and are able to pinpoint the location of a sound more precisely, an ability that continues to improve into their second year (Hillier, Hewitt, & Morrongiello, 1992; Ashmead et al., 1991; Field, 1987).

Newborn infants can also detect the difference between very similar sounds, such as two tones that are only one note apart on the musical scale (Bridger, 1961), and they can distinguish between the human voice and other kinds of sounds. We will see in Chapter 9 that they can also distinguish among various characteristics of human speech. For example, 1-month-old infants can tell the difference between similar sounds such as "pa" and "ba." Interestingly, infants can distinguish between some speech sounds better than adults can. These are sounds that adults "hear" as identical because there is no distinction between them in their native language (Aslin, Pisoni, & Jusczyk, 1983). For example, "ra" and "la" are separate sounds in English but not in Japanese. Japanese infants can distinguish between them, but Japanese adults cannot.

By 6 months the child will have picked up enough information about the language so that it too will begin to "screen out" sounds that it does not use (Kuhl et al., 1992). Thus, human infants appear to be born with perceptual mechanisms that are already tuned to the properties of human speech that will help them in learning language (Eimas, 1975).

Taste and Smell

Infants can discriminate between different tastes shortly after birth. They prefer sweet-tasting liquids over liquids that are salty, bitter, sour, or bland. The characteristic response of the newborn to a sweet liquid is a relaxed expression resembling a slight smile, sometimes accompanied by lip-licking. A sour solution produces pursed lips and a wrinkled nose. In response to a bitter solution, the baby will open its mouth with the corners turned down and stick out its tongue in what appears to be an expression of disgust.

Newborns can also discriminate among odors. They will turn their head toward a sweet smell, and their heart rate and respiration will slow down; these are indicators of attention. Noxious odors, such as those of ammonia or rotten eggs, cause them to turn their head away; their heart rate and respiration accelerate, indicating distress. Infants are even able to discriminate among subtle differences in smells. After nursing for only a few days, an infant will consistently turn its head toward a pad saturated with its mother's milk in preference to one saturated with another mother's milk (Russell, 1976). Only breast-fed babies show this ability to recognize the mother's odor (Cernoch & Porter, 1985). When bottle-fed babies are given a choice between the smell of their familiar formula and that of a lactating breast, they will choose the latter (Porter et al., 1992). Thus, there seems to be an innate preference for the odor of breast milk. In general, the ability to distinguish among smells has a clear adaptive value: It helps infants avoid noxious substances, thereby increasing their chances of survival.

Learning and Memory

It was once thought that infants could neither learn nor remember. This is not the case; evidence for early learning and remembering comes from several studies. In one, infants only a few hours old learned to turn their heads right or left, depending on whether they heard a buzzer or a tone. In order to taste a sweet liquid, the baby had to turn to the right when a tone sounded and to the left when a buzzer sounded. After only a few trials the babies were performing without error—turning to the right when the tone sounded and to the left when the buzzer sounded. The experimenter then reversed the situation so that the infant had to turn the opposite way when either the buzzer or the tone sounded. The babies mastered this new task quickly (Siqueland & Lipsitt, 1966).

By the time they are 3 months old, infants have good memories. When a mobile over an infant's crib was attached to one of the baby's limbs by a ribbon, 3-month-old infants quickly discovered which arm or leg would move the mobile. When the infants were placed in the same situation eight days later, they remembered which arm or leg to move (Hayne, Rovee-Collier, & Borza, 1991; Rovee-Collier & Hayne, 1987) (see Figure 3-1).

More startling is evidence that infants remember sensations they experienced before birth, while still in their mother's uterus. We noted earlier that newborn infants can distinguish the sound of the human voice from other sounds. They also prefer the human voice over other sounds. A few days after birth infants will learn to suck on an artificial nipple in order to turn on recorded speech or vocal music, sucking more vigorously to hear speech sounds than to hear nonspeech sounds or instrumental music (Butterfield & Siperstein, 1972). They also prefer heartbeat sounds and female voices over male voices, and they prefer their mother's voice to those of other women. But they do not prefer their father's voice to those of other men (DeCasper & Prescott, 1984; DeCasper & Fifer, 1980; Brazelton, 1978) (see Figure 3-2).

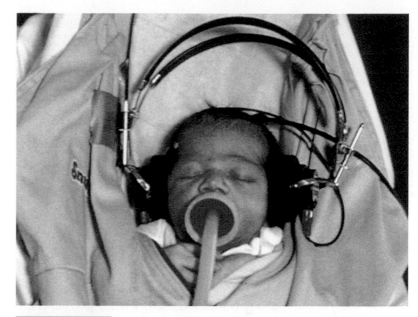

FIGURE 3-2

Preference for Sounds   *A newborn can indicate a preference for certain sounds—such as the mother's voice—by sucking more vigorously on a nipple when it causes the preferred sounds to be played through the earphones.*

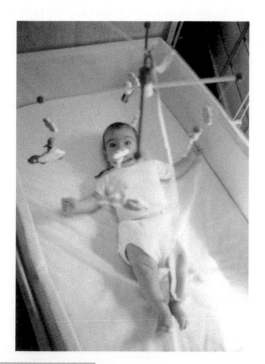

FIGURE 3-1

Early Learning   *If a mobile is attached so that the infant's movements activate the mobile, the infant soon discovers this relationship and seems to delight in activating the mobile with the appropriate kick. Two-month-old babies can learn to do this, but soon forget. Three-month-old babies can remember the correct action for several days.*

These preferences appear to stem from the infant's prenatal experience with sounds. For example, the mother's voice can also be heard in the uterus, which would appear to explain why a newborn infant prefers her voice over others. Perhaps most surprising is evidence that the unborn infant may actually be learning to discriminate among some of the sounds of individual words. In an extraordinary experiment, pregnant women recited passages from children's stories each day during the last six weeks of pregnancy. For example, some women recited the first 28 paragraphs of Dr. Seuss' story *The Cat in the Hat*. Others recited the last 28 paragraphs of the same story, but with the main nouns changed so that it was about the "dog in the fog" instead of the "cat in the hat." By the time the infants were born, they had heard one of the selected stories for a total of about 3½ hours.

Two or three days after the infants were born, they were permitted to suck on a special pacifier wired to record sucking rates (like the apparatus shown in Figure 3-2). Sucking on the pacifier turned on a tape recording of either their mother's voice or an unfamiliar woman's voice reciting either the story the infants had heard before birth or the story they had not heard previously. As in previous experiments, the infants showed by their sucking rates that they preferred their mother's voice to the stranger's. The startling finding, however, was that they also preferred the familiar story over the unfamiliar one—even when the two stories were read by the stranger (DeCasper & Spence, 1986).

In sum, the research we have described challenges the view of the newborn as experiencing the world as "buzzing, blooming confusion" as well as the view that the child enters the world as a "blank slate." Clearly, the infant enters the world well prepared to perceive and learn.

Cognitive Development in Childhood

Although most parents are aware of the intellectual changes that accompany their children's physical growth, they would have difficulty describing the nature of these changes. The ways in which contemporary psychologists describe these changes have been most profoundly influenced by the Swiss psychologist Jean Piaget (1896–1980), who is widely acknowledged to be one of the century's most influential thinkers. Prior to Piaget, psychological thinking about children's cognitive de-

velopment was dominated by the biological-maturation perspective, which gave almost exclusive weight to the "nature" component of development, and by the environmental-learning perspective, which gave almost exclusive weight to the "nurture" component. In contrast, Piaget focused on the interaction between the child's naturally maturing abilities and his or her interactions with the environment. In this section we outline Piaget's stage theory of development and then turn to a critique of that theory and to some more recent approaches. We also discuss the work of Lev Vygotsky, a Russian psychologist whose ideas about cognitive development, originally published in the 1930s, have attracted renewed interest in recent years.

Piaget's Stage Theory

Partly as a result of his observations of his own children, Piaget became interested in the relationship between the child's naturally maturing abilities and his or her interactions with the environment. He saw the child as an active participant in this process, rather than as a passive recipient of biological development or external stimuli. He viewed children as "inquiring scientists" who experiment with objects and events in their environment to see what will happen. ("What does it feel like to suck on the teddy-bear's ear?" "What happens if I push my dish off the edge of the table?") The results of these "experiments" are used to construct **schemas**—*theories about how the physical and social worlds operate.* Upon encountering a novel object or event, the child attempts to *assimilate* it—that is, to understand it in terms of a preexisting schema. If the new experience does not fit the existing schema, the child—like any good scientist—modifies the schema and thereby extends his or her theory of the world. Piaget called this process *accommodation* (Piaget & Inhelder, 1969).

Piaget's first job as a postgraduate student in psychology was as an intelligence tester for Alfred Binet, the inventor of the IQ test (see Chapter 12). In the course of this work he began wondering why children made the kinds of errors they did. What distinguished their reasoning from that of adults? He observed his own children closely as they played, presenting them with simple scientific and moral problems and asking them

Children often are as eager to play with empty boxes as with the toys they contained. Piaget believed that children act as "inquiring scientists," experimenting with objects in their environment to see what will happen.

TABLE 3-1

Piaget's Stages of Cognitive Development *The ages given are averages. They may vary considerably depending on intelligence, cultural background, and socioeconomic factors, but the order of the progression is assumed to be the same for all children. Piaget has described more detailed phases within each stage; only a general characterization of each stage is given here.*

Stage	Characterization
1. Sensorimotor (birth–2 years)	Differentiates self from objects Recognizes self as agent of action and begins to act intentionally; for example, pulls a string to set a mobile in motion or shakes a rattle to make a noise
2. Preoperational (2–7 years)	Learns to use language and to represent objects by images and words Thinking is still egocentric: has difficulty taking the viewpoint of others Classifies objects by a single feature; for example, groups together all the red blocks regardless of shape or all the square blocks regardless of color
3. Concrete operational (7–11 years)	Can think logically about objects and events Achieves conservation of number (age 6), mass (age 7), and weight (age 9) Classifies objects according to several features and can order them in series along a single dimension, such as size
4. Formal operational (11 years and up)	Can think logically about abstract propositions and test hypotheses systematically Becomes concerned with the hypothetical, the future, and ideological problems

to explain how they arrived at their answers. Piaget's observations convinced him that children's ability to think and reason progresses through a series of qualitatively distinct stages. He divided cognitive development into four major stages, each of which has a number of substages. The major stages are the sensorimotor stage, the preoperational stage, the stage of concrete operations, and the stage of formal operations (see Table 3-1).

The Sensorimotor Stage Piaget designated the first two years of life as the **sensorimotor stage,** *a period in which infants are busy discovering the relationships between their actions and the consequences of those actions.* They discover, for example, how far they have to reach to grasp an object and what happens when they push their dish over the edge of the table. In this way they begin to develop a concept of themselves as separate from the external world.

An important discovery during this stage is the concept of **object permanence,** *the awareness that an object continues to exist even when it is not present.* If a cloth is placed over a toy that an 8-month-old is reaching for, the infant immediately stops reaching and appears to lose interest in the toy. The baby seems neither surprised nor

upset, makes no attempt to search for the toy, and acts as if the toy had ceased to exist (see Figure 3-3). In contrast, a 10-month-old will actively search for an object that has been hidden under a cloth or behind a screen. The older baby seems to realize that the object exists even though it is out of sight; thus, the infant has attained the concept of object permanence. But even at this age, search is limited. If the infant has had repeated success in retrieving a toy hidden in a particular place, he or she will continue to look for it in that spot even after watching an adult conceal it in a new location. Not until about 1 year of age will a child consistently look for an object where it was last seen to disappear, regardless of what happened on previous trials.

The Preoperational Stage By about $1\frac{1}{2}$ to 2 years of age, children have begun to use symbols. Words can represent things or groups of things, and one object can represent another. Thus, a 3-year-old may treat a stick as if it were a horse and ride it around the room; a block of wood can become a car; one doll can become a father and another a baby. But although 3- and 4-year-olds can think in symbolic terms, their words and images are not yet organized in a logical manner. During this **preoperational stage** of

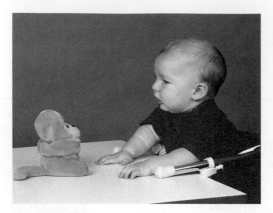
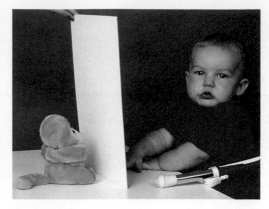

FIGURE 3-3

Object Permanence   *When the toy is hidden by a screen, the infant acts as if the toy no longer exists. From this observation Piaget concluded that the in-fant had not yet acquired the concept of object permanence.*

cognitive development *the child does not yet comprehend certain rules or operations.* An **operation** is *a mental routine for separating, combining, and otherwise transforming information in a logical manner.* For example, if water is poured from a tall, narrow glass into a short, wide one, adults know that the amount of water has not changed because they can reverse the transformation in their minds; they can imagine pouring the water from the short glass back into the tall glass, thereby arriving back at the original state. In the preoperational stage of cognitive development, a child's understanding of

reversibility and other mental operations is absent or weak. As a result, according to Piaget, preoperational children have not yet attained **conservation**—*the understanding that the amount of a substance remains the same even when its form is changed.* Thus, they fail to understand that the amount of water is conserved—that is, remains the same—when it is poured from the tall glass into the short one.

The lack of conservation in preoperational children is also illustrated by a procedure in which a child is given some clay to make into a ball that is equal to another ball of

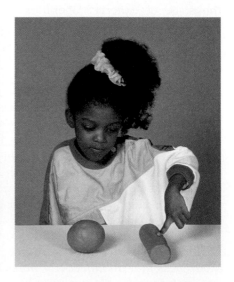

FIGURE 3-4

The Concept of Conservation   *A 4-year-old acknowledges that the two balls of clay are the same size. But when one ball is rolled into a long, thin shape, she says that it contains more clay. Not until she is several years older will she state that the two different shapes contain the same amount of clay.*

the same material. After doing this, the child declares them to be "the same." Then, leaving one ball for reference, the experimenter rolls the other into a long sausage shape while the child watches. The child can plainly see that no clay has been added or subtracted. In this situation, 4-year-olds will say that the two objects no longer contain the same amount of clay: "The longer one contains more" (see Figure 3-4). Not until age 7 do most children say that the amount of clay in the longer object is equal to the amount in the ball.

Piaget believed that preoperational thinking is dominated by visual impressions. A change in the visual appearance of the clay influences the child more than less obvious but more essential qualities, such as mass or weight. This reliance on visual impressions is illustrated by an experiment on the conservation of number. If two rows of checkers are matched one for one against each other, young children will say, correctly, that the rows have the same number of checkers (see Figure 3-5). If the checkers in one row are brought closer together to form a cluster, 5-year-olds say that there are now more checkers in the straight row—even though no checkers have been removed. The visual impression of a long row of checkers over-

rides the numerical equality that was obvious when the checkers appeared in matching rows. In contrast, 7-year-olds assume that if the number of objects was equal before, it must remain equal. At this age, numerical equality has become more significant than visual impression.

Another key characteristic of preoperational children, according to Piaget, is *egocentrism.* Preoperational children are unaware of perspectives other than their own—they believe that everyone else perceives the environment the same way they do (Piaget, 1950). To demonstrate this, Piaget created the "three-mountain problem." A child is allowed to walk around a table on which are arranged three mountains of different heights. Then the child stands on one side of the table while a doll is placed on the table at various locations (and therefore has a different view of the three mountains than the child). The child is asked to choose a photograph that shows what the doll is seeing. Before the age of 6 or 7, most children choose the photograph that illustrates their own perspective on the three mountains (Piaget & Inhelder, 1948/1956).

Piaget believed that egocentrism explains the rigidity of preoperational thought. Because young children cannot appreciate

FIGURE 3-5

Conservation of Number   *When the two rows of seven checkers are evenly spaced, most children report that they contain the same amount. When one row is then clustered into a smaller space, children under age 6 or 7 will say that the original row contains more.*

points of view other than their own, they cannot revise their schemas to take into account changes in the environment. Hence their inability to reverse operations or conserve quantity.

Operational Stages   Between the ages of 7 and 12, children master the various conservation concepts and begin to perform other logical manipulations. They can place objects in order on the basis of a dimension such as height or weight. They can also form a mental representation of a series of actions. Five-year-olds can find their way to a friend's house but cannot direct you there or trace the route with paper and pencil. They can find their own way because they know that they have to turn at certain places, but they have no overall picture of the route. In contrast, 8-year-olds can readily draw a map of the route. Piaget calls this period the **concrete operational stage:** *Although children are using abstract terms, they are doing so only in relation to concrete objects*—that is, objects to which they have direct sensory access.

At about the age of 11 or 12, children arrive at adult modes of thinking. This is the **formal operational stage,** in which *the person is able to reason in purely symbolic terms.* In one test for formal operational thinking, the child tries to discover what determines how long a pendulum will swing back and forth (its period of oscillation). The child is presented with a length of string suspended from a hook, and several weights that can be attached to the lower end. He or she can vary the length of the string, change the attached weight, and alter the height from which the bob is released. In contrast to children who are still in the concrete operational stage—who will experiment by changing some of the variables, but not in a systematic way—adolescents of even average ability will set up a series of hypotheses and test them systematically. They reason that if a particular variable (weight) affects the period of oscillation, the effect will appear only if they change one variable and hold all others constant. If this variable seems to have no effect on the length of time the pendulum will swing, they rule it out and try another. Considering all the possibilities—working out the consequences for each hypothesis and confirming or denying these

consequences—is the essence of formal operational thought.

A Critique of Piaget's Theory

Piaget's theory is a major intellectual achievement; it has revolutionized the way we think about children's cognitive development. However, new, more sophisticated methods of testing the intellectual functioning of infants and preschool children reveal that Piaget underestimated their abilities. Many of the tasks designed to test stage theories actually require several skills, such as attention, memory, and specific factual knowledge. A child may actually have the ability being tested but be unable to perform the task because he or she lacks one of the other required skills.

These points are sharply illustrated by studies of object permanence. As we saw earlier, when infants younger than 8 months are shown a toy that is then hidden or covered while they watch, they act as if the toy no longer exists; they do not attempt to search for it. Note, however, that successful performance on this test requires the child not only to understand that the object still exists but also to remember where the object was hidden and to show through some physical action that he or she is searching for it. Because Piaget believed that early cognitive development depends on sensorimotor activities, he did not consider the possibility that the infant might know that the object still exists but be unable to show this knowledge through searching behavior.

In a study designed to test this possibility, children were not required to actively search for the hidden object. As shown in the top section of Figure 3-6, the apparatus consisted of a screen that was hinged at one edge to the top of a table. At first the screen lay flat on the table. As the infant watched, the screen was slowly rotated away from the infant through a complete 180-degree arc until it was again lying flat on the table. The screen was then rotated in the opposite direction, toward the infant.

When the infants were first shown the rotating screen, they looked at it for almost a full minute, but after repeated trials they lost interest and turned their attention elsewhere. At that point a brightly painted box appeared on the table beyond the hinge, where it would be hidden as the screen moved into its upright position. (The infant was actually seeing a reflected image of a box, not the actual box.) As shown in Figure 3-6, the infants were then shown either a possible event or an impossible event. One group of infants saw the screen rotate from its starting position until it reached the point where it should bump against the box; at that point the screen stopped and then moved back to its starting position. The other group saw the screen rotate to the upright position but then continue to rotate all the way to the other side of the 180-degree arc, just as though there were no box in the way. The investigators reasoned that if the infants thought the box still existed even when it was hidden by the screen, they would be surprised when it seemed to pass through the box—an impossible event—and, hence, would look at the screen longer than they would when the screen seemed to bump into the box before returning to its starting point. This is exactly what happened. Even though the impossible event was perceptually identical to an event that they had seen repeatedly and lost interest in, the infants found it more interesting than a physically possible event that they had never seen before—the screen stopping halfway through the arc and then reversing direction (Baillargeon, Spelke, & Wasserman, 1985).

It should be noted that the infants in this experiment were only 4½ months old; they thus displayed object permanence 4 to 5 months earlier than Piaget's theory predicts. Replications of this study have found that some infants as young as 3½ months display object permanence (Baillargeon, 1987; Baillargeon & DeVos, 1991).

More recent experiments using Piaget's conservation tasks have also yielded evidence that children's mental capacities develop earlier than he thought. In one study of number conservation, two sets of toys were lined up in one-to-one correspondence (as in Figure 3-5, described earlier). The experimenter then said, "These are your soldiers and these are my soldiers. What's more, my soldiers, your soldiers, or are they both the same?" After the child answered this question correctly, the experimenter spread out one of the rows of toys and repeated the question. As Piaget and others

HABITUATION EVENT

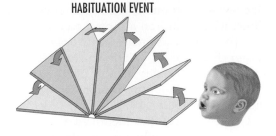

TEST EVENTS

Possible event

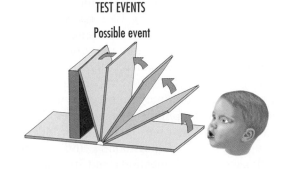

Impossible event

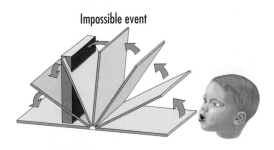

FIGURE 3-6

Testing Object Permanence *Infants are shown a rotating screen until they no longer attend to it. A box is placed where it can be hidden by the screen. The infants then see either a possible event (the screen rotates until it would hit the box and then returns to its starting position) or an impossible event (the screen appears to pass right through the box). Infants attend more to the impossible event, indicating that they realize that the hidden box still exists. (Adapted from Baillargeon)*

had previously reported, 5-year-old children failed to conserve, stating that the spread-out row contained more soldiers. But then the investigator introduced a second set of conditions. Instead of describing the toys as individual soldiers, she said: "This is my army and this is your army. What's more, my army, your army, or are they both the same?" With this simple change of wording, most of the children were able to conserve, judging the two "armies" to be the same size, even when one of them was spread out. Thus, when children are prompted to interpret the display as an aggregate or collection rather than as a set of individual items, their judgments of equality are less likely to be influenced by irrelevant perceptual transformations (Markman, 1979).

Other research has identified a variety of factors that can influence the development of concrete operational thought. For example, specific cultural practices influence children's mastery of Piagetian tasks (Rogoff, 1990). In addition, the experience of going to school seems to promote mastery of those tasks (Artman & Cahan, 1993). This and other evidence suggests that concrete operational reasoning may not be a universal stage of development that emerges during middle childhood but, instead, a product of the cultural setting, schooling, and the specific wording of questions and instructions (Gellatly, 1987; Light & Perrett-Clermont, 1989; Robert, 1989).

Alternatives to Piaget's Theory

Developmental psychologists generally agree that the kinds of findings we have just reviewed show that Piaget underestimated children's abilities, and his theory has been challenged on many grounds. However, there is no consensus on which is the best alternative to pursue. Some psychologists favor information-processing approaches, while others have pursued knowledge acquisition and sociocultural approaches. In this section we look briefly at these alternatives to Piaget's theory.

Information-Processing Approaches We have already noted that many of the experiments challenging Piaget's views were inspired by investigators who view cognitive development as the acquisition of several separate information-processing skills. Accordingly, they believe that the standard Piagetian tasks fail to separate these skills from the skill that the task is allegedly designed to assess. But they disagree among themselves about how exactly their views challenge Piaget's theory. For example, they disagree on the important question of whether development is best understood as a series of qualitatively distinct stages or as a continuous process of change.

Some believe that the entire notion of stages should be abandoned (Klahr, 1982). In their view, the separate skills develop smoothly and continuously rather than in a series of discrete stages. But other information-processing theorists believe that gradual changes in information-processing skills do in fact lead to discontinuous, stagelike changes in children's thinking (Case, 1985). These theorists are sometimes referred to as neo-Piagetians. Other neo-Piagetians agree that there are genuine stages but believe that they occur only within more narrow domains of knowledge. For example, a child's language skills, mathematical understanding, social reasoning, and so forth may all develop in stagelike fashion, but each domain proceeds at its own pace relatively independently of the others (Mandler, 1983).

Knowledge Acquisition Approaches Some developmental psychologists believe that after infancy, children and adults have essentially the same cognitive processes and capacities and that the primary difference between them is the adult's more extensive knowledge base. By *knowledge* they mean not just a larger collection of facts but a deeper understanding of how facts in a particular domain are organized.

The distinction between facts and the organization of facts is illustrated by a study that compared a group of 10-year-olds who were competing in a chess tournament with a group of college students who were chess amateurs. When asked to memorize and recall lists of random numbers, the college students easily outperformed the 10-year-olds. But when tested on their ability to recall actual positions of the chess pieces on the board, the 10-year-old chess experts did better than the 18-year-old chess amateurs (Chi, 1978). Thus, the relevant difference between the two groups is not different stages of cognitive development or different information-processing abilities, but domain-specific knowledge. Because the 10-year-olds had a deeper grasp of the underlying structure of chess, they were able to organize and reconstruct the arrangements from memory by "chunking" the separate pieces of information into larger meaningful units (for example, a king-side attack by white) and eliminating from consideration implausible placements of the pieces. (We discuss experts versus amateur problem solvers in Chapter 9.)

Increasing knowledge of the world, rather than a qualitative shift in cognitive development, may also account for children's increasing ability to solve Piaget's conservation tasks as they grow older. For example, a child who does not know that mass or number is the critical feature that defines what is meant by "more clay" or "more checkers" is likely to judge that the quantity has changed when only its visual appearance has changed. An older child may simply have learned the essential defining feature of "more." If this hypothesis is correct, a child who fails to show conservation in one domain may show conservation in another, depending on his or her understanding of the domain. Evidence in support of this hypothesis was obtained in a study in which kindergarten children were told about a series of "operations" that doctors or scientists had performed. Some operations altered an animal so that it looked like a different animal; other operations altered an animal so that it looked like a plant (see Figure 3-7). For example, the child was told that

FIGURE 3-7

Early Testing of Conservation   *Children are told that doctors or scientists operated on an animal until it looked like a different animal (horse-to-zebra) or until it looked like a plant (hedgehog-to-cactus). Children who say that the animal is "really" the new animal or plant are failing to show conservation; children who say that the animal is still "really" the original animal are showing conservation.*

the doctors took a horse [shows child picture of horse] and did an operation that put black and white stripes all over its body. They cut off its mane and braided its tail. They trained it to stop neighing like a horse, and they trained it to eat wild grass instead of oats and hay. They also trained it to live in the wilds in Africa instead of in a stable. When they were all done, the animal looked just like this [shows picture of zebra]. When they were finished, was this animal a horse or a zebra? (Keil, 1989, p. 307)

On operations that transformed one kind of animal into another, a majority of the children failed to conserve; about 65% agreed that the horse had been genuinely changed into a zebra. But when faced with the transformation of an animal into a plant, only about 25% agreed that a porcupine had been genuinely changed into a cactus (Keil, 1989). Studies like these demonstrate that in some domains, preoperational children can ignore dramatic changes in visual appearance because they have learned that an invisible but essential defining feature of the object has remained unchanged.

Sociocultural Approaches Although Piaget emphasized the child's interactions with the environment, the environment he had in mind was the immediate physical environment. The social and cultural context plays virtually no role in Piaget's theory. Yet much of what children must learn consists of the particular ways in which their culture views reality, what roles different people—and different sexes—are expected to play, and what rules and norms govern social relationships in their particular culture. In these areas there are no universally valid facts or correct views of reality. Thus, according to those who take a sociocultural approach to development, the child should be seen not as a physical scientist seeking "true" knowledge but as a newcomer to a culture who seeks to become a native by learning how to look at social reality through the lens of that culture (Bem, 1993, 1987; Shweder, 1984).

The origins of this view of cognitive development can be seen in the work of the Russian scholar Lev Vygotsky (1934/1986). Vygotsky believed that we develop understanding and expertise primarily through what might be described as apprenticeship—we are guided by more knowledgeable individuals, who help us understand more

According to Vygotsky, children develop understanding and expertise through a form of apprenticeship in which they are guided by more knowledgeable individuals. For example, an older child may help a younger one develop new skills.

and more about our world and develop new skills. He also distinguished between two levels of cognitive development: the child's actual level of development, as expressed in problem-solving ability, and the child's level of potential development, which is determined by the kind of problem solving the child can do when guided by an adult or a more knowledgeable peer. According to Vygotsky, we need to know both the actual and potential levels of development in a particular child if we are to fully understand their level of cognitive development and provide appropriate instruction for them.

Because language is the primary means by which humans exchange social meanings, Vygotsky viewed language development as central to cognitive development; in fact, he regarded the acquisition of language as the most important aspect of children's development (Blanck, 1990). Language plays an important role in developing new skills and knowledge. As adults and peers help children master new tasks, the communication between them becomes part of the children's thinking. The children then use their language ability to guide their own actions as they practice the new skill. Thus, what Piaget referred to as egocentric speech, Vygotsky considered an essential component of cognitive development: Children speak to themselves in order to give themselves guidance and direction. This kind of self-instruction is termed *private speech*. You can observe this process in a child who gives herself instructions about how to perform a task, such as tying her shoes, that she previously heard from an adult (Berk, 1997).

The Development of Moral Judgment

In addition to studying the development of children's thought, Piaget was interested in how children develop moral judgment. He believed that children's understanding of moral rules and social conventions would have to match their overall level of cognitive development. On the basis of observations he made of children of different ages playing games with rules, such as marbles, he proposed that children's understanding of rules develops in a series of four stages (Piaget, 1932/1965). The first stage emerges at the beginning of the preoperational period. Children at this stage engage in "parallel play," in which each child follows his or her own private set of idiosyncratic rules. For example, a child might sort marbles of different colors into groups, or roll all the big ones across the room, followed by all the small ones. These "rules" give the child's play some regularity, but they are frequently changed and serve no collective purpose such as cooperation or competition.

Beginning about age 5, the child develops a sense of obligation to follow rules, treating them as absolute moral imperatives handed down by some authority such as God or the child's parents. Rules are permanent, sacred, and not subject to modification. Obeying them to the letter is more important than any human reason for changing them. For example, children at this stage reject the suggestion that the position of the starting line in the marble game might be changed to accommodate younger children who might want to play.

At this same stage, children judge an act more by its consequences than by the intentions behind it. For example, Piaget told children several pairs of stories. In one pair, a boy broke a teacup while trying to steal some jam when his mother was not home; another boy, who was doing nothing wrong, accidentally broke a whole trayful of teacups. "Which boy is naughtier?" Piaget asked. Preoperational children tended to judge as naughtier the person in the stories who did the most damage, regardless of the intentions or motivation behind the act.

Although young children participate in parallel play with one another, it is only when they become older that they begin to understand the rules that govern social interaction.

In Piaget's third stage of moral development the child begins to appreciate that some rules are social conventions—cooperative agreements that can be arbitrarily decided and changed if everyone agrees. Children's moral realism also declines: When making moral judgments, children now give weight to subjective considerations like a person's intentions, and they see punishment as a human choice rather than as inevitable, divine retribution.

The beginning of the formal operational stage coincides with the fourth and final stage in children's understanding of moral rules. Youngsters now show an interest in generating rules to deal even with situations they have never encountered. This stage is marked by an ideological mode of moral reasoning, which addresses wider social issues rather than just personal and interpersonal situations.

The American psychologist Lawrence Kohlberg extended Piaget's work on moral reasoning to include adolescence and adulthood (Kohlberg, 1976, 1969). He sought to determine whether there are universal stages in the development of moral judgments by presenting research participants with moral dilemmas in the form of stories. For example, in one story a man whose dying wife needs a drug that he cannot afford pleads with a druggist to let him buy the drug at a cheaper price. When the druggist refuses, the man decides to steal the drug. Participants are asked to discuss the man's action.

By analyzing answers to several such dilemmas, Kohlberg arrived at six developmental stages of moral judgment, which he grouped into three levels: *preconventional, conventional,* and *postconventional* (see Table 3-2). The answers are scored on the basis of the reasons given for the decision, not on the basis of whether the action is judged to be right or wrong. For example, agreeing that the man should have stolen the drug because "If you let your wife die, you'll get in trouble" or disagreeing because "If you steal the drug, you'll be caught and sent to jail" are both scored at Stage 1. In both instances the man's actions are evaluated as right or wrong on the basis of anticipated punishment.

Kohlberg believed that all children are at Level I until about age 10, when they begin to evaluate actions in terms of other people's opinions (Level II). Most youngsters can reason at this level by age 13. Following Piaget, Kohlberg argued that only individuals who have achieved formal operational thought are capable of the kind of abstract thinking that is necessary for Level III, postconventional morality. The highest stage, Stage 6, requires the ability to formulate abstract ethical principles and uphold them so as to avoid self-condemnation.

TABLE 3-2

Stages of Moral Reasoning　*Kohlberg believed that moral judgment develops with age according to these stages. (After Kohlberg, 1969)*

Level I:	Preconventional Morality
Stage 1	Punishment orientation (Obeys rules to avoid punishment)
Stage 2	Reward orientation (Conforms to obtain rewards, to have favors returned)
Level II:	**Conventional Morality**
Stage 3	Good-boy/good-girl orientation (Conforms to avoid disapproval of others)
Stage 4	Authority orientation (Upholds laws and social rules to avoid censure of authorities and feelings of guilt about not "doing one's duty")
Level III:	**Postconventional Morality**
Stage 5	Social-contract orientation (Actions guided by principles commonly agreed on as essential to the public welfare; principles upheld to retain respect of peers and, thus, self-respect)
Stage 6	Ethical principle orientation (Actions guided by self-chosen ethical principles, which usually value justice, dignity, and equality; principles upheld to avoid self-condemnation)

Kohlberg reported that fewer than 10% of his adult participants showed the kind of "clear-principled" Stage-6 thinking that is exemplified by the following response of a 16-year-old to the story described earlier: "By the law of society [the man] was wrong. But by the law of nature or of God the druggist was wrong and the husband was justified. Human life is above financial gain. Regardless of who was dying, if it was a total stranger, man has a duty to save him from dying" (Kohlberg, 1969, p. 244). Before he died, Kohlberg eliminated Stage 6 from his theory; Level III is now sometimes simply referred to as *high-stage principled reasoning.*

Kohlberg presented evidence for this sequence of stages in children from several cultures, including the United States, Mexico, Taiwan, and Turkey (Colby, Kohlberg, Gibbs, & Lieberman, 1983; Nisan & Kohlberg, 1982). On the other hand, there is evidence that people use different rules for different situations and that the stages are not sequential (Kurtines & Greif, 1974). The theory has also been criticized for being "male centered" because it places a "masculine" style of abstract reasoning based on justice and rights higher on the moral scale than a "feminine" style of reasoning based on caring and concern for the integrity and continuation of relationships (Gilligan, 1982).

Piaget's assertion that young children cannot distinguish between social conventions (rules) and moral prescriptions has also been challenged. In one study, 7-year-old children were given a list of actions and asked to indicate which ones would be wrong even if there were no rules against them. There was widespread agreement among these children that lying, stealing, hitting, and selfishness would be wrong even if there were no rules against them. In contrast, they thought that there was nothing wrong with chewing gum in class, addressing a teacher by his or her first name, boys entering the girls' bathroom, or eating lunch with one's fingers—as long as there were no rules against these acts (Nuccli, 1981).

Personality and Social Development

First-time parents are often surprised that their newborn seems to have a distinctive personality from the very beginning; when they have a second child, they are often surprised at how different the second is from the first. As early as the first weeks of life, infants show individual differences in activity level, responsiveness to changes in their environment, and irritability. One infant cries a lot; another cries very little. One endures diapering or bathing without much fuss; another kicks and thrashes. One is responsive to every sound; another is oblivious to all but the loudest noises. Infants even differ in "cuddliness": Some seem to enjoy being cuddled and will mold their body to that of the person holding them; others will stiffen and squirm (Korner, 1973). The term **temperament** is used to refer to such *mood-related personality characteristics.*

Temperament

The study of temperament is a very active research area, and there are disagreements over how differing temperaments should be defined, identified, and measured. It also is not clear to what extent temperament in early childhood is reflected in the individual's later personality (Kohnstamm, Bates, & Rothbart, 1989).

The observation that temperamental differences arise early in life challenges the traditional view that all of an infant's behaviors are shaped by its environment. Parents of a fussy baby, for example, tend to blame themselves for their infant's difficulties. But research with newborns has shown that

Some infants are more readily soothed than others. Such differences are due to differences in temperament.

many temperamental differences are inborn and that the relationship between parent and infant is reciprocal—in other words, the infant's behavior also shapes the parent's response. An infant who is easily soothed, who snuggles and stops crying when picked up, increases the parent's feelings of competence and attachment. An infant who stiffens and continues to cry, despite efforts to comfort it, makes the parent feel inadequate and rejected. The more responsive a baby is to the stimulation provided by the parent (snuggling and quieting when held, attending alertly when talked to or played with), the easier it is for parent and child to establish a loving bond.

A pioneering study of temperament began in the 1950s with a group of 140 middle- and upper-class infants. The initial data were gathered through interviews with parents and were later supplemented by interviews with teachers and by scores on tests administered to the children. The infants were scored on nine traits, which were later combined to define three broad temperament types. Infants who were playful, were regular in their sleeping and eating patterns, and adapted readily to new situations were classified as *easy* (about 40% of the sample); infants who were irritable, had irregular sleeping and eating patterns, and responded intensely and negatively to new situations were classified as *difficult* (about 10% of the sample); infants who were relatively inactive, tended to withdraw from new situations in a mild way, and required more time than easy infants to adapt to new situations were classified as *slow to warm up* (about 15% of the sample). The remaining 35% of the infants were not rated high or low on any of the defining dimensions (Thomas et al., 1963).

Of the original sample, 133 individuals have been followed into adult life and have again been assessed on temperament and psychological adjustment. The results provide mixed evidence for the continuity of temperament. On the one hand, temperament scores across the first five years of these children's lives showed significant correlations: Children with "difficult" temperaments were more likely than "easy" children to have school problems later on. Adult measures of both temperament and adjustment were also significantly correlated with measures of childhood temperament obtained at ages 3, 4, and 5. On the other hand, all the correlations were low (about .3), and when considered separately, most of the nine traits measured showed little or no continuity across time (Thomas & Chess, 1986, 1977; Chess & Thomas, 1984).

The researchers emphasize that continuity or discontinuity of temperament is a function of the interaction between the child's genotype (inherited characteristics) and the environment. In particular, they believe that the key to healthy development is a good fit between the child's temperament and the home environment. When parents of a difficult child provide a happy, stable home life, the child's negative, difficult behaviors decline with age (Belsky, Fish, & Isabella, 1991). Thomas and Chess cite the case of Carl, who displayed a very difficult temperament from the first few months of life through age 5. Because Carl's father took delight in his son's "lusty" temperament and allowed for his initial negative reactions to new situations, Carl flourished and became increasingly "easy." At age 23 he was clearly classified into the "easy" temperament group. Nevertheless, Carl's original temperament often emerged briefly when his life circumstances changed. For example, when he started piano lessons in late childhood, he showed an intense negative response, followed by slow adaptability and eventual positive, zestful involvement. A similar pattern emerged when he entered college (Thomas & Chess, 1986).

A recent study provides further evidence of continuity of temperament. Seventy-nine children were categorized at 21 months as either extremely inhibited or uninhibited. At age 13, those who had been categorized as inhibited at 21 months of age scored significantly lower on a test of externalizing, delinquent behavior, and aggressive behavior (Schwartz, Snidman, & Kagan, 1996). Other research has found that the tendency to approach or avoid unfamiliar events, which is an aspect of temperament, remains moderately stable over time (Kagan & Snidman, 1991).

Early Social Behavior

By 2 months of age, the average child will smile at the sight of its mother's or father's face. Delighted with this response, parents will go to great lengths to encourage it. Indeed, the infant's ability to smile at such an early age may have evolved historically precisely because it strengthened the parent-child bond. Parents interpret these smiles to mean that the infant recognizes and loves them, and this encourages them to be even more affectionate and stimulating in response. A mutually reinforcing system of social interaction is thus established and maintained.

Infants all over the world begin to smile at about the same age, suggesting that maturation plays an important role in determining the onset of smiling. Blind babies also smile at about the same age as sighted infants, indicating that smiling is an innate response (Eibl-Eibesfeldt, 1970).

By their third or fourth month, infants show that they recognize and prefer familiar members of the household by smiling or cooing more when seeing these familiar faces or hearing their voices; but they are still fairly receptive to strangers. At about 7 or 8 months, however, many infants begin to show wariness or distress at the approach of a stranger and protest strongly when left in an unfamiliar setting or with an unfamiliar person. Parents are often disconcerted to find that their formerly gregarious infant, who had always happily welcomed the attentions of a babysitter, now cries inconsolably when they prepare to leave—and continues to cry for some time after they have left. Although not all infants show this *stranger anxiety,* the number of infants who do show it increases dramatically from about 8 months of age until the end of the first year. Similarly, distress over separation from the parent reaches a peak between 14 and 18 months and then gradually declines. By the time they are 3 years old, most children are secure enough in their parents' absence to interact comfortably with other children and adults.

The waxing and waning of these two fears appears to be only slightly influenced by conditions of child rearing. The same general pattern has been observed among American children reared entirely at home and among those attending a day-care center. Figure 3-8 shows that although the percentage of children who cry when their mother leaves the room varies in different cultures, the age-related pattern of onset and decline is very similar (Kagan, Kearsley, & Zelazo, 1978).

Infants throughout the world begin to smile at about the same age— as do blind children—implying that maturation is more important than the conditions in which a child is reared in determining the onset of smiling.

How do we explain the systematic timing of these fears? Two factors seem to be important in both their onset and their decline. One is the growth of memory capacity. During the second half of the first year, infants become

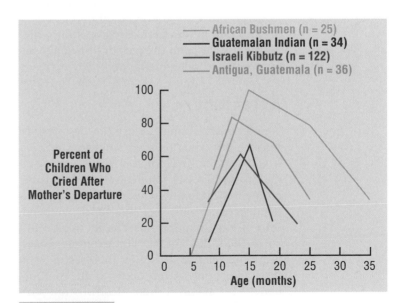

FIGURE 3-8

Children's Stress at Mother's Departure   *Even though the percentages of children who cry when their mothers leave the room varies from one culture to another, the age-related pattern of onset and decline of such distress is similar across cultures.* (From Kagan, Kearsley, & Zelazo, 1978)

better able to remember past events and to compare past and present. This makes it possible for the baby to detect, and sometimes to fear, unusual or unpredictable events. The emergence of stranger anxiety coincides with the emergence of fear of a variety of stimuli that are unusual or unexpected; a weird-looking mask or a jack-in-the-box that brings smiles to a 4-month-old often causes an 8-month-old to look apprehensive and distressed. As children learn that strangers and unusual objects are not generally harmful, such fears gradually diminish.

It also seems reasonable to assume that memory development is involved in separation anxiety. The infant cannot "miss" the parent unless he or she can recall that parent's presence a minute earlier and compare it with the parent's absence now. When the parent leaves the room, the infant is aware that something is amiss, and this can lead to distress. As the child's memory of past instances of separation improves, the child becomes better able to anticipate the return of the absent parent, and anxiety declines.

The second factor is the growth of autonomy. One-year-olds are still highly dependent on the care of adults, but children 2 or 3 years old can head for the snack plate or toy shelf on their own. They can also use language to communicate their wants and feelings. Thus, dependence on caregivers in general and on familiar caregivers in particular decreases, and the parent's presence becomes less critical for the child.

Attachment

The term **attachment** is used to describe *an infant's tendency to seek closeness to particular people and to feel more secure in their presence.* Psychologists at first theorized that attachment to the mother developed because she was the source of food, one of the infant's most basic needs. But some facts did not fit. For example, ducklings and baby chicks feed themselves from birth, yet they still follow their mothers about and spend a great deal of time with them. The comfort they derive from the mother's presence cannot come from her role in feeding. A series of well-known experiments with monkeys showed that there is more to mother-infant attachment than nutritional needs (Harlow & Harlow, 1969).

Infant monkeys were separated from their mothers shortly after birth and placed with two artificial "mothers" constructed of wire mesh with wooden heads. The torso of one mother was bare wire; the other was covered with foam rubber and terry cloth, making it more cuddly and easy to cling to (see Figure 3-9). Either mother could be equipped to provide milk by means of a bottle attached to its chest.

The experiment sought to determine whether the "mother" that was always the source of food would be the one to which the young monkey would cling. The results were clear-cut: No matter which mother provided food, the infant monkey spent its time clinging to the terry-cloth mother. This purely passive but soft-contact mother was a source of security. For example, the obvious fear of the infant monkey placed in a strange environment was allayed if the infant could make contact with the cloth mother. While holding on to the cloth mother with one hand or foot, the

FIGURE 3-9

A Monkey's Response to an Artificial Mother
Although it is fed via a wire mother, the infant spends more time with the terry-cloth mother. The terry-cloth mother provides a safe base from which to explore strange objects.

monkey was willing to explore objects that were otherwise too terrifying to approach.

Although contact with a cuddly, artificial mother provides an important aspect of "mothering," it is not enough for satisfactory development. Infant monkeys raised with artificial mothers and isolated from other monkeys during the first six months of life showed various types of bizarre behavior in adulthood. They rarely engaged in normal interaction with other monkeys later on (either cowering in fear or showing abnormally aggressive behavior), and their sexual responses were inappropriate. When female monkeys that had been deprived of early social contact were successfully mated (after considerable effort), they made poor mothers, tending to neglect or abuse their first-born infants—although they became better mothers with their later-born children. Note, however, that these monkeys were deprived of all social contact. Monkeys with artificial mothers do fine as adults if they are allowed to interact with their peers during the first six months.

Although we should be careful in generalizing from research on monkeys to human development, there is evidence that the human infant's attachment to the primary caregiver serves the same functions. Most of the work on attachment in human infants originated with the psychoanalyst John Bowlby in the 1950s and 1960s. His research convinced him that a child's failure to form a secure attachment to one or more persons in the early years is related to an inability to develop close personal relationships in adulthood (Bowlby, 1973).

Mary Ainsworth, one of Bowlby's associates, made extensive observations of children and their mothers in Uganda and the United States and then developed a laboratory procedure for assessing the security of a child's attachments from about 12 to 18 months of age (Ainsworth, Blehar, Waters, & Wall, 1978). This procedure, called the *strange situation*, consists of a series of episodes in which a child is observed as the primary caregiver leaves and returns to the room (see Table 3-3). Throughout this sequence the baby is observed through a one-way mirror and several observations are recorded: the baby's activity level and play involvement, crying and other distress signs, proximity to and attempts to gain the attention of the mother, proximity to and willingness to interact with the stranger, and so on. On the basis of their behaviors, babies are categorized into one of the following three groups:

Securely attached. Regardless of whether they are upset at the mother's departures (episodes 3 and 5), babies who are classified as securely attached seek to interact with her when she returns. Some are content simply to acknowledge her return from a distance while continuing to play with the toys. Others seek physical contact with her. Still others are completely preoccupied with the mother throughout the entire session, showing intense distress when she leaves. In all, 60–65% of American babies fall into this category.

Insecurely attached: avoidant. These babies avoid interacting with the mother during the reunion episodes. Some ignore her almost entirely; others display mixed attempts to interact and to avoid

---

TABLE 3-3

Episodes in the Strange Situation Procedure

1. A mother and her child enter the room. The mother places the baby on the floor, surrounded by toys, and goes to sit at the opposite end of the room.
2. A female stranger enters the room, sits quietly for a minute, converses with the mother for a minute, and then attempts to engage the baby in play with a toy.
3. The mother leaves the room unobtrusively. If the baby is not upset, the stranger returns to sitting quietly. If the baby is upset, the stranger tries to soothe him or her.
4. The mother returns and engages the baby in play while the stranger slips out of the room.
5. The mother leaves again, this time leaving the baby alone in the room.
6. The stranger returns. If the baby is upset, the stranger tries to comfort him or her.
7. The mother returns and the stranger slips out of the room.

interacting. Avoidant babies may pay little attention to the mother when she is in the room and often do not seem distressed when she leaves. If they are distressed, they are as easily comforted by the stranger as by the mother. About 20% of American babies fall into this category.

Insecurely attached: ambivalent. Babies are classified as ambivalent if they show resistance to the mother during the reunion episodes. They simultaneously seek and resist physical contact. For example, they may cry to be picked up and then squirm angrily to get down. Some act very passive, crying for the mother when she returns but not crawling toward her, and then showing resistance when she approaches. About 10% of American babies fall into this category.

Because some babies did not seem to fit any of these categories, more recent studies have included a fourth category, *disorganized* (Main & Solomon, 1986). Babies in this category often show contradictory behaviors. For example, they may approach the mother while taking care not to look at her, approach her and then show dazed avoidance, or suddenly cry out after having settled down. Some seem disoriented, appear emotionless, or look depressed. About 10–15% of American babies fall into this category, with the percentages much higher among babies who are maltreated or whose parents who are being treated for mental disorders.

In attempting to account for differences in attachment among babies, researchers have directed most of their attention to the behavior of the primary caregiver, usually the mother. The main finding is that a caregiver's "sensitive responsiveness" to the baby's needs produces secure attachment. Mothers of securely attached babies usually respond promptly when the baby cries and behave affectionately when they pick him or her up. They also tailor their responses to the baby's needs (Clarke-Stewart, 1973). In feeding, for example, they use an infant's signals to determine when to begin and end feeding and attend to the baby's food preferences. In contrast, mothers of babies who are insecurely attached respond according to their own needs or moods rather than according to signals from the baby. For example, they will respond to the baby's cries for attention

when they feel like cuddling the baby but will ignore such cries at other times (Stayton, 1973).

Not all developmental psychologists agree that the caregiver's responsiveness is the major cause of an infant's attachment behaviors. They call attention to the baby's own inborn temperament (Kagan, 1984; Campos et al., 1983). For example, perhaps the temperaments that make some babies "easy" also make them more securely attached than do the temperaments of "difficult" babies. And, as noted earlier, a parent's response to a child is often itself a function of the child's own behavior. For example, mothers of difficult babies tend to spend less time playing with them (Green, Fox, & Lewis, 1983). Attachment patterns may reflect this interaction between a baby's temperament and the parents' responsiveness.

In reply, attachment theorists point to evidence that supports the "sensitive responsiveness" hypothesis. For example, it has been found that in the first year of life an infant's crying changes much more than the mother's responsiveness to the crying does. Moreover, the mother's responsiveness over a three-month period predicts the infant's crying over the next three months significantly better than the infant's crying predicts the mother's subsequent responsiveness to crying. In short, the mother appears to influence the infant's crying more than the infant influences the mother's responsiveness to crying (Bell & Ainsworth, 1972). In general, the mother's behavior appears to be the most important factor in establishing a secure or insecure attachment (Isabella & Belsky, 1991).

More recent research may resolve this debate. Recall that the attachment classification is based not on the baby's distress when the mother leaves but on how the baby reacts when she returns. It now appears that an infant's temperament predicts the former but not the latter (Vaughn, Lefever, Seifer, & Barglow, 1989; Frodi & Thompson, 1985). For example, babies with "easy" temperaments typically are not distressed when the mother leaves. When she returns, they either tend to greet her happily—thus showing secure attachment—or show the avoidant type of insecure attachment. Babies with "difficult" temperaments typically are distressed when the mother leaves. When she returns, they either tend to seek her out and cling to her—thus showing secure attachment—or show the ambivalent type of insecure attachment (Belsky & Rovine, 1987). Thus, children's overall reaction to the departure and return of their primary caregiver is a function of both the caregiver's responsiveness to the child and the child's temperament.

Attachment and Later Development

A baby's attachment classification has been found to remain quite stable when retested several years later—unless the family experiences major changes in life circumstances (Main & Cassidy, 1988; Thompson, Lamb, & Estes, 1982). Stressful life changes are likely to affect parental responsiveness to the baby, which, in turn, affects the baby's feelings of security.

Early attachment patterns also appear to be related to how children cope with

Children who were rated as insecure in their attachment relationships at 15 months of age tended to be socially withdrawn and hesitant about participating in activities in later years, when they were in nursery school.

new experiences. For example, in one study, 2-year-olds were given a series of problems requiring the use of tools. Some of the problems were within the child's capacity; others were quite difficult. Children who had been rated as securely attached at 12 months approached the problems with enthusiasm and persistence. When they encountered difficulties, they seldom cried or became angry; rather, they sought help from adults. Children who had earlier been rated as insecurely attached behaved quite differently. They easily became frustrated and angry, seldom asked for help, tended to ignore or reject directions from adults, and quickly gave up trying to solve the problems (Matas, Arend, & Sroufe, 1978).

This and similar studies suggest that children who are securely attached by the time they enter their second year are better equipped to cope with new experiences. However, we cannot be certain that the quality of children's early attachments is directly responsible for their later competence in problem solving. Parents who are responsive to their children's needs in infancy probably continue to provide effective parenting during early childhood—encouraging autonomy and efforts to cope with new experiences, yet ready with help when needed. Thus, the child's competence may reflect the current state of the parent-child relationship rather than the relationship that existed two years earlier. Moreover, children's temperament—which, as we saw earlier, affects their behavior in the strange situation procedure—might also influence their competence as preschoolers. (For a discussion of the effects of day care on attachment, see the Frontiers of Psychological Research feature on page 94.)

Gender Identity and Sex Typing

Most children acquire a **gender identity,** *a firm sense of themselves as either male or female.* But most cultures elaborate the biological distinction between male and female into a sprawling network of beliefs and practices that permeate virtually every domain of human activity. Different cultures may define the socially correct behaviors, roles, and personality characteristics differently from one another, and these may change over time within a culture. But whatever its

FRONTIERS OF PSYCHOLOGICAL RESEARCH

Effects of Day Care

Day care is a controversial subject in the United States because many people have doubts about its effects on very young children; also, many Americans believe that children should be cared for at home by their mothers. But in a society where the vast majority of mothers are in the labor force, day care is a reality; in fact, more 3- and 4-year-olds (43%) attend day care than are cared for in either their own home or another home (35%).

Day care centers that are well equipped and have a high ratio of caregivers to children have been found to have positive effects on children's development.

Many researchers have attempted to discover what effects, if any, day care has on children. One well-known study (Belsky & Rovine, 1988) found that infants who received more than 20 hours of nonmaternal care per week were slightly more likely to be insecurely attached to their mothers; however, this finding applied only to male infants with unresponsive mothers who felt that their infants had a difficult temperament. Similarly, Clarke-Stewart (1989) found that infants receiving nonmaternal care were somewhat less likely to be securely attached to their mothers than infants who were cared for by their mothers (47% versus 53%). Other researchers found that children's development is not affected adversely by good-quality nonmaternal care (Phillips et al., 1987).

In recent years research on day care has focused less on the effects of day care versus maternal care than on the effects of high-quality versus low-quality day care. For example, children who receive high-quality day care from an early age have been found to be more competent socially in elementary school (Andersson, 1992; Field, 1991; Howes, 1990) and more assertive (Scarr & Eisenberg, 1993) than children who enter day care later. On the other hand, poor-quality care may have negative effects on adjustment, particularly in boys, especially if the child comes from a highly stressed home environment (Garrett, 1997). Good-quality day care can reduce the effects of growing up in such an environment (Phillips et al., 1994).

What constitutes good-quality day care? Several factors have been identified. They include the number of children in a single space, the ratio of caregivers to children, low turnover among caregivers, and the caregivers' education and training. Under these conditions caregivers tend to be more attentive to children and sensitive to their needs, as well as more verbally stimulating, and as a result the children perform better on measures of intelligence and social development (Galinsky et al., 1994; Helburn, 1995; Howes, Phillips, & Whitebook, 1992). Other research has found that centers that are well equipped and provide a wide variety of activities have positive effects (Scarr et al., 1993).

A recent large-scale study of more than 1,000 children in 10 day-care centers found that in the better centers (as measured by the qualifications of the caregivers and the amount of individual attention given to the children), children actually made greater gains in language and thinking abilities than children from similar backgrounds who were not receiving high-quality day care. This was especially true of children from lower-income households (Garrett, 1997).

In sum, it appears that children are not significantly affected by nonmaternal care. Any negative effects tend to be emotional in nature, whereas positive effects are more likely to be social; cognitive development is usually affected either positively or not at all. However, these findings apply to day care of reasonable quality. Poor-quality care usually has negative effects on children, regardless of their home environment.

current definition, each culture still strives to transform male and female infants into "masculine" and "feminine" adults.

The term **sex typing** refers to *the acquisition of behaviors and characteristics that a culture considers appropriate to one's sex.* Note that gender identity and sex typing are not the same thing. A girl may have a firm acceptance of herself as female yet not avoid all behaviors that are labeled masculine.

But are gender identity and sex typing simply the product of cultural prescriptions and expectations, or are they partly a product of "natural" development? In this section we will examine four theories that attempt to answer this question.

Psychoanalytic Theory The first psychologist to attempt a comprehensive account of gender identity and sex typing was Sigmund Freud (1933/1964). Psychoanalytic theory and its limitations are discussed in more detail in Chapter 13; here we present a brief overview of aspects of the theory that are relevant to gender identity and sex typing.

According to Freud, children begin to focus on the genitals at about age 3; he called this the beginning of the *phallic stage* of psychosexual development. Specifically, both sexes become aware that boys have a penis and that girls do not. During this same stage, they also begin to have sexual feelings toward their opposite-sex parent and feel jealous and resentful of their same-sex parent; Freud called this the *Oedipal conflict* (after the ancient Greek legend of Oedipus, who killed his father and married his mother). As they mature further, both sexes eventually resolve this conflict by identifying with their same-sex parent, modeling their behaviors, attitudes, and personality attributes on that parent in an attempt to be like him or her—hence, sex typing (Freud, 1925/1961).

Psychoanalytic theory has always been controversial, and many critics have pointed out that there is no empirical evidence to support the conclusion that a child's discovery of genital sex differences or identification with the same-sex parent determines gender identity and sex typing (McConaghy, 1979; Maccoby & Jacklin, 1974; Kohlberg, 1966).

Social-Learning Theory In contrast to psychoanalytic theory, social-learning theory has a much more straightforward account of sex typing. It emphasizes the rewards and punishments that children receive for sex-appropriate and sex-inappropriate behaviors, respectively, and the ways in which children learn sex-typed behavior by observing adults (Bandura, 1986; Mischel, 1966; Perry & Bussey, 1984). Observational learning also enables children to imitate same-sex adults and thereby acquire sex-typed behaviors.

Two broader points about social-learning theory are worth noting. Unlike psychoanalytic theory, social-learning theory treats sex-typed behaviors like any other learned behaviors; no special psychological principles or processes must be proposed to explain how children become sex typed. Second, if there is nothing special about sex-typed behaviors, then sex typing itself is neither inevitable nor unmodifiable. Children become sex typed because sex happens to be the basis on which their culture chooses to base reward and punishment. If a culture becomes less sex typed in its ideology, children will become less sex typed in their behavior.

There is considerable evidence to support the social-learning account of sex typing. Parents do differentially reward and punish sex-appropriate and sex-inappropriate behaviors as well as serve as the child's first models of masculine and feminine behavior. From infancy on, most parents dress boys and girls differently and provide them with different toys (Rheingold & Cook, 1975). Observations made in the homes of preschool children have found that parents reward their daughters for dressing up, dancing, playing with dolls, and simply following them around, but criticize them for manipulating objects, running, jumping, and climbing. In contrast, parents reward their sons for playing with blocks, but criticize them for playing with dolls, asking for help, or even volunteering to be helpful (Fagot, 1978). Parents tend to demand more independence of boys and to have higher expectations of them; they also respond less quickly to boys' requests for help and focus less on the interpersonal aspects of a task. And finally, parents punish boys both verbally and physically more often than girls (Maccoby & Jacklin, 1974).

Some have suggested that in reacting differently to boys and girls, parents may not

Both psychoanalytic theory and social-learning theory propose that children become sex-typed by imitating the behavior of the parent or another adult of the same sex. However, the theories differ markedly in their explanations of this behavior.

be imposing their own stereotypes on them but simply reacting to innate differences between the behaviors of the two sexes (Maccoby, 1980). For example, even as infants, boys demand more attention than girls do, and research suggests that human males are innately more physically aggressive than human females (Maccoby & Jacklin, 1974). This could be why parents punish boys more often than girls. There may be some truth to this, but it is also clear that adults approach children with stereotyped expectations that lead them to treat boys and girls differently. For example, adults viewing newborn infants through the window of a hospital nursery believe that they can detect sex differences. Infants thought to be boys are described as robust, strong, and large featured; identical-looking infants thought to be girls are described as delicate, fine featured, and "soft" (Luria & Rubin, 1974).

Fathers appear to be more concerned with sex-typed behavior than mothers, particularly with their sons. They tend to react more negatively than mothers, interfering with the child's play or expressing disapproval when their sons play with "feminine" toys. Fathers are less concerned when their daughters engage in "masculine" play, but they still show more disapproval than mothers do (Langlois & Downs, 1980). But if parents and other adults treat children in sex-stereotyped ways, children themselves are the real "sexists." Peers enforce sex-stereotyping much more severely than parents. Boys, in particular, criticize other boys when they see them engaged in "girls'" activities. They are quick to call another boy a sissy if he plays with dolls, cries when he is hurt, or shows concern toward another child in distress. In contrast, girls seem not to object to other girls playing with "boys'" toys or engaging in masculine activities. (Langlois & Downs, 1980).

Although social-learning theory plausibly explains many phenomena of sex typing, there are some observations that the theory cannot easily explain. First, it treats the child as a passive recipient of environmental forces: Society, parents, peers, and the media all "do it" to the child. This view of the child is inconsistent with the observation that children themselves construct and enforce their own exaggerated version of society's gender rules more insistently than most of the adults in their world. Second, there is an interesting developmental pattern to the child's view of gender rules. For example, a majority of

4-year-olds and a majority of 9-year-olds believe that there should be no sex-based restrictions on one's choice of occupation: Let women be doctors and men be nurses if they wish. Between these ages, however, children hold more rigid opinions. Thus, about 90% of 6- and 7-year-olds believe that there *should* be sex-based restrictions on occupations (Damon, 1977).

Do these observations sound familiar? If you think these children sound like Piaget's preoperational moral realists, you are right. That is why psychologist Lawrence Kohlberg (1966) developed a cognitive-developmental theory of sex typing based directly on Piaget's theory of cognitive development.

Cognitive-Developmental Theory Although 2-year-olds can identify their own sex in a photograph of themselves and are usually able to identify the sex of a stereotypically dressed man or woman in a photograph, they cannot accurately sort photographs into "boys" and "girls" or predict another child's toy preferences on the basis of sex (Thompson, 1975). At about $2\frac{1}{2}$ years, however, a more conceptual awareness of sex and gender begins to emerge, and it is at this point that cognitive-developmental theory becomes relevant. In particular, the theory proposes that gender identity plays a critical role in **sex typing.** The sequence is: "I am a girl [boy]; therefore I want to do girl [boy] things" (Kohlberg, 1966). In other words, it is the motive to behave consistently with one's gender identity—not to obtain external rewards—that prompts children to behave in sex-appropriate ways. As a result, they willingly take on the task of sex typing themselves—and their peers.

According to cognitive-developmental theory, gender identity itself develops slowly over the years from 2 to 7, in accordance with the principles of the preoperational stage of cognitive development. In particular, preoperational children's overreliance on visual impressions and their resulting inability to conserve an object's identity when its appearance changes becomes relevant to their concept of sex. Thus, 3-year-olds can separate pictures of boys and girls, but many of them cannot say whether they themselves will be a mommy or a daddy when they grow up (Thompson, 1975). The understanding that a person's sex remains

the same despite changes in age and appearance is called *gender constancy* and is analogous to conservation of quantity with water, clay, and checkers.

Earlier we saw that psychologists who adopt a knowledge acquisition approach to cognitive development believe that children often fail conservation tasks because they simply do not possess sufficient knowledge of the relevant domain. We saw, for example, children who conserved on animal-to-plant transformations but failed to conserve on animal-to-animal transformations. Children will ignore dramatic changes in visual appearance only when they understand that some essential defining feature of an object has not changed. This suggests that a child's gender constancy might also depend on his or her understanding of maleness and femaleness. But what do adults know about sex that children do not? One answer is genitalia. For all practical purposes, genitalia constitute the essential defining feature of maleness and femaleness. Can young children who understand this fact conserve on a realistic gender constancy task?

In a study designed to test this possibility, three full-length color photographs of toddlers between the ages of 1 and 2 were used (Bem, 1989). As shown in Figure 3-10, the first photograph showed the toddler completely nude, with the genitalia fully visible. The second photograph showed the same toddler dressed (and the boy bewigged) like a child of the opposite sex; the third photograph showed the toddler dressed normally—like a child of his or her own sex.* Using these six photographs, children between 3 and $5\frac{1}{2}$ years of age were tested for gender constancy. First the experimenter showed the child the photograph of the nude toddler and asked the child to identify the toddler's sex. Next the experimenter showed the child the sex-inconsistent photograph, making sure the

---

*Because of the sensitive nature of child nudity in our culture, each photograph was taken in the toddler's own home with at least one parent present. The parents provided written consent to use the photographs in the research, and the parents of the two children who appear in Figure 3-10 also gave written consent to have these photographs published. Finally, the parents of the children who took part in the study gave written permission for their children to participate in a study in which they would be asked questions about pictures of nude toddlers.

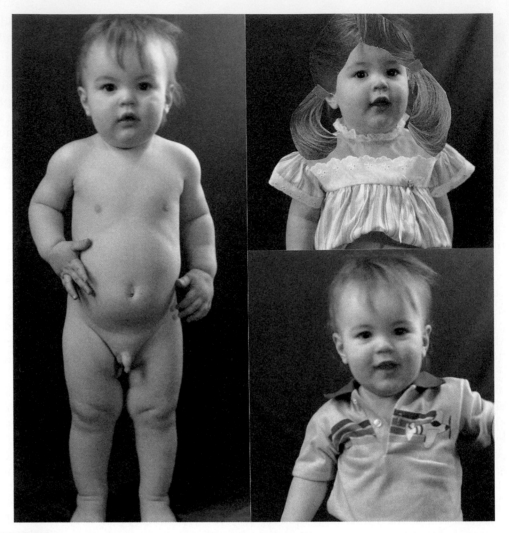

FIGURE 3-10

Testing Gender Constancy   *After seeing the photograph of a nude toddler, children are asked to identify the sex of that toddler from pictures in which the toddler is dressed in sex-inconsistent clothing and in sex-consistent clothing. Children who can correctly identify the toddler's sex in all the pictures have attained gender constancy.* (From Bem, 1989, pp. 653–654)

child realized that this was the same toddler as in the nude photograph. The nude photograph was removed and the child was asked to identify the sex of the toddler while looking only at the sex-inconsistent picture. Finally, the child was asked to identify the sex of the same toddler from the sex-consistent picture. This procedure was then repeated with the other set of three photographs. The children were also asked to explain their answers. A child was considered to have attained gender constancy only if he or she correctly identified the sex of the toddler all six times.

A set of photographs of different toddlers was used to assess whether the children knew that genitalia constitute the defining feature of sex. Again, children were asked to identify the sex of the pictured toddlers and to explain their answers. The most difficult part of the test showed photographs of toddlers who were nude from the waist down but dressed in sex-inconsistent clothes from the waist up. In order to correctly identify the toddler's sex in these photographs, a child would have to know not only that genitalia indicate sex, but that when genital indicators are in conflict with culturally defined

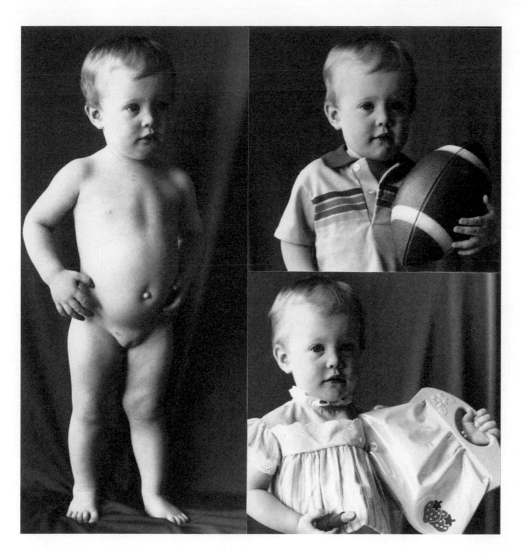

indicators of sex (such as clothing, hairstyles, and toys), the genital indicators have priority.

The results showed that 40% of the 3-, 4-, and early 5-year-old children displayed gender constancy. This is much earlier than predicted by the cognitive developmental theory of Piaget and Kohlberg. More important, a full 74% of those who passed the genital knowledge test displayed gender constancy, compared with only 11% (three children) of those who failed the gender knowledge test. Children who passed the gender knowledge test were also more likely to show personal gender constancy: They correctly answered the question "If you were playing dress-up games one day and you put on a girl's [boy's] wig . . . and girls' [boys'] clothes, what would you really be, a boy or a girl?"

While these results reveal that children are aware of their gender identity at a much earlier age than was previously thought, they also reveal a weakness of social-learning theory: It fails to address why children should organize their self-concepts around their maleness or femaleness in the first place. Why should sex have priority over other potential categories of self-definition? It was this question that the next theory, gender schema theory, was designed to answer (Bem, 1985).

Gender Schema Theory   As we have seen, both social-learning theory and cognitive-developmental theory provide reasonable explanations for how children might acquire information about their culture's' rules and norms regarding sex-appropriate behaviors, roles, and personality characteristics. But the culture is also teaching the child a much deeper lesson—namely, that the distinction between male and female is so important that it should be used as a lens through which all other aspects of culture are viewed. Consider, for example, the child who first enters a day-care center offering a variety of new toys and activities. The child could use many potential criteria in deciding which toys and activities to try. Should she consider indoor or outdoor activities? Does he prefer a toy that involves artistic production or one that requires mechanical manipulation? How about an activity that one can do with other children? Or one that can be done in solitude? But of all the potential criteria, the culture emphasizes one above all others: "Be sure to consider first and foremost whether the toy or activity is appropriate for your sex." At every turn, the child is encouraged to look at the world through the lens of gender—in other words, to view the world in terms of the *gender schema* (Bem, 1993, 1985, 1981).

Parents and teachers do not teach children about the gender schema directly. Instead, the lesson is embedded in the daily practices of the culture. Consider, for example, a teacher who wishes to treat children of both sexes equally. She lines them up at the drinking fountain by alternating boys and girls. If a boy is selected to be hall monitor on Monday, a girl will be hall monitor on Tuesday. Equal numbers of boys and girls must be selected for the class play. This teacher believes that she is teaching her students the importance of gender equality. She is right, but she is also unwittingly teaching them the importance of gender. The students learn that no matter how unrelated to gender an activity might seem, one cannot engage in it without paying attention to the distinction between boys and girls.

Children also learn to apply the gender schema to themselves, to organize their self-concepts around their maleness or femaleness, and to judge their self-worth in terms of their answer to the question, Am I masculine or feminine enough? For these reasons, gender schema theory is a theory of gender identity as well as of sex typing.

Gender schema theory, then, is one possible answer to the question of why children organize their self-concepts around their maleness or femaleness. Like cognitive-developmental theory, gender schema theory views the developing child as an active agent in his or her own socialization. But like social-learning theory, gender schema theory implies that sex typing is neither inevitable nor unmodifiable. According to this theory, children become sex typed because sex happens to be a major focus around which their culture chooses to organize its view of reality. Thus, the theory implies that if the culture becomes less sex typed, children will become less sex typed in their behaviors and self-concepts.

According to gender schema theory, children are constantly encouraged to view the world in terms of the gender schema, which requires them to consider whether a toy or activity is appropriate for their sex.

Adolescent Development

Adolescence refers to *the period of transition from childhood to adulthood.* It extends roughly from age 12 to the late teens, when physical growth is nearly complete. During this period the young person becomes sexually mature and establishes an identity as an individual apart from the family.

Sexual Development   Puberty, *the period of sexual maturation that transforms a child into a biologically mature adult capable of sexual reproduction,* takes place over a period of three or four years. It starts with a period of very rapid physical growth (the so-called adolescent growth spurt) accompanied by gradual development of the reproductive organs and secondary sex characteristics (breast development in girls, beard growth in boys, and the appearance of pubic hair in both sexes).

Menarche, *the first menstrual period,* occurs relatively late in puberty—about 18 months after a girl's growth spurt has reached its peak. The first menstrual periods tend to be irregular, and *ovulation* (the release of a mature egg) does not usually begin until a year or so after menarche. A boy's first ejaculation typically occurs about two years after the growth spurt begins. The first seminal fluid does not contain sperm; the number of sperm and their fertility gradually increase.

There is wide variation in the age at which puberty begins and the rate at which it progresses. Some girls attain menarche as early as 11, others as late as 17; the average age is 12 years, 9 months. Boys, on the average, experience their growth spurt and mature two years later than girls. They begin to ejaculate semen with live sperm sometime between the ages of 12 and 16; the average age is $14\frac{1}{2}$ years. The wide variation in the timing of puberty is strikingly apparent in seventh- and eighth-grade classrooms. Some of the girls may look like mature women with fully developed breasts and rounded hips, while others may still have the size and shape of little girls. Some of the boys may look like gangly adolescents, while others may look much as they did at the age of 9 or 10. (See the discussion of hormonal changes at puberty in Chapter 10.)

Psychological Effects of Puberty Conventional wisdom holds that adolescence is a period of "storm and stress" characterized by moodiness, inner turmoil, and rebellion. But research findings do not support this pessimistic view. One study followed more than 300 adolescents as they progressed from the sixth through the eighth grades,

There is wide variation in the age at which puberty begins and the rate at which it progresses. As a result, some adolescents may be much taller and more physically mature than others of the same age.

assessing them and their parents twice a year by means of interviews and psychological tests. They were assessed again during their last year of high school (Petersen, 1989). Most of the adolescents made it through this period without major turmoil. The data do indicate, however, that puberty has significant effects on body image, self-esteem, moods, and relationships with parents and members of the opposite sex.

Some of these effects may be linked directly to the hormonal changes of puberty (Buchanan, Eccles, & Becker, 1992), but most are related to the personal and social effects of physical changes and, most important, the timing of those changes. Being an early or late maturer (one year earlier or later than average) affects adolescents' satisfaction with their appearance and their body image. In general, seventh- and eighth-grade boys who have reached puberty report positive moods more often than their prepubertal male classmates, and they tend to be more satisfied with their weight and their overall appearance than later-maturing boys—a reflection of the importance of

Developing a personal identity—an answer to the questions "Who am I?" and "Where am I going?"—is a major task of adolescence.

strength and physical prowess for males in our society. But early-maturing boys also tend to have less self-control and emotional stability than later-maturing boys; they are more likely to smoke, drink, use drugs, and get into trouble with the law (Duncan et al., 1985). In contrast, late-maturing boys feel worst about themselves in seventh grade but typically end up as the healthiest group by their senior year in high school (Petersen, 1989).

Early maturation has the opposite effect on the self-esteem of girls. Compared with later maturers, earlier maturers experience more depression and anxiety (Brooks-Gunn & Ruble, 1983), have lower self-esteem (Simmons & Blyth, 1988), and are generally less satisfied with their weight and appearance. They tend to be embarrassed by the fact that their bodies are more womanly in shape than those of their female classmates—particularly since current standards for female attractiveness emphasize a lean look. Although early maturers also achieve early popularity, this is partly because they are seen as sexually precocious. They are also more likely to have conflicts with their parents, to drop out of school, and to have both emotional and behavioral problems (Caspi & Moffitt, 1991; Stattin & Magnusson, 1990).

Again, however, it is important to emphasize that in the study just mentioned, early adolescence was relatively trouble-free for more than 50% of both males and females. About 30% of the group had only intermittent problems. Only 15% were caught in a "downward spiral of trouble and turmoil"; emotional and academic problems that were evident in the eighth grade continued or worsened during the high school years (Petersen, 1989).

Identity Development The psychoanalyst Erik Erikson believed that the major task confronting the adolescent is to develop a sense of identity, to find answers to the questions "Who am I?" and "Where am I going?" Although Erikson coined the term *identity crisis* to refer to this active process of self-definition, he believed that it is an integral part of healthy psychosocial development. Similarly, most developmental psychologists believe that adolescence should be a period of "role experimentation" in which young people can explore various behaviors, interests, and ideologies. Many beliefs, roles, and ways of behaving may be "tried on," modified, or discarded in an attempt to shape an integrated concept of the self.

Adolescents try to synthesize these values and appraisals into a consistent picture. If parents, teachers, and peers project consistent values, the search for identity is easier. In a simple society in which adult models are few and social roles are limited, the task of forming an identity is relatively easy. In a society as complex as ours, it is a difficult task for many adolescents. They are faced with an almost infinite array of possibilities regarding how to behave and what to do in life. As a result, there are large differences among adolescents in how the development of their identity proceeds. Moreover, any particular adolescent's identity may be at different stages of development in different areas of life (for example, sexual, occupational, and ideological).

Ideally, the identity crisis should be resolved by the early or mid-twenties so that the individual can move on to other life tasks. When the process is successful, the individual is said to have achieved an identity; this usually means having arrived at a coherent sense of one's sexual identity, vocational direction, and ideological worldview. Until the identity crisis is resolved, the individual has no consistent sense of self or set of internal standards for evaluating his or her self-worth in major areas of life. Erikson called this unsuccessful outcome *identity confusion.*

Erikson's theory about adolescent identity development has been tested and extended by James Marcia (1980, 1966). On the basis of open-ended interviews, Marcia concluded that there are four identity statuses or positions based on whether the person perceives an identity issue and whether a resolution has been reached:

- *Identity achievement.* Individuals in this status have passed through an identity crisis, a period of active questioning and self-definition. They are committed to ideological positions that they have worked out for themselves, and they have decided on an occupation. They have begun to think of themselves as a future doctor, not just a pre-med chemistry major. They have re-examined their family's religious and po-litical beliefs and discarded those that don't seem to fit their identity.

- *Foreclosure.* Those in this status are also committed to occupational and ideological positions, but they show no signs of having gone through an identity crisis. They have accepted their family's religion without question. When asked about politics, they often say that they have never given it much thought. Some of them seem committed and cooperative, others rigid, dogmatic, and conforming. They give the impression that they would be lost if a major event occurred that challenged their unexamined rules and values.

- *Moratorium.* These young people are in the midst of an identity crisis. They are actively seeking answers but have not resolved the conflicts between their parents' plans for them and their own interests. They may express a set of political or religious beliefs with great intensity for a while, only to abandon them after a period of reconsideration. At best, they seem sensitive, ethical, and open-minded; at worst, they appear anxiety-ridden, self-righteous, and vacillating (Scarr, Weinberg, & Levine, 1986).

- *Identity diffusion.* This is Marcia's term for what Erikson calls identity confusion. Some individuals in this category have had an identity crisis; others have not. But in either case they still have no integrated sense of themselves. They say that it might be "interesting" to go to law school or start a business, but they are not taking steps in either direction. They say that they are not interested in religion or politics. Some seem cynical, others shallow and confused. Some, of course, are still too young to have reached the identity development of adolescence.

As expected, the percentage of adolescents who have attained identity achievement increases steadily from the pre-high school years to the late college years, while the percentage remaining in identity diffusion steadily decreases. The state of identity crisis—moratorium—peaks during the first two years of college. In general, studies show that the level of identity achievement is considerably higher for vocational choice than for political ideology (Waterman, 1985).

How Instrumental Are Parents in the Development of Their Children?

Parents Have No Lasting Influence on the Personality or Intelligence of Their Children

Judith Rich Harris

Your parents took good care of you when you were little. They taught you many things. They are leading players in your memories of childhood. All these things could be true, and yet your parents may have left no lasting impression on your personality or intelligence or on the way you behave when they're not around.

Hard to believe? Try, for a moment, to put aside your preconceptions and consider the evidence. Consider, for example, the studies (discussed in the text) de-

Judith Rich Harris

signed to separate the effects of genes from those of the home environment. These studies show that if you eliminate the similarities due to genes, two people who grew up in the same home are not noticeably more alike in personality or intelligence than two people picked at random from the same population. Almost all the similarities between brothers or sisters reared together are due to the genes they have in common. If they are adoptive siblings, they are no more alike than adopted people reared in different homes. On average, an adopted child reared by agreeable parents is no nicer than one reared by grouches, and one reared by parents who love books is no smarter than one reared by parents who love soap operas.

Because these results don't fit the popular theories of child development, many psychologists ignore

them or try to explain them away. But results that don't fit the theories have been piling up (Harris, 1995, 1998). A recent study showed that children who spent most of their first three years in day-care centers do not differ in behavior or adjustment from children who spent that time at home (NICHD Early Child Care Research Network, 1998). Children who must vie with their siblings for their parents' attention do not differ in personality from only children (Falbo & Polit, 1986). Boys and girls behave as differently today as they did a generation ago, even though today's parents try hard to treat their sons and daughters alike (Serbin, Powlishta, & Gulko, 1993). Children who speak Korean or Polish at home but English with their peers end up as English speakers. The language learned outside the home takes precedence over the one their parents taught them, and they speak it without an accent (Harris, 1998).

But what about the evidence that dysfunctional parents tend to have dysfunctional offspring and that children who are treated with affection tend to turn out better than children who are treated harshly? The trouble with this evidence is that it comes from studies that provide no way to distinguish genetic from environmental influences or causes from effects. Are the offspring's problems due to the unfavorable environment provided by the dysfunctional parents or to personality characteristics inherited from them? Did the hugs cause the child to develop a pleasant personality, or did her pleasant personality make her parents want to hug her? Judging from studies that use more advanced techniques, it appears that the problems were at least partly inherited and that the

child's pleasant personality evoked the hugs (Plomin, Owen, & McGuffin, 1994; Reiss, 1997).

There is no question that parents influence the way their children behave at home, and this is another source of confusion. Is the way children behave at home a good indication of how they'll behave in the classroom or the playground? When researchers discover that children behave differently in different social contexts, they usually assume that the way they behave with their parents is somehow more important or long-lasting than the way they behave elsewhere. But the children who speak Korean or Spanish at home and English outside the home use English as their primary language in adulthood. A boy whose cries evoke sympathy when he hurts himself at home learns not to cry when he hurts himself on the playground, and as an adult he seldom cries. A child who is dominated by her older sibling at home is no more likely than a firstborn to allow herself to be dominated by her peers. Children learn separately how to behave at home and outside the home, and it's their outside-the-home behavior they bring with them to adulthood—which makes sense, since they are not going to spend their adult lives in their parents' house.

The notion that children are in a great hurry to grow up and that they see their own world as a pale imitation of the adult world is an adult-o-centric one. A child's goal is not to be like her mother or his father—it's to be a successful child. Children have to learn how to get along in the world outside the home, and out there the rules are different. Children are not putty in their parents' hands.

The Unquestionable Influence of Parents

Jerome Kagan, *Harvard University*

The development of the skills, values, and social behaviors that maximize adaptation to the society in which a particular child grows requires the orchestration of many relatively independent forces. The most important of these include the temperamental biases that the child inherits; the class, ethnic, and religious affiliations of the child's family; relationships with siblings; the historical era in which childhood is spent; and always the behaviors and personality of the parents.

Parental influences on the child assume two different forms. Parental actions with the child are the most obvious. Parents who regularly talk and read to their children usually produce children with the largest vocabularies, the highest intelligence scores, and the best academic grades (Gottfried, Fleming, & Gottfried, 1998; Ninio, 1980). Parents who reason with their children while making requests for obedience usually end up with more civil children (Baumrind, 1967). The power of the family is seen in the results of a study of over 1,000 children from 10 different cities in the United States who were studied extensively by a team of scientists. Some of these children were raised at home, and some attended daycare centers for varied amounts of time. The main result was that the family had the most important influence on the three-year-old child's personality and character (NICHD Early Child Care Research Network, 1998). One of the most important illustrations of the power of parental behavior is the fact that some children who were orphaned and made homeless by war were able to regain intellectual and social skills they failed to develop during their early privation if they were adopted by nurturant families (Rathbun, DiVirglio, & Waldfogel, 1958).

Parents also influence their children through their own characteristics. Children come to conclusions about themselves, often incorrect, because they assume that since they are the biological offspring of their mother and father, they possess some of the qualities that belong to their parents. This emotionally tinged belief is called identification, and it is the basis for national pride and loyalty to ethnic and religious groups. Thus, if a parent is perceived by her child as affectionate, just, and talented, the child assumes that she, too, probably possesses one or more of these desirable traits and, as a result, feels more confident than she has a right to, given the evidence. By contrast, the child who perceives a parent who is rejecting, unfair in doling out punishment, and without talent feels shame because he assumes that he probably is in possession of some of these undesirable characteristics (Kagan, 1998).

Support for this last claim is fact that all children become upset if someone criticizes their family. The anxiety or anger that follows such criticism is strong because children assume, unconsciously, that any criticism of their parents is also a criticism of them.

The provocative suggestion in Harris's "The Nurture Assumption" that parents have minimal influences on their children's personality and character, while peers have a major influence, is undermined by two sets of facts. First, peers are of little influence until the child is five or six years of age, but six year olds from varied cultures or children living in different historical eras are very different in their behavior and personality. Puritan children living in New England in the 17th century were more obedient than contemporary Boston children because of parental behaviors toward them.

Jerome Kagan

Second, children select friends who share their values and interests. A child who values school work will choose friends with similar interests. If such a child becomes an academically successful adult, it is not logical to assume that this outcome is due to the influence of friends because the child chose that type of friend in the first place.

It is rare to find a belief that all societies, ancient and modern, share. I know of no society that claimed that the family's influence on the child's mind was without much significance. This degree of consensus implies that it might be a universal truth. To declare that parents have little influence on children, in light of the scientific evidence and every parent's daily experiences, is a little like declaring on a foggy September morning that all the trees have disappeared because you cannot see them.

SUMMARY

1. Two central questions in developmental psychology are: (a) How do biological factors ("nature") interact with environmental experiences ("nurture") to determine the course of development? and (b) Is development best understood as a continuous process of change or as a series of qualitatively distinct stages? A related question is: Are there critical or sensitive periods during which specific experiences must occur for psychological development to proceed normally?

2. An individual's genetic heritage is expressed through the process of maturation: innately determined sequences of growth or other changes in the body that are relatively independent of the environment. Motor development, for example, is largely a maturational process because all children master skills such as crawling, standing, and walking in the same sequence and at roughly the same age. But even these can be modified by an atypical or inadequate environment.

3. Infants are born with all of their sensory systems functioning. They are well prepared to learn about their environment. There is even some evidence that newborns respond differentially to sounds they heard while still in the uterus.

4. Piaget's theory describes stages in cognitive development. These proceed from the sensorimotor stage (in which an important discovery is object permanence), through the preoperational stage (when symbols begin to be used), and the concrete operational stage (when conservation concepts develop), to the formal operational stage (when hypotheses are tested systematically in problem solving).

5. New methods of testing reveal that Piaget's theory underestimates children's abilities, and several alternative approaches have been proposed. Information-processing approaches view cognitive development as reflecting the gradual development of processes such as attention and memory. Other theorists emphasize increases in domain-specific knowledge. Still others focus on the influence of the social and cultural context.

6. Piaget believed that children's understanding of moral rules and judgments develops along with their cognitive abilities. Kohlberg extended Piaget's work to include adolescence and adulthood. He proposed three levels of moral judgment: preconventional, conventional, and postconventional.

7. As early as the first weeks of life, infants show individual differences in activity level, responsiveness to change in their environment, and irritability. Such mood-related personality characteristics are called temperaments and appear to be inborn. It is not yet clear to what extent they constitute the building blocks for the individual's later personality. Continuity of temperament across the life span is a function of interactions between the child's inherited characteristics and the environment.

8. Some early social behaviors, such as smiling, reflect innate responses that appear at about the same time in all infants, including blind infants. The emergence of many later social behaviors—including wariness of strangers and distress over separation from primary caregivers—appears to depend on the child's developing cognitive skills.

9. An infant's tendency to seek closeness to particular people and to feel more secure in their presence is called attachment. Attachment can be assessed in a procedure called the strange situation, which consists of a series of episodes in which a child is observed as the primary caregiver leaves and returns to the room. On the basis of the child's reactions, he or she is classified as (a) securely attached; (b) insecurely attached: avoidant; or (c) insecurely attached: ambivalent. Securely attached infants tend to have primary caregivers who respond sensitively to their needs.

10. Gender identity is the degree to which one regards oneself as male or female. It is distinct from sex typing, the acquisition of characteristics and behaviors that society considers appropriate for one's sex. Freud's psychoanalytic theory holds that gender identity and sex typing develop from the children's early discovery of the genital differences between the sexes and children's eventual identification with the same-sex parent. Social-learning theory emphasizes the rewards and punishments that children receive for sex-appropriate and sex-inappropriate behaviors, as well as a process of identification with same-sex adults that is based on observational learning.

11. A cognitive-developmental theory of gender identity and sex typing holds that once children can identify themselves as male or female, they are motivated to acquire sex-typed behaviors. Their understanding of sex and gender corresponds to Piaget's stages of cognitive development, especially their understanding of gender constancy—that is, the realization that a person's sex remains constant despite changes of age and appearance. Like its parent theory, cognitive-developmental theory underestimates children's degree of understanding.

12. Gender schema theory, developed by Sandra Bem, seeks to explain why children base their self-concept on the male-female distinction in the first place. It emphasizes the role of culture in teaching children to view the world through the lens of gender. Like cognitive-developmental theory, gender schema theory sees children as active agents in promoting their own sex typing; like social-learning theory, it rejects the conclusion that traditional sex typing is inevitable and unmodifiable.

13. Puberty has significant effects on an adolescent's body image, self-esteem, moods, and relationships; but most adolescents make it through this period without major turmoil. Compared with their prepubertal classmates, early-maturing boys report greater satisfaction with their appearance and more frequent positive moods; in contrast, early-maturing girls report more depression, anxiety, family conflict, and dissatisfaction with their appearance than do their prepubertal classmates. According to Erikson's theory, forming a personal sense of identity is the major task of the adolescent period.

KEY TERMS

maturation (p. 71)
critical period (p. 72)
schema (p. 76)
sensorimotor stage (p. 77)
object permanence (p. 77)
preoperational stage (p. 77)
operation (p. 78)
conservation (p. 78)
concrete operational stage (p. 80)

formal operational stage (p. 80)
temperament (p. 87)
attachment (p. 90)
gender identity (p. 93)
sex typing (p. 97)
adolescence (p. 100)
puberty (p. 100)
menarche (p. 101)

CRITICAL THINKING QUESTIONS

1. Some psychologists have suggested that our childhood attachment styles can influence the kinds of romantic relationships we form as adults. What forms might the attachment styles discussed in this chapter assume in an adult romantic relationship? Can you relate your own adult "attachment styles" to your childhood attachment style or to features of your childhood environment?

2. What level of moral reasoning seems to be implied by campaigns designed to discourage young people from using drugs or being sexually active? Can you think of campaign themes that would appeal to a higher stage of moral reasoning?

3. Would your parents have characterized your infant personality as easy, difficult, or slow to warm up? Which aspects of your current personality seem to be primarily a reflection of your inborn temperament, which aspects seem to reflect the way you were raised, and which aspects seem to reflect a blend or interaction between "nature" and "nurture"?

4. Using Marcia's categories of identity achievement, foreclosure, moratorium, and identity diffusion, can you identify how and when your religious, sexual, occupational, and political identities have developed and changed over time?

FURTHER READING

Comprehensive textbooks on development include Berk, *Child Development* (4th ed., 1997) and Newcombe, *Child Development: Change Over Time* (8th ed., 1996). A general text on development through the life course is Rice, *Human Development* (3rd ed., 1998). For a discussion of the major approaches to the study of development, see Miller, *Theories of Developmental Psychology* (3rd ed., 1993).

Books focusing on infancy include Osofsky (ed.), *Handbook of Infant Development* (2nd ed., 1987); Lamb and Bornstein, *Development in Infancy: An Introduction* (2nd ed., 1987); and Rosenblith, *In the Beginning: Development from Conception to Age Two Years* (2nd ed., 1992). A four-volume overview of the major theories and research in child development may be found in Mussen (ed.), *Handbook of Child Psychology* (4th ed., 1983).

Cognitive Development (3rd ed., 1992) by Flavell presents a thorough introduction to this topic. *The Development of Memory in Children* (3rd ed., 1989) by Kail provides a readable summary of research on children's memory. *Children's Thinking* (2nd ed., 1991) by Siegler is written from the perspective of information-processing theories. For a brief introduction to Piaget, see Phillips, *Piaget's Theory: A Primer* (1981).

Two books on children's moral and social reasoning are Damon, *Social and Personality Development: From Infancy Through Adolescence* (1983), and Turiel, *The Development of Social Knowledge: Morality and Convention* (1983). Kohnstamm, Bates, and Rothbart (eds.), *Temperament in Childhood* provides a good summary of research in this active area; and Bem, *The Lenses of Gender* (1993) provides a sociocultural approach to issues of sex and gender.

Adolescent development is dealt with in Steinberg, *Adolescence* (4th ed., 1996), and Kimmel and Wiener, *Adolescence: A Developmental Transition* (1985).

Three

Consciousness and Perception

Chapter 4
Sensory Processes

*Y*our face is the most distinctive part of your body. The shape and size of your eyes, ears, nose, and mouth are what make you look so different from everyone else. But the primary purpose of your facial features is not to make you recognizable; it is to enable you to sense the world. Our eyes see it, our ears hear it, our noses smell it, our mouths taste it, and these, along with a few other senses, provide us with most of the knowledge we have about the world. The next time you look at your face in a mirror, think of it as an elaborate sensing system, mounted on the platform you call your body, that allows you to explore the outside world.

The world that we know through our senses is not the same as the world that other species know through their senses. Each of our sense organs is tuned to receive a particular range of stimuli that is relevant to our survival, and is insensitive to stimuli outside this range. Different species have different ranges of sensitivity because they have different survival needs. Dogs, for example, are far more sensitive to smells than we are because they rely heavily on odors for activities that are crucial to their to survival, such as locating food, marking trails, and identifying kin.

In this chapter we discuss some of the major properties of the senses. Some of the research we review deals with psychological phenomena; other studies deal with the biological bases of these phenomena. In virtually no other area of psychology have the biological and psychological approaches worked together so fruitfully.

At both the biological and psychological levels of analysis, a distinction is often made between sensation and perception. At the psychological level, **sensations** are *experiences associated with simple stimuli* (such as a flashing red light), and **perception** involves *the integration and meaningful interpretation of sensations* (for example, "It's a fire engine"). At the biological level, sensory processes involve the sense organs and the neural pathways that emanate from them, which are concerned with the initial stages of acquiring stimulus information. Perceptual processes involve higher levels of the cortex, which are known to be more related to meaning. This distinction is useful for organizing chapters, but it is somewhat arbitrary. Psychological and biological events that occur early in the processing of a stimulus can sometimes affect the way it is interpreted. Moreover, from the perspective of the nervous system, there is no sharp break between the initial uptake of stimulus information by the sense organs and the brain's subsequent use of that information. In fact, one of the most important features of the brain is that, in addition to taking in sensory information, it is constantly sending messages from its highest levels back to the earliest stages of sensory processing. These *back projections* actually modify the way sensory input is processed (Damasio, 1994; Zeki, 1993). Note, therefore, that we employ the sensation-perception distinction, with this chapter discussing sensory processes and Chapter 5 perceptual processes.

This chapter is organized around the different senses: vision, hearing, smell, taste, and touch; the latter includes pressure, temperature, and pain. In everyday life, several senses are often involved in any given act—we see a peach, feel its texture, taste and smell it as we bite into it, and hear the sounds of our chewing. For purposes of analysis, however, we consider the senses one at a time. Before beginning our analysis of individual senses, or *sensory modalities,* we will discuss some properties that are common to all senses.

Characteristics of Sensory Modalities

In this section we consider two characteristics that are common to all sensory modalities. The first one, *sensitivity,* describes sensory modalities at a psychological level, while the second, *sensory coding,* focuses on the biological level.

Sensitivity

One of the most striking aspects about our sensory modalities is that they are extremely sensitive in detecting the presence of, or a change in, an object or event. Some indication of this sensitivity is given in Table 4-1. For five of the senses, we have provided an estimate of the minimal stimulus that they can detect. What is most noticeable about these minimums is how low they are—that is, how sensitive the corresponding sensory modality is. This is particularly true for vision. A classic experiment by Hecht, Shlaer, and Pirenne (1942) demonstrated

TABLE 4-1

Minimum Stimuli *Approximate minimum stimuli for various senses.* (After Galanter, 1962)

Sense	Minimum Stimulus
Vision	A candle flame seen at 30 miles on a dark, clear night
Hearing	The tick of a clock at 20 feet under quiet conditions
Taste	One teaspoon of sugar in 2 gallons of water
Smell	One drop of perfume diffused into the entire volume of six rooms
Touch	The wing of a fly falling on your cheek from a distance of 1 centimeter

that human vision is virtually as sensitive as is physically possible. The smallest unit of light energy is a *quantum*. Hecht and his colleagues showed that a person can detect a flash of light that contains only 100 quanta. Moreover, they showed that only 7 of these 100 quanta actually contact the critical molecules in the eye that are responsible for translating light into vision and that each of these 7 quanta affects a different molecule. The critical receptive unit of the eye (a molecule), therefore, is sensitive to the minimum possible unit of light energy (a quantum).

Absolute Thresholds   Suppose that you came across an alien creature and wanted to determine how sensitive it is to light. What would you do? Perhaps the simplest test would be to determine the minimum amount of light the creature could detect. This is the key idea behind measuring sensitivity. That is, the most common way of assessing the sensitivity of a sensory modality is to determine the **absolute threshold:** *the minimum magnitude of a stimulus that can be reliably discriminated from no stimulus at all*—for

example, the weakest light that can be reliably discriminated from darkness. The procedures used to determine such thresholds are called *psychophysical methods*. In one commonly used method, the experimenter first selects a set of stimuli with magnitudes varying around the threshold (for example, a set of dim lights of varying intensity). The stimuli are presented one at a time in random order, and the participant is instructed to say "yes" if the stimulus is detected and "no" if it is not. Each stimulus is presented many times, and the percentage of "yes" responses is determined for each stimulus magnitude.

Figure 4-1 is a graph of the percentage of "yes" responses as a function of stimulus magnitude (such as intensity of light). The data are typical of those obtained in this kind of experiment; the percentage of "yes" responses rises gradually as intensity is increased. The participant detects some stimuli with intensities as low as three units, yet occasionally fails to detect some with intensities of eight units. When performance is characterized by such a graph, psychologists have agreed to define the absolute threshold as the value of the stimulus at which it is detected 50% of the time. Thus, for the data displayed in Figure 4-1, the absolute threshold is six units. (The absolute threshold may vary considerably from one individual to the next and may also vary within the same individual from time to time, depending on the person's physical and motivational state.)

Detecting Changes in Intensity   The world is constantly changing, and being able to spot the changes has obvious survival value. Not surprisingly, psychologists have devoted a good deal of effort to studying our ability to detect changes in intensity.

The study of change detection focuses on the question: By how much must two stimuli differ for a person to be able to discriminate between them? In a typical study, participants are presented with a pair of stimuli. One of them is the *standard* because it is the one that other stimuli are to be compared with. The others are called *comparison stimuli*. On each presentation of the pair, participants are asked to respond to the comparison stimulus with "more" or "less." What is being measured is the **difference threshold** or **just noticeable difference (jnd),** *the*

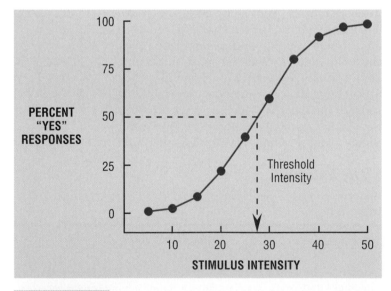

Psychophysical Function From a Detection Experiment   *Plotted on the vertical axis is the percentage of times the participant responds, "Yes, I detect the stimulus"; on the horizontal axis is the measure of the magnitude of the physical stimulus. Such a graph may be obtained for any stimulus dimension to which an individual is sensitive.*

minimum difference in stimulus magnitude necessary to tell two stimuli apart.

Imagine measuring the visual system's sensitivity to changes in the brightness of a light. Typical results are shown in Figure 4-2. In this experiment the standard (a 50-watt bulb) was presented along with each comparison stimulus (ranging from 47 watts to 53 watts, in 1-watt steps) dozens of times. We have plotted the percentage of times in which each comparison stimulus was judged to be "brighter" than the standard. In order to determine the jnd, two points are estimated, one at 75% and the other at 25% on the "brighter than" axis. Psychologists have agreed that half of this distance in stimulus intensity units will be considered to be the just noticeable difference. In this case, then, the estimated jnd is (51 − 49)/2 = 1 watt.

If an individual's sensitivity to change is high, meaning that he or she can notice tiny differences between stimuli, the estimated value of the jnd will be small. On the other

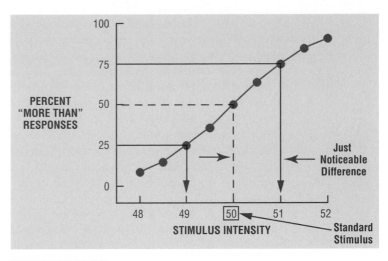

FIGURE 4-2

Results From an Experiment on Change Detection   *Plotted on the vertical axis is the percentage of times the participant responds, "Yes, I detect more than the standard"; on the horizontal axis is the measure of the magnitude of the physical stimulus. The standard stimulus in this example is in the center of the range of stimuli. Such a graph may be obtained for any stimulus dimension for which an individual is sensitive to differences.*

Our sensory modalities are extremely sensitive in detecting the presence of an object—even the faint light of a candle in a distant window. On a clear night, a candle flame can be seen from 30 miles away!

hand, if sensitivity is not as high, the estimated jnd's will be larger. In general, the larger the value of the standard stimulus, the less sensitive the sensory system is to changes in intensity. For example, if a room contained 10 lit candles and you could just detect the addition of one candle, then if the room contained 100 candles it would take an additional 10 candles for you to be able to detect the change reliably. In other words, there is a constant proportional relationship between the jnd and the standard.

This proportional relationship has come to be called the *Weber-Fechner law* because it was first studied carefully by Ernst Heinrich Weber (1834), a physiologist, and then developed more fully by Gustav Fechner (1860), a physicist. Their analyses showed that almost all sensory systems take geometric changes in stimulus intensity (in which increases are multiples of one another— 2, 4, 8, etc.) and convert them into arithmetic changes in sensation (in which increases are simple additions—1, 2, 3, etc.). An example is the sensation of loudness, where increasing the physical amplitude of a sound by 10 times results in an increase in perceived loudness of only about 2 times.

Table 4-2 shows some typical jnd's for different sensory qualities, expressed as the percentage change needed for reliable difference detection. It shows, for example, that we are generally more sensitive to changes in light and sound than we are to changes in taste and smell. These values can be used to predict how much a stimulus will need to be changed from any level of intensity in order for people to notice the changes reliably. For example, if a theater manager wished to produce a subtle but noticeable change in the level of lighting on a stage, he or she might increase the lighting level by 10%. This would mean a 10-watt increase if a 100-watt bulb was being used to begin with, but it would mean a 1,000-watt increase if 10,000 watts were already flooding the stage.

Reaction Time   Notice that we have been discussing situations in which detection is very difficult because stimuli are barely noticeable (absolute threshold) or the differences between stimuli are small (change detection). However, even when stimuli and the differences between them are easy to sense, some detections are easier to make than others. For example, most people can

Just Noticeable Differences (jnd) for Various Sensory Qualities   *(expressed as the percentage change required for reliable change detection)*

Quality	Just Noticeable Difference (jnd)
Light intensity	8%
Sound intensity	5%
Sound frequency	1%
Odor concentration	15%
Salt concentration	20%
Lifted weights	2%
Electric shock	1%

distinguish red from green more easily than from orange, even though we would never actually make an error in discriminating between these colors. Since methods for studying detection depend on participants making errors, they cannot be used in situations in which differences among stimuli are easily perceived. To measure change detection in such situations, psychologists often measure **reaction time,** or *the time between the onset of a stimulus and the beginning of an overt response.* This concept was introduced by the psychologist and physiologist Hermann von Helmholtz (1850), who used reaction time as a crude measure of how quickly nerves conduct information.

There are two types of reaction time. *Simple reaction time* involves pressing a button or making some other simple response, such as an eye movement or a vocal sound, immediately upon detecting a stimulus. These responses are commonly measured in studies of simple detection. A frequent finding is that the less intense a stimulus, the slower the reaction time. Figure 4-3 shows typical average reaction times to the onset of a tone, plotted against the intensity of the tone (Chocolle, 1940). Although the tone is always well above the absolute threshold for hearing, the reaction times are shorter for more intense tones. Similar results are obtained for simple reaction times to the detection of visual or touch stimuli (Coren, Ward, & Enns, 1999).

Choice reaction time involves making one of several different responses, depending on the stimulus presented (for example, press the button on the right in response to a red

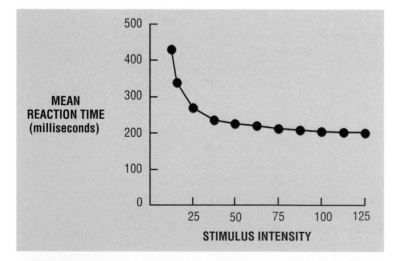

Effects of Stimulus Intensity on Simple Reaction Time   *The average reaction time to all stimulus qualities gets shorter as the intensity of the stimulus to be detected is increased. At some level of intensity, further increases in intensity no longer produce any additional increase in speed of reaction.*

light and the button on the left in response to a green light). It is commonly used in studies of discrimination. As you might expect, the smaller the difference between the stimuli, the longer the choice reaction time (Coren, Ward, & Enns, 1999).

Sensory Coding

Now that we know something about the sensitivity of the different senses, we can explore the biological bases of sensation. We begin with the question of how stimuli are transmitted from the sensory receptors to the brain.

The brain has a formidable problem in sensing the world. Each sense responds to a certain kind of stimulus—light energy for vision, mechanical energy for audition and touch, chemical energy for smell and taste. But the brain understands none of this. It speaks only the language of electrical signals associated with neural discharges. Somehow, each sensory modality must first perform a process termed **transduction**—it must *translate physical energy into electrical signals that can make their way to the brain.* This is accomplished by specialized cells in the sense organs called *receptors.* The receptors for vision, for instance, are located in a thin layer of tissue on the inside of the eye; each visual receptor contains a chemical that reacts to light, and this reaction triggers a series of steps that results in a neural impulse. The receptors for audition are fine hair cells located deep in the ear; vibrations in the air bend these hair cells, thus creating a neural impulse. Similar descriptions apply to the other sensory modalities.

A receptor is a specialized kind of nerve cell or neuron (see Chapter 2); when it is activated, it passes its electrical signal to connecting neurons. The signal travels until it reaches its receiving area in the cortex, with different sensory modalities sending signals to different receiving areas. Somewhere in the brain the electrical signal results in conscious sensory experience. Thus, when we experience a touch, the experience is occurring in our brain, not in our skin. However, the electrical impulses in the brain that mediate the experience of touch are themselves caused by electrical impulses in touch receptors located in the skin. Simi-larly, our experience of a bitter taste occurs in our brain, not in our tongue; but the brain impulses that mediate the taste experience are themselves caused by electrical impulses in taste receptors on the tongue. In this way our receptors play a major role in relating external events to conscious experience. Numerous aspects of our conscious perceptions are caused by specific neural events that occur in the receptors.

Coding of Intensity and Quality   Our sensory systems evolved to pick up information about objects and events in the world. What kind of information do we need to know about an event such as a brief flash of a bright red light? Clearly, it would be useful to know its intensity (bright), quality (red), duration (brief), location, and time of onset. Each of our sensory systems provides some information about these various attributes, although most research has focused on the attributes of intensity and quality.

When we see a bright red color patch, we experience the quality of redness at an intense level; when we hear a faint, high-pitched tone, we experience the quality of the pitch at a nonintense level. The receptors and their neural pathways to the brain must therefore code both intensity and quality. The question is, how do they do this? Researchers who study these coding processes need a way of determining which specific neurons are activated by which specific stimuli. The usual means is to record the electrical activity of single cells in the receptors and neural pathways to the brain while the person being tested is presented with various inputs or stimuli. By such means, one can determine exactly which attributes of a stimulus a particular neuron is responsive to.

A typical single-cell recording experiment is illustrated in Figure 4-4. This is a vision experiment, but the procedure is similar for studying other senses. Before the experiment, the animal (in this case a monkey) has undergone a surgical procedure in which thin wires are inserted into selected areas of its visual cortex. The thin wires are micro-electrodes, insulated except at their tips, that can be used to record electrical activity of the neurons they are in contact with. They cause no pain, and the monkey moves around and lives quite normally. During the

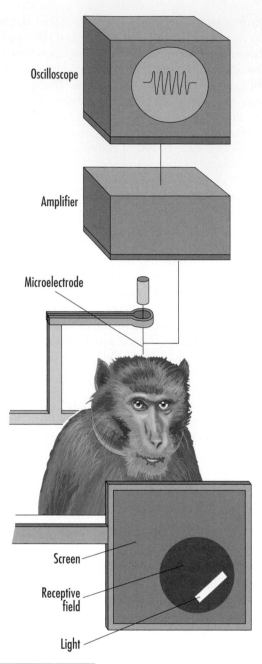

Oscilloscope

Amplifier

Microelectrode

Screen

Receptive field

Light

FIGURE 4-4

Single-Cell Recording. *An anesthetized monkey is placed in a device that holds its head in a fixed position. A stimulus, often a flashing or moving bar of light, is projected onto the screen. A microelectrode implanted in the visual system of the monkey monitors activity from a single neuron, and this activity is amplified and displayed on an oscilloscope.*

experiment, the monkey is placed in a testing apparatus and the microelectrodes are connected to recording and amplifying devices. The monkey is then exposed to various visual stimuli. For each stimulus, the

researcher can determine which neurons respond to it by observing which microelectrodes produce sustained signals. Because the electrical signals are tiny, they must be amplified and displayed on an oscilloscope, which converts the electrical signals into a graph of the changing electrical voltage. Most neurons emit a series of nerve impulses that appear on the oscilloscope as vertical spikes. Even in the absence of a stimulus, many cells will respond at a slow rate (*spontaneous activity*). If a stimulus is presented to which the neuron is sensitive, a fast train of spikes will be seen.

With the aid of single-cell recordings, researchers have learned a good deal about how sensory systems code intensity and quality. The primary means for coding the intensity of a stimulus is in terms of the number of neural impulses in each unit of time, that is, the rate of neural impulses. We can illustrate this point with the sense of touch. If someone lightly touches your arm, a series of electrical impulses are generated in a nerve fiber. If the pressure is increased, the impulses remain the same in size but increase in number per unit of time (see Figure 4-5). The same is true for other modalities. In general, the greater the intensity of the stimulus, the higher the rate of neural firing and the greater the perceived magnitude of the stimulus.

The intensity of a stimulus can also be coded by other means. One alternative is coding by the temporal pattern of the electrical impulses. At low intensities, nerve impulses are further apart in time, and the length of time between impulses is variable. At high intensities, though, the time between impulses may be quite constant (see Figure 4-5). Another alternative is coding by number of neurons activated: The more intense the stimulus, the more neurons are activated.

Coding the quality of a stimulus is a more complex matter. The key idea behind coding quality was proposed by Johannes Müller in 1825. Müller suggested that the brain can distinguish between information from different sensory modalities—such as lights and sounds—because they involve different sensory nerves (some nerves lead to visual experiences, others to auditory experiences, and so on). Müller's idea of *specific nerve energies* received support from subsequent research demonstrating that neural pathways

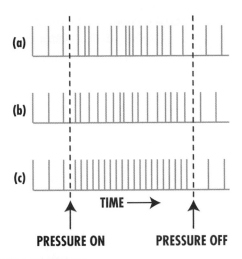

FIGURE 4-5

Coding Intensity   *Responses of a nerve fiber from the skin to (a) soft, (b) medium, and (c) strong pressure applied to the fiber's receptor. Increasing the stimulus strength increases both the rate and the regularity of nerve firing in this fiber.*

originating in different receptors terminate in different areas of the cortex. It is now generally agreed that the brain codes the qualitative differences between sensory modalities according to the specific neural pathways involved.

But what about the distinguishing qualities *within* a sense? How do we tell red from green or sweet from sour? It is likely that, again, the coding is based on the specific neurons involved. To illustrate, there is evidence that we distinguish between sweet and sour tastes by virtue of the fact that each kind of taste has its own nerve fibers. Thus, sweet fibers respond primarily to sweet tastes, sour fibers primarily to sour tastes, and ditto for salty fibers and bitter fibers.

Specificity is not the only plausible coding principle. A sensory system may also use the pattern of neural firing to code the quality of a sensation. While a particular nerve fiber may respond maximally to a sweet taste, it may respond to other tastes as well, but to varying degrees. One fiber may respond best to sweet tastes, less to bitter tastes, and even less to salty tastes; a sweet-tasting stimulus would thus lead to activity in a large number of fibers, with some firing more than others, and this particular pattern of neural activity would be the system's code for a sweet taste. A differ-

ent pattern would be the code for a bitter taste. As we will see when we discuss the senses in detail, both specificity and patterning are used in coding the quality of a stimulus.

Vision

Humans are generally credited with the following senses: (a) vision; (b) audition; (c) smell; (d) taste; (e) touch (or the skin senses); and (f) the body senses (which are responsible for sensing the position of the head relative to the trunk, for example). Since the body senses do not always give rise to conscious sensations of intensity and quality, we will not consider them further in this chapter.

Only vision, audition, and smell are capable of obtaining information that is at a distance from us, and of this group, vision is the most finely tuned in humans. In this section we first consider the nature of the stimulus energy to which vision is sensitive; next we describe the visual system, with particular emphasis on how its receptors carry out the transduction process; and then we consider how the visual modality processes information about intensity and quality.

Light and Vision

Each sense responds to a particular form of physical energy, and for vision the physical stimulus is light. Light is a form of *electromagnetic energy*, energy that emanates from the sun and the rest of the universe and constantly bathes our planet. Electromagnetic energy includes not only light but also cosmic rays, X rays, ultraviolet and infrared rays, and radio and television waves. Think of electromagnetic energy as traveling in waves, with wavelengths (the distance from one crest of a wave to the next) varying tremendously from the shortest cosmic rays (4 trillionths of a centimeter) to the longest radio waves (several miles). Our eyes are sensitive to only a tiny portion of this continuum: wavelengths of approximately 400 to 700 nanometers. Since a nanometer is one-billionth of a meter, visible energy—that is, light—makes up only a very small part of electromagnetic energy.

The Visual System

The human visual system consists of the eyes, several parts of the brain, and the pathways connecting them. (Go back to Figure 2-14 for a simplified illustration of the visual system.) The eye contains two systems, one for forming the image and the other for transducing the image into electrical impulses. The critical parts of these systems are illustrated in Figure 4-6.

The image-forming system works like a camera. Its function is to focus light reflected from objects so as to form an image of the object on the *retina,* a thin layer at the back of the eyeball (see Figure 4-7). The image-forming system itself consists of the cornea, the pupil, and the lens. Without them, we could see light but not pattern. The *cornea* is the transparent front surface of the eye: Light enters here, and rays are bent inward by it to begin the formation of the image. The *lens* completes the process of focusing the light on the retina (see Figure 4-7). To focus on objects at different distances, the lens changes shape. It becomes more spherical for near objects and flatter for far ones. In some eyes, the lens does not become flat enough to bring far objects into focus, although it focuses well on near objects; people with eyes of this type are said to be

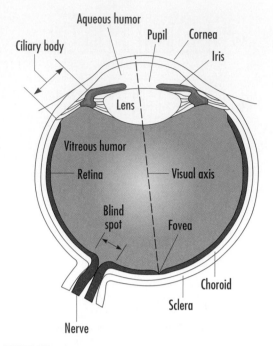

FIGURE 4-6

Top View of the Right Eye   *Light entering the eye on its way to the retina passes through the cornea; the aqueous humor, the lens, and the vitreous humor. The amount of light entering the eye is regulated by the size of the pupil, a small hole toward the front of the eye formed by the iris. The iris consists of a ring of muscles that can contract or relax, thereby controlling pupil size. The iris gives the eyes their characteristic color (blue, brown, and so forth).*

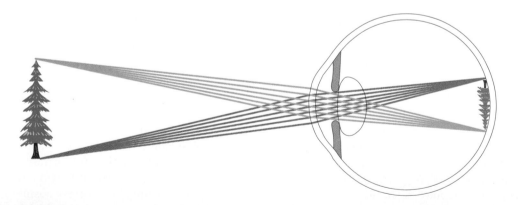

FIGURE 4-7

Image Formation in the Eye   *Each point on an object sends out light rays in all directions, but only some of these rays actually enter the eye. Light rays from the same point on an object pass through different places on the lens. If a sharp image is to be formed, these different rays have to be brought back together (converge) at a single point on the retina. For each point on the object, there will be a matching point in the retinal image. Note that the retinal image is inverted and is generally much smaller than the actual object. Note also that most of the bending of light rays occurs at the cornea.*

myopic (nearsighted). In other eyes, the lens does not become spherical enough to focus on near objects, although it focuses well on far objects; people with eyes of this type are said to be *hyperopic* (farsighted). Such optical defects are common and can easily be corrected with eyeglasses or contact lenses.

The *pupil*, the third component of the image-forming system, is a circular opening that varies in diameter in response to the level of light present. It is largest in dim light and smallest in bright light, thereby ensuring that enough light passes through the lens to maintain image quality at different light levels.

All of these components focus the image on the retina. There the transduction system takes over. The heart of the system is the receptors. There are two types of receptor cells, rods and cones, so called because of their distinctive shapes (see Figure 4-8). The two kinds of receptors are specialized for different purposes. *Rods* are designed for

seeing at night; they operate at low intensities and lead to colorless sensations. *Cones* are best for seeing during the day; they respond to high intensities and result in sensations of color. Curiously, the rods and cones are located in the layer of the retina that is farthest from the cornea (note the direction-of-light arrow in Figure 4-8). The retina also contains a network of neurons, along with support cells and blood vessels.

When we want to see the details of an object, we routinely move our eyes so that the object is projected onto a region at the center of the retina called the *fovea*. The reason we do this has to do with the distribution of receptors across the retina. In the fovea, the receptors are plentiful and closely packed; outside the fovea, on the periphery of the retina, there are fewer receptors. Not surprisingly, the fovea is the region of the eye that is best at seeing details. To get a sense of how your perception of detail changes as an image is moved away from

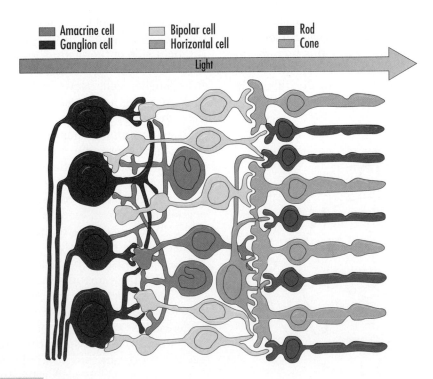

FIGURE 4-8

A Schematic Picture of the Retina *This is a schematic drawing of the retina based on an examination with an electron microscope. The bipolar cells receive signals from one or more receptors and transmit those signals to the ganglion cells, whose axons form the optic nerve. Note that there are several types of bipolar and ganglion cells. There are also sideways or lateral connections in the retina. Neurons called* horizontal cells *make lateral connections at a level near the receptors; neurons called* amacrine cells *make lateral connections at a level near the ganglion cells.* (After Dowling & Boycott, 1966)

your fovea, look at Figure 4-9 and keep your eyes trained on the central letter (A). The sizes of the surrounding letters have been adjusted so that they are all approximately equal in visibility. Note that in order to achieve equal visibility, the letters on the outer circle must be about 10 times larger than the central letter.

Given that light reflected from an object has made contact with a receptor cell, how does the receptor transduce the light into electrical impulses? The rods and cones contain chemicals, called *photopigments,* that absorb light. Absorption of light by the photopigments starts a process that results in a neural impulse. Once this transduction step is completed, the electrical impulses must make their way to the brain via connecting neurons. The responses of the rods and cones are first transmitted to bipolar cells and from there to other neurons called *ganglion cells* (refer to Figure 4-8). The long axons of the ganglion cells extend out of the eye to form the optic nerve to the brain. At the place where the optic nerve leaves the eye, there are no receptors; we are therefore blind to a stimulus in this region (see Figure 4-10). We do not notice this hole in our visual field—known as the blind spot—because the brain automatically fills it in (Ramachandran & Gregory, 1991).

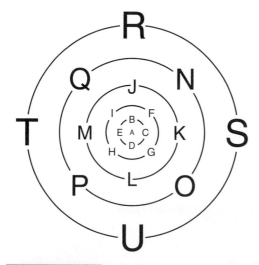

FIGURE 4-9

Visual Acuity Decreases in the Periphery   *Letter sizes have been scaled so that when the central A is looked at directly, all the other letters are approximately equally easy to read.*

Seeing Light

Sensitivity   Our sensitivity to light is determined by the rods and cones. There are three critical differences between rods and cones that explain a number of phenomena involving perceived intensity, or brightness. The first difference is that rods and cones are activated under different levels of light. In broad daylight or in a well-lit room, only the cones are active; the rods send no neural signals. On the other hand, under a full moon or in a dimly lit room, only the rods are active.

A second difference is that cones and rods are specialized for different tasks. This can be seen in the way they are connected to ganglion cells, as illustrated in Figure 4-11. The left side of the figure shows three adjacent cones, each of which is connected to a single ganglion cell. This means that if a cone receives light it will *increase* the activity of its corresponding ganglion cell. Each ganglion cell is connected to its nearest neighbor by a connection that *decreases* the activity of that neighboring cell; it is also connected to the visual area of the brain by a long axon. Together these axons form the optic nerve. The right side of the figure shows three adjacent rods, each of which is connected to three ganglion cells. Here, however, there are no connections among ganglion cells that decrease neural activity.

To see the implications of these differences in wiring, suppose that a single spot of light was presented to either the cones or the rods. When it was presented to the cones, only one of the ganglion cells, corresponding to the location of the spot, would respond. In fact, that cell's connections to neighboring cells would decrease their activity and thus ensure that the signal was very clear in comparison to the signal from surrounding cells. However, when a spot of light was presented only to the rods, it would cause up to three ganglion cells to increase their activity. This combined activity would help ensure that the signal reached the brain, but it would also mean that there would be considerable uncertainty about the exact location of the spot of light. Thus, the connections among ganglion cells associated with cones help ensure detailed form perception under well-lit conditions, whereas the convergence of many rods on a single ganglion cell helps ensure sensitivity to light under low lighting conditions.

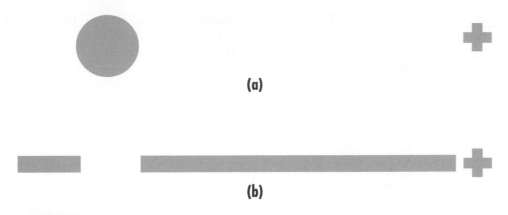

(a)

(b)

FIGURE 4-10

Locating Your Blind Spot   *(a) With your right eye closed, stare at the cross in the upper right-hand corner. Put the book about a foot from your eye and move it forward and back. When the blue circle on the left disappears, it is projected onto the blind spot. (b) Without moving the book and with your right eye still closed, stare at the cross in the lower right-hand corner. When the white space falls in the blind spot, the blue line appears to be continuous. This phenomenon helps us understand why we are not ordinarily aware of the blind spot. In effect, the visual system fills in the parts of the visual field that we are not sensitive to; thus, they appear to be a part of the surrounding field.*

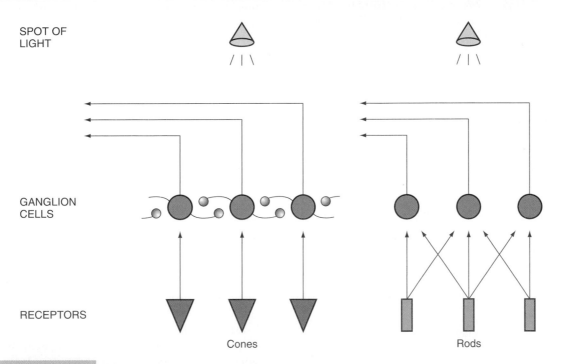

SPOT OF LIGHT

GANGLION CELLS

RECEPTORS

Cones

Rods

FIGURE 4-11

How Cones and Rods Connect to Ganglion Cells   *This diagram shows a single spot of light shining onto a cone and a rod. To simplify matters, we have omitted several other types of cells located between receptors and ganglion cells. Arrows represent a signal to increase neuronal firing. Dots represent a signal to decrease neuronal firing. The long arrows emanating from the ganglion cells are axons that become part of the optic nerve.*

A third difference is that rods and cones are concentrated in different locations on the retina. The fovea contains many cones but no rods. The periphery, on the other hand, is rich in rods but has relatively few cones. We have already seen one consequence of the smaller number of cones in the periphery (see Figure 4-9). A consequence of the distribution of rods can be seen when viewing stars at night. You may

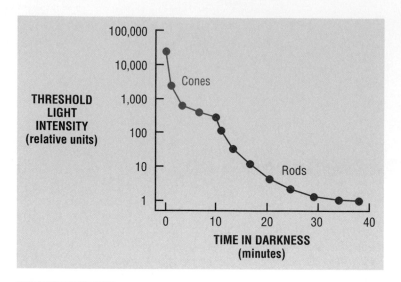

FIGURE 4-12

The Course of Light Adaptation   *Subjects look at a bright light until the retina has become light adapted. When the subjects are then placed in darkness, they become increasingly sensitive to light, and their absolute thresholds decrease. This is called light adaptation. The graph shows the threshold at different times after the adapting light has been turned off. The green data points correspond to threshold flashes whose color could be seen; the purple data points correspond to flashes that appeared white regardless of their wavelength. Note the sharp break in the curve at about 10 minutes; this is called the rod-cone break. A variety of tests show that the first part of the curve is due to cone vision and the second part to rod vision. (Data are approximate, from various determinations.)*

have noticed that in order to see a dim star as clearly as possible it is necessary to look slightly to one side of the star. This ensures that the maximum possible number of rods are activated by the light from the star.

Light Adaptation   A good example of *light adaptation* occurs when you enter a dark movie theater from a bright street. At first you can see hardly anything in the dim

light reflected from the screen. However, in a few minutes you are able to see well enough to find a seat. Eventually you are able to recognize faces in the dim light. When you reenter the bright street, almost everything will seem painfully bright at first. In less than a minute, though, everything will look normal because the eye rapidly adapts to the higher level of light.

Figure 4-12 shows how the absolute threshold decreases with the length of time the person is in darkness. The curve has two limbs. The upper limb is due to the cones and the lower limb to the rods. The rod system takes much longer to adapt, but it is sensitive to much dimmer lights.

Seeing Pattern

Visual acuity refers to *the eye's ability to resolve details.* There are several ways of measuring visual acuity, but the most common measure is the familiar eye chart found in optometrists' offices. This chart was devised by Herman Snellen in 1862. *Snellen acuity* is measured relative to a viewer who does not need to wear glasses. Thus, an acuity of 20/20 indicates that the viewer is able to identify letters at a distance of 20 feet that a typical viewer can read at that distance. An acuity of 20/100 would mean that the viewer can only read letters at 20 feet that are large enough for a typical viewer to read at a distance of 100 feet. In this case, visual acuity is less than normal.

There are a number of reasons why the Snellen chart is not always the best way to measure acuity. First, the method is not good for young children or other people who do not know how to read. Second, the method is designed to test acuity only for objects seen at a distance (20 feet); it does not measure acuity for reading and other tasks involving near distances. Third, the method does not distinguish between **spatial acuity** (*the ability to see details of form*) and **contrast acuity** (*the ability to see differences in brightness*). Figure 4-13 presents examples of typical forms used in tests of visual acuity, with arrows pointing to the critical detail to be detected. Notice that each detail is merely a region of the field where there is a change in brightness from light to dark (Coren, Ward, & Enns, 1999).

The sensory experience associated with viewing a pattern is determined by the way

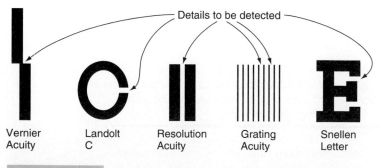

FIGURE 4-13

Some Typical Forms Used in Tests of Visual Acuity   *Arrows point to the details to be discriminated in each case.*

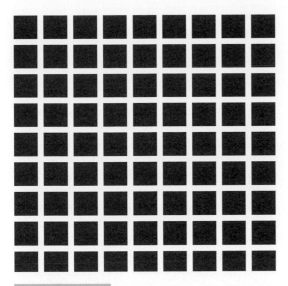

FIGURE 4-14

The Hermann Grid *The gray smudges seen at the white intersections are illusionary. They are seen by your eye and brain but are not on the page. To convince yourself that they are not really there, move your eyes to the different intersections; you will note that there is never a gray smudge at the intersection you are looking at directly. They appear in only intersections that fall on your peripheral visual field.*

and to the left of the intersection). A ganglion cell that is positioned on one of the white rows or columns, on the other hand, will be receiving signals that decrease its rate of firing from neighboring cells on only two sides. As a result, the intersections appear darker than the white rows or columns, reflecting the larger number of signals to decrease the rate of firing being received by ganglion cells centered there.

But why do the smudges appear only off to the side, not at the intersection you are looking at directly? This happens because the range over which the signals are sent is much smaller at the fovea than in the periphery. This arrangement contributes to our having greater visual acuity at the fovea than in the periphery.

Seeing Color

All light is alike except for wavelength. Our visual system does something wonderful with wavelength: It turns it into color, with different wavelengths resulting in different

A prism breaks up light into different wavelengths. Short wavelengths appear blue, medium wavelengths green, and long wavelenghts red.

visual neurons register information about light and dark. The most primitive element of a visual pattern is the *edge*, or *contour*, the region where there is a transition from light to dark or vice versa. One of the earliest influences on the registration of edges occurs because of the way ganglion cells in the retina interact (see Figure 4-11). The effects of these interactions can be observed by viewing a pattern known as the *Hermann grid*, shown in Figure 4-14. You can see gray smudges at the intersections of the white spaces separating the black squares. A disconcerting aspect of this experience is that the very intersection you are gazing at does not appear to be filled with a gray smudge; only intersections that you are not currently gazing at give the illusion of the gray smudge.

This illusion is the direct result of the connections producing decreased activity among the neighbors of active ganglion cells. For example, a ganglion cell that is centered on one of the white intersections of the grid will be receiving signals that decrease its rate of firing from neighboring ganglion cells on four sides (that is, the cells centered in the white spaces above, below, to the right,

colors. For example, short wavelengths (450–500 nanometers) appear blue; medium wavelengths (500–570 nanometers) appear green; and long wavelengths (about 650–780 nanometers) appear red (see Figure 4-15). Our discussion of color perception considers only wavelength. This is adequate for cases in which the origin of a color sensation is an object that emits light, such as the sun or a light bulb. Usually, however, the origin of a color sensation is an object that reflects light when it is illuminated by a light source. In these cases, our perception of the object's color is determined partly by the wavelengths that the object reflects and partly by other factors. One such factor is the surrounding context of colors. A rich variety of other colors in the spatial neighborhood of an object makes it possible for the viewer to see the correct color of an object even when the wavelengths reaching the eye from that object do not faithfully record the object's characteristic color (Land, 1986). Your ability to see your favorite blue jacket as navy despite wide variations in the ambient lighting is called *color constancy.* We will discuss this topic more fully in Chapter 5.

The Appearance of Color Seeing color is a subjective experience in the sense that "color" is a construction of the brain based on an analysis of wavelengths of light. However, it is also objective in that any two viewers with the same kinds of color receptors (cones) appear to construct "color" in the same way. The most common way of referring to the various color experiences of a typical viewer is to organize them on three dimensions: hue, brightness, and saturation. **Hue** refers to *the quality best described by the color's name,* such as red or greenish-yellow. **Brightness** refers to *how much light appears to be reflected from a colored surface,* with white being the brightest possible color and black the dimmest. **Saturation** refers to *the purity of the color,* in that a fully saturated color, such as crimson, appears to contain no gray, while an unsaturated color, such as pink, appears to be a mixture of red and white. Albert Munsell, an artist, proposed a scheme for specifying colored surfaces by assigning them one of 10 hue names and two numbers, one indicating saturation and the other brightness. The colors in the Munsell system are represented by the color solid (see Figure 4-16). (The key characteristics of color and sound are summarized in Table 4-3.)

Given a means of describing colors, we can ask how many colors we are capable of seeing. Within the 400–700 nanometer range to which humans are sensitive, we can discriminate among 150 hues, suggesting that we can distinguish among about 150 wavelengths. This means that, on the average, we can discriminate between two wavelengths that are only 2 nanometers apart; that is, the jnd for wavelengths is 2 nanometers. Given that each of the 150 discriminable colors can have many different values of lightness and saturation, the estimated number of colors among which we can discriminate is over 7 million! Moreover, according to estimates by the National Bureau of Standards, we have names for about 7,500 of these colors. These numbers give some indication of the

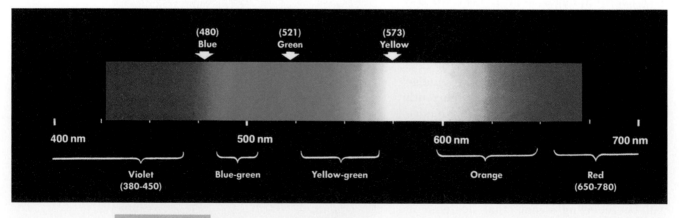

FIGURE 4-15

The Solar Spectrum *The numbers given are the wavelengths of the various colors in nanometers (nm).*

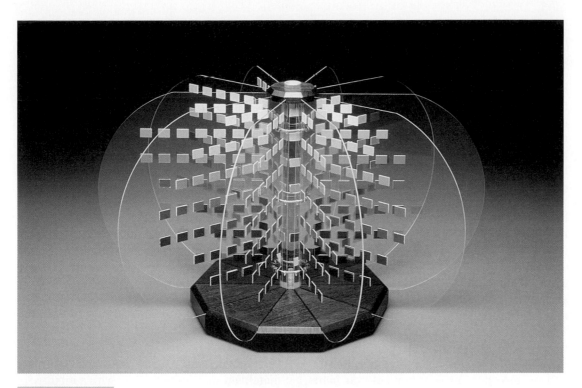

FIGURE 4-16

The Color Solid   *The three dimensions of color can be represented on a double cone. Hue is represented by points around the circumference, saturation by points along the radius, and brightness by points on the vertical axis. A vertical slice taken from the color solid will show differences in the saturation and lightness of a single hue.*

TABLE 4-3

The Physics and Psychology of Light and Sound

Stimulus	Physical Attribute	Measurement Unit	Psychological Experience
Light	Wavelength	Nanometers	Hue
	Intensity	Photons	Brightness
	Purity	Level of Gray	Saturation
Sound	Frequency	Hertz	Pitch
	Amplitude	Decibels	Loudness
	Complexity	Harmonics	Timbre

importance of color to our lives (Coren, Ward, & Enns, 1999).

Color Mixture   Remarkably, all the hues among which we can discriminate can be generated by mixing together only three basic colors. Suppose that we project different-colored lights to the same region of the retina. The result of this light mixture will be a new color. For example, a mixture of 650-nanometer light (red) and 500-nanometer light (green) in the proper proportion will look yellow; in appearance, the mixture will perfectly match a yellow light of 580 nanometers. Other light mixtures besides this particular one can also result in a light that perfectly matches a yellow light of 580 nanometers. Thus, light mixtures whose physical components are grossly different can appear to be identical.

Note that we are referring to mixing *lights* (called an *additive* mixture), not paints or pigments (called a *subtractive* mixture) (see Figure 4-17). The rules of color mixture are different for mixing paints than they are for mixing lights. In mixing paints, the physical stimulus itself is altered—that is, the mixing takes place outside the eye—and hence is a matter of physics. In contrast, in mixing lights, the mixture occurs within the eye and therefore is a matter of psychology.

In general, three wavelengths of light can be combined to match almost any color of light as long as one light is drawn from the long-wave end of the spectrum (red), another is drawn from the middle (green or green-yellow), and the third is from the short end (blue or violet). This finding is sometimes referred to as the *three primaries law.* To illustrate this law, a participant in an experiment on color matching might be asked to match the color of a test light by mixing together three other colored lights. As long as the three lights are drawn from the three widely separated parts of the spectrum—for example, 450 nanometers (blue), 560 (green), and 650 (red)—the person will always be able to match the test light. The participant will not, however, be able to

match any test light if he or she is provided with only two mixture lights—for example, the 450- and 640-nanometer lights. The number three, therefore, is significant.

Because some lights that are grossly different look identical to humans, we have to conclude that we are blind to the differences. Otherwise, color reproduction would be impossible. Realistic color reproduction in television or photography relies on the fact that a wide range of colors can be produced by mixing only a few colors. For example, if you examine your television screen with a magnifying glass you will find that it is composed of tiny dots of only three colors (blue, green, and red). Additive color mixture occurs because the dots are so close together that their images on your retina overlap. (See Figure 4-18 for a way of representing color mixtures.)

Color Deficiency While most people can match a wide range of colors with a mixture of three primaries, others can match a wide range of colors by using mixtures of only two primaries. Such people, referred to as *dichromats,* have deficient color vision, as they confuse some colors that people with normal vision (*trichromats*) can distinguish among.

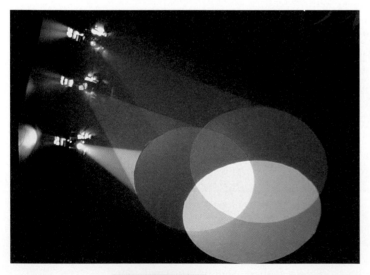

FIGURE 4-17

Additive and Subtractive Color Mixtures   Additive color mixture *(illustrated by the figure at the left)* combines lights. *Red and green lights are mixed to appear yellow; green and purple appear blue; and so on. In the center where the three colors overlap, the mixture appears white.*

Subtractive color mixture (illustrated in the figure at the right) takes place when pigments are mixed or when light is transmitted through colored filters placed one over another. Usually, blue-green and yellow will mix to give green, and complementary colors such as blue and yellow will combine to appear black.

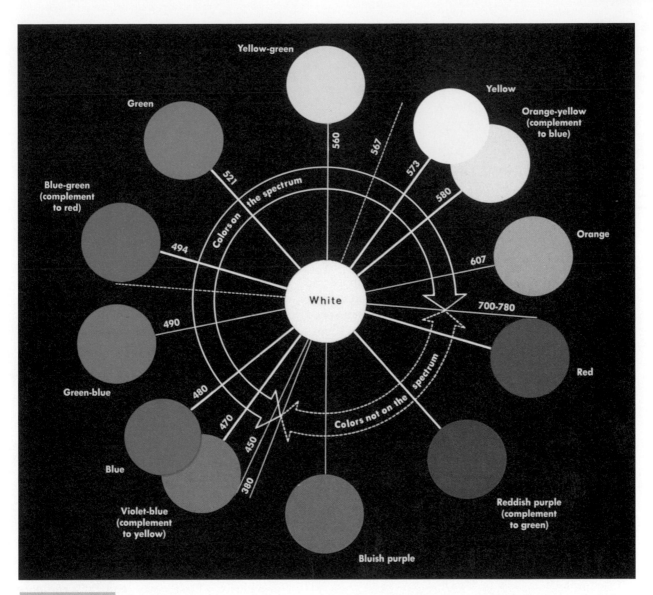

FIGURE 4-18

The Color Circle   *A simple way to represent color mixture is by means of the color circle. The spectral colors (colors corresponding to wavelengths in our region of sensitivity) are represented by points around the circumference of the circle. The two ends of the spectrum do not meet; the space between them corresponds to the nonspectral reds and purples, which can be produced by mixtures of long and short wavelengths. The inside of the circle represents mixtures of lights. Lights toward the center of the circle are less saturated (or whiter); white is at the very center. Mixtures of any two lights lie along the straight line joining the two points. When this line goes through the center of the circle, the lights, when mixed in proper proportions, will look white; such pairs of colors are called* complementary colors.

But dichromats can still see color. Not so for *monochromats,* who are unable to discriminate among different wavelengths at all. Monochromats are truly color-blind. (Screening for color blindness is done with tests like that shown in Figure 4-19, a simpler procedure than conducting color mixture experiments.) Most color deficiencies are genetic in origin.

As noted in Chapter 2, color blindness occurs much more frequently in males (2%) than in females (.03%), because the critical genes for this condition are recessive genes located on the X chromosome (Nathans, 1987).

Theories of Color Vision   Two major theories of color vision have been suggested. The first

FIGURE 4-19

FIGURE 4-19

Testing for Color Blindness *Two plates used in color blindess tests. In the left plate, individuals with certain kinds of red-green blindness will see only the number 5; others see only the 7; still others, no number at all. Similarly, in the right plate, people with normal vision see the number 15, whereas those with red-green blindness see no number at all.*

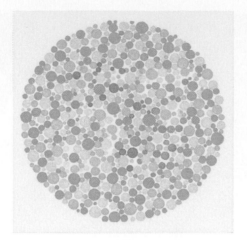

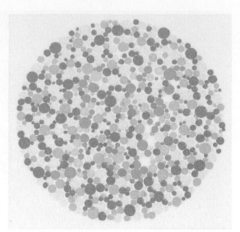

was proposed by Thomas Young in 1807, long before scientists even knew about the existence of cones. Fifty years later, Hermann von Helmholtz further developed Young's theory. According to the Young-Helmholtz or *trichromatic theory,* even though we can discriminate among many different colors, there are only three types of receptors for color. We now know that these are the cones. Each type of cone is sensitive to a wide range of wavelengths but is most responsive within a narrower region. As

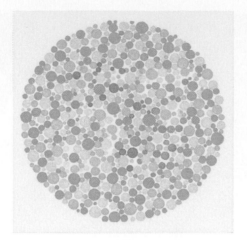

FIGURE 4-20

The Trichromatic Theory *Response curves for the short-, medium-, and long-wave receptors proposed by trichromatic theory. These curves enable us to determine the relative response of each receptor to light of any wavelength. In the example shown here, the response of each receptor to a 500-nanometer light is determined by drawing a line up from 500 nanometers and noting where this line intersects each curve.* Smith, V.C. and J. Porkorny (1975). "Spectral sensitivity of the foveal cone photopigments between 400 and 500 nm." *Vision Research,* 15: 161–171.

shown in Figure 4-20, the short-wavelength cone is most sensitive to short wavelengths (blues), the medium-wavelength cone is most sensitive to medium wavelengths (greens and yellows), and the long-wavelength cone is most sensitive to long wavelengths (reds). The joint action of these three receptors determines the sensation of color. That is, a light of a particular wavelength stimulates the three receptors to different degrees, and the specific ratios of activity in the three receptors leads to the sensation of a specific color. Hence, with regard to our earlier discussion of coding quality, the trichromatic theory holds that the quality of color is coded by the pattern of activity of three receptors rather than by specific receptors for each color.

The trichromatic theory explains the facts about color vision that we mentioned previously. First, we can discriminate among different wavelengths because they lead to different responses in the three receptors. Second, the law of three primaries follows directly from the trichromatic theory. We can match a mixture of three widely spaced wavelengths to any color because the three widely spaced wavelengths will activate the three different receptors, and activity in these receptors results in perception of the test color. (Now we see the significance of the number three.) Third, the trichromatic theory explains the various kinds of color deficiencies by positing that one or more of the three types of receptors is missing: Dichromats are missing one type of receptor, whereas monochromats are missing two of the three types of receptors. In addition to accounting for these long-known facts, trichromatic theory led biological researchers to a successful search for the three kinds of cones that are familiar to us today.

Despite its successes, the trichromatic theory cannot explain some well-established findings about color perception. In 1878 Ewald Hering observed that all colors may be described as consisting of one or two of the following sensations: red, green, yellow, and blue. Hering also noted that nothing is perceived to be reddish-green or yellowish-blue; rather, a mixture of red and green may look yellow, and a mixture of yellow and blue may look white. These observations suggested that red and green form an opponent pair, as do yellow and blue, and that the colors in an opponent pair cannot be perceived simultaneously. Further support for the notion of opponent pairs comes from studies in which a participant first stares at a colored light and then looks at a neutral surface. The participant reports seeing a color on the neutral surface that is the complement of the original one (see Figure 4-21).

These phenomenological observations led Hering to propose an alternative theory of color vision called *opponent-color theory*. Hering believed that the visual system contains two types of color-sensitive units. One type responds to red or green, the other to blue or yellow. Each unit responds in opposite ways to its two opponent colors. The red-green unit, for example, increases its response rate when a red is presented and decreases it when a green is presented. Because a unit cannot respond in two ways at once, if two opponent colors are presented, white is perceived (see Figure 4-18). Opponent-color theory is able to explain Hering's observations about color. The theory accounts for why we see the hues that we do. We perceive a single hue—red or green or yellow or blue—whenever only one type of opponent unit is out of balance, and we perceive combinations of hues when both types of units are out of balance. Nothing is perceived as red-green or as yellow-blue because a unit cannot respond in two ways at once. Moreover, the theory explains why people who first view a colored light and then stare at a neutral surface report seeing the complementary color; if the person first stares at red, for example, the red component of the unit will become fatigued, and consequently, the green component will come into play.

We therefore have two theories of color vision—trichromatic and opponent-color—in which each theory can explain some facts but not others. For decades the two theories were viewed as competing with each other, but eventually, researchers proposed

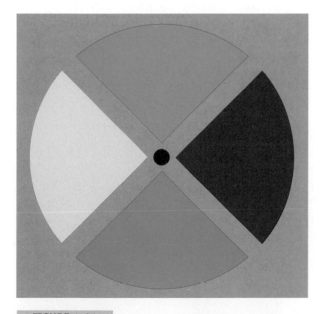

FIGURE 4-21

Complementary Afterimages *Look steadily for about a minute at the dot in the center of the colors, then transfer your gaze to the dot in the gray field at the right. You should see a blurry image with colors that are complementary to the original: The blue, red, green, and yellow are replaced by yellow, green, red, and blue.*

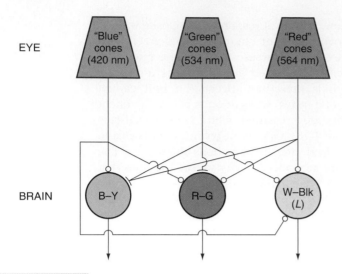

EYE

BRAIN

FIGURE 4-22

How the Trichromatic and Opponent-Process Theories May Be Related
This diagram shows three types of receptors connected to produce opponent-process neural responses at a later stage in processing. The numbers in the cones indicate wavelengths of maximum sensitivity. The lines with arrows represent connections that increase activity; the lines with dots represent connections that decrease activity. Note that this is only a small part of the whole system. Another set of opponent-process units exist that have the reverse arrangement of increasing and decreasing connections.

that they be integrated into a two-stage theory in which the three types of receptors identified by the trichromatic theory feed into the color-opponent units at a higher level in the visual system (Hurvich & Jameson, 1974). This view suggests that there should be neurons in the visual system that function as color-opponent units and operate on visual information after the retina (which contains the three kinds of receptors of trichromatic theory). And in fact such color-opponent neurons have been discovered in the thalamus, a neural waystation between the retina and the visual cortex (DeValois & Jacobs, 1984). These cells are spontaneously active, increasing their activity rate in response to one range of wavelengths and decreasing it in response to another. Thus, some cells at a higher level in the visual system fire more rapidly if the retina is stimulated by a blue light and less rapidly when the retina is exposed to a yellow light; such cells seem to constitute the biological basis of the blue-yellow opponent pair. A summary neural wiring diagram that shows how the trichromatic and opponent-process theories may be related is presented in Figure 4-22.

This research on color vision is a striking example of successful interaction between psychological and biological approaches to a problem. Trichromatic theory suggested that there must be three kinds of color receptors, and subsequent biological research established that there were three kinds of cones in the retina. Opponent-color theory said that there must be other kinds of units in the visual system, and biological researchers subsequently found opponent-color cells in the thalamus. Moreover, successful integration of the two theories required that the trichromatic cells feed into the opponent-color ones, and this, too, was confirmed by subsequent biological research. Thus, on several occasions outstanding work at the psychological level pointed the way for biological discoveries. It is no wonder that many scientists have taken the analysis of color vision as a prototype for the analysis of other sensory systems.

Audition

Along with vision, audition (hearing) is our major means of obtaining information about the environment. For most of us, it is the primary channel of communication as well as the vehicle for music. As we will see, it all comes about because small changes in sound pressure can move a membrane in our inner ear back and forth.

Musical instruments produce complex patterns of sound pressure. These are referred to as the sound's timbre.

Our discussion of audition follows the same plan as our discussion of vision. We first consider the nature of the physical stimulus to which audition is sensitive; then describe the auditory system, with particular emphasis on how the receptors carry out the transduction process; and finally consider how the auditory system codes the intensity of sound and its quality.

Sound Waves

Sound originates from the motion or vibration of an object, as when the wind rushes through the branches of a tree. When something moves, the molecules of air in front of it are pushed together. These molecules push other molecules and then return to their original position. In this way, a wave of pressure changes (a sound wave) is transmitted through the air, even though the individual air molecules do not travel far. This wave is analogous to the ripples set up by throwing a stone into a pond.

A sound wave may be described by a graph of air pressure as a function of time. A pressure-versus-time graph of one type of sound is shown in Figure 4-23. The graph depicts a sine wave (so called because it corresponds to a sine-wave function in mathematics). Sounds that correspond to sine waves are called *pure tones*. They are important in the analysis of audition because more complex sounds can be analyzed into pure tones; that is, they can be decomposed into a number of different sine waves. Pure tones vary in certain ways that determine how we experience the tone. One aspect is the tone's frequency. The **frequency** of a tone is *the number of cycles per second* (called *hertz*), which reflects the rate at which the molecules move back and forth (see Figure 4-23). Frequency is the basis of our perception of pitch, which is one of the most noticeable qualities of a sound.

A second aspect of a pure tone is its **amplitude,** *the difference in pressure between the peak and the trough* in a pressure-versus-time graph (see Figure 4-23). Amplitude underlies our sensation of loudness. Sound amplitude is usually specified in *decibels;* an increase of 10 decibels corresponds to a change in sound power of 10 times; 20 decibels, a change of 100 times; 30 decibels, a change of 1,000 times; and so forth. For example, a soft whisper in a quiet library is approximately 30 decibels, a noisy restaurant may have a level of 70 decibels, a rock concert may be near 120 decibels, and a jet taking off may be over 140 decibels. Consistent exposure to sound levels at or above 100 decibels is associated with permanent hearing loss.

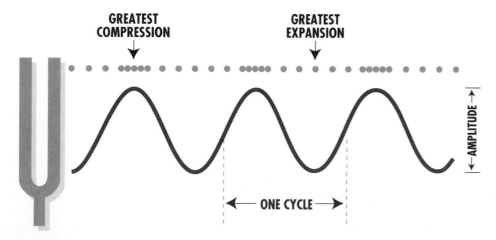

FIGURE 4-23

A Pure Tone   *As the tuning fork vibrates, it produces successive waves of compression and expansion of the air, which correspond to a sine wave. Such a sound is called a pure tone. It can be described by giving its frequency and intensity. If the tuning fork makes 100 vibrations per second, it produces a sound wave with 100 compressions per second and a frequency of 100 hertz. The intensity (or amplitude) of a pure tone is the difference in pressure between the peaks and the troughs. The waveform of any sound can be decomposed into a series of sine waves of different frequencies with various amplitudes and phases. When these sine waves are added together, the result is the original waveform.*

Sitting or standing in front of the speakers at a rock concert can cause permanent hearing loss.

A final aspect of sound is **timbre,** which refers to *our experience of the complexity of a sound.* Almost none of the sounds we hear every day is as simple as the pure tones we have been discussing. (The exceptions are tuning forks and some electronic instruments.) Sounds produced by acoustical instruments, automobiles, the human voice, other animals, and waterfalls are characterized by complex patterns of sound pressure.

The Auditory System

The auditory system consists of the ears, parts of the brain, and the various connecting neural pathways. Our primary concern will be with the ears; this includes not just the appendages on the sides of the head, but the entire hearing organ, most of which lies within the skull (see Figure 4-24).

Like the eye, the ear contains two systems. One system amplifies and transmits the sound to the receptors, whereupon the other system takes over and transduces the sound into neural impulses. The transmission system involves the outer ear, which consists of the external ear (or *pinna*) along with the auditory canal, and the middle ear, which consists of the *eardrum* and a chain of three bones called the *malleus, incus,* and *stapes.* The transduction system is housed in a part of the inner ear called the *cochlea,* which contains the receptors for sound.

Let us take a more detailed look at the transmission system (see Figure 4-25). The outer ear aids in the collection of sound, funneling it through the auditory canal to a taut membrane, the eardrum. The eardrum is the outermost part of the middle ear. It is caused to vibrate by sound waves funneled to it through the auditory canal. The middle ear's job is to transmit these vibrations of the eardrum across an air-filled cavity to another membrane, the *oval window,* which is the gateway to the inner ear and the receptors. The middle ear accomplishes this transmission by means of a mechanical bridge consisting of the malleus, incus, and stapes. The vibrations of the eardrum move the first bone, which then moves the second, which in turn moves the third, which results in vibrations of the oval window. This mechanical arrangement not only transmits the sound wave but greatly amplifies it as well.

Now consider the transduction system. The cochlea is a coiled tube of bone. It is

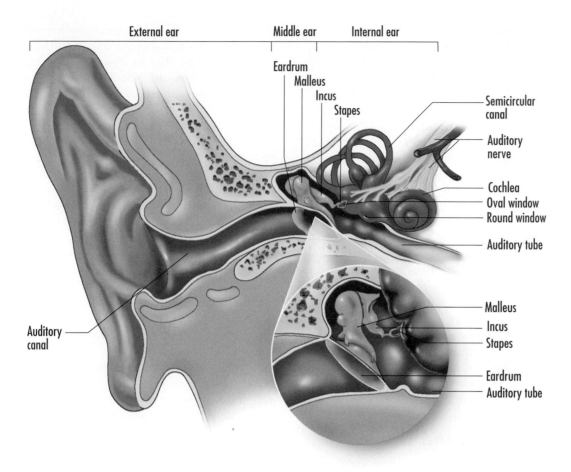

External ear   Middle ear   Internal ear

Eardrum
Malleus
Incus
Stapes

Semicircular canal

Auditory nerve

Cochlea
Oval window
Round window

Auditory tube

Auditory canal

Malleus
Incus
Stapes

Eardrum
Auditory tube

FIGURE 4-24

A Cross-Section of the Ear   *This drawing shows the overall structure of the ear. The inner ear includes the cochlea, which contains the auditory receptors, and the vestibular apparatus (semicircular canals and vestibular sacs), which is the sense organ for our sense of balance and body motion.*

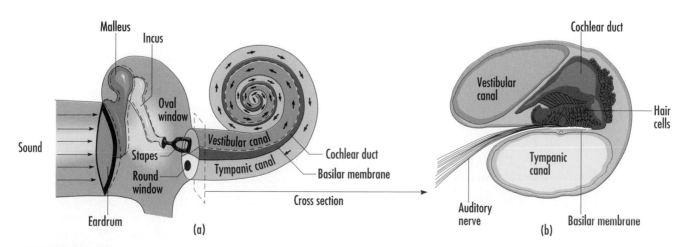

Malleus
Incus
Oval window
Sound
Stapes
Round window
Eardrum
Vestibular canal
Tympanic canal
Cochlear duct
Basilar membrane
Cross section
(a)

Cochlear duct
Vestibular canal
Hair cells
Tympanic canal
Auditory nerve
Basilar membrane
(b)

FIGURE 4-25

A Schematic Diagram of the Middle and Inner Ear   *(a) Movement of the fluid within the cochlea deforms the basilar membrane and stimulates the hair cells that serve as the auditory receptors. (b) A cross-section of the cochlea showing the basilar membrane and the hair cell receptors.*

divided into sections of fluid by membranes, one of which, the *basilar membrane,* supports the auditory receptors (Figure 4-25). The receptors are called *hair cells* because they have hairlike structures that extend into the fluid. Pressure at the oval window (which connects the middle and inner ear) leads to pressure changes in the cochlear fluid, which in turn causes the basilar membrane to vibrate, resulting in a bending of the hair cells and an electrical impulse. Through this complex process, a sound wave is transduced into an electrical impulse. The neurons that synapse with the hair cells have long axons that form part of the auditory nerve. Most of these auditory neurons connect to single hair cells. There are about 31,000 auditory neurons in the auditory nerve, many fewer than the 1 million neurons in the optic nerve (Yost & Nielson, 1985). The auditory pathway from each ear goes to both sides of the brain and has synapses in several nuclei before reaching the auditory cortex.

Hearing Sound Intensity

Recall that our vision is more sensitive to some wavelengths than to others. A similar phenomenon occurs in audition. We are more

sensitive to sounds of intermediate frequency than we are to sounds near either end of our frequency range. This is illustrated in Figure 4-26, which shows the absolute threshold for sound intensity as a function of frequency. Many people have some deficit in hearing and consequently have a threshold higher than those shown in the figure. There are two basic kinds of hearing deficits. In one kind, called *conduction loss,* thresholds are elevated roughly equally at all frequencies as the result of poor conduction in the middle ear. In the other kind, called *sensory-neural loss,* the threshold elevation is unequal, with large elevations occurring at higher frequencies. This pattern is usually a consequence of inner-ear damage, often involving some destruction of the hair cells, which are unable to regenerate. Sensory-neural loss occurs in many older people and explains why the elderly often have trouble hearing high-pitched sounds. Sensory-neural loss is not limited to the elderly, though. It occurs in young people who are exposed to excessively loud sound. Rock musicians, airport-runway crews, and pneumatic-drill operators commonly suffer major, permanent hearing loss. For example, Pete Townsend, the well-known guitarist of the rock group The Who, suffered severe sensory neural loss because of his continuous exposure to loud rock music; since then he has alerted many young people to this danger.

It is natural to assume that the perceived intensity of a sound is the same at both ears, but in fact there are subtle differences. A sound originating on our right side, for example, will be heard as more intense by our right ear than by our left ear. This happens because our head causes a "sound shadow" that decreases the intensity of the sound reaching the far ear. This difference does not interfere with our ability to hear, however; we take advantage of it by using it to localize where the sound is coming from. It is as if we said, "If the sound is more intense at my right ear than at my left ear, it must be coming from my right side." Likewise, a sound originating on the right side will arrive at the right ear a split-second before it reaches the left ear (and vice versa for a sound originating on the left). We also take advantage of this difference to localize the sound ("If the sound arrived at my right ear first, it must be coming from the right").

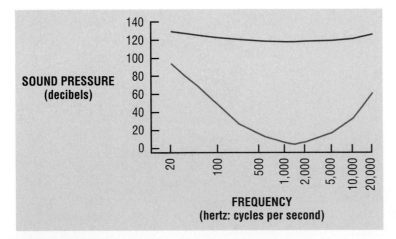

FIGURE 4-26

Absolute Threshold for Hearing   *The lower curve shows the absolute intensity threshold at different frequencies. Sensitivity is greatest in the vicinity of 1,000 hertz. The upper curve describes the threshold for pain. (Data are approximate, from various determinations.)*

Hearing Pitch

One of the primary psychological qualities of a sound is its **pitch**, which is *a sensation based on the frequency of a sound.* As frequency increases, so does pitch, although the correspondence is not one to one. Young adults can detect pure tone frequencies between 20 and 20,000 hertz, with the jnd being less than 1 hertz at 100 hertz and increasing to 100 hertz at 10,000 hertz.

With sound, as with light, we rarely have opportunities to hear pure sensory stimuli. Recall that for the visual system a pure stimulus would be light consisting of only one wavelength. Instead, most colors that we see are a mixture of many wavelengths. A similar situation characterizes the auditory system. We rarely hear a pure tone; instead, we are usually confronted by a sound composed of a mixture of tones. However, here the analogy begins to break down. When we mix wavelengths of light we see an entirely new color, but when we mix pure tones together we often can still hear each of the components separately. This is especially true if the tones are widely separated in frequency. When the frequencies are close together, the sensation is more complex but still does not sound like a single, pure tone. In color vision, the fact that a mixture of three lights results in the sensation of a single color led to the idea of three types of receptors. The absence of a comparable phenomenon in audition suggests that if there are receptors specialized for different frequencies, they must be of many different types.

Theories of Pitch Perception As with color vision, two kinds of theories have been proposed to account for how the ear codes frequency into pitch. The first kind was suggested in 1886 by Lord Rutherford, a British physicist. Rutherford proposed that a sound wave causes the entire basilar membrane to vibrate, and that the rate of vibration determines the rate of impulses of nerve fibers in the auditory nerve. Thus, a 1,000-hertz tone causes the basilar membrane to vibrate 1,000 times per second, which causes nerve fibers in the auditory nerve to fire at 1,000 impulses per second, and the brain interprets this as a particular pitch. Because this theory proposes that pitch depends on how sound varies with time, it is called a *temporal theory*.

Rutherford's hypothesis soon ran into a major problem. Nerve fibers were shown to have a maximum firing rate of about 1,000 impulses per second, so how do we perceive the pitch of tones whose frequency exceeds 1,000 hertz? Weaver (1949) proposed a way to deal with the problem. He argued that frequencies over 1,000 hertz could be coded by different groups of nerve fibers, each group firing at a slightly different pace. If one group of neurons is firing at 1,000 impulses per second, for example, and then 1 millisecond later a second group of neurons begins firing at 1,000 impulses per second, the combined rate of impulses per second for the two groups will be 2,000 impulses per second. This version of temporal theory received support from the discovery that the pattern of nerve impulses in the auditory nerve follows the waveform of the stimulus tone even though individual cells do not respond on every cycle of the wave (Rose, Brugge, Anderson, & Hind, 1967).

However, the ability of nerve fibers to follow the waveform breaks down at about 4,000 hertz—yet we can hear pitch at much higher frequencies. This suggests that there must be another means of coding the quality of pitch, at least for high frequencies. The second kind of theory of pitch perception deals with this question. It dates back to 1683, when the French anatomist Joseph Guichard Duverney proposed that frequency is coded into pitch mechanically by resonance (Green & Wier, 1984). To appreciate this proposal, it is helpful to first consider an example of resonance. When a tuning fork is struck near a piano, the piano string that is tuned to the frequency of the fork will begin to vibrate. To say that the ear works the same way is to say that the ear contains a structure similar to a stringed instrument, with different parts tuned to different frequencies, so that when a frequency is presented to the ear the corresponding part of the structure vibrates. This idea proved to be roughly correct; the structure turned out to be the basilar membrane.

In the 1800s Hermann von Helmholtz developed this hypothesis further, eventually proposing the *place theory* of pitch perception. It holds that each specific place along the basilar membrane will lead to a particular pitch sensation. The fact that there are many such places on the membrane is compatible with there being many different receptors for pitch. Note that place

FRONTIERS OF PSYCHOLOGICAL RESEARCH

Artificial Ears and Eyes

The science fiction fantasy of replacing defective sense organs with artificial ones is becoming a reality. Researchers have been working on artificial replacements (called *prostheses*) for damaged eyes and ears for several years.

Research on auditory prostheses has concentrated on devices that electrically stimulate the auditory nerve. They are designed to aid people whose hair cells have been destroyed but whose auditory nerve is intact and functional. Most of these devices use an electrode, which is inserted through the round window into the cochlea to stimulate the neurons along basilar membrane; this is known as a *cochlear implant*. The implant consists of a series of electrodes placed at different points inside the cochlea. A small microphone is worn by the deaf person, along with a microchip that analyzes the frequencies and sends a small electrical signal to the appropriate place inside the cochlea. This stimulation mimics the way traveling waves stimulate the hair cells for various frequencies (Schindler & Merzenich, 1985).

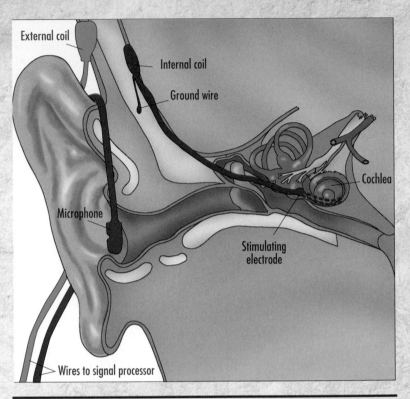

The Cochlear Implant   *This diagram illustrates the auditory prosthesis developed by William House and his associates. Sound is picked up by a microphone and filtered by a signal processor (not shown) worn outside the body. The electrical waveform produced by the processor is transmitted by radio waves through the skull to the electrode inside the brain.*

theory does not imply that we hear with our basilar membrane; rather, the places on the membrane that vibrate most determine which neural fibers are activated, and that determines the pitch we hear. This is an example of a sensory modality coding quality according to the specific nerves involved.

How the basilar membrane actually moves was not established until the 1940s, when Georg von Békésy measured its movement through small holes drilled in the cochleas of guinea pigs and human cadavers. Von Békésy's findings required a modification of place theory: Rather than behaving like a piano with separate strings, the basilar membrane behaves more like a bed sheet being shaken at one end. Specifically, von Békésy

showed that the whole membrane moves for most frequencies, but that the place of maximum movement depends on the specific frequency sounded. High frequencies cause vibration at the near end of the basilar membrane; as frequency increases, the vibration pattern moves toward the oval window (von Békésy, 1960). For this and other research on audition, von Békésy received a Nobel prize in 1961.

Like temporal theories, place theories explain many phenomena of pitch perception, but not all. A major difficulty for place theory arises with low-frequency tones. With frequencies below 50 hertz, all parts of the basilar membrane vibrate about equally. This means that all the receptors are equally acti-

Cochlear implants have now been placed in more than 10,000 profoundly deaf people. Most of the recipients can discriminate among frequencies of sounds quite well (Townshend, Cotter, Van Compernolle, & White, 1987), and many can recognize speech sounds, especially when a specialized speech preprocessor is included on the microchip to isolate certain speech-relevant frequency changes (Blamey et al., 1987). Interestingly, there may be a "critical period" or optimum time to implant these devices. Deaf children who received one before age 5 were able to learn speech more easily than children who received one at a later age (Tye-Murray, Spencer, & Woodworth, 1995). However, among adults, those who have become deaf later in life seem to benefit more than those who have been deaf from an early age (Busby, Tong, & Clark, 1993). The advantage for very young children is probably due to the fact that their brain centers for hearing and speech are still undergoing major developmental changes. In adults, the older they are when they become deaf, the greater the opportunity they have

had to hear a variety of speech sounds, which prepares them to understand the strange new sounds generated by the implant.

There is some promise that cochlear implants will eventually allow a full range of hearing experience for people with this form of deafness (Miller & Spelman, 1990). There is even hope for people who lack a functioning auditory nerve, because more central implants, placed farther along the pathway to the brain, are currently being tested (Shannon & Otto, 1990).

The development of artificial eyes for the blind has not progressed as far as the development of artificial ears. The problem is not a matter of acquiring the optical image; a video camera can do this well. Rather, the problem is how to put the image information into the visual system in a form that the brain can use. Research has focused on direct electrical stimulation of the visual cortex in volunteers who are either blind or undergoing brain surgery. If we know what a person sees when different places in the cortex are electrically stimulated, it should be possible to evoke different visual

experiences by controlling the stimulation. The next step would be to use a video camera to form an image of the scene in front of the blind person and then evoke an experience of that scene in the brain.

Results obtained thus far suggest that we are a long way from developing an artificial eye. When a small region of the visual cortex is stimulated with a weak electrical signal, the person experiences rudimentary visual sensations. These have been described as small spots of light ranging in size from that of a grain of rice to that of a coin. Most are white, but some are colored. If several places in the visual cortex are stimulated simultaneously, the corresponding spots are usually experienced together. Although multiple stimulation of the visual cortex provides the basis for a crude form of pattern vision (Dobelle, Meadejovsky, & Girvin, 1974), it is questionable whether this approach will lead to a successful prosthesis for damaged eyes. The neural input to the visual cortex is so complicated that it is unlikely to be adequately duplicated by artificial means.

vated, which implies that we have no way of discriminating between frequencies below 50 hertz. In fact, though, we can discern frequencies as low as 20 hertz. Hence, place theories have problems explaining our perception of low-frequency tones, while temporal theories have problems dealing with high-frequency tones. This led to the idea that pitch depends on *both* place and temporal pattern, with temporal theory explaining our perception of low frequencies and place theory explaining our perception of high frequencies. It is not clear, however, where one mechanism leaves off and the other takes over. Indeed, it is possible that frequencies between 1000 and 5000 hertz are handled by both mechanisms (Coren, Ward, & Enns, 1999).

Because our ears and eyes are so important to us in our day-to-day lives, many efforts have been made to develop ways to replace them in individuals who suffer irreparable damage to these organs. Some of these efforts are described in the Frontiers of Psychological Research feature above.

Other Senses

Senses other than vision and audition lack the richness of patterning and organization that have led sight and hearing to be called the "higher senses." Still, these other senses are vitally important. Smell (olfaction), for example, is one of the most primitive and most important of the senses. This is probably related to the fact that smell has a more direct route to the brain than any other sense. The receptors, which are in the nasal cavity, are connected to the brain without synapses. Moreover, unlike the receptors for vision and audition, the receptors for smell are exposed directly to the environment— they are right there in the nasal cavity with no protective shield in front of them. (In contrast, the receptors for vision are behind the cornea, and those for audition are protected by the outer and middle ear.) Since smell is clearly an important sensory modality, we begin our discussion of the other senses with smell, also termed *olfaction.*

Olfaction

Olfaction aids in the survival of our species: It is needed for the detection of spoiled food or escaping gas, and loss of the sense of smell can lead to a dulled appetite. Still, smell is even more essential for the survival of many other animals. Not surprisingly, then, a larger area of the cortex is devoted to smell in other species than in our own. In fish, the olfactory cortex makes up almost all of the cerebral hemispheres; in dogs, about one-third; in humans, only about one-twentieth. These variations are related to differences in sensitivity to smell. Taking advantage of the superior smell capability of dogs, both the United States Postal Service and the Bureau of Customs have trained them to check unopened packages for heroin. Specially trained police dogs can sniff out hidden explosives.

Because smell is so well developed in other species, it is often used as a means of communication. Insects and some other animals secrete **pheromones,** *chemicals that float through the air to be sniffed by other members of the species.* For example, a female moth can release a pheromone so powerful that males are drawn to her from a distance of several miles. It is clear that the male moth responds only to the pheromone and not to the sight of the female; the male will be attracted to a female in a wire container even though she is blocked from view, but not to a female that is clearly visible in a glass container from which the scent cannot escape.

Insects use smell to communicate death as well as "love." After an ant dies, the chemicals formed from its decomposing body stimulate other ants to carry the corpse to a refuse heap outside the nest. If a living ant is experimentally doused with the decomposition chemicals, it is carried off by other ants to the refuse heap. When it returns to the nest, it is carried out again. Such premature attempts at burial continue until the "smell of death" has worn off (Wilson, 1963).

Do humans have a vestige of this primitive communication system? Experiments indicate that we can use smell at least to tell ourselves from other people and to distinguish males from females. In one study, participants wore undershirts for 24 hours without showering or using deodorant. The undershirts were collected by the experimenter, who then presented each with three shirts to smell. One was the participant's own shirt, another was a male's, and the third was a female's. Based only on odor, most participants could identify their own shirt and tell which of the other shirts had been worn by a male or a female (Russell, 1976; Schleidt, Hold, & Attili, 1981). Other studies suggest that we may communicate subtler matters by means of odor. Women who live or work together seem to communicate their stage in the menstrual cycle by means of smell, and over time this results in a tendency for their menstrual cycles to begin at the same time (McClintock, 1971; Preti et al., 1986; Russell, Switz, & Thompson, 1980; Weller & Weller, 1993). However, it is important to remember that these are effects on physiological functioning, not behavior. Although menstrual regularity is associated with healthy reproductive functioning and fertility, it does not have a direct influence on human behavior. Indeed, many researchers now believe that the behavioral effects of pheromones on humans are likely to be indirect, since social and learning factors influence our behavior more than they do that of other mammals (Coren, Ward, & Enns, 1999).

The Olfactory System   The volatile molecules given off by a substance are the stimulus for smell. The molecules leave the substance, travel through the air, and enter the nasal passage (see Figure 4-27). The molecules must also be soluble in fat, because the receptors for smell are covered with a fatlike substance.

The olfactory system consists of the receptors in the nasal passage, certain regions of the brain, and interconnecting neural pathways. The receptors for smell are

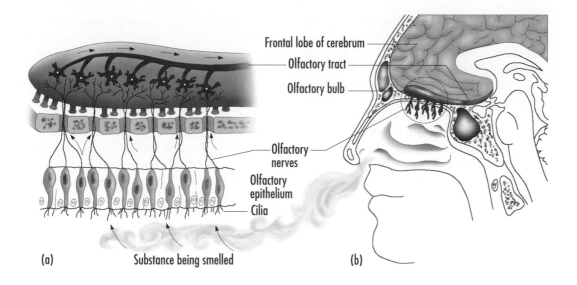

Frontal lobe of cerebrum
Olfactory tract
Olfactory bulb

Olfactory nerves
Olfactory epithelium
Cilia

(a)   Substance being smelled   (b)

FIGURE 4-27

Olfactory Receptors   *(a) Detail of a receptor interspersed among numerous supporting cells. (b) The placement of the olfactory receptors in the nasal cavity.*

located high in the nasal cavity. When the cilia (hairlike structures) of these receptors come into contact with volatile molecules, an electrical impulse results; this is the transduction process. This impulse travels along nerve fibers to the *olfactory bulb,* a region of the brain that lies just below the frontal lobes. The olfactory bulb in turn is connected to the *olfactory cortex* on the inside of the temporal lobes. (Interestingly, there is a direct connection between the olfactory bulb and the part of the cortex known to be involved in the formation of long-term memories; perhaps this is related to the idea that a distinctive smell can be a powerful aid in retrieving an old memory.)

Sensing Intensity and Quality   Human sensitivity to the intensity of a smell depends greatly on the substance involved. Absolute thresholds can be as low as 1 part per 50 billion parts of air. Still, as noted earlier, we are far less sensitive to smell than other species. Dogs, for example, can detect substances in concentrations 100 times lower than those that can be detected by humans (Marshall, Blumer, & Moulton, 1981). Our relative lack of sensitivity is not due to our having less sensitive olfactory receptors. Rather, we just have fewer of them: roughly 10 million receptors for humans versus 1 billion for dogs.

Although we rely less on smell than other species, we are capable of sensing many different qualities of odor. Estimates vary, but a healthy person appears to be able to distinguish among 10,000 to 40,000 different odors, with women generally doing better than men (Cain, 1988). Professional perfumers and whiskey blenders can probably do even better—discriminating

Dogs are far more sensitive to smells than humans, and for this reason they are often used in police work, search-and-rescue operations, and drug and bomb detection, as well as hunting.

among perhaps 100,000 odors (Dobb, 1989). Moreover, we know something about how the olfactory system codes the quality of odors at the biological level. The situation is most unlike the coding of color in vision, for which three kinds of receptors suffice. In olfaction, many kinds of receptors seem to be involved; an estimate of 1,000 kinds of olfactory receptors is not unreasonable (Buck & Axel, 1991). Rather than coding a specific odor, each kind of receptor may respond to many different odors (Matthews, 1972). So quality may be partly coded by the pattern of neural activity, even in this receptor-rich sensory modality.

Gustation

Gustation, or the sense of taste, gets credit for a lot of experiences that it does not provide. We say that a meal "tastes" good; but when our ability to smell is eliminated by a bad cold, food seems to lack taste and we may have trouble telling red wine from vinegar. Still, taste is a sense in its own right. Even with a bad cold, we can tell salted from unsalted food.

In what follows, we will refer to the taste of particular substances, but note that the substance being tasted is not the only factor that determines its taste. Our genetic makeup and experience also affect taste. For example, people vary in their sensitivity to the

bitter taste in caffeine and saccharin, and this difference appears to be genetically determined (Bartoshuk, 1979). The role of experience is illustrated by Indians living in the Karnataka province of India, who eat many sour foods and experience citric acid and quinine (the taste of tonic water) as pleasant tasting. Most Westerners experience the opposite sensations. This particular difference seems to be a matter of experience, for Indians raised in Western countries find citric acid and quinine unpleasant tasting (Moskowitz et al., 1975).

The Gustatory System   The stimulus for taste is a substance that is soluble in saliva. The gustatory system includes receptors that are located on the tongue as well as on the throat and roof of the mouth; the system also includes parts of the brain and interconnecting neural pathways. In what follows, we focus on the receptors on the tongue. These taste receptors occur in clusters, called *taste buds,* on the bumps of the tongue and around the mouth. At the ends of the taste buds are short, hairlike structures that extend outward and make contact with the solutions in the mouth. The contact results in an electrical impulse; this is the transduction process. The electrical impulse then travels to the brain.

Sensing Intensity and Quality   Sensitivity to different taste stimuli varies from place to place on the tongue. While any substance can be detected at almost any place on the tongue (except the center), different tastes are best detected in different regions. Sensitivity to salty and sweet substances is best near the front of the tongue; sensitivity to sour substances along the sides; and sensitivity to bitter substances is best on the soft palate (see Figure 4-28). In the center of the tongue is a region that is insensitive to taste (the place to put an unpleasant pill). While absolute thresholds for taste are generally very low, jnds for intensity are relatively high (Weber's constant is often about 0.2). This means that if you are increasing the amount of spice in a dish, you usually must add more than 20% or you will not taste the difference.

Recent research suggests that "tongue maps," such as the one in Figure 4-28, may be oversimplified in that they suggest that if the nerves leading to a particular region were

Humans vary in their sensitivity to different tastes. Some people, like this coffee taster, are able to discriminate among very subtle differences in the tastes of particular substances.

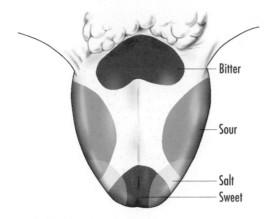

FIGURE 4-28

Taste Areas *Although any substance can be detected anywhere on the tongue—except in the center— different areas are maximally sensitive to different tastes. Thus, the area labeled "sweet" is most sensitive to sweet tastes.*

cut, all sensation would be lost. However, this does not occur because taste nerves inhibit one another. Damaging one nerve abolishes its ability to inhibit others; thus, if you cut the nerves to a particular region, you also reduce the inhibitory effect, and the result is that there is little change in the everyday experience of taste (Bartoshuk, 1993).

There is an agreed-upon vocabulary for describing tastes. Any taste can be described as one or a combination of the four basic taste qualities: sweet, sour, salty, and bitter (McBurney, 1978). These four tastes are best revealed in sucrose (sweet), hydrochloric acid (sour), sodium chloride (salty), and quinine (bitter). When people are asked to describe the tastes of various substances in terms of just the four basic tastes, they have no trouble doing this. Even if they are given the option of using additional qualities of their own choice, they tend to stay with the four basic tastes (Goldstein, 1989).

The gustatory system codes taste in terms of both the specific nerve fibers activated and the pattern of activation across nerve fibers. There appear to be four types of nerve fibers, corresponding to the four basic tastes. While each fiber responds somewhat to all four basic tastes, it responds best to just one of them. Hence, it makes sense to talk of "salty fibers" whose activity signals saltiness to the brain. Thus, there is a remarkable correspondence between our subjective experience of taste and its neural coding.

Pressure and Temperature

Traditionally, touch was thought to be a single sense. Today, it is considered to include three distinct skin senses, one responding to pressure, another to temperature, and the third to pain. This section briefly considers pressure and temperature, and the next discusses pain.

Pressure The stimulus for sensed pressure is physical pressure on the skin. Although we are not aware of steady pressure on the entire body (such as air pressure), we can discriminate among variations in pressure over the surface of the body. Some parts of the body are more effective than others at sensing the intensity of pressure; the lips, nose, and cheek are the most sensitive to pressure, while the big toe is least sensitive. These differences are closely related to the number of receptors that respond to the stimulus at each of these locations. In sensitive regions, we can detect a force as small as 5 milligrams applied to a small area. However, like other sensory systems, the pressure system shows profound adaptation effects. If you hold a friend's hand for several minutes without moving, you will become insensitive to its pressure and cease to feel it.

When we are actively exploring the environment through touch, the motor senses contribute to our experience. Through active touch alone we can readily identify familiar objects, using it to recognize coins, keys, and other small objects that we keep in our pockets and purses (Klatzky, Lederman, & Metzger, 1985).

Temperature The stimulus for temperature is the temperature of our skin. The receptors are neurons just under the skin. In the transduction stage, cold receptors generate a neural impulse when there is a decrease in skin temperature, while warm receptors generate an impulse when there is an increase in skin temperature (Duclauz & Kenshalo, 1980; Hensel, 1973). Hence, different qualities of temperature can be coded primarily by the specific receptors activated. However, this specificity of neural reaction has its limits. Cold receptors respond not only to low temperatures but also to very high temperatures (above 45 degrees centigrade or 113 degrees Fahrenheit). Consequently, a very

After being in a swimming pool for a while, our temperature sense adapts to the change in temperature. However, when first dangling a foot into the water we can detect the cooler temperature.

hot stimulus will activate both warm and cold receptors, as you may have experienced when you accidentally plunged your foot into a very hot bath.

Because maintaining body temperature is crucial to survival, it is important that we be able to sense small changes in our skin temperature. When the skin is at its normal temperature, we can detect a warming of only 0.4 degrees centigrade and a cooling of just 0.15 degrees centigrade (Kenshalo, Nafe, & Brooks, 1961). Our temperature sense adapts completely to moderate changes in temperature, so that after a few minutes the stimulus feels neither cool nor warm. This adaptation explains the strong differences of opinion about the temperature of a swimming pool between those who have been in it for a while and those who are first dangling a foot in it.

Pain

Of all our senses, none captures our attention like pain. We may sometimes take a blasé view of the other senses, but it is hard to ignore pain. Yet for all the discomfort it causes, we would be at risk if we had no sense of pain. It would be difficult for children to learn not to touch a hot stove, or to stop chewing their tongues. In fact, some people are born with a rare genetic disorder that makes them insensitive to pain, and they typically die young, owing to tissue deterioration resulting from wounds that could have been avoided if they had been able to feel pain.

The Pain System Any stimulus that is intense enough to cause tissue damage is a stimulus for pain. It may be pressure, temperature, electric shock, or chemical irritants. Such a stimulus causes the release of chemical substances in the skin, which in turn stimulate distinct high-threshold receptors (the transduction stage). These receptors are neurons with specialized free nerve endings, and researchers have identified several types (Brown & Deffenbacher, 1979). With regard to variations in the quality of pain, perhaps the most important distinction is between the kind of pain we feel immediately upon suffering an injury, called *phasic pain,* and the kind we experience after the injury has occurred, called *tonic pain.* Phasic pain is typically a sharp, immediate pain that is brief in duration (that is, it rapidly rises and falls in intensity), whereas tonic pain is typically dull and long lasting.

To illustrate, if you sprain your ankle, you immediately feel a sharp undulating pain (phasic pain), but after a while you start to feel the steady pain caused by the swelling (tonic pain). The two kinds of pain are mediated by two distinct neural pathways, and these pathways eventually reach different parts of the cortex. (Melzack, 1990).

Nonstimulus Determinants of Pain More than any other sensation, the intensity and quality of pain are influenced by factors other than the immediate stimulus. These factors include the person's culture, expectations, and previous experience. The striking influence of culture is illustrated by the fact that some non-Western societies engage in rituals that seem unbearably painful to Westerners. A case in point is the hook-swinging ceremony practiced in some parts of India:

The ceremony derives from an ancient practice in which a member of a social group is chosen to represent the power of the gods. The role of the chosen man (or "celebrant") is to bless the children and crops in a series of neighboring villages during a particular period of the year. What is remarkable about the ritual is that steel hooks, which are attached by strong ropes to the top of a special cart, are shoved under his skin and muscles on both sides of his back [see Figure 4-29]. The cart is then moved from village to village. Usually the man hangs on to the ropes as the cart is moved about. But at the climax of the ceremony in each village, he swings free, hanging only from the hooks embedded in his back, to bless the children and crops. Astonishingly, there is no evidence that the man is in pain during the ritual; rather, he appears to be in a "state of exaltation." When the hooks are later removed, wounds heal rapidly without any medical treatment other than the application of wood ash. Two weeks later the marks on his back are scarcely visible (Melzak, 1973).

Clearly, pain is as much a matter of mind as of sensory receptors.

Phenomena like the one just described have led to the *gate control theory* of pain (Melzack & Wall, 1982; 1988). According to this theory, the sensation of pain requires not only that pain receptors on the skin be active but also that a "neural gate" in the spinal cord be open and allow the signals from the pain receptors to pass to the brain (the gate closes when critical fibers in the spinal cord are activated). Because the neural gate can be closed by signals sent down from the cortex, the perceived intensity of pain can be reduced by the person's mental state, as in the hook-swinging ceremony. What exactly is the "neural gate"? It appears to involve a region of the midbrain called the *periaqueductal gray*, or PAG for

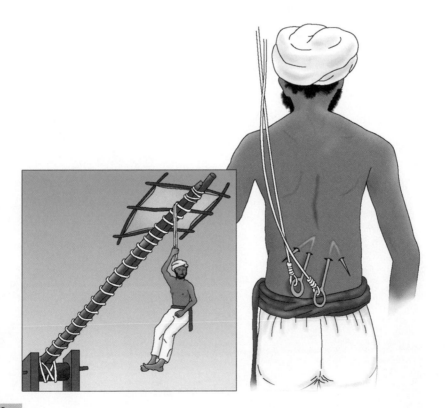

FIGURE 4-29

Culture and Pain   *Right: Two steel hooks are inserted in the back of the celebrant in the Indian hook-swinging ceremony. Left: The celebrant hangs onto the ropes as a cart takes him from village to village. As he blesses the village children and crops, he swings freely suspended by the hooks in his back. (After Kosambi, 1967)*

short; neurons in the PAG are connected to other neurons that inhibit cells that would normally carry the pain signals arising in the pain receptors (Jesell & Kelly, 1991). So when the PAG neurons are active, the gate is closed; when the PAG neurons are not active, the gate is open.

Interestingly, the PAG appears to be the main place where strong painkillers such as morphine affect neural processing. Morphine is known to increase neural activity in the PAG, which, as we have just seen, should result in a closing of the neural gate. Hence, the well-known analgesic effects of morphine fit with the gate control theory. Moreover, our body produces certain chemicals, called *endorphins,* that act like morphine to reduce pain, and these chemicals, too, are believed to create their effect by acting on the PAG in such a way as to close the neural gate.

There are other striking phenomena that fit with gate control theory. One is *stimulation-produced analgesia,* in which stimulation of the PAG acts like an anesthetic. One can perform abdominal surgery on a rat using only PAG stimulation as the anesthetic, with the rat showing no sign of experiencing pain (Reynolds, 1969). A milder version of this phenomenon is familiar to all of us: Rubbing a hurt area relieves pain, presumably because pressure stimulation is closing the neural gate. A phenomenon related to stimulation-produced analgesia is the reduction in pain resulting from *acupuncture,* a healing procedure developed in China in which needles are inserted into the skin at critical points. Twirling these needles has been reported to eliminate pain entirely, making it possible to perform major surgery on a conscious patient (see Figure 4-30). Presumably, the needles stimulate nerve fibers that lead to a closing of the pain gate.

At the psychological level, then, we have evidence that drugs, cultural beliefs, and various nonstandard medicinal practices can dramatically reduce pain. However, all of these factors may stem from a single biological process. Here, then, is a case in which research at the biological level may actually unify findings at the psychological level.

Acupuncture makes use of stimulation-produced analgesia to reduce pain.

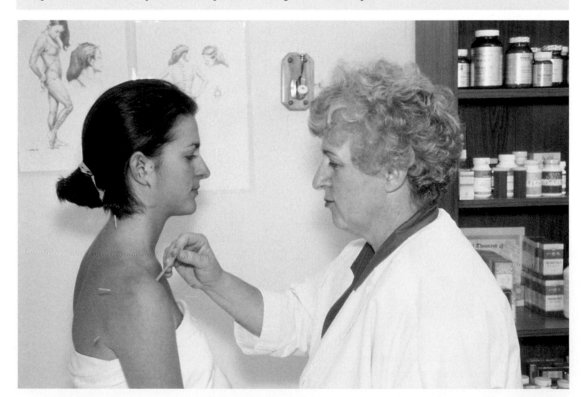

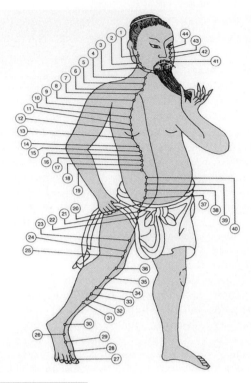

FIGURE 4-30

A Typical Acupuncture Chart   *The numbers indicate sites at which needles can be inserted and then either twisted, electrified, or heated. An impressive analgesia results in many cases.*

The interplay between the psychological and biological research on pain is typical of the successful interaction between these two approaches to sensation. As we commented at the beginning of the chapter, in perhaps no other area of psychology have the biological and psychological approaches worked so well together. Again and again we have seen that neural events occurring in receptors can explain phenomena occurring at the psychological level. Thus, in discussing vision we showed how variations in sensitivity and acuity—which are psychological phenomena—can be understood as the direct consequence of how different kinds of receptors (rods versus cones) connect to ganglion cells. Also with regard to vision, we pointed out how psychological theories of color vision led to discoveries at the biological level (for example, three kinds of cone receptors). In the case of audition, the place theory of frequency perception was initially a psychological theory, and it led to research in the physiology of the basilar membrane. If ever anyone needed justification for intertwining psychological and biological research, the study of sensation provides it.

SHOULD OPIOIDS BE USED FOR TREATING CHRONIC PAIN?

Opioids Are an Appropriate Treatment for Chronic Pain

Robert N. Jamison, *Harvard Medical School*

Pain is a serious problem in the United States and throughout the rest of the world. About one-third of the American population, or more than 80 million people, are severely affected by pain. Pain is the major reason people visit their primary care physicians; in fact, 70 million people see a physician each year because of pain. Chronic pain can affect all aspects of your life, interfering with sleep, employment, social life, and daily activities. Persons who have chronic pain frequently report depression, anxiety, irritability, sexual problems, and decreased energy. A restricted lifestyle causes changes in and concern about finances and the future. The treatments used for short-term pain often do not work well for pain that lasts a long time. Despite medical advances, chronic pain has remained a stubborn, debilitating problem for many individuals (Jamison, 1996).

Controversy remains about the use of opioid analgesics for chronic pain. Most physicians and health-care professionals are reluctant to support the use of opioid medication for patients with chronic pain because of concerns about efficacy, adverse effects, tolerance, diversion, and addiction. It has been suggested that some patients become psychologically dependent after long-term opioid use. Some clinicians believe that opioid analgesics contribute to psychological distress, poor treatment outcome, impaired cognition, and a fostered reliance on the health-care system. The scientific literature has not supported these fears (American Academy of Pain Medicine and American Pain Society, 1996).

Most of the concerns of opioid therapy for chronic pain are based on an ill-founded notion that long-term use of narcotics always causes harm. Researchers and clinicians cite the relatively low incidence of abuse and addiction among patients with chronic pain and report that tolerance appears not to develop in those patients with stable pain pathophysiology (Portenoy, 1990). They suggest that the potential for increased functioning and improved quality of life significantly outweighs the risk of abuse. Investigators have also suggested that chronic opioid therapy may decrease the cost of rehabilitation programs for pain patients while improving outcome.

My colleagues and I initiated a prospective study of opioid therapy for chronic noncancer back pain (Jamison et al.,1998). The aim of this study was to examine the long-term safety and efficacy of chronic opioid therapy in a randomized trial of patients with back pain. All participants were randomly assigned to 1 of 3 treatment regimens: (1) a non-narcotic pain reliever, (2) a few short-acting narcotics a day, or (3) as much short- and long-acting narcotic medication as needed. The patients were followed for a year and then tapered off the medica-tion. The results suggested that opioid therapy had a positive effect on pain and mood. Most importantly, opioid therapy for chronic back pain was used without significant risk of abuse and we found that individuals in the long-term opioid trial were compliant in coming off of the opioid medication without signs of dependency or addiction.

The results of our studies and others point to the overwhelming evidence that addiction rarely occurs when morphine and other opioids are used for pain. This has been found to be true in both human and animal studies. Further studies will help to identify those individuals who benefit the most from opioid therapy. We remain hopeful that future break-throughs will help those who suffer from back pain, headaches, arthritis, and pain associated with cancer. In the meantime, there are millions of people who continue to live and die in needless pain. Many who request medication for their noncancer pain are mistaken as street addicts or drug abusers. Further education is needed to eradicate prejudices about the use of narcotics for pain. We know that when used intelligently, opioids can help to significantly diminish pain. As pointed out by Dr. Ronald Melzack, an internationally recognized psychologist and pain researcher, social action is needed in promoting the use of opioids for pain to attack this "needless tragedy" (Melzack, 1990).

Why Opioids Should Not Be Used for Treating Chronic Pain

Dennis C. Turk, *University of Washington School of Medicine*

Perhaps the earliest mention of the use of opioids for treating pain was contained in the Ebers papyrus dating back to the 4th century B.C. Since then there has been little question as to the effectiveness of opioids for the treatment of acute pain—such as that following surgery. Even the long-term use of opioids was the accepted practice until recently. In the 1960s and 1970s, however, two trends began to challenge the thinking about the medical use of opioids.

Wilbert Fordyce (1976) suggested that it is impossible to know how much pain someone experiences other than by what the person tells you verbally or demonstrates by behaviors. He suggested that these "pain behaviors" were observable and thus capable of being responded to by observers, including family members and physicians. Fordyce also suggested that opioids could serve as a negative reinforcement for pain behaviors. That is, if the patient took opioid medication as is commonly prescribed, "as needed," the pain behaviors would increase in order to obtain the pain-relieving effects of the medication. Fordyce suggested that elimination of the opioid medication would contribute to extinction of the pain behaviors.

We (Turk & Okifuji, 1997) showed that physicians were more likely to prescribe opioids for chronic pain patients if the patients were depressed, complained that pain impacted their lives greatly, and showed a large number of pain behaviors even though there were no differences in physical pathology or pain severity. Thus, the opioids were being prescribed for emotional distress, not specifically for pain, and may reinforce and maintain the patients' complaints.

The second development that challenged the use of opioids for chronic pain was the social movement in the 1970s to combat drug abuse. Unfortunately, the campaign to reduce the inappropriate use of drugs was extended into clinical areas. Thus, even appropriate uses of opioids were influenced by concerns about abuse.

Fears of addiction, tolerance, and side effects became prominent. Addiction is often confused with physical dependence. Addiction refers to a behavioral pattern characterized by overwhelming involvement with the use of a drug, securing of its supply, and tendency to relapse despite physical, psychological, and social harm to the user. Physical dependence is a pharmacological property of a drug characterized by the occurrence of withdrawal following abrupt discontinuation of the substance or administration of a drug antagonist and does not imply an aberrant psychological state or behavior. One concern with the use of opioids is that with long-term use, patients will require escalating doses of the medication to obtain the same level of pain relief.

In the mid-1980s, Melzack (1990), and Portenoy & Foley (1986) questioned the generalization from the illicit to the medical use of drugs. They suggested that if the use of opioids produced symptomatic improvement in chronic pain patients, long-term use might be a reasonable treatment.

A number of studies have evaluated the effectiveness of long-term use of opioids in the treatment of chronic pain (see Turk, 1996). The conclusions from these studies are limited, however, because none have been randomized, controlled trials in which the physician and patient were blind to the medications prescribed. Moreover, the trials have been extended for only one year, the average age of chronic pain patients is 44, and there is no experience with the medical use of opioids for periods that might extend for decades. Finally, although many of the studies report significant reductions in pain severity without significant problems, some have noted particular problems with abuse and intolerable side-effects (Turk, 1996). Even when pain is reduced, no studies have found any significant improvement in physical functioning. Moreover, some studies have reported that both pain severity and physical functioning improve following withdrawal from opioids (Flor, Fydrich, & Turk, 1992).

The results of the available studies raise serious concerns about the long-term use of opioids: 1) There are no research studies where the patients or physicians were blind to the drug being prescribed; 2) no studies have shown any improvement in the patients' functioning; 3) there is no experience with the medical uses of opioids extending over decades; 4) some studies have reported significant problems with addiction and side-effects; and 5) the outcomes of pain clinics have demonstrated *reduction of pain* associated with *reduction of opioids*. The central question is not whether chronic pain should be treated with opioids but, rather, what are the characteristics of patients who are able to reduce pain and improve physical and psychological functioning without significant problems? At the present time it seems premature to recommend that opioids be used on a long-term basis for a significant number of patients.

SUMMARY

1. At the psychological level, sensations are experiences associated with simple stimuli. At the biological level, sensory processes involve the sense organs and connecting neural pathways, and are concerned with the initial stages of acquiring stimulus information. The senses include vision; audition (hearing); olfaction (smell); gustation (taste); the skin senses, which include pressure, temperature, and pain; and the body senses.

2. One property that can be used to describe all senses is sensitivity. Sensitivity to stimulus intensity is measured by the absolute threshold, which is the minimum amount of stimulus energy that can be reliably detected. Sensitivity to a change in intensity is measured by the difference threshold or jnd, the minimum difference between two stimuli that can be reliably detected. The amount of change needed for detection to occur increases with the intensity of the stimulus and is approximately proportional to it (the Weber-Fechner law).

3. Every sense modality must recode or transduce its physical energy into neural impulses. This transduction process is accomplished by the receptors. The receptors and connecting neural pathways code the intensity of a stimulus primarily by the rate of neural impulses and their patterns; they code the quality of a stimulus according to the specific nerve fibers involved and their pattern of activity.

4. The stimulus for vision is light, which is electromagnetic radiation in the range from 400 to 700 nanometers. Each eye contains a system for forming the image (including the cornea, pupil, and lens) and a system for transducing the image into electrical impulses. The transduction system is in the retina, which contains the visual receptors, that is, the rods and cones.

5. Cones operate at high light intensities, lead to sensations of color, and are found mainly in the center (or fovea) of the retina; rods operate at low intensities, lead to colorless sensations, and are found mainly in the periphery of the retina. Our sensitivity to the intensity of light is mediated by certain characteristics of the rods and cones. Of particular importance is the fact that rods connect to a larger number of ganglion cells than do cones. Because of this difference in connectivity, visual sensitivity is greater when it is based on rods than when it is based on cones, but visual acuity is greater when it is based on cones than when it is based on rods.

6. Different wavelengths of light lead to sensations of different colors. The appropriate mixture of three lights of widely separated wavelengths can be made to match almost any color of light. This fact and others led to the development of trichromatic theory, which holds that perception of color is based on the activity of three types of receptors (cones), each of which is most sensitive to wavelengths in a different region of the spectrum.

7. There are four basic color sensations: red, yellow, green, and blue. Mixtures of these make up our experiences of color, except that we do not see reddish-greens and yellowish-blues. This can be explained by the opponent-color theory, which proposes that there are red-green and yellow-blue opponent processes, each of which responds in opposite ways to its two opponent colors. Trichromatic and opponent-color theories have been successfully combined through the proposal that they operate at different neural locations in the visual system.

8. The stimulus for audition (hearing) is a wave of pressure changes (a sound wave). The ear includes the outer ear (the external ear and the auditory canal); the middle ear (the eardrum and a chain of bones); and the inner ear. The inner ear includes the cochlea, a coiled tube that contains the basilar membrane, which supports the hair cells that serve as the receptors for sound. Sound waves transmitted by the outer and middle ear cause the basilar membrane to vibrate, resulting in a bending of the hair cells that produces a neural impulse.

9. Pitch, the most striking quality of sound, increases with the frequency of the sound wave. The fact that we can hear the pitches of two different tones sounded simultaneously suggests that there may be many receptors, which respond to different frequencies. Temporal theories of pitch perception postulate that the pitch heard depends on the temporal pattern of neural responses in the auditory system, which itself is determined by the temporal pattern of the sound wave. Place theories postulate that each frequency stimulates a particular place along the basilar membrane more than it stimulates other places, and that the place where the maximum movement occurs determines which pitch is heard. There is room for both theories, as temporal theory explains perception of low frequencies while place theory accounts for perception of high frequencies.

10. Olfaction (smell) is even more important to non-human species than to humans. Many species use specialized odors (pheromones) for communication, and humans seem to possess a vestige of this system. The stimuli for smell are the molecules given off by a substance. The molecules travel through the air and activate olfactory receptors located high in the nasal cavity. There are many kinds of receptors (on the order of 1,000). A normal person can discriminate among 10,000 to 40,000 different odors, with women generally doing better than men.

11. Gustation (taste) is affected not only by the substance being tasted but also by genetic makeup and experience. The stimulus for taste is a substance that is soluble in saliva; many of the receptors occur in clusters on the tongue (taste buds). Sensitivity varies from one place to another on the tongue. Any taste can be described as one or a combination of the four basic taste qualities: sweet, sour, salty, and bitter. Different qualities of taste are coded partly in terms of the specific nerve fibers activated—different fibers respond best to one of the four taste sensations—and partly in terms of the pattern of fibers activated.

12. Two of the skin senses are pressure and temperature. Sensitivity to pressure is greatest at the lips, nose, and cheeks, and least at the big toe. We are very sensitive to temperature, being able to detect a change of less than one degree centigrade. We code different kinds of temperatures primarily by whether hot or cold receptors are activated.

13. Any stimulus that is intense enough to cause tissue damage is a stimulus for pain. There are two distinct kinds of pain, which are mediated by different neural pathways. Phasic pain is typically brief and rapidly rises and falls in intensity; tonic pain is typically long lasting and steady. Sensitivity to pain is greatly influenced by factors other than the noxious stimulus, including expectations and cultural beliefs. These factors seem to exert their influence by opening or closing a neural gate in the spinal cord and midbrain; pain is felt only when pain receptors are activated and the gate is open.

KEY TERMS

sensation (p. 111)
perception (p. 111)
absolute threshold (p. 112)
difference threshold (p. 112)
just noticeable difference (jnd) (p. 112)
reaction time (p. 114)
transduction (p. 115)
visual acuity (p. 122)
spatial acuity (p. 122)

contrast acuity (p. 122)
hue (p. 124)
brightness (p. 124)
saturation (p. 124)
frequency (p. 131)
amplitude (p. 131)
timbre (p. 132)
pitch (p. 135)
pheromones (p. 138)

CRITICAL THINKING QUESTIONS

1. How might you use measurements of the just noticeable difference (jnd) in loudness to describe the change in the auditory environment caused by the addition of a new airline to those serving your local airport? Would you be able to explain your measurement method to a panel of concerned citizens?

2. Some people have described sensory experiences that cross over between two sensory systems. Called *synesthesia,* this apparently can occur both through natural causes and under the influence of a psychoactive drug. For example, people have reported being able to see the "color" of music, or being able to hear the "tunes" associated with different smells. On the basis of what you know about sensory coding, can you think of what might cause such experiences?

3. From an evolutionary standpoint, can you think of reasons why some animals' eyes consist almost entirely of rods, other animals' eyes have only cones, and those of still others, such as humans, have both cones and rods?

4. How would your life change if you did not have a sense of pain? How would it change if you did not have a sense of smell? Which do you think would be worse, and why?

FURTHER READING

There are several good general texts on sensory processes and perception. A particularly clear one is Coren, Ward, & Enns, *Sensation and Perception* (5th ed., 1999). Other useful texts include Goldstein, *Sensation and Perception* (5th ed., 1999), Barlow & Mollon, *The Senses* (1982), and Sekuler & Blake, *Perception* (1985).

For excellent coverage of the biological basis of vision, see Spillman & Werner, *Visual Perception* (1990); for treatments of color vision, see Boynton, *Human Color Vision* (1979), and Lamb & Bourriau, *Colour: Art & Science* (1995). For introductory coverage of audition, see Moore, *An Introduction to the Psychology of Hearing* (2nd ed., 1982). For olfaction, see Engen, *The Perception of Odors* (1982); for touch, see Shiff & Foulke, *Tactual Perception* (1982); and for pain, see Melzack & Wall, *The Challenge of Pain* (1988).

For reference, there are four multivolume handbooks, each of which has several chapters on sensory systems. They are the *Handbook of Perception* (1974–1978), edited by Carterette and Friedman; the *Handbook of Physiology: The Nervous System:* Section 1, Volume 3, *Sensory Processes* (1984), edited by Darian-Smith; the *Handbook of Perception and Human Performance*: Volume 1, *Sensory Processes and Perception* (1986), edited by Boff, Kaufman, and Thomas; and Stevens's *Handbook of Experimental Psychology: Volume 1* (1988), edited by Atkinson, Herrnstein, Lindzey, and Luce.

Chapter 5
Perception

*I*nformation may enter our senses in bits and pieces, but that is not how we perceive the world. We perceive a world of objects and people, a world that bombards us with integrated wholes, not piecemeal sensations. Only under unusual circumstances, or when we are drawing or painting, do we notice the individual features and parts of stimuli; most of the time we see three-dimensional objects and hear words and music.

Perception is *the study of how we integrate sensory information into percepts of objects, and how we then use those percepts to get around in the world* (a *percept* is a product of a perceptual process). Researchers are increasingly approaching the study of perception by asking what problems the perceptual system is designed to solve. Two general problems are often mentioned. The perceptual system must be able to determine what objects are out there (apples, tables, cats, and so on). It must also know where these objects are (at arm's length on my left, hundreds of yards straight ahead, and so on). The same two problems are involved in auditory perception (What was that sound, a phone or a siren? Where was it coming from, in front or in back?) and in other sensory modalities as well. An unusual example of the complexity of perception is described in the Frontiers of Psychological Research feature on page 153.

In vision, the term **object recognition** refers to *determining the meaning of an object.* Object recognition (or simply *recognition)* is crucial for survival because often we have to know what an object is before we can infer some of its important features. Once we know that an object is an apple, for example, we know that it is edible; once we know that an object is a wolf, we know not to disturb it. **Spatial localization** (or *localization)* refers to *determining where visual objects are.* It is also necessary for survival. We use localization to navigate through our environment.

Without such an ability, we would constantly be bumping into objects, failing to grasp things we are reaching for, and moving into the path of dangerous objects and predators.

In addition to localizing and recognizing objects, another goal of our perceptual system is **perceptual constancy,** that is, *keeping the appearance of objects constant even though their impressions on the retina are constantly changing.*

We begin this chapter by considering how the brain divides its perceptual tasks. Then we turn to what is known about the major goals of perception: localization, recognition, and perceptual constancy. Along the way it will be necessary to discuss the role of attention. Finally, we consider the development of perception. Throughout the chapter we focus primarily on visual perception because this is the area that has been most investigated. Keep in mind, though, that the goals of localization, recognition, and constancy seem to apply to all sensory modalities. With regard to recognition, for example, we can use our hearing to recognize a Mozart sonata, our sense of smell to recognize McDonald's fries, our sense of touch to recognize a quarter in our pants pocket, and our body senses to recognize that we are upright in a dark room.

We use spatial localization to navigate through our environment. Without this ability we would be unable to cross a street safely.

FRONTIERS OF PSYCHOLOGICAL RESEARCH

Ending Pain in an Arm That No Longer Exists

Derek Steen lost his left arm as a result of a motorcycle crash that tore all the nerves that attached the arm to his spine. The arm was hopelessly paralyzed, and a year later it was amputated. But Steen experienced a phenomenon that has been reported by many amputees, known as the "phantom limb." He had the sensation that the missing arm was pressing against his body, and it ached horribly.

Pain or discomfort in a phantom limb is exceedingly difficult to treat. After an amputation, the brain modifies its sensory maps. The region mapping a missing arm no longer receives inputs from the arm, but it does receive stimuli from adjacent body parts, and these stimuli fool the brain into thinking that the arm is still there.

Vilayanus S. Ramachandran, a professor of neuroscience at the University of California at San Diego, began wondering why Steen was experiencing the phantom limb sensation even though the arm had been paralyzed prior to the amputation. He concluded that in the first few weeks after the accident, Steen had developed "learned paralysis"; his brain kept sending signals to the arm, commanding it to move, but although he could see that the arm was there, it did not move. "His brain constantly got information that his arm was not moving, even though it was there," Ramachandran comments.

If paralysis can be learned, is it possible that it can be unlearned? Ramachandran decided to test this idea. Like a magician, he "did it with mirrors." He built a box without a front or a lid and placed a vertical mirror in the middle of it. By placing his right arm in the box, Steen could see a mirror image of his missing left arm.

"I asked him to make symmetric movements with both hands, as if he were conducting an orchestra," Ramachandran said. "He started jumping up and down and said, 'Oh, my God, my wrist is moving, my elbow is moving!'" But when asked to close his eyes, Steen groaned and said. "Oh, no, it's frozen again."

Ramachandran told Steen to take the box home with him and play around with it. Three weeks later Steen called him and said, "Doctor, it's gone!"

According to Ramachandran, the reason the phantom arm disappeared probably has to do with tremendous sensory conflict. "His vision was telling him that his arm had come back and was obeying his commands. But he was not getting feedback from the muscles in his arm. Faced with this type of conflict over a protracted period, the brain says: 'This doesn't make sense. I won't have anything to do with it.'"

Ramachandran emphasizes that his technique needs to be tested further and that his conclusions are speculative. But he has succeeded in treating patients with other kinds of phantom limb pain. These results, along with similar findings in other areas of neuroscience, make it abundantly clear that an individual's perceptions can be quite different from the actual stimuli received from the sensory systems (Ramachandran & Blakeslee, 1998).

Division of Labor in the Brain

In the past decade a great deal has been learned about the neural processes underlying perception. At a general level, the part of the brain that is concerned with vision—the visual cortex—operates according to the principle of division of labor: Different regions of the visual cortex are specialized to carry out different perceptual functions (Kosslyn & Koenig, 1992; Zeki, 1993).

The Visual Cortex

There are over 100 million neurons in the cortex that are sensitive to visual input. Everything we know about them and the way they function has been learned through a small number of techniques. In studies involving animals, what we know is based largely on research in which electrical impulses are recorded (using microelectrodes) from single cells, as discussed in Chapter 4. Modern techniques for conducting such research owe much to the pioneering work done by David Hubel and Torstein Wiesel, who received the Nobel prize in 1981.

In studies involving humans, much of what we know comes from "natural experiments"—that is, cases of brain injury and disease that cast light on how visual behaviors relate to specific regions of the brain. Researchers in this area include neurologists (medical doctors who specialize in the

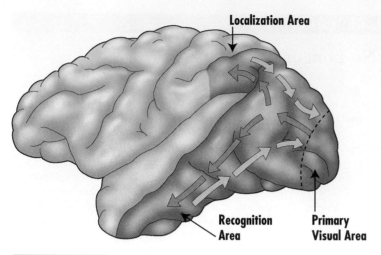

Two Cortical Visual Systems   *The arrows going from the back of the brain toward the top depict the localization system; the arrows going from the back toward the bottom of the brain depict the recognition system.* (After Mishkin, Ungerleider, & Macko, 1983)

brain) and neuropsychologists (psychologists who specialize in treating and studying patients with brain injury). An excellent introduction to this area is presented in Oliver Sacks's (1987) *The Man Who Mistook His Wife for a Hat.*

Today the most exciting discoveries about the human brain are being made by taking pictures of the brain without surgery. This field is called *brain imaging* and includes techniques such as event related potentials (ERPs), positron emission tomography (PET), and functional magnetic resonance imaging (fMRI).

The most important region of the brain for visual processing is the area known as the *primary visual cortex,* or V1. Its location at the back, or posterior, part of the brain is shown in Figure 5-1. This is the first location in the cerebral cortex to which neurons sending signals from the eye are connected. All the other visually sensitive regions of the cortex (more than 30 such locations have been identified) are connected to the eyes through V1.

As has so often been the case, the function of V1 was discovered long before the development of modern recording or imaging techniques. It first became obvious when physicians examined patients who had suffered localized head injuries through acci-

dent or war. Tissue damage (technically referred to as a *lesion*) to a specific part of V1 was linked to blindness in very specific parts of the visual field (technically, a *scotoma*) (see Figure 5-2). Note that this form of blindness is not caused by damage to the eyes or the optic nerve; it is entirely cortical in origin. For example, the very center of the visual field—the fovea—will suffer a scotoma if a lesion occurs at the extreme rear of V1. Scotomas in more peripheral portions of the visual field are caused by lesions farther forward in V1. It is as though a map of the visual field has been stretched over the back of the cortex, with its center directly over the rearmost part of the cortex.

However, the "map" is upside down and mirror reversed. Points in the upper half of the visual field are mapped below a major cortical fold or valley, while locations in the lower half of the visual field are represented just above this fold. The left half of the visual field is mapped onto the right side of V1, while the right half of the visual field is mapped onto the left side.

Neurons in the primary visual cortex are sensitive to many features contained in a visual image, such as brightness, color, orientation, and motion. However, one of the most important features of these neurons is that they are each responsible for analyzing only a very tiny region of the image. In the foveal part of the image, this can be as small as less than 1 millimeter seen at arm's length. These neurons also communicate with one another only in very small regions. The benefit of this arrangement is that the entire visual field can be analyzed simultaneously and in great detail. What is missing from this analysis, however, is the ability to coordinate information that is not close together in the image—that is, to see the "forest" in addition to the "trees."

To accomplish this task, cortical neurons send information from V1 to the many other regions of the brain that analyze visual information. Each of these regions specializes in a particular task, such as analyzing color, motion, shape, and location. These more specialized regions are also in constant contact with V1, so that the neural communication between regions is better thought of as a conversation than as a command (Damasio, 1990; Zeki, 1993). One of the most important divisions of labor in visual analysis by the brain is between localization and recognition, to which we now turn.

Recognition Versus Localization Systems

The idea that localization and recognition are qualitatively different tasks is supported by research findings showing that they are carried out by different regions of the visual cortex. Recognition of objects depends on a branch of the visual system that includes the primary visual cortex and a region near the bottom of the cerebral cortex. In contrast, localization of objects depends on a branch of the visual system that includes the primary visual cortex and a region of the cortex near the top of the brain (see Figure 5-1). Studies with nonhuman primates show that if the recognition branch of an animal's visual system is impaired, the animal can still perform tasks that require it to perceive spatial relations between objects (one in front of the other, for example) but cannot perform tasks that require discriminating between the actual objects—for example, tasks that require discriminating a cube from a cylinder. If the location branch is impaired, the animal can perform tasks that require it to distinguish a cube from a cylinder, but it cannot perform tasks that require it to know where the objects are in relation to each other (Mishkin, Ungerleider, & Macko, 1983).

More recent research has used brain imaging to document the existence of separate object and location systems in the human brain. One widely used technique is PET (discussed in Chapter 2). A participant first has a radioactive tracer injected into her bloodstream and then is placed in a PET scanner while she performs various tasks. The scanner measures increases in radioactivity in various brain regions, which indicate increases in blood flow to those regions. The regions that show the most increase in blood flow are the ones that mediate performance of the task.

In one such study, participants performed two tasks, one a test of face recognition, which depends on the brain region for object recognition, and the other a test of mental rotation, which requires localization. In the face-recognition task, participants saw a target picture with two test faces beneath it

DAMAGE	VISUAL FIELD LOSS
(a) Half-field Lesion 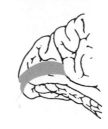	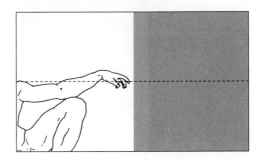
(b) Local lesion 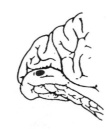	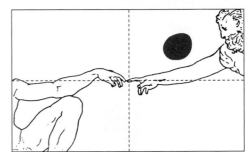
(c) Quarter-field lesion 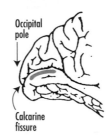Occipital pole Calcarine fissure	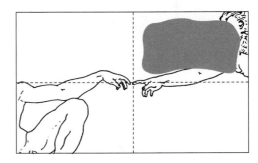

FIGURE 5-2

The visual consequences of various kinds of lesions in the primary visual cortex (V1). *The "map" of the visual field is upside down and mirror reversed.*

during each trial. One of the test faces was the face of the person depicted by the target, except for changes in orientation and lighting; the other was the face of a different person. The participant's task was to decide which test face was the same as the target (see Figure 5-3a). While the participant was engaging in this task, there was an increase in blood flow in the recognition branch of the cortex (the branch terminating near the bottom of the cortex), but not in the localization branch (the branch terminating near the top of the cortex).

Very different results were obtained with the mental rotation task. In this task, on

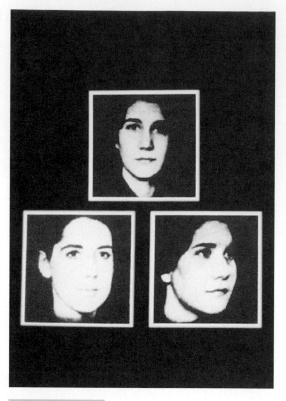
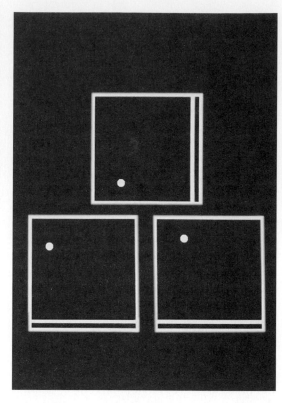

a   b

FIGURE 5-3

Recognition and Localization Tasks   *Sample items from the face-matching (a) and dot-location (b) matching tasks.* (From Grady et al., 1992)

each trial, participants saw a target display of a dot at some distance from a double line; beneath the target were two test displays. One test display was the same as the target, except that it had been rotated; the other test display contained a different configuration of the dot and lines (see Figure 5-3b). While engaging in this task, participants showed an increase in blood flow in the localization branch of the cortex, but not in the recognition branch. Localization and recognition, therefore, are carried out in entirely different regions of the visual cortex (Grady et al., 1992; Haxby et al., 1990).

The division of labor in the visual cortex does not end with the split between localization and recognition. Rather, the different kinds of information that are used in localization—eye movements, motion analysis, and depth perception, for example—are themselves processed by different subregions of the localization branch of the cortex. Similarly, the various kinds of information used in recognition—shape, color, and tex-

ture—also have specialized subregions devoted to their analysis (Livingstone & Hubel, 1988; Zeki, 1993). The upshot of all this is that the visual cortex consists of numerous "processing modules," each of which is specialized for a particular task. The more we learn about the neural basis of other sensory modalities (and other psychological functions as well), the more this modular, or division-of-labor, approach seems to hold.

Localization

To know where the objects in our environment are, the first thing that we have to do is separate the objects from one another and from the background. Then the perceptual system can determine the position of the objects in a three-dimensional world, including their distance from us and their patterns of movement. In this section we discuss each of these perceptual abilities in turn.

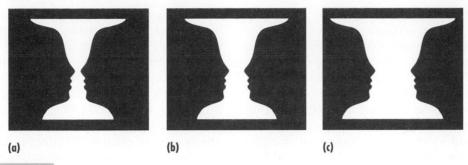

(a)   **(b)**   **(c)**

FIGURE 5-4

Reversible Figure and Ground   *Three patterns in which either a white vase or a pair of black faces can be seen. Note that it is impossible to see both organizations at the same time, even though you know that both are possible percepts. When the white area is smaller (a), the vase is more likely to be seen; when the black area is smaller (c), the faces are more likely to be seen.*

Separation of Objects

The image projected on our retina is a mosaic of varying brightnesses and colors. Somehow our perceptual system organizes that mosaic into a set of discrete objects projected against a background. This kind of organization was of great concern to Gestalt psychologists. (Recall from Chapter 1 that Gestalt psychology was an approach to psychology that began in Germany early in the 20th century.) The Gestalt psychologists emphasized the importance of perceiving whole objects or forms, and proposed a number of principles to explain how we organize objects.

Figure and Ground   In a stimulus that contains two or more distinct regions, we usually see part of it as a *figure* and the rest as *ground* (or background). The regions seen as a figure contain the objects of interest—they appear more solid than the ground and appear in front of it. This is the most elementary form of perceptual organization. Figure 5-4a shows that figure-ground organization can be ambiguous. When you look at this pattern you might see a pair of silhouette faces gazing at each other, or you might see an ornate vase. The vase appears white against a black ground, whereas the faces are black against a white ground. Notice that as you look at Figure 5-4b for a few moments, the two pattern organizations alternate in consciousness, demonstrating that the organization into figure and ground is in your mind, not in the stimulus. Notice, also, that the faces and the vase never appear together. You "know" that both are possible, but you can-

FIGURE 5-5

The Slave Market with a Disappearing Bust of Voltaire   *A reversible figure is in the center of this painting by Salvador Dali (1940). Two nuns standing in an archway reverse to form a bust of Voltaire.*

not "see" both at the same time. Generally speaking, the smaller an area or a shape, the more likely it is to be seen as figure. This is demonstrated by comparing Figures 5-4a, b, and c. It is easier to see the vase when the white area is smaller, and it is easier to see the faces when the black area is smaller (Weisstein & Wong, 1986).

Figure 5-5 illustrates a more complex reversible figure-ground effect. (Note that we can perceive figure-ground relations in senses other than vision. For example, we may hear the song of a bird against a background of outdoor noises, or the melody played by a violin against the harmonies of the rest of the orchestra.)

Grouping of Objects We see not only objects against a ground, but a particular grouping of the objects as well. Even simple patterns of dots fall into groups when we look at them. To illustrate this, begin by looking at the matrix of dots shown in Figure 5-6a. These dots are equally spaced up and down, so they can be seen as being organized in rows or columns, or even as lying along diagonal paths. This is, therefore, an ambiguous pattern that follows similar principles to those illustrated in Figures 5-4 and 5-5. Only one organization is seen at a time, and at intervals this organization will spontaneously switch to another.

The Gestalt psychologists proposed a number of determinants of grouping for these kinds of dot patterns. For instance, if the vertical distance between dots is reduced, as in Figure 5-6b, columns will most likely be seen. This is grouping by *proximity.* If instead of varying the dot distances we vary the color shape of the elements, we can organize the dots on the basis of *similarity* (Figures 5-6c and d). If we move the dots to form two intersecting wave lines of dots, we are grouping by *good continuation* (Figure 5-6e), and if we enclose a space using lines of dots, we will tend to see grouping by *closure.* Note that in this last case we see a diamond positioned between two vertical lines, even though the pattern could be two familiar letters stacked on each other (W on M) or even facing each other (K and a mirror-image K). This illustrates the powerful nature of the Gestalt grouping determinants. These determinants serve to create the most stable, consistent, and simple forms possible within a given pattern.

Modern research on visual grouping has shown that the Gestalt determinants have a strong influence on perception. For example, in one series of studies, visual targets that were part of larger visual groupings based on proximity were much harder to detect than the same targets seen as standing outside the group (Banks & Prinzmetal, 1976; Prinzmetal, 1981). In another set of studies, targets that were dissimilar to nontargets in color and shape were easier to find than targets that were more similar (Triesman, 1986). Even the similarity among the various nontargets has an important effect: Targets are easier to find as the similarity of nontargets increases, allowing the target to "pop out" as a figure distinct from the background (Duncan & Humphreys, 1989). Finally, there are reliable illusions associated with the Gestalt determinants, such that people judge distances among the elements within perceptual groups to be smaller than the same distances when they are between elements in different groups (Coren & Girgus, 1980; Enns & Girgus, 1985). All of these results show that visual groping plays a large role in the way we organize our visual experience.

Although perceptual grouping has been studied mainly in visual perception, the same determinants of grouping appear in

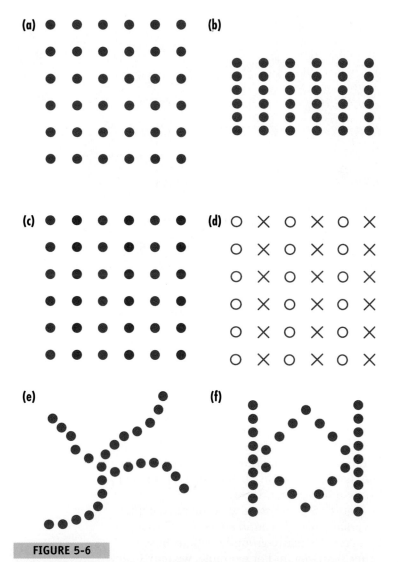

FIGURE 5-6

Gestalt Determinants of Grouping *(a) Equally spaced dots can be seen as rows, columns, or even diagonals; (b) Grouping into columns by proximity; (c) Grouping into columns by color similarity; (d) Grouping into columns by shape similarity; (e) Grouping by good continuation; (f) Grouping by closure.*

audition. Proximity clearly operates in audition (though it is proximity in time rather than in space). For example, four drumbeats with a pause between the second and third beats will be heard as two pairs. Similarity and closure are also known to play important roles in hearing tones and more complex stimuli (Bregman, 1990).

Perceiving Distance

To know where an object is, we must know its distance or depth. Although perceiving an object's depth seems effortless, it is a remarkable achievement given the physical structure of our eyes. In this section we take a closer look at how we perceive distance.

Depth Cues   The retina is a two-dimensional surface. This means that the retinal image is flat and has no depth at all. Therefore, we must use two-dimensional cues or *depth cues* to infer distance in a three-dimensional world. There are a number of cues that combine to determine perceived distance. The cues can be classified as monocular or binocular, depending on whether they involve one or both eyes.

A person using only one eye can perceive depth remarkably well by picking up monocular depth cues. Figure 5-7 illustrates five such cues that can be found in all natural scenes. The first is *relative size*. If an image contains an array of similar objects that differ in size, the viewer interprets the smaller

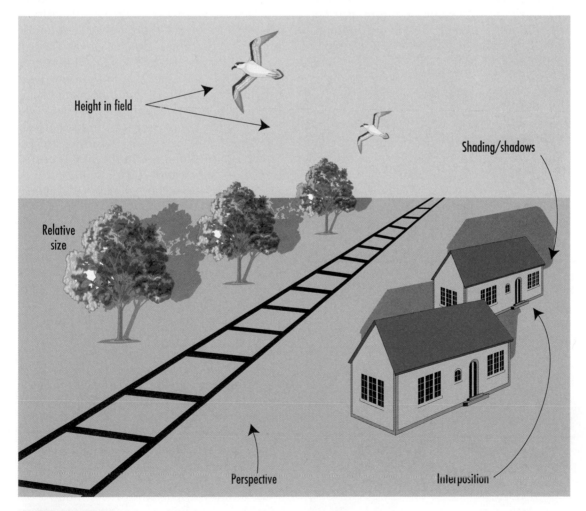

FIGURE 5-7

Monocular Distance Cues in a Picture   *Artists use some or all of these cues in combination to portray depth on a two-dimensional surface. All of these cues are present in a photograph of a natural scene and are also present on the retinal image in our eye.*

objects as being farther away (see the trees in Figure 5-7). A second monocular cue is *interposition*. If one object is positioned so that it obstructs the view of the other, the viewer perceives the overlapping object as being nearer (see the buildings in Figure 5-7). A third cue is *relative height*. Among similar objects, those that appear closer to the horizon are perceived as being farther away (see the birds in Figure 5-7). A fourth cue is *linear perspective*. When parallel lines in a scene appear to converge in the image, they are perceived as vanishing in the distance (see the railroad tracks in Figure 5-7).

A fifth cue is *shading and shadows*. Whenever a surface in a scene is blocked from receiving direct light, a shadow is cast. If that shadow falls on a part of the same object that is blocking the light, it is called an *attached shadow* or simply *shading*. If it falls on another surface that does not belong to the object casting the shadow, it is called a *cast shadow*. Both kinds of shadows are important cues to depth in the scene, giving us information about object shapes, distances between objects, and where the light source is in a scene (Coren, Ward, & Enns, 1999).

These five cues have been known to artists for centuries, and a single painting often uses more than one of the cues.

Another important monocular cue involves motion. Have you ever noticed that if you are moving quickly—perhaps on a fast-moving train—nearby objects seem to move quickly in the opposite direction while more distant objects move more slowly (though still in the opposite direction)? Extremely distant objects, such as the moon, appear not to move at all. The difference in the speeds with which these objects appear to move provides a cue to their distance from us and is termed *motion parallax.*

Seeing with both eyes rather than one gives an important advantage for depth perception. Because the eyes are separated in the head, each eye has a slightly different view of the same scene. You can easily demonstrate this by holding your right index finger close to your face and examining it first with only one eye open and then with only the other eye open. The term **binocular disparity** is used to refer to *the difference in the views seen by each eye.* The disparity is largest for objects that are seen at close range and becomes smaller as the object recedes into the distance. Beyond 3–4 meters (10–12 feet), the difference in the views seen by each eye is so small that binocular disparity loses its effectiveness as a cue for depth. However, for many everyday tasks, such as reaching for objects and navigating around obstacles, the difference in the views seen by each eye is a powerful cue for depth.

In humans and other animals with binocular vision, the visual part of the brain uses binocular disparity to assign objects to various locations in space, depending on how far apart the two images of an object are when compared. If the images of an object are in the same place in the two views, the brain assumes that this is the location on which both eyes are fixating. If the difference between the images is large, as it is for the two views of your finger held close to your face, the brain concludes that the object is much closer.

In addition to helping us see depth in the everyday world, binocular disparity can be used to fool the eye into seeing depth when none is really present. One way this is achieved is by using a device called a *stereoscope,* which displays a different photograph to each eye. In Victorian times these devices were proudly displayed in the sitting rooms of middle-class homes, much as wide-screen television sets might be today. Yet the stereoscope is not just a curious antique. The same principle of binocular disparity is used today in children's "View Master" toys, in "special

The Holmes-Bates stereoscope, invented by Oliver Wendell Holmes in 1861 and manufactured by Joseph Bates, creates a vivid perception of depth.

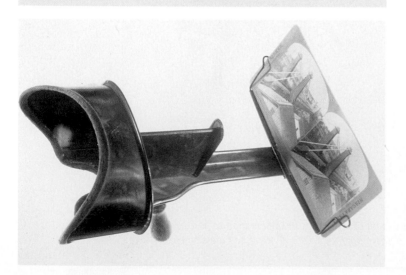

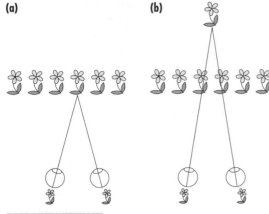

(a)   **(b)**

FIGURE 5-8

The Magic of 3-D Vision in Pictures   *What the eyes normally do when viewing a picture, such as the row of flowers shown in (a), is to converge on the point in space belonging to the picture plane. In this case, both eyes will receive the identical image and the surface will look flat. Every 3-D illusion involving pictures is based on fooling the eyes so that they converge to a different point in space, as shown in (b). In this case, the two eyes will receive slightly different images. If the brain is fooled into thinking that the different images belong to the same scene, either by having similar patterns in the two images (Magic Eye art) or because the images to the eyes have been bent by prisms (View Master toy), small differences (disparity) in the images will be resolved by assigning objects to different locations in depth.*

effects" 3-D movies for which viewers must wear glasses with colored or light-polarizing filters, and in the popular "Magic Eye" poster art. The principle behind all of these illusions is illustrated in Figure 5-8.

Perceiving Motion

If we are to move around our environment effectively, we need to know not only the locations of static objects but also the trajectories of moving ones. We need to know, for example, not only that the object located a few feet in front of us is a softball, but also that it is coming at us at a fast clip. This brings us to the issue of how we perceive motion.

Stroboscopic Motion   What causes us to perceive motion? The simplest idea is that we perceive an object is in motion whenever its image moves across our retina. This answer turns out to be too simple, though, for we can see motion even when nothing moves on our retina. This phenomenon was demonstrated in 1912 by Wertheimer in his studies

To catch the ball and avoid being tackled, football players must be able to perceive motion accurately.

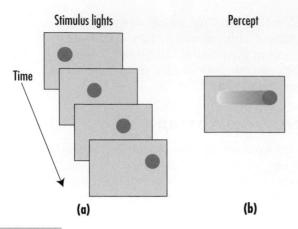

Stimulus lights   Percept

Time

(a)   (b)

Stroboscopic Motion *The sequence of still frames in (a), shown at the appropriate intervals, will result in the percept shown in (b). The illusion of continuous motion resulting from successively viewed still pictures is the basis of motion in movies, video, and television.*

of *stroboscopic motion* (see Figure 5-9). Stroboscopic motion is produced most simply by flashing a light in darkness and then, a few milliseconds later, flashing another light near the location of the first light. The light will seem to move from one place to the other in a way that is indistinguishable from real motion.

The motion that we see in movies is stroboscopic. The film is simply a series of still photographs (or "frames"), each one slightly different from the preceding ones. The frames are projected on the screen in rapid sequence, with dark intervals in between. The rate at which the frames are presented is critical. In the early days of motion pictures, the frame rate was 16 per second, mainly because there was no way to take photographs more rapidly. This rate was too slow, causing movement in these early films to appear too rapid, as well as jerky and disjointed. Today the rate is usually 24–30 frames per second (with each frame typically shown a few times in succession to further reduce jerkiness).

Induced Motion Another case in which we perceive motion in the absence of movement across the retina is the phenomenon of *induced motion*. When a large object surrounding a smaller one moves, the smaller object may appear to be the one that is moving, even if it is static. This phenomenon was first studied by the Gestalt psychologist Duncker in 1929. Participants sat in a darkened room and observed a small luminous

circle inside a larger luminous rectangular frame. When the rectangle was moved to the right, participants reported that the circle appeared to move to the left. This phenomenon can be seen on a windy night when the moon seems to be racing through the clouds. It is also operating when we think that our car is rolling backward at a stoplight, despite the fact that our foot is jammed on the break. In this case, the inducing stimulus is often a large truck, seen out of the corner of our eye, that is slowly rolling forward. The illusory motion is attributed to ourselves and our car, even though there are no vestibular cues for such motion.

Real Motion Of course, our visual system is also sensitive to *real motion*—that is, movement of an object through all intermediate points in space. However, the analysis of such motion under everyday conditions is amazingly complex. Some paths of motion on the retina must be attributed to movements of the eye over a stationary scene (as occurs when we are reading). Other motion paths must be attributed to moving objects (as when a bird enters our visual field). Moreover, some objects whose retinal images are stationary must be seen to be moving (as when we follow the flying bird with our eyes), while some objects whose retinal images are moving must be seen as stationary (as when the stationary background traces motion across the retina because our eyes are pursuing a flying bird).

It therefore is not surprising that our analysis of motion is highly relative. We are much better at detecting motion when we can see an object against a structured background (*relative motion*) than when the background is a uniform color and only the moving object can be seen (*absolute motion*). Certain patterns of relative movement can even serve as powerful cues to the shape and identity of three-dimensional objects. For example, researchers have found that the motion displays illustrated in Figure 5-10 are sufficient to enable viewers to easily identify the activity of a human figure, even though it consists of only 12 (or even fewer) points of light moving relative to one another (Johansson, von Hofsten, & Jansson, 1980). In other studies using these displays, viewers were able to identify their friends and even tell whether the model was male or female after seeing only the lights attached to the ankles (Cutting, 1986).

Another important phenomenon in the study of real motion is *selective adaptation*. This is a loss in sensitivity to motion that occurs when we view motion; the adaptation is selective in that we lose sensitivity to the motion viewed and to similar motions, but not to motion that differs significantly in direction or speed. If we look at upward-moving stripes, for example, we lose sensitivity to upward motion, but our ability to see downward motion is not affected (Sekuler, 1975). As with other types of adaptation, we do not usually notice the loss of sensitivity, but we do notice the aftereffect produced by adaptation. If we view a waterfall for a few minutes and then look at the cliff beside it, the cliff will appear to move upward. Most motions will produce such aftereffects, always in the opposite direction from the original motion.

How does the brain implement the perception of real motion? Some aspects of real motion are coded by specific cells in the visual cortex. These cells respond to some motions and not to others, and each cell responds best to one direction and speed of motion. The best evidence for the existence of such cells comes from studies with animals in which the experimenter records the responses of single cells in the visual cortex while the animal is shown stimuli with different patterns of motion. Such single-cell recording studies have found cortical cells that are tuned to particular directions of movement. There are even cells that are specifically tuned to detect an object moving toward the head, an ability that is clearly useful for survival (Regan, Beverly, & Cynader, 1979). Again, it is striking how the visual cortex distributes its various jobs over different areas and cells.

These specialized motion cells provide a possible explanation for selective adaptation and the motion aftereffect. Presumably, selective adaptation to an upward motion, for example, occurs because the cortical cells that are specialized for upward motion have become fatigued. Because the cells that are specialized for downward motion are functioning as usual, they will dominate the processing and result in the aftereffect of downward motion.

However, there is more to the neural basis of real motion than the activation of specific cells. We can see motion when we track a

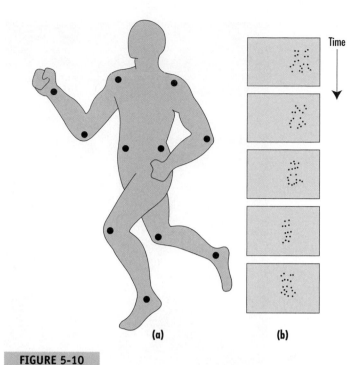

(a)   (b)

FIGURE 5-10

Patterns of Human Motion   *This is an example of the type of displays used by investigators to study patterns of humans in motion. Positions of lights affixed to individuals are indicated in (a). A sequence of movement positions made by a dancing couple is represented in (b).*

luminous object moving in darkness (such as an airplane at night). Because our eyes follow the object, the image is almost motionless on the retina, yet we perceive a smooth, continuous motion. Why? The answer seems to be that information about how our eyes are moving is sent from motor regions in the front of the brain to the visual cortex and influences the motion we see. In essence, the motor system is informing the visual system that it is responsible for the lack of regular motion on the retina, and the visual system then corrects for this lack. In more normal viewing situations, there are both eye movements and large retinal-image movements. The visual system must combine these two sources of information to determine the perceived motion.

Recognition

We turn now to the second major function of perception: recognizing what an object is. Recognizing an object amounts to assigning it to a category—that's a shirt, that's a cat, that's a daisy, and so on. Of

In the early stages of recognition, the perceptual system uses information on the retina to describe the object in terms of primitive components like lines and edges. In later stages, the system compares this description to those of various categories of objects stored in the visual memory, such as "dogs."

course, we can also recognize people, which amounts to assigning the visual input to a particular individual—that's Ben Murphy, this is Irene Paull. In either case, recognition allows us to infer many hidden properties of the object: If it's a shirt, it's made of cloth and I can wear it; if it's a cat, it may scratch me if I pull its tail; if it's Ben Murphy, he'll want to tell me about his baseball exploits; and so on.

What attributes of an object do we use to recognize it—shape, size, color, texture, orientation? While all of these attributes may make some contribution, shape appears to play the most critical role. We can recognize a cup, for example, regardless of whether it is large or small (a variation in size), brown or white (a variation in color), smooth or bumpy (a variation in texture),

or presented upright or tilted slightly (a variation in orientation). In contrast, our ability to recognize a cup is strikingly affected by variations in shape; if part of the cup's shape is hidden, we may not recognize it at all. One piece of evidence for the importance of shape is that we can recognize many objects about as well from simple line drawings, which preserve only the shapes of the objects, as from detailed color photographs, which preserve many other attributes of the objects as well (Biederman & Ju, 1988).

The critical question then becomes: How do we use the shape of an object to assign it to its appropriate category? In dealing with this question, we first focus on simple objects like letters of the alphabet and then consider natural objects like animals and furniture.

Early Stages of Recognition

Many researchers distinguish between early and late stages in recognizing an object. We will characterize these stages by what they accomplish. In early stages, the perceptual system uses information on the retina, particularly variations in intensity, to describe the object in terms of primitive components like lines, edges, and angles. The system uses these components to construct a description of the object. In later stages, the system compares this description to those of various categories of objects stored in visual memory and selects the best match. To recognize a particular object as the letter B, for example, is to say that the object's shape matches that of B's better than it matches that of other letters.

Feature Detectors in the Cortex Much of what is known about the primitive features of object perception comes from biological studies of other species (such as cats and monkeys) using single-cell recordings in the visual cortex. These studies examine the sensitivity of specific cortical neurons when different stimuli are presented to the regions of the retina associated with those neurons; such a retinal region is called a *receptive field*.

These single-cell studies were pioneered by Hubel and Wiesel (1968). They identified

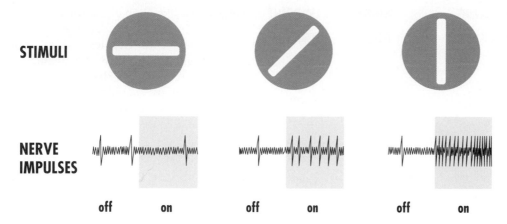

STIMULI

NERVE
IMPULSES

off   on   off   on   off   on

FIGURE 5-11

The Response of a Simple Cell   *This figure illustrates the response of a simple cortical cell to a bar of light. The stimulus is on the top, the response on the bottom; each vertical spike on the bottom corresponds to one nerve impulse. When there is no stimulus, only an occasional impulse is recorded. When the stimulus is turned on, the cell may or may not respond, depending on the position and orientation of the light bar. For this cell, a horizontal bar produces no change in response, a bar at 45 degrees produces a small change, and a vertical bar produces a very large change.*

three types of cells in the visual cortex that can be distinguished by the features to which they respond. *Simple cells* respond when the eye is exposed to a line stimulus (such as a thin bar or straight edge between a dark and a light region) at a particular orientation and position within its receptive field. Figure 5-11 illustrates how a simple cell will respond to a vertical bar and to bars tilted away from the vertical. The largest response is obtained for a vertical bar, and the response decreases as the orientation varies from the optimal one. Other simple cells are tuned to other orientations and positions. A *complex cell* also responds to a bar or edge in a particular orientation, but it does not require that the stimulus be at a particular place within its receptive field. It will respond continuously as the stimulus is moved across that field. *Hypercomplex cells* require not only that the stimulus be in a particular orientation, but also that it be of a particular length. If a stimulus is extended beyond the optimal length, the response will decrease and may cease entirely. Since Hubel and Wiesel's initial reports, investigators have found cells that respond to shape features other than single bars and edges; for example, there are hypercomplex cells that respond to corners or angles of a specific length (DeValois & DeValois, 1980; Shapley & Lennie, 1985).

All of the cells described above are referred to as *feature detectors*. Because the edges, bars, corners, and angles to which these detectors respond can be used to approximate many shapes, the feature detectors might be thought of as the building blocks of shape perception. As we will see later, though, this proposal seems to be more true of simple shapes like letters than of complex shapes like those of tables and tigers.

Relationships Between Features   There is more to a description of a shape than just its features: The relationships between features must also be specified. The importance of such relationships is illustrated in Figure 5-12. For example, the features of a right angle and a diagonal line must be combined in a specific way to result in a triangle. A Y-intersection and a hexagon must be specifically aligned to result in the drawing of a cube. It was these kinds of relationships between features that Gestalt psychologists had in mind when they emphasized that "the whole is different from the sum of its parts."

One way the whole is different is that it creates new perceptual features that cannot be understood by simply examining the component parts. Figure 5-12 shows four such *emergent features*. These features emerge from very specific spatial relationships among more elementary features. Nevertheless, they often

COMPONENT	COMPONENT	WHOLE	EMERGENT
FEATURE A	+ FEATURE B =	OBJECT	PROPERTY

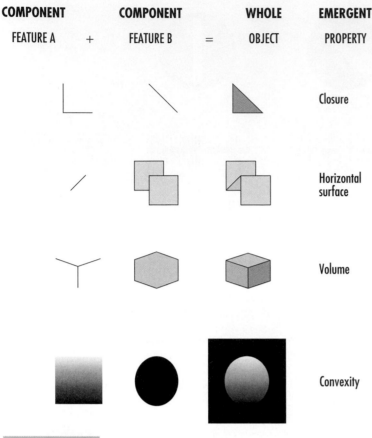

Closure

Horizontal surface

Volume

Convexity

FIGURE 5-12

Relationships Between Features *When simple two-dimensional features such as lines, angles, and shapes are combined, the resulting pattern is highly dependent on the spatial relations between the component features. In addition, new features are created. These emergent features have a perceptual reality even though they involve complex spatial relations.*

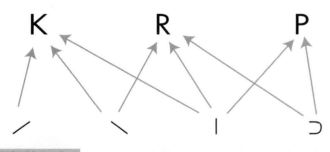

FIGURE 5-13

A Simple Network *The bottom level of the network contains the features (ascending diagonal, descending diagonal, vertical line, and right-facing curve), the top level contains the letters, and a connection between a feature and a letter means that the feature is part of the letter. Because the connections are excitatory, when a feature is activated, the activation spreads to the letter.*

behave just like simpler features in perceptual tasks such as target detection and visual search (Enns & Resnick, 1990; Enns & Prinzmetal, 1984; He & Nakayama, 1992). These results indicate that the visual system performs many sophisticated analyses of shape before the results of these analyses are made available to consciousness.

Later Stages of Recognition

Now that we have some idea of how an object's shape is described, we can consider how that description is matched to shape descriptions stored in memory to find the best match.

Simple Networks Much of the research on the matching stage has used simple patterns, specifically handwritten or printed letters or words. Figure 5-13 illustrates a proposal about how we store shape descriptions of letters. The basic idea is that letters are described in terms of certain features, and that knowledge about what features go with what letter is contained in a network of connections. Such proposals are referred to as *connectionist models.* What is appealing about these models is that it is easy to conceive how these networks could be realized in the brain with its array of interconnected neurons. Thus, connectionism offers a bridge between psychological and biological models.

The bottom level of the network in Figure 5-13 contains the features: ascending diagonal, descending diagonal, vertical line, and right-facing curve. The top level contains the letters themselves. We will refer to each of these features and letters as a *node* in the network. A connection between a feature and a letter node means that the feature is part of the letter. The fact that the connections have arrowheads at their ends means that they are excitatory connections; if the feature is activated, the activation spreads to the letter (in a manner analogous to the way electrical impulses spread in a network of neurons).

To see how this network can be used to recognize (or match) a letter, consider what happens when the letter K is presented. It will activate the features of ascending diagonal,

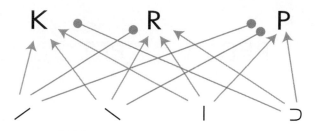

descending diagonal, and vertical line. All three of these features will activate the node for K; two of them—the descending diagonal and vertical line—will activate the node for R; and one of them—the vertical line—will activate the node for P. Only the K node has all of its features activated, and consequently it will be selected as the best match.

This model is too simple to account for many aspects of recognition, however. Consider what happens when the letter R is presented. It activates the features of descending diagonal, vertical line, and right-facing curve. Now the nodes for both R and P have all their features activated, and the model has no way of deciding which of the two categories provides a better match. What the model needs to know is that the presence of a descending diagonal means that the letter cannot be a P. This kind of negative knowledge is included in the augmented network in Figure 5-14. This network has everything the preceding one had, plus inhibitory connections (symbolized by solid circles at their ends) between features and letters that do not contain those features. When a feature is connected to a letter by an inhibitory connection, activating the feature decreases activation of the letter. Thus, when R is presented to the network in Figure 5-14, the descending diagonal inhibits the P node, thereby decreasing its overall level of activation; now the R node will receive the most activation and, consequently, will be selected as the best match.

Networks With Feedback The basic idea behind the model we just considered—that a letter must be described by the features it lacks as well as by the features it contains—does not explain why a letter is easier to perceive when it is presented as part of a word than when it is presented alone. Thus, if individuals are briefly presented with a display containing either the single letter K or the word WORK, and are then asked whether the last letter was a K or a D, they are more accurate when the display contained a word than when it contained only a letter (see Figure 5-15).

To account for this result, our network of feature-letter connections has to be altered in a few ways. First, we have to add a level of words to our network, and along with it

---

FIGURE 5-14

An Augmented Network *The network contains inhibitory connections between features and letters that do not contain these features, as well as excitatory connections.*

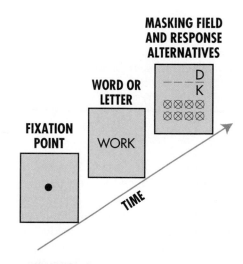

FIGURE 5-15

Perception of Letters and Words *This figure illustrates the sequence of events in an experiment that compares the perceptibility of a letter presented alone or in the context of a word. First, participants saw a fixation point, followed by a word or a single letter, which was present for only a few milliseconds. Then the experimenter presented a stimulus that contained a visual mask in the positions where the letters had been, plus two response alternatives. The task was to decide which of the two alternatives occurred in the word or letter presented earlier. (After Reicher, 1969)*

---

excitatory and inhibitory connections that go from letters to words (see Figure 5-16). In addition, we have to add excitatory connections that go from words down to letters; these top-down feedback connections explain why a letter is more perceptible when presented briefly in a word than

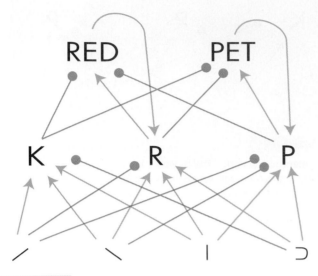

FIGURE 5-16

A Network with Top-Down Activation   *The network contains excitatory and inhibitory connections between letters and words (as well as between features and letters), and some of the excitatory connections go from words to letters.*

when presented briefly alone. When R is presented alone, for example, the features of vertical line, descending diagonal, and right-facing curve are activated, and this activation spreads to the node for R. Because the letter was presented very briefly, not all the features may have been fully activated, and the activation culminating at the R node may not be sufficient for recognition to occur. In contrast, when R is presented in RED, there is activation not only from the features of R to the R node, but also from the features of E and D to their nodes; all of these partially activated letters then partially activate the RED node, which in turn feeds back activation to its letters via its top-down connections.

The upshot is that there is an additional source of activation for R when it is presented in a word—namely, activation coming from the word—and this is why it is easier to recognize a letter in a word than when it is presented alone. Many other findings about letter and word patterns have been shown to be consistent with this connectionist model (McClelland & Rumelhart, 1981). Models like these have also been used successfully in machines designed to read handwriting and recognize speech (Coren, Ward, & Enns, 1999).

Recognizing Natural Objects and Top-Down Processing

We know quite a bit about the recognition of letters and words, but what about more natural objects—animals, plants, people, furniture, and clothing? In this section we examine how we recognize such objects.

Features of Natural Objects   The shape features of natural objects are more complex than lines and curves, and more like simple geometric forms. These features must be such that they can combine to form the shape of any recognizable object (just as lines and curves can combine to form any letter). The features of objects must also be such that they can be determined or constructed from more primitive features, such as lines and curves, because, as noted earlier, primitive features are the only information available to the system in the early stages of recognition.

It has been suggested that the features of objects include a number of geometric forms, such as cylinders, cones, blocks, and wedges, as illustrated in Figure 5-17a. These features, referred to as *geons* (short for "geometric ions"), were identified by Biederman (1987). Biederman argues that a set of 36 geons, such as those in Figure 5-17a, combined according to a small set of spatial relations, is sufficient to describe the shapes of all objects that people can possibly recognize. To appreciate this point, note that the number of possible objects composed of just two geons is 36×36 (you can form an object by combining any two geons—see Figure 5-17b), while the number of possible three-geon objects is $36 \times 36 \times 36$. The sum of these two numbers is already on the order of 30,000, and we have yet to consider objects made up of 4 or more geons. Moreover, geons like those in Figure 5-17a can be distinguished solely in terms of primitive features. For example, geon 2 in Figure 5-17a (the cube) differs from geon 3 (the cylinder) in that the cube has straight edges but the cylinder has curved edges; straight and curved edges are primitive features.

Evidence that geons are features comes from experiments in which participants try to recognize pictured objects that are presented

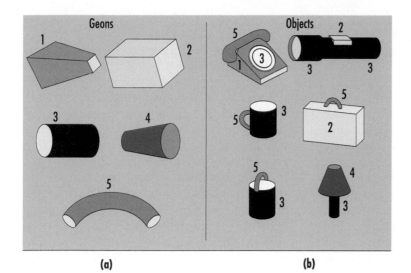

(a)   (b)

FIGURE 5-17

A Possible Set of Features (Geons) for Natural Objects *(a) Wedges, cubes, cylinders, and cones may be features of complex objects. (b) When the features (geons) are combined, they form natural objects. Note that when the arc (geon 5) is connected to the side of the cylinder (geon 3), it forms a cup; when connected to the top of the cylinder, it forms a pail. (After Biederman, 1990)*

briefly. The general finding is that recognition of an object is good to the extent that the geons of the object are perceptible. In one study, part of the shape of an object was deleted in such a way that the deletion either interfered with recovering the geons (see the right column of Figure 5-18) or did not (see the middle column). Recognition of the objects was much better when there was no interference with the geons.

As usual, the description of an object includes not just its features but also the relationships among them. This is evident in Figure 5-17b. When the arc is connected to the side of the cylinder, it forms a cup; when it is connected to the top of the cylinder, it forms a pail. Once the description of an object's shape is constructed, it is compared to an array of geon descriptions stored in memory to find the best match. This matching process between the description of an object's shape and the descriptions stored in memory resembles the process described earlier for letters and words (Hummel & Biederman, 1992).

The Importance of Context   A key distinction in perception is that between bottom-up and top-down processes. *Bottom-up processes* are driven solely by the input, whereas *top-down processes* are driven by a person's knowledge and expectations. To illustrate, recognizing the shape of an object solely on the basis of its geon description involves only bottom-up processes; one starts with primitive features of the input, determines the geon configuration of the input, and then

FIGURE 5-18

Object Recognition and Geon Recovery   *Items used in experiments on object recognition. The left column shows the original intact versions of the objects. The middle column shows versions of the objects in which regions have been deleted, but the geons are still recoverable. The right column shows versions of the objects in which regions have been deleted and the geons are not recoverable. Recognition is better for the middle versions than for the rightmost versions. (After Biederman, 1987)*

makes this description available to shape descriptions stored in memory. In contrast, recognizing that the object is a lamp partly on the basis of its being on a night table next to a bed involves some top-down processes; other information is used besides the input regarding shape. While most of the processes considered thus far in this chapter are bottom-up ones, top-down processes also play a major role in object perception.

Top-down processes underlie the powerful effects of context on our perception of objects and people. You expect to see your chemistry lab partner, Sarah, every Tuesday at 3 P.M., and when she enters the lab at that moment you hardly need to look to know it is she. Your prior knowledge has led to a powerful expectation, and little input is needed for recognition. But should Sarah suddenly appear in your hometown during Christmas vacation, you may have trouble recognizing her. She is out of context—your expectations have been violated, and you must resort to extensive bottom-up processing to tell that it is in fact she (we experience this as "doing a double take"). As this example makes clear, when the context is appropriate (that is, it predicts the input object),

it facilitates perception; when the context is inappropriate, it impairs perception.

The effects of context are particularly striking when the stimulus object is ambiguous—that is, can be perceived in more than one way. An ambiguous figure is presented in Figure 5-19; it can be perceived either as an old woman or as a young woman. If you have been looking at unambiguous pictures that resemble the young woman in the figure (that is, if young women are the context), you will tend to see the young woman first in the ambiguous picture. This effect of temporal context is illustrated with another set of pictures in Figure 5-20. Look at the pictures as you would at a comic strip, from left to right and top to bottom. The pictures in the middle of the series are ambiguous. If you view the figures in the sequence just suggested, you will tend to see the ambiguous pictures as a man's face. If you view the figures in the opposite order, you will tend to see the ambiguous pictures as a young woman.

The stimulus object need not be ambiguous in order to demonstrate the effect of context. Suppose that a person is first shown a picture of a scene and is then briefly given a picture of an unambiguous object to identify. Identification will be more accurate if the object is appropriate to the scene. For example, after looking at a kitchen scene, the person will correctly identify a briefly presented loaf of bread more often than a briefly presented mailbox (Palmer, 1975).

Because of top-down processing, our motives and desires can affect our perceptions. If we are very hungry, a quick glance at a red ball on our kitchen table may register as an apple. Our desire for food has led us to think about food, and these expectations have combined with the input (a red, round object) to yield the percept of an apple. Motives can also have a negative effect on perception. If we believe a man to be a child molester, for example, we are more likely to misperceive his innocent touching of a child as sexual in nature.

Context effects and top-down processing also occur with letters and words, and play a major role in reading. When we read, we do not scan a line of text in a smooth, continuous motion. Rather, our eyes are still for a brief period, then jump to another position on the line, are still for another brief period, then jump again (perhaps to a different line),

An Ambiguous Stimulus   *An ambiguous drawing that can be seen either as a young woman or as an old woman. Most people see the old woman first. The young woman is turning away, and we see the left side of her face. Her chin is the old woman's nose, and her necklace is the old woman's mouth.* (After Boring, 1930)

FIGURE 5-20

Effects of Temporal Context *What you see here depends on the order in which you look at the pictures. The pictures in the middle of the series are ambiguous. If you have been looking at pictures of a man's face, they will appear to be distorted faces. If you have been looking at pictures of a woman, they will look like a woman.* (After Fisher, 1967)

and so on. It is during the periods when the eyes are still, called *fixations,* that the visual system extracts information. Both the number of fixations we make and the durations of these fixations are greatly influenced by how much we know about the text—and, hence, by the amount of top-down processing we can invoke. When the material is unfamiliar, there is little top-down processing. In such cases we tend to fixate on every word, except for function words like "a," "of," "the," and so on. As the material becomes more familiar, we can bring our prior knowledge to bear on it, and our fixations become shorter and more widely spaced (Just & Carpenter, 1980; Rayner, 1978).

Top-down processing occurs even in the absence of context if the input is sufficiently sparse or degraded. Suppose that at a friend's apartment you enter her dark kitchen and see a smallish black object in the corner. You think the object could be your friend's cat, but the perceptual input is too degraded to convince you of this, so you think of a particular feature of the cat, such as its tail, and selectively attend to the region of the object that is likely to contain that feature if it is indeed a cat (Kosslyn & Koenig, 1992). This processing is top-down, because you have used specific knowledge—the fact that cats have tails—to generate an expectation, which is then combined with the visual input. Situations like this are common in everyday life. Sometimes, however, the input is very degraded and the expectations we form are way off the mark, as when we finally realize that our would-be cat in the kitchen is really our friend's purse.

Breakdown of Recognition

Recognizing an object is usually so automatic and effortless that we take it for granted. But the process sometimes breaks down when people suffer brain damage (due to accidents or diseases such as strokes). **Agnosia** is *the general term for breakdowns or disorders in recognition.*

Of particular interest is a type of agnosia called *associative agnosia.* This is a syndrome in which patients with damage to temporal lobe regions of the cortex have difficulty recognizing objects only when they are presented visually. For example, the patient may be unable to name a comb when presented with a picture of it, but can name it when allowed to touch it. The deficit is exemplified by the following case:

> For the first three weeks in the hospital the patient could not identify common objects presented visually and did not know what was on his plate until he tasted it. He identified objects immediately on touching them [but] when shown a stethoscope, he described it as "a long cord with a round thing at the end," and asked if it could be a watch. He identified a can opener as "could be a key." Asked to name a cigarette lighter, he said, "I don't know." He said he was "not sure" when shown a toothbrush. Asked to identify a comb, he said, "I don't know." For a pipe, he said, "some type of utensil, I'm not sure." Shown a key, he said, "I don't know what that is; perhaps a file or a tool of some sort." (Reubens & Benson, 1971)

What aspects of object recognition have broken down in associative agnosia? Since these patients often do well on visual tasks other than recognition—such as drawing objects or determining whether two pictured objects match—the breakdown is likely to be in the later stages of recognition, in which the input object is matched to stored object descriptions. One possibility is that the stored object descriptions have been lost or obscured in some way (Damasio, 1985).

Some patients with associative agnosia have problems recognizing certain categories but not others. These *category-specific deficits* are of considerable interest because they may tell us something new about how normal recognition works. The most frequent category-specific deficit is loss of the ability to recognize faces, called *prosopagnosia*. (We discussed this condition briefly in Chapter 1.) When this deficit occurs, there is always brain damage in the right hemisphere and often some damage in homologous regions of the left hemisphere as well. The condition is illustrated by the following case:

> He could not identify his medical attendants. "You must be a doctor because of your white coat, but I don't know which one you are. I'll know if you speak." He failed to identify his wife during visiting hours. . . . He failed to identify pictures of Churchill, Hitler, and Marilyn Monroe. When confronted with such portraits he would proceed deductively, searching for the "critical" detail which would yield the answer. (Pallis, 1955)

A second kind of category deficit is loss of the ability to recognize words, called *pure alexia* (typically accompanied by damage in the left occipital lobe). Patients with this deficit typically have no difficulty recognizing natural objects or faces. They can even identify individual letters. What they cannot do is recognize visually presented words. When presented with a word, they attempt to read it letter by letter. It can take as much as 10 seconds for them to recognize a common word, with the amount of time needed increasing with the number of letters in the word (Bub, Blacks, & Howell 1989).

Other types of category-specific deficits involve impairment in the ability to recognize living things such as animals, plants, and foods. In rare cases patients are unable to recognize nonliving things such as household tools (Warrington & Shallice, 1984).

Some of the suggested explanations of category-specific deficits have implications for normal recognition. One hypothesis is that the normal recognition system is organized around different classes of objects—one subsystem for faces, another for words, a third for animals, and so on—and these subsystems are localized in different regions of the brain. If a patient suffers only restricted brain damage, he or she may show a loss of one subsystem but not others. Damage in a specific part of the right hemisphere, for example, might disrupt the face-recognition subsystem but leave the other subsystems intact (Damasio, 1990; Farah, 1990).

Attention

Our discussions of localization and recognition presuppose the presence of **attention,** *the ability to select some information for more detailed inspection, while ignoring other information.* To determine the motion of an airplane, one must attend to its path; to recognize a particular object, one must first attend to its shape and color; and to determine whether that black thing in your friend's kitchen has a tail, one must attend to the appropriate location of the object.

Attention involves selectivity. Most of the time we are bombarded with so many stimuli that we are unable to recognize all of them. As you sit reading, stop for a moment, close your eyes, and attend to the various stimuli that are reaching you. Notice, for example, the tightness of your left shoe. What sounds do you hear? Is there an odor in the air? You probably were not aware of these stimuli before, because you had not selected them for recognition. The process by which we select is called *selective attention.*

Selective Looking and Listening

How exactly do we direct our attention to objects of interest? The simplest means is by physically reorienting our sensory receptors. For vision, this means moving our eyes until the object of interest falls on the most sensitive region of the retina.

Studies of visual attention often involve observing a participant looking at a picture or scene. If we watch the person's eyes, it is evident that they are not stationary; rather, they are scanning. As in the case of reading, scanning a scene is not a smooth, continuous motion; rather, it involves successive fixations. There are a number of techniques for recording these eye movements. One involves monitoring the eyes with a television camera in such a way that what the eye sees is superimposed on an image of a cursor, showing where the eye is currently aimed. From this superimposed image, the experimenter can determine the point in the scene on which the eye is fixated.

The eye movements used in scanning a picture ensure that different parts of the picture will fall on the fovea so that all of its details can be seen. (As noted in the preceding chapter, the fovea has the best resolution.) The points on which the eyes fixate are not random. They tend to be the ones that convey the most information about the picture, places where important features are located. For example, in scanning a photograph of a face, many fixations occur in the regions corresponding to the eyes, nose, and mouth (see Figure 5-21).

We can also selectively attend to something without moving our eyes. In experiments that demonstrate this, participants have to detect when an object occurs. On each trial, the person stares at a blank field, then sees a cue presented briefly, and then sees an object. The interval between the cue and object is too brief for participants to move their eyes, yet they can detect the object faster when it occurs in the cued location than elsewhere. Presumably, they are attending to the cued location even though they cannot move their eyes there (Posner & Raichle, 1994).

In the case of audition, the closest thing to eye movements is moving the head so that the ears are directed at the source of interest. This mechanism is of limited use in many situations, though. Consider a crowded party. The sounds of many voices bombard our ears, and their sources are not far enough apart to allow us to selectively follow one conversation by reorienting our ears. However, we can use purely mental means to selectively attend to the desired message. Some of the cues that we use to do this are the direction the sound is coming from, the speaker's lip movements, and the particular characteristics of the speaker's voice (pitch and intonation). Even in the absence of any of these cues, we can (though with difficulty) select one of two messages to follow on the basis of its meaning.

Research on what is called the *cocktail party phenomenon* indicates that we remember very little about auditory messages that we do not attend to. A common procedure in this research is to put earphones on a participant and play one message through one ear and another message through the other ear. The person is asked to repeat (or "shadow") one of the messages as it is heard.

 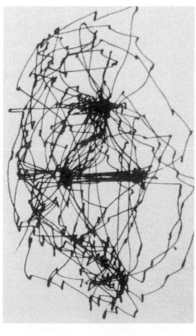

FIGURE 5-21

Eye Movements in Viewing a Picture. *Next to the picture of the young girl is a record of the eye movements made by an individual inspecting the picture.* (After Yarbus, 1967)

Although we may hear a number of conversations around us, as at a cocktail party, we remember very little of what we do not attend to. This is known as selective listening.

After a few minutes the messages are turned off and the listener is asked about the unshadowed message. The listener's remarks about the message are usually limited to the physical characteristics of the sound in the unshadowed ear—whether the voice was high or low, male or female, and so forth; he or she can say almost nothing about the content of the message (Moray, 1969).

The fact that we can report so little about auditory messages that we do not attend to initially led researchers to the idea that nonattended stimuli are filtered out completely (Broadbent, 1958). However, there is now considerable evidence that our perceptual system processes nonattended stimuli to some extent (in vision as well as audition), even though those stimuli rarely reach consciousness. One piece of evidence for partial processing of nonattended stimuli is that we are very likely to hear the sound of our own name, even when it is spoken softly in a nonattended conversation. This could not happen if the entire nonattended message were lost at lower levels of the perceptual system. Hence, lack of attention does not block messages entirely; rather, it attenuates them, much like a volume control that is turned down but not off (Treisman, 1969).

The Neural Basis of Attention

In the past few years there have been breakthroughs in our understanding of the neural basis of attention, particularly visual attention. The research of interest has concerned two major questions: (1) What brain structures mediate the psychological act of selecting an object to attend to? and (2) How does the subsequent neural processing differ for attended and nonattended stimuli? Let's consider each of these questions in turn.

It appears that the brain contains two separate systems that mediate selective attention. One system represents the perceptual features of an object, such as its location in space, its shape, and its color. It is responsible for selecting one object among many on the basis of the features associated with that object. This is referred to as the *posterior system* because the brain structures involved—the parietal and temporal cortex, along with some subcortical structures—are located in the back of the brain.

The other system is designed to control when and how these features will be used for selection. It is referred to as the *anterior system* because the structures involved—the frontal cortex and a subcortical structure—are located in the front of the brain. In short, we can select an object for attention by focusing on its location, its shape, or its color. Although the actual selection of these features will occur in the posterior part of the brain, the selection process will be guided by the anterior part of brain. Because of this function, some researchers refer to the anterior system as the "chief executive officer" or CEO of selective attention.

Some critical findings regarding the posterior system come from PET scans of humans while they are engaged in selective-attention tasks. When participants are instructed to shift their attention from one location to another, the cortical areas that show the greatest increase in blood flow—and, hence, neural activity—are the parietal lobes of both hemispheres (Corbetta, Miezin, Shulman, & Petersen, 1993). Moreover, when people with brain damage in these regions are tested on attentional tasks, they have great difficulty shifting attention from one location to another (Posner, 1988). Hence, the regions that are active when a normal brain accomplishes the task turn out to be the same areas that are damaged when a patient cannot do the task. Moreover, when single-cell recording studies are done with nonhuman primates, cells in the same brain regions are found to be active when attention must be switched from one location to the next (Wurtz, Goldberg, & Robinson, 1980). Taken together, these findings strongly indicate that activity in parietal regions of the brain mediates attending to locations. There is comparable evidence for the involvement of temporal regions in attending to the color and shape of objects (Moran & Desimone, 1985).

Once an object has been selected for attention, what changes in neural processing occur? Consider an experiment in which a set of colored geometric objects is presented and the participant is instructed to attend only to the red ones and to indicate when a triangle is presented. The anterior system will direct the posterior system to focus on color, but what else changes in the neural processing of each stimulus? The answer is that the regions of the visual cortex that process color become more active than they would be if the partici-

pant were not selectively attending to color. More generally, the regions of the brain that are relevant to the attribute being attended to (be it color, shape, texture, motion, and so forth) will show amplified activity (Posner & Dehaene, 1994). There is also some evidence that brain regions that are relevant to unattended attributes will be inhibited (La Berge, 1995; Posner & Raichle, 1994).

Some of the best evidence for this amplification of attributes that are attended to again comes from PET studies. In one experiment (Corbetta et al., 1991), participants whose brains were being scanned viewed moving objects of varying color and form. In one condition, the individuals were instructed to detect changes among the objects in motion, while in other conditions they were instructed to detect changes among the objects in color or shape; hence, motion is the attribute attended to in the first condition, color or shape in the other conditions. Even though the physical stimuli were identical in all the conditions, posterior cortical areas known to be involved in the processing of motion were found to be more active in the first condition, whereas areas involved in color or shape processing were more active in the other conditions (see Figure 5-22). Attention, then, amplifies

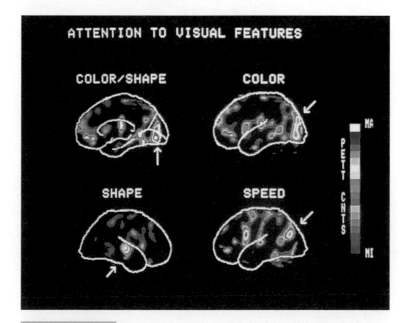

FIGURE 5-22

PET Images Reveal Differences in Cortical Activity *The image on the top right is from the condition in which participants attended to changes in color, whereas the images in the bottom row are from the conditions in which individuals attended to changes in shape or speed.*

what is relevant, not only psychologically but biologically as well.

Perceptual Constancies

In addition to localization and recognition, the perceptual system has another goal: to keep the appearance of objects constant. We have evolved so that in general we represent—and experience—objects as they really are in the world (real objects are constant in shape, size, color, and brightness), not as their images appear on the retina.

By and large, we perceive an object as remaining relatively constant regardless of changes in lighting, the position from which we view it, or its distance from us. Your car does not appear to grow larger as you walk

toward it, become distorted in shape as you walk around it, or change in color when you view it in artificial light, even though the image on your retina undergoes these changes. The term *perceptual constancy* refers to the tendency for the appearance of objects to remain constant even though their impressions on the retina are changing. Although constancy is not perfect, it is a salient aspect of visual experience.

Perceptual constancy also has important implications for our earlier discussion of the goals of localization and recognition. In general, constancies make the tasks of localization and recognition easier. If an object appeared to change its location every time we moved our eyes, determining its depth (an important part of localization) might be exceedingly difficult. If the shape and color of an object changed every time either we or it moved, the description of the object that we construct in the early stages of recognition would also change, and recognition might become an impossible task.

Lightness and Color Constancy

When an object is illuminated, it reflects a certain amount of the light. The amount reflected is related to the apparent lightness of the object. The term *lightness constancy* refers to the fact that the perceived lightness of a particular object may barely change, even when the amount of reflected light changes dramatically. Thus, a black velvet shirt can look just as black in sunlight as in shadow, even though it reflects thousands of times more light when it is directly illuminated by the sun.

Although this effect holds under normal circumstances, a change in surroundings can destroy it. Suppose that the black shirt is put behind an opaque black screen and you view the shirt through a peephole in the screen. The screen reduces what you see through the opening to just the actual light reflected from the shirt, independent of its surroundings. Now, when it is illuminated, the shirt looks white because the light that reaches your eye through the hole is more intense than the light from the screen itself. This demonstration provides a clue as to why the lightness of an object usually remains constant. When we perceive objects in natural

Perceptual constancy enables us to determine how far away objects are.

settings, several other objects are usually visible. Lightness constancy depends on the relationships among the intensities of light reflected from the different objects. Thus, normally we continue to see black velvet as black even in sunlight because the velvet continues to reflect a lesser percentage of its light than its surroundings do. It is the *relative* percentage of light reflected that determines its brightness (Gilchrist, 1988).

Similar principles apply to color. The tendency for an object to remain roughly the same color under different light sources is called *color constancy*. Like lightness constancy, color constancy can be eliminated by removing the object from its background. For example, if you look at a ripe tomato through a tube that obscures the surroundings and the nature of the object, the tomato may appear any color—blue, green, or pink—depending on the wavelengths being reflected from it. Hence, both color constancy and lightness constancy depend on a heterogeneous background (Lland, 1977; Maloney & Wandell, 1986).

Shape and Location Constancy

When a door swings toward us, the shape of its image on the retina goes through a series of changes (see Figure 5-23). The door's rectangular shape produces a trapezoidal image, with the edge toward us wider than the hinged edge; then the trapezoid grows thinner, until finally all that is projected on the retina is a vertical bar the thickness of the door. Nevertheless, we perceive an unchanging door swinging open. The fact that the perceived shape is constant while the retinal image changes is an example of *shape constancy.*

Still another form of perceptual constancy involves the locations of objects. Despite the fact that a series of changing images strike the retina as we move, the positions of fixed objects appear to remain constant. We tend to take this *location constancy* for granted, but it requires that the visual system take account both of our movements and of the changing retinal images. We discussed this kind of "accounting" earlier in connection with the perception of motion. Essentially, the visual system must receive information from the motor system telling it

that the eyes are moving, and take this information into account in interpreting the motion of images. Thus, if your visual system is informed that your eyes just moved 5 degrees to the left, it subtracts this movement from the visual signal.

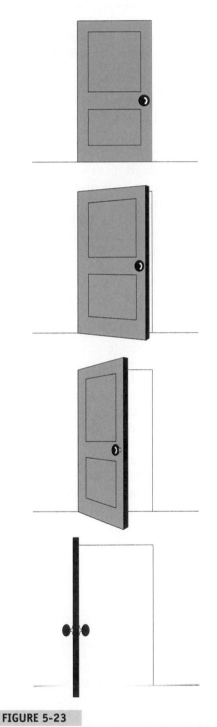

FIGURE 5-23

Shape Constancy *The various retinal images produced by an opening door are quite different, yet we perceive a door of constant rectangular shape.*

Size Constancy

The most thoroughly studied of all the perceptual constancies is *size constancy,* the fact that an object's perceived size remains relatively constant no matter how far away it is. As an object moves farther away from us, we generally do not see it as decreasing in size. Hold a quarter 1 foot in front of you and then move it out to arm's length. Does it appear to get smaller? Not noticeably. Yet the retinal image of the quarter when it is 24 inches away is less than half the size of its retinal image when it is 12 inches away (see Figure 5-24).

Dependence on Depth Cues   The example of the moving quarter indicates that when we perceive the size of an object, we consider something in addition to the size of the retinal image. That additional something is the perceived distance of the object. As long ago as 1881, Emmert was able to show that size judgments depend on distance. Emmert used an ingenious method that involved judging the size of afterimages.

Participants were first asked to fixate on the center of an image for about a minute (see Figure 5-25 for an example of such an image). Then they looked at a white screen and saw an afterimage of what they had just seen. Their task was to judge the size of the afterimage; the independent variable was how far away the screen was. Because the retinal size of the afterimage was the same regardless of the distance of the screen, any variations in judgments of the size of the afterimage had to be due to its perceived dis-

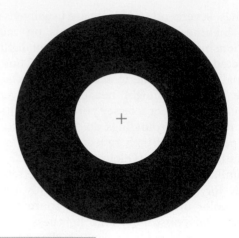

FIGURE 5-25

Emmert's Experiment.   *Hold the book at normal reading distance under good light. Fixate on the cross in the center of the figure for about a minute, then look at a distant wall. You will see an afterimage of the two circles that appears larger than the stimulus. Then look at a piece of paper held close to your eyes; the afterimage will appear smaller than the stimulus. If the afterimage fades, blinking can sometimes restore it.*

tance. When the screen was far away, the afterimage looked large; when the screen was near, the afterimage looked small. Emmert's experiment is so easy to do that you can perform it on yourself.

On the basis of such experiments, Emmert proposed that the perceived size of an object increases with both the retinal size of the object and the perceived distance of the object. This is known as the *size-distance invariance principle*. It explains size constancy as follows: When the distance to an object increases, the object's retinal size decreases; but if distance cues are present, perceived distance will increase. Hence, the perceived size will remain approximately constant. To illustrate: When a person walks away from you, the size of her image on your retina becomes smaller but her perceived distance becomes larger; these two changes cancel each other out, and your perception of her size remains relatively constant.

Illusions   The size-distance principle seems to be fundamental to understanding a number of size illusions. (An **illusion** is *a percept that is false or distorted.*) An example is the *moon illusion:* When the moon is near the horizon, it looks as much as 50% larger than

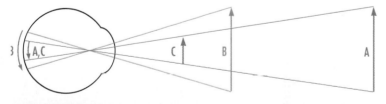

FIGURE 5-24

Retinal Image Size.   *This figure illustrates the geometric relationship between the physical size of an object and the size of its image on the retina. Arrows A and B represent objects of the same size, but one is twice as far from the eye as the other. As a result, the retinal image of A is about half the size of the retinal image of B. The object represented by arrow C is smaller than that of A, but its location closer to the eye causes it to produce a retinal image the same size as A.*

FIGURE 5-26

The Ames Room   *A view of how the Ames room looks to an observer viewing it through the peephole. The sizes of the boy and the dog depend on which one is in the left-hand corner of the room and which one is in the right-hand corner. The room is designed to wreak havoc with our perceptions. Because of the perceived shape of the room, the relative sizes of the boy and the dog seem impossibly different. Yet the same boy and dog appear in both photographs.*

when it is high in the sky, even though in both locations its retinal image is the same size. One explanation of this illusion is that the perceived distance to the horizon is judged to be greater than the distance to the zenith; hence, it is the greater perceived distance that leads to the greater perceived size (Kaufman & Rock, 1989). One way to reduce the effectiveness of the depth cues that indicate that the horizon moon is far away is to view the moon upside down. This can be done by placing your back to the moon, bending over, and viewing it through your legs. If you have a photo of the moon on the horizon, it can be done by simply turning the picture upside down (Coren, 1992).

Another size illusion is created by the *Ames room* (named after its inventor, Adelbert Ames). Figure 5-26 shows how the Ames room looks to an observer seeing it through a peephole. When the boy is in the left-hand corner of the room (see the photograph on the left), he appears much smaller than when he is in the right-hand corner (see the photograph on the right). Yet it is the same boy in both pictures! Here we have a case in which size constancy has broken down. Why? The reason lies in the construction of the room. Although the room looks like a normal rectangular room

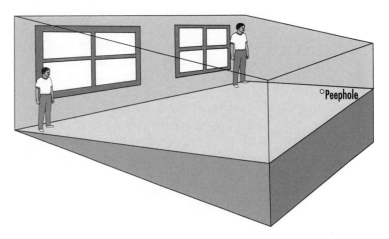

FIGURE 5-27

The True Shape of the Ames Room   *This figure shows the true shape of the Ames room. The boy on the left is actually almost twice as far away as the boy on the right; however, this difference in distance is not detected when the room is viewed through the peephole. (After Goldstein, 1984)*

to an observer seeing it through the peephole, it is in fact shaped so that its left corner is almost twice as far away as its right corner (see the diagram in Figure 5-27). Hence, the boy on the left is much farther away than the one on the right, and consequently projects a smaller retinal image. We do not correct for this difference in distance, though, because the lines in the room

The moon looks much larger when it is near the horizon than when it is high in the sky, even though in both locations its retinal image is the same size.

lead us to believe that we are looking at a normal room and therefore assume that both boys are the same distance from us. In essence, our assumption that the room is normal blocks our application of the size-distance invariance principle, and consequently size constancy breaks down.

Although all the examples of constancy that we have described are visual, constancies also occur in the other senses. For example, a person will hear the same tune even if the frequencies of all its notes are doubled. Whatever the sensory modality, constancies depend on relationships between features of the stimulus—between retinal size and distance in the case of size constancy, between the intensity of two adjacent regions in the case of lightness constancy, and so forth.

Perceptual Development

An age-old question about perception is whether our abilities to perceive are learned or innate—the familiar nature-versus-nurture problem. Contemporary psychologists no longer believe that this is an "either-or" question. No one doubts that both genetics and

learning influence perception; rather, the goal is to pinpoint the contribution of each and to spell out their interactions. For the modern researcher, the question "Must we learn to perceive?" has given way to more specific questions: (a) What discriminatory capacities do infants have (which tells us something about inborn capacities), and how does this capacity change with age under normal rearing conditions? (b) If animals are reared under conditions that restrict what they can learn (referred to as *controlled stimulation*), what effects does this have on their later discriminatory capacity? (c) What effects does rearing under controlled conditions have on perceptual-motor coordination? We will address each of these issues in turn.

Discrimination by Infants

Perhaps the most direct way to find out what human perceptual capacities are inborn is to see what capacities an infant has. At first, you might think that this research should consider only newborns, because if a capacity is inborn it should be present from the first day of life. This idea turns out to be too simple, though. Some inborn capacities, such as perception of form, can appear only after other more basic capacities, such as the ability to register details, have developed. Other inborn capacities may require that there be some kind of environmental input for a certain length of time in order for the capacity to mature. Thus, the study of inborn capacities traces perceptual development from the first minute of life through the early years of childhood.

Methods of Studying Infants It is hard for us to know what an infant perceives because it cannot talk or follow instructions, and has a fairly limited set of behaviors. To study infant perception, a researcher needs to find a form of behavior through which an infant indicates what it can discriminate. One such behavior is an infant's tendency to look at some objects more than at others; psychologists make use of this behavior in a technique known as the *preferential looking method* (see Figure 5-28). Two stimuli are presented to the infant side by side. The experimenter, who is hidden from the infant's view, looks through a partition behind the stimuli and, by watching the infant's eyes, measures the amount of time that the infant looks at each stimulus. (Usually the experimenter uses a television camera to record the infant's viewing pattern.) During the experiment the positions of the stimuli are switched randomly. If an infant consistently looks at one stimulus more than at the other, the experimenter concludes that the infant can tell them apart—that is, discriminate between them.

A related technique is called the *habituation method* (Frantz, 1966; Horowitz, 1974). It takes advantage of the fact that although infants look directly at novel objects, they soon become bored with the same object— that is, they habituate. Suppose that an object is presented for a while and then replaced by a new object. To the extent that the second object is perceived as identical or highly similar to the first one, the infant should spend little time looking at it; conversely, to the extent that the second object is perceived as substantially different from the first one, the infant should spend a lot of time staring at it. By these means, an experimenter can determine whether two physical displays look the same to an infant.

Using these techniques, psychologists have studied a variety of perceptual capacities in infants. Some of these capacities are needed to perceive forms, and hence are used in the task of recognition; others, particularly depth perception, are involved in the task of localization; and still others are

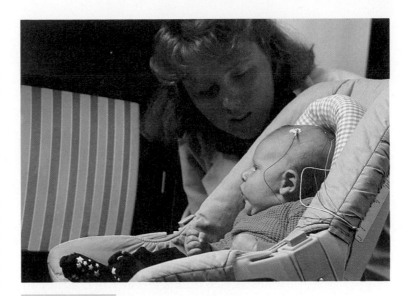

FIGURE 5-28

Testing the Visual Preferences of an Infant

involved in the task of keeping the appearance of perceived objects constant.

Perceiving Forms To be able to perceive an object, a person must first be able to discriminate one part of it from another, an ability referred to as *visual acuity*. Acuity is often assessed by varying both the *contrast* in a pattern (the difference in brightness between dark and light regions) and the *spatial frequency* of the pattern (the number of times a pattern is repeated within a given area). For any particular level of contrast there are always some spatial frequencies that cannot be resolved by the visual system because they are too fine. At the other extreme, there are other spatial frequencies that cannot be seen because they change over too large an area.

The method typically used in studying acuity in infants is preferential looking, with a pattern of stripes as one stimulus and a uniform gray field as the other. Initially the stripes are relatively wide, and the infant prefers to look at the pattern rather than at the uniform field. Then the researcher decreases the width of the stripes until the infant no longer shows a preference. Presumably at this point the infant can no longer discriminate a stripe from its surroundings, so that the pattern of stripes no longer has perceptible parts and looks like a uniform field. When first studied at about 1 month of age, infants can see some patterns, but their acuity is very low. Acuity increases rapidly over the first 6 months of life; then it increases more slowly, reaching adult levels between 1 and 2 years of age (Courage & Adams, 1990; Teller & Moushon, 1986).

What do studies like this tell us about the infant's perceptual world? At 1 month, infants can distinguish among relatively large objects but cannot distinguish fine details. Such vision is sufficient to perceive some general characteristics of an object, including some of the features of a face (which create something like a pattern of dark and light stripes). Figure 5-29 uses the results of acuity experiments to simulate what 1-, 2-, and 3-month-old infants see when viewing a woman's face from a distance of 6 inches. At 1 month, acuity is so poor that it is difficult to perceive facial expressions (and indeed newborns look mostly at the outside contours of a face). By 3 months, acuity has improved to the point where an infant can decipher facial expressions. No wonder that infants seem so much more socially responsive at 3 months than at 1 month.

Being able to discriminate dark from light edges is essential for seeing forms, but what about other aspects of object recognition? Our sensitivity to some of the shape features of objects is manifested very early in life. When presented with a triangle, even a 3-day-old infant will direct its eye movements toward the edges and vertices rather than looking randomly over the form (Salapatek, 1975). Also, infants find some shapes more interesting than others. As noted in Chapter 3, they tend to look more at forms that resemble human faces, a tendency that appears to be based on a preference for some of the features of faces, such as curved rather than straight contours (Fantz, 1970; 1961). By 3 months an infant can recognize something about the mother's face, even in a photograph, as revealed by an infant's preference to look at a photograph of the mother rather than one of an unfamiliar woman (Barrera & Maurer, 1981).

Perceiving Depth   Depth perception begins to appear at about 3 months but is not fully established until about 6 months. Thus, at around 4 months infants will begin to reach for the nearer of two objects, where nearness is signaled by binocular disparity (Granrud, 1986). A month or two later they will begin to reach for objects that are apparently nearer on the basis of monocular depth cues such as relative size, linear perspective, and shading cues (Coren, Ward, & Enns, 1999).

Further evidence of the development of monocular depth perception comes from studies using the *visual cliff* (see Figure 5-30). This consists of a board placed across a sheet of glass, with a surface of patterned material located directly under the glass on the shallow side and at a distance of a few feet below the glass on the deep side. (The appearance of depth in Figure 5-30—the "cliff"—is created by an abrupt change in the texture gradient.) An infant who is old enough to crawl (6–7 months) is placed on the board; a patch is placed over one eye to eliminate binocular depth cues. When the mother calls or beckons from the shallow side, the infant will consistently crawl toward her; but when the mother beckons from the deep side, the infant will not cross the "cliff." Thus, when an infant is old

FIGURE 5-29

Visual Acuity and Contrast Sensitivity   *Simulations of what 1-, 2-, and 3-month-old infants see when they look at a woman's face from a distance of about six inches; the bottom right photograph is what an adult sees. The simulations of infant perception were obtained by first determining an infant's contrast sensitivity and then applying this contrast-sensitivity function to the photograph on the bottom right. (After Ginsberg, 1983)*

enough to crawl, depth perception is relatively well developed.

Perceiving Constancies   Like the perception of form and depth, the perceptual constancies start to develop in the first few months of life. This is particularly true of shape and size constancy (Kellman, 1984). Consider an experiment on size constancy that used the habituation method. Four-month-old infants were first shown one teddy bear for a while and then shown a second one. The second bear was either (a) identical in physical size to the original one, but presented at a different distance so that it produced a different-sized retinal image, or (b) different in physical size from the original bear. If the infants had developed size constancy, they should perceive bear "a" (same physical size) as identical to the one they saw originally, and hence spend little time looking at it compared to the amount of time spent looking at bear "b" (which was actually bigger than the original). And this is exactly what happened (Granrud, 1986).

Controlled Stimulation

We turn now to the question of how specific experiences affect perceptual capacities. To answer this question, researchers have systematically varied the kind of perceptual experiences a young organism has, and then looked at the effects of this experience on subsequent perceptual performance.

Absence of Stimulation   The earliest experiments on controlled stimulation sought to determine the effects of rearing an animal in the total absence of visual stimulation. The experimenters kept animals in the dark for several months after birth, until they were mature enough for visual testing. The idea behind these experiments was that if animals have to learn to perceive, they would be unable to perceive when first exposed to the light. The results turned out as expected: Chimpanzees that were reared in darkness for their first 16 months could detect light but could not discriminate among patterns (Riesen, 1947). However, subsequent studies

FIGURE 5-30

The Visual Cliff   *The "visual cliff" is an apparatus used to show that infants and young animals are able to see depth by the time they are able to move about. The apparatus consists of two surfaces, both displaying the same checkerboard pattern and covered by a sheet of thick glass. One surface is directly under the glass; the other is several feet below it. When placed on the center board between the deep side and the shallow side, the kitten refuses to cross to the deep side but will readily move off the board onto the shallow side. (After Gibson & Walk, 1960)*

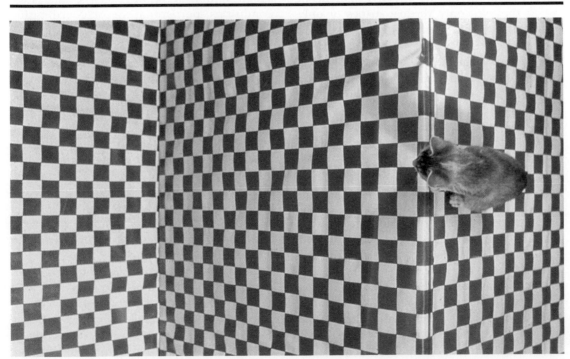

showed that prolonged rearing in the dark does more than prevent learning; it causes deterioration of neurons in various parts of the visual system. It turns out that a certain amount of light stimulation is necessary to maintain the visual system. Without any light stimulation, nerve cells in the retina and visual cortex begin to atrophy (Binns & Salt, 1997; Movshon & Van Sluyters, 1981).

Although these findings do not tell us much about the role of learning in perceptual development, they are important in themselves. In general, when an animal is deprived of visual stimulation from birth, the longer the period of deprivation, the greater the deficit. Adult cats, on the other hand, can have a patch over one eye for a long period without losing vision in that eye. These observations led to the idea that there is a critical period for the development of inborn visual capacities. (A *critical period* is a stage in development during which the organism is optimally ready to acquire certain abilities.) Lack of stimulation during a critical period for vision can permanently impair the visual system (Cynader, Timney, & Mitchell, 1980).

Limited Stimulation Researchers no longer deprive animals of stimulation for a long time; instead, they study the effects of rearing animals that receive stimuli in both eyes, but only certain kinds of stimuli. Researchers have raised kittens in an environment in which they see only vertical stripes or only horizontal stripes. The kittens become blind to stripes in the orientation—horizontal or vertical—that they do not experience. And single-cell recording studies show that many cells in the visual cortex of a "horizontally reared" cat respond to horizontal stimuli and none responds to vertical stimuli, whereas the opposite pattern is found in the visual cortex of "vertically reared" cat (Blake, 1981; Moushon & Van Sluyters, 1981). This blindness seems to be caused by the degeneration of cells in the visual cortex.

Of course, researchers do not deprive humans of normal visual stimulation, but sometimes this happens naturally or as a consequence of medical treatment. For example, after eye surgery the eye that was operated on is usually covered with a patch. If this happens to a child in the first year of life, the acuity of the patched eye is reduced (Awaya et al., 1973). This suggests that there is a critical period early in the development of the human visual system similar to that in animals; if stimulation is restricted during this period, the system will not develop normally. The critical period is much longer in humans than in animals. It may last as long as eight years, but the greatest vulnerability occurs during the first two years of life (Aslin & Banks, 1978).

None of these facts indicates that we have to learn to perceive. Rather, the facts show that certain kinds of stimulation are essential for the maintenance and development of perceptual capacities that are present at birth. But this does not mean that learning has no effect on perception. For evidence of such effects, we need only consider our ability to recognize common objects. The fact that we can recognize a familiar object more readily than an unfamiliar one—a dog versus an aardvark, for example—must certainly be due to learning. If we had been reared in an environment rich in aardvarks and sparse in dogs, we could have recognized the aardvark more readily than the dog.

Active Perception When it comes to coordinating perceptions with motor responses, learning plays a major role. The evidence for this comes from studies in which participants receive normal stimulation but are prevented from making normal responses to that stimulation. Under such conditions, perceptual-motor coordination does not develop.

For example, in one classic study, two kittens that had been reared in darkness had their first visual experience in the "kitten carousel" illustrated in Figure 5-31. As the active kitten walked, it moved the passive kitten riding in the carousel. Although both kittens received roughly the same visual stimulation, only the active kitten had this stimulation produced by its own movement. And only the active kitten successfully learned sensory-motor coordination; for example, when picked up and moved toward an object, only the active kitten learned to put out its paws to ward off a collision.

Similar results have been obtained with humans. In some experiments, people wear prism goggles that distort the directions of objects. Immediately after putting on these goggles, they temporarily have trouble reaching for objects and often bump into things. If

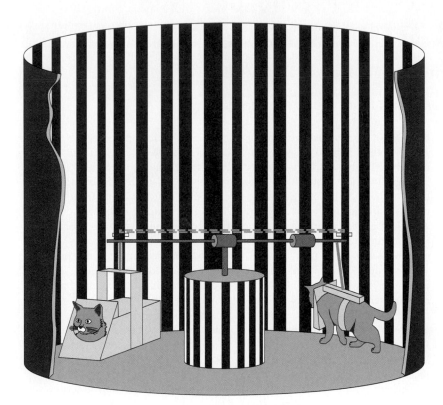

FIGURE 5-31
The Importance of Self-Produced Movements
Both kittens received roughly the same visual stimulation, but only the active kitten had this stimulation produced by its own movement. (After Held & Hein, 1963)

they move about and attempt to perform motor tasks while wearing the goggles, they learn to coordinate their movements with the actual location of objects rather than with their apparent locations. On the other hand, if a person is pushed in a wheelchair he or she does not adapt to the goggles. Apparently, self-produced movement is essential to prism adaption (Held, 1965).

In sum, the evidence indicates that we are born with considerable perceptual capacities. The natural development of some of these capacities may require years of normal input from the environment. But there clearly are learning effects on perception as well; these are particularly striking when perception must be coordinated with motor behavior.

This chapter, like the preceding one, includes many examples of the interplay between psychological and biological approaches. Throughout the chapter we have encountered cases in which specific psychological functions are implemented by specific cells or brain regions. We have seen that specialized cells are used to perceive motion and that separate parts of the brain are used to register the visual features of location, shape, and color. Still other regions of the brain are involved in determining which of these features will be used to control behaviors and actions. These and other examples illustrate how significant the findings of biological research can be in the study of psychological processes.

IS PERCEPTUAL DEVELOPMENT AN INNATE OR SOCIALLY ACQUIRED PROCESS?

Perceptual Development Is an Intrinsic Process

Elizabeth S. Spelke, *Massachusetts Institute of Technology*

Elizabeth S. Spelke

Human beings have a striking capacity to learn from one another. This capacity already is evident in the 1-year-old child, who can learn the meaning of a new word by observing just a few occasions of its use and who can learn the functions of a new object simply by watching another person act on it. The rapid and extensive learning that occurs in early childhood suggests that much of what humans come to know and believe is shaped by our encounters with other things and people. But is our very ability to perceive things and people itself the result of learning? Or, does perception originate in intrinsically generated growth processes and develop in relative independence of one's encounters with things perceived?

For two millennia, most of the thinkers who have pondered this question have favored the view that humans learn to perceive, and that the course of development proceeds from meaningless, unstructured sensations to meaningful, structured perceptions. Research on human infants nevertheless provides evidence against this view. For example, we now know that newborn infants perceive depth and use depth information as adults do, to apprehend the true sizes and shapes of objects. Newborn infants divide the speech stream into the same kinds of sound patterns as do adults, focusing in particular on the set of sound contrasts used by human languages. Newborn infants distinguish human faces from other patterns and orient to faces preferentially. Finally, newborn infants are sensitive to many of the features of objects that adults use to distinguish one thing from another, and they appear to combine featural information in the same kinds of ways as do adults.

How does perception change after the newborn period? With development, infants have been found to perceive depth, objects, and faces with increasing precision. Infants also come to focus on the speech contrasts that are relevant to their own language in preference to speech contrasts relevant to other languages. (Interestingly, this focus appears to result more from a decline in sensitivity to foreign language contrasts than from an increase in sensitivity to native language contrasts.) Finally, infants become sensitive to new sources of information about the environment, such as stereoscopic information for depth, configural information for object boundaries, and new reference frames for locating objects and events. These developments bring greater precision and richness to infants' perceptual experience, but they do not change the infant's world from a meaningless flow of sensation to a meaningful, structured environment.

The findings from studies of human infants gain further support from studies of perceptual development in other animals. Since the pioneering work of Gibson and Walk, we have known that depth perception develops without visual experience in every animal tested: Innate capacities for perceiving depth allow newborn goats to avoid falling off cliffs, and they allow dark-reared rats and cats to avoid bumping into approaching surfaces. More recent studies reveal that newborn chicks perceive the boundaries of objects much as human adults do, and they even represent the continued existence of objects that are hidden. Studies of animals' developing brains reveal that both genes and intrinsically structured neural activity are crucial to the development of normally functioning perceptual systems, but encounters with the objects of perception—external things and events—play a much lesser role. As with human infants, normal visual experience enriches and attunes young animals' perceptual systems, and abnormal visual experience may greatly perturb their functioning. Like human infants, however, other animals do not need visual experience to transform their perceptual world from a flow of unstructured sensations into a structured visual layout.

In sum, perception shows considerable structure at birth and continuity over development. This continuity may help to explain why young human infants are so adept at learning from other people. Consider an infant who watches an adult twist a lid off a jar while saying, "Let's open it." If the infant could not perceive the lid and jar as distinct movable and manipulable objects, she would not be able to make sense of the adult's action. If she could not perceive the sounds that distinguish "open" from other words, she could not begin to learn about this distinctive utterance. And if she could not perceive the person as an agent in some way like herself, then watching the person's action and listening to his speech would reveal nothing about what the infant herself could learn to do or say. Infants' prodigious abilities to learn, therefore, may depend critically on equally prodigious, unlearned abilities to perceive.

Perceptual Development Is an Activity-Dependent Process

Mark Johnson, *University of London*

Most developmental scientists now agree that both nature and nurture are essential for the normal development of perception. However, there is still much dispute about the extent to which either nature or nurture is the more important factor. Points of view on this issue are more than just philosophical musings; they affect the kinds of experiments that are undertaken. In this essay I will argue that classifying particular aspects of perceptual development as being either innate or learned presents us with an overly passive view in which either genes or environment impose structure on the developing brain. In contrast, I suggest that perceptual development is better characterized as an activity-dependent process involving complex and subtle interactions at many levels.

To begin to illustrate my point, let's consider some recent neurobiological work on the prenatal development of the visual cortex in rodents. The neurons studied in these experiments are those involved in binocular vision. Experiments show that the prenatal tuning of these neurons arises through their response to internally generated waves of electrical activity from the main inputs to the visual cortex, the LGN and eye (Katz & Shatz, 1996). In other words, the response properties of these visual cortical neurons are shaped by a kind of "virtual environment" generated by cells elsewhere in the brain and eye. While it is possible to stretch the term *innate* to cover this example of development, we could equally well describe this process as the cortical cells "learning" from the input provided by their cousins in the LGN and eye. Further, after birth the same cortical neurons continue to be tuned in the same way, except that now their

input also reflects the structure of the world outside the infant. Thus, when we examine development in detail it becomes harder to argue, as some theorists do (Spelke, 1998), that "innate knowledge" is fundamentally different from learning.

Another example of the role of activity-dependent processes in perceptual development comes from the ability to detect and recognize faces. Since it is known that there are regions of the human cortex specialized for processing faces, some have argued that this ability is innate. However, experiments with infants reveal a more complex story (Johnson, 1997). The tendency for newborns to look more toward faces turns out to be based on a very primitive reflex-like system that is triggered by a stimulus as simple as three high-contrast blobs in the approximate locations of the eyes and mouth. This simple bias is sufficient to ensure that newborns look much more at faces than at other objects and patterns over the first weeks of life. One consequence of this is that developing circuits on the visual recognition pathway of the cortex get more input related to faces and thus are shaped by experience with this special type of visual stimulus. We can now study this process by using new brain imaging methods. Such studies have shown that the brains of young infants show less localized and less specialized processing of faces in the cortex than do the brains of adults. It is not until 1 year old that infants show the same patterns of brain specialization for processing faces as adults, by which time they have had as much as 1,000 hours of exposure to human faces.

Another example comes from the study of infants' eye movements to visual targets. While newborns are capable of some primitive

reflexive eye movements, it is not until much later in the first year that they can make most of the kinds of complex and accurate saccades seen in adults. One view is that the very limited ability present in newborns is just sufficient to allow them to practice and develop new brain circuits for the more complex integration of visual and motor information necessary for adult eye movements. And practice they do! Even by 4 months, babies have already made over 3 million eye movements. Once

Mark Johnson

again, it appears that infants actively contribute to their own subsequent development.

These considerations should make us skeptical about the many claims for innate perceptual abilities based on experiments with babies of 4 months and older. In fact, it has often turned out that when the same experiments were done with younger infants, quite different results were obtained, suggesting dramatic changes in perceptual abilities over the first few weeks and months after birth (Haith, 1998).

To conclude, infants are not passively shaped by either their genes or their environment. Rather, perceptual development is an activity-dependent process in which, during postnatal life, the infant plays an active role in generating the experience it needs for subsequent development.

SUMMARY

1. The study of perception deals with two major functions of the perceptual system: localization, or determining where objects are, and recognition, or determining what objects are. The study of perception also deals with how the perceptual system keeps the appearance of objects constant, even though their retinal images are changing. Another area of study is how our perceptual capacities develop.

2. The visual cortex operates according to the principle of division of labor. Localization and recognition are carried out by different regions of the brain, with localization mediated by a region near the top of the cortex and recognition by a region near the bottom of the cortex. Recognition processes are further subdivided into separate modules: for example, color, shape, and texture.

3. To localize objects we must first separate them from one another and then organize them into groups. These processes were first studied by Gestalt psychologists, who proposed several principles of organization. One such principle is that we organize a stimulus into regions corresponding to figure and ground. Other principles concern the bases that we use to group objects together, including proximity, closure, similarity, good continuation, and closure.

4. Localizing an object requires that we know its distance from us. This form of perception, known as depth perception, is usually thought to be based on depth cues. Monocular depth cues include relative size, interposition, relative height, linear perspective, shading, and motion parallax. A binocular depth cue is binocular disparity, which results from the fact that any object produces slightly different images on the two retinas.

5. Localizing an object sometimes requires that we know the direction in which an object is moving. Motion perception can be produced in the absence of an object moving across our retina. One example of this phenomenon is stroboscopic motion, in which a rapid series of still images induces apparent movement; another example is induced motion, in which movement of a large object induces apparent movement of a smaller stationary object. Perception of real motion (movement of a real object through space) is implemented by specific cells in the visual system, as indicated by single-cell recordings and experiments on selective adaptation.

6. Recognizing an object amounts to assigning it to a category and is based mainly on the shape of the object. In early stages of recognition, the visual system uses retinal information to describe the object in terms of features like lines and angles; neurons that detect such features (feature detectors) have been found in the visual cortex. In later stages of recognition, the system matches the description of the object with shape descriptions stored in memory to find the best match.

7. Matching can be explained by a connectionist model or network. The bottom level of the network contains features and the next level contains letters; an excitatory connection between a feature and a letter means that the feature is part of a letter, while an inhibitory connection means that the feature is not part of the letter. When a letter is presented, it activates some features in the network, which pass their activation or inhibition up to letters; the letter that receives the most activation is the best match to the input. The network can be expanded to include a level of words and to explain why a letter is easier to recognize when presented in a word than when presented alone.

8. The shape features of natural objects are more complex than lines; they are similar to simple geometric forms such as cylinders, cones, blocks, and wedges. A limited set of such forms may be sufficient in combination to describe the shapes of all objects that people can recognize.

9. Bottom-up recognition processes are driven solely by the input, whereas top-down recognition processes are driven by a person's knowledge and expectations. Top-down processes underlie context effects in perception: The context sets up a perceptual expectation, and when this expectation is satisfied, less input information than usual is needed for recognition.

10. Selective attention is the process by which we select some stimuli for further processing while ignoring others. In vision, the primary means of directing our attention are eye movements. Most eye fixations are on the more informative parts of a scene. Selective attention also occurs in audition. Usually we are able to selectively listen by using cues such as the direction from which the sound is coming and the voice characteristics of the speaker. Our ability to selectively attend is mediated by processes that occur in the early stages of recognition as well as by processes that occur only after the message's meaning has been determined.

11. Two separate brain systems seem to mediate the psychological act of selecting an object to attend to. In the posterior system, objects are selected on the basis of location, shape, or color. The anterior system is responsible for guiding this process, depending on the goals of the viewer. PET studies further show that once an object has been selected, activity is amplified in the posterior regions of the brain that are relevant to the attribute being attended to.

12. Another major function of the perceptual system is to achieve perceptual constancy—that is, to keep the appearance of objects the same in spite of large changes in the stimuli received by the sense organs. Lightness constancy refers to the fact that an object appears equally light regardless of how much light it reflects, and color constancy means that an object looks roughly the same color regardless of the light source illuminating it. In both cases, constancy depends on relationships between the object and elements of the background. Two other well-known perceptual constancies are shape and location constancy.

13. Size constancy refers to the fact that an object's apparent size remains relatively constant no matter how far away it is. The perceived size of an object increases with both the retinal size of the object and the perceived distance of the object, in accordance with the size-distance invariance principle. Thus, as an object moves away from the perceiver, the size of its retinal image decreases but the perceived distance increases, and the two changes cancel each other out, resulting in constancy. This principle can be used to explain certain kinds of perceptual illusions.

14. Research on perceptual development is concerned with the extent to which perceptual capacities are inborn and the extent to which they are learned through experience. To determine inborn capacities, researchers study the discrimination capacities of infants using methods such as preferential looking and habituation. Acuity, which is critical to recognition, increases rapidly during the first 6 months of life and then increases more slowly. Depth perception begins to appear at about 3 months but is not fully established until about 6 months. Perceptual constancies begin to develop as early as 6 months.

15. Animals raised in darkness suffer permanent visual impairment, and animals raised with a patch over one eye become blind in that eye. Adult animals do not lose vision even when deprived of stimulation for long periods. These results suggest that there is a critical period early in life during which lack of normal stimulation produces deficiency in an innate perceptual capacity. If stimulation early in life is controlled in such a way that certain kinds of stimuli are absent, both animals and people become insensitive to the stimuli of which they have been deprived; again, this effect does not have much to do with learning. Perceptual-motor coordination must be learned, however. Both animals and people require self-produced movement to develop normal coordination.

KEY TERMS

perception (p. 151)
object recognition (p. 152)
spatial localization (p. 152)
perceptual constancy (p. 152)

binocular disparity (p. 160)
agnosia (p. 171)
attention (p. 172)
illusion (p. 178)

CRITICAL THINKING QUESTIONS

1. Why do you think the brain seems to solve many problems by dividing the work among specialized regions? What advantages may be gained by this approach? What problems might be caused by this division of labor?

2. Imagine what your visual experience might be like if you suddenly became unable to see motion. How does motion perception contribute to your experience of a coherent world?

3. Some people are skeptical about the value of studying perception and behavior from a biological perspective. Given what you have learned about vision and visually guided behavior, how would you argue against such skeptics?

4. How does selective attention aid perception under everyday circumstances? What would it be like to drive a car in a city where no one had the ability to attend selectively?

5. In what way is the behavior of a visual artist influenced by color and shape constancy? Can you think of ways in which perceptual constancies actually make the artist's task more difficult than it would be without constancy?

FURTHER READING

Many of the textbooks listed under "Further Reading" in Chapter 4 also pertain to the topics considered in this chapter. Several additional sources are appropriate as well.

General treatments of perception are available in Coren, Ward and Enns, *Sensation and Perception* (5th ed., 1999), in Gregory, *Eye and Brain* (5th ed., 1997), and in Kosslyn, *Invitation to Cognitive Science (Vol. 2): Visual Cognition* (2nd ed., 1995). Marr's distinctive cognitive-science approach to visual perception is presented in *Vision* (1982). A more elementary introduction to some of Marr's work may be found in the early chapters of Johnson-Laird, *The Computer and the Mind* (1988).

Studies of brain mechanisms involved in recognition are discussed in Farah, *Visual Agnosia* (1990), and Zeki, *A Vision of the Brain* (1993). Recent advances in the study of selective attention and its neural basis are discussed in Posner and Reichle, *Images of the Mind* (1994). The issue of constancy in perception is reviewed in a very readable fashion in Pinker, *How the Mind Works* (1997). The connectionist approach to problems of recognition and localization is presented in an advanced two-volume work by Rumelhart and McClelland, *Parallel Distributed Processing* (1986). The cognitive neuroscience approach is presented in Gazzaniga, *The Cognitive Neurosciences* (1995).

Chapter 6
Consciousness

*A*s you read these words, are you awake or dreaming? Hardly anyone is confused by this question. We all know the difference between an ordinary state of wakefulness and the experience of dreaming. We also recognize other states of consciousness, including those induced by drugs such as alcohol and marijuana.

A person's conscious awareness is readily subject to change. At this moment, your attention may be focused on this book; in a few minutes, you may be deep in reverie. To most psychologists, an altered state of consciousness exists whenever there is a change from an ordinary pattern of mental functioning to a state that *seems* different to the person experiencing the change. Although this is not a very precise definition, it reflects the fact that states of consciousness are personal and therefore subjective. Altered states of consciousness can vary from the distraction of a vivid daydream to the confusion and perceptual distortion caused by drug intoxication. In this chapter we will look at some altered states of consciousness that are experienced by everyone (sleep and dreams) as well as some that result from special circumstances (meditation, hypnosis, and the use of drugs).

Aspects of Consciousness

Discussions about the nature of conscious experience and the functions of consciousness will appear throughout this book as we consider perception, memory, language, problem solving, and other topics. At this point it would be helpful to present a general theory of consciousness that provides a framework for considering these various topics. Such an approach, however, is not feasible because there is no generally agreed-upon theory. Rather, there are almost as many theories of consciousness as there are individuals who have theorized about the topic. This state of affairs may be discouraging for some readers, particularly those whose prior exposure to science has been in areas where the facts are crystal clear and the theories are well established. Yet what can be more exciting or more challenging than venturing into territory that is still uncharted? As important discoveries are being made—in neurophysiology, evolutionary biology, genetics, and various fields of psychology—many observers believe that an explanation of consciousness is tantalizingly close (Crick, 1994). In the absence of a general theory, our discussion of consciousness can do little more than introduce some terms and concepts that will provide a perspective on the topic as it surfaces in later chapters.

What is consciousness? The early psychologists equated "consciousness" with "mind." They defined psychology as "the study of mind and consciousness" and used the introspective method to study consciousness. As noted in Chapter 1, both introspection as a method for investigation and consciousness as a topic for investigation fell from favor with the rise of behaviorism in the early 1900s. John Watson and his followers believed that if psychology were to become a science, its data must be objective and measurable. Behavior could be publicly observed and various responses could be objectively measured. In contrast, an individual's private experiences might be revealed through introspection, but could not be directly observed by others or objectively measured. If psychology dealt with overt behavior, it would be dealing with public events rather than private events, which are observable only to the person experiencing them.

Behaviorism did not require as radical a change as its pronouncements seemed to imply. The behaviorists themselves dealt with private events when their research required them to do so. They accepted verbal responses as a substitute for introspection when the participant's own experiences were studied. What participants said was objective, regardless of the underlying subjective condition. Still, many psychologists continued to believe that when people said they experienced a series of colored afterimages after staring at a bright light, they probably did see colors in succession. That is, their words were not the whole story. While behaviorists could deal with many phenomena in terms of verbal responses, their preoccupation with observable behavior caused them to neglect interesting psychological problems (such as dreaming, meditation, and hypnosis) because the subjective aspects made those topics irrelevant to them (Ericsson & Simon, 1993).

By the 1960s, psychologists began to recognize that various aspects of consciousness are too pervasive and important to be neglected. This does not mean that psychology must again be defined exclusively as the study of consciousness; it means only that it cannot afford to neglect consciousness. Confining psychology to the study of observable behavior is too limiting. If one can theorize about the nature of consciousness, and that theory leads to testable predictions about behavior, then such theorizing is a valuable contribution to understanding how the mind works.

Consciousness

Many textbooks define consciousness as the individual's current awareness of external and internal stimuli—that is, of events in the environment and of body sensations, memories, and thoughts. This definition identifies only one aspect of consciousness and ignores the fact that we are also conscious when we try to solve a problem or deliberately select one course of action over others in response to environmental circumstances and personal goals. Thus, we are conscious not only when we monitor our environment (internal and external) but also when we seek to control ourselves and our environment. In short, **consciousness** involves (a) *monitoring ourselves and our environment so that percepts, memories, and thoughts are represented in awareness,* and (b) *controlling ourselves and our environment so that we are able to initiate and terminate behavioral and cognitive activities* (Kihlstrom, 1984).

Monitoring   Processing information from the environment is the main function of the body's sensory systems. It leads to awareness of what is going on in our surroundings as well as within our own bodies. However, we could not possibly attend to all of the stimuli that impinge on our senses; if we did, we would experience an information overload. Our consciousness, therefore, focuses on some stimuli and ignores others. Often the information selected has to do with changes in our external or internal worlds. While concentrating on this paragraph, for example, you are probably unaware of numerous background stimuli. But should there be a change—the lights dim, the air begins to smell smoky, or the noise of the air conditioner ceases—you would suddenly be aware of such stimuli.

Our attention is selective; some events take precedence over others in gaining access to consciousness and in initiating action. Events that are important to survival usually have top priority. If we are hungry, it is difficult for us to concentrate on studying; if we experience a sudden pain, we push all other thoughts out of consciousness until we do something to make the pain go away.

When we concentrate, we are unaware of background stimuli such as other people's conversations. This ability to select stimuli to focus on enables us to avoid information overload.

Controlling Another function of consciousness is to plan, initiate, and guide our actions. Whether the plan is simple and readily completed (such as meeting a friend for lunch) or complex and long-range (such as preparing for a career), our actions must be guided and arranged so as to coordinate with events around us. In planning, events that have not yet occurred can be represented in consciousness as future possibilities; we may envision alternative "scenarios," make choices, and initiate the appropriate activities (Johnson-Laird, 1988).

Not all actions are guided by conscious decisions, nor are the solutions to all problems carried out at a conscious level. One of the tenets of modern psychology is that mental events involve both conscious and nonconscious processes and that many decisions and actions are conducted entirely outside of consciousness. The solution to a problem may occur "out of the blue" without our being aware that we have been thinking about it. And once we have the solution, we may be unable to offer an introspective account of how the solution was reached. One can cite many examples of decision making and problem solving that occur at a nonconscious level, but this does not mean that all such behaviors occur without conscious reflection. Consciousness not only monitors ongoing behavior but plays a role in directing and controlling that behavior as well.

Preconscious Memories

As just noted, we cannot focus on everything that is going on around us at any given time, nor can we examine our entire store of knowledge and memories of past events. At any given moment we can focus attention on only a few stimuli. We ignore, select, and reject all the time, so that the contents of consciousness are continually changing. Nevertheless, objects or events that are not the focus of attention can still have some influence on consciousness. For example, you may not be aware of hearing a clock strike the hour. But after a few strokes you become alert; then you can go back and count the strokes that you did not know you heard. Another example of peripheral attention (or nonconscious monitoring) is the lunch-line effect (Farthing, 1992). You are talking with a friend in a cafeteria line, ignoring other voices and general noise, when the sound of your own name in another conversation catches your attention. Clearly, you would not have detected your name in the other conversation if you had not, in some sense, been monitoring that conversation; you were not consciously aware of the other conversation until a special signal drew your attention to it. A considerable body of research indicates that we register and evaluate stimuli that we do not consciously perceive (Greenwald, 1992; Kihlstrom, 1987). These stimuli are said to influence us *subconsciously*, or to operate at a nonconscious level of awareness.

Many memories and thoughts that are not part of your consciousness at this moment can be brought to consciousness when needed. At this moment you may not be conscious of your vacation last summer, but the memories are accessible if you wish to retrieve them; then they become part of your consciousness. The term **preconscious memories** is used to refer to *memories that are accessible to consciousness.* They include specific memories of personal events as well as the information accumulated over a lifetime, such as one's knowledge of the meaning of words, the layout of the streets of a city, or the location of a particular country. They also include knowledge about learned skills like the procedures involved in driving a car or the sequence of steps in tying a shoelace. These procedures, once mastered, generally operate outside conscious awareness, but when our attention is called to them we are capable of describing the steps involved.

The Unconscious

One of the earliest theories of consciousness—and one that has been subject to considerable criticism over the years—is the psychoanalytic theory of Sigmund Freud. Freud and his followers believed that there is a portion of the mind, the **unconscious,** that *contains some memories, impulses, and desires that are not accessible to consciousness.* Freud believed that some emotionally painful memories and wishes are *repressed*—that is, diverted to the unconscious, where they may continue to influence our actions even though we are not aware of them. Repressed thoughts and impulses cannot enter our consciousness, but they can affect us in indirect or disguised ways—through dreams, irrational behaviors, mannerisms, and slips of the tongue. The term "Freudian slip" is commonly used to refer to unintentional remarks that are assumed to reveal hidden impulses. Saying "I'm sad you're better," when intending to say "I'm glad you're better," is an example of such a slip.

Freud believed that unconscious desires and impulses are the cause of most mental illnesses. He developed the method of *psychoanalysis,* which attempts to draw the repressed material back into consciousness and, in so doing, cure the individual (see Chapter 16). Most psychologists accept the idea that there are memories and mental processes that are inaccessible to introspection and accordingly may be described as unconscious. However, many would argue that Freud placed undue emphasis on the emotional aspects of the unconscious and not enough on other aspects. They would include in the unconscious a large array of mental processes that we depend on constantly in our everyday lives but to which we have no conscious access (Kihlstrom, 1987). For example, during perception, the viewer may be aware of two objects in the environment but have no awareness of the mental calculations that she performed almost instantaneously to determine that one is closer or larger than the other (see Chapter 5). Although we have conscious access to the outcome of these mental processes—in that we are aware of the size and distance of the object—we have no conscious access to their operations (Velmans, 1991).

A study of the stereotypes people hold about the elderly (for example, that they are

slow and weak) provided a striking demonstration of how cues from the environment can influence our behavior without our conscious knowledge. Participants were first given a "language test" in which they had to decipher a number of scrambled sentences. Some participants were given sentences that contained words such as *forgetful, Florida,* and *bingo*—words that the researchers believed would subconsciously evoke or "prime" the elderly stereotype in their minds; control participants saw sentences that did not contain these words. After the language test was completed, each participant was thanked and allowed to leave. A research assistant—who did not know whether the participant was in the experimental group or the control group—surreptitiously measured how long it took the participant to walk down the 40-foot hallway to the exit. The researchers found that participants who had been primed with the elderly stereotype words walked more slowly than control participants. (The word *slow* had not appeared in the sentences.) Interviews with the participants showed that they had no awareness of this influence on their behavior (Bargh, Chen, & Burrows, 1996).

Automaticity and Dissociation

An important function of consciousness is control of our actions. However, some activities are practiced so often that they become habitual or automatic. Learning to drive a car requires intense concentration at first. We have to concentrate on coordinating the different actions (shifting gears, releasing the clutch, accelerating, steering, and so forth) and can scarcely think about anything else. However, once the movements become automatic, we can carry on a conversation or admire the scenery without being conscious of driving—unless a potential danger quickly draws our attention to the operation of the car. This habituation of responses that initially required conscious attention is termed **automaticity**.

Skills like driving a car or riding a bike, once they are well learned, no longer require our attention. They become automatic, thereby allowing a relatively uncluttered consciousness to focus on other matters. Such automatic processes may have

Drawing by Dana Fradon; (c)1979 The New York Magazine, Inc.

"Good morning, beheaded—uhm I mean beloved."

For experienced drivers, the actions involved in driving have become so automatic that they can carry on a phone conversation while driving.

negative consequences on occasion—for example, when a driver cannot remember landmarks passed along the way.

The more automatic an action becomes, the less it requires conscious control. Another example is the skilled pianist who carries on a conversation with a bystander while performing a familiar piece. The pianist is exercising control over two activities—playing and talking—but does not think about the music unless a wrong key is hit, alerting her attention to it and temporarily disrupting the conversation. You can undoubtedly think of other examples of well-learned, automatic activities that require little conscious control. One way of interpreting this is to say that the control is still there (we can focus on automatic processes if we want to) but has been *dissociated* from consciousness.

The French psychiatrist Pierre Janet (1889) originated the concept of **dissociation,** in which *under certain conditions some thoughts and actions become split off, or dissociated, from the rest of consciousness and function outside of awareness.* Dissociation differs from Freud's concept of repression because the dissociated memories and thoughts are accessible to consciousness. Repressed memories, in contrast, cannot be brought to consciousness; they have to be inferred from signs or symptoms such as slips of the tongue.

When faced with a stressful situation, we may temporarily put it out of our minds in order to be able to function effectively; when bored, we may lapse into reverie or daydreams. These are mild examples of dissociation; they involve dissociating one part of consciousness from another. More extreme examples of dissociation are demonstrated by cases of dissociative identity disorder, or multiple personality, which is discussed in detail in Chapter 15.

Sleep and Dreams

We begin our discussion of consciousness with a state that seems to be its opposite: sleep. But while sleep might seem to have little in common with wakefulness, there are similarities between the two states. The phenomenon of dreaming indicates that we think while we sleep, although the type of thinking we do in dreams differs in various ways from the type we do while awake. We form memories while sleeping, as we know from the fact that we can remember dreams. Sleep is not entirely quiescent: Some people walk in their sleep. People who are asleep are not entirely insensitive to their environment: Parents are awakened by their baby's cry. Nor is sleep entirely planless: Some people can decide to wake at a given time and do so. In this section we explore several facets of sleep and dreaming.

Stages of Sleep

Some people are readily roused from sleep; others are hard to wake. Research begun in the 1930s (Loomis, Harvey, & Hobart, 1937) has produced sensitive techniques for measuring the depth of sleep and determining when dreams are occurring (Dement & Kleitman, 1957). This research uses devices that measure electrical changes on the scalp associated with spontaneous brain activity during sleep, as well as eye movements that occur during dreaming. The graphic recording of the electrical changes, or brain waves, is called an *electroencephalogram,* or EEG (see Figures 6-1 and 6-2). The EEG measures the rapidly fluctuating average electrical

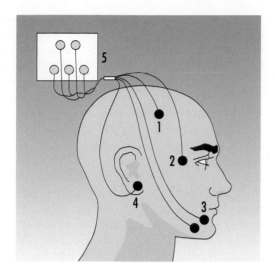

FIGURE 6-1

Arrangement of Electrodes for Recording the Electrophysiology of Sleep   *This diagram shows the way in which electrodes are attached to the person's head and face in a typical sleep experiment. Electrodes on the scalp (1) record the patterns of brain waves. Electrodes near the person's eyes (2) record eye movements. Electrodes on the chin (3) record tension and electrical activity in the muscles. A neutral electrode on the ear (4) completes the circuit through amplifiers (5) that produce graphical records of the various patterns.*

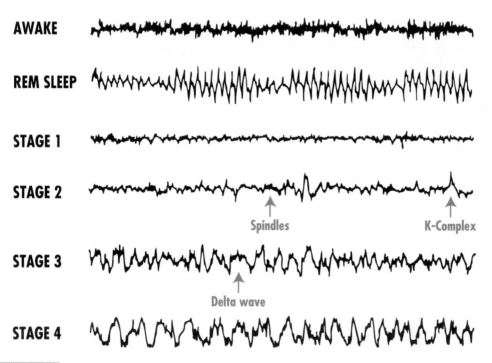

FIGURE 6-2

Electrophysiological Activity During Sleep   *This figure presents EEG recordings during wakefulness and during the various stages of sleep. The Awake Stage (relaxed with eyes closed) is characterized by alpha waves (8–12 hertz). Stage 1 is basically a transition from wakefulness to the deeper stages of sleep. Stage 2 is defined by the presence of sleep spindles (brief bursts of 12–16 hertz waves) and K-complexes (a sharp rise and fall in the brain-wave pattern). Stages 3 and 4 are marked by the presence of delta waves (1–2 hertz), and the only difference between these two stages is the amount of delta waves found. Stage 3 is scored when 20% to 50% of the record contains delta waves, and Stage 4 when the percentage of delta waves is 50% or more.*

potential of thousands of neurons lying on the surface of the cortex under the electrode; it is a rather crude measure of cortical activity, but it has proved very useful in sleep research.

Analysis of the patterns of brain waves suggests that there are five stages of sleep: four differing depths of sleep and a fifth stage, known as rapid eye movement (or REM) sleep. When a person closes her eyes and relaxes, the brain waves characteristically show a regular pattern of 8 to 12 hertz (cycles per second); these are known as *alpha waves*. As the individual drifts into Stage 1 sleep, the brain waves become less regular and are reduced in amplitude. Stage 2 is characterized by the appearance of *spindles*—short runs of rhythmical responses of 12 to 16 hertz—and an occasional sharp rise and fall in the amplitude of the whole EEG (referred to as a *K-complex*). The still deeper Stages 3 and 4 are characterized by slow waves (1 to 2 hertz), which are known as *delta waves*. Generally, it is hard to awaken the sleeper during Stages 3 and 4, although she can be aroused by something personal, such as a familiar name or a child crying. A more impersonal disturbance, such as a loud sound, may be ignored.

Succession of Sleep Stages   After an adult has been asleep for an hour or so, another change occurs. The EEG becomes very active (even more so than when the person is awake), but the person does not awaken. The electrodes placed near the person's eyes detect rapid eye movements; these are so pronounced that one can even watch the sleeper's eyes move around beneath the closed eyelids. This stage is known as **REM sleep;** the other four stages are known as **non-REM (or NREM) sleep.**

These various stages of sleep alternate throughout the night. Sleep begins with the NREM stages and consists of several sleep cycles, each containing some REM and some NREM sleep. Figure 6-3 illustrates a typical night's sleep for a young adult. As you can see, the person goes from wakefulness into a deep sleep (Stage 4) very rapidly. After about 70 minutes, Stage 3 recurs briefly, immediately followed by the first REM period of the night. Notice that the deeper stages (3 and 4) occurred during the first part of the night, whereas most REM sleep occurred in the last part. This is the typical pattern: The deeper stages tend to disappear in the second half of the night as REM becomes more prominent. There are usually four or five distinct REM periods over the course of an 8-hour night, with an occasional brief awakening as morning arrives.

The pattern of the sleep cycles varies with age. Newborn infants, for instance, spend about half their sleeping time in REM sleep. This proportion drops to 20% to 25% of total sleep time by age 5 and remains fairly constant until old age, when it drops to 18% or less. Older people tend to experience less Stage 3 and 4 sleep (sometimes these stages disappear) and more frequent and longer nighttime awakenings. A natural kind of insomnia seems to set in as people grow older (Gillin, 1985).

REM and NREM Compared   The two types of sleep, REM and NREM, are as different from

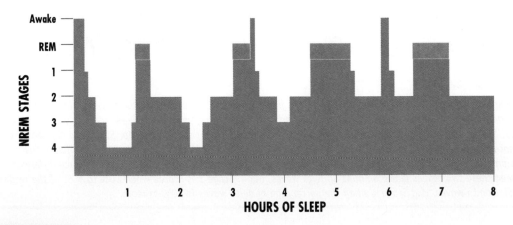

FIGURE 6-3

The Succession of Sleep Stages   *This graph provides an example of the sequence and duration of sleep stages during a typical night. The individual went successively through Stages 1 to 4 during the first hour of sleep. He then moved back through Stage 3 to REM sleep. Thereafter he cycled between NREM and REM periods, with two brief awakenings at about 3½ and 6 hours of sleep.*

each other as each is from wakefulness. Indeed, some investigators consider REM not to be sleep at all, but rather a third state of existence in addition to wakefulness and NREM sleep. During NREM sleep, eye movements are virtually absent, heart and breathing rates decrease markedly, the muscles are relaxed, and the brain's metabolic rate decreases 25% to 30% compared with wakefulness. In contrast, during REM sleep, very rapid eye movements occur in bursts lasting 10 to 20 seconds, the heart rate increases, and the brain's metabolic rate increases somewhat compared with wakefulness. Further, during REM sleep we are almost completely paralyzed—only the heart, diaphragm, eye muscles, and smooth muscles (such as the muscles of the intestines and blood vessels) are spared. To summarize, NREM sleep is characterized by an idle brain in a very relaxed body, whereas REM sleep is characterized by a brain that appears to be wide awake in a virtually paralyzed body.

Physiological evidence indicates that in REM sleep the brain is largely isolated from its sensory and motor channels; stimuli from other parts of the body are blocked from entering the brain, and there are no motor outputs. Nevertheless, the brain is still very active, being spontaneously driven by the discharge of giant neurons that originate in the brain stem. These neurons extend into parts of the brain that control eye movements and motor activities. Thus, during REM sleep the brain registers the fact that the neurons normally involved in walking and seeing are activated, even though the body itself is doing neither of these things (Hobson, 1994).

Sleepers who are awakened during REM sleep almost always report having a dream, but when awakened during NREM sleep they will report a dream only about 50% of the time (Antrobus, 1983; Cavallero et al., 1992; Foulkes & Schmidt, 1983). The dreams reported when a person is roused from REM sleep tend to be visually vivid and have emotional and illogical features—they represent the type of experience we typically associate with the word "dream." The longer the period of REM sleep before being aroused, the longer and more elaborate the reported dream. In contrast, NREM dreams are neither as visual nor as emotionally charged as REM dreams, and more directly related to what is happening in the person's waking life. Thus, mental activity is different in REM and NREM periods, as indicated by the types of dreams we report and the frequency of reporting a dream.

Sleep Theory

Why are we awake at certain times and asleep at others? Two leading sleep researchers, Dale Edgar and William Dement (1992), have proposed an *opponent-process model* of sleep and wakefulness. According to this model, the brain possesses two opponent processes that govern the tendency to fall asleep or remain awake. They are the homeostatic sleep drive and the clock-dependent alerting process.

The homeostatic sleep drive is a physiological process that strives to obtain the amount of sleep required for a stable level of daytime alertness. It is active throughout the night, but it also operates during the daytime. Throughout the day the need to sleep is continuously building. If we have slept too little the previous night, the tendency to fall asleep during the day will be significant.

The clock-dependent alerting process is controlled by the so-called *biological clock*, which consists of two tiny neural structures located in the center of the brain. This "clock" controls a series of psychological

In an experiment by noted sleep researcher William Dement, a narcoleptic dog suddenly falls asleep. About one in 1,000 humans suffers from this debilitating sleep disorder.

and physiological changes, including rhythms of alertness, that are termed **circadian rhythms** because they occur approximately every 24 hours (the term comes from the Latin words *circa,* meaning "around," and *dies,* "day"). The biological clock is affected by exposure to light: Daylight signals it to stop the secretion of melatonin, a hormone that induces sleep.

The two opponent processes—homeostatic sleep drive and the clock-dependent alerting process—interact to produce our daily cycle of sleep and wakefulness. Whether we are asleep or awake at any given time depends on the relative strength of the two processes. During the day the clock-dependent alerting process usually overcomes the drive for sleep, but during the evening our alertness decreases as the urge to sleep becomes stronger. Late in the evening the biological clock becomes inactive and we fall asleep.

Sleep Disorders

About 90% of adults sleep 6 to 9 hours per night, with the largest number sleeping $7\frac{1}{2}$ to 8 hours. While some people sleep only 6 to 7 hours, most of these people have measurable signs of sleepiness during the daytime, even if they do not realize it. It appears that most adults require 8 to 9 hours of sleep to be free from daytime sleepiness (Kripke & Gillin, 1985). A **sleep disorder** exists *when inability to sleep well produces impaired daytime functioning or excessive sleepiness.* In this section we look at some common types of sleep disorders.

Deprivation   Whether they are aware of it or not, most people occasionally or chronically deprive themselves of adequate sleep. Consider a few examples:

■ Thirty percent of high-school and college students fall asleep in class at least once a week.

■ Thirty-one percent of all drivers have fallen asleep at the wheel at least once in their lifetime.

■ Fatigue is the primary factor that detrimentally affects the ability of pilots.

■ The nuclear accidents at Chernobyl and Three Mile Island occurred in the early morning hours, when night-shift workers were fatigued and missed, or were con-

fused by, warning signals on their control panels (Gallup Organization, 1995; Maas, 1998; Pasztor, 1996).

Recent Gallup surveys have found that 56% of the adult population reports daytime drowsiness as a problem. According to a leading sleep researcher, many of these individuals are "waking zombies" carrying years of accumulated "sleep debt." He points out that "a one-hour sleep loss every night for an entire week is equivalent to having pulled one all-nighter" (Maas, 1998, p. 53). A common sign of sleep deprivation is inability to get through the day without a temporary loss in energy and alertness, usually occurring in mid-afternoon. Many people attribute this state to a heavy meal, a low dose of alcohol, or environmental conditions such as sitting in a warm room and listening to a dull lecture. But these factors do not cause sleepiness—they merely reveal the presence of sleep debt. With adequate sleep, a normal person is alert throughout the day, even when engaged in nonstimulating, sedentary activities.

Sleep researchers have demonstrated that alertness significantly increases when people who normally get eight hours of sleep get an additional two hours of sleep. While most people can operate satisfactorily on eight hours of sleep, they are not at their best. Moreover, they lack a "safety margin" to make up for the times when they get less than that amount of sleep. The loss of as little as an hour of sleep increases the likelihood of inattentiveness, mistakes, illness, and accidents (Maas, 1998).

Even if you cannot arrange to get 10 hours of sleep a night, you can avoid excessive sleep debt by getting 8 or 9 hours of restful sleep. Table 6-1 suggests a variety of techniques that can be used to ensure a good night's sleep.

Insomnia   The term **insomnia** refers to complaints about a symptom, namely, *dissatisfaction with the amount or quality of one's sleep.* Whether or not a person has insomnia is a largely subjective matter. Many people who complain of insomnia are found to have perfectly normal sleep when studied in a sleep laboratory, whereas others who do not complain of insomnia have detectable sleep disturbances (Trinder, 1988). This

TABLE 6-1

Advice for a Good Night's Sleep   *There is considerable agreement among researchers and clinicians on how to avoid sleep problems. These recommendations are summarized in the table; some are based on actual research, and others are simply the best judgments of experts in the field.*

Regular Sleep Schedule   Establish a regular schedule of going to bed and getting up. Set your alarm for a specific time every morning and get up at that time no matter how little you may have slept. Be consistent about naps. Take a nap every afternoon or not at all; when you take a nap only occasionally, you probably will not sleep well that night. Waking up late on weekends can also disrupt your sleep cycle.

Alcohol and Caffeine   Having a stiff drink of alcohol before going to bed may put you to sleep, but it disturbs the sleep cycle and can cause you to wake up early the next day. In addition, stay away from caffeinated drinks like coffee or cola for several hours before bedtime. Caffeine works as a stimulant even on those people who claim they are not affected by it, and the body needs 4 to 5 hours to halve the amount of caffeine in the bloodstream at any one time. If you must drink something before bedtime, try milk; there is evidence to support the folklore that a glass of warm milk at bedtime induces sleep.

Eating Before Bedtime   Don't eat heavily before going to bed, since your digestive system will have to do several hours of work. If you must eat something before bedtime, have a light snack.

Excercise   Regular exercise will help you sleep better, but don't engage in a strenuous workout just before going to bed.

Sleeping Pills   Be careful about using sleeping pills. All of the various kinds tend to disrupt the sleep cycle, and long-term use inevitably leads to insomnia. Even on nights before exams, avoid using a sleeping pill. One bad night of sleep tends not to affect performance the next day, but hangover from a sleeping pill may.

Relax   Avoid stressful thoughts before bedtime and engage in soothing activities that help you relax. Try to follow the same routine every night before going to bed; it might involve taking a warm bath or listening to soft music for a few minutes. Find a room temperature at which you are comfortable and maintain it throughout the night.

When all fails   If you are in bed and have trouble falling asleep, don't get up. Stay in bed and try to relax. But if that fails and you become tense, then get up for a brief time and do something restful that reduces anxiety. Doing push-ups or some other form of exercise to wear yourself out is not a good idea. (After Pion, 1991)

does not mean that insomnia is not a real condition, only that subjective reports of sleeplessness do not always correlate well with more objective measures.

A perplexing feature of insomnia is that people seem to overestimate the amount of sleep lost. One study that monitored the sleep of people who identified themselves as insomniacs found that only about half of them were actually awake as much as 30 minutes during the night (Carskadon, Mitler, & Dement, 1974). The problem may be that some people remember only time spent awake and think they have not slept because they have no memory of doing so.

Narcolepsy and Apnea   Two relatively rare but severe sleep disorders are narcolepsy and apnea. A person with **narcolepsy** *has recurring, irresistible attacks of drowsiness and may fall asleep at any time*—while writing a letter, driving a car, or carrying on

a conversation. If a student falls asleep while a professor is lecturing, that may be perfectly normal; but if a professor falls asleep while lecturing, he or she may be suffering from narcolepsy. Such episodes can occur several times a day in severe cases, and last from a few seconds to 15–30 minutes. Narcoleptics have difficulty keeping jobs because of their daytime sleepiness, and are potentially dangerous if they are driving a car or operating machinery when an attack occurs. Approximately one in a thousand individuals suffers from debilitating narcolepsy, and the incidence of milder, unrecognized cases may be much higher.

Essentially, narcolepsy is the intrusion of REM episodes into daytime hours. During attacks, victims go quickly into a REM state, so rapidly in fact that they may lose muscle control and collapse before they can lie down. Moreover, many report experiencing hallucinations during an attack as reality is replaced by vivid REM dreams. Narcolepsy runs in families, and there is evidence that a specific gene or combination of genes makes an individual susceptible to the disorder (Hobson, 1988).

In **apnea,** *the individual stops breathing while asleep.* There are two reasons for apnea attacks. One reason is that the brain fails to send a "breathe" signal to the diaphragm and other breathing muscles, thus causing breathing to stop. The other reason is that muscles at the top of the throat become too relaxed, allowing the windpipe to partially close and thereby forcing the breathing muscles to pull harder on incoming air, which causes the airway to completely collapse. During an apnea episode, the oxygen level of the blood drops dramatically, leading to the secretion of emergency hormones. This reaction causes the sleeper to awaken in order to begin breathing again.

Most people have a few apnea episodes each night, but people with severe sleep problems may have several hundred episodes per night. With each one, they wake up in order to resume breathing, but these arousals are so brief that the person generally is unaware of them. The result is that people who suffer from apnea can spend 12 or more hours in bed each night and still be so sleepy the next day that they cannot function and may even fall asleep in the middle of a conversation (Ancoli-Israel, Kripke, & Mason, 1987).

Sleep apnea is common among older men. Sleeping pills, which make arousal more difficult, lengthen periods of apnea (during which the brain is deprived of oxygen) and may prove fatal. Failure to awaken, and thereby terminate a period of apnea, is probably one of the main reasons that some people die in their sleep.

Dreams

Dreaming is *an altered state of consciousness in which remembered images and fantasies are temporarily confused with external reality.* Investigators do not yet understand why people dream at all, much less why they dream what they do. However, modern methods of study have answered a great many questions about dreaming. Some of them are explored here.

Does Everyone Dream? Although many people do not recall their dreams in the morning, evidence from studies of REM sleep suggests that nonrecallers do as much dreaming as recallers. If you take people who have sworn that they never dreamed in their life, put them in a dream research laboratory, and wake them from REM sleep, they will recall dreams at rates comparable to those of other people. If someone says "I never dream," what they mean is "I can't recall my dreams."

Researchers have proposed several hypotheses to account for differences in dream recall. One possibility is that nonrecallers simply have more difficulty than recallers in remembering their dreams. Another hypothesis suggests that some people awaken relatively easily in the midst of REM sleep and therefore recall more dreams than those who sleep more soundly. The most generally accepted model of dream recall supports the idea that what happens on awakening is the crucial factor. According to this hypothesis, unless a distraction-free waking period occurs shortly after dreaming, the memory of the dream is not consolidated—that is, the dream cannot be stored in memory (Hobson, 1988; Koulack & Goodenough, 1976).

If upon awakening we make an effort to remember what we were dreaming at the time, some of the dream content will be recalled at a later time. Otherwise, the dream will fade quickly; we may know that we have had a dream but will be unable to remember its content. If you are interested in remembering your dreams, keep a notebook and pencil beside your bed. Tell yourself that you want to wake up when you have a dream. When you do, immediately try to recall the details and write them down. As your dream recall improves, look for patterns. Underline anything that strikes you as odd and tell yourself that the next time something similar happens, you are going to recognize it as a sign that you are dreaming. (Of course, you will lose some sleep if you follow this regimen!)

How Long Do Dreams Last? Some dreams seem almost instantaneous. The alarm clock rings, and we awaken to complex memories of a fire breaking out and fire engines arriving with their sirens blasting. Because the alarm is still ringing, we assume that the sound must have produced the dream. Research suggests, however, that a ringing alarm clock or other sound merely reinstates a complete scene from earlier memories or dreams. This experience has its parallel during wakefulness, when a single cue may tap a rich memory. The length of a typical dream can be inferred from a REM study in which participants were awakened and asked to act out what they had been dreaming (Dement & Wolpert, 1958). The time it took them to pantomime the dream was almost the same as the length of the REM sleep period, suggesting that the incidents in dreams commonly last about as long as they would in real life.

Do People Know When They Are Dreaming? The answer to this question is "sometimes yes." People can be taught to recognize that they are dreaming, yet their awareness does not interfere with the spontaneous flow of the dream. For example, people have been trained to press a switch when they notice that they are dreaming (Salamy, 1970).

Some people have *lucid dreams,* in which events seem so normal (lacking the bizarre and illogical character of most dreams) that the dreamers feel as if they are awake and conscious. Lucid dreamers report doing various "experiments" within their dreams to determine whether they are awake or dreaming. They also report an occasional "false awakening" within a dream. For example, one lucid dreamer discovered that he was dreaming and decided to call a taxicab as an indication of his control over events. When he reached into his pocket to see if he had some change to pay the driver, he thought that he woke up. He then found the coins scattered about the bed. At this point he really awoke and found himself lying in a different position and, of course, without any coins (Brown, 1936). Note, however, that relatively few people achieve lucidity with any regularity (Squier & Domhoff, 1998).

Can People Control the Content of Their Dreams? Psychologists have demonstrated that some control of dream content is possible by making suggestions to people in the presleep period and then analyzing the content of their dreams. In a carefully designed study of an implicit predream suggestion, researchers tested the effect of wearing red goggles for several hours before going to sleep. Although the researchers made no actual suggestion and the participants did not understand the purpose of the experiment, many participants reported that their visual dream worlds were tinted red (Roffwarg et al., 1978). In a study of the effect of an overt predream suggestion, participants were asked to try to dream about a personality characteristic that they wished they had. Most of the participants had at least one dream in which the intended trait could be recognized (Cartwright, 1974). Despite these findings, however, there is little evidence that dream content can actually be controlled (Domhoff, 1985).

Theories of Dream Sleep

One of the earliest theories of the function of dream sleep was suggested by Sigmund Freud. In *The Interpretation of Dreams* (1900), Freud proposed that dreams provide a "royal road to a knowledge of the unconscious activities of the mind." He believed that dreams are a disguised attempt at wish fulfillment. By this he meant that the dream touches on wishes, needs, or ideas that the individual finds unacceptable and have been repressed to the unconscious (for example, Oedipal longings for the parent of the opposite sex). These wishes and ideas are the *latent content* of the dream. Freud used the metaphor of a censor to explain the conversion of latent content into *manifest content* (the characters and events that make up the actual narrative of the dream). In effect, Freud said, the censor protects the sleeper, enabling him or her to express repressed impulses symbolically while avoiding the guilt or anxiety that would occur if they were to appear consciously in undisguised form.

According to Freud, the transformation of latent content into manifest content is done by "dream work," whose function is to code and disguise material in the unconscious in such a way that it can reach consciousness. However, sometimes dream work fails, and the resulting anxiety awakens the dreamer. The dream essentially expresses the fulfillment of wishes or needs that are too painful or guilt-inducing to be acknowledged consciously (Freud, 1933, 1965).

Subsequent research challenged several aspects of Freud's theory. After surveying dozens of studies of dreaming, Fisher and Greenberg (1977, 1996) concluded that while there is good evidence that the content of dreams has psychological meaning, there is none that supports Freud's distinction between manifest and latent content. Thus, while most psychologists would agree with Freud's general conclusion that dreams focus on emotional concerns, they question the concept of "dream work" and the idea that dreams represent wish fulfillment.

Since Freud's time, a variety of theories have been advanced to explain the role of sleep and dreams. Evans (1984), for example, views sleep, particularly REM sleep, as a period when the brain disengages from the external world and uses this "off-line" time to sift through the information that was input during the day and to incorporate it into memory. We are not consciously aware of the processing that occurs during REM sleep. During dreaming, however, the brain comes back on-line for a brief time and the conscious mind observes a small sample of the modification and reorganization of information that is taking place. The brain attempts to interpret this information the same way it would interpret stimuli coming from the outside world, giving rise to the kinds of pseudo-events that characterize dreams. Thus, according to Evans, dreams are nothing more than a small subset of the vast amount of information that is being scanned and sorted during REM sleep, a momentary glimpse by the conscious mind that we remember if we awaken. Evans believes that dreams can be useful in making inferences about the processing that occurs during REM sleep, but that they represent an extremely small sample on which to base such inferences. (Additional research on memory processing during REM sleep is presented in the Frontiers of Psychological Research feature on the following page.)

Other researchers take different approaches. Hobson (1997), for example, notes that dreaming is characterized by formal visual imagery (akin to hallucination), inconstancy of time, place, and person (akin to disorientation), and inability to recall (akin to amnesia). Dreaming thus resembles delirium. It has also been suggested that dreams may have a problem-solving function (Cartwright,

1978, 1992, 1996), but this theory has been challenged on methodological grounds (Antrobus, 1993; Foulkes, 1993). Moreover, the content of dreams tends to differ according to the culture, gender, and personality of the dreamer, suggesting that dreams have some psychological meaning (Domhoff, 1996; Hobson, 1988). That is, dream content may *reflect* personal conflicts, but this does not mean that dreams function to *resolve* those conflicts (Squier & Domhoff, 1998).

In this regard, it is worth noting that only about half of all dreams include even one element related to events of the previous day (Botnam & Crovitz, 1992; Hartmann, 1968; Nielson & Powell, 1992). Moreover, systematic analyses of dream content have found that rates of aggression are higher than rates of friendly interactions; in fact, the murder rate in dreams is 2,226 per 100,000 characters, far above real-world rates (Hall & Van de Castle, 1966)! In addition, there are more negative than positive emotions. Thus, dreams cannot be viewed as simple extensions of the activities of the previous day. On the other hand, researchers have repeatedly found great consistency in what people dream about over years or decades. G. William Domhoff and Adam Schneider (1998) report that

> Our analyses of lengthy dream journals reveal that there is an astonishing degree of consistency in what a person dreams about over several months or years, even 40 or 50 years in the two longest dream series analyzed to date. There are also striking continuities between dream findings and waking life, making possible accurate predictions about the concerns and interests of the dreamers. These findings suggest that dreams have "meaning."

Analyses of dreams have also found significant age, gender, and cross-cultural similarities and differences in their content, leading some theorists to propose that dreaming is a cognitive process (Antrobus, 1991; Domhoff, 1996; Foulkes, 1985). An early researcher in this field pointed out that dreams seem to express conceptions and concerns (Hall, 1947, 1953). However, dreaming differs from waking thought in that it lacks intentionality and reflectiveness (Blagrove, 1992, 1996; Foulkes, 1985). Thus, in the view of these theorists it is unlikely that dreaming has a problem-solving function. Instead, it is a

FRONTIERS OF PSYCHOLOGICAL RESEARCH

Memory Consolidation During REM Sleep

Our ability to store incoming information in memory for retrieval at later times is called *memory consolidation*. Researchers have long hypothesized that REM sleep facilitates the consolidation of long-term memories. Several studies with rats have demonstrated that being deprived of REM sleep interferes with the animal's performance on a task that was learned the previous day. And when rats are given intensive training on a difficult maze-learning task, the amount of time spent in REM sleep increases significantly. However, until recently, studies designed to test for similar effects in humans either failed to do so or were at best equivocal (Dujardin, Guerrien, & Leconte, 1990; Horne & McGrath, 1984). The breakthrough with human participants was achieved by Karni et al., (1994) using a unique type of learning task. On each trial a line segment is briefly flashed in the participant's peripheral field of vision; the participant's task is to correctly identify the orientation (angle) of the line. It is a very difficult task because the flash is extremely brief, but with daily

practice sessions—involving many trials—participants eventually become quite proficient. However, the course of learning is atypical: Participants show little improvement during a practice session, but when they return the next day, they are clearly better than they were at the end of the preceding session. Thus, while performance steadily improves over the course of several days, the improvement is not evident within a practice session but only from one day's session to the next. This is an ideal task to determine whether memory consolidation occurs during a specific stage of sleep.

Participants were trained on the task in the evening before going to sleep in the laboratory. Some participants were awakened by an electric bell every time the EEG showed that they were entering REM sleep. Other participants had their sleep interrupted the same number of times, but during NREM sleep Stages 3 and 4 (what is called slow-wave sleep). The following day all participants were tested. Those with REM deprivation showed no improvement at all; their perfor-

mance was the same as the night before. On the other hand, participants who were awakened during slow-wave sleep improved significantly over the night.

This work, taken together with earlier research, tends to support the idea that REM sleep plays a role in the consolidation of memory. However, we still have a great deal to learn about the specific mechanisms involved and whether REM sleep by itself, or REM sleep in conjunction with other sleep stages, is the critical factor (Wilson & McNaughton, 1994; Winson, 1990). REM sleep is probably not a necessary condition for memory consolidation, but it may greatly facilitate the process. And it may be more important for the consolidation of complex skills and memories than it is for simple learning tasks. The consolidation of memory undoubtedly requires the meshing of new information with old memories, a process that could explain why dreams often involve a mix of life's current difficulties and past experiences (Ramachandran et al., 1996).

cognitive activity, as is evidenced by the continuity between dream content and waking thoughts and behavior. As Domhoff notes, "The concerns people express in their dreams are the concerns they have in waking life. What they dream about is also what they think about or do when they are awake" (1996, p. 8). Parents dream of their children; aggressive dream content is more common among people under age 30 than in older people; and women are more often victims of aggression. These patterns support what Domhoff and others refer to as the "continuity theory" of dreaming, in which dreaming is an imaginative process that reflects the individual's conceptions, concerns, and emotional preoccupations.

Meditation

Meditation refers to *achieving an altered state of consciousness by performing certain rituals and exercises*. These include controlling and regulating breathing, sharply restricting one's field of attention, eliminating external stimuli, assuming yogic body positions, and forming mental images of an event or symbol. The result is a pleasant, mildly altered subjective state in which the individual feels mentally and physically relaxed. After extensive practice, some individuals may have mystical experiences in which they lose self-awareness and gain a sense of being involved in a wider consciousness, however defined. The belief

The rituals of meditation include regulating breathing, restricting one's field of attention, eliminating external stimuli, and forming mental images of an event or symbol. Traditional forms of meditation follow the practices of yoga.

that such meditative techniques may cause a change in consciousness goes back to ancient times and is represented in every major world religion. Buddhists, Hindus, Sufis, Jews, and Christians all have literature describing rituals that induce meditative states.

Traditional forms of meditation follow the practices of *yoga,* a system of thought based on the Hindu religion, or *Zen,* which is derived from Chinese and Japanese Buddhism. Two common meditation techniques are *opening-up meditation,* in which the person clears his or her mind in order to receive new experiences, and *concentrative meditation,* in which the benefits are obtained by actively attending to some object, word, or idea. Following is a typical description of opening-up meditation:

> This approach begins with the resolve to do nothing, to think nothing, to make no effort of one's own, to relax completely and let go of one's mind and body . . . stepping out of the stream of ever-changing ideas and feelings which your mind is in, watch the onrush of the stream. Refuse to be submerged in the current. Changing the metaphor . . . watch your ideas, feelings, and wishes fly across the firmament like a flock of birds. Let them fly freely. Just keep a watch. Don't let the birds carry you off into the clouds. (Chauduri, 1965, pp. 30–31)

Here is a corresponding statement for concentrative meditation:

> The purpose of these sessions is to learn about concentration. Your aim is to concentrate on the blue vase. By concentration I do not mean analyzing the different parts of the vase, but rather, trying to see the vase as it exists in itself, without any connections to other things. Exclude all other thoughts or feelings or sounds or body sensations. (Deikman, 1963, p. 330)

After a few sessions of concentrative meditation, people typically report a number of effects: an altered, more intense perception of the vase; some time shortening, particularly in retrospect; conflicting perceptions, as if the vase fills the visual field and does not fill it; decreasing effectiveness of external stimuli (less distraction and eventually less conscious registration); and an impression of the meditative state as pleasant and rewarding.

Experimental studies of meditation provide only limited insight into the alterations of consciousness that a person can achieve when meditative practice and training extend over many years. In his study of the Matramudra, a centuries-old Tibetan Buddhist text, Brown (1977) has described the complex training required to master the technique. He has also shown that cognitive changes can be expected at different levels of meditation. (In this type of meditation, people proceed through five levels until they reach a thoughtless, perceptionless, selfless state known as *concentrative samadhi*.)

Some research evidence suggests that meditation may reduce arousal (especially in easily stressed individuals) and may be valuable for people suffering from anxiety and tension.

Hypnosis

Of all the altered states of consciousness discussed in this chapter, none has raised more questions than hypnosis. Once associated with the occult, hypnosis has become the subject of rigorous scientific investigation. As in all fields of psychological investigation, uncertainties remain, but by now many facts have been established. In this section we explore what is known about this controversial phenomenon.

Induction of Hypnosis

In **hypnosis,** *a willing and cooperative individual* (the only kind that can be hypnotized under most circumstances) *relinquishes some control over his or her behavior to the hypnotist and accepts some distortion of reality.* The hypnotist uses a variety of meth-

ods to induce this condition. For example, the person may be asked to concentrate all his or her thoughts on a small target (such as a thumbtack on the wall) while gradually becoming relaxed. The hypnotist may suggest that the person is becoming sleepy because, like sleep, hypnosis is a relaxed state in which a person is out of touch with ordinary environmental demands. But sleep is only a metaphor. The person is told that he or she will not really go to sleep but will continue to listen to the hypnotist.

The same state can be induced by methods other than relaxation. A hyperalert hypnotic trance is characterized by increased tension and alertness. For example, in one study, participants riding a stationary bicycle while receiving suggestions of strength and alertness were as responsive to hypnotic suggestions as conventionally relaxed participants (Banyai & Hilgard, 1976). This result denies the common equation of hypnosis with relaxation, but it is consistent with the trance-induction methods used by the whirling dervishes of some Muslim religious orders.

Modern hypnotists do not use authoritarian commands. Indeed, with a little training, people can hypnotize themselves (Ruch, 1975). The person enters the hypnotic state when the conditions are right; the hypnotist merely helps set the conditions. The following

A therapist induces a hypnotic state. Not all individuals are equally responsive to hypnosis.

changes are characteristic of the hypnotized state:

- Planfulness ceases. A deeply hypnotized individual does not like to initiate activity and would rather wait for the hypnotist to suggest something to do.

- Attention becomes more selective than usual. A person who is told to listen only to the hypnotist's voice will ignore any other voices in the room.

- Enriched fantasy is readily evoked. People may find themselves enjoying experiences at places that are distant in time and space.

- Reality testing is reduced and reality distortion accepted. A person may uncritically accept hallucinated experiences (for example, conversing with an imagined person who is believed to be sitting in a nearby chair) and will not check to determine whether that person is real.

- Suggestibility is increased. An individual must accept suggestions in order to be hypnotized at all, but whether suggestibility is increased under hypnosis is a matter of some dispute. Careful studies have found some increase in suggestibility following hypnotic induction, though less than is commonly supposed (Ruch, Morgan, & Hilgard, 1973).

- Posthypnotic amnesia is often present. When instructed to do so, an individual who is highly responsive to hypnotism will forget all or most of what took place during the hypnotic session. When a

prearranged release signal is given, the memories are restored.

Not all individuals are equally responsive to hypnosis, as Figure 6-4 indicates. Roughly 5% to 10% of the population cannot be hypnotized even by a skilled hypnotist, and the remainder show varying degrees of susceptibility. However, if a person is hypnotized on one occasion, he or she probably will be equally susceptible on another occasion (Hilgard, 1965; Piccione, Hilgard, & Zimbardo, 1989).

Hypnotic Suggestions

Suggestions given to a hypnotized individual can result in a variety of behaviors and experiences. The person's motor control may be affected, new memories may be lost or old ones reexperienced, and current perceptions may be radically altered.

Control of Movement   Many hypnotized individuals respond to direct suggestion with involuntary movement. For example, if a person stands with arms outstretched and hands facing each other and the hypnotist suggests that the person's hands are attracted to each other, the hands will soon begin to move together and the person will feel propelled by some external force. Direct suggestion can also inhibit movement. If a suggestible individual is told that an arm is stiff (like a bar of iron or an arm in a splint) and then is asked to bend the arm, it will not

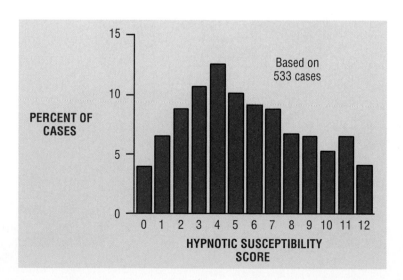

FIGURE 6-4

Individual Differences in Hypnotizability   *After using a standard procedure designed to induce hypnosis, researchers administered 12 test suggestions from the Stanford Hypnotic Susceptibility Scale to 533 participants. The object of the experiment was to test the appearance of hypnotic responses such as those described in the text (for example, being unable to bend one's arm or separate interlocked fingers when the hypnotist suggests these possibilities). The response was scored as present or absent, and the present responses were totaled for each participant to yield a score ranging from 0 (totally unresponsive) to 12 (most responsive). Most individuals fell in the middle ranges, with a few very high and a few very low. (After Hilgard, 1965)*

bend, or more effort than usual will be needed to make it bend. This response is less common than suggested movement.

People who have been roused from hypnosis may respond with movement to a prearranged signal by the hypnotist. This is called a *posthypnotic response*. Even if the suggestion has been forgotten, they will feel a compulsion to carry out the behavior. They may try to justify such behavior as rational even though the urge to perform it is impulsive. For example, a young man searching for a rational explanation of why he opened a window when the hypnotist took off her glasses (the prearranged signal) remarked that the room felt a little stuffy.

Posthypnotic Amnesia   At the suggestion of the hypnotist, events occurring during hypnosis may be "forgotten" until a signal from the hypnotist enables the individual to recall them. This is called *posthypnotic amnesia*. People differ widely in their susceptibility to posthypnotic amnesia, as Figure 6-5 shows. The items to be recalled in this study were 10 actions that the participants performed while hypnotized. A few participants forgot none or only one or two items; most participants forgot four or five items. However, a sizable number of participants forgot all 10 items. Similar results have been found in many studies of posthypnotic amnesia. The group of participants with the higher recall is larger and presumably represents the average hypnotic responders; the smaller group, the participants who forgot all 10 items, has been described as "hypnotic virtuosos."

Differences in recall between the two groups do not appear to be related to differences in memory capacity: Once the amnesia is canceled at a prearranged signal from the hypnotist, highly amnesic participants remember as many items as those who are less amnesic. Some researchers have suggested that hypnosis temporarily interferes with the person's ability to retrieve a particular item from memory but does not affect actual memory storage (Kihlstrom, 1987).

Positive and Negative Hallucinations   Some hypnotic experiences require a higher level of hypnotic talent than others. The vivid and convincing perceptual distortions of hallucinations, for instance, are relatively rare in hypnotized individuals. Two types of sug-

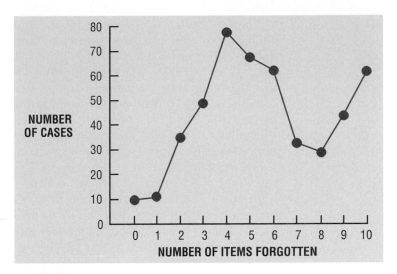

FIGURE 6-5

The Distribution of Posthypnotic Amnesia   *Individuals performed 10 actions while hypnotized and were then given posthypnotic amnesia instructions. When asked what occurred during hypnosis, these individuals varied in the number of actions they failed to recall: The level of forgetting for a given individual ranged from 0 to 10 items. The experiment involved 491 people, and the graph plots the number of people at each level of forgetting. The plot shows a bimodal distribution for posthypnotic amnesia, with peaks at 4 and 10 items forgotten. (After Cooper, 1979)*

gested hallucinations have been documented: *positive hallucinations*, in which the person sees an object or hears a voice that is not actually present; and *negative hallucinations*, in which the person does not perceive something that normally would be perceived. Many hallucinations have both positive and negative components. For example, in order not to see a person sitting in a chair (a negative hallucination), an individual must see the parts of the chair that would ordinarily be blocked from view (a positive hallucination).

Hallucinations can also occur as a result of posthypnotic suggestion. For example, individuals may be told that upon being aroused from the hypnotic state they will find themselves holding a rabbit that wants to be petted and that the rabbit will ask, "What time is it?" Seeing and petting the rabbit will seem natural to most people. But when they find themselves giving the correct time of day, they are surprised and try to provide an explanation for the behavior: "Did I hear someone ask the time? It's funny, it seemed to be the rabbit asking, but rabbits can't talk!"

Negative hallucinations can be used to control pain. In many cases hypnosis eliminates pain even though the source of the pain—a severe burn or a bone fracture, for example—continues. The failure to perceive something (pain) that would normally be perceived qualifies this response as a negative hallucination. The pain reduction need not be complete in order for hypnosis to be useful in giving relief. Reducing pain by 20% can make the patient's life more tolerable. Experimental studies have shown that the amount of pain reduction is closely related to the degree of measured hypnotizability (Crasilneck & Hall, 1985; Hilgard & Hilgard, 1975).

The Hidden Observer

The concept of a **hidden observer** originated with Hilgard's (1986) observation that in many hypnotized individuals *a part of the mind that is not within awareness seems to be watching the person's experience as a whole.* This finding has been described as follows:

> The circumstances of Hilgard's discovery of a doubled train of thought in hypnosis were suitably dramatic. He was giving a classroom demonstration of hypnosis using an experienced subject who, as it happened, was blind. Hilgard induced deafness, telling him that he would be able to hear when a hand was put on his shoulder. Cut off from what was going on around him, he became bored and began to think of other things. Hilgard showed the class how unresponsive he was to noise or speech, but then the question arose as to whether he was as unresponsive as he seemed. In a quiet voice, Hilgard asked the subject whether, though he was hypnotically deaf, there might be "some part of him" that could hear; if so, would he raise a forefinger? To the surprise of everyone—including the hypnotized subject—the finger rose.
>
> At this, the subject wanted to know what was going on. Hilgard put a hand on his shoulder so he could hear, promised to explain later, but in the meantime asked the subject what he remembered. What he remembered was that everything had become still, that he was bored and had begun thinking about a problem in statistics. Then he felt his forefinger rise, and he wanted to know why.
>
> Hilgard then asked for a report from "that part of you that listened to me before and

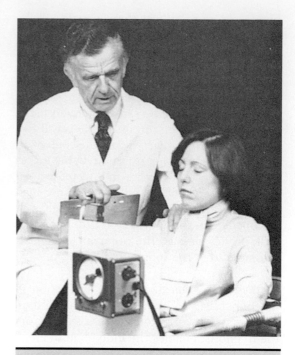

Previously when her hand was in the icewater the woman felt no pain following suggestions of hypnotic anesthesia. By placing a hand on her shoulder, however, Dr. Hilgard tapped a "hidden observer" that reported the pain that the subject had felt at some level.

> made your finger rise," while instructing the hypnotized subject that he would not be able to hear what he himself said. It turned out that this second part of the subject's awareness had heard all that went on and was able to report it. Hilgard found a suitable metaphor to describe this detached witness—the hidden observer. (Hebb, 1982, p. 53)

Thus, the hidden-observer metaphor refers to a mental structure that monitors everything that happens, including events that the hypnotized individual is not consciously aware of perceiving. The presence of the hidden observer has been demonstrated in many experiments (Kihlstrom, 1985; Zamansky & Bartis, 1985). In studies of pain relief, for example, participants are able to describe how the pain feels, using automatic writing or speaking, at the same time that their conscious system accepts and responds to the hypnotist's suggestion of pain relief. Hilgard and his colleagues have compared this phenomenon to everyday experiences in which an individual divides attention between two tasks, such as driving a car and conversing at the same time or making a speech and simultaneously evaluating one's performance as an orator.

Although hidden-observer experiments have been replicated in many laboratories and clinics, they have been criticized on methodological grounds. Skeptics argue that implied demands for compliance may have produced the results (see, for example, Spanos, 1986; Spanos & Hewitt, 1980). In an experiment designed to determine the role of compliance, researchers have shown that it is possible to distinguish the responses of the truly hypnotized from those of the merely compliant. They asked participants of proven low hypnotizability to simulate hypnosis while highly responsive participants behaved naturally. The experimenter did not know to which group each participant belonged. The simulators did conform to the implied demands in the way they were expected to, but their reports of the subjective experiences differed significantly from those of individuals who were actually hypnotized (Hilgard et al., 1978; Zamansky & Bartis, 1985).

Psychoactive Drugs

In addition to meditation and hypnosis, drugs can be used to alter a person's state of consciousness. Since ancient times people have used drugs to stimulate or relax, to bring on sleep or prevent it, to enhance ordinary perceptions, or to produce hallucinations. The word *drug* can be used to refer to any substance (other than food) that chemically alters the functioning of an organism. The term **psychoactive drugs** refers to *drugs that affect behavior, consciousness, and/or mood.* These drugs include not only illegal "street" drugs such as heroin and marijuana but also legal drugs such as tranquilizers

Although alcohol and tobacco are legal, they are included in the category of psychoactive drugs because they affect behavior, consciousness, and mood.

and stimulants. Familiar, widely used drugs such as alcohol, nicotine, and caffeine are also included in this category.

It should be noted that whether use of a particular drug is legal or not does not reflect the risks and dangers associated with the drug. For example, caffeine (coffee) is totally accepted, and its use is unregulated; nicotine (tobacco) is minimally regulated and at present is not even under the jurisdiction of the Food and Drug Administration; alcohol is subject to numerous regulations but is legal; and marijuana is illegal. Yet it could be argued that of all these substances nicotine is the most harmful, since it is responsible for about 360,000 deaths per year. One could well ask whether nicotine would even be made a legal drug if someone tried to introduce it today.

Table 6-2 lists and classifies the psychoactive drugs that are most frequently used and abused. Drugs that are used to treat mental disorders (see Chapter 16) also affect mood and behavior and thus might be considered psychoactive. They are not included here, however, because they are seldom abused. By and large, their effects are not immediate and usually are not experienced as particularly pleasant. An exception would be the minor tranquilizers, which may be prescribed for the treatment of anxiety disorders and are sometimes abused. Caffeine and nicotine are also listed in the table. While both substances are stimulants and can have negative effects on health, they do not significantly alter consciousness and hence are not discussed in this section.

The use of illegal drugs such as marijuana, particularly among young people, was not common before the 1950s, but since then there have been major changes in patterns of drug use. Beginning in the 1960s, drug use increased steadily, peaking in the late 1970s. In the 1980s, however, drug use gradually declined, a trend that continued until 1992 (see Figure 6-6). Efforts to educate young people about the hazards of drug use contributed to this

TABLE 6-2

Psychoactive Drugs That Are Commonly Used and Abused   *Only a few examples of each class of drug are given. The generic name (for example, psilocybin) or the brand name (Xanax for alprazolam; Seconal for secobarbital) is used, depending on which is more familiar.*

Depressants (Sedatives)	Stimulants
Alcohol (ethanol)	Amphetamines
Barbiturates	Benzedrine
Nembutal	Dexedrine
Seconal	Methedrine
Minor tranquilzers	Cocaine
Miltown	Nicotine
Xanax	Caffeine
Valium	
Inhalants	**Hallucinogens**
Paint thinner	
Glue	LSD
	Mescaline
Opiates (Narcotics)	Psilocybin
	PCP (Phencyclidine)
Opium and its derivatives	
Codeine	**Cannabis**
Heroin	
Morphine	Marijuana
Methadone	Hashish

decline. The turnaround that occurred in 1992 is a cause for concern because the percentage of teenagers who disapprove of drug use appears to have decreased (Bachman, Johnston, & O'Malley, 1998).

The drugs listed in Table 6-2 are assumed to affect behavior and consciousness because they act on the brain in specific biochemical ways. With repeated use, an individual can become dependent on any of them. **Drug dependence** has three key characteristics: (1) *tolerance*—with continued use, the individual must take more and more of the drug to achieve the same effect; (2) *withdrawal*—if use of the drug is discontinued, the person experiences unpleasant physical and psychological reactions; and (3) *compulsive use*—the individual takes more of the drug than intended, tries to control his or her drug use but fails, and spends a great deal of time trying to obtain the drug.

The degree to which tolerance develops and the severity of withdrawal symptoms vary from one drug to another. Tolerance for opiates, for example, develops fairly quickly, and heavy users can tolerate a dosage that would be lethal to a nonuser; in contrast, marijuana smokers seldom build up much tolerance. Withdrawal symptoms are common and easily observed following heavy and sustained use of alcohol, opiates, and sedatives. They are common, but less apparent, for stimulants, and nonexistent after repeated use of hallucinogens (American Psychiatric Association, 1994).

Although tolerance and withdrawal are the primary characteristics of drug dependence, they are not necessary for a diagnosis. A person who shows a pattern of compulsive use without any signs of tolerance or withdrawal, as some marijuana users do, would still be considered drug dependent.

Drug dependence is usually distinguished from **drug abuse**, *continued use of a drug by a person who is not dependent on it (that is, shows no symptoms of tolerance, withdrawal, or compulsive craving), despite serious consequences.* For example, an individual whose overindulgence in alcohol results in repeated accidents, absence from work, or marital problems (without signs of dependence) would be said to abuse alcohol. In this section we look at several types of psychoactive drugs and the effects they may have on those who use them.

Depressants

Depressants are *drugs that depress the central nervous system.* They include tranquilizers, barbiturates (sleeping pills), inhalants (volatile solvents and aerosols), and ethyl alcohol. Of these, the one that is most frequently used and abused is alcohol, and we will focus on it here.

Alcohol and Its Effects People in most societies, whether primitive or industrialized, consume alcohol in some form. Alcohol can be produced by fermenting a wide variety of materials: grains such as rye, wheat, and corn; fruits such as grapes, apples, and plums; and vegetables such as potatoes. Through the process of distillation, the alcoholic content of a fermented beverage can be increased so as to obtain "hard liquors" such as whiskey or rum.

The alcohol used in beverages is called ethanol and consists of relatively small molecules that are easily and quickly absorbed

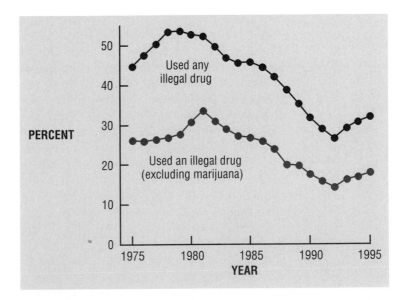

FIGURE 6-6

Illegal Drug Use *The percentage of American high-school seniors who reported using an illegal drug in the 12-month period prior to graduation. Drugs included in the upper curve are marijuana, hallucinogens, cocaine, heroin, and any nonprescribed use of opiates, stimulants, sedatives, and tranquilizers. The lower curve excludes marijuana. (After Johnston, O'Malley, & Bachman, 1995)*

A device called a Breathalyzer is used to determine whether a driver has been drinking. It measures the amount of alcohol in the air the driver exhales, providing an index of the amount of alcohol in the blood.

into the body. Once a drink is swallowed, it enters the stomach and small intestine, where there is a heavy concentration of small blood vessels. These give the ethanol molecules ready access to the blood. Once they enter the bloodstream, they are rapidly carried throughout the body and to all of its organs. Although the alcohol is fairly evenly distributed through the whole body, its effects are likely to be felt most immediately in the brain because a substantial portion of the blood that the heart pumps at any given time goes to the brain and the fatty tissue in the brain absorbs alcohol very well (Kuhn, Swartzwelder, & Wilson, 1998).

Measuring the amount of alcohol in the air we exhale (as in a breath analyzer) gives a reliable index of the amount of alcohol in the blood. Consequently, it is easy to determine the relationship between blood alcohol concentration (BAC) and behavior. At concentrations of .03% to .05% in the blood (30 to 50 milligrams of alcohol per 100 milliliters of blood), alcohol produces light-headedness, relaxation, and release of inhibitions. People say things that they might not ordinarily say and tend to become more sociable and expansive. Self-confidence may increase, but motor reactions will begin to slow. In combination, these effects make it dangerous to drive after drinking.

At a BAC of .10%, sensory and motor functions become noticeably impaired. Speech becomes slurred, and people have difficulty coordinating their movements. Some people tend to become angry and aggressive; others grow silent and morose. At a level of .20% the drinker is seriously incapacitated, and a level above .40% may cause death. In most states, the legal definition of intoxication is a BAC of .10% (one-tenth of 1%).

How much can a person drink without becoming legally intoxicated? The relationship between BAC and alcohol intake is not a simple one. It depends on a person's sex, body weight, and speed of consumption. Age, individual metabolism, and experience with drinking are also factors. Although the effects of alcohol intake on BAC vary a great deal, the average effects are shown in Figure 6-7. Moreover, it is not true that beer or wine is less likely to make someone drunk than so-called hard drinks. A 4-ounce glass of wine, a 12-ounce can of beer, and 1.2 ounces

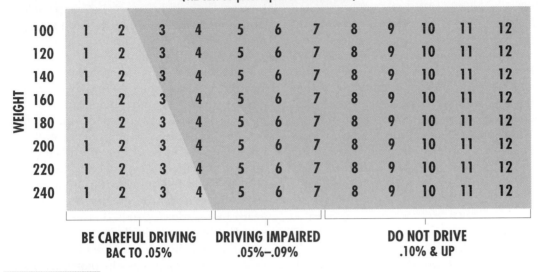

DRINKS IN A TWO-HOUR PERIOD
(1.2 ozs. 80-proof liquor or 12 ozs. beer)

WEIGHT												
100	1	2	3	4	5	6	7	8	9	10	11	12
120	1	2	3	4	5	6	7	8	9	10	11	12
140	1	2	3	4	5	6	7	8	9	10	11	12
160	1	2	3	4	5	6	7	8	9	10	11	12
180	1	2	3	4	5	6	7	8	9	10	11	12
200	1	2	3	4	5	6	7	8	9	10	11	12
220	1	2	3	4	5	6	7	8	9	10	11	12
240	1	2	3	4	5	6	7	8	9	10	11	12

BE CAREFUL DRIVING   **DRIVING IMPAIRED**   **DO NOT DRIVE**
BAC TO .05%   .05%–.09%   .10% & UP

FIGURE 6-7

BAC and Alcohol Intake *Approximate values of blood-alcohol concentration as a function of alcohol consumption in a 2-hour period. For example, if you weigh 180 pounds and had 4 beers in 2 hours, your BAC would be between .05% and .09% and your driving ability would be seriously impaired. Six beers in the same 2-hour period would give you a BAC of over .10%—the level accepted as proof of intoxication.* (After National Highway Traffic Safety Administration)

of 80-proof whiskey have about the same alcohol content and will have about the same effect.

Alcohol Usage Many college students view drinking as an integral part of social life. It promotes conviviality, eases tension, releases inhibitions, and generally adds to the fun. Nevertheless, social drinking can create problems in terms of lost study time, poor performance on exams on "the morning after," and arguments or accidents while intoxicated. Clearly the most serious problem is accidents: Alcohol-related automobile accidents are the leading cause of death among 15- to 24-year-olds. When the legal drinking age was lowered from 21 to 18 in a number of states, traffic fatalities among 18- and 19-year-olds increased by from 20% to 50%. All states have since raised their minimum drinking age, and the number of traffic accidents has decreased significantly.

About two thirds of American adults report that they drink alcohol. At least 10% of them have social, psychological, or medical problems resulting from alcohol use. Probably half of that 10% are dependent on alcohol. Heavy or prolonged drinking can lead to serious health problems. High blood pressure, stroke, ulcers, cancers of the mouth, throat, and stomach, cirrhosis of the liver, and depression are some of the conditions associated with regular use of substantial amounts of alcohol.

Despite the fact that it is illegal for anyone under age 21 to purchase alcoholic beverages, experience with alcohol is almost universal among young people (67% of eighth graders have tried it, 81% of high-school seniors, and 91% of college students). More disturbing is the widespread occurrence of "binge drinking" (having five or more drinks in a row). In national surveys, 28% of high-school seniors and 44% of college students report binge drinking (Wechsler et al., 1994, 1998). Lost study time, missed classes, injuries, engaging in unprotected sex, and trouble with police are some of the problems reported by college students who engage in binge drinking. Because of these problems, an increasing number of universities no longer permit alcohol on campus. The Drug Free School and Campuses Act, passed by Congress in 1989, requires institutions to make alcohol education programs and counseling services available to students and employees.

Alcohol can also cause damage to a developing fetus. Pregnant women who drink heavily are twice as likely to suffer repeated miscarriages and to produce low birth-weight babies. A condition called **fetal alcohol syndrome,** characterized by *mental retardation and multiple deformities of the infant's face and mouth,* is caused by drinking during pregnancy. The amount of alcohol needed to produce this syndrome is unclear, but it is thought that as little as a few ounces of alcohol a week can be detrimental (Streissguth, Clarren, & Jones, 1985).

Opiates

Opium and its derivatives, collectively known as **opiates,** are *drugs that diminish physical sensation and the capacity to respond to stimuli by depressing the central nervous system.* (These drugs are commonly called narcotics, but *opiates* is the more accurate term; the term *narcotics* is not well defined and covers a variety of illegal drugs.) Opiates are used in medical settings to reduce pain, but their ability to alter mood and reduce anxiety has led to widespread illegal consumption. Opium, which is the air-dried juice of the opium poppy, contains a number of chemical substances, including morphine and codeine. Codeine, a common ingredient in prescription pain-killers and cough suppressants, is relatively mild in its effects (at least at low doses).

Drug users who share needles increase their risk of contracting AIDS.

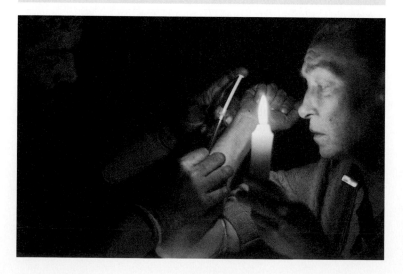

Morphine and its derivative, heroin, are much more potent. Most illegal opiate use involves heroin because, being more concentrated, it can be concealed and smuggled more easily than morphine.

All opiate drugs bind to the same molecules in the brain, known as opiate receptors. The differences among them depend on how quickly they reach the receptors and how much it takes to activate them—that is, their potency. The rate at which opiates enter the body depends on how they are taken. When opiates are smoked or injected, they reach peak levels in the brain within minutes. The faster this occurs, the greater the danger of death by overdose. Drugs that are "snorted" are absorbed more slowly because they must pass through the mucous membranes of the nose to the blood vessels beneath (Kuhn, Swartzwelder, & Wilson, 1998).

Heroin Usage Heroin can be injected, smoked, or inhaled. At first it produces a sense of well-being. Experienced users report a special thrill, or "rush," within a minute or two after an intravenous injection. Some describe this sensation as intensely pleasurable, similar to an orgasm. Young people who sniff heroin report that they forget everything that troubles them. Following this, the user feels "fixed," or gratified, and has no awareness of hunger, pain, or sexual urges. The person may "go on the nod," alternately waking and drowsing while comfortably watching television or reading a book. Unlike a person who is intoxicated by alcohol, a heroin user can readily produce skilled responses to tests of agility and intelligence tests and seldom becomes aggressive or assaultive.

The changes in consciousness produced by heroin are not very striking; there are no exciting visual experiences or feelings of being transported elsewhere. It is the change in mood—the feeling of euphoria and reduced anxiety—that prompts people to start using the drug. However, heroin is very addictive; even a brief period of usage can create physical dependence. After a person has been smoking or "sniffing" (inhaling) heroin for a while, tolerance builds up, and this method no longer produces the desired effect. In an attempt to re-create the original high, the individual may progress to "skin popping" (injecting under the skin) and then to "mainlining" (injecting into a vein). Once the user starts mainlining, stronger and stronger doses are required to produce the high, and the physical discomforts of withdrawal from the drug become intense (chills, sweating, stomach cramps, vomiting, headaches). Thus, additional motivation to continue using the drug stems from the need to avoid physical pain and discomfort.

The hazards of heroin use are many; the average age at death for frequent users is 40 (Hser, Anglin, & Powers, 1993). Death is caused by suffocation resulting from depression of the brain's respiratory center. Death from an overdose is always a possibility because the concentration of street heroin fluctuates widely. Thus, the user can never be sure of the potency of the powder in a newly purchased supply. Heroin use is generally associated with a serious deterioration of personal and social life. Because maintaining the habit is costly, the user often becomes involved in illegal activities to acquire money to purchase the drug.

Additional dangers of heroin use include AIDS (acquired immune deficiency syndrome), hepatitis, and other infections associated with unsterile injections. Sharing needles used to inject drugs is an extremely easy way to be infected with the AIDS virus; blood from an infected person can be trapped in the needle or syringe and injected directly into the bloodstream of the next person who uses the needle. Sharing of needles and syringes by people who inject drugs is the primary means by which the AIDS virus is spreading today.

Opioid Receptors   In the 1970s, researchers made a major breakthrough in understanding opiate dependence with the discovery that opiates act on very specific neuroreceptor sites in the brain. Neurotransmitters travel across the synaptic junction between two neurons and bind to neuroreceptors, triggering activity in the receiving neuron (see Chapter 2). The molecular shape of the opiates resembles that of a group of neurotransmitters called *endorphins*. Endorphins bind to opioid receptors, producing sensations of pleasure as well as reducing discomfort (Julien, 1992). Heroin and morphine relieve pain by binding to opioid receptors that are unfilled (see Figure 6-8). Repeated heroin use causes a drop in endorphin pro-

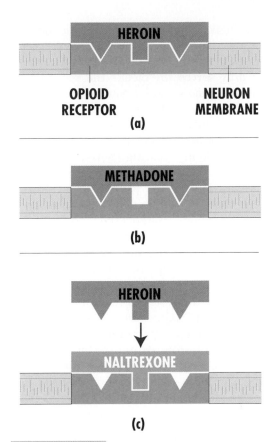

FIGURE 6-8

Drug-Abuse Medications   *(a) Heroin binds to opioid receptors and produces a feeling of pleasure, mimicking the action of the body's naturally occurring endorphins. (b) Methadone, an agonist drug, will also bind to opioid receptors and produce a pleasant sensation. The drug reduces both the craving for heroin and the associated withdrawal symptoms. (c) Naltrexone, an antagonist drug, acts to block the opioid receptors so that heroin cannot gain access to them. The craving for heroin is not satisfied, and the drug has not proved generally effective as a treatment method.*

duction; the body then needs more heroin to fill the unoccupied opioid receptors in order to reduce pain. The person experiences painful withdrawal symptoms when heroin is discontinued because many opioid receptors are left unfilled. In essence, the heroin has replaced the body's own natural opiates (Koob & Bloom, 1988).

These findings have led to the development of new drugs that operate by modulating the opioid receptors. These drugs are of two basic types: agonists and antagonists. *Agonists* bind to the opioid receptors to produce a feeling of pleasure, thereby reducing the craving for opiates; but they cause less psychological and physiological impairment than the opiates. *Antagonists* also lock onto the opioid receptors, but in a way that does not activate them; the drug serves to "block" the receptors so that the opiates cannot gain access to them. Thus, there is no feeling of pleasure and the craving is not satisfied (see Figure 6-8).

Methadone is the best-known agonist drug used in treating heroin-dependent individuals. It is addictive in its own right, but it produces less psychological impairment than heroin and has few disruptive physical effects. When taken orally in low doses, it suppresses the craving for heroin and prevents withdrawal symptoms. Naltrexone, an antagonist drug, blocks the action of heroin because it has a greater affinity for the opioid receptors than does heroin itself. Naltrexone is often used in hospital emergency rooms to reverse the effects of a heroin overdose, but it has not proved generally effective as a treatment for heroin dependence. Interestingly, naltrexone does reduce the craving for alcohol. Alcohol causes the release of endorphins, and naltrexone, by blocking opioid receptors, reduces the pleasurable effects of alcohol and, hence, the desire for it (Winger, Hoffman, & Woods, 1992).

Stimulants

In contrast to depressants and opiates, **stimulants** are *drugs that increase alertness and general arousal.* They increase the amount of monoamine neurotransmitters (norepinephrine, epinephrine, dopamine, and serotonin) in the synapse; the effects resemble what would happen if every one of the neurons that released a monoamine fired at once. The result is to arouse the body both physically, by increasing heart rate and blood pressure, and mentally, causing the person to become hyperalert (Kuhn, Swarzwelder, & Wilson, 1998).

Amphetamines *Amphetamines* are powerful stimulants; they are sold under such trade names as Methedrine, Dexedrine, and Benzedrine and known colloquially as "speed," "uppers," and "bennies." The immediate effects of consuming such drugs are an increase in alertness and a decrease in feelings of fatigue and boredom. Strenuous activities that require endurance seem easier after taking amphetamines. As with other drugs, the ability of amphetamines to alter mood and increase self-confidence is the principal reason for their use. People also use them to stay awake.

Low doses that are taken for limited periods to overcome fatigue (for example, when driving at night) seem to be relatively safe. However, as the stimulating effects of amphetamines wear off, there is a period during which the user feels depressed, irritable, and fatigued, and may be tempted to take more of the drug. Tolerance develops quickly, and the user needs increasingly larger doses to produce the desired effect. Since high doses can have dangerous side effects—agitation, confusion, heart palpitations, and elevated blood pressure—medications containing amphetamines should be used with caution.

When tolerance develops to the point at which oral doses are no longer effective, many users inject amphetamines into a vein. Large intravenous doses produce an immediate pleasant experience (a "flash" or "rush"); this sensation is followed by irritability and discomfort, which can be overcome only by an additional injection. If this sequence is repeated every few hours over a period of days, it will end in a "crash," a deep sleep followed by a period of lethargy and depression. The amphetamine abuser may seek relief from this discomfort by turning to alcohol or heroin.

Long-term amphetamine use is accompanied by drastic deterioration of physical and mental health. The user, or "speed freak," may develop symptoms that are indistinguishable from those of acute schizophrenia (see Chapter 15), including persecutory delusions (the false belief that people are persecuting you or out to get you) and visual or auditory hallucinations. The delusions may lead to unprovoked violence. For example, during an epidemic of amphetamine use in Japan in the early 1950s (when amphetamines were sold without prescription and advertised for "elimination of drowsiness and repletion of the spirit"), 50% of the murders that occurred in a two-month period were related to amphetamine abuse (Hemmi, 1969).

Cocaine Like other stimulants, *cocaine,* or "coke," a substance obtained from the dried leaves of the coca plant, increases energy and self-confidence; it makes the user feel witty and hyperalert. Early in the twentieth century cocaine was widely used and easy to obtain; in fact, it was an ingredient in the original recipe of Coca-Cola. Its use then declined, but recently its popularity has been increasing, even though it is now illegal.

Cocaine can be inhaled or "snorted," or made into a solution and injected directly into a vein. It can also be converted into a flammable compound known as "crack," which is smoked.

One of the earliest studies of the effects of cocaine was conducted by Freud (1885). In an account of his own use of cocaine, he was at first highly favorable to the drug and encouraged its use. However, he changed his mind about the drug after using it to treat a friend, with disastrous results. The friend developed severe dependence on the drug, demanded ever-larger dosages, and was debilitated until his eventual death.

Despite earlier reports to the contrary, and as Freud soon discovered, cocaine is highly addictive. In fact, it has become more addictive and dangerous in recent years with the emergence of crack. Tolerance develops with repeated use, and withdrawal effects, while not as dramatic as those associated with opiates, do occur. The restless irritability that follows the euphoric high becomes, with repeated use, a feeling of depressed anguish. The down is as bad as the up was good and can be alleviated only by more cocaine (see Figure 6-9).

Heavy cocaine users can experience the same abnormal symptoms as people who use amphetamines heavily. A common visual hallucination is flashes of light ("snow lights") or moving lights. Less common—but more disturbing—is the feeling that bugs ("cocaine bugs") are crawling under one's skin. The hallucination may be so strong that the individual will use a knife to cut out the bugs. These experiences occur because cocaine is causing the sensory neurons to fire spontaneously (Weiss, Mirin, & Bartel, 1994).

Hallucinogens

Hallucinogens, or *psychedelics,* are *drugs whose main effect is to change perceptual experience.* They typically change the user's perception of both the internal and the external world. Usual environmental stimuli are experienced as novel events—for example, sounds and colors seem dramatically

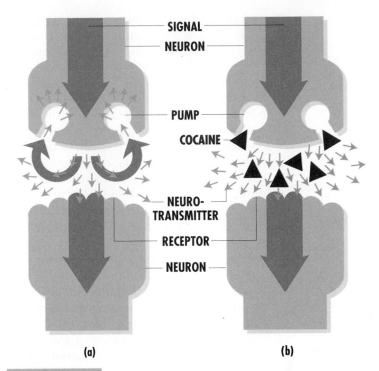

(a)   (b)

FIGURE 6-9

Molecular Effects of Cocaine   *(a) A nerve impulse causes the release of neurotransmitters that carry the signal across the synapse to a receiving neuron. Some of the neurotransmitters are then reabsorbed into the originating neuron (reuptake process), while the rest are broken up chemically and made inactive (degradation process). These processes are discussed in Chapter 2. (b) Research findings indicate that cocaine blocks the reuptake process for three neurotransmitters (dopamine, serotonin, and norepinephrine) that are involved in the regulation of mood. With reuptake hampered by cocaine, the normal effects of these neurotransmitters are amplified; in particular, an excess of dopamine is associated with feelings of euphoria. However, prolonged cocaine use produces a shortage of these neurotransmitters because their reuptake for later use is blocked; that is, the body degrades them at a faster rate than it can manufacture them. With the normal supply depleted by repeated cocaine use, euphoria is replaced by anxiety and depression.*

different. Time perception is so altered that minutes may seem like hours. The user may experience auditory, visual, and tactile hallucinations and reduced ability to differentiate between self and surroundings.

Some hallucinogenic drugs are derived from plants, such as mescaline from cactus and psilocybin from mushrooms. Others are synthesized in the laboratory, such as LSD (lysergic acid diethylamide) and PCP (phencyclidine).

LSD   LSD, or "acid," is a colorless, odorless, tasteless substance that is often sold dissolved on sugar cubes or pieces of paper. It is a potent drug that produces hallucinations at very low doses. Some users have vivid hallucinations of colors and sounds, and others have mystical or semireligious experiences. Anyone can have an unpleasant, frightening reaction (or "bad trip"), even those who have had many pleasant LSD experiences. Another adverse LSD reaction is the *flashback,* which may occur days, weeks, months, or even years after the last use of the drug. During a flashback the individual experiences illusions or hallucinations similar to those experienced when using the drug. Since LSD is almost completely eliminated from the body within 24 hours after it is taken, the flashback is probably a restoration of memories of the prior experience.

More threatening to the LSD user is the loss of reality orientation that can be caused by the drug. This alteration in consciousness can lead to an irrational and disoriented behavior and, occasionally, to a panic state in which users feel that they cannot control what they are doing or thinking. People have jumped from high places to their deaths when in this state. LSD was popular during the 1960s, but its use subsequently declined, probably as a result of widespread reports of severe drug reactions. There are, however, some indications of renewed interest in LSD and other hallucinogens (Johnston, O'Malley, & Bachman, 1995).

PCP Although it is sold as a hallucinogen (under such street names as "angel dust," "Shermans," and "superacid"), PCP is technically classified as a dissociative anesthetic. It may cause hallucinations, but it also makes the user feel dissociated or apart from the environment. PCP was first synthesized in 1956 for use as a general anesthetic. It had the advantage of eliminating pain without producing a deep coma. However, its legal manufacture was discontinued when doctors found that the drug produced agitation, hallucinations, and a psychotic-like state resembling schizophrenia in many patients. Because the ingredients are cheap and the drug is relatively easy to manufacture in a kitchen laboratory, PCP is widely used as an adulterant in other, more expensive street drugs. Much of what is sold as THC (the active ingredient of marijuana) is really PCP.

PCP can be taken in liquid or pill form, but more often it is smoked or snorted. In low doses it produces insensitivity to pain and an experience similar to a moderately drunken state—one characterized by confusion, loss of inhibition, and poor psychomotor coordination. Higher doses produce a disoriented, comalike condition. Unlike the person who experiences LSD, the PCP user is unable to observe his or her drug-induced state and frequently has no memory of it.

Cannabis

The cannabis plant has been harvested since ancient times for its psychoactive effects. The dried leaves and flowers are used to produce *marijuana,* the form in which it is most often used in this country, while the solidified resin of the plant, called *hashish* ("hash"), is commonly used in the Middle East. Marijuana and hashish are usually smoked but may also be taken orally mixed with tea or food. The active ingredient in both substances is THC (tetrahydrocannabinol). Taken orally in small doses (5–10 milligrams), THC produces a mild high; larger doses (30–70 milligrams) produce severe and longer-lasting reactions that resemble those of hallucinogenic drugs. As with alcohol, the reaction often has two stages: a period of stimulation and euphoria followed by a period of tranquility and sleep.

When marijuana is smoked, THC is rapidly absorbed by the rich blood supply of the lungs. Blood from the lungs goes directly to the heart and then to the brain, causing a high within minutes. However, THC also accumulates in other organs, such as the liver, kidneys, spleen, and testes. The amount of THC reaching the body varies according to how the user smokes: A cigarette allows for the transfer of 10% to 20% of the THC in the marijuana, whereas a pipe allows about 40% to 50% to transfer. A water pipe, or bong, traps the smoke until it is inhaled and therefore is a highly efficient means of transferring THC. Once in the brain, the THC binds to cannabinoid receptors, which are especially numerous in the hippocampus. Since the hippocampus is involved in the formation of new memories, it is not surprising that marijuana use inhibits memory formation (Kuhn, Swartzwelder, & Wilson, 1998).

Regular users of marijuana report a number of sensory and perceptual changes: a general euphoria and sense of well-being, some distortions of space and time, and changes in social perception. Not all marijuana experiences are pleasant. Sixteen percent of regular users report anxiety, fearfulness, and confusion as a "usual occurrence," and about one third report that they occasionally experience such symptoms as acute panic, hallucinations, and unpleasant distortions in body image. Individuals who use marijuana regularly (daily or almost daily) often report both physical and mental lethargy; about a third show mild forms of depression, anxiety, or irritability (American Psychiatric Association, 1994). It should be noted that marijuana smoke contains even larger amounts of known carcinogens than tobacco (but since marijuana users tend to smoke less than cigarette smokers, the total intake of these substances is lower).

Marijuana use interferes with performance on complex tasks. Motor coordination is significantly impaired by low to moderate doses; and reaction time for automobile braking and the ability to negotiate a twisting road course are adversely affected (Institute of Medicine, 1982). These findings make it clear that driving under the influence of the drug is dangerous. The number of automobile accidents related to marijuana use is difficult to determine because, unlike alcohol, THC declines rapidly in the blood, quickly going to the fatty tissues and organs of the body. A blood analysis performed two hours after a heavy dose of marijuana may show no signs of THC, even though an observer would judge the person to be clearly impaired. It is estimated that one fourth of all drivers involved in accidents are under the influence of marijuana, either alone or in combination with alcohol (Jones & Lovinger, 1985).

The effects of marijuana may persist long after the subjective feelings of euphoria or sleepiness have passed. A study of aircraft pilots using a simulated flight-landing task found that performance was significantly impaired as much as 24 hours after smoking one marijuana cigarette containing 19 milligrams of THC—despite the fact that the pilots reported no awareness of any aftereffects on their alertness or performance (Yesavage et al., 1985). These findings have led to concern about marijuana use by people whose jobs affect public safety.

It is well known that marijuana disrupts memory functions. Marijuana has two clear effects on memory: (1) It makes short-term memory more susceptible to interference. For example, people under the influence of marijuana may lose the thread of a conversation or forget what they are saying in the middle of a sentence because of momentary distractions (Darley et al., 1973a). (2) Marijuana disrupts learning; that is, it interferes with the transfer of new information from short-term to long-term memory (Darley et al., 1977; Darley et al., 1973b). These findings suggest that it is not a good idea to study while under the influence of marijuana; later recall of the material will be poor.

Table 6-3 summarizes the effects of the major psychoactive drugs described in this

TABLE 6-3

Effects of Major Psychoactive Drugs

Alcohol	Lightheadedness, relaxation, release of inhibitions
	Increased self-confidence
	Slowing of motor reactions
Heroin	Sense of well-being
	Feeling of euphoria
	Reduced anxiety
Amphetamines	Drowsiness
	Increased alertness
	Decreased fatigue and boredom
Cocaine	Increased energy and self-confidence
	Euphoric high
	Restless irritability
	High likelihood of dependence
LSD	Hallucinations
	Mystical experiences
	"Bad trips"
	Flashbacks
PCP	Feelings of dissociation from the environment
	Insensitivity to pain
	Confusion
	Loss of inhibition
	Poor coordination
Cannabis	Stimulation and euphoria followed by tranquility and sleep
	Sense of well-being
	Distortions of space and time
	Changes in social perception
	Impaired motor coordination
	Disruption of memory

section. By and large, these are short-term effects. The long-term effects of most drugs other than nicotine and alcohol are largely unknown. However, the history of these two common drugs should lead us to be cautious in the use of any drug over a long period.

Psi Phenomena

A discussion of consciousness would not be complete without considering some esoteric and mystical claims about the mind that have long attracted widespread public attention. Of particular interest are questions about whether or not human beings (a) can acquire information in ways that do not involve stimulation of the known sense organs or (b) can influence physical events by purely mental means. These questions are the source of controversy over the existence of **psi**, a term used to refer to *processes of information and/or energy exchange that are not currently explicable in terms of known science* (in other words, known physical mechanisms). The phenomena of psi are the subject matter of **parapsychology** (which means *phenomena that are "beside psychology"*) and include the following:

1. *Extrasensory perception (ESP)*. Response to external stimuli without any known sensory contact.

    a. *Telepathy*. Transference of thought from one person to another without the mediation of any known channel of sensory communication (for example, identifying a playing card that is merely being thought of by another person).

    b. *Clairvoyance*. Perception of objects or events that do not provide a stimulus to the known senses (for example,

identifying a concealed playing card whose identity is unknown to anyone).

    c. *Precognition*. Perception of a future event that could not be anticipated through any known inferential process (for example, predicting that a particular number will come up on the next throw of a pair of dice).

2. *Psychokinesis (PK)*. Mental influence over physical events without the intervention of any known physical force (for example, willing that a particular number will come up on the next throw of a pair of dice).

Experimental Evidence

Most parapsychologists see themselves as scientists applying the usual rules of scientific inquiry to admittedly unusual phenomena. Yet the claims for psi are so extraordinary, and so similar to what are widely regarded as superstitions, that some scientists consider psi to be impossible and reject the legitimacy of parapsychological inquiry. Such a priori judgments are out of place in science; the real question is whether the empirical evidence is acceptable by scientific standards. Many psychologists who are not yet convinced that psi has been demonstrated are nonetheless open to the possibility that new evidence might emerge that would be more persuasive. For their part, many parapsychologists believe that several recent experimental procedures either provide that evidence already or hold the potential for doing so. We shall examine the most promising of these, the ganzfeld procedure.

The *ganzfeld procedure* tests for telepathic communication between a participant who serves as the "receiver" and another participant who serves as the "sender." The receiver is sequestered in an acoustically isolated room and placed in a mild form of perceptual isolation: Translucent ping-pong ball halves are taped over the eyes and headphones are placed over the ears; diffuse red light illuminates the room, and white noise is played through the headphones. (*White noise* is a random mixture of sound frequencies similar to the hiss made

by a radio tuned between stations.) This homogeneous visual and auditory environment is called the ganzfeld, a German word meaning "total field."

The sender sits in a separate acoustically isolated room, and a visual stimulus (picture, slide, or brief videotape sequence) is randomly selected from a large pool of similar stimuli to serve as the "target" for the session. While the sender concentrates on the target, the receiver attempts to describe it by providing a continuous verbal report of his or her mental imagery and free associations. Upon completion of the session, the receiver is presented with four stimuli, one of which is the target, and asked to rate the degree to which each matches the imagery and associations experienced during the ganzfeld session. A "direct hit" is scored if the receiver assigns the highest rating to the target stimulus.

More than 50 experiments have been conducted since this procedure was introduced in 1974; the typical experiment involves about 30 sessions in which a receiver attempts to identify the target transmitted by the sender. An overall analysis of 28 studies (comprising a total of 835 ganzfeld sessions conducted by investigators in 10 different laboratories) reveals that participants were able to select the correct target stimulus 38%

of the time. Because a participant must select the target from 4 alternatives, we would expect a success rate of 25% if only chance were operating. Statistically, this result is highly significant; the probability that it could have arisen by chance is less than one in a billion (Bem & Honorton, 1994).

The Debate Over the Evidence

In 1985 and 1986 the *Journal of Parapsychology* published an extended examination of the ganzfeld studies, focusing on a debate between Ray Hyman, a cognitive psychologist and critic of parapsychology, and Charles Honorton, a parapsychologist and major contributor to the ganzfeld database. They agree on the basic quantitative results but disagree on its interpretation (Honorton, 1985; Hyman, 1994, 1985; Hyman & Honorton, 1986). In what follows, we use their debate as a vehicle for examining the issues involved in evaluating claims of psi.

The Replication Problem In scientific research, a phenomenon is not considered established until it has been observed repeatedly by several researchers. Accordingly, the most serious criticism of parapsychology

The receiver (left) and the sender (right) in a ganzfeld experiment.

is that it has failed to produce a single reliable demonstration of psi that can be replicated by other investigators. Even the same investigator testing the same individuals over time may obtain statistically significant results on one occasion but not on another. The ganzfeld procedure is no exception; fewer than half (43%) of the 28 studies analyzed in the debate yielded statistically significant results.

The parapsychologists' most effective response to this criticism actually comes from within psychology itself. Many statisticians and psychologists are dissatisfied with psychology's focus on statistical significance as the sole measure of a study's success. As an alternative, they are increasingly adopting **meta-analysis**, *a statistical technique that treats the accumulated studies of a particular phenomenon as a single grand experiment and each study as a single observation.* Thus, any study that obtains positive results—even though it may not be statistically significant itself—contributes to the overall strength and reliability of the phenomenon rather than simply being dismissed as a failure to replicate (Glass, McGaw, & Smith, 1981; Rosenthal, 1984).

From this perspective, the ganzfeld studies provide impressive replicability: 23 of the 28 studies obtained positive results, an outcome whose probability of occurring by chance is less than one in a thousand.

The ability of a particular experiment to replicate an effect also depends on how strong the effect is and how many observations are made. If an effect is weak, an experiment with too few participants or observations will fail to detect it at a statistically significant level—even though the effect actually exists. In the ganzfeld situation, if the effect actually exists and has a true direct-hit rate of 38%, then statistically we should expect studies with 30 ganzfeld sessions (the average for the 28 studies discussed earlier) to obtain a statistically significant psi effect only about one third of the time (Utts, 1986).

In short, it is unrealistic to demand that any real effect be replicable at any time by any competent investigator. The replication issue is more complex than that, and meta-analysis is proving to be a valuable tool for dealing with some of those complexities.

Inadequate Controls   The second major criticism of parapsychology is that many, if not most, of the experiments have inadequate controls and safeguards. Flawed procedures that would permit a participant to obtain the communicated information in normal sensory fashion, either inadvertently or through deliberate cheating, are particularly fatal. This is called the problem of *sensory leakage.* Inadequate procedures for *randomizing* (randomly selecting) target stimuli are another common problem.

Methodological inadequacies plague all sciences, but the history of parapsychology is embarrassingly full of promising results that collapsed when the procedures were examined from a critical perspective (Akers, 1984). One common charge against parapsychology is that whereas preliminary, poorly controlled studies often obtain positive results, as soon as better controls and safeguards are introduced, the results disappear.

Once a flaw is discovered in a completed experiment, there is no persuasive way of arguing that the flaw did not contribute to a positive outcome; the only remedy is to redo the experiment correctly. In a database of several studies, however, meta-analysis can evaluate the criticism empirically by checking to see whether, in fact, the more poorly controlled studies obtained more positive results than the better controlled studies did. If there is a correlation between a procedural flaw and positive results across the studies, there is a problem. In the case of the ganzfeld database, both critic Hyman and parapsychologist Honorton agree that flaws of inadequate security and possible sensory leakage do not correlate with positive results. Hyman claimed to find a correlation between flaws of randomization and positive results, but both Honorton's analysis and two additional analyses by nonparapsychologists dispute his conclusion (Harris & Rosenthal, 1988; Saunders, 1985). Moreover, a series of 11 new studies designed to control for flaws identified in the original database yielded results consistent with the original set of 28 studies (Bem & Honorton, 1994).

The File-Drawer Problem   Suppose that each of 20 investigators independently decides to conduct a ganzfeld study. Even if there were no genuine ganzfeld effect, there is a reasonable probability that at least one of these investigators would obtain a statistically significant result by pure chance. That lucky investigator would then publish a report of the experiment, but the other 19 investigators—all of whom obtained "null" results—would become discouraged, put their data in a file drawer, and move on to something more promising. As a result, the scientific community would learn about the one successful study but have no knowledge of the 19 null studies buried in file drawers. The database of known studies would thus be seriously biased toward positive studies, and any meta-analysis of that database would arrive at similarly biased conclusions. This is known as the *file-drawer problem*.

The file-drawer problem is a tricky one because by definition it is impossible to know how many unknown studies are languishing in file drawers. Nevertheless, parapsychologists offer two defenses against the charge that this problem constitutes a serious challenge to their findings. First, they point out that the *Journal of Parapsychology* actively solicits and publishes studies that report negative findings. Moreover, the community of parapsychologists is relatively small, and most investigators are aware of ongoing research in the field. When conducting meta-analysis, parapsychologists scout out unpublished negative studies at conventions and through their personal networks.

But their major defense is statistical, and again meta-analysis provides an empirical approach to the problem. By knowing the overall statistical significance of the known database, it is possible to compute the number of studies with null results that would have to exist in file drawers to cancel out that significance. In the case of the ganzfeld database, there would have to be more than 400 unreported studies with null results—the equivalent of 12,000 ganzfeld sessions—to cancel out the statistical significance of the 28 studies analyzed in the debate (Honorton, 1985). It is generally agreed, therefore, that the overall significance of the ganzfeld studies cannot reasonably be explained by the file-drawer effect (Hyman & Honorton, 1986).

Rather than continue their debate, Hyman and Honorton issued a joint communiqué in which they set forth their areas of agreement and disagreement and made a series of suggestions for the conduct of future ganzfeld studies (Hyman & Honorton,

1986). Their debate and the subsequent discussion provide a valuable model for evaluating disputed domains of scientific inquiry.

Anecdotal Evidence

In the public's mind, the evidence for psi consists primarily of personal experiences and anecdotes. From a scientific standpoint such evidence is unpersuasive because it suffers from the same problems that jeopardize the experimental evidence—nonreplicability, inadequate controls, and the file-drawer problem.

The replication problem is acute because most such evidence consists of single occurrences. A woman announces a premonition that she will win the lottery that day—and she does. You dream about an unlikely event, which actually occurs a few days later. A "psychic" correctly predicts the assassination of a public figure. Such incidents may be subjectively compelling, but there is no way to evaluate them because they are not repeatable.

The problem of inadequate controls and safeguards is decisive because such incidents occur under unexpected and ambiguous conditions. There is thus no way of ruling out alternative interpretations such as coincidence (chance), faulty memories, and deliberate deception.

Finally, the file-drawer problem also occurs with anecdotal evidence. The lottery winner who announced ahead of time that she would win is prominently featured in the news. But the thousands of others with similar premonitions who did not win are never heard from; their "evidence" remains in the file drawer. It is true that the probability of this woman's winning the lottery was very low. But the critical criterion in evaluating this case is not the probability that she would win but the probability that any one of the thousands who thought they would win would do so. That probability is much higher. Moreover, this woman has a personal file drawer that contains all the past instances in which she had similar premonitions but did not win.

The same reasoning applies to *precognitive dreams* (dreams that anticipate an unlikely event, which actually occurs a few days later). We tend to forget our dreams unless, and until, an event happens to remind us of them. We thus have no way of evaluating how often we might have dreamed of similar unlikely events that did not occur. We fill our database with positive instances and unknowingly exclude the negative instances.

Perhaps the fullest file drawers belong to the so-called psychics who make annual predictions in the tabloid newspapers. Nobody remembers the predictions that fail, but everybody remembers the occasional direct hits. In fact, these psychics are almost always wrong (Frazier, 1987; Tyler, 1977).

Skepticism About Psi

If some of the experimental evidence for psi is as impressive as it seems, why hasn't it become part of established science? Why do most scientists continue to be skeptical?

Extraordinary Claims   Most scientists believe that extraordinary claims require extraordinary evidence. A study reporting that students who study harder get higher grades will be believed even if the study was seriously flawed because the data fit well with our understanding of how the world works. But the claim that two people in a ganzfeld study communicate telepathically is more extraordinary; it violates most people's a priori beliefs about reality. We therefore rightly demand a higher measure of proof from parapsychologists because their claims, if true, would require us to radically revise our model of the world—something that we should not undertake lightly. In this way, science is justifiably conservative. Many open-minded nonparapsychologists are genuinely impressed by the ganzfeld studies, for example, but it is reasonable for them to ask for more evidence before committing themselves to the reality of psi.

Extraordinariness is a matter of degree. Telepathy seems less extraordinary to most of us than precognition because we are already familiar with the invisible transmission of information through space. We may not understand how television pictures get to our living rooms, but we know that they do so. Why should telepathy seem that much more mysterious? Precognition, on the other hand, seems more extraordinary because there are no familiar phenomena in which information flows backward in time.

Skepticism on the Part of Psychologists   Psychologists are a particularly skeptical group. A survey of more than 1,000 college professors found that about 66% believe that ESP is either an established fact or a likely possibility. Moreover, these favorable views were expressed by a majority of professors in the natural sciences (55%), the social sciences excluding psychology (66%), and the arts, humanities, and education (77%). The comparable figure for psychologists was 34% (Wagner & Monnet, 1979).

There are several reasons for the skepticism of psychologists. First, they are familiar with past instances of extraordinary claims that turned out to be based on flawed experimental procedures, faulty inference, or even fraud and deception. Over the history of research on parapsychology, there have been a number of cases in which research claims have later proved to be based on fraudulent data. Those who follow developments in this field have so often encountered charlatans—some of whom are very clever—that they have good reason to be skeptical of new claims (Gardner, 1981; Randi, 1982).

Second, psychologists know that popular accounts of psychological findings are frequently exaggerated. For example, the remarkable findings of research on asymmetries in the human brain have spawned a host of pop-psychology books and media reports containing unsubstantiated claims about left-brained and right-brained individuals. Irresponsible reports about states of consciousness—including hypnosis and psi— appear daily in the media. It is worth noting, therefore, that when the college professors in the survey cited earlier were asked to name the sources for their beliefs about ESP, the frequently cited sources were reports in newspapers and magazines.

Finally, research in cognitive and social psychology has sensitized psychologists to the biases and shortcomings in our abilities to draw valid inferences from our everyday experiences (see Chapter 18). This makes them particularly skeptical of anecdotal reports of psi, where, as discussed earlier, our judgments are subject to many kinds of errors. Thus, it is clear that much of the skepticism of psychologists toward psi is well founded. Some of it is not, however. The research using the ganzfeld procedure has withstood considerable scrutiny and warrants serious consideration.

Subjective Sleepiness

Harvey Babkoff, *Bar-Ilan University*

Rating subjective sleepiness is only one of a number of measures used by researchers to assess the tendency to change from a state of arousal/awareness to that of sleep/unconsciousness. Although other tests of "sleepiness" (e.g., sleep latency as measured by the multiple sleep latency test, MSLT) (Carskadon, 1989) are, prime facie, more objective, and one might consider dispensing with ratings of subjective sleepiness as a serious measure of sleepiness, nevertheless, the latter does make an important contribution to our understanding the dynamics of moving from a state of arousal/awareness to that of sleep/ unconsciousness. First, rating subjective sleepiness has intuitive appeal, as it certainly seems to be a more direct way of tapping a variable that is of interest to all of us, as we all have experienced and will continue to experience "sleepiness". Second, sleepiness and sleep quality may influence general health (Briones et al., 1996). "Excessive sleepiness" is one of the complaints included in a primary diagnosis of "dyssomnia", so that knowing the dynamics of subjective sleepiness in healthy individuals can contribute to a better understanding of certain sleep pathologies. Third, although the test of sleep latency presumably reflects the physiological pressure for sleep directly, it is limited when used to track sleepiness over long periods of wakefulness. The MSLT fails to show any further significant changes after 24–36 hours of wakefulness, even when sleep deprivation continues for much longer, whereas subjective sleepiness continues to change over long periods of sleep loss.

This leads us to the question of what drives subjective sleepiness? The answer is complicated and depends upon a variety of factors, including, e.g., the length of time since the last sleep period, the duration of the last lengthy sleep period, and the phase of the individual's endogenous circadian rhythm.

Analyses of the free-running sleep-wake cycle indicate that human sleep is timed by at least two processes. It is now generally accepted that one of these is oscillatory and is generated by the mammalian circadian pacemaker, located in the suprachiasmic nucleus of the hypothalamus. The second process, the physiologic pressure for sleep, most probably represents the alternation between the monotonic increase in sleep tendency that occurs during consolidated wakefulness, and its relief by sleep. The impact of the two generators on sleepiness cannot be easily illustrated by tracking subjective sleepiness only during the waking hours of a normal day in which individuals sleep 7 to 8 of the 24-hours. A much clearer illustration of the dynamically changing contributions of these processes over time can be made by tracking subjective sleepiness over longer periods of sleeplessness (see Figure 1).

Ratings of subjective sleepiness increase monotonically but also show clear rhythmic oscillations, whose amplitude appears to increase over time, especially after the first 24 hours (Figure 1). The circadian remodulate, which is a best-fit model of the 24-hour cyclicity as analyzed by time-series analysis (complex demodulation) (Babkoff et al., 1991) is shown in the lower part of Figure 1. Delaying the relief of physiological sleep-pressure by 72 hours results in a

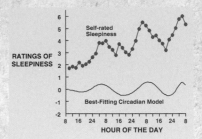

Figure 1

very distinctive monotonic component, which accounts for 45–48% of the overall variance. The circadian cycle, which reflects the endogenous circadian rhythm, accounts for 24% of the overall variance. However, the contributions of these two major components change over time. Contrast the size of the circadian cycle on the first day with that of the second and third days of sleep loss. Note how the amplitude of the circadian component grows over the three days of sleep loss, implying the increasing contribution of the endogenous circadian rhythm as a "driver" of subjective sleepiness. This means that the "oscillation" in sleepiness becomes more pronounced as the individual becomes more sleep deprived. The sleepiness rating at 0400 in the morning of the *first* day of sleep loss is higher than the rating at 1800 in the evening of the *third* day, 38 hours later! These swings may seem counterintuitive, but they clearly illustrate the point that despite the continuing build-up of the physiologic pressure to sleep, the endogenous circadian generator becomes a *stronger* driver of subjective sleepiness as the individual becomes more sleep deprived. Practically, this means that time of day, or more correctly, the phase of the individual's circadian rhythm, is a very potent determinant of his/her sleepiness, most especially when he/she has not had sufficient sleep.

The Paradoxes of Sleepiness

Derk-Jan Dijk, *Harvard Medical School*

The alarm clock wakes you up at 7 a.m. You are very sleepy despite a good night's sleep. It is 10 p.m., and you have been awake the entire day; yet you don't feel sleepy. How paradoxical! Aren't we hungry before dinner and satiated after the meal?

Sleep and biological rhythm researchers have struggled to understand these simple observations for many decades. The real challenge is not to understand how sleepy we are after three days without sleep but to understand the time course of sleepiness during a normal waking day and to explain why only moderate sleep loss can jeopardize performance and safety on the job at some times of day while at other times our performance is near optimal despite sleep loss.

The time course of subjective sleepiness in healthy young adults awake for 40 hours, without knowledge of clock time, is shown in Figure 2. During the first hours after awakening, sleepiness gradually declines. This phenomenon is called sleep inertia. Thereafter sleepiness remains more or less stable until, very close to habitual bedtime, sleepiness suddenly increases. During the next 8–9 hours sleepiness increases, cresting at

Figure 2

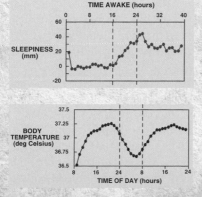

around 8–10 a.m., followed by a small reduction of sleepiness during the second day of wakefulness. Please note that body temperature exhibits a very robust circadian rhythm under these constant conditions and that the nadir in alertness occurs just after the nadir of the body temperature rhythm, which in young healthy subjects is—on average—located at 6 a.m., that is, close to habitual wake time. The data show that after a night without sleep we are more sleepy. That is because there is a process called sleep homeostasis that keeps track of how much we have slept and how long we have been awake. Time of day or—more precisely—the circadian clock also influences sleepiness.

In our 40-hour sleep deprivation the two processes, that is, sleep homeostasis (time awake) and circadian phase (clock time), change simultaneously, and the interaction of these two processes cannot be quantified. To quantify this interaction researchers have used a forced desynchrony protocol in which the sleep-wake cycle is desynchronized from the endogenous circadian cycle by scheduling subjects to go to sleep and wake up four hours later every "day," that is, they live on a 28-hour day. The circadian clock cannot synchronize to this 28-hour period, and the episodes of sleep and wakefulness will now occur at many circadian phases. Thus on some "days" the waking episode will start at the temperature nadir, on other "days" it will start close to the temperature crest, and so on. We can now look at virtually every combination of time awake and circadian phase and quantify the interaction between the homeostatic and circadian process.

The circadian rhythm of sleepiness has its crest located in the early morning, close to habitual wake time, and its nadir in the evening hours, close to habitual bedtime. It furthermore turns out that the homeostatic drive for sleep builds up rather quickly, even within a normal range of wake durations, that is, 0–18 hours. We do not experience this progressive increase in sleepiness during a normal waking day because the (nonlinear) interaction between the two processes is such that during the first 16 hours of a waking day starting at around 7 a.m. the progressive homeostatic increase in the drive for sleep is offset by the progressive reduction in the circadian drive for sleep. This works just fine as long as the sleep-wake cycle and the circadian cycle are in the correct phase relationship. Problems arise in situations in which this phase relationship is changed, such as in night-shift work. The night-shift worker wakes up at around 1 p.m. and will go to work at 11 p.m. He feels fine because he has been awake for only 10 hours and the circadian clock still does not promotes sleepiness but promotes wakefulness instead. However, throughout the night the circadian drive for sleepiness will become stronger as well as the homeostatic drive for sleep. At 6 a.m. homeostatic sleep pressure has been building up for 17 hours and the circadian clock maximally promotes sleep. No wonder the night-shift worker is very sleepy—and now he has to drive home.

SUMMARY

1. A person's perceptions, thoughts, and feelings at any given moment constitute that person's consciousness. An altered state of consciousness is said to exist when mental functioning seems changed or out of the ordinary to the person experiencing the state. Some altered states of consciousness, such as sleep and dreams, are experienced by everyone; others result from special circumstances such as meditation, hypnosis, or the use of drugs.

2. The functions of consciousness are (a) monitoring ourselves and our environment so that we are aware of what is happening within our bodies and in our surroundings, and (b) controlling our actions so that they are coordinated with events in the outside world. Not all events that influence consciousness are at the center of our awareness at a given moment. Memories of personal events and accumulated knowledge, which are accessible but are not currently part of one's consciousness, are called preconscious memories. Events that affect behavior, even though we are not aware of perceiving them, influence us subconsciously.

3. According to psychoanalytic theory, some emotionally painful memories and impulses are not available to consciousness because they have been repressed—that is, diverted to the unconscious. Unconscious thoughts and impulses influence our behavior even though they reach consciousness only in indirect ways—through dreams, irrational behavior, and slips of the tongue.

4. The notion of automaticity refers to the habituation of responses that initially required conscious attention, such as driving a car.

5. Sleep, an altered state of consciousness, is of interest because of the rhythms evident in sleep schedules and in the depth of sleep. These rhythms are studied with the aid of the electroencephalogram (EEG). Patterns of brain waves show four stages (depths) of sleep, plus a fifth stage characterized by rapid eye movements (REMs). These stages alternate throughout the night. Dreams occur more often during REM sleep than during the other four stages (NREM sleep).

6. The opponent-process model of sleep proposes that two opposing processes—the homeostatic sleep drive and the clock-dependent alerting process—interact to determine our tendency to fall asleep or remain awake. Whether we are asleep or awake at any given time depends on the relative forces exerted by the two processes. There are a variety of sleep disorders, including sleep deprivation, insomnia, narcolepsy, and apnea.

7. Freud attributed psychological causes to dreams, distinguishing between their manifest and latent content and suggesting that dreams are wishes in disguise. Other theories see dreaming as a reflection of the information processing that the brain is doing while asleep. Recently some theorists have concluded that dreaming is a cognitive process that reflects the individual's conceptions, concerns, and emotional preoccupations.

7. Meditation represents an effort to alter consciousness by following planned rituals or exercises such as those of yoga or Zen. The result is a somewhat mystical state in which the individual is extremely relaxed and feels divorced from the outside world.

9. Hypnosis is a responsive state in which individuals focus their attention on the hypnotist and his or her suggestions. Some people are more readily hypnotized than others, although most people show some susceptibility. Characteristic hypnotic responses include enhanced or diminished control over movements, distortion of memory through posthypnotic amnesia, and positive and negative hallucinations. Reduction of pain is one of the beneficial uses of hypnosis.

10. Psychoactive drugs have long been used to alter consciousness and mood. They include depressants, such as alcohol, tranquilizers, and inhalants; opiates, such as heroin and morphine; stimulants, such as amphetamines and cocaine; hallucinogens, such as LSD and PCP; and cannabis, such as marijuana and hashish.

11. Repeated use of any of these drugs can result in drug dependence, which is characterized by tolerance, withdrawal, and compulsive use. Drug abuse refers to continued use of a drug, despite serious consequences, by a person who has not reached the stage of dependence.

12. There is considerable controversy over psi, the idea that people can acquire information about the world in ways that do not involve stimulation of known sense organs, or can influence physical events by purely mental means. The phenomena of psi include extrasensory perception (ESP) in its various forms (telepathy, clairvoyance, precognition) and psychokinesis, movement of objects by the mind.

13. A number of carefully controlled studies (called ganzfeld experiments) have been conducted to evaluate ESP via telepathy. Unlike many previous reports of psi phenomena, these experiments seem to withstand the criticisms that they are not replicable, have inadequate controls, or are subject to the file drawer problem. Nevertheless, most psychologists remain skeptical about psi and would, at the least, insist on many more successful replications before concluding that the existence of psi has been demonstrated.

KEY TERMS

consciousness (p. 193)
preconscious memories (p. 194)
unconscious (p. 194)
automaticity (p. 195)
dissociation (p. 196)
REM sleep (p. 198)
non-REM sleep (or NREM sleep) (p. 198)
circadian rhythm (p. 200)
sleep disorder (p. 200)
insomnia (p. 200)
narcolepsy (p. 201)
apnea (p. 202)
dreaming (p. 202)
meditation (p. 205)

hypnosis (p. 207)
hidden observer (p. 210)
psychoactive drugs (p. 211)
drug dependence (p. 213)
drug abuse (p. 213)
depressants (p. 213)
fetal alchohol syndrome (p. 216)
opiates (p. 216)
stimulants (p. 218)
hallucinogens (p. 219)
psi (p. 222)
parapsychology (p. 222)
meta-analysis (p. 224)

CRITICAL THINKING QUESTIONS

1. Many amateur pianists memorize a piece for a recital by playing it over and over again until they can play it automatically, without paying attention to it. Unfortunately, they still often get stuck or forget parts of it during the actual recital. In contrast, some professional pianists deliberately memorize the music away from the piano, so that their "mind, not just their fingers" knows the piece. What does this imply about automatic processes and the controlling function of consciousness?

2. Laws that criminalize some psychoactive drugs (marijuana, cocaine) but not others (alcohol, to-bacco) do not seem well matched to the drugs' actual dangers. If you were to redesign our country's drug policies from scratch, basing them only on current scientific knowledge, which drugs would you want to discourage most vigorously (or criminalize)? Which drugs would you worry least about?

3. It has recently been demonstrated that the ancient Asian medical practice of acupuncture, in which needles are inserted into the skin at different "acupuncture points," stimulates the brain's production of endorphins. How might this explain why acupuncture seems to help people overcome dependence on heroin?

FURTHER READING

Farthing, *The Psychology of Consciousness* (1992), provides a very readable overview of the problems of consciousness and its alterations. See also Hobson, *The Chemistry of Conscious States* (1994). For philosophical/psychological discussions of consciousness, see Jackendoff, *Consciousness and the Computational Mind* (1990), and Churchland, *The Engine of Reason, the Seat of the Soul* (1995).

Useful books on sleep and dreams include Booztin, Kihlstrom, and Schacter (eds.), *Sleep and Cognition* (1990); Anch et al., *Sleep: A Scientific Perspective* (1988); and Hobson, *The Dreaming Brain* (1988). Maas, *Power Sleep* (1998) gives detailed advice on getting sufficient restful sleep.

There are a number of books on hypnosis. Presentations that include methods, theories, and experimental results are Hilgard, *The Experience of Hypnosis* (1968), and Gheorghiu et al. (eds.), *Suggestion and Suggestibility: Theory and Research* (1989).

General books on drugs include Julien, *A Primer of Drug Action* (6th ed., 1992); Goldstein, *Addiction: From Biology to Drug Policy* (1994); and Winger, Hofmann, and Woods, *A Handbook on Drug and Alcohol Abuse* (3rd ed., 1992). For a discussion of cocaine, see Weiss, Mirin, and Bartel, *Cocaine* (2nd. ed., 1994). *Buzzed*, by Kuhn, Swartzwelder, and Wilson (1998), is an excellent, straightforward presentation of the known facts about psychoactive drugs.

For a review of parapsychology, see Wolman, Dale, Schmeidler, and Ullman (eds.), *Handbook of Parapsychology* (1986); Radin, *The Conscious Universe* (1997); and Broughton, *Parapsychology* (1991).

Four

Learning, Remembering, and Thinking

Chapter 7
Learning and Conditioning

*L*earning pervades our lives. It is involved not only in mastering a new skill or academic subject but also in emotional development, social interaction, and even personality development. We learn what to fear, what to love, how to be polite, how to be intimate, and so on. Given the pervasiveness of learning, it is not surprising that we have already discussed many instances of it—how, for example, children learn to perceive the world around them, to identify with their own sex, and to control their behavior according to adult standards. Now, however, we turn to a more systematic analysis of learning.

Learning may be defined as *a relatively permanent change in behavior that occurs as the result of practice; behavior changes that are due to maturation or to temporary conditions* of the organism (such as fatigue or drug-induced states) are not included. Not all cases of learning are the same, though. There are four basic kinds of learning: habituation, classical conditioning, operant conditioning, and complex learning. *Habituation,* the simplest kind of learning, amounts to learning to ignore a stimulus that has become familiar and has no serious consequences—for example, learning to ignore the ticking of a new clock. This form of learning, along with a related form, sensitization, is discussed in the final section of the chapter. *Classical* and *operant conditioning* both involve forming associations—that is, learning that certain events go together. In classical conditioning, an organism learns that one event follows another; for example, a baby learns that the sight of a breast will be followed by the taste of milk. In operant conditioning, an organism learns that a response it makes will be followed by a particular consequence; for example, a young child learns that striking a sibling will be followed by disapproval from his or her parents. *Complex learning* involves something in addition to forming associations—for example, applying a strategy when solving a problem, or constructing a mental map of one's environment.

There are other forms of learning as well; they include imprinting, modeling and imitation, and vicarious learning. These are discussed in later chapters. In this chapter we focus primarily on conditioning and complex learning. First, though, we need to consider how the various perspectives on psychology have been applied to the study of learning.

Perspectives on Learning

Recall from Chapter 1 that three of the most important perspectives on psychology are the behavioristic, cognitive, and biological perspectives. As much as any area in psychology, the study of learning has involved all three of these perspectives.

Much of the early work on learning, particularly conditioning, was done from a behaviorist perspective. Researchers studied how nonhuman organisms learn an association between stimuli or an association between a stimulus and a response. The focus was on external stimuli and responses, in keeping with the behaviorist dictum that behavior is better understood in terms of external causes than mental ones. The behaviorist approach to learning made other key assumptions as well. One was that simple associations of the classical or operant kind are the building blocks of all learning. Thus, something as complex as acquiring a language is presumably a matter of learning many associations (Staats, 1968). Another assumption was that the same basic laws of learning operate regardless of what is being learned or who is doing the learning—be it a rat learning to run a maze or a child mastering long division (Skinner, 1971; 1938). These views led behaviorists to focus on how the behaviors of nonhuman organisms, particularly rats and pigeons, are influenced by rewards and punishments in simple laboratory situations.

This work uncovered a wealth of findings and phenomena that continue to form the basis of much of what we know about associative learning. But as we will see, the behaviorist assumptions have had to be modified in light of subsequent work. Understanding conditioning, not to mention complex learning, requires us to consider what the organism knows about the relations between stimuli and response (even when the organism is a rat or a pigeon), thereby ushering in the cognitive perspective. Also, in cases of complex learning, strategies, rules, and the

Learning may be defined as a relatively permanent change in behavior that occurs as a result of practice. Both humans and animals are able to learn through practice.

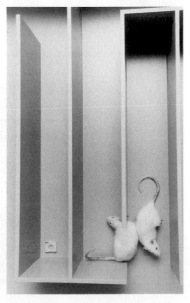

like must be considered in addition to associations, and again this requires us to adopt a cognitive approach. Moreover, it now appears that there is no single set of laws underlying learning in all situations and by all organisms. In particular, different mechanisms of learning seem to be involved in different species, thereby ushering in the biological perspective. The upshot is that the contemporary study of learning requires an integrated approach in which all three of the perspectives just mentioned are considered.

Classical Conditioning

Classical conditioning is *a learning process in which a previously neutral stimulus becomes associated with another stimulus through repeated pairing with that stimulus.* The study of classical conditioning began in the early years of the 20th century when Ivan Pavlov, a Russian physiologist who had already won the Nobel prize for research on digestion, turned his attention to learning. While studying digestion, Pavlov noticed that a dog began to salivate at the mere sight of a food dish. While any dog will salivate when food is placed in its mouth, this dog had learned to associate the sight of the dish with the taste of food. Pavlov had happened upon a case of *associative learning,* and he decided to see whether a dog could be taught to associate food with other things, such as a light or a tone.

Pavlov's Experiments

In Pavlov's basic experiment, a researcher first attaches a *fistula* or tube to the dog's salivary gland to measure salivary flow. Then the dog is placed in front of a pan into which meat powder can be delivered automatically. A researcher turns on a light in a window in front of the dog (or, in some forms of the experiment, rings a bell or sounds a tone). After a few seconds, some meat powder is delivered to the pan and the light is turned off. The dog is hungry, and the recording device registers copious salivation. This salivation is an **unconditioned response,** or UCR, for no learning is involved; by the same token, the meat powder is an **unconditioned stimulus,** or UCS. (See Table 7-1.) The procedure just described is repeated a number of times. At this point the dog will salivate in response to the light even if no meat powder is delivered. This salivation is a **conditioned response,** or CR, while the light is a **conditioned stimulus,** or CS. Although

Ivan Pavlov with his assistants.

TABLE 7-1

Elements of Classical Conditioning

Unconditioned stimulus (UCS)	A stimulus that automatically elicits a response, typically via a reflex, without prior conditioning.
Unconditioned response (UCR)	The response originally given to the unconditioned stimulus, used as the basis for establishing a conditioned response to a previously neutral stimulus.
Conditioned stimulus (CS)	A previously neutral stimulus that comes to elicit a conditioned response through association with an unconditioned stimulus.
Conditioned response (CR)	The learned or acquired response to a stimulus that did not evoke the response originally (i.e., a conditioned stimulus).

the light was originally a neutral stimulus—that is, one that would not ordinarily trigger a response—the dog has been taught, or *conditioned,* to associate the light with food and to respond to it by salivating. Pavlov's experiment is diagrammed in Figure 7-1.

Experimental Variations Over the years, psychologists have devised many variations of Pavlov's experiments. To appreciate these variations, we need to note some critical aspects of the conditioning experiment. Each paired presentation of the conditioned stimulus (CS) and the unconditioned stimulus (UCS) is called a *trial.* The trials during which the organism is learning the association between the two stimuli is the *acquisition stage* of conditioning. During this stage repeated pairings of the CS (light) and UCS (food) strengthen the association between the two, as illustrated in the left-hand curve of Figure 7-2. If the UCS is omitted repeatedly, the response will gradually diminish; this is called *extinction* and is illustrated by the right-hand curve in Figure 7-2.

Acquisition and extinction make intuitive sense if we view classical conditioning as learning to predict what will happen next. (This is the heart of the cognitive approach to conditioning, which we will later consider.) When the prediction is successful (reinforced), the animal learns to keep making that prediction (acquisition); when

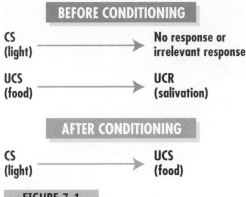

FIGURE 7-1

A Diagram of Classical Conditioning *The association between the unconditioned stimulus and the unconditioned response exists at the beginning of the experiment and does not have to be learned. The association between the conditioned stimulus and the unconditioned stimulus is learned. It arises through the pairing of the conditioned and unconditioned stimuli. (An association may also be learned between the conditioned stimulus and the conditioned response.)*

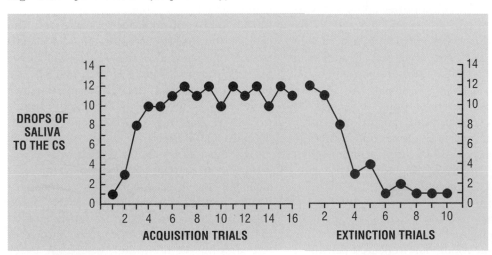

FIGURE 7-2

Acquisition and Extinction of a Conditioned Response *The curve in the panel on the left depicts the acquisition phase of an experiment. Drops of salivation in response to the conditioned stimulus (prior to the onset of the UCS) are plotted on the vertical axis; the number of trials is plotted on the horizontal axis. After 16 acquisition trials the experimenter switched to extinction; the results are presented in the panel at the right. (After Pavlov, 1927)*

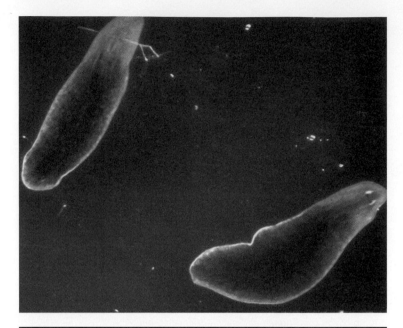

Flatworms—primitive organisms that are flat, soft-bodied, and symmetrical—are often used in biological experiments.

things change so that the prediction is outdated (not reinforced), the animal learns to inhibit that prediction (extinction).

Conditioning in Different Species Classical conditioning is pervasive in the animal kingdom and can occur with organisms as primitive as the flatworm. Flatworms contract their bodies when subjected to a mild electric shock, and if they experience sufficient pairings of shock (the UCS) and light (the CS), eventually they will contract their bodies in response to the light alone (Jacobson, Fried, & Horowitz, 1967). Numerous human responses can also be classically conditioned. Many of these are involuntary responses. To illustrate, consider the plight of cancer patients who are undergoing chemotherapy to stop the growth of their tumors. Chemotherapy involves injecting toxic substances into the patient, who as a result often becomes nauseated. After a number of chemotherapy sessions, patients sometimes become nauseated and sick upon entering the treatment room. The repeated pairing of the chemotherapy (the UCS) and the sight of the treatment room (the CS) has led them to associate the room with the chemotherapy, which results in the patients' experiencing intestinal upset before their treatment even

begins. A related phenomenon arises with young cancer patients who are given ice cream before the chemotherapy session. The ice cream may have been intended to lighten the child's distress about the impending treatment, but unfortunately, the ice cream becomes conditioned to the chemotherapy experience—that is, now the ice cream is the CS and the chemotherapy the UCS. The result is that the children become less likely to eat ice cream even outside the chemotherapy setting (Bernstein, 1978).

Phenomena and Applications

A number of phenomena greatly increase the generality of classical conditioning and make it an important kind of learning. Here we take a brief look at some of them.

Second-Order Conditioning Thus far in our discussion of conditioning, the UCS has always been a biologically significant stimulus such as food or shock. However, other stimuli can acquire the power of a UCS by being consistently paired with a biologically significant UCS. Recall the example of a dog exposed to a light (CS) followed by food (UCS), where the light comes to elicit a conditioned response. Once the dog is conditioned, the light acquires the power of a UCS. Thus, if the dog is now put in a situation in which it is exposed to a tone followed by the light (but no food) on each trial, the tone alone will eventually elicit a conditioned response even though it has never been paired with food. (There must also be other trials in which the light is again paired with food; otherwise, the originally conditioned relation between light and food will be extinguished.)

The existence of such *second-order conditioning* greatly increases the scope of classical conditioning, especially for humans, for whom biologically significant UCSs occur relatively frequently. Now all that is needed for conditioning to occur is the pairing of one stimulus with another, where the latter has previously been paired with a biologically significant event. Consider again the example of chemotherapy. Suppose that for a particular patient the sight of the treatment room has become conditioned to the side effects of chemotherapy, such as nausea (a biologically significant event). If the patient is repeatedly presented with a neutral stimulus, such as a tone, followed by a picture of the treatment room, the patient may start to experience some unpleasant feeling in response to the tone alone.

Generalization and Discrimination When a conditioned response has been associated with a particular stimulus, other similar stimuli will evoke the same response. Suppose that a person is conditioned to have a mild emotional reaction to the sound of a tuning fork producing a tone of middle C. (The emotional reaction is measured by the *galvanic skin response,* or GSR, which is a change in the electrical activity of the skin that occurs during emotional stress.) The person will also show a change in GSR in response to higher or lower tones without further conditioning (see Figure 7-3). *The more similar the new stimuli are to the original CS, the more likely they are to evoke the conditioned* response. This principle, called **generalization,** accounts in part for an individual's ability to react to novel stimuli that are similar to familiar ones.

A process that is complementary to generalization is discrimination. Whereas generalization is a reaction to similarities, **discrimination** is *a reaction to differences.* Conditioned discrimination is brought about through differential association, as shown in Figure 7-4. Instead of just one tone, for instance, now there are two. The low-pitched tone, CS_1, is always followed by a shock, and the high-pitched tone, CS_2, is not. Initially, participants will show a GSR to both tones. During the course of conditioning, however, the amplitude of the conditioned response to CS_1 gradually increases while the amplitude of the response to CS_2 decreases. Through this process of differential reinforcement, participants are conditioned to discriminate between the two tones. The high-pitched tone, CS_2, has become a signal to inhibit the learned response.

Generalization and discrimination occur frequently in everyday life. A young child who has learned to associate the sight of her pet dog with playfulness may initially approach all dogs. Eventually, through discrimination, the child may expect playfulness

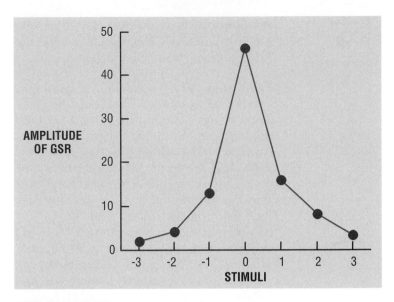

FIGURE 7-3

The Gradient of Generalization *Stimulus 0 denotes the tone to which the galvanic skin response (GSR) was originally conditioned. Stimuli +1, +2, and +3 represent test tones of increasingly higher pitch; stimuli −1, −2, and −3 represent tones of lower pitch. Note that the amount of generalization decreases as the difference between the test tone and the training tone increases.*

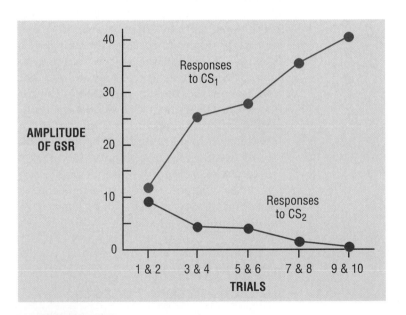

FIGURE 7-4

Conditioned Discrimination *The discriminative stimuli were two tones of clearly different pitch (CS_1 = 700 hertz and CS_2 = 3,500 hertz). The unconditioned stimulus, an electric shock applied to the left forefinger, occurred only on trials when CS_1 was presented. The strength of the conditioned response, in this case the GSR, gradually increased following CS_1 and extinguished following CS_2. (After Baer & Fuhrer, 1968)*

only from dogs that look like hers. The sight of a threatening dog has come to inhibit the child's response of approaching dogs.

Conditioned Fear Classical conditioning plays a role in emotional reactions like fear. Suppose that a rat is placed in an enclosed compartment in which it is periodically subjected to electric shock (by electrifying the floor). Just before the shock occurs, a tone sounds. After repeated pairings of the tone (the CS) and the shock (the UCS), the tone alone will produce reactions in the rat that indicate fear, including stopping in its tracks and crouching; in addition, its blood pressure increases. The rat has been conditioned to be fearful when exposed to what was previously a neutral stimulus.

Humans, too, can be conditioned to be fearful, particularly in early childhood (Watson & Raynor, 1920; Jacobs & Nadel, 1985). Perhaps the best evidence that they can be classically conditioned is that some of these fears, especially irrational ones known as *phobias,* can be eliminated using therapeutic techniques based on classical-conditioning principles. A person with an intense fear of cats, for example, may overcome the fear by being gradually and repeatedly exposed to cats. Presumably, a long time ago a cat was a CS for some noxious UCS, such as getting scratched, but now, when the person repeatedly experiences the CS without the UCS, the conditioned fear is extinguished. Note that if the person were not treated, he or she would simply avoid cats; consequently, extinction would not occur and the phobia would persist. (See Chapter 15 for a discussion of conditioning and phobias and Chapter 16 for conditioning therapies.)

Predictability and Cognitive Factors

Up to this point we have analyzed classical conditioning solely in terms of external or environmental events—one stimulus is consistently followed by another, and the organism comes to associate them with each other. Although this behaviorist view was dominant for many years, some researchers argued that the critical factor behind conditioning is what the animal knows (Tolman, 1932). In this cognitive view, classical conditioning gives an organism new knowledge about the relationship between two stimuli; given the CS, the organism has learned to expect the UCS. In what follows, we consider the role played by cognitive factors in classical conditioning.

Contiguity Versus Predictability Since Pavlov's time, researchers have tried to determine the critical factor needed for classical conditioning to occur. Pavlov believed that the critical factor was *temporal contiguity* of the CS and UCS—that is, the two stimuli must occur close together in time in order for an association to develop. However, an alternative view is that the CS must be a reliable predictor of the UCS. In other words, for conditioning to occur, there must be a *higher probability* that the UCS will occur when the CS has been presented than when it has not; that is, the UCS must be predictable.

In an important experiment, Rescorla (1967) contrasted contiguity and predictability. On certain trials he exposed dogs to shock (the UCS), and on some of these trials he preceded the shock with a tone (the CS). The procedures for two of the groups in the experiment are illustrated in Figure 7-5. The number of temporally contiguous pairings of tone and shock was the same in both groups. The independent variable was that all shocks were preceded by tones in Group A, whereas in Group B shocks were as likely to be preceded by no tones as by tones, so the tone had no real predictive power.

The predictive power of the tone proved to be critical: Dogs in Group A rapidly became conditioned, whereas those in Group B did not (as determined by whether or not the dog responded to the tone in such a way as to avoid the shock). In other groups in the experiment (not shown in Figure 7-5), the strength of the conditioning was directly related to the predictive value of the CS in signaling the occurrence of the UCS. Subsequent experiments support the conclusion that the predictive relationship between the CS and the UCS is more important than either temporal contiguity or the frequency with which the CS and UCS are paired (Rescorla, 1972).

What a dog is doing in the preceding experiment may be compared with what a scientist usually does. Confronted with the

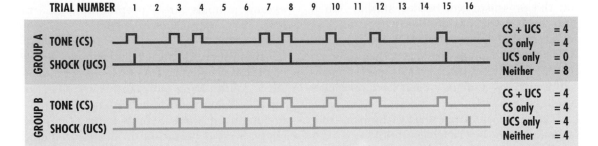

TRIAL NUMBER	1	2	3	4	5	6	7	8	9	10	11	12	13	14	15	16		

GROUP A
TONE (CS)
SHOCK (UCS)

CS + UCS = 4
CS only = 4
UCS only = 0
Neither = 8

GROUP B
TONE (CS)
SHOCK (UCS)

CS + UCS = 4
CS only = 4
UCS only = 4
Neither = 4

FIGURE 7-5

Rescorla's Experiment   *This figure presents a schematic representation of two groups from Rescorla's study. For each group, the events for 16 trials are presented. Note that on some trials the CS occurs and is followed by the UCS (CS$_1$ UCS); on other trials the CS or UCS occurs alone; and on still other trials, neither the CS nor the UCS occurs. The boxes to the far right give a count of these trial outcomes for the two groups. The number of CS$_1$ UCS trials is identical for both groups, as is the number of trials on which only the CS occurs. But the two groups differ in the number of trials on which the UCS occurred alone (never in Group A and as frequently as any other type of trial in Group B). Thus, for Group A the experimenter established a situation in which the tone was a useful (but not perfect) predictor that shock would follow shortly, whereas for Group B the tone was of no value in predicting subsequent shock. A conditioned response to CS developed readily for Group A but did not develop at all for Group B.*

possibility of an important negative occurrence such as a thunderstorm, a meteorologist tries to find something that predicts the event. It cannot be something that merely occurs at the same time as thunderstorms, because many innocuous events can do so (such as clouds and even the presence of trees). Rather, the meteorologist must search for events that are predictive of thunderstorms in that they tend to occur prior to thunderstorms but not at other times. Likewise, when a dog in the preceding experiment has to deal with the occurrence of shock, it, too, tries to find some event that can predict it. And like the meteorologist, the dog does not focus on events that merely occur along with shock (such as the sight of the experimental apparatus, or the tone heard by dogs in Group B); rather, the dog looks for an event that tends to occur prior to any shock but not at other times (the tone heard by dogs in Group A) and therefore is truly predictive of the shock.

Predictability and Emotion   Predictability is also important for emotional reactions. If a particular CS reliably predicts that pain is coming, the absence of that CS predicts that pain is *not* coming and the organism can relax. The CS therefore is a "danger" signal, and its absence is a "safety" signal. When such signals are erratic, the emotional toll

When a person knows when to expect pain, anxiety is reduced.

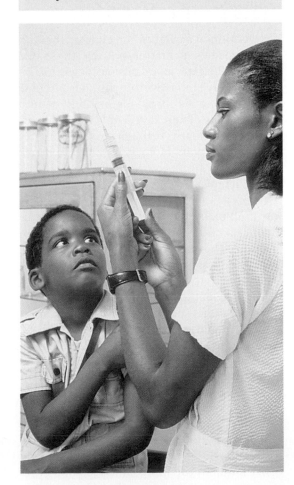

on the organism can be devastating. When rats have a reliable predictor that shock is coming, they respond with fear only when the danger signal is present; if they have no reliable predictor, they appear to be continually anxious and may even develop ulcers (Seligman, 1975).

There are clear parallels to human emotionality. If a dentist gives a child a danger signal by telling him or her that a procedure will hurt, the child will be fearful until the procedure is over. In contrast, if the dentist always tells a child that "it won't hurt" when in fact it sometimes does, the child has no danger or safety signals and may become terribly anxious whenever in the dentist's office. As adults, many of us have experienced the anxiety of being in a situation where something disagreeable is likely to happen but no warnings exist for us to predict it. Unpleasant events are, by definition, unpleasant, but unpredictable unpleasant events are downright intolerable. (Further discussion of this point is included in Chapter 14.)

Biological Constraints

We mentioned earlier in the chapter that different species sometimes learn the same thing by different mechanisms. These mechanisms were discovered by researchers studying animals' behavior in their natural environment. They reveal that what an organism can learn through conditioning is constrained by its biology.

The Ethological Approach   Ethologists, like behaviorists, are concerned with the behavior of animals, but ethologists place greater emphasis on evolution and genetics than on learning. This emphasis has led them to take a distinctive approach to learning, namely, to assume that it is rigidly constrained by an animal's genetic endowment and to show that different species will learn different things in different ways. (Early behaviorists, on the other hand, assumed that the laws of learning were the same for all species.) As ethologists put it, when an animal learns, it must conform to a genetically determined "behavioral blueprint"; just as an architectural blueprint imposes constraints on the kinds of functions that a building may serve, so a behavioral blueprint imposes genetic constraints on the kinds of associations that an organism may learn. That is, to some

extent animals are "preprogrammed" to learn particular things in particular ways.

Constraints on Classical Conditioning   Some of the best evidence for constraints on classical conditioning comes from studies of taste aversion. Consider first the basic phenomenon of taste aversion. In a typical study, a rat is permitted to drink a flavored solution—say, vanilla. After drinking it, the rat is mildly poisoned and made ill. When the rat recovers, it is again presented with the vanilla solution. Now the rat scrupulously avoids the solution because it has learned to associate the vanilla taste with feeling ill. There is good evidence that such avoidance is an instance of classical conditioning: The initial taste of the solution is the CS, the feeling of being sick is the UCS, and after conditioning the taste signals that sickness is on its way.

According to early behaviorist ideas, a light or a sound might be expected to play the same signaling role as taste. That is, if a light is as effective a stimulus as taste, then an association between a light and feeling sick should be no more difficult to establish than one between a taste and feeling sick. But the facts turn out to be otherwise. This is shown by the experiment diagrammed in Table 7-2. In the first stage of the experiment, an experimental group of rats is allowed to lick at a tube that contains a flavored solution; each time the rat licks the tube, a click and a light are presented. Thus, the rat experiences three stimuli simultaneously—the taste of the solution as well as the light and the click. In the second stage of the experiment, rats in the experimental group are mildly poisoned. The question is: What stimuli—the taste or the light-plus-click—will become associated with feeling sick? To answer this, in the third and final stage, rats in the experimental group are again presented with the tube; sometimes the solution in the tube has the same flavor as before but there is no light or click, while at other times the solution has no flavor but the light and click are presented. The animals avoid the solution when they experience the taste, but not when the light-plus-click is presented; hence, the rats have associated only taste with feeling sick. These results cannot be attributed to taste being a more potent CS than light-plus-click, as shown by the control condition of the experiment, which is diagrammed at the bottom of Table 7-2. In the

TABLE 7-2

An Experiment on Constraints and Taste Aversion *The design of an experiment showing that taste is a better signal for sickness than shock, where as light-plus-sound is a better signal for shock than sickness.* (After Garcia & Koelling, 1966)

	Stage 1	Stage 2	Stage 3
Experimental group	Taste and light + click	Sickness	Taste → Avoid Light + click →Don't avoid
Control group	Taste and light + click	Shock	Taste → Don't avoid Light + click → Avoid

second stage, instead of being mildly poisoned the rat is shocked. In the final stage, the animal avoids the solution only when the light-plus-click is presented, not when it experiences the taste alone (Garcia & Koelling, 1966).

Thus, taste is a better signal for sickness than for shock, and light-plus-click is a better signal for shock than for sickness. Why does this selectivity of association exist? It does not fit with the early behaviorist idea that equally potent stimuli can be substituted for one another; since taste and light-plus-click can both be effective CSs, and since being sick and being shocked are both effective UCSs, it should have been possible for either CS to become associated with either UCS. On the other hand, selectivity of association fits perfectly with the ethological perspective and its emphasis on an animal's evolutionary adaptation to its environment. In their natural habitat, rats rely on taste to select their food. Consequently, there may be a genetically determined relationship between taste and intestinal reactions, which fosters an association between taste and sickness but not between light and sickness. Moreover, in a rat's natural environment pain resulting from external factors like cold or injury is invariably due to external stimuli. Consequently, there may be a built-in relationship between external stimuli and "external pain," which fosters an association between light and shock but not one between taste and shock.

If rats learn to associate taste with sickness because it fits with their natural means of selecting food, another species with a different means of selecting food might have trouble learning to associate taste with sickness. This is exactly what happens. Birds naturally select their food on the basis of

looks rather than taste, and they readily learn to associate a light with sickness but not to associate a taste with sickness (Wilcoxin, Dragoin, & Kral, 1971). Here, then, is a perfect example of different species learning the same thing—what causes sickness—by different means. In short, if we want to know what may be conditioned to what, we cannot consider the CS and UCS in isolation; rather, we must focus on the two in combination and consider how well that combination reflects built-in relationships. This conclusion differs considerably from the assumption that the laws of learning are the same for all species and situations.

Operant Conditioning

In classical conditioning, the conditioned response often resembles the normal response to the unconditioned stimulus: Salivation, for example, is a dog's normal response to food. But when you want to teach an organism something novel—such as teaching a dog a new trick—you cannot use classical conditioning. What unconditioned stimulus would make a dog sit up or roll over? To train the dog, you must first persuade it to do the trick and afterward reward it with either approval or food. If you keep doing this, eventually the dog will learn the trick. Much real-life learning occurs by this means, which is referred to as operant conditioning.

In **operant conditioning,** *certain responses are learned because they operate on, or affect, the environment.* That is, an organism does not just react to stimuli, as in classical conditioning, but also behaves in ways designed to produce certain changes in its environment. Alone in a crib, a baby may kick and twist and coo spontaneously. When left by itself in a room, a dog may pad back and forth; sniff; or perhaps pick up a ball, drop it, and play with it. Neither organism is responding to a specific external stimulus. Rather, they are *operating on* their environment. Once the organism performs a certain behavior, however, the likelihood that the action will be repeated depends on its consequences. The baby will coo more often if each such occurrence is followed by parental attention, and the dog will pick up the ball more often if this action is followed by petting or a treat. If we think of the baby as having parental attention as a goal and the dog as having food as a goal, operant conditioning amounts to learning that a particular behavior leads to attaining a particular goal (Rescorla, 1987).

The Law of Effect

The study of operant conditioning began at the turn of the century with a series of experiments by E. L. Thorndike (1898). Thorndike, who was greatly influenced by Darwin's theory of evolution, was trying to show that learning in animals is continuous, as with learning in humans. A typical experiment proceeded as follows. A hungry cat is placed in a cage whose door is held fast by a simple latch, and a piece of fish is placed just outside the cage. Initially, the cat tries to reach the food by extending its paws through the bars. When this fails, the cat moves about the cage, engaging in a variety of behaviors. At some point it inadvertently

hits the latch, frees itself, and eats the fish. The researchers then place the cat back in its cage and put a new piece of fish outside. The cat goes through roughly the same set of behaviors until once more it happens to hit the latch. The procedure is repeated again and again. Over a number of trials the cat eliminates many of its irrelevant behaviors, and eventually it opens the latch and frees itself as soon as it is placed in the cage. The cat has learned to open the latch in order to obtain food.

It may sound as if the cat is acting intelligently, but Thorndike argued that there is little "intelligence" operating here. There is no moment in time at which the cat seems to have an insight about the solution to its problem. Instead, the cat's performance improves gradually over a series of trials. The cat appears to be engaging in trial-and-error behavior, and when a reward immediately follows one of those behaviors, the learning of the action is strengthened. Thorndike referred to this strengthening as the *law of effect*. He argued that in operant learning, the law of effect selects from a set of random responses only those that are followed by positive consequences. The process is similar to evolution, in which the law of survival of the fittest selects from a set of random mutations only those that promote survival of the species (Schwartz, 1989).

Skinner's Experiments

B. F. Skinner was responsible for a number of changes in how researchers conceptualize and study operant conditioning. His method of studying operant conditioning is simpler than Thorndike's—there is only one response involved, for instance—and it has been widely accepted.

Experimental Variations In a Skinnerian experiment, a hungry animal—usually a rat or a pigeon—is placed in a box like the one shown in Figure 7-6, which is popularly called a "Skinner box" or operant chamber. The inside of the box is bare except for a protruding bar with a food dish beneath it. A small light above the bar can be turned on at the experimenter's discretion. Left alone in the box, the rat moves about, exploring. Occasionally it inspects the bar and presses it. The rate at which the rat first presses the bar is the *baseline level*. After establishing

B. F. Skinner was a pioneer in the study of operant conditioning.

the baseline level, the experimenter activates a food magazine located outside the box. Now, every time the rat presses the bar, a small food pellet is released into the dish. The rat eats the food pellet and soon presses the bar again; the food reinforces

FIGURE 7-6

Apparatus for Operant Conditioning *This photograph shows a Skinner box with a magazine for delivering food pellets. The computer is used to control the experiment and record the rat's responses.*

bar pressing, and the rate of pressing increases dramatically. If the food magazine is disconnected so that pressing the bar no longer delivers food, the rate of bar pressing diminishes. Hence, an operantly conditioned response (or, simply, an *operant*) that is not reinforced undergoes extinction just as a classically conditioned response does.

Thus, operant conditioning increases the likelihood of a response by following the behavior with a reinforcer (often something like food or water). Because the bar is always present in the Skinner box, the rat can respond to it as frequently or infrequently as it chooses. The organism's rate of response is therefore a useful measure of the operant's strength; the more frequently the response occurs during a given time interval, the greater its strength.

It is worth noting the relationship between the terms *reward* and *punishment* on the one hand, and *positive* and *negative reinforcement* on the other. *Reward* can be used synonymously with *positive reinforcer*—an event whose occurrence after a particular behavior increases the probability of that behavior. But a punishment is not the same as a negative reinforcer. Negative reinforcement refers to the termination of an aversive event after a particular behavior is performed; like positive reinforcement, it increases the probability of that behavior. Punishment has the opposite effect: It *decreases* the probability of the punished behavior. Punishment also can be both positive (presentation of an unpleasant stimulus) or negative (removal of a pleasant stimulus). (See Table 7-3.)

TABLE 7-3

Types of Reinforcement and Punishment

Type	Definition	Effect	Example
Positive reinforcement	A pleasant stimulus that follows a desired behavior	Increases the likelihood of the desired behavior	A high grade on an exam
Negative reinforcement	Removal of an unpleasant stimulus after a desired behavior occurs	Increases the likelihood of the desired behavior	Allowing a child to leave his or her room when no longer having a temper tantrum
Positive punishment	Presentation of an unpleasant stimulus after an undesired behavior occurs	Decreases the likelihood of the undesired behavior	A low grade on an exam
Negative punishment	Removal of a pleasant stimulus after an undesired behavior occurs	Decreases the likelihood of the undesired behavior	Canceling TV viewing privileges for a child who misbehaves

A child's tendency to have temper tantrums can be reduced if the behavior is not reinforced with parental attention.

Implications for Child Rearing Although rats and pigeons have been the favored experimental subjects, operant conditioning applies to many species, including our own. Indeed, operant conditioning has a good deal to tell us about child rearing. A particularly illuminating example is the following case. A young boy had temper tantrums if he did not get enough attention from his parents, especially at bedtime. Since the parents eventually responded to the tantrums, their attention probably reinforced the boy's behavior. To eliminate the tantrums, the parents were advised to go through the normal bedtime ritual and then ignore the child's protests, painful though that might be. If the reinforcer (attention) was withheld, the behavior should be extinguished—which is just what happened. The time the child spent crying at bedtime decreased from 45 minutes to not at all over a period of only 7 days (Williams, 1959).

Another application of operant conditioning to child rearing focuses on the temporal relationship between a response and its reinforcer. Laboratory experiments have shown that immediate reinforcement is more effective than delayed reinforcement; the more time that elapses between an operant response and a reinforcer, the weaker the response. Many developmental psychologists have noted that delay of reinforcement is an important factor in dealing with young children. If a child acts kindly to a pet, for example, the behavior can best be strength-ened by praising the child immediately rather than waiting until later. Similarly, if a child hits someone without provocation, this aggressive behavior is more likely to be eliminated if the child is punished immediately.

Shaping Suppose that you want to use operant conditioning to teach your dog a trick—for instance, to press a buzzer with its nose. You cannot wait until the dog does this naturally and then reinforce it, because you may wait forever. When the desired behavior is truly novel, you have to condition it by taking advantage of natural variations in the animal's actions. To train a dog to press a buzzer with its nose, you can give the animal a food reinforcer each time it approaches the buzzer, requiring it to move closer and closer to the desired spot for each reinforcer until finally the dog's nose is touching the buzzer. This technique, called **shaping,** consists of *reinforcing only variations in response that deviate in the direction desired by the experimenter.*

Animals can be taught elaborate tricks and routines by means of shaping. Two psychologists and their staff trained thousands of animals of many species for television shows, commercials, and county fairs (Breland & Breland, 1966). One popular show featured "Priscilla, the Fastidious Pig." Priscilla turned on the TV set, ate breakfast at a table, picked up dirty clothes and put them in a hamper, vacuumed the floor, picked out her favorite food, and took part in a quiz program, answering questions from the audience by flashing lights that indicated yes or no. She was not an unusually bright pig; in fact, because pigs grow so fast, a new "Priscilla" was trained every 3 to 5 months. The ingenuity was not the pig's but the experimenters', who used operant conditioning and shaped the pig's behavior so as to produce the desired result. Shaping has been used to train pigeons to locate people lost at sea (see Figure 7-7), and porpoises have been trained to retrieve underwater equipment.

Phenomena and Applications

There are a number of phenomena that greatly increase the generality of operant conditioning and show its applications to human behavior. Here we look briefly at some of them.

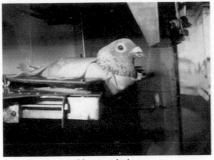

Pigeon sitting

Pigeon pecking key

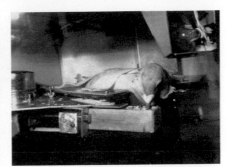

Pigeon rewarded

FIGURE 7-7

Search and Rescue by Pigeons   *The Coast Guard has used pigeons to search for people lost at sea. Shaping methods are used to train the pigeons to spot the color orange—the international color for life jackets. Three pigeons are strapped into a plexiglass chamber attached to the underside of a helicopter. The chamber is divided into thirds so that each bird faces in a different direction. When a pigeon spots an orange object, or any other object, it pecks a key that buzzes the pilot. The pilot then heads in the direction indicated by the bird that responded. Pigeons are better suited than people for the task of spotting distant objects at sea. They can stare over the water for a long time without suffering eye fatigue; they have excellent color vision; and they can focus on a 60- to 80-degree area, whereas a person can focus only on a 2- to 3-degree area. (After Simmons, 1981)*

Conditioned Reinforcers   Most of the reinforcers we have discussed are called *primary* because they satisfy basic drives. If operant conditioning occurred only with primary reinforcers, it would not occur very often because primary reinforcers are not that common. However, virtually any stimulus can become a *secondary* or *conditioned reinforcer* by being consistently paired with a primary reinforcer.

A minor variation in the typical operant-conditioning experiment illustrates how conditioned reinforcement works. When a rat in a Skinner box presses a lever, a tone sounds momentarily and is followed shortly by delivery of food (the food is a primary reinforcer; the tone will become a conditioned reinforcer). After the animal has been conditioned in this way, the experimenter begins the extinction process, so that when the rat presses the lever neither the tone nor the food occurs. In time the animal ceases to press the lever. Then the tone is reconnected but not the food magazine. When the animal discovers that pressing the lever turns on the tone, its rate of pressing increases markedly, overcoming the extinction even though no food is delivered. The tone has acquired a reinforcing quality of its own through classical conditioning; because the tone was reliably paired with food, it came to signal food.

Our lives abound with conditioned reinforcers. Two of the most prevalent are money and praise. Presumably, money is a powerful reinforcer because it has been paired so frequently with so many primary reinforcers—we can buy food, drink, and comfort, to mention just a few of the obvious things. And mere praise can sustain many activities without even the promise of a primary reinforcer.

Generalization and Discrimination   Again, what was true for classical conditioning holds for operant conditioning as well: Organisms generalize what they have learned, and generalization can be curbed by discrimination training. If a young child is reinforced by her parents for petting the family dog, she will soon generalize this petting response to other dogs. Since this can be dangerous (the neighbors might have a vicious watchdog), the child's parents may provide some discrimination training so that she is reinforced when she pets the family dog but not the neighbor's.

Discrimination training will be effective to the extent that there is a discriminative stimulus (or set of them) that clearly distinguishes cases in which the response should be made from those in which it should be suppressed. Our young child will have an easier time learning which dog to pet if her parents can point to an aspect of dogs that signals friendliness (a wagging tail, for example). In general, a discriminative stimulus will be useful to the extent that its presence predicts that a response will be followed by reinforcement while its absence predicts that the response will not be followed by reinforcement (or vice versa). Just as in classical conditioning, the predictive power of a stimulus seems to be critical to conditioning.

Schedules of Reinforcement   In real life, not every instance of a behavior is reinforced. For example, sometimes hard work is followed by praise, but often it goes unacknowledged. If operant conditioning occurred only

Praise is an effective reinforcer for many people.

with continuous reinforcement, it might play a limited role in our lives. It turns out, however, that once a behavior is established, it can be maintained when it is reinforced only a fraction of the time. This phenomenon is known as *partial reinforcement,* and it can be illustrated in the laboratory by a pigeon that learns to peck at a key for food. Once this operant is established, the pigeon continues to peck at a high rate even if it receives only occasional reinforcement. In some cases, pigeons that were rewarded with food an average of once every 5 minutes (12 times an hour) pecked at the key as often as 6,000 times per hour—500 pecks per pellet of food received! Moreover, extinction following the maintenance of a response on partial reinforcement is much slower than extinction following the maintenance of a response on continuous reinforcement. This phenomenon is known as the *partial-reinforcement effect.* It makes intuitive sense because there is less difference between extinction and maintenance when reinforcement during maintenance is only partial.

When reinforcement occurs only some of the time, we need to know exactly how it is scheduled—after every third response? After every five seconds? It turns out that the schedule of reinforcement determines the pattern of responding. Some schedules are called **ratio schedules,** because *reinforcement depends on the number of responses the organism makes.* It's like being a factory worker who gets paid for piecework. The ratio can be either fixed or variable. On a **fixed ratio schedule** (called an FR schedule), *the number of responses that has to be made is fixed at a particular value.* If the number is 5 (FR 5), 5 responses are required for reinforcement; if it is 50 (FR 50), 50 responses are required; and so on. In general, the higher the ratio, the higher the rate at which the organism responds, particularly when the organism is initially trained on a relatively low ratio (say, FR 5) and then is continuously shifted to progressively higher ratios, culminating, say, in FR 100. It is as if our factory worker initially got 5 dollars for every 5 hems sewn, but then times got tough and he needed to do 100 hems to get 5 dollars. But perhaps the most distinctive aspect about behavior under an FR schedule is that there is a pause in responding right after the reinforcement occurs (see the left side of Figure 7-8). It is hard for the factory worker to start on a new set of hems right after he has just finished enough to obtain a reward.

On a **variable ratio schedule** (a VR schedule), the organism is still reinforced only after making a certain number of responses, but that number varies unpredictably. Thus, in a VR 5 schedule, the number of responses needed for reinforcement may sometimes be 1, at other times 10, with an average of 5. Unlike the behavior that occurs under FR schedules, there are no pauses when the organism is operating under a VR schedule (see the left side of Figure 7-8), presumably because the organism has no way of detecting how far it is from a reinforcement. A good example of a VR schedule in everyday life is the operation of a slot machine. The number of responses (plays) needed for reinforcement (payoff) keeps varying, and the operator has no way of predicting when reinforcement will occur. VR schedules can generate very high rates of responding (as casino owners appear to have figured out).

Other schedules of reinforcement are called **interval schedules,** because under these schedules *reinforcement is available only after a certain time interval has elapsed* (and the animal makes a response). Again, the schedule can be either fixed or variable. On a **fixed interval schedule** (an FI schedule), *the organism is reinforced for its first response after a certain amount of time has passed since its last reinforcement.* On an FI 2 (minutes) schedule, for example, reinforcement is available only when 2 minutes have elapsed since the last reinforced response; responses made during that 2-minute interval have no effect. One distinctive aspect of responding on an FI schedule is a pause that occurs immediately after reinforcement. (This post-reinforcement pause can be even longer than the one that occurs under FR schedules.) Another distinctive aspect of responding on an FI schedule is an increase in the rate of responding as the end of the interval approaches, producing a pattern often described as a scallop (see the right side of Figure 7-8). A good example of an FI schedule in everyday life is mail delivery, which comes just once a day (FI 24 hours), or in some places twice a day (FI 12 hours). Thus, right after your mail is delivered you would not check it again, but as the end of the mail-delivery interval approaches you will start checking again.

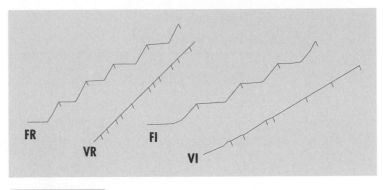

FIGURE 7-8

Typical Patterns of Responding on the Four Basic Schedules of Reinforcement *Each curve plots an animal's cumulative number of responses as a function of time; the slope of the curve thus indicates the animal's rate of responding. The curves on the left are for ratio schedules. In the curve for the FR schedule, note the horizontal segments—these correspond to pauses (they show no increase in the cumulative number of responses). The curves on the right are for interval schedules. In the curve for the FI schedule, again the horizontal segments correspond to pauses.* (Adapted from Schwartz, 1989)

On a **variable interval schedule** (a VI schedule), *reinforcement still depends on a certain interval having elapsed, but the interval's duration varies unpredictably.* In a

Gamblers who play the slot machines are reinforced with payoffs on a variable ratio schedule. Such a schedule can generate very high rates of responding.

TABLE 7-4

Schedules of Reinforcement

Ratio Schedules	
Fixed ratio schedule	Reinforcement is provided after a certain amount of time has elapsed since the last reinforcement.
Variable ratio schedule	Reinforcement is provided after a certain amount of time has elapsed since the last reinforcement, with the duration of the interval varying unpredictably.
Interval Schedules	
Fixed interval schedule	Reinforcement is provided after a fixed number of responses.
Variable interval schedule	Reinforcement is provided after a certain number of responses, with the number varying unpredictably.

VI 10 (minute) schedule, for example, sometimes the critical interval may be 2 minutes, sometimes 20 minutes, and so on, with an average of 10 minutes. Unlike the variations in responding found under an FI schedule, organisms tend to respond at a uniform high rate when the schedule is a VI 1 (see the right side of Figure 7-8). For an example of a VI schedule in everyday life, consider redialing a phone number after hearing a busy signal. In order to receive reinforcement (getting your call through), you have to wait some time interval after your last response (dialing), but the length of that interval is unpredictable. (See Table 7-4.)

Aversive Conditioning

We have talked about reinforcement as if it were almost always positive (food, for example). But negative or aversive events, such as shock or a painful noise, are often used in conditioning. There are different kinds of aversive conditioning, depending on whether the aversive event is used to weaken an existent response or to learn a new response.

Punishment In **punishment** training, *a response is followed by an aversive stimulus or event, which results in the response being weakened or suppressed on subsequent occasions.* Suppose that a young child who is learning to use crayons starts drawing on the wall (this is the undesirable response); if he is slapped on the hand when he does this (the punishment), he will learn not to do so. Similarly, if a rat that is learn-

ing to run a maze is shocked whenever it chooses a wrong path, it will soon learn to avoid its past mistakes. In both cases, punishment is used to decrease the likelihood of an undesirable behavior.

Although punishment can suppress an unwanted response, it has several disadvantages. First, its effects are not as informative as the results of reward. Reward essentially says, "Repeat what you have done"; punishment says, "Stop it!" but fails to give an alternative. As a result, the organism may substitute an even less desirable response for the punished one. Second, the by-products of punishment may be unfortunate. Through classical conditioning, punishment often leads to dislike or fear of the punishing person (parent, teacher, or employer) and the situation (home, school, or office) in which it occurred. Finally, an extreme or painful punishment may elicit aggressive behavior that is more serious than the original undesirable behavior.

These cautions do not mean that punishment should never be employed. It can effectively eliminate an undesirable response if it is consistent and is delivered immediately after the undesired response, and if an alternative response is rewarded. Rats that have learned to take the shorter of two paths in a maze to reach food will quickly switch to the longer one if they are shocked when taking the shorter path. The temporary suppression produced by punishment provides an opportunity for the rat to learn to take the longer path. In this case, punishment is an effective means of redirecting behavior because it is informative, and this seems to be the key to the humane and effective use of punishment. A child who gets a shock from an electrical appliance may learn which connections are safe and which ones are hazardous.

Escape and Avoidance Aversive events can also be used in the learning of new responses. Organisms can learn to make a response in order to terminate an ongoing aversive event, as when a child learns to turn off a faucet to stop hot water from flowing into the bathtub. This is called *escape learning.* Organisms can also learn to make a response in order to prevent an aversive event from even starting, as when we learn to stop at red lights to prevent accidents (and traffic tickets). This is called *avoidance learning.*

Often, escape learning precedes avoidance learning. This is illustrated by the following experiment. A rat is placed in a box consisting of two compartments divided by a barrier. On each trial the animal is placed in one of the compartments. At some point a warning tone is sounded, and 5 seconds later the floor of that compartment is electrified; to get away from the shock, the animal must jump over the barrier into the other compartment. Initially the rat jumps over the barrier only when the shock starts—this is escape learning. But with practice it learns to jump upon hearing the warning tone, thereby avoiding the shock entirely—this is avoidance learning.

Avoidance learning has generated a great deal of interest, in part because there is something very puzzling about it. What exactly is reinforcing the avoidance response? In the experiment just described, what reinforces the animal for jumping over the barrier? Intuitively, it seems to be the absence of shock, but this is a nonevent. How can a nonevent serve as a reinforcer? One solution to this puzzle holds that there are two stages in the learning taking place. The first stage involves classical conditioning: Through repeated pairings of the warning (the CS) and the punishing event or shock (the UCS), the animal learns a fear response to the warning. The second stage involves operant conditioning: The animal learns that a particular response (jumping over the barrier) removes an aversive event, namely fear. In short, what first appears to be a nonevent is actually fear, and we can think of

The threat of punishment is an effective motivator.

avoidance as escape from fear (Mowrer, 1947; Rescorla & Solomon, 1967).

Control and Cognitive Factors

Our analysis of operant conditioning has tended to emphasize environmental factors—a response is consistently followed by a reinforcing event, and the organism learns to associate the response with the reinforcement. However, the cognitive theory of avoidance suggests that cognitive factors may play an important role in operant conditioning just as they do in classical conditioning. As we will see, it is often useful to view the organism in an operant conditioning situation as acquiring new knowledge about relationships between responses and reinforcers.

Contingency Versus Control As with classical conditioning, we want to know what factor is critical for operant conditioning to occur. Again, one of the options is temporal contiguity: An operant behavior is conditioned whenever it is immediately followed by reinforcement (Skinner, 1948). A more cognitive option, closely related to predictability, is that of control: An operant is conditioned only when the organism interprets the reinforcement as being controlled by its response. Some important experiments by

Maier and Seligman (1976) provide more support for the control view than for the temporal contiguity view. (See also the discussion of control and stress in Chapter 15.) Their basic experiment includes two stages. In the first stage, some dogs learn that whether they receive a shock or not depends on (is controlled by) their behavior, while other dogs learn that they have no control over the shock. Think of the dogs as being tested in pairs. Both members of a pair are in a harness that restricts their movements, and occasionally they receive an electric shock. One member of the pair, the "control" dog, can turn off the shock by pushing a nearby panel with its nose; the other member of the pair, the "yoked" dog, cannot exercise any control over the shock. Whenever the control dog is shocked, so is the yoked dog; and whenever the control dog turns off the shock, the yoked dog's shock is also terminated. The control and yoked dogs therefore receive the same number of shocks.

To find out what the dogs learned in the first stage, a second stage is needed. In this stage, the experimenter places both dogs in a new apparatus—a box divided into two compartments by a barrier. On each trial a tone is first sounded, indicating that the compartment the animal currently occupies is about to be subjected to an electric shock; to avoid the shock, the animal must learn to jump the

barrier into the other compartment when it hears the warning tone. Control dogs learn this response rapidly. But the yoked dogs are another story. Initially the yoked dogs make no movement across the barrier, and as trials progress, their behavior becomes increasingly passive, finally lapsing into utter helplessness. Why? Because during the first stage the yoked dogs learned that shocks were not under their control, and this belief in noncontrol made conditioning in the second stage impossible. If a belief in noncontrol makes operant conditioning impossible, a belief in control may be what makes it possible. Many other experiments support the notion that operant conditioning occurs only when the organism perceives reinforcement as being under its control (Seligman, 1975). See Chapter 15 for a detailed discussion of learned helplessness.

Contingency Learning We can also talk about these findings in terms of contingencies. We can say that operant conditioning occurs only when the organism perceives a *contingency* between its responses and reinforcement. In the first stage of the preceding study, the relevant contingency is between pushing a panel and the absence of shock; perceiving this contingency amounts to determining that the likelihood of avoiding shock is greater when the panel is pushed

Operant conditioning and shaping are used in training animals to perform tricks of various kinds.

than when it is not. Dogs that do not perceive this contingency in the first stage of the study appear not to look for any contingency in the second stage. This contingency approach makes it clear that the results of research on operant conditioning fit with the findings about the importance of predictability in classical conditioning: Knowing that a CS predicts a UCS can be interpreted as showing that the organism has detected a contingency between the two stimuli. Thus, in both classical and operant conditioning, what the organism seems to learn is a contingency between two events: In classical conditioning, a behavior is contingent on a particular stimulus; in operant conditioning, a behavior is contingent on a particular anticipated response.

Our ability to learn contingencies develops very early, as shown by the following study of 3-month-old infants. Each infant in the experiment was lying in a crib with its head on a pillow. Beneath each pillow was a switch that closed whenever the infant turned its head. For infants in the control group, whenever they turned their heads and closed the switch, a mobile on the opposite side of the crib was activated. For these infants, there was a contingency between head turning and the mobile moving—the mobile being more likely to move with a head turn than without. These infants quickly learned to turn their heads, and they reacted to the moving mobile with signs of enjoyment (they smiled and cooed). The situation is quite different for infants in the experimental group. For these infants, the mobile was made to move roughly as often as it did for infants in the control group, but whether it moved or not was not under their control: There was no contingency between head turning and the mobile moving. These infants did not learn to turn their heads more frequently. Moreover, after a while they showed no signs of enjoying the moving mobile. The mobile appears to have gained its reinforcing character when its movement could be controlled and lost it when its movement could not be controlled.

Biological Constraints

As with classical conditioning, biology imposes constraints on what may be learned through operant conditioning. These constraints involve relationships between responses and reinforcers. To illustrate, consider pigeons in two experimental situations: reward learning, in which the animal acquires a response that is reinforced by food, and escape learning, in which the animal acquires a response that is reinforced by the termination of shock. In the case of reward, pigeons learn much faster if the response is pecking a key than if it is flapping their wings. In the case of escape, the opposite is true: Pigeons learn faster if the response is wing flapping than if it is pecking (Bolles, 1970).

These seem inconsistent with the assumption that the same laws of learning apply to all situations, but they make sense from an ethological perspective. The reward case with the pigeons involved eating, and pecking (but not wing flapping) is part of the bird's natural eating activities. Hence, a genetically determined connection between pecking and eating is reasonable. Similarly, the escape case involved a danger situation, and the pigeon's natural reactions to danger include flapping its wings (but not pecking). Birds are known to have a small repertoire of defensive reactions, and they will quickly learn to escape only if the relevant response is one of these natural reactions.

The ethological research just discussed reveals a new way in which biological and psychological approaches can interact. Ethological concepts help us make sense of previous psychological findings. In this case, they explain why pigeons learn faster in a reward learning situation if the response is pecking, but learn faster in an escape learning situation if the response is wing flapping.

Complex Learning

According to the cognitive perspective, the crux of learning—and of intelligence in general—lies in an organism's ability to mentally represent aspects of the world and then operate on these mental representations rather than on the world itself. In many cases, what is mentally represented is an association between stimuli or events; these cases correspond to classical and operant conditioning. In other cases, what is represented seems more complex. It might be a map of one's environment or an abstract concept like the notion of cause. Also, there are cases in which the operations performed on mental representations are more complex than associative processes. The operations may take the form of a mental trial and error, in which the organism tries out different possibilities in its mind. Or the operations may consist of a strategy in which we take some mental steps only because they make possible subsequent steps. The idea of a strategy in particular seems at odds with the assumption that complex learning is built out of simple associations. In what follows, we consider some learning phenomena that point to the need to consider nonassociative representations and operations. Some of these phenomena involve animals, whereas others involve humans performing tasks that are similar to conditioning.

Cognitive Maps and Abstract Concepts

An early advocate of the cognitive approach to learning was Edward Tolman, whose research dealt with the problem of rats learning their way through complex mazes (Tolman, 1932). In his view, a rat running through a complex maze was not learning a sequence of right- and left-turning responses but rather was developing a **cognitive map**—*a mental representation of the layout of the maze.*

More recent research provides strong evidence for this view. Consider the maze diagrammed in Figure 7-9. It consists of a central platform with eight identical arms radiating outward. On each trial the researcher places food at the end of each arm; the rat needs to learn to visit each arm (and obtain the food there) without returning to those it has already visited. Rats learn to do so remarkably well; after 20 trials they will virtually never return to an arm that they have already visited. (Rats will do this even when the maze has been doused with aftershave lotion to mask the odor cues about which arms still have food.) Most important, a rat rarely employs the strategy that would occur to humans—such as always going through the arms in an obvious order (say, clockwise). Instead, the rat visits the arms randomly, indicating that it has not learned a

rigid sequence of responses. What, then, has it learned? Probably it has developed a map-like representation of the maze that specifies the spatial relations between arms, and on each trial it makes a mental note of which arm it has visited (Olton, 1979; 1978).

More recent studies using primates provide even stronger evidence for complex mental representations. Particularly striking are studies showing that chimpanzees can acquire abstract concepts that were once believed to be the sole province of humans. In a typical study, chimpanzees learn to use plastic tokens of different shapes, sizes, and colors as words. For example, they might learn that one token refers to "apples" and another to "paper," even though there is no physical resemblance between the token and the object. The fact that chimpanzees can learn these references suggests that they understand concrete concepts such as "apple" and "paper." More impressive, they can also learn abstract concepts such as "same," "different," and "cause." Thus, chimpanzees can learn to use their "same" token when presented with either two "apple" tokens or two "orange" ones, and

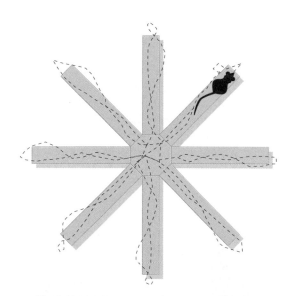

FIGURE 7-9

A Maze for Studying Cognitive Maps   *With food placed at the end of every arm, the rat's problem is to find all the food without retracing its steps. The pattern shown here reflects perfect learning: This rat visited each arm of the maze only once, eating whatever it found there; it did not go back to an empty arm even one time.*

their "different" token when presented with one "apple" and one "orange" token. Likewise, chimpanzees seem to understand causal relations. They will apply the token for "cause" when shown scissors and some cut paper but not when shown scissors and some intact paper (Premack, 1985a; Premack & Premack. 1983).

Insight Learning

While many early researchers tried to study complex learning with species far removed from humans, such as rats and pigeons, others assumed that the best evidence for complex learning would come from research using primates. Wolfgang Köhler's work with chimpanzees, carried out in the 1920s, remains particularly important. The problems that Köhler set for his chimpanzees left some room for insight, because no parts of the problem were hidden from view. (In contrast, the workings of a food dispenser in a Skinner box are hidden from the animal's view.) Typically, Köhler placed a chimpanzee in an enclosed area with a desirable piece of fruit, often a banana, out of reach. To obtain the fruit, the animal had to use a nearby object as a tool. Usually the chimpanzee solved the problem in a way that suggested that the animal had some insight. The following description by Köhler is typical:

> Sultan [Köhler's most intelligent chimpanzee] is squatting at the bars but cannot reach the fruit which lies outside by means of his only available short stick. A longer stick is deposited outside the bars, about two meters on one side of the object and parallel with the grating. It cannot be grasped with the hand, but it can be pulled within reach by means of the small stick. [See Figure 7-10 for an illustration of a similar multiple-stick problem.] Sultan tries to reach the fruit with the smaller of the two sticks. Not succeeding, he tears at a piece of wire that projects from the netting of his cage, but that too is in vain. Then he gazes about him (there are always in the course of these tests some long pauses, during which the animals scrutinize the whole visible area). He suddenly picks up the little stick once more, goes up to the bars directly opposite to the long stick, scratches it towards him with the "auxiliary," seizes it, and goes with it to the point opposite the objective (the fruit), which he secures. From the moment that his eyes fall upon the long stick, his procedure

Using the technique developed by Premack, an experimenter tests a chimpanzee's ability to use language by manipulating plastic chips that represent specific words.

FIGURE 7-10

The Multiple Stick Problem   Using the shorter sticks, the chimpanzee pulls in a stick long enough to reach the piece of fruit. It has learned to solve this problem by understanding the relationship between the sticks and the piece of fruit.

forms one consecutive whole, without hiatus, and although the angling of the bigger stick by means of the smaller is an action that could be complete and distinct in itself, yet observation shows that it follows, quite suddenly, on an interval of hesitation and doubt—staring about—which undoubtedly has a relation to the final objective, and is immediately merged in the final action of the attainment of the end goal. (Köhler, 1925, pp. 174–75)

In several respects, the performance of these chimpanzees is unlike those of Thorndike's cats or Skinner's rats and pigeons. For one thing, the solution was sudden rather than being the result of a gradual trial-and-error process. Another point is that once a chimpanzee solved a problem, thereafter it would solve the problem with few irrelevant moves. This is most unlike a rat in a Skinner box, which continues to make irrelevant responses for many trials. Also, Köhler's chimpanzees could readily transfer what they had learned to a novel situation. For example, in one problem Sultan was not caged, but some bananas were placed too high for him to reach, as shown in Figure 7-11. To solve the problem, Sultan stacked some boxes that were strewn around him, climbed the "platform," and grabbed the bananas. In subsequent problems, if the fruit was again too high to reach, Sultan found other objects to use in constructing a platform; in some cases,

FIGURE 7-11

A Chimpanzee Constructing a Platform   *To reach the bananas hanging from the ceiling, the chimpanzee stacks boxes to form a platform.*

"Deep Blue," IBM's chess-playing computer, applied artificial intelligence to defeat chess master Garry Kasparov. Kasparov believed that the computer had actually learned to formulate strategy rather than simply following the rules for playing chess that were programmed into it.

Sultan used a table and a small ladder, and in one case Sultan pulled Köhler himself over and used the experimenter as a platform!

There are, therefore, three critical aspects of the chimpanzee's solution: its suddenness, its availability once discovered, and its transferability. These aspects are at odds with trial-and-error behaviors of the type observed by Thorndike, Skinner, and their students. Instead, the chimpanzee's solutions may reflect a mental trial and error. That is, the animal forms a mental representation of the problem, manipulates components of the representation until it hits upon a solution, and then enacts the solution in the real world. The solution appears sudden because the researchers do not have access to the chimpanzee's mental processes. The solution is available thereafter because a mental representation persists over time. And the solution is transferable because the representation is either abstract enough to cover more than the original situation or malleable enough to be extended to a novel situation.

Köhler's work suggests that complex learning often involves two phases. In the initial phase, problem solving is used to arrive at a solution; in the second phase, the solution is stored in memory and retrieved whenever a similar problem situation presents itself. Hence, complex learning is intimately related to memory and thinking (the topics of the next two chapters). Moreover, this two-phase structure characterizes not just chimpanzee learning but many cases of complex learning in humans. Indeed, it has recently been incorporated into artificial intelligence programs that try to simulate human learning (Rosenbloom, Laird, & Newell, 1991).

Prior Beliefs

Research on animal learning has tended to emphasize the learning of perfectly predictable relations. For example, in most studies of classical conditioning, the CS is followed by the UCS 100% of the time. But in real life the relationships between stimuli or events usually are less than perfectly predictable. The study of associative learning with less than perfect relationships has been conducted mainly with humans. Many of these studies have used tasks that are quite novel and do not make much contact with the learner's prior beliefs. In such cases, participants are very sensitive to the degree of the objective relationship between the stimuli (Shanks & Dickinson, 1987; Wasserman, 1990). But our concern here is with studies that use tasks that *do* make contact with the learner's prior beliefs. These studies show that prior beliefs can determine what is learned, which indicates that learning involves processes in addition to those that form associations between inputs.

In these studies, a different pair of stimuli—say, a picture and a description of a person—is presented on each trial, and the participant's task is to learn the relationship between the members of the pairs—say, that pictures of tall men tend to be associated with brief descriptions. Some striking evidence for the role of prior beliefs comes from cases in which, objectively, there is no relationship between the stimuli, yet participants "learn" such a relationship. In one experiment participants were concerned with the possible relationship between the drawings that mental patients made and the symptoms the patients displayed. On each trial, participants were presented with a patient's drawing of a person and one of six symptoms, including "suspiciousness of other people" and "concerned with being taken care of." The participant's task was to determine whether any aspects of the drawings were associated with any of the symptoms. In fact, the six symptoms had been randomly paired with the drawings so that there was no association between them. Yet participants consistently reported such associations, and the relationships they reported were ones that they probably believed before participating in the experiment—for example, that large eyes are associated with suspiciousness, or that a large mouth is associated with a desire to be taken care of by others. These nonexistent but plausible relationships are referred to as *spurious associations* (Chapman & Chapman, 1969).

In the preceding study, prior beliefs about the stimuli determined what was "learned."

Since prior beliefs are part of one's knowledge, these results attest to the cognitive nature of such learning. However, the study does not say anything about how learning proceeds when there is in fact an objective association to be learned. This issue was analyzed in the following research.

On each of a set of trials, participants were presented with two measures of an individual's honesty taken from two completely different situations. For example, one measure might have been how often a young boy copied another student's homework in school, and the second might have been an indication of how often that same boy was dishonest at home. It is well known that most people believe (erroneously) that two measures of the same trait (such as honesty) will always be highly correlated. This is the critical prior belief. In fact, the objective relationship between the two measures of honesty varied across different conditions of the experiment, sometimes being quite low, and the participants' task was to estimate the strength of this relationship by choosing a number between 0 (which indicated no relation) and 100 (a perfect relation). The results showed that participants consistently overestimated the strength of the relationship. Their prior belief that an honest person is honest in all situations led them to see more than was there (Jennings, Amabile, & Ross, 1982).

In the preceding study, sometimes the learner's prior beliefs were not in agreement with the objective association to be learned. In these cases beliefs and data were in conflict. In such situations people typically go with their prior beliefs. If they believe that two different measures of an individual's honesty should be highly related, for example, they may "detect" such a relationship even when there is no objective association. However, as the data (the objective association) are made increasingly salient, our prior beliefs are overcome and we learn what is in fact there (Alloy & Tabachnik, 1984).

The results of these studies are reminiscent of what we called top-down processing in perception (see Chapter 5). Recall that top-down processing refers to situations in which a perceiver combines his expectation of what he is likely to see with the actual input to yield a final percept. In top-down processing in learning, the learner combines her prior belief about an associative relationship with the objective input about that relationship to yield a final estimate of the strength of that relationship.

The effects of prior beliefs on learning have important implications for education. In particular, when teaching someone about a topic—for example, the biology of digestion—one cannot ignore his or her prior beliefs about the subject matter. The student will often try to assimilate the new information to the earlier beliefs. Educationally, it may be best to get these prior beliefs out in the open so that they can be confronted by the instructor if they are in fact erroneous (Genter & Stevens, 1983).

In sum, this line of research demonstrates the importance of prior beliefs in human learning, thereby strengthening the case for a cognitive approach to learning. In a way, however, the research also has a connection to the ethological approach to learning. Just as rats and pigeons may be constrained to learn only associations that evolution has prepared them for, so we humans seem to be constrained to learn associations that our prior beliefs have prepared us for. Without prior constraints of some sort, perhaps there would simply be too many potential associations to consider, and associative learning would be chaotic if not impossible.

The Neural Basis of Learning

The biology of neurons and their interconnections, which proved so important in our analysis of sensation and perception, is also relevant to the study of learning, especially classical conditioning and simple forms of learning such as habituation. In what follows, we briefly discuss some of the key ideas behind this expanding research frontier.

Structural Changes

Researchers believe that the neural basis of learning consists of structural changes in the nervous system, and increasingly they are looking for these changes at the level of neural connections. To appreciate their ideas, you need to recall from Chapter 2 the basic structure of a neural connection and how it transmits an impulse. An impulse is transmitted from one neuron to another by the axon of the sending neuron. Because the axons are separated by the synaptic gap, the sender's axon secretes a neurotransmitter, which diffuses across the gap and stimulates the receiving neuron. More precisely, when the neural impulse travels down the sender's axon, it triggers terminals at the end of the axon to release the neurotransmitter, and this neurotransmitter is picked up by receptors on the receiving neuron. This entire structure is called a synapse. The key ideas regarding learning are (1) that some structural change in the synapse is the neural basis of learning, and (2) that the effect of this structural change is to make the synapse more efficient.

What would constitute evidence for this proposal? One approach would be to demonstrate that after a learning episode a synapse becomes more efficient, that is, fires more readily when stimulated again. At present, this is difficult to demonstrate with organisms of any complexity—if you recorded from some specific neurons, how could you find a learning task that affects exactly those neurons? Instead, researchers have devised a procedure that consists of first electrically stimulating a particular set of neurons (presumably this simulates learning) and then checking for an increase in the rate of activity of these neurons when subsequently stimulated. Such increases have been found in a number of regions of the rabbit brain, and the increases can last for several months. This phenomenon is referred to as *long-term potentiation,* and it provides indirect support for the structural-change view of learning (Berger, 1984; Bliss & Lomo, 1973).

Cellular Changes in Simple Learning

We have not been very specific about what kinds of structural changes increase synaptic efficiency. There are several possibilities. One is that learning results in an increase in the amount of neurotransmitter secreted by the sending neuron, perhaps because of an increase in the number of axon terminals that

FRONTIERS OF PSYCHOLOGICAL RESEARCH

Neural Systems in Fear Conditioning

Much recent research on the neural bases of learning focuses on neuroanatomical structures (which can be composed of hundreds or thousands of individual neurons) and the pathways that connect these structures. A good example of this kind of research involves the neural bases of fear conditioning.

For over 60 years it has been suspected that the key brain structure involved in learning to be fearful is the *amygdala,* an almond-shaped group of nuclei buried deep within the temporal lobes (*amygdala* is a Greek word meaning "almond") (Klüver & Bucy, 1937). Recent research has turned up detailed evidence that the amygdala is critically involved in learning and expressing fear.

In species ranging from rats to primates, damage to the amygdala leads to a reduction of fearful behavior in general and to difficulties in fear conditioning in particular. Rats whose amygdalas have been surgically removed show fewer signs of fear—that is, fewer fear-based responses such as freezing and crouching—when exposed to aversive stimuli, and have great difficulty acquiring a classically conditioned fear response (Aggleton & Passingham, 1981). In normal rats with intact amygdalas, learning of a conditioned fear response is accompanied by increased neuronal firing in certain regions of the amygdala (e.g., Quirk, Repa, & LeDoux, 1995). And when normal organisms are given a drug that blocks amygdala functioning, fear conditioning is disrupted (Maren & Fanselow, 1995). Taken together, these findings build a strong case that in mammals the amygdala is the primary brain structure involved in learning to be fearful.

A recent study shows that what holds for other mammals applies to humans as well (Bechara et al., 1995). This study involved a human patient, referred to as S.M., who had a rare disorder (Urbach-Wiethe disease) that results in degeneration of the amygdala. S.M. was exposed to a fear-conditioning situation in which a neutral visual stimulus (the CS) was predictably followed by the sound of a loud horn (the US). Despite repeated trials, S.M. showed no evidence of fear conditioning. Yet S.M. had no trouble recalling the events associated with the fear conditioning, including the relationship between the conditioned and unconditioned stimuli. Another patient, who had a normal amygdala but had suffered damage to a brain structure involved in the learning of factual material, showed normal fear conditioning but was unable to recall the events associated with the conditioning. Thus, the two patients had the opposite problems, indicating that the amygdala is involved in the learning of fear, not learning in general.

---

secrete the neurotransmitter. Alternatively, there may be no increase in the amount of neurotransmitter sent, but there may be an increase in the amount of neurotransmitter taken up by the receiving neuron, perhaps because of an increase in the number of receptors. Other possibilities are that the synapse could change in size, or that entirely new synapses could be established (Carlson, 1998). Several possibilities may be correct, with different kinds of structural changes underlying different kinds of learning.

To study learning processes at this level of neural detail, researchers have to work with elementary forms of learning and with organisms that have simple nervous systems. One kind of elementary learning that we mentioned at the beginning of the chapter is **habituation.** This is *the process by which an organism learns to weaken its reaction to a weak stimulus that has no serious consequences.* A related case of learning is **sensitization,** *the process by which an organism learns to strengthen its reaction to a stimulus if a threatening or painful stimulus follows.* Habituation and sensitization are found at virtually all levels of the animal kingdom, but our present concern is with the snail. Snails have a simple and accessible nervous system, which makes them well suited for studying structural changes in the synapse that accompany elementary learning.

When a snail is repeatedly touched lightly it initially responds, but within about 10 trials it habituates to the touch. Researchers have shown that this habituation learning is accompanied by a decrease in the amount of neurotransmitter secreted by a sending neuron. This snail also manifests sensitization.

After a few trials of a procedure in which a light touch to the body is accompanied by a strong stimulus to the tail, the snail's response to the touch becomes more pronounced. Sensitization learning has been shown to be mediated by an increase in the amount of neurotransmitter secreted by the sending neuron (Kandel, Schwartz, & Jessel, 1991). These findings provide relatively direct evidence that elementary learning is mediated by structural changes at the neuronal level. (For further discussion of the neural basis of learning, see the Frontiers of Psychological Research feature on page 260.)

What about associative learning? Do structural changes like the one just described mediate classical conditioning? The fact that classical conditioning is similar to sensitization—both involve changing one's response to a weak stimulus on the basis of another stronger stimulus—suggests that the two kinds of learning might have a similar neural basis. Indeed, researchers have proposed a neural model of classical conditioning that is remarkably similar to that for sensitization (Hawkins & Kandel, 1984).

Conditioning Sensitizes a Preexisting Fear

N. J. Mackintosh, *University of Cambridge*

John Watson, the founding father of behaviorism, believed that the human infant had only a handful of innate fears—two of the main ones being a fear of loud noises and of loss of support. All other fears, he argued, were learned as a result of conditioning. And to prove his point, Watson and his student, Rosalie Rayner, demonstrated the conditioning of fear in an 11-month infant, Albert B (Watson & Rayner, 1920). Albert was initially happy to reach out and touch any small animal brought close to him, but after seven conditioning trials on which a white rat (the CS) was presented and, if Albert reached toward it, a steel bar was sharply struck immediately behind him (the UCS), Albert began to cry and withdraw from the rat. The fear conditioned to the rat generalized to other stimuli—a rabbit, a dog, and a sealskin coat. Since then, hundreds of laboratory experiments have shown that the pairing of an arbitrary and initially neutral CS with an aversive event, such as a brief electric shock or very loud noise, will establish a conditioned fear reaction to that CS.

Watson and Rayner's study has often been cited (see Harris, 1979) as evidence that adult phobias, whether of snakes or spiders, open spaces or confined places, are based on one or more past episodes of conditioning, in which, for example, a snake has been associated with some aversive consequence. There are several difficulties with this simple application of conditioning theory—one of which, it is worth noting (if only to defend Watson and Rayner against a charge of gross cruelty), is that little Albert never showed much more than mild fretting and withdrawal, even when the rat was allowed to crawl over him, and that even this modest level of fear showed little generalization when he was tested in a different room.

Studies of "vicarious conditioning" have shown that the mere sight of a conspecific showing a fear reaction to a particular CS can act as a sufficient UCS to reinforce the conditioning of fear to that CS. Wildborn rhesus monkeys tend to be afraid of snakes. This is not an innate fear, since laboratory-born infant rhesus monkeys show no such fear. But a single experience of watching an adult displaying a fear reaction to a snake will condition a fear of snakes in the infant (Mineka, 1987). Here, then, may be one way in which parents can, unwittingly, influence the behavior of their children.

The traditional behaviorist view was that any detectable stimulus can become associated with any consequence. On the face of it, this implies another serious problem for a conditioning account of phobias, since by far the most common phobias are those directed toward animals or social situations, rather than to the myriad other objects or events (electrical outlets, the sight of one's own blood) that are more likely to have been associated with painful consequences. Does this mean that the predisposition to phobias is genetically determined? Not if that is taken to imply that we are all born with an innate fear of spiders—or else we would all have a spider phobia. Surely, it is at least in part the differences among our individual experiences that cause one person to develop a phobia of spiders, another, one of snakes, and another, none at all. But why just of spiders, snakes, and so on? Some conditioning experiments have suggested some answers to this question.

In a series of studies, Ohman and his colleagues have shown that conditioned GSRs in people are more resistant to extinction when the CS is a picture of a snake or spider than when it is a picture of flowers or mushrooms (Ohman, 1986). Cook and Mineka (1990) have provided evidence of similar selective fear in monkeys. Infant monkeys developed a fear of snakes after watching a video clip of an adult monkey displaying fear reactions to a snake, but showed no fear of flowers after watching a cleverly edited video clip showing an adult monkey apparently having a panic attack at the sight of a flower.

Results such as these have been widely interpreted as evidence of a biological predisposition to associate certain classes of stimuli with certain consequences: In the evolutionary history of early hominids or other African primates, snakes and spiders were potentially dangerous, while flowers and mushrooms were not. For the learning theories, there are other questions left unanswered. Ohman's experiments have established only that fear of snakes extinguishes more slowly than fear of flowers, not that it is acquired more rapidly in the first place. Other experiments have shown that pictures of snakes are just as easily established as safety signals as are pictures of flowers (McNally & Reiss, 1984). Cook and Mineka's infant monkeys, having watched a video of adults showing fear reactions to flowers but not to snakes, *did* then show significant fear of a live snake (although no fear of flowers). Some of these findings suggest that what is happening is sensitization of a pre-existing fear to certain classes of stimuli under conditions of stress or threat, rather than more rapid conditioning of fear (Lovibond, Siddle, & Bond, 1993).

Phobias Are an Innate Defense Mechanism

Michael S. Fanselow, *University of California, Los Angeles*

The emotional experience of fear can be overwhelmingly powerful. Why does it exist? The reason must lie in the fact that fear serves some biologically important function. Fear in the face of a serious threat organizes our resources to protect against that threat. From such a vantage fear becomes a behavioral system that evolved for the purpose of defense against environmental threats. For many animal species one of the most serious threats is becoming the food of another species. If one fails to defend against a predator, the ability for future contributions to the gene pool is nil. Thus it is not surprising that very effective systems for defending against a predator have evolved. Certain brain regions are dedicated to this function, and those brain regions serve fear in species ranging from at least mice and rats to monkeys and humans. If natural selection is responsible for fear, it seems reasonable that genetic factors shape this experience.

So fear is in part defined by its biological function. But to be useful to a behavioral scientist, there need to be two other aspects to the definition. The conditions that give rise to fear must be specified—what turns on the defensive behavioral system. Also, the behaviors that result as a consequence of fear must be detailed. Natural selection has shaped the answer to these questions with genetic encoding of what we are born to fear, what we come to fear, and how we behave when afraid.

Defending against predation is urgent; you must react quickly with effective behavior. Slow, trial-and-error learning by reinforcement simply will not do. A species that relied on such learning would likely be the subject of a paleontologist rather than a psychologist. First, you must recognize threats quickly. Animals have an uncanny ability to recognize their natural predators. In one study, deermice were trapped on two sides of the Cascade Mountains of Washington. Snakes are a natural predator of the eastern mice but not of the western mice. On the other hand, western mice have to contend with weasels. The mice were bred for one generation in the laboratory, and their offspring were tested for fear of a range of predators and nonpredators. While these animals had no experience outside the lab and had never encountered a predator before, they displayed defensive responses specifically to the predators of their parent's habitat. This innate "phobia" is not lost when selection pressure is eased; even the highly domesticated laboratory rat shows fear on its first encounter with a cat. While it is not possible to perform such experiments with humans, the fact that phobias are far more common for some stimuli than others suggests that we have similar dispositions.

This is not to say that fear of environmental stimuli is never learned. But this learning is genetically constrained and specialized. Learning of fear is rapid and occurs with a single aversive experience, reflecting the evolutionary urgency of defense. Despite the rapidity of this learning, the sort of stimuli we learn to fear is heavily constrained. In the famous "little Albert study" described by Dr. Mackintosh, Watson and Rayner conditioned a baby boy to fear a white rat by pairing it with a loud noise. But while fear of a rat is easily acquired, the same methods do not result in conditioned fear to many other stimuli. Similar predispositions are found in other primates, for as Dr. Mackintosh also explained, monkeys readily learn to become afraid of snakes but not of flowers. Even when a researcher chooses a domesticated laboratory rat and uses a seemingly arbitrary stimulus such as electric shock, there is selectivity in association formation. Rats more readily learn to fear noises than lights, which fare better as safety signals.

If fear has to protect us against a very imminent threat, we are unlikely to have the opportunity to learn what behaviors are effective and what behaviors are not. The trial-and-error learner is doomed. Rather, specialized defensive behaviors are already programmed into the species; they are executed as soon as fear is activated. A rat freezes the first time it encounters a cat—cats are attracted to moving targets. These are responses to fear, as the rat will show the same freezing response to a noise that has been paired with shock. Although rats are known to be adept lever pressers when asked to work for food, they are horrendous if asked to make the same response to avoid shock. Of course, manipulation of small objects probably never did much for the rats' ancestors when they were faced with a predator. Similarly, I speculate that I would be more likely to solve a complex calculus problem if the inducement was a fine wine rather than avoidance of an armed attacker.

SUMMARY

1. Learning may be defined as a relatively permanent change in behavior that is the result of practice. There are four basic kinds of learning: (a) habituation, in which an organism learns to ignore a familiar and inconsequential stimulus; (b) classical conditioning, in which an organism learns that one stimulus follows another; (c) operant conditioning, in which an organism learns that a particular response leads to a particular consequence; and (d) complex learning, in which learning involves more than the formation of associations.

2. Early research on learning was done from a behaviorist perspective. It often assumed that behavior is better understood in terms of external causes than internal ones, that simple associations are the building blocks of all learning, and that the laws of learning are the same for different species and different situations. These assumptions have been modified in light of subsequent work. The contemporary analysis of learning includes cognitive factors and biological constraints as well as behaviorist principles.

3. In Pavlov's experiments, if a conditioned stimulus (CS) consistently precedes an unconditioned stimulus (UCS), the CS comes to serve as a signal for the UCS and will elicit a conditioned response (CR) that often resembles the unconditioned response (UCR). Stimuli that are similar to the CS also elicit the CR to some extent, although such generalization can be curbed by discrimination training. These phenomena occur in organisms as diverse as flatworms and humans.

4. Cognitive factors also play a role in conditioning. For classical conditioning to occur, the CS must be a reliable predictor of the UCS; that is, there must be a higher probability that the UCS will occur when the CS has been presented than when it has not.

5. According to ethologists, what an animal learns is constrained by its genetically determined "behavioral blueprint." Evidence for such constraints on classical conditioning comes from studies of taste aversion. While rats readily learn to associate the feeling of being sick with the taste of a solution, they cannot learn to associate sickness with a light. Conversely, birds can learn to associate light and sickness but not taste and sickness.

6. Operant conditioning deals with situations in which the response operates on the environment rather than being elicited by an unconditioned stimulus. The earliest systematic studies were performed by Thorndike, who showed that animals engage in trial-and-error behavior and that any behavior that is followed by reinforcement is strengthened; this is known as the law of effect.

7. In Skinner's experiments, typically a rat or pigeon learns to make a simple response, such as pressing a lever, to obtain reinforcement. The rate of response is a useful measure of response strength. Shaping is a training procedure that is used when the desired response is novel; it involves reinforcing only variations in response that deviate in the direction desired by the experimenter.

8. A number of phenomena can increase the generality of operant conditioning. One is conditioned reinforcement, in which a stimulus associated with a reinforcer acquires its own reinforcing properties. Other relevant phenomena are generalization and discrimination; organisms generalize responses to similar situations, although this generalization can be brought under the control of a discriminative stimulus. Finally, there are schedules of reinforcement. Once a behavior is established, it can be maintained when it is reinforced only part of the time. Exactly when the reinforcement comes is determined by its schedule; the basic types of reinforcement schedules are fixed ratio, variable ratio, fixed interval, and variable interval schedules.

9. There are three different kinds of aversive conditioning. In punishment, a response is followed by an aversive event, which results in the response being suppressed. In escape, an organism learns to make a response in order to terminate an ongoing aversive event. In avoidance, an organism learns to make a response in order to prevent the aversive event from even starting.

10. Cognitive factors play a role in operant conditioning. For operant conditioning to occur, the organism must believe that reinforcement is at least partly under its control; that is, it must perceive a contingency between its responses and the reinforcement. Biological constraints also play a role in operant conditioning. There are constraints on what reinforcers can be associated with what responses. With pigeons, when the reinforcement is food, learning is faster if the response is pecking a key rather than flapping the wings; but when the reinforcement is termination of shock, learning is faster when the response is wing flapping rather than pecking a key.

11. According to the cognitive perspective, the crux of learning is an organism's ability to represent aspects of the world mentally and then operate on these mental representations rather than on the world itself. In complex learning, the mental representations depict more than associations, and the mental operations may constitute a strategy. Studies of complex learning in animals indicate that rats can develop a cognitive map of their environment as well as acquire abstract concepts such as cause. Other studies demonstrate that chimpanzees can solve problems through insight and then generalize the solutions to similar problems.

12. When learning relationships between stimuli that are not perfectly predictive, people often invoke prior beliefs. This can lead to the detection of rela-tionships that are not objectively present (spurious associations). When the relationship is objectively present, having a prior belief about it can lead to overestimating its predictive strength; when an objective relationship conflicts with a prior belief, the learner may favor the prior belief. These effects demonstrate top-down processing in learning.

KEY TERMS

learning (p. 234)
classical conditioning (p. 236)
unconditioned response (p. 236)
unconditioned stimulus (p. 236)
conditioned response (p. 236)
conditioned stimulus (p. 236)
generalization (p. 239)
discrimination (p. 239)
operant conditioning (p. 243)
shaping (p. 246)

ratio schedules (p. 248)
fixed ratio schedule (p. 248)
variable ratio schedule (p. 249)
interval schedules (p. 249)
fixed interval schedule (p. 249)
variable interval schedule (p. 249)
punishment (p. 250)
cognitive map (p. 254)
habituation (p. 260)
sensitization (p. 260)

CRITICAL THINKING QUESTIONS

1. People sometimes say, "So-and-so is the way he is because of his biological nature" or "because of what he's learned." They do not suggest that both influences are at work. Is there really a dichotomy between biology and learning?

2. Suppose that you are taking care of an 8-year-old who won't make his bed and, in fact, doesn't seem to know how to begin the task. How might you use operant-conditioning techniques to teach him to make his bed?

3. Sometimes a person may be fearful of a neutral object, such as loose buttons, but not know why. How could you explain this phenomenon in terms of prin-ciples presented in this chapter?

4. Do you believe that there are differences between how we learn facts and how we learn motor skills? If so, what are some of those differences?

FURTHER READING

Pavlov's *Conditioned Reflexes* (1927) is the definitive work on classical conditioning. Skinner's *The Behav-ior of Organisms* (1938) is the corresponding state-ment on operant conditioning. The major points of view about conditioning and learning, presented in their historical settings, are summarized in Bower and Hilgard, *Theories of Learning* (5th ed., 1981).

For a general introduction to learning, a number of textbooks are recommended. Schwartz's *Psychology of Learning and Behavior* (3rd ed., 1989) is a particularly well-balanced review of conditioning, including discus-sion of ethology and cognition. Other useful textbooks include Gordon's *Learning and Memory* (1989), Schwartz and Reisberg's *Learning and Memory* (1991),

and Domjan and Burkhard's *The Principles of Learning and Behavior* (1985). At the advanced level, the six-volume Estes (ed.), *Handbook of Learning and Cogni-tive Processes* (1975–1978), covers most aspects of learning and conditioning; and Honig and Staddon (eds.), *Handbook of Operant Behavior* (1977), provides a comprehensive treatment of operant conditioning.

The early cognitive approach is well described in two classics: Tolman's *Purposive Behavior in Animals and Men* (1932; reprinted 1967) and Köhler's *The Men-tality of Apes* (1925; reprinted 1976). For a more recent statement of the cognitive approach to animal learning, see Roitblat's *Introduction to Comparative Cognition* (1986).

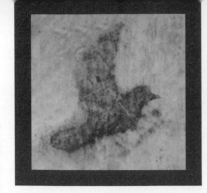

Chapter 8
Memory

It seems . . . that we owe to memory almost all that we either have or are; that our ideas and conceptions are its work, and that our everyday perception, thought, and movement is derived from this source. Memory collects the countless phenomena of our existence into a single whole; and, as our bodies would be scattered into the dust of their component atoms if they were not held together by the attraction of matter, so our consciousness would be broken up into as many fragments as we had lived seconds but for the binding and unifying force of memory. (Hering, 1920)

*H*ering's words, spoken in a lecture to the Vienna Academy of Sciences many years ago, attest to the importance of memory in mental life. As Hering's comments about consciousness suggest, it is memory that gives us the sense of continuity on which our very notion of a self depends. When we think of what it means to be human, we must acknowledge the centrality of memory. To appreciate the scientific study of memory, however, we need to understand how researchers divide the field into manageable units, such as short-term (or *working*) memory and long-term memory. After describing the key distinctions, we will review the major findings about working memory, long-term memory, and what is called implicit memory (the kind of memory involved in learning a skill). Then we will take up a question of universal interest: How can memory be improved? We will conclude with a discussion of situations in which our memories are partly constructed.

Three Important Distinctions

Psychologists today make three major distinctions about memory. The first concerns the three stages of memory: encoding, storage, and retrieval. The second deals with different memories for storing information for

FIGURE 8-1

Three Stages of Memory   *Theories of memory attribute forgetting to a failure at one or more of these stages.* (After Melton, 1963)

short and long periods. The third distinction is about different memories being used to store different kinds of information (for example, one system for facts and another for skills). For each of these distinctions, there is evidence that the entities being distinguished—say, working versus long-term memory—are mediated in part by different structures in the brain.

Three Stages of Memory

Suppose that you are introduced to another student and told that her name is Barbara Cohn. That afternoon you see her again and say something like, "You're Barbara Cohn.

Memory has three stages. The first stage, encoding, consists of placing a fact in memory; this occurs when we study. The second stage is storage, in which the fact is retained in memory. The third stage, retrieval, occurs when the fact is recovered from storage—for example, when taking an exam.

We met this morning." Clearly, you have remembered her name. But how exactly did you remember it?

Your minor memory feat can be broken into three stages (see Figure 8-1). First, when you were introduced, you somehow entered Barbara Cohn's name into memory; this is the **encoding** stage. You transformed a physical input (sound waves) that corresponds to her spoken name into the kind of code or representation that memory accepts, and you "placed" that representation in memory. Second, you retained—or stored—the name during the time between the two meetings; this is the **storage** stage. And third, you recovered the name from storage at the time of your second meeting; this is the **retrieval** stage.

Memory can fail at any of these three stages. Had you been unable to recall Barbara's name at the second meeting, this could have reflected a failure in encoding, storage, or retrieval. Much of current research on memory attempts to specify the mental operations that occur at each of the three stages of memory and explain how these operations can go awry and result in memory failure.

Argentinian pianist Daniel Barenboim in concert. Recent evidence indicated that we use a different long-term memory for storing skills like the ability to play the piano than we do for retaining facts.

A number of recent studies suggest that the different stages of memory are mediated by different structures in the brain. The most striking evidence comes from brain-scanning studies. These experiments involve two parts. In Part 1, which focuses on encoding, participants study a set of verbal items—for example, pairs consisting of categories and uncommon instances (furniture-sideboard); in Part 2, which focuses on retrieval, participants have to recognize or recall the items when cued with the category name. In both parts, positron emission tomography (PET) measures of brain activity are recorded while participants are engaged in their task. The most striking finding is that during encoding most of the activated brain regions are in the left hemisphere, whereas during retrieval most of the activated brain areas are in the right hemisphere (Shallice et al., 1994; Tulving et al., 1994). Thus, the distinction between encoding and retrieval has a clear-cut biological bias.

Working Memory Versus Long-Term Memory

The three stages of memory do not operate the same way in all situations. Memory seems to differ between situations that require us to store material for a matter of seconds and those that require us to store material for longer intervals—from minutes to years. The former situations are said to tap working memory, while the latter reflect long-term memory.

We can illustrate this distinction by amending our earlier story about meeting Barbara Cohn. Suppose that during the first meeting, as soon as you had heard her name, a friend came up and you said, "Have you met Barbara Cohn?" In this case, remembering Barbara's name would be an example of working memory: You retrieved the name after only a second or two. Remembering her name at the time of your second meeting would be an example of long-term memory, because then retrieval would take place hours after the name was encoded. When we recall a name immediately after encountering it, retrieval seems effortless, as if the name were still active, still in our consciousness. But when we try to recall the same name hours later, retrieval is often difficult because the name is no longer in our consciousness and, in some sense, has to be brought back.

It is worth noting the existence of another short-term storage system, one that differs from working memory in that it holds a detailed sensory image of any stimulus that has just been presented, but only for a few hundred milliseconds. For example, if a set of 12 letters is briefly flashed on a screen, a person will have a detailed visual image of *all* the letters for a few hundred milliseconds (e.g., Sperling, 1960). It is believed that there is a separate sensory memory store for each sensory system (vision, hearing, taste, and so on), although only those for vision and hearing have been studied extensively. Sensory or **iconic memory** is clearly useful in extending the duration of briefly presented stimuli, but it plays far less of a role in thought and conscious recollection than do the memory systems that we focus on in this chapter.

It has been known for some time that working memory and long-term memory are implemented by somewhat different brain structures. In particular, the hippocampus, a structure located near the middle of the brain beneath the cortex, is critical for long-term memory but not for working memory. Much of the relevant evidence comes from experiments with rats and other nonhuman species. In some experiments, one group of rats is first subjected to damage to the hippocampus and the surrounding cortex, and a second group is subjected to damage in a completely different region, the front of the cortex. Both groups of rats then have to perform a delayed-response task. On each trial, first one stimulus (such as a square) is presented and then, after a delay, a second stimulus (such as a triangle) is presented; the animal has to respond only when the second stimulus differs from the first. How well the animal performs on this task depends on the kind of brain damage it has suffered and the length of the delay between the two stimuli.

When the delay is long (15 seconds or more), animals with damage to the hippocampus perform poorly, but those with damage in the front of the cortex perform relatively normally. Because a long delay between stimuli requires long-term memory for storage of the first stimulus, these results fit with the idea that the hippocampus is critical for long-term memory. When the

delay between the two stimuli is short (just a few seconds), the opposite results occur: Now animals with damage in the front of the cortex perform poorly and those with hippocampal damage perform relatively normally. Because a short delay between stimuli requires working memory for storage of the first stimulus, these results indicate that regions in the frontal cortex are involved in working memory. Hence, different regions of the brain are involved in working memory and long-term memory (Goldman-Rakic, 1987; Zola-Morgan & Squire, 1985).

What evidence is there for this distinction in humans? Patients who happen to have suffered damage in certain brain regions provide an "experiment of nature." Specifically, some patients have suffered damage to the hippocampus and surrounding cortex, and consequently show a severe memory loss; because the hippocampus is located in the middle of the temporal lobe, these patients are said to have *medial-temporal lobe amnesia*. Such patients have profound difficulty remembering material for long intervals but rarely have any trouble remembering material for a few seconds. Thus, a patient with medial-temporal lobe amnesia may be unable to recognize his doctor when she enters the room—even though the patient has seen this doctor every day for years—yet will have no trouble repeating the physician's name when she is reintroduced (Milner, Corkin, & Teuber, 1968). Such a patient has a severe impairment in long-term memory but a normal working memory.

Other patients, however, show the opposite problem. They cannot correctly repeat a string of even three words, yet they are relatively normal when tested on their long-term memory for words. Such patients have an impaired working memory but an intact long-term memory. And their brain damage is never in the medial temporal lobe (Shallice, 1988). Thus, for humans as well as for other mammals, working memory and long-term memory are mediated by different brain structures.

Recent research using brain-scanning techniques has revealed that neurons in the prefrontal lobes, just behind the forehead, hold information for short-term use, such as a phone number that is about to be dialed.

These neurons appear to act like a computer's random access memory (RAM) chips, which hold data temporarily for current use and switch quickly to other data as needed. These cells are also able to draw information from other regions of the brain and retain it as long as it is needed for a specific task (Goldman-Rakic, cited in Goleman, 1995).

Different Memories for Different Kinds of Information

Until about a decade ago, psychologists generally assumed that the same memory system was used for all kinds of memories. For example, the same long-term memory was presumably used to store both one's recollection of a grandmother's funeral and the skills one needs to ride a bike. Recent evidence indicates that this assumption is wrong. In particular, we seem to use a different long-term memory for storing facts (such as who the current president is) than we do for retaining skills (such as how to ride a bicycle). The evidence for this difference, as usual, includes both psychological and biological findings; these are considered later in the chapter.

The kind of memory situation that we understand best is one in which a person consciously recollects an event in the past, where this recollection is experienced as occurring in a particular time and place. This kind of memory, called *explicit memory,* will be the focus of most sections of the chapter. The next two sections consider the nature of encoding, storage, and retrieval in working and long-term explicit memory. Then we will examine what is known about another kind of memory, which includes memory for skills and is referred to as *implicit memory.*

Working Memory

As noted earlier, **working memory** consists of *memories that are stored for only a few seconds.* However, even in situations in which we must remember information only briefly, memory involves the three stages of encoding, storage, and retrieval. Let us look more closely at each of these stages as they relate to working memory.

Encoding

To encode information into working memory, we must attend to it. Since we are selective about what we attend to (see Chapter 5), our working memory will contain only what has been selected. This means that much of what we are exposed to never even enters working memory and, of course, will not be available for later retrieval. Indeed, many "memory problems" are really lapses in attention. For example, if you bought some groceries and someone later asked you the color of the checkout clerk's eyes, you might be unable to answer, not because of a failure of memory but because you had not paid attention to the clerk's eyes in the first place.

Phonological Coding   When information is encoded into memory, it is entered in a certain code or representation. For example, when you look up a phone number and retain it until you have dialed it, in what form do you represent the digits? Is the representation visual—a mental picture of the digits? Is it *phonological*—the sounds of the names of the digits? Or is it *semantic* (based on meaning)—some meaningful association that the digits have? Research indicates that we can use any of these possibilities to encode information into working memory, although we favor a phonological code when we are trying to keep the information active through *rehearsal*—that is, by repeating an item over and over. Rehearsal is a particularly popular strategy when the information consists of verbal items such as digits, letters, or words. So in trying to remember a phone number, we are most likely to encode the number as the sounds of the digit names and to rehearse these sounds to ourselves until we have dialed the number.

In a classic experiment that provided evidence for a phonological code, researchers briefly showed participants a list of six consonants (for example, RLBKSJ); when the letters were removed, they had to write all six letters in order. Although the entire procedure took only a second or two, participants occasionally made errors. When they did, the incorrect letter tended to be similar in sound to the correct one. For the list mentioned, a participant might have written RLTKSJ, replacing the B with the similar-sounding T (Conrad, 1964). This finding supports the hypothesis that the participants encoded each letter phonologically (for example, "bee" for B), sometimes lost part of this code (only the "ee" part of the sound remained), and then responded with a letter ("tee") that was consistent with the remaining part of the code. This hypothesis also explains why it is more difficult to recall the items in order when they are acoustically similar (for example, TBCGVE) than when they are acoustically distinct (RLTKSJ).

Visual Coding   If need be, we can also maintain verbal items in a visual form. Experiments indicate that while we can use a visual code for verbal material, the code fades quickly. When a person must store nonverbal items (such as pictures that are difficult to describe and therefore difficult to rehearse phonologically), the visual code becomes more important. While most of us can maintain some kind of visual image in working memory, a few people are able to maintain images that are almost photographic in clarity. This ability occurs mainly in children. Such children can look briefly at

When you look up a phone number and retain it until you have dialed it, do you retain it visually, phonologically, or semantically?

FIGURE 8-2

Testing for Eidetic Images   *This test picture was show to elementary-school children for 30 seconds. After the picture was removed, one boy saw his eidetic image "about 14" stripes in the cat's tail. The painting, by Marjorie Torrey, appears in Lewis Carroll's* Alice in Wonderland, *abridged by Josette Frank.*

a picture and, when it is removed, still experience the image before their eyes. They can maintain the image for as long as several minutes and, when questioned, provide a wealth of detail, such as the number of stripes on a cat's tail (see Figure 8-2). Such children seem to be reading the details directly from an *eidetic* (or photographic) *image* (Haber, 1969). Eidetic imagery is very rare, though. Some studies with children indicate that only about 5% report visual images that are long-lasting and possess sharp detail. Moreover, when the criteria for possessing true photographic imagery are made more stringent—for example, being able to read an imaged page of text as easily from the bottom up as from the top down—the frequency of eidetic imagery becomes minuscule, even among children (Haber, 1979).

The visual code in working memory, then, is something short of a photograph.

Two Working Memory Systems The existence of both phonological and visual codes had led researchers to argue that working memory consists of two distinct stores or buffers. One is a *phonological buffer,* which briefly stores information in an acoustic code; the second is a *visual-spatial buffer,* which briefly stores information in a visual or spatial code (Baddeley, 1986). Some recent brain-scanning studies indicated that the two buffers are mediated by different brain structures.

In one experiment, on every trial participants saw a sequence of letters in which both the identity and the position of the letter varied from one item to another (see Figure 8-3). On some trials, participants had to attend only to the identity of the letters; their task was to determine whether each letter presented was identical to the one presented three back in the sequence. On other trials, participants had to attend only to the position of the letters; their task was to deter-

mine whether each letter's position was identical to the position of the letter presented three back in the sequence (see Figure 8-3). Thus, the actual stimuli were identical in all cases; what varied was whether the participants were storing verbal information (the identities of the letters) or spatial information (the positions of the letters). Presumably, the verbal information was being kept in the acoustic buffer and the spatial information in the visual-spatial buffer.

On both the identity and the spatial trials, PET measures of brain activity were recorded. The results indicated that the two buffers are in different hemispheres. On trials in which participants had to store verbal information (acoustic buffer), most of the brain activity was in the left hemisphere; on trials in which participants had to store spatial information (visual-spatial buffer), most of the brain activity was in the right hemisphere. The two buffers seem to be distinct systems (Smith, Jonides, & Koeppe, 1996). This finding is not very surprising, considering the brain's tendency toward hemispheric specialization as discussed in Chapter 2.

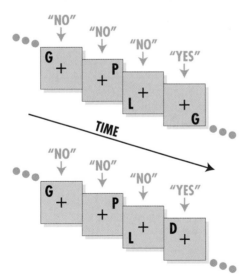

FIGURE 8-3

An Experiment on Acoustic and Visual Buffers
Participants had to decide whether each item was identical to the one three back in the sequence. The top half of the figure shows a typical sequence of events in which participants had to attend only to the identity of the letters, along with the responses required to each item. The bottom half of the figure shows the trial events when individuals had to attend only to the position of the letters, along with the responses required to each item. (After Smith et al., 1995)

Storage

Perhaps the most striking fact about working memory is that its capacity is very limited. On the average, the limit is 7 items, give or take two (7 ± 2). Some people store as few as five items; others can retain as many as nine. It may seem strange to give such an exact number to cover all people when it is clear that individuals differ greatly in memory ability. These differences, however, are due primarily to long-term memory. For working memory, most normal adults have a capacity of 7 ± 2. This constancy has been known since the earliest days of experimental psychology. Hermann Ebbinghaus, who began the experimental study of memory in 1885, reported results showing that his own limit was seven items. Some 70 years later, George Miller (1956) was so struck by the consistency of this finding that he referred to it as the "magic number seven," and we now know that the limit holds in non-Western cultures as well as Western ones (Yu et al., 1985).

Psychologists determined this number by showing people various sequences of unrelated items (digits, letters, or words) and asking them to recall the items in order. The items are presented rapidly, and the individual does not have time to relate them to information stored in long-term memory; hence, the number of items recalled reflects only the storage capacity of the individual's working memory. On the initial trials, participants have to recall just a few items—say, three or four digits—which they can easily do. In subsequent trials, the number of digits increases until the experimenter determines the participant's **memory span**—*the maximum number of items (almost always between five and nine) that the participant can recall in perfect order.* This task is so simple that you can easily try it yourself. The next time you come across a list of names (a directory in a business or university building, for example), read through the list once and then look away and see how many names you can recall in order. It will probably be between five and nine.

Chunking   As just noted, the memory-span procedure discourages individuals from connecting the items to be remembered to information in long-term memory. When such connections are possible, performance on the memory-span task can change substantially. To illustrate this change, suppose that you were presented with the letter string SRUOYYLERECNIS. Because your memory span is 7 ± 2, you would probably be unable to repeat the entire letter sequence since it contains 14 letters. If, however, you noticed that these letters spell the phrase SINCERELY YOURS in reverse order, your task would become easier. By using this knowledge, you have decreased the number of items that must be held in working memory from 14 to 2 (the 2 words). But where did this spelling knowledge come from? From long-term memory, where knowledge about words is stored. Thus, you can use long-term memory to perform what is known as **chunking,** or *recoding new material into larger, more meaningful units and storing those units in working memory.* Such units are called *chunks,* and the capacity of working memory is best expressed as 7 ± 2 chunks (Miller, 1956). Chunking can occur with numbers as well. The string 149-2177-619-96 is beyond our capacity, but 1492-1776-1996 is well within it. The general principle is that we can boost our working memory by regrouping sequences of letters and digits into units that can be found in long-term memory (Bower & Springston, 1970).

Forgetting   We may be able to hold on to seven items briefly, but in most cases they will soon be forgotten. Forgetting occurs either because the items "decay" over time or because they are displaced by new items.

Information in working memory may simply decay as time passes. We may think of the representation of an item as a trace that fades within a matter of seconds. One of the best pieces of evidence for this hypothesis is that our working memory span holds fewer words when the words take longer to say; for example, the span is less for long words such as "harpoon" and "cyclone" than for shorter words such as "bishop" and "pewter" (try saying the words to yourself to see the difference in duration). Presumably this effect arises because as the words are presented we say them to ourselves, and the longer it takes to do this, the more likely it is that some of the words' traces will have faded before they can be recalled (Baddeley, Thompson, & Buchanan, 1975).

The other major cause of forgetting in working memory is the displacement of old items by new ones. The notion of displacement fits with the idea that working memory has a fixed capacity. Being in working memory may correspond to being in a state of activation. The more items we try to keep active, the less activation there is for any one of them. Perhaps only about seven items can be simultaneously maintained at a level of activation that permits all of them to be recalled. Once seven items are active, the activation given to a new item will be taken away from items that were presented earlier; consequently, those items may fall below the critical level of activation needed for recall (Anderson, 1983).

Retrieval

Let us continue to think of the contents of working memory as being active in consciousness. Intuition suggests that access to this information is immediate. You do not have to dig for it; it is right there. Retrieval, then, should not depend on the number of items in consciousness. But in this case intuition is wrong.

Research has shown that the more items there are in working memory, the slower retrieval becomes. Most of the evidence for this comes from a type of experiment introduced by Sternberg (1966). On each trial of the experiment, a participant is shown a set of digits, called the *memory list,* that he or she must temporarily maintain in working memory. It is easy for the participant to do so because the memory list contains between one and six digits. The memory list is then removed from view and a probe digit is presented. The participant must decide whether the probe was on the memory list. For example, if the memory list is 3 6 1 and the probe is 6, the participant should respond "yes"; given the same memory list and a probe of 2, the participant should respond "no." Participants rarely make an error on this task; what is of interest, however, is the decision time, which is the elapsed time between the onset of the probe and the participant's pressing of a "yes" or a "no" button. Figure 8-4 presents data from such an experiment, indicating that decision time increases directly with the length of the

memory list. What is remarkable about these decision times is that they fall along a straight line. This means that each additional item in working memory adds a fixed amount of time to the retrieval process—approximately 40 milliseconds, or 1/25 of a second. The same results are found when the items are letters, words, auditory tones, or pictures of people's faces (Sternberg, 1975).

These results have led some researchers to hypothesize that retrieval requires a search of working memory in which the items are examined one at a time. This search presumably operates at a rate of 40 milliseconds per item, which is too fast for people to be aware of it (Sternberg, 1966). However, thinking of working memory as a state of activation leads to a different interpretation of the results. Retrieval of an item in working memory may depend on the activation of that item reaching a critical level. That is, one decides that a probe is in working memory if it is above a critical level of activation, and the more items are in working memory, the less activation there is for any one of them (Monsell, 1979). Such activation models have been shown to accurately predict many aspects of retrieval from working memory (McElree & Doesher, 1989).

Working Memory and Thought

Working memory plays an important role in thought. When consciously trying to solve a problem, we often use working memory to store parts of the problem as well as information accessed from long-term memory that is relevant to the problem. To illustrate, consider what it takes to multiply 35 by 8 in your head. You need working memory to store the given numbers (35 and 8), the nature of the operation required (multiplication), and arithmetic facts such as $8 \times 5 = 40$ and $8 \times 3 = 24$. Not surprisingly, performance on mental arithmetic declines substantially if you have to remember simultaneously some words or digits; try doing the mental multiplication just described while remembering the phone number 745-1739 (Baddeley & Hitch, 1974). Because of its role in mental computations, researchers often conceptualize working memory as a kind of blackboard on which the mind performs computations and posts the partial results for later use (Baddeley, 1986).

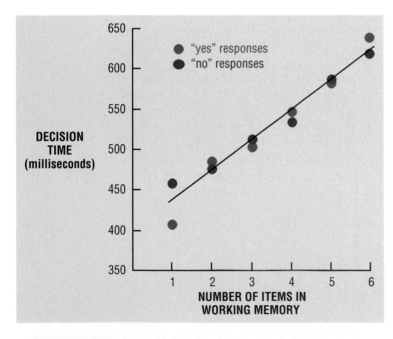

FIGURE 8-4

Retrieval as a Search Process   *Decision times increase in direct proportion to the number of items in short-term memory. Green circles represent "yes" responses; purple circles, "no" responses. The times for both types of decision fall along a straight line. Because the decision times are so fast, they must be measured with equipment that permits accuracy in milliseconds (thousandths of a second). (After Sternberg, 1966)*

Other research shows that working memory is used not only in doing numerical problems but also in solving a wide range of complex problems. An example of such problems is geometric analogies, which are sometimes used in tests of intelligence (e.g., Ravens, 1965). An illustration of a geometric analogy is presented in Figure 8-5. Try to solve it; this will give you an intuitive idea of the role of working memory in problem solving. You may note that you need working memory to store (a) the similarities and differences that you observe among the forms in a row, and (b) the rules that you come up with to account for these similarities and differences and that you then use to select the correct answer. It turns out that the larger one's working memory, the better one does on problems like these (even though there is relatively little variation among people in the capacity of their working memory). Moreover, when computers are programmed to simulate people solving problems such as the one in Figure 8-5, one of the most important determinants of how well the program does is the size of the working memory created by the programmer. There seems to be little doubt that part of the difficulty of many complex problems is the load they place on working memory (Carpenter, Just, & Shell, 1990).

Working memory is also crucial for language processes like following a conversation or reading a text. When reading for understanding, often we must consciously relate new sentences to some prior material in the text. This relating of new to old seems to occur in working memory because people who have more working-memory capacity score higher than others on reading compre-

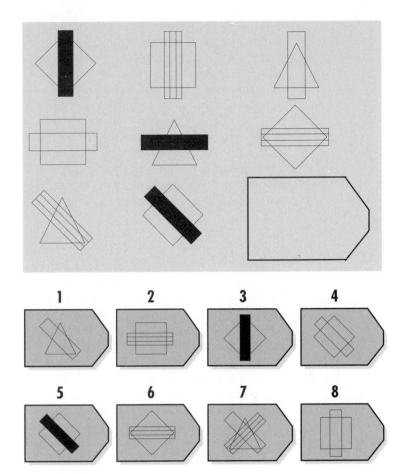

FIGURE 8-5

Illustration of a Geometric Analogy *The task is to inspect the forms in the 3 × 3 matrix, in which the bottom right entry is missing, and to determine which of the 8 alternatives given below is the missing entry. To do this, you have to look across each row and determine the rules that specify how the forms vary, and then do the same thing for each column. (After Carpenter, Just, & Shell, 1990)*

hension tests (Daneman & Carpenter, 1980; Just & Carpenter, 1992).

Transfer From Working Memory to Long-Term Memory

From what we have seen so far, working memory serves two important functions: It stores material that is needed for short periods, and it serves as a work space for mental computations. Another possible function is serving as a way station to long-term memory. That is, information may reside in working memory while it is being encoded or transferred into long-term memory (Atkinson & Shiffrin, 1971; Raaijmakers & Shiffrin,

"Can we hurry up and get to the test? My short-term memory is better than my long-term memory."

©1985, reprinted courtesy of Bill Hoest and *Parade Magazine*.

1992). While there are a number of different ways to implement the transfer, one way that has been the subject of considerable research is **rehearsal,** *the conscious repetition of information in working memory.* Rehearsal apparently not only maintains the item in working memory but also causes it to be transferred to long-term memory. Thus, the term *maintenance rehearsal* is used to refer to active efforts to hold information in working memory; *elaborative rehearsal* refers to efforts to encode information in long-term memory.

Some of the best evidence for the "way-station" function of working memory comes from experiments on free recall. In a *free-recall experiment,* participants first see a list of perhaps 40 unrelated words that are presented one at a time. After all the words have been presented, participants must immediately recall them in any order (hence the designation "free"). The results from such an experiment are shown in Figure 8-6. The chance of correctly recalling a word is graphed as a function of the word's position in the list. The part of the curve to the left in the graph is for the first few words pre-sented, and the part to the right is for the last few words presented.

Presumably, at the time of recall the last few words presented are still likely to be in working memory, whereas the remaining words are in long-term memory. Hence, we would expect recall of the last few words to be high because items in working memory can be retrieved easily. Figure 8-6 shows that this is indeed the case. But recall for the first words presented is also quite good. Why is this? This is where rehearsal enters the picture. When the first words were presented, they were entered into working memory and rehearsed. Since there was little else in working memory, they were rehearsed often and therefore were likely to be transferred to long-term memory. As more items were presented, working memory quickly filled up and the opportunity to rehearse and transfer any given item to long-term memory decreased. So only the first few items presented enjoyed the extra opportunity for transfer, which is why they were later recalled so well from long-term memory.

In sum, working memory is a system that can hold roughly 7 ± 2 chunks of information in either a phonological or a visual format. Information is lost from working memory through either decay or displacement, and is retrieved from this system by a process that is sensitive to the total number of items being kept active at any given time. Lastly, working memory is used to store and process information that is needed during problem solving, and therefore is critical for thought.

Long-Term Memory

Long-term memory is involved *when information has to be retained for intervals as brief as a few minutes* (such as a point made earlier in a conversation) *or as long as a lifetime* (such as an adult's childhood memories). In experiments on long-term memory, psychologists have generally studied forgetting over intervals of minutes, hours, or weeks, but a few studies have involved years or even decades. Experiments that use intervals of years often involve the recall of personal experience (called *autobiographical memory*) rather than the recall of laboratory materials. In what follows, studies using both kinds of material are

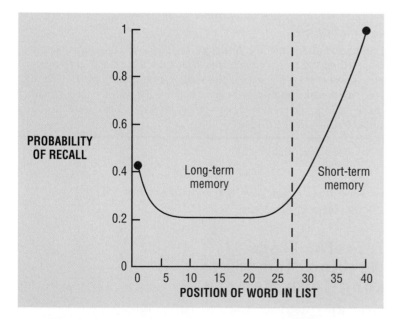

FIGURE 8-6

Results of a Free-Recall Experiment *The Probability of recall varies with an item's position in a list, with the probability being highest for the last five or so positions, next highest for the first few positions, and lowest for the intermediate positions. Recall of the last few items is based on short-term memory, whereas recall of the remaining items is based on long-term memory. (After Glanzer, 1972; Murdock, 1962)*

intermixed because they seem to reflect many of the same principles.

Our discussion of long-term memory will again distinguish among the three stages of memory—encoding, storage, and retrieval—but this time there are two complications. First, unlike the situation with working memory, important interactions between encoding and retrieval occur in long-term memory. In view of these interactions, we will consider some aspects of retrieval in our discussion of encoding and present a separate discussion of interactions between encoding and retrieval. The other complication is that it is often difficult to know whether forgetting from long-term memory is due to a loss from storage or to a failure in retrieval. To deal with this problem, we will delay our discussion of storage until after we have considered retrieval so that we have a clearer idea of what constitutes good evidence for a storage loss.

Encoding

Encoding Meaning   For verbal material, the dominant long-term memory representation is neither acoustic nor visual; instead, it is based on the meanings of the items. Encoding items according to their meaning occurs even when the items are isolated words, but it is more striking when they are sentences. Several minutes after hearing a sentence, most of what you can recall or recognize is the sentence's meaning. Suppose that you heard the sentence, "The author sent the committee a long letter." The evidence indicates that two minutes later you would do no better than chance in telling whether you had heard that sentence or one that has the same meaning: "A long letter was sent to the committee by the author" (Sachs, 1967).

Encoding of meaning is pervasive in everyday memory situations. When people report on complex social or political situations, they may misremember many of the specifics (who said what to whom, when something was said, who else was there) yet can accurately describe the basic situation. Thus, in the Watergate scandal of the early 1970s, the chief government witness (John Dean) was subsequently shown to have made many mistakes about what was said in particular situations, yet his overall testimony is generally thought to accu-

rately describe the events that occurred (Neisser, 1982).

Although meaning may be the dominant way of representing verbal material in long-term memory, we sometimes code other aspects as well. We can, for example, memorize poems and recite them word for word. In such cases we have coded not only the meaning of the poem but the exact words themselves. We can also use a phonological code in long-term memory. When you get a phone call and the other party says "Hello," you often recognize the voice. In a case like this, you must have coded the sound of that person's voice in long-term memory. Visual impressions, tastes, and smells are also coded in long-term memory. Thus, long-term memory has a preferred code for verbal material (namely, meaning), but other codes can be used as well.

Adding Meaningful Connections   Often the items that we need to remember are meaningful but the connections between them are not. In such cases memory can be improved by creating real or artificial links between the items. For example, people who are learning to read music must remember that the five lines in printed music are referred to as EGBDF; although the symbols themselves are meaningful (they refer to notes on a keyboard), their order seems arbitrary. What many learners do is convert the symbols into the sentence "Every Good Boy Does Fine"; the first letter of each word names each symbol, and the relationships between the words in the sentence supply meaningful connections between the symbols. These connections aid memory because they provide retrieval paths between the words: Once the word "Good" has been retrieved, for example, there is a path or connection to "Boy," the next word that must be recalled.

One of the best ways to add connections is to *elaborate* on the meaning of the material while encoding it. The more deeply or elaborately one encodes the meaning, the better the resulting memory will be (Craik & Tulving, 1975). Thus, if you have to remember a point made in a textbook, you will recall it better if you concentrate on its meaning rather than on the exact words. And the more deeply and thoroughly you expand on its meaning, the better you will recall it.

An experiment by Bradshaw and Anderson (1982) illustrates some of these points. Participants read facts about famous people that they would later have to recall, such as "At a critical point in his life, Mozart made a journey from Munich to Paris." Some facts were elaborated according to either their causes or their consequences, as in "Mozart wanted to leave Munich to avoid a romantic entanglement." Other facts were presented alone. Later the participants were tested on their memory of just the facts (not the elaborations). Participants recalled more facts that had been given elaborations than facts that had been presented alone. Presumably, in adding the cause (or consequence) to their memory representation, they set up a retrieval path from the cause to the target fact in the following manner:

Mozart journeyed from Munich to Paris.

cause

Mozart wanted to avoid a romantic entanglement in Munich.

At the time of recall, participants could either retrieve the target fact directly or retrieve it indirectly by following the path from its cause. Even if they forgot the target fact, they could infer it if they retrieved the cause.

When we forget information in long-term memory, it doesn't mean that the information itself is lost. We may be able to retrieve the information if something reminds us of it. This is one reason that families maintain photograph albums.

Results like these establish an intimate connection between understanding and memory. The better we understand some material, the more connections we see between its parts. Because these connections can serve as retrieval links, the better we understand items and the more we remember.

Retrieval

Many cases of forgetting from long-term memory result from loss of access to the information rather than from loss of the information itself. That is, poor memory often reflects a retrieval failure rather than a storage failure. (Note that this is unlike working memory, in which forgetting is a result of decay or displacement and retrieval is thought to be relatively error free.) Trying to retrieve an item from long-term memory is like trying to find a book in a large library. Failure to find the book does not necessarily mean that it is not there; you may be looking in the wrong place, or the book may simply be misfiled.

Evidence for Retrieval Failures Our everyday experience provides considerable evidence for retrieval failures. At some point all of us have been unable to recall a fact or experience, only to have it come to mind later. How many times have you taken an exam and not been able to recall a specific name, only to remember it later? Another example is the "tip-of-the-tongue" phenomenon, in which a particular word or name lies tantalizingly outside our ability to recall it (Brown & McNeill, 1966). We may feel quite tormented until a search of memory (dredging up and then discarding words that are close but not quite right) finally retrieves the correct word.

A more striking example of retrieval failure occurs when a person undergoing psychotherapy retrieves a memory that had previously been forgotten. Although we lack firm evidence for such occurrences, they suggest that some seemingly forgotten memories are not lost but merely difficult to get at.

For stronger evidence that retrieval failures can cause forgetting, consider the following experiment. Participants were asked to memorize a long list of words. Some of the words were names of animals, such as dog, cat, horse; some were names of fruits, such as apple, orange, pear; some were names of furniture; and so on (see Table 8-1). At the time of recall, the participants were divided into two groups. One group was supplied with retrieval cues such as "animal," "fruit," and so on; the other group, the control group, was not. The group that was given the retrieval cues recalled more words than the control group. In a subsequent test, when both groups were given the retrieval cues, they recalled the same number of words. Hence, the initial difference in recall between the two groups must have been due to retrieval failures.

In sum, the better the retrieval cues available, the better our memory. This principle explains why we usually do better on a recognition test of memory than on a recall test. In a *recognition test,* we are asked whether we have seen a particular item before (for example, "Was Bessie Smith one of the people you met at the wedding?"). The test item itself is an excellent retrieval cue for our memory of that item. In contrast, in a *recall test,* we have to produce the memorized items using minimal retrieval cues (for example, "Recall the name of the woman you met at the party"). Since the retrieval cues in a recognition test are generally more useful than those in a recall test, performance is usually better on recognition tests (such as multiple-choice exams) than on recall tests (such as essay exams) (Tulving, 1974).

Interference Among the factors that can impair retrieval, the most important is *interference.* If we associate different items with the same cue, when we try to use that cue to retrieve one of the items (the target item), the other items may become active and interfere with our recovery of the target. For example, if your friend Dan moves and you finally learn his new phone number, you will find it difficult to retrieve the old number. Why? Because you are using the cue "Dan's phone number" to retrieve the old number, but instead this cue activates the new number, which interferes with recovery of the old one. (This is referred to as *retroactive interference.*) Or suppose that your reserved space in a parking garage, which you have used for a year, is changed. At first you may find it difficult to retrieve your new parking location from memory. Why? Because you are trying to learn to associate your new location with the cue "my parking place," but this cue retrieves the old location, which interferes with the learning of the new one (*proactive interference*). In both examples, the power of retrieval cues ("Dan's phone number" or "my parking place") to activate particular target items decreases with the number of other items associated with those cues. The more items are associated with a cue, the more overloaded it becomes and the less effective it is in aiding retrieval.

Interference can operate at various levels, including the level of whole facts. In one experiment, participants first learned to associate various facts with the names of

TABLE 8-1

Examples From a Study of Retrieval Failures
Participants who were not given the retrieval cues recalled fewer words from the memorized list than other participants who were given the cues. This finding shows that problems at the retrieval stage of long-term memory are responsible for some memory failures. (After Tulving & Pearlstone, 1966)

List to Be Memorized		
dog	cotton	oil
cat	wool	gas
horse	silk	coal
cow	rayon	wood
apple	blue	doctor
orange	red	lawyer
pear	green	teacher
banana	yellow	dentist
chair	knife	football
table	spoon	baseball
bed	fork	basketball
sofa	pan	tennis
knife	hammer	shirt
gun	saw	socks
rifle	nails	pants
bomb	screwdriver	shoes
Retrieval Cues		
animals	cloth	fuels
fruit	color	professions
furniture	utensils	sports
weapons	tools	clothing

professions. For example, they learned the following associations:

The banker:

(1) was asked to address the crowd,

(2) broke the bottle, and

(3) did not delay the trip.

The lawyer:

(1) realized that the seam was split, and

(2) painted an old barn.

The occupational names "banker" and "lawyer" were the retrieval cues. Since "banker" was associated with three facts and "lawyer" was associated with just two, "banker" should have been less useful than "lawyer" in retrieving any of its associated facts ("banker" was the more overloaded cue). When participants were later given a recognition test, they did take longer to recognize any one of the facts learned about the banker than any one of those learned about the lawyer. In this study, then, interference slowed the speed of retrieval. Many other experiments show that interference can lead to a complete retrieval failure if the target items are weak or the interference is strong (Anderson, 1983). Indeed, it has long been thought that interference is a major reason why forgetting from long-term memory increases with time: The relevant retrieval cues become more and more overloaded with time (see Figure 8-7).

Models of Retrieval   In attempting to explain interference effects, researchers have developed a variety of models of retrieval. As with retrieval from short-term memory, some models of long-term-memory retrieval are based on a search process whereas others are based on an activation process.

The interference effects in the banker-lawyer experiment fit nicely with the idea that retrieval from long-term memory may be thought of as a search process (e.g., Raaijmakers & Shiffrin, 1981). To illustrate, consider how the sentence "The banker broke the bottle" might be recognized (see Figure 8-8). The term "banker" accesses its representation in memory, which localizes the search to the relevant part of long-term memory. There, three paths need to be searched to verify that "broke the bottle" was one of the facts learned about the banker. In contrast, if the test sentence is "The lawyer painted an old barn," there are only two paths to be searched. Since the duration of a search increases with the number of paths to be considered, retrieval will be slower for the "banker" sentence than for the "lawyer" one.

An alternative way to think about the retrieval process is in terms of activation. When trying to recognize "The banker broke the bottle," for example, the participant activates the representation for "banker" and the activation then spreads simultaneously along the three paths emanating from "banker" (see Figure 8-8). When sufficient activation reaches "broke the bottle," the sentence can be recognized. Interference arises because the activation from the banker representation must be subdivided among the paths emanating from it. Hence, the more facts are associated with "banker,"

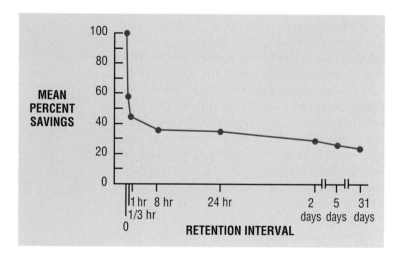

FIGURE 8-7

Forgetting as a Function of Time   *A forgetting curve graphs the decline in recall as a function of time. This forgetting curve, the first ever reported, comes from the work of Ebbinghaus (1885). He studied lists of 13 syllables, which he repeated until he was able to recall the list without error on two successive trials. Then, after intervals ranging from 20 minutes to 31 days, he tested himself by determining how long it took him to relearn the list to the original level; the less the forgetting, the fewer trials should be needed to relearn the list. The figure plots a measure of ease of relearning (called* savings*) as a function of time; it suggests that one forgets a lot about an event within the first few hour but that after that the rate of forgetting slows down. While this curve is representative of memory for unrelated verbal materials, different kinds of curves are found with different kinds of material (Bahrick & Phelphs, 1987). In all cases, interference is thought to play some role in the changes in forgetting with time.*

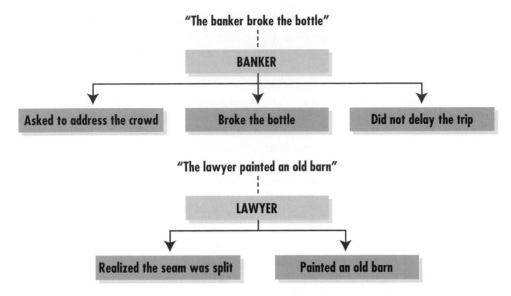

FIGURE 8-8

Retrieval as a Search Process Versus an Activation Process   *When the sentence, "The banker broke the bottle" is presented, the term "banker" accesses the banker representation in long-term memory; once at this representation, there are three paths to be searched. When the sentence "The lawyer painted an old barn" is presented, "lawyer" accesses the lawyer representation; from which there are two paths to be searched. Alternatively, the term "banker" may activate the banker representation, this activation then spreads simultaneously along the three paths (and similarly for the "lawyer" example).*

the thinner the activation will be on each path and the longer it will take for sufficient activation to reach any particular fact. Thus, thinking of retrieval in terms of spreading activation can also account for why interference slows retrieval (Anderson, 1983).

Storage

The fact that *some* forgetting is due to retrieval failures does not imply that *all* forgetting is. It seems most unlikely that everything we ever learned is still there in memory waiting for the right retrieval cue. Some information is almost certainly lost from storage (Loftus & Loftus, 1980).

Some evidence of storage loss comes from people who receive electroconvulsive therapy to alleviate severe depression (a mild electric current applied to the brain produces a brief epilepticlike seizure and momentary unconsciousness; see Chapter 16). In such cases the patient loses some memory for events that occurred in the months just prior to the shock, but not for earlier events (Squire & Fox, 1980). These memory losses are unlikely to be due to retrieval failures because if the shock disrupted retrieval,

all memories should be affected, not just the recent ones. More likely, the shock disrupts storage processes that *consolidate* new memories over a period of months or longer, and information that is not consolidated is lost from storage.

Most research on storage in long-term memory is done at the biological level. Researchers have made substantial progress in determining the neuroanatomical bases of consolidation. It appears that the critical brain structures involved are the hippocampus and the cortex surrounding the hippocampus (which includes the *enthorhinal, perirhinal,* and *parahippocampal* cortices; they are involved in the exchange of information between the hippocampus and much of the cerebral cortex). The hippocampus's role in consolidation seems to be that of a cross-referencing system, linking together aspects of a particular memory that are stored in separate parts of the brain (Squire, 1992). While a global memory loss in humans usually occurs only when the surrounding cortex as well as the hippocampus is impaired, damage to the hippocampus alone can result in severe memory disturbance. This fact was demonstrated by a study that started with an analysis of a particular patient's memory problems (due to complications from coronary bypass surgery) and ended with a detailed autopsy of his brain after his death; the autopsy revealed that the hippocampus was the only brain structure that was damaged (Zola-Morgan, Squire, & Amaral, 1989).

A study using monkeys provides the best evidence we have that the function of the hippocampus is to consolidate relatively new memories. A group of experimental monkeys learned to discriminate between items in 100 pairs of objects. For each pair, there was food under one object, which the monkey got only if it chose that object. Since all the objects differed, the monkeys essentially learned 100 different problems. Twenty of the problems were learned 16 weeks before the researchers removed the monkeys' hippocampus; additional sets of 20 problems were learned either 12, 8, 4, or 2 weeks before the hippocampal surgery. Two weeks after the surgery, the researchers tested the monkeys' memory with a single trial of each of the 100 pairs. The key finding was that the experimental monkeys remembered discriminations that they had learned 8, 12, or 16 weeks before surgery as well as normal control monkeys did, but remembered the discriminations learned 2 or 4 weeks before surgery less well than the control monkeys did. Moreover, the experimental monkeys actually remembered less about the discriminations learned 2 to 4 weeks before surgery than about the discriminations learned earlier. These results suggest that memories need to be processed by the hippocampus for a period of a few weeks, for it is only during this period that memory is impaired by removal of the hippocampus. Permanent long-term memory storage is almost certainly localized in the cortex, particularly in the regions where sensory information is interpreted (Squire, 1992; Zola-Morgan & Squire, 1990).

Interactions Between Encoding and Retrieval

In describing the encoding stage, we noted that operations carried out during encoding, such as elaboration, make retrieval easier. Two other encoding factors also increase the chances of successful retrieval: (a) organiz-

ing the information at the time of encoding and (b) ensuring that the context in which information is encoded is similar to that in which it will be retrieved.

Organization The more we organize the material we encode, the easier it is to retrieve. Suppose that you were at a conference at which you met various professionals—doctors, lawyers, and journalists. When you later try to recall their names, you will do better if you initially organize the information by profession. Then you can ask yourself, "Who were the doctors I met? Who were the lawyers?" and so forth. A list of names or words is far easier to recall when we encode the information into categories and then retrieve it on a category-by-category basis (e.g., Bower, Clark, Winzenz, & Lesgold, 1969).

Context It is easier to retrieve a particular fact or episode if you are in the same context in which you encoded it (Estes, 1972). For example, it is a good bet that your ability to retrieve the names of your classmates in the first and second grades would improve if you were to walk through the corridors of your elementary school. Similarly, your ability to retrieve an emotional moment with a close friend—for example, an argument with her in a restaurant—would be greater if you were back in the place where the incident occurred. This may explain why we are sometimes overcome with a torrent of memories when we visit a place where we once lived. The context in which an event was encoded is one of the most powerful retrieval cues (see Figure 8-9).

Context is not always external to the individual. It can include what is happening inside us when we encode information—that is, our internal state. For example, individuals who learned a list of words while under the influence of marijuana recalled more of the words when tested in the same drug-induced state than when tested in a nondrugged state, and individuals who learned the list in a nondrugged state recalled more words when tested in a nondrugged state than when tested in a drug-induced state (Eich, 1980). Such cases are referred to as **state-dependent learning** because *memory is partly dependent on the internal state prevailing during learning*. It is thought

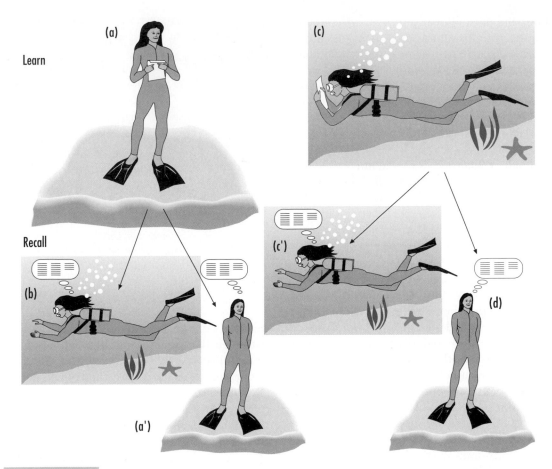

FIGURE 8-9

Effects of Environmental Context on Retrieval   *In an experiment to demonstrate how context affects retrieval, one group of deep-sea divers learned a list of words while they were on the beach (panel a), whereas another group of divers learned the list while they were beneath 15 feet of water (panel c). Later, each group was divided in half and tried to recall the words either in the same environment in which they had learned them (panels a′ and c′) or in a different environment (panels b and d). Whether the divers originally learned the words on land or under water had no overall effect. But divers who were tested in an environment different from the one in which they learned the words recalled 40% less than divers who learned and recalled in the same environment. (Godden & Baddeley, 1975)*

that feelings evoked by the altered state serve as cues for retrieving information encoded while in that state. The evidence for this phenomenon is controversial, but it does suggest that memory does improve when our internal state during retrieval matches our internal state during encoding (Eich, 1980).

Emotional Factors in Forgetting

So far we have treated memory as if it were entirely separate from emotion. But don't we sometimes remember or forget material because of its emotional content? There has been a great deal of research on this ques-

tion. The results suggest that emotion can influence long-term memory in five distinct ways: rehearsal, flashbulb memories, retrieval interference via anxiety, context effects, and repression.

Rehearsal   The simplest idea is that we tend to think about emotionally charged situations, negative as well as positive, more than we think about neutral ones. We rehearse and organize exciting memories more than we do blander ones. For example, you may forget where you saw this or that movie; but if a fire breaks out while you are in a theater, that incident will dominate your thoughts for a while and you will describe the setting over and over to friends as well as think about the setting over and over to yourself, thereby rehearsing and organizing it. Since we know that rehearsal and organization can improve retrieval from long-term memory, it is not surprising that many researchers have found that memory is better for emotional situations than for unemotional ones (Neisser, 1982; Rapaport, 1942).

Flashbulb Memories   The second way emotion can affect memory is via flashbulb memories. A **flashbulb memory** is *a vivid and relatively permanent record of the circumstances in which one learned of an emotionally charged, significant event*. An example is the explosion of the space shuttle *Challenger* in 1986, which was witnessed by millions of people on television. Many people in their 20s remember exactly where they were when they learned of the *Challenger* disaster and exactly who told them about it, even though these are the kinds of details that we usually forget quickly. Americans age 30 or older may have flashbulb memories of the assassination attempt on Ronald Reagan in 1981, while those age 40 or older may have such memories of the assassinations of John F. Kennedy and Martin Luther King, Jr., in the 1960s. There is a published report indicating that a century ago Americans had flashbulb memories of the assassination of Abraham Lincoln. When Colegrove (1899) interviewed 179 people, 127 of them were able to give full particulars as to where they were and what they were doing when they heard of Lincoln's assassination.

What causes such vivid memories? According to Brown and Kulik (1977), extraordinarily important events trigger a special memory mechanism, one that makes a permanent record of everything the person is experiencing at the moment. It is as if we took a picture of the moment, which is why the recollection is dubbed a "flashbulb memory." (The term comes from the flashbulbs formerly used by news photographers.) The idea of a special mechanism for emotional memories is controversial, however. Critics point out that flashbulb memories, like normal long-term memories, become less retrievable over time. In a study carried out a few days after the *Challenger* explosion, people were asked where they were and what they were doing when they heard of the disaster; nine months later, the same

Many people can remember exactly where they are and what they were doing when they heard about the shocking death of Lady Diana, Princess of Wales.

people were asked the same questions. Although they had unusually detailed memories of the event nine months after it occurred, some forgetting had occurred in the interim (McCloskey, Wible, & Cohen, 1988). Results like these suggest that memory for national tragedies could be an instance of normal memory. The reason we remember the events so vividly is that we keep on hearing and talking about them, just as we do in the case of other emotionally charged situations.

Researchers who favor the idea of a special mechanism for emotional memories can cite evidence to support their view. Perhaps the most striking evidence comes from a recent study that focused on the biological bases of memory. The key idea is that storage of emotional memories involves the hormones adrenaline and noradrenaline, whereas storage of normal memories does not. Consequently, if the biochemical effects of these two hormones are blocked, people should have trouble remembering emotional material but no problems remembering nonemotional material. These ideas were tested in the following experiment. Participants watched a slide presentation accompanied by either an emotional narration (about a boy being taken to a hospital for emergency surgery) or a neutral narration (about a boy going to a hospital to visit his father, who works there). Before hearing the stories, half the participants were given a drug (propranolol) known to block the effects of adrenaline and noradrenaline, and the other half were given a placebo (that is, a substance that appears to be a drug but has no effect). One week later all the participants were given a memory test for the stories. The participants who had taken the hormone-blocking drug recalled less information about the emotional story than did the participants who had taken the placebo, but the two groups of participants showed no difference in ability to recall the neutral story. These results imply that emotional material is indeed stored by a different mechanism from that used to store neutral memories (Cahill et al., 1994).

We know what hormones are involved, but what neural structures are being affected by these hormones? In Chapter 7 we noted that the amygdala is involved in emotional learning. It turns out that the same structure is involved in emotional memory. The evidence for this comes from recent brain-scanning studies. While their brains were being scanned, participants viewed slides that were accompanied by an emotional narration. The amygdala was activated, but the degree of activation differed from one participant to another. The more activation a participant displayed, the better he or she recalled the emotional information later. This is good evidence that the amygdala is indeed mediating memory for emotional material (Cahill et al., 1995).

Retrieval Interference via Anxiety   There are also cases in which negative emotions hinder retrieval, which brings us to the third way emotion can affect memory. An experience that many students have at one time or another illustrates this process:

> You are taking an exam about which you are not very confident. You can barely understand the initial question, let alone answer it. Signs of panic appear. Although the second question really isn't hard, the anxiety triggered by the previous question spreads to this one. By the time you look at the third question, it wouldn't matter whether it only asked for your phone number. There's no way you can answer it. You're in a complete panic.

What is happening to memory here? Failure to deal with the first question produced anxiety. Anxiety is often accompanied by extraneous thoughts, such as "I'm going to flunk out" or "Everybody will think I'm stupid." These thoughts fill our consciousness and interfere with attempts to retrieve information that is relevant to the question; this may be why memory fails. According to this view, anxiety does not directly cause memory failure; rather, it causes, or is associated with, extraneous thoughts, and these thoughts cause memory failure by interfering with retrieval (Holmes, 1974).

Context Effects   Emotion may also affect memory through a context effect. As noted earlier, memory is best when the context at the time of retrieval matches that at the time of encoding. Since our emotional state during learning is part of the context, if the material we are learning makes us feel sad, perhaps we can best retrieve that material when we feel sad again. Experimenters have demonstrated such an emotional-context effect. Participants agreed to keep diaries for a week, recording every emotional incident that occurred and noting whether it was pleasant or unpleasant. One week after they handed in their diaries, the participants returned to the laboratory and were hypnotized. Half the participants were put in a pleasant mood and the other half in an unpleasant mood. All were asked to recall the incidents recorded in their diaries. For participants in a pleasant mood, most of the incidents they recalled had been rated as pleasant at the time that they were experienced; for participants in an unpleasant mood at retrieval, most of the incidents recalled had been rated as unpleasant at the time that they were experienced. As expected, recall was best when the dominant emotion during retrieval matched that during encoding (Bower, 1981).

Repression   Thus far, all of the means by which emotions can influence memory rely on principles already discussed—namely, rehearsal, interference, and context effects. Another view of emotion and memory, Freud's theory of the unconscious, brings up new principles. Freud proposed that some emotional experiences in childhood are so traumatic that allowing them to enter consciousness many years later would cause the individual to be totally overwhelmed by anxiety. Such traumatic experiences are said to be *repressed,* or stored in the unconscious, and they can be retrieved only when some of the emotion associated with them is defused. Repression, therefore, represents the ultimate retrieval failure: Access to the target memories is actively blocked. This notion of active blocking makes the repression hypothesis qualitatively different from the ideas about forgetting discussed earlier. (For a discussion of Freud's theory, see Chapter 13.)

Repression is such a striking phenomenon that we would of course like to study it in the laboratory, but it has proved difficult to do this. To induce true repression in the laboratory, the experimenter must cause the participant to experience something extremely traumatic, but this obviously would be unethical. The studies that have been done have exposed participants to mildly upsetting experiences, and the results have been mixed (Baddeley, 1990; Erdelyi, 1985).

In sum, long-term memory is a system that can hold information for days, years, or decades, typically in a code based on meaning, although other codes are possible. Retrieval of information from this system is sensitive to interference; many apparent "storage losses" are really retrieval failures. Storage in this system involves consolidation, a process that is mediated by the hippocampal system. Many aspects of long-term memory can be influenced by emotion; such influences may reflect selective rehearsal, retrieval interference, the effects of context, or two special mechanisms: flashbulb memories and repression.

Implicit Memory

Thus far, we have been concerned mainly with situations in which people remember personal facts. In such cases memory is a matter of consciously recollecting the past, and is said to be expressed *explicitly.* But there seems to be another kind of memory, one that is often manifested in skills and shows up as an improvement in the performance of some perceptual, motor, or cognitive task without conscious recollection of the experiences that led to the improvement. For example, with practice we can steadily improve our ability to recognize words in a foreign language, but at the moment that we are recognizing a word, and thereby demonstrating our skill, we need not have any conscious recollection of the

lessons that led to our improvement. In such cases, memory is expressed *implicitly* (Schacter, 1989).

Memory in Amnesia

Much of what is known about implicit memory has been learned from people who suffer **amnesia,** or *partial loss of memory.* Amnesia may result from very different causes, including accidental injuries to the brain, strokes, encephalitis, alcoholism, electroconvulsive shock, and surgical procedures (for example, removal of the hippocampus to reduce epilepsy). Whatever its cause, the primary symptom of amnesia is a profound inability to remember day-to-day events and, hence, to acquire new factual information; this is referred to as *anterograde amnesia,* and it can be extensive. There is an intensively studied patient, identified as N.A., who is unable to participate in a normal conversation because at the least distraction he loses his train of thought. Another patient, identified as H.M., reads the same magazines over and over and continually needs to be reintroduced to doctors who have been treating him for decades.

H.M. is the most famous of the brain-damaged patients whose memory functioning has been studied extensively (Milner, 1970; Squire, 1992). At the age of 27, H.M., who suffered from severe epilepsy, underwent surgery to remove portions of the temporal lobe and limbic system on both sides of his brain. The surgery left him unable to form new memories, although he could remember events that had occurred prior to the surgery.

H.M. can retain new information as long as he focuses on it, but as soon as he is distracted he forgets the information, and he is unable to recall it later. On one occasion, for example, he kept the number 584 in mind for 15 minutes, using the following mnemonic system:* "5, 8, 4 add to 17. You remember 8, subtract from 17 and it leaves 9. Divide 9 by half and you get 5 and 4, and there you are—584" (quoted in Milner, 1970). A few minutes later, however, H.M.'s attention shifted and he could no longer remember either the number or his method for remembering it.

---

*Mnemonic systems, or systems for aiding memory, are discussed later in the chapter.

A secondary symptom of amnesia is inability to remember events that occurred prior to the injury or disease. The extent of such *retrograde amnesia* varies from one patient to another. Aside from retrograde and anterograde memory losses, the typical amnesiac appears relatively normal: He or she has a normal vocabulary, the usual knowledge about the world (at least before the onset of the amnesia), and generally no loss of intelligence.

Skills and Priming A striking aspect of amnesia is that not all kinds of memory are disrupted. Thus, while amnesiacs generally are unable to either remember old facts about their lives or learn new ones, they have no difficulty remembering and learning perceptual and motor skills. This suggests that there is a different memory for facts than for skills. More generally, it suggests that explicit and implicit memory (which encode facts and skills, respectively) are different systems.

The skills that are preserved in amnesia include motor skills, such as tying one's shoelaces or riding a bike, and perceptual skills, such as normal reading or reading words that are projected into a mirror (and hence reversed). Consider the ability of reading mirror-reversed words. To do this well takes a bit of practice (try holding this book in front of a mirror and reading it). Amnesiacs improve with practice at the

Memory for skills such as tying one's shoelaces is referred to as implicit memory.

same rate as normal participants, although they may have no memory of having participated in earlier practice sessions (Cohen & Squire, 1980). They show normal memory for the skill but virtually no memory for the learning episodes that developed it (the latter being facts).

A similar pattern emerges in situations in which prior exposure to a stimulus facilitates or *primes* later processing of that stimulus. This pattern is illustrated in the experiment outlined in Table 8-2. In Stage 1 of the experiment, amnesiac and normal participants were given a list of words to study. In Stage 2, stems of words on the list and stems of words not on the list were presented, and the participants tried to complete them (see Table 8-2). The normal participants performed as expected, completing more stems when they were drawn from words on the list than when they were drawn from words not on the list. This difference is referred to as *priming* because the words presented in Stage 1 facilitated or primed performance on the stem completion problems presented in Stage 2. Significantly, amnesiacs also completed more stems in Stage 2 when they were drawn from words on the list than when they were drawn from words not on the list. In fact, the degree of priming for amnesiacs was exactly the same as for normals. This finding indicates that when memory is manifested implicitly, as in priming, amnesiacs perform normally.

TABLE 8-2

Procedure for an Experiment to Study Implicit Memory in Amnesia (After Warrington & Weiskrantz, 1978)

Stage 1	Example
Present list of words for study	MOTEL
Stage 2	
Present stems of list words and nonlist words for completion. Number of list words completed minus number of nonlist words completed = Priming	MOT BLA
Stage 3	
Present original list of words plus new words for recognition	MOTEL STAND

In Stage 3 of the experiment, the original words were presented again along with some novel words, and participants had to recognize which words had appeared on the list. Now amnesiacs remembered far fewer words than normals. Thus, when memory is tested explicitly, as in recognition, amnesiacs perform far below normals.

There is an interesting variation of the preceding study that further strengthens its conclusion. Suppose that in Stage 2 participants are instructed that they will perform better on the stem-completion task if they try to think of the words presented earlier. This instruction makes stem completion into an explicit memory task (because conscious recollection is being emphasized). Now amnesiacs show substantially less priming than normal participants (Graf & Mandler, 1984).

Childhood Amnesia One of the most striking aspects of human memory is that everyone suffers from a particular kind of amnesia: Virtually no one can recall events from the first years of life, even though this is the time when experience is at its richest.

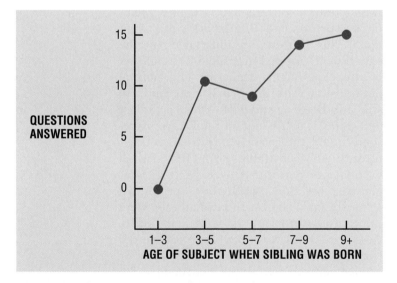

FIGURE 8-10

Recall of an Early Memory *In an experiment on childhood amnesia, college-age individuals were asked 20 questions about the events surrounding the birth of a younger sibling. The average number of questions answered is plotted as a function of the individual's age when the sibling was born. If the birth occurred before the fourth year of life, no individual could recall a thing about it; if the birth occurred after that, recall increased with age at the time of the event.* (After Sheingold & Tenney, 1982)

This curious phenomenon was first discussed by Freud (1905), who called it *childhood amnesia.*

Freud discovered the phenomenon by observing that his patients were generally unable to recall events from their first 3 to 5 years of life. At first you might think that there is nothing unusual about this, because memory for events declines with time, and for adults there has been a lot of intervening time since early childhood. But childhood amnesia cannot be reduced to normal forgetting. Most 30-year-olds can recall a good deal about their high school years, but it is a rare 18-year-old who can tell you anything about his or her third year of life; yet the time interval—about 15 years—is roughly the same in each case.

In some studies, people have been asked to recall and date their childhood memories. For most people, their first memory is of something that occurred when they were age 3 or older; a few individuals will report memories prior to the age of 1. A problem with these reports, however, is that we can never be sure that the "remembered" event actually occurred (the person may have reconstructed what he or she thought happened). This problem was overcome in an experiment in which participants were asked a total of 20 questions about a childhood event that was known to have occurred—the birth of a younger sibling— the details of which could be verified by another person. The questions asked of each participant dealt with events that occurred when the mother left to go to the hospital (for example, "What time of day did she leave?"), when the mother was in the hospital ("Did you visit her?"), and when the mother and infant returned home ("What time of day did they come home?"). The participants were college students, and their ages at the time that their siblings were born varied from 1 to 17 years. The results are shown in Figure 8-10. The number of questions answered is plotted as a function of the participant's age when the sibling was born. If the sibling was born before the participant was 3 years old, the person could not recall a thing about it. If the birth occurred after that, recall increased with age at the time of the event. These results suggest almost total amnesia for the first 3 years of life. More recent research, however, suggests that such

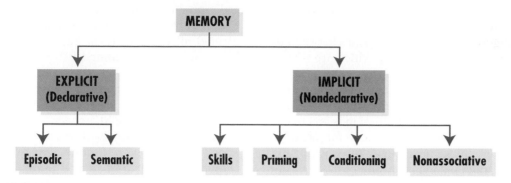

FIGURE 8-11

A Proposed Classification of Memory Stores *Squire et al. (1990) propose that there are several different memory systems. The basic distinction is between explicit and implicit memory (which they refer to as* declarative *and* nondeclarative, *respectively). There are at least four known kinds of implicit memory, corresponding to the memory involved in skills, priming, conditioning, and certain nonassociative phenomena (such as habituating to a repeated stimulus). There are two kinds of explicit memory, corresponding to semantic and episodic memory.*

recall may be improved if more cues are given and the cues are more specific (Fivush & Hamond, 1991). Still, the bulk of the evidence indicates that we should be skeptical about reports of memory from the first few years of life.

What causes childhood amnesia? A generally accepted explanation is that childhood amnesia is due to a massive difference between how young children encode experience and how adults organize their memories. Adults structure their memories in terms of categories and schemas ("She's that kind of person," "It's that kind of situation"), while young children encode their experiences without embellishing them or connecting them to related events. Once a child begins to form associations between events and to categorize those events, early experiences become lost (Schachtel, 1982).

What causes the shift from early childhood to adult forms of memory? One factor is biological development. The hippocampus, which is known to be involved in consolidating memories, is not mature until roughly a year or two after birth. Therefore, events that take place in the first 2 years of life cannot be sufficiently consolidated and consequently cannot be recalled later. Other causes of the shift to adult memory are better understood at the psychological level. These include cognitive factors, particularly the development of language and the beginning of schooling. Both language and the kind of thinking emphasized in school pro-

vide new ways of organizing experiences, ways that may be incompatible with the way the young child encodes experiences. Interestingly, language development reaches an early peak at age 3, while schooling often begins at age 5; and the age span from 3 to 5 is the time when childhood amnesia seems to end.

A Variety of Memory Stores

On the basis of work with various brain-damaged patients, researchers have proposed that both explicit and implicit memory come in various forms. One such proposal is presented in Figure 8-11. The basic distinction is between explicit and implicit memory. (Recall that explicit memory involves consciously recollecting the past, while implicit memory shows up as improved performance of a skill without conscious recollection of the lessons that led to it.) With regard to implicit memory, a further distinction is made between perceptual-motor skills, such as reading mirror-reversed words, and priming, as occurs in word-stem completions. The reason for assuming that skills and priming may involve different memory stores is that there are patients with brain damage (individuals in the early stages of Alzheimer's disease) who are able to learn motor skills but show less priming than normal. In contrast, there are other brain-damaged patients (individuals with Huntington's disease) who show normal priming but have difficulty learning new motor skills (Schacter, 1989).

Figure 8-11 also distinguishes between two kinds of explicit memory, which are referred to as *episodic* and *semantic.* Episodic facts refer to personal episodes and semantic facts to general truths. To illustrate, your memory of your high-school graduation is an episodic fact, and so is your memory for what you had for dinner last night. In each of these cases, the episode is encoded with respect to you, the individual (*your* graduation, *your* dinner, and so on), and often with respect to a specific time and place as well. In contrast, semantic facts, such as your memory or knowledge that the word "bachelor" means an unmarried man and that September has 30 days, is encoded in relation to other knowledge rather than in relation to yourself, and there is no coding of time and place (Tulving, 1985). This distinction between semantic and episodic memory fits with the fact that although amnesiacs have severe difficulty remembering personal episodes, they seem relatively normal in their general knowledge.

Implicit Memory in Normal Individuals

Studies using normal individuals also suggest that there are separate systems for explicit and implicit memories. There seem to be fundamental differences in how these two kinds of memories are implemented in the brain. The critical evidence comes from brain-scanning experiments (PET). In one experiment (Squire et al., 1992), participants first studied a list of 15 words and then were exposed to three different conditions. The implicit-memory condition was the stem-completion task. Half the stems were drawn from the 15 words originally studied and the other half were new; participants were instructed to complete the stems with the first words that came to mind. The second condition of interest involved explicit memory. Again word stems were presented, but now participants were instructed to use them to recall words from the initial list of 15. The third condition was a control. Word stems were presented, and participants were instructed to complete them with the first words that came to mind, but now none of the stems were drawn from the words ini-

tially studied. The control condition therefore requires no memory. Participants performed all three of these tasks while their brains were being scanned.

Consider first what the brain is doing during the explicit-memory task. From the material presented in the first section of this chapter, we might expect that (1) the hippocampus is involved (remember, this structure is critical in forming long-term memories) and (2) most of the brain activity will be in the right hemisphere (because the task emphasized retrieval, and long-term retrieval involves mainly right-hemisphere processes). This is exactly what was found. More specifically, when brain activity in the explicit-memory condition was compared with that in the control condition, there was increased activation of hippocampal and frontal regions in the right-hemisphere.

Now consider the implicit-memory condition. Compared with the control condition, it showed decreases in activation rather than increases. That is, priming is reflected in less-than-usual neural activity, as if there has been a "greasing of the neural wheels." Implicit memory, then, has the opposite neural consequences of explicit memory, demonstrating a biological difference between the two kinds of memory.

This evidence points up once again the interconnections between biological and psychological research. In fact, throughout this chapter we have seen instances of the role of biological evidence in explaining psychological phenomena. In many cases the psychological evidence was obtained first and used to direct subsequent biological research. For example, the cognitive distinction between short-term and long-term memory was made in papers published about a century ago, but only relatively recently have biologically oriented researchers been able to demonstrate some of the neural bases for this key distinction. Biological research is contributing to other areas of the study of memory as well. We now know something about the biological basis of storage in explicit long-term memory and about storage in the visual and verbal buffers of short-term memory. Such knowledge is not only useful in its own right but may also prove helpful in combating the ravages of memory brought about by diseases of aging such as stroke and Alzheimer's.

Improving Memory

Having considered the basics of working memory and long-term memory, we are ready to tackle the question of how memory can be improved, focusing primarily on explicit memory. First we will consider how to increase the working memory span. Then we will turn to a variety of methods for improving long-term memory; these methods work by increasing the efficiency of encoding and retrieval. (A possible herbal remedy for memory loss is discussed in the Frontiers of Psychological Research feature on page 292.)

Chunking and Memory Span

For most of us, the capacity of working memory cannot be increased beyond 7 ± 2 chunks. However, we can enlarge the size of a chunk and thereby increase the number of items in our memory span. We demonstrated this point earlier: Given the string 149-2177-619-96, we can recall all 12 digits if we recode the string into three chunks—1492-1776-1996—and store them in working memory. Although recoding digits into familiar dates works nicely in this example, it will not work with most digit strings because we have not memorized enough significant dates. But if a recoding system could be developed that worked with virtually any string, working memory span for numbers could be dramatically improved.

Psychologists have studied an individual who discovered such a general-purpose recoding system and used it to increase his memory span from 7 to almost 80 random digits (see Figure 8-12). This person, referred to as S.F., had average memory abilities and average intelligence for a college student. For a year and a half he engaged in a memory-span task for about 3 to 5 hours per week. During this extensive practice S.F., a good long-distance runner, devised the strategy of recoding sets of four digits into running times. For example, S.F. would recode 3492 as "3:49.2—world class time for the mile," which for him was a single chunk. Since S.F. was familiar with many running times (that is, he had them stored in long-term memory), he could readily chunk most sets of four digits. In cases in which he could not (for example, 1771 cannot be a running time because the third digit is too large), he

tried to recode the four digits into either a familiar date or the age of some person or object known to him.

Use of these recoding systems enabled S.F. to increase his memory span from 7 to 28 digits (because each of S.F.'s 7 chunks contains 4 digits). He then built up his memory span to nearly 80 digits by organizing the running times in a hierarchy. Thus, one chunk in S.F.'s working memory might have pointed to 3 running times; at the time of recall, S.F. would go from this chunk to the first running time and produce its 4 digits, then move to the second running time in the chunk and produce its digits, and so on. One chunk was therefore worth 12 digits. In this way S.F. achieved his remarkable memory span. The expansion of his memory capacity was due to increasing the size of a chunk (by relating the items to information in long-term memory), not to increasing the number of chunks that working memory can hold. When he switched from digits to letters, his memory span went back to 7—that is, 7 letters (Ericsson, Chase, & Faloon, 1980).

This research on working memory is fairly recent. Interest in expanding long-term memory has a longer history and is the focus of the rest of this section. We will look

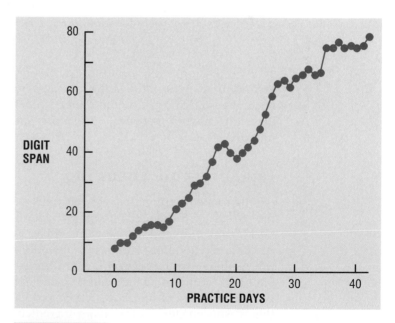

Number of Digits Recalled by S.F. *S.F. greatly increased his memory span for digits by devising a recoding system using chunking and hierarchical organization. Total practice time was about 215 hours. (After Ericsson, Chase, & Faloon, 1980)*

FRONTIERS OF PSYCHOLOGICAL RESEARCH

A Herbal Remedy for Memory Loss?

It has been called "the elixir of youth" and "memory mate." It has been found effective by both ancient healers and modern scientists. These days it is receiving a great deal of attention in the medical journals as well as the popular press.

This much-heralded substance is an extract from the ginkgo tree, an ornamental tree often planted along city streets. The Chinese have used ginkgo nuts for thousands of years to increase sexual energy and as a remedy for diseases ranging from venereal disease to cancer. Modern medical researchers have found evidence that ginkgo extract can be effective in treating a variety of ailments, including asthma, depression, impotence, and retinal damage. Perhaps most significant is the potential of gingko for the treatment of memory loss due to Alzheimer's disease, multi-infarct dementia (mini-strokes), and normal aging.

Much of the research on the health benefits of gingko extract has

been conducted in Europe, where herbal medicine is more accepted than in the United States. Laboratory studies have found that gingko extract improves brain functioning and prevents or treats circulatory disorders such as stroke. These benefits stem largely from ginkgo's effects on the blood: It thins blood viscosity and lowers platelet adhesiveness, thereby increasing blood flow to the brain and extremities; it also regulates blood vessel elasticity. Because of these effects, it can counteract some of the most common conditions associated with aging, particularly decreased blood flow to the brain, which can adversely affect memory, concentration, and intellectual ability.

Laboratory studies of the effects of ginkgo extract on memory are usually set up as double-blind studies in which some participants receive ginkgo extract while others receive a placebo. The results have shown small but significant positive effects of ginkgo extract on short-term memory, degenerative demen-

tia of the Alzheimer type, and multi-infarct dementia. One group of researchers concluded that ginkgo "was safe and appears capable of stabilizing and, in a substantial number of cases, improving the cognitive performance and the social functioning of demented patients for 6 months to 1 year" (Le Bars et al., 1997, p.1327).

Some experts warn against excessive enthusiasm for ginkgo extract. They note that it is beneficial in the *early* treatment of Alzheimer's disease and that it can cure dementia only when the condition is caused by lack of blood flow to the brain. Claims that ginkgo extract is an "elixir of youth" are clearly overstated. Others note that ginkgo extract has not been subjected to extensive clinical trials, nor has it received approval from the Food and Drug Administration. Nevertheless, the evidence from controlled research lends support to the ancient Chinese belief that ginkgo can increase health and longevity.

first at how material can be encoded to make it easier to retrieve and then consider how the act of retrieval itself can be improved.

Imagery and Encoding

We mentioned earlier that we can improve the recall of unrelated items by adding meaningful connections between them at the time of encoding, for these connections will facilitate later retrieval. Mental images have been found to be particularly useful for connecting pairs of unrelated items, and for this reason imagery is the major ingredient in many **mnemonic systems,** or *systems for aiding memory.*

A well-known mnemonic system is the *method of loci* (*loci* is the Latin word for "places"). This method works especially well with an ordered sequence of arbitrary items

FIGURE 8-13

A Mnemonic System   *The method of loci aids memory by associating items (here, entries on a shopping list) with an ordered sequence of places.*

such as unrelated words. The first step is to commit to memory an ordered sequence of places—such as the locations you would come upon during a slow walk through your house. You enter through the front door into a hallway, move next to the bookcase in the living room, then to the television in the living room, then to the curtains at the window, and so on. Once you can easily take this mental walk, you are ready to memorize as many unrelated words as there are locations on your walk. You form an image that relates the first word to the first location, another image that relates the second word to the second location, and so on. If the words are items on a shopping list—for example, "bread," "eggs," "beer," "milk," and "bacon"—you might imagine a slice of bread nailed to your front door, an egg hanging from the light cord in the hallway, a can of beer in the bookcase, a milk commercial playing on your television, and curtains made from giant strips of bacon (see Figure 8-13). Once you have memorized the items in this way, you can easily recall them in order by simply taking your mental walk again. Each location will retrieve an image, and each image will retrieve a word. The method clearly works and is a favorite

Caballo → eye → Horse

Pato → pot → Duck

FIGURE 8-14

Foreign Language Learning *Mental images can be used to associate spoken Spanish words with corresponding English words. Here, possible images for learning the Spanish words for "horse" and "duck" are illustrated.*

among people who perform memory feats professionally.

Imagery is also used in the *key-word method* for learning words in a foreign language. (See Table 8-3.) Suppose that you had to learn that the Spanish word *caballo* means "horse." The key-word method has two steps. The first is to find a part of the foreign word that sounds like an English word. Since caballo is pronounced, roughly, "cob-eye-yo," "eye" could serve as the key word. The next step is to form an image that connects the key word and the English equivalent—for example, a giant eye being kicked by a horse (see Figure 8-14). This should establish a meaningful connection between the Spanish and English words. To recall the meaning of *caballo,* you would first retrieve the key word "eye" and then the stored image that links it to "horse." The key-word method may sound complicated, but studies have shown that it is very helpful in learning the vocabulary of a foreign language (Atkinson, 1975; Pressley, Levin, & Delaney, 1982).

TABLE 8-3

The Key-Word Method *Examples of key words used to link Spanish words to their English translations. For example, when the Spanish word* muleta *is pronounced, part of it sounds like the English word "mule." Thus, "mule" could be used as the key word and linked to the English translation by forming an image of a mule standing erect on a crutch.*

Spanish	Key Word	English
caballo	(eye)	horse
charco	(charcoal)	puddle
muleta	(mule)	crutch
clavo	(claw)	nail
lagartija	(log)	lizard
payaso	(pie)	clown
hiio	(cel)	thread
tenaza	(tennis)	pliers
jabon	(bone)	soap
carpa	(carp)	tent
pato	(pot)	duck

Elaboration and Encoding

We have seen that the more we elaborate items, the more we can subsequently recall or recognize them. This phenomenon arises because the more connections we establish between items, the larger the number of retrieval possibilities. The practical implications of these findings are straightforward: If you want to remember a particular fact, expand on its meaning. To illustrate, suppose you read a newspaper article about an epidemic in Brooklyn that health officials are trying to contain. To expand on this, you could ask yourself questions about the causes and consequences of the epidemic: Was the disease carried by a person or by an animal? Was it transmitted through the water supply? To contain the epidemic, will officials go so far as to stop outsiders from visiting Brooklyn? How long is the epidemic likely to last? Questions about the causes and consequences of an event are especially effective because each question sets up a meaningful connection, or retrieval path, to the event.

Context and Retrieval

Since context is a powerful retrieval cue, we can improve our memory by restoring the context in which the learning took place. If your psychology class always meets in a particular room, your recall of the lecture material may be better when you are in that room than when you are in a different building because the context of the room serves as a cue for retrieving the lecture material. Most often, though, when we have to remember something we cannot physically return to the context in which we learned it. If you are having difficulty remembering the name of a high-school classmate, you are not about to go back to your high school just to recall it. However, you can try to re-create the context mentally. To retrieve the long forgotten name, you might think of different classes, clubs, and other activities that you participated in during high school to see whether any of these bring to mind the name you are seeking. When participants used these techniques in an actual experiment, they were often able to recall the names of high-school classmates that they were sure they had forgotten (Williams & Hollan, 1981).

Organization

We know that organization during encoding improves subsequent retrieval. This principle can be put to great practical use: We are capable of storing and retrieving a massive amount of information if we organize it appropriately.

Some experiments have investigated organizational devices that can be used to learn many unrelated items. In one study, participants memorized lists of unrelated words by organizing the words in each list into a story, as illustrated in Figure 8-15. When tested for 12 such lists (a total of 120 words), participants recalled more than 90% of the words. Control participants, who did not use an organizational strategy, recalled only about 10% of the words! The performance of the experimental participants appears to be a remarkable memory feat, but anyone armed with an organizational strategy can do it.

At this point you might concede that psychologists have devised some ingenious techniques for organizing lists of unrelated items. But, you argue, what you have to remember are not lists of unrelated items but stories you were told, lectures you have heard, and readings like the text of this chapter. Isn't this kind of material already organized, and doesn't this mean that the previously mentioned techniques are of limited value? Yes and no. Yes, this chapter is more than a list of unrelated sentences, but—and this is the essential point—there is always a problem of organization with any lengthy material. Later you may be able to recall that elaborating meaning aids learning, but this may not bring to mind anything about, for example, acoustic coding in short-term memory. The two topics do not seem to be intimately related, but there is a relationship between them: Both deal with encoding phenomena. The best way to see that relationship is to note the headings and subheadings in the chapter, because these show how the material in the chapter is organized.

An effective way to study is to keep this organization in mind. You might, for example, try to capture part of the chapter's organization by sketching a hierarchical tree like the one shown in Figure 8-16. You can use this hierarchy to guide your memory search whenever you have to retrieve information

FIGURE 8-15

Organizing Words Into a Story   *Three examples in which a list of 10 unrelated words is turned into a story. The capitalized items are the words on the list.* (After Bower & Clark, 1969)

HEDGE past a COLONY of DUCKs. He tripped on some FURNITURE, tearing his STOCKING while hastening toward the PILLOW where his MISTRESS lay.

A VEGETABLE can be a useful INSTRUMENT for a COLLEGE student. A carrot can be a NAIL for your FENCE or BASIN. But a MERCHANT of the QUEEN would SCALE that fence and feed the carrot to a GOAT.

One night at DINNER I had the NERVE to bring my TEACHER. There had been a FLOOD that day, and the rain BARREL was sure to RATTLE. There was, however, a VESSEL in the HARBOR carrying this ARTIST to my CASTLE.

about this chapter. It may be even more helpful, though, to make your own hierarchical outline of the chapter. Memory seems to benefit most when the organization is done by the person who needs to remember the material.

Practicing Retrieval

Another way to improve retrieval is to practice it—that is, to ask yourself questions about what you are trying to learn. Suppose that you have 2 hours in which to study an assignment that can be read in approxi-

mately 30 minutes. Reading and rereading the assignment four times is generally less effective than reading it once and asking yourself questions about it. You can then reread selected parts to clear up points that were difficult to retrieve the first time around, perhaps elaborating these points so that they become well connected to one another and to the rest of the assignment. Attempting retrieval is an efficient use of study time. This was demonstrated long ago by experiments using material similar to that actually learned in courses (see Figure 8-17).

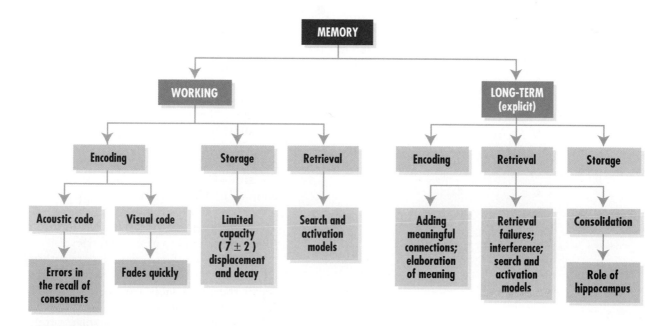

FIGURE 8-16

A Hierarchical Tree   *Creating hierarchical trees of chapters in textbooks can help students retrieve information about those chapters. This tree represents the organization of part of this chapter.*

A procedure akin to practicing retrieval may be useful in implicit memory situations. The procedure, referred to as *mental practice,* consists of imagining the rehearsal of a perceptual motor skill without actually moving any part of the body. For example, you might imagine yourself swinging at a tennis ball, making mental corrections when the imagined swing seems faulty, without moving your arm. Such mental practice can improve performance of the skill, particularly if the mental practice is interspersed with actual physical practice (Swets & Bjork, 1990).

The PQRST Method

One of the best-known techniques for improving memory is the *PQRST method.* It is designed to improve students' ability to study and remember material presented in a textbook (Thomas & Robinson, 1982). The method takes its name from the first letters of its five stages: Preview, Question, Read, Self-Recitation, and Test. We can illustrate the method by showing how it would apply to studying a chapter in this textbook.

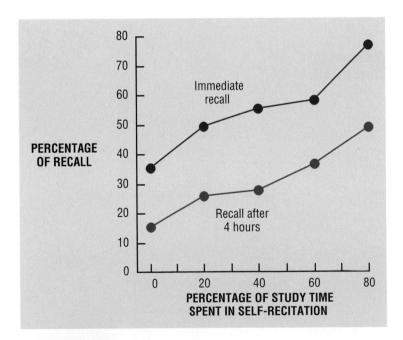

FIGURE 8-17

Practicing Retrieval   *Recall can be improved by spending a large proportion of study time attempting retrieval rather than silently studying. Results are shown for tests given immediately and four hours after completing study.* (After Gates, 1917)

In the first stage, students preview the material in the chapter to get an idea of its major topics and sections. Previewing involves reading the outline at the beginning of the chapter, skimming through the chapter while paying special attention to the headings of main sections and subsections, and carefully reading the summary at the end of the chapter. This kind of preview induces students to organize the chapter, perhaps even leading to the rudiments of a hierarchical organization like that discussed earlier. As we have repeatedly noted, organizing material increases the ability to retrieve it.

The second, third, and fourth stages (Question, Read, and Self-Recitation) apply to each major section of the chapter as it is encountered. In this book, for example, a chapter typically has five to eight major sections, and students would apply the Question, Read, and Self-Recitation stages to each section before going on to the next one. In the Question stage, students carefully read the section and subsection headings and turn these into questions. In the Read stage, students read the section with an eye toward answering those questions. And in the Self-Recitation stage, the reader tries to recall the main ideas in the section and recites the information (either mentally or, preferably, aloud). For example, if you were applying these stages to this section, you might look at the headings and make up questions like "How much can the short-term memory span be increased?" or "What exactly is the PQRST method?" Next you would read the section and try to answer your questions (for example, "One person was able to increase his short-term memory span to nearly 80 digits"). Then you would try to recall the main ideas (for example, "You can increase the size of a chunk but not the number of chunks"). The Question and Read stages induce students to elaborate the material while encoding it; the Self-Recitation stage induces students to practice retrieval.

The fifth, or Test, stage occurs after the entire chapter has been read. Students try to recall the main facts from what they have read and to understand how those facts relate to one another. This stage prompts elaboration and offers further practice at retrieval. In sum, the PQRST method relies on three basic principles for improving memory: organizing the material, elaborating the material, and practicing retrieval. (For a more in-depth description of the method, see "A Word to the Student," which appears just before Chapter 1.)

Constructive Memory

In earlier chapters we distinguished between bottom-up and top-down processes; bottom-up processes are driven by the input, whereas top-down processes are driven by the person's prior knowledge and expectancies. This distinction can be applied to memory as well. Bottom-up processes work only on the input information, the actual items that have to be remembered, whereas top-down processes bring other knowledge to bear on the task. Most of the material we have covered in this chapter deals with bottom-up processes. In this final section, however, we consider top-down processes, which add information to the input and result in **constructive memory,** or *memory that is constructed from inferences as well as input information.*

When we hear a sentence or story, we often take it as an incomplete description of a real event and use our general knowledge about how the world works to construct a more detailed description of the event. How do we do this? By adding to the input sentences statements that are likely to follow from them. For example, upon hearing "Mike broke the bottle in a barroom brawl," we are likely to infer that it was a beer or whiskey bottle, not a milk or soda bottle. We add this inference to our memory of the sentence itself. Our total memory therefore goes beyond the original information given. We fill in the original information by using our general knowledge about what goes with what (for example, that beer bottles go with bars). We do this because we are trying to explain to ourselves the events we are hearing about. Constructive memory thus is a by-product of our need to understand the world. Many, if not most, real-life memory situations are constructive ones.

Simple Inferences

Often when we read a sentence we draw inferences from it and store them along with the sentence. This tendency is particularly strong when reading text because inferences are often needed to connect different lines. To illustrate, consider the following story, which was presented to participants in an experiment.

1. Provo is a picturesque kingdom in France.
2. Corman was heir to the throne of Provo.
3. He was so tired of waiting.
4. He thought arsenic would work well.

When reading this story, participants draw inferences at certain points. At line 3, they infer that Corman wanted to be king, which permits them to connect line 3 to the preceding line. But this is not a necessary inference (Corman could have been waiting for the king to receive him). At line 4, participants infer that Corman had decided to poison the king, so they can connect this line to what preceded it. Again, the inference is not a necessary one (there are people other than the king to poison, and there are other uses of arsenic). When participants' memories were later tested for exactly which lines had been presented, they had trouble distinguishing the story lines from the inferences we just described. It is hard to keep what was actually presented separate from what we added to it (Seifert, Robertson, & Black, 1985).

Inferences can also affect memory for visual scenes. This point is strikingly illustrated in the following study. Participants were shown a film of a traffic accident and then asked questions about their memory of the accident. One question about the speed of the vehicles was asked in two different ways. Some participants were asked, "How fast were the cars going when they smashed into each other?" whereas others were asked, "How fast were the cars going when they hit each other?" Participants who were asked the "smashed" question might infer that the accident was a very destructive one, perhaps more destructive than they had actually remembered. These participants were likely to use this inference to alter their memory of the accident to make it more destructive (see Figure 8-17). Participants who were asked the "hit" question, however, should be less likely to do this, since "hit" implies a less severe accident than does "smashed."

In remembering what happened in a traffic accident, we may use general knowledge (such as our knowledge of rules of the road or of the meaning of traffic signals) to construct a more detailed memory.

This line of reasoning was supported by the results of a memory test administered a week later. In this test, participants were asked, "Did you see any broken glass?" There was no broken glass in the film of the accident, but participants who had been asked the "smashed" question were more likely to say that there had been glass than were participants who had been asked the "hit" question. The "smashed" question may have led to reconstruction of the memory for the accident, and the reconstructed memory contained details, such as broken glass, that were never actually part of the accident (Loftus, Schooler, & Wagenaar, 1985).

These results have important implications for eyewitness testimony: A question phrased in a particular way ("smashed" rather than "hit") can alter the witness's memory structures that an attorney is trying to probe. The results also have implications for the controversy about whether traumatic memories that are "recovered" many years later are true memories or reconstructions.

Stereotypes

Another means by which we fill in, or construct, memories is through the use of social stereotypes. A **stereotype** is *a set of infer-* *ences about the personality traits or physical attributes of a whole class of people.* We may, for example, have a stereotype of the typical German (intelligent, meticulous, serious) or of the typical Italian (artistic, carefree, fun loving). These descriptions rarely apply to many people in the class and can often be misleading guides for social interaction. Our concern here, however, is not with the effects of stereotypes on social interaction (see Chapter 18 for a discussion of this) but with their effects on memory.

When presented with information about a person, we sometimes stereotype that person (for example, "He's your typical Italian") and combine the information presented with that in our stereotype. Our memory of the person thus is partly constructed from the stereotype. To the extent that our stereotype does not fit the person, our recall can be seriously distorted. A British psychologist provides a firsthand account of such a distortion:

In the week beginning 23 October, I encountered in the university, a male student of very conspicuously Scandinavian appearance. I recall being very forcibly impressed by the man's nordic, Viking-like appearance—his fair hair, his blue eyes, and long bones. On several occasions, I recalled his appearance in connection with a Scandinavian correspondence

I was then conducting and thought of him as the "perfect Viking," visualizing him at the helm of a longship crossing the North Sea in quest of adventure. When I again saw the man on 23 November, I did not recognize him, and he had to introduce himself. It was not that I had forgotten what he looked like but that his appearance, as I recalled it, had become grossly distorted. He was very different from my recollection of him. His hair was darker, his eyes less blue, his build less muscular, and he was wearing spectacles (as he always does). (Hunter, 1974, pp. 265–66)

The psychologist's stereotype of Scandinavians seems to have so overwhelmed any information he actually encoded about the student's appearance that the result was a highly constructed memory. It bore so little resemblance to the student that it could not even serve as a basis for recognition.

Schemas

Psychologists use the term **schema** to refer to *a mental representation of a class of people, objects, events, or situations.* Stereotypes are a kind of schema because they represent classes of people (for example, Italians, women, athletes). Schemas can also be used to describe our knowledge about how to act in certain situations. For example, most adults have a schema for how to eat in a restaurant (enter the restaurant, find a table, get a menu from the waiter, order food, and so on). Perceiving and thinking in terms of schemas enables us to process large amounts of information swiftly and economically. Instead of having to perceive and remember all the details of each new person, object, or event we encounter, we can simply note that it is like a schema already in our memory and encode and remember only its most distinctive features. The price we pay for such "cognitive economy," however, is that an object or event can be distorted if the schema used to encode it does not fit well.

Bartlett (1932) was perhaps the first psychologist to systematically study the effects of schemas on memory. He suggested that

The stereotype of the "typical jock" may interfere with our encoding of information about these college students, who could have entirely different characteristics from those included in the stereotype.

memory distortions much like those that occur when we fit people into stereotypes can occur when we attempt to fit stories into schemas. Research has confirmed Bartlett's suggestion. For example, after reading a brief story about a character going to a restaurant, people are likely to recall statements about the character eating and paying for a meal even though those actions were never mentioned in the story (Bower, Black, & Turner, 1979).

Situations in which memory is driven by schemas seem a far cry from the simpler situations discussed earlier in the chapter. Consider, for example, memory for a list of unrelated words: Here memory processes appear more bottom-up; that is, they function more to preserve the input than to construct something new. However, there is a constructive aspect even to this simple situation, for techniques such as using imagery add meaning to the input. Similarly, when we read a paragraph about a schema-based activity we must still preserve some of its specifics if we are to recall it correctly. Thus, the two aspects of memory—to preserve and to construct—may always be present, although their relative emphasis may depend on the exact situation.

Repressed Memories—A Dangerous Belief?

Elizabeth F. Loftus, *University of Washington*

In a land transformed by science, pseudoscientific beliefs live on. It was a set of wild, wacky, and dangerous beliefs that led to serious problems for Nadean Cool, a 44-year-old nurse's aide in Appleton, Wisconsin. Nadean had sought therapy in late 1986 to help her cope with her reaction to a traumatic event that her daughter had experienced. During therapy, her psychiatrist used hypnosis and other methods to dig out allegedly buried memories of abuse. In the process his patient became convinced that she had repressed memories of being in a satanic cult, of eating babies, of being raped, of having sex with animals, of being forced to watch the murder of her 8-year-old friend. She came to believe that she had over 120 separate personalities—children, adults, angels, and even a duck—all because, she was told, she had experienced such severe childhood sexual and physical abuse. In addition to hypnosis and other suggestive techniques, the psychiatrist also performed exorcisms on Nadean, one of which lasted five hours, replete with the sprinkling of holy water and screams for Satan to leave Nadean's body. When Nadean came to realize that false memories had been planted, she sued for malpractice; her case settled, mid-trial, in early 1997, for $2.4 million dollars (see Loftus, 1997 for more cases like Nadean's).

Hundreds of people, mostly women, have developed memories in therapy of extensive brutalization that they claimed they repressed, and they later retracted these. How do we know that the abuse memories aren't real and the retractions false? One clue is that the women would sometimes develop memories that were psychologically or biologically impossible, such as detailed memories of abuse occurring at the age of 3 months or memories of being forced to abort a baby by coat hanger when physical evidence confirmed virginity.

How is it possible for people to develop such elaborate and confident false memories? In the early 1970s, when I began to do studies on the "misinformation effect." When people witness an event and are later exposed to new and misleading information about that event, their recollections often become distorted. The misinformation invades us, like a Trojan horse, precisely because we do not detect its influence.

Later studies showed that suggestive information not only can alter the details of a recent experience, but also can plant entirely false beliefs and memories in the minds of people (Loftus & Pickrell, 1995; Hyman et al., 1995; Porter, 1998). In some studies as many as half the individuals who underwent suggestive interviewing came to develop either full or partial false childhood memories. Hypnotic interventions have been particularly successful ways of feeding people suggestive material and getting them to accept it (e.g., Orne et al., 1984). Inducing people to briefly imagine that something occurred to them in childhood can increase people's belief that something similar to the imagined experience happened to them (Garry, Manning, Loftus, & Sherman, 1996).

It might be tempting to dismiss these studies because they are so unlike the therapy world. However, some recent efforts have taken great pains to mimic a therapy environment (Mazzoni & Loftus, 1998). In this research subjects reported on their very early childhood experiences on two separate occasions. In between, some subjects underwent dream interpretation with a clinical psychologist. Regardless of the content of the dream, the clinician suggestively interpreted their dream to mean that they had had a particular experience before age 3 (e.g., lost for an extended time in a public place, faced a great danger to their lives). Weeks later when subjects were again questioned about their childhoods, most of them had become more confident that they had been lost or had faced a great danger. Their confidence was sometimes quite high, even though they had initially denied having the experience, and even though it would be relatively unlikely that they would have concrete, detailed episodic memories for experiences that actually had happened to them this early in life (cf. childhood amnesia).

Of course, simply because we can plant false childhood memories in subjects in no way implies that memories that arise after suggestion, or imagination, or dream interpretation are all necessarily false. In no way does this invalidate the experiences of the many thousands of individuals who have truly been abused and are later in life reminded of the experience. We do need to keep in mind, however, that without corroboration, there is little that even the most experienced evaluator can use to differentiate the true memories from those suggestively planted. Apart from bearing on the controversy about repressed memories that has plagued our society for more than a decade, the modern research does reveal important ways in which our memories are malleable, and it reveals much about the rather flimsy curtain that sometimes separates memory and imagination.

Recovered Memories or False Memories?

by Kathy Pezdek, *Claremont Graduate University*

In recent years, a number of critical questions have been raised regarding the credibility of adults' memory for their childhood experiences. At the heart of these claims is the view that it is relatively easy to plant memories for events that did not occur.

Let me say up front that surely there have been some false memories for incest, and surely some therapeutic techniques are more likely to foster false memories than others. Further, it is surely possible to find some individuals who are so highly suggestible that one could readily get them to believe anything. However, the claim by those who promote the suggestibility explanation for recovered memories assumes an extremely strong construct of memory suggestibility. The truth is that the cognitive research on the suggestibility of memory simply does not support the existence of a suggestibility construct that is sufficiently robust to explain this phenomenon.

How do cognitive psychologists study the suggestibility of memory? This text refers to an experiment by Loftus, Schooler, & Wagenaar (1985) in which participants were more likely to think that they saw broken glass in the film of a traffic accident (broken glass was not present in the film) if they had been asked a previous question that included the word *smashed* rather than *hit*. This finding is real, but it involves an insignificant detail of an insignificant event, and even so, across a number of studies using this paradigm, the difference in the rate of responding positively to the question about the broken glass, for example, in the control (*hit*) versus the misled (*smashed*) condition is typically only 20%–30%. Thus, although this suggestibility effect is a real one, it is neither large nor robust.

What evidence supports the conclusion that a memory can be planted for an event that never occurred? The most frequently cited study in this regard is the "lost in the mall" study by Loftus and Pickrell, 1995. These researchers had 24 volunteers suggest to offspring or younger siblings that they had been lost in a shopping mall as a child. Six of the 24 participants reported full or partial memory of the false event. However, these results would not be expected to generalize to the situation of having a therapist plant a false memory for incest. Being lost while shopping is not such a remarkable memory implant. Children are often warned about the dangers of getting lost, have fears about getting lost, are commonly read classic tales about children who get lost (e.g., Hansel and Gretel, Pinocchio), and, in fact, do get lost, if only for a few frightening minutes. Therefore, it would be expected that most children would have a pre-existing script for getting lost that would be accessed by the suggestion of a particular instance of getting lost in the Loftus study. In sharp contrast, it is hardly likely that most children would have a pre-existing script for incestuous sexual contact.

My graduate students and I recently conducted a study to test whether Loftus's findings regarding planting a false memory generalize to less plausible events (Pezdek, Finger, & Hodge, 1997). In this study, 20 volunteers read descriptions of one true event and two false events to a younger sibling or close relative. The plausible false event described the relative being lost in a mall while shopping; the implausible false event described the relative receiving a rectal enema. After being read each event, participants were asked what they remembered about the event. Only three of the false events were "remembered" by any of the participants, and all were the plausible event regarding being lost in the mall. No one believed the implausible false event. Implausible events such as parent-child intercourse or receiving an enema are simply unlikely to be suggestively planted in memory because children do not have pre-existing scripts for these events.

Kathy Pezdek

At a broader level, it is also important to consider that although the "false memory debate" most often concerns reported memories for childhood sexual abuse, this is only one of the many sources of psychogenic amnesia for which memory recovery has been reported. It is well documented that combat exposure and other violent events can produce psychogenic amnesia (for a review, see Arrigo & Pezdek, 1997). Those who doubt the reality of repressed memory for sexual abuse need to explain psychogenic amnesia for these other types of trauma as well.

In conclusion, cognitive research offers no support for the claim that implausible false events such as childhood sexual abuse are easily planted in memory. Although there are some techniques that can be used to suggestively plant bizarre false memories in some highly suggestive individuals, there is no evidence that this is a widespread phenomenon.

SUMMARY

1. There are three stages of memory: encoding, storage, and retrieval. Encoding refers to the transformation of information into the kind of code or representation that memory can accept; storage refers to retention of the encoded information; and retrieval refers to the process by which information is recovered from memory. The three stages may operate differently in situations that require us to store material for a matter of seconds (working memory) and in situations that require us to store material for longer intervals (long-term memory). Moreover, different long-term memory systems seem to be involved in storing facts, which are part of explicit memory, and skills, which are part of implicit memory.

2. There is increasing biological evidence for these distinctions. Recent brain-scanning studies of long-term memory indicate that most of the brain regions activated during encoding are in the left hemisphere and that most of the regions activated during retrieval are in the right hemisphere. Evidence from both animal studies and studies of humans with brain damage indicates that different brain regions may mediate working memory and long-term memory. In particular, in both humans and other mammals, damage to the hippocampal system impairs performance on long-term memory tasks but not on working memory tasks.

3. Information in working memory tends to be encoded acoustically, although we can also use a visual code. The most striking fact about working memory is that its storage capacity is limited to 7 ± 2 items, or chunks. While we are limited in the number of chunks we can remember, we can increase the size of a chunk by using information in long-term memory to recode incoming material into larger meaningful units. Information can be lost or forgotten from working memory. One cause of forgetting is that information decays with time; another is that new items displace old ones.

4. Retrieval slows down as the number of items in working memory increases. Some have taken this result to indicate that retrieval involves a search process, whereas others have interpreted the result in terms of an activation process.

5. Working memory is used in solving various kinds of problems, such as mental arithmetic, geometric analogies, and answering questions about text. However, working memory does not seem to be involved in the understanding of relatively simple sentences.

Working memory may also serve as a way station to permanent memory, in that information may reside in working memory while it is being encoded into long-term memory.

6. Information in long-term memory is usually encoded according to its meaning. If the items to be remembered are meaningful but the connections between them are not, memory can be improved by adding meaningful connections that provide retrieval paths. The more one elaborates the meaning of material, the better memory of that material will be.

7. Many cases of forgetting in long-term memory are due to retrieval failures (the information is there but cannot be found). Retrieval failures are more likely to occur when there is interference from items associated with the same retrieval cue. Such interference effects suggest that retrieval from long-term memory may be accomplished through a sequential search process or a spreading activation process.

8. Some forgetting from long-term memory is due to a loss from storage, particularly when there is a disruption of the processes that consolidate new memories. The biological locus of consolidation includes the hippocampus and surrounding cortex. Recent research suggests that consolidation takes a few weeks to be completed.

9. Retrieval failures in long-term memory are less likely when the items are organized during encoding and when the context at the time of retrieval is similar to the context at the time of encoding. Retrieval processes can also be disrupted by emotional factors. In some cases, anxious thoughts interfere with retrieval of the target memory; in others, the target memory may be actively blocked (repressed). In still other cases, emotion can enhance memory, as in flashbulb memories.

10. Explicit memory refers to the kind of memory manifested in recall or recognition, in which we consciously recollect the past. Implicit memory refers to the kind of memory that manifests itself as an improvement on some perceptual, motor, or cognitive task, with no conscious recollection of the experiences that led to the improvement. While explicit memory—particularly recall and recognition of facts—breaks down in amnesia, implicit memory is usually spared. This suggests that there may be separate storage systems for explicit and implicit memory.

11. Research with normal individuals also suggests that there may be separate systems for explicit and implicit memory. Much of this research has relied on a measure of implicit memory called priming (for example, the extent to which prior exposure to a list of words later facilitates completing stems of these words). Some studies reveal that an independent variable that affects explicit memory (amount of elaboration during encoding) has no effect on priming, while other studies show that a variable that affects implicit memory has no effect on explicit memory. Brain-scanning studies with normal individuals show that explicit memory is accompanied by increased neural activity in certain regions whereas implicit memory is accompanied by a decrease in neural activity in critical regions.

12. Although we cannot increase the capacity of working memory, we can use recoding schemes to enlarge the size of a chunk and thereby increase the memory span. Long-term memory for facts can be improved at the encoding and retrieval stages. One way to improve encoding and retrieval is to use imagery, which is the basic principle underlying mnemonic systems such as the method of loci and the key-word method.

13. Other ways to improve encoding (and subsequent retrieval) are to elaborate the meaning of the items and to organize the material during encoding (hierarchical organization seems preferable). The best ways to improve retrieval are to attempt to restore the encoding context at the time of retrieval and to practice retrieving information while learning it. Most of these principles for improving encoding and retrieval are incorporated into the PQRST method, whose five stages are Preview, Question, Read, Self-Recitation, and Test.

14. Memory for complex materials, such as stories, is often constructive. We tend to use our general knowledge of the world to construct a more elaborate memory of a story or event. Construction can involve adding simple inferences to the material presented; it can also involve fitting the material into stereotypes and other kinds of schemas (mental representations of classes of people, objects, events, or situations).

KEY TERMS

encoding (p. 268)
storage (p. 268)
retrieval (p. 268)
iconic memory (p. 269)
working memory (p. 270)
memory span (p. 273)
chunking (p. 273)
rehearsal (p. 276)
long-term memory (p. 276)
flashbulb memory (p. 284)
amnesia (p. 286)
mnemonic system (p. 292)

constructive memory (p. 297)
stereotype (p. 298)
schema (p. 299)

CRITICAL THINKING QUESTIONS

1. How might an increase in the size of your working memory affect your performance on a standardized test of comprehension like the SAT? Try to explain how underlying comprehension processes might be affected.

2. We reviewed various proposals about how emotion affects explicit long-term memory. Some of these proposals imply that emotion helps memory, whereas others suggest that emotion hurts memory. How can you reconcile these apparent differences?

3. On the basis of what you have learned about explicit long-term memory, how would you go about studying for an exam that emphasizes factual recall?

4. We noted that childhood amnesia is related to the development of the hippocampus. What psychological factors might also contribute to childhood amnesia? (Think of things that change dramatically around age 3.)

FURTHER READING

There are several recent introductory books on memory and cognition that are readable and up-to-date: Baddeley, *Human Memory* (1990); Anderson, *Cognitive Psychology and Its Implications* (3rd ed., 1990), Barsalou, *Cognitive Psychology for Cognitive Scientists* (1992); Medin and Ross, *Cognitive Psychology* (1992); Haberlandt, *Cognitive Psychology (1993);* and Best, *Cognitive Psychology* (1992). In addition to these textbooks, Neisser (ed.), *Memory Observed* (1982), provides a survey of remembering in natural contexts.

For an advanced treatment of theoretical issues in memory, see Anderson, *The Architecture of Cognition* (1983); Tulving, *Elements of Episodic Memory* (1983); the second volume of Atkinson, Herrnstein, Lindzey, and Luce (eds.), *Stevens' Handbook of Experimental Psychology* (2nd ed., 1988); and Baddeley, *Working Memory* (1986).

For a review of research on the biological bases of memory and learning, see Squire and Butters (eds.), *The Neuropsychology of Memory* (1984); and Squire, *Memory and Brain* (1987).

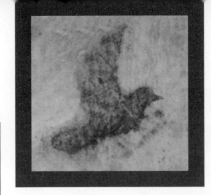

Chapter 9
Language and Thought

*T*he greatest accomplishments of our species stem from our ability to entertain complex thoughts, to communicate them, and to act on them. Thinking includes a wide range of mental activities. We think when we try to solve a problem that has been presented to us in class; we think when we daydream while waiting for a class to begin. We think when we decide what groceries to buy, plan a vacation, write a letter, or worry about a troubled relationship.

We begin this chapter with a discussion of language, the means by which thoughts are communicated. Then we consider the development or acquisition of language. The remaining sections of this chapter discuss major topics in propositional thinking. We begin by focusing on concepts, which are the building blocks of thought, and discuss their use in classifying objects; this is the study of concepts and categorization. Then we consider how thoughts are organized in order to arrive at a conclusion; this is the study of reasoning. Next we turn to the imaginal mode of thought, and in the final section we discuss thought in action—the study of problem solving—and consider the uses of both propositional and imaginal thought.

Language and Communication

Language is our primary means of communicating thought. Moreover, it is universal: Every human society has a language, and every human being of normal intelligence acquires his or her native language and uses it effortlessly. The naturalness of language sometimes lulls us into thinking that language use requires no special explanation. Nothing could be further from the truth. Some people can read, and others cannot; some can do arithmetic, and others cannot; some can play chess, and others cannot. But virtually everyone can master and use an enormously complex linguistic system. Why this should be so is among the fundamental puzzles of human psychology.

Levels of Language

Language use has two aspects: **production** and **comprehension.** In producing language, we start with a thought, somehow translate it into a sentence, and end up with sounds that express the sentence. In comprehending language, we start by hearing sounds, attach meanings to the sounds in the form of words, combine the words to create a sentence, and then somehow extract meaning from it. (For a discussion of brain regions involved in production and comprehension, see the Frontiers of Psychological Research feature on p. 308.) Thus, language use seems to involve moving through various levels, as shown in Figure 9-1. At the highest level are sentence units, including sentences and phrases. The next level is that of words and parts of words that carry meaning (the prefix "non" or the suffix "er," for example). The lowest level contains speech sounds. The adjacent levels are closely related: The

> **SENTENCE UNITS**
>
> **WORDS, PREFIXES, AND SUFFIXES**
>
> **SPEECH SOUNDS**

FIGURE 9-1

Levels of Language *At the highest level are sentence units, including phrases and sentences. The next level is that of words and parts of words that carry meaning. The lowest level contains speech sounds.*

phrases of a sentence are built from words and prefixes and suffixes, which in turn are constructed from speech sounds. Language therefore is a multilevel system for relating thoughts to speech by means of word and sentence units (Chomsky, 1965).

There are striking differences in the number of units at each level. All languages have only a limited number of speech sounds; English has about 40 of them. But rules for combining these sounds make it possible to produce and understand thousands of words (a vocabulary of 40,000 words is not unusual for an adult). Similarly, rules for combining words make it possible to produce and understand millions of sentences (if not an infinite number of them). Thus, two of the basic properties of language are that it is structured at multiple levels and that it is productive: Rules allow us to combine units at one level into a vastly greater number of units at the next level. Every human language has these two properties.

Language Units and Processes

Let us now consider the units and processes involved at each level of language. In surveying the relevant material, we usually take the perspective of a person comprehending language, a listener, though occasionally we switch to that of a language producer, or speaker.

Speech Sounds If you could attend to just the sounds someone makes when talking to you, what would you hear? You would not perceive the person's speech as a continuous stream of sound, but rather as a sequence of

phonemes, or *discrete speech categories.* For example, the sound corresponding to the first letter in "boy" is an instance of a phoneme symbolized as /b/. (Note that while phonemes may correspond to letters, they are speech sounds, not letters.) In English we divide all speech sounds into about 40 phonemes.

We are good at discriminating among different sounds that correspond to different phonemes in our language, but poor at discriminating among different sounds that correspond to the same phoneme. Consider, for example, the sound of the first letter in "pin" and the sound of the second letter in "spin" (Liberman, Cooper, Shankweiler, & Studdert-Kennedy, 1967); they are the same phoneme, /p/, and they sound the same to us even though they have different physical characteristics. The /p/ in "pin" is accompanied by a puff of air, but the /p/ in "spin" is not (try holding your hand a short distance from your mouth as you say the two words). Thus, our phonemic categories act as filters in that they convert a continuous stream of speech into a sequence of familiar phonemes.

Every language has a different set of phonemes, which is one reason why we often have difficulty learning to pronounce foreign words. Another language may use phonemes that do not appear in ours. It may take us a while even to hear the new phonemes, let alone produce them. For example, in Hindi the two different /p/ sounds just described correspond to two different phonemes. Another language may not make a distinction between two sounds that our language treats as two phonemes. For example, in Japanese the English sounds corresponding to "r" and "l" (/r/ and /l/) are perceived as the same phoneme—hence the frequent confusion between words like "rice" and "lice."

When phonemes are combined in the right way, we perceive them as words. Each language has its own rules about which phonemes can follow others. In English, for example, /b/ cannot follow /p/ at the beginning of a word (try pronouncing "pbet"). The influence of such rules is revealed when we listen. We are more accurate in perceiving a string of phonemes whose order conforms to the rules of our language than a string whose order violates these rules. The influence of these rules is even more striking when we take the perspective of a speaker. For example, we have no difficulty pronouncing the plurals of nonsense words that we have never heard before. Consider "zuk" and "zug." In accordance with a simple rule, the plural of "zuk" is formed by adding the phoneme /s/, as in "hiss." In English, however, /s/ cannot follow "g" at the end of a word, so to form the plural of "zug" we must use another rule—one that adds the phoneme /z/, as in "fuzz." We may not be aware of these differences in forming plurals, but we have no difficulty producing them. It is as if we "know" the rules for combining phonemes even though we are not consciously aware of the rules: We conform to rules that we cannot verbalize.

Word Units What we typically perceive when listening to speech are not phonemes but words. Unlike phonemes, **words** are *units of speech that carry meaning.* However, they are not the only smallish linguistic units that convey meaning. Suffixes such as "ly," or prefixes such as "un," also carry meaning; they can be added on to words to form more complex ones with different meanings, as when "un" and "ly" are added on to "time" to form "untimely." The term **morpheme** is used to refer to *any small linguistic unit that carries meaning.*

Most morphemes are themselves words. Most words denote some specific content, such as "house" or "run." A few words, however, primarily serve to make sentences grammatical; such grammatical words, or grammatical morphemes, include what are commonly referred to as articles and prepositions, such as "a," "the," "in," "of," "on," and "at." Some prefixes and suffixes also play primarily a grammatical role. These grammatical morphemes include the suffixes "ing" and "ed."

Grammatical morphemes may be processed differently than content words. One piece of evidence for this is that there are forms of brain damage in which the use of grammatical morphemes is impaired more than the use of content words (Zurif, 1990). Also, as we will see later, grammatical morphemes are acquired in a different way than content words.

The most important aspect of a word is, of course, its meaning. A word can be viewed

FRONTIERS OF PSYCHOLOGICAL RESEARCH

Localization of Language in the Brain

Recall from Chapter 2 that there are two regions of the left hemisphere of the cortex that are critical for language: Broca's area, which lies in the frontal lobes, and Wernicke's area, which lies in the temporal region. Damage to either of these areas leads to specific kinds of aphasia.

The disrupted language of a patient with Broca's aphasia is illustrated by the following interview, in which "E" designates the interviewer and "P," the patient:

E: Were you in the Coast Guard?

P: No, er, yes, yes . . . ship . . . Massachu . . . chusetts . . . Coast Guard . . . years. [Raises hands twice with fingers indicating "19"]

E: Oh, you were in the Coast Guard for 19 years.

P: Oh . . . boy . . . right . . . right.

E: Why are you in the hospital?

P: [Points to paralyzed arm] Arm no good. [Points to mouth] Speech . . . can't say . . . talk, you see.

E: What happened to make you lose your speech?

P: Head, fall, Jesus Christ, me no good, str, str . . . oh Jesus . . . stroke.

E: Could you tell me what you've been doing in the hospital?

P: Yes sure. Me go, er, uh, P. T. nine o'cot, speech . . . two times . . . read . . . wr . . . ripe, er, rike, er, write . . . practice . . . get-ting better. (Gardner, 1975, p. 61)

The speech is very disfluent (halting and hesitant). Even in simple sentences, pauses and hesitations are plentiful. This is in contrast to the fluent speech of a patient with Wernicke's aphasia:

Boy, I'm sweating, I'm awful nervous, you know, once in a while I get caught up. I can't mention the tarripoi, a month ago, quite a little, I've done a lot well, I impose a lot, while, on the other hand, you know what I mean, I have to run around, look it over, trebin and all that sort of stuff. (Gardner, 1975, p. 68)

In addition to fluency, there are other marked differences between Broca's and Wernicke's aphasias. The speech of a Broca's aphasic consists mainly of content words. It contains few grammatical morphemes and complex sentences and, in general, has a telegraphic quality that is reminiscent of the two-word stage of language acquisition. In contrast, the language of a Wernicke's aphasic preserves syntax but is remarkably devoid of content. There are clear problems in finding the right noun, and occa-

sionally words are invented for the occasion (as in the use of "tarripoi" and "trebin"). These observations suggest that Broca's aphasia involves a disruption at the syntactic stage, while Wernicke's aphasia involves a disruption at the level of words and concepts.

These characterizations of the two aphasias are supported by research findings. In a study that tested for a syntactic deficit, participants had to listen to a sentence on each trial and show that they understood it by selecting a picture (from a set) that the sentence described. Some sentences could be understood without using much syntactic knowledge. For example, given "The bicycle the boy is holding is broken," one can figure out that it is the bicycle that is broken and not the boy, solely from one's knowledge of the concepts involved. Understanding other sentences requires extensive syntactic analysis. In "The lion that the tiger is chasing is fat," one must rely on syntax (word order) to determine that it is the lion who is fat and not the tiger. On the sentences that did not require much syntactic analysis, Broca's aphasics did almost as well as normal participants, scoring close to 90% correct. But with sentences that required extensive analysis, Broca's aphasics fell to the level of guessing (for example, given the sentence about the lion

as the name of a concept; hence, its meaning is the concept it names. Some words are ambiguous because they name more than one concept. "Club," for example, names both a social organization and an object used for striking. Sometimes we may be aware of a word's ambiguity, as when hearing the sentence "He was interested in the club." In most cases, however, the sentence context makes the meaning of the word suf-

ficiently clear that we do not consciously experience any ambiguity—for example, "He wanted to join the club." Even in these cases, though, there is evidence that we unconsciously consider both meanings of the ambiguous word for a brief moment. In one experiment, a participant was presented a sentence such as "He wanted to join the club," followed immediately by a test word that the participant had to read aloud as

and tiger, they were as likely to select the picture with a fat tiger as the one with the fat lion). In contrast, the performance of Wernicke's aphasics did not depend on the syntactic demands of the sentence. Thus, Broca's aphasia, but not Wernicke's, seems to be partly a disruption of syntax (Caramazza & Zurif, 1976). The disruption is not total, though, in that Broca's aphasics are capable of handling certain kinds of syntactic analysis (Grodzinski, 1984).

Other experiments have tested for a conceptual deficit in Wernicke's aphasia. In one study, participants were presented with three words at a time and asked to select the two that were most similar in meaning. The words included animal terms, such as "dog" and "crocodile," as well as human terms, such as "mother" and "knight." Normal participants used the distinction between humans and animals as the major basis for their selections; given "dog," "crocodile," and "knight," for example, they selected the first two. Wernicke's patients, however, ignored this basic distinction. Although Broca's aphasics showed some differences from normals, their selections at least respected the human-animal distinction. A conceptual deficit thus is more pronounced in Wernicke's aphasics than in Broca's aphasics (Zurif et al., 1974).

In addition to Broca's and Wernicke's aphasias, there are numerous other kinds of aphasias (Benson, 1985). One of these is referred to as *conduction aphasia*. In this condition, the aphasic seems relatively normal in tests of both syntactic and conceptual abilities but has severe problems when asked to repeat a spoken sentence. A neurological explanation of this curious disorder is that while the brain structures mediating basic aspects of comprehension and production are intact, the neural connections between these structures are damaged. Hence, the patient can understand what is said because Wernicke's area is intact, and can produce fluent speech because Broca's area is intact, but cannot transmit what was understood to the speech center because the connecting links between the areas are damaged (Geschwind, 1972).

This research presupposes that each kind of aphasia is caused by damage to a specific area of the brain. This idea may be too simple; in reality, the particular region mediating a particular linguistic function may vary from one person to another. The best evidence for such individual differences comes from findings of neurosurgeons preparing to operate on patients with incurable epilepsy. The neurosurgeon needs to remove some brain tissue but first has to be sure that this tissue is not mediating a critical function such as language. Accordingly, prior to surgery and while the patient is awake, the neurosurgeon delivers small electric charges to the area in question and observes their effects on the patient's ability to name things. If electrical stimulation disrupts the patient's naming, the neurosurgeon knows to avoid this location during the operation.

These locations are of great interest to students of language. Within a single patient these language locations seem to be highly localized. A language location might be less than one centimeter in all directions from locations where electrical stimulations do not disrupt language. But—and this is the crucial point—different brain locations have to be stimulated to disrupt naming in different patients. For example, one patient's naming may be disrupted by electrical stimulation to locations in the front of the brain but not by stimulation in the back of the brain, whereas another patient might show a different pattern (Ojemann, 1983). If different areas of the brain mediate language in different people, presumably the areas associated with aphasias will also vary from one person to another.

quickly as possible. Participants read the test word faster if it was related to either meaning of "club" (for example, "group" or "struck") than if it was unrelated to either meaning (for example, "apple"). This suggests that both meanings of "club" were activated during comprehension of the sentence, and that either meaning could prime related words (Swinney, 1979; Tanenhaus, Leiman, & Seidenberg, 1979).

Sentence Units As listeners, we usually effortlessly combine words into sentence units, which include sentences as well as phrases. An important property of these units is that they can correspond to parts of a thought, or *proposition*. Such correspondences allow a listener to "extract" propositions from sentences.

To understand these correspondences, first you have to appreciate that any proposition can be divided into a subject and a predicate (a description). In the proposition "Audrey has curly hair," "Audrey" is the subject and "has curly hair" is the predicate. In the proposition "The tailor is asleep," "the tailor" is the subject and "is asleep" is the predicate. And in "Teachers work too hard," "teachers" is the subject and "work too hard" is the predicate. It turns out that any sentence can be broken into phrases in such a way that each phrase corresponds either to the subject or the predicate of a proposition or to an entire proposition. For example, intuitively we can divide the simple sentence "Irene sells insurance" into two phrases, "Irene" and "sells insurance." The first phrase, which is called a noun phrase because it centers on a noun, specifies the subject of an underlying proposition. The second phrase, a verb phrase, gives the predicate of the proposition. For a more complex example, consider the sentence "The serious scholar reads books." This sentence can be divided into two phrases, the noun phrase "serious scholar" and the verb phrase "reads books." The noun phrase expresses an entire proposition, "scholars are serious"; the verb phrase expresses part (the predicate) of another proposition, "scholars read books" (see Figure 9-2). Again, sentence units correspond closely to proposition units, which provides a link between language and thought.

Thus, when listening to a sentence, people seem to first divide it into noun phrases, verb phrases, and the like, and then extract propositions from these phrases. There is a good deal of evidence for our dividing sentences into phrases and treating the phrases as units, with some of the evidence coming from memory experiments. In one study, participants listened to sentences such as "The poor girl stole a warm coat." Immediately after each sentence was presented, participants were given a probe word from the sentence and asked to say the word that came after it. People responded faster when the probe and the response words came from the same phrase ("poor" and "girl") than when they came from different phrases ("girl" and "stole"). Thus, each phrase acts as a unit in memory. When the probe and response are from the same phrase, only one unit needs to be retrieved (Wilkes & Kennedy, 1969).

Analyzing a sentence into noun and verb phrases, and then dividing these phrases into smaller units like nouns, adjectives, and verbs, is called *syntactic analysis* (**syntax** deals with *the relationships between words in phrases and sentences*). In the course of understanding a sentence we usually perform such an analysis effortlessly and unconsciously. Sometimes, however, our syntactic analysis goes awry and we become aware of the process. Consider the sentence, "The horse raced past the barn fell." Many people have difficulty understanding this sentence. Why? Because on first reading, we assume that "The horse" is the noun phrase and "raced past the barn" is the verb phrase, which leaves us with no place for the word "fell." To understand the sentence correctly, we have to repartition it so that the entire phrase "The horse raced past the barn" is the noun phrase and "fell" is the verb phrase

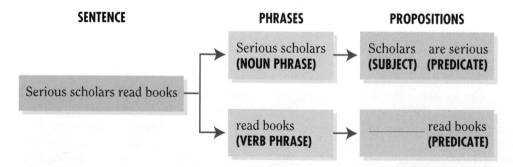

SENTENCE   PHRASES   PROPOSITIONS

Serious scholars read books → Serious scholars **(NOUN PHRASE)** → Scholars **(SUBJECT)**   are serious **(PREDICATE)**

→ read books **(VERB PHRASE)** → _____   read books **(PREDICATE)**

FIGURE 9-2

Phrases and Propositions   *The first step in extracting the propositions from a complex sentence is to decompose the sentence into phrases. This decomposition is based on rules like "Any sentence can be divided into a noun phrase and a verb phrase."*

(that is, the sentence is a shortened version of "The horse who was raced past the barn fell") (Garrett, 1990).

Effects of Context on Comprehension and Production

Figure 9-3 presents an amended version of our levels description of language. It suggests that producing a sentence is the inverse of understanding a sentence.

To understand a sentence, we hear phonemes, use them to construct the morphemes and phrases of the sentence, and finally extract the proposition from the sentence unit. We work from the bottom up. To produce a sentence, we move in the opposite direction: We start with a propositional thought, translate it into the phrases and morphemes of a sentence, and finally translate these morphemes into phonemes.

Although this analysis describes some of what occurs in sentence understanding and production, it is oversimplified because it does not consider the *context* in which language processing occurs. Often the context makes what is about to be said predictable. After comprehending just a few words, we jump to conclusions about what we think the entire sentence means (the propositions behind it), and then use our guess about the propositions to help understand the rest of

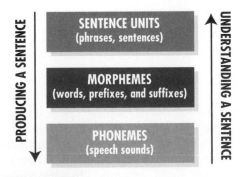

FIGURE 9-3

Levels of Understanding and Producing Sentences
In producing a sentence, we translate a propositional thought into the phrases and morphemes of a sentence and translate these morphemes into phonemes. In understanding a sentence, we go in the opposite direction—we use phonemes to construct the morphemes and phrases of a sentence and from these units extract the underlying propositions.

the sentence. In such cases, understanding proceeds from the highest level down as well as from the lowest level up (Adams & Collins, 1979).

Indeed, there are cases in which language understanding is nearly impossible without some context. To illustrate, try reading the following paragraph:

> The procedure is actually quite simple. First you arrange things into different groups. Of course, one pile may be sufficient, depending on how much there is to do. If you have to go somewhere else due to lack of facilities, that is the next step; otherwise you are pretty well set. It is important not to overdo things. That is, it is better to do too few things at once than too many. In the short run this may not seem important, but complications can easily arise. A mistake can be expensive as well. At first the whole procedure will seem complicated. Soon, however, it will become just another facet of life. (After Bransford & Johnson, 1973)

In reading the paragraph, you no doubt had difficulty understanding exactly what it was about. But given the context of "washing clothes," you can now use your knowledge about washing clothes to interpret all the cryptic parts of the passage. The "procedure" referred to in the first sentence is that of "washing clothes"; the "things" referred to in the first sentence are "clothes"; the "different groups" are "groups of clothing of different colors"; and so on. Your understanding of the paragraph, if you reread it, should now be excellent.

Perhaps the most salient part of the context, though, is the other person (or persons) we are communicating with. In understanding a sentence, it is not enough to understand its phonemes, morphemes, and phrases; we must also understand the speaker's intention in uttering that particular sentence. For example, when someone at dinner asks you, "Can you pass the potatoes?" you usually assume that the speaker's intention was not to find out whether you are physically capable of lifting the potatoes but, rather, to induce you to actually pass the potatoes. However, had your arm been in a sling, given the identical question you might assume that the speaker's intention was to determine your physical capability. In both cases the sentence (and proposition) is the same; what changes is the speaker's intention

Language production depends on context. You would probably use different language when giving directions to a group of tourists than when telling a neighbor where a particular restaurant or store is located

in uttering that sentence (Grice, 1975). There is abundant evidence that people determine the speaker's intention as part of the process of comprehension (Clark, 1984).

There are similar effects in the production of language. If someone asks you, "Where is the Empire State Building?" you will say different things depending on the physical context and the assumptions you make about the questioner. If the question is asked of you in Detroit, for example, you might answer "In New York"; if the question is asked in Brooklyn, you might say "Near Midtown Manhattan"; and if the question is asked in Manhattan, you might say "On 34th Street." In speaking, as in understanding, one must determine how the utterance fits the context.

The Development of Language

Our discussion of language should indicate the immensity of the task confronting children. They must master all levels of language—not only the proper speech sounds

but also how those sounds are combined into thousands of words and how those words can be combined into sentences to express thoughts. It is a wonder that virtually all children in all cultures accomplish so much of this in a mere 4 to 5 years. We will first discuss what is acquired at each level of language and then consider how it is acquired—specifically, the roles played by learning and innate factors.

What Is Acquired?

Development occurs at all three levels of language. It starts at the level of phonemes, proceeds to the level of words and other morphemes, and then moves on to the level of sentence units, or syntax. In what follows, we adopt a chronological perspective, tracing the child's development in both understanding and producing language.

Phonemes and Combinations of Phonemes Recall that adult listeners are good at discriminating among different sounds that correspond to *different* phonemes in their language, but poor at discriminating among different sounds that correspond to *the same* phoneme in their language. Remarkably, children come into the world able to discriminate among different sounds that correspond to different phonemes in any language. What changes over the first year of life is that infants learn which phonemes are relevant to their language and *lose* their ability to discriminate between sounds that correspond to the same phoneme in their language. (In essence, they lose the ability to make distinctions that will be of no use to them in understanding and producing their language.) These remarkable facts were determined through experiments in which infants were presented with pairs of sounds in succession while sucking on pacifiers. Since infants suck more in response to a novel stimulus than in response to a familiar one, their rate of sucking can be used to tell whether they perceive two successive sounds as the same or different. Six-month-old infants increase their rate of sucking when the successive sounds correspond to different phonemes in any language, whereas 1-year-olds increase their rate of sucking only when the successive sounds correspond to different phonemes in their own language. Thus, a 6-month-old Japanese child can distinguish /l/ from /r/ but loses this ability by the end of the first year of life (Eimas, 1985).

While children learn which phonemes are relevant during their first year of life, it takes several years for them to learn how phonemes can be combined to form words. When children first begin to talk, they occasionally produce "impossible" words like "dlumber" for "lumber." They do not yet know that in English /l/ cannot follow /d/ at the beginning of a word. By age 4, however, children have learned most of what they need to know about phoneme combinations.

Words and Concepts At about 1 year of age children begin to speak. One-year-olds already have concepts for many things (including family members, household pets, food, toys, and body parts), and when they begin to speak, they are mapping these concepts onto words that adults use. The beginning vocabulary is roughly the same for all children. Children 1 to 2 years old talk mainly about people ("Dada," "Mama," "baby"), animals ("dog," "cat," "duck"), vehicles ("car," "truck," "boat"), toys ("ball,"

"block," "book"), food ("juice," "milk," "cookie"), body parts ("eye," "nose," "mouth"), and household implements ("hat," "sock," "spoon").

While these words name some of the young child's concepts, they by no means name them all. Consequently, young children often have a gap between the concepts they want to communicate and the words they have at their disposal. To bridge this gap, children aged 1 to 2½ years old **overextend** their words; that is, they *apply words to neighboring concepts.* For example, a 2-year-old child might use the word "doggie" for cats and cows as well as dogs. (The child is not unsure of the word's meaning—if presented with pictures of various animals and asked to pick the "doggie," the child makes the correct choice.) Overextensions begin to disappear at about age 2½, presumably because the child's vocabulary begins to increase markedly, thereby eliminating many of the gaps (Clark, 1983; Rescorla, 1980).

Thereafter, the child's vocabulary development virtually explodes. At 1½ years, a child might have a vocabulary of 25 words; at 6 years, the child's vocabulary is around 15,000 words. To achieve this incredible growth, children have to learn new words at the rate of almost 10 per day (Miller & Gildea, 1987; Templin, 1957). Children seem to be attuned to learning new words.

Children between 18 and 30 months of age learn to combine words in phrases and sentences.

When they hear a word they do not know, they may assume that it maps onto one of their concepts that is not yet labeled, and they use the context in which the word was spoken to find that concept (Clark, 1983; Markman, 1987).

From Primitive to Complex Sentences

Between the ages of $1\frac{1}{2}$ and $2\frac{1}{2}$, the acquisition of phrase and sentence units, or syntax, begins. Children start to combine single words into two-word utterances such as "There cow" (in which the underlying proposition is "There's the cow"), "Jimmy bike" ("That's Jimmy's bike"), or "Towel bed" ("The towel's on the bed"). There is a telegraphic quality about this two-word speech. The child leaves out the grammatical words (such as "a," "an," "the," and "is"), as well as other grammatical morphemes (such as the suffixes "ing," "ed," and "s") and puts in only the words that carry the most important content. Despite their brevity, these utterances express most of the basic intentions of speakers, such as locating objects and describing events and actions.

Children progress rapidly from two-word utterances to more complex sentences that express propositions more precisely. Thus, "Daddy hat" may become "Daddy wear hat" and finally "Daddy is wearing a hat." Such expansions of the verb phrase appear to be the first complex constructions that occur in children's speech. The next step is the use of conjunctions like "and" and "so" to form compound sentences ("You play with the doll and I play with the blocks") and the use of grammatical morphemes like the past tense "ed." The sequence of language development is remarkably similar for all children.

Learning Processes

How do children acquire language? Clearly, learning must play a role; that is why children raised in English-speaking households learn English while children raised in French-speaking households learn French. Innate factors must also play a role; that is why all the children in a household learn language but none of the pets do (Gleitman, 1986). In this section we discuss learning; innate factors are considered in the next section. In both discussions we emphasize sentence units and syntax, for it is at this level of language that the important issues about language acquisition are illustrated most clearly.

Imitation and Conditioning   One possibility is that children learn language by imitating adults. While imitation plays some role in the learning of words (a parent points to a telephone, says "phone," and the child tries to repeat the word), it cannot be the principal means by which children learn to produce and understand sentences. Young children constantly utter sentences that they have never heard an adult say, such as "All gone milk." Even when children in the two-word stage of language development try to imitate longer sentences (for example, "Mr. Miller will try"), they produce their usual telegraphic utterances ("Miller try"). In addition, the mistakes children make (for instance, "Daddy taked me") suggest that they are trying to apply rules, not simply trying to copy what they have heard adults say (Ervin-Tripp, 1964).

A second possibility is that children acquire language through conditioning. Adults may reward children when they produce a grammatical sentence and reprimand them when they make mistakes. For this to work, parents would have to respond to every detail in a child's speech. However, Brown, Cazden, and Bellugi (1969) found that parents do not pay attention to how the child says something as long as the statement is comprehensible. Also, attempts to correct a child (and, hence, apply conditioning) are often futile. Consider an example:

CHILD: Nobody don't like me.
MOTHER: No, say, "nobody likes me."
CHILD: Nobody don't like me.
MOTHER: No, now listen carefully; say "nobody likes me."
CHILD: Oh! Nobody don't LIKES me.
   (McNeill, 1966, p. 49)

Hypothesis Testing   The problem with imitation and conditioning is that they focus on specific utterances. However, children often learn something general, such as a rule; they seem to form a hypothesis about a rule of language, test it, and retain it if it works.

Consider the morpheme "ed." As a general rule in English, "ed" is added to the present tense of verbs to form the past tense (as in "cook-cooked"). Many common verbs, however, are irregular and do not follow this rule ("go-went," "break-broke"). Many of these irregular verbs express concepts that children use from the beginning. So at an early point, children use the past tense of some irregular verbs correctly (presumably because they learned them by imitation). Then they learn the past tense for some regular verbs and discover the hypothesis "add 'ed' to the present tense to form the past tense." This hypothesis leads them to add the "ed" ending to many verbs, including irregular ones. They say things like "Annie goed home" and "Jackie breaked the cup," which they have never heard before. Eventually they learn that some verbs are irregular and stop overgeneralizing their use of "ed."

How do children generate these hypotheses? There are a few operating principles that all children use as a guide to forming hypotheses. One is to pay attention to the ends of words. Another is to look for prefixes and suffixes that indicate a change in meaning. A child armed with these two principles is likely to hit upon the hypothesis that "ed" at the end of verbs signals the past tense, since "ed" is a word ending associated with a change in meaning. A third operating principle is to avoid exceptions, which explains why children initially generalize their "ed"-equals-past-tense hypothesis to irregular verbs. Some of these principles appear in Table 9-1, and they seem to hold for all of the 40 languages studied by Slobin (1985; 1971).

In recent years there has been a challenge to the idea that learning a language involves learning rules. Some researchers argue that the mere fact that a regular pattern is overextended does not guarantee that these errors are caused by following a rule. Marcus (1996), for example, believes that children's grammar is structured similarly to adults'. But because children have had less exposure to correct forms, their memories for irregular forms like "broke" are weaker. Whenever they cannot recall such a form, they add "ed," producing an overextension. Other researchers have argued that what looks like an instance of learning a single rule may in fact be a case of learning numerous associa-

TABLE 9-1

Operating Principles Used by Young Children
Children from many countries seem to follow these principles in learning to talk and to understand speech. (After Slobin, 1971)

1. Look for systematic changes in the form of words.
2. Look for grammatical markers that clearly indicate changes in meaning.
3. Avoid exceptions.
4. Pay attention to the ends of words.
5. Pay attention to the order of words, prefixes, and suffixes.
6. Avoid interruption or rearrangement of constituents (that is, sentence units).

tions. Consider again a child learning the past tense of verbs in English. Instead of learning a rule about adding "ed" to the present tense of a verb, perhaps children are learning associations between the past tense ending "ed" and various phonetic properties of verbs that can go with "ed." The phonetic properties of a verb include properties of the sounds that make up the verb, such as whether it contains an "alk" sound at the end. Thus, a child may unconsciously learn that verbs containing an "alk" sound at the end—such as "talk," "walk," and "stalk"—are likely to take "ed" as a past tense ending. This proposal has in fact been shown to account for some aspects of learning verb endings, including the finding that at some point in development children add the "ed" ending even to irregular verbs (Rumelhart & McClelland, 1987).

However, other aspects of learning verb endings cannot be explained in terms of associations between sounds. For example, the word "break" and the word "brake" (meaning to a stop a car) are identical in sound, but the past tense of the former is "broke" whereas that of the latter is "braked." So a child must learn something in addition to sound connections. This additional knowledge seems best cast in terms of rules (for example, "If a verb is derived from a noun—as in the case of 'brake'—always add 'ed' to form the past tense"). Language learning thus seems to involve rules as well as associations (Pinker, 1991; Pinker & Prince, 1988).

Innate Factors

As noted earlier, some of our knowledge about language is inborn, or innate. There are, however, some controversial questions about the extent and nature of this innate knowledge. One question concerns its richness. If our innate knowledge is very rich or detailed, the process of language acquisition should be similar for different languages even if the opportunities for learning differ among cultures. A second question about innate factors involves critical periods. Innate behavior will be acquired more readily if the organism is exposed to the right cues during a critical time period. Are there such critical periods in language acquisition? A third question concerns the possible uniqueness of our innate knowledge about language: Is the ability to learn a language system unique to the human species? We will consider these three questions in turn.

The Richness of Innate Knowledge   All children, regardless of their culture and language, seem to go through the same sequence of language development. At age 1, the child speaks a few isolated words; at about age 2, the child speaks 2- and 3-word sentences; at age 3, sentences become more grammatical; and at age 4, the child's speech sounds much like that of an adult. Because cultures differ markedly in the opportunities they provide for children to learn from adults, the fact that this sequence is so consistent across cultures indicates that our innate knowledge about language is very rich.

Indeed, our innate knowledge of language seems to be so rich that children can go through the normal course of language acquisition even when there are no language users around them to serve as models or teachers. A group of researchers studied six deaf children of hearing parents who had decided not to have their children learn sign language. Before the children received any instruction in lip reading and vocalization, they began to use a system of gestures called *home sign*. Initially their home sign was a kind of simple pantomime, but eventually it took on the properties of a language. For example, it was organized at both the morphemic and syntactic levels, including individual signs and combinations of signs. In addition, these deaf children (who essen-

tially created their own language) went through the same stages of development as normal hearing children. Thus, the deaf children initially gestured one sign at a time and later put their pantomimes together into two- and three-concept "sentences." These striking results attest to the richness and detail of our innate knowledge (Feldman, Goldin-Meadow, & Gleitman, 1978).

Critical Periods   Like other innate behaviors, language learning has some critical periods. This is particularly evident when it comes to acquiring the sound system of a new language—that is, learning new phonemes and the rules for combining them. We have already noted that infants less than 1 year old can discriminate among phonemes of any language but lose this ability by the end of their first year. Hence, the first months of life are a critical period for homing in on the phonemes of one's native language. There also seems to be a critical period for acquiring the sound system of a second language. After a few years of learning a second language, young children are more likely than adults to speak it without an accent, and they are better able to understand the language when it is spoken in noisy conditions (Snow, 1987; Lenneberg, 1967).

More recent research indicates that there is also a critical period for learning syntax. The evidence comes from studies of deaf people who know American Sign Language (ASL), which is a full-blown language and not a pantomime system. The studies of interest involved adults who had been using ASL for 30 years or more but varied in the age at which they had learned the language. Although all the participants were born to hearing parents, some were native signers who were exposed to ASL from birth, others first learned ASL between ages 4 and 6 when they enrolled in a school for the deaf, and still others did not encounter ASL until after they were 12 (their parents had been reluctant to let them learn a sign language rather than a spoken one). If there is a critical period for learning syntax, the early learners should have shown greater mastery of some aspects of syntax than the later learners, even 30 years after acquisition. This is exactly what the researchers found. Thus, with respect to understanding and producing words with multiple morphemes—such

Research has shown that there is a critical period for learning syntax. Deaf people can use American Sign Language more effectively if they learn it at an early age.

as "untimely," which consists of the morphemes "un," "time," and "ly"—native signers did better than those who learned ASL when entering school, who in turn did better than those who learned ASL after age 12 (Meier, 1991; Newport, 1990).

Indirect evidence for the existence of a critical period for language acquisition can be seen in cases of children who have experienced extreme isolation. A famous case of social isolation in childhood is that of Genie, a girl whose father was psychotic and whose mother was blind and highly dependent. From birth until she was discovered by child welfare authorities at age 11, Genie was strapped to a potty chair in an isolated room of her parents' home.

Before she was discovered, Genie had had almost no contact with other people. She had virtually no language ability. Efforts to teach her to speak had limited results. She was able to learn words, but she could not master the rules of grammar that come naturally to younger children. Although tests showed that she was highly intelligent, her language abilities never progressed beyond those of a third-grader (Curtiss, 1977; Rymer, 1992a, b).

Can Another Species Learn Human Language?

Some experts believe that our innate capacity to learn language is unique to our species (Chomsky, 1972). They acknowledge that other species have communication systems but argue that these are qualitatively different from ours. Consider the communication system of the chimpanzee. Chimpanzees' vocalizations and gestures are limited in number, and the productivity of their communication system is very low compared with that of human language, in which a relatively small number of phonemes can be combined to create thousands of words, which in turn can be combined to create an unlimited number of sentences.

Another difference is that human language is structured at several levels, whereas chimpanzee communications are not. In particular, in human language there is a clear distinction between the level of words or morphemes, which have meaning, and the level of sounds, which do not. There is no hint of such a duality of structure in chimpanzee communication; every symbol carries meaning.

Still another difference is that chimpanzees do not vary the order of their symbols in order to vary the meaning of their messages as we do. For instance, for us "Jonah ate the whale" means something quite different from "The whale ate Jonah"; there is no evidence for a comparable difference in chimpanzee communications.

The fact that chimpanzee communication is impoverished compared with our own does not prove that chimpanzees lack the capacity for a more productive system. Their system may be adequate for their needs. To determine whether chimpanzees have the same innate capacity we do, we must see whether they can learn our language.

In one of the best-known studies of the teaching of language to chimps, Gardner and Gardner (1972) taught a female chimpanzee named Washoe signs adapted from American Sign Language. Sign language was used because chimps lack the vocal equipment to pronounce human sounds. Training began when Washoe was about 1 year old and continued until she was 5. During this time Washoe's caretakers communicated with her only by means of sign language. They first taught her signs by means of shaping procedures, waiting for her to make a gesture that resembled a sign and then reinforcing her. Later, Washoe learned signs simply by observing and imitating. By age 4 Washoe could produce 130 different signs and understand even more. She could also generalize a sign from one situation to another. For example, she first learned the sign for "more" in connection with "more tickling" and then generalized it to indicate "more milk."

Other chimpanzees have acquired comparable vocabularies. Some studies used methods of manual communication other than sign language. For example, Premack (1985; 1971) taught a chimpanzee named Sarah to use plastic symbols as words and to communicate by manipulating these symbols. In a series of similar studies, Patterson (1978) taught sign language to a gorilla named Koko, starting when Koko was 1 year old. By age 10 Koko had a vocabulary of more than 400 signs (Patterson & Linden, 1981).

Do these studies prove that apes can learn human language? There seems to be little doubt that the apes' signs are equivalent to our words and that the concepts behind some of the signs are equivalent to ours. But many experts question whether these stud-

ies show that apes can learn to combine signs in the same way that humans combine words into a sentence. For example, not only can we combine the words "snake," "Eve," "killed," and "the" into the sentence "The snake killed Eve," but we can also combine the same words in a different order to produce a sentence with a different meaning, "Eve killed the snake." Although the studies just described provide some evidence that apes can combine signs into a sequence resembling a sentence, there is little evidence that apes can alter the order of the signs to produce a different sentence (Brown, 1986; Slobin, 1979).

Even the evidence that apes can combine signs into a sentence has come under attack. In their early work, researchers reported cases in which an ape produced what seemed to be a meaningful sequence of signs, such as "Gimme flower" and "Washoe sorry" (Gardner & Gardner, 1972). As data accumulated, however, it became apparent that, unlike human sentences, the utterances of an ape are often highly repetitious. An utterance like "You me banana me banana you" is typical of the signing chimps but would be most odd for a human child. In the cases in which an ape utterance is more like a sentence, the ape may simply have imitated the sequence of signs made by its human teacher. Thus, some of Washoe's most sentencelike utterances occurred when she was answering a question; for example, the teacher signed "Washoe eat?" and Washoe signed "Washoe eat time." Washoe's combination of signs may have been a partial imitation of her teacher's combination, which is not how human children learn to combine words (Terrace et al., 1979).

The evidence considered thus far supports the conclusion that, although apes can develop a humanlike vocabulary, they cannot learn to combine their signs in the systematic way in which humans do so. However, a relatively recent study seems to challenge this conclusion (Greenfield & Savage-Rumbaugh, 1990). The researchers worked with a pygmy chimpanzee, whose behavior is thought to be more like that of humans than the behavior of the more widely studied common chimpanzee. The pygmy chimpanzee, a 7-year-old named Kanzi, communicated by manipulating symbols that stand for words. Unlike the case in previous studies, Kanzi learned to manipulate the symbols in a relatively natural way, for example, by listening to his caretakers as they uttered English words while pointing to the symbols. Most important, after a few years of language training, Kanzi demonstrated some ability to vary word order to communicate changes in meaning. For example, if Kanzi was going to bite his half-sister Mulika he would signal "bite Mulika"; but if his sister bit him he would sign "Mulika bite." Kanzi thus seems to have some syntactic knowledge, roughly that of a 2-year-old human.

These results are tantalizing, but they need to be interpreted with caution. For one thing, so far Kanzi is among the few chimpanzees who have shown any syntactic ability; hence, one may question how general the results are. For another thing, although Kanzi may have the linguistic ability of a 2-year-old, it took him substantially longer to get to that point than it does a human; also, we do not yet know whether Kanzi, or any other chimpanzee, can get much beyond that point. But perhaps the main reason to be skeptical about the possibility of any ape's developing comparable linguistic abilities to a human has been voiced by Chomsky (1991):

> If an animal had a capacity as biologically advantageous as language but somehow hadn't used it until now, it would be an evolutionary miracle, like finding an island of humans who could be taught to fly.

Concepts and Categorization: The Building Blocks of Thought

Thought can be conceived of as a "language of the mind." Actually, there may be more than one language. One mode of thought corresponds to the stream of sentences that we seem to "hear in our mind"; this is referred to as **propositional thought** because *it expresses a proposition or claim.* Another mode, **imaginal thought,** corresponds to *images, particularly visual ones, that we can "see" in our mind.* Finally, there may be a third mode, **motoric thought,** that corresponds to *sequences of "mental movements"* (Bruner, Olver, Greenfield et al., 1966). While studies of cognitive development have paid some attention to motoric thought in children, research on thinking in adults has emphasized the other two modes, particularly the propositional mode.

We can think of a **proposition** as *a statement that expresses a factual claim.*

The chimpanzee on the left has been trained to communicate using a keyboard. The one on the right has learned a kind of sign language; here he makes the sign for "toothbrush."

"Mothers are hard workers" is one proposition; "Cats are animals" is another. It is easy to see that such a thought consists of concepts—such as "mothers" and "hard workers" or "cat" and "animal"—combined in a particular way. To understand propositional thought, however, we first need to understand the concepts that compose it.

Functions of Concepts

A **concept** represents an entire class—it is *the set of properties that we associate with a particular class.* Our concept of "cat," for example, includes the properties of having four legs and whiskers. Concepts serve some major functions in mental life. One of those functions is to divide the world into manageable units (this is referred to as *cognitive economy).* The world is full of so many different objects that if we treated each one as distinct we would soon be overwhelmed. For example, if we had to refer to every single object we encountered by a different name, our vocabulary would have to be gigantic—so immense that communication might become impossible. (Think of what it would be like if we had a separate name for each of the 7 million colors among which we can discriminate!) Fortunately, we do not treat each object as unique; rather, we see it as an instance of a concept. Thus, many different objects are seen as instances of the concept "cat," many others as instances of the concept "chair," and so on. By treating different objects as members of the same concept, we reduce the complexity of the world that we have to represent mentally.

Categorization refers to *the process of assigning an object to a concept.* When we categorize an object, we treat it as if it has many of the properties associated with the concept, including properties that we have not directly perceived. Hence, a second major function of concepts is that they allow us to predict information that is not readily perceived (this is referred to as *predictive power).* For example, our concept of "apple" is associated with such hard-to-perceive properties as having seeds and being edible, as well as with readily perceived properties like being round, having a distinctive color, and being found on trees. We may use the visible properties to categorize some object as an "apple" (the object is red, round, and hangs from a tree) and then infer that the object has the less visible properties as well (it has seeds and is edible). Concepts thus enable us to go beyond directly perceived information (Bruner, 1957).

We also have concepts of activities, such as "eating"; of states, such as "being old"; and of abstractions, such as "truth," "justice," or even the number 2. In each case we know something about the properties that are common to all members of the concept. Widely used concepts like these are generally associated with a one-word name. This allows us to communicate quickly about experiences that occur frequently. We can also make up concepts on the spot to serve some specific goal. For example, if you are planning an outing, you might generate the concept "things to take on a camping trip." These kinds of goal-driven concepts facilitate planning. While such concepts are used relatively infrequently, and accordingly have relatively long names, they still provide us with some cognitive economy and predictive power (Barsalou, 1985).

Prototypes

The properties associated with a concept seem to fall into two sets. One set of properties makes up the **prototype** of the concept; they are *the properties that describe the best examples of the concept.* In the concept "bachelor," for example, your prototype might include such properties as a man who is in his 30s, lives alone, and has an active social life. The prototype is what usually comes to mind when we think of the concept. But while the prototype properties may be true of the typical examples of a bachelor, they clearly are not true of all instances (think of an uncle in his 60s who boards with his sister and rarely goes out). This means that a concept must contain something in addition to a prototype; this additional something is a **core** that comprises *the properties that are most important for being a member of a concept.* Your core of the concept "bachelor" would probably include the properties of being adult, male, and unmarried; these properties are essential for being a member of the concept (Armstrong, Gleitman, & Gleitman, 1983).

As another example, consider the concept "bird." Your prototype likely includes the properties of flying and chirping—which works for the best examples of "bird," such as robins and blue jays, but not for other examples, such as ostriches and penguins. Your core would likely specify something about the biological basis of birdhood—the fact that it involves having certain genes or, at least having parents that are birds.

Note that in both our examples—"bachelor" and "bird"—the prototype properties are salient but not perfect indicators of concept membership, whereas the core properties are more central to concept membership. However, there is an important difference between a concept like "bachelor" and a concept like "bird." The core of "bachelor" is a definition, and it is easily applied. Thus, anyone who is adult, male, and unmarried must be a "bachelor," and it is relatively easy to determine whether someone has these defining properties. Concepts like this one are said to be *well defined*. Categorizing a person or object into a well-defined category involves determining whether it has the core or defining properties. In contrast, the core of "bird" is hardly a definition—we may know only that genes are somehow involved, for example—and the core properties are hidden from view. Thus, if we happen upon a small animal we can hardly inspect its genes or inquire about its parentage. All we can do is check whether it does certain

things, such as fly and chirp, and use this information to decide whether it is a bird. Concepts like "bird" are said to be *fuzzy*. Deciding whether an object is an instance of a fuzzy concept often involves determining its similarity to the concept's prototype (Smith, 1989). Most natural concepts seem to be fuzzy—they lack true definitions, and categorization of these concepts relies heavily on prototypes.

Some instances of fuzzy concepts will have more prototype properties than other instances. Among birds, for example, a robin will have the property of flying, whereas an ostrich will not. The more prototype properties an instance has, the more typical of the concept it is considered to be. Thus, in the case of "bird," most people rate a robin as more typical than a chicken, and a chicken as more typical than an ostrich; in the case of "apple," they rate red apples as more typical than green ones (since red seems to be a property of the concept "apple"); and so on. The degree to which an instance is typical has a major effect on its categorization. When people are asked whether or not a pictured animal is a "bird," a robin produces an immediate "yes," whereas a chicken requires a longer decision time. When young children are asked the same question, a robin will almost inevitably be classified correctly, whereas a chicken will often be declared a nonbird. Typicality also determines

Do flying and chirping make a bird? Your prototype for "bird" probably includes these features; however, they do not apply to certain kinds of birds, such as penguins and ostriches.

Most people in our culture would probably agree on the hue represented by the concept "fire engine red."

what we think of when we encounter the name of the concept. Hearing the sentence, "There is a bird outside your window," we are far more likely to think of a robin than a vulture, and what comes to mind will obviously influence what we make of the sentence (Rosch, 1978).

Universality of Prototypes   Are our prototypes determined mainly by our culture, or are they universal? For some concepts, such as "bachelor," culture clearly has a major impact on the prototype. But for other, more natural concepts, prototypes are surprisingly universal.

Consider color concepts such as "red." This is a fuzzy concept (no ordinary person knows its defining properties) and one with a clear prototype: People in our culture agree on which hues are typical reds and which hues are atypical. People in other cultures agree with our choices. Remarkably, this agreement is found even among people whose language does not include a word for "red." When speakers of these languages are asked to pick the best example from an array of red hues, they make the same choices we would. Even though the range of hues for what they would call "red" may differ from ours, their idea of a typical red is the same as ours (Berlin & Kay, 1969).

Other research suggests that the Dani, a New Guinea people whose language has terms only for "black" and "white," perceive color variations in exactly the same way as English-speaking people, whose language has terms for many colors. Dani individuals were given a set of red color patches to remember; the patches varied in how typical they were of "red." Later the participants were presented with a set of color patches and asked to decide which ones they had seen before. Even though they had no word for "red," they recognized more typical red colors better than less typical ones. This is exactly what American participants do when performing a comparable task (Rosch, 1974). Color prototypes thus appear to be universal.

More recent experiments suggest that prototypes for animal concepts may also be universal. The experiments compared U.S. students and Maya Itza participants. (Maya Itza is a culture of the Guatemalan rainforest that is relatively insulated from Western influences.) The U.S. participants were from southeastern Michigan, which happens to have a number of mammalian species that are comparable to those found in the Guatemalan rainforest. Both groups of participants were presented with the names of these species. They were first asked to group them into sets that go together, then to group those sets into higher-order groups that were related, and so on until all the species were in one group corresponding to "mammals." These groupings were determined by the similarity of the prototypes: In the first pass, participants would group together only species that seemed very similar. By making these groupings, each participant created a kind of tree, with the initial groupings at the bottom and "mammal" at the top; this tree reflects the taxonomy of animals.

The trees or taxonomies created by the Maya Itza were quite similar to those created by the U.S. students; in fact, the correlation between the average Itza and U.S. trees was about +.60. Moreover, both the Itza and U.S. taxonomies were highly correlated with the actual scientific taxonomy. Apparently, all people base their prototypes of animals on properties that they can easily observe (overall shape, or distinctive features like coloring, a bushy tail, or a particular movement pattern). These properties are indicators of the evolutionary history of the species, on which the scientific taxonomy is based (Lopez et al., 1997).

Hierarchies of Concepts

In addition to knowing the properties of concepts, we also know how concepts are related to one another. For example, "apples" are members (or a subset) of a larger concept, "fruit"; "robins" are a subset of "birds," which in turn are a subset of "animals." These two types of knowledge (properties of a concept and relationships between concepts) are represented in Figure 9-4 as a hierarchy. Such a hierarchy allows us to infer that a concept has a particular property even when it is not associated directly with that concept. Suppose that you do not directly associate the property of being sweet with "Golden Delicious apple." If you were asked, "Is a Golden Delicious apple sweet?" presumably you would enter your mental hierarchy at "Golden Delicious apple" (see Figure 9-4), trace a path from "Golden Delicious apple" to "fruit," find the property of being sweet stored at "fruit," and respond "yes." This idea implies that the time needed to establish a relationship between a concept and a property should increase with the distance between them in the hierarchy. This prediction has been confirmed in experiments in which participants were asked questions such as, "Is an apple sweet?" and "Is a Golden Delicious apple sweet?" Participants took longer to answer the second question than the first because the distance in the hierarchy between "Golden Delicious apple" and "sweet" is greater than that between "apple" and "sweet" (Collins & Loftus, 1975).

As the hierarchy in Figure 9-4 makes clear, an object can be identified at different levels. The same object is at once a "Golden Delicious apple," an "apple," and a "fruit." However, in any hierarchy one level is the "basic" or preferred one for classification; this is the level at which we first categorize an object. For the hierarchy in Figure 9-4, the level that contains "apple" and "pear" would be the basic one. Evidence for this

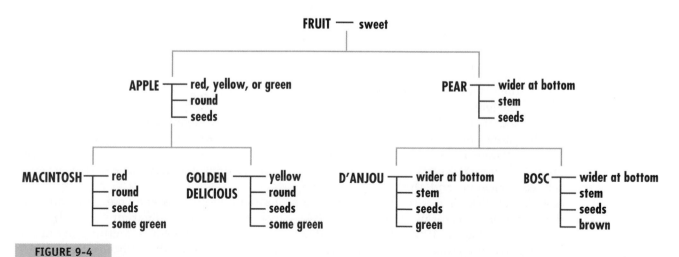

A Hierarchy of Concepts *Words in capital letters represent concepts; lowercase words depict properties of these concepts. The blue lines show relationships between concepts, and the red lines connect properties and concepts.*

claim comes from studies in which people are asked to name pictured objects with the first names that come to mind. People are more likely to call a pictured Golden Delicious apple an "apple" than either a "Golden Delicious apple" or a "fruit."

It seems, then, that we first divide the world into basic-level concepts (Mervis & Rosch, 1981). What determines which level is basic? The answer appears to be that the basic level is the one that has the most distinctive properties. In Figure 9-4, "apple" has several properties that are distinctive—they are not shared by other kinds of fruit (for example, red and round are not properties of "pear"). In contrast, "Golden Delicious apple" has few distinct properties; most of its properties are shared by "MacIntosh apple," for example. And "fruit," which is at the highest level of Figure 9-4, has few properties of any kind. Thus, we first categorize the world at what turns out to be the most informative level (Murphy & Brownell, 1985).

Different Categorization Processes

We are constantly making categorization decisions: We categorize every time we recognize an object, every time we diagnose a problem ("That's a power failure"), and so on. How do we use concepts to categorize our world? The answer depends on whether the concept is well defined or fuzzy.

For well-defined concepts like "bachelor" or "grandmother," we may determine how similar a person is to our prototype ("She's sixtyish and has white hair, so she looks like a grandmother"). But if we are trying to be accurate, we can determine whether the person has the defining properties of the concept ("Is she the female parent of a parent?"). The latter amounts to applying a rule: "If she's the female parent of a parent, she's a grandmother." There have been many studies of such *rule-based categorization* of well-defined concepts, and they show that the more properties there are in the rule, the slower and more error-prone the categorization process (Bourne, 1966). This may be due to processing the properties one at a time.

For fuzzy concepts like "bird" and "chair," we do not know enough defining properties to use rule-based categorization, so we rely on *similarity* instead. As already mentioned,

one thing we may do is determine the similarity of an object to the prototype of the concept ("Is this object similar enough to my prototype to call it a chair?"). The evidence that people categorize objects in this fashion involves three steps (Smith, 1995):

1. First the researcher determines the properties of a concept's prototype and of various instances of that concept. (The researcher might ask one group of participants to describe the properties of their prototypical chair and of various pictures of chairs.)

2. Then the researcher determines the similarity between each instance (each pictured chair) and the prototype by identifying their shared properties. This results in a *similarity-to-prototype score* for each instance.

3. Finally, the researcher shows that the similarity-to-prototype score is highly correlated with how accurately and quickly participants can correctly categorize that instance. This shows that similarity to prototype plays a role in categorization.

There is another kind of similarity calculation that we can use to categorize objects. We can illustrate this with our chair example. Since we have stored in long-term memory some specific instances or *exemplars* of chairs, we can determine whether an object is similar to our stored chair exemplars; if it is, we can declare that it is a chair. Thus, we have two means of categorization based on similarity: similarity to prototypes and similarity to stored exemplars.

Acquiring Concepts

How do we acquire the multitude of concepts that we know about? Some concepts, such as the concepts of "time" and "space," may be inborn. Others have to be learned.

Learning Prototypes and Core   We can learn about a concept in different ways: Either we are explicitly taught something about the concept or we learn it through experience. Which way we learn depends on what we are learning. Explicit teaching is likely to be the means by which we learn cores of concepts, while experience seems to be the usual means by which we acquire prototypes. Thus, someone explicitly tells a child that a "robber" is someone who takes another person's possessions with no intention of returning them (the core), while the child's experiences may lead him or her to expect robbers to be shiftless, disheveled, and dangerous (the prototype).

Children must also learn that the core is a better indicator of concept membership than the prototype is, but it takes a while for them to learn this. In one study, children aged 5 to 10 were presented with descriptions of items and asked to decide whether or not they belonged to particular well-defined concepts. We can illustrate the study with the concept of "robber." One description given for "robber" depicted a person who matched its prototype but not its core:

> A smelly, mean old man with a gun in his pocket who came to your house and takes your TV set because your parents didn't want it anymore and told him he could have it.

Another description given for "robber" was of a person who matched its core but not its prototype:

> A very friendly and cheerful woman who gave you a hug, but then disconnected your toilet bowl and took it away without permission and no intention to return it.

The younger children often thought that the prototypical description was more likely than the core description to be an instance of the concept. Not until age 10 did children show a clear shift from the prototype to the core as the final arbitrator of concept decisions (Keil & Batterman, 1984).

Learning Through Experience There are at least three different ways in which one can learn a concept through experience. The simplest way is called the *exemplar strategy,* and we can illustrate it with a child learning the concept of "furniture." When the child encounters a known instance or exemplar—for example, a table—she stores a representation of it. Later, when she has to decide whether or not a new item—say, a desk—is an instance of "furniture," she determines the new object's similarity to stored exemplars of "furniture," including tables. This strategy seems to be widely used by children, and it works better with typical

Parents can teach children to name and classify objects. Later, when the child sees another object, she may determine whether it is in the same category as the stored exemplar.

instances than with atypical ones. Because the first exemplars a child learns tend to be typical ones, new instances are more likely to be correctly classified to the extent that they are similar to typical instances. Thus, if a young child's concept of "furniture" consisted of just the most typical instances (say, table and chair), he could correctly classify other instances that looked similar to the learned exemplars, such as desk and sofa, but not instances that looked different from the learned exemplars, such as lamp and bookshelf (Mervis & Pani, 1981). The exemplar strategy remains part of our repertory for acquiring concepts, as there is substantial evidence that adults often use it in acquiring novel concepts (Estes, 1994).

But as we grow older we start to use another strategy, *hypothesis testing.* We inspect known instances of a concept, searching for properties that are relatively common to them (for example, many pieces of "furniture" are found in living spaces), and we hypothesize that these common properties are what characterize the concept. We then analyze novel objects for these critical properties, maintaining our hypothesis if it leads to a correct categorization about the novel object and revamping it if it leads us astray. This strategy thus focuses on **abstractions**—*properties that characterize sets of instances rather than just single instances*—and is tuned to finding core properties, since they are the ones that are common to most instances (Bruner, Goodenow, & Austin, 1956).

Both the exemplar and hypothesis-testing strategies are driven solely by the input, the known instances, and give little weight to the learner's prior knowledge. In earlier chapters we have referred to such strategies as *bottom-up* and contrasted them with *top-down* strategies, in which people make extensive use of their prior knowledge. In a top-down strategy of concept learning, people use their prior knowledge along with the known instances to determine the critical properties of a concept. An example is provided by the following study.

Category 1

Category 2

FIGURE 9-5

Top-Down Concept Learning   *In an experiment on concept learning, one group of participants was told that Category 1 drawings had been done by creative children and Category 2 drawings by noncreative children, while another group was told that Category 1 drawings had been done by city children and Category 2 drawings by farm children. The two groups offered different kinds of descriptions of the categories. Moreover, the same feature (for example, the pointed-to object in the fourth figure in Category 1) was sometimes interpreted differently by the two groups* (After Wisniewski & Medin, 1991)

Two groups of adult participants were presented with the children's drawings shown in Figure 9-5. Their task was to describe the properties that characterized each category. One group of participants was told that Category 1 drawings were done by creative children while Category 2 drawings were done by noncreative children; the other group of participants was told that Category 1 drawings were done by city children while Category 2 drawings were done by farm children. The two groups of participants therefore differed in the kind of prior knowledge they would bring to bear on their task: either knowledge about creativity or knowledge about city versus farm living. This difference showed its effect in the descriptions of the categories generated by the two groups of participants. The creative-noncreative group produced more descriptions of the two categories that emphasized the amount of detail in the drawing; for example, "Creative kids will draw more detail—like eyelashes, teeth, curly hair, shading and coloring. Noncreative kids draw more stick-figurish people." In contrast, the farm-city group generated more descriptions of the two categories that emphasized the clothing in the drawings; for example, "Farm kids will draw people with overalls, straw or farm hats. City kids will draw people with ties, suits."

Thus, learners with different prior knowledge focused on different properties of the drawings. Moreover, in some cases differences in prior knowledge seem to have determined how the learners interpreted the properties in the first place. To illustrate, consider the object pointed to in the fourth figure of Category 1 (see Figure 9-5). Some participants in the creative-noncreative group interpreted this object as a pocket and mentioned it as evidence of greater detail. Some participants in the farm-city group interpreted the object as a purse and mentioned it as evidence of an urban background. Prior knowledge therefore may affect every aspect of concept attainment (Wisniewski & Medin, 1991).

Neural Bases of Concepts and Categorization

While we have emphasized the difference between well-defined and fuzzy concepts, research at the neurological level indicates

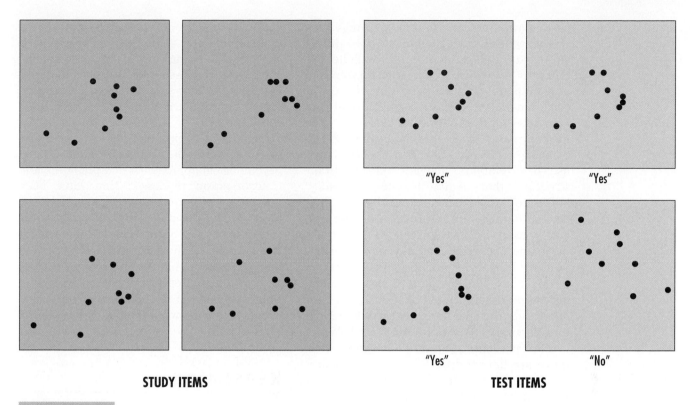

STUDY ITEMS   TEST ITEMS

FIGURE 9-6

Examples of Dot Patterns Used to Study Categorization in Amnesiac Patients   *Individuals learned that the study items all belonged to one category and then had to decide whether each of the test items belonged to that category.* (Adapted from Squire & Knowlton, 1995)

that there are important differences just among fuzzy concepts. In particular, the brain seems to store concepts of animals and concepts of artifacts in different neural regions. We mentioned some of the evidence for this in our discussion of perception in Chapter 5. There we noted that there are patients who are impaired in their ability to recognize pictures of animals but relatively normal in their recognition of pictured artifacts such as tools, whereas there are other patients who show the reverse pattern. Recent research shows that what holds for pictures holds for words as well. Many of the patients who are impaired in naming pictures also cannot tell what the corresponding word means. For example, a patient who cannot name a pictured giraffe also cannot tell you anything about giraffes when presented with the word "giraffe." The fact that the deficit appears for both words and pictures indicates that it has to do with concepts: The patient has lost part of the concept "giraffe" (Farah & McClelland, 1991).

Other research has focused on processes of categorization. One line of research shows that determining the similarity between an object and a concept's prototype involves different brain regions than determining the similarity between an object and stored exemplars of the concept. The logic behind these studies is as follows: The exemplar process involves retrieving items from long-term memory; as we saw in Chapter 8, such retrieval depends on brain structures in the medial temporal lobe. It follows that a patient with damage in these regions of the brain will be unable to effectively categorize objects using a process that involves exemplars, although the patient might be relatively normal in the use of prototypes. This is exactly what researchers have found.

One study tested patients with medial-temporal-lobe damage as well as normal individuals on two different tasks. One task required participants to learn to sort dot patterns into two categories (see Figure 9-6 for examples); the other task required participants to learn to sort paintings into two categories corresponding to two different artists. Independent evidence indicated that only the painting task relied on retrieval of exemplars. The patients learned the dot pattern concepts as easily as the normal participants, but they performed far worse than the normal participants in acquiring the painting concepts (Kolodny, 1994). Thus, use of exemplars depends on the brain structures that mediate long-term memory, but use of prototypes in categorization must depend on other structures. Other research has focused on a patient who is essentially incapable of committing *any* new information to long-term memory, yet performs normally on the dot pattern task. Clearly, prototype-based categorization does not depend on the structures that mediate long-term memory (Squire & Knowlton, 1995).

The preceding discussion shows that there are neural differences between categorization based on prototypes and categorization based on stored exemplars. What about categorization based on rules? A recent study shows that rule use involves different neural circuits than similarity processes. Two groups of participants were taught to categorize imaginary animals into two categories corresponding to whether the animals were from Venus or Saturn. One group learned to categorize the animals on the basis of a complex rule—for example, "An animal is from Venus if it has antennae ears, curly tail, and hoofed feet; otherwise it's from Saturn." The second group learned to categorize the animals by relying solely on their memory. (The first time they saw an animal, they would have to guess, but on subsequent trials they would be able to remember its category.) Then both groups were given novel animals to categorize while having their brains scanned. The rule group continued to categorize by rule, but the memory group had to categorize a novel animal by retrieving the stored exemplar that was most similar to it and then selecting the category associated with that exemplar.

For the memory group, most of the brain areas that were activated were in the visual cortex at the back of the brain. This fits with the idea that these participants were relying on retrieval of visual exemplars. Participants in the rule group also showed activation in the back of the brain, but they showed activation in some frontal regions as well. These regions are often damaged in patients who have trouble doing rule-based tasks. Hence, categorization based on rules relies in different neural circuitry than does categorization based on similarity (Smith, Patalano, & Jonides, 1998).

This research provides yet another example of the interplay between biological and psychological approaches to a phenomenon. Categorization processes that have been viewed as different at the psychological level—such as using exemplars versus using rules—have now been shown to involve different brain mechanisms. This example follows a pattern that we have encountered several times in earlier chapters: A distinction first made at the psychological level is subsequently shown to hold at the biological level as well.

Reasoning

When we think in terms of propositions, our sequence of thoughts is organized. Sometimes our thoughts are organized by the structure of long-term memory. A thought about calling your father, for example, leads to a memory of a recent conversation you had with him in your house, which in turn leads to a thought about cleaning out the attic. But memory associations are not the only means we have of organizing thought. The kind of organization of interest to us here manifests itself when we try to reason. In such cases, our sequence of thoughts often takes the form of an **argument,** in which one proposition corresponds to *a claim, or conclusion, that we are trying to draw.* The remaining propositions are reasons for the claim or premises for the conclusion.

Deductive Reasoning

Logical Rules According to logicians, the strongest arguments are **deductively valid,** meaning that *it is impossible for the conclusion of the argument to be false if its premises are true* (Skyrms, 1986). An example of such an argument is the following.

1. a. If it's raining, I'll take an umbrella.

   b. It's raining.

   c. Therefore, I'll take an umbrella.

How does the reasoning of ordinary people line up with that of the logician? When asked to decide whether or not an argument is deductively valid, people are quite accurate in their assessments of simple arguments. How do we make such judgments? Some theories of deductive reasoning assume that we operate like intuitive logicians and use logical rules in trying to prove that the conclusion of an argument follows from the premises. To illustrate, consider the following rule:

> If you have a proposition of the form "If *p* then *q*," and another proposition *p*, then you can infer the proposition *q*.

Presumably, adults know this rule (perhaps unconsciously) and use it to decide that the previous argument is valid. Specifically, they identify the first premise ("If it's raining, I'll take an umbrella") with the "If *p* then *q*" part of the rule. They identify the second premise ("It's raining") with the *p* part of the rule, and then they infer the *q* part ("I'll take an umbrella").

Rule following becomes more conscious if we complicate the argument. Presumably, we apply our sample rule twice when evaluating the following argument:

2. a. If it's raining, I'll take an umbrella.

    b. If I take an umbrella, I'll lose it.

    c. It's raining.

    d. Therefore, I'll lose my umbrella.

Applying our rule to propositions a and c allows us to infer "I'll take an umbrella," and applying our rule again to proposition b and the inferred proposition allows us to infer "I'll lose my umbrella," which is the conclusion.

One of the best pieces of evidence that people are using rules like this is that the number of rules an argument requires is a good predictor of the argument's difficulty. The more rules are needed, the more likely it is that people will make an error and the longer it will take them when they do make a correct decision (Rips, 1983, 1994).

Effects of Content   Logical rules do not capture all aspects of deductive reasoning. Such rules are triggered only by the logical form of propositions, yet our ability to evaluate a deductive argument often depends on the *content* of the propositions as well. We can

illustrate this point with the following experimental problems. Participants are presented four cards. In one version of the problem, each card has a letter on one side and a digit on the other (see the top half of Figure 9-7). The participant must decide which cards to turn over to determine whether the following claim is correct: "If a card has a vowel on one side, then it has an even number on the other side." While most participants correctly choose the "E" card, fewer than 10% of them also choose the "7" card, which is the other correct choice. (To see that the "7" card is critical, note that if it has a vowel on its other side, the claim is disconfirmed.)

Performance improves dramatically, however, in another version of the problem (see the bottom half of Figure 9-7). Now the claim that participants must evaluate is "If a person is drinking beer, he or she must be over 19." Each card has a person's age on one side and what he or she is drinking on the other. This version of the problem is logically equivalent to the preceding version (in particular, "Beer" corresponds to "E" and "16" corresponds to "7"); but now most participants make the correct choices (they turn over the "Beer" and "16" cards). Thus, the content of the propositions affects their reasoning.

Results like these imply that we do not always use logical rules when solving

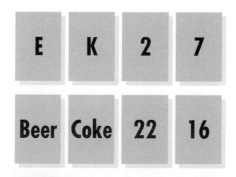

FIGURE 9-7

Content Effects in Deductive Reasoning   *The top row illustrates a version of the problem in which participants had to decide which two cards should be turned over to test the hypothesis, "If a card has a vowel on one side, it has an even number on the other side." The bottom row illustrates a version of the problem in which participants had to decide which cards to turn over to test the hypothesis, "If a person is drinking beer, he or she must be over 19."*   (After Griggs & Cox, 1982; Wason & Johnson-Laird, 1972)

deduction problems. Rather, sometimes we use rules that are less abstract and more relevant to everyday problems; these are called *pragmatic rules.* An example is the permission rule, which states that "If a particular action is to be taken, often a precondition must be satisfied." Most people know this rule and use it when presented with the drinking problem in the bottom half of Figure 9-7; that is, they would think about the problem in terms of permission. Once activated, the rule would lead people to look for failures to meet the relevant precondition (that is, being under age 19), which in turn would lead them to choose the "16" card. In contrast, the permission rule would not be triggered by the letter-number problem in the top half of Figure 9-7, so there is no reason for people to choose the "7" card. Thus, the content of a problem affects whether or not a pragmatic rule is activated, which in turn affects the correctness of reasoning (Cheng, Holyoak, Nisbett, & Oliver, 1986).

In addition to applying rules, participants may sometimes solve the drinking problem by setting up a concrete representation of the situation; this is called a *mental model.* They may, for example, imagine two people, each with a number on his back and a drink in his hand. They may then inspect this mental model and see what happens, for example, if the drinker with "16" on his back has a beer in his hand. According to this idea, we reason in terms of mental models that are suggested by the content of the problem (Johnson-Laird, 1989).

The two procedures just described—applying pragmatic rules and constructing mental models—have one thing in common. They are determined by the content of the problem. This is in contrast to the application of logical rules, which should not be affected by problem content. Hence, our sensitivity to content often prevents us from operating as logicians in solving a problem.

Inductive Reasoning

Logical Rules   Logicians have noted that an argument can be good even if it is not deductively valid. Such arguments are **inductively strong,** meaning that *it is improbable that the conclusion is false if the premises are*

true (Skyrms, 1986). An example of an inductively strong argument is as follows:

> 3. a. Mitch majored in accounting in college.
>
>   b. Mitch now works for an accounting firm.
>
>   c. Therefore, Mitch is an accountant.

This argument is not deductively valid (Mitch may have tired of accounting courses and taken a night-watchman's job). Inductive strength, then, is a matter of probabilities, not certainties; and (according to logicians) inductive logic should be based on the theory of probability.

We make and evaluate inductive arguments all the time. In doing so, do we rely on the rules of probability theory as a logician or mathematician would? One relevant probability rule is the *base-rate rule,* which states that the probability of something being a member of a class (such as Mitch being a member of the class of accountants) is greater the more class members there are (that is, the higher the base rate of the class). Thus, our sample argument about Mitch being an accountant can be strengthened by adding the premise that Mitch joined a club in which 90% of the members are accountants.

Another relevant probability rule is the *conjunction rule:* The probability of a proposition cannot be less than the probability of that proposition combined with another proposition. For example, the probability that "Mitch is an accountant" cannot be less than the probability that "Mitch is an accountant and makes more than $40,000 a year." The base-rate and conjunction rules are rational guides to inductive reasoning—they are endorsed by logic—and most people will defer to them when the rules are made explicit. However, in the rough-and-tumble of everyday reasoning, people frequently violate these rules, as we are about to see.

Heuristics   A **heuristic** is *a short-cut procedure that is relatively easy to apply and can often yield the correct answer, but not inevitably so.* People often use heuristics in everyday life because they have found them to be useful. However, as the following discussion shows, they are not always dependable.

In a series of ingenious experiments, Tversky and Kahneman (1983; 1973) have shown that people violate some basic rules of probability theory when making inductive judgments. Violations of the base-rate rule are particularly common. In one experiment, one group of participants was told that a panel of psychologists had interviewed 100 people—30 engineers and 70 lawyers—and written personality descriptions of them. These participants were then given a few descriptions and asked to indicate the probability that the person described was an engineer. Some descriptions were prototypical of an engineer (for example, "Jack shows no interest in political issues and spends his free time on home carpentry"); others were neutral (for example, "Dick is a man of high ability and promises to be quite successful"). Not surprisingly, these participants rated the prototypical description as more likely to be that of an engineer.

Another group of participants was given the identical instructions and descriptions, except they were told that the 100 people were 70 engineers and 30 lawyers (the reverse of the first group). The base rate of engineers therefore differed greatly between the two groups. This difference had virtually no effect: Participants in the second group gave essentially the same ratings as those in the first group. For example, participants in both groups rated the neutral description as having a 50-50 chance of being that of an engineer (whereas the rational move would have been to rate the neutral description as more likely to be in the profession with the higher base rate). Participants completely ignored the information about base rates (Tversky & Kahneman, 1973).

People pay no more heed to the conjunction rule. In one study, participants were presented with the following description:

Linda is 31 years old, single, outspoken, and very bright. In college, she majored in philosophy . . . and was deeply concerned with issues of discrimination.

Participants then estimated the probabilities of the following two statements:

4. Linda is a bank teller.
5. Linda is a bank teller and is active in the feminist movement.

Statement 5 is the conjunction of statement 4 and the proposition "Linda is active in the feminist movement." In flagrant violation of the conjunction rule, most participants rated statement 5 as more probable than statement 4. This is a fallacy because every feminist bank teller is a bank teller, but some female bank tellers are not feminists, and Linda could be one of them (Tversky & Kahneman, 1983).

Participants in this study based their judgments on the fact that Linda seems more similar to a feminist bank teller than to a bank teller. Although they were asked to estimate probability, participants instead estimated the similarity of Linda to the prototype of the concepts "bank teller" and "feminist bank teller." Thus, estimating similarity is used as a heuristic for estimating probability. People use the similarity heuristic because similarity often relates to probability yet is easier to calculate. Use of the similarity heuristic also explains why people ignore base rates. In the engineer-lawyer study described earlier, participants may have considered only the similarity of the description to their prototypes of "engineer" and "lawyer." Hence, given a description that matched the prototypes of "engineer" and "lawyer" equally well, participants judged that engineer and lawyer were equally probable. Reliance on the similarity heuristic can lead to errors even by experts.

Reasoning by similarity shows up in another common reasoning situation, that in which we know some members of a category have a particular property and have to decide whether other members of the category have that property as well. In one study, participants had to judge which of the following two arguments seemed stronger:

6. a. All robins have sesamoid bones.
   b. Therefore all sparrows have sesamoid bones.
   versus
7. a. All robins have sesamoid bones.
   b. Therefore all ostriches have sesamoid bones.

Not surprisingly, participants judged the first argument to be stronger, presumably because robins are more similar to sparrows than they are to ostriches. This use of similarity appears rational, inasmuch as it fits with the idea that things that have many known properties in common are likely to have unknown properties in common as well. But the veneer of rationality fades when we consider participants' judgments on another pair of arguments:

7. a. All robins have sesamoid bones.

    b. Therefore all ostriches have sesamoid bones (same as the preceding argument).

    versus

8. a. All robins have sesamoid bones.

    b. Therefore all birds have sesamoid bones.

Participants judged the second argument to be stronger, presumably because robins are more similar to the prototype of birds than they are to ostriches. But this judgment is a fallacy: On the basis of the same evidence (that robins have sesamoid bones), it cannot be more likely that all birds have some property than that all ostriches do, because ostriches are in fact birds. Again, our similarity-based intuitions can sometimes lead us astray (Osherson et al., 1990).

Similarity is not our only strong heuristic; another is the causality heuristic. People estimate the probability of a situation by the strength of the causal connections between the events in the situation. For example, people judge statement 10 to be more probable than statement 9:

9. Sometime during the year 2000 there will be a massive flood in California in which more than 1,000 people will drown.

10. Sometime during the year 2000, there will be an earthquake in California, causing a massive flood in which more than 1,000 people will drown.

Judging statement 10 to be more probable than statement 9 is another violation of the conjunction rule (and hence another fallacy). This time, the violation arises because in statement 10 the flood has a strong causal connection to another event, the earthquake; whereas in statement 9 the flood alone is mentioned and hence has no causal connections.

Thus, our reliance on heuristics often leads us to ignore some basic rational rules,

including the base-rate and conjunction rules. But we should not be too pessimistic about our level of rationality. For one thing, the similarity and causality heuristics probably lead to correct decisions in most cases. Another point is that under the right circumstances we can appreciate the relevance of certain logical rules to particular problems and use them appropriately (Nisbett et al., 1983). For example, in reading and thinking about this discussion, you were probably able to see the relevance of the base-rate and conjunction rules to the problems at hand.

Imaginal Thought

Earlier we mentioned that, in addition to propositional thought, we can also think in an imaginal mode, particularly in terms of visual images. In this section we take a closer look at such visual thinking.

We seem to do some of our thinking visually. Often we retrieve past perceptions, or parts of them, and operate on them the way we would operate on a real percept. To appreciate this point, try to answer the following three questions:

1. What shape are a German shepherd's ears?

2. What new letter is formed when an uppercase N is rotated 90 degrees?

3. How many windows are there in your parents' living room?

When answering the first question, most people report that they form a visual image of a German shepherd's head and "look" at the ears to determine their shape. When answering the second question, people report first forming an image of a capital N and then mentally "rotating" it 90 degrees and "looking" at it to determine its identity. And when answering the third question, people report imagining the room and then "scanning" the image while counting the windows (Kosslyn, 1983; Shepard & Cooper, 1982).

These examples are based on subjective impressions, but they and other evidence suggest that imagery involves the same representations and processes that are used in perception (Finke, 1985). Our images of objects and places have visual detail: We see the German shepherd, the N, or our parents' living room in our "mind's eye." Moreover, the mental operations that we perform on these images seem to be analogous to the operations we carry out on real visual objects: We scan the image of our parents' room in much the same way that we would scan a real room, and we rotate our image of the N the way we would rotate the real object.

The Neural Basis of Imagery

Perhaps the most persuasive evidence for imagery being like perception would be demonstrations that the two are mediated by the same brain structures. In recent years a substantial amount of evidence of this sort has accumulated.

Some of the evidence comes from studies of brain-damaged patients and shows that any problem the patient has in visual perception is typically accompanied by a parallel problem in visual imagery (Farah, Hammond, & Levine, 1988). A particularly striking example is seen in patients who suffer damage in the parietal lobe of the right hemisphere and as a result develop visual neglect of the left side of the visual field. Though not blind, these patients ignore everything on the left side of their visual field. A male patient, for example, may neglect to shave the left side of his face. The Italian neurologist Bisiach (Bisiach & Luzzatti, 1978) found that this visual neglect extends to imagery. He asked patients with visual neglect to imagine a familiar square in their native Milan as it looks while standing in the square facing the church. The patients reported most objects on their right but few on their left. When asked to imagine the scene from the opposite perspective, while standing in front of the church and looking out into the square, the patients neglected the objects they had previously reported (which were now on the left side of the image). Thus, these patients manifested the same kind of neglect in imagery that they did in perception, which suggests that the damaged brain structures normally mediate imagery as well as perception.

Some recent studies have used brain-scanning methods to demonstrate that in normal individuals the parts of the brain involved in perception are also involved in imagery. In one experiment, participants performed both a mental arithmetic task ("Start at 50 and count down, subtracting by 3s") and a visual imagery task ("Visualize a walk through your neighborhood, making alternating right and left turns starting at your door"). While a participant was doing each task, the amount of blood flow in various areas of his or her cortex was measured. There was more blood flow in the visual cortex when participants engaged in the imagery task than when they engaged in the mental arithmetic task. Moreover, the pattern of blood flow found during the imagery task was like that normally found in perceptual tasks (Roland & Friberg, 1985).

A PET experiment by Kosslyn et al. (1993) provides a striking comparison of the brain structures involved in perception and imagery. While having their brains scanned, participants performed two different tasks, a perception task and an imagery task. In the perception task, first a block capital letter was presented on a background grid and then an X was presented in one of the grid cells; the participant's task was to decide as quickly as possible whether or not the X fell on part of the block letter (see Figure 9-8). In the imagery task, the background grid was again presented, but without a block capital letter. Under the grid was a lowercase

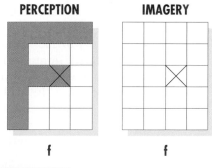

PERCEPTION   IMAGERY

f   f

FIGURE 9-8

Imagery and Perception *Tasks used to determine whether visual imagery involves the same brain structures as visual perception. In the perception task, participants must decide whether or not the X fell on part of the block letter. In the imagery task, participants generate an image of the block letter and then decide whether or not the X fell on part of the (image of the) block letter. The person knows which letter to image because the lowercase version of it is presented below the grid (the lowercase version is also presented in the perception task, just to keep things comparable).* (After Kosslyn et al., 1993)

letter, and participants had been previously instructed to generate an image of the capital version of the lowercase letter and project it onto the grid. Then an *X* was presented in one of the grid cells, and participants were asked to determine whether or not the *X* fell on part of the imagined block letter. Not surprisingly, the perception task resulted in heightened neural activity in parts of the visual cortex. But so did the imagery task. Indeed, the imagery task resulted in increased activity in brain structures that are among the first regions of the cortex to receive visual information.

Thus, imagery is like perception from the early stages of cortical processing. Moreover, when the neural activations from the two tasks were directly compared, there was more activation in the imagery task than in the perception task, presumably reflecting the fact that the imagery task required more "perceptual work" than the perception task. These results leave little doubt that imagery and perception are mediated by the same neural mechanisms. Here again biological research has provided evidence to support a hypothesis that was first proposed at the psychological level.

Imaginal Operations

We have noted that the mental operations performed on images seem to be analogous to those that we carry out on real visual objects. Numerous experiments provide objective evidence for these subjective impressions.

One operation that has been studied intensively is mental rotation. In a classic experiment, participants saw the capital letter R on each trial. The letter was presented either normally or backward, and either in its usual vertical orientation or rotated by various degrees (see Figure 9-9). The participants had to decide whether the letter was normal or backward. The more the letter had been rotated from its vertical orientation, the longer it took the participants to make the decision (see Figure 9-10). This finding suggests that participants made their decisions by mentally rotating the image of the letter until it was vertical and then checking to determine whether it was normal or backward.

Another operation that is similar in imagery and perception is that of scanning an object or array. In an experiment on

scanning an image, participants first studied the map of a fictional island that contained seven key locations. The map was removed, and participants were asked to form an image of it and fixate on a particular location (for example, the tree in the southern part of the island—see Figure 9-11). Then the experimenter named another location (for example, the tree at the northern tip of the island). Starting at the fixated location, the participants were to scan their images until they found the named location and to push a button upon "arriving" there. The greater the distance between the fixated location and the named one, the longer the participants took to respond. This suggests that they were scanning their images in much the same way that they scan real objects.

Another commonality between imaginal and perceptual processing is that both are

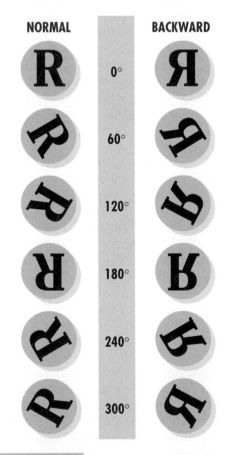

FIGURE 9-9

A Study of Mental Rotation *Shown are examples of the letters presented to participants in studies of mental rotation. On each presentation, participants had to decide whether the letter was normal or backward. Numbers indicate deviation from the vertical in degrees. (After Cooper & Shepard, 1973)*

limited by grain size. On a television screen, for instance, the grain of the picture tube determines how small the details of a picture can be and still remain perceptible. While there is no such screen in the brain, we can think of our images as occurring in a mental medium whose grain limits the amount of detail we can detect in an image. If this grain size is fixed, smaller images should be more difficult to inspect than larger ones. A good deal of evidence supports this claim. In one experiment, participants first formed an image of a familiar animal—for example, a cat. Then they were asked to decide whether or not the imaged object had a particular property. Participants made decisions faster for larger properties, such as the head, than for smaller ones, such as the claws. In another study, participants were asked to image an animal at different relative sizes—small, medium, or large. They were then asked to decide whether their images had a particular property. Their decisions were faster for larger images than smaller ones. Thus, in imagery as in perception, the larger the image, the more readily we can see the details of an object (Kosslyn, 1980).

Visual Creativity

There are innumerable stories about scientists and artists producing their most creative work through visual thinking (Shepard & Cooper, 1982). Although they are not solid evidence, these stories are among the best indicators we have of the power of visual thinking. It is surprising that visual thinking appears to be quite effective in highly abstract areas such as mathematics and physics. Albert Einstein, for example, said that he rarely thought in words; rather, he worked out his ideas in terms of "more or less clear images which can be 'voluntarily' reproduced and combined." Thus, Einstein claimed that he had his initial insight into the theory of relativity when he thought about what he "saw" when he imagined that he was chasing after and matching the speed of a beam of light.

Perhaps the most celebrated example of visual thinking occurred in the field of chemistry. Friedrich Kekule von Stradonitz was trying to determine the molecular structure of benzene (which turned out to have a ring structure). One night he dreamed that a

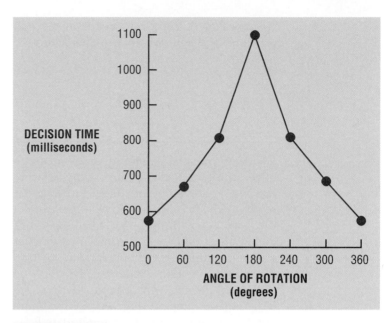

FIGURE 9-10

Decision Times in the Mental Rotation Study   *The time taken to decide whether a letter had normal or reversed orientation was greatest when the rotation was 180° so that the letter was upside down.* (After Cooper & Shepard, 1973)

FIGURE 9-11

Scanning Mental Images   *The person scans the image of the island from south to north, looking for the named location. It appears as though the individual's mental image is like a real map and that it takes longer to scan across the mental image if the distance to be scanned is greater.* (After Kosslyn, Ball, & Reiser, 1978)

writing, snakelike figure suddenly twisted into a closed loop, biting its own tail. The structure of the snake proved to be the structure of benzene. A dream image had provided the solution to a major scientific problem.

Thought in Action: Problem Solving

For many people, solving a problem epitomizes thinking itself. When solving a problem, we are striving for a goal but have no ready means of obtaining it. We must break the goal down into subgoals, and perhaps divide these subgoals further into smaller subgoals, until we reach a level that we have the means to obtain (Anderson, 1990).

We can illustrate these points with a simple problem. Suppose that you need to figure out the combination of an unfamiliar lock. You know only that the combination has four numbers and that whenever you come across a correct number you will hear a click. Your overall goal is to find the combination. Rather than trying four numbers at random, most people divide the overall goal into four subgoals, each corresponding to finding one of the four numbers in the combination. Your first subgoal is to find the first number, and you have a procedure for accomplishing this—namely, turning the lock slowly while listening for a click. Your second subgoal is to find the second number, for which you can use the same procedure, and so on for the remaining subgoals.

The strategies that people use to decompose goals into subgoals is a major issue in the study of problem solving. Another issue is how people represent a problem mentally, because this also affects how readily we can solve the problem. The following discussion considers both of these issues.

Problem-Solving Strategies

Much of what we know about strategies for breaking down goals derives from the research of Newell and Simon (1972). Typically the researchers ask participants to think aloud while trying to solve a difficult problem; they then analyze the participants' verbal responses for clues to the underlying strategy. A number of general-purpose strategies have been identified in this way.

One strategy is to reduce the difference between our current state in a problem situation and our goal state, in which a solution is obtained. Consider again the combination lock problem. Initially our current state includes no knowledge of any of the numbers, while our goal state includes knowledge of all four numbers. We therefore set up the subgoal of reducing the difference between these two states; identifying the first number accomplishes this subgoal. Our current state now includes knowledge of the first number. There is still a difference between our current state and our goal state; we can reduce this difference identifying the second number, and so on for the third and fourth numbers. Thus, the key idea behind difference reduction is that we set up subgoals that, when obtained, put us in a state that is closer to our goal.

A similar but more sophisticated strategy is *means-ends analysis*. We compare our current state to the goal state in order to find the most important difference between them; eliminating this difference becomes our main subgoal. We then search for a means or procedure to achieve this subgoal. If we find such a procedure but discover that something in our current state prevents us from applying it, we introduce a new subgoal of eliminating this obstacle. Many common-sense problem-solving situations involve this strategy. Here is an example:

> I want to take my son to nursery school. What's the [most important] difference between what I have and what I want? One of distance. What [procedure] changes distance? My automobile. My automobile won't work. What is needed to make it work? A new battery. What has new batteries? An auto repair shop. (After Newell & Simon, 1972, as cited in Anderson, 1990, p. 232)

Means-ends analysis is more sophisticated than difference reduction because it allows us to take action even if it results in a temporary decrease in similarity between our current state and the goal state. In the example just presented, the auto repair shop may be in the opposite direction from the nursery school. Going to the shop temporarily increases the distance from the goal, yet this step is essential for solving the problem.

Another strategy is to work backward from the goal. This is particularly useful in solving mathematical problems like the one illustrated in Figure 9-12. The problem is this: Given that ABCD is a rectangle, prove that

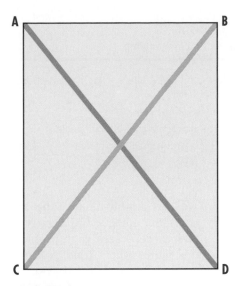

FIGURE 9-12

An Illustrative Geometry Problem   *Given that ABCD is a rectangle, prove that the line segments AD and BC are the same length.*

AD and BC are the same length. In working backward, one might proceed as follows:

> What could prove that AD and BC are the same length? I could prove this if I could prove that the triangles ACD and BDC are congruent. I can prove that ACD and BDC are congruent if I could prove that two sides and an included angle are equal. (After Anderson, 1990, p. 238)

We reason from the goal to a subgoal (proving the triangles congruent), from that subgoal to another subgoal (proving the sides and angle equal), and so on, until we reach a subgoal that we have a ready means of obtaining.

The three strategies that we have considered—difference reduction, means-ends analysis, and working backward—are extremely general and can be applied to virtually any problem. These strategies, which are often referred to as *weak methods,* do not rest on any specific knowledge and may even be innate. People are especially likely to rely on these weak methods when they are first learning about an area and are working on problems whose content is unfamiliar. When people gain expertise in an area, they develop more powerful *domain-specific procedures* (and representations), which come to dominate the weak methods (Anderson, 1987).

Representing the Problem

Being able to solve a problem depends not only on our strategy for breaking it down but also on how we represent it. Sometimes a propositional representation works best; at other times a visual representation or image is more effective. To illustrate, consider the following problem:

> One morning, exactly at sunrise, a monk began to climb a mountain. A narrow path, a foot or two wide, spiraled around the mountain to a temple at the summit. The monk ascended at varying rates, stopping many times along the way to rest. He reached the temple shortly before sunset. After several days at the temple, he began his journey back along the same path, starting at sunrise and again walking at variable speeds with many pauses along the way. His average speed descending was, of course, greater than his average climbing speed. Prove that there exists a particular spot along the path that the monk will occupy on both trips at precisely the same time of day. (Adams, 1974, p. 4)

In trying to solve this problem, many people start with a propositional representation. They may even try to write out a set of equations. The problem is far easier to solve when it is represented visually. All you need do is visualize the upward journey of the monk

Learning aids help students visualize a math problem.

superimposed on the downward journey. Imagine one monk starting at the bottom and the other at the top. No matter what their speed, at some time and at some point along the path the two monks will meet. Thus, there must be a spot along the path that the monk occupied on both trips at precisely the same time of day. (Note that the problem did not ask you where the spot was.)

Some problems can be readily solved by manipulating either propositions or images. We can illustrate this point with the following simple problem: "Ed runs faster than David but slower than Dan; who's the slowest of the three men?" To solve this problem in terms of propositions, note that we can represent the first part of the problem as a proposition that has "David" as subject and "is slower than Ed" as predicate. We can represent the second part of the problem as a proposition with "Ed" as subject and "is slower than Dan" as predicate. We can then deduce that David is slower than Dan, which makes David the slowest. To solve the problem by means of imagery, we might imagine the three men's speeds as points on a line, like this:

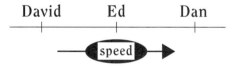

TABLE 9-2

Steps in Problem Solving

1. Represent the problem as a proposition or in visual form.
2. Determine the goal.
3. Break down the goal into subgoals.
4. Select a problem-solving strategy and apply it to achieve each subgoal.

Then we can simply "read" the answer directly from the image. Apparently some people prefer to represent such problems as propositions while others tend to represent them visually (Johnson-Laird, 1985).

In addition to the issue of propositions versus images, there are questions about what is represented. Often we have difficulty with a problem because we fail to include something important in our representation or because we include something in our representation that is not an important part of the problem. We can illustrate this point with an experiment. One group of participants was given the problem of supporting a candle on a door, using only the materials depicted in Figure 9-13. The solution was to tack the box to the door and use the box as a platform for the candle. Most participants had difficulty with the problem, presumably because they represented the box as a container, not as a platform. Another group of participants was given the identical problem except that the contents of the box were removed. These participants had more success in solving the problem, presumably because they were less likely to include the box's container property in their representation and more likely to include its supporter property. Studies like this provide an inkling of why many experts believe that arriving at a useful representation of a problem is half the battle in solving the problem. (The steps in problem solving are listed in Table 9-2.)

Experts Versus Novices

In a given content area (physics, geography, or chess, for instance), experts solve problems qualitatively differently than novices do. These differences are due to differences in the representations and strategies used by experts and novices. Experts have many

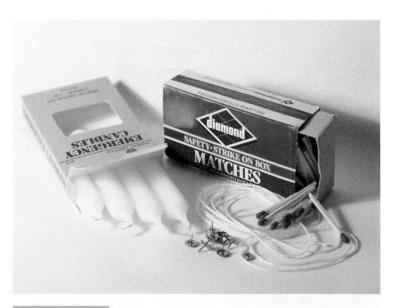

FIGURE 9-13

Materials for the Candle Problem *Given the materials depicted, how can you support a candle on a door? The solution is shown on page 340.* (After Glucksberg & Weisberg, 1966)

more specific representations stored in memory that they can bring to bear on a problem. A master chess player, for example, can look for 5 seconds at a configuration of over 20 pieces and reproduce it perfectly; a novice in this situation can reproduce only the usual 7 ± 2 items (see Chapter 8). Experts can accomplish this memory feat because through years of practice they have developed representations of many possible configurations of chess pieces; these representations permit them to encode a complex configuration in just a few chunks. Further, these representations are presumably what underlies their superior chess game. A master may have stored as many as 50,000 configurations and has learned what to do when each one arises. Thus, master chess players can essentially "see" possible moves; they do not have to think them out the way novices do (Chase & Simon, 1973; Simon & Gilmartin, 1973).

Even when they are confronted with a novel problem, experts represent it differently than novices do. This point is illustrated by studies of problem solving in physics. An expert (say, a physics professor) represents a problem in terms of the physical principle that is needed for solution: For example, "this is one of those every-action-has-an-equal-and-opposite-reaction problems." In contrast, a novice (say, a student taking a first course in physics) tends to represent the same problem in terms of its surface features: For example, "this is one of those inclined-plane problems" (Chi, Glaser, & Rees, 1982).

Experts and novices also differ in the strategies they employ. In studies of physics problem solving, experts generally try to formulate a plan for attacking the problem before generating equations, whereas novices typically start writing equations with no general plan in mind (Larkin, McDermott, Simon, & Simon, 1980). Another difference is that experts tend to reason from the givens of a problem toward a solution, while novices tend to work in the reverse direction (the working-backward strategy). This difference in the direction of reasoning

Experts solve problems in qualitatively different ways than novices do. Experts such as chess masters have many more specific representations stored in memory that they can bring to bear on a problem.

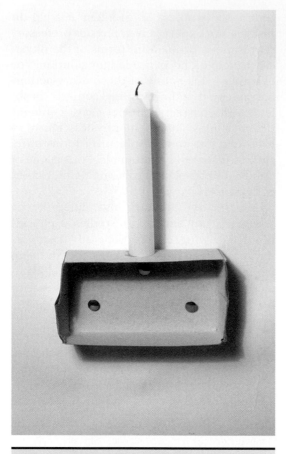

The solution to the candle problem.

has also been found in studies of how physicians solve problems. More expert physicians tend to reason in a forward direction—from symptom to possible disease—while the less expert tend to reason in a backward direction—from possible disease to symptom (Patel & Groen, 1986).

The characteristics of expertise just discussed—a multitude of representations, representations based on principles, planning before acting, and working forward—make up some of the domain-specific procedures that come to dominate the weak methods of problem solving discussed earlier.

Computer Simulation

To study how people solve problems, researchers often use computer simulation. After having people think aloud while solving a complex problem, the researchers use their verbal reports as a guide in programming a computer to solve the problem. The

output can be compared with aspects of people's performance on the problem—for example, the sequence of moves—to see whether they match. If they match, the computer program offers a theory of some aspects of problem solving. Computer simulation has played a major role in the study of weak methods of problem solving as well as of expert procedures.

Why use computers in this way to learn about people? Perhaps the most interesting answer is Simon's claim: "The reason human beings can think is because they are able to carry out with neurons the simple kinds of processes that computers do with tubes or chips" (1985, p. 3). These processes include reading, outputting, storing, and comparing symbols; we do one thing if the symbols match and another if they differ. To the extent that we can simulate human problem solving on a computer, which uses just these simple processes, we have support for Simon's claim.

Consider what is involved in trying to write a computer program that simulates the way many of us solve simple algebraic equations. When confronted with the equation $3X + 4 = X + 10$, you might have learned to reason as follows:

> The solution of the equation looks like an X followed by an $=$ sign followed by a number—not any number, it has to be one that will fit the equation if I substitute it back in. If I start out with something that has a number on the left side where I don't want it, then I'd better get rid of it. So given $3X + 4 = X + 10$, I subtract the 4 (I know I have to subtract it from both sides). Then I have a new equation, $3X = X + 6$. But I don't want an X on the right side of the equation. So I subtract it and now have $2X = 6$. Now I don't want a $2X$, but instead just a plain X on the left side of the equation, so I divide by 2. Then I have $X = 3$. (After Simon, 1985, p. 6)

This reasoning can be captured by four rules:

1. If there is a number on the left side of the equation, subtract it from both sides.

2. If there is an X or a multiple of X on the right side of the equation, subtract it from both sides.

3. If there is a number in front of the X on the left side of the equation, divide both sides of the equation by it.

4. If you arrive at an equation that looks like "X = Number," quit and check your answer.

Although you probably do not articulate these rules, they may underlie your ability to solve algebraic equations. These rules (often referred to as *algorithms*) can readily be translated into a computer program. A program is simply a detailed set of instructions (written in a language designed for a computer) that specifies every step the machine must take. Our rules can be treated as such instructions. Thus, simulation requires that we first be precise about the knowledge involved and then translate it into the language of a computer.

Some critics have challenged the analogy between computers and people: Computers, they say, can do only what they have been programmed to do. However, it is quite possible that humans also can do only what heredity and experience have "programmed" them to do. The analogy between computers and human minds remains appealing because these two kinds of entities are the most complex information-processing systems that we know of. Moreover, as computer scientists continue to design computers to function more like people, the mind-computer analogy will grow even stronger.

How Language Can Direct Thought: Linguistic Relativity and Linguistic Determinism

Dan I. Slobin, *University of California, Berkeley*

Dan I. Slobin

No one would disagree with the claim that language and thought interact in many significant ways. There is disagreement, however, about the proposition that each language has its own influence on the thought and action of its speakers. On the one hand, anyone who has learned more than one language is struck by the many ways in which languages differ from one another. On the other hand, we expect human beings everywhere to have similar ways of experiencing the world.

There are two issues here: linguistic relativity and linguistic determinism. Relativity is easy to demonstrate. While speaking any language, you have to pay attention to the meanings that are grammatically marked in that language. For example, in English you must mark the verb to indicate the time of occurrence of an event you are speaking about: "It's raining"; "It rained"; and so forth. Turkish, however, like many Native-American languages, has more than one past tense, depending on one's source of knowledge of the event. There are two past tenses—one to report direct experience and the other to report events that you know about only by inference or hearsay. Thus, if you were out in the rain last night, you will say, "It rained last night," using the form that indicates you were a witness to the rain; but if you wake up in the morning and see the wet street and garden, you are obliged to use the other past-tense form—the one

that indicates that you were not a witness to the rain itself.

Differences of this sort have long fascinated linguists and anthropologists, who have provided hundreds of facts about "exotic" languages—for example, that the form of a verb of handling can depend on the shape of an object that is being handled (Navajo). But it must be pointed out that "nonexotic" languages also have their surprises. For example, in English it is not appropriate to say, "Richard Nixon has worked in Washington," but it is perfectly okay to say, "George Bush has worked in Washington." Why? English restricts the present-perfect tense ("has worked") to assertions about people who are alive. Exotic!

Proponents of linguistic determinism argue that such differences between languages influence the ways people think—perhaps the ways in which whole cultures are organized. Among the strongest statements of this position are those by Benjamin Lee Whorf and his teacher, Edward Sapir, in the first half of the 20th century—hence the label, "The Sapir-Whorf Hypothesis," for the theory of linguistic relativity and determinism. How can such bold claims be substantiated? If one takes the hypothesis seriously, it should be possible to show that Turks are more sensitive to evidence than are Americans, but that Americans are more aware of death than Turks. Clearly, the hypothesis cannot be supported on so grand a level. Rather, experimental psychologists and cognitive anthropologists have sought to find small differences, on controlled tasks, between speakers of various languages.

The results have been mixed. In most cases, human thought and action are overdetermined by an

array of causes, so the structure of language may not play a central causal role. Linguistic determinism can best be demonstrated in situations in which language is the principal means of drawing people's attention to particular aspects of experience. Some of the most convincing empirical research demonstrating some degree of linguistic determinism is being conducted under the direction of Stephen C. Levinson. For example, Levinson and his collaborators distinguish between languages that describe spatial relations in terms of the body (such as English "right/left," "front/back") and those that orient to fixed points in the environment (such as "north/south/east/west" in some aboriginal Australian languages). In a language of the second type one would refer, for example, to "your north shoulder" or "the west end of the table"; in narrating a past event, one would have to remember how the actions related to the compass points. Thus, in order to speak this type of language, you always have to know where you are with respect to the compass points, whether you are speaking or not. And Levinson's group has shown, in extensive cross-linguistic and cross-cultural studies, that this is, in fact, the case.

Much more research needs to be done, but it is evident that language is only one of the factors shaping human thought and action. However, because language is so pervasive—and because we must always make cognitive decisions while speaking—the hypothesis of linguistic determinism will continue to attract scientific attention. (For a lively debate on many of these issues, read Gumperz and Levinson, 1996.)

The Influence of Thought on Language

Eleanor Rosch, *University of California, Berkeley*

Are we trapped by our language into a particular view of the world? According to the most dramatic form of the hypothesis of linguistic determinism (Whorf, 1956), the grammar of each language embodies a complete metaphysic. For example, while English has nouns and verbs, Nootka has only verbs, and Hopi divides the world into the two principles of manifest and unmanifest. Whorf claims that such linguistic differences mold the minds of speakers into mutually incomprehensible ways of thinking.

What evidence do we have for the effect of linguistic differences on thought? At the level of metaphysic, Whorf used bizarre-sounding literal translations from Native American languages to make his case. But *literal* translations from any language, even familiar ones such as French or German, sound equally strange. At the level of whole societies, language, culture, and thought cannot be separated experimentally. Even in the case where a difference in world view or "metaphysic" has been documented, such as in the Eastern meditation traditions, peoples' ability to understand those traditions has been found to depend on the practices they do, not on the languages they speak or learn (Rosch, 1997).

A less-sweeping Whorfian claim is that grammatical form classes (such as nouns and verbs in English or shape classifiers in Navajo) affect aspects of thought such as classification or memory. Here one can do experiments, but the findings have been largely negative. For example, grammatical classes do not aid memory the way semantic classes (meaning units such as *plants* or *animals*) do. And speaking a language with shape classifiers does not assure that one will prefer to classify items by shape rather than color. Perhaps grammatical form classes become so automatically processed that they lose much of their semantic meaningfulness for speakers. Or perhaps there is a separate module of thinking, specifically for speaking, which does not necessarily interact with the rest of the meaning system (Slobin, 1997).

Most research on the language and thought issue has been at the still narrower level of vocabulary items. Do the Inuit really have many words for snow, and do the words as such, rather than the snow, affect their thought? But even vocabulary is not easy to isolate from other factors. Languages have names for things in their environments (such as *microchip*); words that map important social and cultural distinction (such as separate terms for *older brother* and *younger brother*); ways of referring to distinctions not encoded by single vocabulary items (skiers find many ways to refer to different kinds of snow); and changes in vocabulary to reflect social change (the disappearance of the polite *you* and familiar *thou* distinction in English). Color categories were once thought to be an ideal domain for vocabulary research since one can measure both color (using the physics of light) and aspects of thought (such as color memory) independently of language. However, the findings have suggested that most facts about both color vocabulary and cognition are determined by the human visual system, with only a secondary role played by language (Hardin & Maffi, 1997; Rosch, 1974). As Slobin (this volume) has indicated, location words are the domain in which there is the most persuasive evidence for effects of a linguistic reference system on thinking. But note that this is a circumscribed domain and that the prag-

Eleanor Rosch

matics of location (finding objects and finding one's way around) are adequately conveyed by all systems.

What can we learn from all this? Certainly language differences are intriguing and important, but they do not exist in *isolation*. Posing scientific questions as a dichotomy of isolated extremes on which contributors must take adversarial positions, as in a courtroom or political debate, may be more a matter of our culture (Peng & Nisbett, in press; Tannen, 1998) than of good science that leads to lasting knowledge. We need to learn to think about the relation of language and thought, as well as other polarities in psychology, in terms of interesting, but complex, mutually determining units.

SUMMARY

1. Language, our primary means for communicating thoughts, is structured at three levels. At the highest level are sentence units, including phrases that can be related to thoughts or propositions. The next level is that of words and parts of words that carry meaning. The lowest level contains speech sounds. The phrases of a sentence are built from words (and parts of words), whereas the words themselves are constructed from speech sounds.

2. A phoneme is a category of speech sounds. Every language has its own set of phonemes and rules for combining them into words. A morpheme is the smallest unit that carries meaning. Most morphemes are words; others are prefixes and suffixes that are added to words. A language also has syntactic rules for combining words into phrases and phrases into sentences. Understanding a sentence requires not only analyzing phonemes, morphemes, and phrases but also using context and understanding the speaker's intention.

3. Language development occurs at three different levels. Infants come into the world preprogrammed to learn phonemes, but they need several years to learn the rules for combining them. When children begin to speak, they learn words that name familiar concepts. In learning to produce sentences, they begin with one-word utterances, progress to two-word telegraphic speech, and then elaborate their noun and verb phrases.

4. Children learn language at least partly by testing hypotheses. Children's hypotheses appear to be guided by a small set of operating principles, which call the children's attention to critical characteristics of utterances, such as word endings. Innate factors also play a role in language acquisition.

5. Our innate knowledge of language seems to be very rich and detailed, as suggested by the fact that all children seem to go through the same stages in acquiring a language. Like other innate behaviors, some language abilities are learned only during a critical period. It is a matter of controversy whether or not our innate capacity to learn language is unique to our species. Many studies suggest that chimpanzees and gorillas can learn signs that are equivalent to our words, but they have difficulty learning to combine these signs in the systematic way in which humans combine words.

6. Thought occurs in different modes, including propositional, imaginal, and motoric. The basic component of a proposition is a concept, the set of properties that we associate with a class. Concepts provide cognitive economy by allowing us to code many different objects as instances of the same concept, and also permit us to predict information that is not readily perceptible.

7. A concept includes both a prototype (properties that describe the best examples) and a core (properties that are most essential for being a member of the concept). Core properties play a major role in well-defined concepts like "bachelor"; prototype properties dominate in fuzzy concepts like "bird." Most natural concepts are fuzzy. Concepts are sometimes organized into hierarchies; in such cases, one level of the hierarchy is the basic or preferred level for categorization.

8. Children often learn the prototype of a concept by following an exemplar strategy. With this technique, a novel item is classified as an instance of a concept if it is sufficiently similar to a known exemplar of the concept. As children grow older, they use hypothesis testing as another strategy for learning concepts. Different categorization processes have been shown to involve different brain mechanisms.

9. In reasoning, we organize our propositions into an argument. Some arguments are deductively valid: It is impossible that the conclusion of the argument is false if its premises are true. When evaluating a deductive argument, we sometimes try to prove that the conclusion follows from the premises by using logical rules. Other times, however, we use heuristics—rules of thumb—that operate on the content of propositions rather than on their logical form.

10. Some arguments are inductively strong: It is improbable that the conclusion is false if the premises are true. In generating and evaluating such arguments, we often ignore some of the principles of probability theory and rely instead on heuristics that focus on similarity or causality.

11. Not all thoughts are expressed in propositions; some are manifested as visual images. Such images contain the kind of visual detail found in perceptions. Imagery seems to be like perception because it is mediated by the same parts of the brain. Thus, brain damage that causes certain perceptual problem, visual neglect, also causes comparable problems in imagery. Experiments using brain scanning techniques indicate that the specific brain regions involved in an imagery task are the same as those involved in a perceptual task. In addition, the mental operations performed on images (such as scanning and rotation) are like the operations carried out on perceptions.

12. Problem solving requires breaking down a goal into subgoals that are easier to obtain. Strategies for doing this include reducing differences between the current state and the goal state; means-ends analysis (eliminating the most important differences between the current and goal states); and working backward. Some problems are easier to solve by using a propositional representation; for other problems, a visual representation works best.

13. Expert problem solvers differ from novices in four basic ways: They have more representations to bring to bear on the problem; they represent novel problems in terms of solution principles rather than surface features; they form a plan before acting; and they tend to reason forward rather than working backward. A useful method for studying problem solving is computer simulation, in which one tries to write a computer program that solves problems the same way people do.

KEY TERMS

production (p. 306)
comprehension (p. 306)
phoneme (p. 307)
word (p. 307)
morpheme (p. 307)
syntax (p. 310)
overextension (p. 313)
propositional thought (p. 319)
imaginal thought (p. 319)
motoric thought (p. 319)

proposition (p. 319)
concept (p. 320)
categorization (p. 320)
prototype (p. 320)
core (p. 320)
abstraction (p. 326)
argument (p. 328)
deductive validity (p. 328)
inductive strength (p. 330)
heuristic (p. 330)

CRITICAL THINKING QUESTIONS

1. Now that you have some idea of the units and levels of language (e.g., phonemes, words, semantics, syntax, speaker's intentions), apply these notions to learning a second language. Which components do you think will be easiest and hardest to learn? Why?

2. In this chapter we considered cases in which prototypes seem to be universal, that is, largely unaffected by culture. Can you think of cases in which prototypes would be greatly influenced by culture? If so, give some examples.

3. In this chapter we focused on visual imagery. By analogy, how would you find evidence for auditory imagery?

4. Think of some activity (an academic subject, a game, a sport or hobby) in which you have gained some expertise. How would you characterize the changes that you went through in improving your performance? How do these changes line up with those described in the chapter?

FURTHER READING

Numerous books deal with the psychology of language. See Osherson and Lasnik, *Invitation to Cognitive Science (Vol. 1): Language* (1990); Tartter, *Language Processes* (1986); and Carroll, *Psychology of Language* (1985). For a more advanced treatment, particularly of issues related to Chomsky's theory of language and thought, see Chomsky, *Rules and Representations* (1980); and Fodor, Bever, and Garrett, *The Psychology of Language* (1974). For an introduction to early language development (and other aspects of language), see Pinker, *The Language Gene* (1994).

A useful general resource on cognition is Wilson and Keil (eds.), *The MIT Encyclopedia of the Cognitive Sciences* (1999).

Two relatively recent introductions to the psychology of thinking are Osherson and Smith, *Invitation to Cognitive Science (Vol. 3): Thinking* (1990) and Garnham and Oakhill, *Thinking and Reasoning* (1994). The study of concepts is reviewed in Smith and Medin, *Categories and Concepts* (1981). Research on reasoning is reviewed by Kahneman, Slovic, and Tversky, *Judgment Under Uncertainty: Heuristics and Biases* (1982); for more advanced treatments of reasoning, see Holland, Holyoak, Nisbett, and Thagard, *Induction: Processes of Inference, Learning, and Discovery* (1986), Johnson-Laird and Byrne, *Deduction* (1991), and Rips, *The Psychology of Proof* (1994).

For an introduction to the study of imagery, see Kosslyn, *Ghosts in the Mind's Machine* (1983). For more advanced treatments of imagery, see Kosslyn, *Image and Mind* (1980), Shepard and Cooper, *Mental Images and Their Transformations* (1982), and Kosslyn, *The Resolution of the Imagery Debate* (1994).

For an introduction to problem solving, see Anderson, *Cognitive Psychology and Its Implications*, 3rd ed. (1990), Hayes, *The Complete Problem Solver*, 2nd ed. (1989), and Mayer, *Thinking, Problem Solving, and Cognition* (1983); for an advanced treatment, see the classic by Newell and Simon, *Human Problem Solving* (1972).

Five

Motivation and Emotion

Chapter 10
Basic Motives

*Y*ou're driving along the highway, trying to get to an important job interview on time. You were running late this morning, so you skipped breakfast; now you are starving. It seems as if every billboard on the highway is advertising food—egg and ham muffins, juicy hamburgers, cool sweet juice. Your stomach rumbles and you try to ignore it, but that is impossible. Every mile you go, you are that much hungrier. You nearly rear-end the car in front of you as you stare at a billboard advertising pizza. In short, you have been overwhelmed by the motivational state known as hunger.

A **motivation** is *a condition that energizes behavior and gives it direction*. It is experienced subjectively as a conscious desire—the desire for food, for drink, for sex. Most of us

348

can choose whether or not to act on our desires. We can force ourselves to forgo what we desire, and we can make ourselves do what we would rather not do. Perhaps we can even deliberately choose not to think about the desires that we refuse to act on. But it is considerably more difficult—perhaps impossible—to control our motivations directly. When we are hungry, it is hard not to want food. When we are hot and thirsty, we cannot help wanting a cool breeze or a cold drink. Conscious choice appears to be the consequence, rather than the cause, of our motivational states. So what does control motivation, if not rational choice?

The causes of motivation range from physiological events within the brain and body to our culture and social interactions with other individuals who surround us. This chapter will discuss the control of basic motivations such as thirst, hunger, and sex. To a large extent these motivations arise from our biological heritage and reveal general principles about how motivation and reward work to give direction to behavior. Social aspirations and cultural influences on motivation will be discussed later.

For basic motivations like hunger, thirst, and sex, psychologists have traditionally distinguished between two types of theories of motivation. The difference concerns where the motivation comes from, what causes it, and how the motivation controls behavior. On the one hand are *drive theories,* which stress the role of internal factors in motivation. Some internal drives, such as those related to hunger or thirst, have been said to reflect basic physiological needs. For motivations like sex or aggression, drive factors seem less tied to absolute physiological needs. After all, does one ever need to aggressively attack another in the same way that one needs to eat or drink? Still, aggression and sex have been said to have drive aspects, both in the sense that internal factors such as hormonal state often appear important and in the sense that they may have evolved originally to fulfill basic ancestral needs.

On the other hand are *incentive theories* of motivation, which stress the motivational role of external events or objects of desire. Food, drink, sexual partners, targets of attack, relationships with others, esteem, money and the rewards of success—all are incentives. Incentives are the objects of motivation. After all, our motivations don't operate in a vacuum—when we want, we want

The causes of motivation range from physiological events such as thirst to social aspirations and cultural influences such as those that create the desire to excel.

something. The nature of that something pulls us in one direction or another. The goal might be tasty food, water to drink, a partner for interaction, expulsion of an intruder, or possession of a disputed resource. Many incentives are rewards. They can produce pleasure and reinforce behavior that leads to them.

Some incentives are primary reinforcers, able to act as rewards independently of prior learning. For example, a sweet taste or a sexual sensation may be pleasant the first time it is experienced. Other incentives are secondary reinforcers, which have gained their status at least partly through learning about their relationship to other events. For example, money or a good grade can be effective incentives, based on our cultural experience with them and with what they represent. For animals, a conditioned stimulus that has been paired with food can serve as an effective reward. In every case, learning is crucial to the formation of secondary reinforcers. Though less important, learning may even play a part in modulating the effectiveness of some primary reinforcers. For example, you may have been hungry when you were born—but you weren't born with any idea of the foods that are now your favorites. Incentive theories of motivation focus especially on the relationship of learning and experience to the control of motivation.

Incentive and drive theories provide different perspectives on the control of motivation. But the difference between the theoretical perspectives is primarily in their points of view; there actually is no conflict between the two. It is widely acknowledged that both types of processes exist for almost every kind of motivation (Toates, 1986). But it is easier to focus on one type of control so as to thoroughly understand it before switching to another. For this reason, we will first consider incentive processes and then turn to drive processes. Note, however, that both incentive and drive factors operate together in real life, and they often interact (see Figure 10-1). For example, drive factors can enhance the motivational effect of incentives. The taste of food becomes more pleasant to most people when they are hungry (Cabanac, 1979). Have you ever skipped lunch so that you would better enjoy an evening feast? Or been scolded for snacking because it would "ruin your dinner"? Conversely, incentive factors can awaken drive states. Have you ever walked by the delicious aroma from a bakery or restaurant and suddenly realized that you were hungry?

Reward and Incentive Motivation

Motivation typically directs behavior toward a particular incentive that produces pleasure or alleviates an unpleasant state: food, drink, sex, and so forth. In other words, incentive motivation is characterized by **affect**, *the production of pleasure or displeasure.* The pervasiveness of affect in our experience of life has led some to suggest that pleasure has evolved to serve a basic psychological role (Cabanac, 1992). That role is to shape behavior by serving as a psychological "common currency" that reflects the value of each action we perform. Pleasure tends to be associated with stimuli that increase our ability to survive or our offspring's ability to survive. These include tasty food, refreshing drink, and sexual reproduction. Painful or frustrating consequences are associated with events that threaten our survival: physical damage, illness, or loss of resources. The rewarding consequences of an action, in other words, generally reflect whether the action is worth repeating. Pleasure may have evolved as a

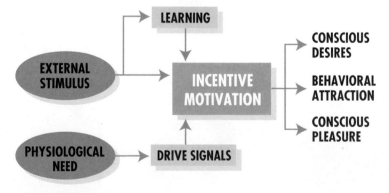

FIGURE 10-1

A Model of Basic Motives *An external stimulus, such as the sight of food, is compared to the memory of its past reward value. At the same time, physiological signals of hunger and satiety modulate the potential value at the moment. These two types of information are integrated to produce the final incentive motivation for the external stimulus, which is manifested in behavior and conscious experience.* (Adapted from Toates, 1986)

way for the brain to keep track of the good or bad consequences of past action, in order to better guide action in the future.

If pleasure is a kind of common currency for the value of diverse events, it makes sense that the brain should have a way of translating different pleasures into the equivalent "dollar value." There is indeed evidence that the brain may have a neural "common currency" for reward. It is even possible that all incentives are rewarding precisely because they activate the same brain reward system. This neural currency appears to be related to the level of activity within the mesolimbic dopamine system (see Figure 10-2). The neurons of this system lie in the upper brain stem and send their axons up to the forebrain. As their name implies, these neurons use the neurotransmitter dopamine to convey their message.

The mesolimbic dopamine system is activated by many kinds of natural rewards, such as tasty food or drink or a desired sexual partner. The same neurons are also activated by many drugs that humans and animals find rewarding: for example, cocaine, amphetamine, and heroin. The ability of virtually every reward, whether natural or artificial, to activate these neurons has led some psychologists to conclude that activity in this neural system constitutes the brain's "common currency" for reward (Wise, 1982).

The functioning of the mesolimbic dopamine system seems to be especially important to the motivational property of rewards. Rather than creating a sensation of pleasure per se, its activity appears to dispose individuals to want to repeat the event that caused the increase by seeking out and acquiring familiar incentives (Berridge & Valenstein, 1991). This may occur when a

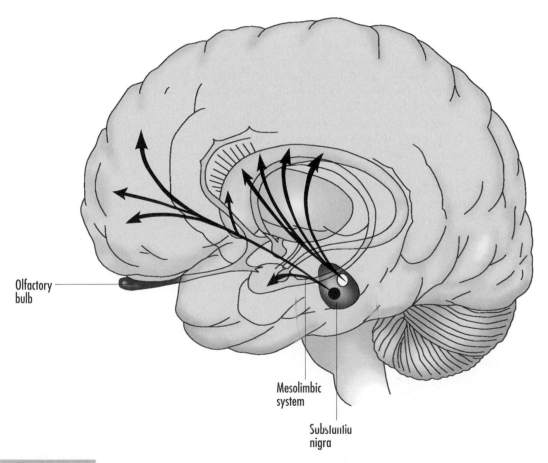

Olfactory bulb

Mesolimbic system

Substantia nigra

FIGURE 10-2

Two Major Dopamine Pathways   *The mesolimbic system apparently is responsible for the symptoms of schizophrenia; the path to the basal ganglia is responsible for tardive dyskinesia, which sometimes results from use of neuroleptic drugs.* (Adapted from Valzelli, 1980)

nibble of food whets your appetite for more. Even artificial activation of dopamine neurons can have the same effect. For example, activation of the system by a stimulating electrode motivates animals to eat, drink, or engage in sex if the opportunity to do these things is available. Activation of the mesolimbic dopamine system by an electrode (or by a drug) is also rewarding by itself. Animals will work to repeat the event that activates the system. In the opposite way, if animals are given drugs that suppress the activity of the mesolimbic dopamine system, they behave as if they do not want food, water, sex, or other natural incentives anymore. They also seem not to want artificial incentives such as cocaine or rewarding electrical brain stimulation. Thus, the mesolimbic dopamine system seems to be used by the brain to create desires for a diverse array of natural and artificial incentives.

Drug Addiction and Reward

Addiction is a powerful motivation for some people. The craving for certain drugs, such as opiates (heroin or morphine), psychostimulants (amphetamine or cocaine) or synthetic "street versions" of these drugs, and certain other drugs (alcohol, nicotine), can become overwhelming (Leshner, 1997). Addicts may crave their drug so strongly that they will sacrifice job, family life and relationships, home, and even freedom to obtain it.

Taking a drug once, or even once in a while, does not constitute addiction. Many Americans have sampled at least one of the drugs just mentioned without becoming addicted. Even regular use (for example, often drinking wine with dinner) need not reflect addiction. **Addiction** occurs only when *a pattern of compulsive and destructive drug-taking behavior* has emerged; often the person compulsively craves the drug. What causes the transformation from "trying out" a drug, or engaging in social or recreational use, into addiction?

Some drugs are especially powerful in their ability to produce addiction. Three major factors operate together to make psychoactive drugs more addictive than other incentives, although not all of these factors need be present for addiction to occur. The first is the ability of most addictive drugs to overactivate reward systems in the brain. Because drugs act directly on brain neurons, they can produce levels of activity in the mesolimbic dopamine system that far surpass those produced by natural incentives. Drug-induced euphoria can be a super-reward because drugs can cause super-activation of brain reward systems. Euphoric drugs activate both pleasure (liking) and motivational (wanting) reward systems, perhaps because they activate both opiate and dopamine neural systems. Once experienced, the memory of such intense pleasure is a potent temptation to regain it again and again.

But the memory of pleasure by itself would not be sufficient to produce addiction, at least for many people, if it were not for additional factors. The second factor is the ability of addictive drugs, if taken repeatedly, to produce unpleasant withdrawal syndromes. As a drug is taken again and again, the pleasure systems that it activates may become increasingly resistant to activation in an effort to regain their normal balanced state. This is, in part, the cause of **tolerance** *(the need for a greater amount of a drug to achieve the same euphoria).* In addition, after repeated exposure to the drug the brain may activate processes that have consequences exactly opposite to those of the drug. These processes may help the brain remain in a balanced state when the drug is taken, but by themselves they are unpleasant. If the addict stops using the drug, the lack of activity in resistant pleasure systems and the activation of unpleasant drug-opposite processes can produce withdrawal. The aversive withdrawal state presents addicts with another motive to resume taking the drug, at least for as long as the withdrawal state lasts—typically several weeks.

Finally, addictive drugs may produce permanent changes in brain reward systems that cause craving even after withdrawal is over. Repeated use of drugs like cocaine, heroin, or amphetamine, which activate the mesolimbic dopamine system, causes these neurons to become hyperactive or sensitized. Neural sensitization may be permanent, and it means that these neurons will be activated more highly by drugs and drug-related stimuli. Since the mesolimbic dopamine brain system appears to mediate the motivational properties of reward (wanting) more than the pleasurable properties (liking), its hyperactivation in addicts may cause exaggerated craving for the drug (Robinson & Berridge, 1993). Neural sensitization lasts much longer than withdrawal. This may be a reason why recovered addicts are in danger of relapse into drug use even after they have completed detoxification programs.

The combination of these factors sheds light on why psychoactive drugs, more than many other incentives, are able to produce addictions. These drugs directly activate brain pleasure mechanisms to unmatched levels, produce withdrawal syndromes that drive a recovering addict back to the drug, and perhaps permanently hyperactivate the brain systems that cause drug rewards to be desired. This combination is hard to resist.

Homeostasis and Drives

Our lives depend on keeping certain things the same. If the temperature of your brain were to change by more than several degrees, you would quickly become unconscious. If the proportion of water in your body were to rise or fall by more than a few percent, your brain and body could not function and you would risk death. Humans and animals walk a tightrope of balance between physiological extremes. Like delicate and finely tuned machines, we cannot work unless our internal environment is in balance. But unlike most machines, we've been designed to maintain this balance ourselves. Even when the outside world changes, our internal states remain relatively stable.

A great deal of basic motivation is directed toward helping to maintain our internal balance. In order to keep our internal world within the narrow limits of physiological survival, we have active control processes to maintain **homeostasis,** that is, *a constant internal state* (*homeo* means "equal" and *stasis* means "static" or "constant"). A homeostatic control process is a system that actively works to maintain a constant state (that is, homeostasis).

Homeostatic control processes can be psychological, physiological, or mechanical. A familiar example is the thermostat that runs your furnace or air conditioner. Thermostats are designed to maintain temperature homeostasis. When you set your thermostat to a particular temperature, that temperature is the goal value or set point. A *set point* is the value that the homeostatic system tries to maintain. If the winter room temperature falls below the value you set, the thermostat is triggered: The discrepancy between its goal and the actual temperature causes it to activate the furnace. If the summer room temperature rises above the thermostat's set temperature for cooling, the thermostat activates the air conditioner. A thermostat coupled to both furnace and air conditioner can be used to keep your room at a stable temperature even as the seasons change. Many physiological processes work like thermostats: They activate motivations that help maintain homeostasis.

Temperature and Homeostasis

If the temperature of your brain dropped by 10°C, you would lose consciousness. If your brain temperature were to rise more than 10°C above normal, you would die. Even though you may have been in very hot or cold weather, your brain remained largely protected within a narrow range of several degrees centigrade. Homeostatic control systems, both physiological and psychological, are the reason for this constancy.

Physiological responses such as sweating and shivering are part of the reason your brain temperature remains so constant: These physiological responses provide cooling in the form of evaporation and heating in the form of muscle activity. Psychological reactions also come into play as you begin to feel uncomfortably hot. You may find yourself wanting to shed clothing, have a cool drink, or find shade. But what turns on these physiological and psychological responses?

When you are under a hot sun, your entire body begins to become hot. Conversely, if you remain too long unprotected in the cold, your entire body becomes hypothermic (too cold). But it is only within your brain that the change of temperature is actually detected. Neurons at several sites in the brain, especially within the preoptic (front) region of the hypothalamus at the base of the brain, are essentially neural thermostats (Satinoff, 1983). They begin to operate differently as their own temperature changes. These neurons serve as both the thermometer and the homeostatic set point within your body. When their temperatures diverge from their normal levels, their metabolism alters, and this changes their activity or firing patterns. This triggers physiological reactions such as perspiration or shivering, which help correct your body temperature. In addition, it triggers your sensation of being too hot or too cold, which makes you want to seek shade or put on a coat, a behavioral solution to the same problem.

When you are too hot, a cool breeze can feel good. Likewise, when you are too cold, a hot bath feels pleasant. But as your own internal temperature changes, your perception of these outside events also changes. Although ordinarily your entire body changes temperature by a degree or two when you are in situations that make you feel very hot or cold, it is only the slight change in your brain temperature that causes the change in the way you feel. The brain can be "fooled" into feeling hot or cold by merely changing the temperature of a relatively few neurons in the hypothalamus. For example, cooling of the hypothalamus alone (by painlessly pumping cold liquid through a small loop of tubing that has been surgically implanted into the hypothalamus) motivates a rat to press a bar to turn on a heat lamp that warms its skin—even though its overall body temperature has not been lowered (Satinoff, 1964). The hypothalamic neurons have detected a change in their own temperature away from the normal set point.

Most of us have experienced a temporary change in set point. An illness can temporarily raise brain set points to several degrees above normal. Then the temperature they "seek" becomes higher, and a fever results. Physiological reactions that elevate body temperature are activated. You shiver, and your body temperature begins to rise above normal. But in spite of the rise in temperature, you may still feel cold—even in a warm room—until your hypothalamic neurons rise all the way to their elevated set point.

Thirst as a Homeostatic Process

Satisfying thirst is an important homeostatic process. **Thirst** is *the psychological manifestation of the need for water,* which is essential for survival. What controls this process?

After going without water or exercising intensively, the body begins to deplete two kinds of fluid reservoirs as water is gradually eliminated through perspiration, respiration, or urination. The first type of reservoir is made up of water contained within the cells. This water is mixed with the protein, fat, and carbohydrate molecules that form the structure and contents of the cell. The water inside your cells is your *intracellular reservoir.* The second type of reservoir is made up of water that is outside the cells. This water is contained in blood and other body fluids and is called the *extracellular reservoir.*

Extracellular thirst results when our bodies lose water because we have gone without drinking or have exercised intensively. Water is extracted from the body by the kidneys in the form of urine, excreted by sweat glands in the skin, or breathed out of the lungs as vapor, and in each case it comes most directly from the blood supply. The loss reduces the volume of extracellular fluid that remains; in turn, the loss of blood volume produces a reduction in blood pressure. You will not feel this slight change in blood pressure, but pressure receptors within your kidneys, heart, and major blood vessels detect it and activate sensory neurons that relay a signal to the brain. Neurons in the hypothalamus next send an impulse to the pituitary gland, causing it to release antidiuretic hormone (ADH) into the bloodstream. ADH causes the kidneys to retain water from the blood as they filter it. Rather than send this water on to become urine, the kidneys deliver it back to the blood. This happens whenever you go without drinking for more than several hours. For example, you may have noticed that your urine appears more concentrated in color at such times (for instance, when you wake up after a night's sleep). In addition, the brain sends a neural signal to the kidneys that causes them to release the hormone renin. Renin interacts chemically with a substance in the blood to produce yet another hormone, angiotensin, which activates neurons deep within the brain, producing the desire to drink.

You may recall that this entire chain of events is triggered by a drop in blood pressure caused by dehydration. Other events that cause dramatic loss of blood pressure can also produce thirst. For example, soldiers wounded on the battlefield or injured people who have bled extensively may feel intense thirst. The cause of their craving is the activation of pressure receptors, which triggers the same chain of renin and angiotensin production, resulting in the experience of thirst (Fitzsimons, 1990).

Intracellular thirst is caused by osmosis—the tendency of water to move from zones where it is plentiful to zones where it is relatively rare. It is primarily the concentration of "salt" ions of sodium, chloride, and potassium that determine whether water is plentiful or rare. As the body loses water, these concentrations begin to rise in the bloodstream. In essence, the blood becomes saltier. The higher concentrations within the blood cause water to migrate from the relatively dilute insides of body cells—including neurons—toward the blood. In a process something like sucking up a puddle of water with a paper towel, water is pulled out of the neurons and other cells. Neurons within the hypothalamus become activated when higher salt concentrations in the blood pulls water from them, causing them to become dehydrated. Their activation produces "osmotic" or intracellular thirst, producing the desire to drink. Drinking replaces water in the blood, reducing the concentration of salt, which in turn allows water to return to neurons and other cells. That is why people become thirsty after eating salty food—even though they might not have lost water.

Hunger

The control of hunger involves many of the same homeostatic concepts as thirst, but eating is much more complex than drinking. When we're thirsty, we generally need only water, and our thirst is directed toward anything that will provide it. But there are lots of different things to eat. We need to eat a number of different kinds of things (proteins, carbohydrates, fats, minerals) in order to be healthy. We need to select the proper balance of foods that contain these things. Evolution has given our brains ways of helping us select the foods we need (and avoid eating things that might poison us). Some of these ways involve the basic taste preferences we were born with. Others involve mechanisms for learning preferences for particular foods and aversions to others.

Most bar owners know that salty foods trigger osmotic thirst and thus induce customers to drink more.

Flavor is the most important factor in food preferences. Flavor contains both taste and odor components, but taste has been more important in human evolution. Humans are born "programmed" with likes and dislikes for particular tastes. Even infants respond to sweet tastes with lip-smacking movements and facial expressions indicative of pleasure (Steiner, 1979). They respond to bitter tastes by turning away and pulling up their faces into expressions of disgust. Apes, monkeys, and a number of other species respond in the same way. Food manufacturers capitalize on our natural "sweet tooth" to devise sweet foods that spur many people to overeat.

Why do we find sweet foods and drinks so attractive? Evolutionary psychologists have suggested that it is because sweetness is an excellent "label" that told our ancestors, foraging among unknown plants, that a particular food or berry was rich in sugar, a class of digestible carbohydrate. Eating sweet foods is an excellent way to gain calories, and calories were not abundant in our evolutionary past. A similar labeling explanation has been advanced for our dislike of bitterness. The naturally bitter compounds that occur in certain plants can make those plants toxic to humans. Bitterness, in other words, is a label for a natural type of poison that occurs commonly. Ancestors who avoided bitter plants may have been more successful at avoiding such poisons (Rozin & Schulkin, 1990).

A second way of developing food preferences is through an array of learning and social learning mechanisms. One of these is preference based on the consequences of ingesting food with a particular taste. Experience with the nourishing consequences of a food leads to gradual liking for its taste through a process that is essentially a form of classical conditioning (Booth, 1991). Experience with other forms of taste-consequence pairings may also be the basis for developing preferences for tastes that are initially not pleasant, such as alcohol or caffeine. In other words, the positive psychological or physical effects of alcohol or caffeine may cause us to develop preferences for these foods, even if we initially do not like their taste. The same kind of process can work in the opposite direction to produce strong dislike or conditioned aversion for a particular food. If your first sample of a tasty food or drink is followed by nausea, you may find that the food is not tasty the next time you try it. The food hasn't changed, but you have, because of your new associative memories, which cause the food to subsequently be experienced as unpleasant.

Interactions Between Homeostasis and Incentives

Whatever the particular foods we choose, it is clear that we must eat in order to maintain energy homeostasis. Body cells burn fuel to produce the energy required for the tasks they perform. Physical exercise causes muscle cells to burn extra fuel in order to meet the metabolic needs placed on them by energetic movement. By burning more fuel, they draw upon stores of calories that have been deposited as body fat or other forms of "stored energy." As you read this, the neurons of your brain are also burning fuel in order to meet the metabolic needs created as they fire electrical impulses and make and release neurotransmitters. The main fuel used by these neurons is glucose, a simple sugar. Without fuel, neurons cannot work. Unfortunately, your brain doesn't use more glucose when you "exercise it" by thinking hard. Those neurons are always active, and always consuming glucose, whether you are thinking hard or not. Concentrated thought or other psychological events may slightly alter the pattern of glucose use, but not the total amount.

Glucose is present in many fruits and other foods. It can also be manufactured by the liver out of other sugars or carbohydrates. Once you've eaten a meal, a great deal of glucose will be absorbed into your bloodstream through the process of digestion. Even more will be created by your liver as it converts other forms of nutrients. In this way, a meal replenishes the fuel needed by your brain neurons and your body's other cells.

Because our cells need fuel, we might expect hunger to be solely a homeostatic motivation controlled entirely by the need to keep sufficient sources of energy available. Indeed, homeostasis is the dominant principle operating in the control of hunger. Deficits in available fuels can trigger hunger, and surpluses can inhibit it. But even though homeostasis is crucial to understanding the control of hunger, incentive factors are equally important. In fact, we can't understand hunger unless we look at the interaction between homeostasis and incentives.

The importance of interactions between homeostatic drive reduction and the taste and other incentive stimuli of food was made clear by a classic experiment by Miller and Kessen (1952). These investigators trained rats to run down a short path for a milk reward. In one case, the rats received milk as a reward in the ordinary way: They drank it. In the other case, the rats received exactly the same amount of milk, but in a more direct way: The milk was gently pumped into their stomachs through a tube passed into an artificial opening, or *fistula*, that had been implanted weeks before. Both of these rewards provided exactly the same number of calories. Both reduced the rats' fuel deficit to the same degree. But the rats learned to run for the milk reward much better when they were allowed to drink it. The milk was not a powerful motivator when it was pumped directly into the stomach, even though it reduced hunger just as well as when it went into the mouth. The rats needed to both taste the reward and have it reduce hunger.

The importance of such interactions between oral incentives and drive reduction has been demonstrated in many ways since that original experiment (Toates, 1986).

Food that bypasses the normal route of voluntary tasting and swallowing is not strongly motivating for either animals or humans. For example, people who are fed entirely by means of intravenous or intragastric infusions of nutrients often find these "meals" unsatisfying. They may feel an intense desire to have some food that they can put into their mouth—even if they are required to spit it out again after chewing it. The strong desire for oral stimulation—above and beyond the satisfaction of caloric needs—is also reflected in our widespread use of artificial sweeteners, which provide flavor without calories. Food incentives, in the form of the sensory experience involved in eating palatable foods and drinks, thus are as crucial to appetite as caloric drive reduction.

Learning is an important part of the interaction between physiological hunger signals and the incentive stimuli of eating. Dramatic demonstrations can be seen in animals in which the act of eating is "uncoupled" from the ordinary caloric consequences by the implantation of a stomach fistula, which allows food to leave the stomach as well as to be put into it. If the fistula cap is removed, whatever is eaten will fall out rather than be digested. This is called *sham feeding* because the meal is a sham in the sense that it provides no calories. Sham-fed animals eat normal amounts and then stop. Why do they stop rather than continue eating? The answer becomes clear if one observes food intake during subsequent meals: The animals gradually increase the amount eaten as they learn that the meal conveys fewer calories than it once did (Van Vort & Smith, 1987). If the fistula cap is replaced so that everything is digested as it normally would be, the animals eat the "too large" amount for their next few meals. Gradually, their meal size declines to normal levels as they learn that the food apparently is rich in calories once again. These observations have led to the hypothesis of *conditioned satiety*—that the fullness we feel after a meal is at least in part a product of learning (Booth, 1987).

Humans also are capable of conditioned satiety. In one experiment, people were asked to eat several meals of a distinctive food that was rich in calories and of another food that was low in calories. Later, when the participants were again given the two foods, which were apparently the same as

before but with the caloric content made equal, they found the food that had originally been higher in calories more satiating (Booth, 1990).

A final form of interaction between food incentives and homeostatic drive is the phenomenon called *alliesthesia* (Cabanac, 1979), in which food (especially sweet food) tastes better when one is hungry. For example, when people are asked to rate the palatability of sweet drinks either after a meal or after several hours without food, they give higher palatability ratings to the same drink when they are hungry than when they have recently eaten.

Physiological Hunger Cues

You may have noticed that when you are hungry your stomach sometimes growls. At such moments the stomach walls are engaged in muscular contractions, creating the burbling movements of its contents that you hear. Stomach contractions are most frequent when you are hungry and likely to feel that your stomach is empty. The association of these contractions with feelings of hunger led early investigators to hypothesize that pressure sensors in the stomach detect emptiness and trigger both contractions and the psychological experience of hunger. Later, psychologists and physiologists found that this coincidence is really just that—a coincidence. Stomach sensations from contractions are not the real cause of hunger. In fact, people who have had their stomachs surgically removed for medical reasons, so that food passes directly to the intestines, can still have strong feelings of hunger.

The stomach does have receptors that are important to changes in hunger, but these receptors are primarily chemical in nature. They have more to do with feelings of satiety—they are activated by sugars and other nutrients in stomach contents and send a neural signal to the brain—than with feelings of hunger.

The physiological signal for hunger is more directly related to the real source of calories for neurons and other cells: levels of glucose and other nutrients in the body. The brain itself is its own sensor for deficiencies in available calories. You may remember that neurons in the brain use glucose as their principal source of energy. Neurons in particular parts of the brain, especially the brain stem and hypothalamus, are especially sensitive to glucose levels. When the level falls too low, the activity of these neurons is disrupted. This signals the rest of the brain, producing hunger. Such hunger can be produced artificially in laboratory animals even if they have recently eaten. If chemicals that prevent neurons from burning glucose as a fuel are infused into an animal's brain, the animal will suddenly seek out food. Its brain has been fooled into sensing a lack of glucose, even though glucose was actually present, because the neurons have been disrupted in the same way as if glucose were low.

Peripheral Signals To some degree, hunger is what we feel when we have no feeling of satiety. As long as caloric food is in our stomach or intestine, or calorie stores are high within our body, we feel relatively sated. When these decline, hunger ensues. The control of hunger is therefore the reverse of the control of satiety.

Many physical systems contribute to the feeling of satiety after a meal. The first system is made up of the parts of the body that process food first: the stomach and intestine. Both the physical expansion of the stomach and the chemicals within the food activate receptors in the stomach's walls. These receptors relay their signal to the brain through the *vagus nerve,* which carries signals from many other body organs as well. A second kind of satiety message comes from the *duodenum,* the part of the intestines that receives food directly from the stomach. This signal is sent to the brain as a chemical rather than through a nerve. When food reaches the duodenum, it causes it to release a hormone (cholecystokinin, or CCK) into the bloodstream. CCK helps promote physiological digestion, but it also has a psychological consequence. It travels through the blood until it reaches the brain, where it is detected by special receptors. This produces feelings of satiety. Hungry animals can be fooled into false satiety if microscopic amounts of CCK are infused into their brains shortly after they have begun a meal (Smith & Gibbs, 1994).

Perhaps surprisingly, the brain's most sensitive signal of nutrient availability comes from neuronal receptors that are separate both from the brain and from food: the liver (Friedman, 1990). Receptors in the liver are highly sensitive to changes in blood nutrients after digestion. These signals are also sent to the brain through the vagus nerve. A hungry animal will stop eating almost immediately after a tiny infusion of nutrients into the blood supply that goes directly to the liver.

Why should the brain rely on nutrient signals from the liver rather than on its own detectors? The answer may be that the liver can more accurately measure the various types of nutrients used by the body. The brain detects chiefly glucose, but other forms of nutrients, such as complex carbohydrates, proteins, and fats, can be measured, stored, and sometimes converted into other nutrients by the liver. Its role as a general "currency exchange" for nutrients may allow the liver to make the best estimate of the total energy stores available to the body.

Integration of Hunger Signals

Signals for hunger and satiety are processed by the brain in two stages to produce the motivation to eat. First, signals from hunger receptors in the brain itself and satiety signals relayed from the stomach and liver are added together in the brain stem to detect the overall level of need (Grill & Kaplan, 1990). This "integrated hunger assessment" is also connected in the brain stem to the sensory neural systems that process taste. Taste neurons in the brain stem may change their responsiveness during some forms of hunger and satiety (Scott & Mark, 1986). This may be part of the reason food tastes more palatable when we are hungry.

In order to become the conscious experience we know as hunger, and in order to stimulate the seeking of food, the hunger signal of the brain stem must be processed further in the forebrain. A key site for this processing is the hypothalamus (see Figure 10-3). Hunger is affected in two dramatically different ways by manipulations of two parts of the hypothalamus: the lateral hypothalamus (the parts on each side) and the ventromedial hypothalamus (the lower ["ventral"] and middle [medial] portion). Destruction of the lateral hypothalamus produces an apparent total lack of hunger, at least until the rest of the brain recovers (Teitelbaum & Epstein, 1962).

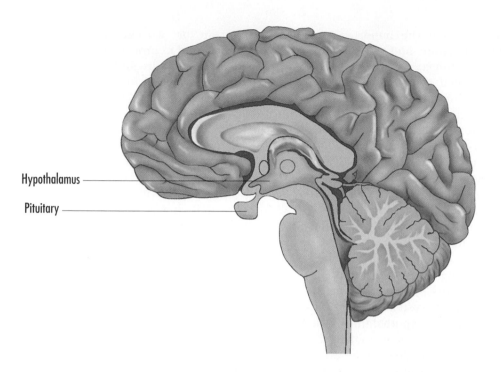

FIGURE 10-3
The Hypothalamus and Pituitary

Hypothalamus

Pituitary

This phenomenon is called the *lateral hypothalamic syndrome.* Animals that have had small lesions made in their lateral hypothalamus may simply ignore food. They may even reject it as though it tasted bad (for example, they will grimace and vigorously spit it out). Unless they are fed artificially, they will starve to death. Nearly the exact opposite pattern of behavior, the *ventromedial hypothalamic syndrome,* is produced by a lesion of the ventromedial hypothalamus. Animals with such lesions eat voraciously and consume large quantities of food, especially if it is palatable. Not surprisingly, they gain weight until they become quite obese, up to double their normal body weight (see Figure 10-4).

Other manipulations of these brain sites also appear to change hunger. For example, electrical stimulation of the lateral hypothalamus produces overeating: the exact opposite of a lesion of the lateral hypothalamus (and the same effect as a lesion of the ventromedial hypothalamus). An animal with a stimulating electrode in its lateral hypothalamus may begin to look for food and eat as soon as the stimulation begins, and to stop eating once it ends. Conversely, stimulation of the ventromedial hypothalamus will stop ordinary eating by a hungry animal.

Neurochemical stimulation of the hypothalamus works in similar ways. For example, certain compounds, such as neuropeptide Y, or opiate drugs such as morphine, can stimulate feeding when they are injected into the ventromedial hypothalamus. These drugs may temporarily stimulate hunger or make food taste better. Other drugs, such as amphetamines, can halt feeding when injected into parts of the lateral hypothalamus. Many prescription diet drugs are chemically similar to amphetamines. Such drugs might inhibit appetite by acting on neurons in the hypothalamus.

FIGURE 10-4

Damage to the ventromedial hypothalamus produces overeating and obesity.

Around 1960, when the importance of the lateral hypothalamus and ventromedial hypothalamus to hunger were discovered, psychologists tended to view these sites simply as hunger or satiety centers. Since then, it has become clear that the concepts of "hunger center" or "satiety center" are too simplistic, for a number of reasons. One is that these sites are not the sole centers for hunger or satiety in the brain. They interact with many other brain systems to produce their effects. In fact, some of the same effects can be produced by manipulating related brain systems instead of the hypothalamus. For example, many of the effects of manipulating the lateral hypothalamus can be duplicated by manipulating the mesolimbic dopamine system, which simply passes through the hypothalamus. Like lateral hypothalamic lesions, lesions in this dopamine-containing bundle of axons eliminate feeding. In fact, many early studies of lateral hypothalamic lesions actually destroyed both the mesolimbic dopamine system and neurons in the lateral hypothalamus itself. Conversely, the elicitation of feeding by electrical stimulation and by many drugs also depends partly on activation of the mesolimbic system. Thus, rather than just one or two centers, many neuroanatomical and neurotransmitter systems are involved in appetite and satiety.

One consequence of having many neural systems for appetite is that it is not possible to abolish eating by destroying just one site. Even in animals with lateral hypothalamic lesions, appetite will return eventually. If the rats are artificially fed for several weeks or months after the lesion, they will begin to eat again, but they will eat only enough to maintain their lower body weight. They seem to have reached homeostasis at a lower set point. In fact, rats can be "protected" from the usual loss of eating that would follow a lateral hypothalamic lesion if they are put on a diet before the lesion that lowers their body weight (see Figure 10-5). This indicates that hypothalamic lesions don't actually destroy hunger. Instead, they may raise or lower the homeostatic set point for body weight that ordinarily controls hunger. Changing the set point is like resetting a thermostat: The system attempts to achieve the new body weight. The effect of ventromedial hypothalamic lesions also conform to this idea. Animals with those lesions do not gain weight infinitely. Eventually they stop at a new, obese body weight. At that point they eat only enough to maintain the new set point. But if they are put on a diet and drop below that set point, they will resume overeating in order to regain that body weight when they are finally given the opportunity (see Figure 10-6). Once they regain that level of obesity, they will halt once again.

Obesity

We have emphasized homeostatic processes in hunger, but eating behavior shows several departures from homeostasis. Some people's body weight is not as constant as the homeostatic viewpoint suggests. The most frequent deviation from homeostatic regulation of eating—at least for humans—is **obesity.** Roughly 25% of Americans are obese, a condition often defined as *being 30% or more in excess of one's appropriate body weight.* The prevalence of obesity varies among different groups. Physical obesity occurs about equally in both sexes, but the psychological perception of being overweight is more common among women. More than 50% of American

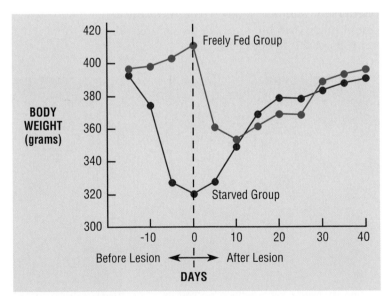

FIGURE 10-5

Body Weight and the Lateral Hypothalamus *Before lesioning of the lateral hypothalamus, one group of rats was starved and another group was allowed to feed freely. After surgery, the starved animals increased their food intake and gained weight while the freely fed group lost weight. Both groups stabilized at the same weight level.* (After Powley & Keesey, 1970)

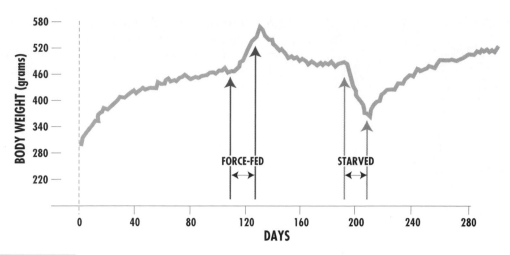

FIGURE 10-6

Effects of Forced Feeding and Starvation on Rats with VMH Lesions   *Following lesioning of the ventromedial hypothalamus, the rat overeats and gains weight until it stabilizes at a new, obese level. Forced feeding or starvation alters the weight level only temporarily; the rat returns to its stabilized level.* (After Hoebel & Teitelbaum, 1966)

women, compared to more than 35% of men, consider themselves overweight (Brownell & Rodin, 1994; Horm & Anderson, 1993). In the United States, obesity is more prevalent in lower-class socioeconomic groups than in higher-class ones; however, in developing countries the reverse is true: The higher people's socioeconomic status, the more likely they are to be obese (Logue, 1991; Stunkard, 1996).

Obesity is a major health hazard. It contributes to a higher incidence of diabetes, high blood pressure, and heart disease. As if this were not bad enough, in our culture obesity can also be a social stigma, as obese people are often perceived as being indulgent and lacking in willpower. This allegation can be most unfair since, as we will see, in many cases obesity is due to genetic factors rather than overeating. Given the problems associated with obesity, it is not surprising that each year millions of people spend billions of dollars on diets and drugs to lose weight.

Most researchers agree that obesity is a complex problem that can involve metabolic, nutritional, psychological, and sociological factors. Obesity probably is not a single disorder but a variety of disorders that all have fatness as their major symptom (Rodin, 1981). Asking how one becomes obese is like asking how one gets to Pittsburgh—there are many ways to do it, and which one you "choose" depends on where

you are coming from (Offir, 1982). In what follows, we will divide the factors that lead to weight gain into two broad classes: (a) genetics and (b) calorie intake (overeating). Roughly speaking, people may become obese because they are genetically predisposed to metabolize nutrients into fat even if they don't eat more than other people (metabolic reasons), or because they eat too much (for psychological or sociological reasons). Both factors may be involved in some cases of obesity, while in other cases genetics or overeating alone may be the culprit.

Genetic Factors   It has long been known that obesity runs in families. In families in which neither parent is obese, only about 10% of the children will be obese; if one parent is obese, about 40% of the children will also be obese; and if both parents are obese, approximately 70% of the children will also be obese (Gurney, 1936). These statistics suggest a biological basis of obesity, but other interpretations are possible—for example, perhaps the children are simply imitating their parents' eating habits. Recent findings, however, strongly support a genetic basis for obesity.

Twin Studies   One way to get evidence about the role of genetics in obesity is to study identical twins. Since identical twins have the same genes, and since genes supposedly play a role in weight gain, identical

Recent findings provide strong evidence of a genetic basis for obesity.

twins should be alike in their patterns of weight gain.

In one experiment, 12 pairs of identical twins (all males) agreed to stay in a college dormitory for 100 days. The intent of the experiment was to get the twins to gain weight. Each man ate a diet that contained 1,000 extra calories per day. Also, the men's physical activity was restricted; they were not allowed to exercise and instead spent much of their time reading, playing sedentary games, and watching television. By the end of the 100 days, all of the men had gained weight, but the amount gained ranged from 9 to 30 pounds. However—and this is the key point—there was hardly any variation in the amount gained by the members of each pair of twins (the variation occurred between pairs of twins). In other words, identical twins gained almost identical amounts. Moreover, identical twins tended to gain weight in the same places. If one member of a pair of twins gained weight in his middle, so did the other; if one member of another pair of twins gained weight on his hips and thighs, so did the other (Bouchard et al., 1990).

These results make it clear that both calorie intake and genetics contribute to weight gain. The fact that all the men in the study gained weight shows that increased calories translates into increased weight; this is hardly surprising. The fact that the amount of weight gained varied from one pair of twins to another but did not vary *within* a pair of twins suggests that genetic factors determine how much we gain when we increase our calorie intake.

The results also make it clear why we should not assume that obese people necessarily eat more than nonobese people. Despite eating roughly the same amount (1,000 extra calories), the amount of weight gained by different pairs of twins varied. This difference seems to arise from how their bodies metabolized the extra calories. Some people's bodies tend to convert a larger proportion of calories into fat stores, while others are likely to burn off the same calories through different metabolic processes, regardless of how much is eaten (Ravussin et al., 1988).

A critic might object to making too much of the study just described. Identical twins not only have identical genes but also grow up in very similar environments. Perhaps environmental factors were responsible for the identical twins being alike in weight gain. We need to study identical twins who have been reared apart and see how similar the members of a pair are in weight gain. This was done in a study conducted in Sweden (Stunkard et al., 1990). The researchers studied the weights of 93 pairs of identical twins reared apart, as well as that of 153 pairs of identical twins reared together. Members of a pair of twins reared apart were found to be remarkably similar in weight; indeed, they were as similar in weight as members of pairs of twins reared together. Clearly, genes are a major determinant of weight and weight gain.

Fat Cells Given that genes play a role in weight gain, we want to know some details of that role. In particular, what are the digestive and metabolic processes that are affected by genes and that mediate weight gain? One answer involves fat cells, where all body fat is stored. There are between 30 billion and 40 billion fat cells in the bodies of most normal adults, but the degree of excess weight carried by ordinary American adults varies by more than the 25% to 33% this figure would suggest. The additional variation comes from the size, rather than the mere number, of fat cells: The more calories one eats and fails to burn off, the larger existing fat cells become.

In one study, obese participants were found to have three times as many fat cells as normal participants (Knittle & Hirsch, 1968). In other studies, researchers have shown that rats that have double the usual number of fat cells tend to be twice as fat as control rats. And when researchers cut some of the fat cells out of young rats so that they had only half as many fat cells as their littermates, those rats grew up to be only half as fat as their littermates (Faust, 1984; Hirsch & Batchelor, 1976). Hence, there is a link between genes and the number of fat cells, and another link between the number of fat cells and obesity; through this chain, genes are connected to obesity.

Dieting and Set Points When people take diet drugs, a variety of things can happen. The drug might suppress appetite directly; this would reduce the feeling of hunger. Another drug might suppress the **set point**—*the point at which body weight is set and that the body strives to maintain*—rather than suppress appetite directly. For example, it has been suggested that diet drugs such as fenfluramine have this effect (Stunkard, 1982). Such an effect would be equivalent to direct appetite suppression as long as body weight was higher than the lowered set point. Once body weight fell to the lower level, appetite would return to just the degree needed to remain at that weight. When a person stopped taking the drug, the set point would return to its higher level and the person would regain the weight he or she had lost. Finally, some drugs, such as nicotine, may help people lose weight by elevating the metabolic rate of cells, causing them to burn more calories than they ordinarily would.

One reason that the set point hypothesis has become popular among psychologists is the strong tendency for obese adults, both humans and animals, to return to their original body weight after ceasing dieting. In contrast to the young rats just described, even surgical removal of fat deposits by liposuction appears not to produce permanent weight loss when it is performed on adult rats: The adults regain the fat elsewhere. This also appears to be true of liposuction performed on obese human adults (Vogt & Belluscio, 1987).

Some investigators have suggested that once adult levels of fat tissue have been reached, they are maintained at that level.

The brain may detect changes in the level of body fat and influence hunger accordingly (Weigle, 1994). For example, an "obesity gene" in mice is thought to control the ability of fat cells to produce a chemical "satiety signal" (Zhang et al., 1994). Mice that lack this gene become obese. Ordinarily, the more body fat one has, the more satiety signal is released into the blood. Whether human obesity involves a disruption in this satiety factor or gene is not yet known. But the possibility that the level of fat stores is kept constant may help explain why some obese people find it difficult not to regain weight that they lost through dieting.

In sum, there are various routes by which genes can be responsible for excessive weight gain, including having many and large fat cells, having a high set point, and having a low metabolic rate.

Overeating While physiological factors such as fat regulation and metabolic rate are important determinants of body weight, there is no question that overeating can also cause obesity. The psychological factors that characterize eating by people who are trying to lose weight include breakdown of conscious restraints, and emotional arousal.

Breakdown of Conscious Restraints Some people stay obese by going on eating binges after dieting. An obese man may break a two-day diet and then overeat so much that he eventually consumes more calories than he would have had he not dieted at all. Since the diet was a conscious restraint, the breakdown of control is a factor in increased calorie intake.

To gain a more detailed understanding of the role of conscious restraints, researchers have developed a questionnaire that asks about diet, weight history, and concern with eating (for example, How often do you diet? Do you eat sensibly in front of others, yet overeat when alone?). The results show that almost everyone—whether thin, average, or overweight—can be classified into one of two categories: people who consciously restrain their eating and people who do not. In addition, regardless of their actual weight, the eating behavior of restrained eaters is closer to that of obese individuals than to that of unrestrained eaters (Herman & Polivy, 1980; Ruderman, 1986).

A laboratory study shows what happens when restraints are dropped. Restrained and unrestrained eaters (both of normal weight) were required to drink either two milkshakes, one milkshake, or none; they then sampled several flavors of ice cream and were encouraged to eat as much as they wanted (Herman & Mack, 1975). The more milkshakes the unrestrained eaters were required to drink, the less ice cream they consumed later. In contrast, the restrained eaters who had been preloaded with two milkshakes ate more ice cream than did those who drank one milkshake or none. Thus, individuals who are trying to restrain their eating, ignoring their ordinary impulse to eat more, may also come to ignore the feelings of satiety that would ordinarily halt their desire to eat.

Emotional Arousal   Overweight individuals often report that they tend to eat more when they are tense or anxious, and experimental results support these reports. Obese participants eat more in a high-anxiety situation than they do in a low-anxiety situation, while normal-weight participants eat more in situations of low anxiety (McKenna, 1972). Other research indicates that any kind of emotional arousal seems to increase food intake in some obese people. In one study, overweight and normal-weight participants saw a different film in each of four sessions. Three of the films aroused various emotions: one was distressing, one amusing, and one sexually arousing. The fourth film was a boring travelogue. After viewing each of the films, the participants were asked to taste and evaluate different kinds of crackers. The obese participants ate significantly more crackers after viewing any of the arousing films than they did after seeing the travelogue. Normal-weight individuals ate the same amount of crackers regardless of which film they had seen (White, 1977).

The ability of emotional stress to elicit eating has been observed in other animals, too. This may mean that stress can activate basic brain systems that, under some conditions, result in overeating (Rowland & Antelman, 1976).

Dieting and Weight Control   Although genetic factors may limit the amount of weight we can comfortably lose, overweight people can still lose weight by following a weight control program. For a program to be successful, though, it must involve something other than just extreme dieting.

Limitations of Dieting   Unfortunately, most dieters are not successful, and those who succeed in shedding pounds often gain weight again after ceasing dieting. This state of affairs seems to be partly due to two deep-seated reactions to a temporary deprivation of food (which is what a diet is). The first reaction is that deprivation per se can lead to subsequent overeating. In some experiments, rats were first deprived of food for four days, then allowed to feed until they regained their normal weights, and finally allowed to eat as much food as they wanted. These rats ate more than control rats with no history of deprivation. Thus, prior deprivation leads to subsequent overeating, even after the weight lost as a result of the deprivation has been regained (Coscina & Dixon, 1983).

The second reaction of interest is that deprivation decreases metabolic rate, and as you may recall, the lower one's metabolic rate, the fewer calories expended and the higher one's weight. Consequently, the calorie reduction during dieting is partly offset by the lowered metabolic rate, making it difficult for dieters to meet their goal. The reduced metabolic rate caused by dieting may also explain why many people find it harder and harder to lose weight with each successive diet: The body responds to each bout of dieting with a reduction in metabolic rate (Brownell, 1988).

Both reactions to dieting—binge eating and lowered metabolic rate—are understandable in evolutionary terms. Until very recently in human history, whenever people experienced deprivation it was because of a scarcity of food in the environment. One adaptive response to such scarcity is to overeat and store in our bodies as much food as possible whenever it is available. Hence, natural selection may have favored the ability to overeat following deprivation. This explains the overeating reaction. A second adaptive response to a scarcity of food in the environment is for organisms to decrease the rate at which they expend their limited calories; hence, natural selection may have favored the ability to lower one's metabolic rate during deprivation. This explains the second reaction of interest. These two reactions have served our species well in times of famine, but once famine is not a concern, they prevent obese dieters from losing weight permanently (Polivy & Herman, 1985).

Weight Control Programs   To lose weight and keep it off, it seems that overweight individuals need to establish a new set of permanent eating habits (as opposed to temporary dieting) and engage in a program of exercise. Some support for this conclusion is provided by the following study, which compared various methods for treating obesity (Craighead, Stunkard, & O'Brien, 1981; Wadden et al., 1997).

For six months, obese individuals followed one of three treatment regimens: (a) behavior modification of eating and exercise habits, (b) drug therapy using an appetite suppressant (fenfluramine), and (c) a combination of behavior modification and drug therapy. Participants in all three treatment groups were given information about exercise and extensive nutritional counseling, including a diet of no more than 1,200 calories per day. Participants in the behavior modification groups were taught to become aware of situations that prompted them to overeat, to change the conditions associated with their overeating, to reward themselves for appropriate eating behavior, and to develop a suitable exercise regimen. In addition to the three treatment groups, there were two control groups: One consisted of participants waiting to take part in the study, and the other of participants who saw a physician for traditional treatment of weight problems.

Table 10-1 presents the results of the study. The participants in all three treatment groups lost more weight than the participants in the two control groups, with the group combining behavior modification and drug therapy losing the most weight and the behavior-modification-only group losing the least. However, during the year after treatment, a striking reversal developed. The behavior-modification-only group regained far less weight than the two other treatment groups; these participants maintained an average weight loss of 19.8 pounds by the end of the year, whereas the weight losses for the

TABLE 10-1

Weight Loss Following Different Treatments   *Weight loss in pounds at the end of six months of treatment and on a follow-up one year later. Participants in the two control groups were not available for the one-year follow-up.* (After Craighead, Stunkard, & O'Brien, 1981)

	Weight Loss After Treatment	Weight Loss One Year Later
Treatment groups		
Behavior modification only	24.0	19.8
Drug therapy only	31.9	13.8
Combined treatment	33.7	10.1
Control groups		
Waiting list	2.9 (gain)	—
Physician office visits	13.2	—

drug-therapy-only group and the combined-treatment group averaged only 13.8 and 10.1 pounds each.

What caused this reversal? An increased sense of self-efficacy or self-control may have been a factor. Participants who received the behavior-modification-only treatment could attribute their weight loss to their own efforts, thereby strengthening their resolve to continue controlling their weight after the treatment ended. Participants who received an appetite suppressant, on the other hand, probably attributed their weight loss to the medication and hence did not develop a sense of self-control. Another possible factor stems from the fact that the medication had decreased the participants' feelings of hunger, or temporarily lowered their set point, and consequently participants in the drug-therapy-only group and the combined-treatment group may not have been sufficiently prepared to cope with the increase in hunger they felt when the medication was stopped.

Anorexia and Bulimia

While obesity is the most common eating problem, the opposite problem has also surfaced in the form of anorexia nervosa and bulimia. Both of these disorders involve a pathological desire not to gain weight.

Anorexia nervosa is characterized by *extreme, self-imposed weight loss—at least 15% of the individual's minimum normal weight.* Some anorexics in fact weigh less than 50% of their normal weight. Despite the extreme loss of weight and the resulting problems, the typical anorexic denies that there is a problem and refuses to gain weight. In fact, anorexics frequently think that they look too fat. For females to be diagnosed as anorexic, in addition to the weight loss they must also have stopped menstruating. The weight loss can lead to a number of dangerous side effects, including emaciation, susceptibility to infection, and other symptoms of undernourishment. In extreme cases the side effects can lead to death.

Anorexia is relatively rare; its incidence in the United States is about 1% (Fairburn, Welch, & Hay, 1993). However, this incidence represents more than a doubling since the 1960s, and the frequency may still be rising (McHugh, 1990). Anorexia is 20 times more likely to occur in women than in men; the majority of anorexics are young women between their teens and their thirties. Typically, anorexics are entirely focused on food, carefully calculating the amount of calories in anything they might consume. Sometimes this concern reaches the point of obsession, as when one anorexic commented to her therapist, "Of course I had breakfast; I ate my Cheerio," or when another said, "I won't lick a postage stamp—one never knows about calories" (Bruch, 1973). The obsession with food and possible weight gains leads some anorexics to become compulsive exercisers, sometimes exercising vigorously several hours a day (Logue, 1991).

Bulimia is characterized by *recurrent episodes of binge eating (rapid consumption of a large amount of food in a discrete period of time), followed by attempts to purge the excess by means of vomiting or laxatives.* The binges can be frequent and extreme. A survey of bulimic women found that most women binged at least once per day (usually in the evening) and that an average binge involved consuming some 4800 calories (often sweet or salty carbohydrate foods). However, because of the purges that follow the binges, a bulimic person's weight may stay relatively normal; this allows bulimics to keep their eating disorder hidden. But this behavior can have a high physiological cost; vomiting and use of laxatives can disrupt the balance of potassium in the body, which can result in problems like dehydration, cardiac arrhythmias, and urinary infections.

Like anorexia, bulimia primarily afflicts young women. But bulimia is more frequent than anorexia, with an estimated 5 to 10% of American women affected to some degree. Rather than being restricted to the upper classes, bulimia is found in all racial, ethnic, and socioeconomic groups in our society.

Researchers have suggested a variety of causes for anorexia and bulimia, including social, biological, and personality or family factors. It is probably necessary for several of these factors to occur together for any individual to develop an eating disorder.

Many psychologists have proposed that social factors play a major role in anorexia and bulimia. In particular, they point to our society's emphasis on thinness in women. This emphasis has increased markedly in the past 40 years, which fits with the claim that the incidence of eating disorders has also increased during that period. An indication of this trend is the change in what people regard as a "perfect" woman's figure. Figure 10-7 places a photo of Jayne Mansfield, who was widely thought to have an ideal figure in the 1950s, next to a photo of actress Julia Roberts, who reflects today's ideal. Roberts is clearly much thinner than Mansfield. Presumably these "perfect" figures influence women's views of their own bodies, and as a result many women feel that their figure is much heavier than the ideal (Garner & Garfinkel, 1980; Logue, 1991).

Clearly, not everyone who is exposed to these societal pressures develops an eating disorder. Certain biological vulnerabilities may increase the tendency to develop eating disorders. One hypothesis is that anorexia is caused by malfunctions of the hypothalamus, the part of the brain that helps regulate eating. Anorexic individuals show lowered functioning of the hypothalamus and abnormalities in several of the neurochemicals that are important to the functioning of the hypothalamus (Fava et al., 1989). With regard to bulimia, there may be a deficiency in the neurotransmitter serotonin, which plays a role in both mood regulation and appetite (Mitchell & deZwann, 1993).

Personality and family factors may also play a role in anorexia and bulimia. Many

FIGURE 10-7

Jayne Mansfield (left) represented a perfect figure for the 1950s, whereas Julia Roberts (right) was considered the perfect figure for the 1990s.

young women with eating disorders come from families that demand "perfection" and extreme self-control but do not allow expressions of warmth or conflict (Bruch, 1973; Minuchin, Rosman, & Baker, 1978). Some young women may seek to gain some control over, and expressions of concern from, their parents by controlling their eating habits, eventually developing anorexia. Others may turn to binge eating when they feel emotionally upset or painfully aware of their low self-esteem (Polivy & Herman, 1993).

Therapies designed to help people with eating disorders regain healthy eating habits and deal with the emotional issues they face have proven useful (Agras, 1993; Fairburn & Hay, 1992). Drugs that regulate serotonin levels can also be helpful, particularly for people with bulimia (FNBC Study Group, 1992). Anorexia and bulimia are serious disorders, however, and people with these disorders often continue to have significant problems for several years.

Gender and Sexuality

Like thirst and hunger, sexual desire is a powerful motivation. There are, however, some important differences. Sex is a social motive—it typically involves another person—whereas the survival motives concern only the individual. In addition, sex does not involve an internal deficit that needs to be regulated and remedied for the organism to survive. Consequently, social motives do not lend themselves to a homeostatic analysis.

With regard to sex, two critical distinctions should be kept in mind. The first stems from the fact that, although we begin to mature sexually at puberty, the basis for our sexual identity is established in the womb. We therefore distinguish between adult sexuality (that is, beginning with changes at puberty) and early sexual development. The second distinction is between the biological and environmental determinants of sexual behaviors and feelings. For many aspects of sexual development and adult sexuality, a fundamental question is the extent to which the behavior or feeling in question is a product of biology (particularly hormones), environment and learning (early experiences and cultural norms), or interactions between biological and environmental factors.

Early Sexual Development

To have gratifying social and sexual experiences as adults, most individuals need to develop an appropriate **gender identity,** in which *males come to think of themselves as males and females as females.* This development is quite complex and actually begins before birth. For the first couple of months after conception, only the chromosomes of a human embryo indicate whether it will develop into a boy or girl. Up to this stage, both sexes are identical in appearance and have tissues that will eventually develop into testes or ovaries, as well as a genital tubercle that will become either a penis or a clitoris. But between two and three months a primitive sex gland, or *gonad,* develops into testes if the embryo is genetically male or into ovaries if the embryo is genetically female

If the embryonic sex glands produce enough androgen, the fetus will develop male genitals. Shown here is a fetus 4 months after conception.

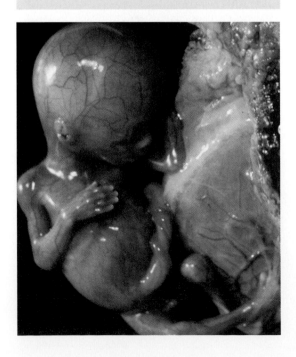

(see Chapter 2). Once testes or ovaries develop, they produce the sex hormones, which then control the development of the internal reproductive structures and the external genitals. The sex hormones are even more important for prenatal development than they will be for the expression of adult sexuality.

The critical hormone in genital development is androgen. If the embryonic sex glands produce enough androgen, the newborn will have male genitals; if there is insufficient androgen, the newborn will have female genitals even if it is genetically male. Conversely, if androgens are added artificially, the newborn will have male genitals even if it is genetically female. In other words, the presence or absence of a male (Y) chromosome normally influences sexual development simply by determining whether the embryo will secrete androgens. The anatomical development of the female embryo does not require female hormones, only the absence of male hormones. In short, nature will produce a female unless androgen intervenes.

The influence of androgen, called *androgenization,* extends far beyond anatomy. After it has molded the genitals, androgen begins to operate on the brain cells. Studies with rats provide evidence that prenatal androgen changes the volume and detailed structure of cells in the fetus's hypothalamus, an organ that regulates motivation in humans as well as in rats (Money, 1988). These effects of androgen essentially masculinize the brain and may be responsible for some masculine traits and behaviors that appear months or years later, such as higher levels of aggressiveness.

In a series of experiments, pregnant monkeys were injected with androgen and their female offspring were observed in detail. These offspring showed some anatomical changes (penises instead of clitorises) and also acted differently than normal females. They were more aggressive in play, more masculine in sexual play, and less intimidated by approaching peers (Goy, 1968; Phoenix, Goy, & Resko, 1968). These findings indicate that some gender-typical behaviors (such as greater aggression in males) are partly hormonally determined in nonhuman animals.

Early hormonal abnormalities can also have the opposite consequence; they can "feminize" the later sexual behavior of males. A striking example is "maternal stress": a change in the sexual behavior of male rats whose mothers experienced high emotional stress during pregnancy (Ward, 1992). High levels of stress in a pregnant mother rat triggers hormonal events that result in a decrease in the amount of androgens produced by the male embryo's testes. That, in turn, results in a reduction of androgen reaching the developing brain. The hypothalamus and other brain regions appear to develop differently in such embryos. When these male rats become adults, they show less male sexual behavior and may even show female patterns of copulation movement if they are mounted by another male.

It is not known whether similar effects on brain development or behavior occur in humans. Although some believe that these experiments may provide insights into the basis of human heterosexual versus homosexual orientation, there are differences between the results of these animal experiments and human behavior. For example, male rats born to maternally stressed mothers tend to show less sexual behavior of any kind than ordinary male rats, but this is not true of gay men compared to heterosexual men. Nevertheless, these examples illustrate the importance of early hormonal environment for the later sexual behavior of nonhuman animals, and they raise the possibility that prenatal hormones may be important for human sexual motivation as well.

Hormones Versus Environment

In humans, much of what is known about the effects of prenatal hormones and early environment has been uncovered by studies of individuals who, for various reasons, were exposed to the prenatal hormones that would ordinarily be experienced by one sex but then were raised in a social role that would ordinarily typify the opposite sex. In most such cases, the assigned label and the sex role in which the individual is raised have a much greater influence on gender identity than the individual's genes and hormones.

For example, many thousands of women born during the 1950s and 1960s were exposed to an antimiscarriage drug, diethyl-stilbestrol, that had unexpected hormone-like effects on brain development. Ordinarily the testosterone (the major androgen) secreted by a male embryo's testes is converted in the brain into a substance similar to diethylstilbestrol. Pregnant women who took the drug therefore unknowingly exposed their fetus to a chemical environment similar to that experienced by the developing brain of a normal male. For male fetuses, this would have little consequence: Their brains were already exposed to male patterns of chemical stimulation. But the female fetuses were exposed to an opposite-sex or malelike chemical stimulation for the period during which their mothers took the drug. For the overwhelming majority of these daughters, the prenatal exposure had no detectable effect. Most girls who were exposed prenatally to diethylstilbesterol went on to grow up similarly to other girls and to become indistinguishable from women with normal prenatal experience. Social environment, in other words, appears to have had a much greater influence on the sexual and gender development of these women than prenatal hormones.

But this is not to say that prenatal chemical environment had absolutely no effect. Researchers have detected several subtle differences that characterize at least some of the women exposed to diethylstilbestrol. For example, a slightly higher proportion of these women appear to be homosexual or bisexual than would ordinarily be expected. Sexual orientation is not identical to gender identity, but in this case a slight effect of prenatal hormones on both may be reflected. (Sexual orientation is discussed in detail later in this section.) Similarly, these women show slightly lower ratings on some measures of "maternal interest," such as finding infants attractive, even though they are not different from other women by most other measures of parental, sexual, or social behavior and attitudes (Ehrhardt et al., 1989). Such studies suggest that although prenatal hormonal events may have some subtle consequences for later sexual and social development, their effect is much weaker in humans than in nonhuman animals. For humans, social and cultural factors appear to be dominant (Money, 1980).

There are, however, some studies that point to the opposite conclusion. The most famous of these occurred several years ago in remote villages of the Dominican Republic. It involved 18 genetic males who, owing to a condition known as *androgen insensitivity,* were born with internal organs that were clearly male but with external genitals that were closer to those of females, including a clitoris-like sex organ. In androgen insensitivity, the gonads develop as normal testes and begin to secrete testosterone and other androgens. However, the receptor systems that would be activated by androgens are missing from at least some of the body tissues that would ordinarily be masculinized by the hormones. Even though androgens are secreted and are present in the bloodstream of such a boy, they do not produce the male pattern of genital and physical development. All 18 of the infants studied had been raised as girls, which was at odds with both their genes and their prenatal hormonal environment. When they reached puberty, the surge of male hormones produced the usual bodily changes and turned their clitoris-like sex organs into penis-like organs. The vast majority of these males-reared-as-females rapidly turned into males. They seemed to have little difficulty adjusting to a male gender identity; they went off to work as miners and woodsmen, and some found female sexual partners. In this case, biology triumphed over environment (Imperato-McGinley et al., 1979).

There is controversy, however, about these Dominican boys who appeared to be girls. They do not seem to have been raised as ordinary girls (which is not surprising, since they had ambiguous genitals). Rather, they seemed to have been treated as half-girl, half-boy, which could have made their subsequent transition to males easier (Money, 1987).

In other cases, the results of conflict between prenatal hormones and social rearing are less clear. In the most dramatic example, identical twin boys had a completely normal prenatal environment. But at the age of 8 months one of the boys had his penis completely severed in what was supposed to be a routine circumcision. Ten months later the parents authorized surgery to turn their child into a little girl—the testes were removed and a vagina was given preliminary shape. The child was then given female sex hormones and raised as a girl. Within a few years the child seemed to have assumed a female gender identity: She preferred more feminine clothes, toys, and activities than her twin brother did. Because she appeared to be a normal girl in many ways, most investigators concluded that this was a case in which social environment had won out.

However, studies of the child at the time that she reached puberty revealed that the outcome was more complex (Diamond, 1982). As a teenager, she was unhappy and appeared to be confused about her sexuality, even though she had not been told about her original sex or the sex-change operation she had undergone. In interviews she refused to draw a picture of a woman and instead would draw only a man. Aspects of her body language, such as her walking gait and patterns of posture and movement, were masculine in appearance. Socially, she had considerably more than the usual degree of difficulty in forming relationships with her peers.

A recent follow-up on this individual found that he eventually rejected the female gender identity and has successfully lived as a male since then (Diamond & Sigmundson, 1997). Thus, the attempt to control his gender identity through socialization, and to raise him as a "normal girl," was unsuccessful in the long run. It is difficult to know the precise source of the difficulty he experienced in emotional and social adjustment at puberty. Explanations include the possibility that his early brain development as a male placed constraints on his later ability to adapt to a female gender identity.

What can we conclude about gender identity? Clearly, prenatal hormones and environment are both major determinants of gender identity and typically work in harmony. When they clash, as they do in some individuals, most experts believe that environment will dominate. But this is a controversial area, and expert opinion may change as additional data are gathered.

Adult Sexuality

Changes in body hormone systems occur at puberty, which usually begins between the ages of 11 and 14 (see Figure 10-8). The hypothalamus begins to secrete chemicals called gonadotropin releasing factors; these stimulate the pituitary gland, which lies immediately below the hypothalamus. The pituitary secretes sex hormones, called gonadotropins, into the bloodstream. These circulate through the body and reach the gonads—ovaries in females and testes in males—which generate egg or sperm cells. Gonadotropins activate the gonads, causing them to secrete additional sex hormones into the bloodstream.

In women, the hypothalamus releases its gonadotropin releasing factors on a monthly cycle, rising and falling approximately every 28 days. This stimulates the pituitary to secrete two gonadotropins: follicle stimulating hormone (FSH) and luteinizing hormone (LH), also on a monthly cycle. These hormones activate the ovaries. Follicle stimulating hormone stimulates the ovaries to generate *follicles,* clusters of cells in the ovaries that allow fertile eggs to develop. Once a follicle is generated, it begins to secrete the female hormone, estrogen. Estrogen is released into the bloodstream to affect the body's sexual development and, in many species of animals, to activate sexual motivation in the brain. The second gonadotropin, luteinizing hormone, is released from the pituitary slightly later than follicle stimulating hormone. Luteinizing hormone causes **ovulation,** *the release of a mature fertile egg cell from the follicle.* When the follicle releases its egg, it also secretes a second female hormone, progesterone, which prepares the uterus for implantation of a fertilized egg and, in some species of animals, also activates sexual motivation in the brain.

In men, the hypothalamus secretes gonadotropin releasing factor in a constant fashion rather than in a monthly cycle. This causes the male pituitary to constantly release its gonadotropin, called interstitial cell stimulating hormone (ICSH), into the bloodstream. ICSH causes male testes to produce mature sperm cells and dramatically boost secretion of androgens, especially testosterone. Testosterone and other androgens stimulate the development of male physical characteristics and, in most species of animals, act on the brain to activate sexual desire.

Effects of Hormones on Desire and Arousal

In many species, sexual arousal is closely

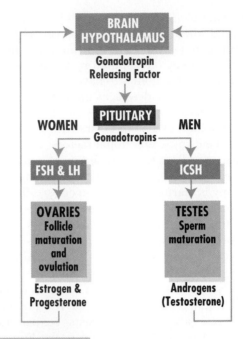

FIGURE 10-8

The Hormonal System Involved in Sex   *By way of hormones, the hypothalamus directs the pituitary, which in turn directs the gonads to secrete the sex hormones.*

tied to variations in hormonal levels; in humans, however, hormones play less of a role. One way to assess the contribution of hormones to sexual arousal is to study the effects of removing the gonads, a procedure called *gonadectomy.* (In males, removal of the testes is called *castration.*) In experiments with animals such as rats and guinea pigs, castration results in rapid decline and eventual disappearance of sexual activity. For humans, of course, there are no controlled experiments; psychologists rely instead on observations of males with serious illnesses (such as cancer of the testes) who have undergone chemical castration (use of synthetic hormones to suppress or block the use of androgen). These studies typically show that some men lose interest in sex while others continue to lead a normal sex life (Money et al., 1976; Walker, 1978). Apparently androgen contributes to sexual desire only in some cases.

Another way to measure the contribution of hormones to sexual desire and arousal in men is to look for a relationship between hormonal fluctuation and sexual interest.

For example, is a man more likely to feel aroused when his testosterone level is high? It turns out that testosterone level may have no effect on copulatory function—as indicated by the ability to have an erection—but does increase desire, as indicated by sexual fantasies (Davidson, 1988). The major determinants of sexual desire in men, however, seem to be emotional factors; thus, for males as well as females, the most common cause of low desire in couples seeking sex therapy is marital conflict (Goleman, 1988).

Sexual desire is even less dependent on hormones in women. This contrasts with nonprimate species, in which female sexual behavior is highly dependent on sexual hormones. In all other animals, removal of the ovaries results in cessation of sexual activity. A castrated female ceases to be receptive to the male and usually resists sexual advances. The major exception is the human female; following menopause (when the ovaries have ceased to function), most women do not experience diminished sexual desire. In fact, some women show increased interest in sex after menopause, possibly because they are no longer concerned about becoming pregnant. There is evidence to indicate that women's sexual desire is facilitated by trace amounts of sex hormones in the bloodstream (Sherwin, 1988). However, the level required is so low that it may be exceeded in most women and hence not play a significant role in changes in desire.

Studies of the relationship between hormonal fluctuation and sexual arousal in premenopausal females lead to a similar conclusion: Normal changes in hormones control arousal in other animals but not in humans. In female mammals, hormones fluctuate cyclically, with accompanying changes in fertility. During the first part of the mammalian cycle (while the egg is being prepared for fertilization), the ovaries secrete estrogen, which prepares the uterus for implantation and also tends to arouse sexual interest. After ovulation occurs, both progesterone and estrogen are secreted. This fertility or *estrous cycle* is accompanied by a variation in sexual motivation in most mammalian species. Most female animals are receptive to sexual advances by a male only during the period of ovulation, when the estrogen level is at its highest; during this time the female is said to be "in heat." Among primates, however, sexual activity is less strongly influenced by the fertility cycle; monkey, ape, and chimpanzee females copulate during all phases of the cycle, although ovulation is still the period of most intense sexual activity. In the human female, sexual desire and arousal seem to be affected much more by social and emotional factors.

In sum, the degree of hormonal control over sexual behavior is lower in humans than in other animals. Still, even for humans there may be some hormonal control, as witnessed by the relationship between testosterone levels and sexual desire in men.

Neural Control   In one sense, the primary sex organ is the brain. The brain is where sexual desire originates and where sexual behavior is controlled. In humans the sexual function of the brain extends to the control of sexual thoughts, images, and fantasies. Within the brain, sexual hormones can influence neural function in adult individuals. Next, we discuss how sexual hormones also influence the physical growth and connection patterns of neurons in early life for all mammalian species, including humans, and in adults for at least some species (Breedlove, 1994).

The nervous system is affected by sexual hormones at many levels. At the level of the spinal cord, neural circuits control the movements of copulation. In males, these include erection of the penis as well as pelvic movements and ejaculation. All of these actions can be elicited in a reflex fashion in men whose spinal cords have been severed by injury and who have no conscious body sensations. Similarly, clinical studies of women with spinal injury indicate that vaginal secretions in response to genital stimulation and pelvic movements may be controlled by neural reflex circuits within the spinal cord (Offir, 1982).

Higher levels of the brain, especially the hypothalamus, contain the neural systems that are important to more complex aspects of sexual behavior. For example, sexual pursuit and copulation can be elicited in both males and females of many animal species by electrical stimulation of hypothalamic regions. Even in humans, stimulation of brain regions near the hypothalamus has been reported to induce intense sexual feelings and desire (Heath, 1972). Conversely, lesions of the hypothalamus can eliminate sexual behavior in many species, including humans.

Early Experiences   The environment also influences adult sexuality. Early experience is a major determinant of the sexual behavior of many mammals and can affect specific sexual responses. For instance, in their play, young monkeys exhibit many of the postures required later for copulation. When wrestling with their peers, infant male monkeys display hindquarter grasping and thrusting responses that are components of adult sexual behavior. Infant female monkeys retreat when threatened by an aggressive male infant and stand steadfastly in a posture similar to the stance required to support the weight of the male during copulation. These presexual responses appear as early as 60 days of age and become more frequent and refined as the monkey matures. Their early appearance suggests that they are innate responses to specific stimuli, and the modification and refinement of these responses through experience indicates that learning plays a role in the development of the adult sexual pattern.

Experience also affects the interpersonal aspect of sex. Monkeys raised in partial isolation (in separate wire cages, where they can see other monkeys but cannot have contact with them) are usually unable to copulate at maturity. The male monkeys are able to perform the mechanics of sex: They masturbate to ejaculation at about the same frequency as normal monkeys. But when confronted with a sexually receptive female, they do not seem to know how to assume the correct posture for copulation. They are aroused, but they aimlessly grope the female or their own bodies. Their problem is not just a deficiency of specific responses. These monkeys have social or affectional problems: Even in nonsexual situations, they are unable to relate to other monkeys, exhibiting either fear and flight or extreme aggression. Apparently, normal heterosexual behavior in primates depends not only on hormones and the development of specific sexual responses but also on an affectional bond with a member of the opposite sex. This bond is an outgrowth of earlier interactions with the mother and

Sexual play among snow monkeys. Normal heterosexual behavior in primates depends not only on hormones and the development of specific sexual responses but also on an affectional bond with a member of the opposite sex.

peers, through which the young monkey learns to trust, to expose its delicate parts without fear of harm, to accept and enjoy physical contact with others, and to be motivated to seek the company of others (Harlow, 1971).

Although we must be cautious about generalizing these findings to human sexual development, clinical observations of human infants suggest certain parallels. Human infants develop their first feelings of trust and affection through a warm and loving relationship with the mother or primary caretaker (see Chapter 3). This basic trust is a prerequisite for satisfactory interactions with peers. And affectionate relationships with other youngsters of both sexes lay the groundwork for the intimacy required for sexual relationships among adults.

Cultural Influences   Culture also influences the expression of sexual desire. Unlike that of other primates, human sexual behavior is strongly determined by culture. For example, every society places some restrictions on sexual behavior. Incest (sexual relations within the family) is prohibited in almost all cultures. Other aspects of sexual behavior—sexual activity among children, homosexuality, masturbation, and premarital sex—are permitted in varying degrees by different societies. Among preliterate cultures acceptable sexual activity varies widely. Some very permissive societies encourage auto-erotic activities and sex play among children of both sexes and allow them to observe adult sexual activity. The Chewa of Africa, for example, believe that if children are not allowed to exercise themselves sexually, they will be unable to produce offspring later. The Sambia of New Guinea have institutionalized bisexuality: From prepuberty until marriage, a boy lives with other males and engages in homosexual practices (Herdt, 1984).

In contrast, very restrictive societies try to control preadolescent sexual behavior and prevent children from learning about sex. The Cuna of South America believe that children should be totally ignorant about sex until they are married; they do not even permit their children to watch animals give birth.

While the most obvious way to study cultural differences is to investigate practices in different countries, one can also look at culture changes that occur within a country. One such change occurred in the United States and other Western countries between the 1940s and the 1970s. In the 1940s and 1950s, the United States and most other Western countries would have been classified as sexually restrictive. Traditionally, the existence of prepubertal sexuality had been ignored or denied. Marital sex was considered the only legitimate sexual outlet, and other forms of sexual expression (homosexual activities, premarital and extramarital sex) were generally condemned and often prohibited by law. Of course, many members of these societies engaged in such activities, but often with feelings of shame.

Over the years, sexual activities became less restricted. Premarital intercourse became more acceptable and more frequent. Among American college-educated individuals interviewed in the 1940s, 27% of the women and 49% of the men had engaged in premarital sex by age 21 (Kinsey et al., 1953; Kinsey, Pomeroy, & Martin, 1948). In contrast, several surveys of American college students conducted in the 1970s reported percentages ranging from 40% to over 80% for both males and females (Hunt, 1974; Tavris & Sadd, 1977). Over the past several decades there has been a gradual trend toward initiating sex at an earlier age. Roughly 50% of both men and women report having had sexual intercourse by age 16 or 17 (Laumann et al., 1994). Figure 10-9 gives the reported incidence of premarital intercourse in studies conducted over a 35-year span. Note that the change in sexual behavior was greater among women than among men and that the biggest changes occurred in the late 1960s. These changes led many observers of the social scene in the 1970s to conclude that a "sexual revolution" had occurred.

Today it seems that the sexual revolution has been stymied by the fear of sexually transmitted diseases, particularly AIDS. Moreover, the "revolution" may have involved behavior more than feelings. In interviews of American college-student couples in the 1970s, only 20% thought that sex between casual acquaintances was completely acceptable (Peplau, Rubin, & Hill, 1977). In a similar vein, while women are becoming more like men with regard to sexual behavior, they continue to differ from men in certain attitudes toward sex before marriage. The majority of women who engage in premarital sex do so with only one or two partners with whom they are emotionally involved. Men, in contrast, are more likely to seek sex with multiple partners (Laumann et al., 1994). However, within a given five-year period, the majority of both men and women are likely to have no more than one sexual partner (Laumann et al., 1994).

Sex Differences   Studies of heterosexuals have shown that young men and women differ in their attitudes about sex; women are more likely than men to view sex as part of a loving relationship. Related to this, differences between women and men have been reported in the nature of the type of event that is most likely to elicit sexual jealousy: emotional infidelity or sexual infidelity. Whether measured by self-reports or by autonomic reactions such as heart rate, women react more strongly to the prospect of emotional infidelity (the prospect of their partner's forming a romantic relationship with someone else), regardless of whether the infidelity involves an actual sexual act. By contrast, men react more strongly to the prospect of sexual infidelity, regardless of whether their partner's sexual liaison involves an emotional commitment (Buss et al., 1992).

Differences between the sexes apply to behavior as well as to attitudes. Women who engage in premarital sex are likely to have fewer sexual partners than men. Differences between male and female patterns of sexual behavior persist regardless of sexual orientation. For example, lesbian couples are likely to have sex less frequently than heterosexual couples, and gay male couples have sex more often than heterosexual couples. Such differences can be viewed as reflecting a continuum that extends from female-typical characteristics to male-typical characteristics (Buss, 1994).

Sexual Orientation

An individual's **sexual orientation** is the *degree to which he or she is sexually attracted to persons of the opposite sex and/or to persons of the same sex.* Like Alfred Kinsey, the pioneering sex researcher of the 1940s, most behavioral scientists conceptualize sexual orientation as a continuum, ranging from exclusive heterosexuality to exclusive homosexuality. For example, on Kinsey's own 7-point scale, individuals who are attracted exclusively to persons of the opposite sex and who engage in sexual behavior only with such persons are at the heterosexual end of the scale (category 0); those who are attracted exclusively to persons of the same sex and who engage in sexual behavior only with such persons are at the homosexual end of the continuum (category 6). Individuals in categories 2–4 are usually defined as bisexual.

This oversimplifies the situation, however, because sexual orientation comprises several distinct components, including erotic attraction or sexual desire, sexual behavior, romantic attraction, and self-identification as a heterosexual, homosexual, or bisexual person. It is not uncommon for an individual to be at different points on the scale for different components. For example, many people who are sexually attracted to persons of the same sex have never participated in any homosexual behaviors; many who have had frequent homosexual encounters do not identify

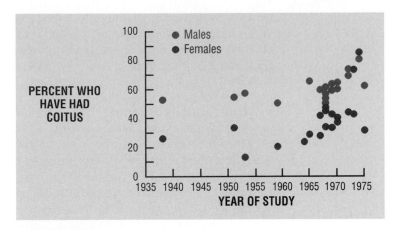

FIGURE 10-9

Reported Incidence of Premarital Coitus *Each data point represents findings from a study of the incidence of premarial sex among college men and women. Note the marked upward trend starting in the 1960s.* (After Hopkins, 1977)

themselves as homosexual or bisexual persons. To further complicate matters, individuals may shift over time on one or more of the components.

Frequency of Different Sexual Orientations In a survey of sexuality in the United States, 10.1% of adult men and 8.6% of adult women in a national random sample reported at least one of the following: (a) they were currently attracted "mostly" or "only" to persons of their own sex; (b) they found having sex with someone of the same sex "somewhat" or "very" appealing; or (c) they had engaged in sexual behavior with a person of the same sex since age 18 (Laumann et al., 1994). These percentages are similar to the percentage of people who are left-handed (about 8%). In terms of self-identification, 2.8% of the men and 1.4% of the women identified themselves as homosexual (or gay or lesbian) or bisexual—similar to the percentage of people in the United States who identify themselves as Jewish (2–3%).

As the authors of the survey acknowledge, these percentages must be regarded as underestimates because many people are reluctant to report desires or behaviors that are still considered by some to be immoral or pathological. The problem was particularly acute in this survey because the interviews were conducted in the respondents' own homes, and other family members, including children, were also in the home at the time, although not necessarily in the room, during more than 20% of the interviews.

Causes of Sexual Orientation   The common question "What causes homosexuality?" is scientifically misconceived because it implicitly assumes either that heterosexuality needs no explanation or that its causes are self-evident. Those who have thought about it at all are likely to conclude that because only heterosexual behavior results in reproduction, it must be the "natural" outcome of evolution, and hence only deviations from heterosexuality (such as homosexuality) pose a scientific puzzle. Freud himself did not agree: "[heterosexuality] is also a problem that needs elucidation and is not a self-evident fact based upon an attraction that is ultimately of a chemical nature" (1905/1962, pp. 11–12). It is because we agree with Freud that we have called this section of the chapter "sexual orientation" and not "homosexuality."

At issue once again is the nature-nurture question, which we introduced in the chapter on development (Chapter 3) and discuss in detail in the chapter on individual differences (Chapter 12): To what extent is an adult's sexual orientation determined by earlier life experiences or to innate biological influences, such as genes or prenatal hormones?

The best data on earlier life experiences comes from an intensive, large-scale interview study of approximately 1,000 homosexual and 500 heterosexual men and women living in the San Francisco Bay area (Bell, Weinberg, & Hammersmith, 1981a). The study uncovered one—and only one—major factor that predicted a homosexual orientation in adulthood for both men and women: childhood gender nonconformity. As shown in Table 10-2, when asked what play activities they had or had not enjoyed as children, gay men and lesbians were significantly more likely than heterosexual men and women to report that they had not enjoyed activities typical of their sex and significantly more likely to report that they had enjoyed ativities typical of the other sex. Gay men and lesbians were also more likely than their heterosexual counterparts to report that they had not been masculine (for men) or feminine (for women) as children. In addition to this gender nonconformity, gay men and lesbians were more likely to have had more friends of the opposite sex.

Two features of the data in Table 10-2 are worth noting. First, the findings are quite strong and similar for men and women: 63% of both gay men and lesbians had not enjoyed childhood activities typical of their sex, compared with only 10% to 15% of their heterosexual counterparts. Second, it is clear that women are more likely than men to have enjoyed activities typical of the opposite sex during childhood and to have had more childhood friends of the opposite sex. In fact, a majority of both the

TABLE 10-2

Gender Nonconformity in Childhood   *In a large-scale interview study, gay men and lesbians were more likely than heterosexual men and women to report that they were gender nonconforming during childhood.* (After Bell, Weinberg, & Hammersmith, 1981b)

Gender Nonconforming Preferences and Behaviors	Men		Women	
	Gay	Heterosexual	Lesbian	Heterosexual
Had not enjoyed sex-typical activities	63%	10%	63%	15%
Had enjoyed sex-atypical activities	48%	11%	81%	61%
Atypically sex-typed (masculinity/femininity)	56%	8%	80%	24%
Most childhood friends were opposite sex	42%	13%	60%	40%

lesbians and the heterosexual women in this study were "tomboys"—that is, enjoyed boys' activities as children. It is the nonenjoyment of sex-typical activities that appears to be the best predictor of an adult homosexual orientation for both men and women. The overall finding that childhood gender nonconformity predicts an adult homosexual outcome has now been confirmed in several other studies (Bailey & Zucker, 1995), including several that followed gender nonconforming boys into adolescence and adulthood and assessed their sexual orientations (Green, 1987; Zucker, 1990).

In addition to the gender nonconformity finding, the San Francisco study also yielded many negative findings that were important because they disconfirmed common theories about the antecedents of a homosexual orientation. For example:

- A person's identification with the opposite-sex parent while growing up appears to have no significant impact on whether he or she turns out to be homosexual or heterosexual. This fails to confirm Freud's psychoanalytic theory (discussed in Chapter 13) as well as other theories based on the dynamics of the person's childhood family.

- Gay men and lesbians were no more likely than their heterosexual counterparts to report having their first sexual encounter with a person of the same sex. Moreover, they neither lacked heterosexual experiences during their childhood and adolescent years nor found such experiences unpleasant.

- A person's sexual orientation is usually determined by adolescence, even though he or she might not yet have become sexually active. Gay men and lesbians typically experienced same-sex attractions about 3 years before they had engaged in any "advanced" sexual activity with persons of the same sex.

These last two sets of findings indicate that, in general, homosexual *feelings,* not homosexual *behaviors,* are the crucial antecedents of an adult homosexual orientation. They thus disconfirm any simple behavioral learning theory of sexual orientation, including the popular, laypersons' version which asserts that an individual can become gay by being "seduced" by a person of the same sex or by having an admired, openly gay teacher, parent, or clergyperson. Cross-cultural data are also consistent with this conclusion. For example, in the Sambian culture of New Guinea, cited earlier, all boys engage in exclusively homosexual behaviors from pre-puberty through late adolescence. At that point, virtually all of them marry and become exclusively heterosexual (Herdt, 1984, 1987).

Finally, it is clear from all the studies that one's sexual orientation is not something that one simply chooses. Gay men and lesbians do not choose to have erotic feelings toward persons of the same sex any more than heterosexual persons choose to have erotic feelings toward persons of the opposite sex. As the accompanying Contemporary Voices discussion illustrates, behavioral scientists do disagree over the nature-nurture question—whether the major determinants of sexual orientation are rooted in biology or experience—but the public often misconstrues the question to be whether sexual orientation is determined by variables beyond the individual's control or is freely chosen. That is not the same question.

Because most of the major theories of homosexuality based on childhood or adolescent experiences have not been supported by the evidence, many scientists now believe that the origins of both childhood gender nonconformity and adult homosexual orientation may lie in an individual's biology, possibly in the genes or prenatal hormones. The Contemporary Voices discussion presents two contrasting views of the current biological evidence.

Biological Factors Because the results of the San Francisco study disconfirmed virtually all the major theories of homosexuality based on childhood or adolescent experiences, the investigators speculate that the origins of both childhood gender nonconformity and adult homosexual orientation may lie in biological factors in the individual, including hormones and genes.

As noted earlier, sex hormones—especially androgens—are involved in sexual motivation. This observation suggested to many early researchers the hypothesis that gay men might have lower androgen or testosterone levels than heterosexual men. But this hypothesis was not confirmed. Most studies showed no differences, and those that did failed to control for other factors that are known to suppress androgen levels, such as stress or recreational drug use. Moreover, when gay men are given additional testosterone, their sexual motivation increases—as it does for men in general—but their sexual orientation does not change.

The role of hormones in prenatal development suggested a different hormonal hypothesis. Reasoning from research on rats in which prenatal testosterone "masculinizes" the brain and influences subsequent male-like mating responses, some researchers hypothesized that human males who get substantially below-average amounts of testosterone at a critical point in prenatal development will be predisposed toward a homosexual orientation in adult life. Similarly, female fetuses exposed to substantially above-average amounts of testosterone may also be slightly predisposed toward a homosexual orientation in adult life (Ellis & Ames, 1987).

It is difficult to test hypotheses about prenatal hormones in humans, and most of the relevant studies have methodological flaws that prevent any firm conclusions (Adkins-Regan, 1988; Ehrhardt & Meyer-Bahlburg, 1981). For example, a well-known study followed girls who were exposed to extremely high levels of prenatal testosterone. The girls were born with ambiguous genitalia, which were surgically corrected soon after birth. In interviews in middle childhood, these girls and their mothers reported that they were more likely to be "tomboys" than girls in a control group (Money & Ehrhardt, 1972). In early adulthood, they were more likely than girls in the control group to have same-sex fantasies (Money, Schwartz, & Lewis, 1984). These results have often been interpreted as demonstrating that the testosterone had "masculinized" the girls' brains during the prenatal period.

But other interpretations are possible. For example, these girls were also taking cortisone medication, which could make them more physically active and, hence, more tomboyish. This might influence their interactions with other girls, with boys, and with adults, and possibly change the way those individuals behave toward them. For this and other reasons, the study does not clearly demonstrate a direct link between prenatal hormones and adult sexual orientation.

Similar methodological problems make it difficult to interpret other findings relevant to the prenatal hormone hypothesis. For example, it has been reported that the hypothalamus of gay men differs in a small structural detail from that of heterosexual men (LeVay, 1993, 1991). As noted earlier, the hypothalamus is intimately involved with sexual hormones and sexual behavior. But this finding is based on an examination of brains of men who had died. The gay men had all died from complications of AIDS, but most of the control group of heterosexual men had died of other causes. We do not know whether the disease process itself might have affected the brain, although there is some evidence suggesting that AIDS is probably not the cause of the structural difference (LeVay, 1993; see also Bem, 1996; Zucker & Bradley, 1995).

In contrast to the ambiguity of the hormonal evidence, the evidence for a link between genetic factors and adult homosexual orientation is well established—even if its interpretation is not. The most compelling data come from studies of identical and fraternal twins. In a study of gay men who were identical twins, it was found that 52% of their twin brothers were also gay, compared with only 22% of fraternal twin brothers (Bailey & Pillard, 1991). In a comparable study of lesbians, 48% of their identical twin sisters were also lesbian, compared with only 16% of fraternal twin sisters. Moreover, only 6% of these women's adoptive sisters were lesbian, a further indication that genes are involved (Bailey, Pillard, Neale, & Agyei, 1993). A subsequent study of nearly 5,000 twins who had been systematically drawn from a twin registry confirmed the heritability of sexual orientation for men but not for women (Bailey & Martin, 1995). Finally, an analysis of 114 families of gay men, in conjunction with a chromosomal analysis of 40 families in which there were two gay brothers, showed evidence of a genetic marker for homosexuality on the X chromosome, the chromosome that males receive from their mothers. Gay men had more gay male relatives on the mother's side than on the father's side of the family (Hamer & Copeland, 1994; Hamer et al., 1993).

The Exotic-Becomes-Erotic Theory A recently proposed experience-based theory attempts to integrate the findings we have reviewed. It is called the *exotic-becomes-erotic (E-B-E) theory* of sexual orientation (Bem, 1995.) The theory proposes, first, that genetic and possibly other biological factors do not influence adult sexual orientation per se but that they influence a child's temperament and personality traits. As we will see in Chapter 12, about half of the variation among individuals in most personality traits can be attributed to genetic differences. In other words, there is solid evidence that most personality traits have a strong genetic or heritable component, including temperaments such as emotionality, sociability, and activity level (Buss & Plomin, 1984, 1975).

Temperament predisposes a child to enjoy some activities more than others: One child will enjoy rough-and-tumble play and competitive team sports; another will prefer to socialize quietly or play jacks or hopscotch. Some of these activities are more male-typical; others are more female-typical. Thus, depending on the sex of the child, he or she will be genetically predisposed to be gender conforming or gender nonconforming. As shown in Table 10-2, children also tend to have friends who share their activity preferences; for example, the child—male or female—who shuns competitive team sports will avoid playing with boys and seek out girls as playmates. Accordingly, gender-conforming children will feel most similar to and most comfortable with children of their own sex; gender-nonconforming children will feel most similar to and most comfortable with children of the opposite sex.

The theory next proposes that dissimilarity and discomfort produce general (nonsexual) arousal. For the female-typical child, this arousal may be experienced as mild fear or apprehension in the presence of boys; for the male-typical child, it may be felt as antipathy or contempt in the presence of girls ("girls are yucky"). The clearest case is the "sissy" boy who is teased and tormented by other boys for his gender nonconformity and hence is likely to experience the strong arousal created by fear and suppressed anger in their presence. The "tomboy" girl who is shunned by

According to Bem's exotic-becomes-erotic theory, a gender-nonconforming child will feel most similar to and most comfortable with children of the opposite sex.

her female peers may experience similar emotionally toned arousal. The most common case, however, is probably the child who experiences the mild arousal produced by being in the presence of dissimilar peers.

Finally, the theory proposes that in later years this general arousal is transformed into erotic arousal or sexual attraction—after the original cause of the arousal may have diminished or disappeared. Evidence for this last step in the process comes, in part, from laboratory studies in which male participants were physiologically aroused in one of several nonsexual ways (for example, by running in place or watching a videotape of a comedy routine or a grisly killing). When these men subsequently watched a videotape of an attractive woman, they found her more attractive and expressed more interest in dating and kissing her than did men who had not been physiologically aroused. Moreover, it did not matter what caused the initial arousal. This general finding has now been replicated in several studies (Allen, Kenrick, Linder, & McCall, 1989; Dutton & Aron, 1974; White & Kight, 1984; White, Fishbein, & Rutstein, 1981). In short, general physiological arousal can be subsequently experienced as, interpreted as, or actually transformed into sexual arousal.

FRONTIERS OF PSYCHOLOGICAL RESEARCH

Imprinting

Some motivations appear to be instinctively directed toward their incentive targets. The concept of *instinct*—an innate propensity to behave in a particular way—has a long and controversial history. In the nineteenth and early twentieth centuries psychologists drew up long lists of instincts (18 according to one prominent theorist) to explain human behavior (McDougall, 1908). Beginning in the 1920s, the concept fell into disrepute among American psychologists, partly because the explanation was usually circular (for example, we might explain that birds build nests because they have an instinct to do so, but the only evidence we have of such an instinct is that birds build nests); partly because every type of behavior seemed to qualify for its own instinct, which led to ever longer lists (do you have an instinct to take psychology courses?); and partly because the emergence of behaviorism made psychologists look more to learning for explanations of behavior. The study of instinctive behavior, however, persisted among a group of European zoologists known as ethologists (*ethology* is the branch of zoology that studies animal behavior), and beginning

The phenomenon of imprinting is so strong that it has been used to train endangered species to learn appropriate migration routes. Here, young sandhill and whooping cranes follow an ultralight plane piloted by wildlife biologist Kent Clegg.

in the 1950s ethological concepts of instinct began to be incorporated into psychology.

In the ethological sense, a pattern of behavior may be called instinctive if it is (a) species-specific—that is, it appears in all members of a species regardless of the environment in which they grew up and without being specifically learned; (b) a fixed action pattern—that is, it has a very stereotyped and predictable organization;

and (c) innately released—that is, it can be triggered by some natural stimulus the first time the stimulus is encountered. A young child crawling or walking for the first time, a young squirrel opening a nut for the first time, and a newborn human smiling or crying are all exhibiting instinctive behavior patterns.

One of the most successful applications of the ethological approach has been the study of

Conversely, the theory implies that when children interact with peers with whom they are quite comfortable, no arousal occurs. Thus, gender-conforming children will come to have comfortable but nonerotic friendships with members of the same sex while gender-nonconforming children will come to have comfortable but nonerotic friendships with members of the opposite sex. Thus, only the exotic becomes erotic. Indirect evidence for this comes from the observation that boys and girls raised collectively on communes (kibbutzim) in Israel rarely

marry one another because they feel too much like brothers and sisters (Shepher, 1971).

The same process explains why virtually all Sambian men turn out to be predominantly heterosexual in adulthood despite having spent their entire adolescence engaging in homosexual activities. Although the majority of Sambian boys enjoy their homosexual activity, the context of close male bonding in which it occurs does not produce strongly charged homoerotic or romantic feelings; meanwhile, the boys

imprinting, the early rapid learning that allows a newborn or newly hatched animal to develop an attachment to its mother (see Chapter 7). Within the first hours of life, infants of many species are "programmed" to learn an emotional attachment to the closest social figure. Normally this would be their mother, but if a newly hatched duckling sees only a human being or even a moving inanimate object, such as a wooden hunting decoy, instead of its real mother, it will imprint on the person or object instead. Within the "critical period" during which imprinting can occur, exposure to an object for as little as 10 minutes is enough to establish an emotional attachment that will persist until the animal is grown. A duckling will follow the decoy if it is the first object it sees, will then attempt to remain close to the decoy even under adverse circumstances, and later will prefer to be near the decoy even if given a choice between it and a live duck (Hess, 1972). This propensity is so strong that it has recently been used to train endangered species to follow light aircraft in order to learn appropriate migration routes (Line, 1998).

Imprinting has several other consequences. The development of the bond between a mother and her offspring is called *maternal imprinting*. Another form of imprinting is *sexual imprinting,* which is learned at the same time as maternal imprinting but isn't expressed in behavior until later in life, when the animal chooses a mate. In sexual imprinting, the infant learns from its parents what a "proper adult" should look like and then, as an adult, chooses a mate of similar appearance. For example, a male duckling raised by its natural mother will later choose a mate that resembles her, but a male raised by a foster mother of a different duck species will choose a mate that resembles the foster mother rather than its biological mother. The greatest preference is for mates that resemble but are not identical to the sexual imprinting target. A mate that is just slightly different from the target is perceived as most desirable (Bateson, 1978). Ethologists have interpreted this phenomenon as a psychological mechanism that evolved to allow the chooser to pick a mate of the appropriate species while at the same time preventing inbreeding. A

When imprinting studies go awry

mate that looks identical to the imprinting target is likely to be a close relative; a mate that is just slightly different would be a better choice. Some psychologists have suggested that this mechanism may be related to why human romantic attachments rarely develop between members of the same family.

Are humans capable of imprinting? Imprinting is strongest in species that are born and hatched already able to walk around and that mature quickly. Humans, by comparison, are born helpless and are slow to mature. Although traces of imprinting persist in humans, these are minor compared to the influence of culture.

are taught that women are inferior and dangerous—which enhances the erotic appeal of women. More generally, the theory implies that across time and cultures, heterosexuality will be the predominant outcome because virtually all societies establish a sex-based division of labor that sets men and women apart and makes them dissimilar, exotic, and, hence, erotic to one another.

Other writers have also proposed that although similarity and familiarity may promote friendship and compatibility, it is

dissimilarity, unfamiliarity, and a sense of the exotic that sparks sexual arousal and/or romantic feelings (Bell, 1982; Tripp, 1987). Ethologists have even noted the effects of dissimilarity in the mating choices of nonhuman animals. As discussed in the Frontiers of Psychological Research feature above, some species prefer mates that resemble, but are not identical to, the sexual imprinting target they encountered prior to sexual maturity; a mate that is just slightly different from the target is perceived as the most desirable. Ethologists speculate that this preference prevents in-breeding because a mate that looks identical to the imprinting target is likely to be a close relative.

The more general point here is that just because a behavior might be advantageous from the standpoint of reproduction, it does not follow that evolution has "hardwired" it into the species. Consider again the ducks described in the Frontiers of Psychological Research feature. Clearly, it would be reproductively advantageous for ducks to mate with other ducks. Yet if they are raised by a foster mother of another species, they will prefer a mate that resembles her to another duck. They will even prefer a human if he or she was the first moving object they saw after they were hatched. As long as the environment supports or promotes the reproductively advantageous behavior often enough, it will not necessarily get programmed into the genes. And just as baby ducks will encounter mother ducks most of the time, so, too, human societies see to it

that men and women will see each other as dissimilar often enough to ensure that the species will not perish from the earth. It has even been proposed that by nurturing their nephews and nieces, lesbian aunts and gay uncles help the species along (Wilson, 1978).

Throughout this chapter we have seen that psychological and biological causes are so closely intertwined in the control of many motivations that they merge into one stream of events. Not only can biological causes control psychological motivations like hunger and thirst, but psychological processes and experiences control motivation and may feed back to control physiological responses. For example, repeated use of an addictive drug may permanently change particular brain systems. More commonly, the particular foods and drinks we desire are established as objects of choice largely by learning, and even the degree of satiety produced by a stomach full of food is influenced by previous experience. Our social attachments are determined largely by the consequences of earlier social interactions with particular individuals. When it comes to many motivational processes, biology and psychology are not separate domains but, rather, two aspects of control that continually interact to direct motivational processes.

Evidence Favors "Born" Over "Made"

J. Michael Bailey, *Northwestern University*

J. Michael Bailey

For many years, most psychologists assumed that homosexuality was a product of nurture, caused by pathological parent-child relationships or atypical conditioning experiences. However, scientific studies of these possibilities did not provide much support for them. (e.g., Bell, Weinberg, & Hammersmith, 1981). Parents of homosexual people were not very different from those of heterosexual people (and when they were, the direction of causation was unclear). Most homosexual people had homosexual desire long before they had any sexual experiences that could plausibly have led to unusual conditioning. As scientists became disenchanted with social explanations, their attention turned to theories that located the origins of sexual orientation within the person.

The best-established correlate of adult homosexuality is childhood gender nonconformity (Bailey & Zucker, 1995). On average, gay men were feminine boys and lesbians were masculine girls. Childhood gender nonconformity emerges in early childhood apparently despite, rather than because of, socialization pressures. Indeed, extremely feminine boys, who usually become gay men (Green, 1987), often suffer due to reactions to their atypical behavior. The association between sexual orientation and childhood gender nonconformity appears cross-culturally universal (Whitam & Mathy, 1986; Whitam & Mathy, 1991). Although we do not know the precise causes of childhood gender nonconformity, the general picture implicates innateness rather than learning.

More direct evidence comes from studies of siblings, including twins. Gay men tend to have more gay brothers compared with heterosexual men, and lesbians tend to have more lesbian sisters compared with heterosexual women (Bailey & Pillard, 1995). Studies of twins suggest that these patterns reflect genetic influences rather than the environment shared by family members. Identical twins tend to be more similar in their sexual orientations than fraternal twins (Bailey & Pillard, 1995). On the other hand, at least half the time if one identical twin is homosexual, the other twin is heterosexual. Although this establishes an important role for environment in sexual orientation development, environmental influences need not be social. Biological factors can also cause twin differences (Martin, Boomsma, & Machen, 1997). When identical twins have different sexual orientations, they often remember being different as children, implicating early environmental factors. The precise nature of the relevant environmental influences remains unclear, however.

More direct evidence for genetic influences has come from linkage studies that actually look at DNA (Hamer et al., 1993). Pairs of gay brothers tend to have inherited the same piece of the X chromosome, Xq28, more often than would be expected by chance. This suggests that a gene in that region affects male sexual orientation. Supporting this possibility, heterosexual men tend not to have inherited the same version of Xq28 as their gay brothers (Hu et al.,1995).

The most influential theory hypothesizes that there is an area of the brain that affects sexual orientation and that the development of this sexual orientation center depends on the early effects of hormones (Levay, 1996). Thus, according to the theory, gay men have feminine sexual orientation centers, and lesbians have masculine centers. Two cases of boys whose penises were accidentally destroyed early in life and who were subsequently reared as females are also relevant. As adults, both individuals were primarily attracted to women, consistent with their prenatal biology rather than postnatal rearing (Bradley, Oliver, Chernick, & Zuckner, 1998; Diamond & Sigmundson, 1996). One study actually compared the brains of gay men to those of heterosexual men and women, and found that one nucleus (a clump of related cells) was larger in the brains of heterosexual men than in those of gay men, whose brains looked like those of heterosexual women (LeVay, 1991). This nucleus was in the hypothalamus, which is known to be important for sexual behavior. The hypothalamus probably develops very early in humans, and thus this difference between gay and heterosexual men was unlikely to be caused by different experiences.

The origins of sexual orientation remain controversial, and there is much work to be done. Many of the most important findings (e.g., Hamet et al., 1993; LeVay, 1991) need to be replicated. At this point, a role for the social environment cannot be excluded, although little if any empirical research has supported such a role. In contrast, the scientific search for innate origins has produced a steady stream of findings.

Sexual Orientation Is Not Inherent

by Daryl J. Bem, *Cornell University*

Dr. Bailey and I agree on the evidence showing a link or correlation between biological variables and sexual orientation. But, I propose an alternative interpretation of the biological evidence: the Exotic-Becomes-Erotic (EBE) theory of sexual orientation (Bem, 1996). The path proposed by this theory is illustrated in the figure.

A →B The theory proposes, first, that genetic, hormonal, and possibly other biological factors do not directly influence adult sexual orientation itself but, rather, influence a child's temperament and personality traits. Many personality traits have a strong genetic or heritable component, including such childhood temperaments as aggression and activity level.

B →C Temperaments such as these predispose a child to enjoy some activities more than others: A more aggressive or active child will enjoy rough-and-tumble play (boy-typical activities); another will prefer to socialize quietly (girl-typical activities). Thus, depending on the sex of the child, he or she will be genetically predisposed to be gender conforming or gender nonconforming. As shown in Table 10-2, children also tend to have friends who share their activity preferences; for example, the child—male or female—who shuns competitive team sports will avoid playing with boys and seek out girls as playmates.

C →D Accordingly, gender conforming children will feel more different from children of the opposite sex; gender nonconforming children will feel more different from children of the opposite sex—that is, to see them as relatively more "exotic" than children of their own sex.

D →E This feeling of being different creates heightened arousal. For the male-typical child, it may be felt as antipathy or contempt in the presence of girls ("girls are yucky"); for the female-typical child, it may be felt as timidity or apprehension in the presence of boys. For most children, however, this arousal will probably not be consciously felt.

E →F This arousal is transformed in later years into sexual arousal or erotic attraction: Exotic becomes erotic. Evidence for this last step comes, in part, from studies in which heterosexual male participants who had been physiologically (but nonsexually) aroused were found to be more sexually attracted to a woman than were men who had not been physiologically aroused. In other words, general physiological arousal can be subsequently experienced as, interpreted as, or actually transformed into sexual arousal.

Evidence for the theory's claim that childhood gender nonconformity intervenes between biological variables and sexual orientation actually comes from the same studies that Dr. Bailey cites as showing the link between the two. For example, the studies of twins that he cites also found that pairs of identical twins were more similar than pairs of fraternal twins on childhood gender nonconformity. Similarly, the DNA studies found that pairs of gay brothers who share the same piece of the X chromosome are also more alike on gender nonconformity than are gay brothers who do not share it. In short, the studies showing a link between biological variables and an adult homosexual orientation are consistent with EBE theory's assertion that the biology leads first to gender-nonconforming interests and preferences in childhood and, only subsequently, to the adult homosexual orientation. Nevertheless, the studies do not prove that the theory is correct; Only additional research can help us to decide.

Finally, it should be noted that EBE theory applies as much to heterosexuality as to homosexuality. Because most societies emphasize the differences between males and females, most boys and girls will grow up feeling different from their opposite-sex peers and, hence, will come to be erotically attracted to them later in life. This is why heterosexuality is the most common orientation across time and culture.

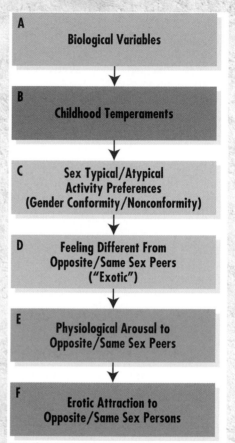

A — Biological Variables

B — Childhood Temperaments

C — Sex Typical/Atypical Activity Preferences (Gender Conformity/Nonconformity)

D — Feeling Different From Opposite/Same Sex Peers ("Exotic")

E — Physiological Arousal to Opposite/Same Sex Peers

F — Erotic Attraction to Opposite/Same Sex Persons

SUMMARY

1. Motivational states direct and activate behavior. They arise from two sources: internal drive factors and external incentive factors.

2. Incentive factors are goals in the outside world, such as food, water, sexual partners, and drugs. Incentives are the target of motivated behavior and are typically rewarding. Although some incentives—such as a sweet food when we are hungry—are powerful motivators by themselves, most incentives are established through learning.

3. Many types of natural rewards may activate the mesolimbic dopamine system. Activity in these neurons may constitute the neural basis for all rewards. Artificial activation of these neurons by rewarding drugs or electrical brain stimulation causes increased motivation for both natural and artificial incentives. Changes in this system, produced by repeatedly taking drugs that activate it, may partly cause the compulsive craving of addiction.

4. Drive factors tend to promote homeostasis: the preservation of a constant internal state. Homeostasis involves several components: a goal value or set point for the ideal internal state, a sensory signal that measures the actual internal state, a comparison between the goal value and the sensory signal, and finally, a response that brings the actual internal state closer to the goal value.

5. Regulation of temperature is an example of homeostasis. The regulated variable is the temperature of the blood, and sensors for this are located in various parts of the body, including the hypothalamus. Adjustments are either automatic physiological responses (for example, shivering) or voluntary behavioral ones (such as putting on a sweater).

6. Thirst is another homeostatic motive. There are two regulated variables, intracellular fluid and extracellular fluid. Loss of intracellular fluid is detected by osmotic sensors, neurons in the hypothalamus that respond to dehydration. Loss of extracellular fluid is detected by blood-pressure sensors, neurons in major veins and organs that respond to a drop in pressure. Intracellular and extracellular signals act together to produce thirst.

7. Hunger has evolved to allow us to select an array of nutrients. Humans have innate taste preferences, such as for sweetness, and innate aversions, such as for bitterness, that guide our choice of foods. In addition, we may develop a wide variety of learned preferences and aversions. Homeostatic hunger signals, which arise when the body is low in calorie-containing fuels such as glucose, produce appetite partly by causing the individual to perceive food incentives as more attractive and pleasant.

8. Hunger is largely controlled by homeostatic deficit and satiety signals. Certain neurons in the brain, especially in the brain stem and hypothalamus, detect shortages in glucose and trigger hunger. Other nutrient detectors, especially in the liver, detect increasing energy stores and trigger satiety. A satiety signal, in the form of the hormone cholecystokinin, is released from the intestines to help stop hunger and eating.

9. Two regions of the brain are critical to hunger: the lateral hypothalamus and the ventromedial hypothalamus. Destruction of the lateral hypothalamus leads to undereating; destruction of the ventromedial hypothalamus leads to overeating. Although these regions were originally thought to be centers for hunger and satiety, hunger is not destroyed by any lesion. Another interpretation of these effects is that the two regions of the hypothalamus exert reciprocal effects on the homeostatic set point for body weight. Damage to the lateral hypothalamus may lower the set point, and damage to the ventromedial hypothalamus may raise the set point. Diet drugs that alter appetite may work partly by affecting neurons in these regions of the hypothalamus.

10. People become obese primarily because: (a) they are genetically predisposed to be overweight or (b) they overeat (for psychological reasons). The influence of genes is mediated by their effect on fat cells, metabolic rate, and set points. As for overeating and obesity, obese people tend to overeat when they break a diet, eat more when emotionally aroused, and are more responsive to external hunger cues than normal-weight individuals. In treating obesity, extreme diets appear ineffective because the deprivation leads to subsequent overeating and to a lowered metabolic rate. What seems to work best is to establish a new set of permanent eating habits and engage in a program of exercise.

11. Anorexia nervosa is characterized by extreme, self-imposed weight loss. Bulimia is characterized by recurrent episodes of binge eating, followed by attempts to purge the excess by means of vomiting and laxatives. Possible causes of these eating disorders include personality factors such as low self-esteem; social factors such as a cultural emphasis on thinness; and biological factors such as low serotonin levels.

12. Prenatal hormones contribute to sexual development. If the embryonic sex glands produce enough androgen hormones, the embryo will have a male pattern of genital and brain development. If androgens are low or missing, the embryo will have a female pattern of genital and brain development. For nonhuman animals, prenatal hormones appear to be powerful determinants of adult sexual behavior. For humans, prenatal hormones appear to be much less important, although they may still play a role in later sexual behavior. In cases in which the hormonal exposure of the embryo is typical of one sex but the social role and gender after birth is more typical of the opposite sex (due to hormone imbalance, prenatal drugs, or a postnatal accident), the individual's development seems to correspond most closely to the postnatal social gender.

13. The female hormones (estrogen and progesterone) and male hormones (androgens) are responsible for the changes in the body that occur at puberty, but they play a limited role in human sexual arousal. In contrast, in other animals there is substantial hormonal control over sex. Early social experiences with parents and peers have a large influence on adult sexuality in primates and humans. For humans, other environmental determinants of adult sexuality include cultural norms. Although Western society has become increasingly flexible regarding female and male sex roles, men and women may still differ in their attitudes toward sex and relationships.

14. Recent studies have bolstered the claim that biological, genetic, hormonal, or neural factors may partly determine whether an individual will be heterosexual or homosexual, but the evidence is not conclusive. It is also unknown whether biological factors may influence sexual orientation directly or whether they instead contribute to other traits, such as gender conformity, that indirectly influence the development of sexual orientation.

KEY TERMS

motivation (p. 348)
affect (p. 350)
addiction (p. 352)
tolerance (p. 352)
homeostasis (p. 353)
thirst (p. 354)
obesity (p. 360)

set point (p. 363)
anorexia nervosa (p. 365)
bulimia (p. 366)
gender identity (p. 368)
ovulation (p. 371)
sexual orientation (p. 375)

CRITICAL THINKING QUESTIONS

1. To what extent do you think your own eating patterns are driven by your body's physiological needs? To what extent are they driven by genetic factors? To what extent by environmental factors?

2. Why do you think many people believe that sexual desire and activity in humans is strongly influenced by hormones when the evidence suggests that it is not?

FURTHER READING

An overview of biological factors in motivation can be found in Rosenzweig, *Biological Psychology* (1996), and in Carlson, *Physiology of Behavior* (5th ed., 1994). The neural substrates of reward are discussed in detail by Hoebel in Stevens' *Handbook of Experimental Psychology* (2nd ed., 1988). For analyses of factors controlling eating and drinking, see E. M. Stricker (ed.), *Neurobiology of Food and Fluid Intake, Handbook of Behavioral Neurobiology* 10 (1990). For a variety of viewpoints on eating disorders, see Szmukler, Dare, and Treasure, *Handbook of Eating Disorders* (1994), and Garner and Garfinkel, *Handbook of Treatment for Eating Disorders* (2nd ed., 1997). For personal accounts of young women with eating disorders, see Pipher, *Reviving Ophelia* (1994). A discussion of diverse aspects of human sexuality can be found in McWhirter et al. (eds.), *Homosexuality/ Heterosexuality* (1990); and in LeVay, *The Sexual Brain* (1994).

Chapter 11
Emotion

*T*he most basic feelings that we experience include not only motives such as hunger and sex but also emotions such as joy and anger. Emotions and motives are closely related. Emotions can activate and direct behavior in the same way that basic motives do. They may also accompany motivated behavior: Sex, for example, is not only a powerful motive but a potential source of joy.

Despite their similarities, we need to distinguish between motives and emotions. One distinction is that emotions are triggered from the outside, whereas motives are activated from within. That is, emotions are usually aroused by external events, and emotional reactions are directed toward these events; motives, in contrast, are often aroused by internal events (such as a homeostatic imbalance) and are naturally directed toward particular objects in the environment (such as food, water, or a mate). Another distinction between motives and emotions is that a motive is usually elicited by a specific need, whereas an emotion can be elicited by a wide variety of stimuli (think of all the different things that can make you angry).

These distinctions are not absolute. An external source can sometimes trigger a motive, as when the sight of food triggers hunger. And the discomfort caused by a homeostatic imbalance—severe hunger, for example—can arouse emotions. Nevertheless, emotions and motives are different enough in their sources, subjective experience, and effects on behavior that they merit separate treatment.

Components of Emotion

Emotion is *a complex condition that arises in response to certain affectively toned experiences.* An intense emotion has at least six components (Fridja, 1986; Lazarus, 1991). The component that we most frequently recognize is the subjective experience of the emotion—the *affective state* or feelings associated with the emotion. A second component is bodily reaction. When angered, for example, you may sometimes tremble or raise your voice, even though you don't want to. A third component is the collection of thoughts and beliefs that accompany the emotion and seem to come to mind automatically. Experiencing joy, for example, often involves thinking about the reasons for the joy ("I did it—I was accepted into college!"). A fourth component of an emotional experience is facial expression. When you experience disgust, for example, you probably frown, often with your mouth open wide and your eyelids partially closed. A fifth component concerns global reactions to the emotion; for example, a negative emotion may darken your outlook on the world. A sixth component is the action tendencies associated with the emotion—the set of behaviors that people tend to engage in when experiencing a certain emotion. Anger may lead you to aggression, for instance.

Thus, our list of the components of an emotion includes the following:

1. The subjective experience of the emotion

2. Internal bodily responses, particularly those involving the autonomic nervous system

3. Cognitions about the emotion and associated situations

4. Facial expression

5. Reactions to the emotion

6. Action tendencies

None of these components by itself is an emotion. They all come together to create a particular emotion. In addition, each of these components can influence the other components. For example, your cognitive appraisal of a situation can lead to a specific emotion: If you believe that a store clerk is trying to cheat you, you are likely to experience anger. But if you enter that situation already angry, you will be even more likely to appraise the clerk's behavior as dishonest.

Emotion theorists are moving toward a systems perspective on emotion, in which the components of an emotion are seen as having reciprocal effects on each other (see Figure 11-1). The critical questions in modern theories of emotion concern the detailed nature of each of these components and the specific mechanisms by which they influence each other. For example, one set of questions concerns how responses of the autonomic nervous system (see Chapter 2), beliefs and cognitions, and facial expressions contribute to the intensity of an experienced emotion. For example, do you feel angrier when you experience more arousal of your autonomic nervous system? Indeed, could you even feel angry if you had no autonomic arousal? Similarly, does the intensity of your anger depend on your having a certain kind of thought, or a certain kind of facial expression? In contrast to these questions about the intensity of an emotion, there are also questions about which components of an emotion are responsible for making the different emotions feel different. To appreciate the difference between questions about intensity and questions about differentiation, consider the possibility that autonomic arousal greatly increases the intensity of our emotions, but that the pattern of arousal is roughly the same for several emotions; if this were the case, autonomic arousal could not differentiate among emotions.

These questions will guide us in this chapter as we consider autonomic arousal,

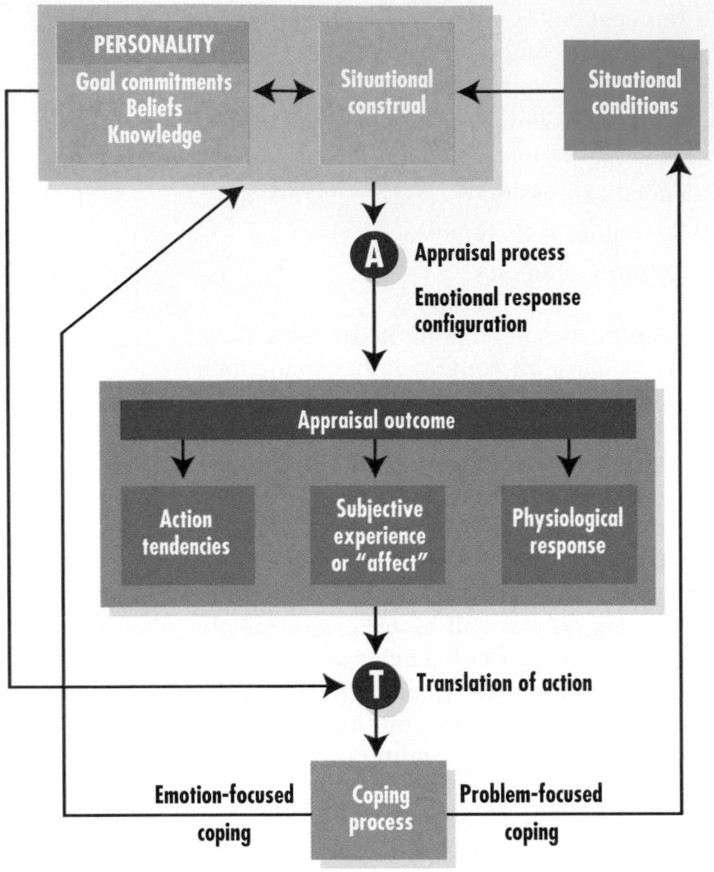

FIGURE 11-1

One Model of How the Components of Emotion Affect Each Other in a Dynamic System (After Lazarus, 1991)

cognitive appraisal, and facial expression. We will then turn our attention to general reactions to being in an emotional state. In the final section we will focus on an action tendency of an emotion, using aggression as an illustration. Throughout, we will be concerned primarily with the more intense affective states—those involved in happiness, sadness, anger, fear, and disgust—although the ideas and principles that will emerge in our discussion are relevant to a variety of feelings.

Arousal and Emotion

When we experience an intense emotion, such as fear or anger, we may be aware of a number of bodily changes—including rapid heartbeat and breathing, dryness of the throat and mouth, perspiration, trembling, and a sinking feeling in the stomach (see Table 11-1). Most of the physiological changes that take place during emotional arousal result from activation of the sympathetic division of the autonomic nervous system as it prepares the body for emergency action (see Chapter 2). The sympathetic system is responsible for the following changes (which need not all occur at once):

1. Blood pressure and heart rate increase.
2. Respiration becomes more rapid.
3. The pupils dilate.
4. Perspiration increases while secretion of saliva and mucus decreases.
5. Blood-sugar level increases to provide more energy.
6. The blood clots more quickly in case of wounds.
7. Blood is diverted from the stomach and intestines to the brain and skeletal muscles.
8. The hairs on the skin become erect, causing goose pimples.

The sympathetic system thus gears up the organism for energy output. As the emotion subsides, the parasympathetic system—the energy-conserving system—takes over and returns the organism to its normal state.

These activities of the autonomic nervous system are themselves triggered by activity in certain regions of the brain, including the hypothalamus (which, as we saw in the last chapter, plays a major role in many biological motives) and parts of the limbic system. Impulses from these areas are transmitted to nuclei in the brain stem that control the functioning of the autonomic nervous system. The autonomic nervous system then acts directly on the muscles and internal organs to initiate some of the bodily changes described earlier. It also acts indirectly by stimulating the adrenal hormones to produce other bodily changes.

Note that the kind of heightened physiological arousal we have described is characteristic of emotional states such as anger and fear, during which the organism must prepare for action—for example, to fight or flee. (The role of this fight-or-flight response in threatening or stressful situations is discussed further in Chapter 14.) Some of the same responses may also occur during joyful excitement or sexual arousal. During emotions such as sorrow or grief, however, some bodily processes may be depressed, or slowed down. (See the Frontiers of Psychological Research feature on pages 392–393 for a discussion of the use of autonomic arousal to determine whether a person is lying.)

Intensity of Emotions

What is the relationship between heightened physiological arousal and the subjective experience of an emotion? In particular, is our perception of our own arousal part of the experience of the emotion? To answer this question, researchers have studied the emotional life of individuals with spinal cord injuries. When the spinal cord is severed or lesioned, sensations below the point of injury cannot reach the brain. Since some of these sensations arise from the sympathetic nervous system, the injuries reduce the contributions of autonomic arousal to the experience of emotion.

In one study, army veterans with spinal cord injuries were divided into five groups according to the location on the spinal cord at which the lesion occurred. In one group, the lesions were near the neck (at the *cervical* level), with no feedback from the sympathetic system to the brain. In another group, the lesions were near the base of the spine (at the *sacral* level), with at least partial feedback from the sympathetic nerves possible. The other three groups fell between these two extremes. The five groups thus represented a continuum of bodily sensation: The higher the lesion on the spinal cord, the less the feedback of the autonomic nervous system to the brain (Hohmann, 1962).

The participants were interviewed to determine their feelings in situations of fear, anger, grief, and sexual excitement. Each person was

TABLE 11-1

Symptoms of Fear in Combat Flying *Based on reports of combat pilots during World War II.* (After Shafer, 1947)

During combat missions did you feel...?	Sometimes	Often	Total
A pounding heart and rapid pulse	56%	30%	86%
That your muscles were very tense	53	30	83
Easily irritated or angry	58	22	80
Dryness of the throat or mouth	50	30	80
Nervous perspiration or cold sweat	53	26	79
Butterflies in the stomach	53	23	76
A sense of unreality—that this could not be happening to you	49	20	69
A need to urinate frequently	40	25	65
Trembling	53	11	64
Confused or rattled	50	3	53
Weak or faint	37	4	41
That right after a mission you were unable to remember the details of what had happened	34	5	39
Sick to the stomach	33	5	38
Unable to concentrate	32	3	35
That you had wet or soiled your pants	4	1	5

asked to recall an emotion-arousing incident prior to the injury and a comparable incident following the injury, and to compare the intensity of their emotional experience in each case. The data for states of fear and anger are shown in Figure 11-2. The higher the lesion on

FIGURE 11-2

The Relationship Between Spinal Cord Lesions and Emotionality *People with spinal cord lesions compared the intensity of their emotional experiences before and after injury. Their reports were coded according to the degree of change: 0 indicates no change; a mild change ("I feel it less, I guess") is scored -1 for a decrease or +1 for an increase; and a strong change ("I feel it a helluva lot less") is scored -2 or +2. Note that the higher the lesion, the greater the decrease in emotionality following injury.* (After Schachter, 1971; Hohmann, 1962)

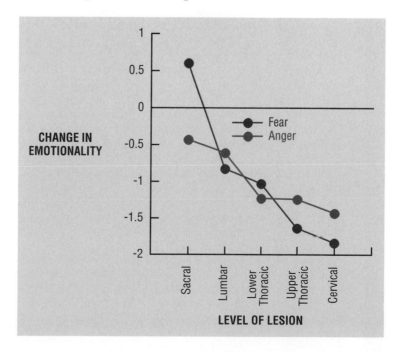

FRONTIERS OF PSYCHOLOGICAL RESEARCH

Using Arousal to Detect Lies

If autonomic arousal is a component of emotion, and if experiencing an emotion is a likely consequence of lying, we should be able to use the presence of autonomic arousal to infer that a person is lying. This is the theory behind the lie-detector test, in which a machine called a *polygraph* (meaning "many writings") simultaneously measures several physiological responses (see Figure 1). The most frequently recorded measures are changes in heart rate, blood pressure, respiration, and galvanic skin response or GSR (a change in the electrical conductivity of the skin that occurs with emotional arousal).

In operating a polygraph, the standard procedure is to make the first recording while the individual is relaxed; this recording serves as a baseline for evaluating subsequent responses. The examiner then asks a series of carefully worded questions that the person has been instructed to answer with a "yes" or "no" response. Some of the questions are "critical," which means that a guilty person is likely to lie in response to them (for example, "Did you rob Bert's Cleaners on December 11?"). Other questions are "controls"; even innocent people are somewhat likely to lie in response to these questions (for example, "Have you ever taken something that didn't belong to you?"). Still other questions are "neutral" (for example, "Do you live in San Diego?"). Critical questions are interspersed with control and neutral ones; enough time is allowed between questions for the polygraph measures to return to normal. Presumably, only a guilty person will show greater physiological responses to the critical questions than to the others. Lie detection essentially rests on a "con game" of sorts, in which the examiner works hard to convince the individual that any attempt to deceive the machine will be very obvious (Saxe, Dougherty, & Cross,

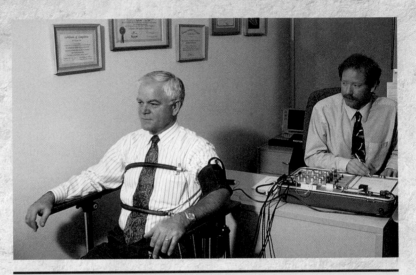

In a polygraph, the arm cuff measures blood pressure and heart rate, the pneumograph around the rib cabe measures rate of breathing, and the finger electrodes measure GSR.

1985). Instilling this belief may be more important than the pen tracings themselves.

However, the use of the polygraph in detecting lies is far from foolproof. A response to a question may show that a subject is aroused but not why he or she is aroused. An innocent person may be very tense, or may react emotionally to certain words in the questions, and therefore appear to be lying when actually telling the truth. On the other hand, a practiced liar may show little arousal when lying. And a knowledgeable individual may be able to "beat" the machine by thinking about something exciting or by tensing muscles during neutral questions, thereby creating a baseline comparable to reactions to the critical questions.

The recording in Figure 1 shows the responses to an actual lie and a simulated lie. In this experiment, the participant picked a number and then tried to conceal its identity from the examiner. The number was 27, and a marked change in heart rate and GSR can be seen when the participant denies having picked number 27. The participant simulates lying in response to

number 22 by tensing his toes, producing noticeable changes in heart rate and GSR.

Because of these and other problems, most state and federal courts will not admit polygraph test results as evidence; the courts that do admit such evidence generally require that both sides agree to the use of the evidence. However, polygraph tests are frequently used in preliminary criminal investigations and by employers interviewing applicants for trusted positions.

Representatives of the American Polygraph Association claim an accuracy rate of 90% or better for polygraph tests conducted by a skilled operator. Critics, however, consider the accuracy rate to be much lower. For example, Lykken (1984) claims that in studies involving real-life situations the lie-detector test is correct only about 65% of the time and that an innocent person has a 50-50 chance of failing the test. He argues that the polygraph detects not only the arousal that accompanies lying but also the stress that an honest person experiences when strapped to the equipment. Also, some guilty people may be less aroused while

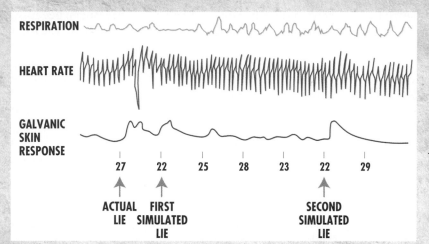

RESPIRATION

HEART RATE

GALVANIC SKIN RESPONSE

27   22   25   28   23   22   29

ACTUAL   FIRST   SECOND
LIE   SIMULATED   SIMULATED
LIE   LIE

FIGURE 1

An Actual Lie and a Simulated Lie Recorded by a Polygraph *This recording shows the physiological responses of an individual as he lies and as he simulates lying. The respiratory trace (top line) shows that he held his breath as he prepared for the first simulation. He was able to produce sizable changes in heart rate and GSR in the second simulation.* (After Kubis, 1962)

lying (Saxe, Dougherty, & Cross, 1985). Nevertheless, many businesses believe that the benefits of these tests outweigh the risks, and polygraph tests are often used in private industry. They are also widely used in law enforcement. The FBI administers several thousand polygraph tests per year, mostly to follow up leads and verify facts—areas in which, experts agree, the polygraph is more useful. In criminal and private cases, anyone has the legal right to refuse a polygraph test. However, this is hardly a safeguard for a person whose refusal, for whatever reason, may endanger a career or job opportunity.

Another type of lie detector measures changes in a person's voice that are undetectable to the human ear. All muscles, including those controlling the vocal cords, vibrate slightly when in use. This tremor, which is transmitted to the vocal cords, is suppressed by the autonomic nervous system when a speaker is under stress. When a tape recording of a person's voice is played through a device called a *voice-stress analyzer,* a visual representation of the voice can be produced on a strip of graph paper. The tremors of the vocal cords in the voice of a relaxed speaker resemble a series of waves (see the left-hand graph in Figure 2). When a speaker is under stress, the tremors are suppressed (see the right-hand graph in Figure 2).

The voice-stress analyzer is used in lie detection in essentially the same way as a polygraph: Neutral questions are interspersed with critical questions, and recordings of the participant's responses to both are compared. If answers to the critical questions produce the relaxed wave form, the person is probably telling the truth (as far as we know, vocal cord tremors can-

not be controlled voluntarily). A stressed wave form, on the other hand, indicates only that the individual is tense or anxious, not necessarily that he or she is lying.

There are, however, two serious problems with the use of the voice-stress analyzer in detecting lies. First, since the analyzer can work over the telephone, from radio or television messages, or from tape recordings, there is potential for unethical use of this device. The second concern is accuracy. Some investigators claim that the voice-stress analyzer is as accurate as the polygraph in distinguishing between guilty and innocent individuals; others claim that it is no more accurate than chance. Much more research is required to determine the relationship between voice changes and other physiological measures of emotion (Lykken, 1980; Rice, 1978).

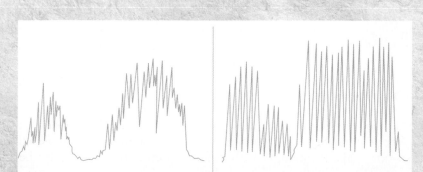

FIGURE 2

Effects of Stress on Voice Patterns *A voice-stress analyzer produces graphic records of speech. The voice printout for a relaxed speaker resembles a series of waves such as those shown on the left. The waves are produced by tiny tremors of the vocal cords. Under stress, the tremors are suppressed, producing a printout similar to that shown on the right.* (After Holden, 1975)

the individual's spinal cord (that is, the less feedback coming from the autonomic nervous system), the greater the decrease in emotionality following injury. The same relationship was true for states of sexual excitement and grief. A reduction in autonomic arousal resulted in a reduction in the intensity of experienced emotion.

Comments by patients with the highest spinal cord lesions suggested that they could react emotionally to arousing situations but that they did not really *feel* emotional. For example, "It's sort of a cold anger. Sometimes I act angry when I see some injustice. I yell and cuss and raise hell, because if you don't do it sometimes, I've learned people will take advantage of you; but it doesn't have the heat to it that it used to. It's a mental kind of anger." Or, "I say I am afraid, like when I'm going into a real stiff exam at school, but I don't really feel afraid, not all tense and shaky with the hollow feeling in my stomach, like I used to."

The study just described is important, but it is not entirely objective—the emotional situations varied from one participant to another, and participants rated their own experiences. A follow-up study was more objective: All of the participants were exposed to the same situations, and their emotional experiences were rated by independent judges. Male participants with spinal cord injuries were presented with pictures of clothed and nude females and told to imagine that they were alone with each woman. Participants reported their "thoughts and feelings," which then were rated by judges for expressed emotion. Patients who had higher lesions were rated as experiencing less sexual excitement than those whose lesions were lower on the spine (Jasmos & Hakmiller, 1975). Again, the less feedback coming from the autonomic system to the brain, the less intense the emotion.

Differentiation of Emotions

Clearly, autonomic arousal contributes to the intensity of emotional experience. But does it differentiate the emotions? In other words, is there one pattern of physiological activity for joy, another for anger, still another for fear, and so on? This question dates back to a paper written by William James over a century ago (James, 1884), in which he proposed that the perception of bodily changes actually *is* the subjective experience of an emotion: "We are afraid because we run"; "we are angry because we strike." The Danish physiologist Carl Lange arrived at a similar conclusion at about the same time, but for him the bodily changes included autonomic arousal. This view has come to be known as the *James-Lange theory,* and it runs as follows: Because the perception of autonomic arousal (and perhaps of other bodily changes) constitutes the experience of an emotion, and because different emotions feel different, there must be a distinct pattern of autonomic activity for each emotion. The James-Lange theory therefore holds that autonomic arousal differentiates the emotions.

This theory (particularly the part dealing with autonomic arousal) came under severe attack in the 1920s. The attack was led by the physiologist Walter Cannon (1927), who offered three major criticisms:

1. Since the internal organs are relatively insensitive structures and are not well supplied with nerves, internal changes occur too slowly to be a source of emotional feeling.

2. Artificially inducing the bodily changes associated with an emotion, for example, injecting a drug such as epinephrine, does not produce the experience of a true emotion.

3. The pattern of autonomic arousal does not seem to differ much from one emotional state to another; for example, while anger makes our heart beat faster, so does the sight of a loved one.

The third argument, then, explicitly denies that autonomic arousal can differentiate the emotions.

Psychologists have tried to rebut Cannon's third point while developing increasingly accurate measures of the components of autonomic arousal. Although a few experiments in the 1950s reported distinct physiological patterns for different emotions (Ax, 1953; Funkenstein, 1955), until the 1980s most studies had found little evidence for different patterns of arousal being associated with different emotions. A study by Levenson, Ekman, and Friesen (1990), however, provides strong evidence that there are autonomic patterns that are distinct to different emotions. Participants produced emotional expressions for each of six emotions—surprise, disgust, sadness, anger, fear, and happiness—by following instructions about which particular facial muscles to contract. While they held an emotional expression for 10 seconds, the researchers measured their heart rate, skin temperature, and other indicators of autonomic arousal. A number of these measures revealed differences among the emotions (see Figure 11-3). Heart rate was faster for the negative emotions of anger, fear, and sadness than for happiness, surprise, and disgust; and the former three emotions themselves could be partially distinguished by the fact that skin temperature was higher in anger than in fear or sadness. Thus, even though both anger and the sight of a loved one make our heart beat faster, only anger makes it beat much faster; and although anger and fear have much in common, anger is hot and fear cold (no wonder people describe their anger as their "blood boiling," and their fear as "bone-chilling" or as "getting cold feet").

In a similar study, 32 female undergraduates were presented with varied, mildly stressful incentives while the temperatures of their face and hands were recorded. There was an increase in hand skin temperature in response to film clips intended to generate a happy affect, but a cooling in response to threatening personal questions (Rimm-Kaufman & Kagan, 1996).

Other research suggests that these distinctive arousal patterns may be universal. Levenson, Ekman, and colleagues studied the Minangkabau of Western Sumatra, a culture very different from ours. Again, participants produced facial expressions for various emotions—fear, anger, sadness, and disgust—while measures were taken of their heart rate, skin temperature, and other indicators of arousal. Although the magnitude of the physiological changes was less than that of the changes reported earlier for American individuals, the patterns of arousal for the different emotions were the same: Heart rate was faster for anger, fear, and sadness than for disgust, and skin temperature was highest for anger (Levenson et al., 1992).

These results are important, but they do not provide unequivocal support for the James-Lange theory or for the claim that autonomic arousal is the only component that differentiates the emotions. The studies we have described demonstrated that there are some physiological differences between emotions (though some researchers question this; see Cacioppo et al., 1993), not that those differences are perceived and experienced as qualitative differences between emotions. Even if autonomic arousal does help differentiate some emotions, it is unlikely that it differentiates all emotions; the difference between contentment and pride, for example, is unlikely to be found in autonomic reactions. Also, Cannon's first two arguments against the James-Lange theory still stand: Autonomic arousal is too slow to differentiate emotional experiences, and artificial induction of arousal does not yield a true emotion. For these reasons, many psychologists still believe that something other than autonomic arousal must be involved in differentiating the emotions. That something else (or part of it) is usually thought to be the individual's cognitive appraisal of the situation.

FIGURE 11-3

Differences in Arousal for Different Emotions
Changes in heart rate (purple) and right finger temperature (green). For heart rate, the changes associated with anger, fear, and sadness were all significantly greater than those for happiness, surprise, and disgust. For finger temperature, the change associated with anger was significantly different from that for all other emotions.
(After Ekman, Levenson, & Friesen, 1990)

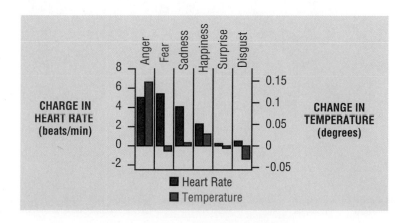

Cognition and Emotion

When we experience an event or action, we interpret it with respect to our personal goals and well-being ("I won the match and I feel happy" or "I failed the test and I feel depressed"). This interpretation is known as a **cognitive appraisal.** It helps determine the type of emotion we feel as well as its intensity.

Intensity and Differentiation of Emotions

Clearly, our appraisal of a situation can contribute to the intensity of our emotional experience. If we are in a car that starts to roll down a steep incline, we experience fear, if not terror; but if we know that the car is part of a roller coaster, the fear is usually much less. If we are told by someone that he or she cannot stand the sight of us, we may feel very angry or hurt if that person is a friend, but not feel very perturbed if the person is someone whom we have never met before. In these cases and countless others, our cognitive appraisal of the situation determines the intensity of our emotional experience (Lazarus, 1991; Lazarus, Kanner, & Folkman, 1980).

Cognitive appraisal may also be largely responsible for differentiating the emotions.

Our cognitive appraisal of a situation helps determine the type of emotion we feel as well as its intensity. Cognitive appraisal contributed to the different ways in which people reacted to the verdict in the murder trial of O.J. Simpson.

Unlike autonomic arousal, appraisals are varied enough to distinguish among many different kinds of feelings, and the appraisal process itself may be fast enough to account for the speed with which some emotions arise. Also, we often emphasize cognitive appraisals when we describe the quality of an emotion. We say, "I felt angry because she was unfair" or "I felt frightened because I was abandoned"; unfairness and abandonment are clearly beliefs that result from a cognitive process. These observations suggest that cognitive appraisals are often sufficient to determine the quality of emotional experience. This in turn suggests that if people could be induced to be in a neutral state of autonomic arousal, the quality of their emotion would be determined solely by their appraisal of the situation. Schachter and Singer (1962) first tested this claim in an experiment that had a major impact on theories of emotion for the next two decades.

Participants were given an injection of epinephrine, which typically causes autonomic arousal—an increase in heart and respiration rates, muscle tremors, and a jittery feeling. The experimenter then manipulated the information that the participants were given regarding the effects of epinephrine. Some participants were correctly informed about the arousal consequences of the drug; others were given no information about the drug's physiological effects. Thus, the informed participants had an explanation of their arousal while the uninformed participants did not. Schachter and Singer predicted that how the uninformed participants interpreted their symptoms would depend on the situation they were placed in. Participants were left in a waiting room with another person, ostensibly another participant but actually a confederate of the experimenter; this confederate created either a happy situation (by making paper airplanes, playing basketball with wads of paper, and so on) or an angry situation (by complaining about the experiment, tearing up a questionnaire, and so on). The uninformed participants placed in the happy situation rated their feelings as happier than the informed participants in that situation did, and the uninformed participants in the angry situation rated their feelings as angrier than the informed participants in that situation did. In other words, participants who had a physiological explanation for their arousal were less influenced by the situation than participants who did not have the explanation.

The Schachter and Singer experiment was extremely influential, but that influence may not have been justified. The pattern of results in the study did not strongly support the experimenters' hypotheses, in that the differences between critical groups did not reach statistical significance and a control group did not react in a manner consistent with the hypotheses. In addition, the autonomic arousal may not have been the same in the happy and angry situations, and it certainly was not neutral. Follow-up experiments have found that participants rate their experiences more negatively (less happy, or more angry) than the situation warrants, suggesting that the physiological arousal produced by epinephrine is experienced as somewhat unpleasant. Also, these experiments have sometimes had difficulty reproducing the results obtained by Schachter and Singer (Marshall & Zimbardo, 1979; Maslach, 1979). Hence, we need further evidence that completely neutral arousal may be mistakenly attributed to a particular emotion.

Another study supplied such evidence. Participants first engaged in strenuous physical exercise and then participated in a task during which they were provoked by a confederate of the experimenter. The exercise induced physiological arousal that was neutral and that persisted until the participant was provoked; this arousal should have combined with any arousal elicited by the provocation, resulting in a more intense experience of anger. In fact, participants who exercised responded more aggressively to the provocation than participants who did not (Zillman & Bryant, 1974).

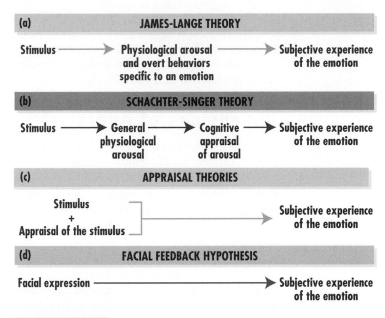

FIGURE 11-4

Major Theories of Emotion *Different theories of emotion propose different relationships between the components of an emotion.*

The conclusions that emerge from this line of research are that an event typically results in both autonomic arousal and cognitive appraisal. The perceived arousal and cognitive appraisal are not experienced as independent; rather, the arousal is attributed to the appraisal—"My heart is racing because I'm so angry about what Mary said." These studies indicate that both arousal and appraisal contribute to the intensity of experience—and that sometimes appraisal alone can determine the quality of experience. While research indicates that arousal may aid in differentiating emotions, it seems to play less of a role than appraisal.

The top two sections of Figure 11-4 summarize how the components of an emotion interact for the two major theories we have discussed so far. Although each of these theories has been supported to some extent, they oversimplify the emotion process. The components, autonomic arousal and cognitive appraisal, are themselves complex events that involve subcomponents, and these subcomponents do not all occur at the same time. For example, suppose that an acquaintance says something insulting to you. You may first be aware of the unpleasantness of the remark, then feel a tinge of arousal, next appraise the remark more in

Physical arousal may intensify feelings of anger.

detail while experiencing more arousal, and so on. Thus, autonomic arousal and cognitive appraisal are stretched out over time, and their subcomponents can occur simultaneously (Ellsworth, 1991).

Dimensions of Appraisal

In the third section of Figure 11-4 is another major theory of emotion, which we have labeled *appraisal theory*. Actually, this is a group of theories that suggest that people's *appraisals of situations* (not their appraisals of physiological arousal) lead to the subjective experience of emotion and the arousal associated with it. These appraisal theories can be divided into (a) theories that identify primary or fundamental emotions and specify the types of situations and appraisals that elicit those emotions, and (b) theories that identify the primary dimensions of appraisals and the specific emotions resulting from them.

According to the first group of appraisal theories, there is a relatively small set of "primary" emotions, each of which is elicited by specific appraisals of an event. Table 11-2 lists several emotions (such as fear) and the appraisals that trigger them (threat). These primary emotions can be found in every human culture and throughout the animal kingdom. Some events may be appraised the same way by everyone. For example, large hissing snakes tend to be appraised as threats by most animals and

TABLE 11-2

Primary Emotions and Their Causes   *Eight primary emotions and their associated appraisals.* (After Plutchik, 1980)

Emotion	Appraisal
Grief (sorrow)	Loss of loved one
Fear	Threat
Anger	Obstacle
Joy	Potential mate
Trust	Group member
Disgust	Gruesome object
Anticipation	New territory
Surprise	Sudden novel object

TABLE 11-3

Primary Appraisal Dimensions and Their Consequences   *Combinations of two appraisal dimensions and their associated emotions.* (After Roseman, 1984; 1979)

	Occur	Not Occur
Desirable	Joy	Sorrow
Undesirable	Distress	Relief

humans. The types of threats that elicit the appraisals listed in Table 11-2 may differ across species and human cultures, however (Mesquita & Frijda, 1992). Among humans, for example, many Americans would be shocked to walk onto a beach and discover that everyone there is nude, but many Brazilians would be unmoved by such a scene because nude sunbathing is more common in Brazil than in the United States.

The second group of appraisal theories is concerned with specifying primary dimensions of appraisals (rather than a primary set of emotions) and the emotional consequences of these dimensions. An example is given in Table 11-3. One dimension is the desirability of an anticipated event, and another is whether or not the event occurs. When we combine these two dimensions, we get four possible appraisals, each of which seems to produce a distinct emotion. (We are using only four emotions in our example in order to keep things simple.) When a desired event (such as falling in love) occurs, we experience joy; when a desired event does not occur (the person we are in love with does not love us), we experience sorrow; when an undesired event (such as doing poorly on an exam) occurs, we experience distress; and when an undesired event does not occur (not doing poorly on an exam), we experience relief.

The preceding example makes use of only two dimensions, but most theories of cognitive appraisal assume that numerous dimensions are involved. For example, Smith and Ellsworth (1987; 1985) found that at least 6 dimensions were needed to describe 15 different emotions (including, for example, anger, guilt, and sadness). These dimensions included (a) the desirability of the situation (pleasant or unpleasant); (b) the amount of effort the person anticipates spending on the situation; (c) the certainty of the situation; (d) the amount of attention the person wants to devote to the situation; (e) the degree of control the person feels he or she has over the situation; and (f) the degree of control the person attributes to nonhuman forces in the situation. To illustrate how the last two dimensions operate, anger is associated with an unpleasant situation caused by another person, guilt is associated with an unpleasant situation brought about by oneself, and sadness is associated with an unpleasant situation controlled by circumstances. Thus, if you and your friend miss a concert that you had your heart set on hearing, you will feel anger if you missed it because your friend carelessly misplaced the tickets, guilt if you misplaced the tickets, and sadness if the performance is canceled because of a performer's illness. The virtue of this kind of approach is that it specifies the appraisal process in detail and accounts for a wide range of emotional experiences.

Some Clinical Implications

The fact that cognitive appraisals can differentiate emotions helps make sense of a puzzling clinical observation. Sometimes a patient appears to be experiencing an emotion but is not conscious of it. That is, the patient has no subjective experience of the emotion, yet reacts in a manner consistent with the emotion—for example, although the patient may not *feel* angry, he acts in a hostile manner. Also, at a later point he may experience the emotion and agree that in some sense he must have been having it earlier. Freud (1915/1976) thought that this phenomenon involved repression of painful ideas, and the findings of modern research on appraisal and emotion are consistent with his hypothesis. Because one's belief about a situation usually gives the emotion its quality, preventing that belief from entering consciousness (repression) prevents one from experiencing the quality of the emotion.

Another point of contact between clinical analysis and experimental research concerns emotional development. Clinical work suggests that a person's sensations of pleasure and distress do not change as he or she matures; what does change, however, are the ideas associated with the sensations (Brenner, 1980). Thus, the sensation of joy may be the same when we are 3 or 30, but what makes us joyous is very different. This developmental pattern fits perfectly with the facts about emotion discussed earlier.

The sensation of joy may be the same whether we are 3 or 30 years old.

Sensations of pleasure and distress are probably due to feedback from autonomic arousal, and the nature of this arousal may not change much over the life span. In contrast, ideas associated with sensations are simply emotional beliefs, and they should show the same kind of development as other aspects of cognition.

Finally, the research on appraisal fits with a phenomenon that is familiar not just to clinicians but to all of us: The extent to which a situation elicits an emotion depends on our experience. When confronted with an overly critical employer, some people will be merely annoyed while others will be enraged. Why the difference? Presumably because of differences in past experience: Perhaps those who are enraged experienced a hypercritical authority figure in the past, while those who are only annoyed had no such experience. A possible link between past experience and current emotion is the appraisal process; that is, our past experience affects our beliefs about the current situation, and these beliefs influence the emotion we experience.

Emotion Without Cognition

Are there cases of emotion in which no cognitive appraisal is involved? When a rat receives an electric shock for the first time, for example, presumably its emotional reaction is devoid of cognitive activity. Similarly, if you are suddenly punched in the face, you may experience an emotion before you interpret the event.

The preceding examples suggest that there may be two kinds of emotional experiences: those that are based on cognitive appraisal and those that precede cognition (Zajonc, 1984; 1980). This dichotomy is supported by research on the brain structures involved in emotion. One such structure is the amygdala, a small, almond-shaped mass that is located in the lower brain and is known to register emotional reactions. Until recently it was thought that the amygdala receives all its inputs from the cortex and, hence, that those inputs always involve cognitive appraisal. But newer research with rats has uncovered connections between sensory channels and the amygdala that do not go through the cortex; these direct connections may be the biological basis of **pre-cognitive emotions,** or *emotions that are not based on appraisal.* Thus, the amygdala is capable of responding to an alarming situation before the cortex does, which suggests that sometimes we can feel before we can think. To illustrate, if from the corner of your eye you see something shaped like a snake, your amygdala will send an alarm signal that makes you jump before your cortex can determine that the object in question is in fact a harmless piece of rope. Although this research is based on rats, there is reason to believe that the neural pathways involved exist in humans as well (Le Doux, 1989).

While we can have emotional experiences without conscious and deliberate cognitive appraisal, such experiences may be restricted to undifferentiated positive or negative feelings. If we define cognitive appraisal broadly to include primitive or automatic evaluations of situations that we have acquired through evolution, we may be able to say that almost all emotions involve some type of appraisal (Lazarus, 1991).

Expression and Emotion

The facial expression that accompanies an emotion clearly serves to communicate that emotion. Since the publication of Charles Darwin's 1872 classic, *The Expression of Emotion in Man and Animals,* psychologists have regarded the communication of emotion as an important function, one that has survival value for the species. Thus, looking frightened may warn others that danger is present, and perceiving that someone is angry tells us that he or she may be about to act aggressively. More recent research suggests that, in addition to their communicative function, emotional expressions contribute to the subjective experience of emotion, just as arousal and appraisal do. This theory is depicted in the bottom panel of Figure 11-4.

Communication of Emotion Through Facial Expressions

Certain facial expressions seem to have a universal meaning, regardless of the culture in which an individual is raised. The universal expression of anger, for example, involves a flushed face, brows lowered and drawn together, flared nostrils, a clenched jaw, and bared teeth. When people from five countries (the United States, Brazil, Chile, Argentina, and Japan) viewed photographs showing facial expressions typical of happiness, anger, sadness, disgust, fear, and surprise, they had little difficulty identifying the emotion that each expression conveyed. Even members of remote groups that had had virtually no con-

tact with Western cultures (the Fore and Dani peoples in New Guinea) were able to identify the emotions represented by facial expressions of people from Western cultures. Likewise, American college students who viewed videotapes of facial expressions of Fore natives identified the associated emotions accurately, although they sometimes confused fear and surprise (Ekman, 1982).

Facial expressions are universal in the emotions they convey. Photographs of people from New Guinea and from the United States demonstrate that specific emotions are conveyed by the same facial expressions. Shown here are, from left to right, happiness, sadness, and disgust.

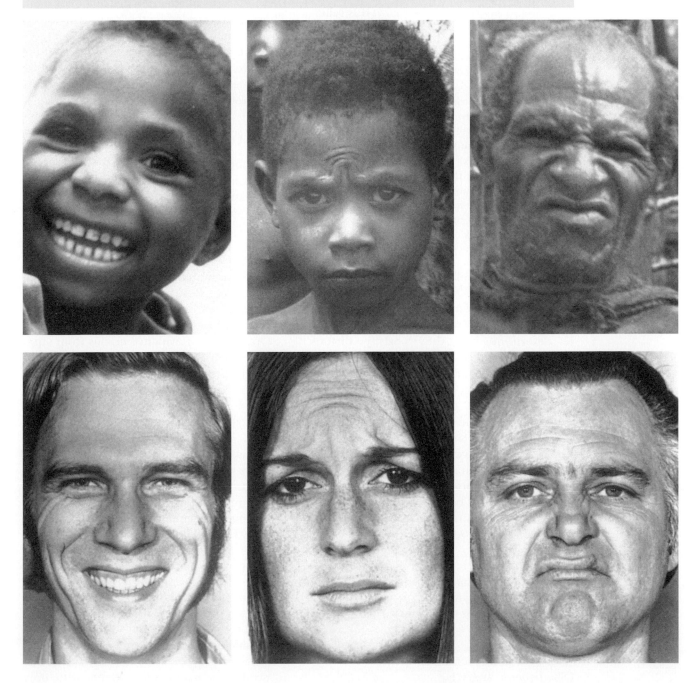

The universality of certain emotional expressions supports Darwin's claim that they are innate responses with an evolutionary history. According to Darwin, many of the ways in which we express emotion are inherited patterns that originally had some survival value. For example, the expression of disgust or rejection is based on the organism's attempt to rid itself of something unpleasant that it has ingested. To quote Darwin (1872),

> The term "disgust," in its simplest sense, means something offensive to the taste. But as disgust also causes annoyance, it is generally accompanied by a frown, and often by gestures as if to push away or to guard oneself against the offensive object. Extreme disgust is expressed by movements around the mouth identical with those preparatory to the act of vomiting. The mouth is opened widely, with the upper lip strongly retracted. The partial closure of the eyelids, or the turning away of the eyes or of the whole body, are likewise highly expressive of disdain. These actions seem to declare that the despised person is not worth looking at, or is disagreeable to behold. Spitting seems an almost universal sign of contempt or disgust; and spitting obviously represents the rejection of anything offensive from the mouth.

While some facial expressions and gestures seem to be innately associated with particular emotions, others are learned. One psychologist reviewed Chinese novels to determine how they portray various human emotions. Many of the bodily changes that occur when a person experiences an emotion (for example, flushing, trembling, goose pimples) represent the same emotions in Chinese fiction as in Western writing. Other bodily expressions, however, convey very different emotions in Chinese fiction than they do in the West. The following quotations from Chinese novels would surely be misinterpreted by an American reader unfamiliar with the culture (Klineberg, 1938):

"They stretched out their tongues."
(They showed signs of surprise.)
"He clapped his hands."
(He was worried or disappointed.)
"He scratched his ears and cheeks."
(He was happy.)
"Her eyes grew round and opened wide."
(She became angry.)

Each culture has its own set of rules for displaying emotion. These rules specify the types of emotions people should experience in certain situations and the behaviors appropriate for particular emotions. As an example, in some cultures people who lose a loved one are expected to feel sad and to express their sadness by openly crying and wailing for the loved one to return. In other cultures, bereaved people are expected to sing, dance, and be merry. In Europe, two men greeting each other on the street may embrace and kiss, but in the United States these gestures of affection are taboo for men. Thus, superimposed on the basic expressions of emotion, which appear to be universal, are conventional forms of expressions—a kind of language of emotion that is recognized by other members of the culture but often misunderstood by people from other cultures.

Localization in the Brain

The emotional expressions that are universal (for example, those associated with joy, anger, and disgust) are also highly specific: Particular muscles are used to express particular emotions. This combination of universality and specificity suggests that a specialized neurological system may have evolved in humans to interpret emotional expressions. Research evidence indicates that there is indeed such a system and that it is located in the right cerebral hemisphere.

One source of evidence comes from studies in which pictures of emotional expressions are presented briefly to either the left side or the right side of the participant's visual field. Recall from Chapter 2 that a stimulus presented to the left visual field projects to the right hemisphere, while a stimulus presented to the right visual field projects to the left hemisphere. When participants have to decide which of two emotions a picture portrays, they are faster and more accurate when the picture is projected to their right hemisphere. In addition, when the two halves of the face convey different emotions (one half may be smiling while the other half is frowning), the expression projected to the right hemisphere has a greater impact on the participant's decision.

Other evidence about the localization of emotional expressions comes from studies of patients who have suffered brain damage due to strokes or accidents. Patients with only right-hemisphere damage have more difficulty recognizing facial expressions of emotion than patients with only left-hemisphere damage (Etcoff, 1985).

Our system for recognizing emotional expressions seems to be highly specialized. In particular, it is distinct from our ability to recognize faces. Consider a prosopagnosic, a person who, because of damage to his cortex, has such extreme difficulty recognizing familiar faces that he sometimes fails to recognize his own face. He can, however, recognize emotional expressions: He can tell you that a particular person is happy even when he does not know that the person is his wife (Bruyer, Laterre, & Seron, 1983). The abilities to recognize faces and to recognize emotions also are differentially affected by electrical stimulation of various regions of the right hemisphere: Face recognition is disrupted by stimulation in the region between the parietal and occipital lobes, whereas emotion recognition is disrupted by stimulation of a particular region in the temporal lobe (Fried, 1982).

In addition to being communicated by facial expressions, emotions are expressed by variations in voice patterns (particularly variations in pitch, timing, and stress). Some of these variations appear to be universal and specific: A sharp increase in pitch indicates fear, for example. The specialized neurological system for perceiving these emotional clues is located in the right cerebral hemisphere, and the evidence for this is similar to that for facial expressions. Participants are more accurate in identifying the emotional tone of a voice presented to the left ear (which projects information primarily to the right hemisphere) than one presented to the right ear (which projects primarily to the left hemisphere). And patients with only right-hemisphere damage have more trouble identifying emotions from voice clues than patients with only left-hemisphere damage (Ley & Bryden, 1982).

Intensity and Differentiation of Emotions

The Facial Feedback Hypothesis   The idea that facial expressions, in addition to their communicative function, also contribute to our experience of emotions is sometimes called the *facial feedback hypothesis* (Tomkins,

1962). According to this hypothesis, just as we receive feedback about (or perceive) our autonomic arousal, so we receive feedback about our facial expression, and this feedback combines with the other components of emotion to produce a more intense experience. This implies that if you make yourself smile and hold the smile for several seconds, you will begin to feel happier; if you scowl, you will feel tense and angry.

In support of the facial feedback hypothesis, participants who exaggerate their facial reactions to emotional stimuli report more emotional response than participants who do not. In one study, participants judged the pleasantness of various odors while either smiling or frowning. Participants who smiled perceived the odors as more pleasant; those who frowned perceived the odors as less pleasant (Kraut, 1982). In another experiment, participants rated cartoons for funniness while holding a pen either in their teeth or in their lips. Holding a pen in one's teeth forces your face into a smile, while holding it in one's lips forces your face into a frown. (Try it.) As expected, the cartoons were rated as funnier when the pen was held in the teeth than when held in the lips (Strack, Martin, & Stepper, 1988).

In addition to these studies, which show a direct connection between expression and felt emotion, other experiments indicate that facial expressions may have an indirect effect on emotion by increasing autonomic arousal. Such an effect was demonstrated in the experiment discussed earlier in which producing particular emotional expressions led to changes in heartbeat and skin temperature (Levenson, Ekman, & Freisen, 1990). We therefore need to add emotional expression to our list of factors that contribute to emotional experience.

Some researchers also believe that facial expressions can determine the quality of emotions. Since the expressions for the primary emotions are distinct and occur rapidly, they are at least plausible candidates for contributing to the differentiation of emotions. Tomkins (1980) has proposed that the feedback from a facial expression is inherently positive or negative, thereby suggesting a means by which facial expressions can distinguish positive from negative emotions. Should this suggestion prove true, we are back (in part) to the James-Lange theory, which holds that emotion is the perception of certain bodily changes.

Blood Flow and Brain Temperature Exactly which aspects of a facial expression make it inherently positive or negative? A possible answer may be found in the fact that contraction of certain facial muscles can affect the blood flow in neighboring blood vessels. This, in turn, may affect cerebral blood flow, which can determine brain temperature, which in turn can facilitate and inhibit the release of various neurotransmitters—and the latter may be part of the cortical activity that underlies emotion. For example, when we smile, the configuration of the facial muscles may lead to a lowering of the temperature in a region of the brain in which the neurotransmitter serotonin is released; this temperature change may block the release of the neurotransmitter, resulting in a positive feeling. The critical path, then, may move from facial expression to blood flow to brain temperature to emotional experience (Zajonc, Murphy, & Inglehart, 1989).

This path from expression to emotion is supported by experimental research. One study takes advantage of the fact that pronunciation of the German vowel "ü" (as in Für) requires extending a facial muscle that is contracted when smiling. This suggests that the facial expression associated with pronouncing ü can lead to a negative feeling. To test this hypothesis, German participants read aloud stories that contained either many words with ü or no words with ü; the stories were similar in content and emotional tone. When asked how much they liked the stories, participants rated those with ü words as less pleasing than those with no ü words. Also, while participants read the stories, the temperature of their foreheads was measured to provide an estimate of brain temperature. Temperatures rose during stories with ü words but not during stories without such words. Thus, the facial expression needed to produce ü led to both increased facial temperature and negative feeling, and perhaps also to increased brain temperature (Zajonc, Murphy, & Inglehart, 1989).

General Reactions to Being in an Emotional State

At the beginning of the chapter we noted that one of the major components of emotion is the way a person reacts to being in an emotional state. Although some reactions are specific to the emotion experienced—approaching someone when happy or withdrawing when frightened, for example— others seem to apply to emotions in general. In particular, being in an emotional state can (a) determine what we attend to and learn and (b) determine what kinds of judgments we make about the world.

Attention and Learning: Mood Congruence

A *mood* is an enduring emotional state. We tend to pay more attention to events that fit our mood than to events that do not. As a consequence, we learn more about the events that fit, or are congruent with, our mood. One experiment that demonstrates these phenomena involved three stages. In the first stage, participants were hypnotized and induced to be in either a happy or a sad mood. In the second stage, the hypnotized participants read a brief story about an encounter between two men—a happy character and a sad one. The story vividly described the events of the two men's lives and their emotional reactions. After reading the story, participants were asked who they thought the central character was and whom they identified with. Participants who had been induced to be happy identified more with the happy character and thought the story contained more statements about him; participants who had been induced to be sad identified more with the sad character and thought the story contained more statements about him. These results indicate that participants paid more attention to the character and events that were congruent with their moods than to those that were not (Bower, 1981).

The third stage of this experiment provided evidence that participants also learned more about mood-congruent events than about mood-incongruent ones. One day after reading the story the participants, now in a neutral mood, returned to the laboratory, where they were asked to recall the story. Participants recalled more about the character they had identified with: For the previously happy participants, 55% of the facts they recalled were about the happy character; for the previously sad participants, 80% of the facts they recalled were about the sad character (Bower, 1981).

Exactly how does the congruence between one's mood and some new material affect the learning of that material? We know that we can learn new material better if we can relate it to information already in memory. One's mood during learning may increase the availability of memories that fit that mood, and such memories will be easier to relate to new material that also fits that mood. Suppose that you hear a story about a student flunking out of school. If you are in a bad mood when you hear the story, some of your memories about failure experiences (particularly academic failures) may be easily accessible, and the similarity of these memories to the new fact of someone flunking out of school will make it easy to relate them. In contrast, if you are in a good mood when you hear the story, your most accessible memories may be too dissimilar to a school failure to foster a relationship between the old memories and the new fact. Thus, our mood influences what memories are more accessible, and those memories influence what is easy for us to learn at the moment (Isen, 1985; Bower, 1981).

Evaluation and Estimation: Mood Effects

Our mood can affect our evaluation of other people. Everyday experiences provide numerous examples of this. When we are in a good mood, a friend's habit of constantly checking his appearance in a mirror may seem just an idiosyncrasy; when we are in a bad mood, we may dwell on how vain our friend is. Our mood affects our evaluation of inanimate objects as well. In one experiment, participants were asked to evaluate their major possessions. Participants who had just been put in a good mood by receiving a small gift rated their televisions and cars more positively than did control participants who were in a neutral mood (Isen et al., 1978).

Our mood also affects our judgments about the frequency of various risks. Bad moods lead us to see risks as more likely; good moods lead us to see them as less likely. In an experiment dealing with estimating risks, participants in the experimental group first read a newspaper story that recounted a tragic death and thus were put in a negative mood. Control participants read a bland newspaper story, which put them in a neutral mood. Then all the participants were asked to estimate the frequencies of various types of fatalities, including death from diseases like leukemia and heart disease and from accidents like fires and floods. Participants who were in a negative mood estimated the frequencies of these types of fatalities to be almost twice as great as did participants in a neutral mood. Further, all that mattered for estimating frequencies was the participant's mood, not the content of the story that had put them in that mood. The tragic story that some experimental participants read involved a case of leukemia, and the story that other experimental participants read involved a death due to fire; both groups of participants overestimated the frequencies of deaths due to leukemia and fire to the same degree. The similarity between the story and the risk had no effect on the estimate of frequency. It is as if the affect was separated from the content of the story, and only the mood or affect guided subsequent estimates. Comparable results were obtained for the effects of being in a good mood. Reading a story about a person's good fortune led participants to make relatively low estimates about the frequencies of various fatalities, and the extent to which participants did this did not depend on the similarity between the story and the risk being evaluated (Johnson & Tversky, 1983).

Specific moods may have specific effects on our judgments of the world and of other people. In one study, participants were put into either a sad mood or an angry mood by imagining themselves experiencing either a sad event or an angry one. They then were asked to evaluate the possible causes of hypothetical events, such as missing an important flight or losing money. Participants who were in an angry mood tended to attribute the hypothetical events to the mistakes of other people, but participants in a sad mood tended to attribute them to situations (for example, traffic congestion was the reason for missing a flight). So the angry participants were more ready to blame someone for negative events, while the sad participants were more willing to acknowledge that an unlucky situation might have caused the events (Keltner, Ellsworth, & Edwards, 1992).

Being in a bad mood, then, makes the world seem more dangerous. Such a perception can reinforce the bad mood. Also, as noted earlier, being in a bad mood leads us to selectively attend to and learn negative-toned facts; this too can reinforce a bad mood. A similar analysis applies to a good mood. It makes the world seem less risky and leads us to attend to and learn positively toned material. Thus, the general consequences of a mood serve to perpetuate that mood.

Aggression as an Emotional Reaction

Emotions cause not only general reactions but specific action tendencies as well. We may laugh when happy, withdraw when frightened, become aggressive when angry, and so forth. Among these typical action tendencies, psychologists have singled out one—aggression—for extensive study. This special attention is partly due to the social significance of aggression. At the societal level, in an age when nuclear weapons are widely available, a single aggressive act can spell disaster. At the individual level, many people experience aggressive thoughts and impulses frequently, and how they handle these thoughts will have major effects on their health and interpersonal relations. Another reason psychologists have focused on aggression is that two major theories of social behavior make quite different assumptions about the nature of aggression. Freud's psychoanalytic theory views aggression as a drive, whereas social-learning theory views it as a learned response. Research

Is aggression a drive or a learned response?

on aggression helps us evaluate these competing theories.

In the following discussion we first describe these different views, along with related research, and then consider how they differ with respect to the effects of portrayals of aggression in the mass media. Keep in mind that what we mean by **aggression** is *behavior that is intended to injure another person (physically or verbally) or to destroy property.* The key concept in this definition is intent. If a person accidentally steps on your foot in a crowded elevator and immediately apologizes, you would not interpret the behavior as aggressive; but if someone walks up to you as you sit at your desk and steps on your foot, you would not hesitate to label the act as aggressive.

Aggression as a Drive

According to Freud's psychoanalytic theory, many of our actions are determined by instincts, particularly the sexual instinct. When expression of these instincts is frustrated, an aggressive drive is induced. Later, psychoanalytic theorists broadened this *frustration-aggression hypothesis,* proposing that whenever a person's effort to reach any goal is blocked, an aggressive drive is induced that motivates behavior intended to injure the obstacle (person or object) causing the frustration (Dollard et al., 1939). This proposal has two critical aspects. One is that the usual cause of aggression is frustration; the other is that aggression has the properties of a basic drive—being a form of energy that persists until its goal is satisfied, as well as being an inborn reaction like hunger or sex. As we will see, it is the drive aspect of the frustration-aggression hypothesis that has been particularly controversial.

Aggression in Other Species If aggression is really a basic drive like hunger, we would expect other mammalian species to exhibit patterns of aggression that are similar to ours (just as they exhibit patterns of hunger that are similar to ours). The evidence for this has changed over the years. In the 1960s, early ethological research suggested that there was a major difference between humans and other species—namely, that animals have evolved mechanisms to control their aggressive instincts but humans have not (Ardrey, 1966; Lorenz, 1966). Subsequent research suggested, however, that animals may be no less aggressive than we are. The incidence of murder, rape, and infanticide among animals was shown to be much greater than previously thought.

One kind of murder occurs in border wars between chimpanzees (Goodall, 1978). In one well-documented case in the Gombe Stream National Park in Tanzania, a gang of five male chimpanzees defended their territory against any strange male that wandered into it. If the gang encountered a group of two or more strangers, their response would be raucous but not deadly; but if there was only one intruder, one member of the gang might hold his arm, another a leg, while a third pounded the intruder to death. Or a couple of members of the gang would drag the intruder over the rocks until he died. In another chimpanzee border war observed during the 1970s, a tribe of about 15 chimpanzees destroyed a smaller neighboring group by killing the males one at a time. Female primates engage in as many aggressive acts as males, although their encounters are less deadly because their teeth are shorter and less sharp (Smuts, 1986).

While observations like these bring animal aggression more in line with human aggression, there still are many differences. Humans wage wide-scale wars, for example.

The Biological Basis of Aggression in Other Species Findings on the biological basis of aggression in animals provide evidence for an aggressive drive in at least some species. Some studies show that mild electrical stimulation of a specific region of the hypothalamus produces aggressive, even deadly, behavior in animals. When a cat's hypothalamus is stimulated via implanted electrodes, the animal hisses, its hair bristles, its pupils dilate, and it will strike at a rat or other objects placed in its cage. Stimulation of a different area of the hypothalamus produces quite different behavior: Instead of exhibiting any of these rage responses, the cat coldly stalks and kills a rat.

Similar techniques have produced aggressive behavior in rats. A laboratory-bred rat that has never killed a mouse, nor seen a wild rat kill one, may live quite peacefully in the same cage with a mouse. But if the rat's hypothalamus is stimulated, the animal will pounce on its cagemate and kill it with exactly the same response that is exhibited by a wild rat (a hard bite to the neck that severs the spinal cord). The stimulation seems to trigger an innate killing response that was previously dormant. Conversely, if a neurochemical blocker is injected into the same brain site that induces rats to spontaneously kill mice on sight, the rats become temporarily peaceful (Smith, King, & Hoebel, 1970). In these cases, then, aggression has some properties of a drive, since it involves inborn reactions.

In some mammals, such instinctive patterns of aggression are controlled by the cortex and therefore are influenced more by experience. Monkeys living in groups establish a dominance hierarchy: One or two males become leaders, and the others position themselves at various lower levels in the hierarchy. When the hypothalamus of a dominant monkey is electrically stimulated, the monkey attacks subordinate males but not females. When a low-ranking monkey is stimulated in the same way, it cowers and behaves submissively (see Figure 11-5). Thus, aggressive behavior in a monkey is not automatically elicited by stimulation of the hypothalamus; the monkey's environment and past experiences also play a role. Humans are similar. Although we are equipped with neurological mechanisms that are tied to aggression, activation of these mechanisms is usually under cortical control (except in some cases of brain damage). Indeed, in most individuals the frequency with which aggressive behavior is expressed, the forms it takes, and the situations in which it is displayed are determined largely by experience and social influences.

Biological Bases of Aggression in Humans One biological factor that may be related to aggression in human males is testosterone level. Recall from Chapter 10 that testosterone is a male sex hormone that is responsible for many male bodily characteristics and has been linked to aggression in monkeys. Studies suggest that in humans as well, higher levels of testosterone are associated with higher levels of aggression. One large-scale study involved more than 4,400 male U.S. veterans. The men were given various psychological tests, some of which measured aggressiveness; they also provided blood samples so that

FIGURE 11-5

Brain Stimulation and Aggression *A mild electrical current is delivered to electrodes implanted in the monkey's hypothalamus via remote radio control. The animal's response (attack or flight) depends on its position in the dominance hierarchy of the colony.*

their testosterone levels could be determined. Men with higher levels of testosterone were more likely to have a history of aggression. Since aggressive behavior in males can sometimes lead to antisocial behavior, we might expect that high testosterone would be an impediment to success in American life. Indeed, men with extremely high testosterone levels were more likely to have low-status jobs than men with lower testosterone levels (Dabbs & Morris, 1990).

These findings provide some evidence for a biological basis of aggression in humans and, hence, for the view that aggression is like a drive. Still, in these studies the link between testosterone and aggression is often tenuous; large numbers of participants are needed to find the effect. This suggests that we need to look elsewhere for other determinants of aggression.

Aggression as a Learned Response

Social-learning theory is concerned with human social interaction, but it has its origins in behaviorist studies of animal learning such as those discussed in Chapter 7. It focuses on the behavior patterns that people develop in response to events in their environment. Some social behaviors may be rewarded while others may produce unfavorable results; through the process of differential reinforcement, people eventually select the more successful behavior patterns. Social-learning theory differs from strict behaviorism, however, in that it stresses cognitive processes. Because people can represent situations mentally, they are able to foresee the likely consequences of their actions and alter their behavior accordingly.

Social-learning theory further differs from strict behaviorism in that it stresses the role of vicarious learning, or learning by observation. Many behavior patterns are learned by watching the actions of others and observing the consequences. A child who observes the pained expression of an older sibling in the dentist's chair will probably be fearful when the time comes for his or her first dental appointment. Social-learning theory emphasizes the role of models in transmitting both specific behaviors and emotional responses. It focuses on such questions as what types of models are most effective and what factors determine whether the observed behavior will actually be performed (Bandura, 1986; 1973).

With this emphasis on learning, it is no surprise that social-learning theory rejects the concept of aggression as a frustration-produced drive; the theory proposes instead that aggression is similar to any other learned response. Aggression can be learned through observation or imitation, and the more often it is reinforced, the more likely it is to occur. A person who is frustrated by a blocked goal or disturbed by a stressful event experiences an unpleasant emotion. The response that this emotion elicits will differ, depending on the kinds of responses the individual has learned to use in coping with stressful situations. The frustrated individual may seek help from others, behave aggressively, withdraw, try even harder to surmount the obstacle, or resort to drug or alcohol use. The chosen response will be the one that has relieved frustration most successfully in the past. According to this view, frustration provokes aggression mainly in people who have learned to respond to adverse situations with aggressive behavior (Bandura, 1977).

Figure 11-6 shows how social-learning theory differs from psychoanalytic theory (that is, the frustration-aggression hypothesis) in conceptualizing aggression. Social-learning theory assumes that (a) aggression is just one of several reactions to the aversive experience of frustration and (b) aggression is a response with no drivelike properties, and consequently is influenced by the anticipated consequences of behavior.

Imitation of Aggression One source of evidence for social-learning theory is research showing that aggression, like any other response, can be learned through imitation. Nursery-school children who observed an adult expressing various forms of aggression toward a large inflated doll subsequently imitated many of the adult's actions, including unusual ones (see Figure 11-7). The experiment was expanded to include two filmed versions of aggressive modeling: one showing an adult behaving aggressively toward the doll, the other showing a cartoon character displaying the same aggressive behavior. The results were equally striking. Children who watched either of the two films behaved as aggressively toward the doll as children who had observed a live model displaying aggression. Figure 11-8 shows the measures of aggressive behavior for each of the groups and for two control groups who observed either no model or a nonaggressive model.

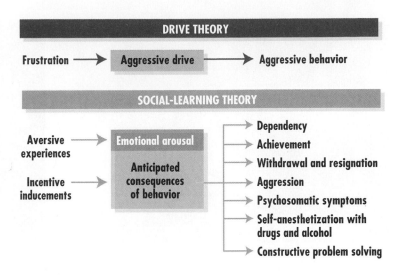

FIGURE 11-6

Two Views of Aggression *This diagram schematically represents the determinants of aggression according to psychoanalytic theory (the frustration-aggression hypothesis) and social-learning theory. From the viewpoint of social-learning theory, the emotional arousal caused by unpleasant experiences can lead to any number of different behaviors, depending on the behavior that has been reinforced in the past.*

The conclusion of such studies is that observation of either live or filmed models of aggression increases the likelihood of aggression in the viewer. This may be part of the reason that children whose parents punish them severely are likely to be more aggressive than average; the parents provide the model (Eron, 1987).

Reinforcement of Aggression Another piece of evidence for social-learning theory is that aggression is sensitive to reinforcement contingencies in the same manner that other learned responses are. A number of studies show that children are more likely to express the aggressive responses they learned by watching aggressive models when they are reinforced for such actions or when they observe aggressive models being reinforced. In one study, investigators observed children for 10 weeks, recording instances of aggression and the events that immediately followed them, such as positive reinforcers (the victim winced or cried), punishment of the aggression (the victim counterattacked), or neutral reactions (the victim ignored the aggressor). For the children who showed the highest overall level of aggression, the most

FIGURE 11-7

Children's Imitation of Adult Aggression *Nursery-school children observed an adult expressing various forms of aggressive behavior toward an inflated doll. After watching the adult, both boys and girls behaved aggressively toward the doll, performing many of the detailed acts of aggression that the adult had displayed, including lifting and throwing the doll, striking it with a hammer, and kicking it.*

common reaction to their aggressive act was positive reinforcement. For the children who showed the least aggression, punishment was a common reaction. Children who initially were not aggressive but who occasionally succeeded in stopping attacks through counteraggression gradually began to initiate attacks of their own (their aggression was being positively reinforced). Clearly, the consequences of aggression play an important role in shaping behavior (Patterson, Littman, & Bricker, 1967).

Aggressive Expression and Catharsis

Studies that try to distinguish between aggression as a drive and aggression as a learned response often focus on **catharsis**, or *purging an emotion by experiencing it intensely.* If aggression is a drive, expression of aggression should be cathartic, resulting in a reduction in the intensity of aggressive feelings and actions (analogous to the way eating leads to a reduction of hunger-based feelings and actions). On the other hand, if aggression is a learned response, expression of aggression could result in an increase in such actions (if the aggression is reinforced). The available evidence favors the learned-response view.

Acting Aggressively Psychologists have conducted numerous laboratory studies to determine whether or not aggression decreases once it has been partially expressed. Studies of children indicate that participation in aggressive activities either increases aggressive behavior or maintains it at the same level. Experiments with adults produce similar results. When given repeated opportunities to shock another person (who cannot retaliate), college students become more and more punitive. Participants who are angry become even more punitive in successive attacks than participants who are not angry. If aggression were cathartic, the angry participants should reduce their aggressive drive by acting aggressively and become less punitive the more they engage in aggression (Berkowitz, 1965).

Some evidence about catharsis comes from real-life situations. In one case, California aerospace workers who had been laid off were interviewed about how they felt about their companies and supervisors, and subsequently asked to describe their feelings in writing. If aggression were cathartic, men who expressed a lot of anger in the interviews should have expressed relatively little in the written reports. The results, however, showed otherwise: The men who let out anger in conversation expressed even more anger in their reports. The expression of anger may have advanced their aggression still further. Another study looked at the relationship between the hostility of a country (vis-à-vis its neighboring countries) and the kinds of sports its citizens play. More belligerent cultures were found to play more combative games. Again, aggression seems to breed more aggression rather than dissipate it (Ebbesen, Duncan, & Konecni, 1975).

These results argue against aggression being cathartic. However, there are circumstances in which the expression of aggression may decrease its incidence. For example, behaving aggressively may arouse feelings of anxiety that inhibit further aggression, particularly if the aggressors observe that their actions have led to injuries. But in these instances the effect on aggressive behavior can be explained without concluding that an aggressive drive is being reduced. Also, although expressing hostile feelings in action does not usually reduce the aggression, it may make the person feel better. But this may happen because the person feels more powerful and more in control, rather than because the person has reduced an aggressive drive.

Viewing Violence   Most of the studies we have discussed deal with the consequences of directly expressing aggression. What about the

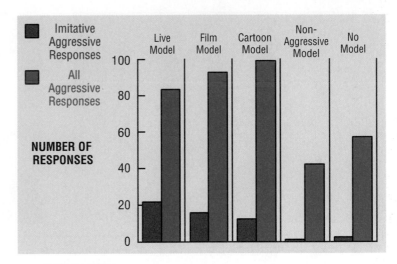

FIGURE 11-8

Imitation of Aggression   *Observing aggressive models (either live or on film) greatly increases the amount of aggressive behavior displayed by children, compared to observing a nonaggressive model or no model at all. Note that observation of the live model results in imitation of more specific aggressive acts, whereas observation of filmed (either real-life or cartoon) models instigates more aggressive responses of all kinds.* (After Bandura, 1973)

effects of indirectly or vicariously expressing aggression by watching violence on television or in the movies? Is viewing violence cathartic, providing fantasy outlets for an aggressive drive? Or does it elicit aggression by modeling violent behavior? We have already seen that children will imitate live or filmed aggressive behavior in an experimental setting, but how will they react in more natural settings? The amount of media violence to which children are exposed makes this an important question.

Several experimental studies have controlled children's viewing of television. In one study, one group of children watched violent cartoons for a specified amount of time each day; another group watched nonviolent cartoons for the same amount of time. The amount of aggression the children showed in their daily activities was carefully recorded. The children who watched violent cartoons became more aggressive in their interactions with peers, whereas the children who viewed nonviolent cartoons showed no change in interpersonal aggression (Steuer, Applefield, & Smith, 1971).

The study just described involves an experimental group and a control group. However, most studies that deal with children's viewing habits are correlational; they determine the relationship between amount of exposure to televised violence and the degree to which children use aggressive behavior to solve

Children often imitate what they see on television.

interpersonal conflicts. This correlation is clearly positive (Singer & Singer, 1981), even for children in Finland, which has a limited number of violent programs (Lagerspetz, Viemero, & Akademi, 1986). Correlations, however, do not imply causal relationships. It may be that children who are aggressive prefer to watch violent television programs—that is, having an aggressive nature causes one to view violence, rather than vice versa.

To evaluate this alternative hypothesis, a study traced television viewing habits over a 10-year period. More than 800 children between the ages of 8 and 9 were studied. Investigators collected information about each child's viewing preferences and aggressiveness (as rated by schoolmates). Boys who preferred programs that contain a considerable amount of violence were found to be much more aggressive in their interpersonal relationships than boys who preferred programs that contain little violence. So far, the evidence is similar to that found in previous studies. But 10 years later, more than half of the original participants were interviewed regarding their television preferences, given a test that measured delinquent tendencies, and rated by their peers for aggressiveness. Figure 11-9 shows that high exposure to violence on television at age 9 is positively related to aggressiveness in boys at age 19. Most important, the correlation remains significant even when statistical methods are used to control for degree of childhood aggressiveness, thereby reducing the possibility that the initial level of aggression

determines both childhood viewing preferences and adult aggressiveness.

It is interesting that the results showed no consistent relationship between the television viewing habits of girls and their aggressive behavior at either age. This agrees with the results of other studies indicating that girls tend to imitate aggressive behavior much less than boys do unless they are specifically reinforced for doing so. In our society, girls are less likely to be reinforced for behaving aggressively. And since most of the aggressive roles on television are male, females are less likely to find aggressive models to imitate. For boys, however, the majority of studies point to the conclusion that viewing violence does increase aggressive behavior, particularly in young children. Indeed, this conclusion is supported by a review of 28 studies of this issue (Wood, Wang, & Chachere, 1991). These findings argue against the idea of aggression as catharsis and the view that aggression is a drive.

The results of research on viewing of television violence provide strong support for efforts to reduce the amount of aggression in children's programming. They also carry a message for parents. Not only should responsible parents closely monitor the type of television programs their children view, but they should avoid praising aggressive actions, either by their children or by television characters. They also need to be aware of their powerful role in modeling behavior—if they behave aggressively, their children are likely to do so as well.

Our survey of aggression has by no means considered all of its possible causes. Common causes of anger and aggression include loss of self-esteem or a perception that another person has acted unfairly (Averill, 1983); we have not focused on either of these factors in our discussion of aggression as a drive versus aggression as a learned response. Also, many social conditions are involved in the instigation of aggression; poverty, overcrowding, the actions of authorities such as the police, and cultural values are only a few. Some of these social influences will be considered in Chapter 18. In sum, aggression may often occur when a person is frustrated, but it does not always follow frustration; there are many social conditions and cues that either increase or decrease a person's tendency to act aggressively (Berkowitz, 1981).

The study of aggression makes it clear that an emotional reaction is a complex event. Similarly, each component of an emotion that we considered—autonomic arousal, cognitive appraisal, and emotional expression—is itself a complex event involving multiple factors, both biological and psychological. In fact, each of the theories of emotion described in this chapter has addressed how the biological components of emotion (such as physiological arousal and universal facial expressions) and the psychological components of emotion (such as cognitive appraisals) interact to produce the experience of emotion. Taken together, the research reviewed in this chapter suggests that in most cases the biological and psychological components of emotion probably have reciprocal influences on each other in a dynamic process that evolves over time. A situation may initially elicit a mild emotion, but as a person evaluates the situation more deeply, the emotion may intensify and his physiological arousal may increase. The effects of the emotion on his memory for

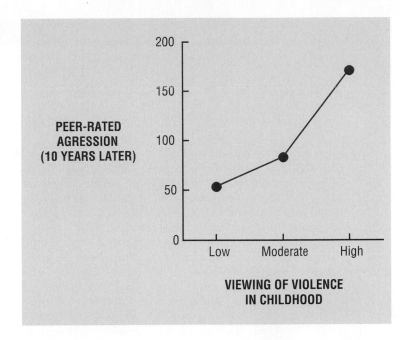

FIGURE 11-9

The Relationship Between Childhood Viewing of Violent Television and Adult Aggression *A preference for viewing violent television programs by boys at age 9 is positively correlated with aggressive behavior at age 19.* (After Eron et al., 1972)

similar events from the past and on his appraisals of this event may further intensify his subjective experience of emotion. Over time, then, feedback loops between the biological and psychological components of an emotion can influence the development of the emotion. We will return to discussions of the feedback between the biological and psychological components of emotion when we discuss stress in Chapter 14 and emotional disorders in Chapters 15 and 16.

The Good in Positive Emotions

Barbara L. Fredrickson, *University of Michigan*

What good are positive emotions? This question seems almost silly because at one level the answer is obvious: Positive emotions feel good. This fact alone makes them rewarding and valuable experiences. End of story, right?

Unfortunately, for many psychologists, this has been the end of the story. Any review of the scientific literature on emotions will reveal an overwhelming focus on negative emotions—like fear, anger, disgust, and shame— and only a tiny focus on positive emotions—

Barbara L. Fredrickson

like joy, contentment, interest, and love. So, although few would argue with Thomas Jefferson's assumption in the United States Declaration of Independence that the pursuit of happiness is a worthy goal, few have pursued positive emotions scientifically.

In my view, this is a big mistake. Common sense (and a bit of research) suggests that positive emotions contribute richly to the quality of our lives (Myers & Diener, 1995). But how? In which domains? These questions warrant scientific attention. To jumpstart research in this area, I have advanced a new model to describe the form and function of a subset of positive emotions, including joy, interest, contentment, and love. These positive emotions, I argue, have beneficial repercussions beyond simply feeling good (Fredrickson, 1998).

Positive Emotions Broaden Our Thinking and Actions. One virtue of negative emotions is that they spark strong urges to act in specific ways: to fight when angry, to flee when afraid, or to spit when disgusted (Frijda, Kuipers, & Schure 1989; Lazarus, 1991). Put differently, negative emotions narrow our thinking and actions. Positive emotions seem to have a complementary effect; they broaden our thinking and actions: Joy creates the urge to play, interest the urge to explore, contentment the urge to savor, and love a recurring cycle of each of these urges. The virtue here is that positive emotions expand our typical ways of thinking and being in the world, pushing us to be more creative, more curious, or more connected to others (Fredrickson, 1998; Isen, 1987).

Positive Emotions Build our Personal Resources. Although emotions themselves are short-lived, they can have lasting effects on us. By momentarily broadening our thinking and actions, positive emotions promote discovery of novel and creative ideas, actions, and social bonds. Playing, for instance, can build our physical and social skills, exploring can generate knowledge, and savoring can set our life priorities. Importantly, these outcomes often endure long after the initial positive emotion has vanished. In this way, positive emotions build up our store of resources to draw on in times of trouble, ranging from physical resources (e.g., the ability to outmaneuver a predator), to intellectual resources (e.g., a cognitive map for way-finding), and social resources (e.g., someone to turn to for help).

Emotions are Evolved Adaptations. Psychologists often cast emotions as evolved psychological adaptations, or tendencies that helped early humans live long enough to reproduce and become our ancestors (Levenson, 1994; Tooby & Cosmides, 1990). The adaptive value of negative emotions has been linked to the narrowed action tendencies they trigger. These specific actions (e.g., fight, flee, spit) represent those that worked best when our ancestors faced threats to life and limb. I believe that the adaptive value of positive emotions can be linked to the broaden-and-build model that I've sketched here. Those of our ancestors who succumbed to the urges sparked by positive emotions (e.g., play, explore, savor) would have by consequence accrued more physical, intellectual, and social resources. When these same ancestors later faced inevitable threats to life and limb, these resources would have translated into increased odds of survival. To the extent, then, that the capacities to experience positive and negative emotions are genetically encoded, these capacities, through the process of natural selection, are likely to have become part of our universal human nature.

So, positive emotions may do more for us than we typically acknowledge. Feeling good may broaden our typical ways of thinking and acting and, in turn, build our personal resources, making us more complex and resilient people than we would be otherwise. So next time you're laughing with friends, pursuing an interest, or enjoying a walk through the park, consider that you may be cultivating more than just fleeting good feelings; you may also be optimizing your own long-term health and well-being (Fredrickson, in press).

The Good in Feeling Bad

Gerald L. Clore, *University of Illinois, Champaign*

Feeling afraid, sad, guilty, or angry is unpleasant. In an ideal world, surely there would be no such negative emotions. Wouldn't it be wonderful never to feel sad, afraid, guilty, or mad again? Or would it? Think twice before you answer, because feeling bad turns out to have many virtues. Three of these are described below:

1. Negative Feelings Motivate Us. Each negative emotion has an important role to play. Fear and anxiety, for example, are endlessly useful. Without fear, we would all go around like puppies or toddlers, quite content to wander into onrushing traffic and embrace fierce dogs. We would stand up for a big presentation without having prepared something to say. Guilt, too, is a useful and important emotion. For example, experiments show that mild feelings of guilt can spark cooperative behavior even in people who would otherwise exploit others (Ketelaar & Au, 1999). Anger also may have benefits. Anger motivates us to seek justice when we are short-changed or treated unfairly. When angry, we may stand up for our principles even when there is little immediate gain for doing so. Indeed, the unpleasantness of negative emotions like anger may have evolved precisely for this purpose—to bring into the present a small part of the delayed but much larger unpleasantness that inaction would bring (Frank, 1988).

2. Negative Feelings Inform Us. One of the virtues of negative emotions is that they are informative (Clore, 1992), and indeed they are far more informative than positive ones. There are many distinctive negative emotions, including fear, anger, sadness, shame, disgust, and on and on. Each of them conveys specific information. Sadness signals a loss, fear a threat, and anger alerts one to blameworthy action (Ortony, Clore, & Collins, 1988). But the positive emotions all seem to be merely variations on happiness, which simply signals that things are fine. The precision of pain and the blurriness of joy can be seen in the fact that people can describe their physical and psychological pains with great precision, but an astronaut floating in space, tethered to his space ship, could only say, "Great, wonderful, I have no words" (Amachai, 1999).

3. Negative Feelings Help Us Learn. We constantly evaluate the situations in which we find ourselves. Affect-as-information theory (e.g., Schwarz & Clore, 1996) maintains that the feelings that result from these evaluations provide feedback about the environment and about our resources for coping with it. Negative feelings indicate that we have a problem and often trigger systematic thought aimed at solving the problem. Negative feelings lead us to gather new information and to change something about our approach.

This relationship between affect and whether we use what we already know is entirely reasonable. When we are succeeding at a task, we feel good and continue doing whatever appears to be working. But when we are not succeeding, we feel bad, so we try to change, focusing on new information from the environment instead of old information that is not working. Philosophers of education (Dewey, 1916), learning theorists (McDougall, 1923), and modern studies of brain waves (Donchin, 1982) agree that learning occurs primarily when one has the experience of being wrong. Even in rats, behavior is guided by old habits when they experience reward and by new learning when they experience negative consequences (Gray, 1971).

Research in social psychology also suggests that positive feelings lead people to rely on their existing beliefs, while negative feelings lead them to place a priority on new information from

Gerald L. Clore

the environment. For example, several experiments have shown that people in happy moods are more likely to use stereotypes and first impressions when making judgments of others, whereas those in sad moods are more likely to make judgments on the basis of what people actually do (Isbell, Clore, & Wyer, 1999).

With respect to relying on our own prior assumptions, then, positive feelings act like an accelerator and negative feelings like a brake. That is, positive feelings encourage us to pursue our own egocentric beliefs, while negative feelings alert us to problems, show us where our assumptions are not correct, and trigger the process of learning new things. Feeling bad is good when it inhibits our reliance on assumptions long enough to allow us to learn something new.

SUMMARY

1. The components of emotion include the subjective experience of emotion, autonomic arousal, cognitive appraisal, emotional expression, general reactions to the emotion, and action tendencies.

2. Intense emotions usually involve physiological arousal caused by activation of the sympathetic division of the autonomic nervous system. People with spinal cord injuries, which limit feedback from the autonomic nervous system, report experiencing less intense emotions. Autonomic arousal may also help differentiate the emotions, since the pattern of arousal (for example, heartbeat, skin temperature) differs for different emotions.

3. A cognitive appraisal is an analysis of a situation that results in an emotion. Such appraisals affect both the intensity and the quality of an emotion. When people are induced into a state of undifferentiated arousal, the quality of their emotional experience may be influenced by their appraisal of the situation. There are, however, cases of emotion in which no conscious or deliberate cognitive appraisal seems to be involved (for example, fear experiences that were acquired in childhood through classical conditioning). These precognitive emotions appear to be mediated by distinct neural pathways in the brain.

4. The facial expressions that accompany primary emotions have a universal meaning: People from different cultures agree on what emotion a person in a particular photograph is expressing. Cultures may differ in the factors that elicit certain emotions and in rules for the proper display of emotion. The ability to recognize emotional expression is localized in the right cerebral hemisphere and is neurologically distinct from the ability to recognize faces.

5. In addition to their communicative functions, emotional expressions may contribute to the subjective experience of an emotion (the facial feedback hypothesis). In support of this hypothesis, people report a greater emotional experience when they exaggerate their facial reactions to emotional stimuli.

6. A general reaction to being in an emotional state is that we tend to pay more attention to and learn more about events that fit our mood than to events that do not. Another consequence is that our emotional mood affects our evaluation of people and objects, as well as our estimation of what will happen in the future. When in a bad mood, we estimate various risks to be relatively frequent; when in a good mood, we estimate these risks to be relatively infrequent.

7. Aggression is a typical action tendency in response to anger (although it can occur for other reasons as well). According to psychoanalytic theory, aggression is a drive produced by frustration; according to social-learning theory, aggression is a learned response.

8. The hypothesis that aggression is a basic drive receives some support from studies showing a biological basis for aggression. In some animals, aggression is controlled by neurological mechanisms in the hypothalamus. Stimulation of the hypothalamus of a rat or cat can lead to a rage or killing response. In humans and certain other mammals, aggressive behavior is largely under cortical control and hence is affected by past experiences and social influences. Even in humans, though, there may be some biological bases of aggression.

9. In keeping with the social-learning theory of aggression, aggressive responses can be learned through imitation and increase in frequency when positively reinforced. Children are more likely to express aggressive responses when they are reinforced for such actions than when they are punished for the actions.

10. Evidence indicates that aggression either increases subsequent aggressive behavior or maintains it at the same level. Thus, when given repeated opportunities to shock another person (who cannot retaliate), college students become more and more punitive. The indirect or vicarious expression of aggression has similar effects: There is a positive relationship between the amount of television violence to which children are exposed and the extent to which they act aggressively.

KEY TERMS

emotion (p. 389)
cognitive appraisal (p. 396)
precognitive emotions (p. 400)

aggression (p. 406)
catharsis (p. 410)

CRITICAL THINKING QUESTIONS

1. Assuming that emotions evolved because they serve useful purposes, what purposes (if any) might be served by extreme manifestations of emotion, such as severe depression or chronic anger?

2. In recent years the notion of emotional intelligence—the ability to understand and regulate one's emotions—has become popular. What do you think it means to be emotionally intelligent in our society? How do you think emotional intelligence might vary across cultures?

FURTHER READING

For an introduction to various views on emotion, some chapters in Mook, *Motivation* (1987) are very useful. For a more technical treatment of emotion, see Lazarus, *Emotion and Adaptation* (1991); Frijda, *The Emotions* (1986); Mandler, *Mind and Emotion* (1982); and Plutchik and Kellerman (eds.), *Emotion: Theory, Research, and Experience* (1980). The role of cognition in emotion is discussed in detail in Ortony, Clore, and Collins, *The Cognitive Structure of Emotions* (1988).

Interesting books on facial expressions and emotion include Ekman's *Emotion in the Human Face* (2nd ed., 1982) and his *Telling Lies: Clues to Deceit in the Marketplace, Politics and Marriage* (1985).

For a review and critical analysis of lie detection procedures, see Lykken, *A Tremor in the Blood: Uses and Abuses of the Lie Detector* (1980).

The psychoanalytic theory of emotion is presented in two books by Freud: *Beyond the Pleasure Principle* (1920/1975) and *New Introductory Lectures on Psychoanalysis* (1933/1965). For the social-learning approach, see Bandura, *Social Learning Theory* (1977). Books on aggression include Bandura, *Aggression: A Social Learning Analysis* (1973); Tavris, *Anger: The Misunderstood Emotion* (1984); Hamburg and Trudeau (eds.), *Biobehavioral Aspects of Aggression* (1981); and Averill, *Anger and Aggression: An Essay on Emotion* (1982).

Personality
and Individuality

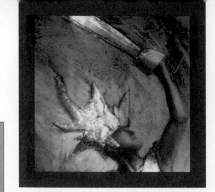

Chapter 12
Individual Differences

Oskar Stohr and Jack Yufe are identical twins who were born in Trinidad and separated shortly after birth. Oskar was taken to Germany by his mother, where he was raised by his grandmother as a Catholic and a Nazi. Jack remained in Trinidad with his Jewish father, was raised as a Jew, and spent part of his youth on an Israeli kibbutz. The two families never corresponded.

When they were in their late forties, Oskar and Jack were brought together by researchers at the University of Minnesota who were studying sets of twins who had been raised apart. Although Oskar and Jack had met only once before, they showed some remarkable similarities. Both showed up for the study wearing mustaches, wire-rimmed glasses, and blue double-breasted suits. Their mannerisms and temperaments were similar, and they shared certain idiosyncrasies: Both liked spicy foods and sweet liqueurs, were absent-minded, flushed the toilet before using it, like to dip buttered toast in their coffee, and enjoyed surprising people by sneezing in elevators.

Many other sets of identical twins studied by the Minnesota researchers also displayed similarities. For example, the twins shown in the accompanying photo were separated at birth and not reunited until they were 31 years old, by which time both had become firefighters. What causes such similarities? Surely there aren't firefighting genes or genes for dipping toast or surprising people in elevators; such similarities reflect the inherited components of more basic personality characteristics. Indeed, both similarities *and* differences among individuals provide challenges for psychology.

In many ways every person is like every other person. The biological and psychological processes discussed in this book—development, consciousness, perception, learning, remembering, thinking, motivation, and emotion—are basically the same for all of us. But in other ways every person is different from every other person. Each of us has a distinctive pattern of abilities, beliefs, attitudes, motivations, emotions, and personality traits that makes us unique. In this section of the book we take a close look at the qualities that make each of us an individual. In this chapter, we discuss the biological and environmental factors that produce individual differences and survey some of the methods for measuring intellectual abilities and personality. In Chapter 13, we review formal theories of personality and discuss the philosophies of human nature underlying them.

We also return to a major theme that we introduced in Chapter 3: the interaction between nature and nurture. In that chapter we discussed how innate biological factors interact with events in an individual's environment to determine the course of development, focusing particularly on factors that make us all alike. We considered, for example, how innately determined sequences of maturation cause all children to go through the same stages of development in the same sequence, regardless of differences in their environments. In this chapter we focus on

These twins, separated at birth, showed remarkable similarities in interests and habits when they first met at age 31.

the biological and environmental factors that make us different from one another—in other words, the factors that create individuality.

Sources of Individual Differences

If you were asked why one person is taller than another, you would probably give a "nature" explanation: The taller person has inherited taller "height genes" from his or her parents than the shorter person. Even though health and nutrition can affect a person's growth, you would be correct in assuming that, in general, environmental factors play a very minor role in determining a person's height. If, however, you were asked why one person prefers classical music to rock music but another person has the opposite preference, you would be much more inclined to give a "nurture" (environmental) explanation: The different preferences probably developed as a result of exposure to different kinds of music at home or in school; the possibility that there might be genes for musical preference seems unlikely.

But might there be genes for musical talent? Or intelligence, sociability, or sexual orientation? Here the answers are not obvious. Moreover, advocates of particular political positions and social policies frequently invoke one answer or another in support of their viewpoint (for example, Herrnstein &

Murray, 1994; also see the discussion of sexual orientation in Chapter 10). Because these debates reveal widespread public misunderstanding about the empirical issues involved, we will describe in some detail the reasoning and methods that behavioral scientists use to assess how genetic and environmental factors contribute to individual differences.

We begin with Table 12-1, which lists (in descending order) the scores of a hypothetical examination taken by two groups of six students each. As shown in the last row, the average (mean) score of the students within each group is 82.0. But we can also see that the scores from Class A are much more spread out—that is, more variable—than the scores from Class B. In other words, the students in Class A are more different from one another than the students in Class B. As explained in the Appendix, the degree to which a set of scores differ from one another can be expressed mathematically by a quantity called their *variance*.

Now consider the scores for Class A. Why are they different from one another? Why do some students do better than others? What accounts for the variance we observe? One obvious possibility is that some students studied for the exam longer than other students did. To find out whether and to what extent this is true, we could conduct a hypothetical experiment in which we "controlled for" the variable of study time by requiring all students to study exactly three hours for the exam, no more and no less. If study time really does affect students' scores, what would happen to the variance of those scores?

TABLE 12-1

Hypothetical Examination Scores of Two Groups of Students

	Group A		Group B
Alice	100	Greta	89
Bob	95	Harold	88
Carol	89	Ilene	83
Dan	83	John	80
Emily	67	Karen	77
Fred	58	Leon	75
Average	82.0	Average	82.0

First, some of the students who would have studied longer than three hours and done quite well will now do less well. For example, if Alice—who might have studied for six hours to achieve her perfect score of 100—had been permitted to study for only three hours, her score might have been more like Greta's score of 89. Second, some of the students who would have studied less than three hours and not done very well will now do better. Fred—who only had time to skim the reading for the exam—might have obtained a score higher than 58 if he had studied for three hours. Like Leon, he might at least have obtained a score of 75. In other words, if we controlled the study time of Class A, the students' scores would bunch closer together, looking more like Class B's scores; in other words, the variance of their scores would decrease. If we actually did this experiment and observed that the variance in Class A's scores decreased by, say, 60%, we could claim that study time had accounted for 60% of the variance in the original scores for this class. In this hypothetical example, then, a major reason the exam scores differed so much from one another in Class A is that students differed in the amount of time they spent studying.

Theoretically, we could test for other potential sources of variance in the same way. If we think that having a good breakfast might affect students' scores, we could feed all the students the same breakfast (or deny breakfast to all the students) and observe whether the variance of their scores is reduced as a result. In general, holding constant any variable that "makes a difference" will reduce the variance of the scores. In the extreme case, if we held all the relevant variables constant, the variance would diminish to zero: Every student would obtain the same score.

It is important to note, however, that we cannot say what will happen to the mean of the scores when we hold a variable constant. For example, if the students in Class A had originally studied for the exam for only two hours on the average, by requiring them all to study for three hours we will raise the class average. If, however, the students had studied for four hours on the average, we will lower the class average by limiting everybody to only three hours of study time.

Heritability

We are now prepared to ask the "nature" question: To what extent do some students do better than others on the exam because they are genetically more capable? To put it another way, what percentage of the variance in exam scores is accounted for by genetic differences among the students? In general, *the percentage of the variance in any trait that is accounted for by genetic differences among the individuals in a population* is the trait's **heritability.** The more individual differences on a trait are due to genetic differences, the closer the heritability is to 100%. For example, height is heavily influenced by genetics: Its heritability ranges from about 85% to 95% across different studies.

Now, however, we face a practical difficulty. We cannot experimentally determine how much of the variance in exam scores is accounted for by genetic differences the way we did for study time because that would require holding the genetic variable constant—that is, turning all the students into genetic clones. But we can take advantage of the fact that nature sometimes produces genetic clones in the form of identical twins. To the extent that identical twins are more alike on a trait than fraternal twins, we can infer that the trait has a genetic or heritable component (assuming that other factors, such as differential parental treatment, can be ruled out).

For example, across many studies the mean correlation between intelligence test scores for identical twins was .86; the comparable correlation for fraternal twins was .60. Mathematically, a difference of this magnitude implies that about 52% of the variance in intelligence test scores in the tested population is due to genetic differences (Bouchard & McGue, 1981). Similar studies have examined the heritability of personality traits. One large Swedish study assessed the traits of extraversion (sociability) and emotional stability in a sample of more than 12,000 pairs of adult twins. On both traits the estimate of heritability was about 60% (Floderus-Myred, Petersen, & Rasmuson, 1980).

One difficulty in interpreting the results of twin studies is that identical twin pairs may be treated more alike than fraternal twin pairs, which may account for the greater similarity of their personalities. This is one reason that researchers at the University of Minnesota decided to study sets of twins who had been reared apart (Bouchard, 1984).

The participants in the Minnesota Study of Twins Reared Apart were assessed on a number of ability and personality measures. In addition, they participated in lengthy interviews during which they were asked questions about such topics as childhood experiences, fears, hobbies, musical tastes, social attitudes, and sexual interests. A number of startling similarities were found. The twins with the most dramatically different backgrounds are Oskar Stohr and Jack Yufe, described at the beginning of the chapter. Another pair of twins with fairly different backgrounds are both British homemakers. They were separated during World War II and raised by families that differed in socioeconomic status. Both twins, who had never met before, arrived for their interviews wearing seven rings on their fingers.

These studies reveal that twins reared apart are just as similar to each other across a wide range of personality characteristics as twins reared together, permitting us to conclude with greater confidence that identical twins are more similar to each other on personality characteristics than fraternal twins because they are more similar genetically (Bouchard et al., 1990; Lykken, 1982; Tellegen et al., 1988).

For the most part, the correlations found in the Minnesota studies are in accord with results from many other twin studies. In general, the highest levels of heritability are found in measures of abilities and intelligence (60%–70%); the next highest levels are typically found in measures of personality (about 50%); and the lowest levels are found for religious and political beliefs and vocational interests (30%–40%).

Misunderstandings About Heritability The recurring public debate over nature-nurture questions reveals widespread misunderstanding about the concept of heritability. Therefore, it is important to be clear about the following points:

- Heritability refers to a *population,* not to individuals.

The heritability of a trait refers to differences among individuals within a population, not to percentages of a trait within an individual. To say that height has a heritability of 90% does not mean that 90% of your height came from your genes and 10% came from the environment. It means that 90% of the differences in height among individuals observed in a particular population is due to genetic differences among those individuals.

■ The heritability of a trait is not a single, fixed number.

Heritability refers to an attribute of a trait in a particular population at a particular point in time. If something happens to change the variance of a trait in a population, the heritability of the trait will also change. For example, if everyone in our society were suddenly given equal educational opportunities, the variance of intellectual performance in the society would decrease; scores on standardized measures of intellectual ability would be more similar. (This is what happened in our hypothetical experiment in which everyone had to study the same length of time for the exam.) And because heritability is the percentage of variance that is due to inherited differences among individuals, the heritability would actually increase because the percentage of the variance due to an important environmental factor, education, would have decreased.

■ Heritability does not tell us about the source of mean differences between groups.

One of the most contentious and recurring debates in American society is over the question of whether average differences in the intelligence test scores of different ethnic groups are due to genetic differences between the groups. In the early twentieth century the debate concerned the relatively low intelligence scores obtained by Hungarian, Italian, and Jewish immigrants when they were tested upon arrival in the United States. The test scores of these immigrants led some researchers to conclude that the majority were "feebleminded" (Kamin, 1974). Today the debate concerns the lower scores obtained by African-American and Hispanic-Americans compared with white Americans (Herrnstein & Murray, 1994).

In these debates, the heritability of intelligence is often used to support the genetic argument. But this claim is based on a logical fallacy, as illustrated by the following "thought experiment":

> We fill a white sack and a black sack with a mixture of different genetic varieties of corn seed. We make certain that the proportions of each variety of seed are identical in each sack. We then plant the seed from the white sack in fertile Field A, while the seed from the black sack is planted in barren Field B. We will observe that within Field A, as within Field B, there is considerable variation in the height of individual corn plants. This variation will be due largely to genetic factors (differences in the seed). We will also observe, however, that the average height of plants in Field A is greater than that of plants in Field B. That difference will be entirely due to environmental factors (the soil). The same is true of IQs: Differences in the average IQ of various human populations could be entirely due to environmental differences, even if within each population all variation were due to genetic differences (Eysenck & Kamin, 1981, p. 97).

■ Heritability does not tell us about the effects of environmental changes on the average level of a trait.

Another incorrect claim about heritability is that a trait with high heritability cannot be changed by a change in the environment. For example, it has been argued that it is futile to use preschool intervention programs to help disadvantaged children enhance their intellectual abilities because those abilities have high levels of heritability. But between 1946 and 1982 the height of young adult males in Japan increased by 3.3 inches, mainly owing to improved nutrition (Angoff, 1988). And yet height is one of the most heritable traits we possess. Then, as now, taller Japanese parents have taller children than do shorter Japanese parents. Similarly, a survey covering 14 countries has shown that the average IQ test score has risen significantly in recent years (Flynn, 1987). In sum, heritability is about variances, not average levels.

Interactions Between Personality and Environment

Genotype-Environment Correlation In shaping an individual's personality, genetic and environmental influences are intertwined from the moment of birth. Parents give their biological offspring both their genes and a home environment, and both are functions of the parents' own genes. As a result, there is a built-in correlation between the child's inherited characteristics (genotype) and the environment in which he or she is raised. For example, because general intelligence is partially heritable, parents with high intelligence are likely to have children with high intelligence. But parents with high intelligence are also likely to provide an intellectually stimulating environment for their children—both through their interactions with them and through the books, music lessons, trips to museums, and other intellectual experiences. Because the child's genotype and environment are positively correlated in this way, he or she will get a double-dose of intellectual advantage. Similarly, children born to parents with low intelligence are likely to encounter a home environment that exacerbates whatever intellectual disadvantage they may have inherited directly.

Some parents may deliberately construct an environment that is negatively correlated with the child's genotype. For example, introverted parents may encourage participation in social activities in order to counteract the child's likely introversion: "We make an effort to have people over because we don't want Chris to grow up to be as shy as we are." Parents of a very active child may try to provide interesting quiet activities. But whether the correlation is positive or nega-

tive, the point is that the child's genotype and environment are not simply independent sources of influence that add together to shape the child's personality.

In addition to being correlated with the environment, a child's genotype shapes the environment in certain ways (Bouchard et al., 1990; Plomin, DeFries, & Loehlin, 1977; Scarr, 1988; Scarr & McCartney, 1983). In particular, the environment becomes a function of the child's personality through three forms of interaction: *reactive, evocative,* and *proactive.*

Reactive Interaction Different individuals who are exposed to the same environment interpret it, experience it, and react to it differently. An anxious, sensitive child will experience and react to harsh parents differently than will a calm, resilient child; the sharp tone of voice that provokes the sensitive child to tears might pass unnoticed by his sister. An extraverted child will attend to people and events around her; her introverted brother will ignore them. A brighter child will get more out of being read to than a less bright child. In other words, each child's personality extracts a subjective psychological environment from the objective surroundings, and it is that subjective environment that shapes personality development. Even if parents provided exactly the same environment for all their children—which they usually do not—it will not be psychologically equivalent for all of them. Reactive interaction occurs throughout life.

Environmental factors such as parental encouragement can influence intellectual ability and personality traits—even though these traits have high heritabilities.

One person will interpret a hurtful act as the product of deliberate hostility and react to it quite differently than a person who interprets the same act as the result of unintended insensitivity.

Evocative Interaction   Every individual's personality evokes distinctive responses from others. An infant who squirms and fusses when picked up will evoke less nurturance from a parent than one who likes to be cuddled. Docile children will evoke a less controlling style of child rearing from parents than will aggressive children. For this reason, we cannot simply assume that an observed correlation between the child-rearing practices of a child's parents and his or her personality reflects a simple cause-and-effect sequence. Instead, the child's personality can shape the parents' child-rearing style, which, in turn, further shapes his or her personality. Evocative interaction also occurs throughout life: Gracious people evoke gracious environments; hostile people evoke hostile environments.

Proactive Interaction   As children grow older, they can move beyond the environments provided by their parents and begin to select and construct environments of their own. These environments, in turn, further shape their personalities. A sociable child will choose to go to the movies with friends rather than stay home alone and watch television; her sociable personality prompts her to select an environment that reinforces her sociability. And what she cannot select she will construct: If nobody invites her to the movies, she will organize the event herself. As the term implies, proactive interaction is a process through which individuals become active agents in the development of their own personality.

The relative importance of these three kinds of personality-environment interaction shifts over the course of development (Scarr, 1988; Scarr & McCartney, 1983). The built-in correlation between a child's genotype and his or her environment is strongest when the child is young and confined almost exclusively to the home environment. As the child grows older and begins to select and construct his or her own environment, this initial correlation decreases and the influence of proactive interaction increases. As we have noted, reactive and evocative interactions remain important throughout life.

Some Unsolved Puzzles   Studies of twins have produced a number of puzzling patterns that still are not completely understood. For example, the estimate of heritability for IQ is higher when it is based on identical twin pairs reared apart than it is when based on a comparison of identical and fraternal twins pairs reared together. Moreover, the striking similarities of identical twins do not seem to diminish across time or separate rearing environments. In contrast, the similarities of fraternal twins (and nontwin siblings) diminish from childhood through adolescence, even when they are reared together; the longer they live together in the same home, the less similar they become (Scarr, 1988; Scarr & McCartney, 1983).

Some of these patterns would emerge if the genes themselves interact so that inheriting all one's genes in common (as identical twins do) is more than twice as effective as inheriting only half one's genes in common (as fraternal twins and nontwin siblings do). This could come about if a trait depends on a particular combination of genes. Consider, for example, the trait of having blue eyes (which we will oversimplify a bit to make the point). Suppose that two parents each have a blue-eye gene and a brown-eye gene. For

---

We display proactive interaction when we select friends and spouses who share our interests and personality traits.

one of their children to get blue eyes, he or she must inherit a blue gene from the father and a blue gene from the mother; the three other combinations (brown-brown, brown-blue, blue-brown) will give the child brown eyes. In other words, any child of theirs has a one-in-four chance of getting blue eyes. But because identical twins inherit identical genes from their parents, they will also inherit the same combination of genes; if one gets blue eyes, so will the other. In contrast, if a fraternal twin inherits a blue gene from both parents, the chances that the other twin will also do so is still only one out of four-not one out of two. Thus, in this example, inheriting all one's genes in common is more than twice as effective as inheriting only half one's genes in common. There is evidence for this kind of gene-gene interaction for some personality traits, especially extraversion (Lykken et al., 1992; Pedersen et al., 1988). But personality-environment interactions could also be partially responsible for these patterns.

Consider identical twins. Because they have identical genotypes, they also react to situations in similar ways (reactive interaction); they evoke similar responses from others (evocative interaction); and their similar, genetically guided talents, interests, and motivations lead them to seek out and construct similar environments (proactive interaction). The important point is that these processes all operate whether the twins are reared together or apart. For example, two identical twins who were separated at birth will still be treated in similar ways by other people because they evoke similar responses from others.

Proactive interaction operates in the same way. Each twin's personality prompts him or her to select friends and environments that happen to be similar to the friends and environments chosen by the other twin. But friends and environments that are similar will treat each twin in similar ways. And so it goes. Because the twins begin with identical genotypic personalities, all the processes of personality-environment interaction act together to promote and sustain their similarity across time—even if they have not met since birth.

In contrast, the environments of fraternal twins and non-twin siblings increasingly diverge as they grow older—even within the

Because identical twins have identical genotypes, the processes of personality-environment interaction act together to promote and sustain their similarity over time—even if they grow up in different environments.

same home. They are most alike in early childhood, when parents provide the same environment for both. (Although even here, siblings will react somewhat differently and evoke different responses from the parents.) But as soon as they begin to select and construct environments outside the home, their moderately different talents, interests, and motivations will take them down increasingly divergent paths, thereby producing increasingly divergent personalities.

Shared Versus Nonshared Environments
Twin studies allow researchers to estimate not only how much of the variation among individuals is due to genetic variation but also how much of the environmentally related variation is due to aspects of the environment that family members share (for example, socioeconomic status) as compared with aspects of the environment that family members do not share (for example, friends outside the family). Surprisingly, differences due to shared aspects of the environment seem to account for almost none of the environmental variation: After their genetic similarities are subtracted out, two children from the same family seem to be no more alike than two children chosen

randomly from the population (Plomin & Daniels, 1987). This implies that the kinds of variables that psychologists typically study (such as child-rearing practices, socioeconomic status, and parents' education) are contributing virtually nothing to individual differences in personality. How can this be so?

One possible explanation might be that the reactive, evocative, and proactive processes act to diminish the differences between environments as long as those environments permit some flexibility of response. A bright child from a neglecting or impoverished home is more likely than a less bright sibling to absorb information from a television program (reactive interaction), to attract the attention of a sympathetic teacher (evocative interaction), and to go to the library (proactive interaction). This child's genotype acts to counteract the potentially debilitating effects of the home environment, and therefore he or she develops differently than a less bright sibling. Only if the environment is severely restrictive will these personality-driven processes be thwarted (Scarr, 1988; Scarr & McCartney, 1983). This explanation is supported by the finding that the most dissimilar pairs of identical twins reared apart are those in which one twin was reared in a severely restricted environment.

Although this explanation seems plausible, there is no direct evidence that it is correct. In any case, it appears that research will have to shift from the usual comparisons of children from different families to comparisons of children within the same families—with particular attention to the personality-environment interactions within those families. Similarly, more attention must be given to influences outside the family; one writer has suggested that the peer group is a far more important source of personality differences among children than the family (Harris, 1995).

Assessment of Individual Differences

Many industrialized societies rely heavily on objective assessment of individual differences, particularly differences in cognitive or intellectual abilities. Schoolchildren are often placed in instructional groups on the basis of their performances on such tests. Aptitude or ability tests are part of the admissions procedure in many colleges and most professional and graduate schools. In addition, many industries and government agencies select job applicants and place or promote employees on the basis of test scores.

Tests for assessing interests, attitudes, and personality traits are also familiar to most of us. In helping students make career choices, counselors can offer better advice if they know something about the student besides his or her academic ability. In selecting individuals for high-level positions, employers often seek to assess a candidate's interactional style, ability to handle stress, and so on. Decisions about the kind of treatment that will be most beneficial to an emotionally disturbed person or will help rehabilitate a felon also require objective assessment of individual differences.

Beyond these practical concerns, methods of assessment are essential to theory and research on individual differences. In fact, several personality theorists (discussed in Chapter 13) have developed assessment methods tailored to their particular approaches.

Characteristics of a Good Test

Because tests and other assessment instruments play important practical and scientific roles, it is essential that they measure accurately what they are intended to measure. Specifically, they must have reliability and validity. They also must be *standardized,* meaning that the conditions for taking the test are the same for all test-takers. For example, the instructions accompanying the test must be the same for all test-takers.

Reliability   If a test or method of assessment is **reliable,** it will *yield reproducible and consistent results.* If a test yielded different results when it was administered on different occasions or scored by different people, it would be unreliable. A simple analogy is a rubber yardstick. If we did not know how much it stretched each time we took a measurement, the results would be unreliable no matter how carefully we made each measurement.

Reliability is typically assessed by correlating two sets of scores. For example, the same test might be given to the same group of people on two occasions. If the test is reliable, their scores on the first occasion should correlate highly with their scores on the second. If they do, the test is said to have *test-retest reliability* or *temporal stability*.

In practice, of course, one would not usually want to give the same test to the same people twice. But there are many situations in which one would want to give equivalent forms of the same test—for example, when college-bound high school seniors want to take the Scholastic Assessment Test (SAT) more than once. To ensure that two forms of the same test yield equivalent scores, both forms are administered to the same population and the two forms are correlated. If they correlate highly, the test is said to have *alternate form reliability*. Some of the questions on the SAT do not actually count toward the student's score but are being statistically evaluated so they can be used on future, equivalent forms of the test.

Another common measure of reliability is *internal consistency,* the degree to which the separate questions or items on a test measure the same thing. This can be assessed by correlating the scores obtained by a group of individuals on each item with their total scores. Any item that does not correlate with the total score is an unreliable item; it is failing to contribute to what the test is measuring. Discarding unreliable items "purifies" a test by increasing its internal consistency. As the number of reliable items on a test increases, the reliability of the test's total score also increases.

Most tests and assessment instruments are scored objectively, often by computer. But sometimes one must evaluate intellectual performance or social behavior subjectively. An essay examination is a familiar example. To assess the reliability of such subjective judgments, two or more sets of ratings by independent judges are correlated. For example, two observers might independently rate a group of nursery school children for aggression, or two or more judges might be asked to read past U.S. presidential inaugural addresses and rate them for optimism or count the number of negative references to Iraq. If the correlation between raters or judges is high, the method is said to possess *interrater agreement* or *interjudge reliability.*

In general, a well-constructed, objectively scored test of ability should have a reliability coefficient of .90 or greater. For personality tests and subjective judgments, reliability coefficients of .70 can sometimes be satisfactory for research purposes, but inferences about particular individuals must be made with great caution. But as noted earlier, the reliability of a test's total score increases as the number of reliable items on the test increases. One can apply the same reasoning to subjective judgments and increase the reliability of the method by adding more judges, raters, or observers. For example, if ratings by two observers correlate only .50, the researcher can add a third, comparable observer and thereby raise the interjudge reliability of their summed ratings to .75; adding a fourth rater would raise the reliability to .80.

Validity   Reliability assesses the degree to which a test is measuring something, but high reliability does not guarantee that the test is **valid,** that is, that it *measures what it is intended to measure.* For example, if the final examination in your psychology course contained especially difficult vocabulary words or trick questions, it might be a test of your verbal ability or test sophistication rather than of the material learned in the course. Such an examination might be reliable—students would achieve about the same scores on a retest, and the separate items might all be measuring the same thing—but it would not be a valid test of achievement for the course.

In some instances the validity of a test can be assessed by correlating the test score with some external criterion. This correlation is called a validity coefficient. For example, the relatively strong positive correlation between scores on the SAT and freshman grades in college indicates that the test has reasonable validity. This kind of validity is called *criterion* or *empirical validity.* Because of sensitivity to race and sex discrimination, the courts are increasingly requiring companies and government agencies that use tests for personnel selection to provide evidence that those tests correlate with on-the-job performance—in other words, that they have criterion or empirical validity.

A special kind of validity, which applies especially to tests used in personality research, is called *construct validity.* If a researcher is designing a test to measure some concept or construct that is part of a theory, it is not always possible to compute a single coefficient that would indicate its criterion validity because it is not clear what the external criterion should be. How, for example, should a researcher assess the validity of a test for achievement motivation? One can think of a number of possibilities. The test could be given to business executives to see if it correlates with their salaries. Perhaps the test will correlate with teachers' ratings of their students' ambitiousness. The problem is that there is no single criterion that the researcher is willing to accept as the ultimate "true" answer. It would be reassuring if the test correlated with executive salaries, but if it did not, the researcher would not be willing to judge the test to be invalid. This is known as the "criterion problem" in personality psychology: There is no measure of "truth" against which to validate the test. Accordingly, the researcher attempts instead to establish its construct validity.

This is done through the research process itself. The researcher uses his or her theory both to construct the test and to generate predictions from the theory. Studies using the test are then conducted to test those predictions. To the extent that the results of several converging studies confirm the theory's predictions, both the theory and the test are validated simultaneously. Most often, mixed results suggest ways in which both the theory and the test need to be modified. For example, McClelland (1987) proposed a theory of achievement motivation that was supposed to identify and explain ambitious, high-achieving individuals in any area of activity. A test for assessing achievement motivation was designed and used to test predictions from the theory. Results from several studies indicated that the predictions were confirmed for men involved in entrepreneurial activities but not for women or for individuals involved in other kinds of activities, such as academic research. Accordingly, the theory was modified to apply primarily to entrepreneurial achievement, and the test was modified so that it was more valid for women.

Assessment of Intellectual Abilities

The first attempt to develop tests of intellectual ability was made a century ago by Sir Francis Galton. A naturalist and mathematician, Galton developed an interest in individual differences after considering the evolutionary theory proposed by his cousin, Charles Darwin. Galton believed that certain families are biologically superior to others— that is, that some people are innately stronger or smarter than others. Intelligence, he reasoned, is a question of exceptional sensory and perceptual skills, which are passed from one generation to the next. Because all information is acquired through the senses, the more sensitive and accurate an individual's perceptual apparatus, the more intelligent the person. (Galton's belief in the heritability of intelligence led him to propose that the human race's mental capacities could be enhanced through eugenics, or selective breeding. Fortunately, he is remembered more for his application of statistics to the study of intelligence than for his espousal of eugenics.)

In 1884, Galton administered a battery of tests (measuring variables such as head size, reaction time, visual acuity, auditory thresholds, and memory for visual forms) to more than 9,000 visitors at the London Exhibition. To his disappointment, he discovered that eminent British scientists could not be distinguished from ordinary citizens on the basis of their head size and that measurements such as reaction time were not related to other measures of intelligence. Although his test did not prove very useful, Galton did invent the correlation coefficient, which—as we have already seen—plays an important role in psychology.

The first tests resembling modern intelligence tests were devised by the French psychologist Alfred Binet in the late nineteenth century. In 1881, the French government passed a law making school attendance compulsory for all children. Previously, slow learners had usually been kept at home; now teachers had to cope with a wide range of individual differences. The government asked Binet to create a test that would detect children who were too slow intellectually to benefit from a regular school curriculum.

Binet assumed that intelligence should be measured by tasks that required reasoning and problem-solving abilities rather than perceptual-motor skills. In collaboration with another French psychologist, Théophile Simon, Binet published such a test in 1905, revising it in 1908 and again in 1911.

Binet reasoned that a slow or dull child was like a normal child whose mental growth was retarded. On tests, the slow child would perform like a younger normal child, whereas the mental abilities of a bright child were characteristic of older children. Binet devised a scale of test items of increasing difficulty that measured the kinds of changes in intelligence ordinarily associated with growing older. The higher a child could go on the scale in answering items correctly, the higher his or her *mental age* (MA). The concept of mental age was critical to Binet's method; using this method, one could compare the MA of a child with his or her *chronological age* (CA) as determined by date of birth.

The Stanford-Binet Intelligence Scale   The test items originally developed by Binet were adapted for American schoolchildren by Lewis Terman at Stanford University. Terman standardized the administration of the test and developed age-level norms by giving the test to thousands of children of various ages. In 1916 he published the Stanford revision of the Binet tests, now referred to as the *Stanford-Binet Intelligence Scale;* it was revised in 1937, 1960, 1972, and most recently in 1986. Despite its age, the Stanford-Binet is still one of the most frequently used psychological tests.

Terman retained Binet's concept of mental age. Each test item was age-graded at the level at which a substantial majority of the children pass it. A child's mental age could be obtained by summing the number of items passed at each level. In addition, Terman adopted a convenient index of intelligence suggested by the German psychologist William Stern. This index is the **intelligence quotient (IQ),** which expresses intelligence as *a ratio of mental age to chronological age:*

$$IQ = MA/CA \times 100$$

The number 100 is used as a multiplier so that the IQ will have a value of 100 when MA

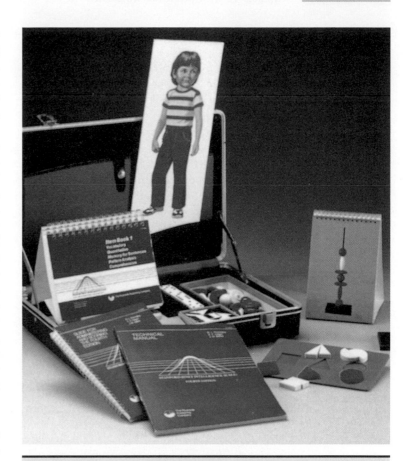

Test materials from the 1986 Stanford-Binet Intelligence Scale.

is equal to CA. If MA is lower than CA, the IQ will be less than 100; if MA is higher than CA, the IQ will be more than 100.

The most recent revision of the Stanford-Binet uses *standard age scores* instead of IQ scores. These can be interpreted in terms of percentiles, which show the percentage of individuals in the standardization group falling above or below a given score (Thorndike, Hagen, & Sattler, 1986). And although the concept of IQ is still used in intelligence testing, it is no longer actually calculated using this equation. Instead, tables are used to convert raw scores on the test into standard scores that are adjusted so that the mean at each age equals 100.

In line with the current view of intelligence as a composite of different abilities, the 1986 revision of the Stanford-Binet groups its tests into four broad areas: verbal reasoning, abstract/visual reasoning, quantitative reasoning, and short-term memory (Sattler, 1988). A separate score is obtained for each area. Table 12-2 gives some examples of items, grouped by area.

The Wechsler Intelligence Scales In 1939, David Wechsler developed a new test because he thought the Stanford-Binet depended too heavily on language ability and was not appropriate for adults. The *Wechsler Adult Intelligence Scale,* or WAIS (1939, 1955, 1981), is divided into two parts—a verbal scale and a performance scale—that yield separate scores as well as a full-scale IQ. The test items are described in Table 12-3. Wechsler later developed a similar test for children, the *Wechsler Intelligence Scale for Children* (WISC) (1958, 1974, 1991).

Items on the performance scale require the manipulation or arrangement of blocks, pictures, or other materials. The Wechsler scales also provide scores for each subtest, so the examiner has a clearer picture of the individual's intellectual strengths and weaknesses. For example, a discrepancy between verbal and performance scores prompts the examiner to look for specific learning problems such as reading disabilities or language handicaps.

Both the Stanford-Binet and the Wechsler scales show good reliability and validity. They have test-retest reliabilities of about .90, and both are fairly valid predictors of achievement in school, with validity coefficients of about .50 (Sattler, 1988).

Group Ability Tests The Stanford-Binet and the Wechsler scales are individual ability tests; that is, they are administered to a single individual by a specially trained tester.

TABLE 12-2

Items From the Stanford-Binet Intelligence Scale   *Typical examples of items from the 1986 Stanford-Binet Intelligence Scale for a 6- to 8-year-old.*

Verbal Reasoning	
Vocabulary	Defines words, such as "dollar" and "envelope."
Comprehension	Answers questions, such as "Where do people buy food?" and "Why do people comb their hair?"
Absurdities	Identifies the "funny" aspect of a picture, such as a girl riding a bicycle on a lake or a bald man combing his hair.
Verbal Relations	Tells how the first three items in a sequence are alike and how they differ from the fourth: scarf, tie, muffler, shirt.
Quantitative Reasoning	
Quantitative	Performs simple arithmetic tasks, such as selecting a die with six spots because the number of spots equals the combination of a two-spot die and a four-spot die.
Number Series	Gives the next two numbers in a series, such as 20 16 12 8 ___ ___.
Equation Building	Builds an equation from the following array: 2 3 5 + =. One correct response would be $2 + 3 = 5$.
Abstract/Visual Reasoning	
Pattern Analysis	Copies a simple design with blocks.
Copying	Copies a geometrical drawing demonstrated by the examiner, such as a rectangle intersected by two diagonals.
Short-Term Memory	
Bead Memory	Shown a picture of different-shaped beads stacked on a stick. Reproduces the sequence from memory by placing real beads on a stick.
Memory for Sentences	Repeats after the examiner sentences such as "It is time to go to sleep" and "Ken painted a picture for his mother's birthday."
Memory for Digits	Repeats after examiner a series of digits, such as 5-7-8-3, forward and backward.
Memory for Objects	Shown pictures of individual objects, such as a clock and an elephant, one at a time. Identifies the objects in the correct order of their appearance in a picture that also includes extraneous objects; for example, a bus, a clown, an *elephant,* eggs, and a *clock.*

TABLE 12-3

Tests Composing the Wechsler Adult Intelligence Scale *The tests of the Wechsler Intelligence Scale for Children are similar, with some modifications.*

Test	Description
Verbal Scale	
Information	Questions tap a general range of information; for example, "What is the capital of Italy?"
Comprehension	Tests practical information and ability to evaluate past experience; for example, "Why do we put stamps on a letter to be mailed?"
Arithmetic	Verbal problems testing arithmetic reasoning.
Similarities	Asks in what way two objects or concepts (for example, *recipe* and *map*) are similar; assesses abstract thinking
Digit Span	A series of digits presented auditorily (for example, 7-5-6-3-8) is repeated in a forward or backward direction; tests attention and rote memory.
Vocabulary	Assesses word knowledge
Letter Number Sequencing	Orally presented letters and numbers presented in a mixed-up order must be reordered and repeated, first with the numbers in ascending order and then with the letters in alphabetical order; assesses working memory.
Performance Scale	
Digit Symbol	A timed coding task in which numbers must be associated with marks of various shapes; assesses speed of learning and writing.
Picture Completion	The missing part of an incompletely drawn picture must be discovered and named; assesses visual alertness, visual memory, and perceptual organization.
Block Design	Pictured designs must be copied with blocks; assesses ability to perceive and analyze patterns.
Picture Arrangement	A series of comic-strip pictures must be arranged in the right sequence to tell a story; assesses understanding of social situations.
Matrix Reasoning	A geometric shape that is similar in some way to a sample shape must be selected from a set of possible alternatives; assesses perceptual organization.
Object Assembly	Puzzle pieces must be assembled to form a complete object; assesses ability to deal with part-whole relationships.
Symbol Search	A series of paired groups of symbols are presented, a target group of two symbols and a search group. Examinee must determine if either target symbol appears in the search group; assesses processing speed.

Group ability tests, in contrast, can be administered to a large number of people by a single examiner and are usually in pencil-and-paper form.

The Scholastic Assessment Test and the American College Test (ACT) are examples of group-administered, general-ability tests that are familiar to most college students in the United States. Virtually all four-year colleges require applicants to take one of these tests as a way of setting a common standard for students from high schools with different curricula and grading standards. The SAT underwent a major revision in 1994 and now includes an essay section and open-ended

(rather than multiple-choice) mathematics questions, among other changes. These changes were made in response to recent high school curriculum trends that place a premium on more sophisticated reading, writing, and mathematics skills.

Correlations between SAT scores and freshman grade point averages vary across studies, with a median correlation of about .38 for the verbal section of the SAT and .34 for the mathematics section (Linn, 1982). When these correlations are corrected for the fact that many students with very low scores do not end up attending college (and hence cannot be included in the calculation of the validity correlation), the resulting correlations are about .50. This means that about 44% of students in the top fifth of the distribution of SAT scores will also be in the top fifth of the distribution of freshman grade point averages, compared with only 4% of students in the bottom fifth of the SAT score distribution. Thus, SAT scores improve prediction considerably, but it is also clear that the freshman grades of students with identical SAT scores will vary widely.

The Factorial Approach Some psychologists view intelligence as a general capacity for comprehension and reasoning that manifests itself in various ways. This was Binet's assumption. Although his test contained many kinds of items, Binet observed that a bright child tended to score higher than dull children on all of them. He assumed, therefore, that the different tasks sampled a basic underlying ability. Similarly, despite the diverse subscales included the WAIS, Wechsler also believed that "intelligence is the aggregate or global capacity of the individual to act purposefully, to think rationally, and

to deal effectively with his environment" (Wechsler, 1958).

Other psychologists, however, question whether there is such a thing as "general intelligence." They believe that intelligence tests sample a number of mental abilities that are relatively independent of one another. One method of obtaining more precise information about the kinds of abilities that determine performance on intelligence tests is *factor analysis,* a statistical technique that examines the intercorrelations among a number of tests and, by grouping those that are most highly correlated, reduces them to a smaller number of independent dimensions, called *factors.* The basic idea is that two tests that correlate very highly with each other are probably measuring the same underlying ability. The goal is to discover the minimum number of factors, or abilities, required to explain the observed pattern of correlations among an array of different tests.

It was the originator of factor analysis, Charles Spearman (1904), who first proposed that all individuals possess a *general intelligence factor* (called *g*) in varying amounts.

Scores on the Scholastic Aptitude Test are used to predict academic achievement in college. The correlation between SAT scores and freshman grade point averages is about .50.

A person could be described as generally bright or generally dull, depending on the amount of g he or she possessed. According to Spearman, the g factor is the major determinant of performance on intelligence tests. In addition, *special factors*, each called s, are specific to particular abilities or tests. For example, tests of arithmetic or spatial relationships would each tap a separate s. An individual's tested intelligence would reflect the amount of g plus the magnitude of the various s factors possessed by that individual. Performance in mathematics, for example, would be a function of a person's general intelligence and mathematical aptitude.

A later investigator, Louis Thurstone (1938), objected to Spearman's emphasis on general intelligence, suggesting instead that intelligence can be broken down into a number of primary abilities using factor analysis. After many rounds of administering tests, factor analyzing the results, purifying the scales, and retesting, Thurstone identified seven factors, which he used to construct his *Test of Primary Mental Abilities.*

Revised versions of this test are still widely used, but its predictive power is no greater than that of general intelligence tests such as the Wechsler scales. Thurstone's hope of discovering the basic elements of intelligence through factor analysis was not fully realized, for several reasons. For one, his primary abilities are not completely independent; indeed, the significant intercorrelations among them provide support for the concept of a general intelligence factor underlying the specific abilities. For another, the number of basic abilities identified by factor analysis depends on the nature of the test items. Other investigators, using different test items and alternative methods of factor analysis, have identified from 20 to 150 factors representing the range of intellectual abilities (Ekstrom, French, & Harman, 1979; Ekstrom, French, Harman, & Derman, 1976; Guilford, 1982).

This lack of consistency in number and kinds of factors raises doubts about the value of the factorial approach. Nevertheless, factor analysis remains an important technique for studying intellectual performance (Carroll, 1993; Comrey & Lee, 1992), and we will encounter it again when we discuss personality traits.

Assessment of Personality

Personality can be defined as *the distinctive and characteristic patterns of thought, emotion, and behavior that define an individual's personal style of interacting with the physical and social environment.* When we are asked to describe an individual's personality, we are likely to use terms referring to personality traits—adjectives such as intelligent, extraverted, conscientious, and so forth. Personality psychologists have attempted to devise formal methods for describing and measuring personality; these go beyond our everyday use of trait terms in three ways. First, they seek to reduce the potential set of trait terms to a manageable set that will still encompass the diversity of human personality. Second, they attempt to ensure that their instruments for measuring personality traits are reliable and valid. Finally, they do empirical research to discover the relationships among traits and between traits and specific behaviors.

One way to begin the task of deriving a comprehensive but manageable number of traits is to consult a dictionary. It is assumed that through the process of linguistic evolution a language will encode most, if not all, of the important distinctions among individuals that make a difference in everyday life. Language embodies the accumulated experience of the culture, and the dictionary is the written record of that experience. In the 1930s two personality psychologists actually undertook this task. They found approximately 18,000 words that refer to characteristics of behavior—nearly 5% of all the words in the dictionary! Next, they reduced the list to about 4,500 terms by eliminating obscure words and synonyms. Finally, they organized the list into psychologically meaningful subsets (Allport & Odbert, 1936).

Subsequent researchers have used such trait terms to obtain personality ratings of individuals. Peers who know an individual well are asked to rate him or her on a scale for each trait. For example, a rater might be asked to rate the person on the trait of friendliness, using a seven-point scale ranging from "not at all friendly" to "very friendly." Often such scales are labeled at the two ends with opposite traits—for example, "domineering-submissive" or "conscientious-unreliable." Individuals can also be asked to rate themselves on the scales.

Raymond Cattell (1966; 1957) condensed the Allport-Odbert list to under 200 traits and obtained both peer and self-ratings for each trait. He then used factor analysis to determine how many underlying personality factors could account for the pattern of correlations among the trait ratings. His analysis yielded 16 factors. A similar procedure was used by the British psychologist Hans Eysenck to arrive at two personality factors: introversion-extraversion and emotional instability-stability, which he calls neuroticism (Eysenck, 1953); he has since added a third. Introversion-extraversion refers to the degree to which a person's basic orientation is turned inward toward the self or outward toward the external world. At the introversion end of the

scale are individuals who are shy and prefer to work alone; they tend to withdraw into themselves, particularly in times of emotional stress or conflict. At the extraversion end are individuals who are sociable and prefer occupations that permit them to work directly with other people; in times of stress, they seek company. Neuroticism (instability-stability) is a dimension of emotionality, with moody, anxious, temperamental, and maladjusted individuals at the neurotic or unstable end, and calm, well-adjusted individuals at the other. Figure 12-1 shows how these two dimensions combine to organize a number of subtraits that are correlated with the factors.

How many basic personality factors are there? Even with a rigorous analytic procedure like factor analysis, there is no definitive answer. Whereas Cattell arrived at 16 factors, Eysenck arrived at only two (or, now, three). Other investigators have come up with different numbers. We encountered a similar situation earlier when we noted that the number of factors defining the concept of intelligence could be one (Spearman's general intelligence factor, *g*), seven (Thurstone's primary mental abilities), or as many as 150 (Guilford, 1982).

Some of the discrepancy occurs because different traits are initially put into the analysis; some occurs because different types of data are being analyzed (for example, peer ratings versus self-ratings); and some occurs because different factor analytic methods are employed. But much of the disagreement is a matter of taste. A researcher who prefers a more differentiated or fine-grained description of personality will set a lower criterion for a factor and thus accept more factors, arguing that important distinctions would be lost if the factors were further merged. Another researcher, like Eysenck, will prefer to merge several lower-level factors into more general ones, arguing that the resulting factors will be more stable (that is, more likely to reemerge in other analyses). For example, when Cattell's 16 factors are factor analyzed, Eysenck's two factors emerge as superfactors. One can therefore think of a hierarchy of traits in which each broad general trait is composed of several subordinate, narrower traits.

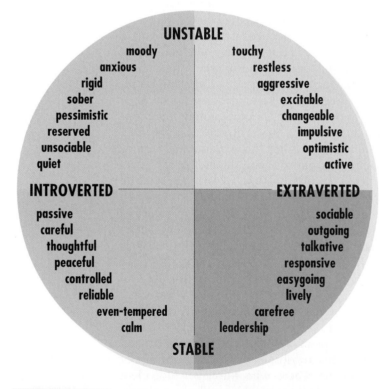

FIGURE 12-1

Eysenck's Personality Factors *This figure shows the two major factors that emerge from factor-analytic studies of the intercorrelations between traits by Eysenck and others. The Stable-Unstable axis defines the neuroticism factor; the Introverted-Extraverted axis defines the extraversion factor. The other terms around the circle indicate where other traits are placed with respect to these two factors. (After Eysenck & Rachman, 1965)*

Despite these disagreements, a consensus is emerging among many trait researchers that five trait dimensions may provide the best compromise (John, 1990). Although the five factors—now called the "Big Five"—were originally identified through a factor analysis of the Allport-Odbert trait list (Norman, 1963), the same five have emerged from a wide variety of personality tests (Digman & Inouye, 1986; McCrae & Costa, 1987). There is still disagreement about how best to name and interpret the factors, but one reasonable way to summarize them is with the acronym OCEAN: Openness to experience, Conscientiousness, Extraversion, Agreeableness, and Neuroticism. Table 12-4 displays some representative examples of the trait scales that characterize each of the five factors. Many personality psychologists consider the discovery and validation of the Big Five to be one of the major breakthroughs of contemporary personality psychology.

Personality Inventories Most personality tests do not actually ask individuals to directly rate themselves on personality trait dimensions. Instead, individuals are asked a set of questions about how they react in certain situations. For example, they might be asked to indicate how much they agree or disagree with the statement "I often try new and foreign foods" or "I really like most people I meet." Such questionnaires—called **personality inventories**—resemble structured interviews in that they ask the same questions of each person, and the answers are usually given in a form that can be easily scored, often by computer. Each item on a personality inventory is composed to exemplify a particular personality trait, and subsets of similar items are summed to give the individual a score on each trait scale. For example, the item "I often try new and foreign foods" is on the Openness to experience scale of one inventory designed to measure the Big Five; the item "I really like most people I meet" is on the Extraversion scale.

Items on most personality inventories are initially composed according to the developer's theory of each trait and then retained or discarded from the final inventory, depending on whether they correlate

TABLE 12-4

Five Trait Factors *This table presents five trait factors that reliably emerge when a wide variety of assessment instruments are factor analyzed. The adjective pairs are examples of trait scales that characterize each of the factors.* (After McCrae & Costa, 1987)

Trait Factor	Representative Trait Scales
Openness	Conventional-Original
	Unadventurous-Daring
	Conservative-Liberal
Conscientiousness	Careless-Careful
	Undependable-Reliable
	Negligent-Conscientious
Extraversion	Retiring-Sociable
	Quiet-Talkative
	Inhibited-Spontaneous
Agreeableness	Irritable-Good natured
	Ruthless-Soft hearted
	Selfish-Selfless
Neuroticism	Calm-Worrying
	Hardy-Vulnerable
	Secure-Insecure

or fail to correlate with other items on the same scale. Often a large number of trial items are placed on a preliminary form of the inventory, which is administered to a large number of people. Their responses are then factor-analyzed to determine which subsets of items intercorrelate and whether these subsets actually belong to the trait scale for which they were originally devised.

A very different method of test construction, called the *criterion-keyed method* or *empirical construction,* was used to develop one of the most popular of all personality inventories, the *Minnesota Multiphasic Personality Inventory* (MMPI). The original MMPI was developed to provide a pencil-and-paper version of a psychiatric interview (Hathaway & McKinley, 1943). It consists of more than 550 statements concerning attitudes, emotional reactions, physical and psychological symptoms, and experiences. The test taker responds to each statement by answering "true," "false," or "cannot say."

Here are four representative items:

- I have never done anything dangerous for the thrill of it.
- I daydream very little.
- My mother or father often made me obey, even when I thought it was unreasonable.
- At times my thoughts have raced ahead faster than I could speak them.

Instead of formulating items on the basis of a theory, designers of the MMPI gave hundreds of test items like these to groups of individuals. Each group was known to differ from the norm on a particular criterion. For example, to develop a scale of items that distinguish between paranoid and normal individuals, the same questions were given to two groups. The criterion group consisted of individuals who had been hospitalized with the diagnosis of paranoid disorder; the control group consisted of people who were similar to the criterion group in age, sex, socioeconomic status, and other important variables but had never been diagnosed as having psychiatric problems. Only the questions that discriminated between the

psychiatric group and the control group were retained on the inventory. Questions that at face value might seem to distinguish normal from paranoid individuals (for instance, "I think that most people would lie to get ahead") may or may not do so when put to an empirical test. In fact, patients diagnosed as paranoid were significantly less likely to respond "true" to this statement than were normal individuals. On the final test, the responses to each item are scored according to the extent to which they correspond to answers given by the different criterion groups.

The MMPI was the first major inventory to incorporate a number of *validity scales* within it. These are scales that attempt to determine whether the person has answered the test items carefully and honestly. If an individual's scores on any of these scales is too high, his or her scores on the content scales must be interpreted with particular caution or disregarded altogether. These scales have been helpful but not completely successful at detecting invalid scores. Table 12-5 lists the 3 validity and 10 content scales usually scored on the MMPI.

TABLE 12-5

MMPI Scales *The first three scales are "validity" scales, which help determine whether the person has answered the test items carefully and honestly. For example, the F (Frequency) scale measures the degree to which infrequent or atypical answers are given. A high score on this scale usually indicates that the individual was careless or confused in responding. (However, high F scores often accompany high scores on the Schizophrenia scale, which measures bizarre thinking.) The remaining "clinical" scales were originally named for categories of psychiatric disorders, but interpretation now emphasizes personality attributes rather than diagnostic categories.*

Scale Name	Scale Abbreviation	Interpretation of High Scores
Lie	L	Denial of common frailties
Frequency	F	Invalidity of profile
Correction	K	Defensive, evasive
Hypochondriasis	Hs	Emphasis on physical complaints
Depression	D	Unhappy, depressed
Hysteria	Hy	Reacts to stress by denying problems
Psychopathic Deviancy	Pd	Lack of social conformity; often in trouble with the law
Masculinity-Femininity	Mf	Feminine orientation (males); masculine orientation (females)
Paranoia	Pa	Suspicious
Psychoasthenia	Pt	Worried, anxious
Schizophrenia	Sc	Withdrawn, bizarre thinking
Hypomania	Ma	Impulsive, excitable
Social Introversion-Extraversion	Si	Introverted, shy

Because the MMPI is derived from differences between criterion and control groups, it does not really matter whether what the person says is true. What is important is the fact that he or she says it. If schizophrenics answer "true" and control participants answer "false" to the statement "My mother never loved me," their answers distinguish the two groups regardless of how their mothers actually behaved. This is an advantage of a test based on the criterion-keyed method over one based on a test constructor's assumption that certain answers indicate specific personality traits. The disadvantage is that one does not really have a theoretical understanding of the connection between the test responses and the personality characteristics they identify.

The MMPI, published in 1943, is based on research that began in 1939. There are now more than 8,000 published studies on the MMPI, and it has been translated into at least 15 languages. There are even several private companies that provide computer-based scoring and interpretation of the inventory.

Over the years the MMPI has been criticized for the weak reliability and validity of some of its scales. It also became evident that the original inventory was getting out of date and should be revised. But the enormous amount of existing data on the original version discouraged most researchers from undertaking such a daunting task. Nevertheless, it has been done. The MMPI-2, published in 1989, incorporates a number of significant revisions while maintaining the basic features of the original, including most of the original items. The new standardization involves a much larger and more diversified sampling that is more representative of the U.S. population (Graham, 1990). The difficult job of assessing the comparability of scores between the new and original versions is now under way.

The MMPI has been most valuable in distinguishing in a general way between abnormal and normal populations and can be used to evaluate the overall severity of a particular individual's disturbance (Meehl & Dahlstrom, 1960). It is less successful, however, in making finer distinctions among various forms of psychopathology (Kleinmuntz, 1985).

Although the MMPI was originally designed to identify people with serious personality disorders, it has been widely used to study normal populations. But because it does not adequately sample some of the traits that are useful in describing the normal personality, the *California Psychological Inventory* (CPI) was devised. The CPI uses many of the same items as the MMPI. Its scales measure such traits as dominance, sociability, self-acceptance, responsibility, and socialization. The comparison groups for some of the scales were obtained by asking high-school and college students to identify classmates whom they would rate high or low on the trait in question. Thus, for the dominance scale, the criterion group consisted of students who were described by their peers as high in dominance (aggressive, confident, self-reliant) and the control group consisted of students who were described by their peers as low in dominance (retiring, lacking in self-confidence, inhibited). Items that revealed a statistically significant difference between the criterion group and the control group formed the dominance scale. The CPI is still one of the most widely validated personality inventories available for use with normal populations (Megargee, 1972).

The Q Sort   A special method for measuring personality traits is called the *Q sort* (The *Q* was chosen arbitrarily and has no particular meaning). In this method, a rater or sorter describes an individual's personality by sorting a set of approximately 100 cards into piles. Each card contains a personality statement (for example, "Has a wide range of interests" and "Is self-defeating"). The rater sorts the cards into nine piles, placing the cards that are least descriptive of the individual in pile one on the left and those that are most descriptive in pile nine on the right. The other cards are distributed in the intermediate piles, with those that seem neither characteristic nor uncharacteristic of the individual going into the middle pile (pile five). Thus, each *Q* item receives a score ranging from one to nine, with higher numbers indicating that the item is more characteristic of the person. (Some *Q* sorts use fewer or more than nine piles, but the technique is the same.)

At first glance, this would seem no different from asking raters to rate an individual on a set of traits, using a nine-point rating

FRONTIERS OF PSYCHOLOGICAL RESEARCH

Studying Personality the Long Way

Only investigators with a strong ability to delay gratification or an unselfish devotion to science undertake longitudinal studies. For studies designed to span many years, the original investigators may not even be around to reap the final rewards; their studies may outlive them. Other practical reasons also deter most would-be investigators. Longitudinal studies are expensive, and funding cannot usually be guaranteed over the required time interval. Second, participants who start out in the study move away, die, decide to discontinue their participation, or cannot otherwise be located for follow-up. In general, the administrative tasks involved in conducting such a study take as much time and effort as collecting the data. For these reasons, many longitudinal studies are conducted under the auspices of research institutes rather than by independent investigators.

In addition to the practical problems, there is a more substantive problem that arises in many long-term longitudinal studies. As the interests of the field change over time, the kinds of data collected in a longitudinal study also change. A study that begins with a focus on academic achievement may fail to gather personality information that later investiga-

tors wish to have. Sometimes assessment methods used early in the study become obsolete and are discarded and replaced by better ones as the study progresses. All of these factors make it difficult to compare later observations with earlier ones.

This was the major problem with two studies that were conducted at the Institute of Human Development (IHD) in Berkeley. Investigators began the Berkeley Guidance Study in 1929 by contacting the parents of every third baby born in Berkeley over an 18-month period and asking them to enroll their newborns in the study; in all, 248 infants and their families were included. The Oakland Growth Study began in 1932 with 212 fifth-grade children in Oakland, California. The children from both samples were studied intensively through adolescence and were interviewed again on several occasions during adulthood. Not only were noncomparable measurements made at different times, but the two studies were themselves not comparable to each other in many ways. These problems were elegantly solved by Jack Block, who used the Q-sort method of personality description to standardize the data (Block, 1961/1978; Block, 1971).

In the Q-sort method a rater (sorter) is given a set of cards, each containing a personality statement (for example, "Is cheerful"), and is asked to describe an individual's personality by sorting the cards into piles. The rater places statements that are least descriptive of the individual in pile one on the left and those that are most descriptive in pile nine on the right. The other statements are distributed in the intermediate piles, thereby assigning each Q item a score ranging from one to nine. In the IHD studies, all the data on a single individual from the junior-high years were placed into a single folder. Two to four clinical psychologists independently examined the folder and prepared Q-sort descriptions of the individual. A different set of sorters did the same thing for the data gathered during the senior high period. And finally, the interviewers and independent clinicians prepared Q-sort descriptions of the individuals when they were interviewed as adults in 1960, 1970, and 1980. This procedure thus converted a bewildering variety of data into a set of independent but standardized personality descriptions on each subject at different ages that could be directly compared with one another.

scale. And in fact, the item scores can be used in this way if the researcher wishes. But there is an important difference. When filling out rating scales, the rater is implicitly comparing the individual with others (for example, a rating of "very friendly" implies that the individual is very friendly compared with other individuals). When performing a Q sort, however, the rater is explicitly comparing each trait with other traits within the same individual (for example, placing the item "friendly" in pile nine implies that, compared with other traits, friendliness

stands out as particularly descriptive of the individual).

Researchers can compare two Q sorts by computing the correlation between them, thereby assessing the degree to which two individuals are similar to one another in their overall personality configurations. If the two Q sorts are descriptions of the same individual at two different times, the correlation assesses the test-retest reliability of the Q sort, or the continuity of the individual's overall personality profile over time. If two Q sorts are descriptions of a single individual made by two raters, the correlation assesses the interjudge reliability of the Q sort, or the degree to which two people perceive the individual in the same way. (For example, in marital counseling, it could be helpful to assess the degree to which two spouses agree or disagree in their perceptions of each other.) Finally, if one of the Q sorts is a description of a hypothetical personality type, the correlation between an individual's Q sort and the hypothetical sort assesses the degree to which the person is similar to that personality type. For example, one researcher asked clinical psychologists to construct Q sorts of the hypothetical "optimally adjusted personality." The correlation between a person's Q sort and this hypothetical sort can be directly interpreted as an adjustment score (Block 1961/1978, 1971).

An innovative use of the Q sort is discussed in the Frontiers of Psychological Research feature. We will see further examples of personality testing methods in Chapter 13, where we discuss theories of personality. In the rest of this chapter we return to the subject of intelligence, examining some recent theories that embody a new approach to the study of intelligence.

Recent Theories of Intelligence

Until the 1960s, research on intelligence was dominated by the factorial approach. However, with the development of cognitive psychology and its emphasis on information-processing models (see Chapter 9), a new approach emerged. This approach is defined somewhat differently by different investigators, but the basic idea is to try to understand intelligence in terms of the cognitive processes that operate when we engage in intellectual activities (Carpenter, Just, & Shell, 1990; Hunt, 1990). The *information-processing approach* asks:

1. What mental processes are involved in the various tests of intelligence?

2. How rapidly and accurately are these processes carried out?

3. What types of mental representations of information do these processes act upon?

Rather than trying to explain intelligence in terms of factors, this approach attempts to identify the mental processes that underlie intelligent behavior. It assumes that individual differences on a given task depend on the specific processes that different individuals bring into play and the speed and accuracy of those processes. The goal is to use an information-processing model of a particular task to identify appropriate measures of the processes used in performing the task. These measures may be as simple as the response to a multiple-choice item, or they may include response speed or the eye movements associated with the response. The idea is to use whatever information is needed to estimate the efficiency of each component process.

Gardner's Theory of Multiple Intelligences

Howard Gardner (1993a) developed his theory of multiple intelligences as a direct challenge to what he calls the "classical" view of intelligence as a capacity for logical reasoning. Gardner was struck by the variety of adult roles in different cultures, roles that depend on a variety of skills and abilities yet are equally important to successful functioning in those cultures. His observations led him to conclude that there is not just one underlying mental capacity, or "g," but a variety of intelligences that work in combination. He defines an intelligence as the "ability to solve problems or fashion products that are of consequence in a particular cultural setting or community" (1993b, p. 15). It is these multiple intelligences that enable human beings to take on such diverse roles as physicist, farmer, shaman, and dancer (Gardner, 1993a).

Gardner is quick to point out that an intelligence is not a "thing," some sort of commodity inside the head, but "a potential, the presence of which allows an individual access to forms of thinking appropriate to specific kinds of content" (Kornhaber & Gardner, 1991, p. 155). He believes that there are seven distinct kinds of intelligence that are independent of one another, each operating as a separate system (or module) in the brain according to its own rules. These are (a) linguistic, (b) musical, (c) logical-mathematical, (d) spatial,

(e) bodily-kinesthetic, (f) intrapersonal, and (g) interpersonal. These are described more fully in Table 12-6.

Gardner analyzes each kind of intelligence from several viewpoints: the cognitive operations involved, the appearance of prodigies and other exceptional individuals, evidence from cases of brain damage, manifestations in different cultures, and the possible course of evolutionary development. For example, certain kinds of brain damage can impair one type of intelligence and have no effect on the others. He notes that the capacities of adults in different cultures represent different *combinations* of the various intelligences. While all normal people can apply all of the intelligences to some extent, each individual is characterized by a unique combination of relatively stronger and weaker intelligences (Walters & Gardner, 1985), which help account for individual differences.

As noted earlier, conventional IQ tests are good predictors of college grades, but they are less valid for predicting later job success or career advancement. Measures of other abilities, such as interpersonal intelligence, may help explain why some people with brilliant college records fail miserably in later life while lesser students become charismatic leaders (Kornhaber, Krechevsky, & Gardner, 1990). Gardner and colleagues therefore call for "intelligence-fair" assessments in schools. These would allow children to demonstrate their abilities by other means besides paper-and-pencil tests, such as putting together gears to demonstrate spatial skills.

Anderson's Theory of Intelligence and Cognitive Development

One criticism of Gardner's theory is that high levels of ability in any of the various intelligences is usually correlated with high ability in the others; that is, no specific intellectual capacity is wholly distinct from the others (Messick, 1992; Scarr, 1985). In addition, psychologist Mike Anderson points out that Gardner's multiple intelligences are ill-defined—they are "sometimes a behavior, sometimes a cognitive process, and sometimes a structure in the brain" (1992, p. 67). Anderson therefore has sought to develop a theory based on the idea of general intelligence proposed by Thurstone and others.

Anderson's theory holds that individual differences in intelligence and developmental changes in intellectual competence are explained by different mechanisms. Differences in intelligence result from differences in the "basic processing mechanism" that implements thinking, which in turn yields knowledge. Individuals vary in the speed at

---

TABLE 12-6

Gardner's Seven Intelligences (Adapted from Gardner, Kornhaber, & Wake, 1996)

1. **Linguistic Intelligence**   The capacity for speech, along with mechanisms dedicated to phonology (speech sounds), syntax (grammar), semantics (meaning), and pragmatics (implications and uses of language in various settings).

2. **Musical Intelligence**   The ability to create, communicate, and understand meanings made of sound, along with mechanisms dedicated to pitch, rhythm, and timbre (sound quality).

3. **Logical-Mathematical Intelligence**   The ability to use and appreciate relationships in the absence of action or objects—that is, to engage in abstract thought.

4. **Spatial Intelligence**   The ability to perceive visual or spatial information, modify it, and re-create visual images without reference to the original stimulus. Includes the capacity to construct images in three dimensions and to move and rotate those images.

5. **Bodily-Kinesthetic Intelligence**   The ability to use all or part of the body to solve problems or fashion products; includes control over fine and gross motor actions and the ability to manipulate external objects.

6. **Intrapersonal Intelligence**   The ability to distinguish among one's own feelings, intentions, and motivations.

7. **Interpersonal Intelligence**   The ability to recognize and make distinctions among other people's feelings, beliefs, and intentions.

According to Gardner's theory of multiple intelligences, these three individuals are displaying different kinds of intelligence: logical-mathematical, musical, and spatial.

which basic processing occurs. Thus, a person with a slower basic processing mechanism is likely to have greater difficulty acquiring knowledge than a person with a faster processing mechanism. This is equivalent to saying that a low-speed processing mechanism produces low general intelligence.

Anderson notes, however, that there are some cognitive mechanisms that show no individual differences. For example, people with Down syndrome may not be able to add 2 plus 2, yet can recognize that other people hold beliefs and may act on those beliefs (Anderson, 1992). The mechanisms that provide these universal capacities are "modules." Each module functions independently, performing complex computations. Modules are not affected by the basic processing mechanism; they are virtually automatic. According to Anderson, it is the maturation of new modules that explains the increase of cognitive abilities in the course

of development. For example, the maturation of a module devoted to language would explain the development of the ability to speak in complete sentences.

In addition to modules, according to Anderson, intelligence includes two "specific abilities." One of these deals with propositional thought (language mathematical expression) and the other with visual and spatial functioning. Anderson suggests that the tasks associated with these abilities are carried out by "specific processors." Unlike modules, which carry out very particular functions, each of the specific processors handles a broad class of problems or knowledge. Also unlike modules, specific processors are affected by the basic processing mechanism. A high-speed processing mechanism enables a person to make more effective use of the specific processors, scoring higher on tests and accomplishing more in the real world.

Anderson's theory of intelligence thus suggests two different "routes" to knowledge. The first involves the using the basic processing mechanism, operating through the specific processors, to acquire knowledge. In Anderson's view, this is what we mean by "thinking," and it accounts for individual differences in intelligence (which, in his view, are equivalent to differences in knowledge). The second route involves the use of modules to acquire knowledge. Module-based knowledge, such as perception of three-dimensional space, comes automatically if the module has matured sufficiently, and this accounts for the development of intelligence.

Anderson's theory can be illustrated by the case of a 21-year-old man known as MA who suffered convulsions as a child and was diagnosed as autistic. As an adult he could not talk and achieved very low scores on psychometric tests. However, he was found to have an IQ of 128 and had an extraordinary ability to detect prime numbers, doing so more accurately than a scientist with a degree in mathematics (Anderson, 1992). Anderson concludes that MA had an intact basic processing mechanism, which allowed him to think about abstract symbols, but had suffered damage to his linguistic modules, which hindered acquisition of everyday knowledge and communication.

Sternberg's Triarchic Theory

In contrast to Anderson's theory, Robert Sternberg's *triarchic theory* addresses experience and context as well as basic information-processing mechanisms. His theory has three parts or subtheories: the componential subtheory, which deals with thought processes; the experiential subtheory, which deals with the effects of experience on intelligence; and the contextual subtheory, which considers the effects of the individual's environment and culture (Sternberg, 1988). The most highly developed of these subtheories is the componential subtheory.

The componental theory considers the components of thought. Sternberg has identified three types of components:

1. Metacomponents, which are used to plan, control, monitor, and evaluate processing during problem solving.

2. Performance components, which carry out problem-solving strategies.

3. Knowledge-acquisition components, which encode, combine, and compare information during the course of problem solving.

These components are intertwined; each comes into play during the problem-solving process, and none of them can operate independently.

Sternberg illustrates the functioning of these components with analogy problems of the following kind:

lawyer is to *client* as *doctor* is to _____

(a) *medicine* (b) *patient*

A series of experiments with such problems led Sternberg to conclude that the critical components were the encoding process and the comparison process. The participant encodes each of the words in the analogy by forming a mental representation of the word—in this case, a list of attributes of the word that are retrieved from long-term memory. For example, a mental representation of the word "lawyer" might include the following attributes: college-educated, versed in legal procedures, represents clients in court, and so on. Once the participant has formed a mental representation for each word in the analogy, the comparison process scans the representations looking for matching attributes that solve the analogy.

Other processes are involved in analogy problems, but Sternberg has shown that individual differences on this task are determined primarily by the efficiency of the encoding and comparison processes. The experimental evidence shows that individuals who score high on analogy problems (skilled performers) spend more time encoding and form more accurate mental representations than do individuals who score low on such problems (less-skilled performers). In contrast, during the comparison stage, the skilled performers are faster than the less-skilled performers in matching attributes, but both are equally accurate. Thus, the better test scores for skilled performers are based on the increased accuracy of their encoding process, but the time they require to solve the problem is a complicated mix of slow encoding speeds and fast comparisons (Galotti, 1989; Pellegrino, 1985).

The componential subtheory by itself does not provide a complete explanation of individual differences in intelligence. The experiential subtheory is needed in order to account for the role of experience in intelligent performance. According to Sternberg, differences in experience affect the ability to solve a given problem. A person who has not previously encountered a particular concept, such as a mathematical formula or an analogy problem, will have more difficulty applying that concept than someone who is experienced in the use of that concept. An individual's experience with a task or problem thus falls somewhere along a continuum that extends from totally novel to completely automatic (that is, totally familiar as a result of long experience).

Of course, a person's exposure to particular concepts depends to a large extent on the environment. This is where the contextual subtheory comes in. This subtheory is concerned with the cognitive activity needed to fit into particular environmental contexts (Sternberg, 1985). It focuses on three mental processes: adaptation, selection, and shaping of real-world environments. According to Sternberg, the individual first looks for ways to adapt, or fit into, the environment. If it is not possible to adapt, the individual tries to select a different environment or to shape the existing environment in order to fit into it better. To illustrate: If a spouse is unhappy in the marriage, it may not be possible to adapt to the current circumstances. He or she may therefore select a different environment (for example, through separation or divorce) or try to shape the existing environment (for example, through counseling) (Sternberg, 1985).

Ceci's Bioecological Theory

Some critics claim that Sternberg's theory has so many parts that it is not coherent (Richardson, 1986). Others note that it does not show how problem solving occurs in everyday contexts. Still others point out that it largely ignores the biological aspects of intelligence. Stephen Ceci (1990) has attempted to address these issues by building on Sternberg's theory while placing much greater emphasis on context and its impact on problem solving.

Ceci proposes that there are "multiple cognitive potentials," rather than a single underlying general intelligence or g. These multiple abilities or intelligences are biologically based and place limits on mental processes. Moreover, they are closely linked to the challenges and opportunities in the individual's environment, or context.

In Ceci's view, context is essential to the demonstration of cognitive abilities. By "context," he means domains of knowledge as well as factors such as personality, motivation, and education. Contexts can be mental, social, or physical (Ceci & Roazzi, 1994). A particular individual or population may appear to lack certain mental abilities, but if given a more interesting and motivating context, the same individual or population can demonstrate a higher level of performance. To take just one example, in a famous longitudinal study of high-IQ children studied by Lewis Terman (Terman & Oden, 1959), high IQ was thought to be correlated with high achievement. But a closer look at the results revealed that children from upper-income families went on to become more successful adults than children from lower-income families. In addition, those who became adults during the Great Depression ended up less successful than those who became adults later, when there were more job opportunities. In Ceci's words, "The bottom line . . . is that the ecological niche one occupies, including individual and historical development, is a far more potent determinant of one's professional and economic success than is IQ" (1990, p. 62).

Ceci also argues against the traditional view that intelligence is related to a capacity for abstract thinking, regardless of the subject area. He believes that the ability to engage in complex thought is tied to knowledge gained in particular contexts or domains. Rather than being endowed with a greater capacity for abstract reasoning, intelligent people have enough knowledge in a particular domain to enable them to think in a complex way about problems in that area of knowledge (Ceci, 1990). In the course of working in a particular domain—for example, computer programming—the individual's knowledge base grows and becomes better organized. Over time, this makes possible more intelligent performances—for example, more efficient programs.

In sum, according to Ceci, everyday or "real-world" intellectual performance cannot be explained by IQ alone or by some biological notion of general intelligence. Instead, it depends on the interaction between multiple cognitive potentials with a rich, well-organized knowledge base.

Theories of Intelligence: A Summary

The four theories of intelligence discussed in this section differ in several ways. Gardner attempts to explain the wide variety of adult roles found in different cultures. He believes that this diversity cannot be explained by a single underlying intelligence and instead proposes that there are at least seven different intelligences, which are present in different combinations in each individual. To Gardner, an intelligence is an ability to solve problems or create products that are of value in a particular culture. In this view, the Polynesian mariner who is skilled at navigating by the stars, the figure skater who can successfully execute a triple axel, and the charismatic leader who can motivate throngs of followers are as "intelligent" as a scientist, mathematician, or engineer.

Anderson's theory attempts to explain several aspects of intelligence—not only individual differences but also the increase of cognitive abilities with development, the existence of specific abilities, and the existence of universal abilities that do not vary from one individual to another, such as the ability to see objects in three dimensions. To explain these aspects, he proposes the existence of a basic processing mechanism, equivalent to Spearman's general intelligence or g, along with specific processors that deal with propositional thought and visual and spatial functioning. The existence of universal abilities is explained by the notion of "modules" whose functioning depends on maturation.

Sternberg's triarchic theory stems from the belief that earlier theories are not wrong, but merely incomplete. It consists of three subtheories: the componential theory, which looks at internal information-processing mechanisms; the experiential subtheory, which takes into account the individual's experience with a task or situation; and the contextual subtheory, which explores the relationship between the external environment and the individual's intelligence.

Ceci's bioecological theory extends Sternberg's theory by examining the role of context in greater depth. Rejecting the idea of a single general capacity for abstract problem solving, Ceci proposes that intelligence rests on multiple cognitive potentials. These potentials are biologically based, but their expression depends on the knowledge an individual has amassed in a particular domain. Thus, knowledge is crucial to intelligence, in Ceci's view.

Despite their differences, these theories have some aspects in common. They all attempt to take into account the biological basis of intelligence, be it a basic processing mechanism or a set of multiple intelligences, modules, or cognitive potentials. In addition, three of the theories place a strong emphasis on the contexts within which individuals operate—that is, environmental factors that influence intelligence. Thus, the study of intelligence continues to explore the complex interaction between biological and environmental factors that is a central focus of psychological research today.

CONTEMPORARY VOICES IN PSYCHOLOGY

DO INTELLIGENCE TESTS ACCURATELY REFLECT APTITUDE?

SATs and GREs Are Accurate Measures of Intelligence

Douglas K. Detterman, *Case Western Reserve University*

How do you know if two measures are really the same thing? You compute a statistic called a correlation (ranging from 0 to 1.0) and the higher the correlation, the more similar two measures are. Mental tests called aptitude, achievement, intelligence, and cognitive ability tests are correlated so highly with one another that many experts believe they are really all the same. What any test of mental ability is called probably has more to do with social acceptability than what the test really measures. It is not surprising that these tests are highly correlated since, from Binet to the most recent computer-administered GRE, they were all designed to predict academic achievement.

A test is nothing more than a sample of behavior hopefully predictive of future behaviors. The easiest thing tests should predict is later behavior on the same test, known as the reliability of a test. Intelligence, aptitude, and achievement tests are the most highly reliable of all psychological tests. Individually administered intelligence tests correlate above .90 with a later administration of the same test. In 1932, a group-administered test was given to every Scottish school child. Recently, the same test was given to some that had taken the original test. The correlation of the two administrations over the 66-year span was .74 (Deary et al.). Compare this with the average reliability of .6 for height, weight, and blood pressure taken in a doctor's office. Most psychological tests of personality, psychopathology, or motivation are lucky to have test-retest reliabilities between .4 and .8.

Do tests predict anything useful? You bet! Anghoff and Johnson correlated the performance of over 20,000 students who had taken the SAT and then later taken the GRE. The correlation was .86. While the addition of gender and major raised the correlation to .93 or higher, college quality mattered little. Paying big bucks for a college education won't help to get you into graduate school, at least as far as test scores are concerned. Other academic criteria like grades or class rank are also predicted by these tests, but less well, because grades and class rank are less reliable themselves. Mental ability tests are highly predictive of many real-world criteria, from flying a jet fighter to becoming a good lawyer or musician. Occupations that have the highest average IQ are also the most socially desirable. Most importantly, mental tests predict academic achievement, the usual doorway to life achievement.

Then why do these tests get so much bad press? First, they are often used improperly. Although nearly all colleges require tests for admission, perhaps 80% of colleges admit nearly everyone who applies. Why do they require tests? I think they want to appear selective. Even for the 20% of colleges that are selective, many other factors than test scores weigh in the decision. Given two students with the same test scores, the one with the best chance of getting in a selective school will have the following characteristics: minority, athlete, attended selective private high school, family income over $70,000 per year and one parent had college education, legacy (a parent attended the college), parent is large donor to college (Bowen & Bok, 1998). Before tests, these sorts of factors were the only thing used for college admission. I think admissions would be fairer at selective schools if only test scores were used.

A second reason that people often get a bad impression of tests is that there are situations in which they cannot predict performance. When applicants are heavily selected for IQ, they will all be very similar in IQ, so IQ cannot contribute to performance. Our educational system selects for intelligence, and each step requires higher levels of academic achievement. You have probably noticed that things are harder in college than they were in high school. Here is the reason. The average IQ of a college graduate is over 110 while the average IQ of those who finish professional or graduate school is over 120. Intelligence will be only a small contributor to performance in medical or graduate school. Other things like hard work and personality will determine differences in success because everyone is smart. You have to be tall to play basketball. The NBA selects players for height and NBA players are much taller than the average person. But the correlation between height and points scored in the NBA is near zero. It is as silly to say that intelligence has nothing to do with performance in medical or graduate school as it is to say height has nothing to do with basketball.

Tests like the SAT and GRE are essentially tests of intelligence. They are highly reliable and predict real-world behaviors better than anything else we know about. Tests have often been misused and are not the measure of the basic worth of a human being. But when used properly, they can make selection decisions fairer and more accurate and can help students in designing their educational future.

Why IQs, SATs, and GREs Are Not Measures of *General* Intelligence

Stephen J. Ceci, *Cornell University*

There is a funny anecdote about a man waiting for a bus. When a woman arrives pushing a pram with her baby in it, the man peers into the pram:

Man: My, what a lovely baby you have!
Woman: Oh don't go by that—you should see her photographs!

We all know individuals who seem more interested in photographs than in reality. For such persons, intelligence test scores (the photos) are more important than the attainments they are supposed to predict (the baby).

Thousands of "validity" studies show that tests of general intelligence predict a wide range of behaviors, imperfectly, but better than anything else we can measure: IQ scores predict freshman grades somewhat better than high-school grades and letters of reference do, and they also predict first-year graduate school grades better than do undergraduate grades and letters. But the prediction from IQ (or SATs or GREs) is modest, and many applicants' grades will differ from expectations based on such scores. Test makers argue that even modest predictability can help admissions officers make better decisions than they would by not using the tests (Hunt, 1995).

For many years I chaired a graduate admissions committee. One of the saddest experiences is discovering the tremendous weight given to test scores such as the GRE. Granted, there are other considerations to distinguish among applicants who are similar in GRE scores and grades; however, at most universities applicants with very low scores won't get admitted unless the school needs to fill seats for financial reasons.

All who serve on admission committees can tell tales—about the applicant with great scores who turned out to be a loser, unable to think creatively and manage work effectively. Or about the occasional applicant with low scores who somehow manages to gain entrance and goes on to disprove the prediction by emerging as the top student. I am not claiming that measures of general intelligence such as the GREs, IQ scores, and SATs are worthless. But they are not perfect, and applicants who excel at them represent but one type of individual who could do well. Other types of applicants (e.g., those with well-honed real-world skills, interpersonal strengths, highly creative) are systematically excluded.

But my most serious complaint about tests of general intelligence is that they do not strike me as measures of general intelligence any more than a math or history achievement test strikes me as one. Like all achievement tests, the SATs, IQs, and GREs are susceptible to external influences, including coaching, quality of school attended, and parental educational level and income. It should come as no surprise to find that the number of math classes taken in school is a predictor of math scores on the SATs and GREs, *even after controlling for initial math aptitude*. This implies that although math scores add to the prediction of college or graduate-school grades, they may not measure inherent math ability any more than a score on a test of Russian proficiency would for someone who attended a school where Russian was not taught. Thus, I view tests of "general intelligence" as often little more than achievement tests, indexing how much knowledge one has gained. They tell us little about actual ability under different circumstances, particularly those situations that require thinking unlike the type required to answer test questions correctly. And such tests tell us little about potentially valuable talents that are not measured, such as creativity, practical intelligence, and the ability to organize, motivate, and manage oneself and others—skills that appear to be somewhat independent of so-called intelligence tests, and which have been demonstrated to predict important educational outcomes.

Stephen J. Ceci

Recently, there has been a spate of studies about the predictive validity of SATs and GREs, and while such measures may predict first-year grades, their predictiveness wanes over the years. One recent study even reported that the GREs did not predict at all after the first year of graduate school—not second-, third-, or fourth-year grades, not creativity or quality of the doctoral research (Sternberg & Williams, 1997), although it's possible there will be a "sleeper effect," and intelligence scores could end up predicting later career achievements and earnings. These de facto achievement tests have many valid uses; however, it is unwise to refer to them as tests of "general intelligence" until they can be shown to tap a far wider array of abilities and achievements than they do. And until their predictiveness gets better, we should not confuse the baby with her photographs.

SUMMARY

1. Behavioral scientists typically quantify the extent to which a group of people differ from one another on some measure of a trait or ability by computing the variance of the scores obtained. The more the individuals in the group differ from one another, the higher the variance. Researchers can then seek to determine how much of that variance is due to different causes. The proportion of variance in a trait that is accounted for (caused by) genetic differences among the individuals is called the heritability of the trait.

2. Heritabilities can be estimated by comparing correlations obtained on pairs of identical twins (who share all their genes) and correlations obtained on pairs of fraternal twins (who, on the average, share about half of their genes). If identical twin pairs are more alike on the trait than fraternal twin pairs, the trait probably has a genetic component. Heritabilities can also be estimated from the correlation between identical twin pairs who have been separated and raised in different environments. Any correlation between such pairs must be due to their genetic similarities.

3. Heritability refers to differences among individuals; it does not indicate how much of a trait in an individual is due to genetic factors. It is not a fixed attribute of a trait: If something happens to change the variability of a trait in a group, the heritability will also change. Heritability indicates the variance within a group, not the source of differences between groups. Heritability does, however, indicate how much possible environmental changes might change the mean level of a trait in a population.

4. In shaping personality, genetic and environmental influences do not act independently but are intertwined from the moment of birth. Because a child's personality and his or her home environment are both a function of the parents' genes, there is a built-in correlation between the child's genotype (inherited personality characteristics) and that environment.

5. Three dynamic processes of personality-environment interaction are (a) reactive interaction—different individuals exposed to the same environment experience it, interpret it, and react to it differently; (b) evocative interaction—an individual's personality evokes distinctive responses from others; and (c) proactive interaction—individuals select or create environments of their own. As a child grows older, the influence of proactive interaction becomes increasingly important.

6. Studies of twins have produced a number of puzzling patterns: Heritabilities estimated from identical twins reared apart are higher than estimates based on comparisons between identical and fraternal twins; identical twins reared apart are as similar to each other as identical twins reared together, but fraternal twins and nontwin siblings become less similar over time, even when they are reared together. These patterns are probably due in part to interactions among genes, so that having all one's genes in common is more than twice as effective as having only half of one's genes in common. Such patterns might also be due in part to the three processes of personality-environment interaction (reactive, evocative, and proactive).

7. After their genetic similarities are subtracted out, children from the same family seem to be no more alike than children chosen randomly from the population. This implies that the kinds of variables that psychologists typically study (such as child-rearing practices and the family's socioeconomic status) contribute virtually nothing to individual differences in personality.

8. Tests for assessing intelligence or personality must yield reproducible and consistent results (reliability) and measure what they are intended to measure (validity).

9. The first successful intelligence tests were developed by the French psychologist Alfred Binet, who proposed the concept of mental age. A bright child's mental age is above his or her chronological age; a slow child's mental age is below his or her chronological age. The concept of the intelligence quotient (IQ), the ratio of mental age to chronological age (multiplied by 100), was introduced when the Binet scales were revised to create the Stanford-Binet. Many intelligence test scores are still expressed as IQ scores, but they are no longer actually calculated according to this formula.

10. Both Binet and Wechsler, the developer of the Wechsler Adult Intelligence Scale (WAIS), assumed that intelligence is a general capacity for reasoning. Similarly, Spearman proposed that a general factor (g) underlies performance on different kinds of test items. Factor analysis is a method for determining the kinds of abilities that underlie performance on intelligence tests.

11. To arrive at a comprehensive but manageable number of personality traits on which individuals can be assessed, investigators first collected all the trait terms found in a dictionary (about 18,000); these were then reduced to a smaller number. Ratings of individuals on these terms were factor-analyzed to determine how many underlying dimensions were needed to account for the correlations among the scales. Although different investigators arrive at different numbers of factors, most now believe that five factors provide the best compromise. These have been labeled the "Big Five" and form the acronym OCEAN: Openness to experience, Conscientiousness, Extraversion, Agreeableness, and Neuroticism.

12. Personality inventories are questionnaires on which individuals report their reactions or feelings in certain situations. Responses to subsets of items are summed to yield scores on separate scales or factors within the inventory. Although items on most inventories are composed or selected on the basis of a theory, they can also be selected on the basis of their correlation with an external criterion—the criterion-keyed method of test construction. The best-known example is the Minnesota Multiphasic Personality Inventory (MMPI), which is designed to identify individuals with psychological disorders.

13. The information-processing approach seeks to understand intellectual behavior in terms of the underlying cognitive processes brought into play when an individual attempts to solve an intelligence test problem.

14. Recent theories of intelligence include Gardner's theory of multiple intelligences, Anderson's theory of intelligence and cognitive development, Sternberg's triarchic theory, and Ceci's bioecological theory. To varying degrees, these theories explore the interaction between biological and environmental factors in determining intellectual performance.

KEY TERMS

heritability (p. 423)
reliability (p. 428)
validity (p. 429)

intelligence quotient (IQ) (p. 431)
personality (p. 435)
personality inventory (p. 437)

CRITICAL THINKING QUESTIONS

1. If you have any siblings, how different are you from them? Can you discern how some of the personality-environment interactions described in this chapter may have contributed to those differences? Can you see ways in which your parents' child-rearing strategies differed from one sibling to another in response to their different personalities?

2. By providing a national yardstick, standardized tests like the SAT enable high-school seniors from any high school to compete equally for openings in the nation's top colleges. Before standardized testing, students rarely had a chance to show that they were qualified, and colleges tended to favor students from well-known high schools or with "family connections." But critics argue that the very success of standardized tests in selecting qualified students has led admissions committees to give them too much weight and has led high schools to gear their curricula toward the tests themselves. In addition, critics argue that standardized tests are biased against certain ethnic groups. On balance, do you think the widespread use of standardized tests has helped or hindered our society in realizing its goal of equal opportunity?

3. How would you rate yourself on the "Big 5" personality traits? Do you think your personality can be accurately described in this way? What important aspect of your personality seems to be left out of such a description? If you and a close friend (or a family member) were to describe your personality, on which characteristics would you be likely to disagree? Why? Are there traits on which you think this other person might actually be more accurate than you in describing your personality? If so, why?

FURTHER READING

Plomin, *Nature and Nurture* (1990) provides an accessible discussion of behavioral genetics, including the twin method of assessing heritability. For a complete discussion of the differences among children from the same family, see Dunn and Plomin, *Separate Lives: Why Siblings Are So Different* (1990). A more advanced treatment of the genetics of intelligence is Plomin, DeFries, and McClearn, *Behavioral Genetics: A Primer* (2nd ed., 1989). Plomin and McClearn (eds.), *Nature, Nurture & Psychology* (1993) provide a collection of essays on the nature-nurture problem in several areas. Harris, *The Nature Assumption* (1998), argues that peers are more important than the family in shaping children's personalities.

For an introduction to individual differences and psychological testing, see Kaplan and Sacuzzo, *Psychological Testing* (3rd ed., 1993); Murphy and Davidshofer, *Psychological Testing: Principles and Applications* (2nd ed., 1991); and Sattler, *Assessment of Children* (1988).

For a more general overview of intellectual abilities, see Gardner, Kornhaber, and Wake, *Intelligence: Multiple Perspectives* (1996); and Brody, *Intelligence* (2nd ed., 1992). A theory of multiple intelligences is presented in Gardner, *Frames of Mind: The Theory of Multiple Intelligence* (1983). Other recent theories may be found in Anderson, *Intelligence and Development: A Cognitive Theory* (1992); Ceci, *On Intelligence . . . More or Less: A Bio-ecological Treatise on Intellectual Development* (1990); Gardner, *Frames of Mind: The Theory of Multiple Intelligences* (1993); and Sternberg, *Metaphors of Mind: Conceptions of the Nature of Intelligence* (1990).

For a historical perspective on intelligence tests and the controversies associated with them, see Fancher, *The Intelligence Men: Makers of the IQ Controversy* (1985). A recent and very controversial book on intelligence in American society is Herrnstein and Murray, *The Bell Curve* (1994). For personality assessment, see Aiken, *Assessment of Personality* (1989) or any of the personality textbooks listed at the end of Chapter 13.

Studies based on the longitudinal archives housed at the Institute of Human Development in Berkeley can be found in Eichorn et al. (eds.), *Present and Past in Middle Life* (1981); and Block, *Lives Through Time* (1971).

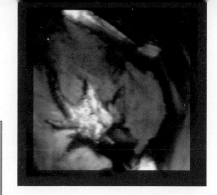

Chapter 13
Personality

*I*n Chapter 12 we defined *personality* as the distinctive and characteristic patterns of thought, emotion, and behavior that define an individual's personal style of interacting with the physical and social environments. Accordingly, one of the first tasks of personality psychology is to describe individual differences—the diverse ways in which individuals differ from one another. In Chapter 12 we described the most common approach to this task, the trait approach. By itself, however, the trait approach is not a theory of personality but a general orientation and set of methods for assessing stable characteristics of individuals. By themselves, personality traits do not tell us anything about the dynamic processes of personality functioning, and trait psychologists who have sought to develop theories of personality have had to look to other approaches to address the second major task of personality psychology: synthesizing the many processes that influence an individual's interactions with the physical and social environments—biology, development, learning, thinking, emotion, motivation, and social interaction—into an integrated account of the total person. This task requires going far beyond the interactions between heredity and environment discussed in Chapter 12 and makes the study of personality one of the most ambitious subfields of psychology.

In this chapter we look at four theoretical approaches that have dominated personality psychology in the twentieth century: the psychoanalytic, behaviorist, humanistic, and cognitive approaches. In doing so, we also raise a question that has never been satisfactorily answered: To what degree are our beliefs, emotions, and actions free and in what ways are they determined by causes beyond our control? Are we basically good, neutral, or evil? Fixed or modifiable? Active or passive in controlling our destinies? What constitutes psychological health or lack of health? These are not empirical questions, and theories of personality do not attempt to answer them explicitly. But each theoretical approach contains implicit answers—a set of distinctive underlying assumptions about human nature. Historically, these more philosophical factors have been as important as the empirical data in provoking controversies and in winning converts for the competing accounts of personality.

The Psychoanalytic Approach

Sigmund Freud, the creator of psychoanalytic theory, is one of the towering intellectual figures of the twentieth century. Whatever its shortcomings as a scientific theory, the psychoanalytic account of personality remains the most comprehensive and influential theory of personality ever created. Its impact extends well beyond psychology, influencing the social sciences, the humanities, the arts, and society generally. Even though psychoanalytic theory plays a less central role in psychology today than it did 50 or 60 years ago, many of its ideas have been absorbed into the mainstream of

psychological thinking. Even parents who have done nothing more than raise their children with the occasional guidance of psychiatrist Benjamin Spock's best-selling *Baby and Child Care* are more like Freudian psychologists than they realize.

Freud began his scientific career as a neurologist, using conventional medical procedures to treat patients suffering from various "nervous" disorders. Because those procedures often failed, he turned to the technique of hypnosis but soon abandoned it. Eventually he discovered the method of **free association,** in which *a patient is instructed to say everything that comes to mind, regardless of how trivial or embarrassing it may seem.* By listening carefully to these verbal associations, Freud detected consistent themes that he believed were manifestations of unconscious wishes and fears. He found similar themes in the recall of dreams and early childhood memories.

Freud compared the human mind to an iceberg. The small part that shows above the surface of the water consists of the **conscious**—*our current awareness*—and the **preconscious,** *all the information that is not currently "on our mind" but that we could bring into consciousness if called upon to do so* (for example, the name of the president of the United States). The much larger mass of the iceberg below the water represents the **unconscious,** a storehouse of *impulses, wishes, and inaccessible memories that affect our thoughts and behavior.* Freud was not the first to discover unconscious mental influences—even Shakespeare includes them in his plays—but he gave them primary importance in the everyday functioning of the normal personality.

Closely allied with Freud's focus on unconscious processes was his belief in the determinism of human behavior. **Psychological determinism** is *the doctrine that all thoughts, emotions, and actions have causes.* Freud maintained not only that all psychological events are caused but that most of them are caused by unsatisfied drives and unconscious wishes. In one of his earliest publications, *The Psychopathology of Everyday Life* (1901), he argued that dreams, humor, forgetting, and slips of the tongue ("Freudian slips") all serve to relieve psychological tension by gratifying forbidden impulses or unfulfilled wishes.

Freud's writings fill 24 volumes. His first major contribution, *The Interpretation of Dreams,* was published in 1900, and his final treatise, *An Outline of Psychoanalysis,* was published in 1940, a year after his death. We can present only the barest outline of Freud's theory of personality here.

Personality Structure

Freud discovered that his iceberg model was too simple to describe the human personality, so he went on to develop a structural model, which divided personality into three major systems that interact to govern human behavior: the id, the ego, and the superego.

The Id   According to Freud, the **id** is *the most primitive part of the personality and the part from which the ego and the superego later develop.* It is present in the newborn infant and consists of the most basic biological impulses or *drives:* the need to eat, to drink, to eliminate wastes, to avoid pain, and to gain sexual (sensual) pleasure. Freud believed that aggression is also a basic biological drive (see Chapter 11). In fact, he believed that the sexual and aggressive drives were the most important instinctual determinants of personality throughout life. The id seeks immediate gratification of these impulses. Like a young child, it operates on the *pleasure principle:* It continually strives to obtain pleasure and to avoid pain, regardless of the external circumstances.

"Very well, I'll introduce you. Ego, meet Id. Now get back to work."

The Ego   Children soon learn that their impulses cannot always be gratified immediately. Hunger will not be alleviated until someone provides food. Relief of bladder or bowel pressure must be delayed until the bathroom is reached. Certain impulses—playing with one's genitals or hitting someone—may be punished. A new part of the personality, the ego, develops as the young child learns to consider the demands of reality. The ego obeys the reality principle: The gratification of impulses must be delayed until the situation is appropriate. The **ego** thus is essentially *the executive of the personality:* It decides which id impulses will be satisfied and in what manner. The ego mediates among the demands of the id, the realities of the world, and the demands of the superego.

The Superego   The third part of the personality is the superego, which judges whether actions are right or wrong. More generally, the **superego** is *the internalized representation of the values and morals of society.* It comprises the individual's conscience as well as his or her image of the morally ideal person (called the *ego ideal*).

The superego develops in response to parental rewards and punishments. Initially, parents control children's behavior directly through reward and punishment. By incorporating parental standards into the superego, a child brings behavior under his or her own control. Children no longer need anyone to tell them it is wrong to steal; their superego tells them. Violating the superego's standards, or even the impulse to do so, produces anxiety—beginning with anxiety over loss of parental love. According to Freud, this anxiety is largely unconscious but may be experienced as guilt. If parental standards are overly rigid, the individual may be guilt-ridden and may inhibit all aggressive or sexual impulses. In contrast, an individual who fails to incorporate any standards for acceptable social behavior will feel few constraints on his or her behavior and may engage in excessively self-indulgent or criminal behavior. Such a person is said to have a weak superego.

The three components of personality are often in conflict: The ego postpones the gratification that the id wants immediately, and the superego battles with both the id and the ego because behavior often falls short of the moral code it represents. In the well-integrated personality, the ego remains in firm but flexible control; the reality principle governs. In terms of his earlier iceberg model, Freud proposed that all of the id and most of the ego and superego are submerged in the unconscious and that small parts of the ego and superego are in either the conscious or the preconscious (See Figure 13-1).

Personality Dynamics

Conservation of Energy Freud was greatly influenced by the German physicist Hermann von Helmholtz, who argued that physiological events could be explained by the same principles that had been so successful in physics. Freud was particularly impressed by the principle of conservation of energy, which states that energy may be changed into different forms but is neither created nor destroyed. He proposed that humans are also closed energy systems. There is a constant amount of psychic energy for any given individual, which Freud called *libido* (Latin

for lust), reflecting his view that the sexual drive was primary.

One corollary of the principle of conservation of energy is that if a forbidden act or impulse is suppressed, its energy will seek an outlet somewhere else in the system, possibly appearing in a disguised form. The desires of the id contain psychic energy that must be expressed in some way, and preventing the expression of those desires does not eliminate them. Aggressive impulses, for example, may be expressed in disguised form by racing sports cars, playing chess, or making sarcastic remarks. Dreams and neurotic symptoms are also manifestations of psychic energy that cannot be expressed directly.

Anxiety and Defense Individuals with an urge to do something forbidden experience anxiety. One way of reducing this anxiety is to express the impulse in a disguised form that will avoid punishment either by society or by its internal representative, the superego. Freud described several additional **defense mechanisms,** or *strategies for preventing or reducing anxiety.* The most basic defense mechanism is **repression,** in which *the ego pushes a threatening thought or forbidden impulse out of awareness into the unconscious;* from the outside it appears that the individual has simply forgotten the thought or impulse. Individuals differ both in their thresholds for anxiety and in the defenses they use to deal with such anxiety. Anxiety and defense mechanisms are central to Freud's theory of psychopathology and will be examined more fully in Chapter 14.

Personality Development

Freud believed that during the first five years of life the individual progresses through several developmental stages that affect his or her personality. Applying a broad definition of sexuality, he called these periods *psychosexual stages.* During each stage the pleasure-seeking impulses of the id focus on a particular area of the body and on activities connected with that area.

Freud called the first year of life the *oral stage* of psychosexual development. During this period, infants derive pleasure from nursing and sucking and begin to put anything they can reach into their mouths. Freud

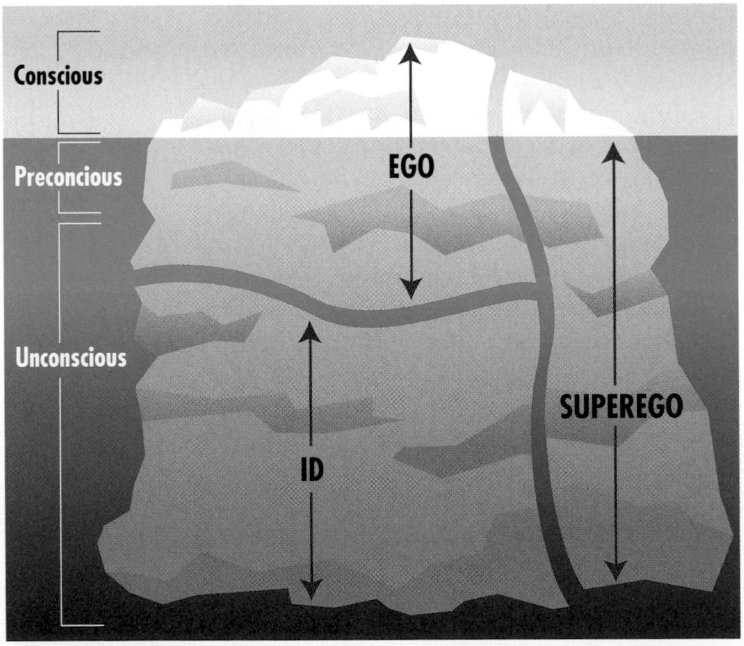

FIGURE 13-1

Freud's Structural Model of the Mind *In Freud's "iceberg" model of the mind, all of the id and most of the ego and superego are submerged in the unconscious. Small parts of the ego and superego are either in the conscious or in the preconscious.*

called the second year of life the beginning of the *anal stage* and believed that during this period children find pleasure both in withholding and in expelling feces. These pleasures come into conflict with parents who are attempting toilet training, the child's first experience with imposed control. In the *phallic stage,* from about age 3 to age 6, children begin to derive pleasure from fondling their genitals. They observe the differences between males and females and begin to direct their awakening sexual impulses toward the parent of the opposite sex.

Around the age of 5 or 6, according to Freud, a boy's sexual impulses are directed toward his mother. This leads him to perceive his father as a rival for his mother's affection. Freud called this situation the *Oedipal conflict,* after the ancient Greek myth in which Oedipus unwittingly kills his father and marries his mother. Freud also believed that the boy fears that his father will retaliate against these sexual impulses by castrating him. He labeled this fear *castration anxiety* and considered it to be the prototype for later anxieties provoked by forbidden internal desires. In a normal case of development, the boy simultaneously reduces this anxiety and vicariously gratifies his feelings toward his mother by *identifying* with his father—that is, by internalizing an idealized perception of his father's attitudes and values. The same process in a girl—resulting in her identifying with her mother—is analogous but more complicated.

Resolution of the Oedipal conflict ends the phallic stage, which is followed by the *latency period.* During this sexually quiescent time, which lasts from about age 7 to age 12, children become less concerned with their bodies and turn their attention to the skills needed for coping with their environment. Finally, adolescence and puberty usher in the *genital stage,* the mature phase of adult sexuality and functioning.

Freud believed that special problems at any stage could arrest, or *fixate,* development and have a lasting effect on personality. The individual's libido would remain attached to the activities appropriate for that stage. Thus, a person who was weaned very early and did not have enough sucking pleasure might become fixated at the oral stage. As an adult, he or she might be excessively dependent on others and overly fond

According to psychoanalytic theory, a child resolves the Oedipal conflict by identifying with the same-sex parent.

of oral pleasures such as eating, drinking, and smoking. Such a person is said to have an *oral personality.* A person fixated at the anal stage of psychosexual development may be abnormally concerned with cleanliness, orderliness, and saving and may tend to resist external pressure. Such a person is said to have an *anal personality.* Inadequate resolution of the Oedipal conflict can lead to a weak sense of morality, difficulties with authority figures, and many other problems.

Modifications of Freud's Theories

Freud modified his theories throughout his life. Like a good scientist, he remained open to new data, revising his earlier positions as new observations accumulated that could not be accommodated by the original theory. For example, quite late in his career he completely revised his theory of anxiety. Freud's theory has been further extended by his daughter Anna, who has played a particularly important role in clarifying the defense mechanisms (1946/1967) and applying psychoanalytic theory to the practice of child psychiatry (1958).

While Freud was open to new data, he was not open to dissenting opinions. He was particularly adamant that his colleagues and followers not question the libido theory and the centrality of sexual motivation in the functioning of personality. This dogmatism forced a break between Freud and many of his most brilliant associates, some of whom went on to develop rival theories that placed more emphasis on motivational processes other than sexuality. These former associates included Carl Jung and Alfred Adler, as well as later theorists such as Karen Horney, Harry Stack Sullivan, and Erich Fromm.

Of those who broke with Freud, perhaps the most famous was Carl Jung. Originally one of Freud's most dedicated followers, Jung eventually came to disagree profoundly with some aspects of Freud's theory and founded his own school of psychology, which he called *analytic psychology.* Jung believed that in addition to the personal unconscious described by Freud, there is a *collective unconscious,* a part of the mind that is common to all humans. The collective unconscious consists of *primordial images* or *archetypes* inherited from our ancestors. Among those archetypes are the mother, the father, the sun, the hero, God, and death. To gather evidence for the presence of these archetypes, Jung examined dreams, myths, and other cultural products, noting that certain images, such as that of a vulture, often appear in dreams and are also found in religious writings and ancient mythologies with which the dreamer is not familiar. Thus, while Jung agreed with Freud on the existence of the unconscious, he believed that Freud's theory failed to explain the presence of common images or archetypes in the unconscious minds of all humans.

Another well-known "neo-Freudian" was the American psychologist Harry Stack Sullivan. Sullivan developed his own theory of personality on the basis of his experience with psychoanalysis. He placed primary emphasis on interpersonal relations, arguing that a personality "can never be isolated from the complex of interpersonal relations in which the person lives and has his being"

(Sullivan, 1953, p. 10). In his view, people's responses to interpersonal experiences cause them to develop *personifications*—mental images of themselves and others. Images of the self fall into three categories: the good-me personification, the bad-me personification, and the not-me. The latter category contains aspects of the self that are so threatening that the individual dissociates them from the self-system and maintains them in the unconscious. This concept is similar to Freud's concept of repression in that it requires a constant effort to keep these aspects of the self in the unconscious.

Like Freud, Sullivan believed that early childhood experiences play an important role in the development of personality. He believed, however, that the personality continues to develop after childhood. He identified seven stages of personality development—infancy, childhood, the juvenile era, preadolescence, early adolescence, late adolescence, and adulthood—and maintained that each stage is largely socially determined. Thus, while a person may go through a stage in a particular way because of certain biological factors, the primary influence is the typical situations he or she experiences at that age. Sullivan's view of development therefore differs considerably from Freud's biologically based theory.

These dissidents and other, more recent psychoanalytic theorists all place greater emphasis on the role of the ego. They believe that the ego is present at birth, develops independently of the id, and performs functions other than finding realistic ways of satisfying id impulses, including learning how to cope with the environment and making sense of experience. Ego satisfactions include exploration, manipulation, and competence in performing tasks. This approach ties the concept of the ego more closely to cognitive processes.

An important part of this new direction is *object relations theory,* which deals with a person's attachments and relationships to other people throughout life. Object relations theorists have not rejected the concept of the id or the importance of biological drives in motivating behavior, but they have an equal interest in such questions as degree of psychological separateness from parents, degree of attachment to and involvement with other people versus preoccupation with

Recent psychoanalytic theorists believe that the ego performs other functions besides finding ways to satisfy id impulses. These include learning how to cope with the environment and making sense of experience.

self, and the strength of the individual's feelings of self-esteem and competence.

Although we did not identify it as such, Erik Erikson's stage theory of development (discussed in Chapter 3) is an example of a revised psychoanalytic theory. Erikson himself was trained as a psychoanalyst by Anna Freud, and he perceived his own views as expanding rather than altering Freudian theory. Instead of viewing developmental stages in terms of their psychosexual functions, Erikson saw them as psychosocial stages involving primarily ego processes. For Erikson, the important feature of the first year of life is not that it focuses on oral gratification but that the child is learning to trust (or mistrust) the environment as a satisfier of needs. The important feature of the second year of life is not that it focuses on anal concerns such as toilet training but that the child is learning autonomy. Toilet training just happens to be a frequent arena of conflict in which the child's striving for autonomy clashes with new demands by parents. Erikson's theory also adds more stages in order to encompass the entire life span.

Projective Tests

Personality psychologists who follow in Freud's psychoanalytic tradition are particularly interested in assessing unconscious wishes, motivations, and conflicts. Accordingly, they prefer tests that resemble Freud's technique of free association, in which the individual is free to say whatever comes to mind. For this reason, they developed projective tests. A **projective test** *presents an ambiguous stimulus to which the person may respond as he or she wishes.* Because the stimulus is ambiguous and does not demand a specific response, it is assumed that the individual *projects* his or her personality onto the stimulus and thus reveals something about himself or herself. Projective tests have also been useful in areas of personality other than psychoanalytic theory. Two of the most widely used projective techniques are the Rorschach Test and the Thematic Apperception Test (TAT).

The Rorschach Test The *Rorschach Test,* developed by the Swiss psychiatrist Hermann Rorschach in the 1920s, consists of a series of 10 cards, each of which displays a rather complex inkblot like the one shown in Figure 13-2. Some of the blots are in color; some are black and white. The person is instructed to look at one card at a time and report everything the inkblot resembles. After the person has finished the 10 cards, the examiner usually goes over each response, asking the person to clarify some responses and indicate which features of the blot gave a particular impression.

The individual's responses may be scored in various ways. Three main categories are location (whether the response involves the entire inkblot or a part of it), determinants (whether the individual responds to the shape of the blot, its color, or differences in texture and shading), and content (what the response represents). Most testers also score responses according to frequency of occurrence; for example, a response is "popular" if many people assign it to the same inkblot.

Several elaborate scoring systems have been devised on the basis of these categories, but most of them have proved to be of limited predictive value. Consequently, many psychologists base their interpretations on an impressionistic evaluation of the response record, as well as on the individual's general reaction to the test situation (for example, whether the person is defensive, open, competitive, cooperative, and so on).

In 1974, a system was introduced that attempted to extract and combine the validated portions of all the scoring systems into one complete system. It has undergone extensive revision and is now supplemented by a computer scoring service and software for microcomputers (Exner, 1986). Although this system looks more promising than previous efforts, not enough studies have accumulated to evaluate its validity with any confidence.

The Thematic Apperception Test   Another popular projective test, the *Thematic Apperception Test* (TAT), was developed at Harvard University by Henry Murray in the 1930s. The participant is shown as many as 20 ambiguous pictures of persons and scenes, similar to the one in Figure 13-3, and asked to make up a story about each picture. The individual is encouraged to give free rein to his or her imagination and to tell whatever story comes to mind. The test is intended to reveal basic themes that recur in a person's imaginings. (*Apperception* is a readiness to perceive in certain ways based on prior experiences.) People interpret ambiguous pictures according to their apperceptions and elaborate stories in terms of preferred plots or themes that reflect personal fantasies. If particular problems are bothering them, those problems may become evident in a number of the stories or in striking deviations from the usual theme in one or two stories. For example, when shown a picture similar to the one in Figure 13-3, a 21-year-old male told the following story:

> She has prepared this room for someone's arrival and is opening the door for a last general look over the room. She is probably expecting her son home. She tries to place everything as it was when he left. She seems like a very tyrannical character. She led her son's life for him and is going to take over again as soon as he gets back. This is merely the beginning of her rule, and the son is definitely cowed by this overbearing attitude of hers and will slip back into her well-ordered way of life. He will go through life plodding down the tracks she has laid down for him. All this represents her complete domination of his life until she dies. (Arnold, 1949, p. 100)

Although the original picture shows only a woman standing in an open doorway looking into a room, the young man's readiness to talk about his relationship with his mother

FIGURE 13-2

A Rorschach Inkblot   *The person is asked to tell what he or she sees in the blot; it may be viewed from any angle.*

FIGURE 13-3

The Thematic Apperception Test *This picture is similar to the pictures used on the Thematic Apperception Test. The pictures usually have elements of ambiguity so that the individual can "read into" them something from personal experience or fantasy.*

led to this story of a woman's domination of her son. Facts obtained later confirmed the clinician's interpretation that the story reflected the man's own problems.

In analyzing responses to TAT cards the psychologist looks for recurrent themes that may reveal the individual's needs, motives, or characteristic way of handling interpersonal relationships.

Problems With Projective Tests Many other projective tests have been devised. Some ask the individual to draw pictures of people, houses, trees, and so on. Others involve completing sentences that start with "I often wish . . . ," "My mother . . . ," or "I feel like quitting when they. . . ." In fact, any stimulus to which a person can respond in an individualistic way could be considered the basis for a projective test. But most projective tests have not been subjected to enough research to establish their usefulness in assessing personality.

In contrast, the Rorschach Test and the TAT have been intensively researched. The results, however, have not always been encouraging. The reliability of the Rorschach Test has been generally poor because the interpretation of responses is too dependent on the clinician's judgment; the same responses may be evaluated quite differently by two trained examiners. And attempts to demonstrate the Rorschach's ability to predict behavior or discriminate between groups have met with limited success. The

new comprehensive system mentioned earlier may prove more successful.

The TAT has fared somewhat better. When specific scoring systems are used (for example, to measure achievement motives or aggressive themes), interscorer reliability is fairly good. But the relationship of TAT scores to overt behavior is complex. People do not necessarily act on their preoccupations. A person who produces a number of stories with aggressive themes may not actually behave aggressively. In fact, the individual may be compensating for a need to inhibit aggressive tendencies by expressing such impulses in fantasies. When inhibitions about expressing aggression and strength of aggressive tendencies are estimated from TAT stories, the relationship to behavior becomes more predictable. Among boys whose tests indicated that they were not very inhibited, the correlation between amount of aggression in the TAT stories and overt aggression was .55. Among boys showing a high degree of inhibition, the correlation between number of aggressive themes and overt aggression was 2.50 (Olweus, 1969).

Defenders of the Rorschach Test and the TAT point out that it is not fair to expect accurate predictions based on test responses alone; responses to inkblots and story themes are meaningful only when considered in light of additional information, such as the person's life history, other test data, and observations of behavior. The skilled clinician uses the results of projective tests to make tentative interpretations about the individual's personality and then verifies or discards them on the basis of additional information. The tests are helpful in suggesting possible areas of conflict to be explored.

A Psychoanalytic Portrait of Human Nature

At the beginning of the chapter we noted that each approach to personality carries with it a distinctive philosophy of human nature. To what extent are our actions free or determined? Good, neutral, or evil? Fixed or modifiable? Active or passive? What constitutes psychological health? Our description of Freud's theory has hinted at many of his views on these matters. Freud is often compared with Copernicus and Darwin. Like them, he was accused of undermining the stature and dignity of humanity. The astronomer Copernicus demoted the earth from its position as the center of the universe to one of several planets moving around a minor star; Darwin demoted the human species to one of numerous animal species. Freud took the next step by emphasizing that human behavior is determined by forces beyond our control, thereby depriving us of free will and psychological freedom. By emphasizing the unconscious status of our motivations, he deprived us of rationality; by stressing the sexual and aggressive nature of those motivations, he dealt the final blow to our dignity.

Psychoanalytic theory also paints a portrait of human nature as basically evil. Without the restraining forces of society and its internalized representative, the superego, humans would destroy themselves. Freud was a deeply pessimistic man. He was forced to flee from Vienna, when the Nazis invaded in 1938, and he died in September 1939 just as World War II began. He saw these events as natural consequences of the human aggressive drive when it is not held in check.

According to psychoanalytic theory, our personalities are basically determined by inborn drives and by events in our environment during the first five years of life. Only extensive psychoanalysis can undo some of the negative consequences of early experiences, and it can do so only in limited ways. We also emerge from psychoanalytic theory

as relatively passive creatures. Although the ego is engaged in an active struggle with the id and superego, we are passive pawns of this drama being played out in our unconscious. Finally, for Freud, psychological health consisted of firm but flexible ego control over the impulses of the id. As he noted, the goal of psychoanalysis was to ensure that "Where id is, there ego shall be" (1933).

An Evaluation of the Psychoanalytic Approach

Psychoanalytic theory is so broad in scope that it cannot simply be pronounced true or false. However, there can be no doubt of its impact on our culture, or of the value of some of its scientific contributions. For example, Freud's method of free association opened up an entirely new database of observations that had never before been explored systematically. In addition, the recognition that our behavior often reflects a compromise between our wishes and our fears accounts for many of the apparent contradictions in human behavior better than any other theory of personality. And Freud's recognition that unconscious processes play an important role in much of our behavior is almost universally accepted—although these processes are often reinterpreted in learning-theory or information-processing terms.

Nevertheless, as a scientific theory the psychoanalytic account has been persistently criticized (Grünbaum, 1984). One of the main criticisms is that many of its concepts are ambiguous and difficult to define or measure objectively. Also, psychoanalytic theory assumes that very different behaviors may reflect the same underlying motive. For example, a mother who resents her child may be abusive, or she may deny her hostile impulses by becoming overly concerned and protective toward the child—what Freud would call a *reaction formation* (see Chapter 14). When opposite behaviors are claimed to result from the same underlying motive, it is difficult to confirm the presence or absence of the motive or to make predictions that can be empirically verified.

A more serious criticism concerns the validity of the observations that Freud obtained through his psychoanalytic procedure. Critics have pointed out that it often is not clear what Freud's patients told him

Freud saw the rise of the Nazis and the outbreak of World War II as natural consequences of the human aggressive drive when it is not held in check.

spontaneously about past events in their lives, what he may have "planted" in their minds, and what he simply inferred. For example, Freud reported that many of his patients recalled being seduced or sexually molested as children. At first he believed them, but then he decided that these reports were not literally true but, rather, reflected the patients' own early sexual fantasies. He regarded this realization as one of his major theoretical insights. But one writer argued that Freud's original assumption about the reality of the seductions was probably more accurate, an argument that seems more reasonable in light of our increased awareness of child sexual abuse (Masson, 1984).

Other critics have gone further and suggested that Freud may have questioned his patients so persistently with leading questions and suggestions that they were led to reconstruct memories of seductions that never occurred—a hypothesis that Freud considered but rejected (Powell & Boer, 1994). (Recall the discussion of reconstructed memories in Chapter 8.) Others charge that in many cases Freud simply

inferred that seduction had occurred even though the patient never reported such an incident; he actually substituted his theoretical expectations for data (Esterson, 1993; Scharnberg, 1993).

When Freud's theories have been empirically tested, the results have been mixed. Efforts to link adult personality characteristics to psychosexually relevant events in childhood have generally met with negative outcomes (Sears, Maccoby, & Levin, 1957; Sewell & Mussen, 1952). When relevant character traits are identified, they appear to be related to similar character traits in the parents (Beloff, 1957; Hetherington & Brackbill; 1963). Thus, even if a relationship were to be found between toilet-training practices and adult personality traits, it could have arisen because both are linked to parental emphasis on cleanliness and order. In such a case, a simple learning-theory explanation—parental reinforcement and the child's imitation of the parents' behavior—would be a more economical explanation of the adult traits than the psychoanalytic hypothesis.

This outcome should also remind us that Freud based his theory on observations of a very narrow range of people—primarily upper-middle-class men and women in Victorian Vienna who suffered from neurotic symptoms. In hindsight, many of Freud's cultural biases are obvious, particularly in his theories about women. For example, his theory that female psychosexual development is shaped largely by "penis envy"—a girl's feelings of inadequacy because she doesn't have a penis—is almost universally rejected as reflecting the sex bias of Freud and the historical period in which he lived. A little girl's personality development during the Victorian era was surely shaped more decisively by her awareness that she lacked the greater independence, power, and social status of her brother than by her envy of his penis.

Despite these criticisms, the remarkable feature of Freud's theory is how well it managed to transcend its narrow observational base. For example, many experimental studies of the defense mechanisms and reactions to conflict have supported the theory in contexts quite different from those in which Freud developed the theory (Blum, 1953; Erdelyi, 1985; Holmes, 1974; Sears, 1944; 1943). The structural theory (ego, id, and superego), the psychosexual theory, and the energy concept have not fared well over the years. Even some psychoanalytic writers are prepared to abandon or to modify them substantially (Kline, 1972; Schafer, 1976; On the other hand, Freud's dynamic theory—his theory of anxiety and the mechanisms of defense—has withstood the test of time, research, and observation. A recent survey of psychoanalytically oriented psychologists and psychiatrists found widespread agreement with a number of ideas that were controversial when Freud first introduced them, including the importance of early childhood experiences in shaping adult personality and the centrality of both conflict and the unconscious in human mental life (Westen, 1998).

The Behaviorist Approach

In contrast to the psychodynamic approach to personality, the behaviorist approach emphasizes the importance of environmental, or situational, determinants of behavior. In this view, behavior is the result of a continuous interaction between personal and environmental variables. Environmental conditions shape behavior through learning; a person's behavior, in turn, shapes the environment. Persons and situations influence each other. To predict behavior, we need to know how the characteristics of the individual interact with those of the situation (Bandura, 1986). Today the behaviorist approach is called the social-learning or social cognitive approach.

Social Learning and Conditioning

Operant Conditioning The effects of other people's actions—the rewards and punishments they provide—are an important influence on an individual's behavior. Accordingly, one of the most basic principles of social-learning theory is operant conditioning and related processes, which we discussed in Chapter 7. The basic tenet of social-learning theory is that people behave in ways that are likely to produce reinforcement and that individual differences in behavior result primarily from differences in the kinds of learning experiences a person encounters in the course of growing up.

Although individuals learn many behavior patterns through direct experience—that is, by being rewarded or punished for behaving in a certain manner—they also acquire many responses through observational learning. People can learn by observing the actions of others and noting the consequences of those actions. It would be a slow and inefficient process indeed if all of our behavior had to be learned through direct reinforcement of our responses. Similarly, the reinforcement that controls the expression of learned behaviors may be direct (tangible rewards, social approval or disapproval, or alleviation of aversive conditions), vicarious (observation of someone receiving reward or punishment for behavior similar to one's own), or self-administered (evaluation of one's own performance with self-praise or self-reproach).

Because most social behaviors are not uniformly rewarded in all settings, the individual learns to identify the contexts in which certain behavior is appropriate and those in which it is not. To the extent that a person is rewarded for the same response in many different situations, *generalization* takes place, ensuring that the same behavior will occur in a variety of settings. Thus, a boy who is reinforced for physical aggression at home, as well as at school and at play, is likely to develop an aggressive personality. More often, aggressive responses are differentially rewarded, and the individual learns to distinguish between situations in which aggression is appropriate and situations in which it is not (for example, aggression is acceptable on the football field but not in the classroom). For this reason, social-learning theorists challenge the usefulness of characterizing individuals with trait terms like "aggressive," arguing that such terms obscure the cross-situational variability of behavior.

Classical Conditioning To account for emotion or affect, social-learning theorists add classical conditioning to their account of personality (see Chapter 7). For example, when a child is punished by a parent for engaging in some forbidden activity, the punishment elicits the physiological responses that we associate with guilt or anxiety. Subsequently, the child's behavior may itself elicit those responses; the child will feel guilty when engaging in the forbidden behavior. In the terminology of classical conditioning, we would say that the behavior becomes a conditioned stimulus by being paired with the unconditioned stimulus of punishment; the anxiety becomes the conditioned response. For the social-learning theorist, it is classical conditioning that produces the internalized source of anxiety that Freud labeled the superego. Like operant conditioning, classical conditioning can also operate vicariously and can generalize to stimuli that have not been directly conditioned.

Cognitive Variables Social-learning theory has come a long way from its roots in early radical behaviorism, which explicitly avoided any reference to internal cognitive processes. The social-learning perspective is aptly summarized in the following comment by Albert Bandura: "The prospects for survival would be slim indeed if one could learn only from the consequences of trial and error. One does not teach children to swim, adolescents to drive automobiles, and novice medical students to perform surgery by having them discover the requisite behavior from the consequences of their successes and failures" (1986, p. 20). According to social-learning theorists, not only do internal cognitive processes influence behavior, but so does observation of the behaviors of others, as well as the environment in which behavior occurs.

As early as 1954, Julian Rotter was introducing cognitive variables into the behaviorist approach (1954, 1982). Rotter proposed the concept of *behavior potential,* meaning the likelihood of a particular behavior occurring in a particular situation—for example, staying up all night to study for an exam. The strength of the behavior potential is determined by two variables: expectancy and reinforcement value. In the case of pulling an all-nighter, the likelihood of engaging in that behavior is greater if the student expects to receive a higher grade as a result. This expectation will depend on what happened the last time the student was in a similar situation. If studying all night resulted in a higher grade last time, the student will expect the same result this time. In other words, the more often the student is reinforced for studying all night, the stronger his or her expectancy that the behavior will be reinforced in the future. As for reinforcement value, it depends on the degree to which we prefer one reinforcer over another. If a student prefers sleeping over receiving a higher grade, the likelihood of pulling an all-nighter decreases.

Bandura, one of the leading contemporary theorists in this area, has taken this approach even further, developing what he calls *social-cognitive theory.* His theory emphasizes *reciprocal determinism,* in which external determinants of behavior (such as rewards and punishments) and internal determinants (such as beliefs, thoughts, and expectations) are part of a system of interacting influences that affect both behavior and other parts of the system (Bandura, 1986). In Bandura's model, not only can the environment affect behavior, but behavior can affect the environment. In fact, the relationship between environment and behavior is a reciprocal one: The

FRONTIERS OF PSYCHOLOGICAL RESEARCH

Neurotransmitters and Personality

There is considerable evidence that certain neurotransmitters play a role in the development and expression of various personality traits. The functioning of the nervous system is affected by the amounts of various neurotransmitters available at any given time, which can vary quite widely. People also seem to differ in their average levels of those transmitters, and these differences seem to be related to particular personality traits.

The most important neurotransmitters from the standpoint of personality are norepinephrine and dopamine. Norepinephrine affects heart rate, blood pressure, and energy level. People with chronically high levels of norepinephrine seem to be more anxious, dependent, and sociable (Gray, 1987), while those with lower levels of this neurotransmitters are less inhibited and more impulsive. Those with chronically low levels are more likely to be socially detached nonconformers (Zuckerman, 1991).

Dopamine plays a role in the control of body movements and is involved in brain systems that cause the person to approach attractive objects and people. It therefore is thought to affect sociability and general activity level. Some researchers suggest that dopamine is related to extraversion and impulsivity (Sacks, 1983; Zuckerman, 1991).

Another important neurotransmitter is serotonin, which seems to be involved in the inhibition of behavioral impulses, including emotional impulses. One author believes that people with abnormally low levels of serotonin suffer from "serotonin depletion" (Metzner, 1994). The symptoms of this condition include irrational anger, hypersensitivity to rejection, pessimism, obsessive worry, and fear of risk-taking.

The popular antidepressant drug Prozac is a selective serotonin reuptake inhibitor; its effect is to raise serotonin levels. According to Peter Kramer, author of *Listening to Prozac,* the drug can actually give people new personalities. It can prevent a person from worrying needlessly and overreacting to minor stresses, thereby giving them a more cheerful outlook on life. People who have taken Prozac often report that they feel like "better people" who get more work done and are more attractive to members of the opposite sex.

Prozac's success has given rise to speculation that personality is actually determined by the presence or absence of certain chemicals in the brain. However, it should be noted that Prozac does not work on people with adequate levels of serotonin (Metzner, 1994). Moreover, Prozac and other drugs that affect serotonin levels have widely varying effects on different individuals; they do not create a predictable new personality in everyone who takes them. Thus, while it seems clear that neurotransmitters affect personality, there is insufficient evidence to conclude that they create it.

---

environment influences our behavior, which then affects the kind of environment we find ourselves in, which may in turn influence our behavior, and so on.

Bandura notes that people use symbols and forethought in deciding how to act. When they encounter a new problem, they imagine possible outcomes and consider the probability of each. Then they set goals and develop strategies for achieving them. This is quite different from the notion of conditioning through rewards and punishments. Of course, the individual's past experiences with rewards and punishments will influence his or her decisions about future behavior.

Bandura also points out that most behavior occurs in the absence of external rewards or punishments. Most behavior stems from internal processes of *self-regulation.* As he expresses it, "Anyone who attempted to change a pacifist into an aggressor or a devout religionist into an atheist would quickly come to appreciate the existence of personal sources of behavioral control" (1977, pp. 128–129).

How do these internal, personal sources of control develop? According to Bandura and other social-learning theorists, we learn how to behave by observing the behavior of others, or reading or hearing about it. We do not have to actually perform the behaviors we observe; instead, we can note whether those behaviors were rewarded or punished and store that information in memory. When new situations arise, we can behave according to the expectations we have accumulated on the basis of our observation of models.

Bandura's social-cognitive theory thus goes beyond classical behaviorism. Rather than focusing only on the ways in which environment affects behavior, it examines the interactions among environment, behavior, and the individual's cognitions. In addition to considering external influences such as rewards and punishments, it considers internal factors such as expectations. And instead of explaining behavior simply in terms of conditioning, it emphasizes the role of observational learning.

Individual Differences   We noted earlier that personality psychology seeks to specify both the variables on which individuals differ from one another and the general processes of personality functioning. Trait approaches have focused on the first task, describing personality differences in detail while saying virtually nothing about personality functioning. Psychoanalytic theory has attempted to do both. In contrast, the social-learning approach has focused primarily on process, devoting little attention to individual differences. Because this approach sees personality as the product of the individual's unique reinforcement history and emphasizes the degree to which behavior varies across situations, it has not attempted to classify individuals into types or to rate them on traits. However, social-learning theorist Walter Mischel has attempted to incorporate individual differences into social learning theory by introducing the following set of cognitive variables:

1. Competencies: What can you do? Competencies include intellectual abilities, social and physical skills, and other special abilities.

2. Encoding strategies: How do you see it? People differ in the way they selectively attend to information, encode (represent) events, and group the information into meaningful categories. An event that is perceived by one person as threatening may be seen by another as challenging.

3. Expectancies: What will happen? Expectations about the consequences of different behaviors will guide the individual's choice of behavior. If you cheat on an examination and are caught, what do you expect the consequences to be? If you tell your friend what you really think of him or her, what will happen to your

relationship? Expectations about our own abilities will also influence behavior: We may anticipate the consequences of a certain behavior but fail to act because we are uncertain of our ability to execute the behavior.

4. Subjective values: What is it worth? Individuals who have similar expectancies may choose to behave differently because they assign different values to the outcomes. Two students may expect a certain behavior to please their professor; however, this outcome is important to one student but not to the other.

5. Self-regulatory systems and plans: How can you achieve it? People differ in the standards and rules they use to regulate their behavior (including self-imposed rewards for success or punishments for failure), as well as in their ability to make realistic plans for reaching a goal. (After Mischel, 1993, 1973)

All of these *person variables* (sometimes referred to as *cognitive social-learning person variables*) interact with the conditions of a particular situation to determine what an individual will do in that situation. (There is also evidence that individual differences in neurotransmitter levels play a role; see the Frontiers of Psychological Research feature on the preceding page.)

A Behaviorist Portrait of Human Behavior

Like the psychoanalytic approach, the behaviorist approach to personality is deterministic. In contrast to the psychoanalytic approach, however, it pays little attention to biological determinants of behavior and focuses on environmental determinants. It has also been strongly influenced by the ideas of Darwin. Just as evolution works through natural selection to shape a species to be adaptive to its environment, so the processes of learning—especially operant conditioning—shape an individual's behavioral repertoire to be adaptive to his or her environment. People are not inherently good or evil but are readily modified by events and situations in their environment. As we noted in Chapter 3, John Watson, the founder of the behaviorist movement in the United States, claimed that he could raise an infant to be anything, regardless of the infant's "talents, penchants, tendencies, abilities, vocations, and race of his [or her] ancestors." Few social-learning theorists would take such an extreme view today. Nevertheless, social-learning theory shares with its behaviorist predecessors a strong optimism about our ability to change human behavior by changing the environment.

The human personality as described by social-learning theorists may be highly modifiable, but it still has a passive quality. We still seem to be shaped primarily by forces beyond our control. This view is changing, however, as social-learning approaches increasingly emphasize the individual's active role in selecting and modifying the environment, thereby permitting the person to become a causal force in his or her own life. As we will see, however, this role is not active enough for humanistic theorists. In particular, they do not believe that it is sufficient to define psychological health merely as optimal adaptation to the environment.

An Evaluation of the Behaviorist Approach

Through its emphasis on specifying the environmental variables that evoke particular behaviors, social-learning theory has made a major contribution to both clinical psychology and personality theory. It has led us to see human actions as reactions to specific environments, and it has helped us focus on the ways in which environments control our behavior and how they can be changed to modify behavior. As we will see in Chapter 16, the systematic application of learning principles has proved successful in changing many maladaptive behaviors.

Social-learning theorists have been criticized for overemphasizing situational influences on behavior (Carlson, 1971), and there is still some merit in this criticism despite the recent modifications of the theories to include cognitive processes and variables. But the learning theorists' findings on the cross-situational consistency of personality have forced other personality psychologists to reexamine their assumptions. The result has been a clearer understanding of the interactions between people and situations and an enhanced appreciation of each person's individuality.

The Humanistic Approach

During the first half of the twentieth century, the psychoanalytic and behaviorist approaches were dominant in psychology. In 1962, however, a group of psychologists founded the Association of Humanistic Psychology. They saw humanistic psychology as a "third force," an alternative to the other two approaches. To define its mission, the association adopted four principles:

1. The experiencing person is of primary interest. Humans are not simply objects of study. They must be described and understood in terms of their own subjective views of the world, their perceptions of self, and their feelings of self-worth. The central question each person must face is "Who am I?" In order to learn how the individual attempts to answer this question, the psychologist must become a partner with that person.

2. Human choice, creativity, and self-actualization are the preferred topics of investigation. People are not motivated only by basic drives like sex or aggression or physiological needs like hunger and thirst. They feel a need to develop their potentials and capabilities. Growth and self-actualization should be the criteria of psychological health, not merely ego control or adjustment to the environment.

3. Meaningfulness must precede objectivity in the selection of research problems. Humanistic psychologists argue that we should study important human and social problems, even if that sometimes means adopting less rigorous methods. And while psychologists should strive to be objective in collecting and interpreting observations, their choice of research topics can and should be guided by values. In this sense, research is not value-free.

4. Ultimate value is placed on the dignity of the person. People are basically good. The objective of psychology is to understand, not to predict or control people.

Psychologists who share these values come from diverse theoretical backgrounds. For example, the trait theorist Gordon Allport was also a humanistic psychologist, and we have already pointed out that several psychoanalysts, such as Carl Jung, Alfred Adler, and Erik Erikson, held humanistic views of motivation that diverged from Freud's views. But it is Carl Rogers and Abraham Maslow whose theoretical views lie at the center of the humanistic movement.

Carl Rogers Like Freud, Carl Rogers (1902–1987) based his theory on work with patients or clients in a clinic (Rogers, 1951; 1959; 1963; 1970). Rogers was impressed with what he saw as the individual's innate tendency to move toward growth, maturity, and positive change. He came to believe that the basic force motivating the human organism is the **actualizing tendency**—*a tendency toward fulfillment or actualization of all the capacities of the* organization. A growing organism seeks to fulfill its potential within the limits of its heredity. A person may not always clearly perceive which actions lead to growth and which ones do not. But once the course is clear, the individual chooses to grow. Rogers did not deny that there are other needs, some of them biological, but he saw them as subservient to the organism's motivation to enhance itself.

Rogers's belief in the primacy of actualization forms the basis of his *nondirective* or *client-centered therapy*. This method of psychotherapy assumes that every individual has the motivation and ability to change and that the individual is best qualified to decide the direction such change should take. The therapist's role is to act as a sounding board while the client explores and analyzes his or her problems. This approach differs from psychoanalytic therapy, during which the therapist analyzes the patient's history to determine the problem and devise a course of remedial action. (See Chapter 16 for a discussion of various approaches to psychotherapy.)

The Self The central concept in Rogers's theory of personality is the self, or self-concept (Rogers uses the terms interchangeably). The **self** (or **real self**) consists of *all the ideas, perceptions, and values that characterize "I" or "me"*; it includes the

Carl Rogers believed that individuals have an innate tendency to move toward growth, maturity, and positive change. He referred to this as the actualizing tendency.

awareness of "what I am" and "what I can do." This perceived self, in turn, influences both the person's perception of the world and his or her behavior. For example, a woman who perceives herself as strong and competent perceives and acts upon the world quite differently than a woman who considers herself weak and ineffectual. The self-concept does not necessarily reflect reality: A person may be highly successful and respected but still view himself or herself as a failure.

According to Rogers, the individual evaluates every experience in relation to his or her self-concept. People want to behave in ways that are consistent with their self-image; experiences and feelings that are not consistent are threatening and may be denied entry into consciousness. This is essentially Freud's concept of repression, although Rogers felt that such repression is neither necessary nor permanent. (Freud would say that repression is inevitable and that some aspects of the individual's experiences always remain unconscious.)

The more areas of experience a person denies because they are inconsistent with his or her self-concept, the wider the gap between the self and reality and the greater the potential for maladjustment. Individuals whose self-concept does not match their feelings and experiences must defend themselves against the truth because the truth will result in anxiety. If the gap becomes too wide, the person's defenses may break down, resulting in severe anxiety or other forms of emotional disturbance. A well-adjusted person, in contrast, has a self-concept that is consistent with his or her thought, experience, and behavior; the self is not rigid but flexible, and can change as it assimilates new experiences and ideas.

Rogers also proposed that each of us has an **ideal self,** *our conception of the kind of person we would like to be.* The closer the ideal self is to the real self, the more fulfilled and happy the individual becomes. A large discrepancy between the ideal self and the real self results in an unhappy, dissatisfied person.

Thus, two kinds of inconsistency can develop: one, between the self and the experiences of reality; the other, between the real self and the ideal self. Rogers proposed some hypotheses about how these inconsistencies may develop. In particular, Rogers believed that people are likely to function more effectively if they are brought up with **unconditional positive regard**—that is, if *they feel themselves valued by parents and others even when their feelings, attitudes, and behaviors are less than ideal.* If parents offer only *conditional* positive regard—valuing the child only when he or she behaves, thinks, or feels correctly—the child's self-concept is likely to be distorted. For example, feelings of competition and hostility toward a younger sibling are natural, but parents disapprove of hitting a baby brother or sister and usually punish such actions. Children must somehow integrate this experience into their self-concept. They may decide that they are bad and feel ashamed. They may decide that their parents do not like them and feel rejected. Or they may deny their feelings and decide they do not want to hit the baby. Each of these attitudes distorts the truth. The third alternative is the easiest for children to accept, but in so doing they deny their real feelings, which then become unconscious. The more people are forced to deny their own feelings and accept the values of others, the more uncomfortable they will feel about themselves. Rogers suggested that the best approach is for the parents to recognize the child's feelings as valid while explaining the reasons that hitting is not acceptable.

Measuring Real-Ideal Self-Congruence In Chapter 12 we described a method of assessment called the Q-sort, in which a rater or sorter is given a set of cards, each containing a personality statement (for example, "Is cheerful"), and asked to describe an individual's personality by sorting the cards into piles. The rater places statements that are least descriptive of the individual in a pile on the left and those that are most descriptive in a pile on the right. The other statements are distributed in the intermediate piles, thereby assigning each Q item a score corresponding to the pile in which it is placed. Researchers can compare two Q-sorts by computing a correlation between their item scores, thereby assessing the degree to which the two sorts are similar.

Rogers pioneered the use of the Q-sort as a way of examining the self-concept. His Q set contains statements like "I am satisfied

According to Rogers, people are likely to function more effectively if they receive unconditional positive regard—that is, if they feel themselves valued by their parents regardless of their feelings, attitudes, and behaviors.

with myself"; "I have a warm emotional relationship with others"; and "I don't trust my emotions." In Rogers' procedure, individuals first sort themselves as they actually are—their real self—and then sort themselves as they would like to be—their ideal self. The correlation between the two sorts reveals the degree of incongruence between the real and ideal selves. A low or negative correlation corresponds to a large discrepancy, implying feelings of low self-esteem and lack of worth.

By repeating this procedure several times during the course of therapy, Rogers could assess the effectiveness of therapy. In one study, correlations between self and ideal Q-sorts of individuals seeking therapy averaged 2.01 before therapy but increased to 1.34 after therapy. Correlations for a matched control group that did not receive therapy did not change (Butler & Haigh, 1954). In other words, the therapy had significantly reduced these individuals' perception of the discrepancy between their real selves and their ideal selves. Note that this could occur in two ways: An individual could change his or her concept of the real self so that it was closer to the ideal self, or change his or her concept of the ideal self so that it was more realistic. Therapy can produce both kinds of changes.

Abraham Maslow The psychology of Abraham Maslow (1908–1970) overlaps with that of Carl Rogers in many ways. Maslow was first attracted to behaviorism and carried out studies of primate sexuality and dominance. He was already moving away from behaviorism when his first child was born, after which he remarked that anyone who observes a baby cannot be a behaviorist. He was influenced by psychoanalysis but eventually became critical of its theory of motivation and developed his own theory. Specifically, he proposed that there is a **hierarchy of needs,** ascending *from the basic biological needs to the more complex psychological motivations that become important only after the basic needs have been satisfied* (see Figure 13-4). The needs at one level must be at least partially satisfied before those at the next level become important motivators of action. When food and safety are difficult to obtain, efforts to satisfy

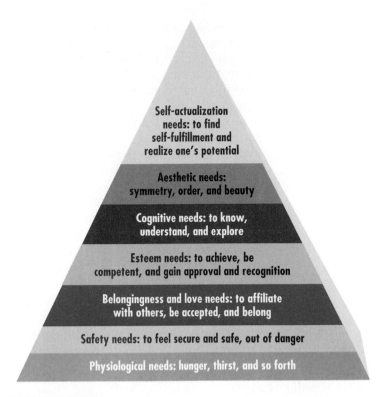

FIGURE 13-4

Maslow's Hierarchy of Needs   *Needs that are low in the hierarchy must be at least partially satisfied before needs that are higher in the hierarchy become important sources of motivation.* (After Maslow, 1970)

those needs will dominate a person's actions, and higher motives will have little significance. Only when basic needs can be satisfied easily will the individual have the time and energy to devote to aesthetic and intellectual interests. Artistic and scientific endeavors do not flourish in societies in which people must struggle for food, shelter, and safety. The highest motive—self-actualization—can be fulfilled only after all other needs have been satisfied.

Maslow decided to study *self-actualizers*—men and women who had made extraordinary use of their potential. He began by studying the lives of eminent historical figures such as Spinoza, Thomas Jefferson, Abraham Lincoln, Jane Addams, Albert Einstein, and Eleanor Roosevelt. In this way he was able to create a composite picture of a self-actualizer. The distinguishing characteristics of such individuals are listed in Table 13-1, along with some of the behaviors that Maslow believed could lead to self-actualization.

Maslow then extended his study to a population of college students. Selecting students who fit his definition of self-actualizers, he found this group to be in the healthiest 1% of the population; these students showed no signs of maladjustment and were making effective use of their talents and capabilities (Maslow, 1970).

Many people experience what Maslow called **peak experiences:** *transient moments of self-actualization.* A peak experience is characterized by happiness and fulfillment— a temporary, nonstriving, non-self-centered state of goal attainment. Peak experiences may occur in different intensities and in various contexts, such as creative activities, appreciation of nature, intimate relationships, aesthetic perceptions, or athletic participation. After asking a large number of college students to describe any experience

that came close to being a peak experience, Maslow attempted to summarize their responses. They spoke of wholeness, perfection, aliveness, uniqueness, effortlessness, self-sufficiency, and the values of beauty, goodness, and truth.

A Humanistic Portrait of Human Nature

As a matter of principle, humanistic psychologists have been quite explicit about the principles underlying their approach to human personality. The four principles set forth by the Association of Humanistic Psychology, which we summarized earlier, draw sharp contrasts between the humanistic portrait of human personality and the portraits drawn by the psychoanalytic and behaviorist approaches.

Most humanistic psychologists do not dispute the claim that biological and environmental variables can influence behavior, but they emphasize the individual's own role in defining and creating his or her destiny, and they downplay the determinism that is characteristic of the other approaches. In their view, individuals are basically good, striving for growth and self-actualization. They are also modifiable and active. Humanistic psychologists set a particularly high criterion for psychological health. Mere ego control or adaptation to the environment is not enough. Only an individual who is growing toward self-actualization can be said to be psychologically healthy. In other words, psychological health is a process, not an end state.

Such assumptions have political implications. From the perspective of humanistic psychology, anything that retards the fulfillment of individual potential—that prevents any human being from becoming all he or she can be—should be challenged. For example, if women in the 1950s were happy and well adjusted to traditional sex roles, the criterion of psychological health defined by behaviorism was satisfied. But from the humanistic perspective, consigning all women to the same role is undesirable—no matter how appropriate that role might be for some women—because it prevents many from reaching their maximum potential. It is no accident that the rhetoric of liberation movements—such as women's liberation

---

TABLE 13-1

Self-Actualization   *Listed here are the personal qualities that Maslow found to be characteristic of self-actualizers and the behaviors he considered important to the development of self-actualization.* (After Maslow, 1967)

Characteristics of Self-Actualizers

Perceive reality efficiently and are able to tolerate uncertainty

Accept themselves and others for what they are

Spontaneous in thought and behavior

Problem-centered rather than self-centered

Have a good sense of humor

Highly creative

Resistant to enculturation, although not purposely unconventional

Concerned for the welfare of humanity

Capable of deep appreciation of the basic experiences of life

Establish deep, satisfying interpersonal relationships with a few, rather than many, people

Able to look at life from an objective viewpoint

Behaviors Leading to Self-Actualization

Experience life as a child does, with full absorption and concentration

Try something new rather than sticking to secure and safe ways

Listen to your own feelings in evaluating experiences rather than to the voice of tradition or authority or the majority

Be honest; avoid pretenses or "game playing"

Be prepared to be unpopular if your views do not coincide with those of most people

Assume responsibility

Work hard at whatever you decide to do

Try to identify your defenses and have the courage to give them up

Albert Einstein and Eleanor Roosevelt were among the individuals Maslow identified as self-actualizers.

and gay liberation—echoes the language of humanistic psychology.

An Evaluation of the Humanistic Approach

By focusing on the individual's unique perception and interpretation of events, the humanistic approach brings individual experience back into the study of personality. More than other theories we have discussed, the theories of Rogers and Maslow concentrate on the whole, healthy person and take a positive, optimistic view of human personality. Humanistic psychologists emphasize that they study important problems even if they do not always have rigorous methods for investigating them. They have a point; investigating trivial problems just because one has a convenient method for doing so does little to advance the science of psychology. Moreover, humanistic psychologists have succeeded in devising new methods for assessing self-concepts and conducting studies that treat the individual as an equal partner in the research enterprise. Nevertheless, critics question the quality of the evidence in support of the humanists' claims. For example, to what extent are the characteristics of self-actualizers a consequence of a

psychological process called self-actualization and to what extent are they merely reflections of the particular value systems held by Rogers and Maslow? Where, they ask, is the evidence for Maslow's hierarchy of needs?

Humanistic psychologists are also criticized for building their theories solely on observations of relatively healthy people. Their theories are best suited to well-functioning people whose basic needs have been met, freeing them to concern themselves with higher needs. The applicability of these theories to malfunctioning or disadvantaged individuals is less apparent.

Finally, some have criticized the values espoused by the humanistic theorists. Many observers believe that Americans are already obsessed with the individual and show little concern for the welfare of the larger society. A psychology that raises individual self-fulfillment and actualization to the top of the value hierarchy may provide a "sanction for selfishness" (Wallach & Wallach, 1983). Although Maslow lists concern for the welfare of humanity among the characteristics of self-actualizers (see Table 13-1) and some of the self-actualizers identified by Maslow—such as Eleanor Roosevelt—clearly possessed this characteristic, it is not included in the hierarchy of needs.

The Cognitive Approach

Today most personality psychologists would not identify themselves as "pure" adherents to any one of the three approaches described so far, and the differences among the approaches are no longer as sharp as they once were. This is because most contemporary personality theorists have joined psychologists in other subfields in becoming more "cognitive." In fact, most contemporary experimental work in personality psychology begins from a cognitive base. The cognitive approach actually is not a "philosophy" of human nature in the way that the other approaches are; rather, it is a general empirical approach and a set of topics related to how people process information about themselves and the world.

For the cognitive theorist, differences in personality stem from differences in the way individuals mentally represent information. These representations are referred to as *cognitive structures*. In this section we look at two types of cognitive structures: personal constructs and schemas.

Kelly's Personal Construct Theory

George Kelly (1905–1966) was one of the first personality psychologists to suggest that cognitive processes play a central role in an individual's functioning. Kelly noted that personality psychologists typically characterized an individual on dimensions that they themselves had constructed. He proposed instead that the goal should be to discover **personal constructs,** *the dimensions that individuals themselves use to interpret themselves and their social worlds*. These dimensions constitute the basic units of analysis in Kelly's *personal construct theory* (1955).

More generally, Kelly believed that individuals should be viewed as intuitive scientists. Like formal scientists, they observe the world, formulate and test hypotheses about

According to Kelly, personal constructs take an either-or form. A new acquaintance is either friendly or unfriendly, intelligent or unintelligent, fun or boring.

it, and make up theories about it. They also categorize, interpret, label, and judge themselves and their world. And, like scientists, individuals can entertain invalid theories, beliefs that hinder them in their daily life and lead to biased interpretations of events and persons, including themselves.

Like scientists trying to make predictions about events, people want to understand the world so that they can predict what will happen to them. Kelly argued that each individual uses a unique set of personal constructs in interpreting and predicting events. Those constructs tend to take an either/or form: A new acquaintance is either friendly or unfriendly, intelligent or unintelligent, fun or boring, and so on. But two people meeting the same individual may use different constructs in evaluating that individual—someone who seems friendly and intelligent to one person may seem unfriendly and unintelligent to another. These differences lead to differences in behavior—one person will respond positively to the new acquaintance while another may avoid him or her. These differences in behavior produce differences in personality.

Because typical trait tests of personality do not meet Kelly's basic criterion that individuals must be assessed in terms of their personal constructs, he devised his own test for eliciting a person's personal constructs, the Role Construct Repertory Test or "Rep Test." On this test, clients fill in a matrix or grid like the one shown in Figure 13-5. Along the top of the grid is a list of people who are important to the individual. These might be supplied by the assessor or the client, but they usually include "myself" and sometimes include "my ideal self." On each line of the grid the assessor circles three of the cells. For example, in the first row of the figure the assessor has circled the cells in the columns labeled "myself," "my mother," and "my best friend." The client is asked to consider these three people and to place an "X" in the cells of the two who are most similar to each other but different from the third. As shown in the first row, this (male) client considers himself and his mother to be the most similar pair. He is then asked, "In what way are you and your mother alike but different from your best friend?" In this case the client has indicated that he and his mother are both witty. This description is

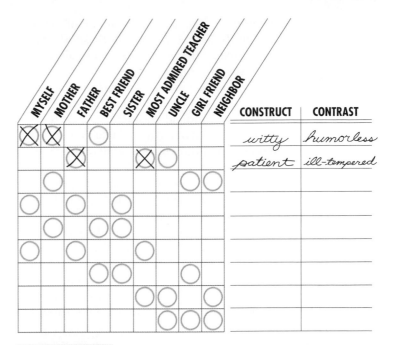

FIGURE 13-5

The Role Construct Repertory Test *In each row, the individual compares three of the people listed at the top of the grid, placing an "X" under the two who are most alike. He or she then describes how they are alike by writing in the construct. Finally, the individual describes how the third person is different from the other two by writing in the contrast. This person indicates that he sees himself and his mother as both being witty and different from his best friend, who is seen as humorless. The procedure is repeated for each row in the matrix.*

his *construct.* Next he is asked, "In what way is your friend different from you and your mother?" He has responded that his friend is humorless. This description is his *contrast.* For this client, then, the dimension witty-humorless is one of the personal constructs he uses to interpret his interpersonal world.

Note that a construct-contrast pair need not constitute logical opposites. For example, this client might have labeled himself and his mother as witty, but then labeled his best friend as serious or introverted or prefers-to-listen-to-humor-rather-than-to-initiate-it. If that is how he construes the two sides of the dimension, then that is what Kelly wanted to know. The Rep Test is designed to assess the individual's constructs, not the psychologist's.

This procedure is repeated with several other triads in the set. By looking at the entire set, the investigator or therapist can explore a number of themes that seem to characterize the individual's interpretation of the world. For example, some clients will reveal through this procedure that they see the entire world in authoritarian terms; dimensions like strong-weak, powerful-powerless, and so forth might appear repeatedly. Or an individual might reveal that she always pairs herself with males on the construct end of dimensions while placing other women on the contrast end.

The Rep Test is a very general procedure and is not restricted to interpretations of other people. For example, an individual may be asked to consider triads of situations or events. (Which two are alike but different from the third? Taking an examination; going out on a blind date; encountering a spider.) The technique has proved valuable both for research on people's constructs and for counseling.

Self-Schemas

A **schema** is *a cognitive structure that helps us perceive, organize, process, and utilize information.* Through the use of schemas, each individual develops a system for identifying what is important in his or her environment while ignoring everything else. Schemas also provide a structure within which to organize and process information. For example, most people have developed a *mother* schema. When asked to describe their mother, it is easy for them to do so because the information is organized into a well-defined cognitive structure. It is easier to describe one's mother than to describe a woman one has heard about but has never met.

Schemas are relatively stable over time and therefore result in stable ways of perceiving and utilizing information. They differ from one individual to another, causing individuals to process information differently and to behave in different ways. They thus can be used to explain differences in personality.

Perhaps the most important schema is the **self-schema**, which consists of *"cognitive generalizations about the self, derived from past experience, that organize and guide the processing of self-related information"* (Markus, 1977, p. 64). From an

early age we all develop a cognitive representation of who we are. The resulting self-schema is made up of the aspects of our behavior that are most important to us and plays a central role in the way we process information and interact with the world around us. For example, two people may both enjoy jogging and literature, but for one person exercise may be an important part of the self-schema, while the other person's self-schema may place greater emphasis on being well-read. Thus, the first person is likely to spend more time jogging than reading, while the reverse is likely to be true of the second person.

The core of the self-schema consists of basic information such as the person's name, physical appearance, and relationships with significant people. But more important from the standpoint of individual differences are *particularistic* features of the self-schema (Markus & Sentis, 1982; Markus & Smith, 1981). For the person whose self-schema includes an emphasis on exercise, for example, exercise is part of "who he or she is" and hence will be a part of his or her daily or weekly routine. For the person who enjoys jogging but does not view it as central to his or her self, an occasional jog around the park will be sufficient. Thus, differences in self-schemas produce differences in behavior.

Self-schemas not only guide the perception and processing of information but also provide a framework for organizing and storing it. As with the *mother* schema mentioned earlier, we would expect people to retrieve information from memory more easily when they have a strong schema for it. This hypothesis was tested in an experiment in which college students were presented with a series of 40 questions on a video screen (Rogers, Kuiper, & Kirker, 1977). The participants were asked to respond to each question by pressing a "yes" or "no" button as quickly as possible. Thirty of the questions could be answered easily without being processed through the self-schema; they asked whether a word was printed in big letters, rhymed with another word, or had the same meaning as another word. The other 10 questions required participants to decide whether a word described them; the

Differences in self-schemas produce differences in behavior. A person whose self-schema includes being physically fit is more likely to exercise regularly.

researchers proposed that in these cases the information had to be processed through the self-schema.

The participants were later asked to recall as many of the 40 words as they could. The results showed that when participants answered questions about themselves they were more likely to remember the information later. The researchers concluded that the participants processed this information through their self-schemas. Because information in the self-schema is easy to access, words referring to the self were easier to remember than words processed in other ways. In subsequent studies, when participants were asked whether a word described the experimenter (Kuiper & Rogers, 1979) or a celebrity (Lord, 1980), they did not recall the words as easily as words describing themselves. In sum, it appears that the superior organization and accessibility of

information about ourselves makes information that is processed through the self-schema more accessible than information that is processed in other ways (Karylowski, 1990; Klein & Loftus, 1988; Klein, Loftus, & Burton, 1989).

Bem's Gender Schema Theory

Another theory stemming from the concept of schemas has been proposed by Sandra Bem. This theory focuses on the use of gender as a way of organizing information.

In most cultures the distinction between male and female tends to organize many features of daily life. Not only are young boys and girls expected to acquire sex-specific skills and behaviors, they are also expected to acquire sex-specific concepts and personality attributes—in other words, to be masculine or feminine as defined by that culture. You will recall from Chapter 3 that the process by which a society teaches children to conform to such expectations is called *sex typing*. Bem (1981) has suggested that in addition to learning the specific concepts and behaviors that the culture associates with being male or female, the child also learns to perceive and organize diverse kinds of information in terms of a **gender schema,** *a mental structure that organizes the person's perceptual and conceptual world into gender categories (male-female, masculine-feminine).*

According to Bem's theory, individuals who are sex-typed use the gender schema more than individuals who are not sex-typed. Bem identifies sex-typed individuals by asking people to rate themselves on a list of sex-typed personality traits. Individuals who rate themselves high on stereotypically masculine traits (such as "assertive," "independent") but low on stereotypically feminine traits (such as "compassionate," "tender") are defined as masculine; individuals with the reverse pattern are defined as feminine; and individuals who describe themselves as having both masculine and feminine traits are defined as *androgynous* (from *andro,* meaning "male," and *gyn,* meaning "female").

Individuals who describe themselves as having both masculine and feminine traits are referred to as androgynous.

In a series of studies, individuals who had been identified as androgynous displayed both masculine independence and feminine nurturance, whereas sex-typed individuals (masculine men and feminine women) tended to display only the behavior considered appropriate for their sex (Bem, 1975; Bem, Martyna, & Watson, 1976).

In one study designed to test whether or not sex-typed individuals use the gender schema to organize information, participants were shown a list of words and later asked to recall as many of the words as they could, in any order. The list included proper names, animal names, verbs, and articles of clothing. Half of the proper names were male and half were female, and one-third of the words in each of the other categories had been rated by judges as masculine (*gorilla, hurling, trousers*), one-third as feminine (*butterfly, blushing, bikini*), and one-third as neutral (*ant, stepping, sweater*). Research on memory has shown that if an individual has encoded a number of words in terms of an underlying schema or network of associations, thinking of one schema-related word enhances the probability of thinking of another. Accordingly, an individual's sequence of recall should reveal "runs" or clusters of words that are linked in memory by the schema. If a participant thinks of an animal word, for example, he or she is likely to think next of another animal word. Note that participants in this experiment could cluster words either according to semantic category (proper names, animals, verbs, clothing) or according to gender.

The participants who were sex-typed showed significantly more gender clustering than those who were not sex-typed. For example, if a sex-typed person happened to recall *butterfly,* he or she was more likely to follow that with another feminine word such as *bikini,* whereas an individual who was not sex-typed was more likely to follow *butterfly* with another animal name. Thus, sex-typed participants were more likely to link words together in memory on the basis of gender; as the theory predicts, they were more likely to use the gender schema to organize information.

Other evidence for the gender schema theory comes from a variety of sources. Sex-typed women, for example, use feminine constructs more often than androgynous women do when placing people into categories on the Rep Test (Tunnell, 1981). Sex-typed people also tend to group statements into masculine and feminine categories when describing themselves (Larsen & Seidman, 1986). And sex-typed people are more likely to identify a person they have read about as either a man or women, even when that information is not relevant (Frable, 1989).

An Evaluation of the Cognitive Approach

The cognitive approach has some strengths as well as some weaknesses. One positive aspect of the approach is that it is based on empirical research. As illustrated by the preceding descriptions of experiments, many cognitive structures have been subjected to extensive study in controlled laboratory experiments. Another strength of cognitive theory is that it goes beyond the trait approach in explaining personality characteristics. Rather than simply identifying traits, cognitive theorists use cognitive structures to explain individual differences in behavior.

On the other hand, a frequent criticism of the cognitive approach is that it employs vague concepts. It is difficult to state specifically what a personal construct is or to be sure when a schema is being used, and it is not entirely clear how a personal construct differs from a schema or how any of these cognitive structures relate to memory and other aspects of information processing. Moreover, behaviorists might ask whether it is really necessary to use these concepts. Perhaps personality can be explained just as well without referring to cognitions.

Freud's Ideas Are Alive and Vibrant

Joel Weinberger, *Adelphi University*

Of course Freud is dead. He died on September 23, 1939. No one asks whether Isaac Newton or William James is dead. For some odd reason this is reserved for Freud. If the question is whether psychoanalysis, the branch of psychology he founded, is dead, the answer is clearly no. Psychoanalysis survived Freud and thrives today. The American Psychological Association's division of psychoanalysis is the second largest division in the association. There now exist several schools of psychoanalysis, some of which Freud would probably not recognize. That is just what you would expect from a discipline whose founder is now 60 years dead.

Are Freud's ideas dead? They certainly are not. They have entered our common vernacular. They have entered and forever changed our culture. Think of the terms of *id, ego, superego, Freudian slip,* and so on. There are psychoanalytic writers, historians, psychiatrists, and of course, psychologists. The real question, I suppose, is whether Freud's ideas are still *valid.* The answer is that some are and some are not. A surprising number remain relevant, even central, to modern psychology. So I suppose the charge is to state which of his ideas remain valid. And that is what I will address.

Let's look at some of Freud's central ideas and see how they stack up with today's psychology. Freud said that all human motives could be traced back to biological sources, specifically to sex and aggression. There is a branch of psychology now termed evolutionary psychology (Buss, 1994); there is also sociobiology (Wilson, 1975) and ethology (Hinde, 1982). All champion the importance of biological factors in our behavior. And all have data to back up their claims. This aspect of Freud's thinking is certainly not dead. As for the importance of sex and aggression? Just look at the best selling books, hit movies, and TV shows around you. What characterizes virtually all of them? Sex and violence. Hollywood and book publishers seem all to be Freudians, and so are the people who sample their wares.

Another idea of Freud's that was very controversial in his time was his notion that children have sexual feelings. Now that is simply commonplace knowledge.

Psychoanalysts have long held that one of the major factors accounting for the effectiveness of psychotherapy is the therapeutic relationship. For many years this was not accepted, particularly by the behaviorist school (Emmelkamp, 1994). We now know that this is a critical factor in therapeutic success (Weinberger, 1996). The related idea that we carry representations of early relationships around in our heads, an idea expanded upon by object relations theory (a school of psychoanalysis) and attachment theory (the creation of a psychoanalyst, John Bowlby), is also now commonly accepted in psychology.

The most central idea usually attributed to Freud is the importance of unconscious processes. According to Freud, we are most often unaware of why we do what we do. For a long while, mainstream academic psychology rejected this notion. Now it seems to have finally caught up to Freud. Modern thinkers now believe that unconscious processes are central and account for most of our behavior. Discussion of unconscious processes permeate research in memory (Graf & Masson, 1993), social psychology (Bargh, 1997), psychology (Baars, 1988), and so on. In fact, it is now a mainstream belief in psychology. More specific notions of Freud's such as his ideas about defense have also received empirical support (Shedler, Mayman, & Manis, 1993; D. Weinberger, 1990). So have some of his ideas about unconscious fantasies (Siegel & Weinberger, 1997). There is even some work afoot to examine Freud's conceptions of transference (Andersen & Glassman, 1996; Crits-Christoph, Cooper, & Luborsky, 1990).

Of course, many of the particulars of Freud's thinking have been overtaken by events and have turned out to be incorrect. What thinker who died over 60 yeas ago has had all of his or her ideas survive intact, without change? In broad outline however, Freud's ideas are not only alive, they are vibrant. We should probably be testing more of them. Any notion that Freud should be ignored because some of his assertions have been shown to be false is just plain silly. It is throwing out the baby with the bath water. And, he is so much fun to read!

Freud's Influence on Psychology Has Been That of a Dead Weight

John F. Kihlstrom, *University of California, Berkeley*

If the 20th century has been "The American Century," it has also been the century of Sigmund Freud (Roth, 1998), because Freud changed our image of ourselves. Copernicus showed that the Earth did not lie at the center of the universe, and Darwin showed that humans were descended from "lower" animals, but Freud claimed to show that human experience, thought, and action was determined not by our conscious rationality, but by irrational forces outside our awareness and control—forces which could only be understood and controlled by an extensive therapeutic process called psychoanalysis.

Freud also changed the vocabulary with which we understand ourselves and others. Before you ever opened this textbook, you already knew something about the id and the superego, penis envy and phallic symbols, castration anxiety and the Oedipus complex. In popular culture, psychotherapy is virtually identified with psychoanalysis. Freudian theory, with its focus on the interpretation of ambiguous events, lies at the foundation of "postmodern" approaches to literary criticism such as deconstruction. More than anyone else, Freud's influence on modern culture has been profound and long-lasting.

Freud's cultural influence is based, at least implicitly, on the premise that his theory is scientifically valid. But from a scientific point of view, classical Freudian psychoanalysis is dead as both a theory of the mind and a mode of therapy (Crews, 1998; Macmillan, 1996). No empirical evidence supports any specific proposition of psychoanalytic theory, such as the idea that development proceeds through oral, anal, phallic, and genital stages, or that little boys lust after their mothers and hate and fear their fathers. No empirical evidence indicates that psychoanalysis is more effective, or more efficient, than other forms of psychotherapy, such as systematic desensitization or assertiveness training. No empirical evidence indicates that the mechanisms by which psychoanalysis achieves its effects, such as they are, are those specifically predicated on the theory, such as transference and catharsis.

Freud lived at a particular period of time, and it might be argued that his theories were valid when applied to European culture at that time, even if they are no longer apropos today. However, recent historical analyses show that Freud's construal of his case material was systematically distorted by his theories of unconscious conflict and infantile sexuality, and that he misinterpreted and misrepresented the scientific evidence available to him. Freud's theories were not just a product of his time: They were misleading and incorrect even as he published them.

Drew Westen (1988), a psychologist at Harvard Medical School, agrees that Freud's theories are archaic and obsolete, but argues that Freud's legacy lives on in a number of theoretical propositions that are widely accepted by scientists: the existence of unconscious mental processes; the importance of conflict and ambivalence in behavior; the childhood origins of adult personality; mental representations as a mediator of social behavior; and stages of psychological development. However, some of these propositions are debatable. For example, there is no evidence that childrearing practices have any lasting impact on personality. More important, Westen's argument skirts the question of whether *Freud's* view of these matters was correct. It is one thing to say that unconscious motives play a role in behavior. It is something quite different to say that our every thought and deed is driven by repressed sexual and aggressive urges; that children harbor erotic feelings toward the parent of the opposite sex; and that young boys are hostile toward their fathers, who they regard as rivals for their mothers' affections. This is what *Freud* believed, and so far as we can tell *Freud* was wrong in every respect. For example, the unconscious mind revealed in laboratory studies of automaticity and implicit memory bears no resemblance to the unconscious mind of psychoanalytic theory (Kihlstrom, 1998).

Westen also argues that psychoanalytic theory itself has evolved since Freud's time, and that it is therefore unfair to bind psychoanalysis so tightly to the Freudian vision of repressed, infantile, sexual and aggressive urges. But again, this avoids the issue of whether *Freud's* theories are correct. Furthermore, it remains an open question whether these "neo-Freudian" theories are any more valid than are the classically Freudian views which preceded them. For example, it is not at all clear that Erik Erikson's stage theory of psychological development is any more valid than Freud's is.

While Freud had an enormous impact on 20th century culture, his influence on psychology has been that of a dead weight. The broad themes that Westen writes about were present in psychology before Freud, or arose more recently independent of his influence. At best, Freud is a figure of only historical interest for psychologists. He is perhaps better studied as a writer than as a scientist.

SUMMARY

1. Personality refers to the distinctive and characteristic patterns of thought, emotion, and behavior that define an individual's personal style of interacting with the physical and social environments. Personality psychology seeks (a) to describe and explain individual differences and (b) to identify the processes that can influence an individual's interactions with the environment and use them to create an integrated account of the total person.

2. Freud's psychoanalytic theory holds that many behaviors are caused by unconscious motivations. Personality is determined primarily by the biological drives of sex and aggression and by experiences that occur during the first five years of life. Freud's theory of personality structure views personality as composed of the id, the ego, and the superego. The id operates on the pleasure principle, seeking immediate gratification of biological impulses. The ego obeys the reality principle, postponing gratification until it can be achieved in socially acceptable ways. The superego (conscience) imposes moral standards on the individual. In a well-integrated personality, the ego remains in firm but flexible control over the id and superego, and the reality principle governs.

3. Freud's theory of personality dynamics proposes that there is a constant amount of psychic energy (libido) for each individual. If a forbidden act or impulse is suppressed, its energy will seek an outlet in some other form, such as dreams or neurotic symptoms. The theory assumes that unacceptable id impulses cause anxiety, which can be reduced by defense mechanisms.

4. Freud's theory of personality development proposes that individuals pass through psychosexual stages and must resolve the Oedipal conflict, in which the young child sees the same-sex parent as a rival for the affection of the opposite-sex parent. Over the years, Freud's theory of anxiety and defense mechanisms has fared better than his structural and developmental theories have.

5. Psychoanalytic theory has been modified by later psychologists, notably Carl Jung and Harry Stack Sullivan. Jung proposed that in addition to the personal unconscious described by Freud, there is a collective unconscious, a part of the mind that is common to all humans. Sullivan suggested that people's responses to interpersonal experiences cause them to develop personifications—mental images of themselves and others.

6. Psychologists who take the psychoanalytic approach sometimes use projective tests, such as the Rorschach Test and the Thematic Apperception Test (TAT). Because the test stimuli are ambiguous, it is assumed that the individual projects his or her personality onto the stimulus, thereby revealing unconscious wishes and motives.

7. Social-learning theory is the contemporary version of the behaviorist approach to personality. It assumes that personality differences result from variations in learning experiences—including learning by observation as well as direct operant or classical conditioning. This approach has become increasingly cognitive over the past few decades and now emphasizes the interaction between external determinants of behavior (such as rewards and punishments) and internal determinants (such as beliefs, thoughts, and expectations).

8. Among the better-known social-learning theorists are Julian Rotter and Albert Bandura. Rotter proposed that the likelihood of a particular behavior occurring in a particular situation is determined by expectancy and reinforcement value. Bandura developed social cognitive theory, which holds that the relationship between environment and behavior is a reciprocal one.

9. The humanistic approach is concerned with the individual's subjective experience. Humanistic psychology was founded as an alternative to psychoanalytic and behaviorist approaches. Humanistic psychologists like Carl Rogers and Abraham Maslow emphasize a person's self-concept and striving for growth, or self-actualization.

10. The cognitive approach to personality is based on the idea that differences in personality stem from differences in the way individuals mentally represent information. George Kelly's personal construct theory focuses on the concepts that individuals use to interpret themselves and their social world. Other theorists focus on schemas, cognitive structures that help us perceive, organize, and store information.

11. Much research has focused on the self-schema, which consists of the aspects of a person's behavior that are most important to that person. Experiments have shown that people perceive information more readily and recall it better when it is relevant to their self-schemas. A related theory is Sandra Bem's gender schema theory, which suggests that individuals who are sex-typed use the gender schema to perceive and organize diverse kinds of information.

KEY TERMS

free association (p. 454)

conscious (p. 454)

preconscious (p. 454)

unconscious (p. 454)

psychological determinism (p. 454)

id (p. 455)

ego (p. 455)

superego (p. 455)

defense mechanisms (p. 456)

repression (p. 456)

projective test (p. 459)

actualizing tendency (p. 469)

self (p. 469)

real self (p. 469)

ideal self (p. 470)

unconditional positive regard (p. 470)

hierarchy of needs (p. 471)

peak experience (p. 472)

personal constructs (p. 474)

schema (p. 476)

self-schema (p. 476)

gender schema (p. 477)

CRITICAL THINKING QUESTIONS

1. Personality psychologists differ in how appealing they find the three major approaches to personality discussed in this chapter. Some prefer to avoid such formal theories and to use the relatively nontheoretical trait approach or the contemporary cognitive approach. What about you? What do you find appealing or unappealing about each of the three historical approaches and the two empirical approaches?

2. As this chapter makes clear, the value of Sigmund Freud's impact on psychology is hotly debated. What is your opinion on the value of Freud's legacy?

3. When it was first introduced, the concept of psychological androgyny—the blending of masculine and feminine traits in a single person—seemed to offer a promising way of liberating individuals from the notion that psychologically healthy men were necessarily masculine and psychologically healthy women were necessarily feminine. But it has been argued that the concept of androgyny is actually more confining than the traditional sex-typed prescriptions because the person has to be both masculine and feminine in order to be considered psychologically healthy; that is, there are now two tests to fail rather than just one. What do you think? Can you suggest a less confining prescription for a psychologically healthy sex role?

FURTHER READING

There are several general textbooks on personality psychology that blend theory and contemporary research. They include Funder, *The Personality Puzzle* (1997); Mischel, *Introduction to Personality* (6th ed., 1998); and Burger, *Personality* (4th ed., 1996). A classic text that compares and contrasts the formal theories of personality is Hall, Lindzey, Loehlin, and Manosevitz, *Introduction to Theories of Personality* (1985).

Among Freud's most readable writings are his *New Introductory Lectures on Psychoanalysis* (1933; reprint ed., 1965) and *Psychopathology of Everyday Life* (1901/1960), in which he discusses "Freudian slips" as well as dreams and humor. An excellent summary of psychoanalytic theory and its development since Freud is Mitchell and Black, *Freud and Beyond: A History of Modern Psychoanalytic Thought* (1995). An unsparingly harsh critique of Freud as both scientist and therapist can be found in Crews (ed.), *Unauthorized Freud: Doubters Confront a Legend* (1998).

The social-learning approach to personality is represented by one of its leading theorists in Bandura, *Social Foundations of Thought and Action: A Social Cognitive Theory* (1985).

Two classic statements of the humanistic viewpoint are Maslow, *Toward a Psychology of Being* (1998) and Rogers, *On Becoming a Person: A Therapists's View of Psychotherapy* (1995). Fadiman and Frager, *Personality and Personal Growth* (4th ed., 1997), focuses on the personality theories that are most concerned with understanding human nature and includes sections on Eastern theories of personality such as yoga, Zen Buddhism, and Sufism—topics that are not usually found in more traditional academic treatments of personality.

Seven

Stress, Psychopathology, and Therapy

Chapter 14
Stress, Health, and Coping

We all experience stress occasionally. Students may be stressed when their relationship with their roommates is not going well, when they must declare a major, or when final exams approach. Today's rapidly paced society creates stress for many of us. We are constantly pressured to accomplish more and more in less and less time. Air and noise pollution, traffic congestion, crime, and excessive workload are increasingly present in our everyday lives. Finally, we sometimes face major stressful events, such as the death of a parent or a natural disaster. Exposure to stress can lead to painful emotions like anxiety or depression. It can also lead to physical illnesses, both minor and severe. But people's reactions to stressful events differ widely: Some people faced with a stressful event develop serious psychological or physical problems, whereas other people faced with the same stressful event develop no problems and may even find the event challenging and interesting. In this chapter we discuss the concept of stress and the effects of stress on the mind and body. We also look at the differences between people's ways of thinking about and coping with stressful events, and how these differences contribute to adjustment.

Stress has become a popular topic. The media often attribute unusual behavior or illness to burn-out due to stress or a nervous breakdown resulting from stress. For example, when a celebrity attempts suicide, it is often said that he or she was burnt out from the pressures of public life. On college campuses, "I'm so stressed out!" is a common claim. But what is stress? In general terms, **stress** refers to *experiencing events that are perceived as endangering one's physical or psychological well-being.* These events are usually referred to as **stressors,** and people's reactions to them are termed **stress responses.**

There are some types of events that most people experience as stressful. We will describe the characteristics of such events and then describe the body's natural reaction to stress. This reaction is adaptive when it is possible to flee from, or attack, a stressor, but it can become maladaptive when a stressor is chronic or uncontrollable. Stress can have both direct and indirect effects on health.

The study of how stress and other social, psychological, and biological factors come together to contribute to illness is known as *behavioral medicine* or *health psychology* (Taylor, 1999). We will review research on how psychosocial factors interact with biological vulnerabilities to affect cardiovascular health and the functioning of the immune system. Finally, we will describe ways of managing stress so as to improve health.

Characteristics of Stressful Events

Countless events create stress. Some are major changes affecting large numbers of people—events such as war, nuclear accidents, and earthquakes. Others are major changes in the life of an individual—for instance, moving to a new area, changing jobs, getting married, losing a friend, suffering a serious illness. Everyday hassles can also be experienced as stressors—losing your wallet, getting stuck in traffic, arguing with your professor, and so on. Finally, the source of stress can be within the individual, in the form of conflicting motives or desires.

Events that are perceived as stressful usually fall into one or more of the following categories: traumatic events outside the usual range of human experience, uncontrollable events, unpredictable events, events that challenge the limits of our capabilities and

The causes of stress vary from one person to the next. What is overwhelming to one person may be exciting and challenging to another.

self-concept, or internal conflicts. In this section we look briefly at each of these categories.

Traumatic Events

The most obvious sources of stress are **traumatic events**—*situations of extreme danger that are outside the range of usual human experience.* These include natural disasters, such as earthquakes and floods; disasters caused by human activity, such as wars and nuclear accidents; catastrophic accidents, such as car or plane crashes; and physical assaults, such as rape or attempted murder.

Many people experience a specific a series of psychological reactions after a traumatic event (Horowitz, 1986). At first, survivors are stunned and dazed, and appear to be unaware of their injuries or of the danger. They may wander around in a disoriented state, perhaps putting themselves at risk for further injury. For example, an earthquake survivor may wander through buildings that are on the verge of collapse. In the next stage, survivors are still passive and unable to initiate even simple tasks, but they may follow orders readily. For example, days after the assault, a rape survivor may not even think to prepare food to eat, but if a friend calls and insists that they go out for food, she will comply. In the third stage, survivors become anxious and apprehensive,

have difficulty concentrating, and may repeat the story of the catastrophe over and over again. The survivor of a car crash may become extremely nervous when near a car, may be unable to go back to work because of inability to concentrate, and may repeatedly tell friends about the details of the crash.

One type of traumatic event that is tragically common in our society is sexual abuse. The impact of rape and other types of sexual violence on the victim's emotional and physical health appears to be great (Koss & Boeschen, 1998). Several studies have found that in the first six months after a rape or other assault, women and men show high levels of depression, anxiety, dismay, and many other indicators of emotional distress (Duncan et al., 1996; Kessler et al., 1997). For some people, this emotional distress declines over time. For others, however, emotional distress is long lasting.

In one study, Burnam and colleagues (1988) found that assault victims were twice as likely as people who had not been assaulted to have a diagnosable depressive disorder, anxiety disorder, or substance abuse disorder at some time after the assault. They were most likely to develop these disorders if they had been assaulted as a child. In fact, people who had been assaulted as children remained at higher risk for developing a psychological disorder throughout their lives.

Fortunately, most of us never experience traumatic events. More common events can lead to stress responses, however. Three characteristics of common events lead to their being perceived as stressful: controllability, predictability, and the extent to which the event challenges our capabilities and self-concept. Of course, the degree to which an event is stressful differs for each individual. That is, people differ in the extent to which they perceive an event as controllable, predictable, and a challenge to their capabilities and self-concept, and it is largely these appraisals that influence the perceived stress-fulness of the event (Lazarus & Folkman, 1984).

Controllability

The more uncontrollable an event seems, the more likely it is to be perceived as stressful (see Chapter 7). Major uncontrollable events include the death of a loved one, being laid

Victims of disasters such as hurricanes and tornados are often stunned and disoriented shortly after the disaster. Later they become more responsive but may still have trouble initiating even simple activities. They may remain anxious and distracted long after the disaster.

off from work, or serious illness. Minor uncontrollable events include such things as having a friend refuse to accept your apology for some misdeed, or being bumped off a flight because the airline oversold tickets. One obvious reason uncontrollable events are stressful is that if we cannot control them, we cannot stop them from happening.

As noted earlier, however, it appears that our *perceptions* of the controllability of events are as important to our assessment of their stressfulness as the *actual* controllability of those events. Consider a study in which participants were shown color photographs of victims of violent deaths. The experimental group could terminate the viewing by pressing a button. The control participants saw the same photographs for the same length of time as the experimental group, but they could not terminate the exposure. The level of arousal or anxiety in both groups was determined by measuring galvanic skin response (GSR), a drop in the electrical resistance of the skin that is widely used as an index of autonomic arousal. The experimental group showed much less anxiety in response to the photographs than the control group, even though the two groups were exposed to the photographs for the same amount of time (Geer & Maisel, 1973).

The belief that we can control events appears to reduce the impact of the events, even if we never exercise that control. This was demonstrated in a study in which two groups of participants were exposed to a loud, extremely unpleasant noise. Participants in one group were told that they could terminate the noise by pressing a button, but they were urged not to do so unless it was absolutely necessary. Participants in the other group had no control over the noise. None of the participants who had a control button actually pressed it, so the noise exposure was the same for both groups. Nevertheless, performance on subsequent problem—solving tasks was significantly worse for the group that had no control, indicating that they were more disturbed by the noise than the group that had the potential for control (Glass & Singer, 1972).

Predictability

Being able to predict the occurrence of a stressful event—even if the individual cannot control it—usually reduces the severity of the stress. As discussed in Chapter 7, laboratory experiments show that both humans and animals prefer predictable aversive events over unpredictable ones. In one study, rats were given a choice between a signaled shock and an unsignaled shock. If the rat pressed a bar at the beginning of a series of shock trials, each shock was preceded by a warning tone. If the rat failed to press the bar, no warning tones sounded during that series of trials. All of the rats quickly learned to press the bar, showing a marked preference for predictable shock (Abbott, Schoen, & Badia, 1984). Humans generally choose predictable over unpredictable shocks, too. They also show less emotional arousal and report less distress while waiting for predictable shocks to occur, and they perceive predictable shocks as less aversive than unpredictable ones of the same intensity (Katz & Wykes, 1985).

How do we explain these results? One possibility is that a warning signal before an aversive event allows the person or animal to initiate some sort of preparatory process that acts to reduce the effects of a noxious stimulus. An animal receiving the signal that a shock is about to happen may shift its feet in such a way as to reduce the experience of the shock. A man who knows he is about to receive a shot in the doctor's office can try to distract himself so as to reduce the pain. A woman who hears warnings of an impending hurricane can board up her windows in an attempt to prevent damage to her house.

Another possibility is that with unpredictable shock, there is no safe period; with predictable shock, the organism (human or animal) can relax to some extent until the signal warns that shock is about to occur (Seligman & Binik, 1977). A real-life example of this phenomenon occurs when a boss who tends to criticize an employee in front of others is out of town on a business trip. The boss's absence is a signal to the employee that it is safe to relax. In contrast, an employee whose boss criticizes him unpredictably throughout the day and never goes out of town may chronically feel stressed.

Some jobs, such as fire fighting and emergency-room medicine, are filled with unpredictability and are considered very stressful. Serious illnesses often are very unpredictable. One of the major problems faced by cancer patients who receive treatment is that they cannot be sure whether or not they have been cured until many years have passed. Every day they must confront the uncertainty of a potentially disastrous future. Even an event as overwhelmingly negative as torture can be affected by the extent to which victims feel that the episodes of torture are predictable. Victims who are able to predict the timing and type of torture they experience while being detained recover better once they are released than victims who perceive the torture as completely unpredictable (Basoglu & Mineka, 1992).

Challenging Our Limits

Some situations are largely controllable and predictable but are still experienced as stressful because they push us to the limits of our capabilities and challenge our views of ourselves. Final-exam week is a good example. Most students work much longer hours during final-exam week than they do during the rest of the year. This physical and intel-

A high level of unpredictability makes firefighting an extremely stressful job.

lectual exertion is experienced as stressful by some people. Some students also find that exams test the limits of their knowledge and intellectual capabilities. Even among students who are capable of doing well on exams, the possibility that they could fail may challenge their view of themselves as competent.

Although we enter some pressure situations enthusiastically and joyfully, they may still be stressful. Marriage is a good example; it entails many adjustments. Individuals are often challenged to the limits of their patience and tolerance as they become accustomed to the habits and idiosyncrasies of their spouse. Arguments over important matters, such as financial decisions, may challenge their belief that they married the right person.

According to Holmes and Rahe (1967), any life change that requires numerous readjustments can be perceived as stressful. In an attempt to measure the impact of life changes, they developed the Life Events Scale shown in Table 14-1. The scale ranks life events from most stressful (death of a spouse) to least stressful (minor violations of the law). To arrive at this scale, the investigators examined thousands of interviews and medical histories to identify the kinds of events that people found stressful. Because marriage appeared to be a critical event for most people, it was placed in the middle of the scale and assigned an arbitrary value of 50. The investigators then asked approximately 400 men and women of varying ages, backgrounds, and marital status to compare marriage with a number of other life events. They were asked such questions as, "Does the event call for more or less readjustment than marriage?" They were then asked to assign a point value to each event on the basis of their evaluation of its severity and the time required for adjustment. These ratings were used to construct the scale in Table 14-1.

Although positive events often require adjustment and hence are sometimes stressful, most research indicates that negative events have a much greater impact on psychological and physical health than positive events. In addition, there are large differences in how people are affected by events. Some of these differences are linked to age and cultural background (Masuda & Holmes,

TABLE 14-1

The Life Events Scale *This scale, also known as the Holmes and Rahe Social Readjustment Rating Scale, measures stress in terms of life changes.* (After Holmes & Rahe, 1967)

Life Event	Value
Death of spouse	100
Divorce	73
Marital separation	65
Jail term	63
Death of close family member	63
Personal injury or illness	53
Marriage	50
Fired from job	47
Marital reconciliation	45
Retirement	45
Change in health of family member	44
Pregnancy	40
Sex difficulties	39
Gain of a new family member	39
Business readjustment	39
Change in financial state	38
Death of a close friend	37
Change to a different line of work	36
Foreclosure of mortgage	30
Change in responsibilities at work	29
Son or daughter leaving home	29
Trouble with in-laws	29
Outstanding personal achievement	28
Wife begins or stops work	26
Begin or end school	26
Change in living conditions	25
Revision of personal habits	24
Trouble with boss	23
Change in residence	20
Change in school	20
Change in recreation	19
Change in church activities	19
Change in social activities	18
Change in sleeping habits	16
Change in eating habits	15
Vacation	13
Christmas	12
Minor legal violations	11

1978). Also, some people do not find major changes or pressure situations stressful. Rather, they experience them as challenging and are invigorated by them. Later we will discuss characteristics of individuals that affect whether they view situations as stressors or as challenges.

Internal Conflicts

So far we have discussed only external events in which something or someone in the environment challenges our well-being. Stress can also be brought about by internal processes—unresolved conflicts that may be either conscious or unconscious. Conflict occurs when a person must choose between incompatible, or mutually exclusive, goals or courses of action. Many of the things people desire prove to be incompatible. You want to play on your college volleyball team but cannot put in the time required and still earn the grades necessary to apply to graduate school. You want to join your friends for a pizza party but are afraid you will fail tomorrow's exam if you don't stay home and study. You don't want to go to your uncle's for dinner, but you also don't want to listen to your parents' complaints if you turn down the invitation. In each case, the two goals are incompatible because the action needed to achieve one automatically prevents you from achieving the other.

Even if two goals are equally attractive—for example, you receive two good job offers—you may agonize over the decision and experience regrets after making a choice. This stress would not have occurred if you had been offered only one job.

Conflict may also arise when two inner needs or motives are in opposition. In our society, the conflicts that are most pervasive and difficult to resolve generally occur between the following motives:

- Independence versus dependence. Particularly when we are faced with a difficult situation, we may want someone to take care of us and solve our problems. But we are taught that we must stand on our own. At other times we may wish for independence, but circumstances or other people force us to remain dependent.

- Intimacy versus isolation. The desire to be close to another person and to share our innermost thoughts and emotions may conflict with the fear of being hurt or rejected if we expose too much of ourselves.

- Cooperation versus competition. Our society emphasizes competition and success. Competition begins in early childhood among siblings, continues through school, and culminates in business and professional rivalry. At the same time, we are urged to cooperate and to help others.

- Expression of impulses versus moral standards. Impulses must be regulated to some degree in all societies. We noted in Chapter 3 that much of childhood learning involves internalizing cultural restrictions on impulses. Sex and aggression are two areas in which our impulses frequently come into conflict with moral standards, and violation of these standards can generate feelings of guilt.

These four areas present the greatest potential for serious conflict. Trying to find a workable compromise between opposing motives can create considerable stress.

Psychological Reactions to Stress

Stressful situations produce emotional reactions ranging from exhilaration (when the event is demanding but manageable) to anxiety, anger, discouragement, and depression (see Table 14-2). If the stressful situation continues, our emotions may switch back and forth among any of these, depending on

TABLE 14-2

Reactions to Stress

Psychological Reactions
Anxiety
Anger and aggression
Apathy and depression
Cognitive impairment
Physiological Reactions
Increased metabolic rate
Increased heart rate
Dilation of pupils
Higher blood pressure
Increased breathing rate
Tensing of muscles
Secretion of endorphins and ACTH
Release of extra sugar from the liver

the success of our coping efforts. Let us take a closer look at some of the more common emotional reactions to stress.

Anxiety

The most common response to a stressor is anxiety. By *anxiety* we mean the unpleasant emotion characterized by such terms as "worry," "apprehension," "tension," and "fear." People who live through events that are beyond the normal range of human suffering (natural disasters, rape, kidnapping) sometimes develop a severe set of anxiety-related symptoms known as *post-traumatic stress disorder* (PTSD). The major symptoms of PTSD include (a) feelings of numbness to the world, estrangement from others, and lack of interest in former activities; (b) a tendency to relive the trauma repeatedly in memories and dreams; and (c) sleep disturbances, difficulty concentrating, and over-alertness. Some individuals also feel guilty about surviving the event when others did not.

Post-traumatic stress disorder may develop immediately after the trauma, or it may be brought on by a minor stress experienced weeks, months, or even years later. And it may last a long time. A study of victims of the 1972 flood that wiped out the community of Buffalo Creek, West Virginia, found that shortly after the flood, 63% of the survivors were suffering from PTSD symptoms. Fourteen years later, 25% still experienced PTSD symptoms (Green et al., 1992). Similarly, a study of Florida children who survived Hurricane Andrew in 1992 found that nearly 20% were still suffering from PTSD a year after the disaster (La Greca et al., 1996).

Traumas caused by humans, such as sexual or physical assault, terrorist attacks, and war, may be even more likely to cause PTSD than natural disasters, for at least two reasons. First, such traumas challenge our basic beliefs about the goodness of life and other people, and when these beliefs are shattered, PTSD is more likely to occur (Janoff-Bulman, 1992). Second, human-caused disasters often strike individuals rather than whole communities, and suffering through a trauma alone seems to increase a person's risk of experiencing PTSD.

A study of survivors of the Holocaust found that almost half were still suffering from PTSD 40 years later (Kuch & Cox, 1992). Those who had been held in concentration camps were three times more likely to experience PTSD than survivors who had not been in the camps. Many still relived the traumas of persecution in their dreams and were afraid that something terrible would happen to their spouse or children whenever they were out of sight.

Studies of rape survivors have found that about 95% experience post-traumatic stress symptoms severe enough to qualify for a diagnosis of the disorder in the first 2 weeks following the rape (see Figure 14-1). About 50% still qualify for the diagnosis three months after the rape. As many as 25% still suffer from PTSD four to five years after the rape (Foa & Riggs, 1995; Resnick, Kilpatrick, Dansky, & Sanders, 1993).

Post-traumatic stress disorder became widely accepted as a diagnostic category because of difficulties experienced by Vietnam War veterans. Although stress reactions to the horrors of battle had been noted in earlier wars (in World War I it was called "shell shock" and in World War II "combat fatigue"), veterans of the Vietnam War seemed especially prone to develop the long-term symptoms we have described. A survey estimated that 15% of Vietnam War veterans have suffered from post-traumatic stress disorder since their discharge (Centers for Disease Control, 1988).

Substance abuse, violence, and interpersonal problems are common correlates of post-traumatic stress disorder. In a study of 713 men who served in Vietnam, 16% reported having problems resulting from drinking heavily, such as trouble at school or work, problems with friends, and passing out. Sixteen percent had been arrested at least once; and 44% said that they had war memories that they were still trying to forget (Yager, Laufer, & Gallops, 1984). The soldiers who fought in Vietnam were young (the average age was 19), and the conditions of warfare were unusual: absence of clear front lines, unpredictable attacks in dense jungle, difficulty distinguishing between Vietnamese allies and enemies, and lack of support for the war among the American public. To this day, some Vietnam veterans still re-experience in memories or in dreams the traumatic events that happened to them. As one veteran wrote, "The war is over in

Post-traumatic stress disorder affects about one-sixth of Vietnam War veterans.

history. But it never ended for me" (Marbly, 1987, p. 193).

Soldiers and noncombatants in more recent wars also suffer PTSD. A study of veterans of the 1991 Persian Gulf War found

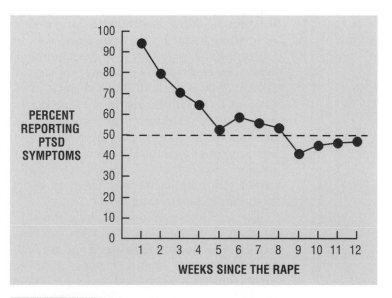

FIGURE 14-1

Post-Traumatic Symptoms in Rape   *Almost all women who have been raped show symptoms of post-traumatic stress disorder severe enough to be diagnosed with PTSD in the first or second week following the rape. Over the three months following the rape, the percentage of women continuing to show PTSD declines. However, almost 50% of women continue to be diagnosed with PTSD three months after a rape. (After Foa & Riggs, 1995)*

that 13% were suffering from PTSD in the year after the war (Sutker, Davis, Uddo, & Ditta, 1995). A study of Bosnian refugees conducted just after they resettled in the United States found that 65% suffered from PTSD (Weine et al., 1995). A follow-up study of these refugees one year later found that 44% were still suffering from PTSD (Weine et al., 1998).

Anger and Aggression

Another common reaction to a stressful situation is anger, which may lead to aggression. Laboratory studies have shown that some animals behave aggressively in response to a variety of stressors, including overcrowding, electric shock, and failure to receive an expected food reward. If a pair of animals is shocked in a cage from which they cannot escape, they begin fighting when the shock starts and stop fighting when it ends.

Children often become angry and exhibit aggressive behavior when they experience frustration. As noted in Chapter 11, the frustration-aggression hypothesis assumes that whenever a person's efforts to reach a goal are blocked, an aggressive drive is induced that motivates behavior designed to injure the object—or person—causing the frustration. While research has shown that aggression is not an inevitable response to frustration, it certainly is a frequent one. When one child takes a toy from another, the second child is likely to attack the first in an attempt to regain the toy. In the late 1980s, some adults frustrated by interminable traffic jams on hot Los Angeles freeways began shooting at one another. Fortunately, adults usually express their aggression verbally rather than physically; they are more likely to exchange insults than blows.

Direct aggression toward the source of frustration is not always possible or wise. Sometimes the source is vague and intangible. The person does not know what to attack but feels angry and seeks an object on which to vent these feelings. Sometimes the individual responsible for the frustration is so powerful that an attack would be dangerous. When circumstances block direct attack on the cause of frustration, aggression may be displaced: The aggressive action may be directed toward an innocent person or object rather than toward the actual cause of the frustration. A man who is reprimanded at work may take out unexpressed resentment on his family. A student who is angry at her professor for an unfair grade may blow up at her roommate. A child frustrated by experiences at school may resort to vandalism of school property.

Apathy and Depression

Although aggression is a frequent response to frustration, the opposite response, withdrawal and apathy, is also common. If the stressful conditions continue and the individual is unable to cope with them, apathy may deepen into depression.

The theory of *learned helplessness* (Seligman, 1975) explains how experience with uncontrollable negative events can lead to apathy and depression (see also Chapter 7). A series of experiments showed that dogs placed in a shuttle box (an apparatus with two compartments separated by a barrier) quickly learn to jump to the opposite compartment to escape a mild electric shock delivered to their feet through a grid on the floor. If a light is turned on a few seconds before the grid is electrified, the dogs can learn to avoid the shock by jumping to the safe compartment when signaled by the light. However, if the dog has previously been confined in another enclosure where shocks were unavoidable and inescapable—so that nothing the animal did terminated the shock—it is very difficult for the dog to learn the avoidance response in a new situation. The animal simply sits and endures the shock in the shuttle box, even though an easy jump to the opposite compartment would eliminate discomfort. Some dogs never learn, even if the experimenter demonstrates the proper procedure by carrying them over the barrier. The experimenters concluded that the animals had learned through prior experience that they were helpless to avoid the shock and therefore gave up trying to do so, even in a new situation. The animals were unable to overcome this learned helplessness (Overmeier & Seligman, 1967).

Some humans also appear to develop learned helplessness, characterized by apathy, withdrawal, and inaction, in response to uncontrollable events. Not all do, however. The original learned helplessness theory has had to be modified to take into account the fact that while some people become helpless after uncontrollable events, others are invigorated by the challenge posed by such events (Wortman & Brehm, 1975). This modified theory will be discussed later in the chapter.

The original learned helplessness theory is useful, however, in helping us understand why some people seem to give up when they are exposed to difficult events. For example, the theory has been used to explain why prisoners in Nazi concentration camps did not rebel against their captors more often: They had come to believe that they were helpless to do anything about their situation and therefore did not try to escape. Similarly, women whose husbands beat them frequently may not try to escape. They often say that they feel helpless to do anything about their situation because they fear what their husband would do if they tried to leave, or because they do not have the economic resources to support themselves and their children.

The theory of learned helplessness may explain why some women remain in abusive relationships even when they have opportunities to leave.

Cognitive Impairment

In addition to emotional reactions, people often show substantial cognitive impairment when faced with serious stressors. They find it hard to concentrate and to organize their thoughts logically. They may be easily distracted. As a result, their performance on tasks, particularly complex tasks, tends to deteriorate.

This cognitive impairment may come from two sources. High levels of emotional arousal can interfere with the processing of information, so the more anxious, angry, or depressed we are after experiencing a stressor, the more likely we are to exhibit cognitive impairment. Cognitive impairment may also result from the distracting thoughts that go through our heads when we are faced with a stressor. We contemplate possible sources of action, worry about the consequences of our actions, and berate ourselves for not being able to handle the situation better. For instance, while trying to complete a test, students who suffer from test anxiety tend to worry about possible failure and about their inadequacies. They can become so distracted by these negative thoughts that they fail to follow instructions and neglect or misinterpret information. As their anxiety mounts, they have difficulty retrieving facts that they have learned well.

Cognitive impairment often leads people to adhere rigidly to behavior patterns because they cannot consider alternative patterns. People have been trapped in flaming buildings because they persisted in pushing against exit doors that opened inward; in their panic, they failed to consider other possible means of escape. Some people resort to old, childlike behavior patterns that are not appropriate to the situation. A cautious person may become even more cautious and withdraw entirely, whereas an aggressive person may lose control and strike out heedlessly in all directions.

Physiological Reactions to Stress

The body reacts to stressors by initiating a complex sequence of responses. If the perceived threat is resolved quickly, these emergency responses subside, but if the stressful situation continues, a different set of internal responses occurs as we attempt to adapt. In this section we examine these physiological reactions in detail.

The Fight-or-Flight Response

Whether you fall into an icy river, encounter a knife-wielding assailant, or are terrified by your first parachute jump, your body responds in similar ways. Regardless of the stressor, your body automatically prepares to handle the emergency. Recall from Chapter 11 that this is called the *fight-or-flight response.* Energy is needed right away, so the liver releases extra sugar (glucose) to fuel the muscles, and hormones are released that stimulate the conversion of fats and proteins into sugar. The body's metabolism increases in preparation for expending energy on physical action. Heart rate, blood pressure, and breathing rate increase, and the muscles tense. At the same time, certain unessential activities, such as digestion, are curtailed. Saliva and mucus dry up, thereby increasing the size of the air passages to the lungs. Thus, an early sign of stress is a dry mouth. The body's natural painkillers, endorphins, are secreted, and the surface blood vessels constrict to reduce bleeding in case of injury. The spleen releases more red blood cells to help carry oxygen, and the bone marrow produces more white corpuscles to fight infection.

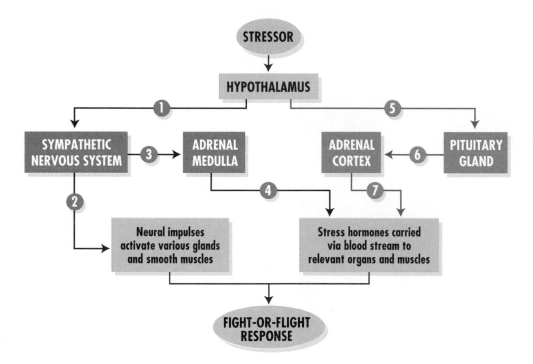

FIGURE 14-2

The Fight-or-Flight Response *A stressful situation activates the hypothalamus, which, in turn, controls two neuroendocrine systems: the sympathetic system (shown in red) and the adrenal-cortical system (shown in green). The sympathetic nervous system, responding to neural impulses from the hypothalamus (1), activates various organs and smooth muscles under its control (2). For example, it increases heart rate and dilates the pupils. The sympathetic nervous system also signals the adrenal medulla (3) to release epinephrine and norepinephrine into the bloodstream (4). The adrenal-cortical system is activated when the hypothalamus secretes CRF, a chemical that acts on the pituitary gland, which lies just below the hypothalamus (5). The pituitary gland, in turn, secretes the hormone ACTH, which is carried via the bloodstream to the adrenal cortex (6), where it stimulates the release of a group of hormones, including cortisol, that regulate blood glucose levels (7). ACTH also signals the other endocrine glands to release some 30 hormones. The combined effects of the various stress hormones carried via the bloodstream plus the neural activity of the sympathetic division of the autonomic nervous system constitute the fight-or-flight response.*

Most of these physiological changes result from activation of two neuroendocrine systems controlled by the hypothalamus: the sympathetic system and the adrenal-cortical system. The hypothalamus has been called the brain's stress center because of its dual function in emergencies. Its first function is to activate the sympathetic division of the autonomic nervous system (see Chapter 2). The hypothalamus transmits nerve impulses to nuclei in the brain stem that control the functioning of the autonomic nervous system. The sympathetic division of the autonomic system acts directly on muscles and organs to produce increased heart rate, elevated blood pressure, and dilated pupils. The sympathetic system also stimulates the inner core of the adrenal glands (the adrenal medulla) to release the hormones epinephrine (adrenaline) and norepinephrine into the bloodstream. Epinephrine has the same effect on the muscles and organs as the sympathetic nervous system (for example, it increases heart rate and blood pressure) and thus serves to perpetuate a state of arousal. Norepinephrine, through its action on the pituitary gland, is indirectly responsible for the release of extra sugar from the liver (see Figure 14-2).

The hypothalamus carries out its second function, activation of the adrenal-cortical system, by signaling the pituitary gland to secrete adrenocorticotrophic hormone (ACTH), the body's "major stress hormone" (see Chapter 2). ACTH stimulates the outer layer of the adrenal glands (the adrenal cortex), resulting in the release of a group of hormones (the major one is cortisol) that regulate the blood levels of glucose and of certain minerals. The amount of cortisol in blood or urine samples is often used as a measure of stress. ACTH also signals other endocrine glands to release about 30 hormones, each of which plays a role in the body's adjustment to emergency situations.

In groundbreaking work that remains influential today, researcher Hans Selye (1978) described the physiological changes we have just discussed as part of a **general adaptation syndrome**, *a set of responses that is displayed by all organisms in response to stress.* The general adaptation syndrome consists of three phases (see Figure 14-3). In the first phase, *alarm,* the body

mobilizes to confront a threat by triggering sympathetic nervous system activity. In the second phase, *resistance,* the organism attempts to cope with the threat by fleeing it or fighting it. The third phase, *exhaustion,* occurs if the organism is unable to flee from or fight the threat and depletes its physiological resources in attempting to do so.

Selye argued that a wide variety of physical and psychological stressors triggers this response pattern. He also argued that repeated or prolonged exhaustion of physiological resources, due to exposure to prolonged stressors that one cannot flee from or fight, is responsible for a wide array of physiological diseases, which he called *diseases of adaptation.* He conducted laboratory studies in which he exposed animals to several types of prolonged stressors, such as extreme cold and fatigue, and found that regardless of the nature of the stressor, certain bodily changes inevitably occurred: enlarged adrenal glands, shrunken lymph nodes, and stomach ulcers. These changes decrease the organism's ability to resist other stressors, including infectious and disease-producing agents. As we will see later, chronic arousal can make both animals and people more susceptible to illness.

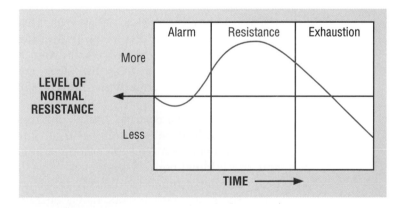

FIGURE 14-3

The General Adaptation Syndrome *According to Hans Selye, the body reacts to a stressor in three phases. In the first phase,* alarm, *the body mobilizes to confront the threat, which temporarily expends resources and lowers resistance. In the* resistance *phase, the body actively confronts the threat and resistance is high. If the threat continues, the body moves into the* exhaustion *phase.*

Stress and Toughness

So far we have focused on the negative aspects of the physiological arousal elicited by stressors. Studies have shown, however, that exposure to intermittent stressors can have benefits in the form of physiological toughness. In essence, intermittent stress (occasional exposure with recovery periods) leads to stress tolerance later on (Dienstbier, 1989). For example, young rats that are removed from their cages and handled daily (a stressor for them) are less fearful when exposed to other stressors as adults, and their stress hormone levels return to normal more quickly (Meaney et al., 1987; Levine, 1960). Similarly, rats that were toughened by having to swim in cold water on 14 consecutive days performed better on a later swim test and showed less depletion of epinephrine and norepinephrine than rats that had received no prior exposure to cold water (Weiss et al., 1975).

The physiological responses that appear to be beneficial involve arousal of the sympathetic system and occur when a person makes active efforts to cope with the stressful situation (Frankenhauser, 1983). Increases in epinephrine and norepinephrine correlate positively with performance on a variety of tasks (from students taking tests to paratroopers engaged in training jumps): High levels of these hormones in blood and urine are related to better performance (Johansson & Frankenhaeuser, 1973; Ursin, 1978). The physiological responses that appear to be harmful involve arousal of the adrenal-cortical system and occur when a person experiences distress but does not actively attempt to cope with the stressful situation.

Research on the positive aspects of stress arousal is still in an exploratory stage. The interaction between the sympathetic system and the adrenal-cortical system is exceedingly complex, and it is difficult to determine their separate effects using current research methods (primarily measures of chemistry of the blood and/or urine). However, the idea that stressors can have beneficial effects under certain circumstances has generated considerable interest among researchers. Indeed, it may be necessary for people to successfully overcome moderate stressors when they are young in order to develop the psychological hardiness described earlier.

How Stress Affects Health

Attempts to adapt to the continued presence of a stressor may deplete the body's resources and make it vulnerable to illness. Chronic stress can lead to physical disorders such as ulcers, high blood pressure, and heart disease. It may also impair the immune system, decreasing the body's ability to fight invading bacteria and viruses. Indeed, doctors estimate that emotional stress plays an important role in more than half of all medical problems.

Psychophysiological disorders are *physical disorders in which emotions are believed to play a central role*. A common misconception is that people with psychophysiological disorders are not really sick and do not need medical attention. On the contrary, the symptoms of psychophysiological illness reflect physiological disturbances associated with tissue damage and pain; a peptic ulcer caused by stress is indistinguishable from an ulcer caused by a factor unrelated to stress, such as long-term heavy usage of aspirin.

Traditionally, research in psychophysiology focused on such illnesses as asthma, hypertension (high blood pressure), ulcers, colitis, and rheumatoid arthritis. Researchers looked for relationships between specific illnesses and characteristic attitudes toward, or ways of coping with, stressful life events. For example, individuals with hypertension were said to feel that life is threatening and that they must therefore be on guard at all times. Those suffering from colitis were believed to be angry but unable to express their anger. However, most studies that reported characteristic attitudes to be related to specific illnesses have not been replicated. Thus, the hypothesis that people who react to stress in similar ways will be vulnerable to the same illnesses has generally not been confirmed. An important exception is research on coronary heart disease and Type A behavior patterns, as we will see shortly.

Direct Effects   The body's physiological response to a stressor may have a direct, negative effect on physical health if it is maintained for a long period. Long-term overarousal of the sympathetic system or the adrenal-cortical system can cause damage to arteries and organ systems. Stress may also have a direct effect on the immune system's ability to fight off disease.

Coronary Heart Disease The overarousal caused by chronic stressors may contribute to coronary heart disease. *Coronary heart disease* (CHD) occurs when the blood vessels that supply the heart muscles are narrowed or closed by the gradual buildup of a hard, fatty substance called *plaque,* blocking the flow of oxygen and nutrients to the heart. This can lead to pain, called *angina pectoris,* that radiates across the chest and arm. When the flow of oxygen to the heart is completely blocked, it can cause a *myocardial infarction* or heart attack.

Coronary heart disease is a leading cause of death and chronic illness. Nearly half of the deaths in the United States every year are caused by coronary heart disease, in many cases before the individual reaches age 65. There seems to be a genetic contribution to coronary heart disease: People with family histories of CHD are at increased risk for the disease. CHD is also linked to high blood pressure, high serum cholesterol, diabetes, smoking, and obesity.

People in high-stress jobs are at increased risk for CHD, particularly if their jobs are highly demanding (in terms of workload, responsibilities, and role conflicts) but provide little control (the worker has little control over the speed, nature, and conditions of work). An example of such a job is an assembly line in which rapid, high-quality production is expected and the work is machine-paced rather than self-paced.

In one study, 900 middle-aged men and women were followed over a 10-year period and examined for the development of heart disease. Two independent methods—occupational titles and the participants' reports of their feelings about their jobs—were used to classify workers along the dimensions of job demand and job control. The results showed that both men and women in occupations classified as "high strain" (high demand combined with low control) had a risk of coronary heart disease 1½ times greater than the risk faced by those in other occupations (Karasek et al., 1981; Karasek et al., 1982; Pickering et al., 1996).

A demanding family life in addition to a stressful job can adversely affect a woman's cardiovascular health. Employed women in general are not at higher risk for CHD than homemakers. However, employed mothers are more likely to develop heart disease. The likelihood of disease increases with the number of children for working women but not for homemakers (Haynes & Feinleib, 1980). Yet women who have flexibility in and control over their work, and a good income so that they can afford to hire help with house cleaning and child-care tasks, seem not to suffer as much either physically or psychologically from their role overload (Lennon & Rosenfield, 1992; Taylor, 1999).

One group that lives in chronically stressful settings and has particularly high rates of high blood pressure is low-income African-Americans. They often do not have adequate financial resources for daily living, may be poorly educated and therefore have trouble finding good jobs, live in violent neighborhoods, and are frequently exposed to racism. All these conditions have been linked to higher blood pressure (Williams, 1995).

Experimental studies with animals have shown that disruption of the social environment can induce pathology that resembles coronary artery disease (Manuck, Kaplan, & Matthews, 1986; Sapolsky, 1990). Some of these experiments have been conducted with a type of macaque monkey whose social organization involves the establishment

People in high-stress jobs (those with high demand and low control) are at greater risk of coronary heart disease than people in low-stress jobs.

of stable hierarchies of social dominance: Dominant and submissive animals can be identified within a given group on the basis of the animals' social behavior. The introduction of unfamiliar monkeys into an established social group is a stressor that leads to increased aggressive behavior as group members attempt to reestablish a social dominance hierarchy (Manuck, Kaplan, & Matthews, 1986).

In these studies, some monkey groups remained stable with fixed memberships; other groups were stressed by the repeated introduction of new members. After about two years under these conditions, the high-ranking or dominant males in the unstable social condition showed more extensive atherosclerosis than the subordinate males (Sapolsky, 1990).

The Immune System A relatively new area of research in behavioral medicine is *psychoneuroimmunology,* the study of how the body's immune system is affected by stress and other psychological variables. By means of specialized cells called *lymphocytes,* the immune system protects the body from disease-causing microorganisms. It affects the individual's susceptibility to infectious diseases, allergies, cancers, and autoimmune disorders (that is, diseases such as

rheumatoid arthritis, in which the immune cells attack the normal tissue of the body). There is no single index of the quality of an individual's immune functioning, or *immunocompetence.* The immune system is a complex one with many interacting components, and different investigators have chosen to focus on different components of the system.

Evidence from a number of areas suggests that stress affects the immune system's ability to defend the body (Taylor, 1999). One study indicates that the common belief that we are more likely to catch a cold when we are under stress is probably correct (Cohen, Tyrel, & Smith, 1991). Researchers exposed 400 healthy volunteers to a nasal wash containing one of five cold viruses or an innocuous salt solution. The participants answered questions about the number of stressful events they had experienced in the past year, the degree to which they felt able to cope with the demands of daily life, and the frequency with which they experienced negative emotions such as anger and depression. Based on these data, each participant was assigned a stress index ranging from 3 (lowest stress) to 12 (highest stress). The volunteers were examined daily for cold symptoms and for the presence of cold viruses or virus-specific antibodies in their upper respiratory secretions.

The majority of the virus-exposed volunteers showed signs of infection, but only about a third actually developed colds. The rates of viral infection and of actual cold symptoms increased in accordance with the reported stress levels. Compared with the lowest-stress group, volunteers who reported the highest stress were significantly more likely to become infected with the cold virus and almost twice as likely to develop a cold (see Figure 14-4). These results held even after controlling statistically for a number of variables that might influence immune functioning, such as age, allergies, cigarette and alcohol use, exercise, and diet. However, the two indicators of immunocompetence that were measured in this study did not show any specific change as a result of stress, so exactly how stress lowered the body's resistance to the cold virus remains to be determined.

This study is unusual in that the participants were exposed to a virus, lived in special quarters near the laboratory for a

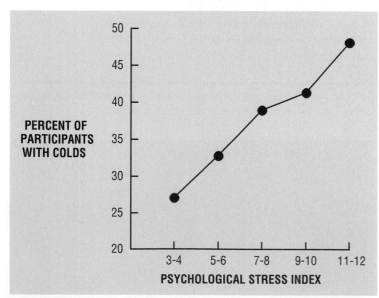

FIGURE 14-4

Stress and Colds   *This graph shows the percentage of virus-exposed people who developed colds as a function of the degree of stress reported.* (After Cohen, Tyrel, & Smith, 1991)

number of days both before and after exposure, and were carefully monitored. Such controlled conditions for studying the effects of stress on health are seldom feasible. Most studies look at individuals undergoing a particularly stressful event—such as academic pressure, bereavement, or marital disruption—and evaluate their immunocompetence (Cohen, 1996). For example, one study found that during examination periods college students have lower levels of an antibody in their blood that defends against respiratory infections (Jemmott et al., 1985), and another found that medical students show lowered immune functioning on a number of blood-sample measures (Glaser et al., 1986). A study of men whose wives had died from breast cancer demonstrated that the responsiveness of their immune system functioning declined significantly within the month following their wife's death and in some cases remained low for a year thereafter (Schleifer et al., 1979). Similarly, a series of studies revealed that individuals of both sexes who have recently been separated or divorced show poorer immune functioning than matched control participants who are still married, even though no significant differences were found between the two groups in health-related behaviors such as smoking and diet (Kiecolt-Glaser et al., 1993).

Psychological factors that reduce stress can diminish these adverse immunological changes. For example, Kiecolt-Glaser and colleagues (1985) trained older adults to use relaxation techniques to reduce stress. These adults showed improvement on a number of measures of immunological functioning, whereas a control group of older adults who received no relaxation training showed no improvement in immunocompetence over the same period.

One factor that appears to be important is the extent to which an individual can control stress. Recall that controllability is one of the variables that determines the severity of stress. A series of animal studies demonstrated that uncontrollable shock has a much greater effect on the immune system than controllable shock (Laudenslager et al., 1983; Visintainer, Volpicelli, & Seligman, 1982). In these experiments, rats were subjected to electric shock. One group could press a lever to turn off the shock. The other animals received an identical sequence of

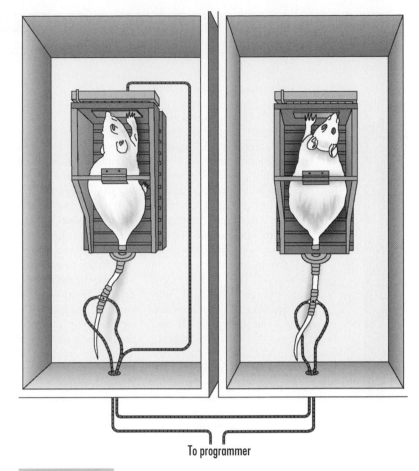

To programmer

FIGURE 14-5

Yoked Controls in a Stress Experiment *A series of electrical shocks are preprogrammed to be delivered simultaneously to the tails of the two male rats. The rat on the left can terminate a shock when it occurs by pressing the lever in front of him. The rat on the right has no control in the situation (his lever is inoperative), but he is yoked to the first rat. That is, when the first rat receives a shock, the yoked rat simultaneously receives the same shock, and the shock remains on until the first rat presses his lever. The lever presses of the yoked rat have no effect on the shock sequence for either animal.*

shocks, but their levers are ineffective (see Figure 14-5). In one study using this procedure, the investigators looked at how readily the rats' T-cells multiplied when challenged by an invader. (T-cells are lymphocytes that secrete chemicals that kill harmful cells, such as cancer cells.) They found that the T-cells from rats that could control the shock multiplied as readily as those from rats that were not stressed at all. T-cells from rats exposed to uncontrollable shock, on the other hand, multiplied only weakly. Thus, shock (stress) interfered with the immune response only in rats that could not control it (Laudenslager et al., 1983).

FRONTIERS OF PSYCHOLOGICAL RESEARCH

Can Psychological Interventions Affect the Course of Cancer?

There is increasing evidence that at least some types of supportive psychological interventions can slow the progress of cancer. David Spiegel and his colleagues (Spiegel, Bloom, Kraemer, & Gottheil, 1989) unintentionally produced some of the best such evidence. Several years ago they began a study in which they randomly assigned women with metastatic breast cancer either to a series of weekly support groups or to no support groups (all of the women were receiving standard medical care for their cancers). The focus of the groups was on facing death and learning to live one's remaining days to the fullest. The researchers had no intention of affecting the course of the cancers—they did not believe that it was possible to do so. They only wanted to improve the quality of life for the women in their study.

The researchers were quite surprised when, 48 months after the study began, all of the women who had not been in the support groups had died of their cancers whereas a third of the women in the support groups were still alive. The average survival time (from the time the study began) for the women in the support groups was about 40 months, compared to about 19 months for the women who were not in the support groups.

There were no differences between the groups, other than their participation in the weekly support meetings, that could explain the differences in average survival time. That is, the two groups did not differ in the initial seriousness of their cancers, the type of therapy received, or other variables that might have affected their survival time. The researchers were forced to conclude that their intervention actually increased the number of months that the women in the support group lived (for similar results, see Richardson et al., 1990).

How did the intervention affect the progress of these women's cancers? It is not clear, but the women in the support groups gained a great deal of psychological strength from the groups, which were intensely emotional and supportive. Members discussed their fear of dying, visited other members in the hospital, grieved when other members died, attended their funerals, and mourned the loss of abilities and friendships. In addition to sharing grief, the women in these groups derived tremendous strength from one another. They came to feel like experts in living, a wisdom that grew from their confrontation with death. They chose new life projects ranging from imparting values to their children to writing books of poetry (Spiegel, 1991). In addition, group members showed lower levels of emotional distress and learned how to control their physical pain better than women who did not participate in the support groups.

Further studies are under way to determine exactly how psychological interventions can affect the course of disease. It may be that reducing distress leads to improved immune system functioning, which slows the course of disease.

In another study, the investigators implanted tumor cells into rats, gave them shocks, and recorded whether the rats' natural defenses rejected the cells or whether they developed into tumors. Only 27% of the rats that were given uncontrollable shocks rejected the tumors, but 63% of the rats that could turn the shocks off rejected the tumors—even though the rats received identical amounts of shock (Visintainer, Volpicelli, & Seligman, 1982).

Perceptions of control also appear to mediate the influence of stress on the immune system in humans. In a study of the effects of marital separation or divorce on immune functioning, the partner who had initiated the separation (the one more in control of the situation) was less distressed, reported better health, and showed better immune system functioning than the other partner (Kiecolt-Glaser et al., 1988). Similarly, a study of women with breast cancer found that those with a pessimistic perspective—that is, who felt that they had little control over events—were the most likely to develop new tumors over a five-year period, even after the physical severity of their diseases was taken into account (Levy & Heiden, 1991). (The value of psychological intervention in treating cancers is discussed in the Frontiers of Psychological Research feature above.)

The immune system is incredibly complicated, employing a number of different weapons that interact to defend the body. Much remains to be discovered about the immune system and even more about its relationship to the nervous system. Scientists once believed that the immune system operated quite independently, isolated from other physiological systems. But current studies are making it increasingly evident that the immune system and the nervous system have numerous anatomical and physiological connections. For example, researchers are discovering that lymphocytes have receptors for a number of different neurotransmitters. Thus, these immune system cells are equipped to receive messages from the nervous system that may alter the way they behave. The discovery of a link between neurotransmitters and the immune system is important because negative emotional states such as anxiety or depression can affect neurotransmitter levels.

In sum, as research on psychoneuroimmunology yields additional information about the links between the nervous and immune systems, we will gain a clearer understanding of how mental attitudes affect health.

Health-Related Behaviors Certain health-related behaviors can greatly increase our susceptibility to illness. Smoking is one of the leading causes of cardiovascular disease and emphysema. A high-fat diet contributes to many forms of cancer as well as cardiovascular disease. People who do not regularly engage in a moderate amount of exercise are at increased risk for heart disease and earlier death (Blumenthal et al., 1991; Paffenberger et al., 1986). Chronic sleep deprivation is associated with a higher mortality rate due to both illness and accidents (Kryger, Roth, & Dement, 1994). Excessive alcohol consumption can lead to liver disease and cardiovascular disease, and may contribute to some cancers. And failure to use condoms during sex significantly increases the risk of contracting HIV. In sum, scientists estimate that most of the diseases people die from in industrialized countries are heavily influenced by health-related behaviors (Taylor, 1999).

When we are stressed, we may be less likely to engage in healthy behaviors. Students taking exams stay up all night, often for several nights in a row. They may skip meals and snack on junk food. Many men whose wives have died do not know how to cook for themselves, and therefore may eat poorly or hardly at all. In their grief, some

Health-related behaviors such as how we eat, how much we exercise, and how much sleep we get influence our body's ability to fight disease.

bereaved men increase their rates of alcohol consumption and smoking. People under stress cease normal exercise routines and become sedentary. Thus, stress may indirectly affect health by reducing rates of positive health-related behaviors and increasing rates of negative behaviors.

Engaging in unhealthy behaviors may also increase a person's subjective sense of stress. Drinking too much alcohol on a regular basis can interfere with cognitive functioning; a person who consumes excessive amounts of alcohol cannot think as clearly or quickly as one who does not drink excessively. Excessive drinking can also induce lethargy, fatigue, and a mild or moderate sense of depression that makes it difficult to overcome stressful situations or just to keep up with the demands of everyday life.

Similarly, people who do not get enough sleep show impairments in memory, learning, logical reasoning, arithmetic skills, complex verbal processing, and decision making. Sleeping for only five hours per night for just two nights significantly reduces performance on math problems and creative thinking tasks. Thus, staying up late to prepare for an exam can actually decrease performance on the test (Dinges & Broughton, 1989).

In contrast, people who engage in a healthy lifestyle—eating a low-fat diet, drinking alcohol in moderation, getting enough sleep, and exercising regularly— often report that stressful events seem more manageable and that they feel more in control of their lives. Thus, engaging in healthy behaviors can help reduce the stressfulness of life as well as reducing the risk of a number of serious diseases.

Mediators of Stress Responses

As noted earlier, events that are uncontrollable or unpredictable, or that challenge our views of ourselves, tend to be experienced as stressful. Some people appear more likely than others to appraise events in these ways. There are three basic theories about why some people are prone to appraise events as stressful; they are the psychoanalytic, behavioral, and cognitive theories.

Psychoanalytic Theory

Psychoanalysts distinguish between *objective anxiety,* which is a reasonable response to a harmful situation, and *neurotic anxiety,* which is out of proportion to the actual danger. Freud believed that neurotic anxiety stems from unconscious conflicts between unacceptable impulses and the constraints imposed by reality (see Chapter 13). Many impulses pose a threat to the individual because they are contradictory to personal or social values. A woman may not consciously acknowledge that she has strong hostile feelings toward her mother because these feelings conflict with her belief that a child should love her parents. If she acknowledged her true feelings, she would destroy her self-concept as a loving daughter and would risk the loss of her mother's love and support. When she begins to feel angry toward her mother, the resulting anxiety serves as a signal of potential danger. Thus, this woman may experience even a minor conflict with her mother, such as a disagreement about where the family should go for vacation or what to have for dinner, as a major stressor. A woman who is not so conflicted in her feelings about her mother would experience such a conflict as a less severe stressor.

According to psychoanalytic theory, we all have some unconscious conflicts. For some people, however, these conflicts are more numerous and severe, and as a result these people experience more events as stressful.

Behavioral Theory

While Freud saw unconscious conflicts as the internal source of stress responses, behaviorists have focused on ways in which individuals learn to associate stress responses with certain situations. People may also react to specific situations with fear and anxiety because those situations caused them harm or were stressful in the past. Some phobias develop through such classical conditioning (see Chapter 7). For example, a person whose car nearly slid off the road on the side of a steep mountain may now experience anxiety every time she is in a high place. Or a student who failed a final exam in a particular classroom may feel anxious the next year when he reenters the room to take another class.

Sometimes fears are difficult to extinguish. If your first reaction is to avoid or escape the anxiety-producing situation, you may not be able to determine when the situation is no longer dangerous. A little girl who has been punished for assertive behavior in the past may never learn that it is acceptable for her to express her wishes in new situations because she never tries to do so. Thus, people can continue to have fears about particular situations because they chronically avoid the situation and therefore never challenge their fears.

Cognitive Theory

A modification of the learned helplessness theory proposed by Abramson, Seligman, and Teasdale (1978) focuses on the attributions or causal explanations people give for important events. These researchers argued that when people attribute negative events to causes that are internal to them ("it's my fault"), are stable in time ("it's going to last forever"), and are global, affecting many areas of their lives, they are likely to show a helpless, depressed response to negative events. For example, if a man whose wife left him attributed the breakup of his marriage to his "bad" personality (an internal, stable, and global attribution), he would tend to lose self-esteem and expect future relationships to fail as well. In turn, he would show lowered motivation, passivity, and sadness. In contrast, if he made a less pessimistic attribution, such as attributing the failure of his marriage to incompatibility between himself and his wife, he would tend to maintain his self-esteem and motivation for the future.

Abramson and colleagues propose that people have consistent **attributional styles,** or *styles of making attributions for the events in their lives,* and that these styles influence the degree to which people view events as stressful and have helpless, depressed reactions to difficult events. A number of studies support this theory (Peterson & Seligman, 1984). In one study, researchers assessed the attributional styles of students a few weeks before a midterm exam. Just before the exam, they also asked the students what grade they would consider a failure and what grade they would be happy with. After the students received their grades, they measured the students' levels of sadness and depression. Among students who received a grade below their standards, those who had a pessimistic attributional style were significantly more depressed than those who had a more optimistic attributional style (Metalsky, Halberstadt, & Abramson, 1987).

A pessimistic attributional style is also linked to physical illness. Students with more pessimistic attributional styles report more illness and make more visits to the health center than students with a more optimistic attributional style. In a 35-year study of men in the Harvard classes of 1939–1940, researchers found that men who had a pessimistic attributional style at age 25 were more likely to develop physical illness over the subsequent years than men with a more optimistic attributional style (Peterson, Seligman, & Vaillant, 1988).

How does attributional style affect health? A pessimistic attributional style has been linked to lowered immune system functioning. For example, a study of older adults found that those who were pessimistic had poorer immune system functioning than those who were optimistic (Kamen-Siegel et al., 1991). A study of gay men who were HIV-positive found that those who blamed themselves for negative events showed more decline in immune functioning

over 18 months than those who engaged in less self-blaming attributions (Segerstrom et al., 1996). Another study of gay men found that among both HIV-positive and HIV-negative men, those who were more pessimistic and fatalistic were less likely to engage in healthy behaviors, such as maintaining a proper diet, getting enough sleep, and exercising (Taylor et al., 1992). This is particularly important for the HIV-positive men, because engaging in these behaviors can reduce the risk of developing AIDS. Thus, a pessimistic outlook may affect health directly, by reducing immune system functioning, or indirectly, by reducing a person's tendency to engage in health-promoting behavior.

Hardiness Another line of research has focused on people who are most resistant to stress—who do not become physically or emotionally impaired even in the face of major stressful events (Kobasa, 1979; Kobasa, Maddi, & Kahn, 1982). This characteristic is referred to as **hardiness.** In one study, more than 600 men who were executives or managers in the same company were given checklists and were asked to describe all of the stressful events and illnesses they had experienced over the previous three years. Two groups were selected for comparison. The first group scored above average on both stressful events and illness; the second group scored equally high on stress but below average on illness. Members of both groups then filled out detailed personality questionnaires. Analysis of the results indicated that the high-stress/low-illness men differed from the men who became ill under stress on three major dimensions: They were more actively involved in their work and social lives, they were more oriented toward challenge and change, and they felt more in control of events in their lives (Kobasa, 1979).

These personality differences could be the result rather than the cause of illness. For example, it is hard for people to be involved in work or in social activity when they are ill. The investigators therefore conducted a longitudinal study that considered the personality characteristics of business executives before they became ill, and then monitored their life stress and the extent of their illnesses for two years. The results showed that the executives whose attitudes toward life could be rated high on involvement, feelings of control, and positive responses to change remained healthier over time than men who scored low on these dimensions (Kobasa, Maddi, & Kahn, 1982). The most important factors appear to be a sense of control and commitment to goals (Cohen & Edwards, 1989). Although this study was conducted with men only, similar results have been found in a study of women (Wiebe & McCallum, 1986).

The personalities of stress-resistant or hardy individuals are characterized by commitment, control, and challenge. These characteristics are interrelated with the factors that influence the perceived severity of stressors. For example, the sense of being in control of life events reflects feelings of competence and also influences the appraisal of stressful events. Challenge also involves cognitive evaluation, the belief that change is normal in life and should be viewed as an opportunity for growth rather than as a threat to security.

TABLE 14-3

Type A Behaviors *Some behaviors that characterize people prone to coronary heart disease.* (After Friedman & Rosenman, 1974)

Thinking of or doing two things at once

Scheduling more and more activities into less and less time

Failing to notice or be interested in the environment or things of beauty

Hurrying the speech of others

Becoming unduly irritated when forced to wait in line or when driving behind a car you think is moving too slowly

Believing that if you want something done well, you have to do it yourself

Gesticulating when you talk

Frequent knee jiggling or rapid tapping of your fingers

Explosive speech patterns or frequent use of obscenities

Making a fetish of always being on time

Having difficulty sitting and doing nothing

Playing nearly every game to win, even when playing with children

Measuring your own and others' success in terms of numbers (number of patients seen, articles written, and so on)

Lip clicking, head nodding, fist clenching, table pounding, or sucking in of air when speaking

Becoming impatient while watching others do things you think you can do better or faster

Rapid blinking or tic-like eyebrow lifting

The Type A Pattern

A behavior pattern or personality style that has received a great deal of attention is the **Type A pattern.** Over the years physicians had noticed that heart attack victims tend to be hostile, aggressive, impatient individuals who were overinvolved in their work. In the 1950s, two cardiologists defined a set of behaviors that seemed to characterize patients with coronary heart disease; these were labeled the *Type A pattern* (Friedman & Rosenman, 1974). People who exhibit this behavior pattern are extremely competitive and achievement oriented; they have a sense of time urgency, find it difficult to relax, and become impatient and angry when confronted with delays or with people whom they view as incompetent. Although outwardly self-confident, they are prey to constant feelings of self-doubt; they push themselves to accomplish more and more in less and less time. Some common Type A behaviors are listed in Table 14-3.

Type B people do not exhibit the characteristics listed for Type A. They are able to relax without feeling guilty and to work without becoming agitated; they lack a sense of time urgency, with its accompanying impatience, and are not easily roused to anger.

To examine the relationship between Type A behavior and coronary heart disease, more than 3,000 healthy, middle-aged men were evaluated by means of a structured interview that was designed to be irritating. The interviewer kept the participant waiting without explanation and then asked a series of questions about being competitive, hostile, and pressed for time, such as "Do you ever feel rushed or under pressure?" "Do you eat quickly?" "Would you describe yourself as ambitious and hard driving or relaxed and easy-going?" "Do you resent it if someone is late?" The interviewer interrupted, asked questions in a challenging manner, and made irrelevant remarks. The interview was scored more on the way the person behaved in answering the questions than on the answers themselves. For example, Type A men spoke loudly in an explosive manner, talked over the interviewer so as not to be interrupted, appeared tense and tight-lipped, and described hostile incidents with great emotional intensity. Type B men sat in a relaxed

Several studies have found that a person's level of hostility is a better predictor of heart disease than his or her overall level of Type A behavior.

manner, spoke slowly and softly, were easily interrupted, and smiled often.

After the participants had been classified as Type A or Type B, they were studied for 8½ years. During that period Type A men had twice as many heart attacks or other forms of coronary heart disease as Type B men. These results held up even after diet, age, smoking, and other variables were taken into account (Rosenman et al., 1976). Other studies confirmed this twofold risk and linked Type A behavior to heart disease in both men and women (Kornitzer et al., 1982; Haynes, Feinleib, & Kannel, 1980). In addition, Type A behavior correlates with severity of coronary artery blockage, as determined at autopsy or in X-ray studies of the inside of coronary blood vessels (Friedman et al., 1968; Williams et al., 1988).

In 1981, the American Heart Association concluded that Type A behavior should be classified as a risk factor for coronary heart disease. However, two subsequent studies failed to find a link between Type A behavior and heart disease (Case et al., 1985; Shekelle et al., 1983). While some researchers attribute this failure to the way Type A individuals were assessed in these studies, others believe that the original definition of Type A behavior is too diffuse. They argue that time urgency and competitiveness are not the most important components; the crucial variable may be hostility.

Several studies have found that a person's level of hostility is a better predictor of heart disease than his or her overall level of Type A behavior (Booth-Kewley & Friedman, 1987; Dembroski et al., 1985; Thoresen, Telch, & Eagleston, 1981). Accordingly, several studies have used personality tests rather than interviews to measure hostility. For example, a 25-year study of 118 male lawyers found that those who scored high in hostility on a personality inventory taken in law school were five times more likely to die before age 50 than classmates who were not hostile (Barefoot et al., 1989). In a similar follow-up study of physicians, hostility scores obtained in medical school predicted the incidence of coronary heart disease as well as mortality from all causes (Barefoot, Williams, & Dahlstrom, 1983). In both studies, this relationship was independent of the effects of smoking, age, and high blood pressure. There is some evidence that when anger is repressed, or held in, it may be even more destructive to the heart than anger that is expressed (Spielberger et al., 1985; Wright, 1988).

How does Type A behavior or hostility lead to coronary heart disease? A possible biological mechanism is the way the sympathetic nervous system responds to stress. When exposed to stressful experimental situations (for example, when faced with the threat of failure, harassment, or competitive task demands), most participants report

Hardy individuals—those who do not become ill when stressed—are more actively involved in their work, are more oriented to challenge and change, and feel more in control of their lives than people who are vulnerable to the effects of stress.

feeling angry, irritated, and tense. However, participants who score high on hostility as a trait show much larger increases in blood pressure, heart rate, and secretion of stress-related hormones than participants with low hostility scores (Raeikkoenen et al., 1999; Suarez et al., 1998). The same results are found when Type A participants are compared with Type B participants. The sympathetic nervous systems of hostile and/or Type A individuals appear to be hyper-responsive to stressful situations. All of these physiological changes can damage the heart and blood vessels.

Hostile and nonhostile people may have fundamentally different nervous systems. When nonhostile individuals are aroused and upset, their parasympathetic nervous systems act like a stop switch to calm them down. In contrast, hostile individuals may have a weak parasympathetic nervous system. When they are angered, their adrenalin fires off and they stay unpleasantly aroused. As a consequence, they interact differently with the world (Suarez et al., 1998).

The good news about the Type A behavior pattern is that it can be modified through well-established therapy programs, and people who are able to reduce their Type A behavior show lowered risk of coronary heart disease. We will discuss this therapy later in the chapter.

Coping Skills

The emotions and physiological arousal created by stressful situations are highly uncomfortable, and this discomfort motivates the individual to do something to alleviate it. The term **coping** is used to refer to *the process by which a person attempts to manage stressful demands,* and it takes two major forms. A person can focus on the specific problem or situation that has arisen, trying to find some way of changing it or avoiding it in the future. This is called *problem-focused coping.* A person can also focus on alleviating the emotions associated with the stressful situation, even if the situation itself cannot be changed. This is called *emotion-focused coping* (Lazarus & Folkman, 1984). When dealing with a stressful situation, most people use both problem-focused and emotion-focused coping.

Problem-Focused Coping

Strategies for solving problems include defining the problem, generating alternative solutions, weighing the alternatives in terms of costs and benefits, choosing among them, and implementing the selected alternative. Problem-focused strategies can also be directed inward: The person can change something about himself or herself instead of changing the environment. Changing levels of aspiration, finding alternative sources of gratification, and learning new skills are examples of inward-directed strategies. How skillfully the individual employs these strategies depends on his or her range of experiences and capacity for self-control.

Suppose you receive a warning that you are about to fail a course required for graduation. You might confer with the professor, devise a work schedule to fulfill the requirements, and then follow it; or you might decide that you cannot fulfill the requirements in the time remaining and sign up to retake the course in summer school. Both of these actions are problem-focused methods of coping.

People who tend to use problem-focused coping in stressful situations show lower levels of depression both during and after the stressful situation (Billings & Moos, 1984). Of course, people who are less depressed may find it easier to use problem-focused coping. But longitudinal studies show that problem-focused coping leads to shorter periods of depression, even taking into account people's initial levels of depression. In addition, therapies that teach depressed people to use problem-focused coping can be effective in helping them overcome their depression and react more adaptively to stressors (Nezu, Nezu, & Perri, 1989).

Emotion-Focused Coping

People engage in emotion-focused coping to prevent their negative emotions from overwhelming them and making them unable to take action to solve their problems. They also use emotion-focused coping when a problem is uncontrollable.

There are many ways in which we try to cope with our negative emotions. Some researchers have divided these into behavioral strategies and cognitive strategies (Moos,

1988). *Behavioral strategies* include engaging in physical exercise, using alcohol or other drugs, venting anger, and seeking emotional support from friends. *Cognitive strategies* include temporarily setting the problem aside ("I decided it wasn't worth worrying about") and reducing the threat by changing the meaning of the situation ("I decided that her friendship wasn't that important to me"). Cognitive strategies often involve reappraising the situation. Obviously, we would expect some behavioral and cognitive strategies to be adaptive and others (such as drinking heavily) to merely cause more stress.

One strategy that appears to help people adjust emotionally and physically to a stressor is seeking emotional support from others. In a study of women who had just undergone surgery for breast cancer, Levy and colleagues (1990) found that those who actively sought social support had higher natural killer cell activity, indicating that their immune system was attacking the cancer more aggressively. Pennebaker (1990) has found that people who reveal personal traumas, such as being raped or having a spouse commit suicide, to supportive others tend to show more positive physical health both shortly after the trauma and in the long run.

The quality of the social support a person receives after experiencing a trauma strongly influences the impact of that support on the individual's health, however (Rook, 1984). Some friends or relatives can be burdens instead of blessings in times of stress. People whose social networks are characterized by a high level of conflict tend to show poorer physical and emotional health after a major stressor such as bereavement (Windholz, Marmar, & Horowitz, 1985). Conflicted social relationships may affect physical health through the immune system. Kiecolt-Glaser and colleagues (1998) found that newlywed couples who became hostile and negative toward each other while discussing a marital problem showed greater decreases in four indicators of immune system functioning than couples who remained calm and nonhostile in discussing marital problems. Couples who became hostile during these

Talking with supportive friends about your problems can be an adaptive coping strategy.

discussions also showed elevated blood pressure for a longer period than those who did not become hostile.

Some people engage in a more maladaptive way of coping with negative emotions: They simply deny that they have any negative emotions and push those emotions out of conscious awareness, a strategy that is referred to as *repressive coping*. People who engage in repressive coping tend to show more autonomic nervous system activity (such as a higher heart rate) in response to stressors than people who do not engage in repressive coping (Brown et al., 1996; Weinberg, Schwartz, & Davidson, 1979). Pushing emotions out of awareness may require real physical work, which results in chronic overarousal and, in turn, in physical illness.

Repressing important aspects of one's identity may also be harmful to one's health. An intriguing study showed that gay men who conceal their homosexual identity may suffer health consequences (Cole et al., 1996). Men who concealed their homosexuality were about three times more likely to develop cancer and certain infectious disease (pneumonia, bronchitis, sinusitis, tuberculosis) over a five-year period than men who were open about their homosexuality (see Figure 14-6). All of these men were HIV-

negative. But another study by the same researchers focused on HIV-positive gay men and found that the disease progressed faster in those who concealed their homosexuality than in those who did not (Cole et al., 1996). The differences in health between the men who were "out" and those who were "closeted" did not reflect differences in health-related behaviors (smoking, exercise). It may be that chronic inhibition of one's identity, like chronic inhibition of emotions, can have direct effects on health.

In contrast, talking about negative emotions and important issues in one's life appears to have positive effects on health. In a large series of studies, Pennebaker (1990) has found that encouraging people to reveal personal traumas in diaries or essays improves their health. For example, in one study, 50 healthy undergraduates were randomly assigned to write either about the most traumatic and upsetting events in their lives or about trivial topics for 20 minutes on four consecutive days. Blood samples were taken from the students on the day before they began writing, on the last day of writing, and six weeks after writing, and tested for several markers of immune system functioning. The number of times the students visited the college health center over the six weeks after the writing task was also recorded and compared to the number of health center visits the students had made before the study. As Figure 14-7 shows, students who revealed their personal traumas in essays showed more positive immune system functioning and visited the health center less frequently than students in the control group (Pennebaker, Kiecolt-Glaser, & Glaser, 1988).

Positive social support may help people adjust better emotionally to stress by leading them to avoid ruminating about the stressor (Nolen-Hoeksema, 1991). *Rumination* involves isolating ourselves to think about how bad we feel, worrying about the consequences of the stressful event or our emotional state, or repeatedly talking about how bad things are without taking any action to change them. One longitudinal study of recently bereaved people found that those who ruminated in response to their grief were depressed for longer periods (Nolen-Hoeksema & Larson, 1999). In addition,

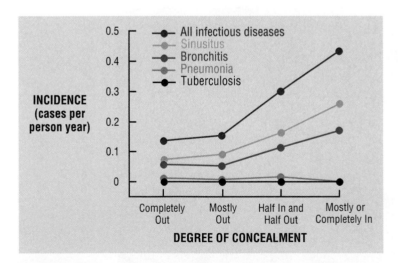

FIGURE 14-6

Infectious Diseases as a Function of Concealing One's Sexual Orientation   *Homosexual men who concealed their homosexuality from others were more prone to several infectious diseases.* (After Cole et al., 1996)

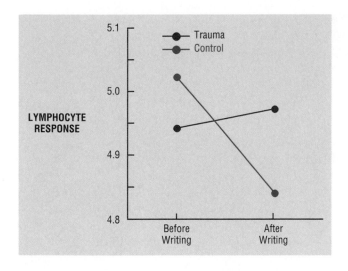

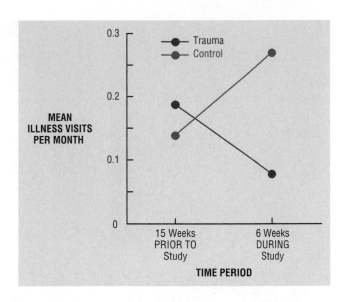

FIGURE 14-7

Students' Health after Writing About Traumas or Trivialities   *Students who revealed personal traumas in a series of essays had stronger immune system functioning and fewer health-care visits than students who wrote about trivial events in their essays.* (After Pennebaker, Krecolt-Glaser, & Glaser, 1988)

those who were more socially isolated or had a lot of conflict in their social networks were most likely to ruminate.

Another longitudinal study was conducted quite by accident. A group of researchers at Stanford University happened to have obtained measures of emotion-focused coping tendencies and levels of depression and anxiety in a large group of students two weeks before the major earthquake that hit the San Francisco Bay area in 1989. They remeasured the students' levels of depression and anxiety ten days and seven weeks following the earthquake. They also estimated how much environmental stress the students experienced as a result of the earthquake (that is, injury to themselves, to their friends or family, and to their homes). The results showed that students who exhibited a ruminative style of coping with emotions before the earthquake were more likely to be depressed and anxious ten days after the earthquake and seven weeks later. This was true even after the students' levels of depression and anxiety before the earthquake were taken into account (Nolen-Hoeksema & Morrow, 1991a). Students who engaged in dangerous activities, such as drinking alcohol, to avoid their negative moods also tended to remain depressed and

anxious. In contrast, students who used pleasant activities to improve their mood and regain a sense of control experienced short and mild periods of depression and anxiety.

You might ask whether people who engage in ruminative coping are more likely to solve their problems. The available evidence suggests that the answer is no. People who engage in ruminative coping are less likely to engage in active problem-solving in response to stressors. In contrast, people who use pleasant activities to take a breather from their negative moods are more likely to turn to active problem-solving to deal with stressors (Nolen-Hoeksema & Larson, 1999; Nolen-Hoeksema & Morrow, 1991a). In addition, people who use ruminative coping may actually do a poorer job of problem-solving when they do try. Two laboratory studies have shown that depressed people who spend ten minutes ruminating and then do a problem-solving task show poorer performance at problem-solving than depressed people who are distracted for ten minutes before attempting the problem-solving task (Lyubomirsky & Nolen-Hoeksema, 1995; Nolen-Hoeksema & Morrow, 1991b). Rumination thus may get in the way of good problem solving.

When confronted with negative emotions, some people isolate themselves and ruminate over the problem; some distract themselves (for example, by exercising); and some avoid the problem by engaging in harmful behaviors such as excessive drinking. How effective is each of these behaviors in coping with negative emotions?

Defense Mechanisms and Coping

The coping strategies we have discussed so far have been the focus of relatively recent research. However, many earlier writings on emotion-focused coping can be found in the psychoanalytic literature (A. Freud, 1946/1967). Freud, for example, used the term **defense mechanisms** to refer to *strategies that people use to deal with anxiety, which are largely unconscious.* These emotion-focused strategies do not alter the stressful situation; they simply change the way the person perceives or thinks about it. Thus, all defense mechanisms involve an element of self-deception.

We all use defense mechanisms at times. They help us over the rough spots until we can deal with stressful situations more directly. Defense mechanisms are maladaptive only when they become the dominant mode of responding to problems. One difference between defense mechanisms and the coping strategies discussed earlier is that the defense mechanisms are unconscious processes, whereas the coping strategies are often engaged in consciously. As we will see shortly, however, some of the unconscious defense mechanisms, when taken to an extreme, may lead an individual to show some of the maladaptive conscious coping strategies described earlier. In this section we take a closer look at several common defense mechanisms; these mechanisms are also listed in Table 14-4.

Repression Freud considered *repression* to be the basic, and most important, defense mechanism. In repression, impulses or memories that are too frightening or painful are excluded from conscious awareness. Memories that evoke shame, guilt, or self-deprecation are often repressed. Freud believed that repression of certain childhood impulses is universal. In later life, individuals may repress feelings and memories that could cause anxiety because they are inconsistent

TABLE 14-4

Major Defense Mechanisms

Repression	Excluding from conscious awareness impulses or memories that are too frightening or painful.
Rationalization	Assigning logical or socially desirable motives to what we do so that we seem to have acted rationally.
Reaction formation	Concealing a motive from ourselves by giving strong expression to the opposite motive.
Projection	Assigning our own undesirable qualities to others in exaggerated amounts.
Intellectualization	Attempting to gain detachment from a stressful situation by dealing with it in abstract, intellectual terms.
Denial	Denying that an unpleasant reality exists.
Displacement	Directing a motive that cannot be gratified in one form into another channel.

with their self-concepts. Feelings of hostility toward a loved one and experiences of failure may be banished from conscious memory.

Repression is different from suppression. *Suppression* is the process of deliberate self-control, keeping impulses and desires in check (perhaps holding them in privately while denying them publicly) or temporarily pushing aside painful memories. Individuals are aware of suppressed thoughts but are largely unaware of repressed impulses or memories.

Freud believed that repression is seldom completely successful. The repressed impulses threaten to break through into consciousness; the individual becomes anxious (though unaware of the reason) and employs several other defense mechanisms to keep the partially repressed impulses from awareness.

In recent years there has been renewed interest in people who habitually repress or suppress painful thoughts and emotions. People with a repressive style appear to have a heightened vulnerability to illness in general, including more coronary heart disease and a more rapid course of cancer (Bonnano & Singer, 1990). Another line of research has shown that people who confide in others about traumatic events and the emotions they feel in reaction to those events tend to be healthier than people who do not confide in others (Petrie et al., 1998). For example, wives of men who died by suicide were more likely to be physically ill during the years following their husband's death if they never confided to others that their husband had committed suicide (Pennebaker & O'Heeron, 1984).

How may repression or suppression contribute to poor physical health? First, as Freud suggested, suppression and repression seldom are completely satisfactory. People who try to suppress thoughts may actually ruminate more about the unwanted thoughts and emotions than people who express them to others. Several studies have shown that trying to suppress thoughts actually leads us to think those thoughts more frequently than when we stop trying to suppress them (Wegner et al., 1987). In other words, there is a rebound effect in which suppressed unwanted thoughts come back with greater force once the person's guard is down. In the study of widows of suicide victims, the researchers found that women who had not told anyone about their husband's suicide actually ruminated more about it than women who had confided in others about the suicide (Pennebaker & O'Heeron, 1984). Thus, people who habitually try to push unwanted thoughts out of their minds might find these thoughts coming back with great force, causing them much distress. In turn, this heightened level of distress and the physiological arousal accompanying it could have negative effects on the body.

Second, the act of suppressing or repressing thoughts may be physically taxing in itself and thus have negative effects on the body. That is, constantly pushing thoughts out of our minds and monitoring whether or not the thoughts are returning may require physical energy and lead to chronic arousal, which damages the body.

Pennebaker (1997) has shown that having people recount traumas and the emotions associated with them, whether in conversations with other people or simply by writing about them in diaries, reduces the tendency to ruminate about the traumas and may lead to better health. Expressing emotion may reduce rumination and improve health in a number of ways. Verbally expressing fears and emotions may make them more concrete and, hence, easier to deal with. When we tell others about our traumas and emotions, the listeners provide social support and validation for our feelings. Finally, talking about a trauma may help us habituate to the trauma—that is, get used to the trauma so it does not create the same level of negative emotion every time we think about it.

Rationalization   When the fox in Aesop's fable rejected the grapes that he could not reach because they were sour, he illustrated a defense mechanism known as *rationalization*. Rationalization does not mean "to act rationally," as we might assume; it refers to the assignment of logical or socially desirable motives to what we do so that we *seem* to have acted rationally. Rationalization serves two purposes: It eases our disappointment when we fail to reach a goal ("I didn't want it anyway"), and it gives us acceptable motives for our behavior. If we act impulsively or on the basis of motives that we do not wish to acknowledge even to ourselves, we rationalize what we have done in order to place our behavior in a more favorable light.

In searching for the good reason rather than the true reason, individuals make a number of excuses. These excuses are usually plausible; they simply do not tell the whole story. For example, "My roommate failed to wake me" or "I had too many other things to do" may be true, but they may not be the real reasons for the individual's failure to perform the behavior in question. Individuals who are really concerned set an alarm clock or find the time to do what they are expected to do.

An experiment involving posthypnotic suggestion (see Chapter 6) demonstrates the process of rationalization. A hypnotist instructs a participant under hypnosis that when he wakes from the trance he will watch the hypnotist; then, when the hypnotist takes off her glasses, the participant will raise the window but will not remember that the hypnotist told him to do this. Aroused from the trance, the participant feels a little drowsy but soon circulates among the people in the room and carries on a normal conversation, furtively watching the hypnotist. When the hypnotist casually removes her glasses, the participant feels an impulse to open the window. He takes a step in that direction but hesitates. Unconsciously, he mobilizes his desire to be a reasonable person; seeking a reason for his impulse to open the window, he says, "Isn't it a little stuffy in here?" Having found the needed excuse, he opens the window and feels more comfortable (Hilgard, 1965).

Reaction Formation   Sometimes individuals can conceal a motive from themselves by giving strong expression to the opposite motive. This tendency is called *reaction formation*. A mother who feels guilty about not wanting her child may become overindulgent and overprotective in order to assure the child of her love and assure herself that she is a good mother. In one case, a mother who wished to do everything for her daughter could not understand why the child was so unappreciative. At great sacrifice, she arranged for the daughter take expensive piano lessons and assisted her in the daily practice sessions. Although the mother thought she was being extremely kind, she was actually being very demanding—in fact, hostile. She was unaware of her own hostility, but when confronted with it she admitted that she had hated piano lessons as a child. Under the conscious guise of being kind, she was unconsciously being cruel to her daughter. The daughter sensed what was going on and developed symptoms that required psychological treatment.

Some people who crusade with fanatical zeal against loose morals, alcohol, and gambling may be manifesting reaction formation. Some of these individuals have experienced these problems themselves, and their zealous crusading may be a means of defending themselves against the possibility of backsliding.

Projection   All of us have undesirable traits that we do not acknowledge, even to ourselves. A defense mechanism known as *projection* protects us from recognizing our own undesirable qualities by assigning them to other people in exaggerated amounts. Suppose that you have a tendency to be critical of or unkind to other people, but you would dislike yourself if you admitted this tendency. If you are convinced that the people around you are cruel or unkind, your harsh treatment of them is not based on your bad qualities—you are simply "giving them what they deserve." If you can assure yourself that everybody else cheats on college examinations, your unacknowledged tendency to take some academic shortcuts seems not so bad. Projection is really a form of rationalization, but it is so pervasive that it merits discussion in its own right.

Intellectualization *Intellectualization* is an attempt to gain detachment from a stressful situation by dealing with it in abstract, intellectual terms. This kind of defense may be a necessity for people who must deal with life-and-death matters in their jobs. A doctor who is continually confronted with human suffering cannot afford to become emotionally involved with each patient. In fact, a certain amount of detachment may be essential for the doctor to function competently. This kind of intellectualization is a problem only when it becomes so pervasive that individuals cut themselves off from all emotional experiences.

Denial When an external reality is too unpleasant to face, an individual may engage in *denial,* denying that the undesired reality exists. The parents of a terminally ill child may refuse to admit that anything is seriously wrong, even though they are fully informed of the diagnosis and the expected outcome. Because they cannot tolerate the pain that acknowledging reality would produce, they resort to denial. Less extreme forms of denial may be seen in individuals who consistently ignore criticism, fail to perceive that others are angry with them, or disregard all kinds of clues suggesting that their spouse is having an affair.

Sometimes, denying facts may be better than facing them. In a severe crisis, denial may give the person time to face the grim facts at a more gradual pace. For example, victims of a stroke or a spinal cord injury might give up altogether if they were fully aware of the seriousness of their condition. Hope gives them an incentive to keep trying.

Soldiers who have faced combat or imprisonment report that denying the possibility of death helped them function. In such situations denial clearly has an adaptive value. On the other hand, the negative aspects of denial are evident when people postpone seeking medical help. For example, a woman may deny that a lump in her breast may be cancerous and hence may delay going to a physician until the condition has become life-threatening.

Displacement Through the mechanism of *displacement,* a motive that cannot be gratified in one form is directed into a new channel. An example of displacement was provided in our discussion of anger that could not be expressed toward the source of frustration and was redirected toward a less threatening object. Freud felt that displacement was the most satisfactory way of handling aggressive and sexual impulses. The basic drives cannot be changed, but we can change the object toward which a drive is directed. Erotic impulses that cannot be expressed directly may be expressed indirectly in creative activities such as art, poetry, and music. Hostile impulses may find socially acceptable expression through participation in contact sports.

It seems unlikely that displacement actually eliminates the frustrated impulses, but substitute activities do help reduce tension when a basic drive is thwarted. For example, the activities of taking care of others or seeking companionship may help reduce the tension associated with unsatisfied sexual needs.

Managing Stress

Thus far we have focused primarily on factors within individuals that influence their perceptions and the impact of stressful events on them. The emotional support and concern of other people also can make stress more bearable. Divorce, the death of a loved one, or a serious illness is usually more devastating if the individual must face it alone. A study of Israeli parents who had lost a son (either through accidents or in the Yom Kippur War) found that bereavement exacted a heavier toll on those who were already widowed or divorced. Their mortality rate in the ten-year period following their loss was higher than the mortality rate for parents who could share their grief with each other (Levav et al., 1988).

Numerous studies indicate that people who have many social ties (spouse, friends, relatives, and group memberships) live longer and are less likely to succumb to stress-related illnesses than people who have few supportive social contacts (Cohen, 1996). Friends and family can provide support in many ways. They can bolster our self-esteem by loving us despite our problems. They can provide information and advice, companionship to distract us from our worries, and financial or material aid. All of these tend to reduce feelings of helplessness and increase our confidence in our ability to cope.

Stress is easier to tolerate when the cause of the stress is shared by others. Community disasters (floods, earthquakes, tornadoes, wars) often seem to bring out the best in people (Nilson et al., 1981). People tend to rally together to support one another and overcome the consequences of the disaster. Individual anxieties and conflicts tend to be forgotten when people are working together against a common enemy or toward a common goal. For example, during the intensive bombing of London in World War II there was a marked decline in the number of people seeking help for emotional problems.

Sometimes, however, family and friends can increase the stress experienced by an individual. Minimizing the seriousness of the problem or giving blind assurance that everything will be all right may produce more anxiety than failing to offer support at all. A study of graduate students facing crucial examinations suggests that spouses who are realistically supportive ("I'm worried, but I know you'll do the best you can") are more helpful than spouses who deny any possibility of failure ("I'm not worried; I'm sure you'll pass). In the latter case, the student has to worry not only about failing the exam but also about losing respect in the eyes of the spouse (Mechanic, 1962). Other people can also make demands and place burdens on an individual at the very time that he or she is dealing with other stressors (Rook, 1984). For example, a person who is caring for a terminally ill parent is more likely to suffer from depression if she is also being criticized and harassed by siblings about the way she is caring for the parent (Nolen-Hoeksema & Larson, 1999).

In addition to seeking positive social support in times of stress, people can learn other techniques to reduce the negative effects of stress on the body and the mind. In this section, we discuss some behavioral and cognitive techniques that have been shown to help people reduce the effects of stress. We then discuss in detail how these techniques are applied to reduce Type A behavior and coronary heart disease.

Behavioral Techniques

Among the behavioral techniques that have been used to help people control their physiological responses to stressful situations are biofeedback, relaxation training, meditation, and aerobic exercise.

Biofeedback In **biofeedback training,** individuals *receive information (feedback) about an aspect of their physiological state and then attempt to alter that state.* For example, in a procedure for learning to control tension headaches, electrodes are attached to the participant's forehead so that any movement in the forehead muscle can be electronically detected, amplified, and fed back to the person as an auditory signal. The signal, or tone, increases in pitch when the muscle contracts and decreases when it relaxes. By learning to control the pitch of the tone, the individual learns to keep the muscle relaxed. (Relaxation of the forehead muscle usually ensures relaxation of scalp and neck muscles as well.) After four to eight weeks of biofeedback training, the participant learns to recognize the onset of tension and to reduce it without feedback from the machine (Thorpe & Olson, 1997).

Relaxation Training Physiological processes that are controlled by the autonomic nervous system, such as heart rate and blood pressure, have traditionally been assumed to be automatic and not under voluntary control. However, laboratory studies have demonstrated that people can learn to modify heart rate and blood pressure (see Figure 14-8). The results of these studies have led to new procedures for treating patients with high blood pressure (hypertension). One procedure is to show patients a graph of their blood pressure while it is being monitored and to teach them techniques for relaxing different muscle groups. The patients are instructed to tense their muscles (for example, to clench a fist or tighten the abdomen), release the tension, and notice the difference in sensation. By starting with the feet and ankle muscles and progressing through the body to the muscles that control the neck and face, the patients learn to modify muscular tension. This combination of biofeedback with relaxation training has proved effective in lowering blood pressure for some individuals (Mukhopadhyay & Turner, 1997).

Reviews of numerous studies using biofeedback and relaxation training to control headaches and hypertension conclude that the most important variable is learning how to relax (Thorpe & Olson, 1997). Some people may learn to relax faster when they receive biofeedback. Others may learn to relax equally well when they receive training in muscle relaxation without any specific biofeedback. The usefulness of relaxation training seems to depend on the individual. Some people who are not conscientious about taking drugs to relieve high blood pressure are more responsive to relaxation training, whereas others who have learned to control their blood pressure through relaxation may eventually drop the procedure because they find it too time-consuming.

Meditation
Meditation is an effective technique for inducing relaxation and reducing physiological arousal. Almost all studies of the phenomenon report a significant lowering of the respiratory rate, a decrease in oxygen consumption, and less elimination of carbon dioxide. The heart rate is lowered, blood flow stabilizes, and the concentration of lactate in the blood is decreased (Dillbeck & Orme-Johnson, 1987). Also, there is a change in the EEG activity; these changes in brain waves suggest that cortical arousal is decreased during meditation, reflecting a reduced level of mental activity (Fenwick, 1987). Meditation has also proved effective in helping people with chronic feelings of anxiety and in improving self-esteem (Snaith, 1998).

However, a leading researcher in this field contends that the same effects can be achieved through simple rest. After a thorough study of the research evidence, he

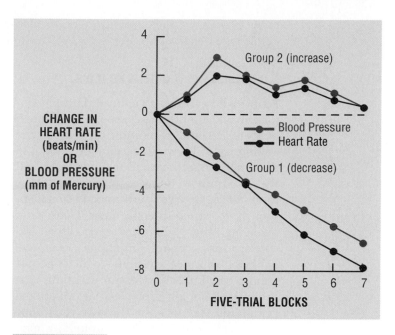

FIGURE 14-8

Operant Conditioning of Blood Pressure and Heart Rate *One group of participants received biofeedback (a light and a tone) whenever their blood pressure and heart rate decreased simultaneously (Group 1); the other group received the same feedback whenever their blood pressure and heart rate increased simultaneously (Group 2). The participants achieved significant simultaneous control of blood pressure and heart rate during a single conditioning session. The group who were reinforced for lowering both functions achieved increasingly greater control over trials; the group who were reinforced for raising both functions was less consistent.* (After Schwartz, 1975)

concludes that there are no consistent differences between meditating and resting participants in heart rate, respiration rate, oxygen consumption, blood flow, and other physiological measures (Holmes, 1984, 1985a, 1985b). Thus, simply resting may produce stress-reflection effects similar to those produced by meditation.

Exercise
Another factor that is important in controlling stress is physical fitness. Individuals who regularly engage in aerobic exercise (any sustained activity that increases heart rate and oxygen consumption, such as jogging, swimming, or cycling) show significantly lower heart rates and blood pressure in response to stressful situations than individuals who do not exercise regularly (Taylor, 1999). In turn, Brown (1991) found that physically fit people were much less likely to become physically ill following stressful events than people who were not fit. Because of these findings,

many stress management programs also emphasize physical fitness.

Cognitive Techniques

People who are able to control their physiological or emotional responses through biofeedback and relaxation training in the laboratory will have more difficulty doing so in actual stressful situations, particularly if they continue to interact in ways that make them tense. Consequently, an additional approach to stress management focuses on changing the individual's cognitive responses to stressful situations. Cognitive behavior therapy attempts to help people identify the kinds of stressful situations that produce their physiological or emotional symptoms and to alter the way they cope with these situations. For example, a man who suffers from tension headaches would be asked to keep a record of their occurrence and rate the severity of each headache and the circumstances in which it occurred. Next he would be taught how to monitor his responses to these stressful events and asked to record his feelings, thoughts, and behavior prior to, during, and following the event. After a period of self-monitoring, certain relationships often become evident among situational variables (for example, criticism by a supervisor or co-worker); thoughts ("I can't do anything

right"); and emotional, behavioral, and physiological responses (depression, withdrawal, and headache).

The next step is trying to identify the expectations or beliefs that might explain the headache reactions (for example, "I expect to do everything perfectly, so the slightest criticism upsets me," or "I judge myself harshly, become depressed, and end up with a headache"). The final and most difficult step is trying to change something about the stressful situation, the individual's way of thinking about it, or the individual's behavior. The options might include finding a less stressful job, recognizing that the need to perform perfectly leads to unnecessary anguish over errors, or learning to behave more assertively in interactions instead of withdrawing.

Biofeedback, relaxation training, exercise, and cognitive therapy have all proved useful in helping people control their physiological and emotional responses to stress. Some research suggests that the improvement is more likely to be maintained over time with a combination of cognitive and behavior therapy (Holroyd, Appel, & Andrasik, 1983). This is not surprising, since the complex demands of everyday life often require flexible coping skills; being able to relax may not be an effective method of coping with some of life's stresses. Programs for stress management frequently employ a combination of biofeedback, relaxation training, exercise, and cognitive modification techniques.

Modifying Type A Behavior

A combination of cognitive and behavioral techniques has been shown to reduce Type A behavior (Friedman et al., 1994). The participants were more than 1,000 individuals who had experienced at least one heart attack. Participants in the treatment group were helped to reduce their sense of time urgency by practicing standing in line (a situation that Type A individuals find extremely irritating) and using the opportunity to reflect on things that they do not normally have time to think about, or to watch people, or to strike up a conversation with a stranger. Treatment also included helping participants learn to express themselves without exploding at people and to alter

In this biofeedback procedure for treating headaches, the sensors measure forehead muscle contractions and finger temperature. Cold fingers are often a sign of tension.

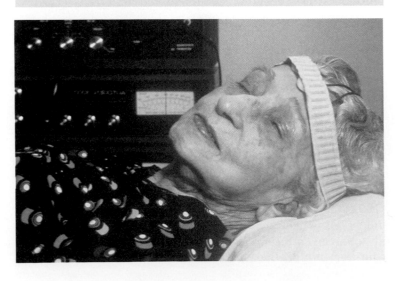

certain specific behaviors (such as interrupting others or talking or eating hurriedly). Therapists helped the participants reevaluate certain beliefs (such as the notion that success depends on the quantity of work produced) that might lead to urgent and hostile behavior. Finally, participants found ways to make their home and work environments less stressful (such as reducing the number of unnecessary social engagements).

The critical dependent variable in this study was the occurrence of another heart attack. By the end of the study $4\frac{1}{2}$ years later, the experimental group had a heart attack recurrence rate almost half that of control participants who were not taught how to alter their lifestyles. Clearly, learning to modify Type A behavior was beneficial to these participants' health (Friedman et al., 1994).

Like other research described in this chapter, this study was based on the premise that the mind and the body influence each other. Simple models of how stress affects health are being replaced by complex models that explain how biological, psychological, and social factors intertwine to create disease or health. As we have seen, the body has characteristic physiological reactions to stress. For people with preexisting biological vulnerabilities, such as a genetic predisposition to heart disease, these physiological reactions to stress can cause deterioration in health. Yet an individual's perception of stress is determined by characteristics of events in the environment and by his or her personal history, appraisals of the event, and coping styles. Thus, the extent to which the individual experiences psychological distress or ill health following potentially stressful situations is determined by the biological and psychological vulnerabilities and strengths he or she brings to these situations.

The Perils of Unrealistic Optimism

Neil D. Weinstein, *Rutgers University*

Neil Weinstein

Are you more likely or less likely to develop a drinking problem than the other people in your psychology class? How about your chances of getting a sexually transmitted disease (STD) or your chances of having a heart attack some day? When asked questions like these, few people admit to having above-average risk. Typically, 50%–70% of a group claim that their risk is below average; another 30%–50% say that their risk is average; but less than 10% acknowledge that their risk is above average.

Obviously, this cannot be correct. Your own risk of heart disease might actually be below average, but the number of people who make such a claim is simply too great for them all to be right. The "average" person has, by definition, an "average" risk. So when the people who claim below-average risk greatly outnumber those who say their risk is higher than average, something must be wrong with their risk judgments.

The data show that most of the individuals whose actions, family history, or environment put them at high risk either don't realize it or won't admit it. In general, we summarize these findings by saying that people are unrealistically optimistic about future risks. This unrealistic optimism is especially strong with risks that are somewhat under our own control, such as alcoholism, lung cancer, and STDs. Apparently, we are quite confident that we will do a better job of avoiding these problems than will our peers.

What unrealistic optimism demonstrates is that we are not impartial and open-minded when it comes to health risk information. Most of us want to be informed and make good decisions, but we also want to feel that our lifestyles are already healthful, that changes are not needed, and that we don't have to worry. Unfortunately, this search for a rosy interpretation can get us into trouble. If everything is okay as is, then we don't need to take precautions. We can continue to get drunk with our friends, eat as much pizza, fries, and hamburgers as we want, and use condoms only with sexual partners whom we know are promiscuous (curiously, we rarely think that any of them are). Most of the time such risky behavior does not get us into trouble, but the odds of getting into trouble are certainly increased. The millions of college students who get STDs every year or who get into automobile accidents after too many beers are clear examples of people doing things that they know are supposed to be risky. But they have concluded that, for them, it will be okay. This is not ignorance; it is unrealistic optimism.

An especially upsetting example is the growing number of college students who smoke cigarettes. They have all kinds of illusions to make them feel comfortable. They will only smoke for a couple of years and then they will quit. (Others may get hooked, but not them.) Their cigarettes are low in tar, or they don't inhale. They exercise a lot, which will counteract the effects of smoking. Smokers don't deny that cigarettes are bad for people. They just think the effects won't be bad for them. Typically, they say that their risk of heart disease, lung cancer, and emphysema is lower than that of other smokers and only "a little" above the risk of the average person.

Optimism does have its advantages. When people already have a severe illness and are coping with it—illnesses such as cancer or AIDS—maintaining optimism is important. It helps people put up with sometimes unpleasant treatments, and a positive mood may itself help by improving the body's ability to resist disease. Even being overly optimistic about the future is unlikely to lead someone who has a life-threatening disease to pretend that he or she is not sick or to stop treatment. However, the perils of unrealistic optimism are greater when the issue is preventing harm from occurring. If you think you can handle a car after a night of drinking, if none of your dates could carry an STD, or if, unlike your classmates, you can stop smoking any time you want, your unrealistic optimism is likely to lead to health consequences you will regret.

Unrealistic Optimism Can Be Good for Your Health

Shelley E. Taylor, *University of California, Los Angeles*

Is unrealistic optimism bad for your health? It seems like it should be. After all, if people believe they are relatively invulnerable to disorders ranging from tooth decay to heart disease, logically, shouldn't that interfere with practicing good health behaviors? Ample evidence suggests that most people are indeed unrealistically optimistic about their health. But, if anything, unrealistic optimism seems to be good for your health.

Consider the practice of health habits, such as wearing a seat belt, getting exercise, and avoiding harmful substances such as tobacco and alcohol. Rather than undermining such habits, as some have assumed, unrealistic optimism may actually lead people to practice better health habits. Aspinwall and Brunhart (1996) found that people with optimistic expectations about their health actually pay *more* attention to personally relevant risk-related information than pessimistic people, apparently so that they can take preventive action to offset those risks (Aspinwall & Brunhart, 1996). People may be optimistic about their health precisely because they practice better health habits than more pessimistic people (Armor & Taylor, 1998).

Perhaps the most persuasive evidence for beneficial health effects of unrealistic optimism has come from studies of gay men with the HIV virus. In one study, men who were unrealistically optimistic about their ability to avoid AIDS (such as believing that their bodies might shake off the virus) practiced *more* health-promoting behaviors than those who were less optimistic (Taylor et al., 1992). Reed, Kemeny, Taylor, Wang, and Visscher (1994) found that, among men diagnosed with AIDS, maintaining an unrealistically optimistic outlook, as opposed to a realistic one, was associated with an increased length of life of nine months. In a parallel finding, Richard Schulz found that pessimistic cancer patients died earlier than those who were more optimistic (Schulz et al., 1994).

Optimists also seem to recover faster from illnesses. Leedham, Meyerowitz, Muirhead, and Frist (1995) found that optimistic expectations among heart transplant patients were associated with better mood, quality of life, and adjustment to illness. Similar findings are reported by Scheier and his associates (Scheier et al., 1989) in their study of people adjusting to coronary artery bypass surgery. What accounts for findings like these?

Optimism is associated with good coping strategies, as well as with good health habits. Optimists are active copers who try to solve problems rather than avoid them (e.g., Scheier & Carver, 1992). Optimistic people are also more interpersonally successful, and so they may do a better job of attracting social support. Social support is known to reduce the likelihood of illness and promote recovery, and so, optimistic people may recruit this special resource for dealing with stress and with illness.

Scientists are now realizing that optimism may create or be associated with a bodily state conducive to health or to rapid recovery from illness. Suzanne Segerstrom and her associates (Segerstrom, Taylor, Kemeny, & Fahey, 1998) studied a group of law students under intense academic stress during the first semester of law school. They found that the optimistic law students showed an immunological profile suggestive of greater resistance to illness and infection. Other studies are showing similar findings (Bower, Kemeny, Taylor, and Fahey, 1998).

Why do some people think that optimism is bad for your health? Some researchers have indicted unrealistic optimism as a culprit that promotes health risk without the evidence. For example, although smokers seemingly underestimate their risk for lung cancer, there is no evidence that their unrealistic optimism led them to smoke or justifies their continued smoking. Indeed, smokers are well aware that they are more vulnerable to lung disorders than are nonsmokers.

Shelley Taylor

Does this mean that unrealistic optimism is always beneficial for your health or is beneficial to all people? Seymour Epstein and his associates (Epstein & Meier, 1989) have suggested that most optimists are "constructive optimists" who take active efforts to protect their health and safety. But a few optimists are "naïve optimists" who believe that everything will turn out all right without any active efforts on their part. If optimists are ever at risk for poorer health habits, it may be this small group of avoidant copers.

Before you write off unrealistic optimism as a state that blinds people to the realistic risks we all face, look at its benefits. It keeps people happier, healthier, and more likely to recover from illness.

SUMMARY

1. Events are often considered stressful when they are traumas outside the range of normal human experience, are perceived as uncontrollable or unpredictable, challenge the limits of our capabilities, and cause internal conflicts between competing goals.

2. Common psychological reactions to stress include anxiety, anger and aggression, apathy and depression, and cognitive impairment (for example, problems in concentration and performance).

3. The body reacts to stress with the fight-or-flight response. The sympathetic nervous system causes increased heart rate, elevated blood pressure, dilated pupils, and the release of extra sugar from the liver. The adrenal-cortical system causes the release of adrenocorticotropic hormone (ACTH), which stimulates the release of cortisol in the blood. These reactions are part of a general adaptation syndrome, a set of responses that is displayed by all organisms in response to stress. The syndrome consists of three phases: alarm, resistance, and exhaustion.

4. Stress may affect health directly by creating chronic overarousal of the sympathetic division of the autonomic nervous system or the adrenal cortical system or by impairing the immune system. People under stress also may not engage in positive health-related behaviors, and this may lead to illness.

5. The way individuals appraise events may influence their vulnerability to illness. For example, peo-
ple who tend to attribute bad events to internal, stable, and global causes are more likely to develop learned helplessness after experiencing such events and to become ill.

6. People with the Type A behavior pattern tend to be hostile, aggressive, impatient individuals who are overinvolved in their work. Studies of men and women show that people who exhibit this pattern are at increased risk for coronary heart disease.

7. Coping strategies are divided into problem-focused strategies and emotion-focused strategies. People who take active steps to solve problems are less likely to experience depression and illness following negative life events. People who use rumination or avoidance strategies to cope with negative emotions show longer and more severe distress after negative events. Psychoanalytic theory describes a number of unconscious strategies (defense mechanisms) that people use to cope with negative emotions; these include repression, reaction formation, denial, and projection.

8. Behavioral techniques such as relaxation training and cognitive techniques such as challenging negative thoughts can help people react more adaptively to stress. Type A behavior can be changed through behavioral and cognitive techniques, resulting in reduced risk of coronary heart disease.

KEY TERMS

stress (p. 485)
stressor (p. 485)
stress response (p. 485)
traumatic event (p. 486)
general adaptation syndrome (p. 497)
psychophysiological disorders (p. 498)

attributional style (p. 505)
hardiness (p. 505)
Type A pattern (p. 506)
coping (p. 508)
defense mechanisms (p. 512)
biofeedback training (p. 516)

CRITICAL THINKING QUESTIONS

1. In what way might the environment in which a child is raised affect the development of his or her coping strategies?

2. How can we help people with a serious disease like cancer change in ways that might slow the progress of the disease without making them feel that they are being blamed for having the disease?

3. What are some of your most unhealthy behaviors? What prevents you from changing them?

4. What might make some cultures more prone to stress-related health problems than others?

FURTHER READING

Stress at Work (1999), by Peterson, describes psychological and sociological approaches to occupational stress. *Psychosocial Processes and Health* (1994), edited by Steptoe, is a reader with chapters by some of the leading researchers in health psychology. *Stress Management for Wellness* (1996), by Schafer, provides practical tips for reducing stress and teaches relaxation techniques.

The developing field of health psychology is described in *Why Zebras Don't Get Ulcers* (1994) by Sapolsky. Pennebaker (1990) summarizes his research on the effect of confiding in others on physical health in *Opening Up: The Healing Powers of Confiding in Others*. For a comprehensive review of the literature on psychology and health, see Taylor's *Health Psychology* (1994).

Chapter 15
Abnormal Psychology

Most of us have periods when we feel anxious, depressed, unreasonably angry, or inadequate in dealing with life's complexities. Trying to lead a satisfying and meaningful life is not easy in an era of rapid social and technological change. Many of our traditional assumptions about work, religion, sex, marriage, and family are being questioned, and the social values that gave our grandparents a sense of security no longer provide clear guidelines for behavior. It is rare for a person to get through life without periods of loneliness, self-doubt, and despair. In fact, nearly half of all Americans will experience a mental or emotional problem at least once during their lifetime that, if diagnosed, would be classified as a mental disorder (Kessler et al., 1994).

A word of warning may be appropriate before we proceed. It is common for students studying abnormal psychology for the first time to see signs of mental disorders in themselves, just as medical students diagnose themselves as suffering from every new disease they read about. Most of us have had some of the symptoms we will be describing, and that is not cause for alarm. However, if you have been bothered by distressing feelings for a long time, it never hurts to talk to someone about them—perhaps someone in your school's counseling service or student health service.

Abnormal Behavior

In this chapter we look at some individuals who have serious mental disorders and some who have developed self-destructive lifestyles. The behaviors we discuss are classified as "abnormal," but as we will see, the dividing line between "normal" and "abnormal" behavior is far from clear.

Defining Abnormality

What do we mean by "abnormal" behavior? By what criteria do we distinguish it from "normal" behavior? There is no general agreement, but most attempts to describe abnormality are based on one or more of the following definitions.

Deviation From Statistical Norms The word *abnormal* means "away from the norm." Many characteristics, such as height, weight, and intelligence, cover a range of values when measured over an entire population. Most people, for example, fall within the middle range of height, while a few are abnormally tall or abnormally short. One definition of abnormality therefore is based on statistical frequency: Abnormal behavior is statistically infrequent or deviant from the norm. But according to this definition a person who is extremely intelligent or extremely happy would be classified as abnormal. Thus, in defining abnormal behavior we must consider more than statistical frequency.

Deviation From Social Norms Every society has certain standards, or *norms,* for acceptable behavior; behavior that deviates markedly from those norms is considered abnormal. Usually, but not always, such behavior is also statistically infrequent in that society. However, several problems arise when deviation from social norms is used as a criterion for defining abnormality. Behavior that is considered normal by one society may be considered abnormal by another. For example, members of some cultures do not consider it unusual to hear voices when no one is actually talking or to see visions when nothing is actually there, but such behaviors are considered abnormal in most societies. Another problem is that the concept of abnormality changes over time within the same society. Forty years ago, most Americans would have considered men wearing earrings abnormal. Today, such behaviors tend to be viewed as differences in life-style rather than as signs of abnormality. Thus, ideas of normality and abnormality differ from one society to another and over time within the same society. Any definition of abnormality must reflect more than social compliance.

Maladaptiveness of Behavior Rather than defining abnormal behavior in terms of deviance from either statistical or societal norms, many social scientists believe that the most important criterion is how the behavior affects the well-being of the individual or the social group. According to this

In defining abnormality, it is important to distinguish maladaptive behavior from behavior that merely deviates from widely accepted social norms.

criterion, behavior is abnormal if it is maladaptive—that is, if it has adverse effects on the individual or on society. Some kinds of deviant behavior interfere with the welfare of the individual (a man who is so fearful of crowds that he cannot ride the bus to work; an alcoholic who drinks so heavily that he or she cannot hold a job; a woman who attempts suicide). Other forms of deviant behavior are harmful to society (an adolescent who has violent aggressive outbursts; a paranoid individual who plots to assassinate national leaders). If we use the criterion of maladaptiveness, all of these behaviors would be considered abnormal.

Personal Distress A fourth criterion considers abnormality in terms of the individual's subjective feelings of distress rather than his or her behavior. Most people who are diagnosed as mentally ill feel acutely miserable. They are anxious, depressed, or agitated, and many suffer from insomnia, loss of appetite, or numerous aches and pains. Sometimes personal distress may be the only symptom of abnormality; the individual's behavior may appear normal to the casual observer.

None of these definitions provides a completely satisfactory description of abnormal behavior. In most instances, all four criteria—statistical frequency, social deviation, maladaptive behavior, and personal distress—are considered in diagnosing abnormality.

What Is Normality?

Normality is even more difficult to define than abnormality, but most psychologists would agree that the characteristics in the following list indicate emotional well-being. (Note that these characteristics do not make sharp distinctions between the mentally healthy and the mentally ill; rather, they represent traits that a normal person possesses to a greater degree than an individual who is diagnosed as abnormal.)

1. *Appropriate perception of reality.* Normal individuals are fairly realistic in appraising their reactions and capabilities and interpreting what is going on in the world around them. They do not consistently misperceive what others say and do, and they do not consistently overrate their abilities and tackle more than they can accomplish, nor do they underestimate their abilities and shy away from difficult tasks.

2. *Ability to exercise voluntary control over behavior.* Normal individuals feel fairly confident about their ability to control their behavior. Occasionally they may act impulsively, but they are able to restrain their sexual and aggressive urges when necessary. They may fail to conform to social norms, but in such instances their decisions are voluntary rather than the result of uncontrollable impulses.

3. *Self-esteem and acceptance.* Well-adjusted people have some appreciation of their own worth and feel accepted by those around them. They are comfortable with other people and are able to react spontaneously in social situations. At the same time, they do not feel obligated to completely subjugate their opinions to those of the group. Feelings of worthlessness, alienation, and lack of acceptance are prevalent among individuals who are diagnosed as abnormal.

4. *Ability to form affectionate relationships.* Normal individuals are able to form close and satisfying relationships with other people. They are sensitive to the feelings of others and do not make excessive demands on others to gratify their own needs. Often, mentally disturbed people are so concerned with protecting their own security that they become extremely self-centered. Preoccupied with their own feelings and strivings, they seek affection but are unable to reciprocate. Sometimes they fear intimacy because their past relationships have been destructive.

5. *Productivity.* Well-adjusted people are able to channel their abilities into productive activity. They are enthusiastic about life and do not need to drive themselves to meet the demands of the day. Chronic lack of energy and excessive susceptibility to fatigue are often symptoms of psychological tension resulting from unsolved problems.

Well-adjusted people are able to channel their abilities into productive activity.

Classifying Abnormal Behaviors

A broad range of behaviors have been classified as abnormal. Some abnormal behaviors are acute and transitory, resulting from particularly stressful events, whereas others are chronic and lifelong. Each person's behavior and emotional problems are unique; no two individuals behave in exactly the same manner or share the same life experiences. However, enough similarities exist for mental health professionals to classify cases into categories.

A good classification system has many advantages. If the various types of abnormal behavior have different causes, we can hope to uncover them by grouping individuals according to similarities in behavior and then looking for other ways in which they may be similar. A diagnostic label also enables those who work with disturbed individuals communicate information more quickly and concisely. The diagnosis of schizophrenia indicates quite a bit about a person's behavior. Knowing that an individual's symp-

toms are similar to those of other patients is also helpful in deciding how to treat the patient. Disadvantages arise, however, if we allow a diagnostic label to carry too much weight. Labeling induces us to overlook the unique features of each case and expect the person to conform to the classification. We may also forget that a label for maladaptive behavior is not an explanation of that behavior; the classification does not tell us how the behavior originated or what causes it to continue.

The classification of mental disorders used by most mental health professionals in the United States is the *Diagnostic and Statistical Manual of Mental Disorders*, 4th edition (DSM-IV for short), which corresponds generally to the international system formulated by the World Health Organization. The major categories of mental disorders classified by DSM-IV are listed in Table 15-1. DSM-IV provides an extensive list of subcategories under each of these headings, as well as a description of the symptoms that must be present for the diagnosis to be applicable.

TABLE 15-1

Categories of Mental Disorders   *Listed here are the main diagnostic categories of DSM-IV. Each category includes numerous subclassifications.* (After American Psychiatric Association, 1994)

1. **Disorders usually first evident in infancy, childhood, or adolescence**	Includes mental retardation, autism, attention deficit disorder with hyperactivity, separation anxiety, speech disorders, and other deviations from normal development.
2. **Delirium, dementia, amnestic, and other cognitive diorders**	Disorders in which the functioning of the brain is known to be impaired, either permanently or transiently; may be the result of aging, degenerative diseases of the nervous system (for example, syphilis or Alzheimer's disease), or the ingestion of toxic substances (for example, lead poisoning or drugs).
3. **Psychoactive substance use disorders**	Includes excessive use of alcohol, barbiturates, amphetamines, cocaine, and other drugs that alter behavior. Marijuana and tobacco are also included in this category, which is controversial.
4. **Schizophrenia**	A group of disorders characterized by loss of contact with reality, marked disturbances of thought and perception, and bizarre behavior. At some phase, delusions or hallucinations almost always occur.
5. **Mood disorders**	Disturbances of normal mood; the person may be extremely depressed, abnormally elated, or may alternate between periods of elation and depression.
6. **Anxiety disorders**	Includes disorders in which anxiety is the main symptom (generalized anxiety or panic disorders) or anxiety is experienced unless the individual avoids feared situations (phobic disorders) or tries to resist performing certain rituals or thinking persistent thoughts (obsessive-compulsive disorders). Also includes post-traumatic stress disorder.
7. **Somatoform disorders**	The symptoms are physical, but no organic basis can be found and psychological factors appear to play the major role. Included are conversion disorders (for example, a woman who resents having to care for her invalid mother suddenly develops a paralyzed arm) and hypochondriasis (excessive preoccupation with health and fear of disease when there is no basis for concern.) Does *not* include psychosomatic disorders that have an organic basis. (See Chapter 14)
8. **Dissociative disorders**	Temporary alterations in the functions of consciousness, memory, or identity due to emotional problems. Included are amnesia (the individual cannot recall anything about his or her history following a traumatic experience) and dissociative identity disorder (better known as multiple personality disorder, involving two or more independent personality systems existing within the same individual).
9. **Sexual Disorders**	Includes problems of sexual identity (for example, transsexualism), sexual performance (for example, impotence, premature ejaculation, and frigidity), and sexual aim (for example, sexual interest in children, sadism, and masochism).
10. **Eating disorders**	Self-induced starvation (anorexia) or patterns of binge eating followed by self-induced purging (bulimia).
11. **Sleep disorders**	Includes chronic insomnia, excessive sleepiness, sleep apnea, sleepwalking, and narcolepsy.
12. **Factitious disorders**	Physical or psychological symptoms that are intentionally produced or feigned. Differs from malingering in that there is no obvious goal, such as disability payments or the avoidance of military service. The best-studied form of this disorder is called Münchausen syndrome: The individual's plausible presentation of factitious physical symptoms results in frequent hospitalizations.
13. **Impulse control disorder**	Includes kleptomania (compulsive stealing of objects not needed for personal use or their monetary value), pathological gambling, and pyromania (setting fires for the pleasure or relief of tension derived thereby).
14. **Personality disorders**	Long-standing patterns of maladaptive behavior that constitute immature and inappropriate ways of coping with stress or solving problems. Antisocial personality disorder and narcissistic personality disorder are two examples.
15. **Other conditions that may be the focus of clinical attention**	This category includes many of the problems for which people seek help, such as marital problems, parent-child difficulties, and academic or occupational problems.

You have probably heard the terms *neurosis* and *psychosis* and may be wondering where they fit into the categories of mental disorders listed in Table 15-1. Traditionally, these terms denoted major diagnostic categories. Neuroses (the plural of *neurosis*) included a group of disorders characterized by anxiety, unhappiness, and maladaptive behavior that were seldom serious enough to require hospitalization. The individual could usually function in society, though not at full capacity. Psychoses (the plural of *psychosis*) included more serious mental disorders. The individual's behavior and thought processes were so disturbed that he or she was out of touch with reality, could not cope with the demands of daily life, and usually had to be hospitalized.

Neither neuroses nor psychoses appear as major categories in DSM-IV. There are several reasons for this departure from earlier classification systems, but the main one concerns precision of diagnosis. Both categories were fairly broad and included a number of mental disorders with quite dissimilar symptoms. Consequently, mental health professionals did not always agree on the diagnosis for a particular case. DSM-IV attempts to achieve greater consensus by grouping disorders according to very specific behavioral symptoms without implying anything about their origins or treatment. The intention is to describe observations of individuals who have psychological problems in a way that ensures accurate communication among mental health professionals. Consequently, DSM-IV includes many more categories than previous editions of the manual.

Although psychosis is no longer a major category, DSM-IV recognizes that people who are diagnosed as having schizophrenia, delusional disorders, and some mood disorders exhibit psychotic behavior at some point during their illness. Their thinking and perception of reality are severely disturbed, and they may have hallucinations (false sensory experiences, such as hearing voices or seeing strange visions) and/or delusions (false beliefs, such as the conviction that all thoughts are controlled by a powerful being from another planet). These issues will become clearer as we look more closely at some of the mental disorders listed in Table 15-1. We will examine anxiety disorders, mood disorders, schizophrenia, and two types of personality disorder. Alcoholism and drug dependence (both classified as psychoactive substance use disorders) are covered in Chapter 6.

Table 15-2 indicates the likelihood of the major mental disorders during one's lifetime. The study on which this table is based found that mental disorders are more common among people under age 45. Although the overall rates of disorders are not different in men and women, there are sex differences in the incidence of specific disorders. For example, men are twice as likely as women to abuse alcohol or other drugs. Antisocial personality disorders affected four times as many men as women, but more women suffered from mood and anxiety disorders.

Many cultures recognize mental disorders that do not correspond to any disorders listed in the DSM-IV (see Table 15-3). Some of these disorders may have the same underlying causes as certain disorders recognized by the DSM-IV but are manifested by different symptoms in other cultures. Other disorders may be truly unique to the cultures in which they are found. The presence of such culture-bound syndromes suggests that the disorders listed in DSM-IV represent only the disorders that occur in mainstream American culture rather than a universal list of disorders to which all humans are susceptible. This supports the views of those who argue that we cannot define abnormality without reference to the norms of a particular culture.

TABLE 15-2

Lifetime Prevalence Rates of Selected Disorders
Listed here are the percentage of individuals in the United States population who have experienced one of these mental disorders during their lifetime. These percentages are based on interviews with a sample of 8,098 individuals, age 18 to 54, all around United States cities. (After Kessler et al., 1994)

Disorder	Rate
Anxiety disorders	24.9
Mood disorders	19.3
Schizophrenia and related disorders	0.7
Antisocial personality	3.5
Substance use disorder	26.6

TABLE 15-3

Culture-Bound Syndromes   *Some cultures have syndromes or mental disorders that are found only in that culture and that do not correspond to any DSM-IV categories.* (Based on Carson & Butcher, 1992, p. 89)

Syndrome	Cultures Where Found	Symptoms
amok	Malaysia, Laos, Philippines, Papua New Guinea, Puerto Rico, Navajos	Brooding, followed by violent behavior, persecutory ideas, amnesia, exhaustion. More often seen in men than in women.
ataque de nervios	Latin America	Uncontrollable shouting, crying, trembling, heat in the chest rising to the head, verbal or physical aggression, seizures, fainting.
ghost sickness	American Indians	Nightmares, weakness, feelings of danger, loss of appetite, fainting, dizziness, hallucinations, loss of consciousness, sense of suffocation.
koro	Malaysia, China, Thailand	Sudden and intense anxiety that the penis (in males) or the vulva and nipples (in females) will recede into body and cause death.
latah	East Asia	Hypersensitivity to sudden fright, trance-like behavior. Most often seen in middle-aged women.
susto	Mexico, Central America	Appetite disturbances, sleep disturbances, sadness, loss of motivation, feelings of low self-worth following a frightening event. Sufferers believe that their soul has left their body.
taijin kyofusho	Japan	Intense fear that one's body displeases, embarrasses, or is offensive to others.

Perspectives on Mental Disorders

Attempts to understand the causes of mental disorders generally fall under one of the approaches to psychology described in Chapter 1. The biological perspective, also called the medical or disease model, suggests that bodily disturbances cause disordered thought, behavior, and emotion. Researchers using this approach look for genetic irregularities that may predispose a person to develop a particular mental disorder. They also look for abnormalities in specific parts of the brain, defects in neurotransmitter systems, or problems in the functioning of the autonomic nervous system. Proponents of this perspective generally favor the use of drugs to treat disorders.

The psychoanalytic perspective on mental disorders emphasizes unconscious conflicts, usually originating in early childhood, and the use of defense mechanisms to handle the anxiety generated by the repressed impulses and emotions. Bringing the unconscious conflicts and emotions into awareness presumably eliminates the need for the defense mechanisms and alleviates the disorder.

The behavioral perspective investigates how fears become conditioned to specific situations and the role of reinforcement in the origin and maintenance of inappropriate behaviors. This approach looks at mental disorders from the standpoint of learning theory and assumes that maladaptive behaviors are learned.

The cognitive perspective suggests that some mental disorders stem from disordered cognitive processes and can be alleviated by changing these faulty cognitions. Rather than stressing hidden motivations, emotions, and conflicts, however, it emphasizes conscious mental processes. The way we think about ourselves, the way we appraise stressful situations, and our strategies for coping with them are all interrelated.

The ideas embodied in these brief summaries will become clearer as we discuss them in relation to specific mental disorders. Each of these approaches has something important to say about mental disorders, but none has the complete answer. One way of integrating these factors is the *vulnerability-stress model,* which considers the interaction between a *predisposition,* which makes a person vulnerable for developing a particular illness, and stressful environmental conditions encountered by that person. At the biological level, vulnerability might stem from genetic factors. This is evident in disorders in which having a close relative with the disorder increases a person's risk of developing it. At the psychological level, a chronic feeling of hopelessness and inadequacy might make an individual vulnerable to depression. Having a predisposition for a particular disorder does not guarantee that the person will develop the disorder. Whether or not the predisposition leads to an actual disorder often depends on the kinds of stressors the individual encounters. These would include poverty, malnutrition, frustration, conflicts, and traumatic life events.

The key point of the vulnerability-stress model is that both vulnerability and stress are necessary. It helps explain why some people become mentally ill when confronted with a minimum of stress while others remain healthy regardless of how difficult their lives may be.

Anxiety Disorders

Most of us feel anxious and tense in the face of threatening or stressful situations. Such feelings are normal reactions to stress. Anxiety is considered abnormal only when it occurs in situations that most people can handle with little difficulty. Anxiety disorders include a group of disorders in which anxiety either is the main symptom (generalized anxiety and panic disorders) or is experienced when the individual attempts to control certain maladaptive behaviors (phobic and obsessive-compulsive disorders). (Post-traumatic stress disorder, which involves anxiety following a traumatic event, was discussed in Chapter 14.) The following passage describes a person suffering from an anxiety disorder:

> Hazel was walking down a street near her home one day when she suddenly felt flooded with intense and frightening physical symptoms. Her whole body tightened up, she began sweating and her heart was racing, she felt dizzy and disoriented. She thought, "I must be having a heart attack! I can't stand this! Something terrible is happening! I'm going to die." Hazel just stood frozen in the middle of the street until an onlooker stopped to help her.

There are four types of symptoms of anxiety, and Hazel was experiencing symptoms of each type. First, she had physiological or somatic symptoms: Her heart was racing, she was perspiring, and her muscles tensed. You may recognize these symptoms as part of the fight-or-flight response discussed in Chapter 14. This is the body's natural reaction to a challenging situation—the physiological changes of the fight-or-flight response prepare the body to fight a threat or to flee from it.

Second, Hazel had cognitive symptoms of anxiety: She was sure she was having a heart attack and dying. Third, Hazel had a behavioral symptom of anxiety: She froze, unable to move until help arrived. Fourth, she had the sense of dread and terror that make up the emotional symptoms of anxiety.

All of these symptoms can be highly adaptive when we are facing a real threat, such as a saber-toothed tiger in prehistoric times or a burglar today. They become maladaptive when there is no real threat to fight against or flee from. Hazel's symptoms were not triggered by a dangerous situation but came "out of the blue." Even when these symptoms do arise in response to some perceived threat, they can be maladaptive when they are out of proportion to the threat or persist after the threat has passed. Many people with anxiety disorders seem to view situations as highly threatening that most of us would consider benign, and they worry about those situations even when they are highly unlikely to occur. For example, people with social phobias are terrified of the possibility that they might embarrass themselves in public; they therefore go to great lengths to avoid social situations.

In one form of anxiety disorder, **generalized anxiety disorder,** the person experiences *a constant sense of tension and dread.* Inability to relax, disturbed sleep, fatigue, headaches, dizziness, and rapid heart rate are the most common physical complaints. In addition, the individual continually worries about potential problems and has difficulty concentrating or making

TABLE 15-4

Generalized Anxiety   *The statements listed in this table are self-descriptions by individuals who have chronically high levels of anxiety.* (After Sarason & Sarason, 1993)

I am often bothered by the thumping of my heart.

Little annoyances get on my nerves and irritate me.

I often become suddenly scared for no good reason.

I worry continuously, and that gets me down.

I frequently get spells of complete exhaustion and fatigue.

It is always hard for me to make up my mind.

I always seem to be dreading something.

I feel nervous and high-strung all the time.

I often feel I cannot overcome my difficulties.

I feel constantly under strain.

decisions. When the individual finally makes a decision, it becomes a source of further worry ("Did I foresee all the possible consequences?"). Some self-descriptions provided by people with chronically high levels of anxiety appear in Table 15-4. Other anxiety disorders, such as panic disorder, phobias, and obsessive-compulsive disorder, are characterized by more focused anxiety and are discussed in more detail in the rest of this section.

Panic Disorders

Hazel's symptoms suggest that she experienced a **panic attack**—*an episode of acute and overwhelming apprehension or terror*. During panic attacks, the individual feels certain that something dreadful is about to happen. This feeling is usually accompanied by such symptoms as heart palpitations, shortness of breath, perspiration, muscle tremors, faintness, and nausea. The symptoms result from excitation of the sympathetic division of the autonomic nervous system (see Chapter 2) and are the same reactions that an individual experiences when extremely frightened. During severe panic attacks, the person fears that he or she will die.

As many as 40% of young adults have occasional panic attacks, especially during times of stress (King et al., 1993). For most of these people, the panic attacks are annoying, but isolated, events and do not change how they live their lives. When panic attacks become a common occurrence and the individual begins to worry about having attacks, he or she may receive a diagnosis of *panic disorder*. Panic disorder is relatively rare: Only about 1.5 to 3.5% of the population will ever develop a panic disorder (American Psychiatric Association, 1994). Usually panic disorder appears sometime between late adolescence and the mid-30s. Without treatment, panic disorder tends to become chronic (Ehlers, 1995).

People with panic disorder may believe that they have a life-threatening illness, such as heart disease or susceptibility to stroke, even after such illnesses have been ruled out by medical examinations. They may go from one physician to another, searching for the one who can diagnose their ailments. They may also believe that they are "going crazy" or "losing control." If their symptoms go untreated, they may become depressed and demoralized.

About one third to one half of people with panic disorder also develop another disorder known as **agoraphobia** (American Psychiatric Association, 1994). People with agoraphobia *fear any place where they might be trapped or unable to receive help in an emergency*. The emergency they most often fear is having a panic attack. The term *agoraphobia* comes from the ancient Greek words meaning "fear of the marketplace." People with agoraphobia fear being in a busy, crowded place such as a mall. They may also fear being in tightly enclosed spaces from which it can be difficult to escape, such as a bus, elevator, or subway, or being alone in wide-open spaces such as a meadow or a deserted beach. All of these places are frightening for people with agoraphobia because if a panic attack or some other emergency were to occur, it would be very difficult for them to escape or get help. They may also fear that they will embarrass themselves when others see that they are having a panic attack, even though other people usually cannot tell when a person is having a panic attack.

People with agoraphobia avoid all the places they fear. They significantly curtail their activities, remaining in a few "safe" places, such as the area within a few blocks of their home. Sometimes they can venture into "unsafe" places if a trusted family member or friend accompanies them. If they attempt to enter "unsafe" places on their own, however, they may experience a great deal of general anxiety beforehand and have a full panic attack when in the unsafe place. Hazel, whom we met earlier in the chapter, provides an example:

> Hazel continued to have panic attacks every few days, sometimes on the same street that she had the first panic attack, but increasingly in places that she'd never had a panic attack before. It seemed she was especially likely to have a panic attack if there were lots of people standing around her, and she became confused about how she would get out of the crowd if she began to panic. The only place Hazel had not had any panic attacks was in her apartment. Thus, she began to spend more and more time in her apartment, and refused to go anyplace she had previously had a panic attack. After a few months, she had called in sick to work so often that she was fired. Yet, Hazel could not bring herself to leave her apartment at all. She had her groceries delivered to her so she wouldn't have to go out to get them. She would only see friends if they would come to her apartment. Hazel's savings were becoming depleted, however, because she had lost her job. Hazel began looking for a job that she could do from her apartment.

Although people can develop agoraphobia without panic attacks, the vast majority of people with agoraphobia do have panic attacks or panic-like symptoms in social situations (Barlow, 1988; McNally, 1994). Agoraphobia usually develops within a year of the onset of recurrent panic attacks. Obviously, the symptoms of agoraphobia can severely interfere with the ability to function in daily life. People with agoraphobia often turn to alcohol and other drugs to cope with their symptoms. Fortunately, we have learned a great deal about the causes of panic and agoraphobia in recent years.

Understanding Panic Disorder and Agoraphobia

Many people who develop panic disorder probably have a genetic or other biological vulnerability to the disorder. Panic disorder runs in families (Fyer et al., 1990, 1993).

This does not mean, of course, that panic disorders are entirely hereditary, since family members live in the same environment. However, the results of twin studies provide firmer evidence for an inherited predisposition for panic disorder. Recall that identical twins share the same heredity; thus, if a disorder is transmitted entirely genetically, when one identical twin suffers from the disorder the other twin should be highly likely to suffer from the disorder. In contrast, fraternal twins are no more alike genetically than ordinary siblings, so that when one twin suffers from the disorder the other twin should not be at greatly increased risk for the disorder. Twin studies have shown than an identical twin is twice as likely to suffer panic disorder if the other twin does than is true for fraternal twins (Kendler et al., 1992, 1993).

One characteristic that may be inherited in people who are prone to panic attacks is an overreactive fight-or-flight response (McNally, 1994). A full panic attack can be induced easily by having such individuals engage in activities that stimulate the initial physiological changes of the fight-or-flight response. For example, when people with panic disorder purposely hyperventilate or breathe into a paper bag or inhale a small amount of carbon dioxide, they experience an increase in subjective anxiety, and many will experience a full panic attack (Rapee et al., 1992). In contrast, people without a history of panic attacks may experience some physical discomfort while performing these activities, but rarely experience a full panic attack.

This overreactive fight-or-flight response may be the result of deficiencies in areas of the brain that regulate this response, especially the limbic system (Deakin & Graeff, 1991; Gray, 1982; Gray & Cosgrove, 1985). Some studies show that people with panic disorder have low levels of the neurotransmitter serotonin in the limbic system and other brain circuits involved in the fight-or-flight response (Bell & Nutt, 1998). Serotonin deficiencies cause chronic hyperactivation of these areas of the brain, putting the individual on the verge of a panic attack most of the time.

An overreactive fight-or-flight response may not be enough to create a full panic disorder, however. Cognitive-behavioral theories of panic and agoraphobia suggest that people who are prone to panic attacks tend to pay very close attention to their bodily sensations, misinterpret bodily sensations in a negative way, and engage in catastrophic thinking (Barlow, 1988; Clark, 1988). Thus, in the case described earlier, when Hazel felt her muscles tightening she began thinking, "I'm having a heart attack! I'm going to die!" Not surprisingly, these thoughts increased her emotional symptoms of anxiety, which in turn made her physiological symptoms worse—her heart rate increased even more and her muscles felt even tighter. Interpreting these physiological changes catastrophically led to a full panic attack. Between attacks, Hazel is hypervigilant, paying close attention to any bodily sensation. Her constant vigilance causes her autonomic nervous system to be chronically aroused, making it more likely that she will have another panic attack (Ehlers & Breuer, 1992).

How does agoraphobia develop out of panic disorder? According to the cognitive-behavioral theory, people with panic disorder remember vividly the places where they have had attacks. They greatly fear those places, and that fear generalizes to all similar places. By avoiding those places, they reduce their anxiety, and their avoidance behavior thus is highly reinforced. They may also find that they experience little anxiety in particular places, such as their own home, and this reduction of anxiety is also highly reinforcing, leading them to confine themselves to these "safe" places. Thus, through classical and operant conditioning, their behaviors are shaped into what we call agoraphobia.

What evidence is there for this theory? Several laboratory studies support the contentions that cognitive factors play a strong role in panic attacks and that agoraphobic behaviors may be conditioned through learning experiences (McNally, 1994). In one study, researchers asked two groups of patients with panic disorder to wear masks through which they would inhale slight amounts of carbon dioxide. Both groups were told that, although inhaling a slight amount of carbon dioxide was not dangerous to their health, it could induce a panic attack. One group was told that they could not control the amount of carbon dioxide that came through their masks. The other group was told that they could control how much carbon dioxide they inhaled by turn-

ing a knob. Actually, neither group had any control over the amount of carbon dioxide they inhaled, and both groups inhaled the same small amount. Eighty percent of the patients who believed that they had no control experienced a panic attack, but only 20% of those who believed that they could control the carbon dioxide had an attack. These results clearly suggest that beliefs about control over panic symptoms play a strong role in panic attacks (Sanderson, Rapee, & Barlow, 1989).

In a study focusing on agoraphobic behaviors, researchers examined whether people with panic disorder could avoid having a panic attack, even after inhaling carbon dioxide, by having a "safe person" nearby. Panic patients who were exposed to carbon dioxide with their safe person present were much less likely to experience the emotional, cognitive, and physiological symptoms of panic than panic patients who were exposed to carbon

Most people feel anxious or tense in the face of stressful situations such as taking an exam. Anxiety is considered abnormal only when it occurs in situations that most people can handle with little difficulty.

dioxide without their safe person present (see Figure 15-1; Carter et al., 1995). These results show that the symptoms of panic become associated with certain situations, and that operant behaviors such as sticking close to a "safe person" can be reinforced by the reduction of panic symptoms.

The biological and cognitive-behavioral theories of panic disorder and agoraphobia thus can be integrated into a vulnerability-stress model (Barlow, 1988) (see Figure 15-2). People who develop panic disorder may have a genetic or biochemical vulnerability to an overreactive fight-or-flight response, so that even with only a slight triggering stimulus, their bodies experience all the physiological symptoms of the response. In order for a full panic disorder to develop, however, it may be necessary for these individuals also to be prone to catastrophizing these symptoms and worrying excessively about having panic attacks. These cognitions further heighten their physiological reactivity, making it even more likely that they will experience a full fight-or-flight response. Agoraphobia develops when they begin to avoid places that they associate with their panic symptoms and confine themselves to places where they experience less anxiety. This vulnerability-stress model has led to exciting breakthroughs in the treatment of panic disorder and agoraphobia, which we will discuss in Chapter 16.

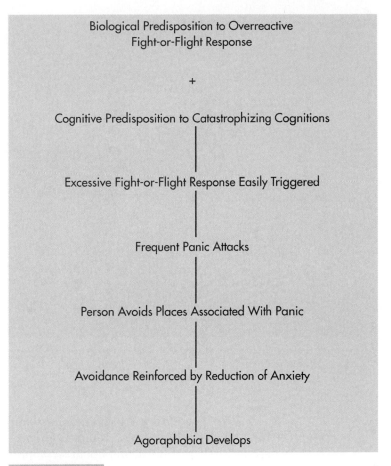

FIGURE 15-2

A Vulnerability-Stress Model of Panic and Agoraphobia   *A combination of biological vulnerability to an overreactive fight-or-flight response plus cognitive vulnerability to catastrophizing cognitions may begin a chain of processes leading to panic and agoraphobia.*

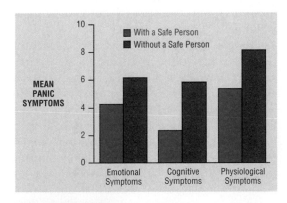

FIGURE 15-1

Panic Symptoms in Panic Patients With and Without a Safe Person Available   *Panic patients were much more likely to show symptoms of panic when a safe person was not with them. (After Carter et al., 1995)*

Phobias

A **phobia** is *intense fear of a stimulus or situation that most people do not consider particularly dangerous.* The individual usually realizes that his or her fear is irrational but still feels anxiety (ranging from strong uneasiness to panic) that can be alleviated only by avoiding the feared object or situation.

Many of us have one or two irrational fears—of snakes, insects, and heights, for example. However, a fear is usually not diagnosed as a phobic disorder unless it interferes considerably with the person's daily life. Examples might include a woman whose fear of enclosed places prevents her from entering elevators, or a man whose fear of crowds prevents him from attending the theater or walking along congested sidewalks.

Sports commentator John Madden rides to sports events in a custom-built bus because he has a phobia of flying.

DSM-IV divides phobic disorders into three broad categories: simple phobias, social phobias, and agoraphobia. A *simple phobia* is a fear of a specific object, animal, or situation. Irrational fears of snakes, germs, enclosed places, and darkness are examples. Some people may develop a simple phobia but be normal in other respects. In more serious cases, the individual has a number of phobias that interfere with many aspects of life and may be intertwined with obsessive or compulsive behavior. People with *social phobias* feel extremely insecure in social situations and have an exaggerated fear of embarrassing themselves. Often they are afraid that they will betray their anxiety by such signs as hand tremors, blushing, or a quavering voice. These fears are usually unrealistic: Individuals who fear that they might shake do not do so; those who fear that they will stutter or quaver actually speak quite normally. Fear of public speaking or of eating in public are the most common complaints of socially phobic individuals.

People with social phobias will go to great length to avoid situations in which others might evaluate them. They may take jobs that are solitary and isolating in order to avoid other people. If they find themselves in a feared social situation, they may begin trembling and perspiring, feel confused and dizzy, have heart palpitations, and eventually have a full panic attack. They are sure that others see their nervousness and are judging them as inarticulate, weak, stupid, or "crazy."

Social phobia is quite common, with about 8% of the U.S. adult population qualifying for the diagnosis in a 12-month period (Schneider et al., 1992). Social phobia typically begins in adolescence (Blazer et al., 1991) and tends to be a chronic problem if it is not treated.

Understanding Phobias

Historically, phobias have been the subject of a major clash between psychodynamic theories and behavioral theories. Freud's theory of the development of phobias was one of his most famous and controversial. Freud argued that phobias result when people displace anxiety over unconscious motives or desires onto objects that symbolize those motives or desires. His classic example was the case of Little Hans, a 5-year-old who developed an intense fear of horses. Freud interpreted the boy's phobia in terms of Oedipal fears (see Chapter 13) through the following analysis: Hans was in love with his mother, jealously hated his father, and wanted to replace him (the Oedipal conflict); he feared that his father would retaliate by castrating him; the anxiety produced by this conflict was enormous because the wishes were unacceptable to the child's conscious mind; the anxiety was displaced onto an innocent object (a large horse that Hans had seen fall down and thrash about violently in the street).

Freud's evidence for his explanation of Hans's horse phobia consisted of Hans's answers to a series of rather leading questions about what he was "really" afraid of, along with the fact that Hans appeared to lose his horse phobia after his conversations with Freud. Freud suggested that Hans had gained insight into the true source of his phobia and that this insight had cured the phobia. Critics pointed out, however, that Hans never provided any spontaneous or direct evidence that his real concern was his father rather than the horse. They also noted that Hans's phobia diminished gradually over time rather than abruptly in response to some sudden insight.

Some of the severest critics of Freud's analysis of phobias were behaviorists (Watson

& Raynor, 1920). They argued that phobias do not develop from unconscious anxieties, but rather from classical and operant conditioning. Many phobias emerge after a traumatic experience—a child nearly drowns and develops a phobia of water, another child is bitten by a dog and develops a phobia of dogs, an adolescent who stumbles through a speech in class is laughed at by peers and develops a phobia of public speaking. In these cases, a previously neutral stimulus (water or dogs or public speaking) is paired with a traumatic event (drowning or biting or embarrassment) that elicits anxiety. Through classical conditioning, the previously neutral stimulus now is able to elicit the anxiety reaction. In addition, many people with such fears avoid the phobic object because avoidance helps reduce their anxiety. Thus, the phobic behavior is maintained through operant conditioning.

While some phobias appear to result from actual frightening experiences, others may be learned vicariously through observation (Bandura, 1969; Mineka et al., 1984). Fearful parents tend to produce children who share their fears. A child who observes his or her parents react with fear to a variety of situations may develop the same reactions to those situations. Indeed, studies find that phobias clearly run in families (Fyer et al., 1993). It is unclear whether this is due largely to children learning phobias from their parents or also partially due to genetic transmission of phobias.

Behavioral theories have led to highly successful treatments for phobias, lending further support to these theories. In contrast, treatments based on psychodynamic theories of phobias tend to be unsuccessful.

Obsessive-Compulsive Disorder

A man gets out of bed several times each night and checks all the doors to make sure they are locked. Upon returning to bed he is tormented by the thought that he may have missed one. Another man takes three or four showers in succession, scrubbing his body thoroughly with a special disinfectant each time, fearful that he may be contaminated by germs. A woman has recurrent thoughts about stabbing her infant and feels panic-stricken whenever she has to handle scissors

or knives. A teenage girl is always late to school because she feels compelled to repeat many of her actions (replacing her brush on the dresser, arranging the school supplies in her book bag, crossing the threshold to her bedroom) a set number of times, usually some multiple of the number four.

All of these people have symptoms of **obsessive-compulsive disorder**: Their lives are dominated by repetitive acts or thoughts. **Obsessions** are *persistent intrusions of unwelcome thoughts, images, or impulses that elicit anxiety*. **Compulsions** are *irresistible urges to carry out certain acts or rituals that reduce anxiety*. Obsessive thoughts are often linked with compulsive acts (for example, thoughts of lurking germs, which lead to the compulsion to wash eating utensils many times before using them). Regardless of whether the repetitive element is a thought (obsession) or an act (compulsion), the central feature of the disorder is the subjective experience of loss of control. The victims struggle mightily to rid themselves of the troublesome thoughts or resist performing the repetitive acts, but are unable to do so.

At times, all of us have persistently recurring thoughts ("Did I leave the gas on?") and urges to perform ritualistic behavior (arranging items on a desk in a precise order before starting an assignment). But for people with obsessive-compulsive disorders such thoughts and acts occupy so much time that they seriously interfere with daily life. These individuals recognize their thoughts as irrational and repugnant but are unable to ignore or suppress them. They realize the senselessness of their compulsive behavior but become anxious when they try to resist their compulsions, and feel a release of tension once the acts are carried out.

Obsessive thoughts cover a variety of topics, but most often they are concerned with causing harm to oneself or others, fear of contamination, and doubt that a completed task has been accomplished satisfactorily (Rachman & Hodgson, 1980; Stern & Cobb, 1978). Interestingly, the content of obsessions changes with the times. In earlier days obsessive thoughts about religion and sex were common—for example, blasphemous thoughts or impulses to shout obscenities in church or expose one's genitals in public. These types of obsessions are less frequent today. And whereas obsessions about contamination used to focus on syphilis, AIDS has now become the object of many contamination fears (Rapaport, 1989).

Some people with an obsessive-compulsive disorder have intrusive thoughts without engaging in repetitious actions. However, the majority of patients with obsessive thoughts also exhibit compulsive behavior (Akhtar et al., 1975). Compulsions take a variety of forms, of which the two most common are washing and checking (Foa & Steketee, 1989). "Washers" are individuals who feel contaminated when exposed to certain objects or thoughts and spend hours performing washing and cleaning rituals. "Checkers" are people who check doors, lights, ovens, or the accuracy of a completed task 10, 20, or 100 times, or repeat ritualistic acts over and over again. They believe that their actions will prevent future "disasters" or punishments. Sometimes these rituals are related to the anxiety-evoking obsessions in a direct way (for example, repeatedly checking to see if the stove has been turned off in order to avoid a possible fire); other rituals are not rationally related to the obsessions (for example, dressing and undressing in order to prevent one's spouse from having an accident). The common theme behind all of these repetitive behaviors is doubt. Obsessive-compulsive individuals cannot trust their senses or their judgment; they can't trust their eyes, even though they see no dirt, or really believe that the door is locked.

Obsessive-compulsive disorders are related to phobic disorders in that both involve severe anxiety and both may appear in the same patient. However, there are important differences. Phobic patients seldom ruminate about their fears, nor do they show ritualistic compulsive behavior. And the two disorders are evoked by different stimuli. Dirt, germs, and harm to others—common obsessive-compulsive preoccupations—seldom cause major problems for phobic individuals.

Obsessive-compulsive disorder often begins at a young age (American Psychiatric Association, 1994; Rasmussen & Eisen, 1990). It tends to be chronic if left untreated. Obsessional thoughts are very distressing, and engaging in compulsive behaviors can take a great deal of time and be highly maladaptive (for example, washing one's hands so often that they bleed). People with this disorder thus are quite psychologically impaired. Between 1.0 and 2.5% of people develop obsessive-compulsive disorder at some time in their lives (Karno & Golding, 1991; Robins et al., 1984).

Understanding Obsessive-Compulsive Disorder

Considerable research evidence suggests that obsessive-compulsive disorder may have biological causes. People with this disorder may have deficiencies in the neurotransmitter serotonin in the areas of the brain that regulate primitive impulses about sex, violence, and cleanliness—impulses that are often the focus of obsessions (Baxter et al., 1992; Rapaport, 1990; Swedo et al., 1992). An elaborate circuit in the brain seems to be involved, beginning with the frontal cortex. Impulses arise here and are carried to a part of the basal ganglia called the caudate nucleus. The strongest impulses then travel to the thalamus, where they may be acted upon. As a result, primitive impulses may break through into consciousness and motivate the execution of stereotyped behaviors much more often in people with obsessive-compulsive disorder than in normal individuals.

PET scans of people with obsessive-compulsive disorder show more activity in the areas of the brain involved in this primitive circuit than do PET scans of people without the disorder (Baxter et al., 1990) (see Figure 15-3). In addition, people with the disorder often get some relief from their symptoms when they take drugs that regulate serotonin levels (Rapaport, 1991). Finally, patients who respond well to these drugs tend to show greater reductions in the rate of activity in these brain areas than patients who do not respond well to these drugs (Baxter et al., 1992; Swedo et al., 1992).

As with panic disorder, however, people may go on to develop a full obsessive-compulsive disorder only if they also have certain cognitive and behavioral vulnerabilities in addition to a biological vulnerability. Cognitive and behavioral theorists suggest that people with obsessive-compulsive disorder have more trouble "turning off" intrusive thoughts because they have a tendency toward rigid, moralistic thinking (Rachman, 1993; Salkovskis, 1989). They are more likely to judge their negative, intrusive thoughts as unacceptable, and they become more anxious and guilty about these thoughts. This anxiety then makes it even harder to dismiss the thought (Clark & de Silva, 1985). People with obsessive-compulsive disorder may also believe that they *should* be able to control all thoughts, and have trouble accepting the fact that everyone has negative thoughts occasionally (Clark & Purdon, 1993; Freeston et al., 1992). They tend to believe that having these thoughts means they are going crazy, or they equate having the thought with actually engaging in the behavior ("If I'm thinking about hurting my child, I'm as guilty as if I actually did hurt my child"). Of course, this just makes them even more anxious when they have thoughts, making it harder to dismiss them.

Compulsions may develop when the obsessional person discovers that some behavior temporarily quells the obsession and the anxiety it arouses. This reduction in anxiety reinforces the behavior, and thus a compulsion is born: Every time the person has the obsession, he or she will feel compelled to engage in the behavior in order to reduce anxiety.

Again, some of the best evidence in favor of cognitive and behavioral perspectives on obsessive-compulsive disorder can be seen in the fact that therapies based on these perspectives are helpful to people with the disorder, as we will discuss in Chapter 16. In contrast, psychodynamic theories of obsessive-compulsive disorder have not led to successful treatments. According to those theories, obsessions are unacceptable impulses (hostility, destructiveness, inappropriate sexual urges) that have been repressed and reappear in a disguised form. The individual feels that they are not a part of himself or herself, and may engage in compulsive acts in order to undo or atone for them. A mother who is obsessed with thoughts of murdering her child may feel compelled to check many times during the night to assure herself that the child is well. Compulsive rituals also serve to keep threatening impulses out of the individual's conscious awareness: A person who is continually busy has little opportunity to think

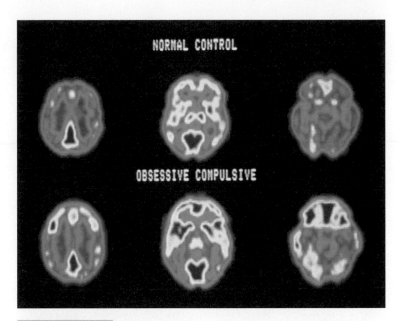

FIGURE 15-3

A Normal Brain Versus an Obsessive-Compulsive Brain   *This PET scan shows the metabolic differences between areas of the brain of a person with obsessive-compulsive disorder and the same areas in the brain of a normal person.*

improper thoughts or commit improper actions. According to psychodynamic theory, bringing the unconscious conflict to light and gaining insight into it should cure an obsessive-compulsive disorder. What little research has been done to test this theory, however, suggests that insight-oriented therapy does not cure obsessive-compulsive disorder in most cases.

In sum, biological and psychological factors probably combine in creating many of the anxiety disorders. Many people who develop these disorders probably have a genetic, neurological, or biochemical vulnerability to anxiety. But it may be necessary for them also to have a tendency toward catastrophizing and engaging in maladaptive avoidant behaviors to reduce anxiety for a full anxiety disorder to develop.

Mood Disorders

Individuals with *mood disorders* may be severely depressed or manic (wildly elated), or may experience periods of depression as well as periods of mania. Mood disorders are divided into **depressive disorders,** in which

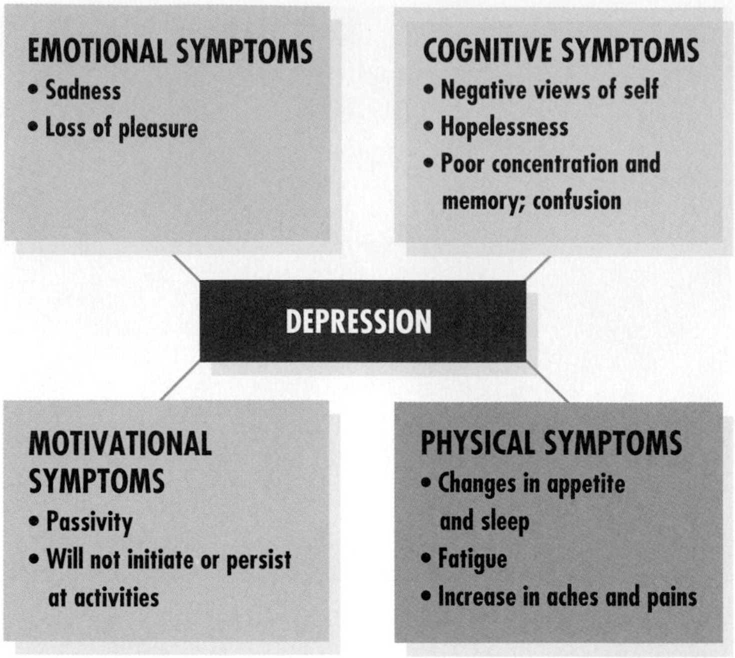

EMOTIONAL SYMPTOMS
- Sadness
- Loss of pleasure

COGNITIVE SYMPTOMS
- Negative views of self
- Hopelessness
- Poor concentration and memory; confusion

DEPRESSION

MOTIVATIONAL SYMPTOMS
- Passivity
- Will not initiate or persist at activities

PHYSICAL SYMPTOMS
- Changes in appetite and sleep
- Fatigue
- Increase in aches and pains

FIGURE 15-4

The Symptoms of Depression   *Depression includes emotional, cognitive, motivational, and physical symptoms.*

the individual has *one or more periods of depression without a history of manic episodes,* and **bipolar disorders,** in which the individual *alternates between periods of depression and periods of mania,* usually with a return to normal mood between the two extremes. Manic episodes without some history of depression are very uncommon.

Depression

Most of us have periods when we feel sad, lethargic, and uninterested in any activities— even pleasurable ones. Mild depressive symptoms are a normal response to many of life's stresses. Among the situations that most often precipitate depressive symptoms are failure at school or at work, the loss of a loved one, and the realization that illness or aging is depleting one's resources. Depression becomes a disorder when the symptoms become so severe that they interfere with normal functioning, and when they continue for weeks at a time. Depressive disorders are relatively common, with about 17% of people having an episode of severe depression at some time in their lives (Kessler et al., 1994).

Although depression is characterized as a mood disorder, there are actually four sets of symptoms (see Figure 15-4). In addition to emotional (mood) symptoms, there are cognitive, motivational, and physical symptoms. A person need not have all of these to be diagnosed as depressed, but the more symptoms he or she has and the more intense they are, the more certain we can be that the individual is suffering from depression.

Sadness and dejection are the most salient emotional symptoms of depression. The individual feels hopeless and unhappy, often has crying spells, and may contemplate suicide. (Depression and suicide are discussed in the Frontiers of Psychological Research on pages 542–543.) Equally pervasive is loss of gratification or pleasure in life. Activities that used to bring satisfaction seem dull and joyless. The depressed person gradually loses interest in hobbies, recreation, and family activities. Most depressed patients report that they no longer derive gratification from former interests, and many report losing interest in and affection for other people.

The cognitive symptoms consist primarily of negative thoughts. Depressed individuals tend to have low self-esteem, feel inadequate, and blame themselves for their failures. They feel hopeless about the future and doubt that they can do anything to improve their life. Motivation is at a low ebb: The depressed person tends to be passive and has difficulty initiating activities. The following conversation between a patient and his therapist illustrates this passivity. The man, who had been hospitalized after a suicide attempt, spent his days sitting motionless in the lounge. His therapist decided to try to engage him in some activities:

THERAPIST: I understand that you spend most of your day in the lounge. Is that true?

PATIENT: Yes, being quiet gives me the peace of mind I need.

THERAPIST: When you sit here, how's your mood?

PATIENT: I feel awful all the time. I just wish I could fall in a hole somewhere and die.

THERAPIST: Do you feel better after sitting for 2 or 3 hours?

PATIENT: No, the same.

THERAPIST: So you're sitting in the hope that you'll find peace of mind, but it doesn't sound like your depression improves.

PATIENT: I get so bored.

THERAPIST: Would you consider being more active? There are a number of reasons why I think increasing your activity level might help.

PATIENT: There's nothing to do around here.

THERAPIST: Would you consider trying some activities if I could come up with a list?

PATIENT: If you think it will help, but I think you're wasting your time. I don't have any interests. (Beck et al., 1979, p. 200)

The physical symptoms of depression include changes in appetite, sleep disturbances, fatigue, and loss of energy. Since a depressed person's thoughts are focused inward rather than toward external events, he or she may magnify minor aches and pains and worry about health.

As we see from this description of its symptoms, depression can be a debilitating disorder. Unfortunately, severe depressions can also be long-lasting. One study of people with severe depressions found that over a nine-year period they were symptom-free only 27% of the time (Judd et al., 1998). Even if they recover from one bout of depression, people remain at high risk for relapses into new episodes. There is some good news, however. Episodes of depression can be greatly shortened, and new episodes prevented, with either drug therapy or psychotherapy, as we will see shortly.

Bipolar Disorder

The majority of depressions occur without episodes of mania. But about 1 or 2 people in 100 will experience both depression and mania, and hence can be diagnosed with bipolar disorder, also known as *manic-depression*. The individual alternates between depression and extreme elation. In some cases the cycle between depressive episodes and manic episodes is swift, with only a brief return to normality in between.

People experiencing manic episodes behave in a way that appears on the surface to be the opposite of depression. During mild manic episodes the individual is energetic, enthusiastic, and full of self-confidence. He

or she talks continually, rushes from one activity to another with little need for sleep, and makes grandiose plans, paying little attention to their practicality. Unlike the kind of joyful exuberance that characterizes normal elation, manic behavior has a driven quality and often expresses hostility more than it does elation.

People experiencing severe manic episodes behave somewhat like the popular concept of a "raving maniac." They are extremely excited and constantly active. They may pace about, sing, shout, or pound the walls for hours. They are angered by attempts to interfere with their activities and may become abusive. Impulses (including sexual ones) are immediately expressed in actions or words. These individuals are confused and disoriented and may experience delusions of great wealth, accomplishment, or power.

> Tony was a middle-aged man, quite ragged in appearance, who was brought to the hospital by his family because he was "out of control" and "going crazy." He had been a sensible, rather subdued man until about a month ago, when his behavior changed dramatically. A bus driver in Philadelphia, Tony had taken to stopping his bus in busy traffic, turning to the passengers, and breaking into song. When

Depression sometimes leads to suicide. Women are more likely to attempt suicide than men, but men more often succeed in killing themselves.

FRONTIERS OF PSYCHOLOGICAL RESEARCH

Depression and Suicide

The most disastrous consequence of depression is suicide. Of the reported 30,000 people who end their lives by suicide in the United States every year, the majority are suffering from depression. However, since suicide deaths are underreported (due to the stigma attached and the fact that many accidental deaths are probably suicides), the number of actual suicides per year may well be closer to 50,000. The number of people who attempt suicide but fail has been estimated at anywhere from two to eight times the number of suicides (Shneidman, 1985).

Women attempt to commit suicide about three times more often than men do, but men succeed more often than women in killing themselves. The greater number of suicide attempts by women is probably related to the greater incidence of depression among women. The fact that men are more successful in their attempts is related to the choice of method. Until recently, women have tended to use less lethal means, such as cutting their wrists or overdosing on sleeping pills; men are more likely to use firearms or carbon monoxide fumes or to hang themselves. However, with the marked increase in the number of women owning guns, suicide by firearms

has now become the woman's method of first choice (Wintemute, Teret, Kraus, & Wright, 1988). Consequently, the fatality rate for women is changing. (Attempted suicides are successful 80% of the time when firearms are involved, while only 10% of drug or poison ingestions are fatal—a powerful argument for not keeping firearms in the home.)

Among the reasons most frequently cited by those who have attempted suicide are depression, loneliness, ill health, marital problems, and financial or job difficulties (Petronis et al., 1990; Shneidman, 1985).

While elderly people have traditionally had the highest rate of suicide, and still do, their rate has been decreasing. In contrast, the suicide rate among adolescents and young adults (traditionally low) has been increasing. In fact, the incidence of suicide among 15- to 24-year-olds in the United States has quadrupled over the past four decades. In a national survey of high-school seniors, 27% reported that they had "thought seriously" about killing themselves, and 1 in 12 said they had actually tried (Centers for Disease Control, 1991).

College students are twice as likely to kill themselves as are non-

students of the same age (Murphy & Wetzel, 1980). The increased suicide rate among college students is found not only in the United States but in European countries, India, and Japan, as well. There are a number of possible reasons for the greater despair among college students: living away from home for the first time and having to cope with new problems; trying to stay at the top academically when the competition is much fiercer than it had been in high school; indecision about a career choice; and loneliness caused by the absence of long-time friends and anxiety about new ones.

A study of the lives and academic records of college students who committed suicide found that they were moodier, drove themselves harder, and were depressed more frequently than their nonsuicidal classmates. They had also given recurrent warnings of their suicidal intent to others. The major precipitating events appear to have been worry about academic work and physical health and difficulties in their relationships with others (Seiden, 1966). However, we cannot be sure whether these factors caused the suicides or whether academic difficulties and interpersonal problems were secondary to a severe depression.

---

asked about these incidents, Tony said he had decided that he wanted to be a nightclub singer and he was glad he had been fired from his bus-driving job because it gave him more time to devote to his singing career. By all accounts, he had a terrible singing voice. Two weeks earlier he had traveled to Las Vegas, where he tried to meet with managers of several casinos to convince them to give him a headline show. He was arrested for making threatening remarks when they threw him out of their offices. He then decided that he

should open his own casino in Philadelphia (although gambling was illegal there) so that he could sing every night. He cashed out the family savings accounts and put the house up for sale to finance his plan.

Manic episodes can occur without depression, but this is very rare. Usually a depressive episode will occur eventually once a person has experienced a manic episode. The depression is similar to what we have already described.

It may be that college students who contemplate suicide never learned how to deal with personal problems and emotions before going to college. One study, for example, found that students with suicidal thoughts were not faced with more stressful situations than other students but had fewer resources for dealing with problems and intense emotions (Carson & Johnson, 1985).

Suicidal college students, on the average, have higher records of academic achievement than their non-suicidal classmates, whereas most adolescents who commit suicide have exceptionally poor high-school records. Suicidal teenagers tend to be dropouts or to have behavior problems in school, although a few are academically gifted students who feel pressure to be perfect and to stay at the top of the class (Leroux, 1986).

The outstanding characteristic of adolescents who attempt suicide is social isolation: They describe themselves as loners, most have parents who were divorced or separated, a large number have alcoholic parents, and they report little parental affection (Berman & Jobes, 1991; Rohn et al., 1977).

A major factor contributing to suicide, in addition to depression, is drug abuse. For example, one study of 283 suicides found that nearly 60% were drug abusers and 84% abused both alcohol and other drugs (Rich et al., 1988). It is not clear whether the drug abuse caused these people to become depressed and kill themselves or whether they turned to drugs as a way of coping with depression and killed themselves when the drugs did not help. But in many of the cases drug abuse appears to have preceded the psychological problems.

Young drug abusers (under age 30) who committed suicide had a greater than expected frequency of intense interpersonal conflict or the loss of a spouse or romantic partner in the weeks prior to killing themselves. They may have felt that they had lost their only source of support. And they might have been able to handle the stress without resorting to suicide had their personal resources not been depleted by drug use.

Some individuals commit suicide because they find their emotional distress intolerable and see no solution to their problems other than death. Their sole motivation is to end their life. In other cases, the person does not really with to die but seeks to impress others with the seriousness of his or her dilemma. The suicide attempt is motivated by a desire to communicate feelings of despair and to change the behavior of other people. Examples would be a woman who takes an overdose of sleeping pills when her lover threatens to leave or a student who does the same when pressured by his parents to achieve beyond his abilities. The suicide attempt is a cry for help.

Some experts use the term *parasuicide* for nonfatal acts in which a person deliberately causes self-injury or ingests a substance in excess of any prescribed or generally recognized therapeutic dosage (Kreitman, 1977). The term *parasuicide* is preferred to *suicide attempt* because it does not necessarily imply a wish to die. As noted earlier, there are many more parasuicides than suicides. However, most people who commit suicidal acts are experiencing such turmoil and stress that their thinking is far from clear. They are not sure whether they want to live or die; they want to do both at the same time, usually one more than the other. Since the best predictor of a future suicide is a prior attempt, all parasuicides should be taken seriously. A person who talks about suicide may actually attempt it. Many communities have established suicide-prevention centers where troubled individuals can seek help, either through telephone contact or in person.

Bipolar disorders are relatively uncommon. Whereas about 21% of adult females and 13% of adult males in the United States have experienced a major depression, less than 2% of the adult population has had a bipolar disorder. Manic-depression, which appears to be equally common in men and women (Kessler et al., 1994), differs from other mood disorders in that it tends to occur at an earlier age, is more likely to run in families, responds to different medications, and almost always recurs if not treated.

Understanding Mood Disorders

As with the anxiety disorders, a combined biological and psychological model may best explain the mood disorders. Most people who develop depression, and particularly bipolar disorder, may have a biological vulnerability to these disorders. But the experience of certain types of life events, along with a tendency to think in negative ways, also clearly increase the likelihood of developing these disorders.

The Biological Perspective A tendency to develop mood disorders, particularly bipolar disorders, appears to be inherited. Family history studies of people with bipolar disorder find that their first-degree relatives (parents, children, and siblings) have at least two to three times higher rates of both bipolar disorder and depressive disorders than relatives of people without bipolar disorder (Gershon; 1990; Keller & Baker, 1991; MacKinnon, Jamison, & De Paulo, 1997). Twin studies of bipolar disorder have also consistently suggested that the disorder has a genetic component (Faraone, Kremen, & Tsuang, 1990; MacKinnon et al., 1997).

The evidence regarding the heritability of depressive disorders is less consistent. Family history studies find higher rates of depression in the first-degree relatives of people with the disorder than in control groups (Gershon, 1990; Keller & Baker, 1991). Interestingly, relatives of depressed people do *not* have any greater risk of developing bipolar disorder than relatives of people with no mood disorder. This suggests that bipolar disorder has a different genetic basis from that of depression. Twin studies have provided mixed evidence concerning the heritability of depression. Some studies find evidence of heritability (Kendler et al., 1992), but others do not (McGuffin, Katz, & Rutherford, 1991; Torgersen, 1986).

The specific role that genetic factors play in mood disorders is unclear. However, it seems likely that a biochemical abnormality is involved. The neurotransmitters norepinephrine and serotonin are believed to play an important role in mood disorders. Recall from Chapter 2 that neurotransmitters and their receptors interact like locks and keys (see Figure 15-5). Each neurotransmitter will fit into a particular type of receptor on the neuronal membrane. If there are the wrong number of receptors for a given type of neurotransmitter, or the receptors for that neurotransmitter are too sensitive or not sensitive enough, the neurons do not efficiently use the available amounts of neurotransmitter. Several studies suggest that people with depression or bipolar disorder may have abnormalities in the number and sensitivity of receptor sites for serotonin and norepinephrine, particularly in areas of the brain that are involved in the regulation of emotion, such as the hypothalamus (Malone & Mann, 1993; McBride et al., 1994). In major depressive disorder, receptors for these neurotransmitters appear to be insensitive or too few in number. The picture is less clear for bipolar disorder, but it is likely that receptors for these neurotransmitters undergo poorly timed changes in sensitivity that are correlated with mood changes (Goodwin & Jamison, 1990).

The Cognitive Perspective Cognitive theories focus primarily on depression. According to these theories, people become depressed because they tend to interpret events in their lives in pessimistic, hopeless ways (Abramson, Metalsky, & Alloy, 1989; Beck et al., 1979; Peterson & Seligman, 1984). One of the most influential cognitive theorists, Aaron Beck, grouped the negative thoughts of depressed individuals into three categories, which he called the *cognitive triad;* these categories consist of negative thoughts about the self, about present experiences, and about the future. Negative thoughts about the self include the depressed person's belief that he or she is worthless and inadequate. The depressed person's negative view of the future is one of hopelessness. Depressed people believe that their inadequacies and defects will prevent them from ever improving their situation.

Beck proposes that the depressed person's negative beliefs about self ("I am worthless," "I can't do anything right") are

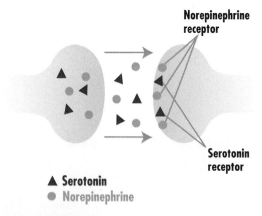

Norepinephrine receptor

Serotonin receptor

▲ **Serotonin**

● Norepinephrine

FIGURE 15-5

Neurotransmission in Depression *The neuronal receptors for norepinephrine and serotonin may not work efficiently in depressed people, so that norepinephrine and serotonin released from one neuron cannot bind to receptor sites on other neurons.*

formed during childhood or adolescence through such experiences as loss of a parent, social rejection by peers, criticism by parents or teachers, or a series of tragedies. These negative beliefs are activated whenever a new situation resembles in some way—perhaps only remotely—the conditions in which the beliefs were learned, and depression may result. Moreover, according to Beck, depressed individuals make some systematic errors in thinking that lead them to misperceive reality in a way that contributes to their negative beliefs about themselves. These cognitive distortions are listed in Table 15-5.

Another cognitive approach to depression, which focuses on the kinds of attributions, or causal explanations, that people make when bad things happen, was discussed in Chapter 14. This theory proposes that people who tend to attribute negative events to causes that are internal ("it's my fault"), are stable over time ("it's going to last forever"), and affect many areas of their lives are more prone to depression than individuals who have a less pessimistic attributional style (Abramson, Metalsky, & Alloy, 1989; Peterson & Seligman, 1984).

Critics of cognitive theories of depression have argued that these negative cognitions are symptoms or consequences of depression rather than causes. While it is clear that depressed people have negative cognitions, there is less evidence that negative cognitive styles precede and cause depressive episodes (Haaga, Dyck, & Ernst, 1991). Also, there is some evidence that depressed people may actually perceive reality more accurately than normal people: When asked to make judgments about how much control they have over situations that are actually uncontrollable, depressed people are quite accurate. In contrast, nondepressed people greatly overestimate the amount of control they have, especially over positive events (Alloy & Abramson, 1979).

A recent study that followed students through their college careers provides strong evidence that negative cognitive styles do precede and predict depression. Researchers measured the students' tendencies toward negative thinking patterns early in their first year of college, and followed them for the next few years. Students who evidenced a negative cognitive triad or a pessimistic attributional style were much more likely to experience episodes of depression during their college years than those who did not, even if they had never been depressed before going to college (Alloy & Abramson, 1997).

TABLE 15-5

Cognitive Distortions in Depression   *According to Beck's theory, these are the principal errors in thinking that characterize depressed individuals.*

Overgeneralization	Drawing a sweeping conclusion on the basis of a single event. For example, a student concludes from his poor performance in one class on a particular day that he is inept and stupid.
Selective Abstraction	Focusing on an insignificant detail while ignoring the more important features of a situation. For example, from a conversation in which her boss praises her overall job performance, a secretary remembers the only comment that could be construed as mildly critical.
Magnification and Minimization	Magnifying small bad events and minimizing major good events in evaluating performance. For example, a woman gets a small dent in her car fender and views it as a catastrophe (magnification), while the fact that she gave an excellent presentation in class does nothing to raise her self-esteem (minimization).
Personalization	Incorrectly assuming responsibility for bad events in the world. For example, when rain dampens spirits at an outdoor buffet, the host blames himself rather than the weather.
Arbitrary Inference	Drawing a conclusion when there is little evidence to support it. For example, a man concludes from his wife's sad expression that she is disappointed in him; if he had checked out the situation, he would have discovered that she was distressed by a friend's illness.

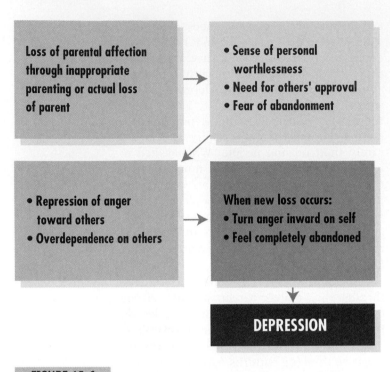

FIGURE 15-6

Psychodynamic Theories of Depression   *Psychodynamic theories suggest that depressed people did not receive enough parental affection in childhood and that subsequent losses in adulthood trigger feelings of dejection and worthlessness.*

The Psychoanalytic Perspective   Psychoanalytic theories interpret depression as a reaction to loss (Figure 15-6). Whatever the nature of the loss (rejection by a loved one, being fired from a job), the depressed person reacts to it intensely because the current situation brings back all the fears of an earlier loss that occurred in childhood—the loss of parental affection. The individual's needs for affection and care were not satisfied in childhood. A loss in later life causes him or her to regress to the helpless, dependent state of childhood, when the original loss occurred. Part of the depressed person's behavior, therefore, represents a cry for love—a display of helplessness and an appeal for affection and security (Bibring, 1953; Blatt, 1974).

Reaction to loss is complicated by angry feelings toward the deserting person. An underlying assumption of psychoanalytic theories is that people who are prone to depression have learned to repress their hostile feelings because they are afraid of alienating those on whom they depend for support. When things go wrong, they turn

their anger inward and blame themselves. For example, a woman may feel extremely hostile toward an employer who fired her. But because her anger arouses anxiety, she internalizes her feelings: She is not angry; rather, others are angry at her. She assumes that the employer had a reason for rejecting her: She is incompetent and worthless.

Psychoanalytic theories suggest that the depressed person's low self-esteem and feelings of worthlessness stem from a childlike need for parental approval. A small child's self-esteem depends on the approval and affection of the parents. But as a person matures, feelings of worth should also be derived from the individual's sense of his or her own accomplishments and effectiveness. The self-esteem of a person prone to depression depends primarily on external sources: the approval and support of others. When these supports fail, the individual may be thrown into a state of depression.

Psychoanalytic theories of depression thus focus on loss, overdependence on external approval, and internalization of anger. They seem to provide a reasonable explanation for some of the behaviors exhibited by depressed individuals, but they are difficult to prove or to refute.

Dissociative Identity Disorder

Dissociative identity disorder, also called multiple personality disorder, is *the existence in a single individual of two or more distinct identities or personalities that alternate in controlling behavior.* Usually, each personality has its own name and age and a specific set of memories and characteristic behaviors. In most cases there is a primary identity that carries the individual's given name and is passive, dependent, and depressed. The alternate identities typically have characteristics that contrast with the primary identity, for example, hostile, controlling, and self-destructive (American Psychiatric Association, 1994). In some cases the personalities may even differ in such characteristics as handwriting, artistic or athletic abilities, and knowledge of a foreign language. The primary identity often has no awareness of the experiences of the other identities. Periods of unexplained **amnesia**—

loss of memory for hours or days each week—can be a clue to the presence of dissociative identity disorder.

One of the most famous cases of multiple personality is that of Chris Sizemore, whose alternative personalities—Eve White, Eve Black, and Jane—were portrayed in the movie *The Three Faces of Eve* (Thigpen & Cleckley, 1957) and later described extensively in her autobiography *I'm Eve* (Sizemore & Pittillo, 1977). Another well-studied case is that of Jonah, a 17-year-old man who was admitted to a hospital complaining of severe headaches that were often followed by memory loss. Hospital attendants noticed striking changes in his personality on different days, and the psychiatrist in charge detected three distinct secondary identities. The relatively stable personality structures that emerged are diagrammed in Figure 15-7 and can be characterized as follows:

- Jonah. The primary personality. Shy, retiring, polite, and highly conventional, he is designated "the square." Sometimes frightened and confused during interviews, Jonah is unaware of the other personalities.

- Sammy. He has the most intact memories. Sammy can coexist with Jonah or set Jonah aside and take over. He claims to be ready when Jonah needs legal advice or is in trouble; he is designated "the mediator." Sammy remembers emerging at age 6, when Jonah's mother stabbed his stepfather and Sammy persuaded the parents never to fight again in front of the children.

- King Young. He emerged when Jonah was 6 or 7 years old to straighten out Jonah's sexual identity after his mother occasionally dressed him in girl's clothing at home and Jonah became confused about boys' and girls' names at school. King Young has looked after Jonah's sexual interests ever since; hence, he is designated "the lover." He is only dimly aware of the other personalities.

- Usoffa Abdulla. A cold, belligerent, and angry person. Usoffa is capable of ignoring pain. It is his sworn duty to watch over and protect Jonah; thus, he is designated "the warrior." He emerged at age 9 or 10, when a gang of boys beat up Jonah without provocation. Jonah was helpless,

but Usoffa emerged and fought viciously against the attackers. He too is only dimly aware of the other personalities.

The four personalities tested very differently on all measures having to do with emotionally laden topics but scored essentially alike on tests relatively free of emotion or personal conflict, such as intelligence or vocabulary tests.

Dissociative identity disorder reflects a failure to integrate various aspects of identity, memory, and consciousness. The dissociation is so complete that several different personalities seem to be living in the same body. Observers note that the switch from one personality to another is often accompanied by subtle changes in posture and tone of voice. The new personality talks, walks, and gestures differently. There may even be changes in physiological processes such as blood pressure and brain activity (Putnam, 1991).

Individuals with dissociative identity disorder frequently report having experienced physical and sexual abuse during childhood.

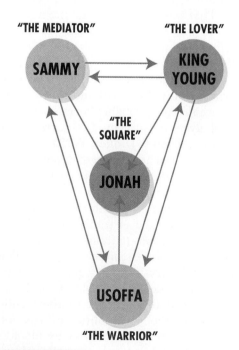

FIGURE 15-7

Jonah's Four Component Identities   *The three personalities on the periphery have superficial knowledge of each other but are intimately familiar with Jonah, who in turn is totally unaware of them.* (After Ludwig et al., 1972)

The accuracy of such reports is controversial, because childhood memories may be subject to distortion and individuals with this disorder tend to be very vulnerable to suggestion. Nevertheless, defense against traumatic childhood experiences forms the basis of a hypothesis about how such disorders develop. The initial dissociation is assumed to occur in response to a traumatic event in childhood (usually between the ages of 4 and 6). The child copes with a painful problem by creating another personality to bear the brunt of the difficulty (Frischholz, 1985). In Jonah's case, Sammy (the mediator) emerged when Jonah had to deal with his mother's attack on his stepfather.

The child presumably learns to defend himself from the pain of abuse by dissociating the memory from consciousness. If the child is severely and repeatedly abused, this method of defense leads over time to dissociative identities in which only one or two subpersonalities are conscious of the abuse while the others have no memory of the pain. It is adaptive for the child to keep the personalities separate in order to keep awareness of the abuse from his or her other selves. That way the feeling and memories of abuse do not continually flood the child's consciousness when he or she cannot handle it—for instance, while at school or playing with friends (Braun, 1986). A large majority of individuals with multiple personalities are female, probably because they are more likely to be subjected to sexual abuse as children (Boon & Draijer, 1993).

Another factor in the development of dissociative identity disorder appears to be an enhanced susceptibility to self-hypnosis, a process by which one is able to put oneself at will into the kind of trance state characteristic of hypnosis. Patients with dissociative identity disorder often make excellent hypnotic subjects, and they report that the trance experience is identical to experiences they have had dating back to their childhood. One of the personalities of a patient said, "She creates personalities by blocking everything from her head, mentally relaxes, concentrates very hard, and wishes" (Bliss, 1980, p. 1392).

Once individuals discover that creating another identity relieves them of emotional pain, they are likely to create other personalities when confronted by emotional problems. Thus, when Jonah was beaten by a gang of boys at age 10, he created another personality, Usoffa Abdulla, to handle the problem. Some dissociative identity patients become so accustomed to defending against problems by means of alternate personalities that they continue the process throughout adulthood, creating new personalities in response to new problems; thus, they may end up with a dozen or more different personalities (Putnam, 1991).

Cases of dissociative identity disorder have always been fascinating but rare. However, recent years have seen a sharp rise in the number of cases reported in the United States. Some believe that this increase reflects increased awareness of the disorder among mental health professionals and, hence, identification of cases that previously were undiagnosed. Others believe that the disorder has been overdiagnosed in individuals who are highly suggestible (American Psychiatric Association, 1994).

Schizophrenia

Schizophrenia is the label applied to *a group of disorders characterized by severe personality disorganization, distortion of reality, and inability to function in daily life.* Schizophrenia occurs in all cultures, even those that are remote from the stresses of industrialized civilization, and appears to have plagued humanity for at least 200 years. The disorder affects about 1% of the population, occurs equally in men and women, and usually appears in late adolescence or early adulthood (in most cases onset is between the ages of 15 and 35).

People who are labeled schizophrenic usually require hospitalization, sometimes for months or years. At any given time this diagnostic group occupies about half of the beds in mental hospitals and constitutes a large proportion of outpatients (Narrow et al., 1993). Sometimes schizophrenia develops slowly as a gradual process of increasing seclusiveness and inappropriate behavior. Sometimes the onset is sudden, marked by intense confusion and emotional turmoil; such acute cases are usually precipitated by a period of stress in individuals whose lives have tended toward isolation, preoccupation with self, and feelings of insecurity.

Characteristics of Schizophrenia

Whether schizophrenia develops slowly or suddenly, the symptoms are many and varied. The primary characteristics of schizophrenia can be summarized under the following headings, although not every person diagnosed as suffering from the disorder will exhibit all of these symptoms.

Disturbances of Thought and Attention In schizophrenia, both the process of thinking and the content of thought may be disordered. The following excerpt from a patient's writings illustrates how difficult it is to understand schizophrenic thinking.

> If things turn by rotation of agriculture or levels in regards and timed to everything; I am referring to a previous document when I made some remarks that were facts also tested and there is another that concerns my daughter she has a lobed bottom right ear, her name being Mary Lou. Much of abstraction has been left unsaid and undone in these products milk syrup, and others, due to economics, differentials, subsidies, bankruptcy, tools, buildings, bonds, national stocks, foundation craps, weather, trades, government in levels of breakages and fuses in electronics too all formerly states not necessarily factuated. (Maher, 1966, p. 395)

By themselves, the words and phrases make sense, but they are meaningless in relation to each other. The juxtaposition of unrelated words and phrases and the idiosyncratic word associations (sometimes called "word salad") are characteristic of schizophrenic writing and speech. They reflect a loosening of associations in which the individual's ideas shift from one topic to another in ways that appear unrelated. Moreover, the train of thought often seems to be influenced by the sound of words rather than by their meaning. The following account by a schizophrenic patient of her thoughts in response to her doctor's questions illustrates this tendency to form associations by rhyming words, referred to as *clang associations:*

> DOCTOR: How about the medication? Are you still taking the Haldol? (an antipsychotic drug)
> Patient Thinks: Foul Wall. (She nods but does not reply.)
> DOCTOR: What about the vitamins?
> Patient Thinks: Seven sins. Has-beens. (She nods.)
> DOCTOR: I don't think you're taking all your meds.
> Patient Thinks: Pencil leads. (North, 1987, p. 261)

The confused thought processes that are the hallmark of schizophrenia seem to stem from a general difficulty in focusing attention and filtering out irrelevant stimuli. Most of us are able to focus our attention selectively. From a mass of incoming sensory information, we are able to select the stimuli that are relevant to the task at hand and ignore the rest. A person who suffers from schizophrenia is receptive to many stimuli at the same time and has trouble making sense of the profusion of inputs, as the following statement by a schizophrenic patient illustrates:

> I can't concentrate. It's diversions of attention that trouble me. I am picking up different conversations. It's like being a transmitter. The sounds are coming through to me, but I feel my mind cannot cope with everything. It's difficult to concentrate on any one sound. (McGhie & Chapman, 1961, p. 104)

A sense of being unable to control one's attention and focus one's thoughts is central to the experience of schizophrenia.

In addition to disorganized thought processes, schizophrenic patients experience disturbances in the *content* of thought. Most individuals suffering from schizophrenia show a lack of insight. When asked what is wrong or why they are hospitalized, they seem to have no appreciation of their condition and little realization that their behavior is unusual. They are also subject to **delusions,** *beliefs that most people would view as misinterpretations of reality.* The most common delusions are beliefs that external forces are trying to control one's thoughts and actions. These *delusions of influence* include the belief that one's thoughts are being broadcast to the world so that others can hear them, that strange thoughts (not one's own) are being inserted into one's mind, or that feelings and actions are being imposed on one by some external force. Also frequent are beliefs that certain people or certain groups are threatening or plotting against one *(delusions of persecution)*. Less common are beliefs that one is powerful and important *(delusions of grandeur)*.

The term **paranoid** is used to refer to *an individual who has delusions of persecution*. Such a person may become suspicious of friends and relatives, fear being poisoned, or complain of being watched, followed, and talked about. So-called motiveless crimes, in which an individual attacks or kills someone for no apparent cause, are sometimes committed by people who are later diagnosed as suffering from paranoid schizophrenia. These incidents are quite rare, however. Most people with schizophrenia are not a danger to others, although their confusion may make them a danger to themselves.

Disturbances of Perception People experiencing acute schizophrenic episodes often report that the world appears different (noises seem louder, colors more intense). Their own bodies may no longer appear the same (their hands may seem too large or too small, their legs overly extended, their eyes dislocated in the face). Some patients fail to recognize themselves in a mirror, or see their reflection as a triple image. The most dramatic disturbances of perception are **hallucinations,** *sensory experiences in the absence of relevant or adequate external stimulation.* Auditory hallucinations (usually voices telling one what to do or commenting on one's actions) are the most common. Visual hallucinations (such as seeing strange creatures or heavenly beings) are somewhat less frequent. Other sensory hallucinations (a bad odor emanating from one's body, the taste of poison in food, the feeling of being pricked by needles) occur infrequently.

Hallucinations are often frightening, even terrifying, as the following example illustrates:

The German psychiatrist Hans Privizhorn has assembled an extensive collection of artwork by mental patients. This painting, by August Neter, illustrates the hallucinations and paranoid fantasies experienced by many schizophrenic patients.

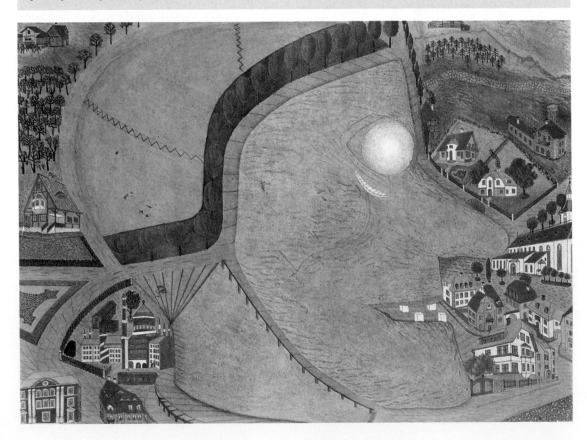

At one point, I would look at my co-workers and their faces would become distorted. Their teeth looked like fangs ready to devour me. Most of the time I couldn't trust myself to look at anyone for fear of being swallowed. I had no respite from the illness. Even when I tried to sleep, the demons would keep me awake, and at times I would roam the house searching for them. I was being consumed on all sides whether I was awake or asleep. I felt I was being consumed by demons. (Long, 1996)

Hallucinations may occur independently or as part of a delusional belief. An example would be a patient who hears voices threatening to kill him and believes that they are part of a plot to eliminate him because of his powers.

In one sense, hallucinations are not far removed from ordinary experiences. We all know what visual hallucinations are like because we have them in dreams. But for most people dreams occur only during sleep. It is possible that some sort of neurotransmitter-mediated process inhibits dreams during the waking state and that this process has failed in schizophrenics who hallucinate (Assad & Shapiro, 1986).

Auditory hallucinations may have their origin in ordinary thought. We often carry on internal dialogues, for example, commenting on our actions or having an imaginary conversation with another person. We may even occasionally talk to ourselves aloud. The voices that schizophrenic patients hear, calling them names or telling them what to do, are similar to internal dialogues. But a patient experiencing an auditory hallucination does not believe that the voices originate within the self or that they can be controlled. The inability to distinguish between external and internal, real and imagined, is central to the schizophrenic experience.

Disturbances of Emotional Expression People suffering from schizophrenia usually fail to exhibit normal emotional responses. They often are withdrawn and unresponsive in situations that should make them sad or happy. For example, a man may show no emotional response when informed that his daughter has cancer. However, this blunting of emotional expression can conceal inner turmoil, and the person may erupt with angry outbursts.

Sometimes individuals with schizophrenia express emotions that are inappropriately linked to the situation or to the thought being expressed. For instance, a patient may smile while speaking of tragic events. Since our emotions are influenced by cognitive processes, it is not surprising that disorganized thoughts and perceptions are accompanied by changes in emotional responses. This point is illustrated in the following comments:

> Half the time I am talking about one thing and thinking about half a dozen other things at the same time. It must look queer to people when I laugh about something that has got nothing to do with what I am talking about, but they don't know what's going on inside and how much of it is running around in my head. You see I might be talking about something quite serious to you and other things come into my head at the same time that are funny and this makes me laugh. If I could only concentrate on one thing at the one time I wouldn't look half so silly. (McGhie & Chapman, 1961, p. 104)

Motor Symptoms and Withdrawal From Reality Patients with schizophrenia often exhibit bizarre motor activity. They may grimace, adopt strange facial expressions, or gesture repeatedly using peculiar sequences of finger, hand, and arm movements. Some may become very agitated and move about in continual activity, as in a manic state. Some, at the other extreme, may become totally unresponsive and immobile, adopting an unusual posture and maintaining it for long periods of time. For example, a patient may stand like a statue with one foot extended and one arm raised toward the ceiling, maintaining this state of *catatonic immobility* for hours. Such an individual, who appears to have completely withdrawn from reality, may be responding to inner thoughts and fantasies.

Decreased Ability to Function Besides the specific symptoms we have described, people with schizophrenia are impaired in their ability to carry out the daily routines of living. If the disorder occurs in adolescence, the individual shows a decreasing ability to cope with school and has limited social skills and few friends. Adults suffering from schizophrenia are often unsuccessful in obtaining or holding

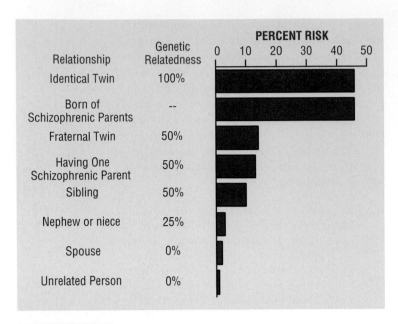

Relationship	Genetic Relatedness
Identical Twin	100%
Born of Schizophrenic Parents	--
Fraternal Twin	50%
Having One Schizophrenic Parent	50%
Sibling	50%
Nephew or niece	25%
Spouse	0%
Unrelated Person	0%

PERCENT RISK 0 10 20 30 40 50

FIGURE 15-8

Genetic Relationships and Schizophrenia   *The lifetime risk of developing schizophrenia is largely a function of how closely an individual is genetically related to a schizophrenic person and not a function of how much their environment is shared. In the case of an individual with two schizophrenic parents, genetic relatedness cannot be expressed in terms of percentage, but the regression of the individual's "genetic value" on that of the parents is 100%, the same as it is for identical twins.* (After Gottesman, 1991; Gottesman & Shields, 1982)

The odds of all four of a set of identical quadruplets being diagnosed as schizophrenic are 1 in 2 billion—yet these quadruplets, the Genain sisters, all suffer from schizophrenia and have been hospitalized at various times since high school.

a job. Personal hygiene and grooming deteriorate, and the individual avoids the company of other people. The signs of schizophrenia are many and varied. Trying to make sense of the variety of symptoms is complicated by the fact that some may result directly from the disorder whereas others may be a reaction to life in a mental hospital or to the effects of medication.

Understanding Schizophrenia

Schizophrenia probably has strong biological roots, but environmental stress may push people who are vulnerable to schizophrenia into more severe forms of the disorder or new episodes of psychosis.

The Biological Perspective   Family studies show that there is a hereditary predisposition for schizophrenia; relatives of people with schizophrenia are more likely to develop the disorder than people from families that are free of schizophrenia (Gottesman, 1991). Figure 15-8 shows the lifetime risk of developing schizophrenia as a function of how closely an individual is genetically related to a person diagnosed as schizophrenic. Note that an identical twin of a schizophrenic is three times more likely than a fraternal twin to develop schizophrenia and 46 times as likely as an unrelated person to develop the disorder. However, fewer than half of identical twins of people with schizophrenia develop schizophrenia themselves, even though they share the same genes. This fact demonstrates the importance of nongenetic variables.

How do the genetic abnormalities that predispose an individual to schizophrenia affect the brain? Current research focuses on two areas: brain structure and biochemistry. Two types of structural deficits have been found in the brains of people with schizophrenia. First, the prefrontal cortex is smaller and shows less activity in some people with schizophrenia compared to people without the disorder (Andreasen et al., 1997; Berman et al., 1992; Buchsbaum et al., 1992) (see Figure 15-9). The prefrontal cortex is the largest region of the brain in human beings, constituting nearly 30% of the total cortex, and has connections to all the other cortical regions as well as to the limbic system, which is involved in emotion and cognition, and the basal ganglia, which is involved in motor movement. The prefrontal cortex plays important roles in language, emotional expression, planning and producing new ideas, and mediating social interactions. Thus, it seems logical that people whose prefrontal cortex is unusually small or inactive would show a wide range of deficits in cognition, emotion, and social interaction, as people with schizophrenia do.

Second, people with schizophrenia have enlarged *ventricles*, fluid-filled spaces in the brain (Andreasen et al., 1990). The presence of enlarged ventricles suggests atrophy or deterioration in other brain tissue. The specific areas of the brain that have deteriorated, resulting in ventricular enlargement, could lead to different manifestations of schizophrenia (Breier et al., 1992).

While neurochemical theories of mood disorders center on norepinephrine and serotonin, the culprit in schizophrenia is believed to be dopamine. Early dopamine theories of schizophrenia held that the disorder was the result of the presence of too much dopamine in key areas of the brain. This view is now considered too simple. The most recent theories suggest that there is a complicated imbalance in levels of dopamine in different areas of the brain (Davis et al., 1991). First, there may be excess dopamine activity in the mesolimbic system, a subcortical part of the brain involved in cognition and emotion, which leads to the "positive" symptoms of schizophrenia—hallucinations, delusions, disordered thought. On the other hand, there may be unusually low dopamine activity in the prefrontal area of the brain, which is involved in attention, motivation, and organization of behavior. Low dopamine activity in the prefrontal area may lead to the "negative" symptoms of schizophrenia—lack of motivation, inability to care for oneself, inappropriate emotional expression.

The Social and Psychological Perspective

Although it is clear that stressful events cannot cause a person to develop the full syndrome of schizophrenia, psychosocial factors may play an important role in deter-

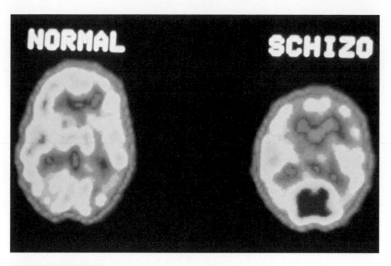

FIGURE 15-9

A Normal Brain Versus a Schizophrenic Brain   *This PET scan shows the metabolic differences between the prefrontal cortex of a schizophrenic individual and the same areas in the brain of a normal individual.*

mining the eventual severity of the disorder in people with a biological predisposition to the disorder, as well as triggering new episodes of psychosis. The type of stress that has received the most attention in recent studies is family-related stress. Members of families that are high in *expressed emotion* are overinvolved with one another, overprotective of the disturbed family member, and, at the same time, critical, hostile, and resentful toward the disturbed member (Brown, Birley, & Wing, 1972; Vaughn & Leff, 1976). People with schizophrenia whose families are high in expressed emotion are three to four times more likely to suffer a new psychotic episode than those whose families are low in expressed emotion (Brown, Birley, & Wing, 1972; Kavanagh, 1992; Leff & Vaughn, 1981; Mintz et al., 1987; Parker & Hadzi-Pavlovic, 1990). Being in a family with high levels of expressed emotion may create stresses that overwhelm the schizophrenic person's ability to cope and trigger new episodes of psychosis.

Critics of the research on expressed emotion argue that the hostility and intrusiveness observed in some families of people with schizophrenia might be the *result* of the symptoms exhibited by the disturbed member, rather than a factor contributing to the disorder (Parker, Johnston, & Hayward,

1988). Although families are often forgiving of positive symptoms like hallucinations, viewing them as uncontrollable, they can be unforgiving of the negative symptoms like lack of motivation (Brewin et al., 1991; Hooley et al., 1987). People with these symptoms may elicit more negative expressed emotion and may be especially prone to relapse.

Another alternative explanation for the link between expressed emotion and relapse comes from evidence that family members who are especially high in expressed emotion are themselves more likely to exhibit some form of psychopathology (Goldstein et al., 1992). Thus, it may be that in such families people with schizophrenia have high rates of relapse because they have a greater genetic predisposition toward psychopathology, as evidenced by the presence of psychopathology in their families, rather than because their families are high in expressed emotion. Perhaps the best evidence that expressed emotion actually influences relapse is that treatments that reduce expressed emotion tend to reduce the relapse rate in schizophrenic family members.

Personality Disorders

Personality disorders are long-standing patterns of maladaptive behavior. In Chapter 13 we described personality traits as enduring ways of perceiving or relating to the environment and thinking about oneself. When personality traits become so inflexible and maladaptive that they significantly impair the individual's ability to function, they are referred to as personality disorders. People with personality disorders experience themselves and the world in ways that are highly distressing to them and/or impair their ability to function in daily life. These experiences begin in childhood or adolescence and persist over time and across situations, affecting most areas of the person's life. The particular emotions, thoughts, and behaviors that an individual experiences vary according to the specific disorder.

Personality disorders constitute immature and inappropriate ways of coping with stress or solving problems. They are usually evident by early adolescence and may continue throughout the life span. Unlike people with mood or anxiety disorders, which also involve maladaptive behavior, people who have personality disorders often do not feel upset or anxious and may not be motivated to change their behavior. They do not lose contact with reality or display marked disorganization of behavior.

DSM-IV lists several personality disorders (see Table 15-6). The characteristics of these disorders tend to overlap, making it difficult to agree on how to classify some individuals. Moreover, it is difficult to say when a person's behavior is simply different from other people's behaviors and when the behavior is so severe that it warrants a diagnosis. The personality disorder that has been studied the most and is the most reliably diagnosed is the *antisocial personality* (formerly termed *psychopathic personality* and sometimes referred to as *sociopathy*). We discuss it in this section, along with borderline personality disorder, a controversial personal disorder that has received much attention in recent years.

Antisocial Personality

People who have antisocial personalities have little sense of responsibility, morality, or concern for others. Their behavior is determined almost entirely by their own needs. In other words, they lack a conscience. Whereas the average person realizes at an early age that some restrictions are placed on behavior and that pleasures must sometimes be postponed in consideration of the needs of others, individuals who have antisocial personalities seldom consider any desires except their own. They behave impulsively, seek immediate gratification of their needs, and cannot tolerate frustration.

Antisocial behavior results from a number of causes, including membership in a delinquent gang or a criminal subculture, the need for attention and status, loss of contact with reality, and inability to control impulses. However, most juvenile delinquents and adult criminals show some concern for others (for example, family or gang members) and adhere to some code of moral conduct (never betray a friend). In contrast, people with antisocial personalities have little feeling for anyone except themselves and seem to experience little

TABLE 15-6

Types of Personality Disorders   *The DSM-IV recognises several different personality disorders.*

Diagnosis	Description
Antisocial Personality Disorder	Impulsive, callous behavior based on disregard for others and lack of respect for social norms.
Borderline Personality Disorder	Chronic instability of mood, relationships, and self-concept; self-destructive impulsiveness.
Histrionic Personality Disorder	Chronic intense need for attention and approval sought by dramatic behavior, seductiveness, and dependence.
Narcissistic Personality Disorder	Frequent grandiosity and obliviousness to others' needs; exploitative behavior; arrogance.
Paranoid Personality Disorder	Chronic and pervasive mistrust of others that is unwarranted.
Schizoid Personality Disorder	Chronic lack of interest in interpersonal relationships; emotional coldness.
Schizotypal Personality Disorder	Chronically inhibited or inappropriate emotional and social behavior; aberrant cognitions; disorganized speech.
Avoidant Personality Disorder	Avoidance of social interactions and restrictiveness in interactions due to chronic worry over being criticized.
Dependent Personality Disorder	Pervasive selflessness, need to be cared for, and fear of rejection.
Obsessive-Compulsive Personality Disorder	Pervasive rigidity in activities and relationships; extreme perfectionism.

guilt or remorse, regardless of how much suffering their behavior may cause. Other characteristics of the antisocial personality (or sociopath) include a great facility for lying, a need for thrills and excitement with little concern for possible injury, and inability to alter behavior as a consequence of punishment. Such individuals are often attractive, intelligent, charming people who are adept at manipulating others—in other words, good con artists. Their façade of competence and sincerity wins them promising jobs, but they have little staying power. Their restlessness and impulsiveness soon lead them into an escapade that reveals their true nature; they accumulate debts, desert their families, squander company money, or commit crimes. When they are caught, their declarations of repentance are so convincing that they often escape punishment and are given another chance. But antisocial personalities seldom live up to these declarations; what they say has little relation to what they feel or do.

The two characteristics that are considered most indicative of an antisocial personality disorder are lack of empathy and

Serial killers like David Berkowitz, the "Son of Sam," display the central characteristics of antisocial personality disorder: lack of empathy and concern for others and lack of shame or guilt.

concern for others and lack of shame or guilt—that is, inability to feel remorse for one's actions, regardless of how reprehensible they may be (Hare, 1980).

Understanding Antisocial Personalities

What factors contribute to the development of an antisocial personality? Current research focuses on biological determinants, the quality of the parent-child relationship, and ways of thinking that promote antisocial behaviors.

Biological Factors Genetic factors appear to play a role in the development of antisocial personality. Twin studies show that if one identical twin has antisocial personality characteristics, the other twin also has these characteristics about 50% of the time. In contrast, among fraternal twins the concordance rate for antisocial personality is only about 20% (Rutter et al., 1990). Adoption studies find that the criminal records of adopted sons are more similar to the records of their biological fathers than to those of their adoptive fathers (Cloninger & Gottesman, 1987; Mednick et al., 1987).

Many studies have argued that people with antisocial personality disorder have low levels of arousability, which may lead them to seek stimulation and sensation through impulsive and dangerous acts (Morey, 1993). For example, one study compared two groups of adolescent male delinquents selected from the detention unit of a juvenile court. One group had been diagnosed as having antisocial personality disorder; the other group was diagnosed as exhibiting adjustment reactions to negative life events. The experimenters measured galvanic skin response, or GSR, under stress (see Chapter 11). Dummy electrodes were attached to each participant's leg, and he was told that in ten minutes he would be given a very strong but not harmful shock. A large clock was visible so that the participant knew precisely when the shock was supposed to occur. No shock was actually administered. The two groups showed no difference in GSR measures during periods of rest or in response to auditory or visual stimulation. However, during the ten minutes of shock anticipation, the group with adjustment reactions showed significantly more tension than the antisocial group. At the moment when the clock indicated the shock was due, most members of the group with adjustment reactions showed GSR responses indicating a sharp increase in anxiety. None of the antisocial participants showed this reaction (Lippert & Senter, 1966). Low arousability to anxiety-provoking stimuli may also make it more difficult for people with antisocial personality disorder to learn from punishment because punishment is less aversive for them than for most people, and they will not be anxious in anticipation of the punishment.

Social Factors Although children who develop antisocial personalities may have a biological predisposition for the disorder, studies suggest that they are unlikely to develop the disorder unless they are also exposed to environments that promote antisocial behavior (Cadoret & Cain, 1980; Cloninger & Gottesman, 1987; Rutter, Quinton, & Hill, 1990). The parents of children with antisocial personalities often appear to be simultaneously neglectful and hostile toward their children. The children are frequently unsupervised for long periods. The parents often are not involved in the children's everyday life, not knowing where they are or who their friends are. But when these parents do interact with their children, the interactions are often characterized by hostility, physical violence, and ridicule (Patterson, DeBaryshe, & Ramsey, 1989). This description does not fit all parents of such children, but parental noninvolvement and hostility are good predictors of children's vulnerability to antisocial personality disorder.

The biological and family factors that contribute to antisocial personality often coincide. Children who behave in antisocial ways often suffer from neuropsychological problems that are the result of maternal drug use, poor prenatal nutrition, pre- and postnatal exposure to toxic agents, child abuse, birth complications, and low birth weight (Moffitt, 1993). Children with these neuropsychological problems are more irritable, impulsive, awkward, overreactive, and inattentive, and they learn more slowly than their peers. This makes them difficult to care for, and they are therefore at increased risk for maltreatment and neglect. In turn, the parents of these children are more likely to be teenagers or to have psychological problems of their own that contribute to ineffective, harsh, or inconsistent parenting. Thus, for these children a biological predisposition to disruptive, antisocial behaviors may be combined with a style of parenting that contributes to these behaviors. In a study of 536 boys, Moffitt (1990) found that those who had both neuropsychological deficits and adverse home environments scored four times higher on an aggression scale than those with neither neuropsychological deficits nor adverse home environments.

Personality Factors Children with antisocial personalities tend to process information about social interactions in ways that promote aggressive reactions to these interactions (Crick & Dodge, 1994). They assume that other children will be aggressive toward them, and they interpret other children's actions in line with these assumptions rather than using cues from the specific situations they actually face. In addition, they tend to believe that any negative action by a peer—such as taking their favorite pencil—are intentional rather than accidental. When deciding what action to take in response to a perceived provocation by a peer, children with antisocial personalities tend to think of a narrow range of responses, usually including aggression. When pressed to consider responses other than aggression, they make ineffective or vague responses and often consider responses other than aggression to be useless or unattractive.

Children who think about their social interactions in this way are likely to engage in aggressive behaviors toward others and may therefore suffer retaliation. Other children will hit them, parents and teachers will punish them, and they will be perceived more negatively by others. These actions may feed their assumptions that the world is against them, causing them to misinterpret future actions by others. In this way a cycle of interactions can be established that maintains and encourages aggressive, antisocial behaviors.

Borderline Personality Disorder

Borderline personality disorder has been the focus of considerable attention in the popular press and in clinical and research writings in psychology in the last couple of decades. The diagnosis of borderline personality disorder was added to the DSM in 1980, but clinicians have long used the label "borderline" to refer to people who seem to teeter between severe neurotic traits (such as emotional instability) and bouts of psychosis (see Millon, 1981).

Instability is a key feature of borderline personality disorder. The mood of individuals with this disorder is unstable, with bouts of severe depression, anxiety, or anger seeming to arise frequently, often without good reason. The self-concept is unstable, with periods of extreme self-doubt and grandiose self-importance. Interpersonal relationships are extremely unstable, and the person can switch from idealizing other people to despising them without provocation. People with borderline personality disorder often feel desperately empty and will initially cling to a new acquaintance or therapist in the hope that he or she will fill the tremendous void they feel in themselves. At the same time, they may misinterpret other people's innocent actions as signs of abandonment or rejection. For example, if a therapist has to cancel an appointment because she is ill, a person with borderline personality disorder might interpret this as a rejection and become extremely depressed or angry. Along with instability of mood, self-concept, and interpersonal relationships comes a tendency toward impulsive self-damaging behaviors, including self-mutilation and suicidal behavior. Self-mutilation often takes the form of burning or cutting oneself. Finally, people with borderline personality disorder are prone to transient episodes in which they feel unreal, lose track of time, and may even forget who they are. The following case describes a person with borderline personality disorder (McGlashan, 1983, pp. 87–88).

Ms. Q was a 28-year-old, white single woman when admitted voluntarily [to a psychiatric hospital]. . . . In late adolescence, Ms. Q became romantically and sexually involved with a young artist. When he informed her that she was "just another woman" in his life, she became morose and moody. She began hallucinating his face on movie screens and newspapers. Shortly after the accidental drowning of a young boy from her neighborhood, Ms. Q started feeling guilty for his death and feared imminent apprehension by the police. In an act later described as a "manipulative gesture," she took an overdose of sleeping medication and was hospitalized briefly.

Over the next five years, Ms. Q attended college sporadically. She moved often between a variety of living situations: alone in hotels or dormitories or with one or the other of her divorced parents. Changes of domicile were often precipitated by quarrels. Although seldom alone, she developed relatively superficial social relationships. The few women whom she befriended tended to be older. She would frequently become attached to their parents and call them "mama and papa." Sexually she had three or four intense affairs, each lasting less than six months and each terminating painfully with one or the other partner refusing to marry. In all of her relationships, Ms. Q was described as manipulative, dependent, masochistic, hostile, and derogatory.

Mood swings between anger and despondency occurred weekly and sometimes daily. She frequently abused alcohol and barbiturates and made numerous manipulative suicidal threats. For the latter she was hospitalized briefly on two more occasions (one month or less in duration). . . .

In her mid-20s, Ms. Q joined the armed services. After an initial honeymoon period, she performed miserably. She cried "for hours over her typewriter and stayed in her room not eating." After ten months, she received a "neuropsychiatric" medical discharge. She began moving around again, trying various jobs, which she was unable to hold for more than a few days. She became more seclusive, even with fellow employees.

At age 26 Ms. Q began two years of intensive psychotherapy (up to four times per week). Her therapist recorded that Ms. Q tried "very hard to be sick" and was intent on causing "trouble with everyone she did not like" by "upsetting everyone during her bad spells."

Her hospitalization at (the psychiatric hospital) arose out of a visit home to her mother. She felt slighted in several ways. First, her mother's welcome was less than "gushing." Second, she felt insulted when her mother's boyfriend showed her a brochure describing a

psychiatric residential treatment facility. Third, she discovered that a certain choice piece of family real estate was being willed to her least favorite sibling. Feeling rejected, she took an overdose of aspirin and was hospitalized at (the psychiatric hospital) shortly thereafter.

People with borderline personality disorder also tend to receive diagnoses of one of the acute disorders, including substance abuse, depression, and generalized anxiety disorder, simple phobias, and agoraphobia, post-traumatic stress disorder, and panic disorder (Fabrega et al., 1991; Weissman, 1993). Longitudinal studies of people with this disorder indicate that about 6% die by suicide (Perry, 1993). The greatest risk of suicide appears to be in the first year or two after receiving a diagnosis of borderline personality disorder. This may be due to the fact that a person is often not diagnosed with this disorder until a crisis brings him or her into therapy.

The lifetime prevalence of borderline personality disorder is between 1 and 2% (Weissman, 1993). The disorder is diagnosed much more often in women than in men (Fabrega et al., 1991; Swartz et al., 1990). People with this disorder tend to have stormy marital relationships, more job difficulties, and a higher rate of physical disability than average.

Understanding Borderline Personalities

Psychoanalytic theorists have provided the most comprehensive explanation of borderline personality disorder. They suggest that individuals with borderline personalities retain a foothold in the real world but rely on primitive defenses such as denial rather than more advanced defenses against their conflicts (Kernberg, 1979). In addition, such individuals have very poorly developed views of self and others, stemming from poor early relationships with caregivers. The caregivers of people with borderline personality disorder are characterized as deriving much gratification from the child's dependence on them early in life. Thus, they do not encourage the child to develop a separate sense of self and may punish his or her attempts at individuation and separation. As a result, people with borderline personality disorder never learn to fully differentiate between their views of self and others. This makes them extremely sensitive to others' opinions of them and to the possibility of being abandoned by others. When others are perceived as rejecting them, they reject themselves and may engage in self-punishment or self-mutilation.

Individuals with borderline personalities also have never been able to integrate the positive and negative qualities of either their self-concept or their concept of others, because their early caregivers were comforting and rewarding when they remained dependent and compliant toward them, but hostile and rejecting when they tried to separate from them. People with borderline personalities therefore tend to see themselves and others as either "all good" or "all bad" and vacillate between these two views. This process is referred to as "splitting." The changeability of borderline individuals' emotions and interpersonal relationships is caused by splitting—their emotions and their perspectives on their relationships reflect their vacillation between the "all good" and the "all bad" self or other.

Other research suggests that many people with borderline personality disorder have a history of physical and sexual abuse during childhood (Perry, 1993). This abuse could lead to the problems in self-concept that most theorists believe to be at the core of this disorder. In addition, a child whose parent alternates between being abusive and being loving could develop a fundamental mistrust of others and a tendency to see others as all good or all bad.

Biological-Psychological Interactions and Mental Disorders

Although some researchers and clinicians who specialize in abnormal psychology still take the perspective that mental disorders are entirely caused by biological factors or entirely caused by psychological factors, many researchers and clinicians believe that most people who develop serious mental disorders probably have both biological and psychological vulnerabilities to these disorders, and that stressful events can trigger new episodes of the disorder. This is especially true of serious anxiety disorders and mood disorders. As we have seen, there is increasing evidence that people who develop serious anxiety or mood disorders in the face of stress differ from people who do not develop these disorders both in their biochemistry and in their ways of thinking about themselves and the world. It is often difficult to tell whether disordered biochemical or thought processes are the cause or the consequence of an anxiety or mood disorder. But it is clear that these disorders are phenomena of the whole person—they affect people at the biological, psychological, and social levels.

In the case of schizophrenia, where the evidence for genetic and biochemical theories of the disorder is strong, it is still clear that environmental stress and family support play a role in triggering new episodes or facilitating recovery. Although we know little about the causes of the personality disorders, the evidence suggests that both biological and psychological factors will be shown to play roles in the development and maintenance of the disorders.

Thus, it seems that advances in our understanding of mental disorders will necessarily involve models that integrate biological and psychological variables. These models may illuminate both how mental disorders are caused and how the mind and body work together in people who are considered mentally healthy.

Insanity as a Legal Defense

Before leaving the subject of mental disorders, we should look briefly at the controversial issue of insanity. How should the law treat a mentally disturbed person who commits a criminal offense? Should individuals whose mental faculties are impaired be held responsible for their actions? These questions are of concern to behavioral and social scientists, members of the legal profession, and others who work with criminal offenders.

Over the centuries, an important part of Western law has been the concept that a civilized society should not punish a person who is mentally incapable of controlling his or her conduct. In 1724 an English court maintained that a man was not responsible for an act if "he doth not know what he is doing, no more than . . . a wild beast." Modern standards of legal responsibility, however, have been based on the M'Naghten decision of 1843. The M'Naghten Rule states that a defendant may be found not guilty by reason of insanity only if he was so severely disturbed at the time of his act that he did not know what he was doing, or if he did know what he was doing, did not know that it was wrong.

The M'Naghten Rule was adopted in the United States, and the distinction of knowing right from wrong remained the basis for most decisions of legal insanity for over a century. Some states added to their statutes the doctrine of "irresistible impulse," which recognizes that some mentally ill individuals may respond correctly when asked if a particular act is morally right or wrong but may be unable to control their behavior.

During the 1970s, a number of state and federal courts adopted a broader legal definition of insanity proposed by the American Law Institute, which states: "A person is not responsible for criminal conduct if at the time of such conduct, as a result of mental disease or defect, he lacks substantial capacity either to appreciate the wrongfulness of his conduct or to conform his conduct to the requirements of the law." The word *substantial* suggests that any incapacity is not enough to avoid criminal responsibility but that total incapacity is not required either. The use of the word *appreciate* rather than *know* implies that intellectual awareness of right or wrong is not enough; individuals must have some understanding of the moral or legal consequences of their behavior before they can be held criminally responsible.

The problem of legal responsibility in the case of mentally disordered individuals became a topic of increased debate in the wake of John Hinckley, Jr.'s, acquittal, by

reason of insanity, for the attempted assassination of President Reagan in 1981. Many Americans were outraged by the verdict and felt that the insanity defense was a legal loophole that allowed too many guilty people to go free. In response, Congress enacted the Insanity Defense Reform Act (1984), which contains a number of provisions designed to make it more difficult to absolve a defendant of legal responsibility. For example, the act changes the American Law Institute's "lacks substantial capacity . . . to appreciate" to "unable to appreciate"; it stipulates that the mental disease or defect be "severe" (the intent being to exclude nonpsychotic disorders such as antisocial personality); and it shifts the burden of proof from the prosecution to the defense (instead of the prosecution having to prove that the person was sane beyond a reasonable doubt at the time of the crime, the defense must prove he or she was not sane, and must do so with "clear and convincing evidence"). This law applies to all cases tried in federal courts and about half the state courts.

Another attempt to clarify the legal defense of insanity is the verdict "guilty but mentally ill." Initially proposed by Michigan, it has been adopted by 11 states. (In some of these states this verdict replaces the not guilty by reason of insanity verdict; in others it is an additional option.) Generally, the laws permit a finding of guilty but mentally ill when a defendant is found to have a substantial disorder of thought or mood that afflicted him at the time of the crime and significantly impaired his judgment, behavior, capacity to recognize reality, or ability to cope with the ordinary demands of life. The effect of this mental illness, however, falls short of legal insanity. The verdict of guilty but mentally ill allows jurors to convict a person whom they perceive as dangerous while attempting also to ensure that he or she receives treatment for the disorder. The individual could be given treatment in prison or be treated in a mental hospital and returned to prison when deemed fit to complete the sentence.

Public concern that the insanity defense may be a major loophole in the criminal law is largely groundless. The defense is rarely used, and actual cases of acquittal by reason of insanity are even rarer. Jurors seem reluctant to believe that people are not morally responsible for their acts, and lawyers, knowing that an insanity plea is likely to fail, tend to use it only as a last resort. Fewer than 1% of defendants charged with serious crimes are found not guilty by reason of insanity.

ADHD Is Overdiagnosed

Caryn L. Carlson, The University of Texas at Austin

Caryn Carlson

The growing public attention to ADHD over the past decade has increased the detection of legitimate cases and led to much-needed research. We must be cautious, however, that we do not allow the diagnostic pendulum to swing too far, since finding answers about ADHD depends on the rigor and integrity of our classification system.

There is reason to believe that ADHD is currently being overdiagnosed in some areas of the United States. Prescriptions of stimulant medications, which are almost exclusively for ADHD, provide a "proxy" for diagnostic rates and afford an examination of trends over time and place. Use of methylphenidate in the United States, already high by worldwide standards (International Narcotics Control Board, 1998), skyrocketed in the early 1990s, more than doubling from 1990 through 1995 (Safer, Zito, & Fine, 1996) and has continued to increase since then. While rates are up for all age groups, the largest increase is for teenagers and adults; among school-age children in one region, the proportion of high school students using stimulant medication tripled from 1991 through 1995 (Safer, Zito, & Fine, 1996). Certainly the true prevalence of ADHD has not increased at this rate, although part of the increase no doubt reflects the detection of previously unrecognized ADHD. While some reports suggest that even now many ADHD children may not be recognized or treated (Wolraich, Hannah, Baumgaertel, & Feurer, 1998), the average rates are now quite high (Safer, Zito, & Fine, 1996).

Part of the dramatic increase probably reflects overdiagnosis, particularly when considered in light of the vast disparities across geographical locales in the United States. The rate of methylphenidate consumption per capita in 1995 was 2.4 times higher in Virginia than in neighboring West Virginia, and nearly 4 times higher than in California (Spanos, 1996). Even more troubling are the high discrepancies across counties within states. For example, although the per capita rate for males of ages 6–12 in 1991 in New York was 4.1% statewide, rates varied by a factor of 10 among counties, ranging up to 14% (Kaufman, 1995).

What factors might lead to overdiagnosis of ADHD? We know from epidemiological research that unreasonable prevalence rates (e.g., up to nearly 23% of school-age boys [Wolraich, Hannah, Baumgaertel, & Feurer, 1998]) are obtained when ADHD is identified based merely on simple ratings from one source, but become much lower when full diagnostic criteria—including age of onset by 7, presence across settings, and confirmation of impairment—are imposed. The wide variability in diagnostic rates across locations suggests that clinicians are applying diagnostic criteria inconsistently. Some clinicians diagnose without assessing all criteria, and often they rely only on parent reports. While underdiagnosis may be occurring in some places, overdiagnosis is occurring in others.

When is overdiagnosis most likely? It seems that the diagnosis of ADHD has become fashionable for those who experience some negative life event—such as school failure or job loss—and desire to attribute such problems to a disorder rather than accept personal responsibility. This tendency is apparent even in more mundane arenas, such as feeling bored or unmotivated—"What a relief: the fact that I find it difficult to pay attention in my 'history of Swedish cartographers' class isn't my fault. I have ADHD."

One safeguard against misdiagnosis is the current criteria that symptoms must onset by age 7. But how early and by what means can we detect ADHD if we agree that it is present from an early age? Since objective measures that can reliably identify ADHD are currently unavailable, we must rely on symptom reports from others. Setting the age of onset at 7 years recognizes that normal behavior patterns may be similar to symptoms of ADHD up to about age 5, when normally activity decreases and attention increases (but not in children with ADHD). Also, impairment may not occur outside the demands of a classroom environment. But if individuals do not have symptoms early but develop them later for a variety of reasons, including life situations or stress, then diagnosis does not seem warranted. Should such problems be recognized? By all means. Should they be treated? Of course, by teaching people organizational and behavior management strategies, and possibly even with medication. But significant problems in living are not the equivalent of disorders, and to call them that will deter us in the search for etiologies of ADHD.

ADHD Is Neither Overdiagnosed nor Overtreated

William Pelham, *SUNY Buffalo*

Because ADHD is the most widely diagnosed mental health disorder of childhood and because its frequency of treatment with medication has been increasing exponentially through the 1990s, it has become fashionable in many quarters—particularly among educators—to argue that it is overdiagnosed and consequently overtreated. Histrionic diatribes aside, there is no solid empirical evidence that ADHD is overdiagnosed or overtreated.

First, consider the accusation that ADHD is only a relatively recent phenomenon. To the contrary, the diagnosis was often widely used in the past but played second fiddle to other diagnoses. For example, one of the more important early studies in treatment of conduct disordered children (Patterson, 1974) noted, almost as an aside that more than two-thirds of the boys had hyperkinesis, an early label for ADHD. Thus while ADHD may well be *diagnosed* more often than in the past 30 years, it is simply being diagnosed more appropriately and given the prominence it deserves.

It is important to note that the major reason for the increasing rate of ADHD identification in the 1990s is a result of the 1991 change in the status of ADHD in the Individuals with Disabilities Education Act (IDEA), the federal law that governs special education throughout the United States. This change included ADHD as a handicapping condition. Further, the U. S. Office of Education sent a memorandum to all state officers of education directing them to consider ADHD as a condition eligible for special education. As a result of this directive, school districts throughout the country for the first time were required to establish screening and diagnostic procedures for ADHD. The increase in diagnosis for ADHD is thus not a conspiracy or a fatal flaw in education or an indictment of current parenting practices, but is instead a natural by-product of a change in federal regulations governing education in the United States.

What about the criticism that ADHD is a disorder with diagnostic rates that vary widely both within North America and across the world? The explanation is that local school districts and states vary dramatically in the degree to which they have implemented the mandated changes in the IDEA. Furthermore, ADHD when similar diagnostic criteria are applied, comparable rates to those in North America exist in a diverse collection of countries that include Italy, Spain, South Africa, Israel, Argentina, and Vietnam.

The most important factor in deciding whether a mental health disorder is overdiagnosed is whether the diagnosed individuals have impairments in daily life functioning sufficient to justify the label. ADHD is a particularly compelling example of this issue because the children suffer from dramatic impairment in relationships with peers, parents, teachers, and siblings, as well as in classroom behavior and academic performance. To take a single example, in one classic study of consecutive referrals to a clinic, 96% of ADHD children were rejected by their peers on sociometric nominations at a rate higher than their class averages (Pelham & Bender, 1982). In the field of child psychopathology, the number of negative nominations received on a classroom peer nomination inventory in elementary school is widely thought to be the best indicator of severe impairment in childhood and poor outcome in adulthood, so this elevated rate of negative nominations highlights the impairment that ADHD children suffer in the peer domain.

A corollary of the argument that many children are inappropriately diagnosed with ADHD is the complaint that these children are being inappropriately treated—usually with medication. In fact, the literature shows that only a small minority of diagnosed ADHD children (or all children with mental health disorders for that matter) receive treatment—medication or otherwise. We should be happy that treatment rates for the disorder are increasing. The dramatic rise in the treatment of ADHD—pharmacological or otherwise—clearly results from the increase in the rates of diagnosis, which are secondary to the change in the IDEA noted above. Notably, one of the studies that supports these arguments regarding impairment and treatment was conducted with children identified using only teacher ratings, which have been the main target for complaints of overdiagnosis (Wolraich et al, 1998).

In summary, ADHD is the most common mental health disorder of childhood, and it is one of the most impairing and refractory, and one with poor long-term prognosis. Current diagnostic rates are in line with scientific views of the nature of the disorder. If anything, we need to accurately identify *more* children with ADHD and provide the evidence-based treatments—both behavioral and pharmacological—that they need.

SUMMARY

1. The diagnosis of abnormal behavior is based on statistical frequency, social norms, adaptiveness of behavior, and personal distress. Characteristics of good mental health include efficient perception of reality, control of behavior, self-esteem, ability to form affectionate relationships, and productivity.

2. DSM-IV classifies mental disorders according to specific behavioral symptoms. Such a classification system helps communicate information and provides a basis for research. However, each case is unique, and diagnostic labels should not be used to pigeon-hole individuals.

3. Theories about the causes of mental disorders and proposals for treating them can be grouped according to the biological, psychoanalytic, behavioral, and cognitive perspectives. The vulnerability-stress model emphasizes the interaction between a predisposition (biological and/or psychological) that makes a person vulnerable to a particular disorder, and stressful environmental conditions encountered by the individual.

4. Anxiety disorders include generalized anxiety (constant worry and tension), panic disorders (sudden attacks of overwhelming apprehension), phobias (irrational fears of specific objects or situations), and obsessive-compulsive disorders (persistent unwanted thoughts, or obsessions, combined with urges, or compulsions, to perform certain acts).

5. Biological theories of anxiety disorders attribute them to genetic predispositions or to biochemical or neurological abnormalities. Most anxiety disorders run in families, and twin studies strongly suggest that panic disorder and obsessive-compulsive disorder have an inherited component. People who suffer panic attacks have an overreactive fight-or-flight response, perhaps because of serotonin deficiencies in the limbic system. People with obsessive-compulsive disorder may have serotonin deficiencies in areas of the brain that regulate primitive impulses.

6. Cognitive and behavioral theorists suggest that people with anxiety disorders are prone to catastrophizing cognitions and to rigid, moralistic thinking. Maladaptive behaviors such as avoidant behaviors and compulsions arise through operant conditioning when the individual discovers that the behaviors reduce anxiety. Phobias may emerge through classical conditioning. Psychodynamic theories attribute anxiety disorders to unconscious conflicts that are disguised as phobias, obsessions, or compulsions.

7. Mood disorders are divided into depressive disorders (in which the individual has one or more periods of depression) and bipolar disorders (in which the individual alternates between periods of depression and periods of elation, or mania). Sadness, loss of gratification in life, negative thoughts, and lack of motivation are the main symptoms of depression.

8. Biological theories attribute mood disorders to genetic factors and to problems in regulation of the neurotransmitters serotonin and norepinephrine. Cognitive theories attribute depression to pessimistic views of the self, the world, and the future, and to maladaptive attributional styles. Psychodynamic theories view depression as a reactivation of loss of parental affection in a person who is dependent on external approval and tends to turn anger inward.

9. In dissociative identity disorder two or more well-developed personalities alternate within the same individual. Many theorists attribute this disorder to child abuse.

10. Schizophrenia is characterized by disturbances in thought, including disorganized thought processes, delusions, and lack of insight. Other symptoms include perceptual disturbances (such as hallucinations), inappropriate emotional expression, bizarre motor activity, withdrawal, and impaired functioning.

11. Schizophrenia clearly is transmitted genetically. People with schizophrenia also have problems in dopamine regulation, as well as two types of brain abnormalities: The prefrontal cortex is smaller and less active, and the ventricles are enlarged. Difficult environments probably cannot cause schizophrenia, but they may worsen the disorder and contribute to relapses.

12. Personality disorders are lifelong patterns of maladaptive behavior that constitute immature and inappropriate ways of coping with stress or solving problems. Individuals with antisocial personalities are impulsive, show little guilt, are concerned only with their own needs, and are frequently in trouble with the law. Antisocial personality disorder probably has genetic and biological roots, but neglectful and hostile parenting may also contribute to the disorder.

13. People with borderline personality disorder show instability in mood, self-concept, and interpersonal relationships. Psychodynamic theories suggest that the caregivers of people with this disorder required their children to be highly dependent and alternated between extreme expressions of love and hostility.

14. Although the use of insanity as a legal defense is a subject of considerable controversy, in reality the defense is rarely used and even more rarely successful.

KEY TERMS

generalized anxiety disorder (p. 531)
panic attack (p. 532)
agoraphobia (p. 532)
phobia (p. 535)
obsessive-compulsive disorder (p. 537)
obsession (p. 537)
compulsion (p. 537)
depressive disorders (p. 539)

bipolar disorders (p. 540)
dissociative identity disorder (p. 546)
amnesia (p. 546)
schizophrenia (p. 548)
delusion (p. 549)
paranoid (p. 550)
hallucination (p. 550)

CRITICAL THINKING QUESTIONS

1. If you were experiencing distressing feelings, thoughts, or behaviors, would you feel better or worse if they were diagnosed as symptoms of a psychological disorder? Explain your answer. What would having a diagnosis mean to you?
2. What are the attitudes of some of your friends and family members toward people with psychological disorders? What theories about the causes of psychological disorders do these attitudes seem to represent?

3. Why might some people become highly anxious when faced with a stressful event while other people, faced with the same event, become highly depressed?
4. If a person with a personality disorder does not want to be treated for the disorder, should he or she be forced to received treatment?
5. Why might psychological disorders be less common in children than in adults?

FURTHER READING

Mending Minds (1992), a paperback by Heston, provides a brief description of the major mental disorders, with case histories and descriptions of treatment options. Also see Torrey, *Out of the Shadows: Confronting America's Mental Illness* (1997).

The hereditary aspects of mental illness are reviewed in Plomin, DeFries, and McClearn, *Behavioral Genetics: A Primer* (2nd ed., 1989). *Schizophrenia Genesis: The Origins of Madness* (1991), a paperback by Gottesman, presents research findings on the genetics of this disorder, a discussion of social and psychological factors, and personal accounts by schizophrenic patients and their families. An important recent work is Torrey, *Schizophrenia and Manic-Depressive Disorder: The Biological Roots of Mental Illness as Revealed by the Landmark Study of Identical Twins* (1994).

Panic: Facing Fears, Phobias, and Anxiety (1985), by Agras, provides an interesting discussion of the way fears develop into phobias. *The Boy Who Couldn't Stop Washing: The Experience and Treatment of Obsessive-Compulsive Disorder* (1989), by Rapaport, provides a fascinating account of this disorder, including descriptions of clinical cases and research findings on treatment.

For a fascinating look at the link between mental illness and creativity, see Jamison, *Touched with Fire: Manic Depressive Illness and the Artistic Temperament* (1996), and *An Unquiet Mind* (1995).

The world of psychosis from the patient's viewpoint is graphically described in Green, *I Never Promised You a Rose Garden* (1971); and in North, *Welcome Silence* (1987). In *Holiday of Darkness* (1982), by Endler, a well-known psychologist, provides an account of his personal battle with depression and discusses the effects of various treatments. *The Three Faces of Eve* gives one of the first and most comprehensive accounts of a person with multiple personality disorder. Donna Williams writes of her childhood experiences with autism in two gripping books, *Nobody Nowhere* (1992) and *Somebody Somewhere* (1994).

People with family members suffering from mental illness will find useful advice in Marsh, Dickens, and Torrey, *How to Cope With Mental Illness in Your Family: A Self-Care Guide for Siblings, Offspring, and Parents* (1998).

Chapter 16
Methods of Therapy

*I*n this chapter we look at methods for treating abnormal behavior. Some of these methods focus on helping individuals gain an understanding of early experiences that may have contributed to their problems, some attempt to modify more current thoughts and behavior, some are biologically based, and some specify ways in which the community can help. The most frequently used methods are listed in Table 16-1. The treatment of mental disorders is linked to theories about the causes of such disorders. A brief history of the treatment of the mentally ill will illustrate how methods have changed along with theories of mental disorder.

TABLE 16-1

Methods of Therapy

Psychological Therapies		
Psychodynamic Therapies	Traditional psychoanalysis	Through free association, dream analysis, and transference, attempts to discover the unconscious basis of the client's current problems so as to deal with them in a more rational way.
	Contemporary psychodynamic therapies (e.g., interpersonal therapy)	More structured and short-term than traditional psychoanalysis; emphasize the way the client is currently interacting with others.
Behavior Therapies	Systematic desensitization	The client is trained to relax and then presented with a hierarchy of anxiety-producing situations and asked to relax while imagining each one.
	In vivo exposure	Similar to systematic desensitization except that the client actually experiences each situation.
	Flooding	A form of in vivo exposure in which a phobic individual is exposed to the most feared object or situation for an extended period without an opportunity to escape.
	Selective reinforcement	Reinforcement of specific behaviors, often through the use of tokens that can be exchanged for rewards.
	Modeling	A process in which the client learns behaviors by observing and imitating others; often combined with behavioral rehearsal (e.g., in assertiveness training).
Cognitive-Behavior Therapies		Treatment methods that use behavior modification techniques but also incorporate procedures designed to change maladaptive beliefs.
Humanistic Therapies (e.g., client-centered therapy)		In an atmosphere of empathy, warmth, and genuineness, the therapist attempts to facilitate the process through which the client works out solutions to his or her own problems.
Biological Therapies	Psychotherapeutic drugs	Use of drugs to modify mood and behavior.
	Electroconvulsive Therapy (ECT)	A mild electric current is applied to the brain to produce a seizure.

Historical Background

Among the earliest beliefs about mental disorders, espoused by the ancient Chinese, Egyptians, and Hebrews, was that a person who behaved in unusual ways was possessed by evil spirits. These demons were removed or *exorcised* through such techniques as prayer, incantation, magic, and the use of purgatives. If these techniques were unsuccessful, more extreme measures were taken to ensure that the body would be an unpleasant dwelling place for the evil spirit. Flogging, starving, burning, and causing the person to bleed profusely were frequent forms of "treatment."

In the Western world, the first progress toward understanding the true causes of mental disorders was made by the Greek physician Hippocrates (circa 460–377 BC), who rejected the notion of demon possession and maintained that unusual behaviors were the result of a disturbance in the balance of bodily fluids. Hippocrates, and the Greek and Roman physicians who followed him, argued for more humane treatment of the mentally ill. They stressed the importance of pleasant surroundings, exercise, proper diet, massage, and soothing baths, as well as some less desirable treatments such as purging and mechanical restraints. Although there were no institutions for the mentally ill, many individuals were cared for with great kindness in temples dedicated to the gods of healing.

This progressive view of mental illness did not continue, however. Primitive superstitions and belief in demon possession were revived during the Middle Ages. The mentally ill were considered to be in league with Satan and to possess supernatural powers with which they could cause floods, pestilence, and injuries to others. Seriously disturbed individuals were treated cruelly: It was believed that beating, starving, and torturing the mentally ill served to punish the devil. This type of cruelty culminated in the witchcraft trials of the fifteenth, sixteenth, and seventeenth centuries, in which thousands of people, many of whom were mentally ill, were sentenced to death.

Philippe Pinel in the courtyard of the hospital of Salpetriere.

Early Asylums

In the late Middle Ages cities created asylums to cope with the mentally ill. These asylums were simply prisons; the inmates were chained in dark, filthy cells and treated more as animals than as human beings. It was not until 1792, when Philippe Pinel was placed in charge of an asylum in Paris, that some improvements were made. As an experiment, Pinel removed the chains that restrained the inmates. Much to the amazement of skeptics who thought Pinel was mad to unchain such "animals," the experiment was a success. When released from their restraints, placed in clean, sunny rooms, and treated kindly, many people who for years had been considered hopelessly insane improved enough to leave the asylum.

By the beginning of the twentieth century the fields of medicine and psychology were making great advances. In 1905, a mental disorder known as *general paresis* was shown to have a physical cause: a syphilis infection acquired many years before the symptoms of the disorder appeared. The syphilis spirochete remains in the body after the initial genital infection disappears, and it gradually destroys the nervous system. The results include a gradual decline in mental and physical functioning, marked changes in personality, and delusions and hallucinations. If the disorder is not treated, death occurs within a few years. At one time, general paresis accounted for more than 10% of all admissions to mental hospitals, but today few cases are reported, owing to the effectiveness of penicillin in treating syphilis (Dale, 1975).

The discovery that general paresis was the result of a disease encouraged those who believed that mental illness has biological causes. Nevertheless, in the early 1900s the public still did not understand mental illness and viewed mental hospitals and their inmates with fear and horror. Clifford Beers undertook the task of educating the public about mental health. As a young man, Beers had developed a bipolar disorder and been confined for three years in several private and state hospitals. At the time, lack of funds made the average state mental hospital—with its overcrowded wards, poor food, and unsympathetic attendants—a highly unpleasant place to live. After his recovery, Beers described his experiences in a book titled *A*

THE CRIB

The crib, a restraining device used in a New York mental institution in 1882.

Mind That Found Itself (1908), which attracted considerable public attention. Beers worked ceaselessly to educate the public about mental illness and helped organize the National Committee for Mental Hygiene. The mental hygiene movement played an invaluable role in stimulating the organization of child-guidance clinics and community mental health centers to aid in the prevention and treatment of mental disorders.

Modern Treatment Facilities

Mental hospitals have been upgraded markedly since Beers's day, but there is still much room for improvement. The best mental hospitals are comfortable and well-kept places that provide a number of therapeutic activities: individual and group psychotherapy, recreation, occupational therapy (designed to teach skills as well as provide relaxation), and educational courses to help patients prepare for a job upon release from the hospital. The worst are primarily custodial institutions where patients lead a boring existence in run-down, overcrowded wards and receive little treatment except for medication. Most mental hospitals fall somewhere between these extremes.

Beginning in the early 1960s, emphasis shifted from treating mentally disturbed individuals in hospitals to treating them in their own communities. This movement toward deinstitutionalization was motivated partly by the recognition that hospitalization has some inherent disadvantages, regardless of how good the facilities may be. Hospitals

remove people from the social support of family and friends and the familiar patterns of daily life; they tend to make people feel "sick" and unable to cope; and they encourage dependence. They are also very expensive.

During the 1950s, psychotherapeutic drugs (discussed later in the chapter) were discovered that could relieve depression and anxiety and reduce psychotic behavior. When these drugs became widely available in the 1960s, it was possible for many hospitalized patients to be discharged and returned home to be treated as outpatients. The Community Mental Health Centers Act of 1963 made federal funds available for the establishment of community treatment centers designed to provide outpatient treatment and a number of other services, including short-term and partial hospitalization. In partial hospitalization, individuals may receive treatment at the center during the day and return home in the evening, or work during the day and spend nights at the center.

As Figure 16-1 shows, the number of patients treated in state and county mental hospitals has decreased dramatically over the past 35 years. For some patients, deinstitutionalization has been successful. The services of mental health centers and private clinicians, along with help from their families and the use of psychotherapeutic drugs, have enabled them to resume a satisfactory life. For others, however, deinstitutionalization has had unfortunate consequences, largely because the facilities in most communities are far from adequate.

Many individuals who improve with hospitalization and could manage on their own

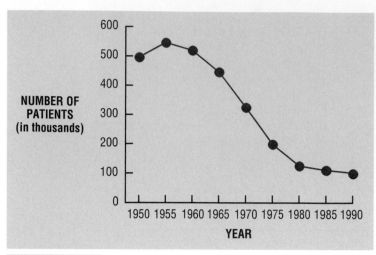

Patients in Mental Hospitals   *The number of patients cared for in the United States's state and county mental hospitals has decreased dramatically over the past 35 years.*

with assistance do not receive adequate follow-up care in terms of outpatient therapy, monitoring of medication, or help in finding friends, housing, and jobs. As a consequence, they lead a "revolving-door" existence, going in and out of institutions between unsuccessful attempts to cope on their own. About half of all patients discharged from state hospitals are readmitted within a year.

Some discharged patients are too incapacitated to even attempt to support themselves or function without custodial care;

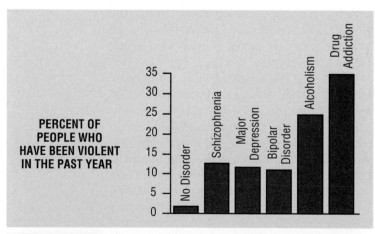

Percentage of People Who Have Been Violent in the Past Year   *People with severe psychiatric disorders do appear to be at increased risk for being violent compared to people with no psychiatric diagnosis.* (After Monahan, 1992)

they often live in dirty, overcrowded housing or on the streets. The disheveled man standing on the corner talking to himself and shouting gibberish may be one victim of deinstitutionalization. The woman with all her possessions in a shopping bag who spends one night in the doorway of an office building and the next in a subway station may be another. At least one third of street people suffer from some sort of mental disorder (Rossi, 1990).

The increasing visibility of homeless mentally ill individuals, particularly in large cities, has aroused public concern and prompted a move toward reinstitutionalization. However, this raises an important ethical issue. If such people are not readjusting to society, should they be involuntarily committed to a mental hospital? One of the most cherished civil rights in a democratic society is the right to liberty. It is essential that any commitment proceedings safeguard this right.

Some experts believe that legal action is warranted only if a person is potentially dangerous to others. The rare, but highly publicized, occasions when a mentally ill person experiencing a psychotic episode attacks an innocent bystander have generated fears for public safety. But dangerousness is difficult to predict (Gardner et al., 1996; Lidz, Mulvey, & Gardner, 1993). Although people with serious mental disorders do appear to commit violent crimes more often than normal people (Monahan, 1992) (see Figure 16-2), experts' opinions regarding whether any individual with a mental disorder will commit violent crimes are wrong as often as they are correct (Monahan & Walker, 1990).

Moreover, our legal system is designed to protect people from preventive detention. A person is assumed to be innocent until proven guilty by the courts, and prisoners are released from penitentiaries even though statistics show that most will commit additional crimes. Should mentally ill individuals not have the same rights? And what about the person who appears to be more dangerous to himself or herself than to others? Should he or she be committed? These complex issues have yet to be resolved.

Aside from the legal issues, the problem of providing care for the mentally ill remains. Many people with mental disorders might voluntarily seek treatment but cannot because they do not have the means to pay for good treatment. Society must be willing to pay the costs of care for such individuals.

Professionals Who Provide Psychotherapy

Whether a person receives therapy in a hospital, a community mental health center, or a private office, several different types of professionals may be involved.

A psychiatrist has an M.D. degree and has completed a three-year residency (after medical school) in a mental health facility, during which he or she received supervision in the diagnosis of abnormal behavior, drug therapy, and psychotherapy. As a physician, the psychiatrist can prescribe medication and, in most states, hospitalization.

The term *psychoanalyst* is reserved for individuals who have received specialized training at a psychoanalytic institute learning the methods and theories derived from Freud. The program usually takes several years, during which the trainees must undergo their own psychoanalysis as well as treat several clients psychoanalytically while under supervision. Until recently, most psychoanalytic institutes required their graduates to have an M.D. degree. Thus, most psychoanalysts are psychiatrists. However, the vast majority of psychiatrists are not psychoanalysts.

Psychologists who work as therapists have obtained graduate training in clinical, counseling, or school psychology. Usually, they hold a Ph.D. (Doctor of Philosophy) or Psy.D. (Doctor of Psychology) degree. The Ph.D. emphasizes training in research as well as diagnosis and therapy. The Psy.D. is a more applied degree, focusing mainly on diagnosis and therapy. Both degrees require four or five years of postgraduate study plus a year or more of internship. In addition, most states require psychologists to pass a licensing or certification examination.

Clinical psychologists work with people suffering from a broad range of mental disorders. Counseling psychologists focus more on problems of adjustment and often concentrate on specific areas such as student, marriage, or family counseling. School psychologists are concerned with young people who have academic difficulties.

Psychiatric social workers have completed a two-year master's degree program (M.S.W.), which includes training in interviewing, therapy, and in extending treatment procedures to the home and community. Some psychiatric social workers also go on to complete a doctorate in social work. A psychiatric social worker is often called on to collect information about a patient's home situation and to assist the patient in getting help from community resources (such as hospitals, clinics, and social agencies).

Sometimes these professionals work as a team. The psychiatrist prescribes psychotherapeutic medications and monitors their effectiveness; the psychologist sees the same client in individual or group psychotherapy; the social worker monitors the home environment and acts as a liaison with community agencies for the client. In mental hospitals a fourth professional is available: the psychiatric nurse. Psychiatric nursing is a field within the nursing profession that requires special training in the understanding and treatment of mental disorders. In our discussion of psychotherapeutic techniques, we will not specify the profession of the psychotherapists; we will assume that they are trained and competent members of any one of these professions.

Techniques of Psychotherapy

Psychotherapy refers to *the treatment of mental disorders by psychological (rather than physical or biological) means.* The term embraces a variety of techniques, all of which are intended to help emotionally disturbed individuals modify their behavior, thoughts, and emotions so that they can develop more useful ways of dealing with stress and with other people. Some psychotherapists (such as psychoanalysts) believe that modification of behavior is dependent on the individual's understanding of his or her unconscious motives and conflicts. Others (such as behavior therapists and cognitive-behavior therapists) focus on changing habitual patterns of thinking and behavior rather than on unconscious conflicts. Despite differences in techniques, most methods of psychotherapy have certain basic features in common. They involve a helping relationship between two people: the client (patient) and the therapist. The client is encouraged to discuss intimate concerns, emotions, and experiences freely without fear of being judged by the therapist or having confidences betrayed. The therapist, in turn, offers empathy and understanding, engenders trust, and tries to help the client develop more effective ways of handling his or her problems.

Psychodynamic Therapies

A key assumption of *psychodynamic therapies* is that a person's current problems cannot be resolved successfully without a thorough understanding of their unconscious basis in early relationships with parents and siblings. The goal of psychoanalysis is to bring conflicts (repressed emotions and motives) into awareness so that they can be dealt with in a more rational and realistic way. The psychodynamic therapies include traditional Freudian psychoanalysis and more recent therapies based on it.

One of the main techniques that psychoanalysts use to recover unconscious conflicts is **free association,** in which *the client is encouraged to give free rein to thoughts and feelings* and to say whatever comes to mind without editing or censoring it. This is not easy to do, however. In conversation we usually try to keep a connecting thread running through our remarks and exclude irrelevant ideas. With practice, free association becomes easier. But even individuals who conscientiously try to give free rein to their thoughts will occasionally find themselves blocked, unable to recall the details of an event or to finish a thought. Freud believed that blocking, or *resistance,* results from the individual's unconscious control over sensitive areas, and that these are precisely the areas that need to be explored.

Another technique often used in traditional psychoanalytic therapy is **dream analysis,** which consists of *talking about the content of one's dreams and then free associating to that content.* Freud believed that dreams are "the royal road to the unconscious"; they represent an unconscious wish or fear in disguised form. He distinguished between dreams' *manifest content* (the obvious, conscious content) and their *latent content* (the hidden, unconscious content). By talking about the manifest content of a dream and then free associating to that content, the analyst and client attempt to discover the dream's unconscious meaning.

As the therapist and client interact during therapy, the client will often react to the therapist in ways that seem exaggerated or inappropriate. The client may become enraged when the therapist must reschedule an appointment, or may be excessively deferential to the therapist. The term **transference** refers to *the tendency for the client to make the therapist the object of emotional responses:* The client expresses attitudes toward the analyst that are actually felt toward other people who are, or were, important in his or her life. By pointing out how their clients are reacting to them, therapists help their clients achieve a better understanding of how they react to others. The following passage illustrates an analyst's use of transference, followed by the use of free association:

CLIENT: I don't understand why you're holding back on telling me if this step is the right one for me at this time in my life.

THERAPIST: This has come up before. You want my approval before taking some action. What seems to be happening here is that one of the conflicts you have with your wife is trying to get her approval of what you have decided you want to do, and that conflict is occurring now between us.

CLIENT: I suppose so. Other people's approval has always been very important to me.

A major technique of psychoanalysis is free association, in which the client is encouraged to give free rein to thoughts and feelings.

THERAPIST: Let's stay with that for a few minutes. Would you free associate to that idea of getting approval from others. Just let the associations come spontaneously—don't force them. (Adapted from Woody & Robertson, 1988, p. 129)

Traditional psychoanalysis is a lengthy, intensive, and expensive process. Client and analyst usually meet for 50-minute sessions several times a week for at least a year, and often for several years. Many people find self-exploration under traditional psychoanalysis to be of value; however, for some people it is unaffordable. In addition, people suffering from acute depression, anxiety, or psychosis typically cannot tolerate the lack of structure in traditional psychoanalysis and need more immediate relief from their symptoms.

In response to these needs, as well as to changes in psychoanalytic theory since Freud's time, newer psychodynamic therapies tend to be more structured and short-term than traditional psychoanalysis. One such therapy is called *interpersonal therapy* (Klerman et al., 1984). Sessions are scheduled less frequently, usually once a week. There is less emphasis on complete reconstruction of childhood experiences and more attention to problems arising from the way the individual is currently interacting with others. Free association is often replaced with direct discussion of critical issues, and the therapist may be more direct, raising pertinent topics when appropriate rather than waiting for the client to bring them up. While transference is still considered an important part of the therapeutic process, the therapist may try to limit the intensity of the transference process. Some research has found interpersonal therapy to be helpful in the treatment of depression, anxiety, drug addiction, and eating disorders (Markowitz & Weissman, 1995).

Still central, however, is the psychoanalytic therapist's conviction that unconscious motives and fears are at the core of most emotional problems and that insight is essential to a cure (Auld & Hyman, 1991). As we will see in the next section, behavior therapists do not agree with these views.

Behavior Therapies

The term *behavior therapy* includes a number of therapeutic methods based on the principles of learning and conditioning (see Chapter 7). Behavior therapists assume that maladaptive behaviors are learned ways of coping with stress and that some of the techniques developed in experimental research on learning can be used to substitute more appropriate responses for maladaptive ones. Whereas psychoanalysis is concerned with understanding how the individual's past conflicts influence behavior, behavior therapy focuses more directly on the behavior itself.

Behavior therapists point out that while the achievement of insight is a worthwhile goal, it does not ensure behavioral change. Often we understand why we behave the way we do in a certain situation but are unable to change our behavior. If you are unusually timid about speaking in class, you may be able to trace this fear to past events (your father criticized your opinions whenever you expressed them, your mother made a point of correcting your grammar, you had little experience in public speaking during high school because you were afraid to compete with your older brother, who was captain of the debate team). Understanding the reasons behind your fear does not necessarily make it easier for you to contribute to class discussions.

In contrast to psychodynamic therapy, which attempts to change certain aspects of the personality, behavior therapies attempt to modify behaviors that are maladaptive in specific situations. In the initial session the therapist listens carefully to the client's statement of the problem. What exactly does the client want to change? Is it a fear of flying or of speaking in public? Difficulty controlling eating or drinking? Feelings of inadequacy and helplessness? Inability to concentrate and get work done? The first step is to define the problem clearly and break it down into a set of specific therapeutic goals. If, for example, the client complains of general feelings of inadequacy, the therapist will try to get the client to describe these feelings more specifically: to pinpoint the kinds of situations in which they occur and the kinds of behaviors associated with them. Inadequate to do what? To speak up in class or in social situations? To get assignments completed on time? To control eating? Once the behaviors that need to be changed have been specified, the therapist and client work out a treatment program, choosing the treatment method that is most appropriate for the particular problem.

Systematic Desensitization and In Vivo Exposure Systematic desensitization and in vivo exposure are two similar but distinct procedures that can both be viewed as deconditioning or counterconditioning processes (Wolpe, 1958). These procedures are highly effective in eliminating fears or phobias. The principle of the treatment is to substitute a response that is incompatible with anxiety—namely, relaxation. (It is difficult to be both relaxed and anxious at the same time.) The client is first trained to relax deeply. One way is to progressively relax various muscles, starting, for example, with the feet and ankles and proceeding up the body to the neck and face. The person learns what muscles feel like when they are truly relaxed and how to discriminate among various degrees of tension. Sometimes drugs and hypnosis are used to help people who cannot relax otherwise.

The next step is to make up a hierarchy of the anxiety-producing situations. The situations are ranked in order from the one that produces the least anxiety to the one that produces the most. In **systematic desensitization,** the *client is then asked to relax and imagine each situation in the hierarchy,* starting with the one that is least anxiety-producing. **In vivo exposure** requires that the *client actually experience the anxiety-producing situations.* In vivo exposure is more effective than simply imagining anxiety-producing situations, but some clients need to begin with imagination and eventually move to actually experiencing feared situations.

An example will make these procedures clearer. Suppose that the client is a woman who suffers from a phobia of snakes. The phobia is so strong that she is afraid to walk in her own back yard, let alone go for a walk in the countryside or on a vacation in a wooded area. Her anxiety hierarchy might begin with a picture of a snake in a book. Somewhere around the middle of the hierarchy might be viewing a snake in a glass cage at the zoo. At the top of the hierarchy would be actually handling a snake. After this woman has learned to relax and has constructed the hierarchy, the therapist begins taking her through her list. In systematic desensitization, she sits with her eyes closed in a comfortable chair while the therapist describes the least anxiety-provoking situation. If she can imagine herself in the situation without any increase in mus-

cle tension, the therapist proceeds to the next item on the list. If the woman reports any anxiety while visualizing a scene, she concentrates on relaxing; the same scene is visualized until all anxiety has been neutralized. This process continues through a series of sessions until the situation that originally provoked the most anxiety now elicits only relaxation. At this point the woman has been systematically desensitized to anxiety-provoking situations through the strengthening of an incompatible response—relaxation.

During in vivo exposure the woman would actually experience each of the situations on her list, beginning with the least feared one, with the coaching of the therapist. Before she actually handled a snake herself, the therapist might model handling the snake without being fearful—the therapist would hold the snake in the client's presence, displaying confidence and no anxiety. Eventually the client would handle the snake herself, allowing it to crawl on her, while using relaxation to control her anxiety. In vivo exposure therapy of this sort has proven extremely effective in the treatment of phobias (Bandura, Blanchard, & Rifter, 1969).

The specific learning process operating in in vivo exposure may be extinction rather than counterconditioning. Exposing oneself to a fear-arousing stimulus and discovering that nothing bad happens extinguishes the conditioned fear response. Relaxation may be merely a useful way to encourage a person to confront the feared object or situation. Indeed, if phobic individuals can force themselves to stay in the feared situation for a long period (for example, a claustrophobic person sits in a closet for hours or someone who fears contamination goes for days without washing), the initial terror gradually subsides. The term **flooding** is used to refer to this procedure, a type of in vivo therapy in which *a phobic individual is exposed to the most feared object or situation for an extended period without an opportunity to escape.* This approach has proved to be particularly effective in the treatment of agoraphobia and obsessive-compulsive disorders (Emmelkamp & Kuipus, 1979; Steketee & White, 1990).

Selective Reinforcement Whether the underlying learning process is counterconditioning or extinction, systematic desensitization and in vivo exposure are based on principles of classical conditioning. **Selective reinforcement,** or *strengthening of specific desired behaviors,* is based on the principles of operant conditioning and has also proved to be an effective method of modifying behavior, especially with children.

The procedure can be illustrated by the case of a third-grade student who was inattentive in school, refused to complete assignments or participate in class, and spent most of her time daydreaming. In addition, her social skills were poor and she had few friends. The behavior to be reinforced was defined as "on task" behavior, which included paying attention to schoolwork or instructions from the teacher, completing reading assignments, and taking part in class discussions. The reinforcement consisted of beans that were used as tokens to be exchanged for special privileges that the girl valued, such as standing first in line (three beans) or being allowed to stay after school to help the teacher with special projects (nine beans). Whenever the teacher observed the student performing on-task behaviors, she placed one bean in a jar.

During the first three months of treatment, the girl completed 12 units of work, compared to none during the previous three months. In the final three months, she completed 36 units and was performing at the same level as the rest of the class. A follow-up the next year showed that the girl was maintaining her academic performance. She also showed marked improvement in social skills and was accepted more by the other children (Walker et al., 1981). This is a common finding: Improving behavior in one area of life often produces benefits in other areas (Kazdin, 1982).

Reinforcement of desirable responses can be accompanied by extinction of undesirable ones. For example, a young boy who habitually shouts to get his mother's attention could be ignored whenever he does so and reinforced by her attention only when he comes to her and speaks in a conversational tone.

Operant conditioning procedures involving rewards for desirable responses and no rewards for undesirable ones have been used successfully in dealing with a broad range of childhood problems, including bed-wetting, aggression, tantrums, disruptive classroom behavior, poor school performance, and social withdrawal. Similar procedures have been used with autistic children, retarded adults, and severely disordered mental patients.

A number of mental hospitals have instituted "token economies" on wards with chronic highly impaired patients to induce socially appropriate behavior. Tokens that can be exchanged for food and privileges such as watching television are given for dressing properly, interacting with other patients, eliminating "psychotic talk," helping on the ward, and so on. Such programs have proved successful in improving both the patients' behavior and the general functioning of the ward (Paul & Lentz, 1977).

Modeling Another effective means of changing behavior is modeling. **Modeling** is *the process by which person learns behaviors by observing and imitating others.* Since observing others is a major way in which humans learn, watching people who are displaying adaptive behavior should teach people with maladaptive responses better coping strategies. Observing the behavior of a model (either live or videotaped) has proved effective in reducing fears and teaching new skills. Figure 16-3 shows the results of a study in which modeling was combined with gradual practice in the treatment of snake phobia.

Modeling is effective in overcoming fears and anxieties because it provides an opportunity to observe someone else go through

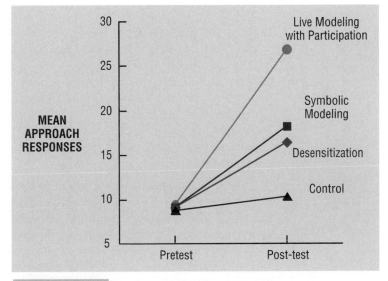

FIGURE 16-3

Treatment of Snake Phobia *The mean number of snake-approach responses by individuals before and after they received different behavior therapy treatments.* (After Bandura, Blanchard, & Ritter, 1969)

the anxiety-provoking situation without getting hurt. Watching videotapes of models enjoying a visit to the dentist or going through various hospital procedures has proved successful in helping both children and adults overcome their fears of such experiences (Melamed & Siegel, 1975; Shaw & Thoresen, 1974).

Behavioral Rehearsal   In a therapy session, modeling is often combined with **behavioral rehearsal,** or *role playing.* The therapist helps the client rehearse or practice more adaptive behaviors. In the following excerpt, a therapist helps a young man overcome his anxieties about asking women for dates. The young man has been pretending to talk to a woman over the phone and finishes by asking for a date.

CLIENT: Um, I was wondering, you wouldn't want to go out on a date Saturday night, or anything, would you?

THERAPIST: Okay, that's a start. Can you think of another way of asking her out that sounds a bit more positive and confident? For example, "There's a concert I'd like to see on Saturday night and I'd like very much to take you, if you are free."

CLIENT: That's great!

THERAPIST: Okay, you try it.

CLIENT: Um, I've got two tickets to the concert Saturday night. If you don't have anything to do, you might want to come along.

THERAPIST: That's better. Try it one more time, but this time try to convey to her that you'd really like her to go.

CLIENT: I've got two tickets for Saturday's concert. It would be great if you'd go with me, if you're not busy.

THERAPIST: Great! Just practice it a couple of more times, and you're ready to pick up the phone.

This example illustrates the use of behavioral rehearsal in a type of behavior therapy known as *assertiveness training.* Like the young man in the example, many people have trouble asking for what they want or refusing to allow others to take advantage of them. By practicing assertive responses (first in role-playing with the therapist and then in real-life situations), the individual not only reduces anxiety but also develops more effective coping techniques. The therapist determines the kinds of situations in which the person is passive and then helps him or her think of and practice some assertive responses that might be effective. The following are examples of situations that might be worked through during a sequence of therapy sessions:

- Someone steps in front of you in line.
- A friend asks you to do something that you do not want to do.
- Your boss criticizes you unjustly.
- You return defective merchandise to a store.
- You are annoyed by the conversation of people behind you in a movie theater.
- The mechanic did an unsatisfactory job of repairing your car.

Most people do not enjoy dealing with such situations, but some are so fearful of asserting themselves that they say nothing and instead build up feelings of resentment and inadequacy. In assertiveness training, the client rehearses with the therapist effective responses that could be made in such situations, and then gradually tries them out in real life. The therapist tries to teach the client to express his or her needs in a way that is straightforward and forceful but is not seen by others as hostile or threatening (see Table 16-2).

Self-Regulation   Because the client and therapist seldom meet more than once per week, the client must learn to control or regulate his or her own behavior so that progress can be made outside the therapy hour. Moreover, if people feel that they are responsible for their own improvement, they are more likely to maintain whatever gains they make. **Self-regulation** involves *monitoring, or observing, one's own behavior* and using various techniques—self-reinforcement, self-punishment, control of stimulus conditions, development of incompatible responses—to change maladaptive behavior. An individual monitors his or her behavior by keeping a careful record of the kinds of situations that elicit the maladaptive behavior and the kinds of responses that are incompatible with it. For example, a person who is concerned with alcohol abuse would note the kinds of situations in which he or she is most tempted to drink and would try to control such situations or devise a response that is incompatible with drinking. A man

TABLE 16-2

Some Elements of an Assertive Response

- Decide what you want to say and stick with it rather than giving into others the minute they disagree with you. For example, when a clerk says you cannot return a defective product, say "This is defective and I want to return it" repeatedly until the clerk allows you to return it or at least calls the manager, whom you tell "This is defective and I want to return it" until you get your money back.

- Ask for small, specific changes in a situation or another person's behavior rather than requesting global changes. For example, rather than saying, "I want you to be more loving," say, "I want you to listen to me when I talk."

- Use "I" phrases instead of accusatory phrases when discussing a difficult situation with another person. Four pieces to an "I" statement are:

  I feel . . .

  when you . . .

  because . . .

  what I want . . .

  For example, *"I feel* angry *when you* don't show up for an appointment *because* it wastes my time. *What I want* is for you to call me and cancel our appointment when you think you won't be able to make it."

who finds it hard not to join his co-workers in a noontime cocktail might plan to eat lunch at his desk, thereby controlling his drinking behavior by controlling his environment. If he is tempted to relax with a drink upon arriving home from work, he might substitute a game of tennis or a jog around the block as a means of relieving tension. Both of these activities would be incompatible with drinking.

Self-reinforcement is rewarding yourself immediately for achieving a specific goal; the reward could be praising yourself, watching a favorite television program, telephoning a friend, eating a favorite food. *Self-punishment* is arranging for an aversive consequence for failing to achieve a goal, such as depriving yourself of something you enjoy (not watching a favorite television program, for instance) or making yourself do an unpleasant task (such as cleaning your room). Depending on the kind of behavior you want to change, various combinations of self-reinforcement, self-punishment, or control of stimuli and responses may be used.

Table 16-3 outlines a program for self-regulation of eating.

Cognitive-Behavior Therapies

The behavior therapy procedures discussed so far have focused on modifying behavior directly; they devote little attention to the individual's thinking and reasoning processes. Initially, behavior therapists discounted the importance of cognition, preferring a strict stimulus-response approach. However, in response to evidence that cognitive factors—thoughts, expectations, and interpretation of events—are important determinants of behavior, many behavior therapists now incorporate cognitions in their approaches to therapy (Bandura, 1986).

Cognitive-behavior therapy is a general term for treatment methods that use behavior modification techniques but also incorporate procedures designed to change maladaptive beliefs. The therapist attempts to help the client control disturbing emotional reactions, such as anxiety and depression, by teaching more effective ways of interpreting and thinking about experiences. For example, as we noted in discussing Beck's cognitive theory of depression (see Chapter 15), depressed individuals tend to appraise events from a negative and self-critical viewpoint. They expect to fail rather than succeed, and they tend to magnify failures and minimize successes in evaluating their performance. In treating depression, cognitive-behavior therapists try to help clients recognize the distortions in their thinking and make changes that are more in line with reality. The following dialogue illustrates how a therapist, through carefully directed questioning, makes a client aware of the unrealistic nature of her beliefs.

THERAPIST: Why do you want to end your life?

CLIENT: Without Raymond, I am nothing. . . . I can't be happy without Raymond. . . . But I can't save our marriage.

THERAPIST: What has your marriage been like?

CLIENT: It has been miserable from the very beginning. . . . Raymond has always been unfaithful. . . . I have hardly seen him in the past five years.

TABLE 16-3

TABLE 16-3

Self-Regulation of Eating *This program illustrates the use of learning principles to help control food intake.* (After Stuart & Davis, 1972; O'Leary & Wilson, 1975)

	Self-Monitoring
Daily Log	Keep a detailed record of everything you eat. Note the amount eaten, the type of food and its caloric value, the time of day, and the circumstances of eating. This record will establish the caloric intake that is maintaining your present weight. It will also help identify the stimuli that elicit and reinforce your eating behavior.
Weight Chart	Decide how much weight you want to lose, and set a weekly weight loss goal. Your weekly goal should be realistic (between 1 and 2 pounds). Record your weight each day on graph paper. In addition to showing how your weight varies with food intake, this visual record will reinforce your dieting efforts as you observe progress toward your goal.

Controlling Stimulus Conditions

Use these procedures to narrow the range of stimuli associated with eating:

1. Eat only at predetermined times, at a specific table, using a special place mat, napkin, dishes, and so forth. Do *not* eat at other times or in other places (for example, while standing in the kitchen).
2. Do *not* combine eating with other activities, such as reading or watching television.
3. Keep in the house only the foods that are permitted on your diet.
4. Shop for food only after having had a full meal; buy only items that are on a previously prepared list.

Modifying Actual Eating Behavior

Use these procedures to break the chain of responses that makes eating automatic.

1. Eat very slowly, paying close attention to the food.
2. Finish chewing and swallowing before putting more food on the fork.
3. Put your utensils down for periodic short breaks before continuing to eat.

Developing Incompatible Responses

When tempted to eat at times other than those specified, find a substitute activity that is incompatible with eating. For example, exercise to music, go for a walk, talk with a friend (preferably one who knows that you are dieting), or study your diet plan and weight graph, noting how much weight you have lost.

Self-Reinforcement

Arrange to reward yourself with an activity that you enjoy (watching television, reading, planning a new wardrobe, visiting a friend) when you have maintained appropriate eating behavior for a day. Plan larger rewards (for example, buying something you want) for a specified amount of weight loss. Self-punishment (other than forgoing a reward) is probably less effective because dieting is a fairly depressing business anyway. But you might decrease the frequency of binge eating by immediately reciting to yourself the aversive consequences or by looking at an unattractive picture of yourself in a bathing suit.

THERAPIST: You say that you can't be happy without Raymond. . . . Have you found yourself happy when you are with Raymond?

CLIENT: No, we fight all the time and I feel worse.

THERAPIST: You say you are nothing without Raymond. Before you met Raymond, did you feel you were nothing?

CLIENT: No, I felt I was somebody.

THERAPIST: If you were somebody before you knew Raymond, why do you need him [in order] to be somebody now?

CLIENT: (puzzled) Hmmm. . . .

THERAPIST: If you were free of the marriage, do you think that men might be interested in you—knowing that you were available?

CLIENT: I guess that maybe they would be.

THERAPIST: Is it possible that you might find a man who would be more constant than Raymond?

CLIENT: I don't know. . . . I guess it's possible. . . .

THERAPIST: Then what have you actually lost if you break up the marriage?

CLIENT: I don't know.

THERAPIST: Is it possible that you'll get along better if you end the marriage?

CLIENT: There is no guarantee of that.

THERAPIST: Do you have a real marriage?

CLIENT: I guess not.

THERAPIST: If you don't have a real marriage, what do you actually lose if you decide to end the marriage?

CLIENT: (long pause) Nothing, I guess. (Beck, 1976, pp. 280–291)

The behavioral component of the treatment comes into play when the therapist encourages the client to formulate alternative ways of viewing her situation and then test the implications of those alternatives. For example, the woman client in the preceding dialogue might be asked to record her moods at regular intervals and then to note how her depression and feelings of self-esteem fluctuate as a function of what she is doing. If she finds that she feels worse after interacting with her husband than when she is alone or is interacting with someone else, this information could serve to challenge her belief that she "can't be happy without Raymond."

A cognitive-behavioral program to help someone overcome agoraphobia might include training in positive thinking, along with in vivo exposure (accompanied excursions that take the individual progressively farther from home). The therapist teaches the client to replace self-defeating internal dialogues ("I'm so nervous, I know I'll faint as soon as I leave the house") with positive self-instructions ("Be calm; I'm not alone; even if I have a panic attack, I can cope"). Table 16-4 describes a program for the treatment of depression that includes techniques for modifying behavior and changing attitudes.

Cognitive-behavior therapists agree that it is important to alter a person's beliefs in order to bring about an enduring change in behavior. Most maintain that behavioral procedures are more powerful than strictly verbal ones in affecting cognitive processes. For example, to overcome anxiety about giving a speech in class, it is helpful to think positively: "I know the material well, and I'm sure I can present my ideas effectively"; "The topic is interesting, and the other students will enjoy what I have to say." But first presenting the speech to a roommate and again before a group of friends will probably do more to reduce anxiety. Successful performance increases our feeling of mastery. In fact, it has been suggested that all therapeutic procedures that are effective give the client a sense of mastery or self-efficacy. Observing others cope and succeed, being verbally persuaded that we can handle a difficult situation, and judging from internal cues that we are relaxed and in control contribute to feelings of self-efficacy. But the greatest sense of efficacy comes from actual performance, from the experience of mastery. In essence, nothing succeeds like success (Bandura, 1995).

Combined cognitive-behavioral therapies have proven highly effective in treating an array of nonpsychotic conditions, including depression, anxiety disorders, eating disorders, drug and alcohol dependence, and sexual dysfunctions (Fairburn et al., 1995; Jacobson & Hollon, 1996; Margraf et al., 1993; Marlatt et al., 1993; Rosen & Lieblum, 1995) (see Figure 16-4). These therapies

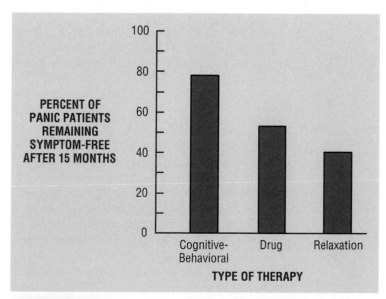

FIGURE 16-4

Percentage of Panic Patients Remaining Symptom-Free After 15 Months
People receiving cognitive-behavioral therapy for panic disorder were more likely to remain symptom-free over 15 months than people receiving only drug therapy or relaxation training. (After Clark et al., 1994)

TABLE 16-4

Coping With Depression   *A program for the treatment of depression that combines behavioral and cognitive techniques. This is a condensed description of a 12-session course used to treat depressed individuals in small groups.* (After Lewnsohn et al., 1984)

Instruction in Self-Change Skills
Pinpointing the target behavior and recording its baseline rate of occurrence; discovering the events or situations that precede the target behavior and the consequences (either positive or negative) that follow it; setting goals for change and choosing reinforcers
Relaxation Training
Learning progressive muscle relaxation to handle the anxiety that often accompanies depression; monitoring tension in daily situations; and applying relaxation techniques.
Increasing Pleasant Activities
Monitoring the frequency of enjoyable activities and planning weekly schedules so that each day contains a balance between negative/neutral activities and pleasant ones.
Cognitive Strategies
Learning methods for increasing positive thoughts and decreasing negative ones; for identifying irrational thoughts and challenging them; and for using self-instructions to help handle problem situations.
Assertiveness Training
Identifying situations in which being nonassertive adds to feelings of depression; learning to handle social interactions more assertively via modeling and role playing.
Increasing Social Interaction
Identifying the factors that are contributing to low social interaction (such as getting into the habit of doing things alone, feeling uncomfortable due to few social skills); deciding on activities that need to be increased (such as calling friends to suggest getting together) or decreased (such as watching television) in order to increase the level of pleasant social interaction.

tend not only to help people overcome troubling thoughts, feelings, and behaviors but also to prevent relapses after therapy has ended.

Humanistic Therapies

Humanistic therapies are based on the humanistic approach to personality discussed in Chapter 13. They emphasize the individual's natural tendency toward growth and self-actualization. Psychological disorders are assumed to arise when circumstances or other people (parents, teachers, spouses) prevent the individual from achieving his or her potential. When this occurs people begin to deny their true desires, and their potential for growth is reduced. Humanistic therapies seek to help people get in touch with their real selves and make deliberate choices regarding their lives and behavior rather than being controlled by external events. The goal of humanistic therapy is to help the client become the person he or she is capable of becoming.

Like the psychoanalyst, the humanistic therapist attempts to increase the client's awareness of underlying emotions and motives. But the emphasis is on what the individual is experiencing in the here and now, rather than in the past. The humanistic therapist does not interpret the client's behavior (as a psychoanalyst might) or try to modify it (as a behavior therapist would), because this would amount to imposing the therapist's views on the patient. The goal of the humanistic therapist is to facilitate exploration of the individual's own thoughts and feelings and to assist the individual in arriving at his or her own solutions. This approach will become clearer as we look at client-centered therapy (also called nondirective therapy), one of the first humanistic therapies.

Client-centered therapy, developed in the 1940s by the late Carl Rogers, is based on the assumption that each individual is the best expert on himself or herself and that people are capable of working out solutions to their own problems. The task of the therapist is to facilitate this process—not to ask probing questions, make interpretations, or suggest courses of action. In fact, Rogers preferred the term "facilitator" to "therapist," and he called the people he worked with "clients" rather than "patients" because he did not view emotional difficulties as indications of an illness to be cured.

The therapist facilitates the client's progress toward self-insight by restating what the client says about his or her needs and emotions. Rogers believed that the most important qualities for a therapist are empathy, warmth, and genuineness. *Empathy* refers to the ability to understand the feelings the client is trying to express and the ability to communicate this understanding to the client. The therapist must adopt the client's frame of reference and strive to see the problems as the client sees them. By *warmth* Rogers meant acceptance of individuals the way they are, including the conviction that they have the capacity to deal constructively with their problems. A therapist who is *genuine* is open and honest and does not play a role or operate behind a professional façade. People are reluctant to reveal themselves to those whom they perceive as phony. Rogers believed that a therapist who possesses these three attributes will facilitate the client's growth and self-exploration (Rogers, 1970).

Rogers was the first therapist to make tape recordings of therapy sessions and permit them to be studied and analyzed. He and his colleagues have contributed much to psychotherapy research. Client-centered therapy has some limitations, however. Like psychoanalysis, it appears to be successful only with individuals who are fairly verbal and are motivated to discuss their problems. For people who do not voluntarily seek help or are seriously disturbed and unable to discuss their feelings, more directive methods are usually necessary. In addition, by using the client's self-reports as the only measure of psychotherapeutic effectiveness, the client-centered therapist ignores behavior outside of the therapy session. Individuals who feel insecure and ineffective in their interpersonal relationships often need more structured help in modifying their behavior.

An Eclectic Approach

There are many variations of psychotherapy besides the ones described here. Several are listed in Table 16-5. Most psychotherapists do not adhere strictly to any single method. Instead, they take an eclectic approach, selecting from the different techniques the ones that they feel are most appropriate given the client's personality and specific symptoms. Although their theoretical orientation may be toward a particular method or school (for example, more psychoanalytic than behaviorist), eclectic psychotherapists feel free to discard concepts that they view as not especially helpful and to select techniques from other schools. In addition, many psychotherapists use both psychotherapeutic techniques and drug therapies in treating clients with more severe problems. (Psychotherapists who are not physicians will work with a psychiatrist who will prescribe drugs for their patients.)

In dealing with a highly anxious individual, for instance, an eclectic psychotherapist might first prescribe tranquilizers or relaxation training to help reduce the client's level of anxiety. (Most psychoanalysts would not take this approach, however, because they believe that anxiety is necessary to motivate the client to explore his or her conflicts.) To help the client understand the origins of his or her problems, the therapist might discuss certain aspects of the patient's history but might consider it unnecessary to explore childhood experiences to the extent that a psychoanalyst would. The therapist might use educational techniques, such as providing information about sex and reproduction to help relieve the anxieties of an adolescent boy who feels guilty about his sexual impulses, or explaining the functioning of the autonomic nervous system to reassure an anxious woman that some of her symptoms, such as heart palpitations and hand tremors, are not indications of a disease.

Recognizing that often no single therapeutic approach deals successfully with all aspects of a problem, more and more therapists are specializing in specific problems. For example, some clinicians specialize in

TABLE 16-5

Other Approaches to Psychotherapy.   *Listed here are several psychotherapies that are not discussed in the text.*

Name	Focus of Therapy	Principal Methods
Gestalt therapy	To become aware of the whole personality by working through unresolved conflicts and discovering aspects of the individual's being that are blocked from awareness. Emphasis is on becoming intensely aware of how one is feeling and behaving at the moment	Therapy in a group setting, but therapist works with one individual at a time. Acting out fantasies, dreams, or the two sides to a conflict are methods used to increase awareness. Combines psychoanalytic emphasis on resolving internal conflicts with behaviorist emphasis on awareness of one's behavior and humanistic concern for self-actualization
Reality therapy	To clarify the individual's values and evaluate current behavior and future plans in relation to these values. To force the individual to accept responsibility.	Therapist helps the individual perceive the consequences of possible courses of action and decide on a realistic solution or goal. Once a plan of action has been chosen, a contract may be signed in which the client agrees to follow through.
Rational-Emotive therapy	To replace irrational ideas (It is essential to be loved and admired by everyone all the time; I should be competent in all respects; People have little control over their sorrow and unhappiness) with more realistic ones. Assumes that cognitive change will produce emotional changes.	Therapist attacks and contradicts the individual's ideas (sometime subtly, sometimes directly) in an attempt to persuade her or him to take a more rational view of the situation. Similar to Beck's cognitive therapy, but the therapist is more direct and confrontive.
Transactional analysis	To become aware of the intent behind the individual's communications; to eliminate subterfuge and deceit so that the individual can interpret his or her behavior accurately.	Therapy in a group setting. Communications between married couples or group members are analyzed in terms of the part of the personality that is speaking—"parent," "child," or "adult" (similar to Freud's superego, id, and ego)—and the intent of the message. Destructive social interactions or "games" are exposed for what they are.
Hypnotherapy	To relieve the symptoms and strengthen ego processes by helping the individual set reality aside and make constructive use of imagery.	Therapist uses various hypnotic procedures in an attempt to reduce conflict and doubt by focusing the individual's attention, to modify symptoms through direct suggestion or displacement, and to strengthen the individual's ability to cope.

sexual dysfunction. They learn all they can about the physiological processes that lead to orgasm; the effects of drugs such as alcohol, tranquilizers, and other medications on sexual performance; and the ways in which such factors as anxiety, sexual traumas, and poor communication between partners contribute to sexual dysfunction. Once they have learned all they can about the variables involved in normal and abnormal sexual functioning, they examine the various therapeutic systems to see what techniques can be applied to specific problems. Although sex therapists may draw upon all of the approaches we have discussed, biological and cognitive-behavioral methods are most often used in treating sexual dysfunctions.

Other therapists specialize in anxiety, depression, alcoholism, and marital problems. Some concentrate on certain age groups, seeking to learn all they can about the problems of children, adolescents, or the aged. Within their area of specialization, therapists generally use an eclectic approach.

Group and Family Therapy

Many emotional problems involve difficulties in relating to others, including feelings of isolation, rejection, and loneliness and

An advantage of group therapy is that participants can observe how other people react to problems similar to theirs.

inability to form meaningful relationships. Although the therapist can help the client work out some of these problems, the final test lies in how well the person can apply the attitudes and responses learned in therapy to relationships in everyday life. *Group therapy* permits clients to work out their problems in the presence of others, observe how other people react to their behavior, and try out new ways of responding when old ones prove unsatisfactory. It is often used as a supplement to individual psychotherapy.

Psychoanalytic, humanistic, and cognitive-behaviorist therapists have modified their techniques so that they can be used with groups. Group therapy has been used in a variety of settings: in hospital wards and outpatient psychiatric clinics, with parents of disturbed children, and with teenagers in correctional institutions, to name a few. Typically, a group consists of a small number of individuals (six to eight is considered optimal) who have similar problems. The therapist usually remains in the background, allowing group members to exchange experiences, comment on one another's behavior, and discuss their own problems as well as those of the other members. However, in some groups the therapist is quite active. For example, in a group desensitization session, people who share the same phobias (such as fear of flying or anxiety about tests) may be led through a systematic desensitization hierarchy. Or in a session for training social skills a group of shy and unassertive

individuals may be coached in a series of role-playing scenes.

Group therapy has several advantages over individual therapy. It uses the therapist's resources more efficiently because one therapist can help several people at once. An individual can derive comfort and support from observing that others have similar, perhaps more severe problems. A person can learn vicariously by watching how others behave, and can explore attitudes and reactions by interacting with a variety of people, not just with the therapist. Groups are

Among the techniques used by Alcoholics Anonymous is detailed instruction about the social impact of alcoholism as well as its physical effects.

particularly effective when they give participants opportunities to acquire new social skills through modeling and to practice these skills in the group.

Most groups are led by a trained therapist. However, the number and variety of **self-help groups**—*groups that are conducted without a professional therapist*—is increasing. Self-help groups are voluntary organizations of people who meet regularly to exchange information and support one another's efforts to overcome a common problem. Alcoholics Anonymous is the best known of these groups. Another well-known self-help group is Recovery, Inc., an organization open to former mental patients. Other groups help people cope with specific stressful situations such as bereavement, divorce, and single parenthood. Table 16-6 lists a variety of self-help groups.

Marital and Family Therapy Problems in communicating feelings, satisfying one's needs, and responding appropriately to the needs and demands of others become intensified in the intimate context of marriage and family life. To the extent that they involve more than one client and focus on interpersonal relationships, marital therapy and family therapy can be considered specialized forms of group therapy.

The high divorce rate and the number of couples seeking help for difficulties in their relationship have made *marital* or *couple therapy* a growing field. Studies show that joint therapy for both partners is more effective in solving marital problems than individual therapy for only one partner (Baucom et al., 1998). Marital therapy can also be very helpful when one partner has a psychological disorder whose symptoms or consequences are disrupting the marriage.

There are many approaches to marital therapy, but most focus on helping the partners communicate their feelings, develop greater understanding and sensitivity to each other's needs, and work on more effective ways of handling their conflicts. Some couples enter marriage with very different, and often unrealistic, expectations about the roles of husband and wife. The therapist can help them clarify their expectations and work out a mutually agreeable compromise. Sometimes the couple negotiates behavioral contracts, agreeing on the behavior changes

TABLE 16-6

Examples of Self-Help Groups *Listed here are some of the self-help groups available in one large community.* (After San Diego Mental Health Association, 1989)

AIDS Counseling Program
AIRS (teenage chemical dependency)
Adult Children of Alcoholics
Adults Molested as Children
Affective Disorders Group (mood disorders)
Al-Anon (families of alcoholics)
Ala-Teen (teenage alcohol abuse)
Alcoholics Anonymous
Alzheimer's Disease Family Support Group
Arthritis Support Group
Battered Women's Support Group
Bi-Polar Support Group (manic-depression)
CREATE (college students recovering from mental illness)
Emotional Health Anonymous
Epilepsy Support Group
Gay Men's Coming-Out Group
Grandmothers' Support Group (mothers of teenage mothers)
Lesbian Support Group
Loss Support (grief recovery)
Make Today Count (breast cancer support)
PMS Association (premenstrual syndrome)
Parent Aid (parents at risk for child abuse)
Parents United (sexual abuse)
Parkinson's Disease Support Group
Pre Ala-Teen (child alcohol dependency)
Project Return (recovering mental patients)
Recovery, Inc.
Phobia Foundation
Single Parent Support Group
Survivors of Suicide
Teen Mothers Support Group
Victims of Homicide (family and loved ones)
Voices (schizophrenic support group)

each person is willing to make in order to create a more satisfying relationship, and specifying rewards and penalties for making, or not making, the desired changes.

Family therapy overlaps with marital therapy but has a somewhat different origin. It developed in response to the discovery that many people who improved in individual therapy away from their families—often in institutional settings—relapsed when they returned home. It became apparent that many of these people came from disturbed family settings that must be modified if the individual's gains were to be maintained. In the case of children with psychological problems it is particularly important that the family be treated. The basic premise of family therapy is that the problem shown by the identified patient is a sign that something is wrong with the entire family; the *family system* is not operating properly. The difficulty may lie in poor communication among family members or in an alliance between some family members that excludes others. For example, a mother whose relationship with her husband is unsatisfactory may focus all her attention on her son. As a result, the husband and daughter feel neglected and the son, upset by his mother's excessive attention and the resentment directed toward him by his father and sister, develops problems in school. While the boy's school difficulties may be the reason for seeking treatment, it is clear that they are only a symptom of a more basic family problem.

In family therapy, the family meets regularly with one or two therapists (usually a male and a female). The therapist observes the interactions among family members and tries to help each member become aware of the way he or she relates to the others and how his or her actions may be contributing to the family's problems. Sometimes videotape recordings are played back to make the family members aware of how they interact. At other times the therapist may visit the family at home to observe conflicts and verbal exchanges as they occur in their natural setting. It often becomes apparent that problem behaviors are being reinforced by the responses of family members. For example, a young child's temper tantrums or a teenager's eating problems may be inadvertently reinforced by the attention they elicit from the parents. The therapist can teach the parents to monitor their own and their children's behavior, determine how their reactions may be reinforcing the problem behavior, and then alter the reinforcement contingencies.

An important application of family therapy is in teaching families of people with schizophrenia to communicate more positively and clearly (Goldstein, 1987). Schizophrenics in families in which conflict and hostility are expressed in hurtful ways and in which family members are overinvolved in each other's lives tend to have more frequent relapses than schizophrenics in families in which conflict and hostility are expressed more calmly and family members respect each other's independence. Training programs that enhance family members' skills in expressing negative emotion and interacting in positive ways can reduce relapse rates for people with schizophrenia.

Special Issues in Treating Children

Every therapy we have described has probably been used at one time or another to treat children and adolescents with psychological disorders. Studies of the effectiveness of psychological and biological therapies generally show that children and adolescents who receive therapy have better outcomes than those who receive no therapy (Weisz et al., 1995). The effectiveness of any specific type of therapy may depend largely on the type of disorder the child or adolescent has.

Designing and applying effective therapies for children and adolescents is made difficult by the need to match the therapy to the child's developmental level; the possibility that a therapy will have long-term negative effects on the child's development; the fact that children are embedded in families, and often the family as well as the child must be treated; and the fact that children and adolescents seldom refer themselves for treatment and hence often are not motivated to engage in therapy.

Unfortunately, most children who could benefit from therapy do not receive it. Treatment facilities specializing in children's problems are not available in many parts of the United States. Perhaps 50% of psychologically disturbed children receive advice or medications only from their family physicians, who are not trained in the assessment and treatment of psychological disorders (Tuma, 1989). The child welfare system sees many troubled children, often the victims of abuse and neglect. Increasingly, such children are placed in long-term foster care rather than given specialized psychological

Selective reinforcement can be used to help children learn to control tantrums.

treatment. Many children in the juvenile justice system suffer from psychological disorders, but few receive long-term intensive treatment (Tuma, 1989). Thus, there is considerable room for the expansion of services to psychologically disturbed children.

The Effectiveness of Psychotherapy

How effective is psychotherapy? Which methods work best? These questions are not easy to answer. Research on the effectiveness of psychotherapy is hampered by several major difficulties. How do we decide whether an individual has improved? What measures of improvement are valid? How do we know what caused the change? In this section we look briefly at research on the effectiveness of various types of therapy.

Evaluating Psychotherapy

It is difficult to evaluate the effectiveness of psychotherapy because so many variables must be considered. For instance, some people with psychological problems get better without any professional treatment. This phenomenon is called *spontaneous remission*. People with some types of mental disorders do improve simply with the passage of time. More often, however, improvement that occurs in the absence of treatment is not spontaneous; rather, it is the result of external events such as the help of another person or changes in the individual's life situation.

Many emotionally disturbed people who do not seek professional assistance are able to improve with the help of a nonprofessional, such as a friend, teacher, or religious adviser. We cannot consider these recoveries to be spontaneous; but since they are not due to psychotherapy, they are included in the rate of spontaneous remission, which ranges from about 30% to 60%, depending on the particular disorder being studied (Bergin & Lambert, 1979). To allow for those who would have improved without treatment, any evaluation of psychotherapy must compare a treated group with an untreated control group. Psychotherapy is judged to be effective if the client's improvement after therapy is greater than any improvement that occurs without therapy over the same period. The ethical problem of allowing someone to go without treatment is usually resolved by composing the control group of individuals on a waiting list. Members of the waiting-list control group are interviewed at the beginning of the study to gather baseline information, but they receive no treatment until after the study. Unfortunately, the longer the study (and time is needed to measure improvement, especially with insight therapies), the harder it is to keep people on a waiting list.

A second major problem in evaluating psychotherapy is measuring the outcome. How do we decide whether a person has been helped by therapy? We cannot always rely on the individual's own assessment. Some people report that they are feeling better simply to please the therapist or to convince themselves that their money was well spent. The therapist's evaluation of the treatment as successful cannot always be considered an objective criterion, either. The therapist has a vested interest in proclaiming that the client is better. And sometimes the changes that the therapist observes during the therapy session do not carry over into real-life situations. Assessment of improvement, therefore, should include at least three independent measures: the client's evaluation of progress; the therapist's evaluation; and the judgment of third parties such as family members and friends or a clinician not involved in the treatment.

Despite these problems, researchers have been able to conduct many psychotherapy evaluation studies. In 1952 the well-known British psychologist Hans Eysenck stunned the field when he reviewed studies evaluating the effectiveness of psychotherapy and concluded that psychotherapy did not work. People who had received psychotherapy apparently fared no better than people who were not treated or were placed on a waiting list. The number and quality of studies evaluating psychotherapies prior to 1952 was limited, however. Not surprisingly, Eysenck's review prompted a great deal of new research. Several reviews of this research over the last five decades have concluded that psychotherapy does indeed have positive effects and is better than no treatment at all or various placebos (Lambert & Bergin, 1994; Luborsky, Singer, & Luborsky, 1975; Smith, Glass, & Miller, 1980; Wampold et al., 1997). In 1980, for example, a group of investigators located 475 published studies that compared at least one therapy group with an untreated control group. Using the statistical procedure known as meta-analysis (see Chapter 6), they determined the magnitude of effect for each study by comparing the average change produced in treatment (on measures such as self-esteem, anxiety, and achievement in work and school) with that experienced by the control group. They concluded that individuals receiving therapy were better off than those who had received no treatment. The average psychotherapy patient showed greater improvement than 80% of the untreated patients (Smith, Glass, & Miller, 1980).

A subsequent review that analyzed a new sample of studies yielded comparable results (Shapiro & Shapiro, 1982). When we look at improvement rates as a function of number of therapy sessions (see Figure 16-5), it is clear that treated groups show a rate of change that is above and beyond spontaneous remission estimates. By the eighth therapy session approximately 50% of patients show a measurable improvement,

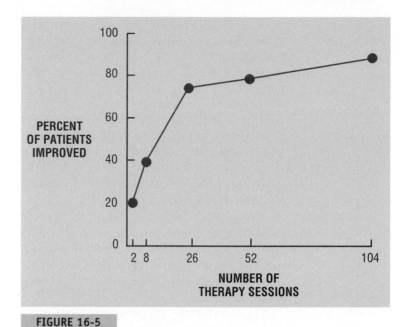

FIGURE 16-5

Improvement with Psychotherapy   *This figure shows the relationship between the number of sessions of individual psychotherapy and the percent of patients who improved. Improvement was rated by independent researchers following termination of treatment.* (After Howard et al.,1986)

and 75% show improvement by the end of six months of weekly psychotherapy.

Comparing Psychotherapies

Psychotherapy produces greater improvement than no treatment, but are the different therapeutic approaches equally effective? A number of reviews have analyzed studies in which the results of different psychotherapies were compared (Bergin & Lambert, 1979; Rachman & Wilson, 1980; Smith, Glass, & Miller, 1980). The conclusion of most of these reviews is that there is little difference in effectiveness between therapies. How can therapies that espouse such different methods produce such similar results? Numerous possible explanations have been suggested (Stiles, Shapiro, & Elliott, 1986). We will discuss two of them here.

Perhaps certain therapies are effective for certain problems or disorders but relatively ineffective for others. When specific therapies are used to treat a wide range of disorders, they may help in some cases but not in others. Thus, averaging results over cases may conceal the special strengths of a particular therapy. We need to know which treatment is effective for which problem (Chambless & Hollon, 1998). Several controlled studies have been done in which different types of psychotherapy were compared to drug therapy or to controls in which people received no therapy for a specific disorder. These studies clearly suggest that certain forms of psychotherapy can be highly effective in the treatment of depression, anxiety disorders, eating disorders, substance abuse disorders, and several childhood disorders (De Rubeis & Crits-Cristoph, 1998; Kazdin & Weisz, 1998; Roth et al., 1996). Psychotherapy can also help reduce symptoms of autism and schizophrenia and lower the risk of relapse in schizophrenia (Hogarty, 1986; Kazdin & Weisz, 1998).

Not all forms of psychotherapy have undergone rigorous empirical tests for effectiveness, however. In general, proponents of behavioral and cognitive approaches have been interested in testing the efficacy of their therapies, so many studies have focused on these types of therapies. In contrast, proponents of psychodynamic and humanistic therapies have been less concerned with empirical tests of their therapies (De Rubeis & Crits-Cristoph, 1998).

Another reason why different psychotherapies may be equally effective in helping clients is because they all share certain factors. It may be these common factors, rather than the specific therapeutic techniques employed, that promote positive change.

Common Factors in Psychotherapies

One school of therapy emphasizes insight; another, modeling and reinforcement; yet another, rational cognitions. But perhaps these variables are not the crucial ones. Other factors that are common to most psychotherapies may be more important (Garfield, 1994; Orlinsky & Howard, 1987). They include a trusting relationship, reassurance and support, desensitization, reinforcement of adaptive responses, and insight.

An Interpersonal Relationship of Warmth and Trust   Regardless of the type of therapy, in a good therapeutic relationship the client and the therapist have mutual respect and regard. The client must believe that the therapist understands and is concerned with his or her problems. A therapist who understands our problems and believes we can solve them earns our trust, which increases our sense of competence and our confidence that we can succeed.

Reassurance and Support   Our problems often seem insurmountable and unique to us. Discussing them with an expert who accepts our difficulties as not unusual and indicates that they can be resolved is reassuring. Having someone help us with problems that we have not been able to solve alone also provides a sense of support and a feeling of hope. In fact, the most successful therapists, regardless of method, are those who form a helpful, supportive relationship with their clients (Luborsky et al., 1985).

Desensitization   We have already talked about *systematic desensitization,* the specific techniques of behavior therapy aimed at helping individuals lose their fear of certain objects or situations. But many types of psychotherapy can encourage a broader kind of desensitization. When we discuss troubling events and emotions in the accepting atmosphere of a therapy session, they gradually lose their threatening quality. Problems that we brood about alone can become magnified beyond proportion; sharing those problems with someone else often makes them seem less serious. Several other hypotheses can also explain how desensitization occurs in psychotherapy. For example, putting disturbing events into words may help us reappraise the situation in a more realistic manner. From the viewpoint of learning theory, repeatedly discussing distressing experiences in the security of a therapeutic setting may gradually extinguish the anxiety associated with them. Whatever the process, desensitization does appear to be common to many kinds of psychotherapy.

Reinforcement of Adaptive Responses   Behavior therapists use reinforcement as a technique to increase positive attitudes and actions. But any therapist who wins the trust of a patient serves as a reinforcing agent; that is, the therapist tends to express approval of behaviors or attitudes that are conducive to better adjustment and while ignoring or expressing disapproval of maladaptive attitudes or responses. Which responses are reinforced depends on the therapist's orientation and therapeutic goals. The use of reinforcement may be intentional or unintentional; in some instances the therapist may be unaware that he or she is reinforcing or failing to reinforce a particular behavior. For example, client-centered therapists believe in letting the client determine what is discussed during the therapy sessions; they do not wish to influence the trend of the client's conversation. However, reinforcement can be subtle; a smile, a nod, or a simple "um hmm" in response to certain statements may increase the likelihood of their recurrence.

Since the goal of all psychotherapies is to bring about a change in the client's attitudes and behaviors, some type of learning must take place in therapy. The therapist needs to be aware of his or her role in influencing the client by means of reinforcement and should use this knowledge to facilitate desired changes.

Understanding or Insight All of the psychotherapies we have been discussing provide an explanation of the client's difficulties—how they arose, why they persist, and how they can be changed. For a patient in psychoanalysis, this explanation may take the form of gradual understanding of repressed childhood fears and the ways in which these unconscious feelings have contributed to current problems. A behavior therapist might inform the client that current fears are the result of previous conditioning and can be conquered by learning responses that are incompatible with the current ones. A client in a cognitive-behavior treatment program might be told that his or her difficulties stem from the irrational belief that one must be perfect or must be loved by everyone.

How can such different explanations all produce positive results? Perhaps the precise nature of the insights and understanding provided by the therapist is relatively unimportant. It may be more important to provide the client with an explanation for the behavior or feelings that he or she finds so distressing and to present a set of activities (such as free association or relaxation training) that both the therapist and the client believe will alleviate the distress. When a person is experiencing disturbing symptoms and is unsure of their cause or how serious they might be, he or she will feel reassured by a professional who seems to know what the problem is and offers ways of relieving it. The knowledge that change is possible gives rise to hope, and hope is an important variable in facilitating change. (See the Frontiers of Psychological Research feature on pages 590–591.)

Our discussion of the factors shared by all forms of psychotherapy is not intended to deny the value of some specific treatment methods. Perhaps the most effective therapist is one who recognizes the importance of these common factors and utilizes them in a planned manner for all patients, but also selects the specific procedures that are most appropriate for each individual case.

Biological Therapies

The biological approach to abnormal behavior assumes that mental disorders, like physical illnesses, are caused by biochemical or physiological dysfunctions of the brain. Biological therapies include the use of drugs and electroconvulsive shock.

Psychotherapeutic Drugs

By far the most successful biological therapy is the use of drugs to modify mood and behavior. The discovery in the early 1950s of drugs that relieved some of the symptoms of schizophrenia represented a major breakthrough in the treatment of severely disturbed individuals. Intensely agitated patients no longer had to be physically restrained by straitjackets, and patients who had been spending most of their time hallucinating and exhibiting bizarre behavior became more responsive and functional. As a result, psychiatric wards became more manageable and patients could be discharged more quickly. A few years later the discovery of drugs that could relieve severe depression had a similar beneficial effect on hospital management and population. We saw in Figure 16-1 the reduction in the number of mental-hospital residents that occurred following the introduction of antipsychotic and antidepressant drugs. At about the same time, drugs were being developed to relieve anxiety.

FRONTIERS OF PSYCHOLOGICAL RESEARCH

The Placebo Response

Placebos are commonly used in research on the effectiveness of drugs. A **placebo** is *an inert substance (known to have no pharmacological effect) that is made to look like an active drug*—in essence, a sugar pill. Placebos are used in drug research as controls (a) for the patients' expectations that the medicine will make them feel better, (b) for the researcher's belief that the medicine is effective, and (c) for the beneficial effects of extra attention from nurses and other personnel that stem from being a research participant. A *double-blind procedure* is usually employed: One group of patients is given the drug and a comparable group is given the placebo, but neither the patients nor the researchers (or whoever judges the results) knows until the end of the study which pills contain the active medication and which are the placebos. If the rate of improvement is greater in those who received the drug, the drug is considered to be therapeutically effective. If both groups of patients show similar improvement, whatever positive response occurs with the drug is considered to be a *placebo effect* and the drug is judged to be ineffective.

All responses that cannot be explained on the basis of actual drug effects are considered to be placebo responses—that is, due to unknown and nonpharmacological causes. Such unknown causes are generally assumed to be psychological in nature.

Placebo responses can be very powerful. For example, 40% of patients who were suffering from a painful heart disease (angina pectoris) reported marked relief from their symptoms after undergoing a diagnostic procedure that they believed was an operation to cure the problem (Beecher, 1961). In treating psychological disorders, placebos are often as effective as medication. For example, a large study of drug therapies and psychotherapies for depression found that patients responded nearly as well to a pill placebo as they did to antidepressant drugs or to psychotherapy (Elkin et al., 1989).

Until the beginning of modern scientific medicine, many medications were placebos. Patients were given every conceivable substance—crocodile dung, lozenges of dried vipers, spermatic fluid of frogs, spiders, worms, and human excrement—prepared in every possible manner. Throughout medical history, patients have been purged, poisoned, leeched, bled, heated, frozen, sweated, and shocked (Shapiro & Morris, 1978).

Since physicians and healers traditionally have held positions of honor and respect, their "treatments" must have helped at least some of their patients. We assume that the effectiveness of the treatments was due to the placebo response. Scientists also attribute documented cases of faith healing and various forms of miraculous cures to placebo effects.

Some clinicians have suggested that the placebo response may be one of the reasons that psychotherapy works (Lieberman & Dunlap, 1979; Wilkins, 1984). According to this view, almost any method of psychotherapy should show positive results if the client believes it will be effective. If this is true, it becomes important for the therapist to convey to the client his or her conviction that the method of treatment will be successful.

The idea that placebo response plays a central role in psychotherapy is disturbing to some clinicians. They feel that it links psychotherapy with quackery or charlatanism and implies that the process is one of self-deception. This is not the case. Physicians and psychotherapists have long known that a patient's attitudes and beliefs are very important in determining the effectiveness of treatment. Any treatment will be

---

Antianxiety Drugs Most drugs that reduce anxiety belong to the family known as *benzodiazepines*. They are commonly known as tranquilizers and are marketed under such trade names as Valium (diazepam), Librium (chlordiazepoxide), and Xanax (alprazolam). Antianxiety drugs reduce tension and cause drowsiness. Like alcohol and the barbiturates, they depress the action of the central nervous system. Family physicians often prescribe tranquilizers to help people cope during difficult periods in their lives. The drugs are also used to treat anxiety disorders, withdrawal from alcohol, and physical disorders related to stress. For example, in the treatment of a phobia, antianxiety drugs may be combined with systematic desensitization to help the individual relax when confronting the feared situation.

Although tranquilizers may be useful on a short-term basis, their overall benefits are debatable and they clearly are overprescribed and misused. Until quite recently (before some of the dangers became apparent), Valium and Librium were the two most widely prescribed drugs in this country (Julien,

more effective if the patient believes in it and is motivated to use it in the proper manner. Rather than deny the importance of the placebo effect, it would be better to continue investigating the variables that contribute to it.

In addition, researchers who wish to demonstrate the effectiveness of a specific therapeutic technique should control for the placebo response. Sophisticated studies do this by including a placebo control group as well as an untreated control group. For example, an experiment designed to test the efficacy of systematic desensitization in reducing anxiety about public speaking included the following groups: systematic desensitization, insight therapy, attention-placebo, and untreated control. The participants in the attention-placebo group met with a sympathetic therapist who led them to believe that a pill would reduce their overall sensitivity to stress. To convince them, the therapist had them listen to a "stress tape" (presumably one used in training astronauts to function under stress) for several sessions after ingesting the "tranquilizer." In reality, the pill was a placebo and the tape contained nonverbal sounds that had been found in other research to be boring rather than stressful. In this way the researcher raised the participants' expectations that their speech anxiety would be lessened by taking a pill. The results of this study revealed that the systematic desensitization group improved (that is, their speech anxiety was reduced) much more than the no-treatment group and more than the attention-placebo and insight therapy groups, who reacted about equally to their forms of therapy. The latter two groups, however, did show significant improvement (Paul, 1967). By including the attention-placebo group, the experimenter was able to conclude that the success of the systematic desensitization procedure was not due solely to the placebo effect.

The mechanism that causes placebo responses is unknown. Numerous hypotheses have been proposed, but so far there is little empirical verification for any of them. One group of explanations focuses on social influence (see Chapter 18). Because patients tend to view physicians and therapists as socially powerful individuals, they may be easily persuaded that the treatments they suggest will have beneficial results. In addition, the role of patient entails certain prescribed behaviors. A "good" patient is one who gets better; getting better justifies the therapist's initial concern and subsequent interest.

Other explanations focus on the individual's expectations. According to neurologist Marcel Kinsbourne,

The brain generates two kinds of activation patterns, which arise from networks of neurons firing together. One type is set in motion by information flowing into the brain from the outside world. . . . At the same time, the cortex draws on memories and feelings to generate patterns of brain activity related to what is expected to happen. . . . The expectations that result are internally generated brain states that can be as real as anything resulting purely from the outside world. (quoted in Blakeslee, 1998, p. F4)

The person who administers a placebo treatment may intentionally or unintentionally communicate expectations about the effects of the treatment. The patients also arrive with certain expectations based on their previous experiences. Expectations that one will get better and a strong desire to do so are the essential ingredients of hope. And hope can have a powerful influence on our emotions and bodily processes.

1992). Tranquilizer overuse gives rise to several dangers. Depending on a pill to relieve anxiety may prevent a person from exploring the cause of the anxiety and learning more effective ways of coping with tension. More important, long-term use of tranquilizers can lead to physical dependence (see Chapter 6). Although tranquilizers are not as addictive as barbiturates, tolerance does develop with repeated use and the individual experiences severe withdrawal symptoms if use of the drug is discontinued. In addition, tranquilizers impair concentration, including driving performance, and can cause death if combined with alcohol.

In recent years, researchers have discovered that certain antidepressant drugs also reduce symptoms of anxiety. This is particularly true of the serotonin reuptake inhibitors (discussed shortly). These drugs may relieve anxiety as well as depression because they affect biochemical disturbances that are common to both conditions.

Antipsychotic Drugs The first drugs that were found to relieve the symptoms of schizophrenia belonged to the family called *phenothiazines.* Examples are Thorazine (chlorpromazine) and Prolixin (fluphenazine). These drugs have been called "major tranquilizers," but this term is not really appropriate because they do not act on the nervous system in the same way as barbiturates or antianxiety drugs. They may cause some drowsiness and lethargy, but they do not induce deep sleep even in massive doses. They also seldom create the pleasant, slightly euphoric feeling associated with low doses of antianxiety drugs. In fact, the psychological effects of the antipsychotic drugs when administered to normal individuals are usually unpleasant. Hence, these drugs are seldom abused.

In Chapter 15 we discussed the theory that schizophrenia is caused by excessive activity of the neurotransmitter dopamine. Antipsychotic drugs block dopamine receptors. Because the drugs' molecules are structurally similar to dopamine molecules, they bind to the postsynaptic receptors of dopamine neurons, thereby blocking the access of dopamine to its receptors. (The drug itself does not activate the receptors.) A single synapse has many receptor molecules. If all of them are blocked, transmission across the synapse will fail. If only some of them are blocked, transmission will be weakened. The clinical potency of an antipsychotic drug is directly related to its ability to compete for dopamine receptors.

Antipsychotic drugs are effective in alleviating hallucinations and confusion and restoring rational thought processes. These drugs do not cure schizophrenia; most patients must continue to use the drugs in order to function outside of a hospital. Many of the characteristic symptoms of schizophrenia—emotional blunting, seclusiveness, difficulties in sustaining attention—remain. Nevertheless, antipsychotic drugs shorten the length of time patients must be hospitalized, and they prevent relapse. Studies of schizophrenics living in the community find that the relapse rate for those taking one of the phenothiazines is typically half the relapse rate for those receiving a placebo (Hogarty et al., 1979).

Unfortunately, antipsychotic drugs do not help all schizophrenic patients. In addition, the drugs have unpleasant side effects—dryness of the mouth, blurred vision, difficulty concentrating—that prompt many patients to discontinue their medication. One of the most serious side effects is a neurological disorder known as **tardive dyskinesia,** which involves *involuntary movements of the tongue, face, mouth, or jaw.* Patients with this disorder may involuntarily smack their lips, make sucking sounds, stick out their tongue, puff their cheeks, or make other bizarre movements, over and over again. Tardive dyskinesia is often irreversible and may occur in over 20% of people who use antipsychotic drugs for long periods (Morganstern & Glazer, 1993).

In recent years, new drugs called *atypical antipsychotics* have been found to reduce symptoms of schizophrenia without causing so many side effects (Wilson & Clausen, 1995). These drugs include clozapine and risperidone. They appear to work by binding to a different type of dopamine receptor than the other drugs, although they also influence several other neurotransmitters, including serotonin.

Antidepressant Drugs Antidepressant drugs help elevate the mood of depressed individuals. These drugs energize rather than tranquilize, apparently by increasing the availability of two neurotransmitters (norepinephrine and serotonin) whose levels are deficient in some cases of depression (see Chapter 15). Antidepressant drugs act in different ways to increase neurotransmitter levels. *Monoamine oxidase* (MAO) *inhibitors* block the activity of an enzyme that can destroy both norepinephrine and serotonin, thereby increasing the concentration of these two neurotransmitters in the brain. *Tricyclic antidepressants* prevent the reuptake of serotonin and norepinephrine, thereby prolonging the action of the neurotransmitter. (Recall that reuptake is the process by which neurotransmitters are drawn back into the nerve terminals that released them.) Both classes of drugs have proved effective in relieving certain types of depression, presumably those caused more by biological factors than by environmental ones.

Like the antipsychotic drugs, the antidepressants can produce some undesirable side effects. The most common of these are dry mouth, blurred vision, constipation, and urinary retention. They can also cause a severe drop in blood pressure upon standing up, and changes in heart rate and rhythm. An overdose of tricyclic antidepressants can be fatal, a serious concern when a depressed patient may be suicidal. The MAO inhibitors can interact with certain foods, including cheese, chocolate, and red wine, to create severe cardiac problems.

The search for drugs that are more effective, have fewer side effects, and act more quickly has intensified in the past few years. As a result, new drugs appear on the market almost daily. Among these newer drugs (called *serotonin reuptake inhibitors*) are several that selectively increase serotonin levels by blocking its reuptake, without affecting norepinephrine. Examples are Prozac (fluoxetine), Anafranil (clomipramine), and Zoloft (sertraline). In addition to relieving depression, these drugs have proved helpful in treating obsessive-compulsive disorder and panic disorder (Lickey & Gordon, 1991). They tend to produce fewer side effects than the other antidepressants, although they can cause inhibited orgasm, nausea and diarrhea, dizziness, and nervousness.

Another drug, *lithium,* has proved very successful in treating bipolar disorder. Lithium reduces extreme mood swings and returns the individual to a more normal emotional state. Although the effectiveness of this drug has been known for more than 40 years, researchers have only recently discovered how its complex action on certain neurotransmitters achieves this normalizing effect.

Between 50% and 60% of patients who take lithium experience significant reductions in symptoms of bipolar disorder (Goodwin & Jamison, 1990). However, many people cannot take lithium because of its side effects, which include abdominal pain, nausea, vomiting, diarrhea, tremors, and twitches (Jamison, 1995). Patients complain of blurred vision and problems in concentration and attention that interfere with their ability to work. Lithium can cause kidney dysfunction, birth defects, and a form of diabetes if taken by women during the first trimester of pregnancy.

Anticonvulsant medications are now commonly used to treat bipolar disorder. These drugs can be highly effective in reducing the symptoms of severe and acute mania but do not seem to be as effective as lithium for long-term treatment of bipolar disorder. The side effects of the anticonvulsants include dizziness, rash, nausea, and drowsiness (Goodwin & Jamison, 1990).

Ritalin Stimulant drugs are used to treat the attentional problems of children with attention deficit hyperactivity disorder (ADHD). One of the most commonly used stimulants has the trade name Ritalin. Although it may seem odd to give a stimulant to a hyperactive child, between 60% and 90% of children with ADHD respond to these drugs with decreases in disruptive behavior and increases in attention (Gadow, 1992). For that matter, children without ADHD also show increases in attention span when they take Ritalin.

The use of Ritalin is a subject of controversy because some schools and physicians have been too quick to diagnose ADHD in schoolchildren and to prescribe Ritalin for them (Hinshaw, 1994). Stimulant drugs have significant side effects, including insomnia, headaches, tics, and nausea (Gadow, 1991, 1992). Thus, it is important that children be accurately diagnosed with ADHD before stimulant drugs are prescribed.

In sum, drug therapy has reduced the severity of some types of mental disorders. Many individuals who would require hospitalization otherwise can function within the community with the help of these drugs. On the other hand, there are limitations to the application of drug therapy. All therapeutic drugs can produce undesirable side effects. Many people with medical problems, and women who are pregnant or nursing, often cannot take psychoactive drugs. In addition, many psychologists feel that these drugs alleviate symptoms without requiring the patient to face the personal problems that may be contributing to the disorder or may have been caused by the disorder (such as marital problems caused by the behaviors of a manic person).

Electroconvulsive Therapy

In **electroconvulsive therapy (ECT)**, also known as electroshock therapy, *a mild electric current is applied to the brain to produce a seizure similar to an epilectic convulsion.* ECT was a popular treatment from about 1940 to 1960, before antipsychotic and antidepressant drugs became readily available. Today it is used primarily in cases of severe depression when the patient has failed to respond to drug therapy.

ECT has been the subject of much controversy. At one time it was used indiscriminately in mental hospitals to treat such disorders as alcoholism and schizophrenia, for which it produced no beneficial results. Before more refined procedures were developed, ECT was a frightening experience for the patient, who was often awake until the electric current triggered the seizure and produced momentary unconsciousness. The patient frequently suffered confusion and memory loss afterward. Occasionally the intensity of the muscle spasms accompanying the brain seizure resulted in physical injuries.

Today, ECT involves little discomfort. The patient is given a short-acting anesthesia and injected with a muscle relaxant. A brief, very weak electric current is applied to the brain, typically to the temple on the side of the nondominant cerebral hemisphere. The minimum current required to produce a brain seizure is administered, since the seizure itself—not the electricity—is therapeutic. The muscle relaxant prevents convulsive muscle spasms. The individual awakens within a few minutes and remembers nothing about the treatment. Four to six treatments are usually administered over a period of several weeks.

The most troublesome side effect of ECT is memory loss. Some patients report a gap in memory for events that occurred up to six months before ECT, as well as impaired ability to retain new information for a month or two after the treatment. However, if very low dosages of electricity are used (the amount is carefully calibrated for each patient to be just sufficient to produce a seizure) and administered only to the nondominant side of the brain, memory problems are minimal (Sackeim et al., 1985).

No one knows how the electrically induced seizures relieve depression. Brain seizures cause massive release of norepinephrine and serotonin, and as noted in Chapter 15, deficiencies of these neurotransmitters may be an important factor in some cases of depression. Currently researchers are trying to determine the similarities and dissimilarities between ECT and antidepressant drugs in terms of the way each affects neurotransmitters. How ever it works, ECT is effective in bringing some people out of severe, immobilizing depression, and it does so faster than drug therapy.

Combining Biological and Psychological Therapies

Although in this chapter we divided therapies into psychological and biological therapies, today there is a movement toward combined biological and psychological treatments. In depression and the anxiety disorders, often both the patient's biochemistry and his or her functioning in social and occupational settings are affected by the disorder, and it can be helpful to provide treatment at both the biological and psychosocial levels. Even in disorders like schizophrenia, whose primary cause is biological, the patient often experiences severe losses in social skills and in his or her ability to function on a job. Supplementing antipsychotic drugs with psychotherapy designed to help the person cope with the consequences of schizophrenia can be very useful.

The fact that a wide range of both psychotherapies and drugs are effective in the treatment of some disorders (especially depression) suggests that intervening at one level of a person's bio-psycho-social system can affect all levels of the system. For example, intervening at the psychological level may cause changes in the patient's biochemistry and in his or her social behaviors. When this occurs, it is because our biochemistry, our personalities and thought processes, and our social behaviors are so thoroughly intertwined that each can affect the other in both positive and negative ways.

Effects of Culture and Gender on Therapy

Each year more than 2 million people in the United States are hospitalized for a mental disorder (Kiesler & Sibulkin, 1987). African-Americans and Native Americans are considerably more likely than white Americans to be hospitalized in an inpatient mental health facility (Snowden & Cheung, 1990). Asian-Americans are much less likely to be hospitalized than members of any other group. These ethnic differences in hospitalization do not appear to be due to ethnic differences in socioeconomic status, which can affect the availability of alternatives to hospitalization such as private care outside a hospital.

Do African-Americans suffer from severe mental disorders that require hospitalization more frequently than members of other groups? The answer seems to be "no." Rates of severe mood disorders and schizophrenia, the disorders that most frequently result in hospitalization, are very similar among African-Americans, whites, and Hispanics (Robins et al., 1984). (Rates of these disorders among Native Americans and Asian-Americans are not available.) African-Americans may be more frequently misdiagnosed as suffering from schizophrenia than whites (Mukherjee et al., 1983). Since this diagnosis often leads to hospitalization, it may explain the overrepresentation of African-Americans among hospitalized mental patients.

Men and women are hospitalized at about the same rate for mental disorders (Narrow et al., 1993), but the types of disorders for which they are hospitalized differ considerably. Men are more often hospitalized for substance abuse than women, but women are more often hospitalized for a mood disorder than men. There are no gender differences in the rate of hospitalization for schizophrenia.

Most people who seek treatment for a psychological disorder are not hospitalized. They are more likely to receive treatment from private-practice psychologists, psychiatrists, or general-practice physicians. In fact, one large study found that people in the United States are twice as likely to seek help for emotional or mental problems from their general-practice physicians than from a mental health professional (Narrow et al., 1993). Women are much more likely than men to talk to their general-practice physicians about mental and emotional problems, and somewhat more likely to seek help from a mental health professional for these problems (Kessler, Brown, & Broman, 1981; Russo & Sobel, 1981).

Hispanics and Asian-Americans appear to be more likely to care for a member of the family who is suffering from a major mental disorder in the home than non-Hispanic whites (Gaw, 1993; Snowden, 1988). These trends may be due both to emphasis on the family as the center of problem solving and to the stigma associated with seeking mental health care. In contrast, African-Americans tend to seek mental health treatment more quickly after the onset of symptoms than members of other groups (Broman, 1987).

Several cross-cultural theorists have made recommendations about the type of psychotherapy that might prove most acceptable to members of specific ethnic groups (see Sue & Zane, 1987). For example, more structured and action-oriented therapies such as behavior or cognitive-behavior therapies have been recommended for Hispanics, African-Americans, and Asian-Americans. Asian-Americans are said to prefer therapists who provide structure, guidance, and direction, rather than nondirective therapies such as psychoanalysis or client-centered therapy (Atkinson, Maruyama, & Matsui, 1978). Most of these assertions have not been thoroughly tested, however (Sue & Zane, 1987). Similarly, although some clinicians have suggested that women find therapies that focus on interpersonal relations and expression of feelings more appealing and helpful than other types of therapies, there is little evidence for or against this assertion (McGrath et al., 1990).

The specific form of therapy may not matter as much as the cultural and gender sensitivity exhibited by the therapist. Members of minority groups are much more likely than whites to drop out of therapy (Sue & Zane, 1987). One study of 13,450 therapy clients found that the dropout rate for Hispanics was 42%, for Native Americans 55%, and for African-Americans 52%, compared to only 30% for whites (Sue, Allen, & Conaway, 1978). In most of these cases the therapist was white. Minority clients may find the suggestions of white therapists strange and unhelpful.

Therapists and clients who are members of the same ethnic or racial group do not necessarily share the same value system,

Therapists and clients who are members of the same ethnic or racial group do not necessarily share the same value system.

however. For example, a fourth-generation Japanese-American who has fully adopted the competitive and individualistic values of U.S. society may clash with a recent immigrant from Japan who adheres to the self-sacrificing, community-oriented values of Japanese culture. Similarly, a woman therapist who has strong feminist values may clash with a woman client who holds traditional sex-role expectations. These value differences among people of the same ethnic/racial group or the same gender may explain why studies show that matching the ethnicity or race or gender of therapist and client does not necessarily lead to a better outcome (Atkinson, 1983; Jones, 1978; Lerner, 1972).

Some clients care deeply about having a therapist of the same ethnic group or gender, but others may only trust a therapist who corresponds to their stereotype of a "doctor" while still others have no preferences regarding the ethnicity or gender of their therapist. For clients who wish to be matched with a therapist of the same ethnic or gender group, this matching may be necessary if the client is to trust the therapist and have faith in the therapy. And as noted earlier, the relationship between client and therapist and the client's beliefs about the likely effectiveness of therapy contribute strongly to the effectiveness of the therapy.

Enhancing Mental Health

The prevention and treatment of mental disorders is a matter of tremendous concern for both the community and the nation. Early in this chapter we noted that the Community Mental Health Centers Act, passed by Congress in 1963, provided funds for the establishment of community mental health centers so that people could be treated close to their family and friends rather than in large psychiatric hospitals. These community centers provide short-term hospitalization, outpatient treatment, and a 24-hour emergency service.

Community Resources and Paraprofessionals

A variety of community resources have been developed to serve the psychological needs of different groups. One such resource is the halfway house, where patients who have been hospitalized can live while making the transition back to independent living in the community. Residential centers are also available for people who are recovering from alcohol and drug problems, for delinquent or runaway youths, and for battered wives. Rap centers, where troubled teenagers can discuss their problems with other teenagers and with sympathetic counselors, play an important role in many communities; youth centers provide job counseling, remedial education, and help with family and personal problems.

Crisis Intervention   Crisis intervention provides immediate help for individuals and families undergoing intense stress. During periods of acute emotional turmoil, people often feel overwhelmed and incapable of dealing with the situation. They may not be able to wait for a therapy appointment, or they may not know where to turn. One form of crisis intervention is provided by 24-hour walk-in services, often in a community mental health center, where a person can receive immediate attention. A therapist helps clarify the problem, provides reassurance, suggests a plan of action, and mobilizes the support of other agencies or family members.

This kind of therapy is usually short-term (five or six sessions) and provides the support the person requires to handle the crisis at hand. Such short-term intervention often makes hospitalization unnecessary.

Another form of crisis intervention is the telephone hot line. Telephone crisis centers are usually staffed by volunteers under the direction of mental health professionals. Some focus specifically on suicide prevention; others help distressed callers find the particular kind of assistance they need. The volunteers usually receive training that emphasizes listening with care, evaluating the potential for suicide, conveying empathy and understanding, providing information about community resources, offering hope and reassurance, and recording the caller's name and phone number before he or she hangs up so that a professional can follow up on the problem. Most major cities in the United States have developed some form of telephone hot line to help people who are undergoing periods of severe stress, as well as specialized hot lines to deal with child abuse, rape victims, battered wives, and run-aways. The phone numbers are widely publicized in the hope of reaching those who need help.

Paraprofessionals as Therapists Most of the community programs we have discussed could not function without the help of paraprofessionals. Because the need for psychological services outstrips the supply of available therapists, concerned citizens can play a valuable role. People of all ages and backgrounds have been trained to work in the field of community mental health. College students have served as companions for hospitalized patients. Older individuals who have raised families have been trained to work with adolescents in community clinics, to counsel parents of youngsters with behavior problems, and to work with schizophrenic children. Former mental patients, recovered drug addicts, and ex-convicts have been trained to help individuals faced with problems similar to the ones they have experienced.

Many residential mental health programs are run by nonprofessionals in consultation with trained therapists. An outstanding

Community resources to serve the psychological needs of different groups include telephone hot lines, usually staffed by volunteers under the direction of mental health professionals.

example is Achievement Place, a home-style facility in Kansas where couples act as surrogate parents for a group of youngsters who have been referred by the courts because of delinquent behavior. Behavior therapy methods are used to extinguish aggressive behavior and reward social skills. Follow-up data show that youths who graduate from Achievement Place have fewer contacts with courts and police and achieve slightly higher grades than youths who are placed on probation or in a traditional institution for delinquents (Fixsen, Phillips, Phillips, & Wolf, 1976). There are numerous other Achievement Places throughout the United States modeled after the original Kansas facility.

Promoting Your Own Emotional Well-Being

Aside from seeking professional help, there are many ways in which we can positively influence our own psychological well-being. By monitoring our feelings and behavior, we can determine the kinds of actions and situations that cause us pain or get us into difficulty, and, conversely, the kinds that benefit us the most. By trying to analyze our motives and abilities, we can enhance our capacity to make active choices in our lives instead of passively accepting whatever happens. The problems that people face vary greatly, and there are no universal guidelines for staying psychologically healthy. However, a few general suggestions have emerged from the experiences of therapists.

Accept Your Feelings Anger, sorrow, fear, and a feeling of having fallen short of ideals or goals are all unpleasant emotions, and we may try to escape anxiety by denying these feelings. Sometimes we try to avoid anxiety by facing situations unemotionally, which leads to a false kind of detachment or "cool" that may be destructive. We may try to suppress all emotions, thereby losing the ability to accept as normal the joys and sorrows that are part of our involvement with other people.

Unpleasant emotions are a normal reaction to many situations. There is no reason to be ashamed of feeling homesick, being afraid when learning to ski, or becoming angry at someone who has disappointed us. These emotions are natural, and it is better to recognize them than to deny them. When emotions cannot be expressed directly (for example, it may not be wise to yell at your boss), it helps to find another outlet for releasing tension. Taking a long walk, pounding a tennis ball, or discussing the situation with a friend can help dissipate anger. As long as you accept your right to feel emotion, you can express it in indirect or alternative ways when direct channels of expression are blocked.

Know Your Vulnerabilities Discovering the kinds of situations that upset you or cause you to overreact may help guard against stress. Perhaps certain people annoy you. You could avoid them, or you could try to understand just what it is about them that disturbs you. Maybe they seem so poised and confident that they make you feel insecure. Trying to pinpoint the cause of your discomfort may help you see the situation in a new light. Perhaps you become very anxious when you have to speak in class or present a paper. Again, you could try to avoid such situations, or you could gain confidence by taking a course in public speaking. (Many colleges offer courses on controlling speech anxiety.) You could also reinterpret the situation. Instead of thinking, "Everyone is waiting to criticize me as soon as I open my mouth," you could tell yourself, "The class will be interested in what I have to say, and I'm not going to let it worry me if I make a few mistakes."

Many people feel especially anxious when they are under pressure. Careful planning and spacing of work can help you avoid feeling overwhelmed at the last minute. The strategy of purposely allowing more time than you think you need to get to classes or appointments can eliminate one source of stress.

Develop Your Talents and Interests People who are bored and unhappy seldom have many interests. Today's college and community programs offer almost unlimited opportunities for people of all ages to explore their talents in many areas, including sports, academic interests, music, art, drama, and crafts. Often, the more you know about a subject, the more interesting it (and life) becomes. In addition, the feeling of competence gained from developing skills can do a great deal to bolster self-esteem.

Become Involved With Other People   Feelings of isolation and loneliness are at the core of most emotional disorders. We are social beings, and we need the support, comfort, and reassurance provided by other people. Focusing all your attention on your own problems can lead to an unhealthy preoccupation with yourself. Sharing your concerns with others often helps you view your troubles in a clearer perspective. Also, being concerned for the welfare of other people can reinforce your feelings of self-worth.

Know When to Seek Help   Although these suggestions can help promote emotional well-being, there are limits to self-understanding and self-help. Some problems are difficult to solve alone. Our tendency toward self-deception makes it hard to view problems objectively, and we may not be aware of all the possible solutions. When you feel that you are making little headway toward gaining control over a problem, it is time to seek professional help from a counseling or clinical psychologist, a psychiatrist, or some other

Developing your talents and interests can do a great deal to promote emotional well-being.

trained therapist. Willingness to seek help is a sign of emotional maturity, not weakness; do not wait until you feel overwhelmed. Obtaining psychological help when it is needed should be as accepted a practice as going to a physician for medical problems.

IS ALCOHOLICS ANONYMOUS (AA) AN EFFECTIVE INTERVENTION FOR ALCOHOL ABUSE?

AA Helps Problem Drinkers

Keith Humphreys, *Stanford University* and *Veterans Affairs Palo Alto Health Care System*

Alcoholics Anonymous (AA) is a worldwide fellowship of approximately 2 million alcohol-dependent individuals who are committed to helping each other permanently abstain from alcohol, as well as become more honest, humble, compassionate, and spiritually serene. In over 50 nations, AA members meet in mutual help groups on a regular basis, where they use AA principles (e.g., the "Twelve Steps") and their personal "experience, strength, and hope" to promote sobriety. In the United States, AA is the most commonly sought source of help for alcohol problems (Weisner, Greenfield, & Room, 1995), far outstripping all professional interventions combined. AA also enjoys an excellent reputation among most treatment professionals. At the same time, some clinicians and researchers doubt AA's effectiveness (Ogborne, 1993), noting that the organization offers a loosely monitored and unstandardized program based primarily on the experience and spiritual outlook of its members rather than a standardized professional treatment derived from objective, scientific research. AA attempts to change many aspects of members' lives, and hence the question of whether AA "works" can be framed in many different ways.

Keith Humphreys

Here, I focus on one of AA's intended benefits—abstinence from alcohol—and describe how recent studies provide credible evidence that AA helps problem drinkers stop consuming alcohol.

For example, Cross and colleagues (Cross, Morgan, Martin, & Rafter, 1990) followed up a sample of 158 alcohol dependent patients 10 years after treatment to determine what factors (e.g., problem severity, age, sex) predicted long-term abstinence from alcohol. Of all the variables examined, only AA involvement increased the likelihood of abstinence. These findings supporting AA's effectiveness were essentially replicated in an 8-year follow-up of a sample of 628 alcohol-abusing individuals conducted by a different research group (Humphreys, Moos, & Cohen, 1997). Although not a study of AA per se, the randomized clinical trial known as Project Match (Project Match Research Group, 1997) demonstrated that counseling facilitating AA involvement is as effective at reducing alcohol consumption as are other established psychotherapies for alcohol-dependent clients.

Because AA attendance is free of charge, the organization is probably the most cost-effective way for alcohol-dependent individuals to become abstinent. One study of 201 alcohol abusers illustrating this point compared 135 individuals who initially chose to attend AA with 66 individuals who initially chose to seek professional outpatient treatment (Humphreys & Moos, 1996). Despite the fact that individuals were not randomly assigned to each condition, at baseline, there were no significant differences between groups on demographic variables, alcohol problems, or psychopathology. By the three-year follow-up, the AA attenders had reduced their daily alcohol intake an average of 75% and had decreased their alcohol dependence symptoms (e.g., blackouts) an average of 71%. Individuals receiving professional treatment improved comparably. However, alcohol-related health care costs over the three-year study were 45% ($1,826 per person) lower in the AA group than in the treated group. Hence, AA not only promotes abstinence, but does so in a cost-effective fashion that probably takes a substantial burden off of the formal health care system.

Research on the effects of AA participation has improved substantially in recent years, but still has considerable room for growth. Confidence in AA's effectiveness would be increased if more studies employed longitudinal designs, included comparison groups, and used biological tests or collateral data sources to confirm self-reports of abstinence. Further, even well-designed studies do not show that AA works for every participant or that its benefits are always substantial. However, the same could be said for virtually every professional psychosocial treatment for alcohol dependence. Therefore, particularly in light of AA's availability and minimal financial cost, it clearly is one of society's more important resources for helping alcohol dependent individuals recover.

AA Is Not the Only Way

G. Alan Marlatt, *University of Washington*

Although Alcoholics Anonymous (AA) is the most well-known self-help group for many people who are recovering from alcoholism, it is not the only way to help many individuals to stop drinking, and for some problem drinkers, AA may be a barrier to successful treatment. Studies show that of every two people who attend their first meeting of AA, only one returns for a second or subsequent meeting.

Why does AA appeal to some and not to others? Although AA is described as a "spiritual fellowship" and is not explicitly identified with any specific religious group, many first-timers are put off by the requirement to admit that one is powerless over one's drinking and that only by turning over personal control to a "higher power," recovery is possible. Others are discouraged by the AA doctrine that alcoholism is basically a physical disease that cannot be cured, only "arrested" by total lifelong abstinence from any alcoholic beverages. For those adherents of the disease model, including almost all AA members, there is no possibility of future moderate or controlled drinking. Once an alcoholic, always an alcoholic, according to AA beliefs.

Research has yet to reveal whether it is the specific teachings (theory) associated with AA, or the group support that the meetings provide that is most effective in helping people change their personal habits. Recent evidence indicates the latter is primarily responsible for AA success, which suggests other groups with different theories or beliefs about alcoholism and recovery can also be effective. In recent years, several new self-help groups for alcoholics have become available, including (1) Rational Recovery, based on rational principles of behavioral change without the need for a "higher power" in order to maintain abstinence; (2) Self Management and Recovery Training (SMART), based on the principles of cognitive-behavioral therapy such as relapse prevention and social skills training; and (3) Women for Sobriety, for women who have problems relating to the mainly masculine flavor of many AA meetings and who could benefit from addressing alcohol problems shared by many women drinkers.

Another alternative to AA is "Moderation Management" self-help groups. After several failed attempts at making AA work for her, Audrey Kishline (1994) developed "Moderation Management," a program of drinking moderation that has been used in many self-help groups in recent years (including some groups that meet on the Internet rather than in person).

Moderate or controlled drinking programs are also known in the addictions treatment field as examples of a "harm-reduction" approach. The goal of harm-reduction programs (such as moderation for heavy drinkers, nicotine replacement therapy for smokers who can't fully kick the habit, etc.) is to reduce the harmful consequences to oneself, one's family, and one's community caused by the drug problem. Although abstinence is accepted as an ideal goal for recovery, any steps toward this goal that reduce harm are considered steps in the right direction toward enhanced health and the prevention of disease.

Harm-reduction programs have been successful in teaching high-risk college students to drink more safely. Alcohol harm-reduction programs are designed to teach the novice drinker skills about drinking behavior and corresponding levels of intoxication. A recent study of high-risk, first-year college students found those who attended the program showed a significant drop in binge drinking, black-outs, severe hangovers, and acts of vandalism, etc. compared with students in a control group who did not receive this training program. Thus for students who choose to drink and are at risk for experiencing serious drinking problems, harm reduction offers a viable alternative to abstinence (see my article in the August 1998 issue of the *Journal of Consulting and Clinical Psychology*).

In AA, if someone does not accept the requirement of total abstinence, he or she is likely to be told to go away and not to come back until having "hit bottom"—in other words, until the person has experienced such profound negative consequences from drinking that he or she sees no other choice but to go back to AA and pursue total abstinence. But what do we do with those drinkers who have not yet "hit bottom," even though they may be experiencing serious harmful consequences? Harm reduction offers a variety of helpful strategies for this group to get them started on the road to recovery.

SUMMARY

1. Treatment of the mentally ill has progressed from the ancient notion that abnormal behavior resulted from possession by evil spirits that needed to be punished, to custodial care in asylums, to modern mental hospitals and community mental health centers. The policy of deinstitutionalization, despite its good intentions, has added to the number of homeless mentally ill individuals, causing concern about civil rights and adequate care.

2. Psychotherapy is the treatment of mental disorders by psychological means. One type of psychotherapy is psychoanalysis, which was developed by Freud. Through the methods of free association and dream analysis, repressed thoughts and feelings are brought to the patient's awareness. By interpreting these dreams and associations, the analyst helps the patient gain insight into his or her problems. Transference, the tendency to express feelings toward the analyst that the client has for important people in his or her life, provides another source of interpretation.

3. Contemporary psychodynamic therapies are briefer than traditional psychoanalysis and place more emphasis on the client's current interpersonal problems (as opposed to a complete reconstruction of childhood experiences).

4. Behavior therapies apply methods based on learning principles to modify the client's behavior. These methods include systematic desensitization (the individual learns to relax in situations that previously produced anxiety), reinforcement of adaptive behaviors, modeling and rehearsal of appropriate behavior, and techniques for self-regulation of behavior.

5. Cognitive-behavior therapies use behavior modification techniques but also incorporate procedures for changing maladaptive beliefs. The therapist helps the client replace irrational interpretations of events with more realistic ones.

6. Humanistic therapies help clients become aware of their real selves and solve their problems with a minimum of intervention by the therapist. Carl Rogers, who developed client-centered psychotherapy, believed that the therapist must have three characteristics in order to promote the client's growth and self-exploration: empathy, warmth, and genuineness.

7. Rather than adhering strictly to any single method, many therapists take an eclectic approach, selecting from the different techniques the ones that are most appropriate for a given client. Some therapists specialize in treating specific problems, such as alcoholism, sexual dysfunction, or depression.

8. Group therapy provides an opportunity for clients to explore their attitudes and behavior in interaction with others who have similar problems. Marital therapy and family therapy are specialized forms of group therapy that help couples, or parents and children, learn more effective ways of relating to one another and handling their problems.

9. The effectiveness of psychotherapy is hard to evaluate because of the difficulty of defining a successful outcome and controlling for spontaneous remission. Research results indicate that psychotherapy does help but that different approaches do not differ greatly in effectiveness. Factors common to the various psychotherapies—a warm and trustful interpersonal relationship, reassurance and support, desensitization, insight, and reinforcement of adaptive responses—may be more important in producing positive change than the specific therapeutic methods used.

10. Biological therapies include electroconvulsive therapy (ECT) and the use of psychotherapeutic drugs. Of the two, drug therapy is by far the most widely used. Antianxiety drugs are used to reduce severe anxiety and help clients cope with life crises. Antipsychotic drugs have proved effective in the treatment of schizophrenia, antidepressants help to elevate the mood of depressed patients, and lithium has been effective in treating bipolar disorders.

11. African Americans and Native Americans are more likely than members of other ethnic groups to be hospitalized for a psychological disorder or to seek outpatient mental health services for a psychological problem. Hispanics and whites have similar hospitalization rates, but Asian-Americans are much less likely than members of other ethnic groups to be hospitalized for psychological problems. These ethnic differences may be caused by differences in attitudes toward hospitalization and in the availability of nonprofessional sources of care. In addition, African-Americans may be overdiagnosed with schizophrenia, which leads to their more frequent hospitalization compared to other groups.

12. Men and women are equally likely to be hospitalized or to seek a mental health professional for psychological problems, but men more frequently seek care for substance abuse than women, and women more frequently seek care for a mood disorder than men. Women are also more likely than men to talk with their general-practice physician about mental health problems.

13. Some clients may wish to work with a therapist of the same culture or gender, but it is unclear whether matching the therapist and the client is necessary for therapy to be effective. It is important for therapists to be sensitive to the influences of culture and gender on a client's attitudes toward therapy and on the acceptability of different types of solutions to their problems.

14. Community resources for the prevention and treatment of mental disorders include halfway houses, residential centers for people who have special problems, and various forms of crisis intervention. We can promote our own emotional health by accepting our feelings as natural, discovering our vulnerabilities, developing talents and interests, becoming involved with others, and recognizing when to seek professional help.

KEY TERMS

psychotherapy (p. 571)
free association (p. 572)
dream analysis (p. 572)
transference (p. 572)
systematic desensitization (p. 574)
in vivo exposure (p. 574)
flooding (p. 574)
selective reinforcement (p. 575)

modeling (p. 575)
behavioral rehearsal (p. 576)
self-regulation (p. 576)
self-help group (p. 584)
placebo (p. 590)
tardive dyskinesia (p. 592)
electroconvulsive therapy (ECT) (p. 594)

CRITICAL THINKING QUESTIONS

1. How might a psychotherapist adapt the therapeutic methods described in this chapter to help a person with schizophrenia? Which methods do you think would be helpful for a person with schizophrenia? Which methods would not be helpful?
2. If a new drug were developed that allowed people who were not suffering from a psychological disorder to feel a little more self-confident, energetic, and creative, while not inducing any significant side effects, do you think the drug should be made widely available? Why or why not?
3. What do you think society's obligations are to people with serious mental disorders? What laws should be enacted to protect the rights of these people?
4. Does society have any right or obligation to see to it that children with serious mental disorders receive treatment even if their parents do not agree to the treatment?

FURTHER READING

Interesting material on the historical treatment of the mentally ill can be found in Veith, *Hysteria: The History of a Disease* (1970); and Grob (1994), *The Mad Among Us.*

A review of the various methods of psychotherapy is provided by Gurman and Messer (eds.) (1995), *Essential Psychotherapies. Psychotherapy: An Eclectic Approach* (1994), by Garfield, describes the process of psychotherapy, the features common to most psychotherapies, and psychotherapy research. Seligman reviews the effectiveness of therapies for a wide range of psychological disorders in *What You Can Change and What You Can't* (1993).

For an introduction to psychoanalytic methods, see Luborsky, *Principles of Psychoanalytic Psychotherapy* (1984) and Auld and Hyman, *Resolution of Inner Conflict: An Introduction to Psychoanalytic Therapy* (1991). For client-centered therapy, see *On Becoming a Person: A Therapist's View of Psychotherapy* (1970) and *Carl Rogers on Personal Power* (1977), both by Rogers. The principles of behavior therapy are presented in Thorpe and Olson (1997*), Behavior Therapy: Concepts, Procedures and Application.* The application of cognitive-behavior therapy to a variety of mental disorders is described in *Cognitive Therapy: Basics and Beyond* (1995), by J. S. Beck.

An overview of group therapy is presented in Yalom, *The Theory and Practice of Group Psychotherapy* (3rd ed., 1985).

Medicine and Mental Illness (1991), a paperback by Lickey and Gordon, presents a very readable summary of biological research on the major mental disorders. It describes symptoms and DSM-III-R diagnostic criteria, evidence of drug effectiveness, and how psychotherapeutic drugs affect the brain. *Blaming the Brain* (1998), by Valenstein, presents a stinging critique of biological theories and treatments of mental disorders.

For ways to modify your own behavior, see Watson and Tharp, *Self-Directed Behavior: Self-Modification for Personal Adjustment* (5th ed., 1989). *Feeling Good* (1981), a paperback by Burns, provides a step-by-step program for using cognitive therapy techniques to understand and to change feelings of depression, anxiety, and anger. *Necessary Losses* (1986) by Viorst, written from a psychoanalytic viewpoint, is a sensitive and wise analysis of how we grow and change through the losses that are an inevitable part of life.

Eight

Social Behavior

Chapter 17
Social Cognition and Affect

Social psychology is *the study of how people think and feel about their social world and how they interact and influence one another.* How do we form our impressions of people and come to interpret their actions? How are our social beliefs and attitudes—including our stereotypes and prejudices—formed and changed? What determines whom we like, love, or choose as a romantic partner? How do we influence one another?

  In seeking answers to such questions, social psychologists begin with the basic observation that human behavior is a function of both the person and the situation. Each individual brings a unique set of personal attributes to a situation, leading different people to act in different ways in the same situation. But each situation also brings a unique set of forces to bear on an individual, leading him or her to act in different ways in different situations. Research has repeatedly shown that situations are more powerful determinants of behavior than our intuitions lead us to believe.

Individuals, however, do not react simply to the objective features of situations but to their subjective interpretations of them. The person who interprets an offensive act as the product of hostility reacts differently than the person who interprets the same act as the product of ignorance. Accordingly, this chapter begins our two-chapter discussion of social behavior by examining the ways in which we think and feel about our social environments. Chapter 18 deals with social interaction and influence.

Intuitive Theories of Social Behavior

We are all psychologists. In attempting to understand people, we act like informal scientists and construct our own intuitive theories of human behavior. In doing so, we face the same basic tasks as the formal scientist (Nisbett & Ross, 1980). First, we collect data ("Jason says women should have the right to obtain abortions"; "Kyoko got the highest score on the math test"). Second, we attempt to detect covariation or correlation, to discern what goes with what ("Do most people who support the right to abortion also oppose the death penalty?" "On the average, do Asians do better in math and science than non-Asians?"). And third, we try to infer cause and effect, to evaluate what causes what ("Does Jason support the right to abortion out of genuine conviction or because of peer pressure to express liberal attitudes?" "Do Asian students excel in math and science because they are inherently smarter or because their families stress the value of education?").

We go through the same processes in trying to understand ourselves: We observe our own thoughts, feelings, or actions ("My heart is pounding"), attempt to detect covariation ("My heart always pounds when I'm with Robin"), and try to infer cause and effect ("Am I in love with Robin, or is it just sexual passion?").

Our intuitive attempts to apply scientific reasoning to everyday life work surprisingly well. Social interaction would be chaos if our informal theories of human behavior did not have substantial validity. But we also make a number of systematic errors in arriving at social judgments, and ironically, our intuitive theories themselves often interfere with making accurate judgments. As we will see in this section, our theories can actually shape our perceptions of data, distort our estimates of covariation, and bias our evaluations of cause and effect.

Schemas

The first difficulty we face as informal scientists is that of collecting data in a systematic and unbiased way. When a survey researcher wants to estimate how many Americans support a woman's right to abortion, he or she takes great care to ensure that a random or *representative sample* of people are contacted so that the numbers of Catholics, Protestants, men, women, and so forth who are interviewed are proportional to the percentages of these groups in the total population. But when, as informal survey researchers, we try to make this estimate intuitively, our major source of data is likely to be the people we know personally. Obviously, this is not a representative sample of the population.

Another major source of data is the mass media, which also provide nonrandom and nonrepresentative samples. For example, the media give more attention to a small number of antiabortion protesters demonstrating at a medical clinic than they do to a larger number of people who silently support the clinic's abortion service. In such cases the media are not biased in the usual sense; they are simply reporting the news. But the data they give us are not a reliable sample from which to estimate public opinion.

A survey researcher also keeps accurate records of data. But in everyday life we constantly accumulate information in memory and attempt to recall it when we are called upon to make some judgment. Thus, not only are the data we collect a biased sample in the first place, but the data we actually bring to bear on our social judgments are further biased by problems of selective recall.

Vividness   One of the factors that influences the information we notice and remember is its vividness. Research has shown that when both vivid and nonvivid information compete for our attention, our estimates and judgments are more likely to be influenced by the vivid information—even when the nonvivid information is more reliable and potentially more informative (Nisbett & Ross, 1980; Taylor & Thompson, 1982).

In one study, students in introductory psychology courses who planned to major in psychology were given information about upper-level psychology courses and asked to indicate which courses they planned to take. The participants either heard two or three students make informal remarks about each course in a face-to-face session or saw a statistical summary of course evaluations by students who had taken the courses. The participants' choices were influenced more by the face-to-face remarks than by the statistical summary—even when the sumary was accompanied by the same remarks in written form. The vivid face-to-face information was more influential than the nonvivid written information even though it was based on less complete and representative data (Borgida & Nisbett, 1977).

The vividness effect is a particular problem with information obtained from the mass media. Even if reporters scrupulously gave equal coverage to both the vivid and nonvivid sides of an issue, our own information-processing tendencies would supply the bias. Thus, even if a television newscast reports the results of a survey showing that a national majority supports abortion rights, we are still more likely to store, and later recall, the vivid pictures of the antiabortion protest when we intuitively try to estimate public opinion.

Even if we could collect data in a systematic and unbiased way, our perceptions of the data might still be biased by our existing expectations and preconceptions. Whenever we perceive any object or event, we compare the incoming information with memories of previous encounters with similar objects and events. In earlier chapters we saw that memories of objects and events are not usually photographlike reproductions of the original stimuli but simplified reconstructions of our original perceptions. As noted in Chapter 8, such representations or memory structures are called **schemas;** they are *organized beliefs and knowledge about people, objects, events, and situations.* The process of searching in memory for the schema that is most consistent with the incoming data is called *schematic processing.* Schemas and schematic processing permit us to organize and process an enormous amount of information very efficiently. Instead of having to perceive and remember all the details of each new object or event, we can simply note that it is like one of our preexisting schemas and encode or remember only its most prominent features. Schematic processing typically occurs rapidly and automatically; usually we are

Vivid events are more likely to influence our judgments than less vivid events.

not even aware that any processing of information is taking place (Fiske, 1993; Fiske & Taylor, 1991).

For example, we have schemas for different kinds of people. When someone tells you that you are about to meet an extravert, you retrieve your "extravert" schema in anticipation of the coming encounter. The extravert schema consists of a set of interrelated traits such as sociability, warmth, and possibly loudness and impulsiveness. As we will see later, general person-schemas like these are sometimes called *stereotypes*. We also have schemas of particular individuals, such as the president of the United States or our parents. And as discussed in Chapter 13, we have a self-schema or schema about ourselves—a set of organized self-concepts stored in memory (Markus, 1977). When you see an advertisement for a peer counselor, you can evaluate the match between your counselor schema and your self-schema to decide whether you should apply for the job.

Research confirms that schemas help us process information. For example, if people are explicitly instructed to remember as much information as they can about a person, they actually remember less than if they are simply told to try to form an impression of him or her (Hamilton, 1979). The instruction to form an impression induces them to search for various person-relevant schemas that help them organize and recall material better. The self-schema also permits us to organize and process information efficiently. For example, as described in Chapter 13, people can recall a list of words better if they are told to decide whether each word describes themselves as they go through the list (Ganellen & Carver, 1985; Rogers, Kuiper, & Kirker, 1977). This has become known as the *self-reference effect* and occurs both because relating each word to the self leads the person to think more deeply and elaborately about it as he or she ponders whether or not it is self-relevant and because the self-schema serves to link in memory what would otherwise be unrelated information (Klein & Loftus, 1989; Klein, Loftus, & Burton, 1989).

Schemas and Perception Without schemas and schematic processing, we would be over-

whelmed by the information that inundates us. We would be very poor information processors. But the price we pay for such efficiency is a bias in both our perception and our memories of the data. Consider, for example, the impression you form of Jim from the following observations of his behavior:

> Jim left the house to get some stationery. He walked out into the sun-filled street with two of his friends, basking in the sun as he walked. Jim entered the stationery store, which was full of people. Jim talked with an acquaintance while he waited to catch the clerk's eye. On his way out, he stopped to chat with a school friend who was just coming into the store. Leaving the store, he walked toward the school. On his way he met the girl to whom he had been introduced the night before. They talked for a short while, and then Jim left for school. After school Jim left the classroom alone. Leaving the school, he started on his long walk home. The street was brilliantly filled with sunshine. Jim walked down the street on the shady side. Coming down the street toward him, he saw the pretty girl whom he had met on the previous evening. Jim crossed the street and entered a candy store. The store was crowded with students, and he noticed a few familiar faces. Jim waited quietly until he caught the counterman's eye and then gave his order. Taking his drink, he sat down at a side table. When he had finished his drink he went home. (Luchins, 1957, pp. 34–35)

What impression do you have of Jim? Do you think of him as friendly and outgoing or as shy and introverted? If you think of him as friendly, you agree with 78% of people who read this description. But examine the description closely; it is actually composed of two very different portraits. Up to the sentence that begins "After school, Jim left . . . ," Jim is portrayed in several situations as fairly friendly. After that point, however, a nearly identical set of situations shows him to be much more of a loner. Whereas 95% of the people who are shown only the first half of the description rate Jim as friendly, only 3% of the people who are shown only the second half do so. Thus, in the combined description Jim's friendliness dominates the overall impression. But when people read the same description with the unfriendly half of the paragraph appearing first, only 18% rate Jim as friendly; his nonfriendly behavior leaves the major impression (see

Table 17-1). In general, *the first information we receive has the greater impact on our overall impressions*. This is known as the **primacy effect**.

The primacy effect has been found repeatedly in several kinds of studies of impression formation, including studies using real rather than hypothetical individuals (Jones, 1990). For example, people who watched a male student attempt to solve a series of difficult multiple-choice problems were asked to assess his general ability (Jones et al., 1968). Although the student always solved exactly 15 of the 30 problems correctly, he was judged more capable if the successes came mostly at the beginning of the series than if they came near the end. Moreover, when asked to recall how many problems the student had solved, participants who had seen the 15 successes bunched at the beginning estimated an average of 21, but participants who had seen the successes at the end estimated an average of 13.

The first information we receive has a greater impact on our overall impressions than later information. This is why people usually wear business suits when being interviewed for a job.

TABLE 17-1

Schematic Processing and the Primacy Effect
Once a schema of Jim has been established, later information is assimilated into it. (After Luchins, 1957)

Conditions	Percentage Rating Jim as Friendly
Friendly description only	95
Friendly first—unfriendly last	78
Unfriendly first—friendly last	18
Unfriendly description only	3

Although several factors contribute to the primacy effect, it appears to be primarily a consequence of schematic processing. When we are first attempting to form our impressions of a person, we actively search in memory for the person-schema or schemas that best match the incoming data. At some point we make a preliminary decision: This person is friendly (or some such judgment). We then assimilate any further information to that judgment and dismiss discrepant information as not representative of the person we have come to know. For example, when asked to reconcile the apparent contradictions in Jim's behavior, participants sometimes say that Jim is really friendly but was probably tired by the end of the day (Luchins, 1957). Our schema of Jim, which has already been established, shapes our perception of all subsequent data about him. More generally, our subsequent perceptions become schema-driven and therefore relatively impervious to new data. There is thus a great deal of truth in the conventional warning that first impressions are important.

Schemas and Memory The way in which schematic processing affects our memories was demonstrated in a study in which participants viewed a videotape of a woman celebrating her birthday by having dinner with her husband. Some of the participants were told that she was a librarian; others were told that she was a waitress. Some of her behaviors were designed to be consistent with the common stereotype of a librarian; for example, she wore glasses, liked classical music, had spent the day reading, and had traveled in Europe. An equal number of behaviors were consistent with a waitress stereotype; for example, she drank beer, liked popular music, and owned a bowling ball.

After viewing the videotape, the participants were given a questionnaire that tested their memories. For example, they were asked whether the woman had drunk beer or wine with her dinner. Participants correctly remembered schema-consistent behaviors 88% of the time but correctly remembered schema-inconsistent behaviors only 78% of the time. Thus, participants who had been told that the woman was a librarian were more likely to remember that she had traveled in Europe than that she owned a bowling ball (Cohen, 1981).

As with the primacy effect, there is more than one possible explanation for memory effects like those just described (Stangor & McMillan, 1992). For example, if participants are unsure about the relevant fact, they may simply use their knowledge that the woman was a librarian or a waitress to make an educated—that is, stereotyped—guess. Another explanation is that our schemas are like folders in a file cabinet. They help us retrieve information by providing a path to the relevant items. Our "waitress" schema (folder) is more likely to contain the "bowling ball" item than the "classical music" item.

Although these findings suggest that we are more likely to remember information that is consistent rather than inconsistent with our schemas, this is not always the case (Stangor & McMillan, 1992). For example, if someone behaves in a way that is startlingly at odds with our expectations (for example, the librarian burns a book), we are likely to remember that behavior even better than behavior that is consistent (she spent the day reading) or only mildly inconsistent (she drank a beer).

Persistence of Schemas Because they affect our perceptions and memories in schema-consistent ways, schemas tend to persist in the face of disconfirming data. If we remember that the librarian spent the day reading but fail to remember that she drank beer at dinner, we will not retain any uncomfortable facts that might prompt us to modify our librarian stereotype.

More elaborate belief-schemas are similarly resistant to data. This was demonstrated in an experiment in which students who held strongly divergent beliefs about whether or not capital punishment (the death penalty) acts as a deterrent against homicide read a summary of two purportedly authentic studies. One of the studies appeared to show that capital punishment is a deterrent; the other appeared to show that it is not. The students also read a critique of each study that criticized its methodology. Not surprisingly, students on each side of the issue found the study supporting their own position to be significantly more convincing and better conducted than the other study. But the more surprising and unsettling result was that after reading all the evidence on both sides, students were *more* convinced about the correctness of their initial position than they were at the beginning of the study (Lord, Ross, & Lepper, 1979). This implies that evidence introduced into public debate in the hope of resolving an issue—or at least moderating extreme views—will tend instead to polarize public opinion even further. Proponents of each side will pick and choose from the evidence so as to bolster their initial opinions (Nisbett & Ross, 1980).

Persistence of Self-Schemas A similar effect has been shown with the self-schema. Participants in an experiment were asked to distinguish between genuine and fake suicide notes. Some of the participants were led to believe that they had done very well at the task; others were led to believe they had done badly. They were then "debriefed"; that is, they were told that the feedback had been manipulated and that the experimenter actually had no idea how well they had done. Despite this, the "successful" participants persisted in the belief that they had probably done quite well and were good at the task; similarly, the "unsuccessful" participants continued to believe that they had done badly and were not good at the task (Ross, Lepper, & Hubbard, 1975). This has been called the *perseverance effect*. Why does it occur?

One compelling explanation is that upon learning that they had done well, participants tried to come up with an explanation for their performance ("Well, I've been a peer counselor, so I'm probably pretty sensitive to other people's moods; it's not surprising that I did well"). Similarly, those who were told that they had done badly might have reviewed their past and discovered reasons for their poor performance ("This person in my dorm who I thought was the picture of mental health had to take medical leave for psychiatric reasons; I guess I'm not very good at spotting someone else's emotional troubles"). When they then learned that, in fact, the experimenter did not know how they had done, they were left with their causal explanations, which still seemed valid, so they continued to predict that they had done well or badly on the basis of their new self-schema for the task (Nisbett & Ross, 1980).

Subsequent research supports this explanation of the perseverance effect. Participants were asked to place themselves in the position of a clinical psychologist and try to explain an event in a person's life on the basis of his or her previous history. All of the participants read an authentic clinical case history of either an unhappy and somewhat neurotic young woman or a chronically unemployed and depressed middle-aged man. Each participant was then told about a later event in the person's life (for example, committing suicide, being involved in a hit-and-run accident, joining the Peace Corps, running for public office) and asked to explain why it might have occurred. The participants were then "debriefed" and told that the later event was purely hypothetical and that in fact there was no available information about the later life of the patient whose history they had read. Each participant was then asked to assess the likelihood of a number of possible events in the patient's later life, including the critical event that had been explained.

Participants predicted that the event they had explained was much more likely to occur than some other event. For example, those who had explained why, on the basis of her earlier case history, the young woman might have joined the Peace Corps now thought it much more likely that she had actually done so than those who had explained why she might have been involved in a hit-and-run accident (Ross et al., 1977).

We will see further evidence of the persistence of schemas in the following section on stereotypes.

Stereotypes

Detecting covariation or correlation—discovering what goes with what—is a fundamental task in every science. Discovering that symptoms of an illness covary with the amount of environmental pollution or correlate with the presence of a virus is the first step toward a cure. And as intuitive scientists we perceive—or think we perceive—such correlations all the time ("People who are against capital punishment seem more likely to hold a pro-choice position on abortion"; "Asians seem to do better in math and science than non-Asians"). **Stereotypes,** or *schemas of classes of people,* are actually mini-theories of covariation: The stereotype of an extravert, a gay person, or a college professor is a theory of what particular traits or behaviors go with certain other traits or behaviors.

Research shows that we are not very accurate at detecting covariations. Once again, our schemas mislead us. When our schemas lead us to expect two things to covary, we overestimate the correlation between them, even seeing illusory correlations that do not exist. But when we do not have a schema that leads us to expect them to covary, we underestimate the correlation, even failing to detect a correlation that is strongly present in the data.

This was demonstrated by two researchers who were intrigued by the fact that clinical psychologists routinely report correlations between their clients' responses to projective tests (see Chapter 13) and their personality characteristics, even though research studies fail to find such correlations. For example, experienced clinicians have often reported that gay men are more likely than heterosexual men to see anal images, feminine clothing, and three other, similar kinds of images in Rorschach inkblots. Controlled studies, however, have not found any of these images to be correlated with a homosexual orientation (Chapman & Chapman, 1969). The researchers hypothesized that psychologists see these correlations because the reported images fit a popular stereotype, or schema, of male homosexuality. Several experiments have confirmed this hypothesis.

In one, college students were asked to study a set of Rorschach cards. Each card contained the inkblot, a description of the image that a client had reported seeing in it, and a statement of two personal characteristics that the client possessed. The images described included the five stereotyped images reported by clinical psychologists to be correlated with male homosexuality plus a number of other unrelated images (for example, images of food). The characteristics reported were either homosexuality ("has sexual feelings toward other men") or unrelated characteristics such as "feels sad and depressed much of the time." The cards were carefully constructed so that no image was systematically associated with homosexuality.

After studying all the cards, participants were asked to report whether they had noticed "any general kind of thing that was seen most often by men" with the different characteristics. The results revealed that the students in this study—like experienced clinical psychologists—erroneously reported a correlation between the stereotyped images and homosexuality. They did not report any correlations between the nonstereotyped images and homosexuality.

The researchers then repeated the study, modifying the cards so that two of the nonstereotyped images (a monster image in one inkblot and an animal-human image in another) always appeared with the characteristic of homosexuality—a perfect correlation. Despite this, participants still reported seeing the nonexistent correlation with the stereotyped images more than twice as often as the perfect, correlation with the nonstereotyped images.

As intuitive scientists, we are schema-driven. We see covariations that our schemas have prepared us to see and fail to see covariations that our schemas have not prepared us to see.

Persistence of Stereotypes Perhaps it is not surprising that the inexperienced students in the study just described are misled by their stereotypes to see nonexistent correlations in the data. But why should this be true of experienced clinical psychologists? Why doesn't their daily contact with real data correct their mistaken perceptions of covariation? More generally, why do our stereotypes persist in the face of nonconfirming data?

We can illustrate some of the factors involved by representing the covariation task as shown in Figure 17-1. The figure displays some hypothetical data relevant to a popular stereotype similar to that explored in the Rorschach inkblot study: the stereotype that gay men display effeminate gestures. The table classifies a hypothetical sample of 1,100 men into the four cells of the table according to whether they have a homosexual or a heterosexual orientation and whether they do or do not display effeminate gestures.

The correct way to assess whether the two factors are correlated is to examine whether the proportion of gay men who display effeminate gestures (the left-hand column) is different from the proportion of heterosexual men who display effeminate gestures (the right-hand column). To do this, we must first add up the two cells in each column to find out how many men with each kind of orientation there are in the sample. When we do this, we see that 10 out of 100, or 10%, of the gay men display effeminate gestures and that 100 out of 1,000, or 10%, of the heterosexual men do so. In other words, these data reveal no correlation between sexual orientation and effeminate gestures.

It is important to note that to assess the correlation we had to take into account all four cells of the table. Now consider what our intuitions would tell us if we encountered these data in daily life—where we do not have the data neatly laid out in front of us.

	HOMOSEXUAL ORIENTATION	HETEROSEXUAL ORIENTATION
EFFEMINATE GESTURES	A 10	B 100
NONEFFEMINATE GESTURES	C 90	D 900
	100	1,000

FIGURE 17-1

Stereotypes as Covariations *To determine whether there is a correlation between sexual orientation and effeminate gestures, we need to know whether the proportion of men with effeminate gestures differs as a function of sexual orientation. This requires taking all four cells into account so that the column totals can be computed. Invalid stereotypes often persist because we attend only to cell A and neglect the other cells. There is, in fact, no correlation between the two factors in these hypothetical data.*

In our society, men with a homosexual orientation are in a minority, as are men who display effeminate gestures. When the two occur together (as in cell A, gay men with effeminate gestures), it is a particularly distinctive occurrence. This has two consequences. First, research has shown that people overestimate the frequency with which they have actually encountered such distinctive combinations (Hamilton & Gifford, 1976; Hamilton & Sherman, 1989). Second, even if we did not overestimate their frequency, we are still most likely to notice and remember instances that fall into cell A and to remain oblivious to the instances that fall into the other cells of the table.

Part of the reason for this is that the relevant information is almost never available to us. In particular, we rarely have the opportunity to assess the frequency of cell C, the number of gay men who do not display effeminate gestures. Cell B also sets a trap for some people. When they observe a man with effeminate gestures, they may assume that he is gay even though they have no knowledge of his actual sexual orientation. He might belong to either cell A or cell B, but through circular reasoning they convert cell B disconfirmations of their stereotype into cell A confirmations. Note that it is the stereotype itself that leads them to make this error—another instance of how our information processing is schema-driven.

But even if the data from cells other than cell A were available to us, it would not typically occur to us that we need to know this other information. We find it particularly difficult to take into account cell D, the frequency of nongay men who do not display effeminate gestures. Why is this difficult?

We noted earlier in the chapter that we are more likely to notice and remember vivid rather than nonvivid information. This is why cell A is noticed, remembered, and overestimated: Gay men with effeminate gestures are distinctive and, hence, vivid. In contrast, there are not many events that are less vivid—and hence, less noticeable and less memorable—than events that do not occur. But this is precisely what cell D events are: nonevents. The nongay man who does not display effeminate gestures does not constitute a psychological event for us. It is difficult to notice or to appreciate the relevance of nonevents in daily life.

This difficulty was cleverly employed by Arthur Conan Doyle in his Sherlock Holmes story, "The Adventure of Silver Blaze," in which the famous detective is asked to discover who stole a prize race horse from its private stable during the night. Holmes draws the police inspector's attention to "the curious incident of the dog in the night time." Puzzled, the inspector says, "The dog did nothing in the night time." To which Holmes replies: "That was the curious incident." Holmes then deduces correctly that the horse was stolen by its own trainer because the dog had not barked and, hence, must have known the intruder (Doyle, 1892/1981, p. 197).

The nonvividness of nonevents also leads the news media to promote and sustain stereotypes. When a gay man commits a murder—especially one with sexual overtones—both the sexual orientation and the murder are featured in the news story; when a heterosexual man commits a murder—even one with sexual overtones—sexual orientation is not mentioned. Thus, cell A events are widely publicized—thereby fueling the stereotype—whereas cell B events are not seen as relevant to sexual orientation. And, of course, cell C and D events—men of any sexual orientation who do not commit murder—are not news. They are nonevents.

Self-Fulfilling Stereotypes Our schemas influence not only our perceptions and inferential processes but also our behavior and social interactions. And this, too, can sustain our stereotypes. In particular, our stereotypes can lead us to interact with those we stereotype in ways that cause them to fulfill our expectations.

In a study illustrating this process, the investigators first noted that white job interviewers displayed a less friendly manner when interviewing African-American applicants than when interviewing white applicants. They hypothesized that this could cause African-American applicants to come off less well in the interviews. To test this hypothesis, they trained interviewers to reproduce both the less friendly and the more friendly interviewing styles. Applicants (all white) were then videotaped while being interviewed by an interviewer using one of these two styles. Judges who viewed the tapes rated applicants who had been interviewed in a less friendly manner significantly lower on their interview performance than those who had been interviewed in the more friendly manner (Word, Zanna, & Cooper, 1974). The study thus confirmed the hypothesis that prejudiced individuals can interact in ways that actually evoke the stereotyped behaviors that sustain their prejudice.

Stereotypes can be self-fulfilling in even more insidious ways, by directly affecting the individual's performance. Just the threat of being identified with the stereotype can raise the individual's anxiety level and thereby degrade his or her performance (Steele, 1997). This effect has been demonstrated both for the stereotype that African-Americans are less intellectually capable than whites and for the stereotype that women are less capable than men in mathematics. In one study, academically talented black and white students from a highly selective university took a test composed of the most difficult items on the verbal Graduate Record Examination. When told that the test was simply a laboratory problem-solving task unrelated to ability, the black students did just as well as the white students. But when told that the test was a test of intellectual ability, the black students performed less well than the white students. A variation of the study revealed that just having the students indicate their race on a questionnaire before taking the test was sufficient to degrade the performance of the black students—even when the test was described as unrelated to ability (Steele & Aronson, 1995).

In a study using the stereotype about women's mathematics ability, female and male college sophomores who were quite good at mathematics were given a very difficult math test. When participants were told before taking the test that men and women generally performed equally well on it, the women did in fact perform as well as the men. But when told that men generally outperformed women, the women performed worse than the men (Spencer, Steele, & Quinn, 1977).

Attributions

At the heart of most sciences is the discovery of causes and effects. Similarly, as intuitive scientists we feel that we truly understand some instance of human behavior when we know why it occurred or what caused it. Suppose, for example, that a famous athlete endorses a breakfast cereal on television. Why does she do it? Does she really like the cereal, or is she doing it for the money? You give a five-dollar donation to Planned Parenthood. Why? Are you altruistic? Were you being pressured? Do you need a tax write-off? Do you believe in the work of the organization?

Each of these cases creates an attribution problem. We see some behavior—perhaps our own—and must decide which of many possible causes the action should be attributed to. Our intuitive attempts to infer the causes of behavior has been a central topic in social psychology for a long time (Heider, 1958; Kelley, 1967).

The Fundamental Attribution Error As the two preceding examples illustrate, one of the major attribution tasks we face is deciding whether an observed behavior reflects something unique about the person (his or her attitudes, personality characteristics, and so forth) or something about the situation in which we observe the person. If we infer that something about the person is primarily responsible for the behavior (for instance, the athlete really loves the cereal), our inference is called an *internal* or *dispositional attribution* ("disposition" here refers to a person's beliefs, attitudes, and personality characteristics). If, however, we conclude that some external cause is primarily responsible for the behavior (money, social norms, threats), it is called an *external* or *situational attribution.*

Fritz Heider, the founder of attribution theory, noted that an individual's behavior is so compelling to us that we take it at face value and give insufficient weight to the circumstances surrounding it (1958). Research has confirmed Heider's observation. We underestimate the situational causes of behavior, jumping too easily to conclusions about the person's disposition. If we observe someone behaving aggressively, we too readily assume that he or she has an aggressive personality, rather than concluding that the situation might have provoked the aggression in anyone. To put it another way, we have a schema of cause and effect for human behavior that gives too much weight to the person and too little to the situation. The term **fundamental attribution error** is used to refer to *the tendency to underestimate situational* *influences on behavior and assume that some personal characteristic of the individual is responsible* (Ross, 1977).

In one of the first studies to reveal this bias, participants read a debater's speech that either supported or attacked Cuban leader Fidel Castro. The participants were explicitly told that the debate coach had assigned each debater one side of the issue or the other; the debater had no choice as to which side to argue. Despite this knowledge, when asked to estimate the debater's actual attitude toward Castro, participants inferred that he or she held a position close to the one argued in the debate. In other words, the participants made a dispositional attribution even though situational forces were fully sufficient to account for the behavior (Jones & Harris, 1967). This effect is quite powerful. Even when the participants themselves designate which side of the issue a speaker is to argue, they still tend to see him or her as actually holding that opinion (Gilbert & Jones, 1986). The effect occurs

Is this woman giving money to the Salvation Army because she supports its work, because she feels pressured, or because she is generally altruistic?

even if the presentations are deliberately designed to be drab and unenthusiastic and the speaker simply reads a transcribed version of the speech in a monotone and uses no gestures (Schneider & Miller, 1975).

An experiment designed as a quiz game illustrates how both participants and observers make the same fundamental attribution error in the same setting. Pairs of male or female participants were recruited to take part in a question-and-answer game testing general knowledge. One member of the pair was randomly assigned to be the questioner and to make up 10 difficult questions to which he or she knew the answers (such as "What is the world's largest glacier?"). The other participant acted as the contestant and attempted to answer the questions. When the contestant was unable to answer a question, the questioner gave the answer. In a reenactment of the study, observers watched the contest. After the game both participants and observers were asked to rate the level of general knowledge possessed by the questioner and the contestant, relative to that possessed by the "average student." It is important to note that participants and observers all knew that the roles of questioner and contestant had been assigned randomly.

As Figure 17-2 shows, questioners judged both themselves and the contestant to be about average in level of general knowledge. But contestants rated the questioner as superior and themselves as inferior to the average student. They attributed the outcome of the game to their (and the questioner's) level of knowledge rather than taking into account the overwhelming situational advantage enjoyed by the questioner, who was able to decide which questions to ask and to omit any questions to which he or she did not know the answer. Observers, aware that the questioner could ask questions that neither they nor the contestant could answer, rated the questioner's level of knowledge even higher. In other words, both contestants and observers gave too much weight to disposition and too little to the situation—the fundamental attribution error (Ross, Amabile, & Steinmetz, 1977).

One implication of this study is that people who select the topics discussed in a conversation will be seen as more knowledgeable than those who passively let others set the agenda, even if everyone is aware of the differential roles being played. This, in turn, has implications for contemporary sex roles. Research has shown that men talk more than women in mixed-sex interactions (Henley, Hamilton, & Thorne, 1985); they interrupt more (West & Zimmerman, 1983); and they are more likely to raise the topics discussed (Fishman, 1983). The questioner-contestant study implies that one consequence of these sex-role patterns is that women leave most mixed-sex interactions thinking themselves less knowledgeable than the men, with bystanders of both sexes sharing this illusion. The moral is clear: The fundamental attribution error can work for or against you. If you want to appear knowledgeable both to yourself and to others, learn how to structure the situation so that you control the choice of topics discussed. Be the questioner, not the contestant.

Self-Attributions In the experiment just described, the contestants made the fundamental attribution error about their own behavior. One social psychologist has proposed that, in general, we make judgments about ourselves using the same inferential processes—and making the same kinds of errors—that we use for making judgments about others. Specifically, this *self-perception theory* proposes that individuals come to know their own attitudes, emotions, and other internal states partially by inferring them from observations of their own behavior and the circumstances in which the behavior occurs. Thus, to the extent that internal cues are weak, ambiguous, or uninterpretable, the individual is like any outside observer who must rely on external cues to infer the individual's inner states (Bem, 1972).

These propositions are illustrated by the common remark, "This is my second sandwich; I guess I was hungrier than I thought." Here the speaker has inferred an internal state by observing his or her own behavior. Similarly, the self-observation "I've been biting my nails all day; something must be bugging me" is based on the same external evidence that might lead a friend to remark, "You've been biting your nails all day; something must be bugging you."

A more formal and surprising illustration of self-perception theory is provided by an induced-compliance experiment originally conducted in order to test Festinger's theory of cognitive dissonance (1957) (discussed

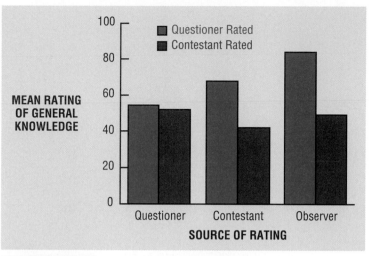

FIGURE 17-2

The Fundamental Attribution Error *Ratings of questioners and contestants after they had participated in a quiz game. The questioner is rated as superior by both the contestant and observers even though the questioner had an overwhelming situational advantage. Both contestants and observers gave too much weight to dispositional causes and too little to situational causes.* (After Ross, Amabile, & Steinmetz, 1977)

later in the chapter). Male college students participated one at a time in an experiment in which they worked on dull, repetitive tasks. After completing the tasks, some participants were offered $1 to tell the next participant that the tasks had been fun and interesting. Others were offered $20 to do this. All of the participants complied with the request. Later they were asked how much they had enjoyed the tasks. As shown in Figure 17-3, participants who had been paid only $1 stated that they had in fact enjoyed the tasks. But participants who had been paid $20 did not find them significantly more enjoyable than did members of a control group who never spoke to another participant (Festinger & Carlsmith, 1959). The small incentive for complying with the experimenter's request—but not the large incentive—led participants to believe what they had heard themselves say. Why should this be so?

Just as we try to decide whether an athlete on television really loves the cereal she endorses or whether she is just saying so for the money, so, too, self-perception theory proposes that participants in this experiment looked at their own behavior (telling another participant that the tasks were interesting) and implicitly asked themselves,

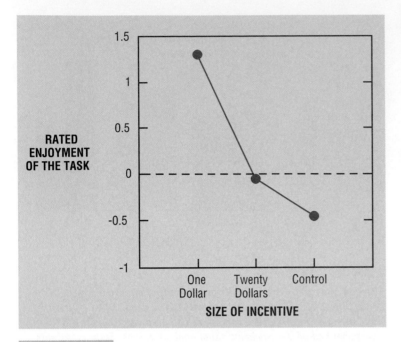

RATED ENJOYMENT OF THE TASK

SIZE OF INCENTIVE

FIGURE 17-3

An Induced-Compliance Experiment *The smaller incentive for agreeing to say that the tasks were interesting led participants to infer that they had actually enjoyed the tasks. The larger incentive did not.* (After Festinger & Carlsmith, 1959)

"Why did I do this?" It further proposes that they sought an answer the same way as an outside observer would, by trying to decide whether to make a dispositional attribution (he did it because he really did enjoy the tasks) or a situational attribution (he did it for the money). When the individual is paid only $1, the observer is more likely to make a dispositional attribution: "He wouldn't be willing to say it for only $1, so he must have actually enjoyed the tasks." But if the individual is paid $20, the observer is more likely to make a situational attribution: "Anyone would have done it for $20, so I can't judge his attitude toward the tasks on the basis of his statement." If the individual follows the same inferential process as this hypothetical outside observer, participants who are paid $1 make a dispositional attribution about their own behavior: "I must think the tasks were enjoyable; otherwise I would not have said so." But participants who are paid $20 attribute their behavior to the money and therefore express the same attitudes toward the tasks as the control participants who made no statements to another participant.

In the experiment just described, all the participants were willing to tell the next par-

ticipant that the tasks were enjoyable—even if they were offered only $1 to do so. But the participants themselves did not know this. Thus, when participants who were paid $1 inferred that they must think the tasks are enjoyable because otherwise they would not have said so, they were wrong. They should have inferred that they talked to the next participant because they were paid $1 to do so. In other words, they made a dispositional attribution about their own behavior when they should have made a situational attribution. They committed the fundamental attribution error.

Theorizing About Oneself   Self-perception theory draws a portrait of two selves in one, a subject-self and a psychologist-self. The subject-self behaves and the psychologist-self attempts to interpret or explain the behavior, displaying the same biases and making the same kinds of errors as any intuitive scientist. We encountered a similar idea in Chapter 6, where we discussed Hilgard's theory of hypnosis. According to this theory, there is a "hidden observer," a mental structure that monitors everything that happens during hypnosis, including events that the individual is not consciously aware of perceiving.

Research in neuropsychology suggests that the concept of an observing self and an observed self may be more than a simple metaphor. In Chapter 2 we discussed research on patients in which the two hemispheres of the brain had been surgically separated for medical reasons. Because the language area of the brain is located in the left hemisphere, such patients cannot verbally describe visual stimuli presented to the right hemisphere. Subsequent experiments have suggested that there is a "left-brain interpreter" that attempts to understand feelings and behaviors originating in other parts of the brain (Gazzaniga, 1985).

In one of those experiments, a picture of a chicken claw was presented to the left hemisphere of a split-brain patient while a picture of a snow scene was presented to the right hemisphere. Under these conditions the left hemisphere does not register the snow scene. The patient was then shown an array of pictures and asked to choose those associated with the pictures presented earlier. The obviously correct associations were a picture of a chicken for the chicken claw and a picture of a shovel for the snow scene. The patient chose both of the correct pictures, pointing to the shovel with the left hand (which is controlled by the right hemisphere) and the chicken with the right hand. When asked why he chose these items, he replied, "Oh, that's simple. The chicken claw goes with the chicken, and you need a shovel to clean out the chicken shed." The left-brain interpreter—ignorant of the snow scene but seeing his hand choose the picture of the shovel—also made up a plausible theory to explain the behavior.

In another experiment, the written command "laugh" was presented to a patient's right hemisphere. The patient laughed, and when asked why, said, "You guys come up and test us every month. What a way to make a living!" When the command "walk" was flashed to the right hemisphere of another patient, he stood up and began to leave, explaining that he had decided to get a Coke.

Understanding our emotions also appears to require the left-brain interpreter. In one experiment, a film depicting a person throwing someone into a fire was shown to the right hemisphere of a split-brain patient. As expected, she could not describe what she saw, but she described herself as feeling kind of scared and jumpy. As an aside to a colleague, she said, "I know I like Dr. Gazzaniga, but right now I'm scared of him for some reason." Denied knowledge of the source of the emotion, the left-brain interpreter came up with a plausible theory to explain the felt emotional state.

In general, when people are asked to account for their preferences, behaviors, and emotional states, they tend to identify causes that seem plausible—even when those causes are not operative—and to overlook actual causes that seem less plausible (Nisbett & Wilson, 1977). For example, several studies have asked individuals to keep daily records of their moods and the factors that might affect them (the day of the week, the weather, how long they slept, and so forth). At the end of each study, the participants were asked to judge how much each of the factors had affected their moods. There was little relationship between their perceptions of how important a factor was and how well it actually correlated with their moods. In fact, participants were no better at esti-

mating how well the day of the week or the weather had predicted their moods than strangers who were simply asked to make plausible intuitive estimates (Wilson, Laser, & Stone, 1982).

Cross-Cultural Differences in Attribution Processes

Most Western industrialized nations have an *individualist* orientation, which values independence and self-assertiveness. In contrast, many non-Western cultures have a more *collectivist* orientation, which stresses people's interdependence with others in the community. This suggests the possibility that some of the attributional effects that we have been discussing may not be universal but instead reflect the individualist orientation of the societies in which most of the research has been conducted. For example, it may be our individualist orientation rather than a universal feature of human information processing that prompts us to describe people in terms of personality traits or to attribute actions to an individual's personality rather than to the situation.

To test this possibility, individuals from Japan (a society with a collectivist orientation) and the United States were asked to respond repeatedly to the question "Who am I?" The Japanese participants listed only one quarter as many psychological traits (for example, "I am optimistic") as the American participants, but they listed three times as many social roles and contexts (for example, "I am a member of the drama club"). Interestingly, when a social context was specified, the Japanese were *more* likely than the Americans to use psychological traits to describe themselves (for example, "at home I am sometimes lazy" or "in school I am hard working"), thereby indicating that they view their behavior as dependent on the situation (Cousins, 1989). Other, similar studies confirm that individuals in Europe and North America are significantly more likely than Asians to describe themselves in dispositional terms (Trafimow, Triandis, & Goto, 1991; Triandis, 1989).

Another cross-cultural study sought to determine whether Americans would be more likely than Hindus to favor dispositional explanations of behavior over situational explanations. Each participant was asked to "describe something a person you know well did recently that you considered a wrong thing to have done" and also to "describe something a person you know well did recently that you considered good for someone else." The participants were then asked to explain why each behavior occurred.

As predicted, American participants offered dispositional explanations (for example, "he is rather careless and inconsiderate") more frequently and situational explanations (for example, "it was hard to see, and the other bicycle was going very fast") less frequently than did Hindu participants. To determine whether these differences were simply due to the kinds of behaviors selected by members of each culture, the American participants were also asked to explain the behaviors mentioned by the Hindu participants. This made no difference; they continued to favor dispositional explanations over situational ones to the same extent (Miller, 1984).

At first glance, these results would seem to imply that individuals in collectivist Asian cultures are less likely to commit the fundamental attribution error than individuals in the United States or other individualist cultures. But it may also be that situational factors actually do play more of a role in determining behavior in collectivist cultures. This is, in fact, the basic assumption of scholars who contrast individualist and collectivist cultures. These explanations are not mutually exclusive, however. Situational influences in collectivist cultures may be more powerful determinants of behavior and, therefore, also more cognitively available as explanations for behavior (Ross & Nisbett, 1991).

Attitudes

So far our discussion has focused on cognitive functioning, the processes of perceiving and thinking. With the concept of attitude, we can begin to incorporate **affect**—*emotions and feelings*—into our discussion of social behavior.

Attitudes are likes and dislikes—*favorable or unfavorable evaluations of and reactions to objects, people, situations, or other aspects of the world*, including abstract ideas and social policies. We often express our attitudes in statements of opinion: "I love oranges" or "I can't abide liberals." But even though attitudes express feelings, they are often linked to cognitions—specifically, to beliefs about the attitude objects ("Oranges contain lots of vitamins"; "Liberals just want to tax and spend"). Moreover, attitudes are sometimes linked to the actions we take with respect to the attitude objects ("I eat an orange every morning"; "I never vote for liberal candidates").

Accordingly, social psychologists usually conceive of attitudes as comprising a *cognitive component*, an *affective component*, and a *behavioral component*. For example, in studying negative attitudes toward groups, social psychologists distinguish between negative stereotypes (negative beliefs and perceptions about a group—the cognitive component), prejudice (negative feelings toward the group—the affective component), and discrimination (negative actions against members of the group—the behavioral component). Some theorists prefer to define an attitude as comprising only the cognitive and affective components; others include only the affective component. But despite differing definitions, all share a concern with the interrelationships among the pertinent beliefs, feelings, and behaviors.

Consistency of Attitudes

Certain attitudes seem to go together. For example, people who support affirmative action seem likely to advocate stronger gun control, oppose capital punishment, and hold a pro-choice position on abortion. On the surface, these diverse attitudes do not seem to follow one another logically. Yet knowing that a person holds one of the attitudes often permits us to guess the others fairly accurately, and there does seem to be a kind of logic involved. The attitudes all appear to stem from a set of underlying values that we might label as "liberal."

The same kind of logic can be discerned among "conservative" attitudes. Many people who oppose affirmative action and gun control laws cite their belief in the value of individual freedom as the basis for their opinions. Even those who disagree with such opinions can appreciate the logic involved. But many such freedom-loving individuals also feel that women belong in the home, that marijuana use should be more heavily penalized, and that homosexual behavior should be illegal. Here the logic is less clear, yet these attitudes, too, seem strangely predictable.

In short, people's attitudes often appear to have a kind of internal logic, but it is not usually a strict, formal logic. Instead, it is a kind of psycho-logic, and it is this psycho-logic that social psychologists have studied under the label *cognitive consistency*. The basic premise of cognitive consistency theories is that we all strive to be consistent in our beliefs, attitudes, and behaviors, and that inconsistency acts as an irritant or a stimulus that motivates us to modify or change them until they form a coherent, if not logical, package. Over the years, consistency theorists have amassed a great deal of evidence for this basic premise (Abelson et al., 1968).

But most of the research on consistency has been conducted with college students in laboratory studies. Psychologists and political scientists who have conducted analyses outside of the laboratory are divided in their views about the ideological coherence of public opinion on social and political issues (Kinder & Sears, 1985). As one of them has said,

> As intellectuals and students of politics we are disposed by training and sensibility to take political ideas seriously. . . . We are therefore prone to forget that most people take them less seriously than we do, that they pay little attention to issues, rarely worry about the consistency of their opinions, and spend little or no time thinking about the values, presuppositions, and implications that distinguish one political orientation from another. (McClosky, quoted by Abelson, 1968)

Examples of such inconsistency have been around for decades. For example, in a national survey conducted by the *New York Times* and CBS News in the late 1970s, a majority of Americans said that they disapprove of "most government-sponsored welfare programs." Yet over 80% said that they supported the government's "program providing financial assistance for children raised in low-income homes where one parent is missing" (Aid to Families with Dependent Children, a major welfare program); the government's program for "helping poor people buy food for their families at cheaper prices" (the essence of the federal food-stamp program); and the government's program for paying for health care for poor people (the Medicaid program).

The level of support for these major welfare programs was similar among all types of people—rich and poor, liberal and conservative, Democrat and Republican. And despite the recent reform of the welfare system, people are still more likely to oppose the general concept of welfare than they are to oppose specific programs.

An early national survey designed to probe this kind of inconsistency found a similar contradiction between ideological conservatism and operational liberalism in attitudes toward welfare. One out of four Americans was conservative on questions concerning the general concept of welfare but simultaneously liberal on questions concerning specific welfare programs (Free & Cantril, 1967).

Despite these findings, we need to be cautious about accusing someone of being inconsistent. The person's attitudes may simply be inconsistent with our own ideological framework. For example, opposition to capital punishment is usually characterized as a liberal position, whereas opposition to legalized abortion is usually thought of as a conservative position. Yet there is a quite logical coherence to the views of a person who, being against all taking of life, opposes both capital punishment and legalized abortion. Another example is provided by libertarians, who are opposed to any government interference in individuals' lives. They are conservative on economic issues—the free market, not the government, should control the economic system—and in their opposition to government—enforced civil rights laws and affirmative action programs. But they are liberal on personal social issues, believing, for example, that the government should not criminalize the use of marijuana or concern itself with private sexual behavior. To libertarians, both conservatives and liberals are inconsistent.

Nevertheless, the evidence suggests that most citizens do not organize their beliefs and attitudes according to any kind of overall ideology; nonconsistency, if not inconsistency, seems to be more prevalent than consistency. This has led one psychologist to propose that many of our attitudes come packaged as "opinion molecules." Each molecule is made up of (a) a belief, (b) an attitude, and (c) a perception of social support for the opinion. In other words, each opinion molecule contains a fact, a feeling, and a following (Abelson,

A person's attitudes are not necessarily consistent. Most people complain bitterly about income taxes, yet at the same time they favor government services that benefit them.

1968). For example: "It's a fact that when my Uncle Charlie had back trouble, he was cured by a chiropractor [fact]"; "You know, I feel that chiropractors have been sneered at too much [feeling], and I'm not ashamed to say so because I know a lot of people who feel the same way [following]."

Opinion molecules serve important social functions. First, they act as conversational units, giving us something coherent to say when a particular topic comes up in conversation. They also give a rational appearance to our unexamined agreement with friends and neighbors on social issues. But most important, they serve to identify us with important social groups, reinforcing our sense of belonging to a social community. Thus, the fact and the feeling are less important ingredients of an opinion molecule than the following.

Functions of Attitudes

Attitudes serve a number of different psychological functions. Different people might hold the same attitude for different reasons, and a person might hold a particular attitude for more than one reason. The functions that an attitude serves for an individual influence how consistent it is with his or her other attitudes and how easily it can be changed. Over the years, attitude theorists have identified several functions of attitudes (Herek, 1986; Katz, 1960; Smith, Bruner, & White, 1956). We discuss five of them here.

The Instrumental Function Attitudes that we hold for practical or utilitarian reasons are said to serve an *instrumental* function. They express specific instances of our general desire to obtain benefits or rewards and avoid punishment. For example, most Americans favor more government services but oppose higher taxes. As this example indicates, such attitudes are not necessarily consistent. To change such attitudes, the person needs only to be convinced that an alternative would bring more benefits.

The Knowledge Function Attitudes that help us make sense of the world, that bring order to the diverse information we must assimilate in our daily lives, are said to serve a *knowledge* function. Such attitudes are essentially schemas that permit us to organize and process diverse information efficiently without having to attend to its details. For example, before 1990, negative attitudes toward the Soviet Union helped many Americans organize and interpret world events in terms of the cold war. The belief that Democrats just want to "tax and spend" or that Republicans care only for the wealthy provides a quick schematic way of interpreting and evaluating the proposals and candidates offered by the two parties. Like other schemas, such attitudes often oversimplify reality and bias our perception of events.

The Value-Expressive Function Attitudes that express our values or reflect our self-concepts are said to serve a *value-expressive* function. For example, a person might have positive attitudes toward gay people because of deeply held values about diversity, personal freedom, and tolerance; another person might have negative attitudes because of deeply held religious convictions that condemn homosexuality. Because value-expressive attitudes are derived from the person's underlying values or self-concept, they tend to be consistent. As noted earlier, broad political values, such as liberalism or conservatism, can serve as a basis for value-expressive attitudes. Such attitudes do not change easily; the individual has to be convinced that an alternative attitude would be more consistent with his or her underlying values or self-concept.

The Ego-Defensive Function Attitudes that protect us from anxiety or from threats to our self-esteem are said to serve an *ego-defensive* function. The concept of ego defensiveness comes from Sigmund Freud's psychoanalytic theory (see Chapter 13). One of the mechanisms of ego defense described by Freud is **projection:** The individual *represses his or her own unacceptable impulses and expresses hostile attitudes toward others who are perceived to possess those impulses.* For example, a person who is fearful of his or her own possible homosexual feelings is likely to deny having such feelings and display hostility toward gay people. In one study, students at a liberal California university were asked to write essays describing their attitudes toward lesbians and gay men. A content analysis of the essays revealed negative attitudes serving an ego-defensive function in about 35% of the essays (Herek, 1987).

The notion that negative attitudes toward minority groups can serve an ego-defensive function is called the *scapegoat theory* of prejudice, because the person's hostility often takes the form of blaming those groups for both personal and societal problems. This theory was tested in the late 1940s by a group of psychologists at the University of California at Berkeley. The researchers sought to discover whether psychoanalytic theory could explain the kind of anti-Semitism and fascist ideology that had emerged in Nazi Germany and whether one could identify individuals who would be particularly susceptible to such an ideology. The research, described in a book titled *The Authoritarian Personality,* has become a classic in social psychology (Adorno et al., 1950).

Using attitude questionnaires, the investigators first confirmed their hypothesis that individuals who were anti-Semitic were also likely to be prejudiced against many groups other than their own—that is, against "outgroups." In interviews such individuals recalled rigidly moralistic parental discipline, a hierarchical family structure, and concern about the family's

Hostile attitudes toward "outgroups" may be serving an ego-defensive function in which the person blames the outgroup for personal and societal problems. This is known as the scapegoat theory of prejudice.

socioeconomic status. According to the investigators, such home environments produce individuals with "authoritarian personalities"—individuals who are submissive and obedient to those they consider their superiors (including authority figures) but contemptuous of and aggressive toward those they consider inferior. As the psychoanalytic theory of prejudice predicts, authoritarian individuals repress knowledge of their own undesirable characteristics, projecting them instead onto members of "inferior" outgroups.

Although the authoritarian personality study has been criticized for a number of shortcomings (Christie & Jahoda, 1954), many of its original conclusions have withstood the test of continued research. In particular, there does appear to be an authoritarian personality type that seems particularly susceptible to a fascist ideology with hostility toward outgroups at its core. More recent research suggests, however, that prejudice and authoritarian attitudes may be acquired more directly through normal learning processes rather than through the more involved psychoanalytic processes described in the original research (Altemeyer, 1988). Also, the specific political content of an authoritarian outlook can differ from one society to another. A survey conducted in 1991 found that highly authoritarian Russians tended to oppose individualism but supported equality (such as free and equal medical care for everybody), a pattern opposite that displayed by authoritarian individuals in the United States (McFarland, Ageyev, & Abalakina-Paap, 1992).

The Social Adjustment Function Attitudes that help us feel that we are part of a social community are said to serve a *social adjustment* function. The "opinion molecules" discussed earlier provide one example. Another example can be seen in people who hold the prescribed beliefs and attitudes of a particular church or political party because their friends, families, and neighbors do; the actual content of the beliefs and attitudes is less important than the social bonds they provide. To the extent that attitudes serve primarily a social adjustment function, they are likely to change if social norms change.

This was demonstrated in striking fashion in the American South during the 1950s,

when legalized racial segregation was being dismantled. Surveys showed that Americans in the South were generally opposed to desegregation and were more likely than Americans in the North to express negative attitudes toward African-Americans. Some psychologists suggested that southern Americans might be more authoritarian than northern Americans-that racial attitudes in the South were serving an ego-defensive function. But Thomas Pettigrew, a social psychologist who specializes in race relations, argued that racial attitudes in the South were being sustained primarily by simple conformity to the prevailing social norms of the region—a social adjustment function (Pettigrew, 1959).

Using the questionnaire developed for measuring authoritarianism, Pettigrew found that southerners were no more authoritarian than northerners (although authoritarian individuals in both regions were more prejudiced against African-Americans than nonauthoritarian individuals). Moreover, southerners who were prejudiced against African-Americans were not necessarily prejudiced against other outgroups—which is contrary to what the theory of authoritarianism predicts. In fact, the South has historically been one of the least anti-Semitic regions in the United States, and one survey done at the time showed southern whites to be unfavorable toward African-Americans but quite favorable toward Jews (Prothro, 1952). Also, veterans from the South—whose military experience had exposed them to different social norms—were considerably less prejudiced than nonveterans, even though veterans from both South and North were more authoritarian than nonveterans.

The subsequent history of desegregation confirmed Pettigrew's analysis. As desegregation progressed, surveys showed that attitudes toward a particular desegregation step tended to be unfavorable just before the change had been implemented but became favorable soon afterward (Pettigrew, 1959). Thus, some communities had accepted the desegregation of public accommodations but were still opposed to school desegregation; other communities showed the reverse pattern. In one study, it was estimated that about 40% of the sample had firm opinions favoring or opposing desegregation, but that the remaining 60%

favored whatever the social norms happened to be at the time (Minard, 1952).

It is often said that one cannot legislate attitudes. In a literal sense this is obviously true. But legislation and judicial decrees change public policies and practices, and these, in turn, frequently lead to changes in social norms. To the extent that a citizen's attitudes are serving a social adjustment function, they, too, will change. Under these conditions the quickest path toward changing "hearts and minds" is to first change behavior by changing social norms.

Attitudes and Behavior

A major reason for studying attitudes is the expectation that they will enable us to predict a person's future behavior. A political candidate is interested in a survey of voters' opinions only if the attitudes expressed relate to voting behavior. The assumption that a person's attitudes determine his or her behavior is deeply ingrained in Western thinking, and in many instances the assumption holds.

But research has shown that the relationship between attitudes and behavior is complex. A classic study conducted during the 1930s was the first to question the link. A white professor traveled across the United States with a young Chinese couple. At that time there was quite strong prejudice against Asians and there were no laws against racial discrimination in public accommodations. The three travelers stopped at over 200 hotels, motels, and restaurants and were served at all the restaurants and all but one of the hotels and motels without a problem. Later, a letter was sent to all of the restaurants and hotels asking them whether or not they would accept a Chinese couple as guests. Of the 128 replies received, 92% said that they would not. In other words, these proprietors expressed attitudes that were much more prejudiced than their behavior (LaPiere, 1934).

This study shows that behavior is determined by many factors other than attitudes, and these other factors affect attitude-behavior consistency. One obvious factor is the degree of constraint in the situation: We must often act in ways that are not consistent with what we feel or believe. As children we ate vegetables that we detested, and

as adults we attend lectures and dinner parties that we considered boring. In the racial discrimination study, the prejudiced proprietors may have found it difficult to act on their prejudices when actually faced with an Asian couple seeking service.

Peer pressure can exert similar influences on behavior. For example, a teenager's attitude toward marijuana is moderately correlated with his or her actual use of marijuana, but the number of marijuana-using friends the teenager has is an even better predictor of his or her marijuana use (Andrews & Kandel, 1979).

In general, attitudes tend to predict behavior best when (a) they are strong and consistent; (b) they are specifically related to the behavior being predicted; (c) they are based on the person's direct experience; and (d) the individual is aware of his or her attitudes. We will look briefly at each of these factors.

Strong and Consistent Attitudes Strong and consistent attitudes predict behavior better than weak or ambivalent ones. Many voters experience ambivalence because they are under pressure from friends and associates who do not agree with one another. For example, a Jewish businessperson belongs to an ethnic group that generally holds liberal political positions, but she also belongs to a business community that frequently holds conservative political positions, particularly on economic issues. When it comes time to vote, she is subjected to conflicting pressures.

Ambivalence and conflict can arise from within the person as well. When the affective and cognitive components of an attitude are not consistent—for example, when we like something that we know is bad for us—it is often difficult to predict behavior (Norman, 1975). In general, when the components are inconsistent, it is the one that is most closely related to the behavior that will best predict it (Millar & Tesser, 1989).

Attitudes Specifically Related to Behavior Relevant to this last point is the frequent finding that attitudes that are specifically related to the behavior being assessed predict the behavior better than attitudes that are only generally related to it. For example in one study, students in the United

States, Britain, and Sweden were asked both about their general attitudes toward nuclear war and about their specific attitudes toward nuclear war, nuclear weapons, and nuclear power plants. Specific attitudes were much better predictors of activist behaviors (such as writing a letter to a newspaper or signing a petition) than more general attitudes (Newcomb, Rabow, & Hernandez, 1992).

Attitudes Based on Direct Experience Attitudes based on direct experience predict behavior better than attitudes formed from reading or hearing about an issue (Fazio, 1990). For example, during a housing shortage at a university, many freshmen had to spend the first few weeks of the term in crowded temporary housing. Researchers measured students' attitudes toward the housing crisis and their willingness to sign and distribute petitions or join committees to study it. For students who actually had to live in the temporary housing, there was a high correlation between their attitude toward the crisis and their willingness to take action to solve it. But for students who had not directly experienced the temporary housing, no such correlation existed (Regan & Fazio, 1977).

Awareness Finally, there is evidence that people who are more aware of their attitudes are more likely to behave in ways that are consistent with those attitudes. This is true of people who are generally more focused on their thoughts and feelings as part of their personalities (Scheier, Buss, & Buss, 1978) as well as of people who are placed in situations designed to make them more aware, such as in front of a mirror or video camera (Carver & Scheier, 1981; Hutton & Baumeister, 1992; Pryor et al., 1977).

Interestingly, however, when people are first asked to ponder the reasons for their attitudes, their attitudes become less predictive of their behavior. Apparently, when we first analyze how we feel, we cognitively "derive" our attitudes on the basis of our intuitive theories of what attitudes should plausibly follow from such reasons. This logically derived attitude is frequently different from our actual feelings (Wilson et al., 1989).

Cognitive Dissonance Theory

We have examined how attitudes might lead to behavior, but it is also possible for behavior to lead to attitudes. The most influential explanation of this sequence of events is Leon Festinger's *cognitive dissonance theory*. Like cognitive consistency theories in general, cognitive dissonance theory assumes that there is a drive toward cognitive consistency; two cognitions that are inconsistent will produce discomfort, which will motivate the person to remove the inconsistency and bring the cognitions into harmony. The term **cognitive dissonance** refers to *the discomfort produced by inconsistent cognitions* (Festinger, 1957).

Although cognitive dissonance theory addresses several kinds of inconsistency, it has been most provocative in predicting that engaging in behavior that is counter to one's attitudes creates pressure to change the attitudes so that they are consistent with the behavior. The theory further states that engaging in such behavior produces the most dissonance, and hence the most attitude change, when there are no consonant (that is, consistent) reasons for engaging in the behavior. This was illustrated in an experiment discussed earlier in the context of self-perception theory, the induced-compliance experiment by Festinger and Carlsmith (1959).

Recall that participants in this study were induced to tell a waiting participant that a series of dull tasks had been fun and interesting. Participants who had been paid $20 to do this did not change their attitudes, but participants who had been paid only $1 came to believe that the tasks had in fact been enjoyable. According to cognitive dissonance theory, being paid $20 provides a very consonant reason for complying with the experimenter's request to talk to the waiting participant, and hence the person experiences little or no dissonance. The inconsistency between the person's behavior and his or her attitude toward the tasks is outweighed by the far greater consistency between the compliance and the incentive for complying. Accordingly, the participants who were paid $20 did not change their attitudes; those who were paid $1, however, had no consonant reason for complying.

Accordingly, they experienced dissonance, which they reduced by coming to believe that they really did enjoy the tasks. The general conclusion is that dissonance-causing behavior will lead to attitude change in induced-compliance situations when the behavior can be induced with a minimum amount of pressure, whether in the form of reward or punishment.

Experiments with children have confirmed the prediction about minimal punishment. If children obey a very mild request not to play with an attractive toy, they come to believe that the toy is not as attractive as they first thought—a belief that is consistent with their observation that they are not playing with it. But if the children refrain from playing with the toy under a strong threat of punishment, they do not change their liking for the toy (Aronson & Carlsmith, 1963; Freedman, 1965).

Over the years, alternative explanations have been offered for some of the findings of cognitive dissonance theory. For example, we have seen that both cognitive dissonance theory and self-perception theory claim to explain the results of induced-compliance studies. In general, each of the alternative theories has generated data that the other theories cannot explain. Some studies find evidence that participants do experience arousal and discomfort when arguing for positions that are contrary to their true beliefs, a finding that is consistent with cognitive dissonance theory but not with self-perception theory (Eliot & Devine, 1994; Elkin & Leippe, 1986). Others have concluded that all the theories may be correct—each under slightly different circumstances—and that the focus of research should be on specifying when and where each theory applies (Baumeister & Tice, 1984; Fazio, Zanna, & Cooper, 1977; Paulhus, 1982).

Interpersonal Attraction

In our discussion of attitudes we distinguished between the cognitive and affective components—thinking and feeling. There is, however, no area of human behavior in which cognitions and affects are intertwined in a more complex way than in interpersonal attraction: liking, loving, and sexual desire. Research in these areas has often confirmed common knowledge, but it has also produced a number of surprises and contradictions. We begin with **liking**—namely, *friendship and the early stages of more intimate relationships.*

Liking

We cannot all be beautiful film stars, but when two such people become a couple, they do illustrate several of the determinants of interpersonal attraction that apply even to us ordinary mortals: physical attractiveness, proximity, familiarity, and similarity. As the high divorce rate among contemporary couples also illustrates, however, these factors are not always sufficient to sustain a long-term relationship.

Physical Attractiveness   To most of us there is something mildly undemocratic about the possibility that a person's physical appearance is a determinant of how well others like him or her. Unlike character and personality, physical appearance is a factor over which we have little control, and hence it seems unfair to use it as a criterion for liking someone. In fact, surveys conducted over a span of several decades have shown that people do not rank physical attractiveness as very important in their liking of other people (Buss & Barnes, 1986; Hudson & Hoyt, 1981; Tesser & Brodie, 1971; Perrin, 1921).

But research on actual behavior shows otherwise (Brehm, 1992). One group of psychologists set up a "computer dance" in which college men and women were randomly paired. At intermission everyone filled out an anonymous questionnaire evaluating his or her date. In addition, the experimenters obtained several personality test scores for each person, as well as an independent estimate of his or her physical attractiveness. The results showed that only physical attractiveness played a role in how much the person was liked by his or her partner. None of the measures of intelligence, social skills, or personality was related to the partners' liking for each other (Walster et al., 1966). This experiment has been replicated many times, and in each case the results have been similar to those just described. Moreover, the importance of physical attractiveness has been found to operate not only on first dates but on subsequent ones as well (Mathes, 1975).

Why is physical attractiveness so important? Part of the reason is that our social standing and self-esteem are enhanced when we are seen with physically attractive companions. Both men and women are rated more favorably when they are with an attractive romantic partner or friend than when they are with an unattractive companion (Sheposh, Deming, & Young, 1977; Sigall & Landy, 1973). But there is an interesting twist to this: Both men and women are rated less favorably when they are seen with a stranger who is physically more attractive than they (Kernis & Wheeler, 1981). Apparently they suffer by comparison with the other person. This effect has been found in other studies. For example, male college students who had just watched a television show starring beautiful young women gave lower attractiveness ratings to a photograph

These neighbors are likely to form a friendship simply because of proximity.

of a more typical-looking woman—as did both men and women who were first shown a photograph of a highly attractive woman (Kendrick & Gutierres, 1980).

Fortunately, there is hope for the unbeautiful among us. First of all, physical attractiveness appears to decline in importance when a permanent partner is being chosen (Stroebe et al., 1971). And as we will see, several other factors can work in our favor.

Proximity   An examination of 5,000 marriage license applications in Philadelphia in the 1930s found that one third of the couples lived within five blocks of each other (Rubin, 1973). Research shows that the best single predictor of whether two people are friends is how far apart they live. In a study of friendship patterns in apartment houses, residents were asked to name the three people they saw socially most often. Residents mentioned 41% of neighbors who lived in the apartment next door, 22% of those who lived two doors away (about 30 feet) and only 10% of those who lived at the other end of the hall (Festinger, Schachter, & Back, 1950). Studies of college dormitories show the same effect. After a full academic year, roommates were twice as likely as floormates to be friends, and floormates were more than twice as likely as dormitory residents in general to be friends (Priest & Sawyer, 1967).

There are cases, of course, in which neighbors and roommates hate one another, and the major exception to the friendship-promoting effect of proximity seems to occur when there are initial antagonisms. In a test of this, a participant waited in a laboratory with a female confederate who treated the participant pleasantly or unpleasantly. When she was pleasant, the closer she sat to the participant the better she was liked; when she was unpleasant, the closer she sat to the participant, the less she was liked. Proximity simply increased the intensity of the initial reaction (Schiffenbauer & Schiavo, 1976). But because most initial encounters probably range from neutral to pleasant, the most frequent result of sustained proximity is friendship.

Those who believe in miracles when it comes to matters of the heart may believe that there is a perfect mate chosen for each of us waiting to be discovered somewhere in the world. But if this is true, the far greater miracle is the frequency with which fate conspires to place this person within walking distance.

Familiarity One of the major reasons that proximity creates liking is that it increases familiarity, and there is now abundant evidence that familiarity all by itself—sheer exposure—increases liking (Zajonc, 1968). This familiarity-breeds-liking effect is a very general phenomenon. For example, rats repeatedly exposed to either the music of Mozart or Schoenberg enhance their liking for the composer they have heard, and humans repeatedly exposed to selected nonsense syllables or Chinese characters come to prefer those they have seen most often. The effect even occurs when individuals are unaware that they have been previously exposed to the stimuli (Bornstein, 1992; Bornstein & D'Agostino, 1992; Moreland & Zajonc, 1979; Wilson, 1979). More germane to the present discussion is a study in which participants were exposed to pictures of faces and then asked how much they thought they would like the person shown. The more frequently they had seen a particular face, the more they said they liked it and thought they would like the person (Zajonc, 1968) (see Figure 17-4). Similar results are obtained when individuals are exposed to one another in real life (Moreland & Beach, 1992).

In one clever demonstration of the familiarity-breeds-liking effect, the investigators took photographs of college women and then prepared prints of both the original face and its mirror image. These prints were then shown to the women themselves, their female friends, and their lovers. The women themselves preferred the mirror-image prints by a margin of 68% to 32%, but the friends and lovers preferred the nonreversed prints by a margin of 61% to 39% (Mita, Dermer, & Knight, 1977). Can you guess why?

The moral is clear. If you are not beautiful or you find your admiration of someone unreciprocated, be persistent and hang around. Proximity and familiarity are your most powerful weapons.

Similarity An old saying declares that opposites attract, and lovers are fond of recounting how different they are from each other: "I love boating, but she prefers mountain climbing." "I'm in engineering, but he's a history major."

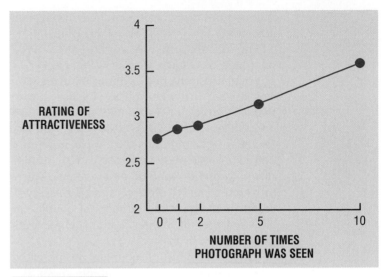

RATING OF ATTRACTIVENESS

NUMBER OF TIMES PHOTOGRAPH WAS SEEN

FIGURE 17-4

Familiarity Breeds Liking *People were asked to rate photographs of unknown faces according to how much they thought they would like the person. The lowest ratings of liking were made by those who had never seen the photograph before; the highest ratings of liking were made by those who had seen the photograph most often.* (After Zajonc, 1968)

What such lovers overlook is that they both like outdoor activities; they are both preprofessionals; they are both Democrats; they are both the same nationality; the same religion; the same social class; the same educational level; and they are probably within three years of each other in age and within five IQ points of each other in intelligence. In short, the old saying is mostly false.

Research dating all the way back to 1870 supports this conclusion. Over 99% of the married couples in the United States are of the same race, and most are of the same religion. Moreover, statistical surveys show that husbands and wives are significantly similar to each other not only in sociological characteristics—such as age, race, religion, education, and socioeconomic class—but also with respect to psychological characteristics like intelligence and physical characteristics such as height and eye color (Rubin, 1973). A study of dating couples finds the same patterns, in addition to finding that couples were also similar in their attitudes about sexual behavior and sex roles. Moreover, couples who were most similar in background at the beginning of the study were most likely to be together a year later (Hill, Rubin, & Peplau, 1976). Of particular pertinence to our earlier discussion is the finding that couples are closely matched on physical attractiveness as well (Feingold, 1988).

For example, in one study, judges rated photographs of each partner of 99 couples for physical attractiveness without knowing who was paired with whom. The physical attractiveness ratings of the couples matched each other significantly more closely than did the ratings of photographs that were randomly paired into couples (Murstein, 1972). Similar results were obtained in a real-life field study in which separate observers rated the physical attractiveness of members of couples in bars and theater lobbies and at social events (Silverman, 1971).

This matching of couples on physical attractiveness appears to come about because we weigh a potential partner's attractiveness against the probability that the person would be willing to pair up with us. Put bluntly, less attractive people seek less attractive partners because they expect to be rejected by someone more attractive than themselves. A study of a video dating service found that both men and women were most likely to pursue a relationship with someone who matched them in physical attractiveness. Only the most attractive people sought dates with the most attractive partners (Folkes, 1982). The overall result of this chilling marketplace process is attractiveness similarity: Most of us end up with partners who are about as attractive as we are.

But similarities on dimensions other than physical attractiveness are probably even more important over the long-term course of a relationship. A longitudinal study of 135 married couples found that spouses who were more similar to each other in personality also resembled each other more in terms of how much they enjoyed similar daily activities like visiting friends, going out for dinner, and participating in community activities and professional meetings. These couples also reported less marital conflict and greater closeness, friendliness, and marital satisfaction than less similar spouses (Caspi & Herbener, 1990).

In an ambitious study of similarity and friendship, male students received free room for the year in a large house at the University of Michigan in exchange for their participation. On the basis of information from tests and questionnaires, some men were assigned roommates who were quite similar to them and others were assigned roommates who were quite dissimilar. The investigator observed the friendship patterns that developed over the course of the year, obtaining more questionnaire and attitude data from the participants at regular intervals. In all other respects the men lived as they would in any dormitory.

Roommates who were initially similar generally liked each other and ended up as better friends than those who were dissimilar. When the study was repeated with a new

Partners in successful long-term relationships tend to be similar to each other in characteristics such as age, race, and education, as well as in their interests, personality traits, and even physical attractiveness.

group of men the next year, however, the familiarity-breeds-liking effect turned out to be even more powerful than similarity. Regardless of whether low or high similarity had been the basis for room assignments, roommates came to like each other (Newcomb, 1961).

One possible reason that similarity produces liking is that people value their own opinions and preferences and enjoy being with others who validate their choices, boosting their self-esteem in the process. But perhaps the major reason that similarity produces liking is that both social norms and situational circumstances throw us together with people who are like us. Most religious groups prefer (or insist) that their members date and mate within the religion, and cultural norms regulate what is considered acceptable in terms of race and age matches—a couple comprising an older woman and a younger man is still viewed as inappropriate. Situational circumstances also play an important role. Many couples meet in college or graduate school, thus ensuring that they will be similar in educational level, general intelligence, and professional aspirations, and probably in age and socioeconomic status. Moreover, tennis players will have met on the tennis courts, political liberals at a pro-choice rally, and gay people at a gay pride parade or a meeting of the Lesbian, Gay, and Bisexual Task Force.

Despite all this, it is often suggested that the saying that opposites attract may still apply to certain complementary personality traits (Winch, Ktsanes, & Ktsanes, 1954). To take the most obvious example, one partner may be quite dominant and therefore require someone who is relatively more submissive. A person with strong preferences may do best with someone who is very flexible or even wishy-washy. But despite the plausibility of this complementarity hypothesis, there is not much evidence for it (Levinger, Senn, & Jorgensen, 1970). In one study, marital adjustment among couples who had been married for up to five years was found to depend more on similarity than on complementarity (Meyer & Pepper, 1977). Attempts to identify the pairs of personality traits that bring about complementarity have not been very successful (Strong et al., 1988).

Romantic/Sexual Attraction and Love

Love is more than just strong liking. Most of us know people whom we like very much but do not love, and some of us have felt passionate attraction for someone whom we did not particularly like. Research confirms these everyday observations. One of the first researchers to study romantic love compiled a number of statements that people thought reflected liking and loving, and constructed separate scales to measure each (Rubin, 1973). Items on the liking scale tap the degree to which the other person is regarded as likable, respected, admired, and having maturity and good judgment. Items on the love scale tap three main themes: a sense of attachment ("It would be hard for me to get along without _____"), a sense of caring for the other person ("I would do almost anything for _____"), and a sense of trust ("I feel that I can confide in _____ about virtually everything"). The two scales are only moderately correlated: .56 for men and .36 for women.

Love and Marriage The concept of romantic love is an old one, but the belief that it has much to do with marriage is more recent and far from universal. In some non-Western cultures, marriage is still considered to be a contractual or financial arrangement that has nothing to do with love. In our own society, the link between love and marriage has actually become stronger over the past 30 years. In 1976, college students were asked, "If a man (woman) had all the other qualities you desired, would you marry this person if you were not in love with him (her)?" About 65% of the men said no, but only 24% of the women said no (only 4% actually said yes; the majority of the women were undecided) (Kephart, 1967). The women's movement had just begun at that time, and it may be that women were more likely than they are now to consider marriage necessary for financial security. When the survey was repeated in 1984, 85% of both men and women said that they would refuse to marry without being in love (Simpson, Campbell, & Berscheid, 1986).

Passionate and Companionate Love Several social scientists have attempted to distinguish among different kinds of love. One of the most widely accepted distinctions is between passionate and companionate love (Hatfield, 1988; Peele, 1988).

Passionate love is defined as *an intensely emotional state in which "tender and sexual feelings, elation and pain, anxiety and relief, altruism and jealousy coexist in a confusion of feelings"* (Berscheid & Walster, 1978, p. 177). It has been suggested that the experience of passionate love combines physiological arousal with the perception that the arousal is evoked by the beloved (Berscheid & Walster, 1974). (See the Frontiers of Psychological Research feature on pages 634–635.)

In contrast, **companionate love** is defined as *"the affection we feel for those with whom our lives are deeply intertwined"* (Hatfield, 1988, p. 205). The characteristics of companionate love are trust, caring, tolerance of the partner's flaws and idiosyncrasies, and an emotional tone of warmth and affection rather than high-pitched emotional passion. As a relationship continues over time, interdependence grows and the potential for strong emotion actually increases. This can be seen when long-time partners experience intense feelings of loneliness and desire when temporarily separated, or in the emotional devastation typically experienced by someone who loses a long-time partner. But, paradoxically, because companionate couples become so

compatible and coordinated in their daily routines, the actual frequency of strong emotions is usually fairly low (Berscheid, 1983).

Many of the young men and women in the survey cited earlier stated that if love disappears from a marriage, that is sufficient reason to end it. Those who equate love with passionate love, however, are likely to be disappointed. Most successful long-term couples emphasize the companionate elements of their relationship, and both theory and research suggest that the intense feelings that characterize passionate love are unlikely to persist over time (Berscheid, 1983; Solomon & Corbit, 1974). As the sixteenth-century writer Giraldi put it, "The history of a love affair is in some sense the drama of its fight against time."

This point is illustrated in a study that compared long-term marriages in the United States—where couples claim to marry for love—with marriages in Japan that had been arranged by the couples' parents. As expected, the American marriages started out with a higher level of expressed love and sexual interest than the Japanese marriages. But the amount of love expressed decreased in both groups until after ten years there were no differences between the two groups. Nevertheless, many couples in this study reported quite gratifying marriages, marriages that had evolved into a deep companionate love characterized by communication between the partners, an equitable division of labor, and equality of decision-making power (Blood, 1967).

The moral is that passionate love might be terrific for starters, but the sustaining forces of a good long-term relationship are less exciting, require more work, and have more to do with equality than with passion. In fact, as we will see shortly, there may even be a built-in incompatibility between passionate and companionate love.

The Triangular Theory of Love   In the years since the distinction between passionate and companionate love was introduced, similar but more differentiated classifications have been proposed. One of these divides love into three components: intimacy, passion, and commitment (Sternberg, 1986). *Intimacy* is the emotional component and involves closeness and sharing of feelings. *Passion,* the motivational component, con-

In later life the passionate component of romantic love tends to become less important than the companionate component.

sists of sexual attraction and the romantic feeling of being "in love." *Commitment* is the cognitive component; it reflects the intention to remain in the relationship. Combining these components in different ways yields the eight kinds of relationships shown in Table 17-2. As can be seen, in this scheme passionate love is split into two types: infatuated love and romantic love. Both are characterized by high passion and low commitment, but infatuated love is low in intimacy whereas romantic love is high in intimacy. Companionate love is characterized by high intimacy and commitment, but low passion.

TABLE 17-2

The Triangular Theory of Love   *The three dimensions of love combine to produce eight types of love relationships.* (After Sternberg, 1986)

	Intimacy	Passion	Commitment
Nonlove	Low	Low	Low
Liking	High	Low	Low
Infatuated love	Low	High	Low
Romantic love	High	High	Low
Empty love	Low	Low	High
Companionate love	High	Low	High
Fatuous love	Low	High	High
Consummate love	High	High	High

Pair Bonding and Mating Strategies

One of the newest approaches to romantic and sexual attraction is also one of the oldest: Darwin's theory of evolution. As noted in Chapter 1, evolutionary psychology is concerned with the origins of psychological mechanisms. The key idea is that, just like biological mechanisms, psychological mechanisms must have evolved over millions of years through a process of natural selection, which means that they have a genetic basis and have proved useful to the human species in the past for solving some problems of survival or increasing the chances of reproducing.

The application of evolutionary principles to social behavior is part of a relatively new discipline known as *sociobiology,* and the renewed interest in evolution among social psychologists has led to a (sometimes controversial) reexamination of several behavioral phenomena. Among these are pair bonding in humans and differences between men and women in sexual behavior and mating strategies.

From an evolutionary perspective, men and women mate in order to produce offspring who will pass their genes along to future generations. To do this, individuals must solve several problems, including (a) winning out over competitors in gaining access to fertile members of the opposite sex; (b) selecting mates with the greatest reproductive potential; (c) engaging in the necessary social and sexual behavior to achieve conception; (d) preventing the mate from defecting or deserting; and (e) ensuring the survival and reproductive success of one's offspring (Buss, 1994). According to sociobiologists, humans have evolved to form intense, long-term bonds with a partner to ensure that human offspring survive to reproductive age. As noted in Chapter 3, the more complex an organism's nervous system is, the longer the time required to reach maturity. A chimpanzee will be a functioning adult member of its species years before a human of the same age is ready to fend for itself. Accordingly, in the history of our species it has been important to have the male stick around to defend, provide for, and help rear the young. In contrast to humans, both male and female chimpanzees are quite promiscuous, and males have little or no involvement in rearing the young.

Sociobiologists further argue that because men and women play different roles in reproduction, the mating tactics and strategies used by the two sexes might also have evolved to be different as well. Because it is theoretically possible for a man to father hundreds of children, it is to his evolutionary advantage to impregnate as many women as possible in order to pass along the greatest number of his own genes. The woman, however, must invest a great deal of time and energy in each birth and can have only a limited number of offspring. Thus, it is to her advantage to select a mate who is most willing and best able to assist in protecting and raising her children, thereby maximizing the likelihood of passing her genes along to future generations. This

FRONTIERS OF PSYCHOLOGICAL RESEARCH

Producing Passion With Extrinsic Arousal

In his handbook *The Art of Love,* the first-century Roman poet Ovid offered advice about romantic conquest to both men and women. Among his more intriguing suggestions for a man was to take a woman in whom he is interested to the gladiatorial contests, where she could be easily aroused to passion. He did not say why this should be so, however. It was not until 1887 that a psychological explanation for this bit of wisdom was offered:

> Love can only be excited by strong and vivid emotion, and it is almost immaterial whether these emotions are agreeable or disagreeable. The Cid wooed the proud heart of Donna Ximene, whose father he had slain, by shooting one after another of her pet pigeons. (Adolf Horwicz, quoted in Finck, 1887, p. 240)

These romantic tactics should strike a familiar chord. As discussed in Chapter 11 and earlier in this chapter, we judge what emotion we are experiencing through a process of cognitive appraisal. Although the physiological arousal of our autonomic nervous system provides the cues that we are experiencing an emotion, the more subtle judgment of precisely which emotion we are experiencing often depends on our cognitive appraisal of the surrounding circumstances.

Ovid and Horwicz thus were suggesting that a person who is physiologically aroused (by whatever means) might attribute that arousal to love or sexual passion—to the advantage of any would-be lover who happens to be at hand. There is now solid experimental evidence for this phenomenon, but psychologists disagree about the process underlying it. In one set of studies, male participants were physiologically aroused by either running in place, hearing an audiotape of a comedy routine, or hearing an audiotape of a grisly killing. They then viewed a taped interview with a woman who was either attractive or unattractive. Finally, they rated the woman on several dimensions, including her attractiveness, her sexiness, and the degree to which they would be interested in dating her and kissing her. The results showed that no matter how the arousal had been elicited, participants were more sexually responsive to the attractive woman and less sexually responsive to the unattractive woman than were control participants who had not been aroused. In other words, the arousal intensified both positive or negative reactions to the woman, depending on which reaction was cognitively appropriate (White, Fishbein, & Rutstein, 1981).

This effect of extrinsic arousal is not limited to the individual's cognitive appraisal of his or her emotional state. In two studies, men or women watched a sequence of two videotapes. The first portrayed either an anxiety-inducing or a nonanxiety-inducing scene; the second videotape portrayed a nude heterosexual couple engaging in sexual foreplay. Preexposure to the anxiety-inducing scene produced greater penile tumescence in men and greater increases in vaginal blood volume in women in

reasoning suggests that evolution would have made men more promiscuous and less discriminating in their choice of sexual partners than women. In fact, it has been documented repeatedly that in most societies men are more promiscuous than women, and societies that permit one man to mate with more than one woman far outnumber those in which one woman may mate with many different men (Wilson, 1978).

Sociobiological theory also predicts that a man should prefer to mate with the most fertile young women available because they are most likely to bear his children. A woman should prefer to mate with a man of high social status and solid material resources, one who can give the children the best chance of surviving to adulthood and reproducing in their turn. As a result, sociobiologists predict that men will prefer younger women (with many more fertile years ahead of them), whereas woman will prefer older men (who have more resources). This sex difference in mate preference was strongly confirmed in a study of 37 cultures (Buss, 1989).

Sociobiological theory has not gone unchallenged. Some critics argue that even if a behavioral pattern appears across many or all cultures, it does not necessarily follow that it is programmed into the genes. For example, some universal cross-cultural sex differences may have arisen simply because women had less upper body strength than men and—until very recently in technological societies—were

There is considerable research evidence that physiological arousal can increase feelings of attraction and passion.

response to the erotic scene than did preexposure to nonanxiety-inducing tapes (Hoon, Wincze, & Hoon, 1977; Wolchik et al., 1980).

Several explanations for this effect have been offered. The *attribution* (or misattribution) explanation is that the individual mistakenly attributes his or her arousal to the target person, thereby interpreting it as romantic or sexual feelings (or possibly as revulsion in the presence of a particularly unattractive person). A second explanation is that the effect reflects *excitation transfer*, in which arousal experienced from one source can carry over to intensify the arousal experienced from a different source. For example, a man will show more aggression when provoked if he has first been exposed to sexually stimulating materials, including nonviolent materials (Zillmann, 1984, 1978; Zillmann & Bryant, 1974). By extension, arousal produced by exercise might carry over to intensify sexual arousal.

A third explanation is *response facilitation*, a well-known phenomenon in psychology. When an organism is aroused, whatever response it is most likely to make in the situation—called the *domi-nant response*—will be facilitated or intensified. If the dominant response is attraction to the woman, this response will be intensified by the additional arousal. If the dominant response in the situation is *not* to be attracted to the woman, the arousal would intensify this negative response. This is exactly what was found in the study just described (Allen, Kenrick, Linder, & McCall, 1989).

Experimental attempts to determine which explanation is most valid have produced mixed results, and the dispute is not yet settled (Allen et al., 1989; McClanahan et al., 1990; White & Kight, 1984). But whatever the specific mechanism, the phenomenon itself appears to be genuine and solidly established. Would-be lovers of both sexes should feel encouraged to buy a pair of tickets to a hockey game.

pregnant or nursing during most of their adult lives. This created sex-based divisions of labor in virtually all societies, which placed political power and decision making in the hands of men and confined women to the domestic sphere (Bem, 1993). Greater sexual freedom for men could easily emerge from such power differences.

It is often instructive to ask whether sociobiological reasoning could also have predicted a different or opposite outcome. For example, we have seen the argument that a male's ability to produce many hundreds of offspring would create an evolutionary push toward male promiscuity. But the need to ensure that one's offspring survive to reproductive age—the same need that presumably gave rise to human pair bonding in the first place—would provide an opposing evolutionary push toward monogamy. In other words, sociobiological theory could be invoked to explain either male promiscuity or male sexual fidelity.

Despite these criticisms, however, there is no doubt that evolutionary thinking has reinvigorated both personality and social psychology. There is probably no other single principle in the behavioral sciences with as much potential explanatory power as the principle of evolution. Moreover, the emergence of sociobiological theorizing shows once again the important role of biological evidence in contemporary psychology. Even social psychologists who study the processes of social cognition now theorize about how and why our strategies for processing social information might have evolved (Nisbett & Ross, 1980).

Evolutionary Origins of Sex Differences in Mate Preferences

David M. Buss, *University of Texas at Austin*

Evolutionary psychology provides a powerful theoretical guide to identifying both commonalities and differences between men and women. The logic stems from understanding the *adaptive problems* the sexes have faced over the long course of human evolutionary history—problems of survival and reproduction. Both sexes have faced many similar survival problems—the need to select food, combat diseases, and fend off predators. Where men and women have confronted similar adaptive problems, evolutionary psychologists predict the sexes will be similar. Both sexes, for example, have similar taste preferences (e.g., sugar, protein, and fat) and similar fears (e.g., snakes).

In reproduction, however, the sexes have faced fundamentally different adaptive problems, and here we expect sex differences in adaptive solutions. Women, for example, bear the burdens and joys of a nine-month minimum obligatory investment (pregnancy) to produce a single child; men's minimum investment is as low as a few hours, a few minutes, or a few seconds.

Much evidence, emerging from varied data sources—self-reports, behavioral studies, and laboratory studies—confirms several sex differences predicted in advance by evolutionary psychologists. One pertains to choosiness. When approached by an opposite-sex stranger, 50% of women agreed to a date, 6% agreed to go back to his apartment, and 0% agreed to sex. In contrast, of the men approached by women, 50% agreed to a date, 69% agreed to go back to her apartment, and 75% agreed to sex (Clarke & Hatfield, 1989). This is one among hundreds of studies that document that women are more selective and discriminating in short-term mating contexts (Buss, 1994). This psychological sex difference stems from a long evolutionary history of an asymmetry between the sexes in parental investment.

Humans, unlike most other primates, also pursue long-term mating. Because of women's heavy parental investment, they are predicted to value mates who are able and willing to invest resources in them and their children. In my study of 10,047 individuals in 37 cultures located on six continents and five islands, from coastal Australia to the Zulu tribe in South Africa, this prediction was soundly supported. Women placed a greater premium on a mate's financial resources, ambition, and industriousness. Women also desired spouses who were roughly three years older.

Sometimes an alternative explanation is proposed—women do not have an evolved desire for resourceful men, but rather are forced to prefer such men because they have been excluded from other means to economic resources (Buss & Barnes, 1986). Although reasonable, the available evidence fails to support it. Women living in more economically equal cultures, such as Sweden and Norway, show just as strong a desire for mates with resources as women in more economically unequal cultures such as Japan or Iran (Buss, 1989). Furthermore, women in the United States who are economically successful place even more emphasis on a man's resources. Although more tests are needed, the available evidence supports the hypothesis that women have an evolved desire for resourceful mates.

Another key sex difference stems from ovulation. Unlike most other primate females, who experience estrus cycles with large red genital swellings, women's ovulation evolved to be cryptic or concealed. This posed a unique adaptive problem for ancestral men—how to identify fertile women in the absence of obvious estrus cues. According to one evolutionary hypothesis, men evolved to value certain features of physical appearance because appearance provides a wealth of cues to a woman's age and health, and hence to her fertility. The 37-culture study supports this explanation. Men worldwide, from Zambia to Austria, value women who are young and physically attractive, precisely as predicted.

Although these findings and their evolutionary explanations are upsetting to some people, there are three important qualifications. First, discoveries that men and women have evolved psychological differences does not justify discrimination based on sex, nor does it excuse behavior some consider immoral, such as sexual infidelity. Second, neither men nor women can be considered superior or inferior; each sex has evolved adaptations to solve its own unique problems. Third, in most psychological domains, the sexes are similar since both sexes have faced similar adaptive problems, such as identifying who will be a good long-term cooperator. Both sexes equally value a potential mate's intelligence, kindness, dependability, creativity, and adaptability. And both sexes in all 37 cultures place a premium on love and mutual attraction, which may be evolution's way of bringing the sexes together over the long term to transcend whatever differences they display.

The Influence of Social Learning and Social Roles on Mate Selection

Janet S. Hyde, *University of Wisconsin, Madison*

A man's attraction to a woman is, on average, powerfully determined by her physical appearance. Women, too, are attracted to good-looking men but, on average, physical appearance is less important to women (Feingold, 1990). Women are more likely to take other characteristics of men—such as success—into account in their attractions. Furthermore, men prefer women who are younger than themselves, and women prefer men who are slightly older than they are. Why do these differences occur?

The answer lies in social roles and social learning. Let's first consider social roles, specifically gender roles (Eagly & Wood, 1999). One key feature of gender roles in American society, as in most other societies around the world, is that women have less power and status than men. In the United States, women earn only 75 cents for every dollar that men earn. Women are sparsely represented in the seats of power such as the U. S. Senate and House of Representatives. According to a 1992 U.S. Department of Labor study of Fortune 1000 companies, only 6.6% of executives were women. A second key feature of gender roles in American society is the gendered division of labor, both in paid work and in home work. Most occupations are highly gender segregated. For example, only 2.3 percent of airline pilots are women, as are 8.5 percent of dentists. Only 2.9 percent of childcare workers are men, as are only 1.4 percent of dental assistants (U.S. Bureau of Labor Statistics, 1993). Women and men, even today, occupy quite different roles. Given the wage gap and women's lesser access to high-paid, high-status occupations, is it any wonder that women, on average, are attracted to men who are successful and earn more? They literally can't afford to do otherwise. Or is it any wonder that men do not take into account women's occupational success or earnings?

A key aspect of the female role is beauty and heterosexual attractiveness. Women's beauty is highly visible in American society and is used to sell everything from mattresses to sportscars. Girls quickly learn that they should be beautiful, and boys learn that they should be associated with beautiful girls. Gender roles also specify that certain age pairings are acceptable. When ads or TV programs show silver-haired men, they are often paired with romantic partners who are much younger than they are. Have you ever seen the reverse pairing?

How and why does each new generation of children generally adopt behaviors that are consistent with gender roles? The answer lies in social learning, particularly reinforcement, punishment, and modeling (Bussey & Bandura, 1999). Gender-role violations typically receive severe punishments, particularly in adolescent culture. Suppose that Ernie, a high school sophomore, invites Ellen, who is pleasant and friendly, to the class dance. Because she is not good looking, Ernie's friends tease him mercilessly for dating a "dog." Ernie won't make that mistake again. Justin, one of Ernie's friends, observed what happened and Justin will be careful to invite only good-looking girls to dances in the future. According to cognitive social learning theory, Justin only needed to observe Ernie's punishment to learn that boys shouldn't date unattractive girls.

Any good psychological theory should be able to specify the processes or mechanisms that pro-

duce the behaviors it seeks to explain. One of the problems with evolutionary psychology is that it does not specify mechanisms. The theory simply says there was evolutionary selection for a predisposition to this behavior and that is why it is present in modern culture. But evolution affects behavior only if genetic factors influence the behavior. Evolution acts through genes. Genes, in turn, have their effect by directing the synthesis of various biochemicals in the body, such as hormones and

Janet Hyde

neurotransmitters. None of this is specified in evolutionary psychology. In contrast, social learning theory tells us exactly the processes that produce human behavior that conforms to gender roles.

A problem with the evidence from evolutionary psychologists is that, although they may have data from many different cultures, all of those cultures have a gender-based division of labor, and the division of labor is generally quite similar to the one in the United States (Eagly & Wood, 1999)—that is, women have more responsibility for caring for the home and children, and men occupy positions of power. Therefore, in regard to gender roles, the other cultures may not be as different from ours as they at first appear.

Gender differences in attraction to romantic partners are quite clearly shaped by gender roles through the process of social learning by reinforcements, punishments, and modeling.

SUMMARY

1. Social psychology is the study of how people perceive, think, and feel about their social world and how they interact and influence one another. Beginning with the premise that human behavior is a function of both the person and the situation, social psychologists emphasize the power of a situation and the importance of the person's interpretation of a situation in determining social behavior.

2. In attempting to understand others and ourselves, we construct intuitive theories of human behavior by performing the same tasks as a formal scientist: collecting data, detecting covariation, and inferring causality. Our theories themselves, however, can shape our perceptions of the data, distort our estimates of covariation, and bias our evaluations of cause and effect. For example, we tend to notice and recall vivid information more than nonvivid information, and this biases our social judgments.

3. Schematic processing is the perceiving and interpreting of incoming information in terms of simplified memory structures called schemas. Schemas are mini-theories about everyday objects and events. They allow us to process social information efficiently by permitting us to encode and remember only the unique or most prominent features of a new object or event.

4. Because schemas simplify reality, schematic processing produces biases and errors in our processing of social information. In forming impressions of other people, for example, we are prone to the primacy effect: The first information we receive evokes an initial schema and, hence, becomes more powerful in determining our impression than does later information. In general, schematic processing produces perceptions that are resistant to change and relatively impervious to new data.

5. We are not very accurate at detecting covariations or correlations between events in everyday life. When our schemas lead us to expect two things to covary, we overestimate their actual correlation; but when we do not have a schema we underestimate their correlation.

6. Stereotypes can be thought of as theories or schemas of covariation. Like other schemas, they are resistant to change. In particular, they lead us to overlook the very data that would disconfirm them. Moreover, they can be self-perpetuating and self-fulfilling because they influence those who hold them to behave in ways that actually evoke the stereotyped behavior.

7. Attribution is the process by which we attempt to interpret and to explain the behavior of other people—that is, to discern the causes of their actions.

One major attribution task is to decide whether someone's action should be attributed to dispositional causes (the person's personality or attitudes) or to situational causes (social forces or other external circumstances). We tend to give too much weight to dispositional factors and too little to situational factors. This bias has been called the fundamental attribution error.

8. Self-perception theory proposes that we make judgments about ourselves using the same inferential processes—and making the same kinds of errors—that we use for making judgments about others. For example, we often commit the fundamental attribution error when interpreting our own behavior.

9. Attitudes are likes and dislikes—favorable or unfavorable evaluations of and reactions to objects, people, events, or ideas. Attitudes have a cognitive component, an affective component, and a behavioral component. A major issue in attitude research is the degree of consistency among a person's attitudes. Despite evidence for attitude consistency in laboratory studies, social scientists are divided in their views about the degree to which individuals hold coherent opinions about social and political issues.

10. Attitudes serve many functions. Attitudes that we hold for practical reasons serve an instrumental function; those that help us make sense of the world serve a knowledge function; those that express our values or reflect our self-concepts serve a value-expressive function; those that protect us from anxiety or threats to our self-esteem serve an ego-defensive function; and those that help us feel that we are a part of a social community serve a social adjustment function.

11. The scapegoat theory of prejudice holds that negative attitudes toward groups sometimes serve an ego-defensive function, leading individuals to repress their own undesirable characteristics and project those characteristics onto other groups. A classic study of the authoritarian personality tested this theory and described the kind of person who would be particularly likely to hold this kind of prejudice.

12. Attitudes tend to predict behavior best when they are (a) strong and consistent; (b) specifically related to the behavior being predicted; and (c) based on the person's direct experience; as well as (d) when the individual is aware of his or her attitudes. Cognitive dissonance theory proposes that when a person's behaviors are inconsistent with his or her attitudes, the discomfort produced by this dissonance leads the person to change the attitudes so that they are consistent with the behavior.

13. Many factors influence whether we will be attracted to a particular individual. The most important are physical attractiveness, proximity, familiarity, and similarity. The old saying that "opposites attract" has not been upheld by research findings.

14. The link between love and marriage is historically recent and far from universal. In our own society the link has become closer over the past few decades, with more women and men refusing to marry someone they do not love. There have been several attempts to classify types of love. Passionate love is characterized by intense and often conflicting emotions, whereas companionate love is characterized by trust, caring, tolerance of the partner's flaws, and an emotional tone of warmth and affection. Even though passionate love decreases over time in long-term relationships, the potential for strong emotion actually increases. But because companionate couples become so compatible in their daily routines, the actual frequency of strong emotions is fairly low. Another classification of love divides it into the components of intimacy, passion, and commitment.

15. Sociobiological theorizing suggests that humans have evolved to form long-term bonds with a partner because historically such pair bonds operated to ensure the survival of offspring to reproductive age. A more controversial sociobiological hypothesis is that men and women have evolved to pursue different mating strategies, with men evolving to be more promiscuous and seek out younger women.

KEY TERMS

social psychology (p. 606)
schema (p. 608)
primacy effect (p. 610)
stereotype (p. 612)
fundamental attribution error (p. 615)
affect (p. 620)

attitude (p. 620)
projection (p. 623)
cognitive dissonance (p. 626)
liking (p. 627)
passionate love (p. 632)
companionate love (p. 632)

CRITICAL THINKING QUESTIONS

1. Suppose that in preparation for buying a new car you carefully read *Consumer Reports'* survey of several thousand car owners and become convinced that a particular model has the highest reliability and owner satisfaction. But then your neighbor tells you that she owned that model and it was a terrible car. Which source of information should be more valid, the survey of several thousand owners or your neighbor? Which source is more influential in your buying decision? If your answer to both questions is not the same, why?

2. How might the fundamental attribution error contribute to the tendency of many people to blame the poor for their condition?

3. In this chapter we describe five different psychological functions that an attitude might serve. Select an attitude that you hold on some controversial social or political issues, such as abortion or gay marriage, and analyze the function or functions it seems to serve for you. Next, analyze the function or functions served by the attitudes of those who oppose your point of view.

FURTHER READING

Three comprehensive textbooks in social psychology are Aronson, Wilson, and Akert, *Social Psychology* (3rd ed. (1998); Baron and Byrne, *Social Psychology* (8th ed., 1997); and Lord, *Social Psychology* (1996). More advanced treatments are available in Gilbert, Fiske, & Lindzey (eds.), *The Handbook of Social Psychology* (4th ed., 1998).

A major theme of this chapter—that people act as informal scientists in arriving at social judgments—is treated in detail in Nisbett and Ross, *Human Inference: Strategies and Shortcomings of Social Judgment* (1980). A delightful extension of this basic theme is presented by Gilovich in *How We Know What Isn't So: The Fallibility of Human Reason in Everyday Life* (1991).

A number of books deal in more depth with other topics discussed in this chapter. Recommended are Aronson, *The Social Animal* (7th ed., 1995); Brehm, *Intimate Relationships* (2nd ed., 1992); and Ross and Nisbett, *The Person and the Situation: Perspectives of Social Psychology* (1991).

Chapter 18
Social Interaction and Influence

*I*n Chapter 17 we discussed the part of social psychology that deals with how people think and feel about their social world—their social cognitions and affects. In this chapter we examine how people interact and influence one another. To most people the term **social influence** connotes *direct and deliberate attempts to change our beliefs, attitudes, or behaviors*. Parents attempt to get their children to eat spinach; television commercials attempt to induce us to buy a particular product or vote for a particular candidate; a religious cult attempts to persuade a person to abandon school, job, or family and serve a "higher" mission.

We react to such social influences in many ways. In some cases— termed **compliance** by psychologists—*we comply with the wishes of* *the influencer but do not necessarily change our beliefs or attitudes.* For example, the child eats the spinach but may continue to dislike it. In other cases, termed **internalization,** *we are convinced that the influencer is correct and change our beliefs and attitudes.* And in some cases we resist the influence, possibly even showing overt rebellion. In this chapter we will see instances of all three types of reactions.

But many forms of social influence are indirect or unintentional; for example, just being with other people can affect us in diverse ways. Even when we are alone we continue to be influenced by **social norms—** *implicit rules and expectations that dictate what we ought to think and how we ought to behave*; these range from the trivial to the profound. Social norms tell us to face forward when riding in an elevator and how long we can gaze at a stranger before being considered rude. More profoundly, social norms can create and maintain racism, sexism, or homophobia. As we will see, compliance with orders or requests often depends on our unwitting allegiance to social norms.

Social interaction and influence are central to communal life. Cooperation, altruism, and love all involve social interaction and influence. But various kinds of social prob-

lems have led social psychologists to focus on the negative effects of social influence. Some of their findings are disturbing, even depressing. But just as the study of psychopathology has led to effective therapies, so too the study of problematic social interactions has led to more effective ways of dealing with them.

The Presence of Others

Social Facilitation

In 1898, while examining the speed records of bicycle racers, the psychologist Norman Triplett noticed that many cyclists achieved better times when they raced against each other than when they raced against the clock. This led him to perform one of social psychology's earliest laboratory experiments. He instructed children to turn a fishing reel as fast as possible for a fixed period. Sometimes two children worked at the same time in the same room, each with his or her own reel. At other times they worked alone. Triplett reported that many children worked faster when another child doing the same task was present (a situation termed *coaction*) than when they worked alone.

In 1898 psychologist Norman Triplett noticed that cyclists achieved better times when they raced against other cyclists than when they raced against the clock. This led him to study the phenomenon of social facilitation.

Since this experiment, many studies have demonstrated the facilitating effects of coaction with both human and animal subjects. For example, worker ants in groups will dig more than three times as much sand per ant than when alone (Chen, 1937); many animals will eat more food if other members of their species are present (Platt, Yaksh, & Darby, 1967); and college students will complete more multiplication problems in coaction than when alone (F. H. Allport, 1920, 1924).

Soon after Triplett's experiment on coaction, psychologists discovered that the presence of a passive spectator—an audience rather than a coactor—also facilitates performance. For example, the presence of an audience had the same facilitating effect on students' multiplication performance as the presence of coactors in the earlier study (Dashiell, 1930). The term **social facilitation** is used to refer to *the effects of coaction and the presence of an audience.*

But even this simple case of social influence turned out to be more complicated than social psychologists first thought. For example, researchers found that people made more errors on the multiplication problems when in coaction or in the presence of an audience than when they performed alone (Dashiell, 1930). In other words, quality of performance declined even though quantity increased. In other studies, however, quality of performance improved when coactors or audiences were present (Cottrell, 1972; Dashiell, 1935). How can these contradictions be reconciled?

In examining the findings, psychologist Robert Zajonc (1980, 1965) noted that simple responses, highly practiced responses, or instinctive responses (such as eating) were typically facilitated in the presence of coactors or audiences, whereas complex or newly learned responses were typically impaired. He proposed that a long-known principle of motivation could account for the findings: A high level of drive or arousal tends to energize the dominant responses of an organism. If the mere presence of another member of the species raises the general arousal or drive level of an organism, the dominant response will be facilitated. For simple or well-learned behaviors, the dominant response is most likely to be the correct response, and performance should

be facilitated. For complex behaviors or behaviors that are just being learned, the dominant or most probable response is likely to be incorrect. On a multiplication problem, for example, there are many wrong responses but only one correct one. Performance therefore should be impaired.

A number of experiments have confirmed these predictions. For example, people learn simple mazes or easy word lists more quickly but learn complex mazes or difficult word lists more slowly when an audience is present than when it is not (Cottrell, Rittle, & Wack, 1967; Hunt & Hillery, 1973). And study using cockroaches found that when attempting to escape light they run an easy route more quickly but a difficult route more slowly if other roaches watch from the sidelines (or run with them) than if they run without other roaches present (Zajonc, Heingartner, & Herman, 1969).

Because social facilitation occurs in nonhuman species, it would not seem to require complex cognitive processes. But one theory suggests that social facilitation in humans is due not to the mere presence of others but to feelings of competition or to concerns about being evaluated, and it is these cognitive concerns that raise the drive level. Even the early studies of coaction found that if all elements of rivalry and competition were removed, social facilitation effects were reduced or eliminated (Dashiell, 1930). Other studies show that audience effects vary depending on how much the person feels that he or she is being evaluated. For example, social facilitation effects are enhanced if an expert watches but are diminished if the audience consists of "undergraduates who want to watch a psychology experiment" (Henchy & Glass, 1968; Paulus & Murdock, 1971). In one study, when the audience wore blindfolds and hence could not watch or evaluate the individual's performance, no social facilitation effects were found (Cottrell et al., 1968).

But participants in these experiments still knew that their performances were being recorded by the experimenter and, accordingly, may still have felt concern about being evaluated even when alone or in the presence of a blindfolded audience. Thus, these studies still leave open the question of whether or not social facilitation effects in humans ever arise purely from the mere presence of others. This problem was overcome in a study in which participants were asked to sit at a computer and provide some "background information before the experiment begins." In the "evaluation" condition, the experimenter stood behind the participant and watched; in the "mere presence" condition, there was a blindfolded person in the room who also wore headphones, faced away from the participant, and was said to be waiting to take part in a sensory deprivation experiment. The computer automatically recorded both how long it took the participant to type his or her name (an easy task) and to type a complex code name (a difficult task). Compared with participants in the alone condition, participants in both the evaluation and mere presence conditions performed the easy task more quickly but the difficult task more slowly, thereby demonstrating that social facilitation in humans can in fact be produced by the mere presence of others (Schmitt et al., 1986).

Two other theories have been proposed to account for social facilitation effects. *Distraction-conflict* theory suggests that the presence of others distracts the person, causing a conflict over how to allocate attention between the others and the task to be performed. It is this attentional conflict—rather than the mere presence of another person or a concern over being evaluated—that raises the drive level and causes social facilitation effects (Baron, 1986; Sanders & Baron, 1975). *Self-presentation theory* proposes that the presence of others enhances the individual's desire to present a favorable image. On easy tasks, this leads to more effort and concentration and thus to improved performance. On difficult tasks, however, this desire magnifies the frustrations imposed by the task and leads to embarrassment, withdrawal, or excessive anxiety, all of which lead to poorer performance (Bond, 1982). There is research evidence to support each of these theories, and it seems likely that all of the proposed processes—mere presence, concern over evaluation, distraction-conflict, and desire to present a favorable image—contribute to social facilitation effects (Sanders, 1984).

Audience effects on performance vary depending on how much the person feels that he or she is being evaluated.

Deindividuation

At about the same time that Triplett was performing his experiment on social facilitation, another observer of human behavior, Gustave LeBon, was also studying the effects of coaction. In *The Crowd* (1895) he complained that "the crowd is always intellectually inferior to the isolated individual. . . . The mob man is fickle, credulous, and intolerant, showing the violence and ferocity of primitive beings . . . women, children, savages, and lower classes . . . operating under the influence of the spinal cord." LeBon believed that the aggressive and immoral behaviors shown by lynch mobs (and, in his view, French revolutionaries) spread through a mob or crowd by contagion, like a disease, breaking down a man's moral sense and self-control. This caused crowds to commit destructive acts that no individuals—except women, children, savages, and members of the lower classes—would commit when acting alone.

People often behave differently in a crowd than when alone. Some researchers believe that in a situation like a riot, individuals experience deindividuation—a feeling that they have lost their personal identities and merged anonymously into the group.

Despite his obvious prejudices, LeBon's observations have some validity. The modern counterpart to his theory is built on the concept of deindividuation, which was first proposed by Festinger, Pepitone, and Newcomb (1952) and extended by Zimbardo (1970) and Diener (1980, 1979). These researchers suggested that certain

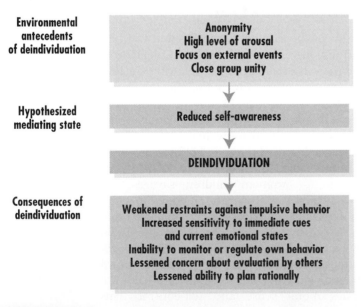

Environmental antecedents of deindividuation	Anonymity High level of arousal Focus on external events Close group unity
Hypothesized mediating state	Reduced self-awareness
	DEINDIVIDUATION
Consequences of deindividuation	Weakened restraints against impulsive behavior Increased sensitivity to immediate cues and current emotional states Inability to monitor or regulate own behavior Lessened concern about evaluation by others Lessened ability to plan rationally

FIGURE 18-1

Antecedents and Consequences of Deindividuation *One explanation of crowd behavior traces it to loss of personal identity in certain group situations.*

conditions that are sometimes present in groups can lead individuals to experience **deindividuation,** *a feeling that they have lost their personal identities and merged anonymously into the group.* This psychological state reduces the normal restraints against impulsive and unruly behavior. The antecedent conditions and the consequences of deindividuation proposed by Diener are illustrated in Figure 18-1. Note that antecedent conditions lead to deindividuation by producing a state of reduced self-awareness.

In one study of deindividuation, groups of four college women were required to deliver electric shocks to another woman who was supposedly participating in a learning experiment. Half of the women were deindividuated by making them feel anonymous. They were dressed in bulky laboratory coats and hoods that hid their faces, and the experimenter spoke to them only as a group, never referring to any of them by name (see Figure 18-2). The remaining women were individuated by having them remain in their own clothes and wear large identification tags. In addition, the women in the second group were introduced to one another by name. During the experiment each woman had a shock button in front of her, which she was to push when the learner made an error. Pushing the button appeared to deliver a shock to the learner. The results showed that the deindividuated women delivered twice as much shock to the learner as the individuated women (Zimbardo, 1970).

Another study was conducted simultaneously at several homes on Halloween. Children out trick-or-treating were greeted at the door by a woman who asked that each child take only one piece of candy. The woman then disappeared into the house briefly, giving the children the opportunity to take more candy. Some of the children had been asked their names, while others remained anonymous. Children who came in groups or who remained anonymous stole more candy than children who came alone or had given their names to the adult (Diener et al., 1976).

These experiments are not definitive, however. For example, you can see from Figure 18-2 that the laboratory coats and hoods in the first study resembled Ku Klux Klan outfits. Similarly, Halloween costumes

FIGURE 18-2

Anonymity Produces Deindividuation *When women were disguised so that they felt anonymous, they delivered more shock to another person than did nondisguised women.*

often represent witches, monsters, or ghosts. These all carry aggressive or negative connotations. It may be that the roles suggested by the costumes, rather than the anonymity they provided, produced the behavior. To test this possibility, the shock experiment was repeated, but this time each participant wore one of three outfits: a Ku Klux Klan-type costume, a nurse's uniform, or the participant's own clothes. The results of the revised experiment did not replicate those of the original study: Wearing a Ku Klux Klan-type costume had only a small effect on the level of shock the participants administered. More significantly, participants wearing nurses' uniforms actually gave fewer shocks than participants who wore their own clothes, suggesting that a uniform encourages the person to play the kind of role it connotes. This study shows that anonymity does not inevitably lead to enhanced aggression (Johnson & Downing, 1979). A more recent study showed that deindividuation led subjects to be both more aggressive and more generous (Spivey & Prentice-Dunn, 1990).

Bystander Intervention

In earlier chapters we noted that people do not react simply to the objective features of a situation but also respond to their subjective interpretations of it. In this chapter we have seen that even social facilitation, a primitive kind of social influence, depends in part on the individual's interpretation of what other people are doing or thinking. But as we will now see, defining or interpreting the situation is often the very mechanism through which individuals influence one another.

In 1964 a young woman named Kitty Genovese was attacked outside her home late at night. She fought back for over half an hour, but in the end she was murdered. At least 38 neighbors heard her screams for help, but nobody came to her aid. No one even called the police.

The American public was horrified by this incident, and social psychologists began to investigate the causes of what at first was termed "bystander apathy." Their research showed that "apathy" was not a very accurate term. It is not indifference that prevents

Although many passers-by have noticed the man lying on the sidewalk, no one has stopped to help—to see if he is asleep, sick, drunk, or dead. Research shows that people are more likely to help if no other bystanders are present.

bystanders from intervening in emergencies. There are realistic deterrents to intervention, such as physical danger. Moreover, getting involved may mean lengthy court appearances or other entanglements. Also, emergencies are unpredictable and require quick, unplanned action; few people are prepared for such situations. Finally, one risks making a fool of oneself by misinterpreting a situation as an emergency when it is not. Researchers concluded that "the bystander to an emergency situation is in an unenviable position. It is perhaps surprising that anyone should intervene at all" (Latané & Darley, 1970, p. 247).

Although we might suppose that the presence of other bystanders would embolden an individual to act despite the risks, research demonstrates the reverse: Often it is the very presence of other people that prevents us from intervening. In fact, by 1980 more than 50 studies of bystander intervention had been conducted; most of them showed that people are less likely to help when others are present (Latané, Nida, & Wilson, 1981). Latané and Darley (1970) suggest that the presence of others deters an individual from intervening by (a) defining the situation as a nonemergency and (b) diffusing the responsibility for acting.

Defining the Situation Many emergencies begin ambiguously. Is the man who is staggering about ill or simply drunk? Is the woman being threatened by a stranger, or is she arguing with her husband? Is that smoke from a fire or just steam pouring out the window? A common way of dealing with such dilemmas is to postpone action, act as if nothing is wrong, and look around to see how other people are reacting. What you are likely to see, of course, are other people who, for the same reasons, are also acting as if nothing is wrong. A state of *pluralistic ignorance* develops—that is, everybody in the group misleads everybody else by defining the situation as a nonemergency. We have all heard about crowds panicking because each person causes everybody else to overreact. The reverse situation—in which a crowd lulls its members into inaction—may be even more common. Several experiments demonstrate this effect.

In one experiment, male college students were invited to an interview. As they sat in a small waiting room, a stream of smoke began to pour through a wall vent. Some participants were alone in the waiting room when this occurred; others were in groups of three. The experimenters observed them through a one-way window and waited 6 minutes to see if anyone would take action or report the situation. Of the participants who were tested alone, 75% reported the smoke within about 2 minutes. In contrast, less than 13% of the participants who were tested in groups reported the smoke within the entire 6-minute period, even though the room was filled with smoke. Those who did not report the smoke subsequently reported that they had decided that it must have been steam, air conditioning vapors, or smog—practically anything but a real fire or an emergency. This experiment thus showed that bystanders can define situations as nonemergencies for one another (Latané & Darley, 1968).

But perhaps these participants were simply afraid to appear cowardly. To check on this possibility, a similar study was designed in which the "emergency" did not involve personal danger. Participants waiting in the testing room heard a female experimenter in the next office climb up on a chair to reach a bookcase, fall to the floor, and yell,

"Oh my God—my foot. . . . I can't move it. Oh . . . my ankle. . . . I can't get this thing off me." She continued to moan for about a minute longer. The entire incident lasted about 2 minutes. Only a curtain separated the woman's office from the testing room, in which participants waited either alone or in pairs. The results confirmed the findings of the smoke study. Of the participants who were alone, 70% came to the woman's aid, but only 40% of those in two-person groups offered help. Again, those who had not intervened claimed later that they were unsure of what had happened but had decided that it was not serious (Latané & Rodin, 1969). In these experiments the presence of others produced pluralistic ignorance; each person, observing the calmness of the others, resolved the ambiguity of the situation by deciding that no emergency existed.

Diffusion of Responsibility Pluralistic ignorance can lead individuals to define a situation as a nonemergency, but this process does not explain incidents like the Genovese murder, in which the emergency is abundantly clear. Moreover, Kitty Genovese's neighbors could not observe one another behind their curtained windows and hence could not tell whether others were calm or panicked. The crucial process here was diffusion of responsibility. When each individual knows that many others are present, the burden of responsibility does not fall solely on him or her. Each can think, "Someone else must have done something by now; someone else will intervene."

To test this hypothesis, experimenters placed participants in separate booths and told them that they would take part in a group discussion about personal problems faced by college students. To avoid embarrassment, the discussion would be held through an intercom. Each person would speak for two minutes. The microphone would be turned on only in the booth of the person speaking, and the experimenter would not be listening. In reality, all the voices except the participant's were tape recordings. On the first round, one person mentioned that he had problems with seizures. On the second round, this individual sounded as if he were actually starting to

have a seizure and begged for help. The experimenters waited to see if the participant would leave the booth to report the emergency and how long it would take. Note that (a) the emergency is not at all ambiguous, (b) the participant could not tell how the bystanders in the other booths were reacting, and (c) the participant knew that the experimenter could not hear the emergency. Some participants were led to believe that the discussion group consisted only of themselves and the seizure victim. Others were told that they were part of a three-person group, and still others that they were part of a six-person group.

Of the participants who thought that they alone knew of the victim's seizure, 85% reported it; of those who thought they were in a three-person group, 62% reported the seizure; and of those who thought they were part of a six-person group only 31% reported it (see Figure 18-3). Interviews showed that all the participants perceived the situation to be a real emergency. Most were very upset by the conflict between letting the victim suffer and rushing for help. In fact, the participants who did not report the seizure appeared more upset than those who did. Clearly, we cannot interpret their

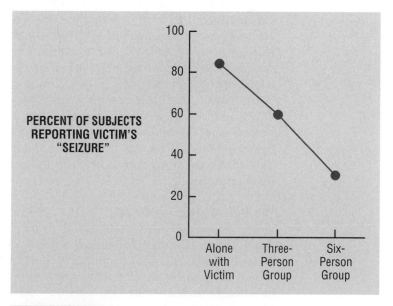

PERCENT OF SUBJECTS REPORTING VICTIM'S "SEIZURE"

FIGURE 18-3

Diffusion of Responsibility *The percentage of individuals who reported a victim's apparent seizure declined as the number of other people the individual believed were in his or her discussion group increased.* (After Darley & Latané, 1968)

nonintervention as apathy or indifference. Instead, the presence of others diffused the responsibility for acting (Darley & Latané, 1968; Latané & Darley, 1968).

If pluralistic ignorance and diffusion of responsibility are minimized, will people help one another? To find out, three psychologists used the New York City subway system as their laboratory (Piliavin, Rodin, & Piliavin, 1969). Two male and two female experimenters boarded a subway train separately. The female experimenters took seats and recorded the results, while the two men remained standing. As the train moved along, one of the men staggered forward and collapsed, remaining prone and staring at the ceiling until he received help. If no help came, the other man finally helped him to his feet. Several variations of the study were tried: The victim either carried a cane (so he would appear ill) or smelled of alcohol (so he would appear drunk). Sometimes the "victim" was white, sometimes black. There was no ambiguity; clearly the victim needed help. Diffusion of responsibility was minimized because each bystander could not continue to assume that someone else was intervening. Therefore, people should help.

The results supported this optimistic expectation. The victim with the cane received spontaneous help on over 95% of the trials, within an average of 5 seconds. The "drunk" victim received help on half of the trials, within an average of two minutes. Both black and white cane victims were aided by black and white bystanders. There was no relationship between the number of bystanders and the speed of help, suggesting that diffusion of responsibility had indeed been minimized.

The Role of Helping Models   In the subway study, as soon as one person moved to help, many others followed. This suggests that just as individuals use other people as models to define a situation as a nonemergency (pluralistic ignorance), they also use other people as models to indicate when to be helpful. This possibility was tested by counting the number of drivers who would stop to help a woman who was parked at the side of a road with a flat tire. It was found that significantly more drivers would stop to help if they had seen another woman with car trouble receiving help about a quarter of a mile earlier. Similarly, people are more likely to donate to a person soliciting for charity if they observe others doing so (Bryan & Test, 1967; Macaulay, 1970). These experiments indicate that others not only help us decide when not to act in an emergency but also serve as models to show us how and when to be good Samaritans.

Even role models on television can promote helping. In one study, 6-year-old children were shown an episode of "Lassie" in which a child rescues one of Lassie's pups from a mine shaft. Children in two control groups saw either a scene from "Lassie" that did not show a rescue or a scene from "The Brady Bunch." Later, when the children were playing a game in which the winner would be given a prize, they were exposed to some whining puppies. Even though helping the puppies would diminish their chances of winning the prize, children who had watched the rescue episode spent more time comforting the puppies than children who had seen the control episodes (Sprafkin, Liebert, & Poulous, 1975). Another study found that children exposed to programs such as "Mister Rogers's Neighborhood" or "Sesame Street" were more likely to behave in giving ways than children who were not exposed to the shows (Forge & Phemister, 1987).

The Role of Information   Now that you have read about the factors that deter bystanders from intervening in an emergency, would you be more likely to act in such a situation? An experiment at the University of Montana suggests that you would. Undergraduates were either given a lecture or shown a film based on the material discussed in this section. Two weeks later, each undergraduate was confronted with a simulated emergency while walking with one other person (a confederate of the experimenters). A male victim was sprawled on the floor of a hallway. The confederate did not react as if the situation were an emergency. Those who had heard the lecture or seen the film were significantly more likely than others to offer help (Beaman, Barnes, Klentz, & McQuirk, 1978).

Related to bystander intervention is the concept of altruism, discussed in the Frontiers of Psychological Research feature on the following page.

FRONTIERS OF PSYCHOLOGICAL RESEARCH

Altruism

The subway riders and the children who helped puppies, discussed in the body of the chapter, illustrate a form of prosocial behavior known as altruism. **Altruism** may be defined as *behavior intended to help others even when no benefits are offered or expected in return.* Much research has been devoted to attempting to discover why people engage in altruistic behavior. One view is that altruistic behavior is not entirely free of benefits; the person who behaves altruistically receives social approval and feels good about himself or herself. This approach, termed *social exchange theory,* holds that the person being helped and the person doing the helping are actually exchanging benefits, and that altruism is not truly selfless.

There are alternative views, however. Some researchers point out that many people display **empathy**; that is, *they feel distress when they see someone else in distress, and experience relief when the other person's suffering ends.* Loving parents, for example, suffer when their children suffer (Miller & Eisenberg, 1988). Thus, while some helpful behavior may be engaged in to gain rewards such as a noble feeling, other helpful acts are intended purely to benefit the person being helped (Batson, 1991). Experiments designed to test this view find that empathy often produces helping behavior only when the helping person believes that the other person will actually receive the help, regardless of whether that person will know who provided the help.

Still other researchers point out that social norms contribute to altruistic behavior. The norm of reciprocity, for example, prescribes that we should help those who have helped us. We recognize, however, that some people are unable to adhere to this norm because of conditions such as poverty or disability. The norm of social responsibility prescribes that we should help people who need help, regardless of whether they will be able to return the favor at a later date.

Psychologists are also interested in the circumstances in which people are most likely to engage in altruistic behavior. We saw in the body of the chapter that the presence of other bystanders diffuses responsibility and thus tends to decrease the potential for helping behavior. Other experiments have focused on nonemergencies such as giving to charity or donating blood (Myers, 1993). They have found that helping behavior often increases when the individual feels guilty and the behavior provides a way to relieve the guilt. The likelihood of helping also increases when we are in a good mood and when we have just observed a helpful model. In addition, deeply religious people are characterized by higher rates of charitable giving and volunteerism than less religious people.

From a biological perspective, there is some evidence that prosocial behavior has a genetic basis. Sociobiologists suggest that behaviors like helping, sharing, and cooperating are rooted in the genetic heritage of our species (Wilson, 1975). Ethologists point out that animals aid other members of their species, often at great risk to themselves. It is believed that in such cases the animal's genetic makeup produces behaviors that protect the social group and thereby contribute to the survival of the species. Exactly how this works is not well understood, but one possibility is that innate emotional reactions are involved. For example, newborns cry when they hear another baby cry, and toddlers react with distress to behaviors that threaten the well-being of others.

Other researchers note, however, that the development of empathy requires a strong caregiving environment and a certain level of cognitive development. They also emphasize the role of cultural factors in producing altruistic behavior. The early Christians, for example, martyred themselves not for the sake of their species but because of their religious beliefs. And many people have risked death in battle for the sake of their honor, not in order to preserve their gene pool. On the other hand, the biological perspective is useful because it reminds us that prosocial behavior can have adaptive value. Concern for the well-being of others contributes to the survival and well-being of the social group as a whole.

According to social exchange theory, a person who helps and the person who is helped are actually exchanging benefits.

Compliance and Resistance

Conformity to a Majority

When we are in a group, we may find ourselves in the minority on some issue. This is a fact of life to which most of us have become accustomed. If we decide that the majority is a more valid source of information than our own experience, we may change our minds and conform to the majority opinion. But imagine yourself in a situation in which you are sure that your own opinion is correct and that the group is wrong. Would you yield to social pressure and conform under those circumstances? This is the kind of conformity that social psychologist Solomon Asch decided to investigate in a series of classic studies (1952, 1955, 1958).

In Asch's standard procedure, a participant was seated at a table with a group of seven to nine others (all confederates of the experimenter). The group was shown a display of three vertical lines of different lengths and asked to judge which line was the same length as a line in another display (see Figure 18-4). Each individual announced his or her decision in turn, and the par-

ticipant sat in the next-to-last seat. The correct judgments were obvious, and on most trials everyone gave the same response. But on several predetermined trials the confederates had been instructed to give the wrong answer. Asch then observed the amount of conformity this procedure would elicit from participants.

The results were striking. Even though the correct answer was always obvious, the average participant conformed to the incorrect group consensus about one third of the time; about 75% of the participants conformed at least once. Moreover, the group did not have to be large to produce such conformity. When Asch varied the size of the group from 2 to 16, he found that a group of 3 or 4 confederates was just as effective at producing conformity as larger groups (Asch, 1958).

Why didn't the obviousness of the correct answer provide support for the participant's independence from the majority? Why isn't a person's confidence in his or her ability to make simple sensory judgments a strong force against conformity? According to one line of argument, it is precisely the obviousness of the correct answer that produces the strong forces toward conformity (Ross, Bierbrauer, & Hoffman, 1976). Disagreements in real life typically involve difficult or subjective judgments, such as which economic policy will best reduce inflation or which of two paintings is more aesthetically pleasing. In these cases, we expect to disagree with others occasionally; we even know that being a minority of one in an otherwise unanimous group is a plausible, if uncomfortable, possibility.

The situation in Asch's experiments is much more extreme. Here the participant is confronted with unanimous disagreement about a simple physical fact, a bizarre and unprecedented occurrence that appears to have no rational explanation. Participants are clearly puzzled and tense. They rub their eyes in disbelief and jump up to look more closely at the lines. They squirm, mumble, giggle in embarrassment, and look searchingly at other members of the group for some clue to the mystery. After the experiment they offer halfhearted hypotheses about optical illusions or suggest that perhaps the first person occasionally made a mistake and each successive person followed suit because of pressure to conform (Asch, 1952).

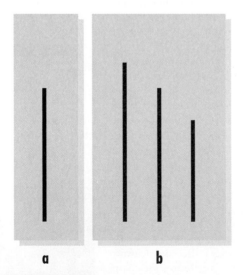

a   b

FIGURE 18-4

A Representative Stimulus in Asch's Study   *After viewing display (a), participants were told to pick the matching line from display (b). The displays shown here are typical in that the correct decision is obvious.* (After Asch, 1958)

In a study of conformity to majority opinion, (top) all of the group members except the man sixth from the left are confederates who have been instructed to give uniformly wrong answers on 12 of the 18 trials. Number 6, who has been told that he is participating in an experiment on visual judgment, therefore finds that he is a lone dissenter when he gives the correct answers. (bottom left) The participant, showing the strain of repeated disagreement with the majority, leans forward anxiously to look at the exhibit in question. (bottom right) This particular participant persists in his opinion, saying that "he has to call them as he sees them." (After Asch, 1958)

Consider what it means to dissent from the majority under these circumstances. Just as the judgments of the group seem incomprehensible to the participant, so the participant believes that his or her dissent will be incomprehensible to the group. Group members will surely judge him or her to be incompetent, even out of touch with reality. Similarly, if the participant dissents repeatedly, this will seem to constitute a direct challenge to the group's competence, a challenge that requires enormous courage when one's own perceptual abilities are suddenly and inexplicably called into question. Such a challenge violates a strong social norm against insulting others. This fear of "What will they think of me?" and "What will they think I think of them?" inhibits dissent and generates the strong pressure to conform in Asch's experiments.

Pressure to conform is far less strong when the group is not unanimous. If even one confederate breaks with the majority, the amount of conformity drops from 32% of the trials to about 6%. In fact, a group of eight containing only one dissenter produces less conformity than a unanimous majority of three (Allen & Levine, 1969; Asch, 1958). Surprisingly, the dissenter does not even have to give the correct answer. Even when the dissenter's answers are more inaccurate than the majority's, their influence is broken and participants are more inclined to give their own, correct judgments (Asch, 1955). Nor does it matter who the dissenter is. An African-American dissenter reduces the conformity rate among racially prejudiced white participants just as effectively as a white dissenter (Malof & Lott, 1962). In a variation that approaches the absurd, conformity was significantly reduced even though the participants thought the dissenter was so visually handicapped that he could not see the stimuli (Allen & Levine, 1971). It seems clear that the presence of just one other dissenter to share the potential disapproval or ridicule of the group permits the participant to dissent without feeling totally isolated.

If Asch's conformity situation is unlike most situations in real life, why did he use a task in which the correct answer was obvious? The reason is that he wanted to study pure public conformity, uncontaminated by the possibility that participants were actually changing their minds about the correct answers. (However, Asch reports that a few participants actually did decide that the group was correct on some of the critical trials.) Several variations of Asch's study have used more difficult or subjective judgments, and although they may reflect life more faithfully, they do not permit us to assess the effects of pure pressure to conform to a majority when we are certain that our own minority judgment is correct (Ross, Bierbrauer, & Hoffman, 1976).

Minority Influence

A number of European scholars have been critical of social psychological research in North America because of its preoccupation with conformity and the influence of the majority on the minority. As they correctly point out, intellectual innovation, social change, and political revolution often occur because an informed and articulate minority begins to convert others to its point of view (Moscovici, 1976). Why not study innovation and the influence that minorities can have on the majority?

To make their point, these European investigators deliberately began their experimental work by setting up a laboratory situation virtually identical to Asch's conformity situation. Participants were asked to make a series of simple perceptual judgments in the face of confederates who consistently gave the incorrect answer. But instead of placing a single participant in the midst of several confederates, these investigators planted two confederates, who consistently gave incorrect responses, in the midst of four real participants. The experimenters found that the minority was able to influence about 32% of the participants to make at least one incorrect judgment. For this to occur, however, the minority had to remain consistent throughout the experiment. If they wavered or showed any inconsistency in their judgments, they were unable to influence the majority (Moscovici, Lage, & Naffrechoux, 1969).

Since this initial demonstration of minority influence, more than 90 related studies have been conducted in both Europe and North America, including several that required groups to debate social and political issues rather than make simple perceptual judgments (Wood et al., 1994). The general finding is that minorities can move majorities toward their point of view if they present a consistent position without appearing rigid, dogmatic, or arrogant. Such minorities are perceived to be more confident and, occasionally, more competent than the majority (Maass & Clark, 1984). Minorities are also more effective if they argue a position that is consistent with the developing social norms of the larger society. For example, in two experiments in which feminist issues were discussed, subjects were moved significantly more by a minority position that was in line with feminist social norms than by one opposed to feminist norms (Paicheler, 1977).

But the most interesting finding of this research is that the majority members in these studies show a change of private attitude—that is, internalization—and not just the public conformity that was found in the Asch experiments. In fact, minorities sometimes cause private attitude change in majority members even when they fail to obtain public conformity.

One investigator has suggested that minorities are able to produce attitude change because they lead majority individuals to rethink the issues. Even when they fail to convince the majority, they broaden the range of acceptable opinions. In contrast, unanimous majorities are rarely prompted to think carefully about their position (Nemeth, 1986).

These findings remind us that majorities typically have the social power to approve and disapprove, to accept or reject, and it is this power that can produce public compliance or conformity. In contrast, minorities rarely have such social power. But if they have credibility they have the power to produce genuine attitude change and, hence, innovation, social change, and even revolution.

Obedience to Authority

In Nazi Germany from 1933 to 1945, millions of innocent people were systematically put to death in concentration camps. The mastermind of this horror, Adolf Hitler, may well have been a psychopathic monster. But he could not have done it alone. What about the people who ran the day-to-day operations, who built the ovens and gas chambers, filled them with human beings, counted bodies, and did the necessary paperwork? Were they all monsters, too?

Not according to social philosopher Hannah Arendt (1963), who observed the trial of Adolf Eichmann, a Nazi war criminal who was found guilty and executed for causing the murder of millions of Jews. She described him as a dull, ordinary bureaucrat who saw himself as a little cog in a big machine. The publication of a partial transcript of Eichmann's pretrial interrogation supports Arendt's view. Several psychiatrists found Eichmann to be quite sane, and his personal relationships were quite normal. In fact, he believed that the Jews should have been allowed to emigrate to a separate territory. Moreover, he had a Jewish mistress in secret—a crime for an SS officer—and a Jewish half-cousin whom he arranged to have protected during the war (Von Lang & Sibyll, 1983).

In her book about Eichmann, subtitled *A Report on the Banality of Evil,* Arendt concluded that most of the "evil men" of the Third Reich were just ordinary people following orders from superiors. This suggests that all of us might be capable of such evil and that Nazi Germany was less wildly alien from the normal human condition than we might like to think. As Arendt put it, "In certain circumstances the most ordinary decent person can become a criminal." This is not an easy conclusion to accept because it is more comforting to believe that monstrous evil is done only by monstrous individuals. In fact, our emotional attachment to this explanation of evil was vividly demonstrated by the intensity of the attacks on Arendt and her conclusions.

The problem of obedience to authority arose again in Vietnam in 1969, when a group of American soldiers, claiming that they were simply following orders, killed a number of civilians in the community of My Lai. Again the public was forced to ponder the possibility that ordinary citizens are willing to obey authority in violation of their own moral consciences.

This issue was explored empirically in a series of important and controversial studies conducted by Stanley Milgram (1963, 1974) at Yale University. Ordinary men and women were recruited through a newspaper ad that offered $4 for one hour's participation

Social change—such as the end of apartheid in South Africa—is sometimes brought about because a few people manage to persuade the majority to change its attitudes.

in a "study of memory." On arriving at the laboratory, the participant was told that he or she would be playing the role of teacher in the study. The participant was to read a series of word pairs to another person and then test that person's memory by reading the first word of each pair and asking him to select the correct second word from four alternatives. Each time the learner made an error, the participant was to press a lever that delivered an electric shock to him.

The participant watched while the learner was strapped into a chair and an electrode was attached to his wrist. The participant was then seated in an adjoining room in front of a shock generator whose front panel contained 30 lever switches in a horizontal line. Each switch was labeled with a voltage rating, ranging in sequence from 15 to 450 volts, and groups of adjacent switches were labeled descriptively, ranging from "Slight Shock" up to "Danger: Severe Shock." When a switch was depressed, an electric buzzer sounded,

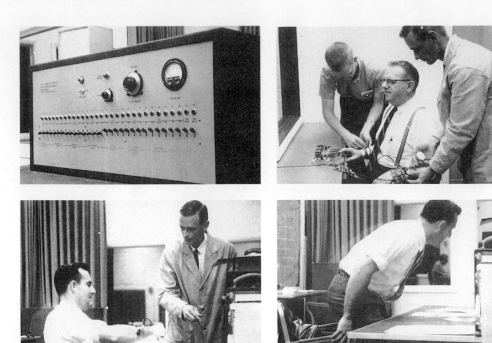

(top left) The "shock generator" used in Milgram's experiment on obedience. (top right) The "learner" is strapped into the "electric chair." (bottom left) A participant receives a sample shock before starting the "teaching session." (bottom right) A participant refuses to go on with the experiment. Most participants became deeply disturbed by the role they were asked to play, whether they remained in the experiment to the end or refused at some point to go on. (From the film *Obedience,* distributed by New York University Film Library, copyright © 1965 by Stanley Milgram)

lights flashed, and the needle on a voltage meter deflected to the right. To illustrate how it worked, the participant was given a sample shock of 45 volts from the generator. As the procedure began, the experimenter instructed the participant to move one level higher on the shock generator after each successive error by the learner (see Figure 18-5).

The learner did not actually receive any shocks. He was a mild-mannered 47-year-old man who had been specially trained for his role. As he began to make errors and the shock levels escalated, he could be heard protesting through the adjoining wall. As the shocks became stronger, he began to shout and curse. At 300 volts he began to kick the wall, and at the next shock level (marked "Extreme Intensity Shock"), he no longer answered the questions or made any noise. As you might expect, many participants began to object to this excruciating procedure, pleading with the experimenter to call a halt. But the experimenter responded with a sequence of prods, using as many as neces-

sary to get the participant to go on: "Please continue"; "The experiment requires that you continue"; "It is absolutely essential that you continue"; and "You have no other choice—you must go on." Obedience to authority was measured by the maximum amount of shock the participant would administer before refusing to continue.

Milgram found that 65% of the participants continued to obey throughout, going all the way to the end of the shock series (450 volts). Not one participant stopped before administering 300 volts, the point at which the learner began to kick the wall (see Figure 18-6). What produces such obedience?

Milgram suggests that the potential for obedience to authority is such a necessary requirement for communal life that it has probably been built into our species by evolution. The division of labor in a society requires that individuals be willing at times to subordinate their own independent actions to serve the goals of the larger social organization. Parents, school systems, and businesses nurture this willingness by reminding the

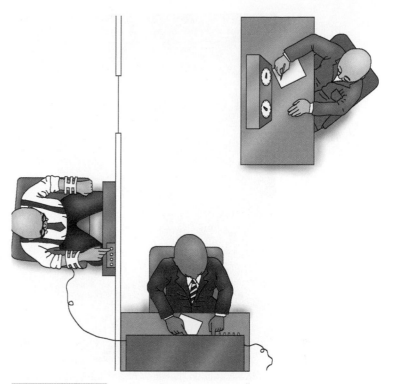

FIGURE 18-5

Milgram's Experiment on Obedience   *The "teacher" was told to give the "learner" a more intense shock after each error. If the "teacher" objected, the experimenter insisted that it was necessary to go on.* (After Milgram, 1974)

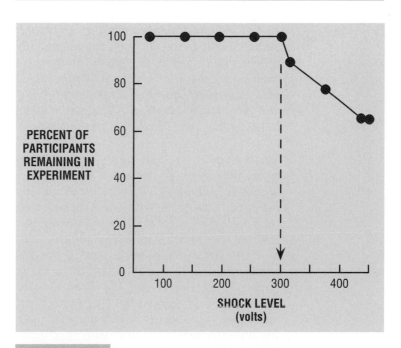

FIGURE 18-6

Obedience to Authority   *The percentage of participants who were willing to administer a punishing shock did not begin to decline until the intensity level of the shock reached 300 volts (the danger level).* (After Milgram, 1963)

Modern warfare allows individuals to distance themselves from the actual killing, giving them the feeling that they are not responsible for enemy deaths.

individual of the importance of following the directives of others who "know the larger picture." To understand obedience in a particular situation, then, we need to understand the factors that persuade individuals to relinquish their autonomy and become voluntary agents of the system. Milgram's experiments illustrate four such factors: social norms, surveillance, buffers, and ideological justification.

Social Norms By replying to the advertisement and agreeing to be in the study, participants in Milgram's experiments implicitly agreed to cooperate with the experimenter, follow the directions of the person in charge, and see the job through to completion. This is a very strong *social norm,* and we tend to underestimate how difficult it is to break such an agreement and go back on our implied word to cooperate. The experiment was designed to reinforce this norm by making it particularly difficult to stop once it had begun. The procedure starts rather innocently as an study of memory and gradually escalates. Once participants begin to give shocks and to raise the shock levels, there is no longer a natural stopping point. By the

time they want to quit, they are trapped. The experimenter makes no new demands, only that they continue to do what they are already doing. In order to break off, they must suffer the guilt and embarrassment of acknowledging that they were wrong to begin at all. And the longer they put off quitting, the harder it is to admit their misjudgment in going as far as they have. It is easier to continue. Imagine how much less obedience there would be if participants had to begin by giving the strongest shock first.

Finally, the potential quitter faces a dilemma over violating a norm of etiquette (not being rude) similar to the one confronting a participant in the Asch experiments. Dissenting in that case implied that the participant thought the group was incompetent. Dissenting in the Milgram experiment is equivalent to accusing the experimenter of being immoral—an even more compelling force that pushes the participant to go along with the experiment.

If social norms like these can produce so much obedience in Milgram's studies, it is easy to imagine how much more powerful the penalties for quitting would be in Nazi

Germany or in military service once one has already "signed on."*

Surveillance An obvious factor in the Milgram experiment is the constant presence or *surveillance* of the experimenter. When the experimenter left the room and issued his orders by telephone, the rate of obedience dropped from 65% to 21% (Milgram, 1974). Moreover, several of the participants who continued under these conditions cheated by administering shocks of lower intensity than they were supposed to.

Buffers Milgram's participants believed that they were committing acts of violence, but there were several buffers that obscured this fact or diluted the immediacy of the experience. For example, the learner was in the next room, out of sight and unable to communicate. The rate of obedience drops from 65% to 40% if the learner is in the same room as the participant. If the participant must personally ensure that the learner holds his hand on a shock plate, obedience declines to 30%. The more direct the participant's experience with the victim—the fewer buffers between the person and the consequences of his or her act—the less the participant will obey.

The most common buffer found in warlike situations is the remoteness of the person from the final act of violence. Thus, Eichmann argued that he was not directly responsible for killing Jews; he merely arranged for their deaths. Milgram conducted an analog to this "link-in-the-chain" role by requiring a subject only to pull a switch that enabled another teacher (a confederate) to deliver the shocks to the learner. Under these conditions the rate of obedience soared: A full 93% of the participants continued to the end of the shock series. In this situation, the participant can shift responsibility to the person who actually delivers the shock.

The shock generator itself served as a *buffer*—an impersonal mechanical agent that actually delivered the shock. Imagine how obedience would have declined if participants were required to hit the learner with their fists. In real life we have analogous technologies that permit us to destroy distant fellow humans by remote control, thereby removing us from the sight of their suffering. Although we probably would all agree that it is worse to kill thousands of people by pushing a button that releases a guided missile than it is to beat one individual to death with a rock, it is still psychologically easier to push the button. Such are the effects of buffers.

Ideological Justification The fourth and most important factor producing voluntary obedience is the individual's acceptance of an *ideology*—a set of beliefs and attitudes—that legitimates the authority of the person in charge and justifies following his or her directives. Nazi officers believed in the primacy of the German state and hence in the legitimacy of orders issued in its name. Similarly, the American soldiers who followed orders to shoot enemy civilians in Vietnam had already committed themselves to the premise that national security requires strict obedience to military commands.

In the Milgram experiments, "the importance of science" is the ideology that legitimates even extraordinary demands. Some critics have argued that the Milgram experiments were artificial, that the prestige of a scientific experiment led participants to obey without questioning the dubious procedures in which they participated, and that in real life people would never do such a thing (Baumrind, 1964). Indeed, when Milgram repeated his experiment in a rundown set of offices and removed any association with Yale University from the setting, the rate of obedience dropped from 65% to 48% (Milgram, 1974).

But this criticism misses the major point. The prestige of science is not an irrelevant artificiality but an integral part of Milgram's demonstration. Science serves the same legitimating role in the experiment that the German state served in Nazi Germany and that national security serves in wartime killing. It is precisely their belief in the importance of scientific research that prompts individuals to subordinate their moral autonomy and independence to those who claim to act on behalf of science.

Ethical Issues Milgram's experiments have been criticized on several grounds. First,

---

*Daniel Goldhagen, the author of the 1996 book *Hitler's Willing Executioners: Ordinary Germans and the Holocaust,* argues that Milgram's studies of obedience do not in fact provide an explanation for Nazi atrocities.

critics argue that Milgram's procedures created an unacceptable level of stress in the participants during the experiment itself. In support of this claim, they quote Milgram's own description:

> Subjects were observed to sweat, tremble, stutter, bite their lips, groan, and dig their fingernails into their flesh. These were characteristic rather than exceptional responses to the experiment. . . . One sign of tension was the regular occurrence of nervous laughing fits. . . . On one occasion we observed a seizure so violently convulsive that it was necessary to call a halt to the experiment. (Milgram, 1963, p. 375)

Second, critics express concern about the long-term psychological effects on participants of having learned that they would be willing to give potentially lethal shocks to a fellow human being. Third, critics argue that participants are likely to feel foolish and "used" when told the true nature of the experiment, thereby making them less trusting of psychologists in particular and of authority in general.

In response to these and other criticisms, Milgram pointed out that after his experiments he conducted a careful "debriefing," explaining the reasons for the procedures and reestablishing positive rapport with the participant. This included a reassuring chat with the "victim" who the participant had thought was receiving the shocks. After the completion of an experimental series, participants were sent a detailed report of the purposes and results and purposes of the experiment. Milgram then conducted a survey, which revealed that 84% of the participants were glad to have taken part in the study; 15% reported neutral feelings; and 1% stated that they were sorry to have participated. These percentages were about the same for those who had obeyed and those who had defied the experimenter. In addition, 74% indicated that they had learned something of personal importance as a result of being in the study.

Milgram also hired a psychiatrist to interview 40 of the participants to determine whether the study had any injurious effects. This follow-up revealed no indications of long-term distress or traumatic reactions (Milgram, 1964).

In Chapter 1 we noted that research guidelines set forth by the United States government and the American Psychological Association emphasize two major principles: minimal risk and informed consent. Milgram's studies were conducted in the early 1960s, before these guidelines were in effect. Despite the importance of the research and the precautions that Milgram took, it seems likely that most of the review boards that must now approve federally funded research projects would not permit these experiments to be conducted today.

Obedience in Everyday Life Because the Milgram experiments have been criticized for being artificial (Orne & Holland, 1968), it is instructive to look at an example of obedience to authority under more ordinary conditions. Researchers investigated whether nurses in public and private hospitals would obey an order that violated hospital rules and professional practice (Hofling et al., 1966). While on regular duty, the participant (a nurse) received a phone call from a doctor whom she knew to be on the staff but had not met: "This is Dr. Smith from Psychiatry calling. I was asked to see Mr. Jones this morning, and I'm going to have to see him again tonight. I'd like him to have had some medication by the time I get to the ward. Will you please check your medicine cabinet and see if you have some Astroten? That's ASTROTEN." When the nurse checked the medicine cabinet, she saw a pillbox labeled:

ASTROTEN
5 mg capsules
Usual dose: 5 mg
Maximum daily dose: 10 mg

After she reported that she had found it, the doctor continued, "Now will you please give Mr. Jones a dose of 20 milligrams of Astroten. I'll be up within 10 minutes; I'll sign the order then, but I'd like the drug to have started taking effect." A staff psychiatrist, posted unobtrusively nearby, terminated each trial by disclosing its true nature when the nurse either poured the medication (actually a harmless placebo), refused to accept the order, or tried to contact another professional.

This order violated several rules: The dose was clearly excessive. Medication orders may not be given by telephone. The medication was unauthorized—that is, it was not on the ward stock list clearing it for use. Finally, the order was given by an unfamiliar person. Despite all this, 95% of the nurses started to give the medication. Moreover, the telephone calls were all brief, and the nurses put up little or no resistance. None of them insisted on a written order, although several sought reassurance that the doctor would arrive promptly. In interviews after the experiment, all the nurses stated that such orders had been received in the past and that doctors became annoyed if the nurses balked.

The Power of Situations

In Chapter 17 we saw that people typically overestimate the role of personal factors and underestimate the role of situational factors in controlling behavior (the *fundamental attribution error*). Studies of conformity and obedience illustrate this point—not through their results but through our surprise at their results. We simply do not expect the situational forces to be as effective as they are. When college students are told about Milgram's procedures (but not given the results) and asked whether they would continue to administer the shocks after the learner begins to pound on the wall, about 99% say that they would not (Aronson, 1995). Milgram himself surveyed psychiatrists at a leading medical school. They predicted that most subjects would refuse to go on after reaching 150 volts, that only about 4% would go beyond 300 volts, and that less than 1% would go all the way to 450 volts. In one study, participants were asked to estimate obedience rates after they had reenacted the entire Milgram procedure, complete with shock apparatus and a tape recording of the protesting learner. Whether they played the role of the actual participant or the role of an observer, all of the participants continued to vastly underestimate the compliance rates actually obtained by Milgram, as shown in Figure 18-7 (Bierbrauer, 1973).

The study involving the administration of medications yielded comparable results. When nurses who had not been participants in the study were given a complete description of the situation and asked how they themselves would respond, 83% reported that they would not have given the medication, and most of them thought that a major-

ity of nurses would also refuse. Twenty-one nursing students who were asked the same question all asserted that they would not have given the medication as ordered.

These studies show that our reactions to conformity and obedience experiments dramatically illustrate a major lesson of social psychology: We seriously underestimate the extent and power of social and situational forces on human behavior. A famous study showing just how powerful situational forces can be is the Stanford Prison Study conducted by Philip G. Zimbardo. Zimbardo and his colleagues were interested in the psychological processes involved in taking the roles of prisoner and prison guard. They created a simulated prison in the basement of a building at Stanford University and placed an ad in a local newspaper for participants to take part in a psychological experiment for pay. From the people who responded to the ad, they selected 24 "mature, emotionally stable, normal, intelligent white male college students

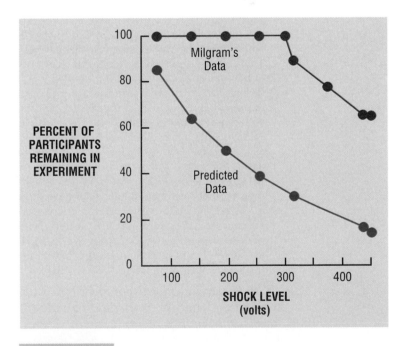

FIGURE 18-7

Predicted and Actual Compliance *The upper curve presents Milgram's data and shows the percentage of participants who remained obedient in the situation, continuing to administer shocks as the voltage increased. The lower curve is from a study in which role-playing participants reenacted the Milgram experiment. The study attempted to predict what percentage of the participants would continue to be obedient as shock increased. The role-playing participants vastly underestimated the magnitude of the situational forces and the likelihood of obedience in Milgram's experimental situation. (After Bierbrauer, 1973)*

from middle-class homes throughout the United States and Canada. None had a prison record, and all seemed very similar in their values. By the flip of a coin, half were assigned to be prison guards and half to be prisoners.

The "guards" were instructed about their responsibilities and made aware of the potential danger of the situation and their need to protect themselves. The "prisoners" were unexpectedly picked up at their homes by a mock police car, handcuffed, and taken blindfolded to the improvised jail, where they were searched, deloused, fingerprinted, given numbers, and placed in "cells" with two other prisoners.

The subjects had signed up for the sake of the money, and all expected to be in the experiment for about two weeks. But by the end of the sixth day the researchers had to cancel the experiment because the results were too frightening to allow them to continue. As Zimbardo explained:

> It was no longer apparent to most of the subjects (or to us) where reality ended and their roles began. The majority had indeed become prisoners or guards, no longer able to clearly differentiate between role playing and self. There were dramatic changes in virtually every aspect of their behavior, thinking, and feeling. In less than a week the experience of imprisonment undid (temporarily) a lifetime of learning; human values were suspended, self-concepts were challenged, and the ugliest, most base, pathological side of human nature surfaced. We were horrified because we saw some boys (guards) treat others as if they were despicable animals, taking pleasure in cruelty, while other boys (prisoners) became servile, dehumanized robots who thought only of escape, of their own individual survival, and of their mounting hatred for the guards. (1972, p. 243)

Far faster and more thoroughly than the researchers thought possible, "the experiment had become a reality."

Rebellion

One reason the experiments on conformity and obedience obtain such high compliance is that the social pressures in these studies are directed toward a lone individual. If the participant were not alone, would he or she be less obedient? We have already seen some data to support this possibility: A participant in the Asch conformity situation is less likely to go along with the group's incorrect judgments if there is at least one other dissenter.

A similar phenomenon occurs in the Milgram obedience situation. In one variation of the procedure, two additional confederates were employed. They were introduced as participants who would also play teacher roles. Teacher 1 would read the list of word pairs; Teacher 2 would tell the learner if he was right or wrong; and Teacher 3 (the participant) would deliver the shocks. The confederates complied with the instructions through the 150-volt shock, at which point Teacher 1 informed the experimenter that he was quitting. Despite the experimenter's insistence that he continue, Teacher 1 got up from his chair and sat in another part of the room. After the 210-volt shock, Teacher 2 also quit. The experimenter then turned to the participant and ordered him to continue alone. Only 10% of the participants were willing to complete the series in this situation. In a second variation, there were two experimenters rather than two additional teachers. After a few shocks, they began to argue. One of them said that they should stop the experiment; the other said that they should continue. Under these circumstances not a single participant would continue despite the orders to do so by the second experimenter (Milgram, 1974).

A more recent experiment examined more directly the possibility that groups of participants might actually be moved to rebel against unjust authority. Citizens from a non-university community were recruited by phone for $10 to spend two hours at a local motel assisting in research on "group standards" sponsored by a fictitious company, the Manufacturer's Human Relations Consultants, or MHRC (Gamson, Fireman, & Rytina, 1982). Nine participants, both male and female, were recruited for each group session. When they arrived, they were given a letter explaining that legal cases sometimes hinge on the notion of community standards and that MHRC collects evidence on such standards by bringing together concerned citizens for group discussions. The participants were then seated in front of video cameras and microphones at a U-shaped table, where they filled out a background questionnaire and signed a "participation agreement" giving MHRC permission to videotape them as they engaged in group discussion. The man in charge, who introduced himself as the coordinator, then read the background of a pending court case. The basic facts were as follows:

A service station manager was suing an oil company because it had canceled the franchise on his service station. The oil company had conducted an investigation of the man and discovered that he was living with a woman to whom he was not married. The company claimed that his lifestyle violated the moral standards of the local community and that he would therefore not be able to maintain good relations with customers; accordingly, they decided to revoke his franchise license. The man sued for breach of contract and invasion of privacy, arguing that the company was out to get him because he had publicly criticized the company's gas pricing policies in a local television interview.

After presenting the case, the coordinator asked the group to discuss it while being videotaped. After a general discussion, the cameras were turned off and the group was given a short break. Before resuming the videotaping, the coordinator requested three of the group members to argue as if they were personally offended by the station manager's lifestyle. This second discussion was taped, there was another break, and three additional individuals were designated to argue in the same way in the next discussion. Finally, the coordinator asked each individual to go on camera alone and voice objections to the station manager's affair, stating an intention to boycott the station and arguing that the manager should lose his franchise. Group members were also told that they would be asked to sign notarized affidavits giving MHRC the right to introduce the tapes as evidence in court after editing them as it saw fit.

As MHRC's motives began to dawn on them, all but one of the 33 groups in this experiment began to dissent: "Can you assure us that the court is going to know these aren't our real opinions?"; "Would you mind leaving the tape on while you give us these instructions, so that it doesn't appear . . ."; "Do these professional people know what you're doing in fact is suborning perjury?" (Gamson, Fireman, & Rytina, 1982, pp. 62, 65). One group even decided to take direct action by gathering up materials from the table and taking them to the local newspaper.

Overall, 16 of the 33 groups rebelled completely—all of their members refused to sign the final affidavit—and in 9 additional groups a majority refused to do so. In the remaining 8 groups only a minority refused, although a number of dissenting comments were voiced. Compared with the Milgram situation, then, obedience to authority had clearly been undermined in this study. But why?

The two studies differ in several respects, so we cannot be certain that the important difference was having a group rather than a lone individual as the target. Nevertheless, this seems to be the most likely factor. In fact, the circumstances producing rebellion in the MHRC study appear to be the same ones that we have seen operating in other group contexts: defining the situation and conformity.

In the bystander intervention studies, we noted that individuals in a group define an ambiguous situation for one another. Participants in the MHRC study were given ample opportunity during the breaks to define and clarify the situation for one another by sharing their suspicions of MHRC's motives. They made comments like the following: "How are people going to know that these aren't our opinions?"; "We don't want to be faced with the situation where you read in the *New York Times* one day that thanks to a new method of litigation [group laughter] that this poor schnook [group laughter] lost his license" (Gamson, Fireman, & Rytina, 1982, pp. 101–102).

The preliminary questionnaires also indicated that 80% to 90% of the participants initially disagreed with the position they were asked to take: They saw nothing wrong with an unmarried man and woman living together; they were critical of large oil companies; and they believed that an employee's private life was none of a company's business. The group members could also share these opinions with one another. The researchers compared the 23 groups in which a majority of the members initially held dissenting opinions with the 10 groups that initially held fewer dissenting opinions. They found that 65% of the former groups produced complete rebellion—nobody signed the affidavits—but only 10% of the latter groups rebelled completely. A majority of the groups also contained some individuals who had been active in past protests and strikes, and these groups were also more likely to rebel than groups without such role models. Lone participants in the Milgram obedience studies obviously had none of these opportunities for sharing information, receiving social support for dissent, or observing role models for disobedience.

Before we congratulate the human species for bold independence and autonomy in the face of social pressure, we should consider the implication of these findings more closely. They suggest that many of the individuals in the groups were not choosing between obedience and autonomy but between obedience and conformity: Obey the coordinator or conform to the group's norm to disobey. As the researchers observed, "Many were uncertain at this point, waiting to see what others would do, delaying decision as long as possible. Ultimately, they were faced with an unavoidable choice—to sign or not to sign—and loyalty to the group became one major factor in their decision." Some who had already signed the affidavit crossed out their names or tore up the form. As one participant told the coordinator, "I didn't personally say anything I didn't believe, but I'm not going to sign this either, if the rest of the group isn't signing" (Gamson, Fireman, & Rytina, 1982, p. 99).

Obeying or conforming may not strike you as a very heroic choice. But these are among the processes that provide the social glue for the human species. Several years before this study was conducted, a social historian noted that "disobedience when it is not criminally but morally, religiously, or politically motivated is always a collective act and it is justified by the values of the collectivity and the mutual engagements of its members" (Walzer, 1970, p. 4).

Internalization

Most studies of conformity and obedience focus on whether or not individuals overtly comply with the influence. In everyday life, however, those who attempt to influence us usually want to change our private attitudes, not just our public behaviors, to obtain changes that will be sustained even after they are no longer on the scene. As noted at the beginning of the chapter, such change is called *internalization*. Certainly the major goal of parents, educators, clergy, politicians, and advertisers is internalization, not just compliance. In general, internalization is obtained by an influence source who either (a) presents a persuasive message that is itself compelling or (b) is perceived as credible, as possessing both expertise and trustworthiness. In this section we examine influence that persuades rather than coerces.

Persuasive Communication

Just as the practices of Nazi Germany under Hitler created interest in obedience to authority, so wartime propaganda efforts prompted social psychologists to study persuasion. Intensive research began in the late

Priests and politicians are among those who seek to present persuasive messages that will be internalized by their audiences.

1940s at Yale University, where investigators sought to determine the characteristics of successful persuasive communicators, successful communications, and the kinds of people who are most easily persuaded (Hovland, Janis, & Kelley, 1953). As research on these topics continued over the years, a number of interesting phenomena were discovered but few general principles emerged. The results became increasingly complex and difficult to summarize, and every conclusion seemed to require several "it depends" qualifications. Beginning in the 1970s, however, interest in information processing gave rise to theories of persuasion that provided a more unified framework for analyzing persuasive communication.

Among the new approaches were several variations of cognitive response theory. This theory proposes that persuasion induced by a communication is actually self-persuasion produced by the thoughts that the person generates while reading, listening to, or even just anticipating the communication. These thoughts can be about the content of the communication itself or about other aspects of the situation, such as the credibility of the communicator. If the communication evokes thoughts that support the position being advocated, the individual will move toward that position; if the communication evokes unsupportive thoughts (such as counterarguments or disparaging thoughts about the communicator), the individual will remain unconvinced or even shift away from the position being advocated (Greenwald, 1968; Petty, Ostrom, & Brock, 1981).

A number of studies support this theory. In one, each participant read a communication containing arguments about a controversial issue and wrote a one-sentence reaction (*cognitive response*) to each argument. One week later the participants were unexpectedly given a memory test asking them to recall both the arguments in the communication and their written reactions to those arguments. Participants' opinions on the issue were assessed before receiving the communication and again at the time of the memory test. The results showed that the amount of opinion change produced by the communication was significantly correlated with both the supportiveness of participants' reactions to the communication and with their later recall of those reactions, but

it was not significantly correlated with their recall of the arguments themselves (Love & Greenwald, 1978). This experiment not only supports the theory but also explains what had previously been a puzzling observation: that the persistence of opinion change is often unrelated to an individual's memory of the arguments that produced that change.

Cognitive response theory also proposes that a persuasive communication will be unsuccessful to the extent that the target individual is motivated to generate counterarguments against the position being advocated and has the ability and opportunity to do so.

Although much research on persuasion has been conducted in laboratories, there has always been an interest in the practical applications of the findings. Cognitive response theory is no exception. An example is an educational program designed to inoculate junior high school students against peer pressure to smoke. High school students conducted sessions in which they taught seventh-graders how to generate counterarguments. For example, in role-playing sessions they were taught to respond to being called "chicken" for not taking a cigarette by saying things like "I'd be a real chicken if I smoked just to impress you." They were also taught to respond to advertisements implying that liberated women smoke by saying, "She's not really liberated if she is hooked on tobacco." Several inoculation sessions were held during seventh and eighth grades, and records were kept of how many of the students smoked from the beginning of the study through the ninth grade. The results showed that inoculated students were half as likely to smoke as students at a matched junior high school that used a more typical smoking education program (McAlister et al., 1980). Similar programs have been designed to inoculate elementary school children against being taken in by deceptive television commercials (Cohen, 1980; Feshbach, 1980).

Central Versus Peripheral Routes of Persuasion
Although research on cognitive response theory has focused primarily on the individual's thoughts about the substantive arguments in a communication, the individual can also respond to other features of the situation, such as cues about the communicator's credibility. Richard Petty and John

Cacioppo have demonstrated the importance of distinguishing between two routes that persuasion can take in producing belief and attitude change (Petty & Cacioppo, 1986, 1981).

Persuasion is said to follow the *central route* when the individual responds to substantive information about the topic. This can be information contained in the persuasive communication itself or information that is part of the individual's preexisting knowledge. Most of the research on cognitive response theory explores this route. Persuasion is said to follow the *peripheral route* when the individual responds to noncontent cues in a communication (such as the sheer number of arguments it contains) or to the context of the communication (such as the credibility of the communicator or the pleasantness of the surroundings).

The central route to persuasion is taken only when the individual is motivated to generate thoughts in response to the substantive content of a communication and has the ability and opportunity to do so. The peripheral route is taken when the individual is unable or unwilling to do the cognitive work required to carefully evaluate the content of the communication. Several factors can influence which route will be taken. One such factor is personal involvement. If a communication addresses an issue in which the individual has a personal stake, he or she is more likely to attend carefully to the arguments. In such a case the individual is also likely to have a rich store of prior information and opinion on the issue. On the other hand, if an issue has no personal relevance for the individual, he or she is not likely to make much of an effort either to support or refute arguments about it. What happens then?

According to one recent theory, when we are unwilling or unable to process the content of a communication, we may use simple rules of thumb—called *heuristics*—to infer the validity of its arguments. Examples of such rules might include "Messages with many arguments are more likely to be valid than messages with few arguments"; "Politicians always lie"; or "College professors know what they are talking about." This special case of cognitive response theory is referred to as the *heuristic theory of persuasion* (Chaiken, 1987, 1980; Eagly & Chaiken, 1984).

The concept of two routes of persuasion has been tested in several studies. In one rather complex study, college undergraduates read an essay allegedly written by the chairperson of a university committee charged with advising the chancellor on changes in academic policy. The essay proposed that the university institute a comprehensive examination that every undergraduate would have to pass before being permitted to graduate. In order to manipulate the students' involvement in the issue, half of them were told that any policy changes adopted by the chancellor would be instituted the next year (high involvement), while the other half were told that any changes would take effect in 10 years (low involvement). Different forms of the essay were also used. Some contained strong arguments, others weak ones. Some contained only three arguments, others nine.

The postcommunication attitudes of students in the high-involvement conditions are shown in Figure 18-8. It can be seen that strong arguments produced more favorable attitudes overall than did weak arguments. But more important, nine strong arguments produced greater agreement with the essay than did three strong arguments, whereas nine weak arguments produced less agreement than did three weak arguments. How do the theories account for these patterns?

The theory of routes of persuasion predicts that students in the high-involvement conditions will be motivated to process the essay's substantive arguments and thus generate topic-relevant cognitive responses. This is the central route of persuasion, and cognitive response theory predicts that strong arguments will evoke more supportive cognitive responses and fewer counterarguments than will weak arguments and hence will produce more agreement with the essay—as, indeed, they did. Moreover, nine strong arguments should be more persuasive than three strong arguments because the more strong arguments the individual encounters, the more supportive cognitive responses he or she will generate. In contrast, nine weak arguments should be less persuasive than three weak arguments because the more weak arguments the individual encounters, the more counterarguments he or she will generate. These predictions are in accordance with the findings displayed in Figure 18-8.

As shown in Figure 18-9, a different pattern emerges for students in the low-involvement conditions. Here the theory of routes of persuasion predicts that students in the low-involvement conditions will not be motivated to scrutinize the essay's arguments closely and will instead rely on simple heuristics to evaluate its merits and form their attitudes. This is the peripheral route, and the heuristic theory of persuasion predicts that an individual in this setting will not even bother to determine whether the arguments are strong or weak but will simply invoke the heuristic rule "Messages with many arguments are more likely to be valid than messages with few arguments." Thus, strong arguments will be no more effective than weak arguments, and nine arguments will be more persuasive than three arguments—regardless of whether they are strong or weak. This is precisely the pattern shown in Figure 18-9: Overall, there were no significant differences between strong and weak arguments, but nine arguments were more effective than three arguments in both conditions (Petty & Cacioppo, 1984).

An experiment that varied the expertise of the communicator rather than the number of arguments found similar results: Participants in the high-involvement conditions were more influenced by the strength of the arguments, but participants in the low-involvement conditions relied more on the heuristic "Arguments made by an expert are more valid than arguments made by a nonexpert" (Petty, Cacioppo, & Goldman, 1981).

Reference Groups and Identification

Nearly every group to which we belong has an implicit or explicit set of beliefs, attitudes, and behaviors that it considers correct. Any member of the group who strays from these social norms risks isolation and social disapproval. Thus, through social rewards and punishments the groups to which we belong obtain compliance from us. In addition, if we respect or admire other individuals or groups, we may obey their norms and adopt their beliefs, attitudes, and behaviors in order to be like them, to identify with them. This process is called **identification.**

Reference groups are *groups with which we identify; we refer to them in order to*

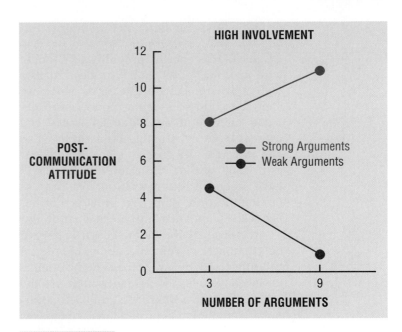

FIGURE 18-8

Postcommunication Attitudes   *When individuals have high involvement in the issue, nine strong arguments produce more agreement with the essay than three strong arguments, but nine weak arguments produce less agreement than three weak arguments.*   (After Cacioppo, 1984)

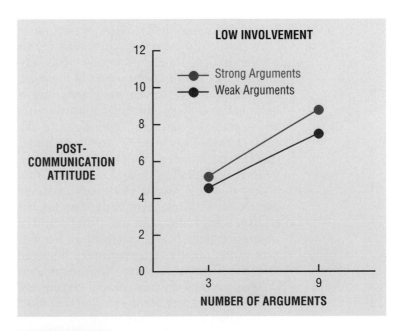

FIGURE 18-9

Postcommunication Attitudes   *When individuals have low involvement in the issue, nine arguments produce more agreement than three arguments, regardless of whether the arguments are strong or weak.*

evaluate and regulate our opinions and actions. Reference groups can also serve as a frame of reference by providing us not only with specific beliefs and attitudes but also with a general perspective from which we view the world—an ideology or set of ready-made interpretations of social issues and events. If we eventually adopt these views and integrate the group's ideology into our own value system, the reference group will have produced internalization. The process of identification, then, can provide a bridge between compliance and internalization.

An individual does not necessarily have to be a member of a reference group in order to be influenced by its values. For example, lower-middle-class individuals often use the middle class as a reference group. An aspiring athlete may use professional athletes as a reference group.

Life would be simple if each of us identified with only one reference group. But most of us identify with several reference groups, which often leads to conflicting pressures. We noted in Chapter 17, for example, that a Jewish businessperson might experience cross-pressures from his or her ethnic and business reference groups. But perhaps the most enduring example of competing reference groups is the conflict that many young people experience between their family reference group and their college or peer reference group. The most extensive study of this conflict is Theodore Newcomb's classic Bennington Study—an examination of the political attitudes of the entire population of Bennington College, a small, politically liberal college in Vermont. The dates of the study (1935–1939) are a useful reminder that this is not a new phenomenon.

Today Bennington College tends to attract liberal students, but in 1935 most students came from wealthy conservative families. (It is also coed today, but in 1935 it was a women's college.) Over two thirds of the parents of Bennington students were affiliated with the Republican party. The Bennington College community was liberal during the 1930s, but this was not the reason that most of the women selected the college.

Newcomb's main finding was that with each year at Bennington, students moved further away from their parents' attitudes and closer to the attitudes of the college community. For example, in the 1936 presidential campaign about 66% of parents favored the Republican candidate, Alf Landon, over the Democratic candidate, Franklin Roosevelt. Landon was supported by 62% of the Bennington freshmen and 43% of the sophomores, but only 15% of the juniors and seniors.

For most of the women, increasing liberalism reflected a deliberate choice between the two competing reference groups. Two women discussed how they made this choice:

> All my life I've resented the protection of governesses and parents. At college I got away from that, or rather, I guess I should say, I changed it to wanting the intellectual approval of teachers and more advanced students. Then I found that you can't be reactionary and be intellectually respectable.
>
> Becoming radical meant thinking for myself and, figuratively, thumbing my nose at my family. It also meant intellectual identification with the faculty and students that I most wanted to be like. (Newcomb, 1943, pp. 134, 131)

Note that the second woman uses the term "identification" in the sense that we have been using it. Note, too, how the women describe a mixture of change produced by social rewards and punishments (compliance) and change produced by attraction to an admired group that they strive to emulate (identification).

From Identification to Internalization As mentioned earlier, reference groups also serve as frames of reference by providing their members with new perspectives on the world. The Bennington community, particularly the faculty, gave students a perspective on the depression of the 1930s and the threat of World War II that their home environments had not, and this began to move them from identification to internalization:

> It didn't take me long to see that liberal attitudes had prestige value. . . . I became liberal at first because of its prestige value; I remain so because the problems around which my liberalism centers are important. What I want now is to be effective in solving problems.
>
> Prestige and recognition have always meant everything to me. . . . But I've sweat[ed] blood in trying to be honest with myself, and the result is that I really know what I want my attitudes to be, and I see what their consequences will be in my own life. (Newcomb, 1943, pp. 136–137)

Many of our most important beliefs and attitudes are probably based initially on identification. Whenever we start to identify with a new reference group, we engage in a process of "trying on" a new set of beliefs and attitudes. What we "really believe" may change from day to day. The first year of college often has this effect on students; many of the views they bring from the family reference group are challenged by students and faculty from very different backgrounds. Students often "try on" the new beliefs with great intensity and strong conviction, only to discard them for still newer beliefs when the first set does not quite fit. This is a natural process of growth. Although the process never really ends for people who remain open to new experiences, it is greatly accelerated during the college years, before the individual has formed a nucleus of permanent beliefs on which to build more slowly and less radically. The real work of college is to evolve an ideological identity from the numerous beliefs and attitudes that are tested in order to move from identification to internalization.

As noted earlier, one advantage of internalization over compliance is that the changes are self-sustaining. The original source of influence does not have to monitor the individual to maintain the induced changes. The test of internalization, therefore, is the long-term stability of the induced beliefs, attitudes, and behaviors. Was the identification-induced liberalism of Bennington women maintained when the students returned to

the "real world"? The answer is yes. Two follow-up studies conducted 25 and 50 years later found the women had remained liberal. For example, in the 1984 presidential election 73% of Bennington alumnae preferred the Democratic candidate, Walter Mondale, over the Republican candidate, Ronald Reagan, compared with less than 26% of women of the same age and educational level. Moreover, about 60% of Bennington alumnae were politically active, most (66%) within the Democratic party (Alwin, Cohen, & Newcomb, 1991; Newcomb et al., 1967).

We never outgrow our need for identification with supporting reference groups. The political attitudes of Bennington women remained stable partly because after college they selected new reference groups that supported the attitudes they had developed in college. Those who married more conservative men were more likely to be politically conservative in later life. As Newcomb noted, we often select our reference groups because they share our attitudes, and our reference groups, in turn, help develop and sustain our attitudes. The relationship is circular. Thus, the distinction between identification and internalization is a useful one for understanding social influence, but in practice it is not always possible to disentangle them.

Collective Decision Making

Many decisions are made not by individuals but by groups. Members of a family jointly decide where to spend their vacation; a jury judges a defendant to be guilty; a city council votes to raise property taxes. How do such decisions compare with those that might have been made by individual decision makers? Are group decisions better or worse, riskier or more cautious? These are the kinds of questions that concern us in this section.

Group Polarization

In the 1950s it was widely believed that decisions made by groups were typically cautious and conservative. For example, it was argued that because business decisions were increasingly being made by committees, the bold, innovative risk-taking of entrepreneurs like Andrew Carnegie was a

As adults we are likely to identify with reference groups that are relevant to the career we have chosen.

thing of the past (Whyte, 1956). James Stoner, then a graduate business student at MIT, decided to test this assumption (1961).

In Stoner's study, participants were asked to consider a number of hypothetical dilemmas. In one, an electrical engineer must decide whether to stick with his present job at a modest but adequate salary or take a job with a new firm offering more money, and a possible partnership in the venture if it succeeds, but no long-term security. In another, a man with a severe heart ailment must seriously curtail his customary way of life or else undergo a medical operation that would either cure him completely or prove fatal. Participants were asked to decide how good the odds of success would have to be before they would advise the person to try the riskier course of action. For example, they could recommend that the engineer take the riskier job if the chances that the new venture would succeed were 5 in 10, 3 in 10, or only 1 in 10. By using numerical odds like these, Stoner was able to compare the riskiness of different decisions quantitatively.

Participants first made their decisions alone, as individuals. They then met in groups and arrived at a group decision for each dilemma. After the group discussion they again considered the dilemmas privately as individuals. When Stoner compared the group's decisions with the average of the individuals' pregroup decisions, he found that the group's decisions were riskier than the individuals' initial decisions. Moreover, this shift reflected genuine opinion change on the part of group members, not just public conformity to the group decision: The private individual decisions made after the group discussion were significantly riskier than the initial decisions.

These findings were replicated by other researchers, even in situations that presented real rather than hypothetical risks (Bem, Wallach, & Kogan, 1965; Wallach, Kogan, & Bem, 1964, 1962). The phenomenon was initially called the *risky shift effect.* This turned out not to be an accurate characterization, however. Even in the early studies, group decisions tended to shift slightly but consistently in the cautious direction on one or two of the hypothetical dilemmas (Wallach, Kogan, & Bem, 1962). After many more studies it became clear that group discussion leads to decisions that are not necessarily

riskier but are more extreme than the individual decisions: If group members are initially inclined to take risks on a particular dilemma, the group's decisions will become riskier; if group members are initially inclined to be cautious, the group will be even more cautious. Accordingly, the phenomenon is now called the **group polarization effect** (Myers & Lamm, 1976).

More than 300 studies of the group polarization effect have been conducted, with a dazzling array of variations. For example, in one recent study, active burglars actually cased houses and then provided individual and group estimates of how easy each would be to burglarize. Compared with the individual estimates, the group estimates were more conservative; that is, they rated the homes to be more difficult to break into successfully (Cromwell et al., 1991).

Group polarization extends beyond issues of risk and caution. For example, group discussion caused French students' initially positive attitudes toward the country's premier to become even more positive and their initially negative attitudes toward Americans to become even more negative (Moscovici & Zavalloni, 1969). Jury decisions can be similarly affected, leading to more extreme verdicts (Isozaki, 1984). Polarization in juries is more likely to occur on judgments concerning values and opinions (such as deciding on an appropriate punishment for a guilty defendant) than on judgments concerning matters of fact (such as the defendant's guilt), and they are most likely to show polarization when they are required to reach unanimous decisions (Kaplan & Miller, 1987).

Many explanations for the group polarization effect have been offered over the years, but the two that have stood up best to intensive testing are informational influence and normative influence (Isenberg, 1986). *Informational influence* occurs when people learn new information and hear novel arguments relevant to the decision under discussion. For example, in discussing whether the electrical engineer should go with the new venture—a decision that almost always shifts in the risky direction—it is quite common for someone in the group to argue that riskiness is warranted because electrical engineers can always find good jobs. A shift in the conservative direction occurred in the burglar study after one member of the group noted that it was nearly 3:00 PM and children would soon be returning from school and playing nearby.

The more arguments are raised in support of a position, the more likely it is that the group will move toward that position. And this is where the bias enters: Members of a group are most likely to present points in support of the position they initially favor and to discuss information they already share (Stasser, Taylor, & Hanna, 1989; Stasser & Titus, 1985). Accordingly, the discussion will be biased in favor of the group's initial position, and the group will move toward that position as more of the group members become convinced. Interestingly, the polarization effect still occurs even when all participants are given an extensive list of arguments before the experiment begins—a finding that some believe casts doubt on the informational explanation (Zuber, Crott, & Werner, 1992).

Normative influence occurs when people compare their own views with the norms of the group. During the discussion they may learn that others have similar attitudes or even more extreme views than they themselves do. If they are motivated to be seen positively by the group, they may conform to the group's position or even express a position that is more extreme than the group's. As one researcher noted, "To be virtuous . . . is to be different from the mean—in the right direction and to the right degree" (Brown, 1974, p. 469).

But normative influence is not simply pressure to conform. Often the group provides a frame of reference for its members, a context within which they can reevaluate their initial positions. This is illustrated by a common and amusing event that frequently occurs in group polarization experiments. For example, in one group a participant began the discussion of the dilemma facing the electrical engineer by confidently announcing, "I feel this guy should really be willing to take a risk here. He should go with the new job even if it has only a 5 in 10 chance of succeeding." Other group members were incredulous: "You think that 5 in 10 is being risky? If he has any guts, he should give it a shot even if there is only 1 chance in 100 of success. I mean, what has he really got to lose?" Eager to reestablish his reputation as a risk-taker, the original

Group polarization often occurs in juries, especially when they are required to reach unanimous decisions.

individual quickly shifted his position further in the risky direction. By redefining "risky," the group moved both its own decision and its members' postdiscussion attitudes further toward the risky extreme of the scale (Wallach, Kogan, & Bem, 1962; from the authors' notes).

As this example illustrates, both informational and normative influence occur simultaneously in group discussions, and several studies have attempted to untangle them. Some studies have shown that the polarization effect occurs if participants simply hear the arguments of the group, without knowing the actual positions of others members of the group (Burnstein & Vinokur, 1977, 1973). This demonstrates that informational influence by itself is sufficient to produce polarization. Other studies have shown that the polarization effect also occurs when people learn others' positions but do not hear any supporting arguments, demonstrating that normative influence by itself is sufficient (Goethals & Zanna, 1979; Sanders & Baron, 1977). Typically, the information effect is greater than the normative effect (Isenberg, 1986).

Groupthink

"How could we have been so stupid?" This was President John Kennedy's reaction to the disastrous failure of his administration's attempt to invade Cuba at the Bay of Pigs in 1961 and overthrow the government of

Fidel Castro. The plan was badly conceived at many levels. For example, if the initial landing were unsuccessful, the invaders were supposed to retreat into the mountains. But no one in the planning group had studied the map closely enough to realize that no army could have gotten through the 80 miles of swamp that separated the mountains from the landing area. As it turned out this didn't matter, because other miscalculations caused the invading force to be wiped out long before the retreat would have taken place.

The invasion had been conceived and planned by the president and a small group of advisers. Writing four years later, one of these advisers, the historian Arthur Schlesinger, Jr., blamed himself

> for having kept so silent during those crucial discussions in the Cabinet Room, though my feelings of guilt were tempered by the knowledge that a course of objection would have accomplished little save to gain me a name as a nuisance. I can only explain my failure to do more than raise a few timid questions by reporting that one's impulse to blow the whistle on this nonsense was simply undone by the circumstances of the discussion. (1965, p. 255)

What were the "circumstances of the discussion" that led the group to pursue such a disastrous course of action? After reading Schlesinger's account, social psychologist Irving Janis proposed a theory of **groupthink**, *a phenomenon in which members of a group are led to suppress their own dissent in the interests of group consensus* (Janis, 1982). After analyzing several other foreign-policy decisions, Janis set forth the circumstances and symptoms of groupthink as well as the symptoms of defective decision making that result from it. These are outlined in Figure 18-10.

As shown in the figure, the stage is set for groupthink when a cohesive group of decision makers assembles in isolation from outside influences and without systematic procedures for considering both the pros and cons of different courses of action. It is further fostered by a directive leader who explicitly favors a particular course of action, and by high stress—often due to an external threat, recent failures, moral dilemmas, and an apparent lack of viable alternatives. Subsequent research has confirmed

that groupthink is particularly likely to develop in situations that involve external threats to the group (McCauley, 1989). All these conditions foster a strong desire to achieve and maintain group consensus and avoid "rocking the boat" by dissenting.

ANTECEDENT CONDITIONS

1. A cohesive group
2. Isolation of the group from outside influences
3. No systematic procedures for considering both the pros and cons of different courses of action
4. A directive leader who explicitly favors a particular course of action
5. High stress

↓

GROUPTHINK

The desire to achieve consensus and avoid dissent

↓

SYMPTOMS OF GROUPTHINK

1. Illusion of invulnerability, morality, and unanimity
2. Pressure on dissenters
3. Self-censorship of dissent
4. Collective rationalization
5. Self-appointed mindguards

↓

FLAWS OF DECISION MAKING PROCESS UNDER GROUPTHINK

1. Incomplete survey of the group's objectives and alternative courses of action
2. Failure to examine the risks of the preferred choice
3. Poor and incomplete search for relevant information
4. Selective bias in processing the information at hand
5. Failure to reappraise rejected alternatives
6. Failure to develop contingency plans in case of failure

FIGURE 18-10

Causes and Consequences of Groupthink (After Janis, 1982)

The symptoms of groupthink include shared illusions of invulnerability, morality, and unanimity. These are achieved by direct pressure on dissenters or, as Schlesinger's account notes, self-censorship. As a result, the group members spend more time rationalizing their decision than realistically examining its strengths and weaknesses. Moreover, there are often self-appointed *mindguards,* group members who actively attempt to prevent the group from considering information that would challenge the effectiveness or morality of its decisions. For example, the attorney general (President Kennedy's brother Robert) privately warned Schlesinger, "The President has made his mind up. Don't push it any further." The secretary of state withheld information that had been provided by intelligence experts who warned against an invasion of Cuba (Janis, 1982). Finally, Figure 18-10 lists the flaws of decision making that follow from groupthink and lead to poor decisions.

Janis has also analyzed two successful group decisions: the Truman administration's decision to implement the Marshall Plan (which helped Europe recover from World War II) and the Kennedy administration's handling of the Soviet Union's attempts to install missiles in Cuba. In later publications Janis spelled out some of the safeguards groups could use to avoid the hazards of groupthink.

First, of course, he believes that group members should be told about groupthink, its causes, and its consequences. Among his more specific suggestions are that the group's leader foster an atmosphere of open debate and not endorse any position before the discussion begins; that one or more members be assigned to play the role of "devil's advocate," actively questioning the group's decisions throughout; that outside experts be brought in to challenge the group and give it fresh perspectives; and finally, once the group has arrived at a consensus, that there be a "second-chance" meeting in which members can rediscuss any lingering doubts or reservations (Janis, 1985, 1982).

There has also been criticism of Janis's theory. First, it is based on historical analysis more than on laboratory experimentation. Experiments have yielded mixed results (Callaway, Marriott, & Esser, 1985; Courtright, 1978; Flowers, 1977; Longley & Pruitt, 1980; McCauley, 1989; Turner et al., 1992). The processes that Janis calls groupthink are clearly quite complex, and recent research has been directed toward trying to integrate it into a more general theory of group decision making (Aldag & Fuller, 1993).

ARE THE EFFECTS OF AFFIRMATIVE ACTION POSITIVE OR NEGATIVE?

Negative Aspects of Affirmative Action

Madeline E. Heilman, *New York University*

Most people would say that rewards should be given according to merit. What happens, then, when people get rewarded not because of their accomplishments but because of who they are or what group they belong to? Many people, perhaps including yourself, react negatively.

Madeline Heilman

This is the heart of the affirmative action dilemma. While created to ensure non-discriminatory treatment of women and minorities, affirmative action has come to be seen as little more than preferential selection and treatment without regard to merit (Kravitz & Platania, 1993). This, of course, may not depict reality, but it is this *perception* of affirmative action that is so problematic. There are a number of detrimental consequences.

First, affirmative action can stigmatize its intended beneficiaries, causing inferences of incompetence. If you believe that someone has been the beneficiary of preferential selection based on non-merit criteria, then you are likely to "discount" that individual's qualifications. In fact, you are likely to make the assumption that this person would not have been selected without the help of affirmative action.

There has been research linking affirmative action with incompetence inferences (Garcia, Erskine, Hawn, & Casmay, 1981; Heilman, Block, & Lucas, 1992). It has been conducted in the labora-

tory, where people review employee records, and in the field, where people are asked to evaluate co-workers in their work units. Inferences of incompetence have been found whether the target beneficiary is a woman or a member of a racial minority, and whether the research participants are male or female, or students or working people (Heilman, Block, & Stathatos, 1997).

A second negative consequence of affirmative action concerns nonbeneficiaries. When women and minorities are believed to be preferentially selected, those who traditionally would have been selected for jobs often feel they are really the more deserving, and consequently, they feel unfairly bypassed (Nacoste, 1987). This has been suggested as a major reason for the "backlash" against affirmative action.

Evidence indicates that there are indeed unfortunate by-products of feeling unfairly bypassed by affirmative action. In one study, male participants were paired with a female who subsequently was preferentially selected for the more desirable task role on the basis of her gender (Heilman, McCullough, & Gilbert, 1996). Those who believed themselves to be more (or even equally) skilled than the female reported being less motivated, more angry, and less satisfied than those who were told the female was the more skilled and therefore the more deserving of the two.

The third negative consequence of affirmative action concerns its potential effect on the intended beneficiary. When people believe that they have been preferentially selected on the basis of irrelevant criteria there can be a chilling effect on self-

view. Ironically, then, affirmative action may sometimes hurt those it was intended to help.

A series of laboratory experiments in which participants were selected for a desired task role (leader) either on the basis of merit or preferentially on the basis of their gender found strong support for the idea that preferential selection can trigger negative self-regard. In repeated studies, women, but not men, who were preferentially selected were found to rate their performance more negatively, view themselves as more deficient in leadership ability, be more eager to relinquish their desirable leadership role, and shy away from demanding and challenging tasks (see Heilman, 1994, for a review of these studies).

Given these consequences, it appears that affirmative action, as it currently is understood, can undermine its own objectives. The stigma associated with affirmative action is apt to fuel rather than discredit stereotypic thinking and prejudiced attitudes. Depriving individuals of the satisfaction and pride that comes from knowing that they have achieved something on their own merits can be corrosive, decreasing self-efficacy and fostering self-views of inferiority. And the frustration resulting from feeling unfairly bypassed for employment opportunities because one does not fit into the correct demographic niche can aggravate workplace tensions and inter-group hostilities. So, paradoxically, despite its success in expanding employment opportunities for women and minorities, affirmative action may contribute to the very conditions that gave rise to the problems it was designed to remedy.

The Benefits of Affirmative Action

Faye J. Crosby, *University of California, Santa Cruz*

To assess the effects of affirmative action, you must first know what affirmative action *is* and what it *is not*. According to the American Psychological Association (APA): "Affirmative action occurs when an organization expends energy to make sure there is no discrimination in employment or education and, instead, equal opportunity exists" (APA, 1995, p. 5). Affirmative action goes beyond reactive policies that passively endorse justice, but waiting until a problem has erupted before enacting measures. Affirmative action requires resources and vigilance. It does not require or endorse quotas, sacrifice standards to diversity, or substitute preference for merit (Turner & Pratkanis, 1994).

For employment, affirmative action law began in earnest in 1965 (Holloway, 1989). Today it applies to all government agencies and most organizations that contract work with the federal government. Chances are that you or someone you know works for an affirmative action employer; one in four employed Americans does (Crosby & Cordova, 1996)!

How does the system work? Think about your professors as employees of your school. Imagine that 10% of the social science professors in your school are women (utilization = 10%). Availability is calculated mostly from the proportion of social science PhDs who are female. If 30% of PhDs in the social sciences are women, while only 10% of the professors are, something is wrong! Detected problems should be corrected. Corrective measures can include flexible goals (not rigid quotas) and realistic timetables.

What are the effects of affirmative action in employment? Economists show that white women

and people of color who work for affirmative action employers benefit in terms of hiring, retention, pay, and promotions (Kravitz et al., 1997). Do men of color and women feel stigmatized by affirmative action? Generally not. Do white men feel resentment or fear? Some do, especially if they are racist or sexist or if they equate affirmative action with quotas (Golden, Hinkle, & Crosby, 1998); but, in fact, most do not. Actually, three quarters of Americans endorse affirmative action (Tomasson, Crosby, & Herzberger, 1996).

Many white men—including heads of some huge corporations—endorse affirmative action out of economic realism. When the game is opened to white women and ethnic minorities, it is also opened to talented white men who previously had no inside track. Affirmative action firms appear to be more profitable than other firms (Reskin, 1998). Like effective fire-fighting units where small people squiggle into small spaces while big people maneuver big equipment, diverse business teams seem to enjoy a competitive edge (Leonard, 1986).

In education, affirmative action also entails the two steps of monitoring and correcting. If monitoring reveals, for example, that Hispanics comprise less of the undergraduate student body than expected from high-school graduation rates, corrective steps (e.g., outreach programs) may be undertaken. Affirmative action in education need not entail lowering standards; but it must result in close, sometimes painful, examination of three provocative questions: (1) What traits do we value in individuals? (2) How can we accurately assess these traits? and (3)

What kinds of teams of individuals do we want to construct?

One misconception is that white women and students of color feel undermined by affirmative action. Nobody likes to be told that he or she is advancing through unjustified preferential treatment, including quotas, rather than merit (Heilman, 1994). Fortunately, most of the direct beneficiaries do not confuse affirmative action with quotas (Truax, Wood, Wright, Cordova & Crosby, 1998), especially if they feel secure in their ethnic identity (Schmermund,

Faye Crosby

Sellers, Mueller, & Crosby, 1998).

A recent landmark study by the former presidents of Harvard and Princeton has fastidiously documented the positive consequences of considering race in college and university admissions. Bowen and Bok (1998) looked at long-term outcomes for hundreds of black students who had been admitted through affirmative action to 24 elite colleges in 1951, 1976, and 1989. The black students graduated from school and obtained advanced degrees at rates comparable to white students. And even more than white alumni/ae, black graduates became civic leaders—giving back to the society that had nurtured them!

What, then, are the overall effects of well-applied affirmative action in education? They are great. Everyone benefits.

SUMMARY

1. To most people the term *social influence* connotes direct and deliberate attempts to change beliefs, attitudes, or behaviors. If we respond to such influence by complying with the wishes of an influencer—without necessarily changing our beliefs or attitudes—our reaction is called compliance. If we change our beliefs and attitudes as well as complying, our reaction is called internalization. Many forms of social influence are indirect or unintentional. Even the presence of other people can affect us. We are also influenced by social norms, implicit rules and expectations about how we ought to think and behave. The success of direct and deliberate social influence often depends on our allegiance to social norms.

2. Both humans and animals respond more quickly when in the presence of other members of their species. This social facilitation occurs whether the others are performing the same task (coactors) or simply watching (an audience). The presence of others appears to raise the organism's drive level. This facilitates the correct performance of simple responses but hinders the performance of complex ones. For humans, cognitive factors such as concern with evaluation also play a role.

3. The uninhibited aggressive behavior sometimes shown by mobs and crowds may be the result of a state of deindividuation, in which individuals feel that they have lost their identities and merged into the group. Anonymity reduces self-awareness and contributes to deindividuation. Some of the consequences of deindividuation are weakened restraints against impulsive behavior, increased sensitivity to immediate cues and current emotional states, and reduced concern with evaluation by others. Being in a group and feeling anonymous do not inevitably lead to increased aggressiveness, however.

4. A bystander to an emergency is less likely to intervene or help if in a group than if alone. Two major factors that deter intervention are defining the situation and diffusion of responsibility. By attempting to appear calm, bystanders may define the situation for one another as a nonemergency, thereby producing a state of pluralistic ignorance. The presence of other people also diffuses responsibility so that no one person feels the necessity to act. Bystanders are more likely to intervene when these factors are minimized, particularly if at least one person begins to help.

5. In a series of classic studies on conformity, Solomon Asch found that a unanimous group exerts strong pressure on an individual to conform to the group's judgments—even when those judgments are clearly wrong. Much less conformity is observed if even one person dissents from the group.

6. In a series of classic studies on obedience, Stanley Milgram demonstrated that ordinary people would obey an experimenter's order to deliver strong electric shocks to an innocent victim. Factors conspiring to produce the high obedience rates include social norms (for example, the implied contract to continue the experiment until completed); surveillance by the experimenter; buffers that distance the person from the consequences of his or her acts; and the legitimating role of science, which leads people to abandon their autonomy to the experimenter. There has been considerable controversy about the ethics of the experiments themselves.

7. Obedience to authority can be undermined, and rebellion provoked, if the individual is with a group whose members have the opportunity to share their opinions, can give each other social support for dissenting, and can provide role models for disobedience. But the individual may then have to choose between obedience to authority and conformity to the group that has decided to rebel.

8. Studies of conformity and obedience reveal that situational factors exert more influence over behavior than most of us realize. We tend to underestimate situational forces on behavior.

9. A minority within a larger group can move the majority toward its point of view if it maintains a consistent dissenting position without appearing to be rigid, dogmatic, or arrogant. Minorities sometimes obtain private attitude change from majority members even when they fail to obtain public conformity.

10. Cognitive response theory proposes that persuasion induced by a communication is actually self-persuasion produced by the thoughts that the person generates while reading or hearing the communication. If the communication evokes thoughts that support the position being advocated, the individual will move toward that position; if the communication evokes nonsupporting thoughts—such as counterarguments or disparaging thoughts about the communicator—the individual will remain unpersuaded.

11. Persuasion can take two routes in producing belief and attitude change: the central route, in which the individual responds to the substantive arguments of a communication, and the peripheral route, in which the individual responds to noncontent cues in a communication (such as the number of arguments) or to context cues (such as the credibility of the communicator or the pleasantness of the surroundings). A communication about an issue of personal relevance is more likely to generate thoughts in response to the communication's substantive arguments. When an issue is of little personal relevance or people are unwilling or unable to respond to the substantive content of a communication, they tend to use simple heuristics—rules of thumb—to judge the merits of the communication.

12. In the process of identification, we obey the norms and adopt the beliefs, attitudes, and behaviors of groups that we respect and admire. We use such reference groups to evaluate and regulate our opinions and actions. A reference group can regulate our attitudes and behavior by administering social rewards and punishments or providing a frame of reference, a ready-made interpretation of events and social issues.

13. Most people identify with more than one reference group, and this can lead to conflicting pressures on beliefs, attitudes, and behaviors. College students frequently move away from the views of their family reference group toward the college reference group. These new views are usually sustained in later life because (a) they become internalized and (b) after college we tend to select new reference groups that share our views.

14. When groups make decisions they often display group polarization: The group decision is in the same direction but is more extreme than the average of the group members' initial positions. This is not just public conformity; group members' private attitudes typically shift in response to the group discussion as well. The effect is due in part to informational influence, in which group members learn new information

and hear novel arguments that are relevant to the decision under discussion. Group members tend to raise more arguments in favor of their initial position than against it, thus biasing the discussion and pushing the final decision further in the direction of the initial positions. Group polarization is also produced by normative influence, in which people compare their own initial views with the norms of the group. They may then adjust their position to conform to that of the majority. In addition, the group can provide a frame of reference that causes its members to perceive their initial position as too weak or too moderate as an expression of their actual attitude.

15. An analysis of disastrous foreign-policy decisions reveals that a cohesive group of decision makers with a directive leader can fall into the trap of groupthink, in which members of the group suppress their own dissenting opinions in the interest of group consensus. This gives rise to a group-shared illusion of invulnerability, morality, and unanimity. This, in turn, produces a flawed decision-making process and bad decisions. It has been suggested that groupthink can be avoided if the leader fosters an atmosphere of open debate and does not endorse any position before discussion begins; some group members are assigned to be "devil's advocates"; outside experts are brought in; and there is a "second-chance" meeting at which members can reconsider any lingering doubts or reservations about their decision.

KEY TERMS

social influence (p. 640)
compliance (p. 640)
internalization (p. 641)
social norms (p. 641)
social facilitation (p. 642)
deindividuation (p. 644)

altruism (p. 649)
identification (p. 665)
reference group (p. 665)
group polarization effect (p. 668)
groupthink (p. 670)

CRITICAL THINKING QUESTIONS

1. If you were a member of a university review board that was asked to consider the risks and benefits of proposed research programs, would you vote to approve Milgram's obedience experiments? Why or why not?

2. Can you identify any changes in your beliefs and attitudes that have come about by being exposed to a new reference group?

3. Discuss the ways in which informational and normative influence might produce group polarization in a jury's deliberations. How might groupthink operate to affect such deliberations? Can you think of a specific trial in which some of these phenomena appear to have been present?

FURTHER READING

The three comprehensive textbooks in social psychology listed at the end of Chapter 17 also cover the topics discussed in this chapter. They are Aronson, Wilson, and Akert, *Social Psychology* (3rd ed., 1998); Baron and Byrne, *Social Psychology* (8th ed., 1997); and Lord, *Social Psychology* (1996). More advanced treatments are available in Gilbert, Fiske, and Lindzey (eds.), *The Handbook of Social Psychology* (4th ed., 1998).

Many of the topics in this chapter are covered in paperback books written for general audiences, often by the original investigators. Milgram, *Obedience to Authority* (1974) is well worth reading, especially before forming an opinion about this controversial series of studies. Latané and Darley, *The Unresponsive Bystander: Why Doesn't He Help?* (1970) is a report by two of the original researchers in that area. Petty and Cacioppo, *Attitudes and Persuasion: Classic and Contemporary Approaches* (1981) is a good summary of both earlier and current work on persuasion written by two major contributors to this field. Janis, *Groupthink: Psychological Studies of Policy Decisions and Fiascoes* (2nd ed., 1982) is the major source for the groupthink phenomenon. And finally, LeBon's classic book, *The Crowd* (1895), is available in several editions.

Appendix
Statistical Methods and Measurement

*M*uch of the work of psychologists calls for making measurements— either in the laboratory or under field conditions. This work may involve measuring the eye movements of infants when first exposed to a novel stimulus, recording the galvanic skin response of people under stress, counting the number of trials required to condition a monkey that has a prefrontal lobotomy, determining achievement test scores for students using computer-assisted learning, or counting the number of patients who show improvement following a particular type of psychotherapy. In all these examples, the *measurement operation* yields numbers; the psychologist's problem is to interpret them and to arrive at some general conclusions. Basic to this task is statistics—the discipline that deals with collecting numerical data and with making inferences from such data. The purpose of this appendix is to review certain statistical methods that play an important role in psychology.

This appendix is written on the assumption that the problems students have with statistics are essentially problems of clear thinking about data. An introductory acquaintance with statistics is not beyond the scope of anyone who understands enough algebra to use plus and minus signs and to substitute numbers for letters in equations.

Descriptive Statistics

Statistics serves, first of all, to provide a shorthand description of large amounts of data. Suppose that we want to study the college entrance examination scores of 5,000 students recorded on cards in the registrar's office. These scores are the raw data. Thumbing through the cards will give us some impressions of the students' scores, but it will be impossible for us to keep all of them in mind. So we make some kind of summary of the data, possibly averaging all the scores or finding the highest and lowest scores. These statistical summaries make it easier to remember and to think about the data. Such summarizing statements are called *descriptive statistics*.

Frequency Distributions

Items of raw data become comprehensible when they are grouped in a *frequency distribution*. To group data, we must first divide the scale along which they are measured into intervals and then count the number of items that fall into each interval. An interval in which scores are grouped is called a *class interval*. The decision of how many class intervals the data are to be grouped into is not fixed by any rules but is based on the judgment of the investigator.

Table 1 provides a sample of raw data representing college entrance examination scores for 15 students. The scores are listed in the order in which the students were tested (the first student tested had a score of 84; the second, 61; and so on). Table 2 shows these data arranged in a frequency distribution for which the class interval has been set at 10. One score falls in the interval

from 50 to 59, three scores fall in the interval from 60 to 69, and so on. Note that most scores fall in the interval from 70 to 79 and that no scores fall below the 50 to 59 interval or above the 90 to 99 interval.

A frequency distribution is often easier to understand if it is presented graphically. The most widely used graph form is the *frequency histogram*; an example is shown in the top panel of Figure 1. Histograms are constructed by drawing bars, the bases of which are given by the class intervals and the heights of which are determined by the corresponding class frequencies. An alternative way of presenting frequency distributions in graph form is to use a *frequency polygon*, an example of which is shown in the bottom panel of Figure 1. Frequency polygons are constructed by plotting the class frequencies at the center of the class interval and connecting the points obtained by straight lines. To complete the picture, one extra class is added at each end of the distribution; since these classes have zero frequencies, both ends of the figure will touch the horizontal axis. The frequency polygon gives the same information as the frequency histogram but by means of a set of connected lines rather than bars.

TABLE 1

Raw Scores *College entrance examination scores for 15 students, listed in the order in which they were tested.*

84	75	91
61	75	67
72	87	79
75	79	83
77	51	69

TABLE 2

A Frequency Distribution *Scores from Table 1, accumulated by class intervals.*

Class Interval	Number of Persons in Class
50–59	1
60–69	3
70–79	7
80–89	3
90–99	1

In practice, we would obtain a much greater number of items than those plotted in Figure 1, but a minimum amount of data is shown in all of the illustrations in this appendix so that you can easily check the steps in tabulating and plotting.

Measures of Central Tendency

A *measure of central tendency* is simply a representative point on our scale—a central point that summarizes important information about the data. Three such measures are commonly used: the *mean*, the *median*, and the *mode*.

The mean is the familiar arithmetic average obtained by adding the scores and dividing by the number of scores. The sum of the raw scores in Table 1 is 1,125. If we divide this by 15 (the number of students' scores), the mean turns out to be 75.

The median is the score of the middle item, which is obtained by arranging the scores in order and then counting into the middle from either end. When the 15 scores in Table 1 are placed in order from highest to lowest, the eighth score from either end turns out to be 75. If the number of cases is even, we simply average the two cases on each side of the middle.

The mode is the most frequent score in a given distribution. In Table 1, the most frequent score is 75; hence, the mode of the distribution is 75.

In a *normal distribution*, in which the scores are distributed evenly on either side of the middle (as in Figure 1), the mean, median, and mode all fall together. This is not true for distributions that are *skewed*, or unbalanced. Suppose we want to analyze the departure times of a morning train. The train usually leaves on time; occasionally it leaves late, but it never leaves early. For a train with a scheduled departure time of 8:00 AM, one week's record might be as follows:

M	8:00	Mean = 8:07
Tu	8:04	Median = 8:02
W	8:02	Mode = 8:00
Th	8:19	
F	8:22	
Sat	8:00	
Sun	8:00	

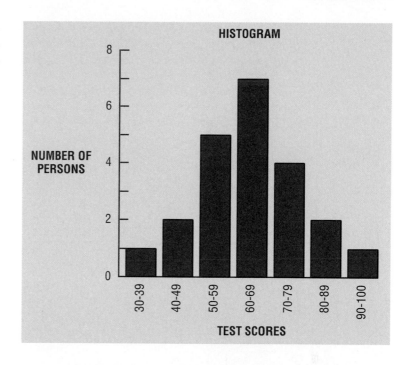

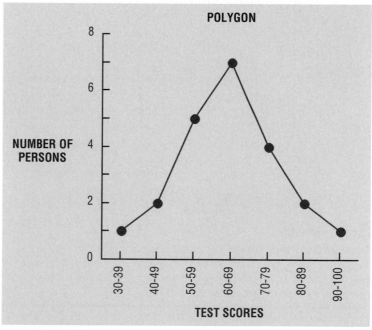

Frequency Diagrams   *The data from Table 2 are plotted here. A frequency histogram is on the top, a frequency polygon on the bottom.*

The distribution of departure times in this example is skewed because of the two late departures; they raise the mean departure time but do not have much effect on the median or the mode.

Skewness is important because, unless it is understood, the differences between the

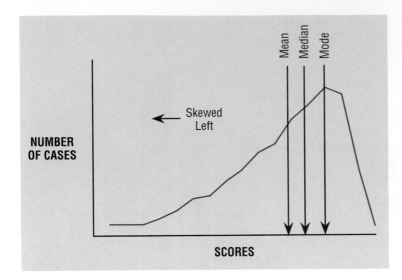

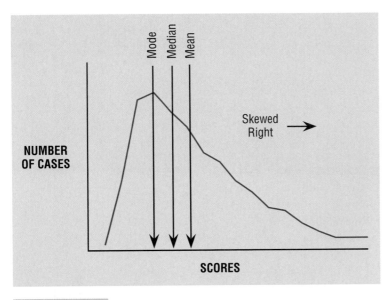

Skewed Distribution Curves   *Note that skewed distributions are designated by the direction in which the tail falls. Also note that the mean, median, and mode are not identical for a skewed distribution; the median commonly falls between the mode and the mean.*

median and the mean may sometimes be misleading (see Figure 2). If, for example, company executives and the company's union are arguing about the prosperity of the company's work force, it is possible for the mean and median incomes to move in opposite directions. Suppose that a company raises the wages of most of its employees, but cuts the wages of its top executives, who were at the extremely high end of the pay scale. The median income of the company might have gone up while the mean went down. The party wanting to show that incomes were getting higher would choose the median, and the party wanting to show that incomes were getting lower would choose the mean.

The mean is the most widely used measure of central tendency, but there are times when the mode or the median is a more meaningful measure.

Measures of Variation

Usually more information is needed about a distribution than can be obtained from a measure of central tendency. For example, we need a measure to tell us whether scores cluster closely around their average or whether they scatter widely. A measure of the spread of scores around the average is called a *measure of variation*.

Measures of variation are useful in at least two ways. First, they tell us how representative the average is. If the variation is small, we know that individual scores are close to it. If the variation is large, we cannot use the mean as a representative value with as much assurance. Suppose that clothing is being designed for a group of people without the benefit of precise measurements. Knowing their average size would be helpful, but it also would be important to know the spread of sizes. The second measure provides a yardstick that we can use to measure the amount of variability among the sizes.

To illustrate, consider the data in Figure 3, which show frequency distributions of entrance examination scores for two classes of 30 students. Both classes have the same mean of 75, but they exhibit clearly different degrees of variation. The scores of all the students in Class I are clustered close to the mean, whereas the scores of the students in Class II are spread over a wide range. Some measure is required to specify more exactly how these two distributions differ. Three measures of variation frequently used by psychologists are the *range*, the *variance*, and the *standard deviation*.

To simplify arithmetic computation, we will suppose that five students from each class seek entrance to college and that their entrance examination scores are as follows:

Student scores from Class I:
73, 74, 75, 76, 77 (mean = 75)

Student scores from Class II:
60, 65, 75, 85, 90 (mean = 75)

We will now compute the measures of variation for these two samples. The range is the spread between the highest score and the lowest score. The range of scores for the five students from Class I is 4 (from 73 to 77); the range of scores from Class II is 30 (from 60 to 90).

The range is easy to compute, but the variance and standard deviation are more frequently used. They are more sensitive measures of variation because they account for every score, not just extreme values as the range does. The variance measures how far the scores making up a distribution depart from that distribution's mean. To compute the variance, first compute the deviation d of each score from the mean of the distribution by subtracting each score from the mean (see Table 3). Then, each of the deviations is squared to get rid of nega-

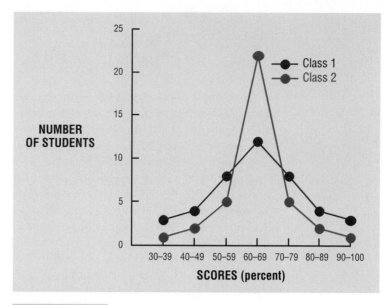

Distributions Differing in Variation   *It is easy to see that the scores for Class I cluster closer to the mean than the scores for Class II, even though the means of the two classes are identical (75). For Class I, all the scores fall between 60 and 89, with most of the scores falling in the interval from 70 through 79. For Class II, the scores are distributed fairly uniformly over a wide range from 40 through 109. This difference in variability between the two distributions can be measured using the standard deviation, which is smaller for Class I than for Class II.*

TABLE 3

Computation of the Variance and Standard Deviation

Class I Scores (Mean = 75)		
	d	d^2
77 − 75 =	2	4
76 − 75 =	1	1
75 − 75 =	0	0
74 − 75 =	−1	1
73 − 75 =	−2	4
		10

Sum of d^2 = 10

Variance = mean of d^2 = 10/5 = 2.0

Standard Deviation (σ) = $\sqrt{2.0}$ = 1.4

Class II Scores (Mean = 75)		
	d	d^2
90−75 =	15	225
85−75 =	10	100
75−75 =	0	0
65−75 =	−10	100
60−75 =	−15	225
		650

Sum of d^2 = 650

Variance = mean of d^2 = 650/5 = 130

Standard Deviation (σ) = $\sqrt{130}$ = 11.4

---

tive numbers. Finally, the deviations are added together and divided by the total number of deviations to obtain the average deviation. This average deviation is the variance. When this is done for the data in Figure 3, we find that the variance for Class I is 2.0 and the variance for Class II is 130. Obviously, Class II has much more variability in its scores than Class I.

One disadvantage of the variance is that it is expressed in squared units of measurement. Thus, to say that Class I has a variance of 2 does not indicate that, on average, scores varied an average of 2 points from the mean. Instead, it indicates that 2 is the average of the squared number of points that scores varied from the mean. In order to obtain a measure of variability that is expressed in the original units of measurement (in this case, points on an exam), simply take the square root of the variance. This is known as the standard deviation. The standard deviation is denoted by the lowercase Greek letter *sigma*, σ, which also is used in several other statistical calculations, as we will discuss shortly. The formula for the standard deviation is:

$$\sigma = \sqrt{\frac{\text{sum of } d^2}{N}}$$

The scores for the samples from the two classes are arranged in Table 3 for easy computation of the standard deviation. The first step involves subtracting the mean from each score (the mean is 75 for both classes). This operation yields positive d values for scores above the mean and negative d values for scores below the mean. The minus signs disappear when the d values are squared in the next column. The squared deviations are added and then divided by N, the number of cases in the sample; in our example, $N = 5$. Taking the square root yields the standard deviation.*

Statistical Inference

Now that we have become familiar with statistics as a way of describing data, we are ready to turn to the processes of interpretation—to the making of inferences from data.

Populations and Samples

First, it is necessary to distinguish between a *population* and a *sample* drawn from that population. The United States Census Bureau attempts to describe the whole population by obtaining descriptive material on age, marital status, and so on from everyone in the country. The word *population* is appropriate to the census because it represents *all* the people living in the United States.

In statistics, the word "population" is not limited to people or animals or things. The population may be all of the temperatures registered on a thermometer during the last decade, all of the words in the English lan-

guage, or all of any other specified supply of data. Often we do not have access to the total population, and so we try to represent it by a sample drawn in a *random* (unbiased) fashion. We may ask some questions of a random fraction of the people, as the Census Bureau has done as part of recent censuses; we may derive average temperatures by reading the thermometer at specified times, without taking a continuous record; we may estimate the number of words in the encyclopedia by counting the words on random pages. These illustrations all involve the selection of a sample from the population. If any of these processes are repeated, we will obtain slightly different results due to the fact that a sample does not fully represent the whole population and therefore contains *errors of sampling*. This is where statistical inference enters.

A sample of data is collected from a population in order to make inferences about that population. A sample of census data may be examined to see whether the population is getting older, for example, or whether there is a trend of migration to the suburbs. Similarly, experimental results are studied to determine what effects experimental manipulations have had on behavior—whether the threshold for pitch is affected by loudness, whether child-rearing practices have detectable effects later in life. To make *statistical inferences*, we have to evaluate the relationships revealed by the sample data. These inferences are always made under some degree of uncertainty due to sampling errors. If the statistical tests indicate that the magnitude of the effect found in the sample is fairly large (relative to the estimate of the sampling error), then we can be confident that the effect observed in the sample holds for the population at large.

Thus, statistical inference deals with the problem of making an inference or judgment about a feature of a population based solely on information obtained from a sample of that population. As an introduction to statistical inference, we will consider the normal distribution and its use in interpreting standard deviations.

The Normal Distribution

When large amounts of data are collected, tabulated, and plotted as a histogram or

---

* For this introductory treatment, we will use sigma (σ) throughout. However, in the scientific literature, the lowercase letter s is used to denote the standard deviation of a sample and σ is used to denote the standard deviation of the population. Moreover, in computing the standard deviation of a sample s, the sum of d^2 is divided by $N - 1$ rather than by N. For reasonably large samples, however, the actual value of the standard deviation is only slightly affected whether we divide by $N - 1$ or N. To simplify this presentation, we will not distinguish between the standard deviation of a sample and that of a population; instead, we will use the same formula to compute both. For a discussion of this point, see Phillips (1992).

polygon, they often fall into a roughly bell-shaped symmetrical distribution known as the *normal distribution*. Most items fall near the mean (the high point of the bell), and the bell tapers off sharply at very high and very low scores. This form of curve is of special interest because it also arises when the outcome of a process is based on a large number of *chance* events all occurring independently. The demonstration device displayed in Figure 4 illustrates how a sequence of chance events gives rise to a normal distribution. The chance factor of whether a steel ball will fall to the left or right each time it encounters a point where the channel branches results in a symmetrical distribution: More balls fall straight down the middle, but occasionally one reaches one of the end compartments. This is a useful way of visualizing what is meant by a chance distribution closely approximating the normal distribution.

The normal distribution (Figure 5) is the mathematical representation of the ideal-

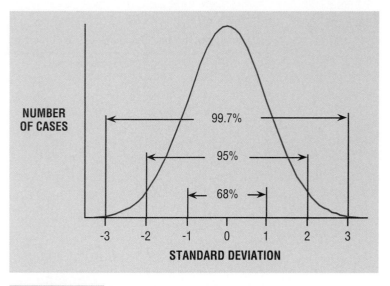

FIGURE 5

The Normal Distribution   *The normal distribution curve can be constructed using the mean and the standard deviation. The area under the curve below -3σ and above $+3\sigma$ is negligible.*

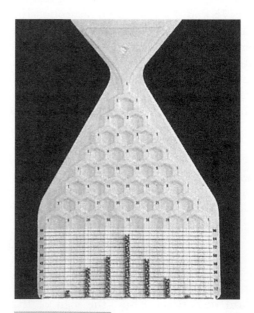

FIGURE 4

A Device to Demonstrate a Chance Distribution
The board is held upside down until all the steel balls fall into the reservoir. Then the board is turned over and held vertically until the balls fall into the nine columns. The precise number of balls falling into each column will vary from one demonstration to the next. On average, however, the heights of the columns of balls will approximate a normal distribution, with the greatest height in the center column and gradually decreasing heights in the outer columns.

ized distribution approximated by the device shown in Figure 4. The normal distribution represents the likelihood that items within a normally distributed population will depart from the mean by any stated amount. The percentages shown in Figure 5 represent the *percentage of the area* lying under the curve between the indicated scale values; the total area under the curve represents the whole population. Roughly two thirds of the cases (68%) will fall between plus and minus one standard deviation from the mean ($\pm 1\sigma$); 95% of the cases within $\pm 2\sigma$ and virtually all cases (99.7%) within $\pm 3\sigma$. A more detailed listing of areas under portions of the normal curve is given in Table 4.

Using Table 4, let us trace how the 68% and 95% values in Figure 5 are derived. We find from Column 3 of Table 4 that between -1σ and the mean lies .341 of the total area and between $+1\sigma$ and the mean also lies .341 of the area. Adding these values gives us .682, which is expressed in Figure 5 as 68%. Similarly, the area between -2σ and $+2\sigma$ is $2 \times 477 = .954$, which is expressed as 95%.

These percentages have several uses. One is in connection with the interpretation of standard scores, to which we turn next. Another is in connection with tests of significance.

TABLE 4

The Area of the Normal Distribution as a Proportion of Total Area

Standard Deviation	(1) Area to the Left of This Value	(2) Area to the Right of This Value	(3) Area Between This Value and Mean
-3.0σ	.001	.999	.499
-2.5σ	.006	.994	.494
-2.0σ	.023	.977	.477
-1.5σ	.067	.933	.433
-1.0σ	.159	.841	.341
-0.5σ	.309	.691	.191
0.0σ	.500	.500	.000
$+0.5\sigma$	.691	.309	.191
$+1.0\sigma$	.841	.159	.341
$+1.5\sigma$	.933	.067	.433
$+2.0\sigma$	.977	.023	.477
$+2.5\sigma$	.994	.006	.494
$+3.0\sigma$	.999	.001	.499

Scaling of Data

In order to interpret a score, we often need to know whether it is high or low in relation to other scores. If a person taking a driver's test requires .500 seconds to brake after a danger signal, how can we tell whether the performance is fast or slow? Does a student who scores 60 on a physics examination pass the course? To answer questions of this kind, we have to derive a scale against which the scores can be compared.

Ranked Data   By placing scores in rank order from high to low, we derive one kind of scale. An individual score is interpreted on the basis of where it ranks among the group of scores. For example, the graduates of West Point know where they stand in their class—perhaps 35th or 125th in a class of 400.

Standard Scores   The standard deviation is a convenient unit to use in scaling because we can interpret how far away 1σ or 2σ is from the mean (see Table 4). A score based on a multiple of the standard deviation is known as a *standard score*. Many scales used in psychological measurement are based on the principle of standard scores.

Table 1 presented college entrance scores for 15 students. Without more information, we do not know whether these scores are representative of the population of all college applicants. On this examination, however, we will assume that the population mean is 75 and the standard deviation is 10.

What, then, is the standard score for a student who had 90 on the examination? We must express how far this score lies above the mean in multiples of the standard deviation.

Standard score for grade of 90:

$$\frac{90-75}{10} = \frac{15}{10} = 1.5\sigma$$

As a second example, consider a student with a score of 53.

Standard score for grade of 53:

$$\frac{53-75}{10} = \frac{-22}{10} = -2.2\sigma$$

In this case, the minus sign tells us that the student's score is below the mean by 2.2 standard deviations. Thus, the sign of the standard score (+ or −) indicates whether the score is above or below the mean, and its value indicates how far from the mean the score lies in standard deviations.

How Representative Is a Mean?

How useful is the mean of a sample in estimating the population mean? If we measure the height of a random sample of 100 college students, how well does the sample mean predict the true population mean (that is, the mean height of *all* college students)? These questions raise the issue of making an *inference* about a population based on information from a sample.

The accuracy of such inferences depends on *errors of sampling*. Suppose we were to select two random samples from the same population and compute the mean for each sample. What differences between the first and the second mean could be expected to occur by chance?

Successive random samples drawn from the same population will have different means, forming a distribution of *sample means* around the *true mean* of the population. These sample means are themselves numbers for which the standard deviation can be computed. We call this standard deviation the standard error of the mean, or σ_M, and can estimate it on the basis of the following formula:

$$\sigma_M = \frac{\sigma}{\sqrt{N}}$$

where σ is the standard deviation of the sample and N is the number of cases from which each sample mean is computed.

According to the formula, the size of the standard error of the mean decreases as the sample size increases; thus, a mean based on a large sample is more trustworthy (more likely to be close to the actual population mean) than a mean based on a smaller sample. Common sense would lead us to expect this. Computations of the standard error of the mean permit us to make clear assertions about the degree of uncertainty in our computed mean. The more cases in the sample, the more uncertainty has been reduced.

The Significance of a Difference

In many psychological experiments, data are collected on two groups of subjects; one group is exposed to certain specified experimental conditions, and the other serves as a control group. The question is whether there is a difference in the mean performance of the two groups, and if such a difference is observed, whether it holds for the population from which these groups of subjects have been sampled. Basically, we are asking whether a difference between two sample means reflects a true difference or whether this difference is simply the result of sampling error.

As an example, we will compare the scores on a reading test for a sample of first-grade boys with the scores for a sample of first-grade girls. The boys score lower than the girls as far as mean performances are concerned, but there is a great deal of overlap; some boys do extremely well, and some girls do very poorly. Thus, we cannot accept the obtained difference in means without making a test of its *statistical significance*. Only then can we decide whether the observed differences in sample means reflect true differences in the population or are due to sampling error. If some of the brighter girls and some of the duller boys are sampled by sheer luck, the difference could be due to sampling error.

As another example, suppose that we have set up an experiment to compare the grip strength of right-handed and left-handed men. The top panel of Table 5 presents hypothetical data from such an experiment. A sample of five right-handed men averaged 8 kilograms stronger than a sample of five left-handed men. In general, what can we infer from these data about left-handed and right-handed men? Can we argue that right-handed men are stronger than left-handed men? Obviously not, because the averages derived from most of the right-handed men would not differ from those from the left-handed men; the one markedly deviant score of 100 tells us we are dealing with an uncertain situation.

Now suppose that the results of the experiment were those shown in the bottom panel of Table 5. Again, we find the same mean difference of 8 kilograms, but we are now inclined to have greater confidence in the results, because the left-handed men scored consistently lower than the right-handed men. Statistics provides a precise way of taking into account the reliability of the mean differences so that we do not have to depend solely on intuition to determine that one difference is more reliable than another.

These examples suggest that the significance of a difference will depend on both the size of the obtained difference and the variability of the means being compared. From the standard error of the means, we can

TABLE 5

The Significance of a Difference   *Two examples that compare the difference between means are shown. The difference between means is the same (8 kilograms) in both the top and bottom panel. However, the data in the bottom panel indicate a more reliable difference between means than do the data in the top panel.*

Strength of Grip in Kilograms, Right-Handed Men	Strength of Grip in Kilograms, Left-Handed Men
40	40
45	45
50	50
55	55
100	60
Sum 290	Sum 250
Mean 58	Mean 50

Strength of Grip in Kilograms, Right-Handed Men	Strength of Grip in Kilograms, Left-Handed Men
56	48
57	49
58	50
59	51
60	52
Sum 290	Sum 250
Mean 58	Mean 50

compute the *standard error of the difference between two means*, σD_M. We can then evaluate the obtained difference by using a *critical ratio*—the ratio of the obtained difference between the means D_M to the standard error of the difference:

$$\text{Critical Ratio} = \frac{D_M}{\sigma D_M}$$

This ratio helps us evaluate the significance of the difference between the two means. As a rule of thumb, a critical ratio should be 2.0 or larger for the difference between means to be accepted as significant. Throughout this book, statements that the difference between means is "statistically significant" indicate that the critical ratio is at least that large.

Why is a critical ratio of 2.0 selected as statistically significant? Simply because a value this large or larger can occur by chance only 5 out of 100 times. Where do we get the 5 out of 100? We can treat the critical ratio as a standard score because it is merely the difference between two means, expressed as a multiple of its standard error. Referring to Column 2 in Table 4, we note that the likelihood is .023 that a standard deviation as high as or higher than +2.0 will occur by chance. Because the chance of deviating in the opposite direction is also .023, the total probability is .046. This means that 46 times out of 1,000, or about 5 times out of 100, a critical ratio as large as 2.0 would be found by chance if the population means were identical.

The rule of thumb that says a critical ratio should be at least 2.0 is just that—an arbitrary but convenient rule that defines the "5% level of significance." Following this rule, we will make fewer than 5 errors in 100 decisions by concluding on the basis of sample data that a difference in means exists when in fact there is none. The 5% level need not always be used; a higher level of significance may be appropriate in certain experiments, depending on how willing we are to make an occasional error in inference.

The computation of the critical ratio calls for finding the *standard error of the difference between two means*, which is given by the following formula:

$$\sigma D_M = \sqrt{(\sigma M_1)^2 + (\sigma M_2)^2}$$

In this formula, σM_1, and σM_2 are the standard errors of the two means being compared.

As an illustration, suppose we wanted to compare reading achievement test scores for first-grade boys and girls in the United States. A random sample of boys and girls would be identified and given the test. We will assume that the mean score for the boys was 70 with a standard error of .40 and that the mean score for the girls was 72 with a standard error of .30. On the basis of these samples, we want to decide whether there is a real difference between the reading achievement of boys and girls in the population as a whole. The sample data suggest that girls do achieve better reading scores than boys, but can we infer that this would have been the case if we had tested all the girls and all the boys in the United States? The critical ratio helps us make this decision.

$$\sigma D_M = \sqrt{(\sigma M_1)^2 + (\sigma M_2)^2}$$
$$= \sqrt{.16 + .09} = \sqrt{.25}$$
$$= .5$$

$$\text{Critical Ratio} = \frac{D_M}{\sigma D_M} = \frac{72 - 70}{.5} = \frac{2.0}{.5} = 4.0$$

Because the critical ratio is well above 2.0, we may assert that the observed mean difference is statistically significant at the 5% level. Thus, we can conclude that there is a reliable difference in performance on the reading test between boys and girls. Note that the sign of the critical ratio could be positive or negative, depending on which mean is subtracted from which; when the critical ratio is interpreted, only its magnitude (not its sign) is considered.

The Coefficient of Correlation

Correlation refers to the parallel variation of two measures. Suppose that a test is designed to predict success in college. If it is a good test, high scores on it will be related to high performance in college and low scores will be related to poor performance. The *coefficient of correlation* gives us a way of stating the degree of relationship more precisely.

Product-Moment Correlation

The most frequently used method of determining the coefficient of correlation is the *product-moment method*, which yields the index conventionally designated by the lowercase letter r. The product-moment coefficient r varies between perfect positive correlation ($r = +1.00$) and perfect negative correlation ($r = -1.00$). Lack of any relationship yields $r = .00$.

The formula for computing the product-moment correlation is:

$$r = \frac{\text{Sum }(dx)(dy)}{N\sigma_x\sigma_y}$$

Here, one of the paired measures has been labeled the x-score; the other, the y-score. The dx and dy refer to the deviations of each score from its mean, N is the number of paired measures, and σ_x and σ_y are the standard deviations of the x-scores and the y-scores.

The computation of the coefficient of correlation requires the determination of the sum of the $(dx)(dy)$ products. This sum, in addition to the computed standard deviations for the x-scores and y-scores, can then be entered into the formula.

Suppose that we have collected the data shown in Table 6. For each subject, we have obtained two scores—the first being a score on a college entrance test (to be labeled

Computation of a Product-Moment Correlation

Student	Entrance Test (x-score)	Freshman Grades (y-score)	(dx)	(dy)	(dx)(dy)
Adam	71	39	6	9	+54
Bill	67	27	2	−3	−6
Charles	65	33	0	3	0
David	63	30	−2	0	0
Edward	59	2	−6	−9	+54
Sum	325	150	0	0	+102
Mean	65	30			

$$\sigma_x = 4$$
$$\sigma_y = 6$$
$$r = \frac{\text{Sum }(dx)(dy)}{N\sigma_x\sigma_y} = \frac{+102}{5 \times 4 \times 6} = +.85$$

arbitrarily the *x*-score) and the second being freshman grades (the *y*-score).

Figure 6 is a *scatter diagram* of these data. Each point represents the *x*-score and *y*-score for a given subject; for example, the uppermost right-hand point is for Adam (labeled A). Looking at these data, we can easily detect that there is some positive correlation between the *x*-scores and the *y*-scores. Adam attained the highest score on the entrance test and also earned the highest freshman grades; Edward received the lowest scores on both. The other students' test scores and grades are a little irregular, so we know that the correlation is not perfect; hence, *r* is less than 1.00.

We will compute the correlation to illustrate the method, although no researcher would consent, in practice, to determining a correlation for so few cases. The details are given in Table 6. Following the procedure outlined in Table 3, we compute the standard deviation of the *x*-scores and then the standard deviation of the *y*-scores. Next, we compute the $(dx)(dy)$ products for each subject and total the five cases. Entering these results in our equation yields an *r* of +.85.

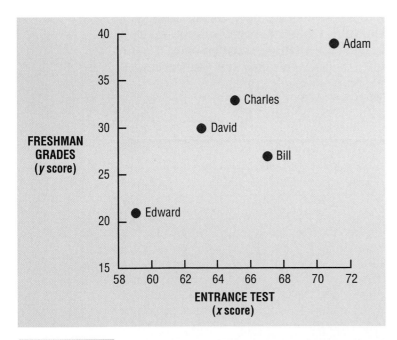

A Scatter Design *Each point represents the x- and y-scores for a particular student. The letters next to the points identify the students in the data table (A = Adam, B = Bill, and so on).*

Interpreting a Correlation Coefficient

We can use correlations in making predictions. For example, if we know from experience that a certain entrance test correlates with freshman grades, we can predict the freshman grades for beginning college students who have taken the test. If the correlation were perfect, we could predict their grades without error. But *r* is usually less than 1.00, and some errors in prediction will be made; the closer *r* is to 0, the greater the sizes of the errors in prediction.

Although we cannot go into the technical problems of predicting freshman grades from entrance examinations or of making other similar predictions, we can consider the meanings of correlation coefficients of different sizes. It is evident that with a correlation of 0 between *x* and *y*, knowledge of *x* will not help to predict *y*. If weight is unrelated to intelligence, it does us no good to know a subject's weight when we are trying to predict his or her intelligence. At the other extreme, a perfect correlation would mean 100% predictive efficiency—knowing *x*, we can predict *y* perfectly. What about intermediate values of *r*? Some appreciation of the meaning of correlations of intermediate sizes can be gained by examining the scatter diagrams in Figure 7.

In the preceding discussion, we did not emphasize the sign of the correlation coefficient, since this has no bearing on the strength of a relationship. The only distinction between a correlation of *r* = +.70 and *r* = −.70 is that increases in *x* are accompanied by increases in *y* for the former, and increases in *x* are accompanied by decreases in *y* for the latter.

Although the correlation coefficient is one of the most widely used statistics in psychology, it is also one of the most widely misused procedures. Those who use it sometimes overlook the fact that *r* does not imply a cause-and-effect relationship between *x* and *y*. When two sets of scores are correlated, we may suspect that they have some causal factors in common, but we cannot conclude that one of them causes the other.

Correlations sometimes appear paradoxical. For example, the correlation between study time and college grades has been found to be slightly negative (about −.10). If

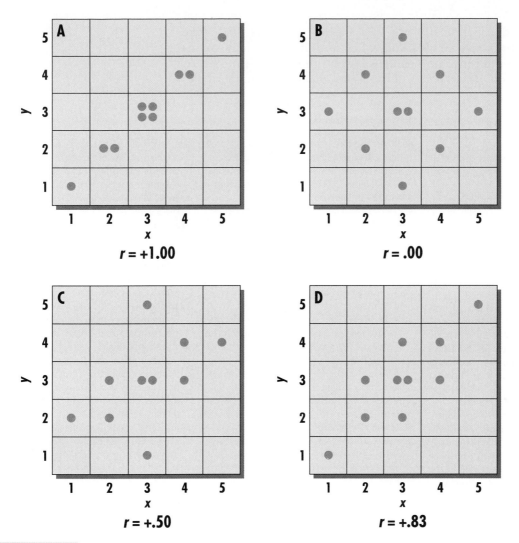

Scatter Diagrams Illustrating Correlations of Various Sizes   *Each dot represents one individual's score on two tests, x and y. In A, all cases fall on the diagonal and the correlation is perfect (r = +1.00); if we know a subject's score on x, we know that it will be the same on y. In B, the correlation is 0; knowing a subject's score on x, we cannot predict whether it will be at, above, or below the mean on y. In both C and D, there is a diagonal trend to the scores, so that a high score on x is associated with a high score on y and a low score on x with a low score on y, but the relationship is imperfect.*

a causal interpretation were assumed, we might conclude that the best way to raise grades would be to stop studying. The negative correlation arises because some students have advantages over others in grade making (possibly due to better college preparation), so that often those who study the hardest are those who have difficulty earning the best grades.

This example provides sufficient warning against assigning a causal interpretation to a coefficient of correlation. It is possible, however, that when two variables are correlated, one may be the cause of the other. The search for causes is a logical one, and correlations can help us by providing leads to experiments that can verify cause-and-effect relationships.

Glossary

The glossary defines the technical words that appear in the text and some common words that have special meanings when used in psychology. No attempt is made to give the range of meanings beyond those used in the text. For fuller definitions and other shades of meaning, consult any standard dictionary of psychology.

A

ability. Demonstrable knowledge or skill. Ability includes aptitude and achievement. See also achievement, aptitude.

abreaction. In psychoanalysis, the process of reducing emotional tension by reliving (in speech or action or both) the experience that caused the tension.

absolute threshold. The minimum magnitude of a stimulus that can be reliably discriminated from no stimulus at all. See also difference threshold, threshold.

abstractions. Properties that characterize sets of instances rather than just single instances.

accommodation. (1) The process by which the lens of the eye varies its focus. (2) In Piaget's theory of cognitive development, the process by which an infant modifies a pre-existing schema in order to include a novel object or event. See also assimilation, schema.

acetylcholine. The most common of the neurotransmitters. It is found in many synapses in the brain and spinal cord, and is particularly prevalent in an area of the brain called the hippocampus, which plays a key role in the formation of new memories. See also neurotransmitter.

achievement. Acquired ability, such as school attainment in spelling. See also aptitude.

achromatic colors. Black, white, and gray. See also chromatic colors.

acoustic buffer. In short-term memory, a hypothesized component of the encoding process which briefly stores information in an acoustic code (i.e., the sound of the digit, letter, or word). See also central executive, encoding, short-term memory, visual buffer.

acquisition. The stage during which a new response is learned and gradually strengthened. See also classical conditioning.

ACTH. See adrenocorticotropic hormone.

action potential. An electrochemical impulse that travels from the dendritic area down to the end of the axon. See also depolarization, graded potentials, resting potential.

activation model. In memory, the proposal that retrieval of an item depends on the activation of that item reaching a critical level.

actualizing tendency. A tendency toward fulfillment or actualization of all the capacities of the organism.

acupuncture. A healing procedure developed in China in which needles are inserted in the skin at critical points and twirled, eliminating pain. See also gate control theory of pain.

addiction. A pattern of compulsive and destructive drug-taking behavior.

additive mixture. The mixture of colored lights; two spotlights of different colors focused on the same spot yield an additive color mixture. See also subtractive mixture.

ADH. See antidiuretic hormone.

adipocytes. Special fat cells in the body. Obese individuals have many more of them and thus, perhaps, a higher body fat base line.

adolescence. The period of transition from childhood to adulthood. See also puberty.

adolescent growth spurt. A period of rapid physical growth that accompanies the onset of puberty.

adrenal gland. One of a pair of endocrine glands located above the kidneys. The medulla of the gland secretes the hormones epinephrine and norepinephrine. The cortex of the gland secretes a number of hormones, collectively called the adrenocortical hormones, which include cortisol. See also endocrine system.

adrenalin. See epinephrine.

adrenal-cortical-system. A neuroendocrine system activated in response to stress. On a signal from the hypothalamus, the pituitary gland secretes a number of hormones. One stimulates the thyroid gland to make more energy available; the other (adrenocorticotropic hormone, ACTH) triggers the outer layer of the adrenal gland (the adrenal cortex) to release some 30 hormones (including cortisol) which play a role in the body's adjustment to emergencies. See also adrenocorticotropic hormone, cortisol.

adrenocorticotropic hormone (ACTH). A hormone released by the pituitary gland in response to stress; known as the body's major "stress" hormone. It is carried by the bloodstream to the adrenal glands and various other organs of the body, causing the release of some 30 hormones, each of which plays a role in the body's adjustment to emergency situations. See also corticotropin-release factor.

aerobic exercise. Any sustained activity that increases oxygen consumption, such as jogging, swimming, cycling, or fast walking.

affect. Emotions and feelings.

affective experience. An emotional experience, whether pleasant or unpleasant, mild or intense. See also emotion.

afferent neuron. See sensory neuron.

afterimage. The sensory experience that remains when a stimulus is withdrawn. Usually refers to visual experience—for example, the negative afterimage of a picture or the train of colored images that results after staring at the sun.

age regression. In hypnosis, the reliving through fantasy of experiences that are based on early memories or that are appropriate to a younger age. See also hypnosis.

aggregated score. A combination of several measures of the same behavior or characteristic.

aggression. Behavior that is intended to injure another person (physically or verbally) or to destroy property.

agnosia. The general term for breakdowns or disorders in recognition. See also associative agnosia, prosopagnosia.

agoraphobia. Fear of places where one might be trapped or unable to receive help in an emergency. See also panic disorder, phobia.

AI. See artificial intelligence.

all-or-none principle. The rule that the nerve impulse in a single neuron is independent of the strength of stimulation; the neuron either responds completely (fires its action potential) or not at all.

alpha waves. See electroencephalogram.

alternate form reliability. The consistency between two or more versions of the same test when given to the same person. See also reliability.

altruism. Behavior intended to help others even when no benefits are offered or expected in return.

ambivalence. Simultaneous liking and disliking of an object or person; the conflict caused by an incentive that is at once positive and negative. See also conflict.

Ames room. A perceptual illusion; specifically, a room that when viewed through a peephole leads to distortions in size judgments. See also size constancy.

amnesia. Partial loss of memory. See also anterograde amnesia, retrograde amnesia.

amphetamines. Central nervous system stimulants that produce restlessness, irritability, anxiety, and rapid heart rate. Dexedrine sulfate ("speed") and methamphetamine ("meth") are two types of amphetamines. See also depressants, stimulants.

amplitude. The difference in pressure between the peak and the trough.

amygdala. A brain structure located below the cerebral cortex that is involved in consolidation of emotional memories. See also diencephalon, hippocampus.

anal stage. The second stage in Freud's psychoanalytic theory of psychosexual development, following the oral stage. The sources of gratification and conflict have to do with the expulsion and retention of feces. See also psychosexual development.

androgen. A male hormone.

androgens. The collective name for male sex hormones, of which testosterone, secreted by the testes, is best known. See also gonads.

angiotensin. A hormone that induces the feeling of thirst as well as an appetite for salt, which leads to behavioral adjustments.

Anorexia nervosa. Self-imposed weight loss—at least 15 percent of the individual's minimum normal weight.

anterior attentional system. Neural structures in the front of the brain that mediate our ability to selectively attend to some attribute of an object (other than its location).

anterograde amnesia. Loss of memory for events and experiences occurring subsequent to an amnesia-causing trauma; the patient is unable to acquire new information, although recall of information learned prior to the onset may be largely unaffected. See also amnesia, retrograde amnesia.

anthropology. The science that studies chiefly preliterate societies. Its main divisions are archaeology (the study of the physical monuments and remains from earlier civilizations), physical anthropology (concerned with the anatomical differences among people and their evolutionary origins), linguistic anthropology, and social anthropology (concerned with social institutions and behavior). See also behavioral sciences.

antianxiety drug. Central nervous system depressant (belonging to the family of drugs called benzodiazapines) that reduces anxiety and tension. Causes some drowsiness but less than barbiturates. Diazepam (Valium) and alprozolam (Xanax) are examples (syn. tranquilizer).

antidepressant. Drug used to elevate the mood of depressed individuals, presumably by increasing the availability of the neurotransmitters norepinephrine and/or serotonin. Examples are imipramine (Tofranil), isocarboxazid (Marplan), and fluoxetine (Prozac).

antidiuretic hormone (ADH). A hormone that regulates the kidneys so they release water back into the bloodstream and form only very concentrated urine.

antipsychotic drug. A drug that reduces psychotic symptoms, used more frequently in the treatment of schizophrenia. The phenothiazines, such as chlorpromazine (Thorazin) and fluphenazine (Prolixin), are examples (syn. neuroleptic drug). See also phenothiazines, psychotic behavior.

antisocial personality. A type of personality disorder marked by impulsivity, inability to abide by the customs and laws of society, and lack of anxiety or guilt regarding behavior (syn. sociopathic personality, psychopathic personality).

anxiety. A state of apprehension, tension, and worry. Synonymous with fear for some theorists, although others view the object of anxiety (such as a vague danger or foreboding) as less specific than the object of a fear (such as a vicious animal). See also neurotic anxiety, objective anxiety.

anxiety disorders. A group of mental disorders characterized by intense anxiety or by maladaptive behavior designed to relieve anxiety. Includes generalized anxiety and panic disorders, phobic and obsessive-compulsive disorders. Major category of DSM-IV covering most of the disorders formerly called neuroses. See also generalized anxiety disorder, neurosis, obsessive-compulsive disorder, panic disorder, phobic disorder, post-traumatic stress disorder.

anxiety hierarchy. A list of situations or stimuli to which a person responds with anxiety ranked in order from the least anxiety-producing to the most fearful. Used by behavior therapists in systematically desensitizing patients to feared stimuli by associating deep relaxation with the situations rather than anxiety. See also behavior therapy, systematic desensitization.

apathy. Listlessness, indifference; one of the consequences of frustration. See also frustration.

aphagia. Inability to eat. See also hyperphagia.

aphasia. Language deficits caused by brain damage.

apnea. The individual stops breathing while asleep.

apparent motion. See phi phenomenon, stroboscopic motion.

appetitive behavior. Seeking behavior. See also aversive behavior.

appraisals. Evaluations of a situation, event, person, or the self.

appraisal theories of emotion. A group of theories of emotions stating that people's cognitive appraisals of situations determine the emotions they experience in response to the situations.

aptitude. The capacity to learn—for instance, a person's typing aptitude prior to practice on a typewriter. Aptitude tests are designed to predict the outcome of training, hence to predict future ability on the basis of present ability. See also achievement.

argument. A claim, or conclusion, that we are trying to draw.

arousal level. The principle according to which people seek an optimal level of drive or arousal.

artificial intelligence (AI). A field of research combining computer science and cognitive psychology; it is concerned with (a) using computers to simulate human thought processes and (b) devising computer programs that act "intelligently" and can adapt to changing circumstances. In essence, it is the science of making machines (computers) do things that are normally done by the human mind. See also cognitive psychology, cognitive science, computer simulation.

assertiveness training. The use of behavioral rehearsal to help an individual learn to express his or her needs in an effective, nonhostile manner. See also behavioral rehearsal.

assimilation. In Piaget's theory of cognitive development, the process by which an infant comprehends a novel object or event in terms of a pre-existing schema. See also accommodation, schema.

association areas. Areas of the cerebral cortex that are not directly concerned with sensory or motor processes; they integrate inputs from various sensory channels and presumably function in learning, memory, and thinking.

associative agnosia. A perceptual disturbance, resulting from damage to specific areas of the cerebral cortex, in which the individual has difficulty recognizing familiar objects presented visually, although he or she can readily name the objects if allowed to touch or hear them. See also agnosia, prosopagnosia.

associative learning. Learning that certain contingencies (or relations) exist between events; learning that one event is associated with another.

astigmatism. In vision, an optical defect that prevents horizontal and vertical contours from being in focus simultaneously. See also strabismus.

attachment. An infant's tendency to seek closeness to particular people and to feel more secure in their presence.

attention. The ability to select some information for more detailed inspection, while ignoring other information. See also orienting reflex.

attitudes. Favorable or unfavorable evaluations of and reactions to objects, people, situations, or other aspects of the world.

attribution. The process by which we attempt to explain the behavior of other people. Attribution theory deals with the rules people use to infer the causes of observed behavior. See also dispositional attribution, situational attribution.

attributional styles. Styles of making attributions for the events in one's life. See also attribution.

auditory area. A brain region located at the top of the temporal lobe of each cerebral hemisphere where auditory signals carried by the acoustic nerve are analyzed. Because nerve fibers from each side of the head cross over at the brain stem before reaching the auditory area, signals from each ear reach both temporal lobes. Thus, damage to one lobe does not produce deafness in one ear.

authoritarian personality. A personality type who is submissive and obedient to superiors but contemptuous of and aggressive toward those he or she considers inferior. Shows prejudice against minority groups. The Authoritarian Personality is a classic social psychological study, based in psychoanalytic theory, which examined this personality type. See also scapegoat theory of prejudice.

autism. A mental disorder, first evident during early childhood, in which the child shows significant deficits in communication, social interaction, and bonding and play activities, and engages in repetitive stereotyped behaviors and self-damaging acts.

automatic writing. Writing that the writer is unaware of (does not know that he or she is producing); familiar in hypnosis. See also hypnosis.

automaticity. The habituation of responses that initially requires conscious attention.

autonomic system. Connects with the internal organs and glands.

autonomic nervous system. The division of the peripheral nervous system that regulates smooth muscle (organ and glandular) activities. It is divided into the sympathetic and parasympathetic divisions. See also parasympathetic system, peripheral nervous system, sympathetic system.

average. See measure of central tendency.

aversive behavior. Avoidance behavior. See also appetitive behavior.

aversive conditioning. A form of conditioning in which an undesirable response is extinguished through association with punishment; has been used in behavior therapy to treat alcoholism, smoking, and sexual problems. See also behavior therapy, counterconditioning.

avoidance learning. Learning to make a response to a warning signal in order to avoid an aversive event. See also escape learning.

awareness. See consciousness.

axon. That portion of a neuron that transmits impulses to other neurons. See also dendrite, neuron.

B

BAC. See blood alcohol concentration.

basal mental age. In individual tests of the Binet type, the highest age level at which, and below which, all tests are passed. See also mental age.

base-rate rule. A rule in probability theory, which states that the probability of something (e.g., a person or object) being a member of a class is greater the more class members there are. People frequently violate this rule when reasoning about real-world situations.

basic level. In a hierarchy of concepts, the level at which one first categorizes an object.

basilar membrane. A membrane of the ear within the coils of the cochlea supporting the organ of Corti. Movements of the basilar membrane stimulate the hair cells of the organ of Corti, producing the neural effects of auditory stimulation. See also cochlea.

behavior. Those activities of an organism that can be observed by another organism or by an experimenter's instruments. Included within behavior are verbal reports made about subjective, conscious experiences. See also conscious processes.

behavior genetics. Combines the methods of genetics and psychology to study the inheritance of behavioral characteristics.

behavior modification. See behavior therapy.

behavior therapy. A method of psychotherapy based on learning principles. It uses such techniques as counterconditioning, reinforcement, and shaping to modify behavior (syn. behavior modification). See also cognitive behavior therapy.

behavioral medicine. The study of how social, psychological, and biological factors interact to contribute to physical illness (syn. health psychology).

behavioral perspective. An approach to psychology that focuses only on observable behavior, and tries to explain it in terms of its relation to environmental events. See also behaviorism.

behavioral rehearsal. Role-playing. See also assertiveness training.

behavioral sciences. The sciences concerned in one way or another with the behavior of humans and lower organisms (especially social anthropology, psychology, and sociology but including some aspects of biology, economics, political science, history, philosophy, and other fields of study.)

behaviorism. A school or system of psychology associated with the name of John B. Watson; it defined psychology as the study of behavior and limited the data of psychology to observable activities. In its classical form it was more restrictive than the contemporary behavioral viewpoint in psychology.

belief-driven learning. A kind of associative learning in which people have prior beliefs about the relation that has to be learned; learning is driven by the beliefs as well as by the input. See also data-driven learning.

benzodiazepines. A class of drugs with similar chemical structures that are effective in reducing anxiety. Examples are diazepam (Valium) and alprazolam (Xanax). See antianxiety drug.

binocular cues. See distance cues.

binocular disparity. The difference in the views seen by each eye.

binocular parallax. A cue to depth perception that arises because any visible point will differ slightly in its direction to the two eyes. See also binocular disparity.

biofeedback training. Receiving information (feedback) about an aspect of one's physiological state and then attempting to alter that state.

biological perspective. An approach to psychology that tries to explain behavior in terms of electrical and chemical events taking place inside the body, particularly within the brain and nervous system.

biological psychologist. A psychologist concerned with the relationship between biological processes and behavior. Same as physiological psychologist.

biological therapy. Treatment of emotional problems or mental disorders by drugs, electric shock, or other methods directly affecting bodily processes. See also psychotherapy.

bipolar cells. Cells in the retina that transmit electrical impulses from photoreceptors to ganglion cells. See also ganglia, photoreceptors, retina.

bipolar disorders. Alternating between periods of depression and periods of mania. (syn. manic-depression). See also depression, mood disorder.

blind spot. An insensitive area of the retina where the nerve fibers from the ganglion cells join to form the optic nerve.

blocking. A phenomenon in classical conditioning: if one conditioned stimulus reliably predicts an unconditioned stimulus, and another conditioned stimulus is added, the relation between the added conditioned stimulus and the unconditioned stimulus will not be learned.

blood alcohol concentration (BAC). The concentration, in milligrams, of alcohol per 100 milliliters of blood. The legal definition of intoxication in most states is a blood alcohol concentration of .10 percent (100 milligrams of alcohol per 100 milliliters of blood).

blood pressure. The pressure of the blood against the walls of the blood vessels. Changes in blood pressure following stimulation serve as one indicator of emotion.

borderline personality disorder. A mental disorder in which the individual has manifested unstable moods, relationships with others, and self-perceptions chronically since adolescence or childhood.

bottom-up processes. Processes in perception, learning, memory, and comprehension that are driven solely by the information input, and that do not involve the organism's prior knowledge and expectations. See also top-down processes.

brain stem. The structures lying near the core of the brain; essentially all of the brain with the exception of the cerebrum and the cerebellum and their dependent parts.

brightness. How much light appears to be reflected from a colored surface.

Broca's area. A portion of the left cerebral hemisphere involved in the control of speech. Individuals with damage in this area have difficulty enunciating words correctly and speak in a slow and labored way; their speech often makes sense, but it includes only key words.

bulimia. Recurrent episodes of binge eating (rapid consumption of a large amount of food in a discrete period of time), followed by attempts to purge the excess by means of vomiting or laxatives.

C

cannabis. The hemp plant from which marijuana is obtained. See also marijuana.

Cannon-Bard theory. A classical theory of emotion proposed by Cannon and Bard. The theory states that an emotion-producing stimulus activates the cortex and bodily responses at the same time; bodily changes and the experience of emotion occur simultaneously. See also cognitive-appraisal theory, James-Lange theory.

cardiac muscle. A special kind of muscle found only in the heart. See also smooth muscle, striate muscle.

case histories. Biographies designed for scientific use. See also longitudinal study.

castration. Surgical removal of the gonads; in the male, removal of the testes; in the female, removal of the ovaries.

catatonic immobility. A fixed posture maintained for long periods with accompanying muscular rigidity and a trance-like state of consciousness. A symptom in some cases of schizophrenia. See also schizophrenia.

categorization. The process of assigning an object to a concept. See also concept.

catharsis. Purging an emotion by experiencing it intensely.

central core. The most central portion of the brain, including structures that regulate basic life processes. See also brain stem, cerebellum, hypothalamus, reticular formation.

central executive. In short-term memory, a hypothesized component of the encoding process that coordinates the acoustic and visual buffers. See also acoustic buffer, encoding, short-term memory, visual buffer.

central fissure. A fissure of each cerebral hemisphere that separates the frontal and parietal lobes (syn. fissure of Rolando).

central nervous system. All the neurons in the brain and spinal cord.

cerebellum. Lobed structure attached to the rear of the brain stem that regulates muscle tone and coordination of intricate movements.

cerebral cortex. The surface layer of the cerebral hemispheres in higher animals, including humans, commonly called gray matter.

cerebral hemisphere. Two large masses of nerve cells and fibers constituting the bulk of the brain in humans and other higher animals. The hemispheres are separated by a deep fissure, but connected by a broad band of fibers, the corpus callosum (syn. cerebrum). See also cerebral cortex, left hemisphere, right hemisphere, split-brain subject.

cerebrum. The brain's two cerebral hemispheres. See cerebral hemisphere.

childhood amnesia. The inability to recall events from the first years of one's life.

chlorpromazine. See antipsychotic drug.

chromatic colors. All colors other than black, white, and gray; for instance, red, yellow, blue. See also achromatic colors.

chromosomes. Structures found in the nucleus of each cell in the body. See also gene.

chronological age (CA). Age from birth; calendar age. See also mental age.

chunking. Recoding new material into larger, more meaningful units and storing those units in working memory. See also short-term memory.

cilia. Hairlike structures that are sometimes parts of receptors.

circadian rhythm. Rhythms of the body that occur approximately every 24 hours.

clairvoyance. Perception of objects or events that do not provide a stimulus to the known senses (for example, identifying a concealed playing card, the identity of which is unknown). See also extrasensory perception, parapsychology, precognition, psi, psychokinesis, telepathy.

classical concept. A concept where an instance must have every property mentioned in the concept. An example is the concept of bachelor; every instance must have the properties of being adult, male, and unmarried. See also fuzzy concept.

classical conditioning. A learning process in which a previously neutral stimulus becomes associated with another stimulus through repeated pairing with that stimulus. See also operant conditioning.

claustrophobia. Fear of closed places. See also phobia.

client-centered therapy. A method of psychotherapy developed by Carl Rogers in which the therapist is nondirective and reflective and does not interpret or advise. The operating assumption is that the client is the best expert on his or her problems and can work them out in a nonjudgmental, accepting atmosphere (syn. nondirective counseling). See also humanistic therapies.

clinical psychologist. A psychologist, usually with a Ph.D. or Psy.D. degree, trained in the diagnosis and treatment of emotional or behavioral problems and mental disorders. See also counseling psychologist, psychiatrist.

cocaine. A central nervous system stimulant derived from leaves of the coca plant. Increases energy, produces euphoria, and in large doses causes paranoia.

cochlea. The portion of the inner ear containing the receptors for hearing. See also basilar membrane.

coding. See encoding.

coding by pattern. Coding the quality of a sensation in terms of the pattern of neural firing. See also coding by specificity.

coding by specificity. Coding the quality of a sensation in terms of the specific neurons involved. See also coding by pattern, specific nerve energies.

coefficient of correlation. A numerical index used to indicate the degree of correspondence between two sets of paired measurements. The most common kind is the product-moment coefficient designated by r.

cognition. An individual's thoughts, knowledge, interpretations, understandings, or ideas. See also cognitive processes.

cognitive appraisal. The interpretation of an event or situation with respect to one's goals and well-being. The cognitive appraisal of an event influences both the quality and intensity of the emotion experienced and the degree of perceived threat.

cognitive-appraisal theory. A theory of emotion that proposes that the subjective emotional state is a function of the individual's appraisal, or analysis, of the emotion-arousing situation. A state of physiological arousal can produce different emotions (even antithetical ones) depending on how the person appraises the situation. See also Cannon-Bard theory, James-Lange theory.

cognitive behavior therapy. A psychotherapy approach that emphasizes the influence of a person's beliefs, thoughts, and self-statements on behavior. Combines behavior therapy methods with techniques designed to change the way the individual thinks about self and events. See also behavior therapy.

cognitive dissonance. The discomfort produced by inconsistent cognitions.

cognitive distortions. In Beck's theory of depression, systematic errors in thinking that lead depressed individuals to misperceive reality in a way that contributes to their negative self-schema. Examples are overgeneralization (drawing a sweeping conclusion on the basis of a single negative event) and selective abstraction (focusing on an insignificant negative detail while ignoring the more important positive features of a situation). See also depression, self-schema.

cognitive map. A hypothetical structure in memory that preserves and organizes information about the various events that occur in a learning situation; a mental picture of the learning situation. See also schema.

cognitive neuroscience. An interdisciplinary approach that combines aspects of cognitive psychology and neuroscience to study how mental activities are executed in the brain.

cognitive perspective. An approach to psychology that focuses on mental processes such as perceiving, remembering, reasoning, deciding, and problem solving, and tries to explain behavior in terms of these mental processes. See also cognitive psychology, cognitive science.

cognitive processes. Mental processes of perception, memory, and information processing by which the individual acquires information, makes plans, and solves problems.

cognitive psychology. A general approach to psychology that stresses the role of mental processes in understanding behavior. The cognitive psychologist explains behavior at the level of mental representations and the mental processes that operate on these representations to produce products (including responses). The approach is not restricted to the study of thought and knowledge; its early concerns with these topics led to the label "cognitive psychology," but in recent years the approach has been generalized to all areas of psychology. See also artificial intelligence, cognitive science, information-processing model, mental representation.

cognitive response theory. A theory that proposes that persuasion induced by a communication is actually self-persuasion produced by the thoughts that the individual generates while receiving or even just anticipating the communication.

cognitive science. A term introduced in the 1970s to focus attention on how humans acquire and organize knowledge; a "new" science dedicated to understanding cognition. In addition to psychology, the disciplines relevant to cognitive science are neuroscience, linguistics, philosophy, mathematics, and computer science (particularly that branch of computer science known as artificial intelligence). See also artificial intelligence, cognitive psychology.

cognitive triad. In Beck's theory, the major concommitant, and possibly cause, of depression. Consists of negative thoughts about the self, the present situation, and the future. See also depression.

color blindness. Defective discrimination of chromatic colors. See also dichromatism, monochromatism, red-green color blindness, trichromatism.

color circle. An arrangement of chromatic colors on the circumference of a circle in the order in which they appear in the spectrum but with the addition of nonspectral reds and purples. The colors are so arranged that those opposite each other are complementaries in additive mixture. See also color solid.

color constancy. The tendency to see a familiar object as of the same color, regardless of changes in illumination on it that alter its stimulus properties. See also perceptual constancy.

color solid. A three-dimensional representation of the psychological dimensions of color, with hue around the circumference, saturation along each radius, and brightness from top to bottom. See also color circle.

color-opponent cells. In color vision, cells that respond only to their two opponent colors. See also opponent-color theory.

companionate love. Contrasted with passionate love. The affection we feel for those with whom our lives are deeply intertwined. See also passionate love.

complementary colors. Two colors that in additive mixture yield either a gray or an unsaturated color of the hue of the stronger component.

complex cell. A cell in the visual cortex that responds to a bar of light or straight edge of a particular orientation located anywhere in the visual field. See also simple cell.

complex learning. Learning that involves more than forming associations; for example, using a strategy to solve a problem or forming a mental map of one's surroundings. Contrasted with habituation and conditioning which are simpler types of learning. See also classical conditioning, habituation, operant conditioning.

compliance. We comply with the wishes of the influencer but do not necessarily change our beliefs or attitudes. See also identification, internalization.

comprehension. Understanding language by hearing sounds, attaching meanings to the sounds in the form of words, combining the words to create a sentence, and then somehow extracting meaning from it.

compulsion. Irresistible urges to carry out certain acts or rituals that reduce anxiety. See also obsession, obsessive-compulsive disorder.

computer program. See program.

computer simulation. The use of a computer to simulate a phenomenon or system in order to study its properties. In psychology, the simulation usually involves an attempt to program a computer to mimic how the mind processes information and solves problems. See also artificial intelligence, cognitive psychology, information-processing model.

computerized axial tomography (CT). A computer-based procedure that analyzes data obtained by a scanning beam of X rays to provide a picture of a cross-sectional slice through the body or brain.

concept. The set of properties that we associate with a particular class. See also classical concept, fuzzy concept.

concrete operational stage. Piaget's third stage of cognitive development (ages 7 to 11 years) during which children become capable of logical thought and conservation. See also conservation.

conditioned emotion. An emotional response acquired by conditioning: one aroused by a stimulus that did not originally evoke it. See also conditioning.

conditioned fear. A fear acquired by classical conditioning. The object that the organism comes to fear was originally neutral, but when it is repeatedly paired with an aversive stimulus it becomes an object of fear.

conditioned reinforcer. A stimulus that has become reinforcing through prior association with a reinforcing stimulus (syn. secondary reinforcer). See also reinforcing stimulus.

conditioned response (CR). The learned or acquired response to a stimulus that did not evoke the response originally (i.e., a conditioned stimulus). See also conditioned stimulus, unconditioned response, unconditioned stimulus.

conditioned stimulus (CS). A previously neutral stimulus that comes to elicit a conditioned response through association with an unconditioned stimulus. See also conditioned response, unconditioned response, unconditioned stimulus.

conditioning. The process by which conditioned responses are learned. See also classical conditioning, operant conditioning.

conduction loss. A hearing deficit in which threshold elevation (loss of sensitivity) occurs equally at all frequencies as the result of poor conduction in the middle ear. See also sensory-neural loss.

cone. In the eye, a specialized cell of the retina found predominantly in the fovea and more sparsely throughout the retina. The cones mediate both chromatic and achromatic sensations. See also fovea, retina, rod.

conflict. The simultaneous presence of opposing or mutually exclusive impulses, desires, or tendencies. See also ambivalence.

conjunction rule. A rule in probability theory, which states that the probability of a proposition cannot be less than the probability of that proposition conjoined with another proposition. People frequently violate the rule when reasoning about real-world situations.

connectionist models. Models of cognitive processes (like perception) that incorporate a network of nodes, with excitatory and inhibitory connections between them.

connotative meaning. The suggestive and emotional meanings of a word or symbol, beyond its denotative meaning. Thus, naked and nude both refer to an unclothed body (denotative meaning), but they have somewhat different connotations. See also denotative meaning.

conscience. An internal recognition of standards of right and wrong by which the individual judges his or her conduct. See also superego.

conscious. Our current awareness. See also preconscious, topographic model, unconscious.

conscious processes. Events such as perceptions, private thoughts, and dreams, of which only the person is aware. They are accessible to others through verbal report or by way of inference from other behavior (syn. experience, awareness).

consciousness. (a) Monitoring ourselves and our environment so that percepts, memories, and thoughts are represented in awareness. (b) controlling ourselves and our environment so that we are able to initiate and terminate behavioral and cognitive activities.

conservation. The understanding that the amount of a substance remains the same even when its form is changed. See also preoperational stage.

construct validity. The ability of a test or assessment instrument to confirm predictions of the theory underlying some theoretical concept or construct. Confirming results validate both the concept and the assessment instrument simultaneously. See also criterion problem, validity.

constructive memory. Memory that is constructed from inferences as well as input information.

contrast acuity. The ability to see differences in brightness.

contrast sensitivity. In visual perception, the ability to discriminate between dark and light stripes under various conditions.

control group. In an experiment, the group in which the condition under study is absent. See also experimental group.

control processes. Regulatory processes that serve to establish equilibrium or monitor goal-directed activities. See also homeostasis.

controlled stimulation. Conditions in which the perceptual experiences of an organism are systematically varied in order to determine the effect on subsequent performance. For example, rearing kittens in an environment where they see only vertical stripes for the first few months of life.

coping. The process by which a person attempts to manage stressful demands.

core. The part of a concept that contains the properties that are more essential for determining membership in the concept. See also prototype.

cornea. The transparent surface of the eye through which light enters and rays are bent inward to begin image formation. See also lens, pupil, retina.

corpus callosum. A large band of nerve fibers connecting the two cerebral hemispheres.

correlation. See correlation coefficient.

correlation coefficient. An estimate of the degree to which two variables are related.

correlational method. A research method used to determine whether some difference that is not under the researcher's control is associated, or correlated, with another difference of interest. See also coefficient of correlation.

corticotropin-release factor (CRF). A substance secreted by neurons in the hypothalamus in response to stress. It, in turn, is carried through a channel-like structure to the pituitary gland, causing ACTH (the body's major "stress" hormone) to be released. See also adrenocorticotropic hormone.

cortisol. One of the steroid hormones produced by the adrenal glands. It has many effects on the body, including the formation of glucose, the reduction of inflammation, and the retention of water. Its level in the blood is used as a measure of stress. See also adrenal gland, adrenal-cortical system.

counseling psychologist. A trained psychologist, usually with a Ph.D. or Psy.D. degree, who deals with personal problems not classified as illness, such as academic, social, or vocational problems of students. He or she has skills similar to those of the clinical psychologist but usually works in a nonmedical setting. See also clinical psychologist, psychiatrist.

counterconditioning. In behavior therapy, the replacement of a particular response to a stimulus by the establishment of another (usually incompatible) response.

CRF. See corticotropin-release factor.

criterion. (a) A set of scores or other records against which the success of a predictive test is verified. (b) A standard selected as the goal to be achieved in a learning task; for example, the number of runs through a maze to be made without error as an indication that the maze has been mastered.

criterion-keyed method of test construction. Selecting items for a test or assessment instrument by comparing the responses of some criterion group (for example, paranoid individuals) with a control group and retaining only those that discriminate between the two groups.

criterion problem. The difficulty that arises in validating a test or assessment instrument when there is no criterion behavior the investigator is willing to accept as the "true" measure of the concept being evaluated. See also construct validity, validity.

criterion validity. The ability of a test or assessment instrument to predict the behavior it is designed to predict (syn. empirical validity). See also criterion, validity.

critical periods. Crucial time periods in a person's life during which specific events occur if development is to proceed normally.

cross-pressure. Conflicting social influences on an individual's beliefs, attitudes, or behaviors. Usually arises when a person identifies with more than one reference group.

cues to distance. See distance cues.

cultural psychology. An interdisciplinary approach involving psychologists, anthropologists, sociologists, and other social scientists that is concerned with how an individual's culture influences his or her mental representations and psychological processes.

cumulative curve. A graphic record of the responses emitted during an operant conditioning session. The slope of the cumulative curve indicates the rate of response.

D

dark adaptation. The increased sensitivity to light when the subject has been continuously in the dark or under conditions of reduced illumination. See also light adaptation.

data-driven learning. A kind of associative learning in which people have no prior beliefs about the relation that has to be learned; learning is driven only by the input or data. See also belief-driven learning.

db. See decibel.

decibel (db). A measure of sound intensity. A change of 10 decibels corresponds to a change in sound power of 10 times; 20 decibels, a change of 100 times; and so forth.

deductive reasoning. Reasoning about arguments in which the conclusion cannot be false if the premises are true. See also inductive reasoning.

deductively valid. It is impossible for the conclusion of the argument to be false if its premises are true.

defense mechanisms. Strategies that people use to deal with anxiety, which are largely unconscious.

degradation. The process in which enzymes in the membrane of a receiving neuron react with a neurotransmitter to break it up chemically and make it inactive; one method (in addition to reuptake) of terminating a neurotransmitter's action. See also neurotransmitter, reuptake.

deindividuation. A feeling that one has lost his or her personal identity and merged anonymously into a group.

delayed conditioning. A classical conditioning procedure in which the CS begins several seconds or more before the onset of the UCS and continues with it until the response occurs. See also trace conditioning.

delta waves. See electroencephalogram.

delusions. Beliefs that most people would view as misinterpretations of reality. See also hallucination, illusion, paranoid schizophrenia.

dendrite. The specialized portion of the neuron that (together with the cell body) receives impulses from other neurons. See also axon, neuron.

denial. A defense mechanism by which unacceptable impulses or ideas are not perceived or allowed into full awareness. See also defense mechanisms.

denotative meaning. The primary meaning of a symbol, something specific to which the symbol refers or points (for example, my street address is denotative; whether I live in a desirable neighborhood is a connotative meaning secondary to the address itself). See also connotative meaning.

deoxyribonucleic acid (DNA). The basic hereditary material of all organisms; a nucleic acid polymer incorporating the sugar deoxyribose. In higher organisms, the great bulk of DNA is located within the chromosomes.

dependent variable. A variable that is hypothesized to depend on the value of the independent variable. See also independent variable.

depolarization. Change in the resting potential of the nerve cell membrane in the direction of the action potential; the inside of the membrane becomes more positive. See also action potential, resting potential.

depressants. Drugs that depress the central nervous system.

depression. A mood disorder characterized by sadness and dejection, decreased motivation and interest in life, negative thoughts (for example, feelings of helplessness, inadequacy, and low self-esteem) and such physical symptoms as sleep disturbances, loss of appetite, and fatigue. See also mood disorder.

depressive disorders. Having one or more periods of depression without a history of manic episodes.

depth perception. The perception of the distance of an object from the observer. See also distance cues.

determinism. See psychological determinism.

developmental psychologist. A psychologist whose research interest lies in studying the changes that occur as a function of the growth and development of the organism, in particular the relationship between early and later behavior.

diathesis-stress model. See vulnerability-stress model.

dichromatism. Color blindness in which either the red-green or the blue-yellow system is lacking. The red-green form is relatively common; the blue-yellow form is the rarest of all forms of color blindness. See also monochromatism, red-green color blindness, trichromatism.

diencephalon. A cluster of nuclei, located below the cerebral cortex, that is involved in memory. See also amygdala, hippocampus.

difference reduction. A problem-solving strategy in which one sets up subgoals that, when obtained, put one in a state closer to the goal. See also means-ends analysis, working backwards.

difference threshold. The minimum difference in stimulus magnitude necessary to tell two stimuli apart.

differential reinforcement. A procedure in conditioning in which reinforcement is given only in the presence of a certain stimulus. The outcome of this procedure is a conditioned discrimination.

diffusion of responsibility. The tendency for persons in a group situation to fail to take action (as in an emergency) because others are present, thus diffusing the responsibility for acting. A major factor in inhibiting bystanders from intervening in emergencies.

disaster syndrome. A three-stage behavior pattern that is a common reaction to a traumatic event. The person is at first dazed and disoriented, then passive but able to respond to instructions, and finally anxious, apprehensive, and unable to concentrate.

discrimination. A reaction to differences. See also prejudice.

discriminative stimulus. A stimulus that becomes an occasion for an operant response; for example, a knock that leads one to open the door. See also operant behavior.

dishabituation. A return in strength of a response following habituation to a repeated stimulus. Indicates renewed attention on the part of the organism to a change in the stimulus situation. See also habituation.

displaced aggression. Aggression against a person or object other than that which was (or is) the source of frustration. See also scapegoat.

displacement. (a) A defense mechanism whereby a motive that may not be directly expressed (such as sex or aggression) appears in a more acceptable form. See also defense mechanism. (b) The principle of loss of items from short-term memory as too many new items are added. See also chunking, short-term memory.

display rules. A culture's rules for the types of emotions people should experience in certain situations, and the behaviors (including facial expressions) appropriate for each emotion.

dispositional attribution. Attributing a person's actions to internal dispositions (attitudes, traits, motives), as opposed to

situational factors. See also situational attribution.

dissociation. Under certain conditions some thoughts and actions become split off, or dissociated, from the rest of consciousness and function outside of awareness.

dissociative identity disorder. The existence in a single individual of two or more distinct identities or personalities that alternate in controlling behavior. Formerly called multiple personality disorder.

dissonance. (a) In music, an inharmonious combination of sounds; contrasted with consonance. (b) In social psychology, Festinger's term for discomfort arising from a perceived inconsistency between one's attitudes and one's behavior. See also cognitive dissonance.

distance cues. (a) In vision, the monocular cues according to which the distance of objects is perceived—such as superposition of objects, perspective, light and shadow, and relative movement—and the binocular cues used in stereoscopic vision. See also stereoscopic vision. (b) In audition, the corresponding cues governing perception of distance and direction, such as intensity and time differences of sound reaching the two ears.

dizygotic (DZ) twins. Twins developed from separate eggs. They are no more alike genetically than ordinary brothers and sisters and can be of the same or different sexes (syn. fraternal twin). See also monozygotic twins.

DNA. See deoxyribonucleic acid.

dominance. The higher status position when social rank is organized according to a dominance–submission hierarchy; commonly found in human societies and in certain animal groups.

dominant gene. A member of a gene pair which, if present, determines that the individual will show the trait controlled by the gene, regardless of whether the other member of the pair is the same or different (that is, recessive). See also recessive gene.

dopamine. A neurotransmitter of the central nervous system believed to play a role in schizophrenia. It is synthesized from an amino acid by the action of certain body enzymes and, in turn, is converted into norepinephrine. See also neurotransmitter, norepinephrine.

dopamine hypothesis. The hypothesis that schizophrenia is related to an excess of the neurotransmitter dopamine; either schizophrenics produce too much dopamine or have an abnormally large number of dopamine receptors. See also dopamine, schizophrenia.

double blind. An experimental design, often used in drug research, in which neither the investigator nor the patients know which subjects are in the treatment and which in the nontreatment condition until the experiment has been completed.

Down's syndrome. A form of mental deficiency produced by a genetic abnormality (an extra

chromosome on pair 21). Characteristics include a thick tongue, extra eyelid folds, and short, stubby fingers (syn. mongolism).

dream analysis. Talking about the content of one's dreams and then free associating to that content.

dreaming. An altered state of consciousness in which remembered images and fantasies are temporarily confused with external reality.

drive. An internal cause for motivation, which arises independent of events outside the individual. Drive theories of motivation stress the role of physiological states and of homeostasis.

drive-reduction theory. The theory that a motivated sequence of behavior can be best explained as moving from an aversive state of heightened tension (or drive) to a goal state in which the drive is reduced. The goal of the sequence, in other words, is drive reduction. See also drive, incentive theory, motive, need.

drug abuse. Continued use of a drug by a person who is not dependent on it (that is. shows no signs of tolerance, withdrawal, or compulsive craving), despite serious consequences. See also drug dependence.

drug dependence. A pattern of compulsive drug use usually characterized by tolerance (the need to take more and more of the drug to achieve the same effect), withdrawal (unpleasant physical and psychological reactions if the drug is discontinued), and compulsive use (taking more of the drug than intended, being unable to control drug use, or spending a great deal of time trying to obtain the drug). See also drug abuse.

DSM-IV. The fourth edition of the Diagnostic and Statistical Manual of the American Psychiatric Association, revised.

dual-memory theory. A theory that distinguishes between a short-term memory of limited capacity and a virtually unlimited long-term memory. Information is encoded into long-term memory via short-term memory. See also long-term memory, short-term memory.

DZ twins. See dizygotic twins.

E

eardrum. The membrane at the inner end of the auditory canal, leading to the middle ear. See also middle ear.

early selection. Selective attention that occurs in the early stages of recognition, when the organism is constructing a description of the input and before the meaning of the input has been determined. See also late selection, selective attention.

educational psychologist. A psychologist whose research interest lies in the application of psychological principles to the education of children and adults in schools. See also school psychologist.

EEG. See electroencephalogram.

efferent neuron. See motor neuron.

ego. The executive of the personality. See also id, reality principle, superego.

ego analyst. A psychoanalyst, who focuses on the integrative, positive functions of the ego (for example, coping with the environment) rather than the functions of the id (for example, gratifying sexual impulses). Heinz Hartman and David Rapaport are considered ego analysts. See also ego, id, psychoanalyst.

eidetic imagery. The ability to retain visual images of pictures that are almost photographic in clarity. Such images can be described in far greater detail than would be possible from memory alone. See also mental imagery.

elaboration. A memory process wherein one expands verbal material so as to increase the number of ways to retrieve the material.

electroconvulsive therapy (ECT). A mild electric current is applied to the brain to produce a seizure similar to an epileptic convulsion. Also known as electroshock therapy.

electroencephalogram (EEG). A record obtained by attaching electrodes to the scalp (or occasionally to the exposed brain). Among the brain waves observed are alpha waves (8–13 Hz), characteristic of relaxed wakefulness; delta waves (1–3 Hz), a slower wave of high amplitude that occurs during deep sleep; and theta waves (4–7 Hz), a pattern characteristic of the EEG of the hippocampus and indicative of behavioral arousal.

electroshock therapy. See electroconvulsive therapy.

emotion. A complex condition that arises in response to certain affectively toned experiences. See also affective experience.

emotion-focused coping. Ways of reducing anxiety or stress that do not deal directly with the emotion-producing situation; defense mechanisms are a form of emotion-focused coping. See also problem-focused coping.

empathy. Feeling distress when one sees someone else in distress, and experiencing relief when the other person's suffering ends.

empirical validity. See criterion validity.

empiricism. The view that behavior is learned as a result of experience. See also nativism.

encoding. Transforming physical input into a representation that the memory accepts and "placing" it into memory.

endocrine system. A system of ductless glands that discharge their secretions (hormones) into the extracellular fluid around capillaries and hence into the bloodstream. The hormones secreted by the endocrine glands are important integrators of bodily functions. See also hormone.

endorphins. Chemicals produced by our own body that act like morphine to reduce pain.

engineering psychologist. A psychologist who specializes in the relationship between people and machines, seeking, for example, to design machines that minimize human error.

epinephrine. The principal hormone secreted by the adrenal medulla in response to stressful situations. Its effects are similar to those brought about by stimulation of the sympathetic division of the autonomic nervous system (for example, arousal, increased heart rate and blood pressure). It is also an excitatory neurotransmitter in the central nervous system (syn. adrenalin). See also adrenal gland, norepinephrine.

episodic memory. A type of memory that stores facts about personal episodes. The fact or episode is encoded with respect to the memorizer, and often with respect to the specific time and place as well. See also semantic memory.

equilibratory senses. The senses that give discrimination of the position of the body in space and of the movement of the body as a whole. See also kinesthesis, semicircular canals, vestibular sacs.

escape learning. Learning to make a response in order to escape from an aversive event. See also avoidance learning.

ESP. See extrasensory perception.

estrogens. A group of female sex hormones produced principally by the ovaries. They are responsible for the development of female body characteristics and hair distribution, and for preparing the reproductive system for pregnancy. See also androgens.

estrous cycle. Recurring episodes of sexual receptivity that precede ovulation in most female mammals. They are characterized by rising and falling levels of estrogens and progesterone in the bloodstream. See also estrogens, progesterone.

ethology. The study of animal behavior in the natural environment.

evocative interaction. The interaction between individuals and their environments that arises because the behavior of different individuals evokes different responses from others. See also proactive interaction, reactive interaction.

evoked potential. An electric discharge in some part of the nervous system produced by stimulation elsewhere. The measured potential is commonly based on response averaging by a computer.

evolutionary psychology. An area of research that studies how psychological processes have evolved by means of natural selection; those behaviors that aided survival or increased the chance of reproduction have tended to persist through the course of evolutionary history.

exemplar strategy. A categorization strategy in which (a) old instances of a concept are memorized and (b) a new item is declared a member of that concept if it is sufficiently similar to the memorized instances.

excitatory synapse. A synapse at which the neurotransmitter changes the membrane permeability of the receiving cell in the direction of depolarization. See also depolarization, inhibitory synapse, synapse.

expectation. An anticipation or prediction of future events based on past experience and present stimuli.

experimental design. A plan for collecting and treating the data of a proposed experiment.

experimental group. In an experiment, the group of subjects given the treatment whose effect is under investigation. See also control group.

experimental method. The method of investigation of natural events that seeks to control the variables involved so as to more precisely define cause-and-effect relationships. Most frequently done in a laboratory, but need not be. See also observational method, variable.

experimental psychologist. A psychologist who uses experimental methods to study how people (and other animals) react to sensory stimuli, perceive the world, learn and remember, reason and respond emotionally.

explicit memory. The kind of memory that underlies a conscious recollection of something in the past. See also implicit memory.

extinction. (a) The experimental procedure, following classical or operant conditioning, of presenting the conditioned stimulus without the usual reinforcement. (b) The reduction in response that results from this procedure. See also reinforcement.

extracellular fluid. Fluid, including the blood, outside the cells; one of the critical variables monitored in the control of thirst.

extracellular reservoir. Water outside the body's cells, including blood.

extrasensory perception (ESP). Response to external stimuli without any known sensory contact. See also clairvoyance, parapsychology, precognition, psi, psychokinesis, telepathy.

F

facial feedback hypothesis. The hypothesis that people's subjective experience of an emotion is determined by feedback from the physiological arousal caused by engaging in specific facial expressions.

factor analysis. A statistical method used in test construction and in interpreting scores from batteries of tests. The method enables the investigator to compute the minimum number of determiners (factors) required to account for the intercorrelations among the scores on the tests making up the battery.

family therapy. Psychotherapy with the family members as a group rather than treatment of the patient alone. See also group therapy.

feature detector. A general term for any perceptual mechanism that detects distinctive features in a complex display. An example is a line (or edge) detector in vision. Since anything we see can be approximated by a series of line segments at angles to each other, feature detectors have been postulated to be the building blocks for recognizing more complex forms.

Fechner's law. The assertion that the perceived magnitude of a stimulus increases in proportion to the logarithm of its physical intensity.

fetal alcohol syndrome. Mental retardation and multiple deformities of the infant's face and mouth due to exposure to alcohol in the womb.

fight-or-flight response. A pattern of bodily responses that prepares the organism for an emergency. Includes increases in pupil size, heart rate, blood pressure, respiration, muscle tension, and the secretion of epinephrine, norepinephrine, ACTH and other hormones; decreases in saliva, mucous, digestive activity, and the size of blood vessels. See also ACTH, adrenal-cortical system, epinephrine, norepinephrine, sympathetic system.

figure-ground organization. Perceiving a pattern as foreground against a background. Patterns are commonly perceived this way even when the stimuli are ambiguous and the foreground–background relationships are reversible.

file-drawer problem. A problem that arises because studies that fail to obtain positive results are less likely to be published than studies that do obtain positive results. (Failed studies are thus said to "go into the file drawer" rather than being published.) The file-drawer effect causes the database of known studies to be biased toward confirming studies.

filter. Any device that allows some things to pass through it and not others; for example, an electronic device that allows only particular sound frequencies to pass or an optical lens that transmits only certain wavelengths of light. Various types of filters are embedded in the sensory system (optical, mechanical, chemical, neural) that pass some signals and not others. A neuron in the sensory system that is preceded by a filter will respond only to signals that pass through the filter; such a neuron is said to be "tuned" to those signals.

fixation. In Freud's psychoanalytic theory, arrested development through failure to pass beyond one of the earlier stages of psychosexual development or to change the objects of attachment (such as fixation at the oral stage or fixation on the mother).

fixed interval schedule. The organism is reinforced for its first response after a certain amount of time has passed since its last reinforcement.

fixed ratio schedule (FR). The number of responses that has to be made before reinforcement is fixed at a particular value.

flashbulb memory. A vivid and relatively permanent record of the circumstances in which one learned of an emotionally charged, significant event.

flooding. A phobic individual is exposed to the most feared object or situation for an extended period without an opportunity to escape. See also behavior therapy.

flow chart. A diagrammatic representation of the sequence of choices and actions in an activity.

forebrain. The structures located in the front, or anterior, part of the brain.

formal operational stage. Piaget's fourth stage of cognitive development in which the child becomes able to use abstract rules.

fovea. In the eye, a small area in the central part of the retina, packed with cones; the most sensitive part of the retina for detail vision and color vision in daylight. See also cone, retina.

fraternal twins. See dizygotic twins.

free association. A patient is instructed to say everything that comes to mind, regardless of how trivial or embarrassing it may seem.

free recall. A memory task in which a subject is given a list of items (usually one at a time) and is later asked to recall them in any order.

frequency. The number of cycles per second.

frequency theory of pitch. Same as temporal theory of pitch.

Freudian slip. In psychoanalytic theory, a mistake or substitution of words in speaking or writing that is contrary to the speaker's conscious intention and presumably expresses wishes or thoughts repressed to the unconscious.

frontal lobe. A portion of each cerebral hemisphere, in front of the central fissure. See also occipital lobe, parietal lobe, temporal lobe.

frustration. (a) As an event, the thwarting circumstances that block or interfere with goal-directed activity. (b) As a state, the annoyance, confusion, or anger engendered by being thwarted, disappointed, defeated.

frustration-aggression hypothesis. The hypothesis that frustration (thwarting a person's goal-directed efforts) induces an aggressive drive, which, in turn, motivates aggressive behavior.

fundamental. The frequency being played in a musical note.

fundamental attribution error. The tendency to underestimate situational influences on behavior and assume that some personal characteristic of the individual is responsible. See also attribution, dispositional attribution, situational attribution.

functionalism. Studying how the mind works so that an organism can adapt to and function in its environment.

fuzzy concept. A concept in which one primarily relies on prototype properties in determining membership, and hence cannot always be sure of one's decisions. See also prototype.

G

GABA. See gamma-aminobutyric acid.

galvanic skin response (GSR). Changes in electrical conductivity of, or activity in, the skin, detected by a sensitive galvanometer. The reactions are commonly used as an emotional indicator.

gamma-aminobutyric acid (GABA). An important inhibitory neurotransmitter.

ganglia (sing. ganglion). A group of neuronal cell bodies found outside the brain and spinal cord. See also nuclei.

gate control theory of pain. According to this theory, the sensation of pain requires not only that pain receptors be activated, but also that a neural gate in the spinal cord allow these signals to continue to the brain. Pressure stimulation tends to close the gate; this is why rubbing a hurt area can relieve pain. Attitudes, suggestions, and drugs may act to close the gate.

gender constancy. A child's realization that a person's sex does not change with age or appearance (e.g., wearing opposite-sex clothes).

gender identity. A firm sense of oneself as either male or female.

gender schema. A mental structure that organizes the person's perceptual and conceptual world into gender categories (male-female, masculine-feminine). See also gender identity, schema, sex typing.

gene. A segment of a deoxyribonucleic acid molecule. See also chromosome, dominant gene, recessive gene.

general adaptation syndrome. A set of responses that is displayed by all organisms in response to stress.

General Problem Solver (GPS). A computer program to simulate human problem solving by setting up subgoals and reducing the discrepancies to each subsequent subgoal. See also simulation.

generalization. (a) In learning, the detection of a characteristic or principle common to a class of objectcs or events. (b) In conditioning, the principle that once a conditioned response has been established to a given stimulus, similar stimuli will also evoke that response.

generalized anxiety disorder. A constant sense of tension and dread. See also anxiety disorders.

genetics. That branch of biology concerned with heredity and the means by which hereditary characteristics are transmitted.

genital stage. In Freud's psychoanalytic theory, the final stage of psychosexual development, beginning at puberty and culminating in mature adult sexuality. See also psychosexual development.

genotype. In genetics, the characteristics that an individual has inherited and will transmit to his or her descendants, whether or not the individual manifests these characteristics. See also phenotype.

geon. In perception, geometric forms (such as cylinders, cones, blocks, and wedges) that comprise the features of objects. Recognition of an object is good to the extent that the geons of the object can be recovered.

Gestalt psychology. A system of psychological theory concerned primarily with perception that emphasizes pattern, organization, wholes, and field properties.

glia cells. Supporting cells (not neurons) composing a substantial portion of brain tissue; recent speculation suggests that they may play a role in neural conduction.

glutamate. An amino acid that serves as an important excitatory neurotransmitter. See also neurotransmitter.

gonads. Sexual organs that secrete sexual hormones and that manufacture reproductive cells. Female gonads, called ovaries, secrete estrogen and produce egg cells. Male gonads, called testes, secrete androgen (especially testosterone) and produce sperm cells.

graded potentials. Potential changes of varying size induced in a neuron's dendrites or cell body by stimulation from synapses from other neurons. When the graded potentials reach a threshold of depolarization, an action potential occurs. See also action potential, depolarization.

group polarization. The tendency of groups to arrive at decisions that are in the same direction but are more extreme than the mean of the pre-discussion decisions of the individuals in the group.

group therapy. A group discussion or other group activity with a therapeutic purpose participated in by more than one client or patient at a time. See also psychotherapy.

groupthink. A phenomenon in which members of a group are led to suppress their own dissent in the interests of group consensus.

GSR. See galvanic skin response.

gustation. The sense of taste.

H

habit. A learned stimulus-response sequence. See also conditioned response.

habituation. The reduction in the strength of a response to a repeated stimulus. See also dishabituation.

habituation method. A technique used to study perception in infants. It is based on the fact that while infants look directly at novel objects they soon tire of doing so (habituation). Hence one can determine the degree to which an infant perceives an object as novel by measuring the time spent looking at it.

hair cells. In audition, hairlike receptors in the cochlea that bend due to vibration of the basilar membrane and then send electrical impulses to the brain. See also basilar membrane, cochlea.

hallucinations. Sensory experiences in the absence of relevant or adequate external stimulation. See also delusion, illusion, schizophrenia.

hallucinogens. Drugs whose main effect is to change perceptual experience (syn. psychedelic drugs).

halo effect. The tendency to bias our perception of another person in the direction of one particular characteristic that we like or dislike.

hardiness. Resistance to becoming physically or emotionally impaired even in the face of major stressful events.

hashish. See marijuana.

health psychology. See behavioral medicine.

heritability. The percentage of the variance in any trait that is accounted for by genetic differences among the individuals in a population.

hermaphrodite. An individual born with genitals that are ambiguous in appearance or that are in conflict with the internal sex glands. See also transsexual.

heroin. An extremely addictive central nervous system depressant derived from opium. See also opiates.

hertz (Hz). The unit used to measure the frequency of a sound wave, specifically the number of cycles per second.

heterosexual. When a person is sexually attracted primarily to members of the opposite sex.

heuristic. A short-cut procedure that is relatively easy to apply and can often yield the correct answer, but not inevitably so.

heuristic theory of persuasion. A theory that proposes that when we are unwilling or unable to process the content of a persuasive communication, we evaluate its validity by utilizing simple rules of thumb (heuristics).

hidden observer. A part of the mind that is not within awareness seems to be watching the person's experience as a whole.

hierarchies of concepts. The relationships among individual concepts. See also concept.

hierarchy of needs. Maslow's way of classifying needs and motives, from the basic biological needs to the more complex psychological motivations that become important only after the basic needs have been satisfied.

hindbrain. All the structures located in the hind, or posterior, part of the brain, closest to the spinal cord.

hippocampus. A brain structure located below the cerebral cortex that is involved in the consolidation of new memories; its role seems to be that of a cross-referencing system, linking together aspects of a particular memory that are stored in separate parts of the brain.

home sign. A system of gestures used by deaf children that initially functions as a kind of simple pantomime but eventually takes on the properties of a language.

homeostasis. The normal level of functioning that is characteristic of the healthy organism (chapter 2); a constant internal state (chapter 10).

homosexual. When a person is sexually attracted primarily to members of the same sex; the term can be applied to a man or a woman.

hormones. Chemicals secreted by the endocrine glands into the bloodstream and transported to other parts of the body, where they have specific effects on cells that recognize their message. See also endocrine system.

hue. The quality best described by the color's name. See also saturation.

humanistic psychology. A psychological approach that emphasizes the uniqueness of human beings; it is concerned with subjective experience and human values. See also phenomenology.

humanistic therapies. A general term for approaches to psychotherapy that emphasize the individual's subjective experiences, free will, and ability to solve his or her own problems. Client-centered therapy and Gestalt therapy are examples. See also client-centered therapy.

hunger drive. A drive based on food deprivation. See also drive, specific hunger.

hypercomplex cell. A cell in the visual cortex that responds to a particular orientation and length. See also complex cell, feature detector, simple cell.

hyperphagia. Pathological overeating. See also aphagia.

hypnosis. A willing and cooperative individual relinquishes some control over his or her behavior to the hypnotist and accepts some distortion of reality.

hypnotic induction. The procedure used in establishing hypnosis in a responsive person. It usually involves relaxation and stimulated imagination. See also hypnosis.

hypnotic trance. The dreamlike state of heightened suggestibility induced in a subject by a hypnotist. See also posthypnotic suggestion.

hypothalamus. A small but very important structure located just above the brain stem and just below the thalamus. Considered a part of the central core of the brain, it includes centers that govern motivated behavior such as eating, drinking, sex, and emotions; it also regulates endocrine activity and maintains body homeostasis. See also lateral hypothalamus, ventromedial hypothalamus.

hypothesis. A statement that can be tested.

hypothesis testing. Gathering information and testing alternative explanations of some phenomenon.

hypothetical construct. One form of inferred intermediate mechanism. The construct is conceived of as having properties of its own, other than those specifically required for the explanation; for example, drive that is inferred from the behavior of a deprived organism and is used in the explanation of later behavior.

Hz. See hertz.

I

iconic memory. Extends the duration of briefly presented stimuli

id. The most primitive part of the personality and the part from which the ego and the superego later develop. See also ego, libido, pleasure principle, superego.

ideal self. Our conception of the kind of person we would like to be.

identical twins. See monozygotic twins.

identification. Respecting or admiring other individuals or groups and obeying their norms and adopting their beliefs, attitudes, and behaviors in order to be like them and identify with them.

identification figures. Adult models (especially parents) copied, partly unconsciously, by the child. See also identification.

identity crisis. In Erikson's theory of psychosocial development, a period of self-doubt and active questioning about one's definition of self ("Who am I?" "Where am I going?") which typically takes place during adolescence. See also identity status, psychosocial stages.

identity status. An individual's position on Erikson's identity-formation continuum, which includes identity achievement, foreclosure, moratorium, and identity diffusion (or confusion). See also identity crisis.

illusion. A percept that is false or distorted. See also delusions, hallucination.

imaginal thought. Images, particularly visual ones, that we can "see" in our mind.

imitation. Behavior that is modeled on or copies that of another. See also identification.

implicit memory. The kind of memory that underlies perceptual and cognitive skills. It is often expressed as an improvement on some perceptual or cognitive task without any conscious recollection of the experiences that led to the improvement. See also explicit memory.

impossible figures. A figure in which recognition is normal when attending to each part, but the parts do not fuse into a single coherent picture.

imprinting. A type of early learning in which a newborn forms an attachment with some kind of model (normally, a parent).

incentive. An external event or stimulus that is the target of a motivation, and that can serve as a reward. Incentive theories of motivation stress the role of external targets in eliciting and satisfying motivational states.

incentive theory. A theory of motivation that emphasizes the importance of negative and positive incentives in determining behavior; internal drives are not the sole instigators of activity. See also drive-reduction theory.

independent variable. A variable that is independent of what the participant does. See also dependent variable.

individual differences. Relatively persistent dissimilarities in structure of behavior among persons or members of the same species.

induced motion. The perception of motion caused when a larger object surrounding a smaller object moves; the smaller object may appear to be the one that is moving even if it is stationary. See also stroboscopic motion.

inductive reasoning. Reasoning about arguments in which it is improbable that the conclusion is false if the premises are true. See also deductive reasoning.

inductive strength. It is improbable that the conclusion is false if the premises are true.

industrial psychologist. A psychologist who is concerned with such problems as selecting people most suitable for particular jobs, developing job training programs, and figuring out the determinants of consumer behavior.

infancy. The period of helplessness and dependency in humans and other organisms; in humans, roughly the first 2 years.

information-processing model. In general, a model based on assumptions regarding the flow of information through a system; usually best realized in the form of a computer program. In cognitive psychology, theories of how the mind functions are often represented in the form of an information-processing model. By simulating the model on a computer, one can study the properties and implications of the theory. See also cognitive psychology, computer simulation, model.

informed consent. The participants must enter a study voluntarily and be permitted to withdraw from it at any time without penalty if they so desire.

inhibitory synapse. A synapse at which the neurotransmitter changes the membrane permeability of the receiving cell in the direction of the resting potential; in other words, keeps it from firing. See also excitatory synapse, synapse.

inner ear. The internal portion of the ear containing, in addition to the cochlea, the vestibular sacs and the semicircular canals. See also cochlea, semicircular canals, vestibular sacs.

insight. (a) In problem-solving experiments the perception of relationships leading to solution. Such a solution can be repeated promptly when the problem is again confronted. (b) In psychotherapy, the discovery by the individuals of dynamic connections between earlier and later events so that they come to recognize the roots of their conflicts.

insomnia. Dissatisfaction with the amount or quality of one's sleep. See also apnea.

instinct. An innately determined behavior that is specific to a certain species and appears in the same form in all members of the species.

insulin. The hormone secreted by the pancreas. See also hormone.

intellectualization. A defense mechanism whereby a person tries to gain detachment from an emotionally threatening situation by dealing with it in abstract, intellectual terms. See also defense mechanisms.

intelligence. (a) That which a properly standardized intelligence test measures. (b) The ability to learn from experience, think in abstract terms, and deal effectively with one's environment. See also intelligence quotient, mental age.

intelligence quotient (IQ). A ratio of mental age to chronological age.

interactionism. (a) Within personality-development theory, a framework in which personality is seen as resulting from the interaction between the child's genotype (inherited characteristics) and the environment in which he or she is raised. (b) In personality theory, a framework in which behavior is seen as resulting from the interaction between consistent personality dispositions or traits and the situations in which people find themselves. See also evocative interaction, proactive interaction, reactive interaction.

interaural intensity difference. The difference in intensity of sounds reaching the two ears; it aids in the localization of sounds at high frequencies. See also interaural time difference.

interaural time difference. The difference in time between the arrival of sound waves at the two ears; it aids in the localization of sounds at low frequencies. See also interaural intensity.

interference. A factor that can impair retrieval from long-term memory. It arises when different items are associated with the same retrieval cue; attempted retrieval of one of these items can be blocked by the inadvertent retrieval of the other item. See also long-term memory, retrieval cue.

interjudge reliability. The consistency achieved by two or more observers when assessing or rating some behavior (for example, in rating the aggressiveness of nursery-school children). Also called interater agreement. See also reliability.

intermittent reinforcement. See partial reinforcement.

internalization. We are convinced that the influencer is correct and change our beliefs and attitudes. See also compliance, identification.

internal consistency. A form of test reliability. Specifically, the homogeneity of a set of items on a test, the degree to which they are all measuring the same variable. See also reliability.

interneurons. Neurons in the central nervous system that receive messages from sensory neurons and send them to other interneurons or to motor neurons. See also motor neuron, sensory neuron.

interpretation. In psychoanalysis, the analyst's calling attention to the patient's resistances in order to facilitate the flow of associations; also the explanation of symbols, as in dream interpretation. See also resistance.

interrater agreement. See interjudge reliability.

interval schedules. Reinforcement is available only after a certain time interval has elapsed. See also ratio schedules.

intervening variable. A process inferred to occur between stimulus and response, thus accounting for one response rather than another to the same stimulus. The intervening variable may be inferred without further specification, or it may be given concrete properties and become an object of investigation.

interview. A conversation between an investigator (the interviewer) and a subject (the respondent) used for gathering pertinent data for the subject's benefit (as in the psychotherapeutic interview) or for information-gathering (as in a sample survey).

intracellular fluid. Water contained within the body's cells; one of the critical variables monitored in the control of thirst.

intracellular reservoir. Water inside the body's cells.

introspection. The observation and recording of one's own perceptions, thoughts, and feelings.

introspective method. See introspection.

introversion–extraversion. The personality dimension first identified by Carl Jung that refers to the degree to which a person's basic orientation is turned inward toward the self or outward toward the external world. At the introversion end are shy individuals who tend to withdraw into themselves; at the extraversion end are sociable individuals who prefer to be with others.

ion channel. A specialized protein molecule that permits specific ions to enter or leave cells. Some ion channels open or close in response to appropriate neurotransmitter molecules; others open or close in response to voltage changes across the cell membrane. This process regulates depolarization and the firing of nerve impulses.

ion pump. A protein molecule that helps to maintain an uneven distribution of electrically charged ions across the cell membrane of a neuron by pumping them into or out of the cell. Ion pumps work with ion channels to regulate depolarization and firing of nerve impulses. See also depolarization, ion channel.

J

James–Lange theory. A classical theory of emotion, named for the two men who independently proposed it. The theory states that the stimulus first leads to bodily responses, and then the awareness of these responses constitutes the experience of emotion. See also Cannon-Bard theory, cognitive-appraisal theory.

jnd. See just noticeable difference.

just noticeable difference (jnd). The minimum difference in stimulus magnitude necessary to tell two stimuli apart.

K

key-word method. A technique for learning vocabulary of a foreign language via an intermediate key word related to the sound of the foreign word and the meaning of the English equivalent. See also mnemonics.

kinesthesis. The muscle, tendon, and joint senses, yielding discrimination of position and movement of parts of the body. See also equilibratory senses.

L

late selection. Selective attention that occurs in the later stages of recognition, after the organism has determined the meaning of the input. See also early selection.

latency. A temporal measure of response, referring to the time delay between the occurrence of the stimulus and the onset of the response. See also psychosexual development.

latency period. In Freud's psychoanalytic theory, a period in middle childhood, roughly the years 6–12, when both sexual and aggressive impulses are said to be in a quiescent state.

latent content. The underlying significance of a dream (such as the motives of wishes being expressed by it) as interpreted from the manifest content. See also manifest content.

lateral fissure. A deep fissure at the side of each cerebral hemisphere, below which lies the temporal lobe (syn. fissure of Sylvius).

lateral hypothalamus (LH). An area of the hypothalamus important to the regulation of food intake. Electrical stimulation of this area will make an experimental animal start to eat; destruction of brain tissue here causes an animal to stop eating. See also hypothalamus, ventromedial hypothalamus.

law of effect. The principle that any behavior that is followed by reinforcement is strengthened; from the infinite pool of possible responses, those that lead to reinforcement are repeated, whereas those that do not are extinguished. See also reinforcement.

learned helplessness. A condition of apathy or helplessness created experimentally by subjecting an organism to unavoidable trauma (such as shock, heat, or cold). Being unable to avoid or escape an aversive situation produces a feeling of helplessness that generalizes to subsequent situations.

learning. A relatively permanent change in behavior that occurs as the result of practice.

learning curve. A graph plotting the course of learning, in which the vertical axis (ordinate) plots a measure of proficiency (amount per unit time, time per unit amount, errors made, and so on), while the horizontal axis (abscissa) represents some measure of practice (trials, time, and so on).

left hemisphere. The left cerebral hemisphere. Controls the right side of the body and, for most people, speech and other logical, sequential activities (syn. major hemisphere). See also cerebral hemispheres, corpus callosum, right hemisphere, split-brain subject.

lens. The part of the eye that helps focus light rays on a single point of the retina. See also cornea, pupil, retina.

lesbian. Female homosexual. See homosexual.

LH. See lateral hypothalamus.

libido. (Latin for lust.) In Freud's psychoanalytic theory, the psychic energy of the id. See also id.

lie detector. See polygraph, voice stress analyzer.

light adaptation. The decreased sensitivity of the eye to light when the subject has been continuously exposed to high levels of illumination. See also dark adaptation.

lightness. In sensory psychology, the degree to which a light appears white (which is different from brightness, in that a dimly lit object can still appear white).

lightness constancy. The tendency to see a familiar object as of the same lightness, regardless of light and shadow that change its stimulus properties. See also perceptual constancy.

liking. Friendship and the early stages of more intimate relationships.

limbic system. A set of structures that are closely interconnected with the hypothalamus and appear to impose additional controls over some of the instinctive behaviors regulated by the hypothalamus and the brain stem.

linear perspective. In perspective, a monocular cue for depth. When parallel lines appear to converge, they are perceived as vanishing in the distance. See also relative height, relative size, superposition.

linguistic relativity hypothesis. The proposition that one's thought processes, the way one perceives the world, are determined by one's language.

lithium carbonate. A compound based on lithium, an element related to sodium. Has been successful in treating bipolar disorders. See also bipolar disorder.

localized functions. Behavior controlled by known areas of the brain; for example, vision is localized in the occipital lobes.

location constancy. The tendency to perceive the place at which a resting object is located as remaining the same even though the relationship to the observer has changed. See also perceptual constancy.

long-term memory (LTM). When information has to be retained for intervals as brief as a few minutes or as long as a lifetime. See also short-term memory.

long-term potentiation. A phenomenon concerning the neural bases of learning. Once stimulated, neurons will show an increase in their rate of activity when subsequently stimulated (at least up to a period of months).

longitudinal study. A research method that studies an individual through time, taking measurements at periodic intervals. See also case history.

loudness. An intensity dimension of hearing correlated with the amplitude of the sound waves that constitute the stimulus. Greater amplitudes yield greater loudnesses. See also pitch, timbre.

LSD. See lysergic acid diethylamide.

LTP. See long-term potentiation.

lucid dream. A dream in which events seem so normal (lacking the bizarre and illogical character of most dreams) that the dreamer believes he or she is awake and conscious.

lunch-line effect. An example of peripheral attention. Even though you may be absorbed in conversation in a room full of people, the sound of your name in another conversation will usually attract your attention; this phenomenon suggests a nonconscious monitoring of that conversation.

lysergic acid diethylamide. A powerful psychoactive drug capable of producing extreme alterations in consciousness, hallucinations, distortions in perception, and unpredictable mood swings.

M

magnetic resonance imaging (MRI). A computer-based scanning procedure that uses strong magnetic fields and radiofrequency pulses to generate a picture of a cross section of the brain or body. Provides greater precision than the CT scanner.

major hemisphere. See left hemisphere.

manic-depression. See bipolar disorder.

manifest content. The remembered content of a dream, the characters, and their actions, as distinguished from the inferred latent content. See also latent content.

mantra. See meditation.

MAO. See monamine oxidase.

MAOI. See monoamine oxidase inhibitor.

marijuana. The dried leaves of the hemp plant (cannabis); also known as hashish, "pot," or "grass." Hashish is actually an extract of the plant material and, hence, is usually stronger than marijuana. Intake may enhance sensory experiences and produce a state of euphoria.

marital therapy. Psychotherapy with both members of a couple aimed at resolving problems in their relationship (syn. couples therapy). See also psychotherapy.

masochism. A pathological desire to inflict pain on oneself or to suffer pain at the hands of others. See also sadism.

maternal drive. The drive, particularly in animals, induced in the female through bearing and nursing young, leading to nestbuilding, retrieving, and other forms of care. See also drive.

maturation. An innately determined sequence of growth and change that is relatively independent of external events.

maze. A device used in the study of animal and human learning, consisting of a correct path and blind alleys.

mean. The technical term for an arithmetic average. See also measure of central tendency.

means-ends analysis. A problem-solving strategy in which one compares one's current state to the goal state in order to find the most important difference between them; eliminating this difference then becomes the main subgoal. See also difference reduction, working backwards.

measurement. A system for assigning numbers to variables.

measure of central tendency. A value representative of a frequency distribution, around which other values are dispersed; for example, the mean, the median, or mode of a distribution of scores. See also mean, median, mode.

measure of variation. A measure of the dispersion or spread of scores in a frequency distribution, such as the range or the standard deviation. See also standard deviation.

mechanisms of defense. See defense mechanisms.

medial-temporal-lobe amnesia. A form of amnesia or memory loss that results from damage to the middle of the temporal lobe of the brain.

median. The score of the middle case when cases are arranged in order of size of score. See also measure of central tendency.

meditation. Achieving an altered state of consciousness by performing certain rituals and exercises.

medulla. The lowest section of the brainstem, a slight enlargement of the spinal cord as it enters the skull; the point at which the major nerve tracts cross over so that the right cerebral hemisphere controls the left side of the body, and the left cerebral hemisphere controls the right side.

memory decay. A major cause of forgetting in short-term memory in which information simply fades with time.

memory span. The maximum number of items (almost always between five and nine) that can be recalled in order. See also chunking, short-term memory.

memory trace. The inferred change in the nervous system that persists between the time something is learned and the time it is recalled.

menarche. The first menstrual period.

mental age (MA). A scale unit proposed by Binet for use in intelligence testing. If an intelligence test is properly standardized, a representative group of children of age 6 should earn an average mental age of 6, those of age 7, a mental age of 7, and so on. A child whose MA is above his or her chronological age (CA) is advanced; one whose MA lags behind is retarded. See also chronological age, intelligence quotient.

mental imagery. Mental representations that are picture-like. Not the same as eidetic imagery. See also eidetic imagery.

mental model. A concrete mental representation of a problem situation that may be useful in solving the problem. See also mental representation.

mental practice. The imagined rehearsal of a perceptual-motor skill in the absence of gross body movements. For example, picturing yourself serving a tennis ball and making mental corrections when the movement seems faulty, without actually moving your arm.

mental representation. A hypothesized "inner representation" of objects and events in human memory. Some theorists endow mental representations with the very properties they are alleged to represent (a "picture of the mind"); others argue that they involve an abstract characterization much like the propositional logic used by mathematicians (the way information is represented in a digital computer); and yet others believe that they are best thought of as a kind of private symbol system that may vary from person to person. The general concept is pervasive in cognitive psychology. See also mental imagery.

mental retardation. Subnormal intellectual functioning with impairment in social adjustment.

mental rotation. The notion that a mental image of an object can be rotated in the mind in fashion analogous to rotating the real object.

mesolimbic dopamine system. A set of neurons in the upper brainstem that is crucial to incentive motivation for food and other rewards. The neurons begin in the midbrain and project their axons upward to limbic structures in the forebrain, where they release dopamine as a neurotransmitter.

meta-analysis. A statistical technique that treats the accumulated studies of a particular phenomenon as a single grand experiment and each study as a single observation.

method of constant stimuli. A psychophysical method for determining sensory thresholds. Stimuli with magnitudes varying around the threshold are presented to a subject many times to see what percentage of the time the subject detects them. See also psychophysical methods.

method of loci. An aid to serial memory. Verbal material is transformed into mental images, which are then located at successive positions along a visualized route, such as an imaged walk through the house or down a familiar street.

midbrain. The middle of the brain.

middle ear. The part of the ear that transmits sound waves from the eardrum to the oval window of the inner ear by means of three tiny connecting bones (malleus, incus, and stapes). See also cochlea, eardrum, inner ear, oval window.

minimal risk. The principle that risks anticipated in the research should be no greater than those ordinarily encountered in daily life.

minor hemisphere. See right hemisphere.

mnemonics. Systems for aiding memory.

mode. The most frequent score in a distribution, or the class interval in which the greatest number or cases fall. See also measure of central tendency.

model. (a) Miniature systems are often constructed according to a logical, mathematical, or physical model. That is, the principles according to which data are organized and made understandable parallel those of the model; for instance, the piano keyboard is a model for understanding the basilar membrane; the thermostat is a model for the feedback principle of homeostasis. (b) In behavior therapy, one who models or performs behaviors that the therapist wishes the patient to imitate.

modeling. The process by which a person learns behaviors by observing and imitating others.

mongolism. See Down's syndrome.

monoamine oxidase (MAO). One of the enzymes responsible for the breakdown of a group of neurotransmitters called biogenic amines (norepinephrine, dopamine, and serotonin are examples); believed to be important in the regulation of emotion. Drugs that inhibit the action of this enzyme (MAO inhibitors) are used in treating depression. See also antidepressant, monamine oxidase inhibitor, neurotransmitter.

monoamine oxidase inhibitor (MAOI). A class of drugs used to treat depression; the drug inhibits the action of an enzyme (monoamine oxidase) that breaks down certain neurotransmitters (such as dopamine, norepinephrine, and serotonin), thereby prolonging the action of these neurotransmitters. See also antidepressant, monoamine oxidase, neurotransmitter.

monochromatism. Total color blindness, the visual system being achromatic. A rare disorder. See also dichromatism, trichromatism.

monocular cues. See distance cues.

monozygotic (MZ) twins. Twins developed from a single egg. They are always of the same sex and commonly much alike in appearance, although some characteristics may be in mirror image; for example one right-handed, the other left-handed (syn. identical twins). See also dizygotic twins.

mood disorder. A mental disorder characterized by disturbances of mood. Depression, mania (exaggerated excitement), and bipolar disorders in which the individual experiences both extremes of mood are examples. See also bipolar disorder, depression.

moon illusion. A perceptual illusion that makes the moon appear as much as 50 percent larger when it is near the horizon than when it is at its zenith, even though at both locations the moon produces the same retinal image.

moral realism. In Piaget's theory of cognitive development, the preoperational child's treatment of social rules as absolute and unchangeable. Also see preoperational stage.

morpheme. Any small linguistic unit that carries meaning. See also phoneme.

motion aftereffect. The illusion of movement in a static object that occurs after viewing motion for an extended period of time; the aftereffect occurs in the opposite direction of the viewed motion.

motion parallax. A monocular cue to depth perception. When you are moving rapidly, nearby objects appear to move more quickly in the opposite direction than distant objects do. This difference in apparent speed provides a cue to the respective depths of the objects.

motivation. A condition that energizes behavior and gives it direction.

motive. Any condition of the organism that affects its readiness to start on or continue in a sequence of behavior.

motor neuron. A neuron, or nerve cell, that conveys messages from the brain or spinal cord to the muscles and glands (syn. efferent neuron). See also sensory neuron.

motoric thought. Sequences of "mental movements."

MRI. See magnetic resonance imaging.

multiple personality. See dissociative identity disorder.

multivariate experiment. A type of experiment that involves the simultaneous manipulation of several independent variables. See also independent variable.

myelin sheath. The fuzzy sheath surrounding certain nerve fibers known as myelinated fibers. Impulses travel faster and with less energy expenditure in myelinated fibers than in unmyelinated fibers.

MZ twins. See monozygotic twins.

N

nREM. The four stages of sleep (excluding REM sleep) in which eye movements are virtually absent, heart and breathing rates decrease markedly, the muscles are relaxed, and the brain's metabolic rate decreases 25 to 30 percent compared to wakefulness.

nanometer (nm). A billionth of a meter. Wavelength of light is measured in nanometers.

narcissism. Self-love; in Freud's psychoanalytic theory, the normal expression of pregenital development.

narcolepsy. Recurring, irresistible attacks of drowsiness with the likelihood of falling asleep at any time.

narcotics. See opiates.

nativism. The view that behavior is innately determined. See also empiricism.

nature-nurture issue. The problem of determining the relative importance of heredity (nature) and the result of upbringing in a particular environment (nurture) on behavior.

need. A physical state involving any lack or deficit within the organism. See also drive, motive.

negative incentive. An object or circumstance away from which behavior is directed when the object or circumstance is perceived or anticipated. See also positive incentive.

negative reinforcement. Reinforcing a response by the removal of an aversive stimulus. See also negative reinforcer.

negative reinforcer. Any stimulus that, when removed following a response, increases the probability of the response. Loud noises, electric shock, and extreme heat or cold classify as negative reinforcers. See also punishment.

negative symptoms. In schizophrenia, behavioral deficits such as flattened affect, apathy, and poverty of speech. Presumed to result from abnormalities in brain structure. See also positive symptoms, schizophrenia.

nerve. A bundle of elongated axons belonging to hundreds or thousands of neurons. See also axon, neuron.

nerve cell. See neuron.

neuroimaging. Newly developed techniques that can create visual images of a brain in action, with an indication of which regions of the brain show the most neural activity during a particular task. One of the most widely used neuroimaging techniques is positron emission tomography (PET).

neuron. A specialized cell that transmits neural impulses or messages to other neurons, glands, and muscles.

neuroreceptor molecule. A protein molecule in a cell membrane that is sensitive to a particular chemical, such as a neurotransmitter. When the appropriate chemical activates a neuroreceptor molecule, changes occur in the cell membrane that either increase or decrease its permeability. Some neurotransmitters have an excitatory effect when locked to their neuroreceptors; others have an inhibitory effect. See also neurotransmitter.

neurosis (pl. neuroses). A mental disorder in which the individual is unable to cope with anxieties and conflicts and develops symptoms that he or she finds distressing, such as obsessions, compulsions, phobias, or anxiety attacks. In Freud's psychoanalytic theory, neurosis results from the use of defense mechanisms to ward off anxiety caused by unconscious conflicts. No longer a diagnostic category of DSM-IV. See also anxiety disorders, obsessive-compulsive disorder, phobia.

neurotic anxiety. Fear that is out of proportion to the actual danger posed (such as stage fright). See also anxiety, objective anxiety.

neuroticism. The name of the emotional instability–stability dimension in Eysenck's factor-analytic theory of personality. Moody, anxious, and maladjusted individuals are at the neurotic or unstable end; calm, well-adjusted individuals are at the other. See also introversion–extraversion.

neurotransmitter. A chemical that diffuses across the synaptic gap and stimulates the next neuron. See also dopamine, epinephrine, norepinephrine, serotonin.

NMDA. See N-methyl D-aspartate receptor.

N-methyl D-aspartate receptor (NMDA receptor). A receptor molecule that requires two successive chemical signals to activate it; the first signal makes the receptor more responsive (a phenomenon known as long-term potentiation) so that when a second chemical signal occurs (the neurotransmitter glutanate), the receptor is activated. NMDA receptors are particularly dense in the hippocampus and may explain how memories are stored by linking neurons to form new neural circuits. See also hippocampus, neurotransmitter, neuroreceptor molecule.

nonconscious processes. A considerable body of research indicates that we register and evaluate stimuli that we are not consciously aware of. The stimuli are said to influence us unconsciously or to operate at an unconscious (or subconscious) level of awareness. See also consciousness.

noradrenaline. See norepinephrine.

norepinephrine. One of the hormones secreted by the adrenal medulla; its action in emotional excitement is similar in some, but not all, respects to that of epinephrine. It is also a neurotransmitter of the central nervous system. Norepinephrine synapses can be either excitatory or inhibitory. Believed to play a role in depression and bipolar disorders (syn. noradrenaline). See also adrenal gland, epinephrine.

normal curve. The plotted form of the normal distribution.

normal distribution. The standard symmetrical bell-shaped frequency distribution, whose properties are commonly used in making statistical inferences from measures derived from samples. See also normal curve.

nuclei (sing. nucleus). A collection of nerve cell bodies grouped in the brain or spinal cord. See also ganglia.

null hypothesis. A statistical hypothesis that any difference observed among treatment conditions occurs by chance and does not reflect a true difference. Rejection of the null hypothesis means that we believe the treatment conditions are actually having an effect.

O

obesity. Being 30 percent or more in excess of one's appropriate body weight.

object constancy. See perceptual constancy.

object permanence. The awareness that an object continues to exist even when it is not present.

object recognition. Determining the meaning of an object.

object relations theory. An outgrowth of psychoanalytic theory that deals with the person's attachments to others over the course of development. Emphasizes ego functioning more than did classical psychoanalytic theory.

object size. The size of an object as determined from measurement at its surface. When size constancy holds, the observer perceives a distant object as being near its object size. See also retinal size.

objective anxiety. Fear that is proportionate to the danger posed.

observational method. Studying events as they occur in nature, without experimental control of variables; for instance, studying the nest-building of birds, or observing children's behavior in a play situation. See also experimental method.

obsessions. Persistent intrusions of unwelcome thoughts, images, or impulses that elicit anxiety. See also compulsion, obsessive-compulsive disorder.

obsessive-compulsive disorder. An anxiety disorder taking one of three forms: (a) persistent intrusions of unwelcome thoughts, images, or impulses that elicit anxiety (obsessions); (b) irresistible urges to carry out

certain acts or rituals that reduce anxiety (compulsions); (c) both of these in combination. See also anxiety disorders.

occipital lobe. A portion of the cerebral hemisphere, behind the parietal and temporal lobes. See also frontal lobe, parietal lobe, temporal lobe.

Oedipal conflict. In Freud's psychoanalytic theory, the conflict that arises during the phallic stage of psychosexual development in which the individual is sexually attracted to the parent of the opposite sex and perceives the same-sex parent as a rival. See also phallic stage, psychosexual development.

olfaction. The sense of smell.

olfactory bulb. A region of the brain involved in olfaction (smell); it is a way station between the receptors in the nasal passage and the olfactory cortex.

olfactory epithelium. The specialized skin within the nasal cavity that contains the receptors for the sense of smell.

operant behavior. Behavior defined by the stimulus to which it leads rather than by the stimulus that elicits it; such as behavior leading to reward (syn. instrumental behavior).

operant conditioning. Certain responses are learned because they operate on, or affect, the environment. See also classical conditioning.

operation. A mental routine for separating, combining, and otherwise transforming information in a logical manner.

opiates. Drugs that diminish physical sensation and the capacity to respond to stimuli by depressing the central nervous system. See also heroin.

opinion molecule. A cognitive unit comprising a belief, an attitude, and a perception of social support for the individual's view on the matter. For example, "I believe that Democrats are compassionate toward the poor" (belief); "I prefer having Democrats in office" (attitude); "And I think the American people agree with me" (perception of social support).

opioid receptors. Neuroreceptor molecules in specific areas of the brain and spinal cord to which a group of neurotransmitters, called endorphins, bind. These molecules also have an affinity for opiates. There are several distinct types of opioid receptors; each has a different affinity for binding with various opiates. See also neurotransmitter, neuroreceptor molecule.

opponent-color theory. A theory of color perception that postulates two types of color-sensitive units that respond in opposite ways to the two colors of an opponent pair. One type of unit responds to red or green, the other to blue or yellow. Since a unit cannot respond in two ways at once, reddish-greens and yellowish-blues cannot occur. See also trichromatic theory, two-stage color theory.

optic chiasma. A cross-over junction of the optic nerves, located near the base of the

brain, where nerve fibers from the inner half of each retina (nearest the nose) cross to the opposite side of the brain. The resulting left optic tract carries data about objects seen in the right-hand side of the field of vision, and the right optic tract carries signals from objects seen on the left.

optic nerve. In vision, a nerve formed out of axons of the ganglion cells, which leads to the brain. See also bipolar cells. ganglia, photoreceptors, retina.

oral stage. In Freud's psychoanalytic theory, the first stage of psychosexual development; pleasure derives from the lips and mouth, as in sucking at the mother's breast. See also psychosexual development.

organizational psychologist. See industrial psychologist.

orienting reflex. (a) A nonspecific response to change in stimulation involving depression of cortical alpha rhythm, galvanic skin response, pupillary dilation, and complex vasomotor responses (a term introduced by Russian psychologists). (b) Head or body movements that orient the organism's receptors to those parts of the environment in which stimulus changes are occurring.

osmoreceptors. Hypothesized cells in the hypothalamus that respond to dehydration by stimulating the release of ADH by the pituitary gland, which, in turn, signals the kidneys to reabsorb water into the bloodstream. See also antidiuretic hormone, volumetric receptors.

otoliths. "Ear stones." See vestibular sacs.

outer ear. The external ear and auditory canal, whose purpose is to funnel sound waves towards the inner ear. See also inner ear, middle ear.

oval window. A membrane on the cochlea of the inner ear that receives vibrations from the ear drum via three connecting bones (malleus, incus, and stapes). Vibrations at the oval window set up similar vibrations in the internal fluid of the cochlea, ultimately activating the hair cells that serve as auditory receptors. See also cochlea, hair cells.

ovarian hormones. See estrogen, progesterone.

overextension. Tendency to apply a new word too widely.

overtone. A higher frequency tone, a multiple of the fundamental frequency, that occurs when a tone is sounded by a musical instrument. See also timbre.

ovulation. The release of a mature fertile egg cell from the follicle.

P

PAG. A region of the midbrain called the perioqueductal gray, or PAG for short, that is involved in sensing pain. When PAG neurons are active, a neural gate is closed and consequently the sensation of pain is diminished.

pancreas. A bodily organ situated near the stomach. As a duct gland, it secretes pancreatic juice into the intestines, but some specialized cells function as an endocrine gland, secreting the hormone insulin into the bloodstream. See also endocrine gland.

panic attack. An episode of acute and overwhelming apprehension or terror.

panic disorder. An anxiety disorder in which the individual has sudden and inexplicable episodes of terror and feelings of impending doom accompanied by physiological symptoms of fear (such as heart palpitations, shortness of breath, muscle tremors, faintness). See also anxiety, anxiety disorders.

parallel processing. A theoretical interpretation of information processing in which several sources of information are all processed simultaneously. See also serial processing.

paranoid. An individual who has delusions of persecution.

paranoid schizophrenia. A schizophrenic reaction in which the patient has delusions of persecution. See also schizophrenia.

paraphilias. Same as sexual perversions. Sexual attraction to unusual objects as well as sexual activities that are unusual in nature. Examples are fetishism (sexual attractions to an inanimate object or some specific nongenital part of a person), exhibitionism (obtaining sexual gratification by exposing one's genitals to an unwilling observer), and pedophilia (a preference for obtaining sexual gratification through contact with youngsters who are legally underage).

parapsychology. Phenomena that are "beside psychology," including telepathy, clairvoyance, precognition, psychokinesis.

parasympathetic system. A division of the automatic nervous system, the nerve fibers of which originate in the cranial and sacral portions of the spinal cord. Active in relaxed or quiescent states of the body and to some extent antagonistic to the sympathetic division, or system. See also sympathetic system.

parathyroid glands. Endocrine glands adjacent to the thyroid gland in the neck, whose hormones regulate calcium metabolism, thus maintaining the normal excitability of the nervous system. Parathyroid inadequacy leads to tetany. See also endocrine system.

parietal lobe. A portion of the cerebral hemisphere, behind the central fissure and between the frontal and occipital lobes. See also frontal lobe, occipital lobe, temporal lobe.

partial reinforcement. Reinforcing a given response only some proportion of the times it occurs (syn. intermittent reinforcement). See also reinforcement, reinforcement schedule.

passionate love. Contrasted with companionate love. An intensely emotional state in which tender and sexual feelings, elation and pain, anxiety and relief, altruism and jealousy coexist in a confusion of feelings. See also companionate love.

path analysis. A correlational procedure that divides an overall correlation between two variables into separate components or paths. For example, path analysis can help to determine whether a link between childhood temper tantrums and later occupational problems is direct or is due to some intervening link like dropping out of school.

pattern recognition. The perceptual process of determining what an object is.

PCP. See phencyclidine.

peak experiences. Transient moments of self-actualization.

percept. The result of the perceptual process; that which the individual perceives.

perception. The study of how we integrate sensory information into percepts of objects, and how we then use those percepts to get around in the world. See also sensory processes.

perceptual constancy. Keeping the appearance of objects constant even though their impressions on the retina are constantly changing. See also color constancy, lightness constancy, location constancy, shape constancy, size constancy.

perceptual defense. The supposed prevention of an individual's conscious perceptual system from recognizing an anxiety-producing situation perceived by the individual's unconscious perceptual system.

perceptual patterning. The tendency to perceive stimuli according to principles such as proximity, similarity, continuity, and closure. Emphasized by Gestalt psychologists. See also figure-ground organization, gestalt psychology.

performance. Overt behavior, as distinguished from knowledge or information not translated into action. The distinction is important in theories of learning.

peripheral nervous system. The nerves connecting the brain and spinal cord to other parts of the body. See also autonomic nervous system, somatic nervous system.

personal construct. The dimensions that individuals themselves use to interpret themselves and their social worlds. See also Role Construct Repertory Test.

personality. The distinctive and characteristic patterns of thought, emotion, and behavior that define an individual's personal style of interacting with the physical and social environment.

personality assessment. The measurement or appraisal of personality.

personality disorders. Ingrained habitual, and rigid patterns of behavior or character that severely limit the individual's adaptive potential; often society sees the behavior as maladaptive whereas the individual does not.

personality inventory. An inventory for self-appraisal, consisting of many statements or questions about personal characteristics and behavior that the person judges to apply or not to apply to him or her. See also projective test.

personality psychologist. A psychologist whose area of interest focuses on classifying individuals and studying the differences between them. This specialty overlaps both developmental and social psychologists to some extent. See also developmental psychologist, social psychologist.

person-centered therapy. See client-centered therapy.

PET scan. See positron emission tomography.

phallic stage. In Freud's psychoanalytic theory, the third stage of psychosexual development in which gratification is associated with stimulation of the sex organs and sexual attachment is to the parent of the opposite sex. See also Oedipal conflict, psychosexual development.

phasic pain. The kind of sharp pain experienced immediately upon suffering an injury; usually brief with a rapid increase in intensity followed by a decrease. See also tonic pain.

phencyclidine (PCP). Originally developed as an anesthetic but discontinued because of the bizarre reactions it produced, this drug causes an insensitivity to pain and makes the users feel dissociated from themselves and from their environments. Overdoses result in prolonged periods of stupor or coma.

phenomenological perspective. An approach to psychology that focuses on subjective experience and tries to describe it from each individual's unique perspective. See also humanistic psychology.

phenomenology. The study of an individual's subjective experience or unique perception of the world. Emphasis is on understanding events from the subject's point of view rather than focusing on behavior. See also humanistic psychology, introspection.

phenothiazines. A group of antipsychotic drugs that relieve the symptoms of schizophrenia by blocking the access of the neurotransmitter dopamine to its receptors. Chlorpromazine (Thorazine) and fluphenazine (Prolixin) are examples. See also antipsychotic drug, dopamine, neurotransmitter.

phenotype. In genetics, the characteristics that are displayed by the individual organism—such as eye color or intelligence—as distinct from those traits that one may carry genetically but not display. See also genotype.

pheromones. Chemicals that float through the air to be sniffed by other members of the species.

phi phenomenon. Stroboscopic motion is its simpler form. Commonly produced by successively turning on and off two separated stationary light sources; as the first is turned off and the second turned on, the subject perceives a spot of light moving from the position of the first to that of the second. See also stroboscopic motion.

phobia. Intense fear of a stimulus or situation that most people do not consider particularly dangerous. See also agoraphobia, claustrophobia.

phobic disorder. An anxiety disorder in which phobias are severe or pervasive enough to interfere seriously with the individual's daily life. See also anxiety disorders, phobia.

phoneme. Discrete speech categories. See also morpheme.

photopigments. Chemicals contained in the rods and cones (the receptor cells in the eye). These chemicals absorb light, which starts a process that results in a neural impulse.

physiology. The study of the functions of the living organism and its parts.

physiological motive. A motive based on an evident bodily need, such as the need for food or water.

physiological psychologist. See biological psychologist.

pitch. A sensation based on the frequency of sound. See also loudness, timbre.

pituitary gland. An endocrine gland joined to the brain just below the hypothalamus. It consists of two parts, the anterior pituitary and the posterior pituitary. The anterior pituitary is the more important part because of its regulation of growth and of other endocrine glands (syn. hypophysis). See also endocrine system.

place theory of pitch. A theory of hearing that associates pitch with the place on the basilar membrane where activation occurs. See also temporal theory of pitch.

placebo. An inert substance (known to have no pharmacological effect) that is made to look like an active drug.

pleasure principle. In Freud's psychoanalytic theory, the strategy followed by the id, seeking to obtain pleasure and to avoid pain regardless of external circumstances. See also id, reality principle.

pluralistic ignorance. The tendency for persons in a group to mislead each other about a situation; for example, to define an emergency as a nonemergency because others are remaining calm and are not taking action.

polygenic traits. Characteristics—intelligence, height, emotional stability—determined by many sets of genes.

polygraph. A device that measures simultaneously several physiological responses that accompany emotion; for instance, heart and respiration rate, blood pressure, and GSR. Commonly known as a "lie detector" because of its use in determining the guilt of a subject through responses while he or she answers questions. See also GSR, voice stress analyzer.

pop-out effect. A phenomenon in perception, wherein when searching for a primitive feature in a large array, the target feature seems to "pop out."

population. The total universe of all possible cases from which a sample is selected. The usual statistical formulas for making inferences from samples apply when the population is appreciably larger than the sample—for instance, 5 to 10 times larger than the sample. See also sample.

positive incentive. An object or circumstance toward which behavior is directed when the object or circumstance is perceived or anticipated. See also negative incentive.

positive reinforcement. Reinforcing a response by the presentation of a positive stimulus. See also positive reinforcer.

positive reinforcer. Any stimulus that, when applied following a response, increases the probability of the response (syn. reward). See also negative reinforcer.

positive symptoms. In schizophrenia, behavioral excesses such as hallucinations and bizarre behavior. Contrasted with negative symptoms and presumed to be caused by irregularities in neural transmission. See also negative symptoms, schizophrenia.

positron emission tomography (PET). A computer-based scanning procedure that measures regional changes in blood flow to map the neural activities of the living brain.

posterior attentional system. Neural structures in the back of the brain that mediate our ability to selectively attend to a particular location.

posthypnotic amnesia. A particular form of posthypnotic suggestion in which the hypnotized person forgets what has happened during the hypnosis until signaled to remember. See also posthypnotic suggestion.

posthypnotic response. See posthypnotic suggestion.

posthypnotic suggestion. A suggestion made to a hypnotized person that he or she will perform in a prescribed way (commonly to a prearranged signal) when no longer hypnotized. The activity, the posthypnotic response, is usually carried out without the subject's awareness of its origin. See also hypnosis.

post-traumatic stress disorder. An anxiety disorder in which a stressful event that is outside the range of usual human experience, such as military combat or a natural disaster, brings in its aftermath such symptoms as a re-experiencing of the trauma and avoidance of stimuli associated with it, a feeling of estrangement, a tendency to be easily startled, nightmares, recurrent dreams, and disturbed sleep. See also anxiety disorder.

PQRST method. A technique for reading and studying information presented in textbook form. The method takes its name from the first letter of the five steps one follows in reading a textbook chapter: Preview, Question, Read, Self-recitation, Test.

pragmatic rules. Rules used in deductive reasoning that are less abstract than logical rules, but still applicable to many different domains of life. An example is the permission rule.

precognition. Perception of a future event that could not be anticipated through any known inferential process (for example, predicting that a particular number will come up on the next throw of dice). See also clairvoyance, extrasensory perception, parapsychology, psi, psychokinesis, telepathy.

precognitive emotions. Emotions that are not based on appraisal.

preconscious. All the information that is not currently "on our mind" but that we could bring into consciousness if called upon to do so. See also conscious, topographic model, unconscious.

preconscious memories. Memories that are accessible to consciousness.

preferential looking method. A method of examining infants' perceptual preferences by presenting them two stimuli simultaneously and noting the amount of time the infants gaze at each object.

prejudice. Negative feelings toward a group. Derived from "pre-judgment," usually implies negative feelings not based on adequate or valid data about the group. See also attitude, discrimination, stereotype.

preoperational stage. Piaget's second stage of cognitive development. The children think in terms of symbols, but does not yet comprehend certain rules or operations. See also conservation.

prepared conditioning. The proposal that humans are biologically predisposed, or prepared, by evolutionary selection to associate fear with objects or situations that were dangerous in earlier times. See also classical conditioning.

primacy effect. The tendency for first information we receive to have a greater impact on our overall impressions.

primary abilities. The abilities, discovered by factor analysis, that underlie intelligence test performance. See also factor analysis.

primary auditory area. A brain region located at the top of the temporal lobe of each cerebral hemisphere where auditory signals carried by the acoustic nerve are analyzed. Because nerve fibers from each side of the head cross over at the brain stem before reaching the auditory area, signals from each ear reach both temporal lobes. Thus, damage to one lobe does not produce deafness in one ear.

primary motor area. A projection area in the brain lying in front of the central fissure. Electrical stimulation commonly results in movement, or motor responses. See also primary somatosensory area.

primary sex characteristics. The structural or physiological characteristics that make possible sexual union and reproduction. See also secondary sex characteristics.

primary somatosensory area. Area in the parietal lobe of the brain that registers sensory experiences, such as heat, cold, touch, and pain (syn. body-sense area). See also primary motor area.

primary visual area. A projection area lying in the occipital lobe. In humans, damage to this area produces blindness in portions of the visual field corresponding to the amount and location of the damage.

priming. The increased accessibility or retrievability of information stored in memory produced by the prior presentation of relevant cues.

proactive interaction. The interaction between individuals and their environments that arises because different individuals choose to enter different situations and to shape those situations differently after entering them. See also evocative interaction, reactive interaction.

proactive interference. The interference of earlier learning with the learning and recall of new material. See also retroactive interference.

probe. In studies of memory, an item from a list to be remembered that is presented as a cue to the subject; for example, the subject could be asked to give the next item in the list.

problem-focused coping. Reducing anxiety or stress by dealing in some way with the anxiety-producing situation. Escaping the situation or finding a way to alter it are examples. See also emotion-focused coping.

problem-solving strategies. The various strategies that can be employed in solving a problem. Of special interest are a class of strategies that involve breaking the solution to a problem into a series of subgoals. The subgoals are to be accomplished as intermediate steps toward ultimately reaching the final goal.

product-moment correlation. See coefficient of correlation.

production. Producing language by starting with a thought that translates into a sentence and ends up with sounds that express the sentence.

progesterone. A female hormone secreted by the ruptured follicle.

program. (a) A plan for the solution of a problem; often used interchangeably with "routine" to specify the precise sequence of instructions enabling a computer to solve a problem. (b) In teaching, a set of materials arranged so as to maximize the learning process.

projection. Repressing one's own unacceptable impulses and expressing hostile attitudes toward others who are perceived to possess those impulses. See also defense mechanisms.

projective test. Presents an ambiguous stimulus to which the person may respond as he or she wishes. See also personality inventory.

prolactin. Pituitary hormone prompting the secretion of milk. See also hormones.

proposition. A statement that expresses a factual claim.

propositional thought. Expresses a proposition or claim.

prosopagnosia. A loss in the ability to recognize faces that results from brain damage.

prototype. The properties that describe the best examples of the concept. See also core.

psi. Processes of information and/or energy exchange that are not currently explicable in terms of known science.

psychedelic drugs. See hallucinogens.

psychiatric nurse. A nurse specially trained to deal with patients suffering from mental disorders.

psychiatric social worker. A social worker trained to work with patients and their families on problems of mental health and illness, usually in close relationship with psychiatrists and clinical psychologists. See also clinical psychologist, psychiatrist.

psychiatrist. A medical doctor specializing in the treatment and prevention of mental disorders both mild and severe. See also clinical psychologist, psychoanalyst.

psychiatry. A branch of medicine concerned with mental health and mental illness. See also psychiatrist, psychoanalyst.

psychoactive drugs. Drugs that affect behavior, consciousness, and/or mood. See also depressants, hallucinogens, stimulants.

psychoanalysis. (a) The method developed by Freud and extended by his followers for treating mental disorders. (b) The theory of personality which grew out of experiences with the psychoanalytic method of treatment. The theory emphasizes the role of unconscious processes in personality development and in motivation.

psychoanalyst. A psychotherapist, usually trained as a psychiatrist, who uses methods related to those originally proposed by Freud for treating neuroses and other mental disorders. See also clinical psychologist, psychiatrist.

psychoanalytic perspective. An approach to psychology that tries to explain certain kinds of behaviors in terms of unconscious beliefs, fears, and desires. See also psychoanalysis.

psychoanalytic psychotherapy. A method of treating mental disorders based on the theories of Freud but briefer and less intense than psychoanalysis. Less emphasis on exploration of childhood experiences and more attention to the client's current interpersonal problems. See also psychoanalysis.

psychoanalytic theory. See psychoanalysis.

psychoimmunology. An area of research in behavioral medicine that studies how the body's immune system is affected by psychological variables. See also behavioral medicine.

psychokinesis (PK). Mental influence over physical events without the intervention of any known physical force (for example, willing that a particular number will come up on the throw of dice). See also clairvoyance, extrasensory perception, parapsychology, precognition, psi, telepathy.

psycholinguistics. The study of the psychological aspects of language and its acquisition.

psychological dependence. Habitual use of a drug to relieve anxiety even though no physical dependence (addiction) has developed.

psychological determinism. The doctrine that all thoughts, emotions, and actions have causes.

psychological motive. A motive that is primarily learned rather than based on biological needs.

psychology. The scientific study of behavior and mental processes.

psychometric function. A curve plotting the percentage of times the subject reports detecting a stimulus against a measure of the physical energy of the stimulus.

psychopathic personality. See antisocial personality.

psychopharmacology. The study of the effects of drugs on behavior.

psychophysical methods. Procedures used to determine thresholds of sensory modalities.

psychophysics. A name used by Fechner for the science of the relationship between mental processes and the physical world. Now usually restricted to the study of the sensory consequences of controlled physical stimulation.

psychophysiological disorder. Physical disorders in which emotions are believed to play a central role.

psychosexual development. In Freud's psychoanalytic theory, the idea that development takes place through stages (oral, anal, phallic, latent, genital), each stage characterized by a zone of pleasurable stimulation and appropriate objects of sexual attachment, culminating in adult sexuality. See also anal stage, genital stage, latency, oral stage, psychosocial stages.

psychosexual stages. See psychosexual development.

psychosis (pl. psychoses). A severe mental disorder in which thinking and emotion are so impaired that the individual is seriously out of contact with reality. No longer a major diagnostic category in DSM-IV. See also psychotic behavior.

psychosocial stages. A modification by Erikson of the psychoanalytic theory of psychosexual development, giving more attention to the social and environmental problems associated with the various stages of development and adding some adult stages beyond genital maturing. See also psychosexual development.

psychosomatic disorder. Physical illness that has psychological causes (syn. psychophysiological disorder).

psychotherapy. The treatment of mental disorders by psychological (rather than physical or biological) means. See also biological therapy.

psychotic behavior. Behavior indicating gross impairment in reality contact as evidenced by delusions and/or hallucinations. May result from damage to the brain or from a mental disorder such as schizophrenia or a bipolar disorder. See also psychosis.

puberty. The period of sexual maturation that transforms a child into a biologically mature adult capable of sexual reproduction. See also adolescent growth spurt, secondary sex characteristics.

punishment. A procedure used to decrease the strength of a response by presenting an aversive stimulus whenever the response occurs. See also negative reinforcer.

pupil. In the eye, a circular opening in the iris (the colored part of the eye) that expands and contracts, varying according to the intensity of light present. See also cornea, lens, retina.

pure alexia. A loss of the ability to recognize words that results from brain damage (in the left occipital lobe).

Q

Q sort. An assessment technique by which a rater provides a systematic description of an individual's personality by sorting a set of personality statements (for example, "Has a wide range of interests") into groups, ranging from those that are least descriptive to those that are most descriptive of the individual.

R

rapid eye movements (REMS). Eye movements that usually occur during dreaming and that can be measured by attaching small electrodes laterally to and above the subject's eye. These register changes in electrical activity associated with movements of the eyeball in its socket.

rapport. (a) A comfortable relationship between the subject and the tester, ensuring cooperation in replying to test questions. (b) A similar relationship between therapist and patient. (c) A special relationship of hypnotic subject to hypnotist.

rating scale. A device by which raters can record their judgments of others (or of themselves) on the traits defined by the scale.

ratio schedules. Reinforcement schedules where reinforcement depends on the number of responses the organism makes. See also interval schedules.

rationalization. A defense mechanism in which self-esteem is maintained by assigning plausible and acceptable reasons for conduct entered on impulsively or for less acceptable reasons. See also defense mechanisms.

reaction formation. A defense mechanism in which a person denies a disapproved motive through giving strong expressions to its opposite. See also defense mechanisms.

reaction time. The time between the onset of a stimulus and the beginning of an overt response. See also latency.

reactive interaction. The interaction between individuals and their environments that arises because different individuals interpret, experience, and react to situations in different ways. See also evocative interaction, proactive interaction.

real self. See self.

reality principle. In Freud's psychoanalytic theory, the strategy followed by the ego, holding back the impulses of the id until they can be satisfied in socially approved ways. See also ego, pleasure principle.

receiver-operating-characteristic curve (ROC curve). The function relating the probability of hits and false alarms for a fixed signal level in a detection task. Factors influencing response bias may cause hits and false alarms to vary, but their variation is constrained to the ROC curve. See also signal detection task.

recency effect. In memory experiments, the tendency for the last words in a list to be recalled more readily than other list words.

receptive field. In vision, a region of the retina that is associated with a specific cortical neuron; when a stimulus appears anywhere in the field, the associated neuron fires. See also feature detector.

receptor. A specialized cell sensitive to particular kinds of stimuli and connected to nerves composed of afferent neurons (such as the retina of the eye). Used more loosely, the organ containing these sensitive portions (such as the eye or the ear).

recessive gene. A member of a gene pair that determines the characteristic trait or appearance of the individual only in the other member of the pair is recessive. If the other member of the pair is dominant, the effect of the recessive gene is masked. See also dominant gene.

recoding. A process for improving short-term memory by grouping items into a familiar unit or chunk.

recognition. To recognize something is to associate it correctly with a category, such as "chair," or with a specific name, such as "John Jones." It is a high-level process that requires learning and remembering.

red-green color blindness. The commonest form of color blindness, a variety of dichromatism. See also color blindness, dichromatism.

reduced stimulation study. An experimental situation in which sensory stimulation is markedly reduced (syn. sensory deprivation study).

reductionism. Reducing psychological notions to biological ones.

reference groups. Groups with which we identify; we refer to them in order to evaluate and regulate our opinions and actions. See also identification.

refractory phase. The period of temporary inactivity in a neuron after it has fired once.

registration. A term to describe receptive processing in which information is processed but not perceived. See also perception.

regression. A return to more primitive or infantile modes of response.

rehearsal. The conscious repetition of information in short-term memory, usually involving speech. The process facilitates the short-term recall of information and its transfer to long-term memory. See also dual-memory theory.

reincarnation. The belief in rebirth; in other words, that a person has lived before.

reinforcement. (a) In classical conditioning, the experimental procedure of following the conditioned stimulus by the unconditioned stimulus. (b) In operant conditioning, the analogous procedure of following the occurrence of the operant response by the reinforcing stimulus. (c) The process that increases the strength of conditioning as a result of these arrangements. See also negative reinforcement, partial reinforcement, positive reinforcement.

reinforcement schedule. A well-defined procedure for reinforcing a given response only some proportion of the time it occurs. See also interval schedules, partial reinforcement, ratio schedules.

reinforcing stimulus. (a) In classical conditioning, the unconditioned stimulus. (b) In operant conditioning, the stimulus that reinforces the operant (typically, a reward) (syn. reinforcer). See also negative reinforcer, positive reinforcer.

relative height. In perception, a monocular cue for depth. Among identical objects, those that are higher in an image are perceived as being farther away. See also distance cues, linear perspective, relative height, superposition.

relative size. In perception, a monocular cue for depth. If an image contains an array of objects of similar shape, the smaller objects are perceived as being farther away. See also distance cues, linear perspective, relative height, superposition.

relaxation training. Training in various techniques for relaxing muscle tension. The procedure is based on Jacobson's progressive relaxation method, in which the person learns how to relax muscle groups one at a time, the assumption being that muscular relaxation is effective in bringing about emotional relaxation.

releaser. A term used by ethologists for a stimulus that sets off a cycle of instinctive behavior. See also ethology, instinct.

reliability. Yielding reproducible and consistent results. See also validity.

REM sleep. The period of sleep during which rapid eye movements occur. See rapid eye movements.

repression. The ego pushes a threatening thought or forbidden impulse out of awareness into the unconscious. See also defense mechanisms, suppression.

Rescorla–Wagner model. A model of classical conditioning. It assumes that the amount of conditioning between a conditioned stimulus and an unconditioned stimulus on any trial depends on the predictability of the unconditioned stimulus; the less predictable the unconditioned stimulus, the greater the amount of conditioning.

resistance. A psychological barrier against bringing unconscious impulses to the level of awareness. See also interpretation, repression.

respondent behavior. A type of behavior corresponding to reflex action, in that it is largely under the control of and predictable from the stimulus (syn. elicited behavior). See also operant behavior.

response. (a) The behavioral result of stimulation in the form of a movement or glandular secretion. (b) Sometimes, any activity of the organism, including central responses (such as an image or fantasy) regardless of whether the stimulus is identified and whether identifiable movements occur. (c) Products of the organism's activity, such as words typed per minute.

resting potential. The electrical potential across the nerve cell membrane when it is in its resting state (in other words, not responding to other neurons); the inside of the cell membrane is slightly more negative than the outside. See also action potential.

reticular formation. A system of ill-defined nerve paths and connections within the brain stem, lying outside the well-defined nerve pathways, and important as an arousal mechanism.

retina. The portion of the eye sensitive to light, containing the rods and the cones. See also cone, rod.

retinal image. The image projected onto the retina by an object in the visual field.

retinal size. The size of the retinal image of an object; retinal size decreases in direct proportion to the object's distance. See also object size.

retrieval. Recovering physical input from storage.

retrieval cue. Anything that can help you retrieve information from memory.

retroactive interference. The interference in recall of something earlier learned by something subsequently learned. See also proactive interference.

retrograde amnesia. Loss of memory for events and experiences occurring in a period of time prior to the amnesia-causing trauma. See also amnesia, anterograde amnesia.

reuptake. The process by which a neurotransmitter is "taken up" again (reabsorbed) by the synaptic terminals from which it had been released. See also neurotransmitter, synaptic terminals.

reward. A synonym for positive reinforcement. See also positive reinforcement.

right hemisphere. The right cerebral hemisphere. Controls the left side of the body and, for most people, spatial and patterned activities (syn. minor hemisphere). See also cerebral hemispheres, corpus callosum, left hemisphere, split-brain subject.

right to privacy. Information about a person acquired during a study must be kept confidential and not made available to others without his or her consent.

ROC curve. See receiver-operating-characteristic curve.

rod. In the eye, an element of the retina mediating achromatic sensation only; particularly important in peripheral vision and night vision. See also cone, retina.

Role Construct Repertory Test. A measuring instrument devised by George Kelly for eliciting a person's constructs. Also called the Rep Test. See also personal construct.

role-playing. A method for teaching attitudes and behaviors important to interpersonal relations by having the subject assume a part in a spontaneous play, whether in psychotherapy or in leadership training.

Rorschach Test. See projective test.

S

saccade. The quick movement of the eyes between eye fixations.

sadism. A pathological motive that leads to inflicting pain on another person. See also masochism.

safety signal hypothesis. The suggestion that the reason organisms prefer predictable to unpredictable aversive events is because predictability provides a safe period.

sample. A selection of scores from a total set of scores known as the "population." If selection is random, an unbiased sample results; if selection is nonrandom, the sample is biased and unrepresentative. See also population.

satiety sensors. Detectors located in different parts of the digestive or thirst systems that signal that the needed nutrients or fluids are on their way and that feeding or drinking can stop.

saturation. The purity of the color. See also hue.

scaling. Converting raw data into types of scores more readily interpreted, such as ranks, centiles, standard scores.

scapegoat. A form of displaced aggression in which an innocent but helpless victim is blamed or punished as the source of the scapegoater's frustration. See also displaced aggression, scapegoat theory of prejudice.

scapegoat theory of prejudice. The theory that some hostility toward minority groups arises because prejudiced individuals repress their own unacceptable impulses and then express hostile attitudes toward others who are perceived to possess those same impulses. The hostility often takes the form of blaming the group for both personal and societal problems.

Schacter-Singer theory. A theory of emotions stating that environmental stimuli lead to general physiological arousal; the individual's cognitive appraisal of the arousal then leads to the subjective experience of a specific emotion.

schedule of reinforcement. The frequency and/or timing with which reinforcement occurs. See also ratio schedules, interval schedules.

schema (pl. schemas). Theory about how the physical and social worlds operate (chapter 3); a mental representation of a class of people, objects, events, or situations (chapter 8); a cognitive structure that helps us perceive, organize, process, and utilize information (chapter 13); organized beliefs and knowledge about people, objects, events, and situations (chapter 17).

schematic processing. The cognitive process of searching for the schema in memory that is most consistent with the incoming information. See also schema.

schizoid. Having some characteristics that resemble schizophrenia but are less severe. Occurs with higher frequency in families of schizophrenics and thus tends to support a genetic basis for schizophrenia. See also schizophrenia.

schizophrenia. A group of disorders characterized by severe personality disorganization, distortion of reality, and inability to function in daily life.

school psychologist. A professional psychologist employed by a school or school system, with responsibility for testing, guidance, research, and so on. See also educational psychologist.

second order conditioning. Conditioning in which the UCS is not biologically significant (such as food, water, or shock) but gains power as a UCS by being consistently paired with a biologically significant UCS. See also classical conditioning, unconditioned stimulus.

secondary sex characteristics. The physical features distinguishing the mature male from the mature female, apart from the reproductive organs. In humans, the deeper voice of the male and the growth of the beard are illustrative. See also primary sex characteristics.

selective adaptation. In perception, a loss of sensitivity to motion that occurs when we view motion. The adaptation is selective because we lose sensitivity to the motion viewed, and to similar motions, but not to motion that differs significantly in direction or speed. Presumably the result of fatigued neurons in the cerebral cortex.

selective attention. The perceptual processes by which we select certain input, but not others, for recognition.

selective breeding. A method of studying genetic influences by mating animals that display certain traits and selecting for breeding from among their offspring those that express the trait. If the trait is primarily determined by heredity, continued selection for a number of generations will produce a strain that breeds true for that trait.

selective reinforcement. Strengthening of specific desired behaviors.

self. All the ideas, perceptions, and values that characterize "I" or "me."

self-actualization. A person's fundamental tendency toward maximal realization of his or her potentials; a basic concept in humanistic theories of personality such as those developed by Maslow and Rogers.

self-concept. The composite of ideas, feelings, and attitudes people have about themselves. For some theorists, self-concept is synonymous with the self.

self-consciousness. A state of heightened self-awareness; the disposition to be self-attentive.

self-help groups. Groups that are conducted without a professional therapist.

self-perception. The individual's awareness of himself or herself; differs from self-consciousness because it may take the form of objective self-appraisal. See also self-consciousness.

self-perception theory. The theory that attitudes and beliefs are influenced by observations of one's own behavior; sometimes we judge how we feel by observing how we act.

self-regulation. Monitoring, or observing, one's own behavior. See also behavior therapy.

self-schema (pl. self-schemas). Cognitive generalizations about the self, derived from past experience, that organize and guide the processing of self-related information. See also schema.

semantic memory. A type of memory that stores general knowledge, such as the meanings of words. Knowledge is encoded in relation to other knowledge rather than in relation to the memorizer. See also episodic memory.

semicircular canals. Three curved tubular canals, in three planes, which form part of the labyrinth of the inner ear and are concerned with equilibrium and motion. See also equilibratory senses.

sensations. Experiences associated with simple stimuli. See critical periods.

sensitization. The process by which an organism learns to strengthen its reaction to a stimulus if a threatening or painful stimulus follows.

sensorimotor stage. A period in which infants are busy discovering the relationships between their actions and the consequences of those actions. See also object permanence.

sensory adaptation. The reduction in sensitivity that occurs with prolonged stimulation and the increase in sensitivity that occurs with lack of stimulation; most noted in vision, smell, taste, and temperature sensitivity. See also dark adaptation, light adaptation.

sensory modalities. The individual senses.

sensory-neural loss. A hearing deficit in which threshold elevation (loss of sensitivity) is greater at high rather than low frequencies. See also conduction loss.

sensory neuron. A neuron, or nerve cell, that conveys messages to the brain or spinal cord from the sense receptors informing the organism about events in the environment or within the body (syn. afferent neuron). See also motor neuron, receptor.

sensory processes. The subprocesses of the perceptual system that are closely associated with the sense organs. Sensory processes provide selectively filtered information about the stimuli that impinge on us; higher-level processes use this information to form a mental representation of the scene. See also filter, perception.

septal area. A portion of the brain deep in the central part, between the lateral ventricles, that appears to yield a state akin to pleasure when stimulated electrically (in a rat, at least).

serial memory search. Comparing a test stimulus in sequence to each item in short-term memory. See also short-term memory.

serial processing. A theoretical interpretation of information processing in which several sources of information are processed in a serial order; only one source being attended to at a time. See also parallel processing.

serotonin. A neurotransmitter in both the peripheral and central nervous systems. It is an inhibitory transmitter whose actions have been implicated in various processes including sleep, the perception of pain, and mood disorders (depression and manic-depression). See also neurotransmitter.

serotonin reuptake inhibitors. A class of antidepressant drugs that work by increasing levels of the neurotransmitter serotonin in the synapse.

set point. The point at which body weight is set and that the body strives to maintain.

sex role. The full complement of attitudes and behaviors that a society considers appropriate for the individual because of his or her sex. See also sex typing.

sex typing. The acquisition of behaviors and characteristics that a culture considers appropriate to one's sex. See also sex role.

sex-linked trait. A trait determined by a gene transmitted on the same chromosomes that determine sex, such as red-green color blindness. See also X, Y chromosome.

sexual orientation. The degree to which an individual is sexually attracted to members of the opposite sex and/or to members of the same sex.

shape constancy. The tendency to see a familiar object as of the same shape regardless of the viewing angle. See also perceptual constancy.

shaping. Reinforcing only variations in response that deviate in the direction desired by the experimenter.

shock therapy. See electroconvulsive therapy.

short-term memory (STM). The component of the memory system has limited capacity and maintains information for only a brief time. See also long-term memory.

sibling. A brother or sister.

signal detection task. A procedure whereby the subject must judge on each trial whether a weak signal was embedded in a noise background. Saying "yes" when the signal was presented is called a hit and saying "yes" when the signal was not presented is called a false alarm. See also receiver-operating-characteristic curve.

signal detection theory. A theory of the sensory and decision processes involved in psychophysical judgments, with special reference to the problem of detecting weak signals in noise. See also signal detection task.

simple cell. A cell in the visual cortex that responds to a bar of light or straight edge of a particular orientation and location in the visual field. See also complex cell.

simple phobia. Excessive fear of a specific object, animal, or situation in the absence of real danger. See also phobia, phobic disorder.

simulation. See computer simulation.

sine wave. A cyclical wave that when plotted corresponds to the plot of the trigonometric sine function. The sound waves of pure tones yield this function when plotted.

situational attribution. Attributing a person's actions to factors in the situation or environment, as opposed to internal attitudes and motives. See also dispositional attribution.

size constancy. The tendency to see a familiar object as of its actual size regardless of its distance. See also perceptual constancy.

size-distance invariance principle. The proposal that the perceived size of an object is equal to the product of the retinal size of the object and the perceived distance of the object.

sleep disorder. When inability to sleep well produces impaired daytime functioning or excessive sleepiness.

smooth muscle. The type of muscle found in the digestive organs, blood vessels, and other internal organs. Controlled via the autonomic nervous system. See also cardiac muscle, striate muscle.

social facilitation. The effects of coaction and the presence of an audience.

social-learning theory. The application of learning theory to the problems of personal and social behavior (syn. social behavior theory).

social norms. Implicit rules and expectations that dictate what we ought to think and how we ought to behave.

social phobia. Extreme insecurity in social situations accompanied by an exaggerated fear of embarrassing oneself. See also phobia, phobic disorder.

social psychologist. A psychologist who studies social interaction and the ways in which individuals influence one another.

socialization. The shaping of individual characteristics and behavior through the training that the social environment provides.

social psychology. The study of how people think and feel about their social world and how they interact and influence one another.

sociology. The science dealing with group life and social organization in literate societies. See also behavioral sciences.

sociopathic personality. See antisocial personality.

somatic nervous system. Carries messages to and from the sense receptors, muscles, and the surface of the body. See also autonomic nervous system, peripheral nervous system.

spatial acuity. The ability to see details of form.

spatial frequency. In perception, the distance between successive dark bars in a grating consisting of alternating dark and light bars. Spatial frequency is a determinant of visual resolution. See also contrast sensitivity.

spatial localization. Determining where visual objects are. See also pattern recognition.

spatial resolution. The ability to see spatial patterns. Visual acuity and the contrast threshold are measures of spatial resolution.

speaker's intention. The speaker's goal in uttering a particular sentence, which is distinct from the actual content of the sentence.

species-specific behavior. See instinct.

specific hunger. Hunger for a specific food incentive, such as a craving for sweets. See also hunger drive.

specific nerve energies. Johannes Müller's proposal that the brain codes qualitative differences between sensory modalities by the specific neural pathways involved.

spindle. An EEG characteristic of Stage 2 sleep, consisting of short bursts of rhythmical responses of 13–16 Hz; slightly higher than alpha. See also electroencephalogram.

split-brain subject. A person who has had an operation that severed the corpus callosum, thus separating the functions of the two cerebral hemispheres. See also cerebral hemispheres, corpus callosum.

spontaneous recovery. A phenomenon in classical conditioning discovered by Pavlov. When an organism undergoes execution of a conditioned response and is then moved to a new context, the conditioned response may reappear.

spontaneous remission. Recovery from an illness or improvement without treatment.

sports psychology. The study of human behavior in sport. The goal of much of the work is to help athletes develop psychological skills that maximize performance and enhance the sport experience. For example, hypnosis and biofeedback have been used to control an athlete's anxiety level during competition and mental imagery has been employed to help perfect the synchrony and flow of certain body movements.

spreading activation. A proposed model of retrieval from long-term memory in which activation subdivides among paths emanating from an activated mental representation.

spurious association. A plausible but nonexistent relation between two stimuli. Human learners frequently report such relations when trying to learn less-than-perfect relations.

S-R psychology. See stimulus-response psychology.

stabilized retinal image. The image of an object on the retina when special techniques are used to counteract the minute movements of the eyeball that occur in normal vision. When an image is thus stabilized it quickly disappears, suggesting that the changes in stimulation of retinal cells provided by the eye movements are necessary for vision.

stages of development. Developmental periods, usually following a progressive sequence, that appear to represent qualitative changes in either the structure or the function of the organism (such as Freud's psychosexual stages, Piaget's cognitive stages).

standard deviation. The square root of the mean of the squares of the amount by which each case departs from the mean of all the cases (syn. root mean square deviation).

state-dependent learning. Learning that occurs during a particular biological state—such as when drugged—so that it can best be demonstrated or is most effective when the person is put in the same state again.

statistical significance. The trustworthiness of an obtained statistical measure as a statement about reality; for example, the probability that the population mean falls within the limits determined from a sample. The expression refers to the reliability of the statistical finding and not to its importance.

statistics. The discipline that deals with sampling data from a population of individuals and then drawing inferences about the population from those data. See also statistical significance.

stereoscopic vision. (a) The binocular perception of depth and distance of an object owing to the overlapping fields of the two eyes. (b) The equivalent effect when slightly unlike pictures are presented individually to each eye in a stereoscope. See also distance cues.

stereotype. A set of inferences about the personality traits or physical attributes of a whole class of people (chapter 8); schemas of classes of people (chapter 17). See also schema.

steroids. Complex chemical substances, some of which are prominent in the secretions of the adrenal cortex and may be related to some forms of mental illness. See also adrenal gland.

stimulants. Drugs that increase alertness and general arousal.

stimulation-produced analgesia. An analgesic effect produced by the stimulation of a region of the midbrain. See also gate control theory of pain.

stimulus (pl. stimuli). (a) Some specific physical energy impinging on a receptor sensitive to that kind of energy. (b) Any objectively describable situation or event (whether outside or inside the organism) that is the occasion for an organism's response. See also response.

stimulus-response (S-R) psychology. A psychological view that all behavior is in response to stimuli and that the appropriate tasks of psychological science are those identifying stimuli, the responses correlated with them, and the processes intervening between stimulus and response.

storage. Retaining and storing the physical input from the encoding stage.

STM. See short-term memory.

strabismus. In vision, a lack of binocular depth perception caused by a person's eyes not pointing in the same direction early in life. See also astigmatism.

stress. Experiencing events that are perceived as endangering one's physical or psychological well-being.

stress responses. Reactions to events an individual perceives as endangering his or her well-being. These may include bodily changes that prepare for emergency (the fight-or-flight response) as well as such psychological reactions as anxiety, anger and aggression, apathy and depression, and cognitive impairment. See also fight-or-flight response.

stressors. Events that an individual perceives as endangering his or her physical or psychological well-being.

striate muscle. Striped muscle; the characteristic muscles controlling the skeleton, as in the arms and legs. Activated by the somatic, as opposed to the autonomic, nervous system. See also cardiac muscle, smooth muscle.

stroboscopic motion. An illusion of motion resulting from the successive presentation of discrete stimulus patterns arranged in a progression corresponding to movement, such as motion pictures. See also phi phenomenon.

structuralism. The analysis of mental structures.

subtractive mixture. Color mixture in which the results differ from additive mixture obtained by mixing projected lights. Subtractive mixture occurs when transparent colored filters are placed one in front of the other and when pigments are mixed. See also additive mixture.

superego. The internalized representation of the values and morals of society. See also conscience, ego, id.

superposition. In perception, a monocular cue for depth. If an object has contours that cut through those of another, obstructing the other object's view, the overlapping object is perceived as being nearer. See also distance cues, linear perceptive, relative height, relative size.

suppression. A process of self-control in which impulses, tendencies to action, and wishes to perform disapproved acts are in awareness but not overtly revealed. See also repression.

survey method. A method of obtaining information by questioning a large sample of people.

symbol. Anything that stands for or refers to something other than itself.

sympathetic system. A division of the autonomic nervous system, characterized by a chain of ganglia on either side of the spinal cord, with nerve fibers originating in the thoracic and lumbar portions of the spinal cord. Active in emotional excitement and to some extent antagonistic to the parasympathetic division. See also parasympathetic system.

synapse. The close functional connection between the axon of one neuron and the dendrites or cell body of another neuron. See also excitatory synapse, inhibitory synapse.

synaptic gap. The space between the presynaptic cell membrane and the post-synaptic cell membrane; the space across a synapse. See also synapse.

synaptic terminals. Small swellings at the end of axon branches that enclose synaptic vesicles containing neurotransmitters. See also neurotransmitter, synapse, synaptic vesicles.

synaptic vesicles. Small spherical or irregularly shaped structures within a synaptic terminal that contain neurotransmitters; when stimulated, they discharge the neurotransmitters. See also neurotransmitter, synapse, synaptic terminals.

syntactic analysis. In language, an analysis that divides a sentence into noun phrases and verb phrases, and then divides these phrases into smaller units like nouns, adjectives, and verbs.

systematic desensitization. A behavior therapy technique in which hierarchies of anxiety-producing situations are imagined (or sometimes confronted in reality) while the person is in a state of deep relaxation. Gradually the situations become dissociated from the anxiety response. See also anxiety hierarchy, behavior therapy, counterconditioning.

systematic reinforcement. A method for modifying behavior by reinforcing desirable responses (with praise or tangible rewards) and ignoring undesirable ones. Used in behavior therapy. See also behavior therapy.

T

tabula rasa. Latin, meaning blank slate. The term refers to the view that human beings are born without any innate knowledge or ideas; all knowledge is acquired through learning and experience. Proposed by the 17th- and 18th-century British empiricists (Locke, Hume, Berkeley, Hartley).

tachistoscope. An instrument for the brief exposure of words, symbols, pictures, or other visually presented material; sometimes called a T-scope.

tardive dyskinesia. Involuntary movements of the tongue, face, mouth, or jaw.

taste buds. Receptors for taste located in clusters on the tongue and around the mouth.

T-cell (thymus-dependent cell). A type of lymphocyte that recognizes and destroys foreign antigens (enzymes, toxins, or other substances) and thus plays an important role in the body's immune response.

telegraphic speech. A stage in the development of speech in which the child preserves only the most meaningful and perceptually salient elements of adult speech. The child tends to omit prepositions, articles, prefixes, suffixes, and auxiliary words.

telepathy. Thought transference from one person to another without the mediation of any known channel of sensory communication (for example, identifying a playing card merely being thought of by another person). See also clairvoyance, extrasensory perception, parapsychology, precognition, psi, psychokinesis.

temperament. Mood-related personality characteristics.

temperature regulation. The process by which an organism keeps its body temperature relatively constant.

temporal lobe. A portion of the cerebral hemisphere, at the side below the lateral fissure and in front of the occipital lobe. See also frontal lobe, occipital lobe, parietal lobe.

temporal stability. See test-retest reliability.

temporal theory of pitch. A theory of pitch perception which assumes that the frequency of neural impulses traveling up the auditory nerve correspond to the frequency of a tone. See also place theory of pitch.

test battery. A collection of tests whose composite scores are used to appraise individual differences.

test profile. A chart plotting scores from a number of tests given to the same individual (or group of individuals) in parallel rows on a common scale, with the scores connected by lines, so that high and low scores can be readily perceived.

test-retest reliability. The consistency of a test when given over successive occasions to the same person (syn. temporal stability). See also reliability.

testosterone. A kind of androgen that is responsible during puberty for the sudden growth of facial, underarm, and pubic hair; it also causes a deepening of the voice, the development of muscles that lead to a more masculine form, and the growth of the external genitals.

texture gradient. A cue for perceiving depth directly. When viewing a surface in perspective, the elements that make up the surface appear to be packed closer and closer together, giving an impression of depth. See also distance cues.

thalamus. Two groups of nerve cell nuclei located just above the brain stem and inside the cerebral hemispheres. Considered a part of the central core of the brain. One area acts as a sensory relay station, the other plays a role in sleep and waking; this portion is considered part of the limbic system. See also hypothalamus.

Thematic Apperception Test (TAT). See projective test.

theory. An interrelated set of propositions about a particular phenomenon.

theta rhythm. See electroencephalogram.

thinking. The ability to imagine or represent objects or events in memory and to operate on these representations.

thirst. The psychological manifestation of the need for water.

three primaries law. A basic law about color vision. Three wavelengths of light can be combined to match almost any color of light, as long as one light is drawn from the long-wave end of the spectrum, another light is drawn from the middle, and the third light is drawn from the short end.

threshold. The transitional point at which an increasing stimulus or an increasing difference not previously perceived becomes perceptible (or at which a decreasing stimulus or previously perceived difference becomes imperceptible). The value obtained depends in part on the methods used in determining it. See also absolute threshold, difference threshold.

thyroid gland. An endocrine gland located in the neck, whose hormone thyroxin is important in determining metabolic rate. See also endocrine gland.

timbre. Our experience of the complexity of a sound. See also overtone.

tip-of-the-tongue phenomenon. The experience of failing to recall a word or a name when we are quite certain we know it.

TM. See meditation.

tolerance. The need for a greater amount of a drug to achieve the same euphoria.

tonic pain. The kind of steady, long-lasting pain experienced after an injury has occurred; usually produced by swelling and tissue damage. In contrast to phasic pain. See also phasic pain.

top-down processes. Processes in perception, learning, memory, and comprehension that are driven by the organism's prior knowledge and expectations, rather than by the input. See also bottom-up processes.

topographic model. Freud's model of the human mind, containing the conscious, preconscious, and the unconscious. See also conscious, preconscious, unconscious.

trace conditioning. A classical conditioning procedure in which the CS terminates before the onset of the UCS. See also delayed conditioning.

tranquilizer. A drug that reduces anxiety and agitation. See antianxiety drug.

transcendental meditation (TM). See meditation.

transducer. A device such as an electrode or gauge that, in psychophysiology, converts physiological indicators into other forms of energy that can be recorded and measured.

transduction. Translate physical energy into electrical signals that can make their way to the brain. See also receptor cells.

transference. The tendency for the client to make the therapist the object of emotional responses.

transsexual. An individual who is physically one sex but psychologically the other. Transsexuals sometimes resort to surgery and hormonal treatment to change their physical appearance. They do not, however, consider themselves to be homosexual. See also homosexual.

traumatic events. Situations of extreme danger that are outside the range of usual human experience.

trichromatic theory. A theory of color perception that postulates three basic color receptors (cones), a "red" receptor, a "green" receptor, and a "blue" receptor. The theory explains color blindness by the absence of one or more receptor types (syn. Young-

Helmholtz theory). See also opponent-color theory, two-stage color theory.

trichromatism. Normal color vision, based on the classification of color vision according to three color systems: black-white, blue-yellow, and red-green. The normal eye sees all three; the colorblind eye is defective in one or two of the three systems. See also dichromatism, monochromatism.

tricyclic antidepressant. A class of antidepressants that relieve the symptoms of depression by preventing the reuptake of the neurotransmitters serotonin and norepinephrine, thereby prolonging their action. Imipramine (brand names, Tofranil and Elavil) is one drug commonly prescribed. See also antidepressant.

two-point threshold. A kind of pressure threshold; it is the minimum distance by which two thin rods touching the skin must be separated before they are felt as two points rather than one.

two-stage color theory. A theory of color vision that postulates three types of cones (in agreement with trichromatic theory) followed by red-green and yellow-blue opponent processes (in agreement with opponent-color theory). This theory accounts for much of what is known about color vision, and serves as a prototype for the analysis of other sensory systems. See also opponent-color theory, trichromatic theory.

type A and type B. Two contrasting behavior patterns found in studies of coronary heart disease. Type As are people who have a sense of time urgency, find it difficult to relax, and become impatient and angry when confronted with delays or with people whom they view as incompetent. Type As are at risk for heart disease. Type Bs are able to relax without feeling guilty and to work without becoming agitated; they lack a sense of time urgency, with its accompanying impatience, and are not easily roused to anger.

U

unconditional positive regard. Feeling that oneself is valued by parents and others even when t heir feelings, attitudes, and behaviors are less than ideal.

unconditioned response (UCR). In classical conditioning, the response given originally to the unconditioned stimulus used as the basis for establishing a conditioned response to a previously neutral stimulus. See also conditioned response, conditioned stimulus, unconditioned stimulus.

unconditioned stimulus (UCS). In classical conditioning, a stimulus that automatically elicits a response, typically via a reflex, without prior conditioning. See also conditioned response, conditioned stimulus, unconditioned response.

unconscious. The thoughts, attitudes, impulses, wishes, motivations, and emotions of which we are unaware (chapter 1); contains some memories, impulses, and desires that are not accessible to consciousness (chapter 6); impulses, wishes, and inaccessible memories that affect our thoughts and behavior (chapter 13). See also conscious, preconscious, repression, topographic model.

unconscious inference. A term used by the German scientist Hermann von Helmholtz to describe the process by which the perceiver progresses from experiencing sensations evoked by an object to recognizing the properties of the object. We make this inference automatically and unconsciously, and eventually we do not even notice the sensations on which it is based. Helmholtz argued that unconscious inference is the basis of many perceptual phenomena, including distance and object perception.

unconscious motive. A motive of which the subject is unaware or aware of in distorted form. Because there is no sharp dividing line between conscious and unconscious, many motives have both conscious and unconscious aspects.

unconscious processes. Memories, impulses, and desires that are not available to consciousness. According to the psychoanalytic theories of Sigmund Freud, painful memories and wishes are sometimes repressed—that is, diverted to the unconscious where they continue to influence our actions even though we are not aware of them. See also conscious, unconscious.

V

validity. Measuring what is intended to be measured. See also criterion, reliability.

validity coefficient. The correlation between a test score and some criterion to which the test is supposed to predict. See also criterion, validity.

variable. Something that can occur with different values. See also dependent variable, independent variable.

variable ratio schedule. The organism is reinforced only after making a certain number of responses, but that number varies unpredictably.

variable interval schedule. Reinforcement still depends on a certain interval having elapsed, but the interval's duration varies unpredictably.

variance. The square of a standard deviation.

ventromedial hypothalamus (VMH). Area of the hypothalamus important to the regulation of food intake. Electrical stimulation of this area will make an experimental animal stop eating; destruction of brain tissue here produces voracious eating, eventually leading to obesity. See also hypothalamus, lateral hypothalamus.

vestibular apparatus. An organ in the inner ear that contains receptors for body movement and kinesthesis.

vestibular sacs. Two sacs in the labyrinth of the inner ear, called the saccule and utricle, which contain the otoliths ("ear stones"). Pressure of the otoliths on the hair cells in the gelatinous material of the utricle and saccule gives us the sense of body tilt or linear acceleration. See also equilibratory senses.

vicarious learning. Learning by observing the behavior of others and noting the consequences of that behavior (syn. observational learning).

visual acuity. The eye's ability to resolve details.

visual area. A projection area lying in the occipital lobe. In humans, damage to this area produces blindness in portions of the visual field corresponding to the amount and location of the damage.

visual buffer. In short-term memory, a hypothesized component of the encoding process that briefly stores information in a visual code (i.e., a visual representation of verbal and nonverbal items). See also acoustic buffer, central executive, encoding, short-term memory.

visual cliff. An experimental apparatus with glass over a patterned surface, one half of which is just below the glass and the other half, several feet below. Used to test the depth perception of animals and human infants.

visual-evoked potentials. A method of studying perception using electrodes placed on the back of the head over the visual cortex. The electrodes record electrical responses related to how well the observer can discriminate a presented stimulus.

visual field. The total visual array acting on the eye when it is directed toward a fixation point.

VMH. See ventromedial hypothalamus.

voice stress analyzer. A device that graphically represents changes in a person's voice associated with emotion. Used in lie detection. See also polygraph.

volumetric receptors. Hypothesized receptors that regulate water intake by responding to the volume of blood and body fluids. Renin, a substance secreted by the kidneys into the bloodstream, may be one volumetric receptor; it constricts the blood vessels and stimulates the release of the hormone, angiotensin, which acts on cells in the hypothalamus to produce thirst. See also osmoreceptors.

voluntary processes. Activities selected by choice and controlled or monitored according to intention or plan. See also control processes.

vulnerability-stress model. An interactive model of physical or mental disorders that proposes that an individual will develop a disorder only when he or she has both some constitutional vulnerability (predisposition) and experiences stressful circumstances. Same as diathesis-stress model.

W

weak methods. General problem-solving strategies that do not depend on specific knowledge of a problem. Examples are difference reduction, means-ends analysis, and working backwards. See also difference reduction, means-ends analysis, and working backwards.

Weber's constant. See Weber's law.

Weber's law. The observation that the difference threshold is a fixed proportion of the stimulus magnitude at which it is measured. The proportion is constant over a wide range of stimulus magnitudes, and is called Weber's constant. The value of Weber's constant depends on the sensory modality; the smaller the constant, the more sensitive the modality. See also difference threshold.

Wernicke's area. A portion of the left cerebral hemisphere involved in language understanding. Individuals with damage in this area are not able to comprehend words; they can hear words, but they do not know their meanings.

withdrawal symptoms. Unpleasant physiological and psychological reactions that occur when a person suddenly stops taking an addictive drug; these range from nausea, anxiety, mild tremors, and difficulty sleeping at low levels of dependence to vomiting, cramps, hallucinations, agitation, and severe tremors or seizures at higher levels. See also drug dependence.

words. Units of speech that carry meaning.

working backwards. A problem-solving strategy in which one works backwards from the goal towards the current state. See also difference reduction, means-ends analysis.

working memory. Memories that are stored for only a few seconds.

working through. In psychoanalytic therapy, the process of reeducation by having patients face the same conflicts over and over in the consultation room, until they can independently face and master the conflicts in ordinary life.

X

X chromosome. A chromosome that, if paired with another X chromosome, determines that the individual will be a female. If it is combined with a Y chromosome, the individual will be a male. The X chromosome transmits sex-linked traits. See also chromosome, sex-linked trait, Y chromosome.

XYY syndrome. An abnormal condition in which a male has an extra Y sex chromosome; reputedly associated with unusual aggressiveness, although the evidence is not conclusive. See also Y chromosome.

Y

Y chromosome. The chromosome that, combined with an X chromosome, determines maleness. See also chromosome, sex-linked trait, X chromosome.

Young-Helmholtz theory. See trichromatic theory.

Z

zygote. A fertilized ovum or egg. See also dizygotic twins, monozygotic twins.

References

Citations in the text are made by author and date of publication.

ABBOTT, B. B., SCHOEN, L. S., & BADIA, P. (1984). Predictable and unpredictable shock: Behavioral measures of aversion and physiological measures of stress. *Psychological Bulletin, 96,* 45–71.

ABELSON, R. P. (1968). Computers, polls, and public opinion—Some puzzles and paradoxes. *Transaction, 5,* 20–27.

ABRAMSON, L. Y., METALSKY, G. I, & ALLOY, L. B. (1989). Hopelessness depression: A theory-based subtype of depression. *Psychological Review, 96,* 358–372.

ABRAMSON, L. Y., SELIGMAN, M. E. P., & TEASDALE, J. (1978). Learned helplessness in humans: Critique and reformulation. *Journal of Abnormal Psychology, 87,* 49–74.

ADAMS, J. L. (1974). *Conceptual blockbusting.* Stanford, CA: Stanford Alumni Association.

ADAMS, M., & COLLINS, A. (1979). A schema-theoretic view of reading. In R. O. Freedle (Ed.), *New Directions Discourse Processing,* Vol. 12. Norwood, NJ: Ablex.

ADKINS-REGAN, E. (1988). Sex hormones and sexual orientation in animals. *Psychobiology, 16,* 335–347.

ADORNO, T. W., FRENKEL-BRUNSWIK, E., LEVINSON, D. J., & SANFORD, R. N. (1950). *The authoritarian personality.* New York: Harper.

AGRAS, W. S. (1993). Short term psychological treatments for binge eating. In C. G. Fairburn & G. T. Wilson (Eds.), *Binge eating: Nature, assessment, and treatment.* New York: Guilford.

AINSWORTH, M. D. S., BLEHAR, M. C., WALTERS, E., & WALL, S. (1978). *Patterns of attachment: A psychological study of the strange situation.* Hillsdale, NJ: Erlbaum.

AKERS, C. (1984). Methodological criticisms of parapsychology. In S. Krippner (Ed.), *Advances in parapsychological research* (Vol. 4). Jefferson, NC: McFarland.

AKHTAR, S., WIG, N. N., VARMA, V. K., PERSHARD, D., & VERMA, S. K. (1975). A phenomenological analysis of symptoms in the obsessive-compulsive neurosis. *British Journal of Psychiatry, 127,* 342–348.

ALBERTS, B., BRAY, D., LEWIS, J., RAFF, M., ROBERTS, K., & WATSON, J. D. (1994). *Molecular biology of the cell* (3rd ed.). New York: Garland.

ALDAG, R. J., & FULLER, S. R. (1993). Beyond fiasco: A reappraisal of the groupthink phenomenon and a new model of group decision processes. *Psychological Bulletin, 113,* 533–552.

ALLEN, J. B., KENRICK, D. T., LINDER, D. E., & MCCALL, A. M. (1989). Arousal and attraction: A response-facilitation alternative to misattribution and negative-reinforcement models. *Journal of Personality and Social Psychology, 57,* 261–270.

ALLEN, V. L., & LEVINE, J. M. (1969). Consensus and conformity. *Journal of Experimental Social Psychology, 5,* 389–399.

ALLEN, V. L., & LEVINE, J. M. (1971). Social support and conformity: The role of independent assessment of reality. *Journal of Experimental Social Psychology, 7,* 48–58.

ALLOY, L., & ABRAMSON, L. Y. (1997, May). The cognitive vulnerability to depression project. Paper presented to the Midwestern Psychological Association, Chicago, IL.

ALLOY, L. B., & ABRAMSON, L. Y. (1979). Judgment of contingency in depressed and nondepressed students: Sadder but wiser? *Journal of Experimental Psychology: General, 108,* 441–485.

ALLOY, L. B., & TABACHNIK, N. (1984). Assessment of covariation by animals and humans: Influence of prior expectations and current situational information. *Psychological Review, 91,* 112–149.

ALLPORT, F. H. (1920). The influence of the group upon association and thought. *Journal of Experimental Psychology, 3,* 159–182.

ALLPORT, F. H. (1924). *Social psychology.* Boston: Houghton Mifflin.

ALLPORT, G. W., & ODBERT, H. S. (1936). Trait-names: A psycholexical study. *Psychological Monographs, 47* (1, Whole No. 211).

ALTEMEYER, B. (1988). *Enemies of freedom: Understanding right-wing authoritarianism.* San Francisco: Jossey-Bass.

ALWIN, D. F., COHEN, R. L., & NEWCOMB, T. M. (1991). *Personality and social change: Attitude persistence and changes over the lifespan.* Madison: University of Wisconsin Press.

AMERICAN PSYCHIATRIC ASSOCIATION (1994). *Diagnostic and statistical manual of mental disorders* (4th ed.). Washington, DC: American Psychiatric Association.

AMERICAN PSYCHOLOGICAL ASSOCIATION (1990). Ethical principles of psychologists. *American psychologist, 45,* 390–395.

ANCH, M. A., BROWMAN, C. P., MITLER, M. M., & WALSH, J. K. (1988). *Sleep: A scientific perspective.* Englewood Cliffs, NJ: Prentice-Hall.

ANCOLI-ISRAEL, S., KRIPKE, D. F., & MASON, W. (1987). Characteristics of obstructive and central sleep apnea in the elderly: An interim report. *Biological Psychiatry, 22,* 741–750.

ANDERSON, J. R. (1983). *The architecture of cognition.* Cambridge, MA: Harvard University Press.

ANDERSON, J. R. (1987). Skill acquisition: Compilation of weak-method problem solutions. *Psychological Review, 94,* 192–210.

ANDERSON, J. R. (1990). *Cognitive psychology and its implications* (3rd ed.). New York: Freeman.

ANDERSON, M. (1992). *Intelligence and development: A cognitive theory.* Oxford: Blackwell.

ANDERSSON, B-E. (1992). Effects of day-care on cognitive and socioemotional competence of thirteen-year-old Swedish schoolchildren. *Child Development, 63,* 20–36.

ANDREASEN, N. C. (1988). Brain imaging: Applications in psychiatry. *Science, 239,* 1381–1388.

ANDREASEN, N. C., FLAUM, M., SCHULTZ, S., DUZYUREK, S., & MILLER, D. (1997). Diagnosis, methodology, and subtypes of schizophrenia. *Neuropsychobiology, 35,* 61–63.

ANDREASEN, N. C., FLAUM, M., SWAYZE, V. W., TYRRELL, G., & ARNDT, S. (1990). Positive and negative symptoms in schizophrenia: A critical reappraisal. *Archives of General Psychiatry, 47,* 615–621.

ANDREWS, K. H., & KANDEL, D. B. (1979). Attitude and behavior. *American Sociological Review, 44,* 298–310.

ANGOFF, W. H. (1988). The nature-nurture debate, aptitudes, and group differences. *American Psychologist, 43,* 713–720.

ANTROBUS, J. (1983). REM and NREM sleep reports: Comparisons of word frequencies by cognitive classes. *Psychophysiology, 20,* 562–568.

ANTROBUS, J. (1991). Dreaming: Cognitive processes during cortical activation and high afferent thresholds. *Psychological Review, 98,* 96–121.

ANTROBUS, J. (1993). Dreaming: Could we do without it? In A. Moffitt, M. Kramer, & R. Hoffman (Eds.), *The functions of dreaming.* Albany: State University of New York Press.

ARDREY, R. (1966). *The territorial imperative.* New York: Dell.

ARENDT, H. (1963). *Eichmann in Jerusalem: A report on the banality of evil.* New York: Viking Press.

ARMSTRONG, S. L., GLEITMAN, L. R., & GLEITMAN, H. (1983). What some concepts might not be. *Cognition, 13,* 263–308.

ARNOLD, M. (1949). A demonstrational analysis of the TAT in a clinical setting. *Journal of Abnormal and Social Psychology, 44,* 97–111.

ARONSON, E. (1995). *The social animal* (7th ed.). San Francisco: Freeman.

ARONSON, E., & CARLSMITH, J. M. (1963). The effect of the severity of threat on the devaluation of forbidden behavior. *Journal of Abnormal and Social Psychology, 66,* 584–588.

ARTMAN, L., & CAHAN, S. (1993). Schooling and the development of transitive inference. *Developmental Psychology, 29,* 753–759.

ASCH, S. E. (1952). *Social psychology.* Englewood Cliffs, NJ: Prentice-Hall.

ASCH, S. E. (1955). Opinions and social pressures. *Scientific American, 193,* 31–35.

ASCH, S. E. (1958). Effects of group pressure upon modification and distortion of judgments. In E. E. Maccoby, T. M. Newcomb, & E. L. Hartley (Eds.), *Readings in social psychology* (3rd ed.). New York: Holt, Rinehart & Winston.

ASHMEAD, D. H., DAVIS, D. L., WHALEN, T., & ODOM, R. D. (1991). Sound localization and sensitivity to interaural time differences in human infants. *Child Development, 62,* 1211–1226.

ASLIN, R. N. (1987). Visual and auditory development in infancy. In J. D. Osofsky (Ed.), *Handbook of infant development* (2nd ed.). New York: Wiley.

ASLIN, R. N., & BANKS, M. S. (1978). Early visual experience in humans: Evidence for a critical period in the development of binocular vision. In S. Schneider, H. Liebowitz, H. Pick, & H. Stevenson (Eds.), *Psychology: From basic research to practice.* New York: Plenum.

ASLIN, R. N., PISONI, D. V., & JUSCZYK, P. W. (1983). Auditory development and speech perception in infancy. In P. H. Mussen (Ed.), *Handbook of child psychology* (Vol. 2). New York: Wiley.

ASSAD, G., & SHAPIRO, B. (1986). Hallucinations: Theoretical and clinical overview. *American Journal of Psychiatry, 143,* 1088–1097.

ATKINSON, D. (1983). Ethnic similarity in counseling psychology: A review of the research. *Counseling Psychologist, 11,* 79–92.

ATKINSON, D., MARUYAMA, M., & MATSUI, S. (1978). The effects of counselor race and counseling approach on Asian Americans' perceptions of counselor credibility and utility. *Journal of Counseling Psychology, 25,* 76–83.

ATKINSON, D. R. (1983). Ethnic similarity in counseling psychology: A review of the research. *Counseling Psychologist, 11,* 79–92.

ATKINSON, R. C. (1975). Mnemotechnics in second-language learning. *American Psychologist, 30,* 821–828.

ATKINSON, R. C., HERRNSTEIN, R. J., LINDZEY, G., & LUCE, R. D. (Eds.) (1988). *Stevens' handbook of experimental psychology* (Vols. 1 and 2). New York: Wiley.

ATKINSON, R. C., & SHIFFRIN, R. M. (1971a). The control of short-term memory. *Scientific American, 225,* 82–90.

ATKINSON, R. C., & SHIFFRIN, R. M. (1971b). Human memory: A proposed system and its control processes. In K. W. Spence (Ed.), *The psychology of learning and motivation: Advances in research and theory* (pp. 89–195). New York: Academic Press.

AULD, F., & HYMAN, M. (1991). *Resolution of inner conflict: An introduction to psychoanalytic therapy.* Washington, DC: American Psychological Association.

AVERILL, J. R. (1983). Studies on anger and aggression: Implications for theories of emotion. *American Psychologist, 38,* 1145–1160.

AWAYA, S., MIYAKE, Y., IMAYUMI, Y., SHIOSE, Y., KNADA, T., & KOMURO, K. (1973). Amblyopia. *Japanese Journal of Ophthalmology, 17,* 69–82.

AX, A. (1953). The physiological differentiation between fear and anger in humans. *Psychosomatic Medicine, 15,* 433–442.

BACHMAN, J. G., JOHNSTON, L. D., & O'MALLEY, M. (1998). Explaining recent increase in students' marijuana use: Impacts of perceived risks and disapproval, 1976 through 1996. *American Journal of Public Health, 88,* 887–892.

BADDELEY, A. (1986). *Working memory.* Oxford: Clarendon.

BADDELEY, A. D. (1990). *Human memory: Theory and practice.* Boston: Allyn and Bacon.

BADDELEY, A. D., & HITCH, G. J. (1974). Working memory. In G. H. Bower (Ed.), *The psychology of learning and motivation* (Vol. 8). New York: Academic Press.

BADDELEY, A. D., THOMPSON, N., & BUCHANAN, M. (1975). Word length and the structure of short-term memory. *Journal of Verbal Learning and Verbal Behavior, 14,* 575–589.

BAER, P. E., & FUHRER, M. J. (1968). Cognitive processes during differential trace and delayed conditioning of the G. S. R. *Journal of Experimental Psychology, 78,* 81–88.

BAHRICK, H. P., & PHELPHS, E. (1987). Retention of Spanish vocabulary over eight years. *Journal of Experimental Psychology: Learning, Memory and Cognition, 13,* 344–349.

BAILEY, J. M., & MARTIN, N. G. (1995, September). A twin registry study of sexual orientation. Paper presented at the twenty-first annual meeting of the International Academy of Sex Research, Provincetown, MA.

BAILEY, J. M., & PILLARD, R. C. (1991). A genetic study of male sexual orientation. *Archives of General Psychiatry, 48,* 1089–1096.

BAILEY, J. M., PILLARD, R. C., NEALE, M. C., & AGYEI, Y. (1993). Heritable factors influence sexual orientation in women. *Archives of General Psychiatry, 50,* 217–223.

BAILLARGEON, R. (1987). Object permanence in 3½- and 4½-month-old infants. *Developmental Psychology, 23,* 655–664.

BAILLARGEON, R., & DEVOS, J. (1991). Object permanence in young infants: Further evidence. *Child Development, 62,* 1227–1246.

BAILLARGEON, R., SPELKE, E. S., & WASSERMAN, S. (1985). Object permanence in five-month-old infants. *Cognition, 20,* 191–208.

BANDURA, A. (1969). *Principles of behavior modification.* New York: Holt, Rinehart and Winston.

BANDURA, A. (1973). *Aggression: A social learning analysis.* Englewood Cliffs, NJ: Prentice-Hall.

BANDURA, A. (1977). *Social learning theory.* Englewood Cliffs, NJ: Prentice-Hall.

BANDURA, A. (1986). *Social foundations of thought and action: A social cognitive theory.* Englewood Cliffs, NJ: Prentice-Hall.

BANDURA, A. (1995). *Self-efficacy in changing societies.* New York: Cambridge University Press.

BANDURA, A., BLANCHARD, E. B., & RITTER, B. (1969). The relative efficacy of desensitization and modeling approaches for inducing behavioral, affective, and attitudinal changes. *Journal of Personality and Social Psychology, 13,* 173–199.

BANKS, W. P., & PRINTZMETAL, W. (1976). Configurational effects in visual information processing. *Perception and Psychophysics, 19,* 361–367.

BANKS, W. P., & SALAPATEK, P. (1983). Infant visual perception. In P. H. Mussen (Ed.), *Handbook of child psychology* (Vol. 2). New York: Wiley.

BANYAI, E. I., & HILGARD, E. R. (1976). A comparison of active-alert hypnotic induction with traditional relaxation induction. *Journal of Abnormal Psychology, 85,* 218–224.

BAREFOOT, J. C., WILLIAMS, R. B., & DAHLSTROM, W. G. (1983). Hostility, CHD incidence and total mortality: A 25-year follow-up study of 255 physicians. *Psychosomatic Medicine, 45,* 59–63.

BARGH, J. A., CHEN, M., & BURROWS, L. (1996). Automaticity of social behavior: Direct effects of trait construct and stereotype activation on action. *Journal of Personality and Social Psychology, 71,* 230–244.

BARKOW, J., COSMIDES, L., & TOOKY, J. (1990). *The adapted mind: Evolutionary psychology and the generation of culture.* Oxford University Press.

BARLOW, D. H. (1988). *Anxiety and its disorders: The nature and treatment of anxiety and panic.* New York: Guilford.

BARLOW, H. B., & MOLLON, J. D. (1982). *The senses.* Cambridge, England: Cambridge University Press.

BARON, R. S. (1986). Distraction-conflict theory: Progress and problems. In L. Berkowitz (Ed.), *Advances in experimental social psychology* (Vol. 19). New York: Academic Press.

BARRERA, M. E., & MAURER, D. (1981). Recognition of mother's photographed face by the three-month-old infant. *Child Development, 52,* 714–716.

BARSALOU, L. W. (1985). Ideals, central tendency, and frequency of instantiation as determinants of graded structure in categories. *Journal of Experimental Psychology: Learning, Memory, and Cognition, 11,* 629–654.

BARSALOU, L. W. (1992). *Cognitive psychology: An overview for cognitive scientists.* Hillsdale, NJ: Erlbaum.

BARTLETT, F. C. (1932). *Remembering: A study in experimental and social psychology.* Cambridge, England: Cambridge University Press.

BARTOSHUK, L. M. (1979). Bitter taste of saccharin: Related to the genetic ability to taste the bitter substance propylthiourial (PROP). *Science, 205,* 934–935.

BARTOSHUK, L. M. (1993). Genetic and pathological taste variation: What can we learn from animal models and human disease? *Ciba Foundation Symposium (D7X), 179,* 251–262.

BASOGLU, M. (Ed.). (1992). *Torture and its consequences: Current treatment approaches.* Cambridge, England: Cambridge University Press.

BATESON, P. (1978). Sexual imprinting and optimal outbreeding. *Nature, 273,* 659–660.

BATSON, C. D. (1991). *The altruism question: Toward a social-psychological answer.* Hillsdale, NJ: Erlbaum.

BAUCOM, D. H., SHOHAM, V., MUESSER, K. T., DAIUTO, A. D., & STICKLE, T. R. (1998). Empirically supported couple and family interventions for marital distress and adult mental health problems. *Journal of Consulting and Clinical Psychology, 66,* 53–88.

BAUMEISTER, R. F., & TICE, D. M. (1984). Role of self-presentation and choice in cognitive dissonance under forced compliance: Necessary or sufficient causes? *Journal of Personality and Social Psychology, 43,* 838–852.

BAUMRIND, D. (1964). Some thoughts on ethics of research: After reading Milgram's "Behavioral study of obedience." *American Psychologist, 19,* 421–423.

BAUMRIND, D. (1971). Current patterns of parental authority. *Developmental Psychology Monographs, 1,* 1–103.

BAXTER, L., SCHWARTZ, J., BERGMAN, K., & SZUBA, M. (1992). Caudate glucose metabolic rate changes with both drug and behavior therapy for obsessive-compulsive disorder. *Archives of General Psychiatry, 49,* 681–689.

BAXTER, L. R., SCHWARTZ, J. M., GUZE, B. H., & BERGMAN, K. (1990). PET imaging in obsessive compulsive disorder with and without depression. *Journal of Clinical Psychiatry, 51*(suppl.), 61–69.

BEAMAN, A. L., BARNES, P. J., KLENTZ, B., & MCQUIRK, B. (1978). Increasing helping rates through information dissemination: Teaching pays. *Personality and Social Psychology Bulletin, 4,* 406–411.

BECHARA, A., TRANEL, D., DAMASIO, H., ADOLPHS, R., ROCKLAND, C., & DAMASIO, A. R. (1995). *Science, 269,* 1115–1118.

BECK, A. T. (1976). *Cognitive therapy and the emotional disorder.* New York: International Universities Press.

BECK, A. T., RUSH, A. J., SHAW, B. F., & EMERY, G. (1979). *Cognitive therapy of depression.* New York: Guilford.

BEECHER, H. K. (1961). Surgery as placebo. *Journal of the American Medical Association, 176,* 1102–1107.

BÉKÉSY, G. VON (1960). *Experiments in hearing* (E. G. Weaver, Trans). New York: McGraw-Hill.

BELL, A. P. (1982, November). Sexual preference: A postscript. *Siecus Report, 11,* 1–3.

BELL, A. P., & WEINBERG, M. S. (1978). *Homosexualities: A study of diversity among men and women.* New York: Simon & Schuster.

BELL, A. P., WEINBERG, M. S., & HAMMER-SMITH, S. K. (1981a). *Sexual preference: Its development in men and women.* Bloomington: Indiana University Press.

BELL, A. P., WEINBERG, M. S., & HAMMER-SMITH, S. K. (1981b). *Sexual preference: Its development in men and women. Statistical appendix.* Bloomington: Indiana University Press.

BELL, C. J., & NUTT, D. J. (1998). Serotonin and panic. *British Journal of Psychiatry, 172,* 465–471.

BELL, S. M., & AINSWORTH, M. D. (1972). Infant crying and maternal responsiveness. *Child Development, 43,* 1171–1190.

BELOFF, H. (1957). The structure and origin of the anal character. *Genetic Psychology Monographs, 55,* 141–172.

BELSKY, J., FISH, M., & ISABELLA, R. A. (1991). Continuity and discontinuity in infant negative and positive emotionality: Family antecedents and attachment consequences. *Developmental Psychology, 27,* 421–431.

BELSKY, J., & ROVINE, M. J. (1987). Temperament and attachment security in the strange situation: An empirical rapprochement. *Child Development, 58,* 787–795.

BELSKY, J., & ROVINE, M. J. (1988). Nonmaternal care in the first year of life and the security of infant-parent attachment. *Child Development, 59,* 157–167.

BEM, D. J. (1972). Self-perception theory. In L. Berkowitz (Ed.), *Advances in experimental social psychology* (Vol. 6). New York: Academic Press.

BEM, D. J. (1995). *Exotic becomes erotic: A developmental theory of sexual orientation.* Unpublished manuscript, Cornell University at Ithaca, New York.

BEM, D. J. (1996). Exotic becomes erotic: A developmental theory of sexual orientation. *Psychological Review, 103,* 320–335.

BEM, D. J., & HONORTON, C. (1994). Does psi exist? Replicable evidence for an anomalous process if information transfer. *Psychological Bulletin, 115,* 4–18.

BEM, D. J., WALLACH, M. A., & KOGAN, N. (1965). Group decision-making under risk of aversive consequences. *Journal of Personality and Social Psychology, 1,* 453–460.

BEM, S. L. (1975). Sex role adaptability: One consequence of psychological androgyny. *Journal of Personality and Social Psychology, 31,* 634–643.

BEM, S. L. (1981). Gender schema theory: A cognitive account of sex typing. *Psychological Review, 88,* 354–364.

BEM, S. L. (1985). Androgyny and gender schema theory: A conceptual and empirical integration. In T. B. Sonderegger (Ed.), *Nebraska symposium on motivation 1984: Psychology and gender* (pp. 179–226). Lincoln, NE: University of Nebraska Press.

BEM, S. L. (1987). Gender schema theory and the romantic tradition. In P. Shaver & C. Hendrick (Eds.), *Review of personality and social psychology* (Vol. 7, pp. 251–271). Newbury Park, CA: Sage.

BEM, S. L. (1989). Genital knowledge and gender constancy in preschool children. *Child Development, 60,* 649–662.

BEM, S. L. (1993). *The lenses of gender: Transforming the debate on sexual inequality.* New Haven, CT: Yale University Press.

BENJAMIN, J., LI, L., PATTERSON, C., GREENBERG, B. D., MURPHY, D. L., & HAMER, D. H. Population and familial association between the D4 dopamine receptor gene and measures of novelty seeking. *Nature Genetics, 12,* 81–84.

BENSON, D. F. (1985). Aphasia in K. M. Heilman & E. Valenstein (Eds.), *Clinical neuropsychology* (2nd ed., pp. 17–47). New York: Oxford University Press.

BERGER, T. W. (1984). Long-term potentiation of hippocampal synaptic transmission affects rate of behavioral learning. *Science, 224,* 627–630.

BERGIN, A. E., & LAMBERT, M. J. (1978). The evaluation of therapeutic outcomes. In S. L. Garfield & A. E. Bergin (Eds.), *Handbook of psychotherapy and behavior change* (2nd ed.). New York: Wiley.

BERGIN, A. E., & LAMBERT, M. J. (1979). Counseling the researcher. *Counseling Psychologist, 8,* 53–56.

BERK, L. E. (1997). *Child development* (4th ed.). Needham Heights, MA: Allyn and Bacon.

BERKOWITZ, L. (1965). The concept of aggressive drive. In L. Berkowitz (Ed.), *Advances in experimental social psychology* (Vol. 2). New York: Academic Press.

BERLIN, B., & KAY, P. (1969). *Basic color terms: Their universality and evolution.* Los Angeles: University of California Press.

BERMAN, A. L., & JOBES, D. A. (1991). *Adolescent suicide assessment and intervention.* Washington, DC: American Psychological Association.

BERMAN, K. F., TORREY, E. F., DANIEL, D. G., & WEINBERGER, D. R. (1992). Regional cerebral blood flow in monozygotic twins discordant and concordant for schizophrenia. *Archives of General Psychiatry, 49,* 927–934.

BERNSTEIN, I. L. (1978). Learned taste aversions in children receiving chemotherapy. *Science, 200,* 1302–1303.

BERRIDGE, K. C., & VALENSTEIN, E. S. (1991). What psychological process mediates feeding evoked by electrical stimulation of the lateral hypothalamus? *Behavioral Neuroscience, 105,* 3–14.

BERSCHEID, E. (1983). Emotion. In H. H. Kelley, E. Berscheid, A. Christensen, J. H. Harvey, T. L. Hutson, G. Levinger, E. McClintock, L. A. Peplau, & D. R. Peterson (Eds.), *Close relationships* (pp. 110–168). New York: Freeman.

BERSCHEID, E., & WALSTER, E. H. (1974). A little bit about love. In T. Huston (Ed.), *Foundation of interpersonal attraction*. New York: Academic Press.

BEST, J. B. (1992). *Cognitive psychology*. New York: West.

BIBRING, E. (1953). The mechanism of depression. In P. Greenacre (Ed.), *Affective disorders* (pp. 13–48). New York: International Universities Press.

BIEDERMAN, I. (1987). Recognition by components: A theory of human image understanding. *Psychological Review, 94*, 115–1947.

BIEDERMAN, I. (1990). Higher-level vision. In D. N. Osherson, S. M. Kossyln, & J. M. Hollerbach (Eds.). *An invitation to cognitive science: Visual cognition and action* (Vol. 2). Cambridge, MA: MIT Press.

BIEDERMAN, I., & JU, G. (1988). Surface versus edge-based determinants of visual recognition. *Cognitive Psychology, 20*, 38–64.

BIERBRAUER, G. (1973). *Attribution and perspective: effects of time, set, and role on interpersonal inference*. Unpublished Ph.D. dissertation, Stanford University.

BILLINGS, A. G., & MOOS, R. H. (1984). Coping, stress, and social resources among adults with unipolar depression. *Journal of Personality and Social Psychology, 46*, 887–891.

BINET, A., & SIMON, T. (1905). New methods for the diagnosis of the intellectual level of subnormals. *Annals of Psychology, 11*, 191.

BINNS, K. E., & SALT, T. E. (1997). Post eye-opening maturation of visual receptive field diameters in the superior colliculus of normal- and dark-reared rats. *Brain Research: Developmental Brain Research, 99*, 263–266.

BISIACH, E., & LUZZATI, C. (1978). Unilateral neglect of representational space. *Cortex, 14*, 129–133.

BLAGROVE, M. (1992). Dreams as a reflection of our waking concerns and abilities: A critique of the problem-solving paradigm in dream research. *Dreaming, 2*, 205–220.

BLAGROVE, M. (1996). Problems with the cognitive psychological modeling of dreaming. *Journal of Mind and Behavior, 17*, 99–134.

BLAKE, R. (1981). Strategies for assessing visual deficits in animals with selective neural deficits. In R. N. Aslin, J. R. Alberts, & M. R. Petersen (Eds.), *Development of perception: Vol. 2. The visual system* (pp. 95–110). New York: Academic Press.

BLAKESLEE, S. (1998, October 13). Placebos prove so powerful even experts are surprised. *New York Times*, pp. F1, F4.

BLAMEY, P. J., DOWELL, R. C., BROWN, A. M., CLARK, G. M., & SELIGMAN, P. M. (1987). Vowel and consonant recognition of cochlear implant patients using formant-estimating speech processors. *Journal of the Acoustical Society of America, 82*, 48–57.

BLANCK, G. (1990). Vygotsky: The man and his cause. In L. C. Moll (Ed.), *Vygotsky and education*. New York: Cambridge University Press.

BLATT, S. J. (1974). Levels of object representation in anaclitic and introjective depression. *Psychoanalytic Study of the Child, 29*, 107–159.

BLAZER, D. G., GEORGE, L., & HUGHES, D. (1991). The epidemiology of anxiety disorders. In C. Salzman & B. Liebowitz (Eds.), *Anxiety disorders in the elderly* (pp. 17–30). New York: Springer-Verlag.

BLISS, E. L. (1980). Multiple personalities: Report of fourteen cases with implications for schizophrenia and hysteria. *Archives of General Psychiatry, 37*, 1388–1397.

BLISS, T. V. P., & LMO, T. (1973). Long-lasting potentiation of synaptic transmission in the dentate area of the anesthetized rabbit following stimulation of the preforant path. *Journal of Physiology, 232*, 331–356.

BLOCK, J. (1961/1978). *The Q-sort method in personality assessment and psychiatric research*. Palo Alto: Consulting Psychologists Press.

BLOOD, R. O. (1967). *Love match and arranged marriage*. New York: Free Press.

BLUM, G. S. (1953). *Psychoanalytic theories of personality*. New York: McGraw-Hill.

BLUM, K., CULL, J. G., BRAVERMAN, E. R., & COMINGS, D. E. (1996). Reward deficiency syndrome. *American Scientist, 84*, 132–145.

BLUMENTHAL, J. A., EMERY, C. F., MADDEN, D. J., SCHNIEBOLK, S., WALSH-RIDDLE, M., GEORGE, L. K., MCKEE, D. C., HIGGINBOTHAM, M. B., COBB, F. R., & COLEMAN, R. E. (1991). Long term effects of exercise on psychological functioning in older men and women. *Journal of Gerontology, 46*, 352–361.

BOFF, K. R., KAUFMAN, L., & THOMAS, J. P. (Eds.) (1986). *Handbook of perception and human performance* (Vol. 1). New York: Wiley.

BOLLES, R. C. (1970). Species-specific defense reactions and avoidance learning. *Psychological Review, 77*, 32–48.

BONANNO, G. A., & SINGER, J. L. (1990). Repressive personality style: Theoretical and methodological implications for health and pathology. In J. L. Singer (Ed.), *Repression and dissociation* (pp. 435–465). Chicago: University of Chicago Press.

BOND, C. F. (1982). Social facilitation: A self-presentational view. *Journal of Personality and Social Psychology, 42*, 1042–1050.

BOON, S., & DRAIJER, N. (1993). Multiple personality disorder in The Netherlands: A clinical investigation of 71 patients. *American Journal of Psychiatry, 150*, 489–494.

BOOTH, D. (1990). Learned role of tastes in eating motivation. In E. D. Capaldi & P. T. L. (Eds.), *Taste, experience, and feeding* (pp. 179–194). Washington, DC: American Psychological Association.

BOOTH, D. A. (1991). Learned ingestive motivation and the pleasures of the palate. In R. C. Bolles (Eds.), *The hedonics of taste* (pp. 29–58). Hillsdale: Erlbaum.

BOOTH-KEWLEY, S., & FRIEDMAN, H. S. (1987). Psychological predictors of heart disease: A quantitative review. *Psychological Bulletin, 101*, 343–362.

BOOTZIN, R. R., KIHLSTROM, J. F., & SCHACTER, D. L. (Eds.) (1990). *Sleep and cognition*. Washington, DC: American Psychological Association.

BORGIDA, E., & NISBETT, R. E. (1977). The differential impact of abstract vs. concrete information on decisions. *Journal of Applied Social Psychology, 7*, 258–271.

BORING, E. G. (1930). A new ambiguous figure. *American Journal of Psychology, 42*, 444–445.

BORNSTEIN, R. F. (1992). Subliminal mere exposure effects. In R. F. Bornstein & T. S. Pittman (Eds.), *Perception without awareness: Cognitive, clinical and social perspectives* (pp. 191–210). New York: Guilford.

BORNSTEIN, R. F., & D'AGOSTINO, P. R. (1992). Stimulus recognition and the mere exposure effect. *Journal of Personality and Social Psychology, 63*, 545–552.

BOTMAN, H., & CROVITZ, H. (1992). Dream reports and autobiographical memory. *Imagination, Cognition and Personality, 9*, 213–214.

BOUCHARD, C., et al. (1990). The response to long-term overeating in identical twins. *New England Journal of Medicine, 322*, 1477–1482.

BOUCHARD, T. J., JR. (1984). Twins reared apart and together: What they tell us about human diversity. In S. Fox (Ed.), *The chemical and biological bases of individuality*. New York: Plenum.

BOUCHARD, T. J., JR. (1995). Nature's twice-told tale: Identical twins reared apart—What they tell us about human individuality. Paper presented at the annual meeting of the Western Psychological Association, Los Angeles.

BOUCHARD, T. J., JR., LYKKEN, D. T., MCGUE, M., SEGAL, N. L., & TELLEGEN, A. (1990). Sources of human psychological differences: The Minnesota study of twins reared apart. *Science, 250*, 223–228.

BOUCHARD, T. J., & MCGUE, M. (1981). Familial studies of intelligence: A review. *Science, 212*, 1055–1059.

BOURNE, L. E. (1966). *Human conceptual behavior*. Boston: Allyn and Bacon.

BOWER, G. H. (1981). Mood and memory. *American Psychologist, 6*, 129–148.

BOWER, G. H., BLACK, J. B., & TURNER, T. R. (1979). Scripts in memory for text. *Cognitive Psychology, 11*, 177–220.

BOWER, G. H., & CLARK, M. C. (1969). Narrative stories as mediators for serial learning. *Psychonomic Science, 14*, 181–182.

BOWER, G. H., CLARK, M. C., WINZENZ, D., & LESGOLD, A. (1969). Hierarchical retrieval schemes in recall of categorized word lists. *Journal of Verbal Learning and Verbal Behavior, 8*, 323–343.

BOWER, G. H., & SPRINGSTON, F. (1970). Pauses as recoding points in letter series. *Journal of Experimental Psychology, 83,* 421–430.

BOWLBY, J. (1973). *Attachment and loss: Separation, anxiety and anger* (Vol. 2). London: Hogarth Press.

BOYNTON, R. M. (1979). *Human color vision.* New York: Holt, Rinehart & Winston.

BRADSHAW, G. L., & ANDERSON, J. R. (1982). Elaborative encoding as an explanation of levels of processing. *Journal of Verbal Learning and Verbal Behavior, 21,* 165–174.

BRANSFORD, J. D., & JOHNSON, M. K. (1973). Considerations of some problems of comprehension. In W. G. Chase (Ed.), *Visual information processing.* New York: Academic Press.

BRAUN, B. G. (1986). *Treatment of multiple personality disorder.* Washington, DC: American Psychiatric Press.

BRAZELTON, T. B. (1978). The remarkable talents of the newborn. *Birth & Family Journal, 5,* 4–10.

BREEDLOVE, S. M. (1994). Sexual differentiation of the human nervous system. *Annual Review of Psychology, 45,* 389–418.

BREGMAN, A. S. (1990). *Auditory scene analysis.* Cambridge, MA: MIT Press.

BREHM, S. S. (1992). *Intimate relationships* (2nd ed.). New York: McGraw-Hill.

BREIER, A., SCHREIBER, J. L., DYER, J., & PICKAR, D. (1992). Course of illness and predictors of outcome in chronic schizophrenia: Implications for pathophysiology. *British Journal of Psychiatry, 161,* 38–43.

BRELAND, K., & BRELAND, M. (1966). *Animal behavior.* New York: Macmillan.

BRENNER, C. (1980). A psychoanalytic theory of affects. In R. Plutchik & H. Kellerman (Eds.), *Emotion: Theory, research, and experience* (Vol. 1). New York: Academic Press.

BREWIN, C. R., MACCARTHY, B., DUDA, K., & VAUGHN, C. E. (1991). Attribution and expressed emotion in the relatives of patients with schizophrenia. *Journal of Abnormal Psychology, 100*(4), 546–554.

BRIDGER, W. H. (1961). Sensory habituation and discrimination in the human neonate. *American Journal of Psychiatry, 117,* 991–996.

BROADBENT, D. E. (1958). *Perception and communication.* London: Pergamon.

BROMAN, C. L. (1987). Race differences in professional help seeking. *American Journal of Community Psychology, 15,* 473–489.

BROOKS-GUNN, J., & RUBLE, D. N. (1983). The experience of menarche from a developmental perspective. In J. Brooks-Gunn & A. C. Petersen (Eds.), *Girls at puberty: Biological and psychological perspectives.* New York: Plenum.

BROWN, A. E. (1936). Dreams in which the dreamer knows he is asleep. *Journal of Abnormal Psychology, 31,* 59–66.

BROWN, D. P. (1977). A model for the levels of concentrative mediation. *International Journal of Clinical and Experimental Hypnosis, 25,* 236–273.

BROWN, E. L., & DEFFENBACHER, K. (1979). *Perception and the senses.* Oxford: Oxford University Press.

BROWN, G. W., BIRLEY, J. L., & WING, J. K. (1972). Influence of family life on the course of schizophrenic disorders: A replication. *British Journal of Psychiatry, 121,* 241–258.

BROWN, J. (1991). Staying fit and staying well: Physical fitness as a moderator of life stress. *Journal of Personality and Social Psychology, 60,* 555–561.

BROWN, J. D. (1986). Evaluations of self and others: Self-enhancement biases in social judgments. *Social Cognition, 4,* 353–376.

BROWN, L. L., TOMKARKEN, A. J., ORTH, D. N., LOOSEN, P. T., KALIN, N. H., & DAVIDSON, R. J. (1996). Individual differences in repressive-defensiveness predict basal salivary cortisol levels. *Journal of Personality and Social Psychology, 70,* 362–371.

BROWN, R. (1973). *A first language: The early stages.* Cambridge, MA: Harvard University Press.

BROWN, R. (1974). Further comment on the risky shift. *American Psychologist, 29,* 468–470.

BROWN, R. (1986). *Social psychology: The second edition.* New York: Free Press.

BROWN, R., CAZDEN, C. B., & BELLUGI, U. (1969). The child's grammar from 1 to 3. In J. P. Hill (Ed.), *Minnesota symposium on child psychology* (Vol. 2). Minneapolis: University of Minnesota Press.

BROWN, R., & KULIK, J. (1977). Flashbulb memories. *Cognition, 5,* 73–99.

BROWN, R. W., & MCNEILL, D. (1966). The "tip-of-the-tongue" phenomenon. *Journal of Verbal Learning and Verbal Behavior, 5,* 325–337.

BROWNELL, K. (1988, January). Yo-yo dieting. *Psychology Today, 22,* 20–23.

BROWNELL, K. D., & RODIN, J. (1994). The dieting maelstrom: Is it possible and advisable to lose weight? *American Psychologist, 49,* 781–791.

BRUCH, H. (1973). *Eating disorders: Obesity, anorexia nervosa, and the person within.* New York: Basic Books.

BRUNER, J. S. (1957). Going beyond the information given. In *Contemporary approaches to cognition: A symposium held at the University of Colorado.* Cambridge, MA: Harvard University Press.

BRUNER, J. S., GOODNOW, J. J., & AUSTIN, G. A. (1956). *A study of thinking.* New York: Wiley.

BRUNER, J. S., OLVER, R. R., GREENFIELD, P. M., & collaborators (1966). *Studies in cognitive growth.* New York: Wiley.

BRUYER, R., LATERRE, C., SERON, X., & collaborators (1983). A case of prosopagnosia with some preserved covert remembrance of familiar faces. *Brain and Cognition, 2,* 257–284.

BRYAN, J. H., & TEST, M. A. (1967). Models and helping: Naturalistic studies in aiding behavior. *Journal of Personality and Social Psychology, 6,* 400–407.

BUB, D., BLACKS, S., & HOWELL, J. (1989). Word recognition and orthographic context effects in a letter-by-letter reader. *Brain and Language, 36,* 357–376.

BUCHANAN, ECCLES, & BECKER (1992). Are adolescents the victims of raging hormones? Evidence for activational effects of hormones on moods and behavior at adolescence. *Psychological Bulletin, 111,* 62–107.

BUCHSBAUM, M. S., HAIER, R. J., POTKIN, S. G., & NUECHTERLEIN, K. (1992). Fronostriatal disorder of cerebral metabolism in never-medicated schizophrenics. *Archives of General Psychiatry, 49,* 935–942.

BUCK, L., & AXEL, R. (1991). A novel multigene family may encode odorant receptors: A molecular basis for odor recognition. *Cell, 65,* 175–187.

BURNAM, M. A., STEIN, J. A., GOLDING, J. M., SIEGEL, J. M., SORENSON, S. B., FORSYTHE, A. B., & TELLES, C. A. (1988). Sexual assault and mental disorders in a community population. *Journal of Consulting and Clinical Psychology, 56,* 843–850.

BURNSTEIN, E., & VINOKUR, A. (1973). Testing two classes of theories about group-induced shifts in individual choice. *Journal of Experimental Social Psychology, 9,* 123–137.

BURNSTEIN, E., & VINOKUR, A. (1977). Persuasive arguments and social comparison as determinants of attitude polarization. *Journal of Experimental Social Psychology, 13,* 315–332.

BUSBY, P. A., TONG, Y. C., & CLARK, G. M. (1993). Electrode position, repetition rate, and speech perception by early- and late-deafened cochlear implant patients. *Journal of the Acoustical Society of America, 93,* 1058–1067.

BUSS, A. H., & PLOMIN, R. (1975). *A temperament theory of personality development.* New York: Wiley.

BUSS, D. M. (1989). Sex differences in human mate preference: Evolutionary hypotheses tested in 37 cultures. *Brain and Behavior Sciences, 12,* 1–49.

BUSS, D. M. (1991). Evolutionary personality psychology. *Annual Review of Psychology, 42,* 459–491.

BUSS, D. M. (1994). *The evolution of desire: Strategies of human mating.* New York: Basic Books.

BUSS, D. M., & BARNES, M. (1986). Preferences in human mate selection. *Journal of Personality and Social Psychology, 50,* 559–570.

BUSS, D. M., LARSEN, R. J., WESTERN, D., & SEMMELROTH, J. (1992). Sex differences in jealousy: Evolution, physiology, and psychology. *Psychological Science, 3,* 251–255.

BUTLER, J. M., & HAIGH, G. V. (1954). Changes in the relation between self-concepts and ideal concepts consequent upon client centered counseling. In C. R. Rogers & R. F. Dymond (Eds.), *Psychotherapy and personality change: Coordinated studies in the client-centered approach* (pp. 55–76). Chicago: University of Chicago Press.

BUTTERFIELD, E. L., & SIPERSTEIN, G. N. (1972). Influence of contingent auditory stimulation on nonnutritional sucking. In J. Bosma (Ed.), *Oral sensation and perception: The mouth of the infant.* Springfield, IL: Charles B. Thomas.

CABANAC, M. (1979). Sensory pleasure. *Quarterly Review of Biology, 54,* 1–29.

CABANAC, M. (1992). Pleasure: The common currency. *Journal of Theoretical Biology, 155,* 173–200.

CACIOPPO, J. T., KLEIN, D. J., BEMSTON, G. G., & HATFIELD, E. (1993). The psychophysiology of emotion. In M. Lewis & J. M. Haviland (Eds.), *The handbook of emotions.* New York: Guilford.

CADORET, R. J., & CAIN, C. A. (1980). Sex differences in predictors of antisocial behavior in adoptees. *Archives of General Psychiatry, 37,* 1171–1175.

CAHILL, L., BABINSKY, R., MARKOWITSCH, H. J., & MCGAUGH, J. L. (1996). The amygdala and emotional memory. *Nature, 377,* 295–296.

CAHILL, L., PRINS, B., WEBER, M., & MCGAUGH, J. L. (1994). Adrenergic activation and memory for emotional events. *Nature, 371.*

CAIN, W. S. (1988). Olfaction. In R. C. Atkinson, R. J. Hernstein, G. Lindzey, & R. D. Luce (Eds.), *Stevens' handbook of experimental psychology* (Vol. 1). New York: Wiley, 409–459.

CALLAWAY, M. R., MARRIOTT, R. G., & ESSER, J. K. (1985). Effects of dominance on group decision making: Toward a stress-reduction explanation of group-think. *Journal of Personality and Social Psychology, 49,* 949–952.

CAMPOS, J. J., BARRETT, K. C., LAMB, M. E., GOLDSMITH, H. H., & STENBERG, C. (1983). Socioemotional development. In P. Mussen (Ed.), *Handbook of child psychology* (Vol. 1, pp. 1–101). New York: Wiley.

CANNON, W. B. (1927). The James-Lange theory of emotions: A critical examination and an alternative theory. *American Journal of Psychology, 39,* 106–124.

CARAMAZZA, A., & ZURIF, E. B. (1976). Dissociation of algorithmic and heuristic processes in language comprehension: Evidence from aphasia. *Brain and Language, 3,* 572–582.

CARDON, L. R., FULKER, D. W., DEFRIES, J. C., & PLOMIN, R. (1992). Continuity and change in general cognitive ability from 1 to 7 years of age. *Developmental Psychology, 28,* 64–73.

CARLSON, N. R. (1998). *Foundations of physiological psychology* (4th ed.). Boston: Allyn and Bacon.

CARLSON, N. R. (1994). *Physiology of behavior* (5th ed.). Boston: Allyn and Bacon.

CARLSON, N. R. (1998). *Foundations of physiological psychology* (4th ed.). Boston: Allyn and Bacon.

CARLSON, R. (1971). Where is the person in personality research? *Psychological Bulletin, 75,* 203–219.

CARLSON, W. R. (1986). *Physiology of behavior* (3rd ed.). Boston: Allyn and Bacon.

CARPENTER, P. A., JUST, M. A., & SHELL, P. (1990). What one intelligence test measures: A theoretical account of the processing in the Raven Progressive Matrices Test. *Psychological Review, 97,* 404–431.

CARROLL, D. W. (1985). *Psychology of language.* Monterey, CA: Brooks/Cole.

CARROLL, J. B. (1988). Individual differences in cognitive functioning. In R. C. Atkinson, R. J. Herrnstein, G. Lindzey, & R. D. Luce (Eds.), *Stevens' handbook of experimental psychology* (Vol. 2). New York: Wiley.

CARROLL, J. B. (1993). *Human cognitive abilities: A survey of factor-analytic studies.* New York: Cambridge University Press.

CARSKADON, M. A., MITLER, M. M., & DEMENT, W. C. (1974). A comparison of insomniacs and normals: Total sleep time and sleep latency. *Sleep Research, 3,* 130.

CARTER, M. M., HOLLON, S. D., CARON, R. S., & SHELTON, R. C. (1995). Effects of a safe person on induced distress following a biological challenge in panic disorder with agoraphobia. *Journal of Abnormal Psychology, 104,* 156–163.

CARTERETTE, E. C., & FRIEDMAN, M. P. (Eds.) (1974–1978). *Handbook of perception* (Vols. 1–11). New York: Academic Press.

CARTWRIGHT, R. (1978, December). Happy endings for our dreams. *Psychology Today,* pp. 66–67.

CARTWRIGHT, R. (1992). Masochism in dreaming and its relation to depression. *Dreaming, 2,* 79–84.

CARTWRIGHT, R. (1996). Dreams and adaptation to divorce. In D. Barrett, (Ed.), *Trauma and dreams.* Cambridge, MA: Harvard University Press.

CARTWRIGHT, R. D. (1974). The influence of a conscious wish on dreams. A methodological study of dream meaning and function. *Journal of Abnormal Psychology, 83,* 387–393.

CARVER, C. S., & SCHEIER, M. F. (1981). *Attention and self-regulation: A control-theory approach to human behavior.* New York: Springer-Verlag.

CASE, R. (1985). *Intellectual development: A systematic reinterpretation.* New York: Academic Press.

CASE, R. B., HELLER, S. S., CASE, N. B., & MOSS, A. J. (1985). Type A behavior and survival after acute myocardial infarction. *The New England Journal of Medicine, 312,* 737.

CASPI, A., & HERBENER, E. S. (1990). Continuity and change: Assortative marriage and the consistency of personality in adulthood. *Journal of Personality and Social Psychology, 58,* 250–258.

CASPI, A., & MOFFIT, T. E. (1991). Individual differences are accentuated during periods of social change: The sample case of girls at puberty. *Journal of Personality and Social Psychology, 61,* 157–168.

CATTELL, R. B. (1957). *Personality and motivation structure and measurement.* Yonkers-on-Hudson, NY: World.

CATTELL, R. B. (1966). *The scientific analysis of personality.* Chicago: Aldine.

CAVALLERO, C., CICOGNA, P., NATALE, V., & OCCIONERO, M. (1992). Slow wave sleep dreaming. *Sleep, 15,* 562–566.

CECI, S. J. (1990). *On intelligence . . . more or less: A bio-ecological treatise on intellectual development.* Englewood Cliffs, NJ: Prentice-Hall.

CECI, S. J., & ROAZZI, A. (1994). The effect of context on cognition: Postcards from Brazil. In R. J. Sternberg & R. K. Wagner (Eds.), *Mind in context: Interactionist perspectives on human intelligence.* Cambridge, England: Cambridge University Press.

CENTERS FOR DISEASE CONTROL (1988). Health status of Vietnam veterans: Psychosocial characteristics. *Journal of the American Medical Association, 259,* 2701–2707.

CERNOCH, J. M., & PORTER, R. H. (1985). Recognition of maternal axillary odors by infants. *Child Development, 56,* 1593–1598.

CHAIKEN, S. (1987). The heuristic model of persuasion. In M. P. Zanna, J. N. Olson, & C. P. Herman (Eds.), *Social influence: The ontario symposium* (Vol. 5, pp. 3–39). Hillsdale, NJ: Erlbaum.

CHAMBLESS, D. L., & HOLLON, S. D. (1998). Defining empirically supported therapies. *Journal of Consulting and Clinical Psychology, 66,* 7–18.

CHAPMAN, L. J., & CHAPMAN, J. P. (1969). Illusory correlation as an obstacle to the use of valid psychodiagnostic signs. *Journal of Abnormal Psychology, 74,* 271–280.

CHASE, W. G., & SIMON, H. A. (1973a). The mind's eye in chess. In W. G. Chase (Ed.), *Visual information processing.* New York: Academic Press.

CHASE, W. G., SIMON, H. A. (1973b.) Perception in chess. *Cognitive Psychology, 4,* 55–81.

CHAUDURI, H. (1965). *Philosophy of meditation.* New York: Philosophical Library.

CHEN, S. C. (1937). Social modification of the activity of ants in nest-building. *Physiological Zoology, 10,* 420–436.

CHEN, X. H., GELLER, E. B., & ADLER, M. W. (1996). Electrical stimulation at traditional acupuncture sites in periphery produces brain opoid-receptor-mediated antinociception in rats. *Journal of Pharmacology and Experimental Therapy, 277,* 654–660.

CHENG, P. W., HOLYOAK, K. J., NISBETT, R. E., & OLIVER, L. (1986). Pragmatic versus syntactic approaches to training deductive reasoning. *Cognitive Psychology, 18,* 293–328.

CHESS, S., & THOMAS, A. (1984). *Origins and evolution of behavior disorders: Infancy to early adult life.* New York: Brunner/Mazel.

CHI, M. (1978). Knowledge structures and memory development. In R. S. Siegler (Ed.), *Children's thinking: What develops?* Hillsdale, NJ: Erlbaum.

CHI, M., GLASER, R., & REES, E. (1982). Expertise in problem solving. In R. Sternberg (Ed.), *Advances in the psychology of human intelligence* (Vol. 1). Hillsdale, NJ: Erlbaum.

CHOCOLLE, R. (1940). Variations des temps de réaction auditifs en fonction de l'intensité à diverses fréquences. *Année Psychologique, 41,* 65–124.

CHOMSKY, N. (1965). *Aspects of the theory of syntax.* Cambridge, MA: MIT Press.

CHOMSKY, N. (1972). *Language and mind* (2nd ed.). New York: Harcourt Brace Jovanovich.

CHOMSKY, N. (1980). *Rules and representations.* New York: Columbia University Press.

CHOMSKY, N. (1991, March). Quoted in *Discover.*

CHORNEY, M. J., CHORNEY, K., SEESE, N., OWEN, M. J., DANIELS, J., MCGUFFIN, P., THOMPSON, L. A., DETTERMAN, D. K., BENBOW, C., LUBINSKI, D., ELEY, T., & PLOMIN, R. (1998). A quantitative trait locus associated with cognitive ability in children. *Psychological Science, 13,* 159–166.

CHRISTIE, R., & JOHODA, M. (Eds.) (1954). *Studies in the scope and method of "the authoritarian personality."* New York: Free Press.

CHURCHLAND, P. M. (1995) *The engine of reason, the seat of the soul.* Cambridge, MA: MIT Press.

CHURCHLAND, P. S., & SEJNOWSKI, T. J. (1988). Perspectives on cognitive neuroscience. *Science, 242,* 741–745.

CLARK, D. A., & DESILVA, P. (1985). The nature of depressive and anxious, intrusive thoughts: Distinct or uniform phenomena? *Behaviour Research & Therapy, 23,* 383–393.

CLARK, D. A., & PURDON, C. (1993). New perspectives for a cognitive theory of obsessions. *Australian Psychologist, 28,* 161–167.

CLARK, D. M. (1988). A cognitive model of panic attacks. In S. Rachman & J. D. Maser (Eds.), *Panic: Psychological perspectives.* Hillsdale, NJ: Erlbaum

CLARK, D. M., SALKOVSKIS, P. M., HACKMANN, A., MIDDLETON, H., and collaborators (1994). A comparison of cognitive therapy, applied, relaxation, and imipramine in the treatment of panic disorder. *British Journal of Psychiatry, 164,* 759–769.

CLARK, E. V. (1983). Meanings and concepts. In P. H. Mussen (Ed.), *Handbook of child psychology* (Vol. 3). New York: Wiley.

CLARK, H. H. (1984). Language use and language users. In G. Lindzey & E. Aronson (Eds.), *The handbook of social psychology* (Vol. 2, 3rd. ed.). New York: Harper & Row.

CLARK, H. H., & CLARK, E. V. (1977). *Psychology and language: An introduction to psycholinguistics.* New York: Harcourt Brace Jovanovich.

CLARKE-STEWART, K. A. (1973). Interactions between mothers and their young children: Characteristics and consequences. *Monographs of the Society for Research in Child Development, 38* (6 & 7, Serial No. 153).

CLARKE-STEWART, K. A. (1989). Infant day care: Maligned or malignant? *American Psychologist, 44,* 266–273.

CLONINGER, C. R., & GOTTESMAN, I. I. (1987). Genetic and environmental factors in antisocial behavior disorders. In S. A. Mednick, T. E. Moffitt, & S. A. Stack (Eds.), *The causes of crime: New biological approaches* (pp. 92–109). New York: Cambridge University Press.

COHEN, C. E. (1981). Person categories and social perception: Testing some boundaries of the processing effects of prior knowledge. *Journal of Personality and Social Psychology, 40,* 441–452.

COHEN, N. J., & SQUIRE, L. R. (1980). Preserved learning and retention of pattern analyzing skill in amnesia: Dissociation of knowing how and knowing that. *Science, 210,* 207–209.

COHEN, S. (1980, September). Training to understand TV advertising: Effects and some policy implications. Paper presented at the American Psychological Association convention, Montreal.

COHEN, S. (1996). Psychological stress, immunity, and upper respiratory infections. *Current Directions in Psychological Science, 5,* 86–90.

COHEN, S., & EDWARDS, J. R. (1989). Personality characteristics as moderators of the relationship between stress and disorder. In R. J. Neufeld (Ed.), *Advances in the investigation of psychological stress* (pp. 235–283). New York: Wiley.

COHEN, S., TYRRELL, D. A. J., & SMITH, A. P. (1991). Psychological stress and susceptibility to the common cold. *The New England Journal of Medicine, 325,* 606–612.

COLBY, A., KOHLBERG, L., GIBBS, J., & LIEBERMAN, M. A. (1983). A longitudinal study of moral judgment. *Monographs of the Society for Research in Child Development, 48,* 1–2.

COLE, M., & COLE, S. R. (1993). *The development of children.* (2nd ed.) New York: Scientific American Books.

COLE, S. W., KEMENY, M. E., TAYLOR, S. E., & VISSCHER, B. R. (1996). Elevated physical health risk among gay men who conceal their homosexual identity. *Health Psychology, 15,* 243–251.

COLE, S. W., KEMENY, M. E., TAYLOR, S. E., VISSCHER, B. R., & FAHEY, J. L. (1996). Accelerated course of human immunodeficiency virus infection in gay men who conceal their homosexual identity. *Psychosomatic Medicine, 58,* 219–238.

COLEGROVE, F. W. (1899). Individual memories. *American Journal of Psychology, 10,* 228–255.

COLLINS, A. M., & LOFTUS, E. G. (1975). A spreading-activation theory of semantic processing. *Psychological Review, 82,* 407–428.

COMREY, A. L., & LEE, H. B. (1992). *A first course in factor analysis* (2nd ed.). Hillsdale, NJ: Erlbaum.

CONRAD, R. (1964). Acoustic confusions in immediate memory. *British Journal of Psychology, 55,* 75–84.

COOPER, L. A., & SHEPARD, R. N. (1973). Chronometric studies of the rotation of mental images. In W. G. Chase (Ed.), *Visual information processing.* New York: Academic Press.

COOPER, L. M. (1979). Hypnotic amnesia. In E. Fromm & R. E. Shor (Eds.), *Hypnosis: Developments in research and new perspectives* (rev. ed.). New York: Aldine.

CORBETTA, M., MIEZIN, F.M., SHULMAN, G. L., & PETERSEN, S. E. (1991). Selective attention modulates extrastriate visual regions in humans during visual feature discrimination and recognition. In D. J. Chadwick & J. Whelan (Eds.), *Ciba Foundation symposium 163, exploring brain functional anatomy with positron tomography* (pp. 165–180). Chichester: Wiley.

CORBETTA, M., MIEZIN, F. M., SHULMAN, G. L., & PETERSEN, S. E. (1993). A PET study of visuospatial attention. *The Journal of Neuroscience, 13,* 1202–1226.

COREN, S. (1992). The moon illusion: A different view through the legs. *Perceptual & Motor Skills, 75,* 827–831.

COREN, S., & GIRGUS, J. S. (1980). Principles of perceptual organization and spatial distortion: The gestalt illusions. *Journal of Experimental Psychology: Human Perception & Performance, 6,* 404–412.

COREN, S., WARD, L. M., & ENNS, J. T. *Sensation and perception* (5th ed.). Fort Worth: Harcourt Brace.

COSCINA, D. V., & DIXON, L. M. (1983). Body weight regulation in anorexia nervosa: Insights from an animal model. In F. L. Darby, P. E. Garfinkel, D. M. Garner, & D. V. Coscina (Eds.), *Anorexia nervosa: Recent developments.* New York: Allan R. Liss.

COTTRELL, N. B. (1972). Social facilitation. In C. G. McClintock (Ed.), *Experimental social psychology.* New York: Holt, Rinehart & Winston.

COTTRELL, N. B., RITTLE, R. H., & WACK, D. L. (1967). Presence of an audience and list type (competitional or noncompetitional) as joint determinants of performance in paired-associates learning. *Journal of Personality, 25,* 425–434.

COTTRELL, N. B., WACK, D. L., SEKERAK, G. J., & RITTLE, R. H. (1968). Social facilitation of dominant responses by the presence of an audience and the mere presence of others. *Journal of Personality and Social Psychology, 9,* 245–250.

COURAGE, M. L., & ADAMS, R. J. (1990a). Visual acuity assessment from birth to three years using the acuity card procedures: Cross-sectional and longitudinal samples. *Optometry and Vision Science, 67,* 713–718.

COURAGE, M. L., & ADAMS, R. J. (1990b). The early development of visual acuity in the binocular and monocular peripheral fields. *Infant Behavioral Development, 13,* 123–128.

COURTRIGHT, J. A. (1978). A laboratory investigation of groupthink. *Communications Monographs, 43,* 229–246.

COUSINS, S. D. (1989). Culture and self-perception in Japan and the U.S. *Journal of Personality and Social Psychology, 56,* 124–131.

CRAIGHEAD, L. W., STUNKARD, A. J., & O'BRIEN, R. M. (1981). Behavior therapy and pharmacotherapy for obesity. *Archives of General Psychiatry, 38,* 763–768.

CRAIK, F. I. M., & TULVING, E. (1975). Depth of processing and the retention of words in episodic memory. *Journal of Experimental Psychology: General, 104,* 268–294.

CRARY, W. G. (1966). Reactions to incongruent self-experiences. *Journal of Consulting Psychology, 30,* 246–252.

CRASILNECK, H. B., & HALL, J. A. (1985). *Clinical hypnosis: Principles and applications* (2nd ed.). Orlando: Grune & Stratton.

CRICK, F. (1994). *The astonishing hypothesis: The scientific search for the soul.* New York: Macmillan.

CRICK, N. R., & DODGE, K. A. (1994). A review and reformulation of social information-processing mechanisms in children's social adjustment. *Psychological Bulletin, 115,* 74–101.

CROMWELL, P. F., MARKS, A., OLSON, J. N., & AVARY, D. W. (1991). Group effects on decision-making by burglars. *Psychological Reports, 69,* 579–588.

CURTISS, S. (1977). *Genie: A psycholinguistic study of a modern-day "wild child."* New York: Academic Press.

CURTISS, S. (1989). The independence and task-specificity of language. In M. H. Bornstein & J. S. Bruner (Eds.), *Interaction in human development.* Hillsdale, NJ: Erlbaum.

CUTLER, W. B., PRETI, G., KRIEGER, A., HUGGINS, G. R., GARCIA, C. R. & LAWLEY, H. J. (1986). Human axillary secretions influence women's menstrual cycles: The role of donor extract from men. *Hormones and Behavior, 20,* 463–473.

CUTTING, J. E. (1986). *Perception with an eye for motion.* Cambridge, MA: MIT Press.

CYANDER, M., TIMNEY, B. N., & MITCHELL, D. E. (1980). Period of susceptability of kitten visual cortex to the effects of monocular deprivation extends beyond 6 months of age. *Brain Research, 191,* 545–550.

DABBS, J. M., & MORRIS, R., JR. (1990). Testosterone, social class, and antisocial behavior in a sample of 4,462 men. *Psychological Science, 1,* 209–211.

DALE, A. J. D. (1975). Organic brain syndromes associated with infections. In A. M., Freeman, H. I. Kaplan, & B. J. Sadock (Eds.), *Comprehensive textbook of psychiatry* (Vol. 2, pp. 1121–1130). Baltimore, MD: Williams & Wilkins.

DAMASIO, A.R. (1985). Disorders of complex visual processing: Agnosia, achromatopsia, Balint's syndrome, and related difficulties of orientation and construction. In M. M. Mesulam (Ed.), *Principles of behavioral neurology* (pp. 259–288). Philadelphia: F. A. Davis.

DAMASIO, A. R. (1990). Category-related recognition defects as a clue to the neural substrates of knowledge. *Trends in Neurosciences, 13,* 95–98.

DAMASIO, A. R. (1994). *Descartes' error.* New York: Putnam.

DAMON, W. (1977). *The social world of the child.* San Francisco: Jossey-Bass.

DAMON, W. (1983). *Social and personality development.* New York: Norton.

DANEMAN, M., & CARPENTER, P. A. (1980). Individual differences in working memory and reading. *Journal of Verbal Learning and Verbal Behavior, 19,* 450–466.

DARIAN-SMITH, I. (Ed.) (1984). *Handbook of physiology: The nervous system: Section 1, vol. 3. Sensory processes.* Bethesda, MD: American Physiological Society.

DARLEY, C. F., TINKLENBERG, J. R., ROTH, W. T., HOLLISTER, L. E., & ATKINSON, R. C. (1973a). Influence of marijuana on storage and retrieval processes in memory. *Memory and Cognition, 1,* 196–200.

DARLEY, C. F., TINKLENBERG, J. R., ROTH, W. T., HOLLISTER, L. E., & ATKINSON, R. C. (1973b). Marijuana and retrieval from short-term memory. *Psychopharmacologia, 29,* 231–238.

DARLEY, C. F., TINKLENBERG, J. R., ROTH, W. T., VERNON, S., & KOPELL, B. S. (1977). Marijuana effects on long-term memory assessment and retrieval. *Psychopharmacology, 52,* 239–241.

DARLEY, J. M., & LATANÉ, B. (1968). Bystander intervention in emergencies: Diffusion of responsibility. *Journal of Personality and Social Psychology, 8,* 377–383.

DARWIN, C. (1859). *On the origin of the species.* London: Murray.

DARWIN, C. (1872). *The expression of emotion in man and animals.* New York: Philosophical Library.

DASHIELL, J. F. (1930). An experimental analysis of some group effects. *Journal of Abnormal and Social Psychology, 25,* 190–199.

DASHIELL, J. F. (1935). Experimental studies of the influence of social situations on the behavior of individual human adults. In C. Murchison (Ed.), *Handbook of social psychology.* Worcester, MA: Clark University.

DAVIS, K. L., KAHN, R. S., KO, G., & DAVIDSON, M. (1991). Dopamine in schizophrenia: A review and conceptualization. *American Journal of Psychiatry, 148,* 1474–1486.

DEAKIN, J. W., & GRAEFF, F. G. (1991). 5-HT and mechanisms of defense. *Journal of Psychopharmacology, 5,* 305–315.

DEARY, I. (1992). Multiple minds. *Science, 259,* 28.

DECASPER, A. J., & FIFER, W. P. (1980). Of human bonding: Newborns prefer their mothers' voices. *Science, 208,* 1174–1176.

DECASPER, A. J., & PRESCOTT, P. A. (1984). Human newborns' perception of male voices: Preference, discrimination and reinforcing value. *Developmental Psychobiology, 17,* 481–491.

DECASPER, A. J., & SPENCE, M. J. (1986). Prenatal maternal speech influences newborns' perception of speech sounds. *Infant Behavior and Development, 9,* 133–150.

DEIKMAN, A. J. (1963). Experimental meditation. *Journal of Nervous and Mental Disease, 136,* 329–373.

DEMBROSKI, T. M., MACDOUGALL, J. M., WILLIAMS, B., & HANEY, T. L. (1985). Components of Type A hostility and anger: Relationship to angiographic findings. *Psychosomatic Medicine, 47,* 219–233.

DEMENT, W. C., & KLEITMAN, N. (1957). The relation of eye movements during sleep to dream activity: An objective method for the study of dreaming. *Journal of Experimental Psychology, 53,* 339–346.

DEMENT, W. C., & WOLPERT, E. (1958). The relation of eye movements, bodily mobility, and external stimuli to dream content. *Journal of Experimental Psychology, 55,* 543–553.

DENNIS, W., & DENNIS, M. (1940). The effects of cradling practices upon the onset of walking in Hopi children. *Journal of Genetic Psychology, 56,* 77–86.

DERUBEIS, R. J., & CRITS-CHRISTOPH, P. (1998). Empirically supported individual and group psychological treatments for adult mental disorders. *Journal of Abnormal Psychology, 101,* 371–382.

DEVALOIS, R. L., & DEVALOIS, K. K. (1980). Spatial vision. *Annual Review of Psychology, 31,* 309–341.

DEVALOIS, R. L., & JACOBS, G. H. (1984). Neural mechanisms of color vision. In I. Darian-Smith (Ed.), *Handbook of physiology* (Vol. 3). Bethesda, MD: American Physiological Society.

DIAMOND, M. (1982). Sexual identity, monozygotic twins reared in discordant sex roles and a BBC follow-up. *Archives of Sexual Behavior, 11,* 181–6.

DIAMOND, M., & SIGMUNDSON, K. (1997). Sex reassignment at birth: Long-term review and clinical implications. *Archives of Pediatric Medicine, 151,* 298.

DIENER, E. (1979). Deindividuation, self-awareness, and disinhibition. *Journal of Personality and Social Psychology, 37,* 1160–1171.

DIENER, E. (1980). Deindividuation: The absence of self-awareness and self-regulation in group members. In P. B. Paulus (Ed.), *The psychology of group influence.* Hillsdale, NJ: Erlbaum.

DIENER, E., FRASER, S. C., BEAMAN, A. L., & KELEM, R. T. (1976). Effects of deindividuation variables on stealing among Halloween trick-or-treaters. *Journal of Personality and Social Psychology, 33,* 178–183.

DIENSTBIER, R. A. (1989). Arousal and physiological toughness: Implications for mental and physical health. *Psychological Review, 96,* 84–100.

DIGMAN, J. M., & INOUYE, J. (1986). Further specification of the five robust factors of personality. *Journal of Personality and Social Psychology, 50,* 116–123.

DILLBECK, M. C., & ORME-JOHNSON, D. W. (1987). Physiological differences between transcendental meditation and rest. *American Psychologist, 42,* 879–881.

DINGES, D. F., & BROUGHTON, R. J. (Eds.) (1989). *Sleep and alertness: Chhronobiological, behavioral, and medical aspects of napping.* New York: Raven.

DOBB, E. (1989, November–December). The scents around us. *The Sciences, 29,* 46–53.

DOBELLE, W. H., MEADEJOVSKY, M. G., & GIRVIN, J. P. (1974). Artificial vision for the blind: Electrical stimulation of visual cortex offers hope for a functional prosthesis. *Science, 183,* 440–444.

DOLLARD, J., DOOB, L. W., MILLER, N. E., MOWRER, O. H., & SEARS, R. R. (1939). *Frustration and aggression.* New Haven, CT: Yale University Press.

DOMHOFF, G. W. (1985). *The mystique of dreams.* Berkeley: University of California Press.

DOMHOFF, G. W. (1996). *Finding meaning in dreams: A quantitative approach.* New York: Plenum.

DOMHOFF, G. W., & SCHNEIDER, A. (1998). The quantitative study of dreams. http://zzyx.ucsc.edu?~dreams/.

DOMJAN, M., & BURKHARD, B. (1986). *The principles of learning and behavior.* Monterey, CA: Brooks/Cole.

DOWLING, J. E., & BOYCOTT, B. B. (1966). Organization of the primate retina. *Proceedings of the Royal Society of London, Series b, 166,* 80–111.

DOYLE, A. C. (1892/1981). *The original illustrated Sherlock Holmes.* Secaucus, NJ: Castle Books. (Originally published in America by Harper & Bros. in *McClure's Magazine,* 1893)

DUCLAUX, R., & KENSHALO, D. R. (1980). Response characteristics of cutaneous warm fibers in the monkey. *Journal of Neurophysiology, 43,* 1–15.

DUJARDIN, K., GUERRIEN, A., & LECONTE, P. (1990). Sleep, brain activation and cognition. *Physiology & Behavior, 47,* 1271–1278.

DUNCAN, J., & HUMPHREYS, G. W. (1989). Visual search and simulus similarity. *Psychological Review, 96,* 433–458.

DUNCAN, P. D., and collaborators (1985). The effects of pubertal timing on body image, school behavior, and deviance. *Journal of Youth and Adolescence, 14,* 227–235.

DUNCAN, R. D., SAUNDERS, B. E., KILPATRICK, D. G., HANSON, R. F., & RESNICK, H. S. (1996). Childhood physical assault as a risk factor for PTSD, depression, and substance abuse: Findings from a national survey. *American Journal of Orthopsychiatry, 66,* 437–448.

DUTTON, D. G., & ARON, A. P. (1974). Some evidence for heightened sexual attraction under conditions of high anxiety. *Journal of Personality and Social Pychology, 30,* 510–517.

EAGLY, A. H., & CHAIKEN, S. (1984). Cognitive theories of persuasion. In L. Berkowitz (Ed.), *Advances in experimental social psychology* (Vol. 17, pp. 267–359). New York: Academic Press.

EBBESEN, E., DUNCAN, B., & KONECNI, V. (1975). Effects of content of verbal aggression on future verbal aggression: A field experiment. *Journal of Experimental Psychology, 11,* 192–204.

EBBINGHAUS, H. (1885). *Uber das gedachthis.* Leipzig: Dunckes and Humbolt.

EDGAR, D. M., & DEMENT, W. C. (1992). Evidence for opponent processes in sleep/wake regulation. *Sleep Research, 20A,* 2.

EHLERS, A. (1995). A 1-year prospective study of panic attacks: Clinical course and factors associated with maintenance. *Journal of Abnormal Psychology, 104,* 164–172.

EHLERS, A., & BREUER, P. (1992). Increased cardiac awareness in panic disorder. *Journal of Abnormal Psychology, 101,* 371–382.

EHRHARDT, A. A., MEYER-BAHLBURG, H. F., ROSEN, L. R., FELDMAN, J. F., VERIDIANO, N. P., ELKIN, E. J., & MCEWEN, B. S. (1989). The development of gender-related behavior in females following prenatal exposure to diethylstilbestrol (DES). *Hormones & Behavior, 23,* 526–541.

EIBL-EIBESFELDT, I. (1970). *Ethology: The biology of behavior* (E. Klinghammer, Trans.). New York: Holt, Rinehart & Winston.

EICH, J. E. (1980). The cue-dependent nature of state-dependent retrieval. *Memory and Cognition, 8,* 157–173.

EIMAS, P. D. (1975). Speech perception in early infancy. In L. B. Cohen & P. Salapatek (Eds.), *Infant perception: From sensation to cognition* (Vol. 2). New York: Academic Press.

EIMAS, P. D. (1985). The perception of speech in early infancy. *Scientific American, 252,* 46–52.

EKMAN, P. (1982). *Emotion in the human face* (2nd ed.). New York: Cambridge University Press.

EKSTROM, R. B., FRENCH, J. W., HARMAN, H. H., & DERMAN, D. (1976). *Manual for kit of factor-referenced cognitive tests, 1976.* Princeton, NJ: Educational Testing Service.

EKSTROM, R. B., FRENCH, J. W., & HARMAN, H. H. (1979). Cognitive factors: Their identification and replication. *Multivariate behavioral research monographs.* Fort Worth: Society for Multivariate Experimental Psychology.

ELKIN, I. SHEA, T., WATKINS, J. T., IMBER, S. D., SOTSKY, S. M., COLLINS, J. F., GLASS, D. R., PILKONIS, P. A., LEBER, W. R., DOCHERTY, J. P., FIESTER, S. J., & PARLOFF, M. B. (1989). National Institute of Mental Health treatment of depression collaborative research program: General effectiveness of treatments. *Archives of General Psychiatry, 46,* 971–982.

ELKIN, R. A., & LEIPPE, M. R. (1986). Physiological arousal, dissonance, and attitude change: Evidence of a dissonance-arousal link and a "don't remind me" effect. *Journal of Personality and Social Psychology, 51,* 55–65.

ELLIOT, A. J., & DEVINE, P. G. (1994). On the motivational nature of cognitive dissonance: Dissonance as psychological discomfort. *Journal of Personality and Social Psychology, 67,* 382–394.

ELLIS, L., & AMES, M. A. (1987). Neurohormonal functioning and sexual orientation: A theory of homosexuality-heterosexuality. *Psychological Bulletin, 2,* 233–258.

ELLSWORTH, P. (1991). Some implications of cognitive appraisals on theories of emotion. In K. T. Strongman (Ed.)., *International review of studies on emotion* (Vol. 1). New York: Wiley.

ELMES, D. G., KANTOWITZ, B. H., & ROEDIGER, H. L. (1989). *Research methods in psychology* (3rd ed.). St. Paul, MN: West.

EMMELKAMP, P., & KUIPERS, A. (1979). Agoraphobia: A follow-up study four years after treatment. *British Journal of Psychiatry, 134,* 352–355.

ENGEN, T. (1982). *The perception of odors.* New York: Academic Press.

ENNS, J. T., & GIRGUS, J. S. (1985). Perceptual grouping and spatial distortion: A developmental study. *Developmental Psychology, 21,* 241–246.

ENNS, J. T., & PRINZMETAL, W. (1984). The role of redundancy in the object-line effect. *Perception & Psychophysics, 35,* 22–32.

ENNS, J. T., & RENSINK, R. A. (1990). Sensitivity to three-dimensional orientation in visual search. *Psychological Science, 1,* 323–326.

ERDELYI, M. H. (1985). *Psychoanalysis: Freud's cognitive psychology.* New York: Freeman.

ERICSSON, K. A., CHASE, W. G., & FALOON, S. (1980). Acquisition of a memory skill. *Science, 208,* 1181–1182.

ERICSSON, K. A., & SIMON, H. A. (1993). *Protocol analysis: Verbal reports as data* (rev. ed.). Cambridge, MA: MIT Press.

ERIKSON, E. H. (1963). *Childhood and society* (2nd ed.). New York: Norton.

ERIKSON, E. H. (1968). *Identity: Youth and crisis*. New York: Norton.

ERON, L. D. (1987). The development of aggressive behavior from the perspective of a developing behaviorism. *American Psychologist, 42*, 435–442.

ERON, L. D., HUESMANN, L. R., LEFKOWITZ, M. M., & WALDER, L. O. (1972). Does television violence cause aggression? *American Psychologist, 27*, 253–263.

ERVIN-TRIPP, S. (1964). Imitation and structural change in children's language. In E. H. Lenneberg (Ed.), *New directions in the study of language*. Cambridge, MA: MIT Press.

ESTERSON, A. (1993). *Seductive mirage: An exploration of the work of Sigmund Freud*. Chicago: Open Court.

ESTES, W. K. (1972). An associative basis for coding and organization in memory. In A. W. Melton & E. Martin (Eds.), *Coding processes in human memory*. Washington, DC: Winston.

ESTES, W. K. (1994). *Classification and cognition*. New York: Oxford University Press.

ESTES, W. K. (Ed.) (1975–1979). *Handbook of learning and cognitive processes* (Vols. 1–6). Hillsdale, NJ: Erlbaum.

ETCOFF, N. L. (1985). The neuropsychology of emotional expression. In G. Goldstein & R. E. Tarter (Eds.), *Advances in clinical neuropsychology* (Vol. 3). New York: Plenum.

EVANS, C. (1984). *Landscapes of the night: How and why we dream*. New York: Viking.

EXNER, J. (1986). *The Rorschach: A comprehensive system* (2nd ed., Vol. 1). New York: Wiley.

EYSENCK, H. J. (1953). *The structure of human personality*. New York: Wiley.

EYSENCK, H. J., & KAMIN, L. (1981). *The intelligence controversy*. New York: Wiley.

FABREGA, H. ULRICH, R. PILKONIS, P., & MEZZICH, J. (1991). On the homogeneity of personality disorder clusters. *Comprehensive Psychiatry, 32*, 373–386.

FAGOT, B. I. (1978). The influence of sex of child on parenteral reactions to toddler children. *Child Development, 49, 459–465.

FAIRBURN, C. G., & HAY, P. J. (1992). Treatment of bulimia nervosa. *Annals of Medicine, 24*, 297–302.

FAIRBURN, C. G., NORMAN, P. A., WELCH, S. L., O'CONNOR, M. E., DOLL, H. A., & PEVELER, R. C. (1995). A prospective study of outcome in bulimia nervosa and the long-term effects of three psychological treatments. *Archives of General Psychiatry, 52*, 304–312.

FAIRBURN, C. G., WELCH, S. L., & HAY, P. J. (1993). The classification of recurrent overeating: The "binge eating disorder" proposal. Fifth International Conference on Eating Disorders (1992, New York). *International Journal of Eating Disorders, 13*, 155–159.

FANTZ, R. L. (1961). The origin of form perception. *Science, 204*, 66–72.

FANTZ, R. L. (1970). Visual perception and experience in infancy: Issues and approaches. In *National Academy of Science, early experience and visual information processing in perceptual and reading disorders* (pp. 351–381). New York: National Academy of Science.

FARAH, M, HAMMOND, K. M., & LEVINE, D. N. (1988). Visual and spatial mental imagery: Dissociable systems of representation. *Cognitive Psychology, 20*, 439–462.

FARAH, M. J., & MCCLELLAND, J. L. (1991). A computational model of semantic memory impairment. *Journal of Experimental Psychology: General, 120*, 339–357.

FARAH, M. J. (1990). *Visual agnosia: Disorders of object recognition and what they tell us about normal vision*. Cambridge, MA: MIT Press.

FARAONE, S. V., and collaborators (1990). Genetic transmission of major affective disorders: Quantitative models and linkage analyses. *Psychological Bulletin, 108*, 109–127.

FARTHING, G. W. (1992). *The psychology of consciousness*. Englewood Cliffs, NJ: Prentice Hall.

FAUST, I. M. (1984). Role of the fat cell in energy balance physiology. In A. T. Stunkard & E. Stellar (Eds.), *Eating and its disorders*. New York: Raven Press.

FAVA, M., COPELAND, P. M., SCHWEIGER, U., & HERZOG, D. B. (1989). Neurochemical abnormalities of anorexia nervosa and bulimia nervosa. *American Journal of Psychiatry, 146*, 963–971.

FAZIO, R. H. (1990). Multiple processes by which attitudes guide behavior: The MODE model as an integrative framework. In M. P. Zanna (Ed.), *Advances in experimental social psychology* (Vol. 23). San Diego: Academic Press.

FAZIO, R., ZANNA, M. P., & COOPER, J. (1977). Dissonance and self-perception: An integrative view of each theory's proper domain of application. *Journal of Experimental Social Psychology, 13*, 464–479.

FECHNER, G. T. (1860/1966). *Elements of psychophysics* (H. E. Adler, Trans.). New York: Holt, Rinehart & Winston.

FEINGOLD, A. (1988). Cognitive gender differences are disappearing. *American Psychologist, 43*, 95–103.

FELDMAN, H., GOLDIN-MEADOW, S., & GLEITMAN, L. R. (1978). Beyond Herodotus: The creation of language by linguistically deprived children. In A. Lock (Ed.), *Action, gesture, and symbol: The emergence of language*. London: Academic Press.

FELDMAN, H., MEYER, & QUENZER. (1997). *Neuropharmacology*. New York: Sinauer.

FENWICK, P. (1987). Meditation and the EEG. In M. A. West (Ed.), *The psychology of meditation*. Oxford, England: Oxford University Press.

FESHBACH, N. D. (1980, September). The child as psychologist and economist: Two curricula. Paper presented at the American Psychological Association convention. Montreal.

FESTINGER, L. (1957). *A theory of cognitive dissonance*. Stanford: Stanford University Press.

FESTINGER, L., & CARLSMITH, J. M. (1959). Cognitive consequences of forced compliance. *Journal of Abnormal and Social Psychology, 58*, 203–210.

FESTINGER, L., PEPITONE, A., & NEWCOMB, T. M. (1952). Some consequences of deindividuation in a group. *Journal of Abnormal and Social Psychology, 47*, 383–389.

FESTINGER, L., SCHACHTER, S., & BACK, K. (1950). *Social pressures in informal groups: A study of human factors in housing*. New York: Harper & Row.

FIELD, J. (1987). The development of auditory-visual localization in infancy. In B. E. McKenzie & R. H. Day (Eds.), *Perceptual development in early infancy*. Hillsdale, NJ: Erlbaum.

FIELD, T. (1991). Quality infant day care and grade school behavior and performance. *Child Development, 62*, 863–870.

FINCK, H. T. (1887). *Romantic love and personal beauty: Their development, causal relations, historic and national pecularities*. London: Macmillan.

FINKE, R. A. (1985). Theories relating mental imagery to perception. *Psychological Bulletin, 98*, 236–259.

FISHER, G. H. (1967). Preparation of ambiguous stimulus materials. *Perception and Psychophysics, 2*, 421–422.

FISHER, S., & GREENBERG, R. (1977). *The scientific credibility of Freud's theories and therapy*. New York: Basic Books.

FISHER, S., & GREENBERG, R. (1996). *Freud scientifically appraised*. New York: Wiley.

FISHMAN, P. (1983). Interaction: The work women do. In B. Thorne, C. Kramarae, & N. Henley (Eds.), *Language, gender, and society*. Rowley, MA: Newbury House.

FISKE, S. T. (1993). Social cognition and social perception. In L. Porter & M. R. Rosenzweig (Eds.), *Annual review of psychology* (Vol. 44, pp. 155–194).

FISKE, S. T., & TAYLOR, S. E. (1991). *Social cognition* (2nd ed.). New York: McGraw-Hill.

FITZSIMONS, J. T. (1969). The role of a renal thirst factor in drinking induced by extra cellular stimuli. *Journal of Physiology, London, 201*, 349–368.

FITZSIMONS, J. T. (1990). Thirst and sodium appetite. In E. M. Stricker (Ed.), *Neurobiology of food and fluid intake* (pp. 23–44). New York: Plenum.

FIVUSH, R., & HAMOND, N. R. (1991). Autobiographical memory across the preschool years: Toward reconceptualizing childhood memory. In R. Fivush & N. R. Hamond (Eds.), *Knowing and remembering in young children*. New York: Cambridge University Press.

FIXSEN, D. L., PHILLIPS, E. L., PHILLIPS, E. A., & WOLF, M. M. (1976). The teaching-family model of group home treatment. In W. E. Craighead, A. E. Kazdin, & M. J. Mahoney (Eds.), *Behavior modification: Principles, issues, and applications*. Boston: Houghton Mifflin.

FLAVELL, J. H. (1992). *Cognitive development* (3rd ed.). Englewood Cliffs, NJ: Prentice Hall.

FLEMING, J., & DARLEY, J. M. (1986). Perceiving intention in constrained behavior: The role of purposeful and constrained action cues in correspondence bias effects. Unpublished manuscript, Princeton University, Princeton, NJ.

FLODERUS-MYRED, B., PETERSEN, N., & RASMUSON, I. (1980). Assessment of heritability for personality based on a short form of the Eysenck Personality Inventory. *Behavior Genetics, 10*, 153–161.

FLOWERS, M. L. (1977). A laboratory test of some implications of Janis's groupthink hypothesis. *Journal of Personality and Social Psychology, 35*, 888–896.

FLUOXETINE BULIMIA NERVOSA STUDY GROUP (1992). Fluoxetine in the treatment of bulimia nervosa: A multi-center, placebo-controlled, double-blind trial. *Archives of General Psychiatry, 49*, 156–162.

FLYNN, J. R. (1987). Massive IQ gains in 14 nations: What IQ tests really measure. *Psychological Bulletin, 101*, 171–191.

FOA, E., & STEKETEE, G. (1989). Obsessive-compulsive disorder. In C. Lindemann (Ed.), *Handbook of phobia therapy*. Northvale, NJ: Jason Aronson.

FOA, E. D., & RIGGS, D. S. (1995). Posttraumatic stress disorder following assault: Theoretical considerations and empirical findings. *Current Directions in Psychological Science, 4*, 61–65.

FODOR, J. A., BEVER, T. G., & GARRETT, M. F. (1974). *The psychology of language: An introduction to psycholinguistics and generative grammar*. New York: McGraw-Hill.

FOLKES, V. S. (1982). Forming relationships and the matching hypothesis. *Personality and Social Psychology Bulletin, 8*, 631–636.

FORGE, K. L., & PHEMISTER, S. (1987). The effect of prosocial cartoons on preschool children. *Child Development Journal, 17*, 83–88.

FOSS, D. J., & HAKES, D. T. (1978). *Psycholinguistics: An introduction to the psychology of language*. Englewood Cliffs, NJ: Prentice-Hall.

FOULKES, D. (1985). *Dreaming: A cognitive-psychological analysis*. Hillsdale, NJ: Erlbaum.

FOULKES, D. (1993). Data constraints on theorizing about dream function. In A. Moffitt, M. Kramer, & R. Hoffman (Eds.), *The functions of dreaming*. Albany: State University of New York Press.

FOULKES, D., & SCHMIDT, M. (1983). Temporal sequence and unit comparison composition in dream reports from different stages of sleep. *Sleep, 6*, 265–280.

FRABLE, D. E. (1989). Sex typing and gender ideology: Two facets of the individual's gender psychology that go together. *Journal of Personality and Social Psychology, 56*, 95–108.

FRANKENHAEUSER, M. (1983). The sympathetic-adrenal and pituitary-adrenal response to challenge: Comparison between the sexes. In T. M. Dembroski, T. H. Schmidt, & G. Blumchen (Eds.), *Biobehavioral bases of coronary heart disease*. Basel: Karger.

FRANKLIN, J. (1987). *Molecules of the mind*. New York: Atheneum.

FRANTZ, R. L. (1966). Pattern discrimination and selective attention as determinants of perceptual development from birth. In A. H. Kikk & J. F. Rivoire (Eds.), *Development of perception: Vol. 2. The visual system* (pp. 143–173). New York: International University Press.

FRAZIER, K. (1987). Psychic's imagined year fizzles (again). *Skeptical Inquirer, 11*, 335–336.

FREE, L. A., & CANTRIL, H. (1967). *The political beliefs of Americans*. New Brunswick, NJ: Rutgers University Press.

FREEDMAN, J. L. (1965). Long-term behavioral effects of cognitive dissonance. *Journal of Experimental Social Psychology, 1*, 145–155.

FREESTON, M. H., LADOUCEUR, R., THIBODEAU, N., & GAGNON, F. (1992). Cognitive intrusions in a non-clinical population: II. Associations with depressive, anxious, and compulsive symptoms. *Behaviour Research and Therapy, 30*, 263–271.

FREUD, A. (1958). Adolescence. *The Psychoanalytic Study of the Child, 13*, 255–278.

FREUD, A. (1946/1967). *The ego and the mechanisms of defense* (rev. ed.). New York: International Universities Press.

FREUD, S. (1885). *Ueber coca*. Vienna: Mortiz Perles. (Translated in Freud, 1974).

FREUD, S. (1885/1974). *Cocaine papers* (edited and introduction by R. Byck; notes by A. Freud). New York: Stonehill.

FREUD, S. (1900/1953). *The interpretation of dreams* (Reprint ed., Vols. 4, 5). London: Hogarth Press.

FREUD, S. (1901/1960). *Psychopathology of everyday life* (Standard ed., Vol. 6). London: Hogarth Press.

FREUD, S. (1905/1948). *Three contributions to theory of sex* (4th ed.; A. A. Brill, Trans.). New York: Nervous and Mental Disease Monograph.

FREUD, S. (1915/1976). Repression. In J. Strachey (Ed. and Trans.), *The complete psychological works: Standard edition* (Vol. 14). London: Hogarth Press.

FREUD, S. (1920/1975). *Beyond the pleasure principle*. New York: Norton.

FREUD, S. (1925/1961). Some psychical consequences of the anatomical distinctions between the sexes. In J. Strachey (Ed. and Trans.), *The complete psychological works: Standard edition* (Vol. 18). London: Hogarth Press.

FREUD, S. (1933/1964). *New introductory lectures on psychoanalysis* (J. Strachey, Ed. and Trans.). New York: Norton.

FREUD, S. (1933/1965). Revision of the theory of dreams. In J. Strachey (Ed. and Trans.), *New introductory lectures on psychoanalysis* (Vol. 22, Lect. 29). New York: Norton.

FREUD, S. (1940). An outline of psychoanalysis. *International Journal of Psychoanalysis, 21*, 27–84.

FRIEDMAN, M., & ROSENMAN, R. H. (1974). *Type A behavior*. New York: Knopf.

FRIEDMAN, M., THORESEN, C. E., GILL, J. J., ULMER, D., POWELL, L. H., PRICE, V., BROWN, B., THOMPSON, L., RABIN, D. D., and collaborators (1994). Alteration of Type A behavior and its effect on cardiac recurrences in post myocardial infarction patients: Summary results of the recurrent coronary prevention project. In A. Steptoe (Ed.), *Psychosocial processes and health: A reader*. Cambridge, England: Cambridge University Press.

FRIEDMAN, M. I. (1990). Making sense out of calories. In E. M. Stricker (Eds.), *Neurobiology of food and fluid intake* (pp. 513–528). New York: Plenum.

FRIJDA, N. H. (1986). *The emotions*. Cambridge, England: Cambridge University Press.

FRISCHHOLZ, E. J. (1985). The relationship among dissociation, hyponosis, and child abuse in the development of multiple personality disorder. In R. P. Kluft (Ed.), *Childhood antecedents of multiple personality*. Washington, DC: American Psychiatric Press.

FRODI, A., & THOMPSON, R. (1985). Infants' affective responses in the strange situation: Effects of prematurity and of quality of attachment. *Child Development, 56*, 1280–1290.

FUNKENSTEIN, D. (1955). The physiology of fear and anger. *Scientific American, 192*, 74–80.

FYER, A. J., MANNUZZA, S., CHAPMAN, T. F., & LIEBOWITZ, M. R. (1993). A direct interview family study of social phobia. *Archives of General Psychiatry, 50*, 286–293.

FYER, A. J., MANNUZZA, S., GALLOPS, M. S., & MARTIN, L. Y. (1990). Familial transmission of simple phobias and fears: A preliminary report. *Archives of General Psychiatry, 47*, 252–256.

GADOW, K. D. (1991). Clinical issues in child and adolescent psychopharmacology. *Journal of Consulting and Clinical Psychology, 59*, 842–852.

GADOW, K. D. (1992). Pediatric psychopharmacotherapy: A review of recent research. *Journal of Child Psychology and Psychiatry*, 153–195.

GALANTER, E. (1962). Contemporary psychophysics. In R. Brown & collaborators (Eds.), *New directions in psychology* (Vol. 1). New York: Holt, Rinehart & Winston.

GALINSKY, E., HOWES, C., KONTOS, S., & SHINN, M. (1994). The study of children in family child care and relative care: Highlights of findings.

GALLUP ORGANIZATION (1995). *Sleep in America: A national survey of U.S. adults.* Poll conducted for the National Sleep Foundation. Princeton, NJ: National Sleep Foundation.

GALOTTI, K. M. (1989). Approaches to studying formal and everyday reasoning. *Psychological Bulletin, 105,* 331–351.

GAMSON, W. B., FIREMAN, B., & RYTINA, S. (1982). *Encounters with unjust authority.* Homewood, IL: Dorsey Press.

GANELLEN, R. J., & CARVER, C. S. (1985). Why does self-reference promote incidental encoding? *Journal of Personality and Social Psychology, 21,* 284–300.

GARCIA, J., & KOELLING, R. A. (1966). The relation of cue to consequence in avoiding learning. *Psychonomic Science, 4,* 123–124.

GARDNER, B. T., & GARDNER, R. A. (1972). Two-way communication with an infant chimpanzee. In A. M. Schrier & F. Stollnitz (Eds.), *Behavior of nonhuman primates* (Vol. 4). New York: Academic Press.

GARDNER, E. L. (1992). Brain reward mechanisms. In J. H. Lowinson, P. Ruiz, & R. B. Millman (Eds.), *Substance abuse: A comprehensive textbook* (2nd ed.). Baltimore, MD: Williams & Wilkins.

GARDNER, H. (1975). *The shattered mind.* New York: Knopf.

GARDNER, H. (1985). *The mind's new science: A history of the cognitive revolution.* New York: Basic Books.

GARDNER, H. (1993a). *Frames of mind: The theory of multiple intelligences.* New York: Basic Books.

GARDNER, H. (1993b). *Multiple intelligences: The theory in practice.* New York: Basic Books.

GARDNER, H. KORNHABER, M. L., & WAKE, W. K. (1996). *Intelligence: Multiple perspectives.* Fort Worth: Harcourt Brace.

GARDNER, M. (1981). *Science: Good, bad, and bogus.* New York: Prometheus.

GARDNER, W., LIDZ, C. W., MULVEY, E. P., & SHAW, E. C. (1996). Clinical versus actuarial predictions of violence in patients with mental illnesses. *Journal of Consulting and Clinical Psychology, 64,* 602–609.

GARFIELD, S. L. (1994). Research on client variables in psychotherapy. In S. L. Garfield & A. E. Bergen (Eds.), *Handbook of psychotherapy and behavior change* (pp. 190–228). New York: Wiley.

GARNER, D. M., & GARFINKEL, P. E. (1980). Socio-cultural factors in the development of anorexia nervosa. *Psychological Medicine, 10,* 647–656.

GARRETT, M. (1997). The effects of infant child care on infant-mother attachment security: Results of the NICHD Study of Early Child Care. *Child Development, 68,* 860–879.

GARRETT, M. F. (1990). Sentence processing. In D. N. Osherson & H. Lasnik, *An invitation to cognitive science: Language* (Vol. 1). Cambridge, MA: MIT Press.

GATES, A. I. (1917). Recitation as a factor in memorizing. *Archives of Psychology,* No. 40.

GAW, A. (1993). *Culture, ethnicity, and mental illness.* Washington, DC: American Psychiatric Press.

GAZZANIGA, M. S. (1985). *The social brain: Discovering the networks of mind.* New York: Basic Books.

GELLATLY, A. R. H. (1987). Acquisition of a concept of logical necessity. *Human Development, 30,* 32–47.

GENTER, D., & STEVENS, A. L. (1983). *Mental models.* Hillsdale, NJ: Erlbaum.

GERSHON, E. S. (1990). Genetics. In F. K. Goodwin & K. R. Jamison (Eds.), *Manic-depressive illness* (pp. 373–401). New York: Oxford University Press.

GESCHWIND, N. (1972). Language and the brain. *Scientific American, 226,* 76–83.

GESCHWIND, N. (1979). Specializations of the human brain. *Scientific American, 241,* 180–199.

GESELL, A., & THOMPSON, H. (1929). Learning and growth in identical twins: An experimental study by the method of co-twin control. *Genetic Psychology Monographs, 6,* 1–123.

GHEORGHIU, V. A., NETTER, P. EYSENCK, H. J., & ROSENTHAL, R. (Eds.) (1989). *Suggestion and suggestibility: Theory and research.* New York: Springer-Verlag.

GIANOULAKIS, C., KRISHNAN, B., & THAVUNDAYIL, J. (1996). Enhanced sensitivity of pituitary ß-endorphin to ethanol in subjects at high risk of alcoholism. *Archives of General Psychiatry, 53,* 250–257.

GIBSON, E. J., & WALK, R. D. (1960). The "visual cliff." *Scientific American, 202,* 64–71.

GILBERT, D. T., & JONES, E. E. (1986). Perceiver-induced constraint: Interpretations of self-generated reality. *Journal of Personality and Social Psychology, 50,* 269–280.

GILCHRIST, A. L. (1988). Lightness contrast and failures of constancy: A common explanation. *Perception & Psychophysics, 43,* 415–424.

GILLGAN, C. (1982). *In a different voice.* Cambridge, MA: Harvard University Press.

GILLIN, J. C. (1985). Sleep and dreams. In G. L. Klerman, M. M. Weissman, P. S. Applebaum, & L. H. Roth (Eds.), *Psychiatry* (Vol. 3). Philadelphia: Lippincott.

GINSBERG, A. (1983). Contrast perception in the human infant. Unpublished manuscript.

GLANZER, M. (1972). Storage mechanisms in recall. In G. H. Bower & J. T. Spence (Eds.), *The psychology of learning and motivation* (Vol. 5). New York: Academic Press.

GLASER, R., RICE, J., SPEICHER, C. E., STOUT, J. C., & KIECOLT-GLASER, J. K. (1986). Stress depresses interferon production by leukocytes concomitant with a decrease in natural killer cell activity. *Behavioral Neuroscience, 100,* 675–678.

GLASS, D. C., & SINGER, J. E. (1972). *Urban stress: Experiments on noise and social stressors.* New York: Academic Press.

GLASS, G. V., MCGAW, B., & SMITH, M. L. (1981). *Meta-analysis in social research.* Beverly Hills, CA: Sage

GLEITMAN, H. (1986). *Psychology* (2nd ed.). New York: Norton.

GLEITMAN, L. R. (1986). Biological predispositions to learn language. In P. Marler & H. S. Terrace (Eds.), *The biology of learning.* New York: Springer-Verlag.

GODDEN, D., & BADDELEY, A. D. (1975). Context-dependent memory in two natural environments: On land and under water. *British Journal of Psychology, 66,* 325–331.

GOETHALS, G. P., & ZANNA, M. P. (1979). The role of social comparison in choice shifts. *Journal of Personality and Social Psychology, 37,* 1469–1476.

GOLDIN-MEADOW, S. (1982). The resilience of recursion: A structure within a conventional model. In E. Wanner & L. R. Gleitman (Eds.), *Language acquisition: The state of the art.* Cambridge, England: Cambridge University Press.

GOLDMAN-RAKIC, P. S. (1987). Circuitry of primate prefrontal corex and regulation of behavior by representational memory. In F. Plum (Ed.), *Handbook of physiology: The nervous system.* Bethesda, MD: American Physiology Society.

GOLDMAN-RAKIC, P. S. (1996). Regional and cellular fractionation of working memory. *Proceedings of the National Academy of Science of the United States of America, 93,* 13473–13480.

GOLDSTEIN, A. (1994). *Addiction: From biology to drug policy.* New York: Freeman.

GOLDSTEIN, E. B. (1989). *Sensation and perception* (3rd ed.). Belmont, CA: Wadsworth.

GOLDSTEIN, M. (1987). Family interaction patterns that antedate the onset of schizophrenia and related disorders: A further analysis of data from a longitudinal prospective study. In K. Hahlweg & M. Goldstein (Eds.), *Understanding major mental disorders: The contribution of family interaction research* (pp. 11–32). New York: Family Process Press.

GOLDSTEIN, M. J., TALOVIC, S. A., NUECHTERLEIN, K. H., & FOGELSON, D. L. (1992). Family interaction versus individual psychopathology: Do they indicate the same processes in the families of schizophrenia? *British Journal of Psychiatry, 161,* 97–102.

GOLEMAN, D. (1995, May 2). Biologists find the site of working memory. *New York Times.*

GOLEMAN, D. J. (1988, October 18). Chemistry of sexual desire yields its elusive secret. *New York Times.*

GOODALL, J. (1978). Chimp killings: Is it the man in them? *Science News, 113,* 276.

GOODGLASS, H., & BUTTERS, N. (1988). Psychobiology of cognitive processes. In R. C. Atkinson, R. J. Hernstein, G. Lindzey, & R. D. Luce (Eds.), *Stevens' handbook of experimental psychology* (Vol. 2). New York: Wiley.

GOODWIN, F. K., & JAMISON, K. R. (1990). *Manic-depressive illness.* New York: Oxford University Press.

GORDON, W. (1989). *Learning & memory.* Pacific Grove, CA: Brooks/Cole.

GOTTESMAN, I. I. (1991). *Schizophrenia genesis: The origins of madness.* New York: W. H. Freeman.

GOY, R. W. (1968). Organizing effect of androgen on the behavior of rhesus monkeys. In R. F. Michael (Ed.), *Endocrinology of human behaviour.* London: Oxford University Press.

GRADY, C. L., HAXBY, J. V., HORWITZ, B., SCHAPIRO, M. B., RAPOPORT, S. I., UNGER-LEIDER, L. G., MISHKIN, M., CARSON, R. E., & HERSCOVITCH, P. (1992). Dissociation of object and spatial vision in human extrastriate cortex: Age-related changes in activation of regional cerebral blood flow measured with [^{15}O] water and positron emission tomography. *Journal of Cognitive Neuroscience, 4,* 23–34.

GRAF, P., & MANDLER, G. (1984). Activation makes words more accessible, but not necessarily more retrievable. *Journal of Verbal Learning and Verbal Behavior, 23,* 553–568.

GRAHAM, J. R. (1990). *The MIMPI-2: Assessing personality and psychopathology.* New York: Oxford University Press.

GRANRUD, C. E. (1986). Binocular vision and spatial perception in 4- and 5-month old infants. *Journal of Experimental Psychology: Human Perception and Performance, 12,* 36–49.

GRAY, E., & COSGROVE, J. (1985). Ethnocentric perception of childbearing practices in protective services. *Child Abuse and Neglect 9,* 389–396.

GRAY, J. (1982). Precis of the neuropsychology of anxiety: An enquiry into the functions of the septo-hippocampal system. *Behavioural & Brain Sciences, 5,* 469–534.

GRAY, J. A. (1987). *The psychology of fear and stress* (2nd ed.). Cambridge, England: Cambridge University Press.

GREEN, B. L., LINDY, J. D., GRACE, M. C., & LEONARD, A. C. (1992). Chronic post-traumatic stress disorder and diagnostic comorbidity in a disaster sample. *Journal of Nervous and Mental Disease, 180,* 760–766.

GREEN, D. M., & WIER, C. C. (1984). Auditory perception. In I. Darian-Smith (Ed.), *Handbook of physiology* (Vol. 3). Bethesda, MD: American Physiological Society.

GREEN, J. G., FOX, N. A., & LEWIS, M. (1983). The relationship between neonatal characteristics and three-month mother-infant interaction in high-risk infants. *Child Development, 54,* 1286–1296.

GREEN, R. (1987). *The "sissy boy syndrome" and the development of homosexuality.* New Haven, CT: Yale University Press.

GREENFIELD, P. M., & SAVAGE-RUMBAUGH, S. (1990). Grammatical combination in *Pan Paniscus:* Processes of learning and invention in the evolution and development of language. In S. Parker & K. Gibson (Eds.), *"Language" and intelligence in monkeys and apes: Comparative developmental perspectives.* New York: Cambridge University Press.

GREENWALD, A. G. (1968). Cognitive learning, cognitive response to persuasion, and attitude change. In A. G. Greenwald, T. C. Brock, & T. M. Ostrom (Eds.), *Psychological foundations of attitudes.* New York: Academic Press.

GREENWALD, A. G. (1992). Unconscious cognition reclaimed. *American Psychologist, 47,* 766–779.

GRICE, H. P. (1975). Logic and conversation. In G. Harman & D. Davidson (Eds.), *The logic of grammar.* Encino, CA: Dickinson.

GRIGGS, R. A., & COX, J. R. (1982). The elusive thematic-materials effect in Watson's selection task. *British Journal of Psychology, 73,* 407–420.

GRILL, H. J., & KAPLAN, J. M. (1990). Caudal brainstem participates in the distributed neural control of feeding. In E. M. Stricker (Eds.), *Neurobiology of food and fluid intake* (pp. 125–149). New York: Plenum Press.

GRODZINSKY, Y. (1984). The syntactic characterization of agrammatism. *Cognition, 16,* 99–120.

GROVES, P. M., & REBEC, G. V. (1992). *Introduction to biological psychology* (4th ed.). Dubuque, IA: Brown.

GRÜNBAUM, A. (1984). *The foundations of psychoanalysis.* Berkeley, CA: University of California Press.

GUILFORD, J. P. (1982). Cognitive psychology's ambiguities: Some suggested remedies. *Psychological Review, 89,* 48–49.

GURNEY, R. (1936). The hereditary factor in obesity. *Archives of Internal Medicine, 57,* 557–561.

HAAGA, D. A. F., DYCK, M. J., & ERNST, D. (1991). Empirical status of cognitive theory of depression. *Psychological Bulletin, 110,* 215–236.

HABER, R. N. (1969). Eidetic images. *Scientific American, 220,* 36–55.

HABER, R. N. (1979). Twenty years of haunting edetic imagery: Where's the ghost? *Behavioral and Brain Sciences, 24,* 583–629.

HABERLANDT, K. (1993). *Cognitive psychology.* Boston, MA: Allyn and Bacon.

HAITH, M. M., BERGMAN, T., & MOORE, M. J. (1977). Eye contact and face scanning in early infancy. *Science, 198,* 853–855.

HALL, C., & VAN DE CASTLE, R. (1966). *The content analysis of dreams.* New York: Appleton-Century-Crofts.

HALL, C. S. (1947). Diagnosing personality by the analysis of dreams. *Journal of Abnormal and Social Psychology, 42,* 68–79.

HALL, C. S. (1953). A cognitive theory of dreams. *Journal of General Psychology, 48,* 169–186.

HAMER, D. H., HU, S., MAGNUSON, V. L., HU, N., & PATTATUCCI, A. M. L. (1993). A linkage between DNA markers on the X chromosome and male sexual orientation. *Science, 261,* 321–327.

HAMER, D., & COPELAND, P. (1994). *The science of desire: The search for the gay gene and the biology of behavior.* New York: Simon & Schuster.

HAMILTON, D. L. (1979). A cognitive-attributional analysis of stereotyping. In L. Berkowitz (Ed.), *Advances in experimental social psychology* (Vol. 12). New York: Academic Press.

HAMILTON, D. L., & GIFFORD, R. K. (1976). Illusory correlation in interpersonal perception: A cognitive basis of stereotypic judgments. *Journal of Experimental Social Psychology, 12,* 392–407.

HAMILTON, D. L., & SHERMAN, S. J. (1989). Illusory correlations: Implications for stereotype theory and research. In D. Bar-Tal, C. F. Gravmann, A. W. Kruglanski, & W. Stroebe (Eds.), *Stereotypes and predjudice: Changing conceptions.* New York: Springer-Verlag.

HARE, R. D. (1980). A research scale for the assessment of psychopathy in criminal populations. *Personality and Individual Differences, 1,* 111–119.

HARLOW, H. F. (1971). *Learning to love.* San Francisco: Albion.

HARLOW, H. F., & HARLOW, M. K. (1969). Effects of various mother-infant relationships on rhesus monkey behaviors. In B. M. Foss (Ed.), *Determinants of infant behavior* (Vol. 4). London: Methuen.

HARRIS, J. R. (1995). Where is the child's environment? A group socialization theory of development. *Psychological Review, 102,* 458–489.

HARRIS, M. J., & ROSENTHAL, R. (1988). *Interpersonal expectancy effects and human performance research.* Washington, DC: National Academy Press.

HARTMANN, E. (1968). The day residue: Time distribution of waking events. *Psychophysiology, 5,* 222.

HATFIELD, E. (1988). Passionate and companionate love. In R. J. Sternberg & M. L. Barnes (Eds.), *The psychology of love* (pp. 191–217). New Haven, CT: Yale University Press.

HATHAWAY, S. R., & MCKINLEY, J. C. (1943). *Manual for the Minnesota Multiphasic Personality Inventory.* New York: Psychological Corporation.

HAWKINS, R. D., & KANDEL, E. R. (1984). Is there a cell-biological alphabet for simple forms of learning? *Psychological Review, 91,* 375–391.

HAXBY, J. V., GRADY, C. L., HORWIZ, B., UNGERLEIDER, L. G., MISHKIN, M., CARSON, R. E., HERSCOVITCH, P., SCHAPIRO, M. B., & RAPOPORT, S. I. (1990). Dissociation of object and spatial visual processing pathways in human extrastriate cortex. *Neurobiology, 88,* 1621–1625.

HAYES, J. R. (1989). *The complete problem solver* (2nd ed.). Hillsdale, NJ: Erlbaum.

HAYES, L. A., & WATSON, J. S. (1981). Neonatal imitation: Fact or artifact. *Developmental Psychology, 17,* 655–660.

HAYNE, H., ROVEE-COLLIER, C., & BORZA, M. A. (1991). Infant memory for place information. *Memory and Cognition, 19,* 378–386.

HAYNES, S. G., & FEINLEIB, M. (1980). Women, work, and coronary heart disease: Prospective findings from the Framingham heart study. *American Journal of Public Health, 70,* 133–141.

HAYNES, S. G., FEINLEIB, M., & KANNEL, W. B. (1980). The relationship of psychosocial factors to coronary heart disease in the Framingham study: Pt. 3. Eight-year incidence of coronary heart disease. *American Journal of Epidemiology, 111,* 37–58.

HE, Z. J., & NAKAYAMA, K. (1992). Surfaces versus features in visual search. *Nature, 359,* 231–233.

HEATH, R. G. (1972). Pleasure and brain activity in man. Deep and surface electroencephalograms during orgasm. *Journal of Nervous and Mental Disease, 154,* 3–18.

HEBB, D. O. (1982). Understanding psychological man: A state-of-the-science report. *Psychology Today, 16,* 52–53.

HECHT, S., SHALER, S., & PIREENE, M. H. (1942). Energy, quanta, and vision. *Journal of General Physiology, 25,* 819–840.

HEIDER, F. (1958). *The psychology of interpersonal relations.* New York: Wiley.

HEILBRUN, K. S. (1982). Silverman's subliminal psychodynamic activation: A failure to replicate. *Journal of Abnormal Psychology, 89,* 560–566.

HELBURN, S. W. (Ed.) (1995). *Cost, quality and child outcomes in child care centers.* Denver: University of Colorado.

HELD, R. (1965). Plasticity in sensory motor systems. *Scientific American, 21,* 84–94.

HELD, R., & HEIN, A. (1963). Movement produced stimulation in the development of visually guided behavior. *Journal of Comparative and Physiological Psychology, 56,* 872–876.

HELLIGE, J. B. (1990). Hemispheric asymmetry. *Annual Review of Psychology, 41,* 55–80.

HELLIGE, J. B. (1993). Unity of thought and action: Varieties of interaction between left and right hemispheres. *Current Directions in Psychological Science, 2,* 21–25.

HEMMI, T. (1969). How we have handled the problem of drug abuse in Japan. In F. Sjoqvist & M. Tottie (Eds.), *Abuse of central stimulants.* New York: Raven Press.

HENCHY, T., & GLASS, D. C. (1968). Evaluation apprehension and social facilitation of dominant and subordinate responses. *Journal of Personality and Social Psychology, 10,* 445–454.

HENLEY, N., HAMILTON, M., & THORNE, B. (1985). Womanspeak and manspeak: Sex differences and sexism in communication, verbal and nonverbal. In A. G. Sargent (Ed.), *Beyond sex roles.* St. Paul, MN: West.

HENSEL, H. (1973). Cutaneous thermoreceptors. In A. Iggo (Ed.), *Handbook of sensory physiology* (Vol. 2). Berlin: Springer-Verlag.

HERDT, G. H. (Ed.) (1984). *Ritualized homosexuality in melanesia.* Berkeley: University of California Press.

HEREK, G. M. (1986). The instrumentality of attitudes: Toward a neofunctional theory. *Journal of Social Issues, 42,* 99–114.

HEREK, G. M. (1987). Can functions be measured? A new perspective on the functional approach to attitudes. *Social Psychology Quarterly, 50,* 285–303.

HERING, E. (1878). *Outlines of a theory of the light sense* (L. M. Hurvich & D. Jameson, Trans.). Cambridge, MA: Harvard University Press.

HERING, E. (1920). Memory as a universal function of organized matter. In S. Butler (Ed.), *Unconscious memory.* London: Jonathon Cape.

HERMAN, C. P., & MACK, D. (1975). Restrained and unrestrained eating. *Journal of Personality, 43,* 647–660.

HERMAN, C. P., & POLIVY, J. (1980). Retrained eating. In A. J. Stunkard (Ed.), *Obesity.* Philadelphia: Saunders.

HERRNSTEIN, R. J., & MURRAY, C. (1994). *The bell curve: Intelligence and class structure in American life.* New York: Free Press.

HESS, E. H. (1972). "Imprinting" in a natural laboratory. *Scientific American, 227,* 24–31.

HETHERINGON, E. M., & BRACKBILL, Y. (1963). Etiology and covariation of obstinacy, orderliness, and parsimony in young children. *Child Development, 34,* 919–943.

HILGARD, E. R. (1965). *Hypnotic susceptibility.* New York: Harcourt Brace Jovanovich.

HILGARD, E. R. (1968). *The experience of hypnosis.* New York: Harcourt Brace Jovanovich.

HILGARD, E. R. (1986). *Divided consciousness: Multiple controls in human thought and action.* New York: Wiley-Interscience.

HILGARD, E. R. (1987). *Psychology in America: A historical survey.* San Diego: Harcourt Brace Javanovich.

HILGARD, E. R., & HILGARD, J. R. (1975). *Hypnosis in the relief of pain.* Los Altos, CA: Kaufmann.

HILGARD, E. R., HILGARD, J. R., MACDONALD, H., MORGAN, A. H., & JOHNSON, L. S. (1978). Covert pain in hypnotic analgesia: Its reality as tested by the real-simulator design. *Journal of Abnormal Psychology, 87,* 655–663.

HILL, C., RUBIN, Z., & PEPLAU, L. A. (1976). Breakups before marriage: The end of 103 affairs. *Journal of Social Issues, 32,* 147–168.

HILLIER, L., HEWITT, K. L., & MORRON-GIELTO, B. A. (1992). Infants' perception of illusions in sound localization: Reaching to sounds in the dark. *Journal of Experimental Child Psychology, 53,* 159–179.

HILLYARD, S. A. (1985). Electrophysiology of human selective attention. *Trends in Neuroscience, 8,* 400–406.

HINSHAW, S. P. (1994). *Attention deficits and hyperactivity in children.* Thousand Oaks, CA: Sage.

HIRSCH, J., & BATCHELOR, B. R. (1976). Adipose tissue cellularity and human obesity. *Clinical Endocrinology and Metabolism, 5,* 299–311.

HOBSON, J. A. (1988). *The dreaming brain.* New York: Basic Books.

HOBSON, J. A. (1989). *Sleep.* New York: Freeman.

HOBSON, J. A. (1994). *The chemistry of conscious states, how the brain changes its mind.* New York: Little, Brown.

HOBSON, J. A. (1997). Dreaming as delirium: A mental status analysis of our nightly madness. *Seminars in Neurology, 1,* 121–128.

HOEBEL, B. G., & TEITELBAUM, P. (1966). Effects of force-feeding and starvation on food intake and body weight on a rat with ventromedial hypothalamic lesions. *Journal of Comparative and Physiological Psychology, 61,* 189–193.

HOFLING, C. K., BROTZMAN, E., DALRYMPLE, S., GRAVES, N., & PIERCE, C. M. (1966). An experimental study in nurse-physician relationships. *Journal of Nervous and Mental Disease, 143,* 171–180.

HOGARTY, G. E. (1986). Family psychoeducation, social skills training, and maintenance chemotherapy in the aftercare treatment of schizophrenia: I. One-year effects of a controlled study on relapse and expressed emotion. *Archives of General Psychiatry, 43,* 633–642.

HOGARTY, G. E., SCHOOLER, N. R., ULRICH, R., MUSSARE, F., FERRO, P., & HERRON, E. (1979). Fluphenazine and social therapy in the after care of schizophrenic patients. *Archives of General Psychiatry, 36,* 1283–1294.

HOHMANN, G. W. (1962). Some effects of spinal cord lesions on experienced emotional feelings. *Psychophysiology, 3,* 143–156.

HOLLAND, J. H., HOLYOAK, K. J., NISBETT, R. E., & THAGARD, P. R. (1986). *Induction: Processes of inference, learning, and discovery.* Cambridge, MA: MIT Press.

HOLMES, D. S. (1974). Investigations of repression: Differential recall of material experimentally or naturally associated with ego threat. *Psychological Bulletin, 81,* 632–653.

HOLMES, D. S. (1984). Meditation and somatic arousal reduction: A review of the experimental evidence. *American Psychologist, 39,* 1–10.

HOLMES, D. S. (1985a). To meditate or rest? The answer is rest. *American Psychologist, 40,* 728–731.

HOLMES, D. S. (1985b). Self-control of somatic arousal: An examination of the effects of meditation and feedback. *American Behavioral Scientist, 28,* 486–496.

HOLMES, T. H., & RAHE, R. H. (1967). The social readjustment rating scale. *Journal of Psychosomatic Research, 11,* 213–218.

HOLROYD, K. A., APPEL, M. A., & ANDRASIK, F. (1983). A cognitive behavioral approach to psychophysiological disorders. In D. Meichenbaum & M. E. Jaremko (Eds.), *Stress reduction and prevention.* New York: Plenum.

HONIG, W. K., & STADDON, J. E. R. (Eds.) (1977). *Handbook of operant behavior.* Englewood Cliffs, NJ: Prentice-Hall.

HONORTON, C. (1985). Meta-analysis of psi ganzfeld research: A response to Hyman. *Journal of Parapsychology, 49,* 51–91.

HOOLEY, J. M., RICHTERS, J. E., WEINTRAUB, S., & NEALE, J. M. (1987). Psychopathology and marital distress: The positive side of positive symptoms. *Journal of Abnormal Psychology, 96,* 27–33.

HOON, P. W., WINCZE, J. P., & HOON, E. F. (1977). A test of reciprocal inhibition: Are anxiety and sexual arousal in women mutually inhibitory? *Journal of Abnormal Psychology, 86,* 65–74.

HOPKINS, J. R. (1977). Sexual behavior in adolescence. *Journal of Social Issues, 33,* 67–85.

HORM, J., & ANDERSON, K. (1993). Who in America is trying to lose weight? *Annals of Internal Medicine, 119,* 672–676.

HORNE, J. A., & MCGRATH, M. J. (1984). The consolidation hypothesis for REM sleep function: Stress and other confounding factors—A review. *Biological Psychology, 18,* 165–84.

HOROWITZ, F. D. (1974). Visual attention, auditory stimulation, and language stimulation in young infants. *Monographs of the Society for Research in Child Development, 31,* Serial No. 158.

HOROWITZ, M. (1986). Stress-response syndromes: A review of postraumatic and adjustment disorders. *Hospital & Community Psychiatry, 37,* 241–249.

HOVLAND, C., JANIS, I., & KELLEY, H. H. (1953). *Communication and persuasion.* New Haven, CT: Yale University Press.

HOWES, C. (1990). Can the age of entry into child care and the quality of child care predict adjustment in kindergarten? *Developmental Psychology, 26,* 292–803.

HOWES, C., PHILLIPS, D. A., & WHITEBOOK, M. (1992). Thresholds of quality: Implications for the social development of children in center-based child care. *Child Development, 63,* 449–460.

HSER, Y. I., ANGLIN, D., & POWERS, K. (1993). A 24-year follow-up of California narcotics addicts. *Archives of General Psychiatry, 50,* 577–584.

HUBEL, D. H., & WIESEL, T. N. (1963). Receptive fields of cells in striate cortex of very young visually inexperienced kittens. *Journal of Neurophysiology, 26,* 994–1002.

HUBEL, D. H., & WIESEL, T. N. (1968). Receptive fields and functional architecture of monkey striate cortex. *Journal of Physiology, 195,* 215–243.

HUDSON, J. W., & HOYT, L. L. (1981). Personal characteristics important in mate preference among college students. *Social Behavior and Personality, 9,* 93–96.

HUMMEL, J. E., & BIEDERMAN, I. (1992). Dynamic binding in a neutral network for shape recognition. *Psychological Review, 99,* 480–517.

HUNT, E. (1990). A modern arsenal for mental assessment. *Educational Psychologist, 25,* 223–241.

HUNT, M. (1974). *Sexual behavior in the 1970's.* Chicago: Playboy Press.

HUNT, P. J., & HILLERY, J. M. (1973). Social facilitation at different stages in learning. Paper presented at the Midwestern Psychological Association Meetings, Cleveland.

HUNTER, I. M. L. (1974). *Memory.* Baltimore: Penguin.

HURVICH, L. M., & JAMESON, D. (1974). Opponent processes as a model of neural organizations. *American Psychologist, 29,* 88–102.

HUTTON, D. C., & BAUMEISTER, R. F. (1992). Self-awareness and attitude change: Seeing oneself on the central route to persuasion. *Personality and Social Psychology Bulletin, 18,* 68–75.

HYMAN, R. (1985). The ganzfield psi experiment: A critical appraisal. *Journal of Parapsychology, 49,* 3–49.

HYMAN, R. (1994). Anomaly or Artifact? Comments on Bem and Honorton. *Psychological Bulletin, 115,* 19–24.

HYMAN, R., & HONORTON, C. (1986). A joint communiqué: The psi ganzfeld controversy. *Journal of Parapsychology, 50,* 351–364.

IMPERATO-MCGINLEY, J., PETERSON, R. E., GAUTIER, T., & STURLA, E. (1979). Androgens and the evolution of male gender identity among male pseudohermaphrodites with 5 alpha reductase deficiency. *New England Journal of Medicine, 300,* 1233–1237.

INSTITUTE OF MEDICINE (1982). *Marijuana and health.* Washington, DC: National Academy Press.

ISABELLA, R. A., & BELSKY, J. (1991). Interactional synchrony and the origins of infant-mother attachment: A replication study. *Child Development, 62,* 373–384.

ISEN, P. M. (1985). The assymmetry of happiness and sadness in effects on memory in normal college students. *Journal of Experimental Psychology: General, 114,* 388–391.

ISEN, P. M., SHALKER, T. E., CLARK, M., & KARP, L. (1978). Affect, accessibility of material in memory, and behavior: A cognitive loop? *Journal of Personality and Social Psychology, 36,* 1–12.

ISENBERG, D. J. (1986). Group polarization: A critical review and meta-analysis. *Journal of Personality and Social Psychology, 50,* 1141–1151.

ISOZAKI, M. (1984). The effect of discussion on polarization of judgments. *Japanese Psychological Research, 26,* 187–193.

JACKENDOFF, R. (1990). *Consciousness and the computational mind.* Cambridge, MA: MIT Press.

JACOBS, W. J., & NADEL, W. (1985). Stress-induced recovery of fears and phobias. *Psychological Review, 92,* 512–531.

JACOBSON, A. L., FRIED, C., & HOROWITZ, S. D. (1967). Classical conditioning, pseudoconditioning, or sensitization in the planarian. *Journal of Comparative and Physiological Psychology, 64,* 73–79.

JACOBSON, N. S., & HOLLON, S. D. (1996). Cognitive-behavior therapy versus pharmacotherapy: Now that the jury's returned its verdict, it's time to present the rest of the evidence. *Journal of Consulting and Clinical Psychology, 64,* 74–80.

JAMES, W. (1884). What is an emotion? *Mind, 9,* 188–205.

JAMISON, K. R. (1995, February). Manic-depressive illness and creativity. *Scientific American.*

JANET, P. (1889). *L'automisme psychologigue.* Paris: Félix Alcan.

JANIS, I. L. (1982). *Groupthink: Psychological studies of policy decisions and fiascoes* (2nd ed.). Boston: Houghton Mifflin.

JANIS, I. L. (1985). Sources of error in strategic decision making. In J. M. Pennings (Ed.), *Organizational strategy and change.* San Francisco: Jossey-Bass.

JANOFF-BULMAN, R. (1992). *Shattered assumptions: Toward a new psychology of trauma.* New York: Maxwell Macmillan International.

JASMOS, T. M., & HAKMILLER, K. L. (1975). Some effects of lesion level and emotional cues on affective expression in spinal cord patients. *Psychological Reports, 37,* 859–870.

JEMMOTT, J. B., III, BORYSENKO, M., MCCELLAND, D. C., CHAPMAN, R., MEYER, D., & BENSON, H. (1985). Academic stress, power motivation, and decrease in salivary secretory immunoglubulin: A secretion rate. *Lancet, 1,* 1400–1402.

JENNINGS, D., AMABILE, T. M., & ROSS, L. (1982). Informal covariation assessment: Data-based vs. theory-based judgments. In A. Tversky, D. Kahneman, & P. Slovic (Eds.), *Judgment under uncertainty: Heuristics and biases.* New York: Cambridge University Press.

JOHANSSON, G., & FRANKENHAEUSER, J. (1973). Temporal factors in sympatho-adrenomedullary activity following acute behavioral activation. *Biological Psychology, 1,* 63–73.

JOHANSSON, G., VON HOFSTEN, C., & JANSON, G. (1980). Event perception. *Annual Review of Psychology, 31,* 27–63.

JOHN, O. P. (1990). The "Big Five" factor taxonomy: Dimension of personality in the natural language and in questionnaires. In L. A. Pervin (Ed.), *Handbook of personality: Theory and research* (pp. 66–100). New York: Guilford.

JOHNSON, R. D., & DOWNING, L. L. (1979). Deindividuation and valence of cues: Effect on prosocial and antisocial behavior. *Journal of Personality and Social Psychology, 37,* 1532–1538.

JOHNSON-LAIRD, P. N. (1985). The deductive reasoning ability. In R. J. Sternberg (Ed.), *Human abilities: An information processing approach.* New York: Freeman.

JOHNSON-LAIRD, P. N. (1988). *The computer and the mind: An introduction to cognitive science.* Cambridge, MA: Harvard University Press.

JOHNSON-LAIRD, P. (1988). A computational analysis of consciousness. In A. J. Marcel & E. Bisiach (Eds.), *Consciousness in contemporary science.* New York: Oxford University Press.

JOHNSON-LAIRD, P. N. (1989). Mental models. In M. I. Posner (Ed.), *Foundations of cognitive science.* Cambridge, MA: MIT Press.

JOHNSON-LAIRD, P. N., & BYRNE, R. M. J. (1991). *Deduction.* Hillsdale, NJ: Erlbaum.

JOHNSTON, L. D., O'MALLEY, P. M., & BACHMAN, J. G. (1995). *National survey results on drug use.* Rockville, MD: National Institute on Drug Abuse.

JONES, E. E. (1978). Effects of race on psychotherapy process and outcome: An exploratory investigation. *Psychotherapy: Theory, Research, and Practice, 15,* 226–236.

JONES, E. E. (1990). *Interpersonal perception.* New York: Freeman.

JONES, E. E., & HARRIS, V. A. (1967). The attribution of attitudes. *Journal of Experimental Social Psychology, 3,* 1–24.

JONES, E. E., ROCK, L., SHAVER, K. G., GOETHALS, G. R., & WARD, L. M. (1968). Pattern of performance and ability attribution: An unexpected primacy effect. *Journal of Personality and Social Psychology, 9,* 317–340.

JONES, H. C., & LOVINGER, P. W. (1985). *The marijuana question and science's search for an answer.* New York: Dodd, Mead.

JUDD, L., AKISKAL, H., MASER, J., ZELLER, P. J., ENDICOTT, J., CORYELL, W., PAULUS, M., KUNOVAC, J., LEON, A., MUELLER, T., RICE, J., & KELLER, M. (1998). A prospective 12-year study of subsyndromal and syndromal depressive symptoms in unipolar major depressive disorders. *Archives of General Psychiatry, 55,* 694–700.

JULIEN, R. M. (1988). *Drugs and the body.* New York: Freeman.

JULIEN, R. M. (1992). *A primer of drug action: A concise, nontechnical guide to the actions, uses, and side effects of psychoactive drugs* (6th ed.). New York: Freeman.

JUST, M. A., & CARPENTER, P. A. (1980). A theory of reading: From eye fixations to comprehension. *Psychological Review, 87,* 329–354.

JUST, M. A., & CARPENTER, P. A. (1992). A capacity theory of comprehension: Individual differences in working memory. *Psychological Review, 99,* 122.

KAGAN, J. (1979). Overview: Perspectives on human infancy. In J. D. Osofsky (Ed.), *Handbook of infant development.* New York: Wiley-Interscience.

KAGAN, J., KEARSLEY, R. B., & ZELAZO, P. (1978). *Infancy: Its place in human development.* Cambridge, MA: Harvard University Press.

KAGAN, J., & SNIDMAN, N. (1991). Temperamental factors in human development. *American Psychologist, 46,* 856–862.

KAGAN, N. (1984). *The nature of the child.* New York: Basic Books.

KAGAN, N., & MOSS, H. A. (1962). *Birth to maturity.* New York: Wiley.

KAHNEMAN, D., SLOVIC, P., & TVERSKY, A. (Eds.) (1982). *Judgment under uncertainty: Heuristics and biases.* New York: Cambridge University Press.

KAIL, R. (1989). *The development of memory in children* (3rd ed.). New York: Freeman.

KAMEN-SIEGEL, L., RODIN, J., SELIGMAN, M. E., & J. D. (1991). Explanatory style and cell-mediated immunity in elderly men and women. *Health Psychology, 10,* 229–235.

KAMIN, L. J. (1974). *The science and politics of IQ.* Hillsdale, NJ: Erlbaum.

KANDEL, E. R., SCHWARTZ, J. H., & JESSELL, T. M. (Eds.) (1991). *Principles of neural science* (3rd ed.). New York: Elsevier.

KAPLAN, M. R., & MILLER, C. E. (1987). Group decision making and normative versus informational influence: Effects of type of issue and assigned decision rule. *Journal of Personality and Social Psychology, 53,* 306–313.

KARASEK, R., BAKER, D., MARXER, F., AHLBOM, A., & THEORELL, T. (1981). Job decision latitude, job demands, and cardiovascular disease: A prospective study of Swedish men. *American Journal of Public Health, 71,* 694–705.

KARASEK, R. A., THEORELL, T. G., SCHWARTZ, J., PIEPER, C., & ALFREDSSON, L. (1982). Job, psychological factors and coronary heart disease: Swedish prospective findings and U.S. prevalence findings using a new occupation inference method. *Advances in Cardiology, 29,* 62–67.

KARNI, A., TANNE, D., RUBENSTEIN, B. S., ASKENASY, J. J. M., & SAGI, D. (1994). Dependence on REM sleep of overnight improvement of a perceptual skill. *Science, 265,* 679–682.

KARNO, M., & GOLDING, J. M. (1991). Obsessive compulsive disorder. In L. R. Robins & D. A. Regier (Eds.), *Psychiatric disorders in America: The epidiologic Catchment area study.* New York: Maxwell Macmillan International.

KARYLOWSKI, J. J. (1990). Social reference points and accessibility of trait-related information in self-other similarity judgments. *Journal of Personality and Social Psychology, 58,* 975–983.

KATZ, D. (1960). The functional approach to the study of attitudes. *Public Opinion Quarterly, 24,* 163–204.

KATZ, R., & WYKES, T. (1985). The psychological difference between temporally predictable and unpredictable stressful events: Evidence for information control theories. *Journal of Personality and Social Psychology, 48,* 781–790.

KAUFMAN, L., & ROCK, I. (1989). The moon illusion thirty years later. In M. Hershenson (Ed.), *The moon illusion* (pp. 193–234). Hillsdale, NJ: Erlbaum.

KAZDIN, A. E. (1982). Symptom substitution, generalization, and response covariation: Implications for psychotherapy outcome. *Psychological Bulletin, 91,* 349–365.

KAZDIN, A. E., & WEISZ, J. R. (1998). Identifying and developing empirically supported child and adolescent treatments. *Journal of Consulting and Clinical Psychology, 66,* 19–36.

KEIL, F. C. (1989). *Concepts, kinds, and cognitive development.* Cambridge, MA: MIT Press.

KEIL, F. C., & BATTERMAN, N. A. (1984). Characteristic-to-defining shift in the development of word meaning. *Journal of Verbal Learning and Verbal Behavior, 23,* 221–236.

KELLER, M. B., & BAKER, L. A. (1991). Bipolar disorder: Epidemiology, course, diagnosis, and treatment. *Bulletin of the Menninger Clinic, 55,* 172–181.

KELLEY, H. H. (1967). Attribution theory in social psychology. In D. Levine (Ed.), *Nebraska symposium on motivation* (Vol. 15). Lincoln: University of Nebraska Press.

KELLMAN, P. J. (1984). Perception of three-dimensional form by human infants. *Perception and Psychophysics, 36,* 353–358.

KELLY, G. A. (1955). *The psychology of personal constructs.* New York: Norton.

KENDLER, K. S., NEALE, M. C., KESSLER, R. C., & HEATH, A. C. (1992). Major depression and generalized anxiety disorder: Same genes, (partly) different environments? *Archives of General Psychiatry, 49,* 716–722.

KENDLER, K. S., NEALE, M. C., KESSLER, R. C., & HEATH, A. C. (1993). Panic disorder in women: A population-based twin study. *Psychological Medicine, 23,* 397–406.

KENDRICK, D. T., & GUTIERRES, S. E. (1980). Contrast effects and judgments of physical attractiveness: When beauty becomes a social problem. *Journal of Personality and Social Psychology, 38,* 131–140.

KENSHALO, D. R., NAFE, J. P., & BROOKS, B. (1961). Variations in thermal sensitivity. *Science, 134,* 104–105.

KEPHART, W. M. (1967). Some correlates of romantic love. *Journal of Marriage and the Family, 29,* 470–474.

KERNBERG, P. F. (1979). Psychoanalytic profile of the borderline adolescent. *Adolescent Psychiatry, 7,* 234–256.

KERNIS, M. H., & WHEELER, L. (1981). Beautiful friends and ugly strangers: Radiation and contrast effects in perception of same-sex pairs. *Journal of Personality and Social Psychology, 7,* 617–620.

KESSLER, R. C., BROWN, R. L., & BROMAN, C. L. (1981). Sex differences in psychiatric help-seeking: Evidence from four large-scale surveys. *Journal of Health and Social Behavior, 22,* 49–64.

KESSLER, R. C., DAVIS, C. G., & KENDLER, K. S. (1997). Childhood adversity and adult psychiatric disorder in the US National Comorbidity Survey. *Psychological Medicine, 27,* 1101–1119.

KESSLER, R. C., MCGONAGLE, K. A., ZHAO, S., NELSON, C., HUGHES, M., ESHLEMAN, S., WITTCHEN, H., & KENDLER, K. (1994). Lifetime and 12-month prevalence of DSM-III-R psychiatric disorders in the United States. *Archives of General Psychiatry, 51,* 8–19.

KIECOLT-GLASER, J. K., and collaborators (1985). Psychosocial enhancement of immunocompetence in a geriatric population. *Health Psychology, 4,* 25–41.

KIECOLT-GLASER, J. K., GLASER, R., CACIOPPO, J. T., & MALARKEY, W. B. (1998). Marital stress: Immunologic, neuroendocrine, and autonomic correlates. In S. M. McCann (Ed.), *Annals of the New York Academy of Sciences, Vol. 840: Neuroimmunomodulation: Molecular aspects, integrative systems, and clinical advances* (pp. 656–663). New York: New York Academy of Sciences.

KIECOLT-GLASER, J. K., KENNEDY, S., MALKOFF, S., FISHER, L., SPEICHER, C. E., & GLASER, R. (1988). Marital discord and immunity in males. *Psychosomatic Medicine, 50,* 213–229.

KIESLER, C. A., & SIBULKIN, A. E. (1987). *Mental hospitalization: Myths and facts about a national crisis.* Newbery Park, CA: Sage.

KIHLSTROM, J. F. (1984). Conscious, subconscious, unconscious: A cognitive view. In K. S. Bowers & D. Meichenbaum (Eds.), *The unconscious: Reconsidered.* New York: Wiley.

KIHLSTROM, J. F. (1985). Hypnosis. *Annual Review of Psychology, 36,* 385–235.

KIHLSTROM, J. F. (1987). The cognitive unconscious. *Science, 237,* 1445–1452.

KIMMEL, D. C., & WEINER, I. B. (1985). *Adolescence: A developmental transition.* Hillsdale, NJ: Erlbaum.

KINDER, D. R., & SEARS, D. O. (1985). Public opinion and political action. In G. Lindzey & E. Aronson, (Eds.), *The handbook of social psychology* (3rd ed., Vol. 2). New York: Random House.

KING, N. J., GULLONE, E, TONGE, B. J., & OLLENDICK, T. H. (1993). Self-reports of panic attacks and manifest anxiety in adolescents. *Behavior Research & Therapy 31,* 111–116.

KINSEY, A. C., POMEROY, W. B., & MARTIN, C. E. (1948). *Sexual behavior in the human male.* Philadelpia: Saunders.

KINSEY, A. C., POMEROY, W. B., & MARTIN, C. E. & GEBHARD, P. H. (1953). *Sexual behavior in the human female.* Philadelphia: Saunders.

KISHLINE, A. (1994). *Moderate drinking.* New York: Three Rivers Press.

KLAHR, D. (1982). Nonmonotone assessment of monotone development: An information processing analysis. In S. Strauss (Ed.), *U-shaped behavioral growth.* New York: Academic Press.

KLATZKY, R. L., LEDERMAN, S. J., & METZGER, V. A. (1985). Identifying objects by touch: An expert system. *Perception and Psychophysics, 37,* 299–302.

KLEIN, S. B., & LOFTUS, J. (1988). The nature of self-referent encoding: The contributions of elaborative and organizational processes. *Journal of Personality and Social Psychology, 55,* 5–11.

KLEIN, S. B., & LOFTUS, J., & BURTON, H. A. (1989). Two self-reference effects: The importance of distinguishing between self-descriptiveness judgments and autobiographical retrieval in self-referent encoding. *Journal of Personality and Social Psychology, 56,* 853–865.

KLERMAN, G. L., WEISSMAN, M. M., ROUNSAVILLE, B., & CHEVRON, E. (1984). *Interpersonal psychotherapy of depression.* New York: Basic Books.

KLINE, P. (1972). *Fact and fancy in Freudian theory.* London: Methuen.

KLINEBERG, O. (1938). Emotional expression in Chinese literature. *Journal of Abnormal and Social Psychology, 33,* 517–520.

KLÜVER, H., & BUCY, P. C. (1937). "Psychic blindness" and other symptoms following temporal lobectomy in rhesus monkeys. *American Journal of Physiology, 119,* 352–353.

KNITTLE, J. L., & HIRSCH, J. (1968). Effect of early nutrition on the development of rat epididymal fat pads: Cellularity and metabolism. *Journal of Clinical Investigation, 47,* 2091.

KOBASA, S. C. (1979). Stressful life events, personality, and health: An inquiry into hardiness. *Journal of Personality and Social Psychology, 37,* 1–11.

KOBASA, S. C., MADDI, S. R., & KAHN, S. (1982). Hardiness and health: A prospective study. *Journal of Personality and Social Psychology, 42,* 168–177.

KOHLBERG, L. (1966). A cognitive-developmental analysis of children's sexrole concepts and attitudes. In E. E. Maccoby (Ed.), *The development of sex differences* (pp. 82–173). Stanford, CA: Stanford University Press.

KOHLBERG, L. (1969). Stage and sequence: The cognitive-developmental approach to socialization. In D. A. Goslin (Ed.), *Handbook of socialization theory and research.* Chicago: Rand McNally.

KOHLBERG, L. (1976). Moral stages and moralization: The cognitive-developmental approach. In T. Lickong (Ed.), *Moral development and behavior.* New York: Holt, Rinehart & Winston.

KOHLER, W. (1925). *The mentality of apes.* New York: Harcourt Brace. (Reprint ed., 1976. New York: Liveright.)

KOHNSTAMM, G. A., BATES, J. E., & ROTHBART, M. K. (Eds.) (1989). *Temperament in childhood.* Chichester: Wiley.

KOLB, B., & WHISHAW, I. Q. (1985). *Fundamentals of human neuropsychology* (2nd ed.). San Francisco: Freeman.

KOLODNY, J. A., (1994). Memory processes in classification learning. *Psychological Science, 5,* 164–169.

KOOB, G. F., & BLOOM, F. E. (1988). Cellular and molecular mechanisms of drug dependence. *Science, 242,* 715–723.

KORNER, A. F. (1973). Individual differences at birth: Implications for early experience and later development. In J. C. Westman (Ed.), *Individual differences in children.* New York: Wiley.

KORNHABER, M., & GARDNER, H. (1991). Critical thinking across multiple intelligences. In S. Maclure & P. Davies (Eds.), *Learning to think: Thinking to learn.* Oxford, England: Pergamon.

KORNHABER, M., KRECHEVSKY, M., & GARDNER, H. (1990). Engaging intelligence. *Educational Psychologist, 25,* 177–199.

KOSAMBI, D. D. (1967). Living prehistory in India. *Scientific American, 215,* 105.

KOSS, M., & BOESCHEN, L. (1998). Rape. In *Encyclopedia of Mental Health,* (Vol. 3). New York: Academic Press.

KOSSLYN, S. M. (1980). *Image and mind.* Cambridge, MA: Harvard University Press.

KOSSLYN, S. M. (1983). *Ghosts in the mind's machine.* New York: Norton.

KOSSLYN, S. M. (1988). Aspects of a cognitive neuroscience of mental imagery: *Science, 240,* 1621–1626.

KOSSLYN, S. M. (1994). *The resolution of the imagery debate.* Cambridge, MA: MIT Press.

KOSSLYN, S. M., ALPERT, N. M., THOMPSON, W. L., MALJKOVIC, V., WEISE, S. B., CHABRIS, C. F., HAMILTON, S. E., RAUCH, S. L., & BUONANNO, F. S. (1993). Visual mental imagery activates topographically organized visual cortex. *Journal of Cognitive Neuroscience, 5,* 263–287.

KOSSLYN, S. M., BALL, T. M., & REISER, B. J. (1978). Visual images preserve metric spatial information: Evidence from studies of image scanning. *Journal of Experimental Psychology: Human Perception and Performance, 4,* 47–60.

KOSSLYN, S. M., & KOENIG, O. (1992). *Wet mind: The new cognitive neuroscience.* New York: Free Press.

KOULACK, D., & GOODENOUGH, D. R. (1976). Dream recall and dream recall failure: An arousal-retrieval model. *Psychological Bulletin, 83,* 975–984.

KRAUT, (1982). Social presence, facial feedback, and emotion. *Journal of Personality and Social Psychology, 42,* 853–863.

KRIPKE, D. F. (1985). Biological rhythms. In G. L. Klerman, M. M. Weissman, P. S. Applebaum, & L. H. Roth (Eds.), *Psychiatry* (Vol. 3). Philadelphia: Lippincott.

KRIPKE, D. F., & GILLIN, J. C. (1985). Sleep disorders. In G. L. Klerman, M. M. Weissman, P. S. Applebaum, & L. N. Roth (Eds.), *Psychiatry* (Vol. 3). Philadelphia: Lippincott.

KRYGER, M. H., ROTH, T., & DEMENT, W. C. (Eds.) (1994). *Principles and practice of sleep medicine.* Philadelphia: Saunders.

KUCH, K., & COX, B. J. (1992). Symptoms of PTSD in 124 survivors of the Holocaust. *American Journal of Psychiatry, 149,* 337–340.

KUHL, P. K., WILLIAMS, K. A., LACERDA, F., STEVENS, K. N., & LINDBLOM, B. (1992). Linguistic experience alters phonetic perception in infants by 6 months of age. *Science, 255,* 606–608.

KUHN, C., SWARTZWELDER, S., & WILSON, W. (1998). *Buzzed: The straight facts about the most used and abused drugs.* New York: Norton.

KUIPER, N. A., MACDONALD, M. R., & DERRY, P. A. (1983). Parameters of a depressive self-schema. In J. Suls & A. G. Greenwald (Eds.), *Psychological perspectives on the self* (Vol. 2). Hillsdale, NJ: Erlbaum.

KUIPER, N. A., OLINGER, L. J., MACDONALD, M. R., & SHAW, B. F. (1985). Self-schema processing of depressed and nondepressed content: The effects of vulnerability on depression. *Social Cognition, 3,* 77–93.

KUIPER, N. A., & ROGERS, T. B. (1979). Encoding of personal information: Self-other differences. *Journal of Personality and Social Psychology, 37,* 499–514.

KUMAN, I. G., FEDROV, C. N., & NOVIKOVA, L. A. (1983). Investigation of the sensitive period in the development of the human visual system. *Journal of Higher Nervous Activity, 33,* 434–441.

KURTINES, W., & GREIF, E. B. (1974). The development of moral thought: Review and evaluation of Kohlberg's approach. *Psychological Bulletin, 81,* 453–470.

LA BERGE, D. (1995). *Attentional processing: The brain's art of mindfulness.* Cambridge, MA: Harvard University Press.

LAGERSPETZ, K., VIEMERO, V., & AKADEMI, A. (1986). Television and aggressive behavior among Finnish children. In L. R. Huesmann & L. D. Eron (Eds.), *Television and the aggressive child.* New York: Erlbaum.

LAGRECA, A. M., SLIVERMAN, W. K., VERNBERG, E. M., & PRINSTEIN, M. J. (1996). Symptoms of posttraumatic stress in children after Hurricane Andrew: A prospective study. *Journal of the American Academy of the Child and Adolescent Psychiatry, 27,* 330–335.

LAMB, M. E., & BORNSTEIN, M. H. (1987). *Development in infancy: An introduction* (2nd ed.). New York: Random House.

LAMBERT, M. J., & BERGIN, A. E. (1994). The effectiveness of psychotherapy. In A. Bergin (Ed.), *Handbook of psychotherapy and behavior change* (4th ed., pp. 143–189). New York: Wiley.

LAND, E. H. (1977). The retinex theory of color vision. *Scientific American, 237,* 108–128.

LAND, E. H. (1986). Recent advances in retinex theory. *Vision Research, 26,* 7–21.

LANGLOIS, J. H., & DOWNS, A. C. (1980). Mothers, fathers, and peers as socialization agents of sex-typed play behaviors in young children. *Child Development, 51,* 1237–1247.

LAPIERE, R. (1934). Attitudes versus actions. *Social Forces, 13,* 230–237.

LARKIN, J. H., MCDERMOTT, J., SIMON, D. P., & SIMON, H. A. (1980). Expert and novice performance in solving physics problems. *Science, 208,* 1335–1342.

LARSEN, R. J., & SEIDMAN, E. (1986). Gender schema theory and sex role inventories: Some conceptual and psychometric considerations. *Journal of Personality and Social Psychology, 50,* 205–211.

LATANÉ, B., & DARLEY, J. M. (1968). Group inhibition of bystander intervention in emergencies. *Journal of Personality and Social Psychology, 10,* 215–221.

LATANÉ, B., & DARLEY, J. M. (1970). *The unresponsive bystander: Why doesn't he help?* New York: Appleton-Century-Crofts.

LATANÉ, B., NIDA, S. A., & WILSON, D. W. (1981). The effects of group size on helping behavior. In J. P. Rushton & R. M. Sorrentino (Eds.), *Altruism and helping behavior: Social personality, and developmental perspectives.* Hillsdale, NJ: Erlbaum.

LATANÉ, B., & RODIN, J. (1969). A lady in distress: Inhibiting effects of friends and strangers on bystander intervention. *Journal of Experimental and Social Psychology, 5,* 189–202.

LAUDENSLAGER, M. L., RYAN, S. M., DRUGAN, R. C., HYSON, R. L., & MAIER, S. F. (1983). Coping and immunosuppression: Inescapable but not escapable shock suppresses lymphocyte proliferation. *Science, 221,* 568–570.

LAUMANN, E. O., GAGNON, J. H. MICHAEL, R. T., & MICHAELS, S. (1994). *The social organization of sexuality: Sexual practices in the United States.* Chicago: University of Chicago Press.

LAZARUS, R. S. (1991a). Cognition and motivation in emotion. *American Psychologist, 46,* 352–367.

LAZARUS, R. S. (1991b). *Emotion and adaptation.* New York: Oxford University Press.

LAZARUS, R. S., & FOLKMAN, S. (1984). *Stress, appraisal, and coping.* New York: Springer.

LAZARUS, R. S., KANNER, A. D., & FOLKMAN, S. (1980). Emotions: A cognitive-phenomenological analysis. In R. Plutchik & H. Kellerman (Eds.), *Emotion: Theory, research, and experience* (Vol. 1). New York: Academic Press.

LE BARS, P. L., KATZ, M. M., BERMAN, N., ITIL, T. M., FREEDMAN, A. M., & SCHATZBERG, A. F. (1997). *A placebo-controlled, double-blind, randomized trial of an extract of ginkgo biloba for dementia.* Tarrytown: New York Institute for Medical Research.

LE BON, G. (1895). *The crowd.* London: Ernest Benn.

LE DEOX, J. E. (1989). Cognitive-emotional interactions in the brain. *Cognition and Emotion, 3,* 267–289.

LEFF, J. P., & VAUGHN, C. E. (1981). The role of maintenance therapy and relatives' expressed emotion in relapse of schizophrenia: A two-year follow-up. *British Journal of Psychiatry, 139,* 102–104.

LENNEBERG, E. H. (1967). *Biological foundations of language.* New York: Wiley.

LENNON, M. C., & ROSENFIELD, S. (1992). Women and mental health: The interaction of job and family conditions. *Journal of Health and Social Behavior, 33,* 316–327.

LERNER, B. (1972). *Therapy in the ghetto: Political impotence and personal disintegration.* Baltimore: Johns Hopkins University Press.

LESHNER, A. I. (1997). Addiction is a brain disease, and it matters. *Science, 278,* 45–47.

LEVAV, I., FRIEDLANDER, Y., KARK, J. D., & PERITZ, E. (1988). An epidemiologic study of mortality among bereaved parents. *New England Journal of Medicine, 319,* 457–461.

LEVAY, S. (1991). A difference in hypothalmic structure between heterosexual and homosexual men. *Science, 253,* 1034–1037.

LEVENSON, R. W., EKMAN, P., & FRIESEN, W. V. (1990). Voluntary facial action generates emotion-specific nervous system activity. *Psychophysiology, 27,* 363–384.

LEVENSON, R. W., EKMAN, P., HEIDER, K., & FRIESIN, W. V. (1992). Emotion and automic nervous system activity in an Indonesian culture. *Journal of Personality and Social Psychology, 62,* 927–988.

LEVINE, S. (1960). Stimulation in infancy. *Scientific American, 202,* 80–86.

LEVINGER, G., SENN, D. J., & JORGENSEN, B. W. (1970). Progress toward permanence in courtship: A test of the Kerckhoff-Davis hypotheses. *Sociometry, 33,* 427–443.

LEVY, J. (1985). Right brain, left brain: Facts and fiction. *Psychology Today, 19,* 38–44.

LEVY, S. M., & HEIDEN, I., (1991). Depression, distress and immunity: Risk factors for infectious disease. *Stress Medicine, 7,* 45–51.

LEVY, S., HERBERMAN, R., WHITESIDE, T., SANZO, K., LEE, J., & KIRKWOOD, J. (1990). Perceived social support and tumor estrogen/progesterone receptor status as predictors of natural killer cell activity in breast cancer patients. *Psychosomatic Medicine, 52,* 73–85.

LEWINSOHN, P. M., MISCHEL, W., CHAPLIN, W., & BARTON, R. (1980). Social competence and depression: The role of illusory self-perceptions. *Journal of Abnormal Psychology, 89,* 203–212.

LEY, R. G., & BRYDEN, M. P. (1982). A dissociation of right and left hemispheric effects for recognizing emotional tone and verbal content. *Brain and Cognition, 1,* 3–9.

LIBERMAN, A. M., COOPER, F., SHANKWEILER, D., & STUDERT-KENNEDY, M. (1967). Perception of the speech code. *Psychological Review, 74,* 431–459.

LICKEY, M. E. & GORDON, B. (1991). *Medicine and mental illness.* New York: Freeman.

LIDZ, C. W., MULVEY, E. P., & GARDNER, W. (1993). The accuracy of predictions of violence to others. *Journal of the American Medical Association, 269,* 1007–1011.

LIEBERMAN, L. R., & DUNLAP, J. T. (1979). O'Leary and Borkovec's conceptualization of placebo: The placebo paradox. *American Psychologist, 34,* 553–554.

LIGHT, P., & PERRETT-CLERMONT, A. (1989). Social context effects in learning and testing. In A. R. H. Gellatly, D. Rogers, & J. Sloboda (Eds.), *Cognition and social worlds.* Oxford: Clarendon Press.

LINE, L. (1998, August–September). Leader of the flock. *National Wildlife,* pp. 20–27.

LINN, R. L. (1982). Ability testing: Individual differences, prediction, and differential prediction. In A. Wigdor & W. Gardner (Eds.), *Ability testing: Uses, consequences, and controversies.* Washington, DC: National Academy Press.

LIPPERT, W. W., & SENTER, R. J. (1966). Electrodermal responses in the sociopath. *Psychonomic Science, 4,* 25–26.

LIVINGSTONE, M., & HUBEL, D. (1988). Segregation of form, color, movement, and depth: Anatomy, physiology, and perception. *Science, 240,* 740–750.

LOFTUS, E. F., & LOFTUS, G. R. (1980). On the permanence of stored information in the human brain. *American Psychologist, 35,* 409–420.

LOFTUS, E. F., SCHOOLER, J. W., & WAGENAAR, W. A. (1985). The fate of memory: Comment on McCloskey and Zaragoza. *Journal of Experimental Psychology: General, 114,* 375–380.

LOGUE, A. W. (1991). *The psychology of eating and drinking: An introduction* (2nd ed.). New York: Freeman.

LONG, P. W. (1996). Internet mental health. http://www.mentalhealth.com/

LONGLEY, J., & PRUITT, D. G. (1980). Groupthink: A critique of Janis's theory. In L. Wheeler (Ed.), *Review of personality and social psychology* (Vol. 1). Beverly Hills, CA: Sage.

LOOMIS, A. L., HARVEY, E. N., & HOBART, G. A. (1937). Cerebral states during sleep as studied by human potentials. *Journal of Experimental Psychology, 21,* 127–144.

LOPEZ, A., ATRAN, S., MEDIN, D. L., COOLEY, J., & SMITH, E. E. (1997). The tree of life: Universals of folkbiological taxonomies and inductions. *Cognitive Psychology, 32,* 251–295.

LORD, C. G. (1980). Schemas and images as memory aids: Two modes of processing social information. *Journal of Personality and Social Psychology, 38,* 257–269.

LORD, C. G., ROSS, L., & LEPPER, M. R. (1979). Biased assimilation and attitude polarization: The effects of prior theories on subsequently considered evidence. *Journal of Personality and Social Psychology, 37,* 2098–2109.

LORENZ, K. (1966). *On aggression.* New York: Harcourt Brace Jovanovich.

LOVE, R. E., & GREENWALD, A. C. (1978). Cognitive responses to persuasion as mediators of opinion change. *Journal of Social Psychology, 104,* 231–241.

LUBORSKY, L. L., MCLELLAN, A. T., WOODY, G. E., O'BRIEN, E. P., & AUERBACH, A. (1985). Therapist success and its determinants. *Archives of General Psychiatry, 42,* 602–611.

LUBORSKY, L. L., SINGER, B., & LUBORSKY, L. (1975). Comparative studies of psychotherapies: Is it true that "everyone has won and all must have prizes"? *Archives of General Psychiatry, 32,* 995–1008.

LUCHINS, A. (1957). Primacy-recency in impression formation. In C. L. Hovland (Ed.), *The order of presentation in persuasion.* New Haven: Yale University Press.

LUNDIN, R. W. (1985). *Theories and systems of psychology* (3rd ed.). Lexington, MA: Heath.

LURIA, Z., & RUBIN, J. Z. (1974). The eye of the beholder: Parents' views on sex of newborns. *American Journal of Orthopsychiatry, 44,* 512–519.

LYKKEN, D. T. (1980). *Tremor in the blood: Uses and abuses of the lie detector.* New York: McGraw-Hill.

LYKKEN, D. T. (1982). Research with twins: The concept of emergenesis. *The Society for Psychophysiological Research, 19,* 361–373.

LYKKEN, D. T. (1984). Polygraphic interrogation. *Nature, 307,* 681–684.

LYKKEN, D. T., MCGUE, M., TELLEGEN, A., & BOUCHARD, T. J., JR. (1992). Emergenesis: Genetic traits that may not run in families. *American Psychologist, 47,* 1565–1577.

LYUBOMIRSKY, S., & NOLEN HOEKSEMA, S. (1995). Effects of self-focused rumination on negative thinking and interpersonal problem solving. *Journal of Personality and Social Psychology, 69,* 176–190.

MAAS, J. B. (1998). *Power sleep: The revolutionary program that prepares your mind for peak performance.* New York: HarperCollins.

MAASS, A., & CLARK, R. D., III (1984). Hidden impact of minorities: Fifteen years of minority influence research. *Psychological Bulletin, 95,* 428–450.

MACAULAY, J. (1970). A shill for charity. In J. Macaulay & L. Berkowitz (Eds.), *Altruism and helping behavior* (pp. 43–59). New York: Academic Press.

MACCOBY, E. E. (1980). *Social development: Psychological growth and the parent-child relationship.* New York: Harcourt Brace Jovanovich.

MACCOBY, E. E., & JACKLIN, C. N. (1974). *The psychology of sex differences.* Stanford, CA: Stanford University Press.

MACKINNON, D., JAMISON, R., & DEPAULO, J. R. (1997). Genetics of manic depressive illness. *Annual Review of Neuroscience, 20,* 355–373.

MAHER, B. A. (1966). *Principles of psychotherapy: An experimental approach.* New York: McGraw-Hill.

MAIER, S. F., & SELIGMAN, M. E. P. (1976). Learned helplessness: Theory and evidence. *Journal of Experimental Psychology: General, 105,* 3–46.

MAIN, M., & CASSIDY, J. (1988). Categories of response to reunion with parents at age 6: Predictable from infant attachment classifications and stable over a 1-month period. *Developmental Psychology, 24,* 415–426.

MAIN, M., & SOLOMON, J. (1986). Discovery of an insecure-disorganized/disoriented attachment pattern: Procedures, findings and implications for the classification of behavior. In T. B. Brazelton, & M. Yogman (Eds.), *Affective development in infancy* (pp. 95–124). Norwood, NJ: Ablex.

MALINOW, R., OTMAKHOV, N., BLUM, K. I., & LISMAN, J. (1994). Visualizing hippocampal synaptic function by optical detection of Ca2+ entry through the N-methyl-D-aspartate channel. *Proceedings of the National Academy of Sciences of the United States of America, 91,* 8170–8174.

MALOF, M., & LOTT, A. J. (1962). Ethnocentrism and the acceptance of Negro support in a group pressure situation. *Journal of Abnormal and Social Psychology, 65,* 254–258.

MALONE, K., & MANN, J. J. (1993). Serotonin and major depression. In J. J. Mann & D. J. Kupfer (Eds.), *Biology of depressive disorders: Part A. A systems perspective* (pp. 29–49). New York: Plenum Press.

MALONEY, L. T., & WANDELL, B. A. (1986). Color constancy: A method for recovering surface spectral reflectance. *Journal of the Optical Society of America, 3,* 29–33.

MANDLER, J. (1983). Representation. In P. H. Mussen (Ed.), *Handbook of child psychology* (Vol. 3). New York: Wiley.

MANUCK, S. B., KAPLAN, J. R., & MATTHEWS, K. A. (1986). Behavioral antecedents of coronary heart disease and atherosclerosis. *Arteriosclerosis, 6,* 1–14.

MARBLY, N. (1987). But you weren't there. In T. Williams (Ed.), *Posttramuatic stress disorders: A handbook for clinicians.* Cincinnati, OH: Disabled American Veterans.

MARCIA, J. E. (1966). Development and validation of ego identify status. *Journal of Personality and Social Psychology, 3,* 551 558.

MARCIA, J. E. (1980). Identity in adolescence. In J. Adelson (Ed.), *Handbook of adolescent psychology.* New York: Wiley.

MARCUS, G. F. (1996). Why do children say "breaked"? *Current Directions in Psychological Science, 5,* 81–85.

MAREN, S., & FANSELOW, M. S. (1996). The amygdala and fear conditioning: Has the nut been cracked? *Neuron, 16,* 237–240.

MARGRAF, J., BARLOW, D. H., CLARK, D. M., & TELCH, M. J. (1993). Psychological treatment of panic: Work in progress on outcome, active ingredients, and follow-up. *Behaviour Research & Therapy, 31,* 1–8.

MARKMAN, E. M. (1979). Classes and collections: Conceptual organization and numerical abilities. *Cognitive Psychology, 11,* 395–411.

MARKMAN, E. M. (1987). How children constrain the possible meanings of words. In U. Neisser (Ed.), *Concepts and conceptual development: Ecological and intellectual factors in categorizations.* New York: Cambridge University Press.

MARKOWITZ, J. C., & WEISSMAN, M. M. (1995). Interpersonal psychotherapy. In E. E. Beckham & W. R. Leber (Eds.), *Handbook of depression* (2nd ed.). New York: Guilford.

MARKUS, H. (1977). Self-schemata and processing information about the self. *Journal of Personality and Social Psychology, 35,* 63–78.

MARKUS, H., & NURIUS, P. (1986). Possible selves. *American Psychologist, 41,* 954–969.

MARKUS, H., & SENTIS, K. (1982). The self in social information processing. In J. Suls (Ed.), *Psychological perspectives on the self* (Vol. 1). Hillsdale, NJ: Erlbaum.

MARKUS, H., & SMITH, J. (1981). The influence of self-schema on the perception of others. In N. Cantor & J. F. Kihlstrom (Eds.), *Personality, cognition, and social interaction.* Hillsdale, NJ: Erlbaum.

MARLATT, G. A., LARIMER, M. E., BAER, J. S., & QUIGLEY, L. A. (1993). Harm reduction for alcohol problems: Moving beyond the controlled drinking economy. *Behavior Therapy, 24,* 461–503.

MARR, D. (1982). *Vision.* San Francisco: Freeman.

MARSHALL, D. A., BLUMER, L., & MOULTON, D. G. (1981). Odor detection curves for n-pentanoic acid in dogs and humans. *Chemical Senses, 6,* 445–453.

MARSHALL, G., & ZIMBARDO, P. G. (1979). Affective consequences of inadequately explained physiological arousal. *Journal of Personality and Social Psychology, 37,* 970–988.

MASLACH, C. (1979). The emotional consequences of arousal without reason. In Izard, C. E. (Ed.), *Emotion in personality and psychopathology.* New York: Plenum.

MASLOW, A. H. (1970). *Motivation and personality* (2nd ed.). New York: Harper and Row.

MASSON, J. M. (1984). *The assault on truth.* New York: Farrar, Straus & Giroux, Inc.

MASTERS, W. H., & JOHNSON, V. E. (1966). *Human sexual response.* Boston: Little, Brown.

MASUDA, M. & HOLMES, T. H. (1978). Life events: Perceptions and frequencies. *Psychosomatic Medicine, 40,* 236–261.

MATAS, L., AREND, R. A., & SROUFE, L. A. (1978). Continuity of adaption in the second year: The relationship between quality of attachment and later competence. *Child Development, 49,* 547–556.

MATHES, E. W. (1975). The effects of physical attractiveness and anxiety on heterosexual attraction over a series of five encounters. *Journal of Marriage and the Family, 37,* 769–773.

MATTHEWS, D. F. (1972). Response patterns of single neurons in the tortoise olfactory epithelium and olfactory bulb. *Journal of General Physiology, 60,* 166–180.

MAYER, R. E. (1983). *Thinking, problem solving and cognition.* New York: Freeman.

MCALISTER, A., PERRY, C., KILLEN, J., SLINKARD, L. A., & MACCOBY, N. (1980). Pilot study of smoking, alcohol and drug abuse prevention. *American Journal of Public Health, 70,* 719–721.

MCBRIDE, P., BROWN, R. P., DEMEO, M., & KEILP, J. (1994). The relationship of platelet 5-HT-sub-2 receptor indices to major depressive disorder, personality traits, and suicidal behavior. *Biological Psychiatry, 35,* 295–308.

MCBURNEY, D. H. (1978). Psychological dimensions and the perceptual analysis of taste. In E. C. Carterette & M. P. Friedman (Eds.), *Handbook of perception* (Vol. 6). New York: Academic Press.

MCCLANAHAN, K. K., GOLD, J. A., LENNEY, E., RYCKMAN, R. M., & KULBERG, G. E. (1990). Infatuation and attraction to a dissimilar other: Why is love blind? *Journal of Social Psychology, 130,* 433–445.

MCCLELLAND, D. C. (1987). *Human motivation.* New York: Cambridge University Press.

MCCLELLAND, J. L., & RUMELHART, D. E. (1981). An interactive model of context effects in letter perception: Pt. 1. An account of basic findings. *Psychological Review, 88,* 375–407.

MCCLINTOCK, M. K. (1971). Menstrual synchrony and suppression. *Nature, 229,* 244–245.

MCCOLSKEY, M., WIBLE, C. G., & COHEN, N. J. (1988). Is there a flashbulb-memory system? *Journal of Experimental Psychology, 117,* 171–181.

MCCONAGHY, M. J. (1979). Gender permanence and the genital basis of gender. Stages in the development of constancy of gender identity. *Child Development, 50,* 1223–1226.

MCCRAE, R. R., & COSTA, P. T., JR. (1987). Validation of the five-factor model of personality across instruments and observers. *Journal of Personality and Social Psychology, 52,* 81–90.

MCDOUGALL, W. (1908). *Social psychology.* New York: Putnam.

MCELREE, B. & DOSHER, B. A. (1989). Serial position and set size in short-term memory. The time course of recognition. *Journal of Experimental Psychology: General, 118,* 346–373.

MCFARLAND, S. G., AGEYEV, V. S., & ABALAKINA-PAAP, M. A. (1992). Authoritarianism in the former Soviet Union. *Journal of Personality and Social Psychology, 63,* 1004–1010.

MCGHIE, A., & CHAPMAN, J. (1961). Disorders of attention and perception in early schizophrenia. *British Journal of Medical Psychology, 34,* 103–116.

MCGLASHAN, T. H. Omnipotence, helplessness, and control with the borderline patient. *American Journal of Psychotherapy, 37,* 49–61.

MCGRATH, E., KEITA, G. P., STRICKLAND, B. R., & RUSSO, N. F. (1990). *Women and depression: Risk factors and treatment issues.* Washington, DC: American Psychological Association.

MCGRAW, M. B. (1975). *Growth: A study of Johnny and Jimmy.* New York: Acno Press. (Originally published 1935)

MCGUFFIN, P., KATZ, R., & RUTHERFORD, J. (1991). Nature, nurture and depression: A twin study. *Psychological Medicine, 21,* 329–335.

MCHUGH, P. R. (1990). Clinical issues in food ingestion and body weight maintenance. In E. M. Stricker (Ed.), *Neurobiology of food and fluid intake* (pp. 531–547). New York: Plenum.

MCKENNA, R. J. (1972). Some effects of anxiety level and food cues on the eating behavior of obese and normal subjects. *Journal of Personality and Social Psychology, 22,* 311–319.

MCNALLY, R. J. (1994). Choking phobia: A review of the literature. *Comprehensive Psychiatry, 35,* 83–89.

MCNEILL, D. (1966). Developmental psycholinguistics. In F. Smith & G. A. Miller (Eds.), *The genesis of language: A psycholinguistic approach.* Cambridge, MA: MIT Press.

MEANEY, M. J., AITKENS, D. H., BERKEL, C., BHATNAGAR, S., SARRIEAU, A., & SAPOLSKY, R. M. (1987). *Post-natal handling attenuates age-related changes in the adrenocortical stress response and spatial memory deficits in the rat.* Paper presented at the 17th Annual Meeting of the Society of Neuroscience, New Orleans.

MECHANIC, D. (1962). *Students under stress.* New York: Free Press.

MEDCOF, J., & ROTH, J. (Eds.) (1988). *Approaches to psychology.* Philadelphia: Open University Press, Milton Keynes.

MEDIN, D. L., & ROSS, B. H. (1992). *Cognitive psychology.* Fort Worth: Harcourt Brace.

MEDNICK, B., REZNICK, C., HOCEVAR, D., & BAKER, R. (1987). Long-term effects of parental divorce on young adult male crime. *Journal of Youth & Adolescence, 16,* 31–45.

MEEHL, P. E., & DAHLSTROM, W. G. (1960). Objective configural rules for discriminating psychotic from neurotic MMPI profiles. *Journal of Consulting Psychology, 24,* 375–387.

MEGARGEE, E. I. (1972). *The California psychological inventory handbook.* San Francisco: Jossey-Bass.

MEIER, R. P. (1991). Language acquisition by deaf children. *American Scientist, 79,* 60–76.

MELAMED, B. G., & SIEGEL, L. J. (1975). Reduction of anxiety in children facing hospitalization and surgery by use of filmed modeling. *Journal of Consulting and Clinical Psychiatry, 43,* 511–521.

MELTON, A. W. (1963). Implications of short-term memory for a general theory of memory. *Journal of Verbal Learning and Verbal Behavior, 1,* 1–21.

MELZAK, R. (1973). *The puzzle of pain.* New York: Basic Books.

MELZAK, R. (1990). The tragedy of needless pain. *Scientific American, 262,* 27–33.

MELZAK, R., & WALL, P. D. (1982, 1988). *The challenge of pain.* New York: Basic Books.

MERVIS, C. B., & PANI, J. R. (1981). Acquisition of basic object categories. *Cognitive Psychology, 12,* 496–522.

MERVIS, C. B., & ROSCH, E. (1981). Categorization of natural objects. In M. R. Rosenz & L. W. Porter (Eds.), *Annual review of psychology* (Vol. 21). Palo Alto, CA: Annual Reviews.

MESQUITA, B., & FRIJDA, N. H. (1992). Cultural variations in emotions: A review. *Psychological Bulletin, 112,* 179–204.

MESSICK, S. (1992). Multiple intelligences or multilevel intelligence? Selective emphasis on distinctive properties of hierarchy: On Gardner's *Frames of mind* and Sternberg's *Beyond IQ* in the context of theory and research on the structure of human abilities. *Journal of Psychological Inquiry, 1,* 305–384.

METALSKY, G. I., HALBERSTADT, L. J., & ABRAMSON, L. Y. (1987). Vulnerability to depressive mood reactions: Toward a more powerful test of the diathesis-stress and causal meditation components of the reformulated theory of depression. *Journal of Personality and Social Psychology, 52,* 386–393.

METZNER, R. J. (1994, March 14). Prozac is medicine, not a miracle. *Los Angeles Times,* p. B7.

MEYER, J. P., & PEPPER, S. (1977). Need compatability and marital adjustment in young married couples. *Journal of Personality and Social Psychology, 8,* 331–342.

MIDDLETON, F. A., & STRICK, P. L. (1994). Anatomic evidence for cerebellar and basal ganglia involvement in higher cognitive function. *Science, 266,* 458–463.

MILGRAM, S. (1963). Behavioral study of obedience. *Journal of Abnormal and Social Psychology, 67,* 371–378.

MILGRAM, S. (1974). *Obedience to authority: An experimental view.* New York: Harper & Row.

MILLAR, M. G., & TESSER, A. (1989). The effects of affective-cognitive consistency and thought on the attitude-behavior relation. *Journal of Experimental Social Psychology, 25,* 189–202.

MILLER, D. T., & ROSS, M. (1975). Self-serving biases in attribution of causality: Fact or fiction? *Psychological Bulletin, 82,* 213–225.

MILLER, G. A. (1956). The magical number seven plus or minus two: Some limits on our capacity for processing information. *Psychological Review, 63,* 81–97.

MILLER, G. A., & GILDEA, P. M. (1987). How children learn words. *Scientific American, 257,* 94–99.

MILLER, J. G. (1984). Culture and the development of everyday social explanation. *Journal of Personality and Social Psychology, 46,* 961–978.

MILLER, J. M., & SPELMAN, F. A. (1990). *Cochlear implants: Models of the electrically stimulated ear.* New York: Springer-Verlag.

MILLER, N. E., & KESSEN, M. L. (1952). Reward effects of food via stomach fistula compared with those of food via mouth. *Journal of Comparative and Physiological Psychology, 45,* 555–564.

MILLER, P. A., & EISENBERG, N. (1988). The relation of empathy to aggressive and externalizing/antisocial behavior. *Psychological Bulletin, 103,* 324–344.

MILLER, P. H. (1993). *Theories of developmental psychology* (3rd ed.). New York: Freeman.

MILLON, T. (1981). *Disorders of personality: DSM-III.* New York: Wiley.

MILNER, B. (1970). Memory and the medial temporal regions of the brain. In K. H. Pribram & D. E. Broadbent (Eds.), *Biology of memory.* New York: Academic Press.

MILNER, B., CORKIN, S., & TUEBER, H. L. (1968). Further analysis of the hippocampal amnesic syndrome: 14-year follow-up study of H. M. *Neuropsychologia, 6,* 215–234.

MINARD, R. D. (1952). Race relations in the Pocahontas coal field. *Journal of Social Issues, 8,* 29–44.

MINEKA, S., DAVIDSON, M., COOK, M., & KEIR, R. (1984). Observational conditioning of snake fear in rhesus monkeys. *Journal of Abnormal Psychology, 93,* 355–372.

MINTZ, L. I., LIEBERMAN, R. P., MIKLOWITZ, D. J., & MINTZ, J. (1987). Expressed emotion: A call for partnership among relatives, patients, and professionals. *Schizophrenia Bulletin, 13,* 227–235.

MINUCHIN, S., ROSMAN, B. L., & BAKER, L. (1978). *Psychosomatic families: Anorexia nervosa in context.* Cambridge, MA: Harvard University Press.

MISCHEL, W. (1966). A social learning view of sex differences in behavior. In E. E. Maccoby (Ed.), *The development of sex differences.* Stanford, CA: Stanford University Press.

MISCHEL, W. (1973). Toward a cognitive social learning reconceptualization of personality. *Psychological Review, 80,* 272–283.

MISCHEL, W. (1993). *Introduction to personality* (5th ed.). Fort Worth: Harcourt Brace Jovanovich.

MISHKIN, M., UNGERLEIDER, L. G., & MACKO, K. A. (1983). Object vision and spatial vision: Two cortical pathways. *Trends in Neuroscience, 6,* 414–417.

MITA, T. H., DERMER, M., & KNIGHT, J. (1977). Reversed facial images and the mere-exposure hypthoses. *Journal of Personality and Social Psychology, 35,* 597–601.

MITCHELL, J. E., & DEZWAAN, M. (1993). Pharmacological treatments of binge eating. In C. E. Fairburn & G. T. Wilson (Eds.), *Binge eating: Nature, assessment, and treatment.* New York: Guilford.

MOFFITT, T. E. (1993). The neuropsychology of conduct disorder. *Development and Psychopathology, 5,* 135–151.

MONAHAN, J. (1992). Mental disorder and violent behavior: Perceptions and evidence. *American Psychologist, 47,* 511–521.

MONAHAN, J., & WALKER, L. (1990). *Social science in law: Cases and materials.* Westbury, NY: Foundation Press.

MONEY, J. (1980). Endocrine influences and psychosexual status spanning the life cycle. In H. M. Van Praag (Ed.), *Handbook of biological psychiatry* (Part 3). New York: Marcel Dekker.

MONEY, J. (1987). Sin, sickness, or status? Homosexual gender identity and psychoneuroendocrinology. *American Psychologist, 42,* 384–400.

MONEY, J., & EHRHARDT, A. A. (1972). *Man and woman, boy and girl: The differentiation and dimorphism of gender identity from conception to maturity.* Baltimore: Johns Hopkins University Press.

MONEY, J., SCHWARTZ, M., & LEWIS, V. G. (1984). Adult heterosexual status and fetal hormonal masculinization and demasculinization: 46, XX congenital virilizing adrenal hyperplasia and 46, XY androgen-insensitivity syndrome compared. *Psychoneuroendocrinology, 9,* 405–414.

MONEY, J., WEIDEKING, C., WALKER, P. A., & GAIN, D. (1976). Combined antiandrogenic and counseling programs for treatment for 46 XY and 47 XXY sex offenders. In E. Sacher (Ed.), *Hormones, behavior and psychopathology.* New York: Raven Press.

MONSELL, S. (1979). Recency, immediate recognition memory, and reaction time. *Cognitive Psychology, 10,* 465–501.

MOORE, B. C. J. (1982). *An introduction to the psychology of hearing* (2nd ed.). New York: Academic Press.

MOOS, R. H. (1988). *Coping responses inventory manual.* Palo Alto, CA: Social Ecology Laboratory, Department of Psychiatry, Stanford University and Veterans Administration Medical Centers.

MORAN, J., & DESIMONE, R. (1985). Selective attention gates visual processing in the extrastriate cortex. *Science, 229,* 782–784.

MORAY, N. (1969). *Attention: Selective processes in vision and hearing.* London: Hutchinson.

MORELAND, R. L., & BEACH, S. R. (1992). Exposure effects in the classroom: The development of affinity among students. *Journal of Experimental Social Psychology, 28,* 255–276.

MORELAND, R. L., & ZAJONC, R. B. (1979). Exposure effects may not depend on stimulus recognition. *Journal of Personality and Social Psychology, 37,* 1085–1089.

MOREY, L. C. (1993). Psychological correlates of personality disorder. *Journal of Personality Disorders* (suppl.), 149–166.

MORGENSTERN, H., & GLAZER, W. M. (1993, September). Identifying risk factors for tardive dyskinesia among long-term outpatients maintained with neuroleptic medications: Results of the Yale tardive dyskinesia study. *Archives of General Psychiatry, 50.*

MOSCOVICI, S. (1976). *Social influence and social change.* London: Academic Press.

MOSCOVICI, S., LAGE, E., & NAFFRECHOUX, M. (1969). Influence of a consistent minority on the responses of a majority in a color perception task. *Sociometry, 32,* 365–379.

MOSCOVICI, S., & ZAVALLONI, M. (1969). The group as a polarizer of attitudes. *Journal of Personality and Social Psychology, 12,* 125–135.

MOSKOWITZ, H. R., KUMRAICH, V., SHARMA, H., JACOBS, L., & SHARMA, S. D. (1975). Cross-cultural difference in simple taste preference. *Science, 190,* 1217–1218.

MOVSHON, J. A., & VAN SLUYTERS, R. C. (1981). Visual neural development. *Annual Review of Psychology, 32,* 477–522.

MOWRER, O. H. (1947). On the dual nature of learning—A reinterpretation of "conditioning" and "problem-solving". *Harvard Educational Review, 17,* 102–148.

MUKHERJEE, S., SHUKLA, S., WOODLE, J., ROSEN, A. M., & OLARTE, S. (1983). Misdiagnosis of schizophrenia in bipolar patients: A multiethnic comparison. *American Journal of Psychiatry, 140,* 1571–1574.

MUKHOPADHYAY, P., & TURNER, R. M. (1997). Biofeedback treatment of essential hypertension. *Social Science International, 13,* 1–9.

MURDOCK, B. B., JR. (1962). The serial position effect in free recall. *Journal of Experimental Psychology, 64,* 482–488.

MURPHY, G. L., & BROWNELL, H. H. (1985). Category differentiation in object recognition: Typicality constraints on the basic category advantage. *Journal of Experimental Psychology, 11,* 70.

MURSTEIN, B. I. (1972). Physical attractiveness and marital choice. *Journal of Personality and Social Psychology, 22,* 8–12.

MUSSEN, P. H. (Ed.) (1983). *Handbook of child psychology* (4th ed.). New York: Wiley.

MYERS, D. G. (1993). *Social psychology* (4th ed.). New York: McGraw-Hill.

MYERS, D. G., & LAMM, H. (1976). The group polarization phenomenon. *Psychological Bulletin, 83,* 602–627.

NARROW, W. E., REGIER, D. A., RAE, D., MANDERSCHEID, R. W., & LOCKE, B. Z. (1993). Use of services by persons with mental and addictive disorders. *Archives of General Psychiatry, 50,* 95–107.

NATHANS, J. (1987). Molecular biology of visual pigments. *Annual Review of Neuroscience, 10,* 163–164.

NEISSER, U. (Ed.) (1982). *Memory observed: Remembering in natural contexts.* New York: Freeman.

NEMETH, C. (1986). Differential contributions of majority and minority influence. *Psychological Review, 93,* 23–32.

NEWCOMB, M. D., RABOW, J., & HERNANDEZ, A. C. R. (1992). A cross-national study of nuclear attitudes, normative support, and activist behavior: Additive and interactive effects. *Journal of Applied Social Psychology, 22,* 780–200.

NEWCOMB, T. M. (1943). *Personality and social change.* New York: Dryden Press.

NEWCOMB, T. M. (1961). *The acquaintance process.* New York: Holt, Rinehart & Winston.

NEWCOMB, T. M., KOENING, K. E., FLACKS, R., & WARWICK, D. P. (1967). *Persistence and change: Bennington College and its students after twenty-five years.* New York: Wiley.

NEWELL, A., & SIMON, H. A. (1972). *Human problem solving.* Englewood Cliffs, NJ: Prentice-Hall.

NEWPORT, E. L. (1990). Maturational constraints on language learning. *Cognitive Science, 14,* 11–28.

NEZU, A. M., NEZU, C. M., & PERRI, M. G. (1989). *Problem-solving therapy for depression: Theory, research, and clinical guidelines.* New York: Wiley.

NIELSON, T., & POWELL, R. (1992). The day-residue and dream-lag effect. *Dreaming, 2,* 67–77.

NILSON, D. C., NILSON, L. B., OLSON, R. S., & MCALLISTER, B. H. (1981). *The planning environment report for the Southern California Earthquake Safety Advisory Board.* Redlands, CA: Social Research Advisory & Policy Research Center.

NISAN, M., & KOHLBERG, L. (1982). Universality and variation in moral judgment: A longitudinal and cross-sectional study in Turkey. *Child Development, 53,* 865–876.

NISBETT, R. E., KRANZ, D. H., JEPSON, D., & KUNDA, Z. (1983). The use of statistical heuristics in everyday inductive reasoning. *Psychological Review, 90,* 339–363.

NISBETT, R. E., & ROSS, L. (1980). *Human inference: Strategies and shortcomings of social judgment.* Englewood Cliffs, NJ: Prentice-Hall.

NISBETT, R. E., & WILSON, T. D. (1977). Telling more than we can know: Verbal reports on mental processes. *Psychological Review, 84,* 231–259.

NOLEN-HOEKSEMA, S. (1991). Responses to depression and their effects on the duration of depressive episodes. *Journal of Abnormal Psychology, 100,* 569–582.

NOLEN-HOEKSEMA, S., & LARSON, J. (1999). *Coping with loss.* Mahwah, NJ: Erlbaum.

NOLEN-HOEKSEMA, S., & MORROW, J. (1991). A prospective study of depression and distress following a natural disaster: The 1989 Loma Prieta earthquake. *Journal of Personality and Social Psychology, 61,* 105–121.

NORTH, C. (1987). *Welcome silence.* New York: Simon and Schuster.

NUCCLI, L. (1981). The development of personal concepts: A domain distinct from moral or societal concepts. *Child Development, 52,* 114–121.

OFFIR, C. (1982). *Human sexuality.* San Diego: Harcourt Brace Jovanovich.

OJEMANN, G. (1983). Brain organization for language from the perspective of electrical stimulation mapping. *Behavioral and Brain Sciences, 6,* 189–230.

OLTON, D. S. (1978). Characteristics of spatial memory. In S. H. Hulse, H. F. Fowler, & W. K. Honig (Eds.), *Cognitive processes in animal behavior.* Hillsdale, NJ: Erlbaum.

OLTON, D. S. (1979). Mazes, maps, and memory. *American Psychologist, 34,* 583–596.

OLWEUS, D. (1969). *Prediction of aggression.* Scandanavian Test Corporation.

ORLINSKY, D. E., & HOWARD, K. I. (1987). A generic model of psychotherapy. *Journal of Integrative and Eclectic Psychotherapy, 6,* 6–27.

ORNE, M. T., & HOLLAND, C. C. (1968). On the ecological validity of laboratory deceptions. *International Journal of Psychiatry, 6,* 282–293.

OSHERSON, D. N., KOSLYN, S. M. & HOLLERBACH, J. M. (1990). *An invitation to cognitive science* (Vol. 2). Cambridge, MA: MIT Press.

OSHERSON, D. N., & LASNIK, H. (1990). *An invitation to cognitive science* (Vol. 1). Cambridge, MA: MIT Press.

OSHERSON, D. N., & SMITH, E. E. (1990). *An invitation to cognitive science* (Vol. 3). Cambridge, MA: MIT Press.

OSHERSON, D. N., SMITH, E. E., WILKIE, O., LOPEZ, A., & SHAFIR, E. B. (1990). Category based induction. *Psychological Review, 97,* 185–200.

OSOFSKY, J. D. (Ed.) (1987). *Handbook of infant development* (2nd ed.). New York: Wiley.

OVERMEIER, J. B., & SELIGMAN, M. E. P. (1967). Effects of inescapable shock upon subsequent escape and avoidance responding. *Journal of Comparative and Physiological Psychology, 63,* 28.

PAFFENBERGER, R. S., HYDE, R. T., WING, A. L., & HSIEH, C. (1986). Physical activity, all-cause mortality, and longevity of college alumni. *New England Journal of Medicine, 314,* 605–613.

PAICHELER, G. (1977). Norms and attitude change: Pt. 1. Polarization and styles of behavior. *European Journal of Social Psychology, 7,* 5–14.

PALLIS, C. A. (1955). Impaired identification of faces and places with agnosia for colors. *Journal of Neurology, Neurosurgery, and Psychiatry, 18,* 218–224.

PALMER, S. E. (1975). The effect of contextual scenes on the identification of objects. *Memory and Cognition, 3,* 519–526.

PARKER, G., JOHNSTON, P., & HAYWARD, L. (1988). Parental "expressed emotion" as a predictor of schizophrenic relapse. *Archives of General Psychiatry, 45,* 806–813.

PARKER, G., & HADZZI-PAVLOVIC, D. (1990). Expressed emotion as a predictor of schizophrenic relapse: An analysis of aggregated data. *Psychological Medicine, 20,* 961–965.

PASZTOR, A. (1996, July 1). An air-safety battle brews over the issue of pilots' rest time. *The Wall Street Journal.*

PATEL, V. L., & GROEN, G. J. (1986). Knowledge based solution strategies in medical reasoning. *Cognitive Science, 10,* 91.

PATTERSON, F. G. (1978). The gestures of a gorilla: Language acquisition in another pongid. *Brain and Language, 5,* 72–97.

PATTERSON, F. G., & LINDEN, E. (1981). *The education of Koko.* New York: Holt, Rinehart & Winston.

PATTERSON, G. R., DEBARSHYE, B. D., & RAMSEY, E. (1989). A developmental perspective on antisocial behavior. *American Psychologist, 44,* 329–335.

PATTERSON, G. R., LITTMAN, R. A., & BRICKER, W. A. (1967). Assertive behavior in children: A step toward a theory of aggression. *Monographs of the Society for Research in Child Development* (Serial No. 113), 5.

PAUL, G. L. (1967). Insight versus desensitization in psychotherapy two years after termination. *Journal of Consulting Psychology, 31,* 333–348.

PAUL, G. L., & LENTZ, R. J. (1977). *Psychosocial treatment of chronic mental patients: milieu versus social learning programs.* Cambridge, MA: Harvard University Press.

PAULHUS, D. (1982). Individual differences, self-presentation, and cognitive dissonance: Their concurrent operation in forced compliance. *Journal of Personality and Social Psychology, 43,* 838–852.

PAULUS, P. B., & MURDOCK, P. (1971). Anticipated evaluation and audience presence in the enhancement of dominant responses. *Journal of Experimental Social Psychology, 7,* 280–291.

PAVLOV, I. P. (1927). *Conditioned reflexes.* New York: Oxford University Press.

PECHURA, C. M., & MARTIN, J. B. (Eds.) (1991). *Mapping the brain and its functions.* Washington, D.C.: National Academy Press.

PEDERSEN, N. L., PLOMIN, R., MCCLEARN, G. E., & FRIBERG, L. (1988). Neuroticism, extraversion and related traits in adult twins reared apart and reared together. *Journal of Personality and Social Psychology, 55,* 905–957.

PEELE, S. (1988). Fools for love: The romantic ideal, psychological theory, and addictive love. In R. J. Sternberg & M. L. Barnes (Eds.), *The psychology of love* (pp. 159–188). New Haven, CT: Yale University Press.

PELLEGRINO, J. W. (1985). Inductive reasoning ability. In R. J. Sternberg (Ed.), *Human abilities: An information-processing approach.* New York: Freeman.

PENNEBAKER, J. W. (1990). *Opening up: The healing power of confiding in others.* New York: William Morrow.

PENNEBAKER, J. W. (1997). *Opening up: The healing power of expressing emotions* (rev. ed.). New York: Guilford.

PENNEBAKER, J. W., KIECOLT-GLASER, J. K., & GLASER, R. (1988). Disclosure of traumas and immune function: Health implications for psychotherapy. *Journal of Consulting and Clinical Psychology, 56,* 239–245.

PENNEBAKER, J. W., & O'HEERON, R. C. (1984). Confiding in others and illness rates among spouses of suicide and accidental-death victims. *Journal of Abnormal Psychology, 93,* 473–476.

PEPLAU, L. A., RUBIN, Z., & HILL, C. T. (1977). Sexual intimacy in dating relationships. *Journal of Social Issues, 33,* 86–109.

PERRIN, F. A. C. (1921). Physical attractiveness and repulsiveness. *Journal of Experimental Psychology, 4,* 203–217.

PERRY, D. G., & BUSSEY, K. (1984). *Social development.* Englewood Cliffs, NJ: Prentice-Hall.

PERRY, J. C. (1993). Longitudinal studies of personality disorders. *Journal of Personality Disorders,* Suppl. 1, 63–85.

PETERSEN, A. C. (1989). Adolescent development. In M. R. Rosenzweig & L. W. Porter (Eds.), *Annual review of psychology* (Vol. 39). Palo Alto, CA: Annual Reviews.

PETERSON, C., & SELIGMAN, M. E. P. (1984). Causal explanations as a risk factor for depression: Theory and evidence. *Psychological Review, 91,* 347–374.

PETRIE, K. J., BOOTH, R. J., & PENNEBAKER, J. W. (1998). The immunological effects of thought suppression. *Journal of Personality and Social Psychology, 75,* 1264–1272.

PETTIGREW, T. F. (1959). Regional differences in anti-Negro prejudice. *Journal of Abnormal and Social Psychology, 59,* 28–36.

PETTY, R. E., & CACIOPPO, J. T. (1981). *Attitudes and persuasion: Classic and contemporary approaches.* Dubuque, IA: Wm. C. Brown.

PETTY, R. E., & CACIOPPO, J. T. (1984). The effects of involvement on responses to argument quantity and quality: Central and peripheral routes to persuasion. *Journal of Personality and Social Psychology, 46,* 69–81.

PETTY, R. E., & CACIOPPO, J. T. (1986). Elaboration likelihood model of persuasion. In L. Berkowitz (Ed.), *Advances in experimental social psychology* (Vol. 19, pp. 123–205). New York: Academic Press.

PETTY, R. E., & CACIOPPO, J. T. & GOLDMAN, R. (1981). Personal involvement as a determinant of argument-based persuasion. *Journal of Personality and Social Psychology, 41,* 847–855.

PETTY, R. E., OSTROM, T. M., & BROCK, T. C. (1981). Historical foundations of the cognitive response approach to attitudes and persuasion. In R. E. Petty, T. M. Ostrom, & T. C. Brock (Eds.), *Cognitive responses in persuasion.* Hillsdale, NJ: Erlbaum.

PHILLIPS, D. A., MCCARTNEY, K., & SCARR, S. (1987). Child-care quality and children's

social development. *Developmental Psychology, 23,* 537–543.

PHILLIPS, D. A., VORAN, M., KISKER, E., HOWES, C., & WHITEBROOK, M. (1994). Child care for children in poverty: Opportunity or inequity? *Child Development, 65,* 472–492.

PHILLIPS, J. L., JR. (1981). *Piaget's theory: A primer.* San Francisco: Freeman.

PHILLIPS, J. L., JR. (1992). *How to think about statistics* (rev. ed.). New York: Freeman.

PHOENIX, C. H., GOY, R. H., & RESKO, J. A. (1968). Psychosexual differentiation as a function of androgenic stimulation. In M. Diamond (Ed.), *Reproduction and sexual behavior.* Bloomington: Indiana University Press.

PIAGET, J. (1932/1965). *The moral judgment of the child.* New York: Free Press.

PIAGET, J. (1950a). *The origins of intelligence in children.* New York: International Universities Press.

PIAGET, J. (1950b). *The psychology of intelligence.* New York: International Universities Press.

PIAGET, J., & INHELDER, B. (1956). *The child's conception of space.* London: Routledge & Kegan Paul. (originally published 1948)

PIAGET, J., & INHELDER, B. (1969). *The psychology of the child.* New York: Basic Books.

PICCIONE, C., HILGARD, E. R., & ZIMBARDO, P. G. (1989). On the degree of stability of measured hyponotizability over a 25-year period. *Journal of Personality and Social Psychology, 56,* 289–295.

PICKERING, T. G., DEVEREUX, R. B., JAMES, G. D., GERIN, W., LANDSBERGIS, P., SCHNALL, P. L., & SCHWARTZ, J. E. (1996). Environmental influences on blood pressure and the role of job strain. *Journal of Hypertension, 14* (Suppl.), S179–S185.

PILIAVIN, I. M., RODIN, J., & PILIAVIN, J. A. (1969). Good Samaritanism: An underground phenomenon: *Journal of Personality and Social Psychology, 13,* 289–299.

PINKER, S. (1984). *Language learnability and language development.* Cambridge, MA: Harvard University Press.

PINKER, S. (1991). Rules of language. *Science, 253,* 530–555.

PINKER, S., & PRINCE, A. (1988). On language and connectionism: Analysis of a parallel distributed processing model of language acquisition. *Cognition, 28,* 71–193.

PION, G. M. (1991). Psychologists wanted: Employment trends over the past decade. In R. R. Kilburg (Ed.), *How to manage your career in psychology.* Washington, D.C.: American Psychological Association.

PLATT, J. J., YAKSH, T., & DARBY, C. L. (1967). Social facilitation of eating behavior in armadillos. *Psychological Reports, 20,* 1136.

PLOMIN, R. (1989). Environment and genes: Determinants of behavior. *American Psychologist, 44,* 105–111.

PLOMIN, R., & DANLIES, D. (1987). Why are children in the same family so different from one another? *Behavioral and Brain Sciences, 10,* 1–60.

PLOMIN, R., DEFRIES, J. C., & LOEHLIN, J. C. (1977). Genotype-environment interaction and correlation in the analysis of human behavior. *Psychological Bulletin, 84,* 309–322.

PLOMIN, R., FULKER, D. W., CORLEY, R., & DEFRIES, J. C. (1997). Nature, nurture, and cognitive development from 1 to 16 years: A parent-offspring adoption study. *Psychological Science, 8,* 442–447.

PLOMIN, R., OWEN, M. J., & MCGUFFIN, P. (1994). The genetic basis of complex human behaviors. *Science, 264,* 1733–1739.

POLIVY, J., & HERMAN, C. P. (1985). Dieting and bingeing: A causal analysis. *American Psychologist, 40,* 193–201.

POLIVY, J., & HERMAN, C. P. (1993). Etiology of binge eating: Psychological mechanisms. In C. E. Fairburn & G. T. Wilson (Eds.), *Binge eating: Nature, assessment, and treatment.* New York: Guilford.

PORTER, R. H., MAKIN, J. W., DAVIS, L. B., & CHRISTENSEN, K. M. (1992). An assessment of the salient olfactory environment of formula-fed infants. *Physiology and Behavior, 50,* 907–911.

POSNER, M. I. (1988). Structures and functions of selective attention. In T. Boll & B. K. Bryant (Eds.), *Clinical neuropsychology and brain function: Research, measurement, and practice.* Washington, DC: American Psychological Association.

POSNER, M. I. (1993). Seeing the mind. *Science, 262,* 673–674.

POSNER, M. I., & DEHAENE, S. (1994). Attentional networks. *Trends in Neuroscience, 17,* 75–79.

POSNER, M. I., & RAICHLE, M. E. (1994). *Images of mind.* New York: Scientific American Library.

POWELL, R. A., & BOER, D. P. (1994). Did Freud mislead patients to confabulate memories of abuse? *Psychological Reports, 74,* 1283–1298.

PREMACK, D. (1971). Language in chimpanzees? *Science, 172,* 808–822.

PREMACK, D. (1985). "Gavagi!" Or the future history of the animal language controversy. *Cognition, 19,* 207–296.

PREMACK, D., & PREMACK, A. J. (1983). *The mind of an ape.* New York: Norton.

PRESSLEY, M., LEVIN, J. R., & DELANEY, H. D. (1982). The mnemonic keyword method. *Review of Educational Research, 52,* 61–91.

PRETI, G., CUTLER, W. B., GARCIA, C. R., HUGGINS, G. R., and collaborators (1986). Human axillary secretions influence women's menstrual cycles: The role of donor extract of females. *Hormones & Behavior, 20,* 474–482.

PRIEST, R. F., & SAWYER, J. (1967). Proximity and peership: Bases of balance in interpersonal attraction. *American Journal of Sociology, 72,* 633–649.

PRINZMETAL, W. (1981). Principles of feature integration in visual perception. *Perception & Psychophysics, 30,* 330–340.

PROTHRO, E. T., (1952). Ethnocentrism and anti-Negro attitudes in the deep South. *Journal of Abnormal and Social Pathology, 47,* 105–108.

PUTNAM, F. W. (1991). Recent research on multiple personality disorder. *Psychiatric Clinics of North America, 14,* 489–502.

QUIRK, G. J., REPA, C., & LEDOUX, J. E. (1995). *Neuron, 15,* 1029–1039.

RAAIJMAKERS, J. G., & SHIFFRIN, R. M. (1981). Search of associative memory. *Psychological Review, 88,* 93–134.

RAAIJMAKERS, J. G., & SHIFFRIN, R. M. (1992). Models for recall and recognition. *Annual Review of Psychology, 43,* 205–234.

RACHMAN, S. (1993). Obsessions, responsibility and guilt. *Behaviour Research & Therapy, 31,* 149–154.

RACHMAN, S. J., & HODGSON, R. J. (1980). *Obsessions and compulsions.* Englewood Cliffs, NJ: Prentice-Hall.

RACHMAN, S. J., & WILSON, G. T. (1980). *The effects of psychological therapy* (2nd ed.). Elmsford, NY: Pergamon Press.

RAEIKKOENEN, K., MATTHEWS, K. A., FLORY, J. D., & OWENS, J. F. (1999). Effects of hostility on ambulatory blood pressure and mood during daily living in healthy adults. *Health Psychology 18,* 44–53.

RAGSDALE, D. S., MCPHEE, J. C., SCHEUER, T., & CATTERALL, W. A. (1994). Molecular determinants of state-dependent block of Na^+ channels by local anesthetics. *Science, 265,* 1724–1728.

RAICHLE, M. E. (1994). Images of the mind: Studies with modern imaging techniques. *Annual Review of Psychology, 45,* 333–356.

RAMACHANDRAN, V. S., & BLAKESLEE, S. (1998). *Phantoms in the brain.* New York: William Morrow.

RAMACHANDRAN, V. S., & GREGORY, R. L. (1991). Perceptual filling in of artificially induced scotomas in human vision. *Nature, 350,* 699–702.

RAMACHANDRAN, V. S., LEVI, L., STONE, L., ROGERS-RAMACHANDRAN, D., and collaborators (1996). Illusions of body image: What they reveal about human nature. In R. R. Llinas & P. S. Churchland (Eds.) et al., *The mind-brain continuum: Sensory processes* (pp. 29–60). Cambridge, MA: MIT Press.

RANDI, J. (1982). *Flim-flam! Psychics, ESP, unicorns and other delusions.* Buffalo: Prometheus Books.

RAPAPORT, D. (1942). *Emotions and memory.* Baltimore: Williams & Wilkins.

RAPAPORT, J. L. (1990). *The boy who couldn't stop washing.* New York: Plume.

RAPAPORT, J. L. (1991). Recent advances in obsessive-compulsive disorder. *Neuropsychopharmacology, 5,* 1–10.

RAPEE, R. M., BROWN, T. A., ANTONY, M. M., & BARLOW, D. H. (1992). Response to hyperventilation and inhalation of 5.5% carbon dioxide-enriched air across the DSM III-R anxiety disorders. *Journal of Abnormal Psychology, 101,* 538–552.

RASMUSSEN, S. A., & EISEN, J. L. (1990). Epidemiology of obsessive compulsive disorder. *Journal of Clinical Psychiatry, 51* (suppl.), 10–13.

RAVENS, J. C. (1965). *Advanced progressive matrices, sets II and II.* London: H. K. Lewis. (Distributed in the U.S. by The Psychological Corporation, San Antonio, TX)

RAVUSSIN, E., and collaborators (1988). Reduced rate of energy expenditure as a risk factor for body-weight gain. *New England Journal of Medicine, 318,* 467–472.

RAY, W. J., & RAVIZZA, R. (1988). *Methods toward a science of behavior and experience* (3rd ed.). Belmont, CA: Wadsworth.

RAYNER, K. (1978). Eye movements, reading and information processing. *Psychological Bulletin, 6,* 618–660.

REGAN, D., BEVERLEY, K. I., & CYNADER, M. (1979). The visual perception of motion depth. *Scientific American, 241,* 136–151.

REGAN, D. T., & FAZIO, R. (1977). On the consistency between attitudes and behavior: Look to the method of attitude information. *Journal of Experimental Social Psychology, 13,* 28–45.

REICHER, G. M. (1969). Perceptual recognition as a function of the meaningfulness of the material. *Journal of Experimental Psychology, 81,* 275–280.

RESCORLA, R. A. (1967). Pavlovian conditioning and its proper control procedures. *Psychological Review, 74,* 71–80.

RESCORLA, R. A. (1972). Informational variables in Pavlovian conditioning. In G. H. Bower (Ed.), *Psychology of learning and motivation* (Vol. 6). New York: Academic Press.

RESCORLA, R. A. (1980). Overextension in early language development. *Journal of Child Language, 7,* 321–335.

RESCORLA, R. A. (1987). A Pavlovian analysis of goal-directed behavior. *American Psychologist, 42,* 119–129.

RESCORLA, R. A. & SOLOMON, R. L. (1967). Two-process learning theory: Relations between Pavlovian conditioning and instrumental learning. *Psychological Review, 74,* 151–182.

RESNICK, H. S., KILPATRICK, D. G., DANSKY, B. S., & SAUNDERS, B. E. (1993). Prevalence of civilian trauma and posttraumatic stress disorder in a representative national sample of women. *Journal of Consulting and Clinical Psychology, 61,* 984–991.

REUBENS, A. B., & BENSON, D. F. (1971). Associative visual agnosia. *Archives of Neurology, 24,* 305–316.

REYNOLDS, D. V. (1969). Surgery in the rat during electrical analgesia induced by focal brain stimulation. *Science, 164,* 444–445.

RHEINGOLD, H. F., & COOK, K. V. (1975). The content of boys' and girls' rooms as an index of parent behavior. *Child Development, 46,* 459–463.

RICE, B. (1978). The new truth machine. *Psychology Today, 12,* 61–78.

RICHARDSON, J. L., SHELTON, D. R., KRAILO, M., & LEVINE, A. M. (1990). The effect of compliance with treatment in survival among patients with hematologic malignancies. *Journal of Clinicial Oncology, 8,* 356.

RICHARDSON, K. (1986). Theory? Or tools for social selection? *Behavioral and Brain Sciences, 9,* 579–581.

RIESEN, A. H. (1947). The development of visual perception in man and chimpanzee. *Science, 106,* 107–108.

RIMM-KAUFMAN, S., & KAGAN, J. (1996). The psychological significance of changes in skin temperature. *Motivation and Emotion, 20,* 63–78.

RIPS, L. J. (1983). Cognitive processes in propositional reasoning. *Psychological Review, 90,* 38–71.

RIPS, L. J. (1994). *The psychology of proof.* Cambridge, MA: MIT Press.

ROBERT, M. (1989). Reduction of demand characteristics in the measurement of certainty during modeled conservation. *Journal of Experimental Child Psychology, 47,* 451–466.

ROBINS, L. N., HELZER, J. E., WEISSMAN, M. M., ORVASCHEL, H., GRUENBERG, E., BURKE, J. D., & REIGIER, D. A. (1984). Lifetime prevalence of specific psychiatric disorders in three sites. *Archives of General Psychiatry, 41,* 949–958.

ROBINSON, T. E., & BERRIDGE, K. C. (1993). The neural basis of drug craving: an incentive-sensitization theory of addiction. *Brain Research Review, 18,* 247–291.

RODIN, J. (1981). Current status of the internal-external hypothesis of obesity: What went wrong? *American Psychologist, 36,* 361–372.

ROFFWARG, H. P., HERMAN, J. H., BOWER-ANDERS, C., & TAUBER, E. S. (1978). The effects of sustained alterations of waking visual input on dream content. In A. M. Arkin, J. S. Antrobus, & S. J. Ellman (Eds.), *The mind in sleep.* Hillsdale, NJ: Erlbaum.

ROGERS, C. R. (1959). A theory of therapy, personality, and interpersonal relationships as developed in the client-centered framework. In S. Koch (Ed.), *Psychology: A study of a science: Vol. 3. Formulations of the person and the social context.* New York: McGraw-Hill.

ROGERS, C. R. (1951). *Client-centered therapy.* Boston: Houghton Mifflin.

ROGERS, C. R. (1963). The actualizing tendency in relation to motives and to consciousness. In M. Jones (Ed.), *Nebraska symposium on motivation* (pp. 1–24). Lincoln: University of Nebraska Press.

ROGERS, C. R. (1970). *On becoming a person: A therapist's view of psychotherapy.* Boston: Houghton Mifflin.

ROGERS, T. B., KUIPER, N. A., & KIRKER, W. S. (1977). Self-reference and the encoding of personal information. *Journal of Personality and Social Psychology, 35,* 677–688.

ROGOFF, B. (1990). *Apprenticeship in thinking.* New York: Oxford University Press.

ROITBLAT, H. L. (1986). *Introduction to comparative cognition.* New York: Freeman.

ROLAND, P. E., & FRIBERG, L. (1985). Localization of cortical areas activated by thinking. *Journal of Neurophysiology, 53,* 1219–1243.

ROOK, K. (1984). The negative side of social interaction: Impact on psychological well-being. *Journal of Personality and Social Psychology, 46,* 1097–1108.

ROSCH, E. (1974). Linguistic relativity. In A. Silverstein (Ed.), *Human communication: Theoretical perspectives.* New York: Halsted Press.

ROSCH, E. (1978). Principles of categorization. In E. Rosch & B. L. Lloyd (Eds.), *Cognition and categorization.* Hillsdale, NJ: Erlbaum.

ROSE, J. E., BRUGGE, J. F., ANDERSON, D. J., & HIND, J. E. (1967). Phase-locked response to lower frequency tones in single auditory nerve fibers of the squirrel monkey. *Journal of Neurophysiology, 390,* 769–793.

ROSEN, R. C., & LEIBLUM, S. R. (1995). Treatment of sexual disorders in the 1990s: An integrated approach. *Journal of Consulting and Clinical Psychology, 63,* 877–890.

ROSENBLITH, J. F. (1992). *In the beginning: Development from conception to age two years* (2nd ed.). Newbury Park, CA: Sage.

ROSENBLOOM, P. S., LAIRD, J. E., NEWELL, A., & MCCARL, R. (1991). A preliminary analysis of the foundations of Soar. *Artificial Intelligence, 47,* 289–325.

ROSENMAN, R. H., BRAND, R. J., JENKINS, C. D., FRIEDMAN, M., STRAUS, R., & WRUM, M. (1976). Coronary heart disease in the Western Collaborative Group Study: Final follow-up experience of 8½ years. *Journal of the American Medical Association, 233,* 878–877.

ROSENTHAL, R. (1984). *Meta-analytic procedures for social research.* Beverly Hills, CA: Sage.

ROSENZWEIG, M. R., & LEIMAN, A. L. (1989). *Physiological psychology* (2nd ed.). Lexington, MA: Heath.

ROSS, L. (1977). The intuitive psychologist and his shortcomings: Distortions in the attribution process. In L. Berkowitz, (Ed.), *Advances in experimental social psychology* (Vol. 10). New York: Academic Press.

ROSS, L., AMABILE, T. M., & STEINMETZ, J. L. (1977). Social roles, social control, and biases in social-perception processes. *Journal of Personality and Social Psychology, 35,* 485–494.

ROSS, L., BIERBRAUER, G., & HOFFMAN, S. (1976). The role of attribution processes in conformity and dissent. Revisiting the Asch situation. *American Psychologist, 31,* 148–157.

ROSS, L., LEPPER, M. R., & HUBBARD, M. (1975). Perseverance in self perception and social perception: Biased attributional processes in the debriefing paradigm. *Journal of Personality and Social Psychology, 32,* 880–892.

ROSS, L., LEPPER, M. R., STRACK, F., & STEINMETZ, J. L. (1977). Social explanation and social expectation: The effects of real and hypothetical explanations upon subjective likelihood. *Journal of Personality and Social Psychology, 35,* 817–829.

ROSS, L., & NISBETT, R. E. (1991). *The person and the situation: Perspectives of social psychology.* New York: McGraw-Hill.

ROSSI, P. (1990). The old homelessness and the new homelessness in historical perspective. *American Psychologist, 45,* 954–959.

ROTH, A., FONAGY, P., PARRY, G., TARGET, M., and collaborators (1996). *What works for whom? A critical review of psychotherapy research.* New York: Guilford.

ROTTER, J. B. (1954). *Social learning and clinical psychology.* Englewood Cliffs, NJ: Prentice-Hall.

ROTTER, J. B. (1982). *The development and applications of social learning theory: Selected papers.* New York: Praeger.

ROVEE-COLLIER, C., & HAYNE, H. (1987). Reactivation of infant memory: Implications for cognitive development. In H. W. Reese (Ed.), *Advances in child development and behavior* (Vol. 20). New York: Academic Press.

ROWLAND, N. E., & ANTELMAN, S. M. (1976). Stress-induced hyperphagia and obesity in rats: A possible model for understanding human obesity. *Science, 191,* 310–12.

ROYCE, J. R., & MOS, L. P. (Eds.) (1981). *Humanistic psychology: Concepts and criticisms.* New York: Plenum.

ROZIN, P. N., & SCHULKIN, J. (1990). Food selection. In E. M. Stricker (Ed.), *Neurobiology of food and fluid intake* (pp. 297–328). New York: Plenum.

RUBIN, Z. (1973). *Liking and loving.* New York: Holt, Rinehart & Winston.

RUCH, J. C. (1975). Self-hypnosis: The result of heterohypnosis or vice versa? *International Journal of Clinical and Experimental Hypnosis, 23,* 282–304.

RUCH, J. C., MORGAN, A. H., & HILGARD, E. R. (1973). Behavioral predictions from hypnotic responsiveness scores when obtained with and without prior induction procedures. *Journal of Abnormal Psychology, 82,* 543–546.

RUDERMAN, A. J. (1986). Dietary restraint: A theoretical and empirical review. *Psychological Bulletin, 99,* 247–262.

RUMELHART, D. E., & MCCLELLAND, J. L. (1987). Learning the past tenses of English verbs: Implicit rules or parallel distributed processing? In B. MacWhinney (Ed.), *Mechanisms of language acquisition.* Hillsdale, NJ: Erlbaum.

RUMELHART, D. E., MCCLELLAND, J. L., & THE PDP RESEARCH GROUP (1986). *Parallel distributed processing: Explorations in the microstructure of cognition. Volume 1: Foundations.* Cambridge, MA: Bradford Books/MIT Press.

RUSSELL, M. J. (1976). Human olfactory communication. *Nature, 260,* 520–522.

RUSSELL, M. J., SWITZ, G. M., & THOMPSON, K. (1980). Olfactory influence on the human menstrual cycle. *Pharmacology, Biochemistry and Behavior, 13,* 737–738.

RUSSO, N. F., & SOBEL, S. B. (1981). Sex differences in the utilization of mental health facilities. *Professional Psychology, 12,* 7–19.

RUTTER, M., MACDONALD, H., CONTEUR, A. L., HARRINGTON, R., BOLTON, P., & BAILEY, A. (1990). Genetic factors in child psychiatric disorders: II. Empirical findings. *Journal of Child Psychology and Psychiatry, 31,* 39–83.

RUTTER, M., QUINTON, D., & HILL, J. (1990). Adult outcome of institution-reared children: Males and females compared. In L. Robins (Ed.), *Straight and devious pathways from childhood to adulthood* (pp. 135–157). Cambridge, England: Cambridge University Press.

RYMER, R. (1992a, April 13). A silent childhood. *New Yorker,* pp. 41–53.

RYMER, R. (1992b, April 20). A silent childhood, pt. II. *New Yorker,* pp. 43–47.

SACHS, J. D. S. (1967). Recognition memory for syntactic and semantic aspects of connected discourse. *Perception and Psychophysics, 2,* 437–442.

SACKS, O. (1985). *The man who mistook his wife for a hat and other clinical tales.* New York: Harper Perennial.

SACKS, O. W. (1983). *Awakenings.* New York: Dutton.

SALAMY, J. (1970). Instrumental responding to internal cues associated with REM sleep. *Psychonomic Science, 18,* 342–343.

SALAPATEK, P. (1975). Pattern perception in early infancy. In L. B. Cohen & P. Salapatek (Eds.), *Infant perception: From sensation to cognition* (Vol. 1). New York: Academic Press.

SALKOVSKIS, P. M. (1989). Cognitive-behavioral factors and the persistence of intrusive thoughts in obsessional problems. *Behaviour Research & Therapy, 27,* 677–682.

SANDERS, G. S. (1984). Self-presentation and drive in social facilitation. *Journal of Experimental Social Psychology, 20,* 312–322.

SANDERS, G. S., & BARON, R. S. (1975). The motivating effects of distraction on task performance. *Journal of Personality and Social Psychology, 32,* 956–963.

SANDERS, G. S., & BARON, R. S. (1977). Is social comparison irrelevant for producing choice shifts? *Journal of Experimental Social Psychology, 13,* 303–314.

SANDERSON, W. C., RAPEE, R. M., & BARLOW, D. H. (1989). The influence of illusion of control on panic attacks induced via inhalation of 5.5% carbon dioxide-enriched air. *Archives of General Psychology, 46,* 157–162.

SAPOLSKY, R. M. (1990). Stress in the wild. *Scientific American, 262,* 116–123.

SATINOFF, E. (1964). Behavioral thermoregulation in reponse to local cooling of the rat brain. *American Journal of Physiology, 206,* 1389–1394.

SATINOFF, E. (1983). A reevaluation of the concept of the homeostatic organization of temperature regulation. In E. Satinoff & P. Teitelbaum (Eds.), *Motivation* (pp. 443–474). New York: Plenum Press.

SAUNDERS, D. R. (1985). On Hyman's factor analyses. *Journal of Parapsychology, 49,* 86–88.

SAXE, L., DOUGHERTY, D., & CROSS, T. (1985). The validity of polygraph testing. *American Psychologist, 40,* 355–366.

SCARR, S. (1985). An author's frame of mind: Review of *Frames of mind,* by Howard Gardner. *New Ideas in Psychology, 3,* 95–100.

SCARR, S. (1988). How genotypes and environments combine: Development and invidual differences. In N. Bolger, A. Caspi, G. Downey, & M. Moorehouse (Eds.), *Persons in context: Developmental processes* (pp. 217–244). New York: Cambridge University Press.

SCARR, S., & EISENBERG, M. (1993). Child care research: Issues, perspectives, and results. *Annual Review of Psychology, 44,* 613–644.

SCARR, S., & MCCARTNEY, K. (1983). How people make their own environments: A theory of genotype-environment effects. *Child Development, 54,* 424–435.

SCARR, S., PHILLIPS, D., MCCARTNEY, K., & ABBOTT-SHIM, M. (1993). Quality of child care as an aspect of family and child care policy in the United States. *Pediatrics, 91,* 182–188.

SCARR, S., WEINBERG, R. A., & LEVINE, A. (1986). *Understanding development.* San Diego: Harcourt Brace Javanovich.

SCHACHTEL, E. G. (1982). On memory and childhood amnesia. In U. Neisser (Ed.), *Memory observed: Remembering in natural contexts.* San Francisco: Freeman.

SCHACHTER, S., & SINGER, J. E. (1962). Cognitive, social and physiological determinants of emotional state. *Psychological Review, 69,* 379–399.

SCHACTER, D. L. (1989). Memory. In M. Posner (Ed.), *Foundations of cognitive science.* Cambridge, MA: MIT Press.

SCHAFER, R. (1976). *A new language for psychoanalysis.* New Haven, CT: Yale University Press.

SCHARNBERG, M. (1993). *The nonauthentic nature of Freud's observations: Vol. 1. The seduction theory.* Philadelphia: Coronet.

SCHEIER, M. F., BUSS, A. H., & BUSS, D. M. (1978). Self-consciousness, self-reports of aggressiveness, and aggressions. *Journal of Research in Personality, 12,* 133–140.

SCHIFF, W., & FOULKE, E. (Eds.) (1982). *Tactual perception: A sourcebook.* Cambridge, England: Cambridge University Press.

SCHIFFENBAUER, A., & SCHIAVO, R. S. (1976). Physical distance and attraction: An intensification effect. *Journal of Experimental Social Psychology, 12,* 274–282.

SCHINDLER, R. A., & MERZENICH, M. M. (Eds.) (1985). *Cochlear implants.* New York: Raven Press.

SCHLEIDT, M., HOLD, B., & ATTILI, G. (1981). A cross-cultural study on the attitude toward personal odors. *Journal of Chemical Ecology, 7,* 19–31.

SCHLEIFER, S. J., KELLER, S. E., MCKEGNEY, F. P., & STEIN, M. (1979, March). The influence of stress and other psychosocial factors on human immunity. Paper presented at the 36th Annual Meeting of the Psychosomatic Society, Dallas.

SCHLESINGER, A. M., JR. (1965). *A thousand days.* Boston: Houghton Mifflin.

SCHMITT, B. H., GILOVICH, T., GOORE, N., & JOSEPH, L. (1986). Mere presence and social facilitation: One more time. *Journal of Experimental Social Psychology, 22,* 242–248.

SCHNEIDER, A. M., & TARSHIS, B. (1986). *An introduction to physiological psychology* (3rd ed.). New York: Random House.

SCHNEIDER, D. J., & MILLER, R. S. (1975). The effects of enthusiasm and quality of arguments on attitude attribution. *Journal of Personality, 43,* 693–708.

SCHNEIER, F. R., JOHNSON, J., HORNIG, C. D., & LIEBOWITZ, M. R. (1992). Social phobia: Comorbidity and morbidity in an epidemiologic sample. *Archives of General Psychiatry, 49,* 282–288.

SCHULTZ, D. (2000). *A history of modern psychology* (7th ed.). Fort Worth: Harcourt.

SCHWARTZ, B. (1989). *Psychology of learning and behavior* (3rd ed.). New York: Norton.

SCHWARTZ, B., & REISBERG, D. (1991). *Learning and memory.* New York: Norton.

SCHWARTZ, B., SNIDMAN, N., & KAGAN, J. (1996). Early childhood temperament as a determinant of externalizing behavior in adolescence. *Development and Psychopathology, 8,* 527–537.

SCOTT, T. R., & MARK, G. P. (1986). Feeding and taste. *Progress in Neurobiology, 27,* 293–317.

SEARS, R. R. (1943). Survey of objective studies of psychoanalytic concepts. *Social Science Research Council Bulletin,* No. 51.

SEARS, R. R. (1944). Experimental analyses of psychoanalytic phenomena. In J. Hunt (Ed.), *Personality and the behavior disorders* (Vol. 1, pp. 306–332). New York: Ronald.

SEARS, R. R., MACCOBY, E. E., & LEVIN, H. (1957) *Patterns of child rearing.* New York: Harper &Row.

SEGERSTROM, S. C., TAYLOR, S. E., KEMENY, M. E., REED, G. M., & VISSCHER, B. R. (1996). Causal attributions predict rate of immune decline in HIV-Seropositive gay men. *Health Psychology, 15,* 485–493.

SEIFERT, C. M., ROBERTSON, S. P., & BLACK, J. B. (1985). Types of inferences generated during reading. *Journal of Memory and Language, 24,* 405–422.

SEKULER, R. (1975). Visual motion perception. In E. C. Carterette & M. Friedman (Eds.), *Handbook of perception: Vol. 5* (pp. 387–433). New York: Academic Press.

SEKULER, R., & BLAKE, R. (1985). *Perception.* New York: Knopf.

SELIGMAN, M. E. P. (1975). *Helplessness*. San Francisco: Freeman.

SELIGMAN, M. E. P. & BINIK, Y. M. (1977). The safety signal hypothesis. In H. Davis & H. Hurwitz (Eds.), *Pavlovian operant interactions*. Hillsdale, NJ: Erlbaum.

SELYE, H. (1978). *The stress of life*. New York: McGraw-Hill.

SEWELL, W. H., & MUSSEN, P. H. (1952). The effects of feeding, weaning, and scheduling procedures on childhood adjustment and the formation of oral symptoms. *Child Development, 23,* 185–191.

SHALLICE, T. (1988). *From neuropsychology to mental structure*. Cambridge, England: Cambridge University Press.

SHALLICE, T., FLETCHER, P., FRITH, C. D., GRASBY, P., FRACKOWIAK, R. S. J., & DOLAN, R. J. (1994). Brain regions associated with acquisition and retrieval of verbal episodic memory. *Nature, 368,* 633–635.

SHANKS, D. R., & DICKINSON, A., (1987). Associative accounts of causality judgment. *The Psychology of Learning and Motivation, 21,* 229–261.

SHANNON, R. V., & OTTO, S. R. (1990). Psychophysical measures from electrical stimulation of the human cochlear nucleus. *Hearing Research, 47,* 159–168.

SHAPIRO, A. K., & MORRIS, L. A. (1978). The placebo effect in medical and psychological therapies. In S. L. Garfield & A. E. Bergin (Eds.), *Handbook of psychotherapy and behavior change* (2nd ed.). New York: Wiley.

SHAPIRO, D. A., & SHAPIRO, D. (1982). Meta-analysis of comparative therapy outcome studies: A replication and refinement. *Psychological Bulletin, 92,* 581–604.

SHAPLEY, R., & LENNIE, P. (1985). Spatial frequency analysis in the visual system. *Annual Review of Neurosciences, 8,* 547–583.

SHAW, D. W., & THORESEN, C. E. (1974). Effects of modeling and desensitization in reducing dentist phobia. *Journal of Counseling Psychology, 21,* 415–420.

SHEINGOLD, K., & TENNEY, Y. J. (1982). Memory for a salient childhood event. In U. Neisser (Ed.), *Memory observed: Remembering in natural contexts*. San Francisco: Freeman.

SHEKELLE, R., NEATON, J. D., JACOBS, D., HULLEY, S., & BLACKBURN, H. (1983). Type A behavior pattern in MRFIT. A paper presented to the American Heart Association Council on Epidemiology Meetings, San Diego.

SHEPARD, R. N., & COOPER, L. A. (1982). *Mental images and their transformations*. Cambridge, MA: MIT Press, Bradford Books.

SHEPHER, J. (1971). Mate selection among second generation kibbutz adolescents and adults: Incest avoidance and negative imprinting. *Archives of Sexual Behavior, 1,* 293–307.

SHEPOSH, J. P., DEMING, M., & YOUNG, L. E. (1977, April). The radiating effects of status and attractiveness of a male upon evaluating his female partner. Paper presented at the an-

nual meeting of the Western Psychological Association, Seattle.

SHERWIN, B. (1988a). A comparative analysis of the role of androgen in human male and female sexual behavior: Behavioral specificity, critical thresholds, and sensitivity. *Psychobiology, 16,* 416–425.

SHERWIN, B. (1988b). Critical analysis of the role of androgens in human male and female sexual behavior: Behavioral specificity, critical thresholds, and sensitivity. *Psychobiology, 16,* 416–423.

SHWEDER, R. A. (1984). Anthropology's romantic rebellion against the enlightenment, or there's more to thinking than reason and evidence. In R. A. Shweder & R. A. LeVine (Eds.), *Culture theory: Essays on mind, self, and emotion* (pp. 27–66). Cambridge, England: Cambridge University Press.

SIEGLER, R. S. (1991). *Children's thinking* (2nd ed.). Englewood Cliffs: NJ: Prentice-Hall.

SIGALL, H., & LANDY, D. (1973). Radiating beauty: The effects of having a physically attractive partner on person perception. *Journal of Personality and Social Psychology, 31,* 410–414.

SILVERMAN, I. (1964). Self-esteem and differential responsiveness to success and failure. *Journal of Abnormal and Social Psychology, 69,* 115–119.

SILVERMAN, I. (1971). Physical attractiveness and courtship. *Sexual Behavior, 1,* 22–25.

SIMMONS, J. V. (1981). *Project sea hunt: A report on prototype development and tests*. Technical Report 746, Naval Ocean Systems Center, San Diego.

SIMMONS, R. G., & BLYTH, D. A. (1988). *Moving into adolescence: The impact of pubertal change and school context*. Hawthorne, NY: Aldine.

SIMON, H. A. (1985, June). Using Cognitive Science to Solve Human Problems. Paper presented at Science and Public Policy Seminar, Federation of Behavioral, Psychological, and Cognitive Sciences.

SIMON, H. A., & GILMARTIN, K. (1973). A simulation of memory for chess positions. *Cognitive Psychology, 5,* 29–46.

SIMPSON, J. A., CAMPBELL, B., & BERSCHEID, E. (1986). The association between romantic love and marriage: Kephart (1967) twice revisited. *Personality and Social Psychology Bulletin, 12,* 363–372.

SINGER, J. L., & SINGER, D. G. (1981). *Television, imagination and aggression*. Hillsdale, NJ: Erlbaum.

SIQUELAND, E. R., & LIPSITT, J. P. (1966). Conditioned head-turning in human newborns. *Journal of Experimental Child Psychology, 3,* 356–376.

SIZEMORE, C. C., & PITTILLO, E. S. (1977). *I'm Eve*. Garden City, NY: Doubleday.

SKINNER, B. F. (1938). *The behavior of organisms*. New York: Appleton-Century-Crofts.

SKINNER, B. F. (1948). "Superstition" in the pigeon. *Journal of Experimental Psychology, 38,* 168–172.

SKINNER, B. F. (1971). *Beyond freedom and dignity*. New York: Knopf.

SKINNER, B. F. (1981). Selection by consequences. *Science, 213,* 501–504.

SKYRMS, B. (1986). *Choice and chance: An introduction to inductive logic*. Belmont, CA: Dickenson.

SLOBIN, D. I. (1971). Cognitive prerequisites for the acquisition of grammar. In C. A. Ferguson & D. I. Slobin (Eds.), *Studies of child language developments*. New York: Holt, Rinehart & Winston.

SLOBIN, D. I. (1979). *Psycholinguistics* (2nd. ed.). Glenville, IL: Scott, Foresman.

SLOBIN, D. I. (Ed.) (1985). *The cross-linguistic study of language acquisition*. Hillsdale, NJ: Erlbaum.

SMITH, C. A., & ELLSWORTH, P. C. (1985). Patterns of cognitive appraisal in emotion. *Journal of Personality and Social Psychology, 48,* 813–848.

SMITH, C. A., & ELLSWORTH, P. C. (1987). Patterns of appraisal and emotion related to taking an exam. *Journal of Personality and Social Psychology, 52,* 475–488.

SMITH, D., KING, M., & HOEBEL, B. G. (1970). Lateral hypothalamic control of killing: Evidence for a cholinoceptive mechanism. *Science, 167,* 900–901.

SMITH, E. E. (1989). Concepts and induction. In M. I. Posner (Ed.), *Foundations of cognitive science*. Cambridge, MA: MIT Press.

SMITH, E. E. (1995). Concepts and categorization. In E. E. Smith & D. Osherson (Eds.), *Invitation to cognitive science, Vol. 3, Thinking* (2nd ed.). Cambridge, MA: MIT Press.

SMITH, E. E., & JONIDES, J. (1994). Neuropsychological studies of working memory. In M. Gazzaniga (Ed.), *The cognitive neurosciences*. Cambridge, MA: MIT Press.

SMITH, E. E., JONIDES, J., & KOEPPE, R. A. (1996). Dissociating verbal and spatial working memory using PET.

SMITH, E. E., & MEDIN, D. L. (1981). *Categories and concepts*. Cambridge, MA: Harvard University Press.

SMITH, E. E., PATALANO, A. L., & JONIDES, J. (1998). Alternative strategies of categorization. *Cognition, 65,* 167–196.

SMITH, G. P., & GIBBS, J. (1994). Satiating effect of cholecystokinin. *Annals of the New York Academy of Sciences, 713,* 236–41.

SMITH, M. B., BRUNER, J. S., & WHITE, R. W. (1956). *Opinions and personality*. New York: Wiley.

SMITH, M. L., GLASS, G. V., & MILLER, T. I. (1980). *The benefits of psychotherapy*. Baltimore: Johns Hopkins University Press.

SMITH, V. C., & POKORNY, J. (1975). Spectral sensitivity of the foveal cones between 400 and 500 nm. *Vision Res.* 15, 161.

SMUTS, B. B. (1986). Gender, aggression, and influence. In B. Smuts, D. Cheney, R. Seyfarth, R. Wrangham, & T. Struhsaker (Eds.), *Primate societies*. Chicago: University of Chicago Press.

SNAITH, P. (1998). Meditation and psychotherapy. *British Journal of Psychiatry, 173*, 193–195.

SNODGRASS, J. G., LEVY-BERGER, G., & HAYDON, M. (1985). *Human experimental psychology*. New York: Oxford University Press.

SNOW, C. (1987). Relevance of the notion of a critical period to language acquisition. In M. H. Bornstein (Ed.), *Sensitive periods in development: Interdisciplinary perspectives*. Hillsdale, NJ: Erlbaum.

SNOWDEN, L. R. (1988). Ethnicity and utilization of mental health services: An overview of current findings. In *Oklahoma Mental Health Research Institute, 1988 professional symposium* (pp. 227–238). Oklahoma City: Oklahoma Mental Health Research Institute.

SNOWDEN, L., & CHEUNG, F. (1990, March). Use of inpatient mental health services by members of ethnic minority groups. *American Psychologist, 45*, 347–355.

SOLOMON, R. L., & CORBIT, J. D. (1974). An opponent-process theory of motivation: I. Temporal dynamics of affect. *Psychological Review, 81*, 119–145.

SONTHEIMER, H. (1995). Glial neuronal interactions: A physiological perspective. *The Neuroscientist, 1*, 328–337.

SPANOS, N. P. (1986). Hypnotic behavior: A social-psychological interpretation of amnesia, analgesia, and "trance logic." *The Behavioral and Brain Sciences, 9*, 449–502.

SPANOS, N. P., & HEWITT, E. C. (1980). The hidden observer in hypnotic analgesia: Discovery or experimental creation? *Journal of Personality and Social Psychology, 39*, 1201–1214.

SPEARMAN, C. (1904). "General intelligence" objectively determined and measured. *American Journal of Psychology, 15*, 201–293.

SPENCER, S., STEELE, C. M., & QUINN, D. (1997). Under suspicion of inability: Stereotype threat and women's math performance. Unpublished manuscript, Stanford University.

SPERLING, G. (1960). The information available in brief visual presentations. *Psychological Monographs, 74*, 329.

SPERRY, R. W. (1968). Perception in the absence of neocortical commissures. In Association for Research in Nervous and Mental Disease, *Perception and its disorders*. New York: Williams & Wilkins.

SPIEGEL, D. (1991). Mind matters: Effects of group support on cancer patients. *Journal of NIH Research, 3*, 61–63.

SPIEGEL, D., BLOOM, J. R., KRAEMER, H. C., & GOTTHEIL, E. (1989). Psychological support for cancer patients. *Lancet, II*, 1447.

SPIELBERGER, C. D., JOHNSON, E. H., RUSSELL, S. F., CRANE, R. S., JACOBS, G. A., & WORDEN, T. J. (1985). The experience and expression of anger: Construction and validation of an anger expression scale. In M. A. Chesney & R. H. Rosenman (Eds.), *Anger and hostility in cardiovascular and behavioral disorders*. New York: Hemisphere/McGraw-Hill.

SPIVEY, C. B., & PRENTICE-DUNN, S. (1990). Assessing the directionality of deindividuated behavior: Effects of deindividuation, modeling, and private self-consciousness on aggressive and prosocial responses. *Basic and Applied Social Psychology, 11*, 387–403.

SPRAFKIN, J. N., LIEBERT, R. M., & POULOUS, R. W. (1975). Effects of a prosocial televised example on children's helping. *Journal of Personality and Social Psychology, 48*, 35–46.

SPRINGER, S. P., & DEUTSCH, G. (1989). *Left brain, right brain* (3rd ed.). San Francisco: Freeman.

SQUIER, L. H., & DOMHOFF, G. W. (1998). The presentation of dreaming and dreams in introductory psychology textbooks: A critical examination. Unpublished paper.

SQUIRE, L. R. (1987). *Memory and brain*. New York: Oxford University Press.

SQUIRE, L. R. (1992). Memory and the hippocampus: A synthesis from findings with rats, monkeys, and humans. *Psychological Review, 99*, 195–231.

SQUIRE, L. R., & BUTTERS, N. (Eds.) (1984). *The neuropsychology of memory*. New York: Guilford.

SQUIRE, L. R., & FOX, M. M. (1980). Assessment of remote memory: Validation of the television test by repeated testing during a seven-day period. *Behavioral Research Methods and Instrumentation, 12*, 583–586.

SQUIRE, L. R., KNOWLTON, B., & MUSEN, G. (1993). The structure and organization of memory. *Annual Review of Psychology, 44*, 453–495.

SQUIRE, L. R., OJEMANN, J. G., MIEZIN, F. M., PETERSEN, S. E., VIDEEN, T. O., & RAICHLE, M. E. (1992). Activation of the hippocampus in normal humans: A functional anatomical study of memory. *Proceedings of the National Academy of Science, 89*, 1837–1841.

SQUIRE, L. R., & ZOLA, S. M. (1996). Ischemic brain damage and memory impairment: A commentary. *Hippocampus, 6*, 546–552.

SQUIRE, L. R., ZOLA-MORGAN, S., CAVE, C. B., HAIST, F., MUSEN, G., & SUZUKI, W. A. (1990). Memory: Organization of brain systems and cognition. In *Symposium on quantiative biology, the brain* (Vol. 55). Cold Spring Harbor, NY: Cold Spring Harbor Laboratory.

STAATS, A. W. (1968). *Language, learning, and cognition*. New York: Holt, Rinehart & Winston.

STANGOR, C., & MCMILLAN, D. (1992). Memory for expectancy-congruent and expectancy-incongruent information: A review of the social and social developmental literature. *Psychological Bulletin, 111*, 42–61.

STASSER, G., TAYLOR, L. A., & HANNA, C. (1989). Information sampling in structured and unstructured discussion of three- and six-person groups. *Journal of Personality and Social Psychology, 57*, 67–78.

STASSER, G., & TITUS, W. (1985). Pooling of unshared information in group decision making: Biased information sampling during discussion. *Journal of Personality and Social Psychology, 48*, 1467–1478.

STATTIN, H., & MAGNUSSON, D. (1990). *Pubertal maturation in female development*. Hillsdale, NJ: Erlbaum.

STAYTON, D. J. (1973, March). Infant responses to brief everyday separations: Distress, following, and greeting. Paper presented at the meeting of the Society for Research in Child Development.

STEELE, C. M. (1997). A threat in the air: How stereotypes shape intellectual identify and performance. *American Psychologist, 52*, 613–629.

STEELE, C. M., & ARONSON, J. (1995). Stereotype threat and the intellectual test performance of African Americans. *Journal of Personality and Social Psychology, 69*, 797–811.

STEINBERG, L. (1996). *Adolescence* (4th ed.). New York: Knopf.

STEINER, J. E. (1979). Human facial expressions in response to taste and smell stimulation. *Advances in Child Development and Behavior, 13*, 257–295.

STEKETEE, G., & WHITE, K. (1990). *When once is not enough*. Oakland, CA: New Harbinger.

STELLAR, J. R., & STELLAR, E. (1985). *The neurobiology of motivation and reward*. New York: Springer-Verlag.

STERN, R. S., & COBB, J. P. (1978). Phenomology of obsessive-compulsive neurosis. *Britis Journal of Psychiatry, 132*, 233–239.

STERNBERG, R. J. (1985). *Beyond IQ: A triarchic theory of human intelligence*. Cambridge, England: Cambridge University Press.

STERNBERG, R. J. (1986). *Intelligence applied: Understanding and increasing your intellectual skills*. San Diego: Harcourt Brace Jovanovich.

STERNBERG, R. J. (1988). *The triarchic mind: A new theory of human intelligence*. New York: Viking.

STERNBERG, S. (1966). Highspeed scanning in human memory. *Science, 153*, 652–654.

STERNBERG, S. (1975). Memory scanning: New findings and current controversies. *Quarterly Journal of Experimental Psychology, 27*, 1–32.

STEUER, F. B., APPLEFIELD, J. M., & SMITH, R. (1971). Televised aggression and the interpersonal aggression of preschool children. *Journal of Experimental Child Psychology, 11*, 422–447.

STEVENSON, H. W., LEE, S., & GRAHAM, T. (1993). Chinese and Japanese kindergartens: Case study in comparative research. In B. Spodek (Ed.), *Handbook of research on the education of young children*. New York: Macmillan.

STILES, W. B., SHAPIRO, D. A., & ELLIOTT, R. (1986). Are all psychotherapies equivalent? *American Psychologist, 41,* 165–180.

STONER, J. A. F. (1961). *A comparison of individual and group decisions involving risk.* Unpublished master's thesis, Massachusetts Institute of Technology.

STRACK, F., MARTIN, L. L., & STEPPER, S. (1988). Inhibiting and facilitating conditions of the human smile: A non-obtrusive test of the facial feedback hypothesis. *Journal of Personality and Social Psychology, 54,* 768–777.

STREISSGUTH, A. P., CLARREN, S. K., & JONES, K. L. (1985). Natural history of the fetal alcohol syndrome: A 10-year follow-up of eleven patients. *Lancet, 2,* 85–91.

STROEBE, W., INSKO, C. A., THOMPSON, V. D., & LAYTON, B. D. (1971). Effects of physical attractiveness, attitude similarity and sex on various aspects of interpersonal attraction. *Journal of Personality and Social Psychology, 18,* 79–91.

STRONG, S. R., HILLS, H. J., KILMARTIN, C. T., DEVRIES, H., LANIER, A, K., NELSON, B. N., STRICKLAND, D., & MEYER, C. W., III (1988). The dynamic relations among interpersonal behaviors: A test of complementarity and anti-complementarity. *Journal of Personality and Social Psychology, 54,* 798–810.

STUNKARD, A. J. (1982). Obesity. In M. Hersen, A. Bellack, & A. Kazdin (Eds.), *International handbook of behavior modification and therapy*. New York: Plenum.

STUNKARD, A. J. (1996). *The origins and consequences of obesity*. Chichester: Wiley.

STUNKARD, A. J., HARRIS, J. R., PEDERSEN, N. L., & MCCLEARN, G. E. (1990). A separated twin study of the body mass index. *The New England Journal of Medicine, 322,* 1483–1487.

SUAREZ, E. C., KUHN, C. M., SCHANBERG, S. M., WILLIAMS, R. B., JR., & ZIMMERMAN, E. A. (1998). Neuroendocrine, cardiovascular, and emotional responses of hostile men: The role of interpersonal challenge. *Psychosomatic Medicine, 60,* 78–88.

SUE, S., ALLEN, D., & CONAWAY, L. (1978). The responsiveness and equality of mental health care to Chicanos and Native Americans. *American Journal of Community Psychology, 6,* 137–146.

SUE, S., & ZANE, N. (1987). The role of culture and cultural techniques in psychotherapy: A critique and reformulation. *American Psychologist, 42,* 37–51.

SULLIVAN, H. S. (1953). *The interpersonal theory of psychiatry*. New York: Norton.

SUTKER, P. B., DAVIS, J. M., UDDO, M., & DITTA, S. R. (1995). Assessment of psychological distress in Persian Gulf troops: Ethnicity and gender comparisons. *Journal of Personality Assessment, 64,* 415–427.

SVENSON, O. (1981). Are we all less risky and

more skillful than our fellow drivers? *Acta Psychologica, 47,* 143–148.

SWARTZ, M., BLAZER, D., GEORGE, L., & WINFIELD, I. (1990). Estimating the prevalence of borderline personality disorder in the community. *Journal of Personality Disorders, 4,* 257–272.

SWEDO, S. PIETRINI, P., & LEONARD, H. (1992). Cerebral glucose metabolism in childhood-onset obsessive-compulsive disorder. *Archives of General Psychiatry, 49,* 690–694.

SWETS, J. A., & BJORK, R. A. (1990). Enhancing human performance: An evaluation of "new age" techniques considered by the U.S. Army. *Psychological Science, 1,* 85–96.

SWINNEY, D. A. (1979). Lexical access during sentence comprehension: Consideration of context effects. *Journal of Verbal Learning and Verbal Behavior, 18,* 645–659.

SYMONS, D. (1992). On the use and misuse of Darwinism in the study of human behavior. In J. H. Barkow & L. Cosmides (Eds.) et al., *The adapted mind: Evolutionary psychology and the generation of culture* (pp. 137–159). New York: Oxford University Press.

TANENHAUS, M. G., LEIMAN, J., & SEIDEN-BERG, M. (1979). Evidence for multiple stages in the processing of ambiguous words in syntactic contexts. *Journal of Verbal Learning and Verbal Behavior, 18,* 427–441.

TARTTER, V. C. (1986). *Language processes*. New York: Holt, Rinehart & Winston.

TAVRIS, C., & SADD, S. (1977). *The Redbook report on female sexuality*. New York: Dell.

TAYLOR, S. (1999). *Health psychology* (4th ed.). Boston: McGraw-Hill.

TAYLOR, S. E., & BROWN, J. D. (1988). Illusion and well-being: A social psychological perspective on mental health. *Psychological Bulletin, 103,* 193–210.

TAYLOR, S., KEMENY, M., ASPINWALL, L., SCHNEIDER, S., RODRIGUEZ, R., & HERBERT, M. (1992). Optimism, coping, psychological distress, and high-risk sexual behavior among men at risk for acquired immunodeficiency syndrome (AIDS). *Journal of Personality and Social Psychology, 63,* 460–473.

TAYLOR, S. E., & THOMPSON, S. C. (1982). Stalking the elusive "vividness" effect. *Psychological Review, 89,* 155–181.

TEITELBAUM, P., & EPSTEIN, A. N. (1962). The lateral hypothalamic syndrome: Recovery of feeding and drinking after lateral hypothalamic lesions. *Psychological Review, 69,* 74–90.

TELLEGEN, A., LYKKEN, D. T., BOUCHARD, T. J., JR., WILCOX, K. J., SEGAL, N. L., & RICH, S. (1988). Personality similarity in twins reared apart and together. *Journal of Personality and Social Psychology, 54,* 1031–1039.

TELLER, D. Y., & MOVSHON, J. A. (1986). Visual development. *Vision Research, 26,* 1483–1506.

TEMPLIN, M. C. (1957). *Certain language skills in children: Their development and interrelationships*. Minneapolis: University of Minnesota Press.

TERMAN, L. M., & ODEN, M. H. (1959). *Genetic studies of genius, Vol. IV: The gifted group at midlife*. Stanford, CA: Stanford University Press.

TERRACE, H. S., PETITTO, L. A., SANDERS, D. J., & BEVER, T. G. (1979). Can an ape create a sentence? *Science, 206,* 891–902.

TESSER, A., & BRODIE, M. (1971). A note on the evaluation of a "computer date." *Psychonomic Science, 23,* 300.

THIGPEN, C. H., & CLECKLEY, H. (1957). *The three faces of eve*. New York: McGraw-Hill.

THOMAS, A., & CHESS, S. (1977). *Temperament and development*. New York: Brunner/Mazel.

THOMAS, A., & CHESS, S. (1986). The New York longitudinal study: From infancy to early adult life. In R. Plomin & J. Dunn (Eds.), *The study of temperament: Changes, continuities and challenges* (pp. 39–52). Hillsdale, NJ: Erlbaum.

THOMAS, A., & CHESS, S., BIRCH, H., HERTZIG, M., & KORN, S. (1963). *Behavioral individuality in early childhood*. New York: New York University Press.

THOMAS, E. L., & ROBINSON, H. A. (1982). *Improving reading in every class*. Boston: Allyn and Bacon.

THOMPSON, R. A., LAMB, M., & ESTES, D. (1982). Stability of infant-mother attachment and its relationship to changing life circumstances in an unselected middle-class sample. *Child Development, 53,* 144–148.

THOMPSON, S. K. (1975). Gender labels and early sex role development. *Child Development, 46,* 339–347.

THOMPSON, W. R. (1954). The inheritance and development of intelligence. *Proceedings of the Association for Research on Nervous and Mental Disease, 33,* 209–231.

THORESEN, C. E., TELCH, M. J., & EAGLESTON, J. R. (1981). Altering Type A behavior. *Psychosomatics, 8,* 472–482.

THORNDYKE, E. L. (1898). Animal intelligence: An experimental study of the associative processes in animals. *Psychological Monographs, 2.*

THORPE, G. L., & OLSON, S. L. (1997). *Behavior therapy: Concepts, procedures, and applications* (2nd ed.). Boston: Allyn and Bacon.

THURSTONE, L. L. (1938). Primary mental abilities. *Psychometric Monographs*, No. 1. Chicago: University of Chicago Press.

TIZARD, B., & REES, J. (1975). The effect of early institutional rearing on the behavioural problems and affectional relationships of four-year-old children. *Journal of Child Psychology and Psychiatry, 16,* 61–73.

TOATES, F. (1986). *Motivational systems*. Cambridge, England: Cambridge University Press.

TOLMAN, E. C. (1932). *Purpose behavior in animals and men*. New York: Appleton-Century-Crofts. (Reprinted 1967. New York: Irvington.)

TOMPKINS, S. S. (1962). *Affect, imagery, consciousness: Vol. 1. The positive affects*. New York: Springer.

TOMPKINS, S. S. (1980). Affect as amplification: Some modifications in theory. In R. Plutchik & H. Kellerman (Eds.), *Emotion: Theory, research and experience* (Vol. 1). New York: Academic Press.

TORGERSEN, S. (1986). Genetic factors in moderately severe and mild affective disorders. *Archives of General Psychiatry, 49,* 690–694.

TOWNSHEND, B., COTTER, N., VAN COMPERNOLLE, D., & WHITE, R. L. (1987). Pitch perception by cochlear implant subjects. *Journal of the Acoustical Society of America, 82,* 106–115.

TRAFIMOW, D., TRIANDIS, H. C., & GOTO, S. G. (1991). Some tests of the distinction between the private self and the collective self. *Journal of Personality and Social Psychology, 60,* 649–655.

TREISMAN, A. (1969). Strategies and models of selective attention. *Psychological Review, 76,* 282–299.

TREISMAN, A. M. (1986). Features and objects in visual processing. *Scientific American, 255,* 114B–125.

TRIANDIS, H. C. (1989). The self and social behavior in different cultures. *Psychological Review, 96,* 506–520.

TRINDER, J. (1988). Subjective insomnia without objective findings: A pseudodiagnostic classification. *Psychological Bulletin, 103,* 87–94.

TRIPP, C. A. (1987). *The homosexual matrix* (2nd ed.). New York: New American Library.

TULVING, E. (1974). Cue-dependent forgetting. *American Scientist, 62,* 74–82.

TULVING, E. (1983). *The elements of episodic memory*. New York: Oxford University Press.

TULVING, E. (1985). How many memory systems are there? *American Psychologist, 40,* 385–398.

TULVING, E., KAPUR, S., CRAIK, F. I. M., MOSCOVITCH, M., & HOULE, S. (1994). Hemispheric encoding/retrieval asymmetry in episodic memory: Positron emission tomography findings. *Proceedings of the National Academy of Science of the United States of America, 91,* 2016–2020.

TULVING, E., KAPUR, S., MARKOWITSCH, H. J., CRAIK, F. I. M., HABIB, R., & HOULE, S. (1994). Neuroanatomical correlates of retrieval in episodic memory: Auditory sentence recognition. *Proceedings of the National Academy of Science of the United States of America, 91,* 2012–2015.

TULVING, E., & PEARLSTONE, Z. (1966). Availability versus accessibility of information in memory for words. *Journal of Verbal Learning and Verbal Behavior, 5,* 381–391.

TUMA, J. M. (1989). Mental health services for children: The state of the art. *American Psychologist, 44,* 188–199.

TUNNELL, G. (1981). Sex role and cognitive schemata: Person perception in feminine and androgynous women. *Journal of Personality and Social Psychology, 40,* 1126–1136.

TURIEL, E. (1983). *The development of social knowledge: Morality and convention*. Cambridge, England: Cambridge University Press.

TURNER, M. E., PRATKANIS, A. R., PROBASCO, P., & LEVER, C. (1992). Threat, cohesion, and group effectiveness: Testing a social identity maintenance perspective in groupthink. *Journal of Personality and Social Psychology, 63,* 781–796.

TVERSKY, A., & KAHNEMAN, D. (1973). On the psychology of prediction. *Psychological Review, 80,* 237–251.

TVERSKY, A., & KAHNEMAN, D. (1983). Extensional versus intuitive reasoning: The conjunction fallacy in probability judgment. *Psychological Review, 90,* 293–315.

TYE-MURRAY, N., SPENCER, L., & WOODWORTH, G. G. (1995). Acquisition of speech by children who have prolonged cochlear implant experience. *Journal of Speech and Hearing Research, 38,* 327–337.

TYLER, H. (1977). The unsinkable Jeane Dixon. *The Humanist, 37,* 6–9.

URSIN, H. (1978). Activation, coping, and psychosomatics. In H. Ursin, E. Baade, & S. Levine (Eds.), *Psychobiology of stress: A study of coping men*. New York: Academic Press.

UTTS, J. (1986). The gansfeld debate: A statistician's perspective. *Journal of Parapsychology, 50,* 393–402.

VAN VORT, W., & SMITH, G. P. (1987). Sham feeding experience produces a conditioned increase of meal size. *Appetite, 9,* 21–29.

VAUGHN, B. E., LEFEVER, G. B., SEIFER, R., & BARGLOW, P. (1989). Attachment behavior, attachment security, and temperament during infancy. *Child Development, 60,* 728–737.

VAUGHN, C. E., & LEFF, J. P. (1976, August). The influence of family and social factors on the course of psychiatric illness: A comparison of schizophrenic and depressed neurotic patients. *British Journal of Psychiatry, 129,* 125–137.

VELMANS, M. (1991). Is human information processing conscious? *Behavioral and Brain Sciences, 14,* 651–726.

VISINTAINER, M. A., VOLPICELLI, J. R., & SELIGMAN, M. E. P. (1982). Tumor rejection in rats after inescapable or escapable shock. *Science, 216,* 437–439.

VOGT, T., & BELLUSCIO, D. (1987). Controversies in plastic surgery: Suction-assisted lipectomy (SAL) and the HCG (human chorionic gonadotropin) protocol for obesity treatment. *Aesthetic Plastic Surgery, 11,* 131–56.

VON LANG, J., & SIBYLL, C. (Eds.) (1983). *Eichmann interrogated* (R. Manheim, Trans.). New York: Farrar, Straus & Giroux.

VYGOTSKY, L. S. (1986). *Thought and language* (A. Kozulin, Trans.). Cambridge, MA: MIT Press. (originally published 1934)

WADDEN, T. A., BERKOWITZ, R. I., VOGT, R. A., STEEN, S. N., STUNKARD, A. J., & FOSTER, G. D. (1997). Lifestyle modification in the pharmacological treatment of obesity: A pilot investigation of a potential primary care approach. *Obesity Research, 5,* 218–226.

WAGNER, W. M., & MONNET, M. (1979). Attitudes of college professors toward extrasensory perception. *Zetetic Scholar, 5,* 7–17.

WALKER, C. E., HEDBERG, A., CLEMENT, P. W., & WRIGHT, L. (1981). *Clinical procedures for behavior therapy*. Englewood Cliffs, NJ: Prentice-Hall.

WALKER, E. (1978). *Explorations in the biology of language*. Montgomery, VT: Bradford.

WALLACH, M. A., KOGAN, N., & BEM, D. J. (1962). Group influence on individual risk taking. *Journal of Abnormal and Social Psychology, 65,* 75–86.

WALLACH, M. A., KOGAN, N., & BEM, D. J. (1964). Diffusion of responsibility and level of risk taking in groups. *Journal of Abnormal and Social Psychology, 68,* 263–274.

WALLACH, M. A., & WALLACH, L. (1983). *Psychology's sanction for selfishness*. San Francisco: Freeman.

WALSTER, E., ARONSON, E., ABRAHAMS, D., & ROTTMAN, L. (1966). Importance of physical attractiveness in dating behavior. *Journal of Personality and Social Psychology, 4,* 508–516.

WALTERS, J., & GARDNER, H. (1985). The development and education of intelligences. In F. Link (Ed.), *Essays on the intellect*. Washington, DC: Curriculum Development Associates/Association for Supervision and Curriculum Development.

WALZER, M. (1970). *Obligations*. Cambridge, MA: Harvard University Press.

WAMPOLD, B. E., MONDIN, G. W., MOODY, M., STICH, F., BENSON, K., & AHN, H. (1997). A meta-analysis of outcome studies comparing bona fide psychotherapies: Empirically, "all must have prizes." *Psychological Bulletin, 122,* 203–215.

WARD, I. L. (1992). Sexual behavior: The products of perinatal hormonal and prepubertal social factors. In A. A. Gerall, H. Motz, & I. L. Ward (Eds.), *Sexual differentiation* (pp. 157–179). New York: Plenum.

WARRINGTON, E. K., & SHALLICE, T. (1984). Category specific semantic impairments. *Brain, 107,* 829–853.

WARRINGTON, E. K., & WEISKRANTZ, L. (1978). Further analysis of the prior learning effect in amnesic patients. *Neuropsychologica, 16,* 169–177.

WASON, P. C., & JOHNSON-LAIRD, P. N. (1972). *Psychology of reasoning: Structure and content*. London: Batsford.

WASSERMAN, E. A. (1990). Detecting response-outcome relations: Toward an understanding of the causal texture of the environment. *Psychology of Learning and Motivation, 26,* 27–82.

WATERMAN, A. S. (1985). Identity in the context of adolescent psychology. In A. S. Waterman (Ed.), *Identity in adolescence: Progress and contents (New directions for child development, no. 30)*. San Francisco: Jossey-Bass.

WATSON, J. B. (1930). *Behaviorism* (rev. ed.). New York: Norton.

WATSON, J. B., & RAYNER, R. (1920). Conditioned emotional reactions. *Journal of Experimental Psychology, 3,* 1–14.

WEAVER, E. G. (1949). *Theory of hearing.* New York: Wiley.

WECHSLER, D. (1958). *The measurement and appraisal of adult intelligence.* Baltimore: Williams.

WECHSLER, H., DAVENPORT, A., DOWDALL, G., MOEYKENS, B., & CASTILLO, S. (1994). Health and behavioral consequences of binge drinking in college, a national survey of students at 140 campuses. *Journal of the American Medical Association, 272,* 1672–1677.

WECHSLER, H., DOWDALL, G. W., MAENNER, G., GLEDHILL-HOYT, J., & LEE, H. (1998). Changes in binge drinking and related problems among American college students between 1993 and 1997. *Journal of American College Health, 47,* 57–68.

WEGNER, D. M., SCHNEIDER, D. J., CARTER, S., III, & WHITE, L. (1987). Paradoxical consequences of thought suppression. *Journal of Personality and Social Psychology, 53,* 1–9.

WEIGLE, D. S. (1994). Appetite and the regulation of body composition. *Faseb Journal, 8,* 302–10.

WEINBERG, M. S., SCHWARTZ, G. E., & DAVIDSON, R. E. (1979). Low-anxious, high-anxious, and repressive coping styles: Psychometric patterns and behavioral and physiological responses to stress. *Journal of Abnormal Psychology, 88,* 369–380.

WEINE, S. M., BECKER, D. F., MCGLASHAN, T. H., LAUB, D., LAZROVE, S., VOJVODA, D., & HYMAN, L. (1995). Psychiatric consequences of "ethnic cleansing": Clinical assessments and trauma testimonies of newly resettled Bosnian refugees. *American Journal of Psychiatry, 152,* 536–542.

WEINE, S. M., VOJVODA, D., BECKER, D. F., MCGLASHAN, T. H., HODZIC, E., LAUB, D., HYMAN, L., SAWYER, M., & LAZROVE, S. PTSD symptoms in Bosnian refugees 1 year after resettlement in the United States. *American Journal of Psychiatry, 155,* 562–564.

WEINSTEIN, N. D. (1980). Unrealistic optimism about future events. *Journal of Personality and Social Psychology, 39,* 806–820.

WEISS, J. M., GLAZER, H. I., POHORECKY, L. A., BRICK, J., & MILLER, N. E. (1975). Effects of chronic exposure to stressors on avoidance-escape behavior and on brain norepinephrine. *Psychosomatic Medicine, 37,* 522–534.

WEISS, R. D., MIRIN, S. M., & BARTEL, R. L. (1994). *Cocaine* (2nd ed.). Washington, DC: American Psychiatric Press, Inc.

WEISSMAN, M. M. (1993). Family genetic studies of panic disorder. Conference on panic and anxiety: A decade of progress. *Journal of Psychiatric Research, 27* (Suppl.), 69–78.

WEISSTEIN, N. A., & WONG, E. (1986). Figure-ground organization and the spatial and temporal responses of the visual system. In E. C. Schwab & H. C. Nusbaum (Eds.), *Pattern recognition by humans and machines. Volume 2. Visual perception* (pp. 31–64). Orlando: Academic Press.

WEISZ, J. R., DONENBERG, G., HAN, S., & KAUNECKIS, D. (1995). Child and adolescent psychotherapy outcomes in experiments versus clinics: Why the disparity? *Journal of Abnormal Child Psychology, 23,* 83–106.

WELLER, L., & WELLER, A. (1993). Human menstrual synchrony: A critical assessment. *Neuroscience & Behavioral Reviews, 17,* 427–439.

WERTHEIMER, M. (1912/1932). Experimentelle studien uber das sehen von beuegung. *Zeitschrift Fuer Psychologie, 61,* 161–265.

WERTHEIMER, M. (2000). *A brief history of psychology* (6th ed.). Fort Worth: Harcourt.

WEST, C., & ZIMMERMAN, D. H. (1983). Small insults: A study of interruptions in cross-sex conversations between unacquainted persons. In B. Thorne, C. Kramarae, & N. Henley (Eds.), *Language, gender, and society.* Rowley, MA: Newbury House.

WESTBROOK, G. L. (1994). Glutamate receptor update. *Current Opinion in Neurobiology, 4,* 337–346.

WESTEN, D. (1998). The scientific legacy of Sigmund Freud: Toward a psychodynamically informed psychological science. *Psychological Bulletin, 124,* 333–371.

WHITE, C. (1977). Unpublished Ph.D. dissertation, Catholic University, Washington, DC.

WHITE, G. L., FISHBEIN, S., & RUTSTEIN, J. (1981). Passionate love and the misattribution of arousal. *Journal of Personality and Social Psychology, 41,* 56–62.

WHITE, G. L., & KIGHT, T. D. (1984). Misattribution of arousal and attraction: Effects of salience of explanations for arousal. *Journal of Experimental Social Psychology, 20,* 55–64.

WHYTE, W. H. (1956). *The organization man.* New York: Simon & Schuster.

WIEBE, D. J., & MCCALLUM, D. M. (1986). Health practices and hardiness as mediators in the stress-illness relationship. *Health Psychology, 5,* 425–438.

WILCOXIN, H. C., DRAGOIN, W. B., & KRAL, P. A. (1971). Illness-induced aversions in rat and quail: Relative salience of visual and gustatory cues. *Science, 171,* 823–828.

WILKES, A. L., & KENNEDY, R. A. (1969). Relationship between pausing and retrieval latency in sentences of varying grammatical form. *Journal of Experimental Psychology, 79,* 241–245.

WILKINS, W. (1984). Psychotherapy: The powerful placebo. *Journal of Consulting and Clinical Psychology, 52,* 570–573.

WILLIAMS, D. C. (1959). The elimination of tantrum behavior by extinction procedures. *Journal of Abnormal and Social Psychology, 59,* 269.

WILLIAMS, M. D., & HOLLAN, J. D. (1981). The process of retrieval from very long-term memory. *Cognitive Science, 5,* 87–119.

WILLIAMS, R. B. (1995). Somatic consequences of stress. In M. J. Friedman (Ed.), *Neurobiological and clinical consequences of stress: From normal adaptation to post-traumatic stress disorder.* Philadelphia: Lippincott-Raven.

WILLIAMS, R. B., JR., BAREFOOT, J. C., HANEY, T. L., HARRELL, F. E., BLUMENTHAL, J. A., PRYOR, D. B., & PETERSON, B. (1988). Type A behavior and angiographically documented coronary atherosclerosis in a sample of 2,289 patients. *Psychosomatic Medicine, 50,* 139–152.

WILSON, E. O. (1975). *Sociobiology.* Cambridge, MA: Harvard University Press.

WILSON, E. O. (1978). *On human nature.* Cambridge, MA: Harvard University Press.

WILSON, E. O. (1963). Pheromones. *Scientific American, 208,* 100–114.

WILSON, M. A., & MCNAUGHTON, B. L. (1994). Reactivation of hippocampal ensemble memories during sleep. *Science, 265,* 676–679.

WILSON, T. D., DUNN, D. S., KRAFT, D., & LISLE, D. J. (1989). Introspection, attitude change, and attitude-behavior consistency: The disruptive effects of explaining why we feel the way we do. In L. Berkowitz (Ed.), *Advances in experimental social psychology* (Vol. 22). San Diego: Academic Press.

WILSON, T. D., LASER, P. S., & STONE, J. I. (1982). Judging the predictors of one's mood: Accuracy and the use of shared theories. *Journal of Experimental Social Psychology, 18,* 537–556.

WILSON, W. H., & CLAUSEN, A. M. (1995). 18-month outcome of clozapine treatment for 100 patients in a state psychiatric hospital. *Psychiatric Services, 46,* 386–389.

WILSON, W. R. (1979). Feeling more than we can know: Exposure effects without learning. *Journal of Personality and Social Psychology, 37,* 811–821.

WINCH, R. F., KTSANES, T., & KTSANES, V. (1954). The theory of complementary needs in mate selection: An analytic and descriptive study. *American Sociological Review, 29,* 241–249.

WINDHOLZ, M. J., MARMAR, C. R., & HOROWITZ, M. J. (1985). A review of the research on conjugal bereavement: Impact on health and efficacy of intervention. *Comprehensive Psychiatry, 26,* 433–447.

WINGER, G., HOFFMAN, F. G., & WOODS, J. H. (1992). *A handbook on drug and alcohol abuse* (3rd ed.). New York: Oxford University Press.

WINSON, J. (1990). The meaning of dreams. *Scientific American, 262,* 86–96.

WISE, R. A. (1982). Neuroleptics and operant behavior: The anhedonia hypothesis. *Behavioral and Brain Sciences,* 539–587.

WISNIEWSKI, E. J., & MEDIN, D. L. (1991). Harpoons and longsticks: The interaction of theory and similarity in rule induction. In D. Fisher, M. Pazzani, & P. Langley (Eds.), *Concept formation: Knowledge and experience in unsupervised learning*. San Mateo, CA: Morgan-Kaufman.

WOLCHIK, S. A., BEGGS, V. E., WINCZE, P. P., SAKHEIM, D. K., BARLOW, D. H., & MAVISSAKALIAN, M. (1980). The effect of emotional arousal on subsequent sexual arousal in men. *Journal of Abnormal Psychology, 89,* 595–598.

WOLMAN, B. B., DALE, L. A., SCHMEIDLER, G. R., & ULLMAN, M. (Eds.) (1986). *Handbook of parapsychology*. New York: Van Nostrand & Reinhold.

WOLPE, J. (1958). *Psychotherapy by reciprocal inhibition*. Stanford, CA: Stanford University Press.

WOOD, G. (1986). *Fundamentals of psychological research* (3rd ed.). Boston: Little, Brown.

WOOD, W., LUNDGREN, S., OUELLETTE, J. A., BUSCEME, S., & BLACKSTONE, T. (1994). Minority influence: A meta-analytic review of social influence processes. *Psychological Bulletin, 115,* 323–345.

WOOD, W., WANG, F. Y. & CHACHERIE, J. G. (1991). Effects of media violence on viewers' aggression in unconstrained social situtions. *Psychological Bulletin, 109,* 371–383.

WOODY, R. H., & ROBERTSON, M. (1988). *Becoming a clinical psychologist*. Madison, CT: International Universities Press.

WORD, C. O., ZANNA, M. P., & COOPER, J. (1974). The nonverbal mediation of self-fulfilling prophecies in interracial interaction. *Journal of Experimental Social Psychology, 10,* 109–120.

WORTMAN, C. B., & BREHM, J. W. (1975). Responses to uncontrollable outcomes: An integration of reactance theory and the learned helplessness model. *Advances in Experimental and Social Psychology, 8,* 277–236.

WRIGHT, L. (1988). The Type A behavior pattern and coronary artery disease, quest for the active ingredients and the elusive mechanism. *American Psychologist, 43,* 2–14.

WURTZ, R. H., GOLDBERG, M. E., & ROBINSON, D. L. (1980). Behavioral modulation of visual responses in monkeys. *Progress in Psychobiology and Physiological Psychology, 9,* 42–83.

YAGER, T., LAUFER, R., & GALLOPS, M. (1984). Some problems associated with war experience in men of the Vietnam generation. *Archives of General Psychiatry, 41,* 327–333.

YARBUS, D. L. (1967). *Eye movements and vision*. New York: Plenum.

YESAVAGE, J. A., LEIER, V. O., DENARI, M., & HOLLISTER, L. E. (1985). Carry-over effect of marijuana intoxication on aircraft pilot performance: A preliminary report. *American Journal of Psychiatry, 142,* 1325–1330.

YOST, W. A., & NIELSON, D. W. (1985). *Fundamentals of hearing* (2nd ed.). New York: Holt, Rinehart & Winston.

YU, B., ZHANG, W., JING, Q., PENG, R., ZHANG, G., & SIMON, H. A. (1985). STM capacity for Chinese and English language materials. *Memory and Cognition, 13,* 202–207.

ZAJONC, R. B. (1965). Social facilitation. *Science, 149,* 269–274.

ZAJONC, R. B. (1968). Attitudinal effects of mere exposure. *Journal of Personality and Social Psychology,* Monograph Supplement 9 (No. 2), 1–29.

ZAJONC, R. B. (1980). Compresence. In P. B. Paulus (Ed.), *Psychology of group influence*. Hillsdale, NJ: Erlbaum.

ZAJONC, R. B. (1984). On the primacy of affect. *American Psychologist, 39,* 117–123.

ZAJONC, R. B., HEINGARTNER, A., & HERMAN, E. M. (1969). Social enhancement and impairment of performance in the cockroach. *Journal of Personality and Social Psychology, 13,* 83–92.

ZAJONC, R. B., MURPHY, S. T., & INGLEHART, M. (1989). Feeling and facial efference: Implications of the vascular theory of emotion. *Psychological Review*.

ZALUTSKY, R. A., & NICOLL, R. A. (1990). Comparison of two forms of longterm potentiation in single hippocampal neurons. *Science, 248,* 1619–1624.

ZAMANSKY, H. S., & BARTIS, S. P. (1985). The dissociation of an experience: The hidden observer observed. *Journal of Abnormal Psychology, 94,* 243–248.

ZEKI, S. (1993). *A vision of the brain*. Boston: Blackwell Scientific Publications.

ZELAZO, P. R., ZELAZO, N. A., & KOLB, S. (1972). Walking in the newborn. *Science, 176,* 314–315.

ZHANG, Y., PROENCA, R., MAFFEI, M., BARONE, M., LEOPOLD, L., & FRIEDMAN, J. M. (1994). Positional cloning of the mouse *obese* gene and its human homologue. *Nature, 372,* 425–431.

ZILLMANN, D. (1984). *Connections between sex and aggression*. Hillsdale, NJ: Erlbaum.

ZILLMANN, D., & BRYANT, J. (1974). Effect of residual excitation on the emotional response to provocation and delayed aggressive behavior. *Journal of Personality and Social Psychology, 30,* 782–791.

ZIMBARDO, P. G. (1970). The human choice: Individuation, reason and order versus deindividuation, impulse and chaos. In W. J. Arnold & D. Levine (Eds.), *Nebraska symposium on motivation* (Vol. 16). Lincoln: University of Nebraska Press.

ZIMBARDO, P. G. (1972). Pathology of imprisonment. *Society, 9,* 4–8.

ZOLA-MORGAN, S., & SQUIRE, L. R. (1985). Medial-temporal lesions in monkeys impair memory on a variety of tasks sensitive to human amnesia. *Behavioral Neuroscience, 99,* 22–34.

ZOLA-MORGAN, S. M., SQUIRE, L. R., & AMARAL, D. G. (1989). Lesions of the hippocampal formation but not lesions of the fornix or the mamalary nuclei produce long-lasting memory impairments in monkeys. *Journal of Neuroscience, 9,* 898–913.

ZOLA-MORGAN, S. M., & SQUIRE, L. R. (1990). The primate hippocampal formation: Evidence for a time-limited role in memory storage. *Science, 250,* 228–290.

ZUBER, J. A., CROTT, H. W., & WERNER, J. (1992). Choice shift and group polarization: An analysis of the status of arguments and social decision schemes. *Journal of Personality and Social Psychology, 62,* 50–61.

ZUCKER, K. J., & BRADLEY, S. J. (1995). *Gender identity disorder and psychosexual problems in children and adolescents*. New York: Guilford.

ZUCKERMAN, M. (1979). *Sensation seeking: Beyond the optimal level of arousal*. Hillsdale, NJ: Erlbaum.

ZUCKERMAN, M. (1991). *Psychobiology of personality*. Cambridge, England: Cambridge University Press.

ZUCKERMAN, M. (1995). Good and bad humors: Biochemical bases of personality and its disorders. *Psychological Science, 6,* 325–332.

ZURIF, E. B., (1990). Language and the brain. In D. N. Osherson & H. Lasnik (Eds.), *An invitation to cognitive science: Language* (Vol. 1). Cambridge, MA: MIT Press.

ZURIF, E. B., CARAMAZZA, A., MYERSON, R., & GALVIN, J. (1974). Semantic feature representations for normal and aphasic language. *Brain and Language, 1,* 167–187.

Copyrights, Acknowledgments, and Illustration Credits

McVav/Tony Stone Images; p. 503, © Tony Freeman/PhotoEdit; p. 507, (bottom) © Mary Kate Denny/PhotoEdit, (top) © Leinwand/Monkmeyer; p. 509, © Amy C. Etra/PhotoEdit; p. 512, (left) © Mary Kate Denny/PhotoEdit, (middle) © Burns/Monkmeyer, (right) © Mimi Forsythe/Monkmeyer; p. 520, Courtesy of Neil D. Weinstein; p. 521, Courtesy of Shelley E. Taylor

Chapter 15

p. 525, © Robert Yager/Tony Stone Images; p. 527, © Steven Peters/Tony Stone Images; p. 534, © Gary A. Conner/PhotoEdit; p. 536, AP/Wide World Photos; p. 539, © Dr. Lewis Baxter/Peter Arnold, Inc.; p. 541, © CORBIS/Reuters; p. 550, Privizhorn Collection, Ruprecht-KarlspUniversitat Heidelberg Klinikum; p. 552, Laboratory of Psychology and Psycholpathology, National Institute of Mental Health; p. 553, © Photo Researchers; p. 555, © Associated Press/AP/World Wide Photos; p. 562, Courtesy of Caryn L. Carlson

Chapter 16

p. 569, CORBIS/Bettmann; p. 572, © Bruce Ayers/Tony Stone Images; p. 583, (top) © David Harry Stewart/Tony Stone Images, (bottom) © LeDuc/Monkmeyer; p. 586, © Comstock; p. 596, © Michael Newman/PhotoEdit; p. 597, © Shackman/Monkmeyer; p. 599, © Richard Hutchings/PhotoEdit; p. 600, Courtesy of Keith Humphreys

Chapter 17

p. 608, © Les Stone/Sygma; p. 610, © Robert Brenner/PhotoEdit; p. 616, © Don Smetzer/Tony Stone Images; p. 622, © Michael Newman/PhotoEdit; p. 623, © Jeffrey Markowitz/Sygma; p. 628, © Cleo/PhotoEdit; p. 630, (left) © Shaefer/Monkmeyer, (right) © Zigy Kaluzny/Tony Stone Images; p. 632, © Comstock; p. 635, © Bob Daemmrich; p. 637, © Office of News and Public Affairs, University of Wisconsin–Madison/Photographer: Jeff Miller

Chapter 18

p. 641, © Tony Stone Images; p. 643, © Mark E. Gibson; p. 644, © SYGMA; p. 645, Philip G. Zimbardo, Inc.; p. 646, © Robert Brenner/PhotoEdit; p. 651, The Asch Study of the Resistance of Majority Opinion from *Scientific American*, November, 1995, Vol. 193, No. 5, by Solomon E. Asch; p. 653, © Jon Jones/Sygma; p. 654, Milgram's "Shock Generator" (four photos): from the film "Obedience," distributed by the New York University Film Library; copyright © 1965 by Stanley Milgram. Reprinted by permission of Alexandra Milgram; p. 656, © Jeff Greenberg/PhotoEdit; p. 662, (left) © Michael Newman/PhotoEdit, (right) David Young-Wolff/PhotoEdit; p. 667, © A. Ramey/PhotoEdit; p. 669, © John Newbauer/PhotoEdit; p. 649, © Tony Freeman/PhotoEdit; p. 672, Courtesy of Madeline E. Heilman; p. 673, Courtesy of Faye J. Crosby

Figures, Boxes, and Tables

Figure 1-2: Sheingold, K. and Tenney, Y. J., (1982) "Recall of An Early Memory," adapted from "Memory for a Salient Childhood Event," from U. Neisser (ed.) *Memory Observed: Remembering in Natural Context,* Copyright © 1982 by W.H. Freeman & Company. Adapted by permission of the publisher. Figure 1-3: Eron, L., et al. (1972) "Does Television Violence Cause Aggression?"

American Psychologist, 27:253–262. Copyright © 1972 by The American Psychological Association. Adapted by permission.

Figures 2-1, 2-2, 2-3: Adapted from *Human Anatomy* by Anthony J. Gaudin and Kenneth C. Jones. Copyright © 1988 by Anthony J. Gaudin and Kenneth C. Jones. Reprinted by permission of the authors. Figure 2-6: Adapted from *Search for the Human Mind* by Robert Sternberg. Copyright © 1994 by Harcourt Brace & Company, reproduced by permission of the publisher. Figure 2-7: Adapted from *Human Anatomy* by Anthony J. Gaudin and Kenneth C. Jones. Copyright © 1988 by Anthony J. Gaudin and Kenneth C. Jones. Reprinted by permission of the authors. Figure 2-9: Adapted from *Psychology,* 3rd edition, by Margaret Matlin. Copyright © 1992 by Harcourt Brace & Company, reproduced by permission of the publisher. Figures 2-11, 2-12, 2-14: Adapted from *Human Anatomy* by Anthony J. Gaudin and Kenneth C. Jones. Copyright © 1988 by Anthony J. Gaudin and Kenneth C. Jones. Reprinted by permission of the authors. Figures 2-15, 2-16: Reprinted from *Neuropsychologia,* Volume 9, by R. D. Nebes and W. Sperry, p. 247. Copyright © 1971, with kind permission of Elsevier Science, Ltd., The Boulevard, Langford Lane, Kidlington, Oxford, OX5 1DX, UK. Figures 2-17, 2-18: Adapted from *Human Anatomy* by Anthony J. Gaudin and Kenneth C. Jones. Copyright © 1988 by Anthony J. Gaudin and Kenneth C. Jones. Reprinted by permission of the authors. Figure 2-21: Reprinted from *Proceedings of the Association for Research in Nervous and Mental Diseases,* Volume 33, by R. W. Thompson, pp. 209–231. Copyright © 1954, with kind permission of Elsevier Science, Ltd., The Boulevard, Langford Lane, Kidlington, Oxford, OX5 1DX, UK.

Table 3-1: from *Review of Child Development Research,* Vol. 1, edited by M. L. Hoffman & L. W. Hoffman. Copyright © 1964 by the Russell Sage Foundation. Reprinted by permission of the Russell Sage Foundation. Figure 3-6: adapted from Balliargeon, R., "Object Permanence in 3 1/2 and 4 1/2 Month Old Infants," from *Developmental Psychology,* 23:655–664. Copyright © 1987. Reprinted by permission of the Academic Press. Table 3-2: Kohlberg, L., (1969) "Stages of Moral Reasoning," from "Stage and Sequence: The Cognitive Developmental Approach to Socialization," in *Handbook of Socialization Theory and Research,* D. A. Goslin (ed.) Reprinted by permission of Rand McNally. Figure 3-8: Reprinted by permission of the publishers from *Infancy: Its Place in Human Development* by Jerome Kagan, Richard B. Kearsley, & Philip R. Zelazo, Cambridge, MA: Harvard University Press. Copyright © 1978 by the President and Fellows of Harvard College.

Table 4-1: Galanter, E. (1962) "Contemporary Psychophysics," from Roger Brown & collaborators (eds.), *New Directions in Psychology,* Vol. 1. Reprinted by permission of Roger Brown. Figure 4-5: from *Sensation and Perception* by E. Bruce Goldstein. Copyright © 1989, 1984, 1980 by Wadsworth Publishing Company. Reprinted by permission of Brooks/Cole Publishing Company, a division of International Thomson Publishing, Inc. Pacific Grove, CA 93950. Figures 4-6, 4-7: Adapted from *Human Color Vision* by Robert M. Boynton, copyright © 1979 by Holt, Rinehart & Winston. Reprinted by permission of Harcourt Brace & Company.

Figure 4-8: Dowling, J. E. and Boycott, B. B. (1969) "Organization of the Primate Retina" from *Proceedings of the Royal Society of London,* Series B, Vol. 166, pp. 80–111. Adapted by permission of the Royal Society of London. Figure 4-20: Wald, G. and Brown, P. K. (1965) "Human Color Vision and Color Blindness," from *Cold Spring Harbor Symposia on Quantitative Biology,* 30:345–359. By permission of the American Psychological Association. Figure 4-24: Adapted from *Human Anatomy and Physiology* by Anthony J. Gaudin, Kenneth C. Jones, James G. Cotanche, & Josephine Ryan. Copyright © 1988 by Anthony J. Gaudin and Kenneth C. Jones. Reprinted by permission of the authors. Figure 4-25: Figure from *Sensation and Perception,* 3rd edition, by Stanley Coren & Laurence Ward, copyright © 1989 by Harcourt Brace & Company. Reproduced by permission of the publisher. Figure 4-28: Erickson, E. H., "Sensory Neural Patterns in Gustation," from Zotterman (ed.) *Olfaction and Taste,* Vol. I, pp. 205–213. Copyright © 1963, with kind permission of Elsevier Science, Ltd., The Boulevard, Langford Lane, Kidlington, Oxford, OX5 1DX, UK. Figure 4-30: Kosambi, D. D., (1967) "Living Prehistory in India," from *Scientific American,* 215:105. Copyright © 1967 by D. D. Kosambi. Reprinted by permission of Dr. Meera Kosambi and Mr. Jijoy B. Surkar.

Figure 5-1: Mishkin, Mortimer, Ungerleider, Leslie G., & Macko, Kathleen A. (1983), "Object vision and spatial vision: two cortical pathways," *Trends in Neurosciences,* 6(10):414–417. Figure 5-15: Reicher, G. M. (1969) "Perception of Letters & Words," from article, "Perceptual Recognition as a Function of the Meaningfulness of the Material," from *Journal of Experimental Psychology,* 81:275–280. Copyright © 1969 by American Psychological Association. Adapted by permission. Figures 5-17, 5-18: Biederman, I. (1987) "Recognition of Components: A Theory of Human Image Understanding," from *Psychological Review,* 94:115–147. Copyright © 1987 by American Psychological Association. Reprinted by permission. Figure 5-19: Boring, E. G. (1930) "A New Ambiguous Figure," from *American Journal of Psychology,* 42:444–445. Copyright © 1930 by the Board of Trustees of the University of Illinois. Used with permission of the University of Illinois Press. Figure 5-20: Fisher, G. H. (1967) "Perception of Ambiguous Stimulus Materials," from *Perception & Psychophysics,* 2:421–422. Reprinted by permission of the Psychonomic Society. Figure 5-27: from *Sensation and Perception* by E. Bruce Goldstein. Copyright © 1989, 1984, 1980 by Wadsworth Publishing Company. Reprinted by permission of Brooks/Cole Publishing Company, a division of International Thomson Publishing, Inc. Pacific Grove, CA 93950. Figure 5-31: Held, R. and Hein, A. (1963) "Movement Produced in the Development of Visually Guided Behavior," from *Journal of Comparative and Physiological Psychology,* 56:872–876. Copyright © 1963 by the American Psychological Association. Adapted with permission.

Table 6-1: Pion, G.M. (1991) "Psychologists Wanted: Employment Trends Over the Past Decade," in R.R. Kilbur (ed.) *How to Manage Your Career in Psychology,* Copyright © 1991 by the American Psychological Association. Reprinted by permission. Figure 6-6: From *Illicit Drug Use, Smoking, and Drinking by America's High School Students, College Students, and Young Adults, 1975–1995,* by

Jerome Johnston, P. M. O'Malley, & Jerald G. Bachman. Rockville, MD: National Institute on Drug Abuse. Figure 6-7: Data from the National Highway and Traffic Safety Administration.

Figure 7-2: Adapted from *Conditioned Reflexes,* by E. P. Pavlov. Copyright © 1927 by Oxford University Press. Reprinted by permission of Oxford University Press. Figure 7-3: "The Sensory Generalization of Conditioned Responses With Varying Frequencies of Tone," from *Journal of General Psychology,* Vol. 17, pp. 125–148, 1937. Reprinted by permission of the Helen Dwight Reid Educational Foundation. Published by Heldref Publications, 1319 18th Street N.W., Washington, DC 20036. Copyright © 1939. Figure 7-4: Adapted from article "Differential Classical Conditioning: Verbalization of Stimulus Contingencies," by M. J. Fuhrer & P. E. Baer, reprinted by permission from *Science,* Vol. 150, December 10, 1965, pp. 1479–1481. Copyright © 1965 by American Association for the Advancement of Science. Figure 7-5: Rescorla, R. A. (1967) "Pavlovian Conditioning & Its Proper Control Procedures," from *Psychological Review,* Vol. 74:71–80. Copyright © 1967 by the American Psychological Association. Adapted by permission. Table 7-1: Kamin, Leon J., "Predictability, Surprise, Attention, & Conditioning," from *Punishment and Aversive Behavior,* edited by B. A. Campbell & R. M. Church. Copyright © 1969. Adapted by permission of Prentice-Hall, Needham Heights, MA. Table 7-2: Garcia, J. and Koelling, R. A. (1966) "The Relation of Cue to Consequence in Avoidance Learning," from *Psychonomic Science,* 4:123–124. Reprinted by permission of the Psychonomic Society. Figure 7-8: Adapted from Schwartz, Barry, *Psychology of Learning and Behavior,* 3rd edition, with the permission of W. W. Norton & Company, Inc. Copyright © 1989, 1984, 1979 by W. W. Norton & Company, Inc. Figure 7-9: From *Brain, Mind and Behavior* by Bloom and Lazerton. Copyright © 1988 by Educational Broadcasting Corporation. Used with permission of W. H. Freeman and Company.

Figure 8-1: Melton, A. W. (1963) "Implication of Short-Term Memory for a General Theory of Memory" from *Journal of Verbal Learning and Verbal Behavior,* 2:1–21. Adapted by permission of the Academic Press. Figure 8-2: From *Alice in Wonderland* by Lewis Carrol, illustrated by Marjorie Torrey. Abridged under the supervision of Josette Frank. Copyright © 1955 and renewed 1983 by Random House, Inc. Reprinted by permission of the publisher. Figure 8-3: Jonides, John, Smith, Edward E., Koeppe, Robert A., and Awh, Edward (1994), "Spatial working memory in humans as revealed by PET," *Nature,* 363:623–625. Reprinted by permission from Nature. Copyright © 1994 by MacMillan Magazines, Ltd. Figure 8-4: Adapted from article "High-Speed Scanning in Human Memory," reprinted with permission from *Science,* Vol. 153, August 5, 1966, pp. 652–654 by S. Sternberg. Copyright © 1966 by the American Association for the Advancement of Science. Figure 8-5: Carpenter, P. A., Just, M. A., and Shell, P. (1990), "What one intelligence test measures: A theoretical account of the processing in the Raven Progressive Matrices Test," *Psychological Review,* 97(3):404–431. Adapted by permission of the American Psychological Association. Figure 8-6: Murdock, B. B. (1962) "The Serial Position Effect in Free Recall," from *Journal*

Name Index

Subject Index